CODE OF VIRGINIA
1950

With Provision for Subsequent Pocket Parts

ANNOTATED

Prepared under the Supervision of
The Virginia Code Commission

BY

The Editorial Staff of the Publishers

VOLUME 6A

1999 REPLACEMENT VOLUME

*(Including Acts of the 1999 Regular Session and annotations
taken from South Eastern Reporter, 2d series,
through Volume 509, page 928.)*

MICHIE
Law Publishers
CHARLOTTESVILLE, VIRGINIA

4904412

ISBN 0-327-09053-7

Scope of Annotations

The annotations of this 1999 Replacement Volume 6A include decisions reported through:

South Eastern Reporter, 2nd Series, through Volume 509, p. 928.
Supreme Court Reporter, through Volume 119, p. 720.
Federal Reporter, 3rd Series, through Volume 158, p. 1383.
Federal Supplement, 2nd Series, through Volume 8, p. 1389.
Federal Rules Decisions, through Volume 182, p. 692.
Bankruptcy Reporter, through Volume 228, p. 922.
Virginia Law Review, through Volume 84, p. 953.
Washington and Lee Law Review, through Volume 54, p. 1336.
William and Mary Law Review, through Volume 39, p. 282.
University of Richmond Law Review, through Volume 32, p. 939.
George Mason University Law Review, through Volume 7, p. 484.

Unpublished Opinions of Court of Appeals. — Some of the annotations contained in this supplement are derived from unpublished opinions of the Court of Appeals of Virginia. These opinions will not appear in the Court of Appeals Reports or any other court reporter. The unpublished opinions can be identified by their citation, which gives the parties' names, a case number, "Ct. of Appeals," and a date. The Court of Appeals has placed the following footnote on all unpublished opinions: "Pursuant to Code § 17.1-413, recodifying § 17-116.010, this opinion is not designated for publication." A copy of the full text of any unpublished opinion can be obtained by contacting: Court of Appeals of Virginia, Attention: Clerk's Assistant (Opinions), 109 North Eighth Street, Richmond, Virginia 23219.

Suggestions, comments, or questions about the Code of Virginia or this Cumulative Supplement are welcome. You may call us toll free at (800) 446-3410, fax us toll free at (800) 643-1280, email us at LLP.Customer.Support@Lexis-Nexis.com, or write Code of Virginia Editor, Lexis Law Publishing, P.O. Box 7587, Charlottesville, Virginia 22906-7587.

For an online bookstore, technical and customer support, and other company information, visit Lexis Law Publishing's Internet home page at **http://www.lexislawpublishing.com.**

User's Guide

In order to assist both the legal profession and the layman in obtaining the maximum benefit from the Code of Virginia, a User's Guide has been included in Volume 1. This guide contains comments and information on the many features found within the Code of Virginia intended to increase the usefulness of this set of laws to the user. See Volume 1 of this set for the complete User's Guide.

Table of Titles

In addition, this publication contains

Constitution of the United States of America.
Constitution of Virginia.
Rules of Supreme Court of Virginia.
Legal Ethics Opinions.
Unauthorized Practice of Law Opinions.
Table of Comparative Sections.
Table of Tax Code Sections.
Table of Reorganization Provisions of 1948.
Table of Acts Through 1948 Not Previously Codified.
Table of Acts Codified Subsequent to 1948.
Table of Sections Amended or Repealed.
Tables of Comparable Sections for Certain Repealed and Revised Titles.

Table of Contents

VOLUME 6A

TITLE 38.

INSURANCE.

[Repealed.]

TITLE 38.1.

INSURANCE.

[Repealed.]

TITLE 38.2.

INSURANCE.

TITLE 39.

JUSTICES OF THE PEACE.

[Repealed.]

TITLE 39.1.

JUSTICES OF THE PEACE.

[Repealed.]

TITLE 40.

LABOR AND EMPLOYMENT.

[Repealed.]

TITLE 40.1.

LABOR AND EMPLOYMENT.

TITLE 41.

LAND OFFICE.

[Repealed.]

TITLE 41.1.

LAND OFFICE.

TITLE 42.

LIBRARIES.

[Repealed.]

TITLE 42.1.

LIBRARIES.

CODE OF VIRGINIA

Title 38.

Insurance.

§§ 38-1 through 38-564: Repealed by Acts 1952, ch. 317.

Cross references. — For new sections covering same subject matter as the repealed sections, see Title 38.2, §§ 38.2-100 through 38.2-4917.

Former §§ 38-308 through 38-315 were reenacted and renumbered by Acts 1952, c. 225, as §§ 2-64.1 through 2-64.8, which have been repealed by Acts 1966, c. 677. See now §§ 2.1-74 through 2.1-81.

Title 38.1.

Insurance.

§§ 38.1-1 through 38.1-971: Repealed by Acts 1986, c. 562.

Cross references. — For new sections covering same subject matter as the repealed sections, see Title 38.2, §§ 38.2-100 through 38.2-4917. See Editor's note under § 38.2-100.

INSURANCE

Title 38.2.

Insurance.

3

CHAPTER 1.

GENERAL PROVISIONS.

4

ARTICLE 1.

Definitions.

§ 38.2-100. Definitions. — As used in this title:

"Alien company" means a company incorporated or organized under the laws of any country other than the United States.

"Commission" means the State Corporation Commission.

"Commissioner" or *"Commissioner of Insurance"* means the administrative or executive officer of the division or bureau of the Commission established to administer the insurance laws of this Commonwealth.

"Company" means any association, aggregate of individuals, business, corporation, individual, joint-stock company, Lloyds type of organization, organization, partnership, receiver, reciprocal or interinsurance exchange, trustee or society.

"Domestic company" means a company incorporated or organized under the laws of this Commonwealth.

"Foreign company" means a company incorporated or organized under the laws of the United States, or of any state other than this Commonwealth.

"Health services plan" means any arrangement for offering or administering health services or similar or related services by a corporation licensed under Chapter 42 (§ 38.2-4200 et seq.) of this title.

"Insurance company" means any company engaged in the business of making contracts of insurance.

"Insurance transaction," "insurance business," and *"business of insurance"* include solicitation, negotiations preliminary to execution, execution of an insurance contract, and the transaction of matters subsequent to execution of the contract and arising out of it.

"Insurer" means an insurance company.

"Medicare" means the *"Health Insurance for the Aged Act,"* Title XVIII of the Social Security Amendment of 1965, as amended.

"Person" means any association, aggregate of individuals, business, company, corporation, individual, joint-stock company, Lloyds type of organization, organization, partnership, receiver, reciprocal or interinsurance exchange, trustee or society.

"Rate" or *"rates"* means any rate of premium, policy fee, membership fee or any other charge made by an insurer for or in connection with a contract or

policy of insurance. The terms "rate" or "rates" shall not include a membership fee paid to become a member of an organization or association, one of the benefits of which is the purchasing of insurance coverage.

"Rate service organization" means any organization or person, other than a joint underwriting association under § 38.2-1915 or any employee of an insurer including those insurers under common control or management, who assists insurers in ratemaking or filing by:

(a) Collecting, compiling, and furnishing loss or expense statistics;

(b) Recommending, making or filing rates or supplementary rate information; or

(c) Advising about rate questions, except as an attorney giving legal advice.

"State" means any commonwealth, state, territory, district or insular possession of the United States.

"Surplus to policyholders" means the excess of total admitted assets over the liabilities of an insurer, and shall be the sum of all capital and surplus accounts, including any voluntary reserves, minus any impairment of all capital and surplus accounts.

Without otherwise limiting the meaning of or defining the following terms, "insurance" shall include fidelity and suretyship, and "insurance contracts" or "insurance policies" shall include contracts of fidelity, indemnity, guaranty and suretyship. (Code 1950, §§ 38-1, 38-194, 38-253.20, 38-253.67; 1952, c. 317, §§ 38.1-1, 38.1-219; 1973, c. 504, § 38.1-279.30; 1980, c. 204, § 38.1-362.12; 1986, c. 562.)

Editor's note. — House Joint Resolution No. 1 of the 1984 Acts of Assembly directed the Virginia Code Commission to make a study of Title 38.1 and report to the Governor and the General Assembly its findings in the form of a revision of that title. In January, 1986, its report, containing a proposed revision of Title 38.1, was sent to the Governor and the General Assembly. The report was published as House Document No. 17 of the 1986 Session and served as the basis for this title, which was enacted by Acts 1986, c. 562, effective July 1, 1986.

In addition to its revision by Acts 1986, c. 562, Title 38.1 was amended by certain other acts during the 1986 Session. These amendments have been incorporated, as appropriate, into comparable provisions of this title, pursuant to § 9-77.11.

Many of the cases cited in the notes under sections of this title were decided under corresponding provisions of former Title 38.1 and earlier statutes.

Law Review. — For article, "The 1952 Revision of the Virginia Life Insurance Laws," see 39 Va. L. Rev. 547 (1953). For note on waiver, election and estoppel in Virginia insurance litigation, see 48 Va. L. Rev. 416 (1962). For survey of the Virginia law on insurance for the year 1961-1962, see 48 Va. L. Rev. 1354 (1962); for the year 1964-1965, see 51 Va. L. Rev. 1432 (1965); for the year 1967-1968, see 54 Va. L. Rev. 1627 (1968); for the year 1968-1969, see 55 Va. L. Rev. 1552 (1969); for the year 1978-1979, see 66 Va. L. Rev. 321 (1980).

Motorists not required to have automobile liability insurance under this title. — Nothing in this title requires any motorist, whether a resident or nonresident of Virginia, to have any automobile liability insurance as a condition to operate or use a motor vehicle in Virginia, and nothing therein requires those who elect to purchase insurance to have any minimum coverage. Reliance Ins. Cos. v. Darden, 217 Va. 694, 232 S.E.2d 749 (1977).

Applied in Northland Ins. Co. v. Virginia Property & Cas. Ins. Guar. Ass'n, 240 Va. 115, 392 S.E.2d 682 (1990).

ARTICLE 2.

Insurance Classified and Defined.

§ 38.2-101. Classification of insurance. — Insurance is classified and defined as set out in subsequent sections of this article. (1952, c. 317, § 38.1-2; 1986, c. 562.)

Law Review. — For survey of Virginia law on insurance for the year 1973-1974, see 60 Va. L. Rev. 1553 (1974).

§ 38.2-102. Life. — *"Life insurance"* means insurance upon the lives of human beings. "Life insurance" includes policies that also provide (i) endowment benefits; (ii) additional benefits in the event of death, dismemberment, or loss of sight by accident or accidental means; (iii) additional benefits to safeguard the contract from lapse or to provide a special surrender value, a special benefit or an annuity, in the event of total and permanent disability of the insured; and (iv) optional modes of settlement of proceeds. As used in this title, unless the context requires otherwise, "life insurance" shall be deemed to include "credit life insurance," "industrial life insurance," "variable life insurance" and "modified guaranteed life insurance." (1952, c. 317, § 38.1-3; 1976, c. 562; 1986, c. 562; 1992, c. 210.)

Difference between life and accident insurance. — It is apparent that life insurance means insurance against death regardless of cause. It is equally apparent that accident and sickness insurance means insurance against death caused only by accident or, where the policy so provides, by accident or sickness, or both. Gudnason v. Life Ins. Co. of N. Am., 231 Va. 197, 343 S.E.2d 54 (1986).

§ 38.2-103. Credit life. — *"Credit life insurance"* means insurance on the life of a debtor pursuant to or in connection with a specific loan or other credit transaction. (1960, c. 67, § 38.1-482.2; 1982, c. 223; 1986, c. 562.)

§ 38.2-104. Industrial life. — *"Industrial life insurance"* means life insurance provided by an individual insurance contract (i) under which premiums are payable at least monthly and (ii) that has the words "industrial policy" printed upon the policy as a part of the descriptive matter. (Code 1950, § 38-433; 1952, c. 317, § 38.1-409; 1986, c. 562.)

§ 38.2-105. Variable life. — *"Variable life insurance"* means any policy or contract of life insurance in which the amount or duration of benefits may vary according to the investment experience of any separate account maintained by the insurer for the policy or contract, as provided for in § 38.2-3113. (1986, c. 562.)

§ 38.2-105.1. Modified guaranteed life insurance. — *"Modified guaranteed life insurance"* means any policy or contract of life insurance in which the benefits are guaranteed if held for specified periods and nonforfeiture values are based upon a market-value adjustment formula if held for shorter periods. The formula may or may not reflect the investment experience of any separate account which may be maintained by the insurer for the policy or contract as provided for in § 38.2-3113.1. (1992, c. 210.)

§ 38.2-106. Annuities. — *"Annuities"* means all agreements to make periodic payments in fixed dollar amounts pursuant to the terms of a contract for a stated period of time or for the life of the person or persons specified in the contract. "Annuities" does not include contracts defined in § 38.2-102 and qualified charitable gift annuities as defined in § 38.2-106.1.

As used in this title, unless the context requires otherwise, "annuity" shall be deemed to include "variable annuity" and "modified guaranteed annuity," and shall be deemed to include a contract under which a lump sum cash settlement is an alternative to the option of periodic payments. (1952, c. 317, § 38.1-4;

1966, c. 289; 1970, c. 532; 1985, c. 312; 1986, c. 562; 1992, c. 210; 1993, c. 764; 1996, c. 425.)

Editor's note. — Acts 1996, c. 425, cl. 2, provides: "[t]hat the provisions of this act amending § 38.2-106, the definition of 'charitable gift annuity' as added by this act in § 38.2-106.1, and subsections A and C in § 38.2-3113.2 as added by this act are declarative of existing law."

The 1996 amendment inserted "and qualified charitable gift annuities as defined in § 38.2-106.1" in the paragraph defining "Annuities."

§ 38.2-106.1. Charitable gift annuities. — For purposes of this title:

"Charitable gift annuity" means an agreement by a charitable organization to make periodic payments in fixed dollar amounts payable over one or two lives, under which the actuarial value of the annuity, as determined for federal tax purposes, is less than the value of the cash or other property transferred by the donor in return therefor and the difference in value constitutes a charitable contribution for federal tax purposes.

"Charitable organization" means an entity described in:
1. § 501 (c) (3) of the Internal Revenue Code of 1986 (26 U.S.C. § 501 (c) (3)); or
2. § 170 (c) of the Internal Revenue Code of 1986 (26 U.S.C. § 170 (c)).

"Qualified charitable gift annuity" means a charitable gift annuity that conforms to the requirements of § 501 (m) (5) of the Internal Revenue Code of 1986 (26 U.S.C. § 501 (m) (5)) and § 514 (c) (5) of the Internal Revenue Code of 1986 (26 U.S.C. § 514 (c) (5)) and that is issued by a charitable organization that on the date of the annuity agreement:
1. Has a minimum of $100,000 in unrestricted cash, cash equivalents, or publicly traded securities, exclusive of the assets contributed by the donor in return for the annuity agreement; and
2. Has been in continuous operation as a charitable organization for at least three years or is a successor or affiliate of a charitable organization that has been in continuous operation as such for at least three years. (1996, c. 425.)

Editor's note. — Acts 1996, c. 425, cl. 2, provides: "[t]hat the provisions of this act amending § 38.2-106, the definition of 'charitable gift annuity' as added by this act in § 38.2-106.1, and subsections A and C in § 38.2-3113.2 as added by this act are declarative of existing law."

§ 38.2-107. Variable annuity. — *"Variable annuity"* means any agreement or contract for an annuity in which the amount or duration of benefits or optional lump sum cash settlement may vary according to the investment experience of any separate account maintained by the insurer for the policy or contract as provided for in § 38.2-3113. Pursuant to the terms of the contract, payments may be made for a stated period of time or for the life of the person or persons specified in the contract. (1986, c. 562; 1993, c. 764.)

§ 38.2-107.1. Modified guaranteed annuity. — *"Modified guaranteed annuity"* means any agreement or contract for an annuity in which the benefits are guaranteed if held for specified periods and nonforfeiture values are based upon a market-value adjustment formula if held for shorter periods. The formula may or may not reflect the investment experience of any separate account which may be maintained by the insurer for the agreement or contract as provided for in § 38.2-3113.1. (1992, c. 210.)

§ 38.2-108. Credit accident and sickness. — *"Credit accident and sickness insurance"* means insurance on a debtor to provide for payments on a

specific loan or other credit transaction while the debtor is disabled as defined in the policy. (1960, c. 67, § 38.1-482.2; 1982, c. 223; 1986, c. 562.)

§ 38.2-109. Accident and sickness.

— A. *"Accident and sickness insurance"* means insurance against loss resulting from sickness, or from bodily injury or death by accident or accidental means, or from a combination of any or all of these perils. As used in this title, unless the context requires otherwise, the term "accident and sickness insurance" shall be deemed to include "credit accident and sickness insurance."

B. The term "accident and sickness insurance" shall also include agreements insuring against losses resulting from health care claims or expenses of health care in excess of a specific or aggregate dollar amount, when such agreements are used to provide coverage to (i) an employee welfare benefit plan or any other plan providing accident and sickness benefits, (ii) a health maintenance organization, or (iii) a provider associated with a managed care network, provided:

1. The agreement clearly discloses the extent and duration of the liability assumed by the insurer once the policyholder's liability has been exceeded; and

2. The insurer maintains reserves in accordance with § 38.2-1314 for the liability it assumes under the agreement.

Such agreements shall not be subject to the requirements of Chapters 34 (§ 38.2-3400 et seq.) and 35 (§ 38.2-3500 et seq.) of this title. (1952, c. 317, § 38.1-5; 1986, c. 562; 1997, c. 28.)

Accident defined. — An accident is an event that takes place without one's foresight or expectation, an undesigned, sudden, and unexpected event; further, it is generally held that if the insured voluntarily provokes or is the aggressor in an encounter, and knows, or under the circumstances should reasonably anticipate, that he will be in danger of death or great bodily harm as the natural or probable consequence of his act or course of action, his death or injury is not caused by an accident within the meaning of such a policy. Harris v. Bankers Life & Cas. Co., 222 Va. 45, 278 S.E.2d 809 (1981).

Difference between life and accident insurance. — It is apparent that life insurance means insurance against death regardless of cause. It is equally apparent that accident and sickness insurance means insurance against death caused only by accident or, where the policy so provides, by accident or sickness, or both. Gudnason v. Life Ins. Co. of N. Am., 231 Va. 197, 343 S.E.2d 54 (1986).

Issue of accident improperly decided by court. — In an action claiming that defendant insurance company breached a contract insuring plaintiff's husband against accidental death or dismemberment, where evidence showed that the husband was stabbed to death by another woman with whom he lived after the husband had disciplined the woman's child and pushed the woman, the trial court erred in deciding as a matter of law that the husband's death was not an accident, since whether the husband should have anticipated that his disciplining the child or his pushing the woman would lead to a violent reaction presented a factual issue dependent on the relationship of the parties and the circumstances of the incident. Harris v. Bankers Life & Cas. Co., 222 Va. 45, 278 S.E.2d 809 (1981).

§ 38.2-110. Fire.

— *"Fire insurance"* means insurance against loss of or damage to any property resulting from fire, including loss or damage incident (i) to extinguishing a fire, or (ii) to the salvaging of property in connection with a fire. (1952, c. 317, § 38.1-6; 1986, c. 562.)

§ 38.2-111. Miscellaneous property.

— *"Miscellaneous property insurance"* means insurance against loss of or damage to property resulting from:

1. Lightning, smoke or smudge, windstorm, tornado, cyclone, earthquake, volcanic eruption, rain, hail, frost and freeze, weather or climatic conditions, excess or deficiency of moisture, flood, the rising of the waters of the ocean or its tributaries; or

2. Insects, blights, or disease of such property other than animals; or

3. Electrical disturbance causing or concomitant with a fire or an explosion; or

4. The ownership, maintenance or use of elevators, except loss or damage by fire. This class of insurance includes the incidental power to make inspections of and to issue certificates of inspection upon any such elevator; or

5. Bombardment, invasion, insurrection, riot, civil war or commotion, military or usurped power, any order of a civil authority made to prevent the spread of a conflagration, epidemic or catastrophe, vandalism or malicious mischief, strike or lockout, collapse from any cause, or explosion; but not including any kind of insurance specified in § 38.2-115, except insurance against loss or damage to property resulting from:

a. Explosion of pressure vessels, except steam boilers of more than fifteen pounds pressure, in buildings designed and used solely for residential purposes by not more than four families;

b. Explosion of any kind originating outside of the insured building or outside of the building containing the insured property;

c. Explosion of pressure vessels not containing steam; or

d. Electrical disturbance causing or concomitant with an explosion; or

6. Any other cause or hazard which may result in a loss or damage to property, if the insurance is not contrary to law or public policy. (1952, c. 317, §§ 38.1-7, 38.1-12; 1986, c. 562.)

§ 38.2-112. Water damage. — *"Water damage insurance"* means insurance against loss or damage to any property by water or other fluid or substance resulting from (i) the breakage or leakage of sprinklers, pumps or other apparatus erected for extinguishing fires or of water pipes or other conduits or containers, or (ii) casual water entering through leaks or openings in buildings or by seepage through building walls, but not including loss or damage resulting from flood or the rising of the waters of the ocean or its tributaries. This class of insurance includes insurance against accidental injury of such sprinklers, pumps, fire apparatus, conduits or containers. (1952, c. 317, § 38.1-8; 1986, c. 562.)

§ 38.2-113. Burglary and theft. — *"Burglary and theft insurance"* means insurance against:

1. Loss of or damage to any property resulting from actual or attempted burglary, theft, larceny, robbery, forgery, fraud, vandalism, malicious mischief, wrongful confiscation or wrongful conversion, disposal or concealment by any person or persons;

2. Loss of or damage to moneys, coins, bullion, securities, notes, drafts, acceptances or any other valuable papers or documents, resulting from any cause, except while in the custody or possession of and being transported by any carrier for hire or in the mail; or

3. The loss of property actually surrendered due to extortion, threat, or demand, involving the actual, alleged or threatened kidnapping of any individual or the threat to do bodily injury to or damage to property of or to wrongfully abduct or detain any individual. (1952, c. 317, § 38.1-9; 1986, c. 562.)

Theft requires intent to deprive owner permanently. — Under the terms of an automobile insurance policy, in order to constitute a theft there must be present an intent permanently to deprive the owner of the vehicle. If it is shown that the alleged thief intended to return the vehicle after using it temporarily, there is no theft. Travelers Indem. Co. v. Ford, 208 Va. 151, 156 S.E.2d 606 (1967).

Taking without requisite intent is not within coverage of theft insurance policy. — The taking of a car, unaccompanied by an intent permanently to deprive the owner of the car, is a crime separate from the crime of larceny. A taking without the requisite intent is not within the coverage of a theft insurance policy. Travelers Indem. Co. v. Ford, 208 Va. 151, 156 S.E.2d 606 (1967).

§ 38.2-114. Glass insurance. — *"Glass insurance"* means insurance against loss of or damage to glass and its appurtenances resulting from any cause. (1952, c. 317, § 38.1-10; 1986, c. 562.)

§ 38.2-115. Boiler and machinery. — *"Boiler and machinery insurance"* means insurance against any liability of the insured and against loss of or damage to any property of the insured resulting from the explosion of or injury to (i) any boiler, heater or other fired pressure vessel; (ii) any unfired pressure vessel; (iii) any pipes or containers connected with any of the boilers or vessels; (iv) any engine, turbine, compressor, pump or wheel; (v) any apparatus generating, transmitting or using electricity; or (vi) any other machinery or apparatus connected with or operated by any of the previously named boilers, vessels or machines. Boiler and machinery insurance includes the incidental power to inspect and to issue certificates of inspection upon any such boilers, pressure vessels, apparatus, and machinery. (1952, c. 317, § 38.1-11; 1986, c. 562.)

§ 38.2-116. Animal. — *"Animal insurance"* means insurance against loss of or damage to any animal resulting from any cause. (1952, c. 317, § 38.1-13; 1986, c. 562.)

§ 38.2-117. Personal injury liability. — *"Personal injury liability insurance"* means insurance against legal liability of the insured, and against loss, damage or expense incident to a claim of such liability, arising out of the death or injury of any person, or arising out of injury to the economic interests of any person as the result of negligence in rendering expert, fiduciary or professional service, but not including any class of insurance specified in § 38.2-119.

Any policy of personal injury liability insurance may include appropriate provisions obligating the insurer to pay medical, hospital, surgical, and funeral expenses arising out of the death or injury of any person, regardless of any legal liability of the insured. (Code 1950, § 38-239; 1952, c. 317, § 38.1-15; 1986, c. 562.)

§ 38.2-118. Property damage liability. — *"Property damage liability insurance"* means insurance against legal liability of the insured, and against loss, damage or expense incident to a claim of such liability, arising out of the loss or destruction of, or damage to, the property of any other person, but not including any class of insurance specified in § 38.2-117 or § 38.2-119. (1952, c. 317, § 38.1-16; 1986, c. 562.)

§ 38.2-119. Workers' compensation and employers' liability. — *"Workers' compensation and employers' liability insurance"* means insurance against the legal liability of any employer for the death or disablement of, or injury to, his or its employee whether imposed by common law or by statute, or assumed by contract.

Employers' liability insurance may include appropriate provisions obligating the insurer to pay medical, chiropractic, hospital, surgical, and funeral expenses arising out of the death or injury of an employee, regardless of any legal liability of the insured. (1952, c. 317, § 38.1-17; 1986, c. 562.)

§ 38.2-120. Fidelity. — *"Fidelity insurance"* means:
1. Indemnifying any person against loss through counterfeit, forgery or alteration of, on, or in any security obligation or other written instrument; or

2. Indemnifying banks, bankers, brokers, financial or moneyed corporations or associations against loss resulting from any cause, of personal property, including fixtures, equipment, safes and vaults on the insured's premises. (1952, c. 317, § 38.1-18; 1986, c. 562.)

§ 38.2-121. Surety. — *"Surety insurance"* means:

1. Becoming surety or guarantor for any person, in any public or private position or place of trust, whether the guarantee is in an individual, schedule or blanket form; or

2. Becoming surety on or guaranteeing the performance of any lawful obligation, undertaking, agreement, or contract, including reinsurance contracts connected therewith, except policies of insurance; or

3. Becoming surety on or guaranteeing the performance of bonds and undertakings required or permitted in all judicial proceedings or otherwise allowed by law, including surety bonds accepted by state and municipal authorities in lieu of deposits as security for the performance of insurance contracts. (1952, c. 317, § 38.1-18; 1986, c. 562.)

§ 38.2-122. Credit. — *"Credit insurance"* means indemnifying merchants or other persons extending credit against loss or damage resulting from the nonpayment of debts owed to them. "Credit insurance" includes the incidental power to acquire and dispose of debts so insured and to collect any debts owed to the insurer or to any persons so insured by the insurer. "Credit insurance" does not include any insurance defined in §§ 38.2-103, 38.2-108, or § 38.2-128. (1952, c. 317, § 38.1-19; 1986, c. 562.)

§ 38.2-122.1. Credit involuntary unemployment insurance. — *"Credit involuntary unemployment insurance"* means insurance on a debtor in connection with a specified loan or other credit transaction to provide payment to a creditor for the installment payments or other periodic payments becoming due while the debtor is involuntarily unemployed. Such term shall not mean any insurance defined in § 38.2-122. (1993, c. 774.)

§ 38.2-123. Title. — *"Title insurance"* means insurance against loss by reason of liens and encumbrances upon property, defects in the title to property, and other matters affecting the title to property or the right to the use and enjoyment of property. "Title insurance" includes insurance of the condition of the title to property and the status of any lien on property. (Code 1950, § 38-233; 1952, c. 317, § 38.1-20; 1986, c. 562.)

§ 38.2-124. Motor vehicle. — A. *"Motor vehicle insurance"* means insurance against:

1. Loss of or damage to motor vehicles, including trailers, semitrailers or other attachments designed for use in connection with motor vehicles, resulting from any cause, and against legal liability of the insured for loss or damage to the property of another resulting from the ownership, maintenance or use of motor vehicles and against loss, damage or expense incident to a claim of such liability; or

2. Legal liability of the insured, and liability arising under subsection A of § 38.2-2206 and against loss, damage, or expense incident to a claim of such liability, arising out of the death or injury of any person resulting from the ownership, maintenance or use of motor vehicles. Motor vehicle insurance does not include any class of insurance specified in § 38.2-119.

B. Any policy of "motor vehicle insurance" covering legal liability of the insured under subdivision 2 of subsection A and covering liability arising under subsection A of § 38.2-2206 may include appropriate provisions obligating the insurer to pay to the covered injured person medical expense and loss of income benefits arising out of the death or injury of any person, as set forth in subsection A of § 38.2-2201. Any such policy of motor vehicle insurance may include appropriate provisions obligating the insurer to pay weekly indemnity or other specific benefits to persons who are injured and specific death benefits to dependents, beneficiaries or personal representatives of persons who are killed, if the injury or death is caused by accident and sustained while in or upon, entering or alighting from, or through being struck by a motor vehicle while not occupying a motor vehicle. These provisions shall obligate the insurer to make payment regardless of any legal liability of the insured or any other person. (1952, c. 317, § 38.1-21; 1956, c. 678; 1962, c. 253; 1983, c. 448; 1984, c. 311; 1986, c. 562; 1991, c. 4; 1996, c. 276.)

Law Review. — For article, "An Overview of Automobile Liability Insurance in Virginia," see 28 U. Rich. L. Rev. 863 (1994).

Policy must provide coverage prescribed by this section. — While this section may constitute the basis upon which an insurer voluntarily writes medical payments insurance, once coverage is provided, it must be written to provide at least the coverage herein prescribed. State Farm Mut. Auto. Ins. Co. v. Seay, 236 Va. 275, 373 S.E.2d 910 (1988).

The language "while in or upon ... a motor vehicle" in B applies to coverage for both medical payments and weekly indemnity benefits. State Farm Mut. Auto. Ins. Co. v. Seay, 236 Va. 275, 373 S.E.2d 910 (1988).

Clause applies only to weekly indemnity or other specific benefits. — The statutory clause mandating coverage for injuries sustained "through being struck by a motor vehicle" applies only with respect to weekly indemnity or other specific benefits. State Farm Mut. Auto. Ins. Co. v. Major, 239 Va. 375, 389 S.E.2d 307 (1990).

Where the medical payments provision of insured's policy did not comply with the requirements of this section, this section would prevail and supersede the inconsistent policy provision; therefore, the term "motor vehicle" was incorporated into the medical payments provision and construed to include a motorcycle, entitling insured to coverage. State Farm Mut. Auto. Ins. Co. v. Seay, 236 Va. 275, 373 S.E.2d 910 (1988).

Section held to supersede conflicting policy provision as to nonoccupancy. — By mandating the use of "while not occupying a motor vehicle" language in the medical payments provisions of automobile liability policies, the State Corporation Commission created an irreconcilable conflict between such provisions and this section, and this section would supersede the conflicting provisions. Virginia Farm Bureau Mut. Ins. Co. v. Jerrell, 236 Va. 261, 373 S.E.2d 913 (1988).

This section extends coverage to injuries sustained through being struck by a motor vehicle, without any qualifications regarding the nonoccupancy of the motor vehicle; therefore, this section superseded an insurance policy provision purporting to limit coverage to injuries sustained "while not occupying a motor vehicle, through being struck by a motor vehicle," making such provision ineffective to limit coverage. Virginia Farm Bureau Mut. Ins. Co. v. Jerrell, 236 Va. 261, 373 S.E.2d 913 (1988).

Applied in State Farm Mut. Auto. Ins. Co. v. Gandy, 238 Va. 257, 383 S.E.2d 717 (1989); Baker v. State Farm Mut. Auto. Ins. Co., 242 Va. 74, 405 S.E.2d 624 (1991).

§ 38.2-125. Aircraft. — *"Aircraft insurance"* means insurance against:

1. Loss of or damage to aircraft and its equipment, resulting from any cause, and against legal liability of the insured for loss of or damage to the property of another resulting from the ownership, maintenance or use of aircraft and against loss, damage or expense incident to a claim of liability; or

2. Legal liability of the insured, and against loss, damage, or expense incident to a claim of liability, arising out of the death or injury of any person resulting from the ownership, maintenance or use of aircraft.

Any policy of "aircraft insurance" covering legal liability of the insured under subdivision 2 of this section may include appropriate provisions obligating the insurer to pay medical, chiropractic, hospital, surgical, and funeral expenses arising out of the death or injury of any person. (1952, c. 317, § 38.1-21; 1956, c. 678; 1962, c. 253; 1983, c. 448; 1984, c. 311; 1986, c. 562.)

Law Review. — For article on the law governing airplane accidents, see 39 Wash. & Lee L. Rev. 1303 (1982).

§ 38.2-126. Marine. — A. *"Marine insurance"* means insurance against any kind of loss or damage to:

1. Vessels, craft, aircraft, vehicles of every kind, excluding vehicles operating under their own power or while in storage not incidental to transportation, as well as all goods, freights, cargoes, merchandise, effects, disbursements, profits, moneys, bullion, precious stones, securities, choses in action, evidences of debt, valuable papers, bottomry and respondentia interests and all other kinds of property and interests therein in respect to any risks or perils of navigation, transit or transportation, including war risks, on or under any seas or other waters, on land or in the air, or while being assembled, packed, crated, baled, compressed or similarly prepared for shipment or while awaiting shipment, or during any delays, storage, transshipment, or reshipment incident to shipment, including marine builders' risks and all personal property floater risks;

2. Persons or property in connection with or appertaining to marine, inland marine, transit or transportation insurance, including liability for loss of or damage to either arising out of or in connection with the construction, repair, operation, maintenance, or use of the subject matter of the insurance. This class of insurance shall not include life insurance, surety bonds or insurance against loss by reason of bodily injury to the person arising out of the ownership, maintenance or use of automobiles;

3. Precious stones, jewels, jewelry, gold, silver and other precious metals used in business, trade, or otherwise and whether or not in transit. This class of insurance shall include jewelers' block insurance;

4. (i) Bridges, tunnels, and other instrumentalities of transportation and communication, excluding buildings, their furniture and furnishings, fixed contents and supplies held in storage, unless fire, tornado, sprinkler leakage, hail, explosion, earthquake, riot, and civil commotion are the only hazards to be covered; (ii) to piers, wharves, docks, and slips, excluding the risks of fire, tornado, sprinkler leakage, hail, explosion, earthquake, riot and civil commotion; and (iii) to other aids to navigation and transportation, including dry docks and marine railways, against all risks.

B. Marine insurance shall also include "marine protection and indemnity insurance," meaning insurance against loss, damage, or expense or against legal liability of the insured for loss, damage, or expense arising out of or incident to ownership, operation, chartering, maintenance, use, repair or construction of any vessel, craft or instrumentality in use in ocean or inland waterways, including liability of the insured for personal injury, illness or death or for loss of or damage to the property of another person.

C. Any policy of "marine insurance" as defined in this section providing protection against bodily injury, sickness or death of another person may include appropriate provisions obligating the insurer to pay medical, hospital, surgical, and funeral expenses arising out of the death or injury of any person, regardless of any legal liability of the insured. (1952, c. 317, § 38.1-22; 1986, c. 562.)

§ 38.2-127. Legal services insurance. — *"Legal services insurance"* means the assumption of a contractual obligation to reimburse the insured against, or pay on behalf of the insured, all or a portion of his fees, costs, and expenses related to services performed by or under the supervision of an attorney licensed to practice in the jurisdiction where the services are performed. (1976, c. 636, § 38.1-22.1; 1978, c. 658; 1986, c. 562.)

Cross references. — As to contracts and plans for future legal services, see § 38.2-4400 et seq.

Law Review. — For survey of Virginia insurance law for the year 1975-1976, see 62 Va. L. Rev. 1446 (1976). For discussion of legislative developments with regard to prepaid legal services in the 1978 Session of the General Assembly, see 12 U. Rich. L. Rev. 759 (1978).

§ 38.2-128. Mortgage guaranty insurance.

— *"Mortgage guaranty insurance"* means indemnifying lenders against financial loss arising from nonpayment of principal, interest, or other sums due under the terms of any evidence of indebtedness secured by a mortgage, deed of trust, or other instrument constituting a lien or charge on real property. (1986, c. 562.)

§ 38.2-129. Home protection insurance.

— *"Home protection insurance"* means any contract or agreement whereby a person undertakes for a specified period of time and for a predetermined fee to furnish, arrange for, or indemnify for service, repair, or replacement of any or all of the structural components, parts, appliances, or systems of any covered residential dwelling caused by wear and tear, deterioration, inherent defect, or by the failure of any inspection to detect the likelihood of failure. (1986, c. 562.)

§ 38.2-130. Homeowners insurance.

— *"Homeowners insurance"* is a combination multi-peril policy written under the provisions of § 38.2-1921 containing fire, miscellaneous property, and liability coverages, insuring primarily (i) owner-occupied residential real property pursuant to § 38.2-2108, (ii) personal property located in residential units, or (iii) any combination thereof. (1986, c. 562.)

§ 38.2-131. Farmowners insurance.

— *"Farmowners insurance"* is a combination multi-peril policy written under the provisions of § 38.2-1921 containing fire, miscellaneous property, and liability coverages, insuring primarily (i) farm and related residential property and improvements to real property owned, leased, or operated as a farm, (ii) personal property located in residential units, (iii) other real or personal property usual or incidental to the operation of a farm, or (iv) any combination thereof. (1986, c. 562.)

§ 38.2-132. Commercial multi-peril insurance.

— *"Commercial multi-peril insurance"* is a combination multi-peril policy written under the provisions of § 38.2-1921 insuring risks incident to a commercial enterprise containing any combination of the classes of insurance set forth in subsection A of § 38.2-1902, except insurance on or with respect to operating properties of railroads. (1986, c. 562.)

§ 38.2-133. Contingent and consequential losses.

— The definition of any class of insurance against loss of or damage to property enumerated in this article may include insurance against contingent, consequential and indirect losses resulting from any of the causes set out in this article. Coverage for these losses shall be included in the specific grouping of the class of insurance where the cause is specified. Insurance against loss of or damage to property may include insurance against loss or damage to all lawful interests in the property, and against loss of use and occupancy, rents, and profits resulting from the loss or damage. (1952, c. 317, § 38.1-23; 1986, c. 562.)

§ 38.2-134. Definitions to include other insurance of same general kind.

— The definition of any class of insurance enumerated in this article shall include insurance against other loss, damage or liability of the same general nature or character, or of a similar kind, if the insurance may reasonably and properly be included in the definition and is not specifically included in the definition of some other class of insurance. (1952, c. 317, § 38.1-24; 1986, c. 562.)

ARTICLE 3.

Classes of Insurance Companies May Write; Reinsurance.

§ 38.2-135. Classes of insurance companies may be licensed to write. — Except as otherwise provided in this title and subject to any conditions and restrictions imposed therein, any insurer licensed to transact the business of insurance in this Commonwealth, other than life insurers and title insurers, may be licensed to write one or more of the classes of insurance enumerated in Article 2 (§ 38.2-101 et seq.) of this chapter that it is authorized under its charter to write, except life insurance, industrial life insurance, credit life insurance, variable life insurance, modified guaranteed life insurance, annuities, variable annuities, modified guaranteed annuities, and title insurance. An insurer licensed to write life insurance shall not be licensed to write any additional class of insurance except modified guaranteed life insurance, variable life insurance, annuities, modified guaranteed annuities, variable annuities, credit life insurance, credit accident and sickness insurance, accident and sickness insurance, and industrial life insurance. An insurer licensed to write title insurance shall not be licensed to write any additional class of insurance. However, any life insurer that has been licensed to write and has been actively engaged in writing life insurance and any additional class of insurance set out in Article 2 (§ 38.2-101 et seq.) of this chapter continuously during a period of twenty years immediately preceding July 1, 1952, may continue to be licensed to write those classes of insurance. No company shall write any class of insurance unless it has a current annual license from the Commission to do so. (Code 1950, §§ 38-159, 38-504; 1952, c. 317, § 38.1-25; 1978, c. 20; 1986, c. 562; 1994, c. 316; 1995, c. 789.)

§ 38.2-136. Reinsurance. — A. Except as otherwise provided in this title, any insurer licensed to transact the business of insurance in this Commonwealth may, by policy, treaty or other agreement, cede to or accept from any insurer reinsurance upon the whole or any part of any risk, with or without contingent liability or participation, and, if a mutual insurer, with or without membership therein.

B. No insurer licensed in this Commonwealth shall cede or assume policy obligations on risks located in this Commonwealth whereby the assuming insurer assumes the policy obligations of the ceding insurer as direct obligations of the assuming insurer to the payees under the policies and in substitution for the obligations of the ceding insurer to the payees, unless: (i) the policyholder has consented to the assumption and (ii) the assuming insurer is licensed in this Commonwealth to write the class or classes of insurance applicable to the policy obligations assumed.

C. Notwithstanding the provisions of subsection B, the transfer of risk under any reinsurance agreement may be effected by entry of an order by the Commission approving the transaction whenever (i) the Commission finds a licensed insurer to be impaired or in hazardous financial condition, (ii) a delinquency proceeding has been instituted against the licensed insurer for the purpose of conserving, rehabilitating, or liquidating the insurer, or (iii) the Commission finds, after giving the insurer notice and an opportunity to be heard, that the transfer of the contracts is in the best interests of the policyholders. In granting any such approval, the Commission shall ensure that policyholders do not lose any rights or claims afforded under their original policies pursuant to Chapter 16 (§ 38.2-1600 et seq.) or 17 (§ 38.2-1700 et seq.) of this title. Prior to granting an approval under clause (iii), the Commission shall consider whether there is a reasonable expectation that the ceding insurer may not be able to meet its obligations to all policyholders; whether the ceding insurer's continued operation in this Commonwealth may become hazardous to policyholders, creditors and the public in this Commonwealth; or whether the ceding insurer may otherwise be unable to comply with the provisions of this title. (Code 1950, §§ 38-160, 38-519; 1952, c. 317, § 38.1-26; 1986, c. 562; 1993, c. 158.)

§ 38.2-137. Flood insurance. — *"Flood insurance"* means insurance against loss or damage to any property caused by flooding or the rising of the waters of the ocean or its tributaries. (1990, c. 916.)

Editor's note. — Repeal of this section by Acts 1997, c. 590 was contingent on funding in the general appropriation act. The funding was not provided, and therefore, the repeal never took effect.

CHAPTER 2.

PROVISIONS OF A GENERAL NATURE.

§ 38.2-200. General powers of the Commission relative to insurance.
— A. The Commission is charged with the execution of all laws relating to insurance and insurers. All companies, domestic, foreign, and alien, transacting or licensed to transact the business of insurance in this Commonwealth are subject to inspection, supervision and regulation by the Commission.

B. All licenses granting the authority to transact the business of insurance in this Commonwealth shall be granted and issued by the Commission under its seal. The licenses shall be in addition to the certificates of authority required of foreign corporations under §§ 13.1-757 and 13.1-919. (Code 1950, § 38-2; 1952, c. 317, § 38.1-29; 1986, c. 562.)

Cross references. — For other provisions as to licenses and certificates of authority, see § 38.2-1024 et seq. See also Va. Const., Art. IX. **Law Review.** — For survey of Virginia law on insurance for the year 1969-1970, see 56 Va. L. Rev. 1356 (1970). For article analyzing ratemaking issues under the SCC, see 14 Wm. & Mary L. Rev. 601 (1973).

§ 38.2-201. Recommendations by Commission to General Assembly.
— The Commission shall make any recommendations to the General Assembly necessary for legislation governing and regulating the classes of companies placed under its supervision by this title. (Code 1950, § 38-128; 1952, c. 317, § 38.1-30; 1986, c. 562.)

§ 38.2-202. Regulation of solicitation of proxies, consents and authorizations.
— The Commission may adopt any rules and regulations regarding the voting equity securities of any domestic stock insurer. These rules and regulations shall cover (i) the solicitation of proxies, (ii) consents, (iii) authorizations, and (iv) any related financial reports. However, these rules and regulations shall not apply to any domestic stock insurer whose equity securities are registered, or required to be registered, pursuant to § 12 of the Securities Exchange Act of 1934, as amended. (1966, c. 262, § 38.1-30.1; 1986, c. 562.)

§ 38.2-203. Management and exclusive agency contracts subject to approval by Commission.
— A. For the purpose of this section, an insurer shall mean a stock or mutual insurer, cooperative nonprofit life benefit company, mutual assessment life, accident and sickness insurer, burial society, fraternal benefit society, mutual assessment property and casualty insurer, home protection company, health maintenance organization, premium finance company or a person licensed under Chapter 42 (§ 38.2-4200 et seq.), 44 (§ 38.2-4400 et seq.) or 45 (§ 38.2-4500 et seq.) of this title, incorporated or organized under the laws of this Commonwealth.

B. No insurer shall make or enter into any contract that provides for the control and management of the insurer, or the controlling or preemptive right to produce substantially all insurance business for the insurer, unless the contract has been filed with and approved by the Commission and approval has not been withdrawn by the Commission. Any approval, disapproval, or withdrawal of approval shall be delivered to the insurer in writing. The notice of disapproval or withdrawal of approval shall state the grounds of such action and shall be delivered to the insurer at least fifteen days before the effective date.

C. The Commission may disapprove or withdraw approval of any contract referred to in this section that:

1. Subjects the insurer to excessive charges for expenses or commissions;
2. Does not contain fair and adequate standards of performance;
3. Extends for an unreasonable length of time; or
4. Contains other inequitable provisions or provisions that may jeopardize the security of policyholders.

D. The provisions of this section shall not affect contracts made before June 30, 1954, but shall apply to all renewals of those contracts made after that date.

E. Any insurer aggrieved by a disapproval or withdrawal of approval under this section may proceed under the provisions of § 38.2-222. (1954, c. 363, § 38.1-29.1; 1986, c. 562; 1998, c. 42.)

The **1998 amendment,** in subsection A, substituted "casualty insurer" for "casualty insurers," deleted "legal services plan or" preceding "home protection company" and inserted "health maintenance organization, premium fi- nance company or a person licensed under Chapter 42 (§ 38.2-4200 et seq.), 44 (§ 38.2-4400 et seq.) or 45 (§ 38.2-4500 et seq.) of this title" following "home protection company."

§§ 38.2-204, 38.2-205: Repealed by Acts 1991, c. 620.

§ 38.2-205.1. Temporary contracts of insurance permitted. — A lender engaged in making or servicing real estate mortgage or deed of trust loans on one to four family residences shall accept as evidence of insurance a temporary written contract of insurance meeting the requirements of § 38.2-2112 and issued by any duly licensed agent, broker, or insurance company. Nothing herein prohibits the lender from disapproving such insurer provided such disapproval is reasonable. Such lender need not accept a binder unless such binder (i) includes the name and address of the insured, name and address of the mortgagee, a description of the insured collateral, and a provision that it may not be cancelled within the term of the binder except upon ten days' written notice to the mortgagee; (ii) is accompanied by a paid receipt for one year's premium, except in the case of the renewal of a policy subsequent to the closing of a loan; and (iii) includes an undertaking of agent to use his best efforts to have the company issue a policy within forty-five days, unless the binder is cancelled. The Bureau of Insurance may by administrative letter require binders to contain such additional information as may be necessary to permit such binders to comply with the reasonable requirements of the Federal National Mortgage Association or Federal Home Loan Mortgage Corporation for purchase of mortgage loans. (1987, c. 10.)

§ 38.2-206. Corporations as members of mutual insurers. — Any public or private corporation in this Commonwealth or elsewhere may apply and enter into agreements for, hold policies in, and be a member of any mutual insurer. (Code 1950, § 38-506; 1952, c. 317, § 38.1-31.1; 1986, c. 562.)

§ 38.2-207. Enforcement of right of subrogation in name of insured. — Except for contracts or plans subject to § 38.2-3405 or § 38.2-2209, when any insurer pays an insured under a contract of insurance which provides that the insurer becomes subrogated to the rights of the insured against any other party the insurer may enforce the legal liability of the other party. This action may be brought in its own name or in the name of the insured or the insured's personal representative. (1952, c. 476, § 38.1-31.2; 1973, c. 28; 1986, c. 562.)

Law Review. — For survey of Virginia law on insurance for the year 1972-1973, see 59 Va. L. Rev. 1535 (1973).

When loss occurs. — While an insurer cannot enforce subrogation rights until after it has made payment under a policy, loss does not occur only after payment by the insurer to the insured or by the insured to a third party whose claim might be covered under the policy. In the context of a policy provision that "the insured shall do nothing after loss to affect such rights" loss occurs when an insured risk causes damage. Insurance Co. of N. Am. v. Abiouness, 227 Va. 10, 313 S.E.2d 663 (1984).

If construction defects existed and caused damage before a release agreement between insured and a subcontractor was signed, and if the agreement released a person or entity allegedly responsible for the damage, then the subrogation rights of the insurers would have been prejudiced and insured would be barred from recovery by a policy provision that the insured not injure the insurer's subrogation rights. Insurance Co. of N. Am. v. Abiouness, 227 Va. 10, 313 S.E.2d 663 (1984).

Where the assured has an uncompen- sated claim for its deductible under the insurance policy the assured is a real party in interest which may properly seek enforcement of its claim for the uncompensated deductible. National Union Fire Ins. Co. v. Hutcherson, 50 Bankr. 845 (Bankr. E.D. Va. 1985).

Subrogation to insured's claim against employee for embezzlement was nondischargeable in bankruptcy. — The creditor's insurer, as subrogee to the creditor (the debtor's employer), was substituted to the rights of the creditor to whom it succeeded in relation to the debt arising out of debtor's embezzlement of his employer's funds. Nothing in the Bankruptcy Code would prevent the insurer, as subrogee, from filing a proof of claim or asserting a nondischargeability complaint. National Union Fire Ins. Co. v. Hutcherson, 50 Bankr. 845 (Bankr. E.D. Va. 1985).

Subrogation under Virginia Consumer Protection Act. — An insurance company has a right to subrogation under the Virginia Consumer Protection Act. Gill v. Rollins Protective Servs. Co., 773 F.2d 592 (4th Cir. 1985), modified on other grounds, 788 F.2d 1042 (4th Cir. 1986).

§ 38.2-208. Limitation of risks generally. — A. Except as otherwise provided in this title, no insurer transacting business in this Commonwealth shall expose itself to any loss on any one risk or hazard in an amount exceeding ten percent of its surplus to policyholders. Any risk or portion of any risk reinsured by an insurer meeting standards of solvency equal to those set forth in § 38.2-1316 shall be deducted in determining the limitation of risk prescribed in this section.

B. For the purpose of this section, the surplus to policyholders shall be determined from (i) the insurer's last sworn statement filed with the Commission or (ii) the Commission's last report of examination, whichever is more recent at the time the risk is assumed.

C. For the purpose of this section, any one risk or hazard (i) in the case of municipal bond insurance shall mean average annual debt service of insured obligations backed by a single revenue source, provided that the insurance policy does not require any accelerated payment of principal by the insurer upon the event of default and (ii) in the case of all other kinds of financial guaranty insurance shall mean the insured unpaid principal with respect to obligations for any one entity, except that any risk or hazard shall be defined by revenue source, if the insured risk or hazard is payable from a specified revenue source or adequately secured by loan obligations or other assets.

D. As used in subsection C above:

"*Municipal bond insurance*" means a kind of financial guaranty insurance providing insurance against loss by reason of nonpayment of principal, interest or other payment obligations pursuant to the terms of municipal bonds.

"*Municipal bond*" means any security, or other instrument under which a payment obligation is created, issued by or on behalf of, or payable or guaranteed by, the United States, Canada, a state, a province of Canada, a municipality or political subdivision of any of the foregoing, or any public agency or instrumentality thereof, or by any other entity provided that such security is eligible for issuance by one of the foregoing.

"*Average annual debt service*" means the amount of insured unpaid principal and interest on an obligation multiplied by the number of such insured obligations, assuming that each obligation represents a $1,000 par value, divided by the amount equal to the aggregate life of all such obligations.

"Financial guaranty insurance" means insurance against loss by reason of the failure of any obligor on any debt instrument or other monetary obligation, including common or preferred stock or capital leases, to pay when due principal, interest, premium, dividend, or purchase price of or on such instrument or obligation, or a fee in connection therewith, when such failure is the result of a financial default or insolvency, regardless of whether such obligation is incurred directly or as a guarantor by or on behalf of another obligor that has also defaulted.

For the purposes of subsection C of this section, the amount of insured unpaid principal shall be reduced by the amount of deposit of (i) cash, or (ii) the market value of obligations rated in the four highest major rating categories by a securities rating agency recognized by the Commission, or (iii) the stated amount of an unconditional, irrevocable letter of credit issued or confirmed by a bank or trust company that (a) is a member of the federal reserve system or chartered by any state or (b) is organized and existing under the laws of a foreign country, has been licensed as a branch or agency by any state or the federal government and is rated in the two highest major rating categories by a securities ratings agency recognized by the Commission or (c) is otherwise acceptable to the Commission or (iv) a conveyance or mortgage of real property, or (v) the scheduled cash flow from obligations rated in the four highest major rating categories by a securities rating agency recognized by the Commission if scheduled to be received on or prior to the date of scheduled debt service on the insured obligations. Such deposit shall be held by the insurer or held in trust for the benefit of the insurer or held in trust for the benefit of holders of the insured obligation whether in the form of debt service, sinking funds or other reserves pursuant to the bond indenture by a trustee acceptable to the Commission.

For the purpose of subsection C of this section, an insurer's surplus to policyholders shall include the amount of any contingency or similar reserve established and maintained by the insurer pursuant to applicable law for the protection of insureds covered by financial guaranty insurance policies against the effect of excessive losses usually occurring during adverse economic cycles.

E. The limitation of risk prescribed in this section for any alien insurer shall apply only to the exposure to risk and the trusteed surplus of the alien insurer's policyholders.

F. This section shall not apply to (i) life insurance, (ii) annuities, (iii) accident and sickness insurance, (iv) insurance of marine risks or marine protection and indemnity risks, (v) workers' compensation or employers' liability risks, or (vi) risks covered by title insurance. (Code 1950, §§ 38-167, 38-168; 1952, c. 317, § 38.1-32; 1986, c. 562; 1987, c. 353; 1988, c. 554.)

Cross references. — As to compliance with this section by reciprocal insurers, see § 38.2-1203.

Editor's note. — Section 38.2-1316, referred to in subsection A, was repealed by Acts 1991, c. 264. For present reinsurance provisions, see § 38.2-1316.1 et seq.

§ **38.2-209. Award of insured's attorney fees in certain cases.** — A. Notwithstanding any provision of law to the contrary, in any civil case in which an insured individual sues his insurer to determine what coverage, if any, exists under his present policy or bond or the extent to which his insurer is liable for compensating a covered loss, the individual insured shall be entitled to recover from the insurer costs and such reasonable attorney fees as the court may award. However, these costs and attorney's fees shall not be awarded unless the court determines that the insurer, not acting in good faith, has either denied coverage or failed or refused to make payment to the insured under the policy. "Individual," as used in this section, shall mean and include any person, group, business, company, organization, receiver, trustee, security, corporation, partnership, association, or governmental body, and this definition is declaratory of existing policy.

B. Nothing in this section shall be deemed to grant a right to bring an action against an insurer by an insured who would otherwise lack standing to bring an action.

C. As used in this section, "insurer" shall include "self-insurer." (1982, c. 576, § 38.1-32.1; 1986, c. 562.)

Purpose. — Statute is both punitive and remedial in nature; it is designed to punish insurer guilty of bad faith in denying coverage or withholding payment and to reimburse insured who has been compelled by insurer's bad-faith conduct to incur expense of litigation. CUNA Mut. Ins. Soc'y v. Norman, 237 Va. 33, 375 S.E.2d 724 (1989) (decided under former § 38.1-32.1).

This section does not create cause of action, but merely permits the award of attorney fees where a private cause of action already exists. Salomon v. Transamerica Occidental Life Ins. Co., 801 F.2d 659 (4th Cir. 1986).

Plaintiff seeking attorney's fees based on common law principles can alternatively seek them under this section. Atlantic Permanent Fed. Sav. & Loan Ass'n v. American Cas. Co., 670 F. Supp. 168 (E.D. Va. 1986).

Bad faith. — In order to recover attorney's fees and costs under this section, a plaintiff must establish that the insurer acted in bad faith by denying coverage or refusing to make payment under the policy. Joseph P. Bornstein, Ltd. v. National Union Fire Ins. Co., 828 F.2d 242 (4th Cir. 1987).

An insured may be awarded attorney's fees generated in a suit against its insurer for a determination of coverage under the policy if it shows that the insurer, not acting in good faith, denied coverage or failed or refused to make payment to the insured under the policy, or an insured may seek the imposition of penalties for insurer's violations of the Unfair Insurance Practices Act. Ryder Truck Rental, Inc. v. UTF Carriers, Inc., 790 F. Supp. 637 (W.D. Va. 1992).

Bad faith analysis. — In evaluating conduct of insurer, courts should apply reasonableness standard; bad-faith analysis generally would require consideration of such questions as whether reasonable minds could differ in interpretation of policy provisions defining coverage and exclusions; whether insurer had made reasonable investigation of facts and circumstances underlying insured's claim; whether evidence discovered reasonably supports denial of liability; whether it appears that insurer's refusal to pay was used merely as tool in settlement negotiations; and whether defense insurer asserts at trial raises issue of first impression or reasonably debatable question of law or fact. CUNA Mut. Ins. Soc'y v. Norman, 237 Va. 33, 375 S.E.2d 724 (1989) (decided under former § 38.1-32.1).

Reliance on reasonable interpretation of policy. — Insurer should not be subjected to tort liability or to liability for insured's costs and fees simply because it refused to defend insured in reliance on its reasonable interpretation of the insurance policy. Joseph P. Bornstein, Ltd. v. National Union Fire Ins. Co., 828 F.2d 242 (4th Cir. 1987).

Insufficient evidence for awarding of attorney fees. — Where plaintiff presented no evidence that defendant acted in bad faith and where defendant's refusal to pay was substantially justified in that the legal and factual issues were unsettled, plaintiff may not recover attorney fees. Rush v. Hartford Mut. Ins. Co., 652 F. Supp. 1432 (W.D. Va. 1987).

No evidence of record was found to support trial judge's conclusion that insurer had not acted in good faith where testimonial and documentary evidence insurer adduced at trial showed that insurer had made thorough investigation of facts and circumstances underlying plaintiff's claim where determination of issue turned upon construction of word "livelihood," where issue was matter of first impression in jurisdiction. CUNA Mut. Ins. Soc'y v. Norman, 237 Va. 33, 375 S.E.2d 724 (1989) (decided under former § 38.1-32.1).

Punitive damages not authorized. — The Virginia legislature has provided for punishment and deterrence without authorizing punitive damages against errant insurance companies. Bettius & Sanderson v. National Union Fire Ins. Co., 839 F.2d 1009 (4th Cir. 1988).

Applied in A & E Supply Co. v. Nationwide Mut. Fire Ins. Co., 798 F.2d 669 (4th Cir. 1986), cert. denied, 479 U.S. 1091, 107 S. Ct. 1302, 94 L. Ed. 2d 158 (1987); Scottsdale Ins. Co. v. Glick, 240 Va. 283, 397 S.E.2d 105 (1990); Allison v. Continental Cas. Ins. Co., 953 F. Supp. 127 (E.D. Va. 1997).

§ 38.2-210. Loans to officers, directors, etc., prohibited. — A. Except as provided in § 38.2-212, no insurer, legal services plan, health services plan, dental or optometric services plan, health maintenance organization, or home protection company, transacting business in this Commonwealth shall make a loan, either directly or indirectly, to any of its officers or directors. No such company shall make a loan to any other corporation or business unit in which any of its officers or directors has a substantial interest. No such officer or director shall accept or receive any such loan directly or indirectly.

B. For the purposes of this section and of § 38.2-211, *"a substantial interest"* in any corporation or business unit means an interest equivalent to ownership or control of at least ten percent of its stock or its equivalent by an officer or director, or the aggregate ownership or control by all officers and directors of the same company. (Code 1950, § 38-4.1; 1952, c. 317, § 38.1-33; 1978, c. 701; 1986, c. 562.)

§ 38.2-211. Other interests and payments to officers, directors, etc., prohibited. — Except as provided in § 38.2-212, no officer or director of any company listed in § 38.2-210 and transacting business in this Commonwealth shall receive, directly, indirectly or through any substantial interest in any other corporation, any compensation for negotiating, procuring, recommending, or aiding in the purchase or sale of property by such company, or in obtaining any loan from the company. No such officer or director shall be pecuniarily interested, either as principal, agent, or beneficiary, in any such purchase, sale or loan. No financial obligation of any such officer or director shall be guaranteed by the company. (Code 1950, § 38-4.2; 1952, c. 317, § 38.1-34; 1978, c. 701; 1986, c. 562.)

§ 38.2-212. Certain compensation not prohibited. — A. Nothing contained in §§ 38.2-210 and 38.2-211 shall prohibit any officer or director of any company listed in § 38.2-210 from receiving usual compensation for services rendered in the ordinary course of his duties as an officer or director, if the compensation is authorized by vote of the board of directors or other governing body of the company. Nor shall the provisions of §§ 38.2-210 and 38.2-211 prohibit the payment to an officer or director of any such company who is a licensed attorney-at-law of a fee in connection with loans made by the company if and when those fees are paid by the borrower and do not constitute a charge against the company.

B. Nothing contained in this chapter shall prohibit a life insurer from making a loan upon a policy of insurance issued by it and held by the borrower. This loan shall not exceed the net cash value of the policy. Nothing contained in this chapter shall prohibit any company from (i) making a loan on real property owned by the officer and improved with a dwelling that is to serve as his residence if the loan qualifies under subdivision 1 of § 38.2-1434 and under § 38.2-1437 or (ii) acquiring the residence of the officer in conformance with subsection D of § 38.2-1441 if the transaction is in connection with the relocation of the place of employment of an officer who is neither a director nor a trustee of the company.

C. Nothing contained in § 38.2-211 shall prohibit a director of any such company from receiving compensation that is usual and customary in the director's business with respect to transactions in the ordinary course of business of the company and of the director. Prior to payment of the compensation, written request for the Commission's approval shall be made. This written request shall set forth under oath complete details concerning the transactions that the company intends to conduct with a director. Any approval given by the Commission shall be in writing. No approval granted under this subsection shall imply that the Commission approves any investment of any company. (Code 1950, § 38-4.3; 1952, c. 317, § 38.1-35; 1977, c. 261; 1978, c. 701; 1981, c. 272; 1983, c. 457; 1986, c. 562; 1992, c. 588.)

§ 38.2-213. Violation of § 38.2-210 or § 38.2-211. — Any company, officer or director violating any provision of § 38.2-210 or § 38.2-211 shall be guilty upon conviction of a Class 1 misdemeanor. Any funds of any company invested or used in violation of either of § 38.2-210 or § 38.2-211 may not be allowed as admitted assets of the company. (Code 1950, § 38-4.4; 1952, c. 317, § 38.1-36; 1986, c. 562.)

Cross references. — As to punishment for Class 1 misdemeanors, see § 18.2-11.

§ 38.2-214. Restrictions upon purchase and sale of equity securities of domestic stock insurers. — A. Each person who is directly or indirectly the beneficial owner of more than ten percent of a class of any equity security of a domestic insurer, or who is a director or an officer of a domestic stock insurer, shall file a statement with the Commission within ten days after becoming a beneficial owner, director or officer. This statement shall be in a form prescribed by the Commission and shall show the amount of all the domestic insurer's equity securities of which he is the beneficial owner. Within ten days after the close of each calendar month, if there has been a change in his ownership during such month, the person shall file with the Commission a statement prescribed by the Commission indicating his ownership at the close of the calendar month and such changes in his ownership as have occurred during such calendar month.

B. To prevent the unfair use of information obtained by any beneficial owner, director or officer, any profit realized by such person within six months from the purchase and sale, or any sale and purchase, of any of the insurer's equity securities shall inure to and be recoverable by the insurer. This provision shall apply regardless of any intention of the beneficial owner, director or officer to hold the equity security purchased or not to repurchase any sold equity security for a period exceeding six months. However, this provision shall not apply if the security was acquired in good faith in connection with a debt previously contracted. The insurer may sue at law or in equity to recover the profit in any court of competent jurisdiction. The owner of any equity security of the insurer may sue in the name and in behalf of the insurer if the insurer fails or refuses to bring suit within sixty days after request or if the insurer fails to diligently prosecute after bringing suit. No suit under this subsection shall be brought more than two years after the date the profit was realized. This subsection shall not be construed to cover any transaction where the person was not the beneficial owner at the time of either the purchase or sale of the equity security involved. The Commission may by rules and regulations exempt from the provisions of this subsection any transaction that is not comprehended within the purpose of this subsection.

C. No beneficial owner, director or officer shall directly or indirectly sell any equity security of the insurer if the person selling the security or his principal (i) does not own the security sold, or (ii) owns the equity security but does not deliver it within twenty days after the sale or does not mail it within five days after the sale. No person shall be deemed to have violated this subsection if he proves that, notwithstanding the exercise of good faith, he was unable to deliver or mail the security within the required time, or that to do so would cause undue inconvenience or expense. Any person violating this subsection shall be guilty upon conviction of a Class 1 misdemeanor.

D. Subsections B and C of this section shall not apply to the transactions of a dealer in an investment account that are conducted in the ordinary course of a dealer's business and incident to the establishment or maintenance of an equity security's primary or secondary market, other than on an exchange defined in the Securities Exchange Act of 1934. The Commission may, by rules and regulations, define and prescribe terms and conditions with respect to equity securities held in an investment account and transactions made in the ordinary course of business and incident to the establishment or maintenance of a primary or secondary market.

E. Subsections A, B, and C of this section shall not apply to foreign or domestic arbitrage transactions unless made in contravention of rules and regulations adopted by the Commission to carry out the purposes of this section.

F. The term *"equity security"* when used in this section means (i) any stock or similar security, (ii) any security that is convertible, with or without consideration, into another security, (iii) any security that carries any warrant or right to subscribe to or purchase a security, or (iv) any warrant, right or other security that the Commission, by rules and regulations, deems to be similar in nature to an equity security and considers the classification necessary or appropriate for protecting the public or an investor's interest.

G. Subsections A, B, and C of this section shall not apply to equity securities of a domestic stock insurer if (i) those equity securities are registered or are required to be registered pursuant to § 12 of the Securities Exchange Act of 1934, as amended; or (ii) the domestic stock insurer does not have any class of its equity securities held of record by 100 or more persons on the last business day of the year immediately preceding the year in which equity securities of the insurer would be subject to subsections A, B, and C of this section.

H. The Commission may adopt rules and regulations pursuant to § 38.2-223 for the execution of the functions vested in it by subsections A through G of this section. The Commission may classify for that purpose any domestic stock insurers, equity securities, and other persons or matters within its jurisdiction. The Commission may exempt from the provisions of this section any officer, director or beneficial owner of equity securities of any domestic stock insurer under the terms and conditions, and for the period of time the Commission considers necessary or appropriate if the Commission finds that the action is consistent with the public interest or the protection of investors. Any such exemption may be accomplished by (i) rules and regulations issued pursuant to § 38.2-223 or (ii) by order, upon application of any interested person, after due notice and an opportunity for hearing has been given. No provision of subsections A, B, and C of this section imposing any liability shall apply to any act done or omitted in good faith in conformity with any rule or regulation of the Commission. Notwithstanding the provisions of this subsection, such rule or regulation may be amended, rescinded or determined by judicial or other authority to be invalid for any reason after the act or omission has occurred. (1966, c. 265, § 38.1-36.1; 1986, c. 562.)

Cross references. — As to punishment for Class 1 misdemeanors, see § 18.2-11.

§ **38.2-215. Liability of president, chief executive officer or directors if insurance issued when insurer insolvent.** — If any insurer is insolvent, and the president, chief executive officer or directors with knowledge of insolvency make or agree to further insurance, they shall be personally liable for any loss under that insurance. (Code 1950, § 38-176; 1952, c. 317, § 38.1-37; 1986, c. 562.)

§ **38.2-216. Restrictions on removal or transfer of property and on reinsurance; penalty.** — A. No domestic insurer shall remove from this

Commonwealth either all or substantially all of its property or business without the written approval of the Commission.

B. No domestic insurer shall transfer or attempt to transfer substantially its entire property, or enter into any transaction the effect of which is to merge substantially its entire property or business into the property or business of any other company, without prior written approval of the Commission.

C. No domestic insurer shall reinsure with any other insurer all or substantially all of its risks without prior written approval of the Commission of the reinsurance and of the contract under which reinsurance is effected.

D. Any director or officer of the insurer consenting to and participating in any violation of this section shall be guilty of a Class 1 misdemeanor. (Code 1950, § 38-6; 1952, c. 317, § 38.1-38; 1986, c. 562.)

Cross references. — As to punishment for Class 1 misdemeanors, see § 18.2-11.

§ 38.2-217. When assets may not be distributed among stockholders. — No domestic insurer shall distribute its assets among its stockholders until all risks have expired or have been cancelled, or have been replaced by the policies of another solvent insurer licensed to transact the business of insurance in this Commonwealth, and until all claims against the insurer have been settled. No insurer shall contract to reinsure its risks for the purpose of distributing its assets without first obtaining the written approval of the Commission. However, nothing in this section shall be construed to prohibit the lawful payment of dividends. (Code 1950, §§ 38-170, 38-171; 1952, c. 317, § 38.1-39; 1986, c. 562.)

§ 38.2-218. Penalties and restitution payments. — A. Any person who knowingly or willfully violates any provision of this title or any regulation issued pursuant to this title shall be punished for each violation by a penalty of not more than $5,000.

B. Any person who violates without knowledge or intent any provision of this title or any rule, regulation, or order issued pursuant to this title may be punished for each violation by a penalty of not more than $1,000. For the purpose of this subsection, a series of similar violations resulting from the same act shall be limited to a penalty in the aggregate of not more than $10,000.

C. Any violation resulting solely from a malfunction of mechanical or electronic equipment shall not be subject to a penalty.

D. 1. The Commission may require a person to make restitution in the amount of the direct actual financial loss:

a. For charging a rate in excess of that provided by statute or by the rates filed with the Commission by the insurer;

b. For charging a premium that is determined by the Commission to be unfairly discriminatory, such restitution being limited to a period of one year from the date of determination; and

c. For failing to pay amounts explicitly required by the terms of the insurance contract where no aspect of the claim is disputed by the insurer.

2. The Commission shall have no jurisdiction to adjudicate controversies growing out of this subsection regarding restitution among insurers, insureds, agents, claimants and beneficiaries.

E. The provisions provided under this section may be imposed in addition to or without imposing any other penalties or actions provided by law. (Code 1950, § 38-24; 1952, c. 317, § 38.1-40; 1986, c. 562.)

An insured may be awarded attorney's fees generated in a suit against its insurer for a determination of coverage under the policy if it shows that the insurer, not acting in good faith, denied coverage or failed or refused to make payment to the insured under the policy, or an insured may seek the imposition of penalties for insurer's violations of the Unfair Insurance Practices Act. Ryder Truck Rental, Inc. v. UTF Carriers, Inc., 790 F. Supp. 637 (W.D. Va. 1992).

§ 38.2-219. Violations; procedure; cease and desist orders. —

A. Whenever the Commission has reason to believe that any person has committed a violation of this title or of any rule, regulation, or order issued by the Commission under this title, it shall issue and serve an order upon that person by certified or registered mail or in any other manner permitted by law. The order shall include a statement of the charges and a notice of a hearing on the charges to be held at a fixed time and place which shall be at least ten days after the date of service of the notice. The order shall require that person to show cause why an order should not be made by the Commission directing the alleged offender to cease and desist from the violation or to show cause why the Commission should not issue any other appropriate order as the nature of the case and the interests of the policyholders, creditors, shareholders, or the public may require. At the hearing, that person shall have an opportunity to be heard in accordance with the Commission's order. In all matters in connection with the charges or hearing, the Commission shall have the jurisdiction, power and authority granted or conferred upon it by Title 12.1 and, except as otherwise provided in this title, the procedure shall conform to and the right of appeal shall be the same as that provided in Title 12.1.

B. If the Commission finds in the hearing that there is about to be or has been a violation of this title, it may issue and serve upon any person committing the violation by certified or registered mail or in any other manner permitted by law (i) an order reciting its findings and directing the person to cease and desist from the violation or (ii) such other appropriate order as the nature of the case and the interests of the policyholders, creditors, shareholders, or the public requires.

C. Any person who violates any order issued under subsection B of this section may upon conviction be subject to one or both of the following:

1. Punishment as provided in § 38.2-218; or

2. The suspension or revocation of any license issued by the Commission. (1952, c. 317, §§ 38.1-54, 38.1-55, 38.1-60 through 38.1-62; 1971, Ex. Sess., c. 1; 1973, c. 505, § 38.1-178.7; 1977, c. 414, § 38.1-178.17; 1977, c. 529; 1980, c. 404; 1982, c. 223, § 38.1-482.14:1; 1986, c. 562.)

§ 38.2-220. Injunctions. —

The Commission shall have the jurisdiction and powers of a court of equity to issue temporary and permanent injunctions restraining acts which violate or attempt to violate provisions of this title and to enforce the injunctions by civil penalty or imprisonment. (Code 1950, § 32-195.17; 1956, c. 268, § 38.1-830; 1978, c. 658, § 38.1-806; 1979, c. 721; 1980, c. 682, § 38.1-911; c. 720, § 38.1-884; 1981, c. 530, § 38.1-946; 1986, c. 562.)

§ 38.2-221. Enforcement of penalties. —

The Commission may impose, enter judgment for, and enforce any civil penalty or other penalty pronounced against any person for violating any of the provisions of this title, subject to the hearing provisions of § 12.1-28. The power and authority conferred upon the Commission by this section shall be in addition to and not in substitution for the power and authority conferred upon the courts by general law to impose civil penalties for violations of the laws of this Commonwealth. (Code 1950, § 38-26; 1952, c. 317, § 38.1-41; 1986, c. 562.)

§ 38.2-222. Appeals generally. — Except as otherwise specifically provided in this title, § 12.1-39 shall apply to the appeal of any final (i) finding, (ii) decision settling the substantive law, (iii) order, or (iv) judgment of the Commission issued pursuant to this title. (1986, c. 562.)

§ 38.2-223. Rules and regulations; orders. — The Commission, after notice and opportunity for all interested parties to be heard, may issue any rules and regulations necessary or appropriate for the administration and enforcement of this title. (1986, c. 562.)

§ 38.2-224. Procedures. — Except as otherwise specifically provided in this title, Chapter 5 (§ 12.1-25 et seq.) of Title 12.1 shall apply to proceedings under this title. (1986, c. 562.)

§ 38.2-225. Disposition of fines and penalties. — A. All fines recovered for criminal violations of this title or for criminal violations of rules, regulations, or orders issued pursuant to this title shall be paid into the state treasury to the credit of the Literary Fund.

B. All penalties and compromise settlements recovered for civil violations of this title or civil violations of rules, regulations, or orders issued pursuant to this title shall be paid into the state treasury. Pursuant to §§ 38.2-1620 and 38.2-1718 these funds shall be credited to the Literary Fund or if the Commission determines a need, to either (i) the Virginia Property and Casualty Insurance Guaranty Association established pursuant to Chapter 16 of this title or (ii) the Virginia Life, Accident and Sickness Insurance Guaranty Association established pursuant to Chapter 17 of this title. (Code 1950, § 38-25; 1952, c. 317, § 38.1-42; 1986, c. 562.)

§ 38.2-226. Provisions of title not to apply to certain mutual aid associations. — This title shall not apply to beneficial, relief, or mutual aid societies, or partnerships, plans, associations, or corporations, established prior to 1935 and formed by churches for the purpose of aiding members who sustain property losses by fire, lightning, hail, storm, flood, explosion, power failure, theft, burglary, vandalism, civil commotion, airplane and vehicular damage, and in which the privileges and memberships in these societies, partnerships, plans, associations, or corporations are confined to members of the churches. (1981, c. 171, § 38.1-42.1; 1985, c. 361; 1986, c. 562.)

§ 38.2-226.1: Expired.

Editor's note. — Acts 1996, c. 628, which enacted this section, provided for its expiration on July 1, 1997, pursuant to clause 2 of the 1996 legislation. Acts 1997, cc. 414 and 475, amended the text of the section, but did not amend the expiration clause. Therefore, at the direction of the Code Commission, this section is now set out as expired.

§ 38.2-226.2. Provisions of title not applicable to certain long-term care health plans. — A. This title shall not apply to pre-PACE long-term care health plans (i) authorized by the United States Health Care Financing Administration pursuant to § 1903 (m) (2) (B) of Title XIX of the United States Social Security Act (42 U.S.C. § 1396b et seq.) and the state plan for medical assistance services as established pursuant to Chapter 10 (§ 32.1-323 et seq.) of Title 32.1 and (ii) which have signed agreements with the Department of Medical Assistance Services as long-term care health plans.

B. This title shall not apply to PACE long-term care health plans (i) authorized as programs of all-inclusive care for the elderly by Subtitle I

(§ 4801 et seq.) of Chapter 6 of Title IV of the Balanced Budget Act of 1997, Pub. L. No. 105-33, 111 Stat. 528 et seq., §§ 4801-4804, 1997, pursuant to Title XVIII and Title XIX of the United States Social Security Act (42 U.S.C. § 1395eee et seq.) and the state plan for medical assistance services as established pursuant to Chapter 10 (§ 32.1-323 et seq.) of Title 32.1 and (ii) which have signed agreements with the Department of Medical Assistance Services as long-term care health plans.

C. Enrollment in a pre-PACE or PACE plan shall be restricted to those individuals who participate in programs authorized pursuant to Title XIX or Title XVIII of the United States Social Security Act, respectively. (1998, c. 318.)

§ **38.2-227. Public policy regarding punitive damages.** — It is not against the public policy of the Commonwealth for any person to purchase insurance providing coverage for punitive damages arising out of the death or injury of any person as the result of negligence, including willful and wanton negligence, but excluding intentional acts. This section declares existing policy. (1983, c. 353, § 38.1-42.2; 1986, c. 562.)

No punitive damages in property damage cases. — This section does not extend to awards of punitive damages in property damage cases. United States Fire Ins. Co. v. Aspen Bldg. Corp., 235 Va. 263, 367 S.E.2d 478 (1988).

§ **38.2-228. Proof of future financial responsibility.** — At the request of a named insured, a licensed property and casualty insurer shall provide without unreasonable delay to the Commissioner of the Department of Motor Vehicles proof of future financial responsibility as required by the provisions of Title 46.2. (1986, c. 562.)

§ **38.2-229. Immunity from liability.** — A. There shall be no liability on the part of and no cause of action against any person for furnishing in good faith to the Commission information relating to the investigation of any insurance or reinsurance transaction when such information is furnished under the requirements of law or at the request or direction of the Commission.

B. There shall be no liability on the part of and no cause of action against the Commission, the Commissioner of Insurance, or any of the Commission's employees or agents, acting in good faith, for investigating any insurance or reinsurance transaction or for the dissemination of any official report related to an official investigation of any insurance or reinsurance transaction. (1986, c. 562.)

§ **38.2-230. Distributions by nonstock corporation.** — No dividend or distribution of income, as used in § 13.1-814, shall be made to a member corporation of a corporation licensed under the provisions of this title unless the corporation has received approval by the Commission prior to the distribution. In approving the distribution, the Commission shall give consideration to the subscribers' or policyholders' best interest. (1985, c. 380, § 38.1-39.1; 1986, c. 562.)

§ **38.2-231. Notice of cancellation, refusal to renew, reduction in coverage or increase in rate of certain liability insurance policies.** — A. 1. No cancellation or refusal to renew by an insurer of a policy of insurance as defined in § 38.2-117 or § 38.2-118 insuring a business entity, or a policy of insurance that includes as a part thereof insurance as defined in § 38.2-117 or § 38.2-118 insuring a business entity, or a policy of motor vehicle insurance against legal liability of the insured as defined in § 38.2-124 insuring a business entity, shall be effective unless the insurer delivers or mails to the named insured at the address shown on the policy a written notice of cancellation or refusal to renew. Such notice shall:

a. Be in a type size authorized under § 38.2-311;

b. State the date, which shall not be less than forty-five days after the delivery or mailing of the notice of cancellation or refusal to renew, on which such cancellation or refusal to renew shall become effective, except that such effective date may not be less than fifteen days from the date of mailing or delivery when the policy is being cancelled or not renewed for failure of the insured to discharge when due any of its obligations in connection with the payment of premium for the policy;

c. State the specific reason or reasons of the insurer for cancellation or refusal to renew;

d. Advise the insured of its right to request in writing, within fifteen days of the receipt of the notice, that the Commissioner of Insurance review the action of the insurer; and

e. In the case of a policy of motor vehicle insurance, inform the insured of the possible availability of other insurance which may be obtained through its agent, through another insurer, or through the Virginia Automobile Insurance Plan.

2. Nothing in this subsection shall apply to any policy of insurance if the named insured or his duly constituted attorney-in-fact has notified orally, or in writing, if the insurer requires such notification to be in writing, the insurer or its agent that he wishes the policy to be canceled or that he does not wish the policy to be renewed, or if, prior to the date of expiration, he fails to accept the offer of the insurer to renew the policy.

B. No insurer shall cancel or refuse to renew a policy of motor vehicle insurance against legal liability of the insured as defined in § 38.2-124 insuring a business entity solely because of lack of supporting business or lack of the potential for acquiring such business.

C. No reduction in coverage for personal injury or property damage liability initiated by an insurer and no increase in the filed rate for such coverage greater than twenty-five percent initiated by an insurer of a policy of insurance defined in § 38.2-117 or § 38.2-118 insuring a business entity, or of a policy of insurance that includes as a part thereof insurance defined in § 38.2-117 or § 38.2-118 insuring a business entity, or a policy of motor vehicle insurance against legal liability of the insured as defined in § 38.2-124 insuring a business entity, and which in the case of a reduction in coverage is subject to § 38.2-1912, shall be effective unless the insurer delivers or mails to the named insured at the address shown on the policy a written notice of such reduction in coverage or rate increase not later than forty-five days prior to the effective date of same. Such notice shall:

1. Be in a type size authorized under § 38.2-311;

2. State the date, which shall not be less than forty-five days after the delivery or mailing of the notice of reduction in coverage or increase in rate, on which such reduction in coverage or increase in rate shall become effective;

3. State the manner in which coverage under an existing policy will be reduced or the amount of such rate increase;

4. State the specific reason or reasons for the reduction in coverage or increase in rate;

5. Advise the insured of its right to request in writing, within fifteen days of receipt of the notice, that the Commissioner of Insurance review the action of the insurer.

D. If an insurer does not provide notice in the manner required in subsection C, coverage shall remain in effect until forty-five days after written notice of reduction in coverage or increase in rate is mailed or delivered to the insured at the address shown on the policy, unless the insured obtains replacement coverage or elects to cancel sooner in either of which cases coverage under the prior policy shall cease on the effective date of the replacement coverage or the elected date of cancellation as the case may be. If the insured fails to accept or rejects the changed policy, coverage for any period that extends beyond the expiration date will be under the prior policy's terms and conditions. If the insured accepts the changed policy, the reduction in coverage or increase in rate shall take effect upon the expiration of the prior policy.

E. Notice of reduction in coverage or increase in rate shall not be required if the insurer, after written demand, has not received, within forty-five days after such demand has been mailed or delivered to the insured at the address shown on the policy, sufficient information from the insured to provide the required notice, or if such notice is waived in writing by the insured.

F. No written notice of cancellation, refusal to renew, reduction in coverage or increase in rate that is mailed by an insurer to an insured in accordance with this section shall be effective unless:

1. a. It is sent by registered or certified mail, or

b. At the time of mailing the insurer obtains a written receipt from the United States Postal Service showing the name and address of the insured stated in the policy; and

2. The insurer retains a copy of the notice of cancellation, refusal to renew, reduction in coverage or increase in rate.

3. If the terms of a policy of motor vehicle insurance insuring a business entity require the notice of cancellation, refusal to renew, reduction in coverage or increase in rate to be given to any lienholder, then the insurer shall mail such notice and retain a copy of the notice in the manner required by this subsection. If the notices sent to the insured and the lienholder are part of the same form, the insurer may retain a single copy of the notice. The registered, certified or regular mail postal receipt and the copy of the notices required by this subsection shall be retained by the insurer for at least one year from the date of termination.

4. Copy, as used in this subsection, shall include photographs, microphotographs, photostats, microfilm, microcard, printouts or other reproductions of electronically stored data, or copies from optical disks, electronically transmitted facsimiles, or any other reproduction of an original from a process which forms a durable medium for its recording, storing, and reproducing.

G. Nothing in this section shall prohibit any insurer or agent from including in a notice of cancellation, refusal to renew, reduction in coverage or rate increase any additional disclosure statements required by state or federal laws.

H. For the purpose of this section the terms (i) *"business entity"* shall mean an entity as defined by subsection B of §§ 13.1-543, 13.1-603 or § 13.1-803 and shall include an individual, a partnership, an unincorporated association, the Commonwealth, a county, city, town, or an authority, board, commission, sanitation, soil and water, planning or other district, public service corporation owned, operated or controlled by the Commonwealth, a locality or other local governmental authority, (ii) "policy of motor vehicle insurance" shall mean a policy or contract for bodily injury or property damage liability insuring a business entity issued or delivered in this Commonwealth covering liability arising from the ownership, maintenance, or use of any motor vehicle, but does not include (a) any policy issued through the Virginia Automobile Insurance Plan, (b) any policy providing insurance only on an excess basis, or (c) any other contract providing insurance to the named insured even though the contract may incidentally provide insurance on motor vehicles, and (iii) "reduction in coverage" shall mean, but not be limited to, any diminution in scope of coverage, decrease in limits of liability, addition of exclusions, increase in deductibles, or reduction in the policy term or duration except a reduction in coverage filed with and approved by the Commission and applicable to an entire line, classification or subclassification of insurance.

I. Within fifteen days of receipt of the notice of cancellation, refusal to renew, reduction in coverage or increase in rate, the insured shall be entitled to request in writing to the Commissioner that he review the action of the insurer. Upon receipt of the request, the Commissioner shall promptly begin a review to determine whether the insurer's notice of cancellation, refusal to renew, reduction in coverage or rate increase complies with the requirements of this section. Where the Commissioner finds from the review that the notice of cancellation, refusal to renew, reduction in coverage or rate increase does not comply with the requirements of this section, he shall immediately notify the insurer, the insured and any other person to whom such notice was required to be given by the terms of the policy that such notice is not effective. Nothing in this section authorizes the Commissioner to substitute his judgment as to underwriting for that of the insurer. Pending review by the Commission, this section shall not operate to relieve an insured from the obligation to pay any premium when due; however, if the Commission finds that the notice required by this section was not proper, the Commission may order the insurer to pay to the insured any overpayment of premium made by the insured.

J. Every insurer shall maintain for at least one year records of cancellation, refusals to renew, reductions in coverage and rate increases to which this section applies and copies of every notice or statement required by subsections A, C and F of this section that it sends to any of its insureds.

K. There shall be no liability on the part of and no cause of action of any nature shall arise against (i) the Commissioner of Insurance or his subordinates, (ii) any insurer, its authorized representative, its agents, or its employees, or (iii) any firm, person or corporation furnishing to the insurer information as to reasons for cancellation, refusal to renew, reduction in coverage or rate increase, for any statement made by any of them in complying with this section or for providing information pertaining thereto. (1986, c. 376, § 38.1-43.01; 1987, c. 697; 1988, c. 189; 1989, c. 728; 1992, c. 160; 1996, c. 237; 1998, c. 142.)

Editor's note. — This section was enacted as § 38.1-43.01 by Acts 1986, c. 376. Pursuant to § 9-77.11, this section has been incorporated into Title 38.2 as § 38.2-231.

The 1998 amendment, in subdivision A 2, inserted "orally, or," and inserted "if the insurer requires such notification to be in writing."

§ 38.2-232. Notice of lapse or pending lapse of certain life and accident and sickness insurance policies.

— Every insurer, health services plan, or health care plan that issues a policy, contract, or plan of insurance or annuity as defined in §§ 38.2-102 through 38.2-109 shall provide the policy owner, contract owner, or plan owner with a written notice prior to the date that the policy, contract, or plan will lapse for failure to pay premiums due.

This section shall not apply (i) to policies, contracts, or plans of group insurance, (ii) where the insurer, health services plan, or health care plan, as a general business practice, provides its policy owners, contract owners, or plan owners with written notices of premiums due, or (iii) where the insurer, health services plan, or health care plan has furnished its policy owner, contract owner, or plan owner with written notice separate from that contained in the policy that the failure to pay premiums in a timely manner will result in a lapse of such policy, contract or plan. (1991, c. 369.)

§ 38.2-233. Credit involuntary unemployment insurance; disclosure and readability. — A. If a creditor makes available to the debtors more than one plan of credit involuntary unemployment insurance as defined in § 38.2-122.1, all debtors must be informed of all such plans for which they are eligible.

B. When elective credit involuntary unemployment insurance is offered, the borrower shall be given written disclosure that purchase of credit involuntary unemployment insurance is not required and is not a factor in granting credit. The disclosure shall also include notice that the borrower has the right to use alternative coverage or to buy insurance elsewhere.

C. If the debtor is given a contract which includes a single premium payment to be charged for elective credit involuntary unemployment insurance, the debtor shall be given:

1. A contract which does not include the elective credit involuntary unemployment insurance premium; or

2. A disclosure form which shall clearly disclose the difference in premiums charged for a contract with credit involuntary unemployment insurance and one without credit involuntary unemployment insurance. This disclosure shall include the difference between the amount financed, the monthly payment and the charge for insurance. The form shall be signed and dated by the debtor and the agent, if any, soliciting the application or the creditor's representative, if any, soliciting the enrollment request. A copy of this disclosure shall be given to the debtor and a copy shall be made a part of the creditor's loan file.

Nothing contained in this subsection shall be construed to prohibit the creditor from combining such disclosure, in order to avoid redundancy, with other forms of disclosure required under state or federal law.

D. If credit involuntary unemployment insurance is required as security for any indebtedness, the debtor shall have the option of (i) furnishing the required amount of insurance through existing policies of insurance owned or controlled by him or (ii) procuring and furnishing the required coverage through any insurer authorized to transact insurance in this Commonwealth. The creditor shall inform the debtor of this option in writing and shall obtain the debtor's signature acknowledging that he understands this option. Nothing contained in this subsection shall be construed to prohibit the creditor from combining such disclosure, in order to avoid redundancy, with other forms of disclosure required under state or federal law.

E. The disclosure requirements set forth in subsections A, B, C and D shall be separately disclosed in another form or forms approved by the Commission. Notwithstanding the provisions of § 38.2-1921, when credit involuntary unemployment insurance is offered with credit life insurance or credit accident and sickness insurance, the disclosure requirements set forth in subsections A, B, C and D of § 38.2-233 and the disclosure requirements set forth in subsections A, B, C and D of § 38.2-3735 may be disclosed together in a form which shall be approved by the Commission.

F. The Commission shall not approve any form providing credit involuntary unemployment insurance unless the policy or certificate is written in nontechnical, readily understandable language, using words of common everyday usage. A form shall be deemed acceptable under this section if the insurer certifies that the form achieves a Flesch Readability Score of forty or more, using the Flesch Readability Formula as set forth in Rudolf Flesch, The Art of Readable Writing (1949, as revised 1974), and certifies compliance with the guidelines set forth in this section.

G. A credit involuntary unemployment insurance policy or certificate which provides truncated or critical period coverage, or any other type of similar coverage that does not provide benefits or coverage for the entire term or amount of the indebtedness, shall be subject to the following requirements:

1. The credit involuntary unemployment insurance policy or certificate shall include a statement printed on the face of the policy or first page of the

certificate which clearly describes the limited nature of the insurance. The statement shall be printed in capital letters and in bold twelve-point or larger type; and

2. The credit involuntary unemployment insurance policy or certificate shall not include any benefits or coverage other than truncated or critical period coverage or any other type of similar coverage that does not provide benefits or coverage for the entire term or amount of the indebtedness.

H. A portion of the premium charged for credit involuntary unemployment insurance may be allowed by the insurer to the creditor for providing and furnishing such insurance, and no such allowance shall be deemed a rebate of premium or as interest charges or consideration or an amount in excess of permitted charges in connection with the loan or other credit transaction.

I. All of the acts necessary to provide and service credit involuntary unemployment insurance may be performed within the same place of business in which is transacted the business giving rise to the loan or other credit transaction.

J. Subsections A, B, C, D, E and K shall not apply to credit involuntary unemployment insurance that will insure open end monthly outstanding balance credit transactions if the following criteria are met:

1. Credit involuntary unemployment insurance that will insure the open end monthly outstanding balance credit transaction is offered to the debtor after the loan or credit transaction it will insure has been approved by the creditor and has been effective at least seven days;

2. The solicitation for the insurance is by mail or telephone. The person making the solicitation shall not condition the future use or continuation of the open end credit upon the purchase of credit involuntary unemployment insurance;

3. The creditor makes available only one plan of credit involuntary unemployment insurance to the debtor;

4. The debtor is provided written confirmation of the insurance coverage within thirty days of the effective date of such coverage. The effective date of such coverage shall begin on the date the solicitation is accepted; and

5. The individual policy or certificate has printed on it a notice stating that if, during a period of at least thirty days from the date the policy or certificate is delivered to the policy owner or certificate holder, the policy or certificate is surrendered to the insurer or its agent with a written request for cancellation, the policy or certificate shall be void from the beginning and the insurer shall refund any premium paid for the policy or certificate. This statement shall be prominently located on the face page of the policy or certificate, and shall be printed in capital letters and in bold face twelve-point or larger type.

K. Subsections A, B, C, D, E and J shall not apply to open end credit transactions by mail, telephone or brochure solicitations that are not excluded from the requirements of subsections A, B, C, D and E by subsection J where the insurer is offering only one plan of credit involuntary unemployment insurance and the following criteria are met:

1. The following disclosures shall be included in solicitations, whether as part of the application or enrollment request or separately:

a. The name and address of the insurer(s) and creditor; and

b. A description of the coverage offered, including the amount of coverage, the premium rate for the insurance coverage offered, and a description of any exceptions, limitations or restrictions applicable to such coverage.

2. The application or enrollment requests shall comply as follows:

a. Notwithstanding requirements set forth elsewhere, the application and enrollment request shall be printed in a type size of not less than eight-point type, one-point leaded;

b. The application or enrollment request shall contain a prominent statement that the insurance offered is optional, voluntary or not required;

c. The application or enrollment request shall contain no questions relating to insurability other than the debtor's age or date of birth and active employment status; and

d. If the disclosures required by subdivision 1 of this subsection are not included in the application or enrollment request, the application and enrollment request shall make reference to such disclosures with sufficient information to assist the reader in locating such disclosures within separate solicitation material.

3. Each insurer proposing to utilize an application or enrollment request in such transactions shall file such form for approval by the Commission. If the insurer anticipates utilizing such application or enrollment form in more than one solicitation, the insurer shall submit, as part of its filing of such form, a certification signed by an officer of the insurer, stating that any such subsequent use of the application or enrollment form will utilize the same form number and will not vary in substance from the wording and format in which the form is submitted for approval. Upon approval of such application or enrollment form by the Commission, the insurer shall be permitted to utilize such form in various solicitation materials provided that the application or enrollment form, when incorporated into such solicitation materials, has the same form number and wording substantially identical to that contained on the approved application or enrollment form. Notwithstanding the provisions of § 38.2-1921, when credit involuntary unemployment insurance is offered with credit life insurance or credit accident and sickness insurance, insurers may file one common form which shall be approved by the Commission and shall incorporate the requirements of subsection K of § 38.2-233 and subsection F of § 38.2-3737, according to the requirements stated in this paragraph and in subdivision F 3 of § 38.2-3737. (1993, c. 774; 1994, c. 306; 1995, c. 167; 1999, c. 586.)

The 1999 amendment, in subsection C, inserted "if any" in two places in the third sentence of sudivision 2, and added the concluding paragraph, added the last sentence in subsection D, in subsection F, added the last sentence, deleted former subdivision 1, which read: "Each insurer is required to test the readability of its policies or certificates by use of the Flesch Readability Formula, as set forth in Rudolf Flesch, The Art of Readable Writing (1949, as revised 1974)," deleted former subdivision 2, which read: "A total readability score of forty or more on the Flesch score is required; and," and deleted former subdivision 3, which read: "All policies or certificates within the scope of this section shall be filed with the Commission, accompanied by a certificate setting forth the Flesch score and certifying compliance with the guidelines set forth in this section," and substituted "the insurance coverage" for "each plan of insurance" in subdivision K 1 b.

Applied in Employers Resource Mgt. Co. v. Shannon, 65 F.3d 1126 (4th Cir. 1995).

§ 38.2-234. Release of information. — Notwithstanding the provisions of subdivision 5 of § 2.1-384, the Commission may share information with databases developed by the National Association of Insurance Commissioners (NAIC) for use by regulators. (1996, c. 32.)

§ 38.2-235. Liability insurance; carbon monoxide exclusions. — No policy of insurance furnishing personal injury liability or property damage liability coverage as defined in §§ 38.2-117 and 38.2-118, including any endorsements thereto, shall be deemed to exclude coverage for the discharge, dispersal, seepage, migration, release, emission, leakage or escape of carbon monoxide from a residential or commercial heating system unless excluded in such policy by explicit reference thereto. (1997, c. 157.)

CHAPTER 3.

PROVISIONS RELATING TO INSURANCE POLICIES AND CONTRACTS.

§ 38.2-300. Scope of chapter. — This chapter shall apply to all classes of insurance except:

1. Ocean marine insurance other than private pleasure vessels;

2. Life insurance policies and accident and sickness insurance policies not delivered or issued for delivery in this Commonwealth;

3. Contracts of reinsurance; or

4. Annuities, except as provided for in §§ 38.2-305, 38.2-316 and 38.2-321. (1952, c. 317, § 38.1-328; 1986, c. 562; 1988, cc. 333, 523.)

Law Review. — For note on insurance contracts and methods of interpretation, see 18 Wash. & Lee L. Rev. 104 (1961). For note on fraud as a defense to insurance contracts, see 18 Wash. & Lee L. Rev. 172 (1961).

§ 38.2-301. Insurable interest required; life, accident and sickness insurance. — A. Any individual of lawful age may procure or effect an insurance contract upon himself for the benefit of any person. No person shall knowingly procure or cause to be procured any insurance contract upon another individual unless the benefits under the contract are payable to (i) the insured or his personal representative, (ii) a beneficiary designated by the insured, or (iii) a person having an insurable interest in the insured at the time when the contract was made.

B. As used in this section and § 38.2-302, *"insurable interest"* means:

1. In the case of individuals related closely by blood or by law, a substantial interest engendered by love and affection;

2. In the case of other persons, a lawful and substantial economic interest in the life, health, and bodily safety of the insured. "Insurable interest" shall not include an interest which arises only or is enhanced by the death, disability or injury of the insured;

3. In the case of employees of corporations, with respect to whom the corporate employer or an employee benefit trust is the beneficiary under an

insurance contract, the lawful and substantial economic interest required in subdivision 2 of this subsection shall be deemed to exist in (i) key employees; and (ii) other employees who have been employed by the corporation for twelve consecutive months, provided that the amount of insurance coverage on such other employees shall be limited to an amount which is commensurate with employer-provided benefits to such employees; and

4. In the case of an organization described in § 501 (c) of the Internal Revenue Code, the lawful and substantial economic interest required in subdivision 2 of this subsection shall be deemed to exist where (i) the insured or proposed insured has either assigned all or part of his ownership rights in a policy or contract to such an organization or has executed a written consent to the issuance of a policy or contract to such organization and (ii) such organization is named in the policy or contract as owner or as beneficiary. (1952, c. 317, § 38.1-329; 1986, c. 562; 1988, c. 831; 1992, cc. 8, 50; 1993, c. 105.)

Editor's note. — Acts 1992, cc. 8 and 50, which amended this section, in cl. 2 provide that the provisions of the 1992 act are declaratory of existing law.

§ 38.2-302. Life, accident and sickness insurance; application required.

— A. No contract of insurance upon a person shall be made or effectuated unless at the time of the making of the contract the individual insured, being of lawful age and competent to contract for the insurance contract (i) applies for insurance, or (ii) consents in writing to the insurance contract. However:

1. A wife or husband may effect an insurance contract upon each other;

2. Any person having an insurable interest in the life of a minor, or any person upon whom a minor is dependent for support and maintenance, may effect an insurance contract upon the life of or pertaining to the minor; or

3. A corporate employer or an employee benefit trust having the insurable interest described in subdivision 3 of subsection B of § 38.2-301, may effect an insurance contract upon the lives of such employees, provided that the employer or trust provides the employee with notice in writing that such insurance has been purchased, the amount of such coverage, and to whom benefits are payable in the event of the employee's death.

B. Nothing in this section shall prohibit a minor from obtaining insurance on his own life as authorized in § 38.2-3105. (1952, c. 317, § 38.1-330; 1986, c. 562; 1988, c. 831; 1993, c. 105.)

Law Review. — For survey of Virginia law on insurance for the year 1972-1973, see 59 Va. L. Rev. 1535 (1973).

Consent in writing. — No valid life insurance contract existed where son filled out and signed life insurance application on the life of his father because father's alleged oral authorization to son and father's participation in medical examination and signing of medical form did not constitute written consent as required by this statute. Hilfiger v. Transamerica Occidental Life Ins. Co., 256 Va. 265, 505 S.E.2d 190 (1998).

§ 38.2-303. Insurable interest required; property insurance.

— A. No insurance contract on property or on any interest therein or arising therefrom shall be enforceable except for the benefit of persons having an insurable interest in the property insured.

B. As used in this section, *"insurable interest"* means any lawful and substantial economic interest in the safety or preservation of the subject of insurance free from loss, destruction or pecuniary damage. (1952, c. 317, § 38.1-331; 1986, c. 562.)

Law Review. — For note, "Insurable Interest in Property in Virginia," see 44 Va. L. Rev. 278 (1958).

Section codifies decision and reasoning in Liverpool & London & Globe Ins. Co. v. Bolling, 176 Va. 182, 10 S.E.2d 518 (1940); Home Ins. Co. v. Dalis, 206 Va. 71, 141 S.E.2d 721 (1965).

Stolen vehicle. — The interest a car dealer acquired for value without notice that the car was stolen property was economic, substantial, and lawful and such interest was insurable. Castle Cars, Inc. v. United States Fire Ins. Co., 221 Va. 773, 273 S.E.2d 793 (1981).

Contractor and architect have interest in preserving building from loss. — Although building was substantially complete and occupied, until final payment was made, the property constituted inchoate security for the payment of contract debts due the contractor and the architect for performance of the entire work. Thus, at the time the loss occurred — three months before the date of final payment — both the contractor and the architect had a substantial economic interest in preserving the building from loss. Blue Cross & Blue Shield v. McDevitt & St. Co., 234 Va. 191, 360 S.E.2d 825 (1987).

§ 38.2-304. Contracts of temporary insurance; duration; what deemed to include. — A. Oral or written binders or other temporary insurance contracts may be made and used for a period not exceeding sixty days pending the issuance of the policy. Unless otherwise provided, oral or written binders or other temporary insurance contracts shall be deemed to include the usual provisions, stipulations and agreements which are commonly used in this Commonwealth in effecting the class of insurance being written.

B. This section shall not apply to:

1. Binders or other contracts referred to in §§ 38.2-2112 and 38.2-4605;
2. Conditional receipts issued by life insurers; or
3. Group insurance policies. (Code 1950, § 38-181; 1952, c. 317, § 38.2-332; 1986, c. 562.)

Law Review. — For survey of Virginia law on insurance for the year 1972-1973, see 59 Va. L. Rev. 1535 (1973).

Generally parties must agree on certain provisions. — While this section specifically permits oral binders of temporary insurance, as a general rule the parties must normally agree upon provisions such as those required by § 38.2-305, although under certain circumstances, some of these elements may be supplied by inference. Dickerson v. Conklin, 218 Va. 59, 235 S.E.2d 450 (1977).

Oral binder consists of usual provisions absent special agreement. — An oral binder or contract for temporary insurance pending issuance of a written policy consists, in the absence of special agreement, of the usual provisions of contracts employed to effect like insurance. First Protection Life Ins. Co. v. Compton, 230 Va. 166, 335 S.E.2d 262 (1985).

Where the parties to a temporary contract for insurance do not specially agree upon all the essential terms, they are presumed to have contemplated the terms, conditions, and limitations of the usual policies covering similar risks. First Protection Life Ins. Co. v. Compton, 230 Va. 166, 335 S.E.2d 262 (1985).

Oral credit insurance contract. — While oral insurance contracts are generally enforceable if the essential elements are adequately proven, this rule does not apply to an oral contract for credit insurance. The statute governing credit accident and sickness insurance requires that all credit insurance be evidenced by a written policy, certificate, or statement and sets forth the required provisions of such instruments. First Protection Life Ins. Co. v. Compton, 230 Va. 166, 335 S.E.2d 262 (1985).

It is apparent that the General Assembly intended to proscribe only oral contracts of insurance never commemorated by a writing, not oral binders, or contracts of temporary credit insurance pending issuance of a written policy. First Protection Life Ins. Co. v. Compton, 230 Va. 166, 335 S.E.2d 262 (1985).

§ 38.2-305. Contents of policies. — A. Each insurance policy or contract shall specify:

1. The names of the parties to the contract;
2. The subject of the insurance;
3. The risks insured against;
4. The time the insurance takes effect and, except in the case of group insurance, title insurance, and insurance written under perpetual policies, the period during which the insurance is to continue;

5. A statement of the premium, except in the case of group insurance and title insurance; and

6. The conditions pertaining to the insurance.

B. Each new or renewal insurance policy, contract, certificate or evidence of coverage issued to a policyholder, covered person or enrollee shall be accompanied by a notice stating substantially:

"IMPORTANT INFORMATION REGARDING YOUR INSURANCE"

"In the event you need to contact someone about this insurance for any reason please contact your agent. If no agent was involved in the sale of this insurance, or if you have additional questions you may contact the insurance company issuing this insurance at the following address and telephone number [Insert the appropriate address and telephone number, toll free number if available, for the company's home or regional office].

Health maintenance organizations shall add the following: We recommend that you familiarize yourself with our grievance procedure, and make use of it before taking any other action.

If you have been unable to contact or obtain satisfaction from the company or the agent, you may contact the Virginia State Corporation Commission's Bureau of Insurance at: [Insert the appropriate address, toll free phone number, and phone number for out-of-state calls for the Bureau of Insurance.]

Written correspondence is preferable so that a record of your inquiry is maintained. When contacting your agent, company or the Bureau of Insurance, have your policy number available."

C. If, under the contract, the exact amount of premiums is determinable only at the termination of the contract, a statement of the basis and rates upon which the final premium is to be determined and paid shall be furnished to any policy-examining bureau having jurisdiction or to the insured upon request.

D. This section shall not apply to surety insurance contracts. (1952, c. 317, § 38.1-333; 1986, c. 562; 1987, c. 519; 1988, c. 333; 1997, c. 688.)

When oral contract enforceable. — An oral contract of insurance may be enforceable, either at law or in equity, if all essential elements are proven by clear and convincing evidence. Dickerson v. Conklin, 218 Va. 59, 235 S.E.2d 450 (1977).

Generally parties must agree on certain provisions. — While § 38.2-304 specifically permits oral binders of temporary insurance, as a general rule, the parties must normally agree upon provisions such as those required by this section, although under certain circumstances, some of these elements may be supplied by inference. Dickerson v. Conklin, 218 Va. 59, 235 S.E.2d 450 (1977).

Court unable to supply essential elements for oral contract of insurance. — Where there was no clear and convincing evidence that there was a meeting of the minds of the plaintiff and defendant on the essential elements necessary to create an oral contract of automobile liability insurance, the court would have had to supply virtually every essential element in order for affirmation to be meaningful and to provide an enforceable contract, and this the court was without authority to do.

Dickerson v. Conklin, 218 Va. 59, 235 S.E.2d 450 (1977).

Each element listed in this section must be proved by clear and convincing evidence in order to establish an oral contract of insurance. Yates v. Whitten Valley Rental Corp., 226 Va. 436, 309 S.E.2d 330 (1983).

Some elements of credit accident or sickness insurance policy may be supplied by inference. — By statute, a policy, certificate, or statement of credit accident or sickness insurance must state, among other things, "a description of the coverage including the amount and term thereof, and any exceptions, limitations, or restrictions." Although the parties normally must expressly agree on each essential element of an insurance contract, some of these elements may be supplied by inference in certain circumstances, including cases involving temporary insurance binders. First Protection Life Ins. Co. v. Compton, 230 Va. 166, 335 S.E.2d 262 (1985).

Insurer's right to void policy for misrepresentation. — The Virginia Supreme Court has specifically upheld provisions in insurance policies that limit the insurer's right to void the

policy for misrepresentation. Atlantic Permanent Fed. Sav. & Loan Ass'n v. American Cas.
Co., 839 F.2d 212 (4th Cir.), cert. denied, 486

U.S. 1056, 108 S. Ct. 2824, 100 L. Ed. 2d 925
(1988).

§ 38.2-306. Additional contents. — A policy or contract may contain
additional provisions that are not substantially in conflict with this title and
that:

1. Are required to be inserted by the laws of the insurer's state or country of
domicile or of the state or country in which the policy is to be delivered or
issued for delivery; or

2. Are necessary to state the rights and obligations of the parties to the
contract because of the manner in which the insurer is constituted or operated.
(Code 1950, § 38-513; 1952, c. 317, § 38.1-334; 1986, c. 562.)

§ 38.2-307. Charter and bylaw provisions in policies. — No policy
shall contain any provision purporting to make any portion of the charter,
bylaws or other organic law of the insurer, however designated, a part of the
contract unless that portion is set out in full in the policy. Any policy provision
in violation of this section shall be invalid. (1952, c. 317, § 38.1-335; 1986, c.
562.)

**§ 38.2-308. Contingent liability provisions in policies issued by cer-
tain mutual insurers.** — Except in the case of nonassessable policies, the
contingent liability of each member of a mutual insurer, other than a life
insurer, shall be clearly stated in the mutual insurer's policies. The contingent
liability may be limited, but such limitation shall not be less than one
additional annual premium on each policy held by the member. (Code 1950,
§ 38-508; 1952, c. 317, § 38.1-335.1; 1986, c. 562.)

**§ 38.2-309. When answers or statements of applicant do not bar
recovery on policy.** — All statements, declarations and descriptions in any
application for an insurance policy or for the reinstatement of an insurance
policy shall be deemed representations and not warranties. No statement in an
application or in any affidavit made before or after loss under the policy shall
bar a recovery upon a policy of insurance unless it is clearly proved that such
answer or statement was material to the risk when assumed and was untrue.
(Code 1950, § 38-7; 1952, c. 317, § 38.1-336; 1986, c. 562.)

Law Review. — For comment on materiality
of ownership in automobile liability policies,
see 19 Wash. & Lee L. Rev. 141 (1962). For
survey of Virginia law on insurance for the year
1969-1970, see 56 Va. L. Rev. 1356 (1970). For

note on automobile liability insurance and the
voluntary-certified policy dichotomy, see 29
Wash. & Lee L. Rev. 426 (1972). For survey of
Virginia law on insurance for the year 1974-
1975, see 61 Va. L. Rev. 1759 (1975).

I. General Consideration.
II. Representation and Warranties.
III. Materiality.
  A. Concepts.
  B. Illustrative Cases.
IV. Effect of Acts of Agents.

I. GENERAL CONSIDERATION.

Purpose of section. — Statutes like this
section have been quite generally enacted to
relieve against the hardships arising from the

strict enforcement at common law of warranties in insurance policies concerning matters of
no real relation to the risk assumed. Jefferson
Std. Life Ins. Co. v. Clemmer, 79 F.2d 724 (4th
Cir. 1935).

While this section does focus on statements made by the applicant, its purpose is not to limit whose statements may be used to challenge a policy; rather, this section modifies the common law fraud standard applied in determining whether a statement bars recovery to a material misrepresentation standard. Nyonteh v. Peoples Sec. Life Ins. Co., 958 F.2d 42 (4th Cir. 1992).

Companies have right to correct information. — It is an accepted practice of insurance companies to issue health and accident policies based upon applications without medical examinations. Such companies have a right to be in possession of the true facts and correct information when they make a determination whether or not a risk should be assumed. Mutual of Omaha Ins. Co. v. Dingus, 219 Va. 706, 250 S.E.2d 352 (1979).

An insurer is entitled to full and truthful disclosure. It is for the insurer, not the insured, to decide whether the true facts are significant or important because it is the insurer which is assuming the risk to which the true facts relate. Parkerson v. Federal Home Life Ins. Co., 797 F. Supp. 1308 (E.D. Va. 1992).

The language of this section is clear and unambiguous. Inter-Ocean Ins. Co. v. Harkrader, 193 Va. 96, 67 S.E.2d 894 (1951).

This section applies only to the application for the policy, and not to the policy itself. North River Ins. Co. v. Atkinson, 137 Va. 313, 119 S.E. 46 (1923).

The provisions of this section relating to answers to interrogatories made by an applicant for a policy of insurance have no application to the warranties contained in the "iron safe clause" of fire insurance policies. Prudential Fire Ins. Co. v. Alley, 104 Va. 356, 51 S.E. 812 (1905).

This section pertains to statements and declarations made in the application for an insurance policy, and not to increases in the hazard under a provision of the policy, suspending coverage "while the hazard is increased by any means within the control of the insured." American Ins. Co. v. Peyton, 272 F.2d 58 (4th Cir. 1959).

It sets forth the circumstances under which a false representation therein bars recovery on a policy. Chitwood v. Prudential Ins. Co. of Am., 206 Va. 314, 143 S.E.2d 915 (1965).

It includes an application for reinstatement. — Where the insured made a willfully false statement in application for reinstatement there could be no recovery on the reinstated policy. New York Life Ins. Co. v. Franklin, 118 Va. 418, 87 S.E. 584 (1916).

This section is applicable to a policy issued pursuant to the Virginia Automobile Assigned Risk Plan. Such a policy is to be distinguished from "certified" policies which the insurer is required to accept pursuant to § 46.1-497 et seq. (now § 46.2-464). Virginia Farm Bureau Mut. Ins. Co. v. Saccio, 204 Va. 769, 133 S.E.2d 268 (1963).

Effect of "declarations" provision in policy. — A provision in the policy that it was issued in reliance upon the truth of representations contained in the declarations in the policy and that the policy "embodies all agreements existing between" insured and insurer did not preclude the company from avoiding the policy because of material and fraudulent misstatements in the application. State Farm Mut. Auto. Ins. Co. v. Butler, 203 Va. 575, 125 S.E.2d 823 (1962).

Question as to "good health." — Plaintiff, who honestly thought her mother was in good health and so stated to defendant's agent in answer to questions in applying for insurance on the mother's life, was not precluded from recovering as beneficiary under the policy because the insured was then suffering from a latent illness of which plaintiff was unaware. The term "good health" means apparent sound health without knowledge to the contrary on the part of the applicant. Gilley v. Union Life Ins. Co., 194 Va. 966, 76 S.E.2d 165 (1953).

Reliance by insurance company on representations made to State agency. — There is no authority authorizing an insurance company to rely on representations made to a State agency when issuing an insurance policy. Utica Mut. Ins. Co. v. Stegall, 293 F. Supp. 199 (W.D. Va. 1968).

Failure to instruct jury as to fraud in misstatements. — It is error to fail to instruct the jury that any misstatements in the application which were relied upon by the defendant must have been fraudulent misstatements in accordance with § 38.2-3503. Sutton v. American Health & Life Ins. Co., 683 F.2d 92 (4th Cir. 1982).

Statement need not be willfully false or fraudulently made. — Under provision of this section that no statement in an application for an insurance policy will bar recovery unless the statement was material and untrue, the statement need not be willfully false or fraudulently made. Insurance Co. of N. Am. v. United States Gypsum Co., 639 F. Supp. 1246 (W.D. Va. 1986).

Burden on insurer to show insured's answers were knowingly false. — It is usually not necessary for an insurer to establish that an untrue representation was willfully false or fraudulently made. However, where the insurer asks the insured to aver only that the representations are true to the best of the insured's knowledge and belief, the insurer must clearly prove that the insured's answers were knowingly false. Parkerson v. Federal Home Life Ins. Co., 797 F. Supp. 1308 (E.D. Va. 1992).

Mere nondisclosure not sufficient for fraud if investigation conducted. — If one conducts an investigation, he cannot hold another in fraud unless material untrue affirmative representations were made. Mere nondisclosures would not be sufficient for fraud if an investigation is conducted. Insurance Co. of N. Am. v. United States Gypsum Co., 639 F. Supp. 1246 (W.D. Va. 1986).

Limitation on general rule regarding jury questions. — Generally, whether a statement is true and whether an untrue statement was knowingly made are questions of fact reserved for the jury. However, where the record shows clearly that the insured gave statements that were not true and correct to the best of his knowledge and belief, the Supreme Court of Virginia has held that a trial court errs in submitting that question to the jury. Parkerson v. Federal Home Life Ins. Co., 797 F. Supp. 1308 (E.D. Va. 1992).

When rescission appropriate. — Rescission of the professional liability insurance policy was appropriate only if insurer clearly proved that an answer or statement in insured-fertility specialist's renewal application for insurance was both (i) material to the risk assumed and (ii) untrue. St. Paul Fire & Marine Ins. Co. v. Jacobson, 826 F. Supp. 155 (E.D. Va. 1993), aff'd, 48 F.3d 778 (4th Cir. 1995).

Whether insurance company can satisfy the settled test for rescission depends on whether it can clearly prove that insured's misrepresentation was material to the risk it assumed in issuing the policy. Breault v. Berkshire Life Ins. Co., 821 F. Supp. 410 (E.D. Va. 1993).

II. REPRESENTATION AND WARRANTIES.

Warranty defined. — A warranty, in the law of insurance, may be defined as a statement or stipulation in the policy as to the existence of a fact or a condition of the subject of the insurance which, if untrue, will prevent the policy from attaching as the contract of the insurer. North River Ins. Co. v. Atkinson, 137 Va. 313, 119 S.E. 46 (1923).

Differentiated from representation. — A warranty is a statement of a fact on the literal truth of which the validity of the contract depends; but, in the case of a representation, the validity of the policy does not depend upon the literal truth of the assertion. In other words, a warranty must be literally true, while a representation need be only substantially true. North River Ins. Co. v. Atkinson, 137 Va. 313, 119 S.E. 46 (1923).

Underlying the whole doctrine of warranties and representations is the fundamental principle that warranties are always a part of the completed contract, while representations precede, are collateral to, and are not necessarily a part of the contract. North River Ins. Co. v. Atkinson, 137 Va. 313, 119 S.E. 46 (1923).

Representations should not only be true but full. — Representations in an application for a policy of insurance should not only be true but full. The insurer has the right to know the whole truth. If a true disclosure is made, it is put on guard to make its own inquiries, and determine whether or not the risk should be assumed. Chitwood v. Prudential Ins. Co. of Am., 206 Va. 314, 143 S.E.2d 915 (1965); Mutual of Omaha Ins. Co. v. Echols, 207 Va. 949, 154 S.E.2d 169 (1967); Mutual of Omaha Ins. Co. v. Dingus, 219 Va. 706, 250 S.E.2d 352 (1979).

A factual representation is material to the risk to be assumed by an insurance company if it would reasonably influence the company's decision whether or not to issue a policy. Breault v. Berkshire Life Ins. Co., 821 F. Supp. 410 (E.D. Va. 1993).

Insured not guilty of misrepresentation of fact material to risk. — Where insured answered the questions in the application in good faith and he did not willfully make an incorrect or misleading statement in order to become eligible for a policy of insurance under the Voluntary Assigned Risk Plan, and if there was any concealment under the facts and circumstances, he was not responsible for it, he was not guilty of misrepresentation of a fact which was material to the risk. Buckeye Union Cas. Co. v. Robertson, 206 Va. 863, 147 S.E.2d 94 (1966).

Where answers are stated to be true to the best knowledge and belief of applicant. — Where the answers in an application for insurance are stated to be true to the best knowledge and belief of the applicant, an incorrect statement innocently made in the belief in its truth will not avoid the policy, although there is also an agreement that any untrue or fraudulent statement shall avoid the policy. Sterling Ins. Co. v. Dansey, 195 Va. 933, 81 S.E.2d 446 (1954).

There was no merit to the company's contention that if insured had diabetes, his misrepresentation of the fact in his application for a policy of health and accident insurance, though innocently made through lack of knowledge, avoided the policy under this section. The company, having provided in the application that the insured's answers must be true and correct to the best of his knowledge and belief, was bound by the terms of its contract, which were not prohibited by this section nor inconsistent with public policy. This section did not prevent the parties from entering into a contract more favorable to the insured. Sterling Ins. Co. v. Dansey, 195 Va. 933, 81 S.E.2d 446 (1954).

No rescission even though memoranda contradicted oral representations. — In case involving two insurers seeking to rescind

part of the contract. North River Ins. Co. v. Atkinson, 137 Va. 313, 119 S.E. 46 (1923).

mortgage insurance coverage which they claimed was procured by fraud, where both insurers had in their possession written memoranda contradicting oral representations as to the availability of rental deficit contribution funds for mortgage payment, rescission could not be accomplished under this section on that account. Foremost Guar. Corp. v. Meritor Sav. Bank, 910 F.2d 118 (4th Cir. 1990) (decided under former § 38.1-336).

Jury question. — Whether a representation is made and the terms on which it is made, are questions of fact for the jury. United States Fid. & Guar. Co. v. Haywood, 211 Va. 394, 177 S.E.2d 530 (1970).

III. MATERIALITY.

A. Concepts.

False statement will not necessarily vitiate policy. — A false statement made in an application for insurance concerning a mere temporary indisposition, not affecting the general health or constitution of the applicant, will not vitiate the policy, unless it be clearly proved that the statement was willfully false, or fraudulently made, or was material. The fact that the answer was merely untrue is not sufficient, under this section, to vitiate the policy. Modern Woodmen of Am. v. Lawson, 110 Va. 81, 65 S.E. 509 (1909); Jefferson Std. Life Ins. Co. v. Clemmer, 79 F.2d 724 (4th Cir. 1935).

One of the purposes of this section is to relieve against the rigorous consequences of the common-law rule that answers to interrogatories in applications for insurance imply that the subject matter of the questions and answers is material, and that if such answers are not true the policy is voidable. Sterling Ins. Co. v. Dansey, 195 Va. 933, 81 S.E.2d 446 (1954); Scott v. State Farm Mut. Auto. Ins. Co., 202 Va. 579, 118 S.E.2d 519 (1961).

One of the purposes of this section is to relieve against the rigorous consequences of the common-law rule that answers to questions in applications for insurance imply that the subject matter of the questions and answers is material, and that if such statements and answers are not true the policy is voidable. Harrell v. North Carolina Mut. Life Ins. Co., 215 Va. 829, 213 S.E.2d 792 (1975).

It is no longer necessary to show that a misrepresentation was willfully false, or fraudulently made, to affect its materiality. A former requirement to the contrary was removed in 1919 from the Code of Virginia, when a general revision of the Code was made, and § 4220, Code of 1919, was enacted, the forerunner of this section. Chitwood v. Prudential Ins. Co. of Am., 206 Va. 314, 143 S.E.2d 915 (1965).

The fact that the statement was not willfully false or fraudulently made does not affect its materiality. Old Republic Life Ins. Co. v. Bales,

213 Va. 771, 195 S.E.2d 854 (1973).

The materiality and falsity of a representation in an insurance application was determinative irrespective of whether the insured acted fraudulently. Gilmore v. Prudential Ins. Co. of Am., 432 F. Supp. 35 (W.D. Va. 1977).

Statement, etc., must be material as well as false. — Under this section no statement, declaration, or description in an application for a policy of insurance shall be allowed to bar a recovery on the policy, or be construed as a warranty, unless it be clearly proved that it was both false and material to the risk. Green v. Southwestern Voluntary Ass'n, 179 Va. 779, 20 S.E.2d 694 (1942).

Recovery will not be barred by a statement in the application for insurance unless such statement is both false and material to the risk. Utica Mut. Ins. Co. v. Stegall, 293 F. Supp. 199 (W.D. Va. 1968).

But material misrepresentations are fatal. — Misrepresentations made in an application for insurance which are material to the risk are fatal. Keeton v. Jefferson Std. Life Ins. Co., 5 F.2d 183 (4th Cir. 1925); Mutual Benefit Health & Accident Ass'n v. Ratcliffe, 163 Va. 325, 175 S.E. 870 (1934).

A misrepresentation of facts material to the risk voids the insurance contract. Inter-Ocean Ins. Co. v. Harkrader, 193 Va. 96, 67 S.E.2d 894 (1951); Hawkeye-Security Ins. Co. v. GEICO, 207 Va. 944, 154 S.E.2d 173 (1967).

Misrepresentations of facts, in an application for insurance, material to the risk when assumed, renders the contract void. Utica Mut. Ins. Co. v. National Indem. Co., 210 Va. 769, 173 S.E.2d 855 (1970).

An insured's answer in an application for insurance which is material to the risk when assumed and untrue avoids the insurer's liability under the policy. Gilmore v. Prudential Ins. Co. of Am., 432 F. Supp. 35 (W.D. Va. 1977).

Suppressed facts need not have causal connection with death. — It is of no consequence that the facts suppressed had no causal connection with the death of the insured, for they affect the very origin of the insurance contract, and, except for them, the contract would not have been made. Such facts cannot, therefore, be said to be immaterial within the meaning of this section. Jefferson Std. Life Ins. Co. v. Clemmer, 79 F.2d 724 (4th Cir. 1935).

Materiality of a fact, in insurance law, is subjective. It concerns rather the impression which the fact claimed to be material would reasonably and naturally convey to the insurer's mind before the event, and at the time the insurance is effected, than the subsequent actual causal connection between the fact, or the probable cause it evidences, and the event. Thus, it is by no means conclusive upon the question of materiality of a fact that it was actually one link in a chain of causes leading to the event. Jefferson Std. Life Ins. Co. v. Clemmer, 79 F.2d 724 (4th Cir. 1935).

Test of materiality. — A fair test of the materiality of a fact is found in the answer to the question whether reasonably careful and intelligent men would have regarded the fact communicated at the time of effecting the insurance as substantially increasing the chances of the loss insured against, so as to bring about a rejection of the risk or the charging of an increased premium. Standard Accident Ins. Co. v. Walker, 127 Va. 140, 102 S.E. 585 (1920); Flannagan v. Northwestern Mut. Life Ins. Co., 152 Va. 38, 146 S.E. 353 (1929), overruled on another point, Gilley v. Union Life Ins. Co., 194 Va. 966, 76 S.E.2d 165 (1953); Buckeye Union Cas. Co. v. Robertson, 206 Va. 863, 147 S.E.2d 94 (1966).

A fact is material to the risk to be assumed by an insurance company if the fact would reasonably influence the company's decision whether or not to issue a policy. Hawkeye-Security Ins. Co. v. GEICO, 207 Va. 944, 154 S.E.2d 173 (1967); Mutual of Omaha Ins. Co. v. Echols, 207 Va. 949, 154 S.E.2d 169 (1967); United States Fid. & Guar. Co. v. Haywood, 211 Va. 394, 177 S.E.2d 530 (1970); Gilmore v. Prudential Ins. Co. of Am., 432 F. Supp. 35 (W.D. Va. 1977); Mutual of Omaha Ins. Co. v. Dingus, 219 Va. 706, 250 S.E.2d 352 (1979).

Misrepresentation of identity by assured concealed the fact that he had an interest in certain machines and prevented inquiry into his background, which would have disclosed the presence of unsatisfied judgments against him, and this misrepresentation was material. United States Fid. & Guar. Co. v. Haywood, 211 Va. 394, 177 S.E.2d 530 (1970).

Burden is on insurer to prove materiality of misrepresentation. — Materiality of a misrepresentation is an affirmative defense, and the burden is upon the insurer to prove it. Virginia Mut. Ins. Co. v. State Farm Mut. Auto. Ins. Co., 204 Va. 783, 133 S.E.2d 277 (1963); Hawkeye-Security Ins. Co. v. GEICO, 207 Va. 944, 154 S.E.2d 173 (1967).

The insurer must "clearly prove" that the misrepresentation is material to the risk. Scott v. State Farm Mut. Auto. Ins. Co., 202 Va. 579, 118 S.E.2d 519 (1961); Buckeye Union Cas. Co. v. Robertson, 206 Va. 863, 147 S.E.2d 94 (1966).

To be entitled to the voidance of the binder, the insurer had the burden of clearly proving that the assured falsely represented his identity and that the representation was material to the risk when assumed. United States Fid. & Guar. Co. v. Haywood, 211 Va. 394, 177 S.E.2d 530 (1970).

In the ordinary case, where an insurance carrier seeks to escape liability for allegedly false statements made in an application for insurance, the proper standard of proof is gleaned from this section. The burden is on the carrier to clearly prove that a statement in an application is material to the risk when assumed and is untrue. Old Republic Life Ins. Co. v. Bales, 213 Va. 771, 195 S.E.2d 854 (1973).

Materiality of a misrepresentation is an affirmative defense. Harrell v. North Carolina Mut. Life Ins. Co., 215 Va. 829, 213 S.E.2d 792 (1975).

Under the explicit mandate of this section, the insurer had the burden of clearly proving that the insured's answers in the application were material to the risk assumed and were untrue. Harrell v. North Carolina Mut. Life Ins. Co., 215 Va. 829, 213 S.E.2d 792 (1975).

The burden of clearly proving the affirmative defense of materiality of a misrepresentation is not carried when the court, to find the fact, must resort to assumption and conjecture. Harrell v. North Carolina Mut. Life Ins. Co., 215 Va. 829, 213 S.E.2d 792 (1975).

Information concerning an applicant's existing disability coverage is clearly material to an insurer's decision to issue a disability policy because it bears on the possibility that the applicant, if overinsured, might feign a disabling illness or seek to avoid returning to work after a legitimate injury. Breault v. Berkshire Life Ins. Co., 821 F. Supp. 410 (E.D. Va. 1993).

Effect of incontestability clause on material misrepresentation. — An insurer must contest a contract's validity for false or fraudulent statements within the period prescribed in the policy, thus, an incontestability clause forecloses untimely challenges based on material misrepresentations in insurance applications. Nyonteh v. Peoples Sec. Life Ins. Co., 958 F.2d 42 (4th Cir. 1992).

Materiality is a question for the court. — Whether a representation is made and the terms on which it is made are questions of fact for the jury, but, when proved, its materiality is a question for the court. North River Ins. Co. v. Atkinson, 137 Va. 313, 119 S.E. 46 (1923); Inter-Ocean Ins. Co. v. Harkrader, 193 Va. 96, 67 S.E.2d 894 (1951); Scott v. State Farm Mut. Auto. Ins. Co., 202 Va. 579, 118 S.E.2d 519 (1961); Chitwood v. Prudential Ins. Co. of Am., 206 Va. 314, 143 S.E.2d 915 (1965); Hawkeye-Security Ins. Co. v. GEICO, 207 Va. 944, 154 S.E.2d 173 (1967); Mutual of Omaha Ins. Co. v. Echols, 207 Va. 949, 154 S.E.2d 169 (1967); Harrell v. North Carolina Mut. Life Ins. Co., 215 Va. 829, 213 S.E.2d 792 (1975). See Jefferson Std. Life Ins. Co. v. Clemmer, 79 F.2d 724 (4th Cir. 1935).

When a misrepresentation is proved, its materiality is a question of law for the court. United States Fid. & Guar. Co. v. Haywood, 211 Va. 394, 177 S.E.2d 530 (1970).

Whether a statement is untrue is a question of fact for the jury, but when its falsity is proved, the question of materiality is for the court. Old Republic Life Ins. Co. v. Bales, 213 Va. 771, 195 S.E.2d 854 (1973); Gilmore v. Prudential Ins. Co. of Am., 432 F. Supp. 35 (W.D. Va. 1977).

The materiality of a misrepresentation, if shown to have been made, is an issue of law to be decided by the courts. Parkerson v. Federal Home Life Ins. Co., 797 F. Supp. 1308 (E.D. Va. 1992).

B. Illustrative Cases.

Recitation of correctness by insured increases burden on insurer. — In the application submitted by the insured it was recited that his answers were correct to the best of his knowledge. Where there is such a recitation, the burden upon the insurance carrier increases from that specified in this section to clear proof that the answer is knowingly false. Old Republic Life Ins. Co. v. Bales, 213 Va. 771, 195 S.E.2d 854 (1973).

Insurance company was not estopped from relying on misrepresentations of material fact because insurance company continued to accept premium payments from plaintiff's husband for 21 months after insurance company's agent was told by husband that he "had just realized he had been diagnosed" as having colon cancer. It could not be said, as a matter of law, that what agent said husband told him should have excited insurance company to inquire further. Further, plaintiff offered no evidence that husband prejudicially relied on any act or inaction of insurance company. Parkerson v. Federal Home Life Ins. Co., 797 F. Supp. 1308 (E.D. Va. 1992).

Warranty that car was new was material. — Where a policy of insurance on an automobile contained a warranty that the car was a new one, it was error to refuse to instruct that the warranty was material and that plaintiff could not recover if in fact the car was not new. North River Ins. Co. v. Atkinson, 137 Va. 313, 119 S.E. 46 (1923).

As was warranty of automobile number. — In the instant case, an action on an insurance policy against loss by fire and theft of an automobile, the warranties were that the factory number of the automobile insured was 87382, and that it was new when purchased. Plaintiff contended that this section destroyed the effect of all such warranties. It was held that it appears from the language used in the section that it had no application to the instant case, as it was clearly proven that the answer or statement as to the number of the automobile and that it was new were material to the risk assumed and were untrue. North River Ins. Co. v. Atkinson, 137 Va. 313, 119 S.E. 46 (1923).

In an action upon an automobile insurance policy, an instruction that if the jury believed from the evidence that the motor number of plaintiff's automobile was 87382 and that he represented to the defendant this number as the factory number of the automobile, instead of the motor number, then such representation is not material, was error. North River Ins. Co. v. Atkinson, 137 Va. 313, 119 S.E. 46 (1923).

Of ownership. — In the instant case, an action against an indemnity company on an automobile insurance policy, the statements in the application as to the ownership of the car were material and untrue. Therefore, this section did not govern the case. The title was clouded by a conditional sales contract, and the one stated to be the owner of the car was not the owner. The answer as to ownership was material to the risk and was untrue, and these untrue statements would have been sufficient to have invalidated the policy but for the fact that defendant's agent who secured the policy knew that these statements were untrue. Moreover, when the company sent its agent to adjust the troubles attendant upon a transfer of the title, it must have known what these troubles were. Royal Indem. Co. v. Hook, 155 Va. 956, 157 S.E. 414 (1931).

Materiality of a misrepresentation as to ownership of an automobile must be clearly proved by the insurer, and materiality will not be assumed or judicially noticed in the absence of such proof. Scott v. State Farm Mut. Auto. Ins. Co., 202 Va. 579, 118 S.E.2d 519 (1961).

That beneficiary was insured's wife. — In a written application for insurance, where the insured is asked to give the name, relationship and residence of the beneficiary, and he states in reply that the beneficiary is his wife, and it turns out that she is not his wife but a woman with whom he is living in illicit cohabitation, such false statement with respect to his relation to the beneficiary avoids the policy. Continental Cas. Co. v. Lindsay, 111 Va. 389, 69 S.E. 344 (1910).

Concealment of physical condition and prior refusal of insurance. — Where, prior to the issuance of preferred accident and health policy, the insured had been twice refused insurance, had undergone an operation for appendicitis, and had been suffering from effects of a vascular disease in his legs, but he made no disclosure of these facts in his application, his representations were untrue and material to the risk, when assumed, and if correct information had been disclosed in his application the policy would not have been issued. Consequently, the insurer, to protect itself against the failure to disclose such material information, had the right to void the policy and return the premiums paid. Inter-Ocean Ins. Co. v. Harkrader, 193 Va. 96, 67 S.E.2d 894 (1951).

Concealment of psychiatric treatment. —A false statement concealing the fact that the applicant was being treated for a psychiatric disorder was proven to be material to the risk.

Fidelity Bankers Life Ins. Corp. v. Wheeler, 203 Va. 434, 125 S.E.2d 151 (1962).

Concealment of treatment for nervous disorder. — In a case in which suicide was charged, a false concealment as to a treatment by a physician for a nervous disorder was material to the risk. Flannagan v. Northwestern Mut. Life Ins. Co., 152 Va. 38, 146 S.E. 353 (1929), overruled on another point, Gilley v. Union Life Ins. Co., 194 Va. 966, 76 S.E.2d 165 (1953). See Jefferson Std. Life Ins. Co. v. Clemmer, 79 F.2d 724 (4th Cir. 1935). But see Williams v. Metropolitan Life Ins. Co., 139 Va. 341, 123 S.E. 509 (1924), wherein it was said that where the insured did not disclose the fact that she had had a cancer and was not asked about it by the insurer, the insured was not bound to tell the medical examiner what she knew about a cancer, and there were no representations or statements of insured in the evidence which it could be said were material to the risk when examined and were not true, within this section.

Concealment of consumption. — The statements of the assured were shot through with fraud. There had been a material change in his weight, which, in his statement, he denied. He was not last sick in 1928, as he stated; his last illness had been for more than a week, as he stated; he had left his work for more than a month on account of illness, though he said he had not; he had consulted physicians other than the physician named by him, and he had within the last five years been to a sanatorium for treatment, which he denied in his statement. He had consumption and he knew it. All of these statements were material to the risk assumed and barred a recovery upon the policy under this section unless the insurance company was estopped to rely upon them. Metropolitan Life Ins. Co. v. Hart, 162 Va. 88, 173 S.E. 769 (1934).

Concealment of terminal illness leading to imminent death was material to the risk assumed by an insurance carrier; thus, the district court's conclusion that leukemia victim and his ex-wife had fraudulently misrepresented the state of his health in both the insurance application and the application for reinstatement was clearly correct. Nyonteh v. Peoples Sec. Life Ins. Co., 958 F.2d 42 (4th Cir. 1992).

Concealment of claims on prior policies. — The failure of an applicant for an accident and health insurance policy to recall some minor payment made upon an accident policy in another company would not be material to the risk assumed, but if an applicant in the preceding nine years had made on other accident and health policies eleven claims, certainly such information would be important. It would tend to show either that the making of claims was a habit or that misfortune had

dogged his footsteps. Mutual Benefit Health & Accident Ass'n v. Ratcliffe, 163 Va. 325, 175 S.E. 870 (1934).

False statement of occupation. — Where the assured in his application said that he was a lawyer, whereas in fact he was at that time in the forbidden railway service as a railroad conductor or brakeman, he warranted his answer as to occupation and made it part of the policy, and it was material to the risk, untrue, and made the contract voidable from its inception. United Sec. Life Ins. & Trust Co. v. Massey, 159 Va. 832, 164 S.E. 529 (1932), rev'd on other grounds, 159 Va. 850 (1933).

Representation of occupation held not false. — The occupation of the insured in an accident policy was that of contractor, whose chief duty was to supervise the work of his servants in brick construction, although he sometimes actually laid bricks, for the purpose of showing inexpert bricklayers how the work was to be done. It was held that his representation that the duties of his occupation were fully described as "Proprietor — supervising only" was not a false representation which induced the company to give him a preferred classification. He was, in fact, a preferred risk, and received the classification to which he was entitled. Standard Accident Ins. Co. v. Walker, 127 Va. 140, 102 S.E. 585 (1920).

Misrepresentation of other insurance held immaterial. — An applicant for accident insurance declared that he had no other accident or sickness insurance as enumerated. The applicant failed to mention that he was a member of a social club, the members of which, among other privileges, were entitled to a weekly sick benefit of $4, and to report that his wife, without his knowledge, had subsequently taken out a weekly sick benefit policy of $5 a week in another company. It was held that under this section, these omissions of the applicant, without any willful purpose to deceive or defraud the company, did not avoid the policy so far as death from accident was concerned. Standard Accident Ins. Co. v. Walker, 127 Va. 140, 102 S.E. 585 (1920).

Witnesses. — Since the agent had the authority to issue and did issue the binder, he was a competent witness to testify on the materiality question that he would have rejected the risk had he known the true facts. United States Fid. & Guar. Co. v. Haywood, 211 Va. 394, 177 S.E.2d 530 (1970).

Misstatement held to be material as a matter of law. — A misstatement was held to be material to the risk as a matter of law where uncontradicted testimony on behalf of defendant insurance company was to the effect that the policy would not have been issued except at a higher premium if the insurance company had known facts which were concealed by the misstatement. Fidelity Bankers Life Ins. Corp. v. Wheeler, 203 Va. 434, 125 S.E.2d 151 (1962).

Insurer's actions held to show false statement not regarded as material. — Though its underwriting superintendent testified the policy would not have been issued had the true facts been known, the company's actions (particularly its issuance of a new policy) after the accident was reported and after the falsity of the answer was known were held to show conclusively that it did not regard the false statement as material. Virginia Mut. Ins. Co. v. State Farm Mut. Auto. Ins. Co., 204 Va. 783, 133 S.E.2d 277 (1963).

IV. EFFECT OF ACTS OF AGENTS.

Where agent inserts in application statements made by insured, and insured has knowledge of statements inserted, the insured is bound by the statements. If the statements are false and material the policy is defeated under this section. Mutual Benefit Health & Accident Ass'n v. Ratcliffe, 163 Va. 325, 175 S.E. 870 (1934).

Where insured truthfully answers questions but insurance agent enters false answers in application and the insured acts without fraud, collusion or actual or constructive knowledge of agent's act in supplying false answers, the insurer is precluded from avoiding liability on the grounds of falsity of answers in the application. Gilley v. Union Life Ins. Co., 194 Va. 966, 76 S.E.2d 165 (1953). See New York Life Ins. Co. v. Eicher, 198 Va. 255, 93 S.E.2d 269 (1956).

Mere knowledge by an applicant that an agent is not putting down complete answers is not a defense to a suit on the policy, unless the evidence goes to show that the applicant knows that the agent in doing so is inserting false statements through mistake, neglect or fraud. There must be conduct upon the part of the applicant that amounts to a wrong. Reserve Life Ins. Co. v. Ferebee, 202 Va. 556, 118 S.E.2d 675 (1961).

A plaintiff who has signed an application for insurance without reading it is not thereby precluded from proving that false answers contained in it were not given by her but were inserted by the insurance agent, she having given true answers and being unaware of their falsification. Gilley v. Union Life Ins. Co., 194 Va. 966, 76 S.E.2d 165 (1953).

The insurer in an action on an insurance policy cannot avoid liability on the ground that false answers appear in the application, if it is shown that: (1) the false answers contained in the application were inserted by an agent of the insurer, and (2) the answers to the interrogations contained in the application were truthfully given without fraud or collusion, and (3) the applicant had no knowledge, actual or constructive, that his application contained false answers. This rule applies even though the insurer attempts to limit the authority of its agent by stipulations inserted in the application and policy, and even though a copy of the application is attached to and made a part of the policy. But the existence of these facts should be taken into consideration with all the other facts and circumstances of the particular case in determining whether the applicant had any knowledge that the answers contained in the application were false. New York Life Ins. Co. v. Eicher, 198 Va. 255, 93 S.E.2d 269 (1956).

The insurer in an action on an insurance policy cannot avoid liability on the ground that false answers appear in the application, if it is shown that: (1) The false answers contained in the application were inserted by an agent of the insurer, and (2) the answers to the interrogations contained in the application were truthfully given without fraud or collusion, and (3) the applicant had no knowledge, actual or constructive, that his application contained false answers. Mutual of Omaha Ins. Co. v. Dingus, 219 Va. 706, 250 S.E.2d 352 (1979).

If the applicant is a party to the fraud or in collusion with the insurer's agent or has actual or constructive knowledge that his application contains false answers material to the risk, neither he nor the beneficiary under the policy will be allowed to profit thereby and the insurer will not be estopped by the knowledge or conduct of its agent from asserting the falsity of such answers as a bar to its liability on the policy. Furthermore, in the absence of peculiar circumstances, there is a presumption that the applicant has read the application which he signed and he is prima facie charged with knowledge of its contents, but this presumption may be rebutted. To rebut the presumption that the insured knew his application contained false answers it is essential to prove that the answers to the interrogations contained in the application were truthfully given by the insured. New York Life Ins. Co. v. Eicher, 198 Va. 255, 93 S.E.2d 269 (1956).

Jury question as to applicant's knowledge. — Where insurance agent filled out an application for insurance and read each question aloud to the applicant and upon the applicant making oral answer thereto made a notation at the appropriate place in the application, and where the evidence was in dispute as to whether the applicant gave truthful oral answers to the questions propounded in the application, a jury question was presented as to whether at the time of applying for insurance the insured knew of certain physical disorders. Quillin v. Prudential Ins. Co. of Am., 280 F.2d 771 (4th Cir. 1960).

§ 38.2-310. All fees, charges, etc., to be stated in policy. — A. All fees, charges, premiums or other consideration charged for the insurance or for the procurement of insurance shall be stated in the policy except in the case of fidelity, surety, title, and group insurance, and except for consulting services as provided in Article 4 (§ 38.2-1837 et seq.) of Chapter 18 of this title. Except as provided in this subsection, no person shall charge or receive any fee, compensation, or consideration for insurance or for the procurement of insurance that is not included in the premium or stated in the policy.

B. Service charges for installment payments of insurance premiums do not need to be stated in the policy if the charges are provided to the insured in writing. (Code 1950, § 38-508; 1952, c. 317, § 38.1-337; 1986, c. 562; 1990, c. 281.)

§ 38.2-311. Type size in which conditions and restrictions to be printed. — Except as otherwise provided in this title, no restriction, condition or provision in or endorsed on any insurance policy shall be valid unless the condition or provision is printed in type as large as eight point type, or is written in ink or typewritten in or on the policy. This section shall not apply to a copy of an application or parts thereof, attached to or made part of an insurance policy. (Code 1950, § 38-9; 1952, c. 317, § 38.1-338; 1986, c. 562.)

Constitutionality. — The provisions of this section relating to the size of type are constitutional. Dupuy v. Delaware Ins. Co., 63 F. 680 (W.D. Va. 1894).

The object of this section is a wise and beneficent one to protect applicants for insurance who are oftentimes inexperienced and unacquainted with the provisions and stipulations usual in policies of insurance, by requiring that such conditions and restrictive provisions shall not constitute a defense unless they are printed in the policy in type of prescribed size. It does not forbid companies to protect themselves by the insertion of conditions, limitations, and restrictions upon their liability, for men usually have the right to contract as they please about their own affairs. If printed in small type these restrictive provisions might easily escape the observation of the unwary, and it has therefore been wisely ordered that they, and not the policy, shall be nugatory unless printed in type of such size as would challenge the attention and be easily read by the ordinary applicant. Sulphur Mines Co. v. Phenix Ins. Co., 94 Va. 355, 26 S.E. 856 (1897).

"Conditions" and "restrictive provisions." — The words "condition" and "restrictive provision," used in this section before the 1952 act, which substituted therefor "restriction, condition or provision," were intended to cover any clause, expression or provision, included in or appended to a policy, whereby the effect of the principal and essential part of the policy is modified, changed, restricted, or otherwise affected, so as to materially influence the rights and liabilities of the insured thereunder. National Life Ass'n v. Berkeley, 97 Va. 571, 34 S.E. 469 (1899).

Before the 1952 act, this section specified "conditions" and "restrictive provisions," which would impose upon the insured the performance of some function the nonperformance of which would defeat a recovery in an action on the policy, provided such "condition" or "restrictive provision" was printed in type of the size required, or was written with pen and ink. Stipulations with respect to the risks insured against, which imposed no onus on the insured, and with respect to which he could not be guilty of any act of omission or commission which could affect his right of recovery, where held not within the statute. Cline v. Western Assurance Co., 101 Va. 496, 44 S.E. 700 (1903).

Section does not apply to bylaws of mutual benefit societies. — This section has no application to the conditions and restrictive provisions contained in the bylaws of an ordinary mutual benefit society made a part of the certificate of membership, which is the contract between it and the member. Fraternities Accident Order v. Armstrong, 106 Va. 746, 56 S.E. 565 (1907).

But may apply to application. — The provision of this section in regard to size of type applies to both application and policy when the application is expressly made a part of the contract of insurance. Burruss v. National Life Ass'n, 96 Va. 543, 32 S.E. 49 (1899).

Whole of provision must fulfill requirements. — The requirement of this section is not satisfied by inserting a figure, word or even a sentence with pen and ink. The whole provision relied on must be in writing or type of the prescribed size, or else it is not available as a defense to an action on the policy. National Life Ass'n v. Berkeley, 97 Va. 571, 34 S.E. 469 (1899).

Beneficiary disclaiming and claiming

under a provision simultaneously. — Where an insurance company is seeking to escape liability for the surrender value of its policy on the ground that the policy was not surrendered within the time prescribed by a provision of the policy, it is not inequitable for the beneficiary, while claiming the surrender value under that same provision, to insist that the time limit fixed by the provision shall be excluded because not printed in type of the required size nor written with pen and ink in or on the policy. Equitable Life Assurance Soc'y v. Wilson, 110 Va. 571, 66 S.E. 836 (1910).

When objection to be raised. — An objection that the conditions of an insurance policy are not printed in the type required by the statute cannot be made for the first time in the appellate court. The company was allowed to rely on the conditions in the policy which rendered it void, and the record fails to disclose that the conditions were not printed in the type prescribed by the statute. Hence, the presumption is that the policy conformed to the statutory requirement. Sulphur Mines Co. v. Phenix Ins. Co., 94 Va. 355, 26 S.E. 856 (1897).

Admissibility of application not part of insurance contract. — Contention that since printed words on application for insurance were in six point type instead of eight point, the application should not have been admitted in evidence by virtue of this section was without merit, where the application did not become a part of an insurance contract or a restriction therein. Peoples Life Ins. Co. v. Parker, 179 Va. 662, 20 S.E.2d 485 (1942).

A jury's verdict as to size of type will be set aside where a different measurement is shown by a recognized device for measuring the size of type. Spicer v. Hartford Fire Ins. Co., 171 Va. 428, 199 S.E. 499 (1938).

§ 38.2-312. Provisions limiting jurisdiction, or requiring construction of contracts by law of other states, prohibited.

— No insurance contract delivered or issued for delivery in this Commonwealth and covering subjects which are located or residing in this Commonwealth, or which are performed in this Commonwealth shall contain any condition, stipulation or agreement:

1. Requiring the contract to be construed according to the laws of any other state or country, except as may be necessary to meet the requirements of the motor vehicle financial responsibility laws of the other state or country; or

2. Depriving the courts of this Commonwealth of jurisdiction in actions against the insurer.

Any such condition, stipulation or agreement shall be void, but such voiding shall not affect the validity of the remainder of the contract. (1952, c. 317, § 38.1-339; 1986, c. 562.)

Purpose of this section is different from that of the long arm statute. August v. HBA Life Ins. Co., 734 F.2d 168 (4th Cir. 1984).

§ 38.2-313. Where certain contracts deemed made.

— All insurance contracts on or with respect to the ownership, maintenance or use of property in this Commonwealth shall be deemed to have been made in and shall be construed in accordance with the laws of this Commonwealth. (Code 1950, § 38-162; 1952, c. 317, § 38.1-340; 1986, c. 562.)

Place of contract governs nature, validity, and interpretation. — The nature, validity, and interpretation of a contract is governed by the law of the place where the contract was made. National Indep. Coal Operators Ass'n v. Old Republic Ins. Co., 544 F. Supp. 520 (W.D. Va. 1982).

§ 38.2-314. Limitation of action and proof of loss.

— No provision in any insurance policy shall be valid if it limits the time within which an action may be brought to less than one year after the loss occurs or the cause of action accrues.

If an insurance policy requires a proof of loss, damage or liability to be filed within a specified time, all time consumed in an effort to adjust the claim shall not be considered part of such time. (Code 1950, § 38-9; 1952, c. 317, § 38.1-341; 1986, c. 562.)

Section applies to policies as to which limitations are not specifically provided. — It seems reasonably clear that the function of this section is to provide a limitation upon the minimum time for bringing suit on policies as to which limitations are not specifically provided, and in such cases the policy may limit the time to not less than one year after the loss or after the cause of action accrues, as the policy may provide. Ramsey v. Home Ins. Co., 203 Va. 502, 125 S.E.2d 201 (1962).

And does not affect rule as to fire policies conforming to § 38.2-2105. — This section does not affect the rule that the twelve-month limitation contained in a fire policy conforming with § 38.2-2105 begins to run at the time of the loss rather than 60 days after proof of loss. Ramsey v. Home Ins. Co., 203 Va. 502, 125 S.E.2d 201 (1962).

First sentence applies to policies in force when section adopted. — The declaration that no provision in any policy of insurance limiting the time within which a suit or action may be brought to less than one year after loss shall be valid applies not only to policies thereafter issued, but also to policies in force when the act was passed and upon which a right of action had not accrued. Smith v. Northern Neck Mut. Fire Ass'n, 112 Va. 192, 70 S.E. 482 (1911).

One-year limitation period in group health plan contract had to be enforced as a valid contractual provision which violated no state or federal public policy. Koonan v. Blue Cross & Blue Shield, 802 F. Supp. 1424 (E.D. Va. 1992).

Filing proof of loss. — This section and § 38.2-320 do not change the rule adopted in North British & Mercantile Ins. Co. v. Edmundson, 104 Va. 486, 52 S.E. 350 (1905), to the effect that failure to file proof of loss within the time specified in the policy does not bar an action on the policy if the proof of loss is filed before suit is brought. Southern Home Ins. Co. v. Bowers, 157 Va. 686, 161 S.E. 914 (1932).

§ 38.2-315. Intervening breach. — If any breach of warranty or condition in any insurance contract covering property located in this Commonwealth occurs prior to a loss under the contract, the breach shall not void the contract nor permit the insurer to avoid liability unless the breach existed at the time of the loss. (Code 1950, § 38-8; 1952, c. 317, § 38.1-342; 1986, c. 562.)

§ 38.2-316. Policy forms to be filed with Commission; notice of approval or disapproval; exceptions. — A. No policy of life insurance, industrial life insurance, variable life insurance, modified guaranteed life insurance, group life insurance, accident and sickness insurance, or group accident and sickness insurance; no annuity, modified guaranteed annuity, pure endowment, variable annuity, group annuity, group modified guaranteed annuity, or group variable annuity contract; no health services plan, legal services plan, dental or optometric services plan, or health maintenance organization contract; and no fraternal benefit certificate nor any certificate or evidence of coverage issued in connection with such policy, contract, or plan issued or issued for delivery in Virginia shall be delivered or issued for delivery in this Commonwealth unless a copy of the form has been filed with the Commission. In addition to the above requirement, no policy of accident and sickness insurance shall be delivered or issued for delivery in this Commonwealth unless the rate manual showing rates, rules, and classification of risks applicable thereto has been filed with the Commission.

B. Except as provided in this section, no application form shall be used with the policy or contract and no rider or endorsement shall be attached to or printed or stamped upon the policy or contract unless the form of such application, rider or endorsement has been filed with the Commission. No individual certificate and no enrollment form shall be used in connection with any group life insurance policy, group accident and sickness insurance policy, group annuity contract, or group variable annuity contract unless the form for the certificate and enrollment form have been filed with the Commission.

C. 1. None of the policies, contracts, and certificates specified in subsection A of this section shall be delivered or issued for delivery in this Commonwealth and no applications, enrollment forms, riders, and endorsements shall be used in connection with the policies, contracts, and certificates unless the forms thereof have been approved in writing by the Commission as conforming to the requirements of this title and not inconsistent with law.

2. In addition to the above requirement, no premium rate change applicable to individual accident and sickness insurance policies, subscriber contracts of health services plans, dental or optometric services plans, or fraternal benefit contracts providing individual accident and sickness coverage as authorized in § 38.2-4116 shall be used unless the premium rate change has been approved in writing by the Commission. No premium rate change applicable to individual or group Medicare supplement policies shall be used unless the premium rate change has been approved in writing by the Commission.

D. The Commission may disapprove or withdraw approval of the form of any policy, contract or certificate specified in subsection A of this section, or of any application, enrollment form, rider or endorsement, if the form:

1. Does not comply with the laws of this Commonwealth;

2. Has any title, heading, backing or other indication of the contents of any or all of its provisions that is likely to mislead the policyholder, contract holder or certificate holder; or

3. Contains any provisions that encourage misrepresentation or are misleading, deceptive or contrary to the public policy of this Commonwealth.

E. Within thirty days after the filing of any form requiring approval, the Commission shall notify the organization filing the form of its approval or disapproval of the form which has been filed, and, in the event of disapproval, its reason therefor. The Commission, at its discretion, may extend for up to an additional thirty days the period within which it shall approve or disapprove the form. Any form received but neither approved nor disapproved by the Commission shall be deemed approved at the expiration of the thirty days if the period is not extended, or at the expiration of the extended period, if any; however, no organization shall use a form deemed approved under the provisions of this section until the organization has filed with the Commission a written notice of its intent to use the form together with a copy of the form and the original transmittal letter thereof. The notice shall be filed in the offices of the Commission at least ten days prior to the organization's use of the form.

F. If the Commission proposes to withdraw approval previously given or deemed given to the form of any policy, contract or certificate, or of any application, rider or endorsement, it shall notify the insurer in writing at least fifteen days prior to the proposed effective date of withdrawal giving its reasons for withdrawal.

G. Any insurer or fraternal benefit society aggrieved by the disapproval or withdrawal of approval of any form may proceed as indicated in § 38.2-1926.

H. This section shall not apply to any special rider or endorsement on any policy, except an accident and sickness insurance policy that relates only to the manner of distribution of benefits or to the reservation of rights and benefits under such policy, and that is used at the request of the individual policyholder, contract holder or certificate holder.

I. The Commission may exempt any categories of such policies, contracts, and certificates and any applicable rate manuals from (i) the filing requirements, (ii) the approval requirements of this section, or (iii) both such requirements. The Commission may modify such requirements, subject to such limitations and conditions which the Commission finds appropriate. In promulgating an exemption, the Commission may consider the nature of the coverage, the person or persons to be insured or covered, the competence of the buyer or other parties to the contract, and other criteria the Commission considers relevant.

J. Pursuant to the authority granted by § 38.2-223, the Commission may promulgate such rules and regulations as it may deem necessary to set standards for policy and other form submissions required by this section or § 38.2-3501. (1952, c. 317, § 38.1-342.1; 1972, c. 836; 1973, c. 504; 1977, c. 325; 1986, c. 562; 1990, c. 332; 1994, c. 316; 1996, c. 12; 1998, c. 17.)

The 1998 amendment, in the second sentence of subsection B, inserted "and no enrollment form," and substituted "and enrollment form have been filed" for "has been filed"; in subdivision 1 of subsection C, inserted "enrollment forms"; and in the introductory language of subsection D, inserted "enrollment form."

Breach of warranty must exist at time of loss. — The Virginia law today is in accord with the common-law doctrine that a breach of a material warranty in an insurance policy will defeat recovery, with the exception that, under the Virginia rule, the breach of warranty must exist at the time the loss occurs. Coleman Furn.

Corp. v. Home Ins. Co., 67 F.2d 347 (4th Cir. 1933), cert. denied, 291 U.S. 669, 54 S. Ct. 453, 78 L. Ed. 1059 (1934).

But it is unnecessary to prove breach contributed to loss. — This section makes it unnecessary for the insurance company to prove that the breach of the warranty contributed to the loss, and under the Virginia rule, as under the federal rule, breach of a material warranty will defeat recovery of the insurance policy whether contributing to the loss or not. Coleman Furn. Corp. v. Home Ins. Co., 67 F.2d 347 (4th Cir. 1933), cert. denied, 291 U.S. 669, 54 S. Ct. 453, 78 L. Ed. 1059 (1934).

§ 38.2-317. Delivery and use of certain policies and endorsements.
— A. No insurance policy or endorsement of the kind to which Chapter 19 (§ 38.2-1900 et seq.) of this title applies shall be delivered or issued for delivery in this Commonwealth unless the policy form or endorsement is filed with the Commission at least thirty days prior to its effective date. The provisions of this section shall not apply to statutory fire insurance policies, standard automobile policy forms and endorsements, workers' compensation and employers' liability insurance as defined in § 38.2-119, or surety insurance as defined in § 38.2-121.

B. The Commission may disapprove or withdraw approval of the policy form or endorsement to which the section applies if the policy form or endorsement:

1. Is in violation of any provision of this title;

2. Contains provisions that are contrary to the public policy of this Commonwealth;

3. Contains or incorporates by reference, even where such incorporation is otherwise permissible, any inconsistent, ambiguous or misleading clauses or exceptions and conditions that deceptively affect the risk purported to be assumed in the general coverage of the policy;

4. Has any title, heading or other indication of its provisions that is misleading;

5. Contains provisions that are so unclear or deceptively worded that they encourage misrepresentation; or

6. Provides coverage of such a limited nature that it is contrary to the public interest of this Commonwealth.

C. Within thirty days after the filing of any policy form or endorsement requiring approval pursuant to this section, the Commission shall notify the insurer or rate service organization filing the policy form or endorsement of its approval or disapproval, and in the event of disapproval, its reason therefor. The Commission, at its discretion, may extend for up to an additional thirty days the period within which it shall approve or disapprove the policy form or endorsement. Any policy form or endorsement received but neither approved nor disapproved by the Commission shall be deemed approved at the expiration of the thirty days if the period is not extended, or at the expiration of the extended period, if any; however, no policy form or endorsement shall be deemed approved under the provisions of this section unless written notice of the intent to use the policy form or endorsement has been filed with the Commission.

D. If the Commission proposes to withdraw approval previously given or deemed given to the policy form or endorsement to which this section applies, it shall notify the insurer in writing at least ninety days prior to the proposed effective date of withdrawal giving its reasons for withdrawal.

E. The policy and endorsement forms referred to in subsection A of this section in use on October 1, 1976, may continue to be used, subject to disapproval by the Commission.

F. The Commission may by rule exempt any person, class of persons, or market segment from any or all of the provisions of this section. In promulgating an exemption, the Commission may consider the nature of the coverage, the person or persons to be insured or covered, the competence of the buyer or other parties to the contract, and other criteria the Commission considers relevant.

G. The policy and endorsement forms referred to in subsection A of this section shall be open to public inspection. Copies may be obtained by any person on request and upon payment of a reasonable charge for the copies.

H. Any insurer whose rate service organization files on behalf of such insurer shall notify the Commission prior to the effective date of any filing if the insurer is not going to accept the filing made on its behalf. (1976, c. 278, § 38.1-279.48:1; 1986, c. 562; 1988, c. 523; 1993, c. 985; 1997, c. 26.)

§ **38.2-318. Validity of noncomplying forms.** — A. Any insurance policy or form containing any condition or provision that is not in compliance with this title shall be valid, but shall be construed and applied in accordance with the conditions and provisions required by this title.

B. As used in this section, *"form"* means any contract, rider, endorsement, amendment, certificate, or application or other instrument providing, modifying, or eliminating insurance coverage. (1952, c. 317, § 38.1-343; 1986, c. 562.)

Statutory provisions supersede inconsistent policy provisions. — If the terms of the policy are inconsistent with statutory provisions, the statutory provisions supersede the inconsistent policy terms. USAA Cas. Ins. Co. v. Yaconiello, 226 Va. 423, 309 S.E.2d 324 (1983).

Superseding provision takes effect only if policy restricts coverage. — Where minor was passenger on uninsured moped which collided with truck, where insurance policy defined uninsured motor vehicle as motor vehicle which lacked effective protection by insurance coverage, and where insurer pointed out that former § 46.1-1(15) (now § 46.2-100) specifically excluded bicycles and mopeds from defini-

tion of term motor vehicle, moped was motor vehicle within terms of uninsured motorist coverage because insurer's policy afforded broader coverage and there is no prohibition against insurer offering broader coverage than minimum prescribed by law; superseding provisions of § 38.2-318 take effect only where insurer seeks, by policy language, to narrow, avoid, vary or restrict coverage legislature has required. Hill v. State Farm Mut. Auto. Ins. Co., 237 Va. 148, 375 S.E.2d 727 (1989).

Applied in State Farm Mut. Auto. Ins. Co. v. Seay, 236 Va. 275, 373 S.E.2d 910 (1988); Virginia Farm Bureau Mut. Ins. Co. v. Jerrell, 236 Va. 261, 373 S.E.2d 913 (1988).

§ **38.2-319. Validity of contracts in violation of law.** — Any insurance contract made in violation of the laws of this Commonwealth may be enforced against the insurer. (Code 1950, §§ 38-32, 38-223; 1952, c. 317, § 38.1-344; 1986, c. 562.)

§ **38.2-320. Insurer to furnish forms for proof of loss.** — Whenever notice of any loss or damage has been given to the insurer or its agent, the insurer shall, upon written request, deliver to the insured or to the person to whom the benefits are payable the forms for such preliminary proof of loss or damage as may be required under the policy. Such forms shall be delivered within fifteen days after written request has been made or mailed to the insurer by the insured or person to whom benefits are payable. The failure or refusal of an insurer or its agent to deliver such forms within fifteen days of written request shall be deemed a waiver of any condition, stipulation or provision in the policy requiring preliminary proof. (Code 1950, § 38-11; 1952, c. 317, § 38.1-345; 1986, c. 562.)

This section is applicable to life insurance contracts containing accidental death benefits. Wharton v. Lincoln Nat'l Life Ins. Co., 134 F. Supp. 558 (E.D. Va. 1955).

It applies only to waiver of preliminary proofs. — This section applies only to waiver of preliminary proofs. It is inapplicable to "amended proofs" and the burden rests upon claimant to supply same. Wharton v. Lincoln Nat'l Life Ins. Co., 134 F. Supp. 558 (E.D. Va. 1955).

This section and § 38.2-314 do not change the rule adopted in North British & Mercantile Ins. Co. v. Edmundson, 104 Va. 486, 52 S.E. 350 (1905), to the effect that failure to file proof of loss within the time specified in the policy does not bar an action on the policy if the proof of loss is filed before suit is brought. Southern Home Ins. Co. v. Bowers, 157 Va. 686, 161 S.E. 914 (1932).

§ 38.2-321. Payment discharges insurer. — A. An insurer shall be fully discharged from all claims under a life insurance policy, accident and sickness insurance policy, or annuity contract:

1. When the proceeds of or payments under a policy or contract become payable in accordance with (i) the terms of the policy or contract or (ii) the exercise of any right or privilege under the contract; and

2. If the insurer makes payments in accordance with the terms of the policy or contract or any written assignment to the person designated in the policy or contract or by assignment as being entitled to the proceeds or payments.

B. An insurer may not be fully discharged from all claims under a life insurance policy, accident and sickness insurance policy, or annuity contract before payment is made and if the insurer has received, at its home office, written notice that some other person claims to be entitled to payment or some interest in the policy or contract. (1952, c. 317, § 38.1-346.1; 1986, c. 562.)

Insurer protected against double payment where insured and his assignee file claims. — This section is designed, not to burden an insurer, but rather to protect it against double payment when both the insured and his assignee file claims for the same ben-

efits. The notice proviso simply withholds that protection when the insurer has the knowledge necessary to protect itself. Kelly Health Care, Inc. v. Prudential Ins. Co. of Am., 226 Va. 376, 309 S.E.2d 305 (1983).

§ 38.2-322. Standardized claims forms. — A. No accident and sickness insurer, health maintenance organization, health services plan, or optometric services plan licensed in the Commonwealth shall refuse to accept, as a standard claims form for physician services or for services provided by chiropractors, optometrists, opticians, professional counselors, psychologists, clinical social workers, podiatrists, physical therapists, clinical nurse specialists who render mental health services, audiologists, and speech pathologists, the standardized HCFA-1500 health insurance claims form, or its successor as it may be amended from time to time. However, nothing in this section shall prohibit an insurer, health maintenance organization, health services plan, or optometric services plan from accepting any other claims form.

B. No accident and sickness insurer, health maintenance organization, or health services plan licensed in the Commonwealth shall refuse to accept as a standard claims form for hospital services the standardized UB-82 claims form, or its successor as it may be amended from time to time. However, nothing in this section shall prohibit an accident and sickness insurer, health maintenance organization, or health services plan from accepting any other claims form.

C. No accident and sickness insurer, health maintenance organization, health services plan, or dental services plan licensed in the Commonwealth shall refuse to accept as a standard claims form for dental services the standardized ADA form prepared by the American Dental Association, or its successor as it may be amended from time to time. However, nothing in this section shall prohibit an accident and sickness insurer, health maintenance organization, health services plan, or dental services plan from accepting any other claims form.

D. The forms specified in this section may be modified as necessary to accommodate the transmission and administration of claims by electronic means.

E. After July 1, 1998, no health maintenance organization authorized to transact business in this Commonwealth and no health insurer, health services plan or preferred provider organization authorized to offer health benefits in this Commonwealth that requires the use of the Physicians' Current Procedural Terminology (CPT) identifying codes published by the American Medical Association for reporting claims for medical services and procedures, including any standardized form, shall refuse to accept and utilize these identifying codes and any appropriate modifiers listed therein when the same are appropriately used for processing such claims for provider services and procedures. (1993, c. 307; 1997, c. 531.)

CHAPTER 4.

ASSESSMENT FOR ADMINISTRATION OF INSURANCE LAWS AND DECLARATIONS OF ESTIMATED ASSESSMENTS BY INSURERS.

§ 38.2-400. Expense of administration of insurance laws borne by licensees; minimum contribution. — A. The expense of maintaining the Bureau of the Commission responsible for administering the insurance laws of this Commonwealth, including a reasonable margin in the nature of a reserve fund, shall be assessed annually by the Commission against all companies and surplus lines brokers subject to this title except premium finance companies and providers of continuing care registered pursuant to Chapter 49 (§ 38.2-4900 et seq.) of this title. The assessment shall be in proportion to the direct gross premium income on business done in this Commonwealth. The assessment shall not exceed one-tenth of one percent of the direct gross premium income and shall be levied pursuant to § 38.2-403. For any year a company is subject to an assessment, the assessment shall not be less than $300.

B. All fees assessed under any provision of this title and paid into the state treasury shall be deposited to a special fund designated "Bureau of Insurance Special Fund — State Corporation Commission," and out of such special fund and the unexpended balance thereof shall be appropriated the sums necessary for the regulation, supervision and examination of all entities subject to regulation under this title. Any references in the Code of Virginia to funds being paid directly into the state treasury and credited to the fund for the maintenance of the Bureau of Insurance shall hereinafter mean the "Bureau of Insurance Special Fund — State Corporation Commission." (Code 1950, § 38-17; 1952, c. 317, § 38.1-44; 1954, c. 231; 1960, c. 294; 1977, cc. 317, 613; 1978, c. 4; 1981, c. 605; 1986, c. 562; 1987, cc. 558, 565, 655; 1994, c. 316.)

Cross references. — As to the application of this article to licensed group self-insurance associations formed by employers subject to Virginia Workers' Compensation Act, see § 65.2-802.

§ 38.2-401. Fire Programs Fund. — A. There is hereby established a Fire Programs Fund which shall be administered by the Department of Fire Programs under policies and definitions established by the Virginia Fire Services Board. The Fund, which includes grants noted herein, shall be created in the state treasury as a special nonreverting fund and shall be established on the books of the Comptroller. Any moneys deposited to or remaining in such Fund during or at the end of each fiscal year or biennium shall not revert to the general fund but shall remain in the Fund. Moneys shall be deposited or transferred to the account as collected by the State Corporation Commission and as coordinated with the Department. Interest earned on all moneys shall remain in the Fund and be credited to it. Interest earned from the Fund shall be set aside to be used for fire service purposes as defined by the Virginia Fire Services Board. The Fund shall consist of any moneys appropriated for this purpose by the General Assembly and any other moneys received for such purpose by the Board or Department. Notwithstanding any other provision of law to the contrary, policies established by the Board for the administration of the Fund, and any grants provided from the Fund, that are not inconsistent with the purposes set out in this section shall be binding upon any locality that accepts such funds or related grants. In order to maintain the Fund, the Commission shall annually assess against all licensed insurance companies doing business in this Commonwealth by writing any type of insurance as defined in §§ 38.2-110, 38.2-111, 38.2-126, 38.2-130 and 38.2-131 and those combination policies as defined in § 38.2-1921 that contain insurance as defined in §§ 38.2-110, 38.2-111 and 38.2-126, an assessment in the amount of one percent of the total direct gross premium income for such insurance. Such assessment shall be apportioned, assessed and paid as prescribed by § 38.2-403. In any year in which a company has no direct gross premium income or in which its direct gross premium income is insufficient to produce at the rate of assessment prescribed by law an amount equal to or in excess of $100, there shall be so apportioned and assessed against such company a contribution of $100. The Commission shall be reimbursed from the Fund for all expenses necessary for the administration of this section.

B. After reserving funds for the grants noted herein, seventy-five percent of the remaining amount collected annually pursuant to this section shall be allocated to the several counties, cities and towns of the Commonwealth providing fire service operations to be used for the improvement of volunteer and career fire services in each of the receiving localities. Funds allocated to the counties, cities and towns pursuant to this subsection shall not be used directly or indirectly to supplant or replace any other funds appropriated by the counties, cities and towns for fire service operations. Such funds shall be used solely for the purposes of training volunteer or career firefighting personnel in each of the receiving localities; funding fire prevention and public safety education programs; constructing, improving and expanding regional or local fire service training facilities; or for purchasing personal protective equipment, vehicles, equipment and supplies for use in the receiving locality specifically for fire service purposes. Notwithstanding any other provision of the Code, when localities use such funds to construct, improve or expand fire service training facilities, fire-related training provided at such training facilities shall be by instructors certified or approved according to policies developed by the Department of Fire Programs and approved by the Virginia Fire Services Board. Distribution of this seventy-five percent of the Fund shall be made on the basis of population as provided for in §§ 4.1-116 and 4.1-117; however, no county or city eligible for such funds shall receive less than $10,000, nor eligible town less than $4,000. In order to remain eligible for such funds, each receiving locality shall report annually to the Department on the use of the funds allocated to it for the previous year and shall provide a completed Fire Programs Fund Disbursement Agreement form. Each receiving locality shall be responsible for certifying the proper use of the funds. If, at the end of any annual reporting period, a satisfactory report and a completed agreement form have not been submitted by a receiving locality, any funds due to that locality for the next year shall be retained until said documents are submitted to the Department.

C. The remainder of this Fund shall be used for the purposes of underwriting the costs of the operation of the Department of Fire Programs which shall include providing funded training and administrative support services for non-funded training to localities.

D. The Fire Services Grant Fund Program is hereby established and will be used as grants to provide regional fire services training facilities, to finance the Virginia Fire Incident Reporting System and to build or repair burn buildings as determined by the Virginia Fire Services Board. Beginning January 1, 1996, one million dollars from the assessments made pursuant to this section shall be distributed each year for the Fire Services Grant Fund to be used as herein provided, and $100,000 shall be distributed annually for continuing the statewide Dry Fire Hydrant Grant Program. All grants provided from this Fund shall be administered by the Department according to the policies and procedures established by the Virginia Fire Services Board.

E. Moneys in the Fund shall not be diverted or expended for any purpose not authorized by this section. (1985, c. 545, § 38.1-44.1; 1986, cc. 60, 562; 1988, c. 336; 1995, cc. 615, 637; 1997, c. 791; 1998, cc. 166, 877.)

Editor's note. — Pursuant to § 9-77.11, effect has been given in this section, as set out above, to Acts 1986, c. 60, which amended former § 38.1-44.1, the comparable provision in former Title 38.1.

Acts 1989, cc. 19 and 103 repealed Acts 1985, c. 545, cl. 3, which had provided an expiration date for Acts 1985, c. 545, the act which enacted

§ 38.1-44.1 (now this section).

The 1998 amendments. — The 1998 amendments by cc. 166 and 877 are identical, and, in subsection D, in the second sentence, substituted "one million dollars" for "$1,000,000," and in the last sentence, substituted "this Fund" for "the fund"; and added subsection E.

§ 38.2-401.1. Flood Prevention and Protection Assistance Fund assessment.
— The Commission shall annually assess against all licensed insurance companies doing business in this Commonwealth by writing any type of flood insurance an assessment in the amount of one percent of the total direct gross premium income for such insurance. Such assessment shall be

apportioned, assessed, and paid as prescribed by § 38.2-403. In any year in which a company has no direct gross premium income from flood insurance or in which its direct gross premium income from flood insurance is insufficient to produce at the rate of assessment prescribed by law an amount equal to or in excess of $100, there shall be so apportioned and assessed against such company a contribution of $100. One hundred percent of the total amount collected annually pursuant to this section shall be paid into the Flood Prevention and Protection Assistance Fund established per § 10.1-603.17. The assessment established by this section shall not apply to premium income for policies written pursuant to the National Flood Insurance Act of 1968 or for policies providing comprehensive motor vehicle insurance coverage. (1990, c. 916.)

Editor's note. — Repeal of this section by Acts 1997, c. 590 was contingent on funding in the general appropriation act. The funding was not provided, and therefore, the repeal never took effect.

§ **38.2-402. Definitions.** — As used in this chapter:

"Assessable year" means the calendar year upon which the direct gross premium income is computed under this chapter. In the case of direct gross premium income for a fraction of a calendar year, the term includes the period in which that direct gross premium income is received or derived from business in this Commonwealth.

"Direct gross premium income" means direct gross premium as defined in § 58.1-2500.

"Estimated assessment" means the company's estimate of the amount imposed by this chapter for the license year.

"License year" means the twelve-month period beginning on July 1 next succeeding the assessable year and ending on June 30 of the subsequent year. This shall also be the year in which annual reports of direct gross premium income are required to be filed under § 38.2-406 and the annual assessment paid under the provisions of this chapter. (1977, c. 317, §§ 38.1-48.1, 38.1-48.2; 1978, c. 4; 1986, c. 562; 1996, c. 22.)

Cross references. — As to the application of this article to licensed group self-insurance associations formed by employer subject to the Virginia Workers' Compensation Act, see § 65.2-802.

§ **38.2-403. Assessment for expenses.** — The Commission shall assess each company annually for its just share of expenses. The assessment shall be in proportion to direct gross premium income for the year immediately preceding that for which the assessment is made. The Commission shall give the companies notice of the assessment which shall be paid to the Commission on or before March 1 of each year for deposit into the state treasury as provided in subsection B of § 38.2-400. Any company that fails to pay the assessment on or before the date herein prescribed shall be subject to a penalty imposed by the Commission. The penalty shall be ten percent of the assessment and interest shall be charged at a rate pursuant to § 58.1-1812 for the period between the due date and the date of full payment. If a payment is made in an amount later found to be in error, the Commission shall, (i) if an additional amount is due, notify the company of the additional amount and the company shall pay the additional amount within fourteen days of the date of the notice or, (ii) if an overpayment is made, order a refund as provided for in subsection B of § 38.2-410. (Code 1950, § 38-18; 1952, c. 317, § 38.1-45; 1977, c. 317; 1978, c. 4; 1986, c. 562; 1994, c. 316.)

§ 38.2-404. Recovery of such assessments; revocation or suspension of license. — If an assessment made under § 38.2-403 is not paid to the Commission by the prescribed date, the amount of the assessment, penalty, and interest may be recovered from the defaulting company on motion of the Commission made in the name and for the use of the Commonwealth in the appropriate circuit court after ten days' notice to the company. The license or certificate of authority of any defaulting company to transact business in this Commonwealth may be revoked or suspended by the Commission until it has paid such assessment. (Code 1950, § 38-19; 1952, c. 317, § 38.1-46; 1978, c. 4; 1986, c. 562.)

§ 38.2-405. Appeal from assessment. — A company aggrieved by the assessment may appeal to the Supreme Court of Virginia in accordance with the Rules of Court applicable to appeals from the State Corporation Commission. If the court is of the opinion that the assessment is either excessive or insufficient, the court shall by its order request the Commission to make appropriate adjustments. If the appellant fails to pay the assessment when due and the court affirms the action of the Commission, judgment shall be entered against the appellant for damages, which are to be paid to the Commission, equal to legal interest upon the amount of the assessment from the time the assessment was payable. If relief is granted in whole or in part, judgment shall be rendered against the Commonwealth for any excess that may have been paid, with legal interest. (Code 1950, § 38-20; 1952, c. 317, § 38.1-47; 1978, c. 4; 1986, c. 562.)

§ 38.2-406. Report of gross premium income and other information. — Each company subject to assessment under this chapter shall report to the Commission by March 1 of each year. The report shall be on forms furnished by the Commission and shall include the company's direct gross premium income, assessments, dues and fees for the preceding calendar year, and any other information the Commission requires. (Code 1950, § 38-21; 1952, c. 317, § 38.1-48; 1977, c. 317; 1978, c. 4; 1986, c. 562.)

§ 38.2-407. Declarations of estimated assessment. — A. Each company subject to the assessment prescribed by § 38.2-400 shall make a declaration of estimated assessment for the assessable year as provided in this chapter. This declaration is required if the assessment imposed by § 38.2-400 can reasonably be expected to exceed $3,000.

B. The declaration shall contain any pertinent information the Commission may require.

C. A company may make amendments of a declaration filed during the assessable year, subject to the requirements of the Commission, not exceeding the number specified in subsection B of § 38.2-408.

D. A company with an assessable year of less than twelve months shall make a declaration in accordance with the requirements of the Commission. (1977, c. 317, § 38.1-48.2; 1986, c. 562; 1998, c. 15.)

The 1998 amendment, effective January 1, 1999, in subsection A, in the first sentence, substituted "the assessment prescribed by § 38.2-400" for "licensure under this title that is required to make a declaration of estimated tax as provided in Article 2 (§ 58.1-2520 et seq.) of Chapter 25 of Title 58.1" and in the second sentence, substituted "§ 38.2-400" for "this chapter."

§ 38.2-408. Time for filing declarations of estimated assessment. —
A. The declaration of estimated assessment required of companies by § 38.2-407 shall be filed as follows:

If the requirements of § 38.2-407 are first met:

1. Before April 1 of the assessable year, the declaration shall be filed on or before April 15 of the assessable year.

2. After March 31 but before June 1 of the assessable year, the declaration shall be filed on or before June 15 of the assessable year.

3. After May 31 but before September 1 of the assessable year, the declaration shall be filed on or before September 15 of the assessable year.

4. After August 31 but before December 1 of the assessable year, the assessment shall be filed on or before December 15 of the assessable year.

B. An amendment of a declaration may be filed in any interval between installment dates prescribed for the assessable year, but only one amendment may be filed in each such interval.

C. The application of this section to assessable years of less than twelve months shall be in accordance with the prescribed requirements of the Commission. (1977, c. 317, § 38.1-48.3; 1986, c. 562.)

§ 38.2-409. Installment payment of estimated assessment. — A. The amount of estimated assessment, as defined in subsection B of § 38.2-407 for which a declaration is required under § 38.2-407 shall be paid in installments as follows:

1. If the declaration is required to be filed by April 15 of the assessable year, twenty-five percent of the estimated assessment shall be paid on April, June, September and December 15 respectively of the assessable year.

2. If the declaration is required to be filed by June 15 of the assessable year, one-third of the estimated assessment shall be paid on June, September and December 15 respectively of the assessable year.

3. If the declaration is required to be filed by September 15 of the assessable year, one-half of the estimated assessment shall be paid on September and December 15 respectively of the assessable year.

4. If the declaration is required to be filed by December 15 of the assessable year, 100 percent of the estimated assessment shall be paid on the same date the declaration is filed.

B. A declaration is timely filed if it is filed on or before the date prescribed by subsection A of § 38.2-408. The timeliness of filing shall be determined without regard to any extension of time for filing the declaration.

C. If the declaration is filed after the time prescribed in subsection A of § 38.2-408, determined without regard to any extension of time for filing the declaration, all estimated assessment installments shall be paid at the time of the filing which would have been payable on or before that time if the declaration had been filed within the prescribed time. The remaining installments shall be paid at the times and in the amounts that would have been payable if the declaration had been filed within the time prescribed.

D. If any amendment of a declaration is filed, the amount of each remaining installment shall be the amount of the last installment due subject to the following adjustment. Each installment shall be increased or decreased by the amount computed by dividing (i) the difference between the current amount of estimated assessment and the amended amount of estimated assessment by (ii) the number of installments remaining to be paid.

E. The Commission shall determine the application of this section to assessable years of less than twelve months.

F. A company may prepay any installment of the estimated assessment.

G. Payment of the estimated assessment or any installment thereof shall be considered payment on account of the assessment imposed by this chapter for the license year.

H. The Commission may grant a reasonable extension of time for (i) payment of estimated assessment, or any installment or (ii) filing any declaration pursuant to this chapter, on condition that interest shall be paid on the amount involved at the rate of three-quarters of one percent per month or fraction thereof from the time the payment was due until the time of payment. Whenever a company, without having been granted an extension, fails to make payment of the estimated assessment or any installment, or fails to file any declaration as required by this chapter, it shall pay interest on the amount involved at the rate of one percent per month or fraction thereof from the time payment was due until the time of payment. (1977, c. 317, § 38.1-48.4; 1986, c. 562.)

§ 38.2-410. Where declarations filed and how payments made; refunding overpayments. — A. As required by this chapter, each company shall file a declaration of estimated assessment with and pay the same to the Commission. All such payments shall be deposited by the Commission into the state treasury.

B. If any company overestimates and overpays the assessment, the Commission shall order a refund of the amount of the overpayment to the company. The overpayment shall be refunded out of the state treasury on the order of the Commission upon the Comptroller. (1977, c. 317, § 38.1-48.5; 1986, c. 562.)

§ 38.2-411. Failure to pay estimated assessment. — A. In case of any underpayment of estimated assessment by a company, except as provided in subsection D of this section, interest shall be added to the assessment for the license year and shall be determined at the rate set forth in § 58.1-15. Interest shall be based on the amount of the underpayment as determined in subsection B for the period of the underpayment as determined in subsection C.

B. For purposes of subsection A of this section the amount of the underpayment shall be the excess of the amount of the installment which would be required to be paid if the estimated assessment were equal to ninety percent of the assessment for the license year, over any amount of the installment paid on or before the last date prescribed for payment.

C. The period of the underpayment shall run from the date the installment was required to be paid to whichever of the following dates is the earlier:

1. The first day of the third month following the close of the assessable year.

2. For any portion of the underpayment, the date on which the portion is paid. For purposes of this subdivision, a payment of estimated assessment on any installment date shall be considered a payment of any previous underpayment only to the extent the payment exceeds the amount of the installment determined under subsection B for that installment date.

D. Notwithstanding the provisions of subsections A, B and C of this section, the addition to the assessment for any underpayment of an installment shall not be charged if the total amount of all estimated assessment payments made prior to the last date prescribed for the payment meets the following conditions. The total shall equal or exceed the amount which would have been required to be paid on or before the last date prescribed for the payment if the estimated assessment were the lesser of:

1. The assessment for the preceding license year which was computed on the basis of an assessable year of twelve months; or

2. An amount equal to the assessment computed at the rate applicable to the license year based on the facts shown on the company's report, and the applicable law for the preceding license year; or

3. a. An amount equal to ninety percent of the assessment measured by direct gross premium income received or derived in the assessable year computed by placing on an annualized basis the assessable direct gross premium income:

(1) For the first three months of the assessable year, in the case of the installment required to be paid in the fourth month;

(2) For the first three months or for the first five months of the assessable year, in the case of the installment required to be paid in the sixth month;

(3) For the first six months or for the first eight months of the assessable year, in the case of the installment required to be paid in the ninth month; and

(4) For the first nine months or for the first eleven months of the assessable year, in the case of the installment required to be paid in the twelfth month of the assessable year.

b. For the purposes of this subsection, the assessable direct gross premium income shall be placed on an annualized basis by (i) multiplying by twelve the assessable direct gross premium income referred to in subdivision 3 a of this subsection, and (ii) dividing the resulting amount by the number of months in the assessable year referred to in subdivision 3 a of this subsection.

E. The Commission shall determine the application of this section to assessable years of less than twelve months. (1977, c. 317, § 38.1-48.6; 1986, c. 562.)

§ **38.2-412. Companies going out of business.** — If a company goes out of business or ceases to be a company in this Commonwealth in any assessable or license year, the company shall remain liable for the payment of the assessment measured by direct gross premium income for the period in which it operated as a company and received or derived direct gross premium income from business in this Commonwealth. (1977, c. 317, § 38.1-48.7; 1986, c. 562.)

§ **38.2-413. Double assessment respecting same direct gross premium income negated.** — This chapter shall not be construed to require including any direct gross premium income used previously in calculating the assessment imposed by this chapter for any license year or fraction thereof, and the assessment paid thereon. (1977, c. 317, § 38.1-48.9; 1986, c. 562.)

§ **38.2-414. Assessments to fund program to reduce losses from motor vehicle thefts.** — A. To provide funds to establish and operate a statewide program to receive and reward information leading to the arrest of persons who commit motor vehicle theft-related crimes in Virginia, each insurer licensed to write insurance coverage as defined in § 38.2-124 shall, prior to March 1 of each year, pay an assessment equal to one-quarter of one percent of the total direct gross premium income for automobile physical damage insurance other than collision written in the Commonwealth during the preceding calendar year.

B. Assessments received pursuant to subsection A of this section, and all other moneys received by the Commission for the same purpose, shall be segregated and placed in a fund to be known as the Help Eliminate Automobile Theft Fund, hereinafter referred to as the HEAT Fund.

C. Any insurer that fails to pay the assessment on or before the date prescribed in subsection A shall be subject to a penalty imposed by the Commission. The penalty shall be ten percent of the assessment and interest shall be charged at a rate pursuant to § 58.1-1812 for the period between the date due and the date of full payment. If a payment is made in an amount later found to be in error, the Commission shall, (i) if an additional amount is due, notify the insurer of the additional amount, which the insurer shall pay within fourteen days of the date of the notice or, (ii) if an overpayment is made, order a refund of the amount of the overpayment, which shall be paid out of the HEAT Fund. The Commission shall be reimbursed from the Fund for all expenses necessary for the administration of this section.

D. The HEAT Fund shall be controlled and administered by the Superintendent of the Department of State Police. The Superintendent shall appoint an advisory committee of seven members to assist in developing and annually reviewing the plan of operation for the HEAT Fund program.

E. Money in the HEAT Fund shall be expended as follows:

1. To pay the costs of establishing and operating a program to receive and reward information leading to the arrest of persons who commit motor vehicle theft-related crimes in Virginia.

2. Any uncommitted funds remaining in the HEAT Fund on the last day of February of each year may be transferred to the Department of State Police, Department of Motor Vehicles, or Department of Criminal Justice Services for the following purposes: (i) providing financial support to state or local law-enforcement agencies for motor vehicle theft enforcement efforts, (ii) providing financial support to local prosecutors or judicial agencies for programs designed to reduce the incidence of motor vehicle theft, and (iii) conducting educational programs to inform vehicle owners of methods of preventing motor vehicle theft. (1991, c. 318; 1993, c. 196.)

§ 38.2-415. (Effective until January 1, 2003) Assessment to fund program to reduce losses from insurance fraud. — A. Each licensed insurer doing business in the Commonwealth by writing any type of insurance as defined in §§ 38.2-110 through 38.2-122.1 and 38.2-124 through 38.2-132 shall pay, in addition to any other assessments provided in this title, an assessment in an amount equal to 0.05 of one percent of the direct gross premium income during the preceding calendar year. The assessment shall be apportioned and assessed and paid as prescribed by § 38.2-403. The Commission shall be reimbursed from the fund for all necessary expenses for the administration of this section.

B. The assessments made by the Commission under subsection A and paid into the state treasury shall be deposited to a special fund designated "Virginia State Police, Insurance Fraud," and out of such special fund and the unexpended balance thereof shall be appropriated the sums necessary for accomplishing the powers and duties assigned to the Virginia State Police under Chapter 9 (§ 52-36 et seq.) of Title 52. All interest earned from the deposit of moneys accumulated in the Fund shall be deposited in the Fund for the same use.

C. The moneys deposited in the Fund shall not be considered general revenue of the Commonwealth but shall be used only to (i) effectuate the purposes enumerated in Chapter 9 (§ 52-36 et seq.) of Title 52 and (ii) reimburse the Commission for its necessary expenses for the administration of this section. The Fund shall be subject to audit by the Auditor of Public Accounts.

D. In the event that the Insurance Fraud Investigation Unit is dissolved by operation of law or otherwise, any balance remaining in the Fund, after deducting administrative costs associated with the dissolution, shall be returned to insurers in proportion to their financial contributions to the Fund in the preceding calendar year. (1998, c. 590; 1999, c. 483.)

Editor's note. — Acts 1998, c. 590, cl. 2 provides: "That the provisions of this act will expire on January 1, 2003."

Effective date. — This section is effective January 1, 1999.

The 1999 amendment deleted "collected" preceding "during the preceding" in the first sentence of subsection A.

CHAPTER 5.

Unfair Trade Practices.

§ **38.2-500. Declaration of purpose.** — The purpose of this chapter is to regulate trade practices in the business of insurance in accordance with the intent of Congress as expressed in the McCarran-Ferguson Act, 15 U.S.C. §§ 1011 through 1015, by defining and prohibiting all practices in this Commonwealth that constitute unfair methods of competition or unfair or deceptive acts or practices. (1952, c. 317, § 38.1-49; 1986, c. 562.)

Federal preemption of state laws in relation to employee benefit plans. — State laws, insofar as they are invoked by beneficiaries claiming relief for injuries arising out of the administration of employee benefit plans, "relate to" such plans and, absent an applicable exemption, are preempted by Employee Retirement Income Security Act, 29 U.S.C. § 1001 et seq. Claims for breach of an implied covenant of good faith and fair dealing and for violations of the Virginia Unfair Trade Practices Act, both of which purport to impose duties on insurers, are not rescued from preemption by an "insurance saving clause," in 29 U.S.C. § 1144(b)(2)(A), since the insurance saving clause is limited by the so-called "deemer clause," which provides that no employee benefit plan shall be deemed to be an insurance company or other insurer or to be engaged in the business of insurance for purposes of any law of any State purporting to regulate insurance companies or insurance contracts. Powell v. C & P Tel. Co., 780 F.2d 419 (4th Cir. 1985), cert. denied, 476 U.S. 1170, 106 S. Ct. 2892, 90 L. Ed. 2d 980 (1986).

Application of the Racketeer Influenced and Corrupt Organization Act (RICO) to afford redress for violation of Chapter 5, would invalidate and impair the regulation sought to be accomplished by Chapter 5 and the enforcement mechanisms of §§ 38.2-218—38.2-220.

Ambrose v. Blue Cross & Blue Shield of Va., Inc., 891 F. Supp. 1153 (E.D. Va. 1995), aff'd, 95 F.3d 41 (4th Cir. 1996).

Because RICO provides for a private cause of action and treble damages, and because these provisions of RICO differ dramatically from the way in which Virginia's insurance code addresses the same conduct, RICO would in effect replace Chapter 5 as the principal means by which to remedy such conduct. It would convert a system of public redress into a system of private redress. The forum for redress would shift from the State Corporation Commission (SCC) to the federal courts. The result of these effects would be that RICO would supersede Virginia's laws. Ambrose v. Blue Cross & Blue Shield of Va., Inc., 891 F. Supp. 1153 (E.D. Va. 1995), aff'd, 95 F.3d 41 (4th Cir. 1996).

The Virginia Unfair Insurance Practices Act does not establish a private cause of action. A & E Supply Co. v. Nationwide Mut. Fire Ins. Co., 798 F.2d 669 (4th Cir. 1986), cert. denied, 479 U.S. 1091, 107 S. Ct. 1302, 94 L. Ed. 2d 158 (1987); Salomon v. Transamerica Occidental Life Ins. Co., 801 F.2d 659 (4th Cir. 1986).

An award of punitive damages may not rest on a jury finding that defendant violated the Unfair Insurance Practices Act. A & E Supply Co. v. Nationwide Mut. Fire Ins.

Co., 798 F.2d 669 (4th Cir. 1986), cert. denied,
479 U.S. 1091, 107 S. Ct. 1302, 94 L. Ed. 2d 158
(1987).

§ 38.2-501. Definitions. — As used in this chapter:

"Insurance policy" or *"insurance contract"* includes annuities and any group
or individual contract, certificate, or evidence of coverage, including, but not
limited to, those issued by a health services plan, health maintenance
organization, legal organization, legal services plan, or dental or optometric
services plan as provided for in Chapters 42 (§ 38.2-4200 et seq.), 43 (§ 38.2-
4300 et seq.), 44 (§ 38.2-4400 et seq.) and 45 (§ 38.2-4500 et seq.) of this title
issued, proposed for issuance, or intended for issuance, by any person.

"Lending institution" means any corporation, company or organization that
accepts deposits from the public and lends money in this Commonwealth,
including banks and savings institutions.

"Person," in addition to the definition in Chapter 1 (§ 38.2-100 et seq.) of this
title, extends to any other legal entity transacting the business of insurance,
including agents, brokers and adjusters. "Person" also means health, legal,
dental, and optometric service plans and health maintenance organizations, as
provided for in Chapters 42, 43, 44 and 45 of this title. For the purposes of this
chapter, such service plans shall be deemed to be transacting the business of
insurance. "Person" also means premium finance companies. (1952, c. 317,
§ 38.1-50; 1977, c. 529; 1980, c. 404; 1986, c. 562; 1989, c. 653; 1992, c. 7.)

**§ 38.2-502. Misrepresentations and false advertising of insurance
policies.** — No person shall make, issue, circulate, cause or knowingly allow
to be made, issued or circulated, any estimate, illustration, circular, statement,
sales presentation, omission, or comparison that:

1. Misrepresents the benefits, advantages, conditions or terms of any
insurance policy;

2. Misrepresents the dividends or share of the surplus to be received on any
insurance policy;

3. Makes any false or misleading statements as to the dividends or share of
surplus previously paid on any insurance policy;

4. Misrepresents or is misleading as to the financial condition of any person
or the legal reserve system upon which any life insurer operates;

5. Uses any name or title of any insurance policy or class of insurance
policies that misrepresents the true nature of the policy or policies;

6. Misrepresents any material fact for the purpose of inducing or tending to
induce the lapse, forfeiture, exchange, conversion, replacement, or surrender
of any insurance policy;

7. Misrepresents any material fact for the purpose of effecting a pledge,
assignment, or loan on any insurance policy; or

8. Misrepresents any insurance policy as being a share of stock. (Code 1950,
§ 38.1-52; 1952, c. 317, § 38.1-52.1; 1977, c. 529; 1978, c. 441; 1979, c. 324;
1980, c. 404; 1986, c. 562; 1990, c. 265.)

Purpose. — The plain meaning of this section, § 38.2-503 and § 38.2-510 show that the primary purpose of these sections is to regulate the performance of insurance contracts by assuring conformity between representations made by the insurer to the insured and the actual performance of the insurance policies. In other words, each statute is designed to regulate the representations made to form, and the practices which comprise, the relationship between insurer and insured and the performance of the insurance contract which is the foundation of that relationship. Ambrose v. Blue Cross & Blue Shield of Va., Inc., 891 F. Supp. 1153 (E.D. Va. 1995), aff'd, 95 F.3d 41 (4th Cir. 1996).

Federal preemption of state laws in relation to employee benefit plans. — State laws, insofar as they are invoked by beneficiaries claiming relief for injuries arising out of the administration of employee benefit plans, "relate to" such plans and, absent an applicable exemption, are preempted by Employee Retirement Income Security Act, 29 U.S.C. § 1001 et seq. Claims for breach of an implied covenant of good faith and fair dealing and for violations of the Virginia Unfair Trade Practices Act, both of which purport to impose duties on insurers, are not rescued from preemption by an "insurance saving clause," in 29 U.S.C. § 1144(b)(2)(A), since the insurance saving clause is limited by the so-called "deemer clause," which provides that no employee benefit plan shall be deemed to be an insurance company or other insurer or to be engaged in the business of insurance for purposes of any law of any State purporting to regulate insurance companies or insurance contracts. Powell v. C & P Tel. Co., 780 F.2d 419 (4th Cir. 1985), cert. denied, 476 U.S. 1170, 106 S. Ct. 2892, 90 L. Ed. 2d 980 (1986).

§ 38.2-503. False information and advertising generally. — No person shall knowingly make, publish, disseminate, circulate, or place before the public, or cause or knowingly allow, directly or indirectly, to be made, published, disseminated, circulated, or placed before the public in a newspaper, magazine or other publication, or in the form of a notice, circular, pamphlet, letter or poster, or over any radio or television station, or in any other way, an advertisement, announcement or statement containing any assertion, representation or statement relating to (i) the business of insurance or (ii) any person in the conduct of his insurance business, which is untrue, deceptive or misleading. (Code 1950, § 38.1-52; 1952, c. 317, § 38.1-52.2; 1977, c. 529; 1978, c. 441; 1979, c. 324; 1980, c. 404; 1986, c. 562.)

Purpose. — The plain meaning of this section, § 38.2-502 and § 38.2-510 show that the primary purpose of these sections is to regulate the performance of insurance contracts by assuring conformity between representations made by the insurer to the insured and the actual performance of the insurance policies. In other words, each statute is designed to regulate the representations made to form, and the practices which comprise, the relationship between insurer and insured and the performance of the insurance contract which is the foundation of that relationship. Ambrose v. Blue Cross & Blue Shield of Va., Inc., 891 F. Supp. 1153 (E.D. Va. 1995), aff'd, 95 F.3d 41 (4th Cir. 1996).

§ 38.2-504. Defamation. — No person shall make, publish, disseminate, or circulate, directly or indirectly, or aid, abet or encourage the making, publishing, disseminating or circulating of any oral or written statement or any pamphlet, circular, article or literature that is false, and maliciously critical of, or derogatory to, any person with respect to the business of insurance or with respect to any person in the conduct of his insurance business and that is calculated to injure that person. (Code 1950, § 38.1-52; 1952, c. 317, § 38.1-52.3; 1977, c. 529; 1978, c. 441; 1979, c. 324; 1980, c. 404; 1986, c. 562.)

§ 38.2-505. Boycott, coercion and intimidation. — No person shall enter into any agreement to commit, or by any concerted action commit, any act of boycott, coercion or intimidation resulting in or tending to result in unreasonable restraint of, or monopoly in, the business of insurance. (Code 1950, § 38.1-52; 1952, c. 317, § 38.1-52.4; 1977, c. 529; 1978, c. 441; 1979, c. 324; 1980, c. 404; 1986, c. 562.)

Boycott requires coercion. — Where a purchaser has a free choice of a product in a competitive market, his acceptance of an offer to deal cannot constitute an antitrust boycott since a "boycott" requires duress or coercion. Anglin v. Blue Shield, 510 F. Supp. 75 (W.D. Va. 1981), aff'd, 693 F.2d 315 (4th Cir. 1982).

§ 38.2-506. False statements and entries. — No person shall:
1. Knowingly file with any supervisory or other public official, or knowingly make, publish, disseminate, circulate, or deliver to any person, or place before the public, or knowingly cause, directly or indirectly, to be made, published,

disseminated, circulated, delivered to any person, or placed before the public, any false material statement of fact as to the financial condition of a person; or

2. Knowingly make any false entry of a material fact in any book, report or statement of any person or knowingly fail to make a true entry of any material fact pertaining to the business of any person in any book, report or statement of that person. (Code 1950, § 38.1-52; 1952, c. 317, § 38.1-52.5; 1977, c. 529; 1978, c. 441; 1979, c. 324; 1980, c. 404; 1986, c. 562.)

§ 38.2-507. Stock operations and advisory board contracts. — No person shall issue or deliver or permit agents, officers, or employees to issue or deliver capital stock, benefit certificates or shares in any corporation, securities, any special or advisory board contracts or any contract promising returns and profits as an inducement to insurance. (Code 1950, § 38.1-52; 1952, c. 317, § 38.1-52.6; 1977, c. 529; 1978, c. 441; 1979, c. 324; 1980, c. 404; 1986, c. 562.)

§ 38.2-508. Unfair discrimination. — No person shall:

1. Unfairly discriminate or permit any unfair discrimination between individuals of the same class and equal expectation of life (i) in the rates charged for any life insurance or annuity contract, or (ii) in the dividends or other benefits payable on the contract, or (iii) in any other of the terms and conditions of the contract;

2. Unfairly discriminate or permit any unfair discrimination between individuals of the same class and of essentially the same hazard (i) in the amount of premium, policy fees, or rates charged for any policy or contract of accident or health insurance, (ii) in the benefits payable under such policy or contract, (iii) in any of the terms or conditions of such policy or contract, or (iv) in any other manner;

3. Refuse to insure, refuse to continue to insure, or limit the amount, extent or kind of insurance coverage available to an individual, or charge an individual a different rate for the same coverage solely because of blindness, or partial blindness, or mental or physical impairments, unless the refusal, limitation or rate differential is based on sound actuarial principles. This paragraph shall not be interpreted to modify any other provision of law relating to the termination, modification, issuance or renewal of any insurance policy or contract;

4. Unfairly discriminate or permit any unfair discrimination between individuals or risks of the same class and of essentially the same hazards by refusing to issue, refusing to renew, cancelling or limiting the amount of insurance coverage solely because of the geographic location of the individual or risk, unless:

a. The refusal, cancellation or limitation is for a business purpose that is not a mere pretext for unfair discrimination; or

b. The refusal, cancellation or limitation is required by law or regulatory mandate;

5. Make or permit any unfair discrimination between individuals or risks of the same class and of essentially the same hazards by refusing to issue, refusing to renew, cancelling or limiting the amount of insurance coverage on a residential property risk, or the personal property contained in a residential property risk, solely because of the age of the residential property, unless:

a. The refusal, cancellation or limitation is for a business purpose that is not a mere pretext for unfair discrimination; or

b. The refusal, cancellation or limitation is required by law or regulatory mandate;

6. Refuse to issue or renew any individual accident and sickness insurance policy or contract for coverage over and above any lifetime benefit of a group accident and sickness policy or contract solely because an individual is insured

under a group accident and sickness insurance policy or contract; provided that medical expenses covered by both individual and group coverage shall be paid first by the group policy or contract to the extent of the group coverage. This subsection shall not apply to individual policies or contracts issued or renewed pursuant to § 38.2-4216.1. (Code 1950, § 38.1-52; 1952, c. 317, § 38.1-52.7; 1977, c. 529; 1978, c. 441; 1979, c. 324; 1980, c. 404; 1986, c. 562; 1993, c. 130.)

This section creates no private cause of action. Salomon v. Transamerica Occidental Life Ins. Co., 801 F.2d 659 (4th Cir. 1986).

Limitations in coverage based on physical or mental disabilities must be based on sound actuarial principles. Lewis v. Aetna Life Ins. Co., 7 F. Supp. 2d 743 (E.D. Va. 1998).

Court could not accept state regulatory body's unelaborated approval of a plan as controlling authority that the plan is non-discriminatory within the meaning of this section. Lewis v. Aetna Life Ins. Co., 7 F. Supp. 2d 743 (E.D. Va. 1998).

§ 38.2-508.1. Unfair discrimination; members of the armed forces. — A. No person shall refuse to issue or refuse to continue a life insurance policy on the life of any member of the United States Armed Forces, the Reserves of the United States Armed Forces or the National Guard due to (i) their status as a member of any such military organization or (ii) their duty assignment while a member of any such military organization.

B. In circumstances where an individual's or family member's coverage under a group life or group health insurance policy or contract was terminated due to such individual's status as a member of the United States Armed Forces, the Reserves of the United States Armed Forces or the National Guard, no person shall refuse to reinstate such coverage, regardless of continuation, renewal, reissue or replacement of the group insurance policy, upon the occurrence of the individual's return to eligibility status under the policy or contract. Such reinstated coverage shall not contain any new preexisting condition or other exclusions or limitations except that the remainder of a preexisting condition requirement that was not satisfied prior to termination of the individual's coverage resulting from such military status may be applied once the individual returns and coverage under the group policy is reinstated. (1991, cc. 663, 678.)

§ 38.2-508.2. Discrimination prohibited. — No person shall refuse to issue or refuse to continue a life insurance policy on the life of any individual solely because of that individual's race, color, religion, national origin or gender. (1993, c. 152.)

§ 38.2-508.3. Consideration of Medicaid eligibility prohibited. — A. No person shall, in determining the eligibility of an individual for coverage under an individual or group accident and sickness policy, health services plan or health maintenance organization contract, consider the eligibility of such individual for medical assistance ("Medicaid") from this Commonwealth or from any other state.

B. No person shall, in determining benefits payable to, or on behalf of an individual covered under an individual or group accident and sickness policy, health services plan or health maintenance organization contract, take into account the eligibility of such individual for medical assistance ("Medicaid") from this Commonwealth or from any other state. (1994, c. 213.)

§ 38.2-508.4. Genetic information privacy. — A. As used in this section:
"Genetic characteristic" means any scientifically or medically identifiable gene or chromosome, or alteration thereof, which is known to be a cause of a disease or disorder, or determined to be associated with a statistically

increased risk of development of a disease or disorder, and which is asymptomatic of any disease or disorder.

"Genetic information" means information about genes, gene products, or inherited characteristics that may derive from an individual or a family member.

"Genetic test" means a test for determining the presence or absence of genetic characteristics in an individual in order to diagnose a genetic characteristic.

B. No person proposing to issue, re-issue, or renew any policy, contract, or plan of accident and sickness insurance defined in § 38.2-109, but excluding disability income insurance, issued by any (i) insurer providing hospital, medical and surgical or major medical coverage on an expense incurred basis, (ii) corporation providing a health services plan, or (iii) health maintenance organization providing a health care plan for health care services shall, on the basis of any genetic information obtained concerning an individual or on the individual's request for genetic services, with respect to such policy, contract, or plan:

1. Terminate, restrict, limit, or otherwise apply conditions to coverage of an individual or restrict the sale to an individual;

2. Cancel or refuse to renew the coverage of an individual;

3. Exclude an individual from coverage;

4. Impose a waiting period prior to commencement of coverage of an individual;

5. Require inclusion of a rider that excludes coverage for certain benefits and services; or

6. Establish differentials in premium rates for coverage.

In addition, no discrimination shall be made in the fees or commissions of an agent or agency for an enrollment, a subscription, or the renewal of an enrollment or subscription of any person on the basis of a person's genetic characteristics which may, under some circumstances, be associated with disability in that person or that person's offspring.

C. Notwithstanding any other provisions of law, all information obtained from genetic screening or testing conducted prior to the repeal of this section shall be confidential and shall not be made public nor used in any way, in whole or in part, to cancel, refuse to issue or renew, or limit benefits under any policy, contract or plan subject to the provisions of this section. (1996, c. 704.)

Editor's note. — Acts 1996, ch. 356, cl. 2, which provided for the expiration of this section on July 1, 1998, was repealed by Acts 1998, ch. 356, cl. 1.

§ 38.2-509. Rebates. — A. Except as otherwise expressly provided by law, no person shall:

1. Knowingly permit, offer, or make any insurance or annuity contract or agreement which is not plainly expressed in the contract issued;

2. Pay, allow or give, or offer to pay, allow or give, directly or indirectly, as inducement to any insurance or annuity contract, any rebate of premium payable on the contract, any special favor or advantage in the dividends or other benefits on the contract, any valuable consideration or inducement not specified in the contract, except in accordance with an applicable rating plan authorized for use in this Commonwealth;

3. Give, sell, purchase, or offer to give, sell or purchase as inducement to insurance, or annuity contracts, or in connection with such contracts, any stocks, bonds, or other securities of any company, any dividends or profits accrued on any stocks, bonds or other securities of any company, or anything of value not specified in the contract; or

4. Receive or accept as inducement to insurance, or annuity contracts, any rebate of premium payable on the contract, any special favor or advantage in

the dividends or other benefit to accrue on the contract, or any valuable consideration or inducement not specified in the contract.

B. Nothing in § 38.2-508 or in this section shall be construed to include within the definition of discrimination or rebates any of the following practices:

1. In the case of any life insurance or annuity contract, paying bonuses to policyholders or otherwise abating their premiums in whole or in part out of surplus accumulated from nonparticipating insurance if the bonuses or abatement of premiums are fair and equitable to policyholders and in the best interests of the insurer and its policyholders;

2. In the case of life or accident and sickness insurance policies issued on the industrial debit plan, making allowance to policyholders who, for a specified period, have continuously made premium payments directly to an office of the insurer in an amount that fairly represents the savings in collection expense;

3. Readjustment of the rate of premium for a group insurance policy based on the loss or expense experience under the policy, at the end of the first or any subsequent policy year of insurance;

4. In the case of insurers, allowing their bona fide employees to receive a reduction on the premiums paid by them on policies or contracts on their own lives and property, and on the lives and property of their spouses and dependent children;

5. Issuing life or accident and sickness policies or annuity contracts on a salary savings or payroll deduction plan at a reduced rate consistent with the savings made by the use of such plan;

6. Paying commissions or other compensation to duly licensed agents or brokers; or

7. Allowing or returning to participating policyholders, members or subscribers, dividends, savings or unabsorbed premium payments. (Code 1950, § 38.1-52; 1952, c. 317, § 38.1-52.8; 1977, c. 529; 1978, c. 441; 1979, c. 324; 1980, c. 404; 1986, c. 562.)

§ **38.2-510. Unfair claim settlement practices.** — A. No person shall commit or perform with such frequency as to indicate a general business practice any of the following:

1. Misrepresenting pertinent facts or insurance policy provisions relating to coverages at issue;

2. Failing to acknowledge and act reasonably promptly upon communications with respect to claims arising under insurance policies;

3. Failing to adopt and implement reasonable standards for the prompt investigation of claims arising under insurance policies;

4. Refusing arbitrarily and unreasonably to pay claims;

5. Failing to affirm or deny coverage of claims within a reasonable time after proof of loss statements have been completed;

6. Not attempting in good faith to make prompt, fair and equitable settlements of claims in which liability has become reasonably clear;

7. Compelling insureds to institute litigation to recover amounts due under an insurance policy by offering substantially less than the amounts ultimately recovered in actions brought by such insureds;

8. Attempting to settle claims for less than the amount to which a reasonable man would have believed he was entitled by reference to written or printed advertising material accompanying or made part of an application;

9. Attempting to settle claims on the basis of an application that was altered without notice to, or knowledge or consent of, the insured;

10. Making claims payments to insureds or beneficiaries not accompanied by a statement setting forth the coverage under which payments are being made;

11. Making known to insureds or claimants a policy of appealing from arbitration awards in favor of insureds or claimants for the purpose of

compelling them to accept settlements or compromises less than the amount awarded in arbitration;

12. Delaying the investigation or payment of claims by requiring an insured, a claimant, or the physician of either to submit a preliminary claim report and then requiring the subsequent submission of formal proof of loss forms, when both contain substantially the same information;

13. Failing to promptly settle claims where liability has become reasonably clear, under one portion of the insurance policy coverage in order to influence settlements under other portions of the insurance policy coverage;

14. Failing to promptly provide a reasonable explanation of the basis in the insurance policy in relation to the facts or applicable law for denial of a claim or for the offer of a compromise settlement; or

15. Failing to comply with § 38.2-3407.13, or to perform any provider contract provision required by that section.

B. No violation of this section shall of itself be deemed to create any cause of action in favor of any person other than the Commission; but nothing in this subsection shall impair the right of any person to seek redress at law or equity for any conduct for which action may be brought.

C. 1. No insurer shall prepare or use an estimate of the cost of automobile repairs based on the use of an after market part, as defined herein, unless:

The insurer discloses to the claimant in writing either on the estimate or in a separate document attached to the estimate the following information:

"THIS ESTIMATE HAS BEEN PREPARED BASED ON THE USE OF AUTOMOBILE PARTS NOT MADE BY THE ORIGINAL MANUFACTURER. PARTS USED IN THE REPAIR OF YOUR VEHICLE BY OTHER THAN THE ORIGINAL MANUFACTURER ARE REQUIRED TO BE AT LEAST EQUAL IN LIKE KIND AND QUALITY IN TERMS OF FIT, QUALITY AND PERFORMANCE TO THE ORIGINAL MANUFACTURER PARTS THEY ARE REPLACING."

2. "After market part" as used in this section shall mean an automobile part which is not made by the original equipment manufacturer and which is a sheet metal or plastic part generally constituting the exterior of a motor vehicle, including inner and outer panels. (Code 1950, § 38.1-52; 1952, c. 317, § 38.1-52.9; 1977, c. 529; 1978, c. 441; 1979, c. 324; 1980, c. 404; 1986, c. 562; 1988, c. 29; 1999, cc. 709, 739.)

The 1999 amendments. — The 1999 amendments by cc. 709 and 739 are identical, and in subsection A, deleted "or" at the end of subdivision 13, inserted "or" at the end of subdivision 14, and added subdivision 15.

Law Review. — For comment, "Insurers' Liability for Excess Judgments in Virginia: Negligence or Bad Faith," see 15 U. Rich. L. Rev. 153 (1980).

Purpose. — The plain meaning of this section, § 38.2-502 and § 38.2-503 shows that the primary purpose of these sections is to regulate the performance of insurance contracts by assuring conformity between representations made by the insurer to the insured and the actual performance of the insurance policies. In other words, each statute is designed to regulate the representations made to form, and the practices which comprise, the relationship between insurer and insured and the performance of the insurance contract which is the foundation of that relationship. Ambrose v. Blue Cross & Blue Shield of Va., Inc., 891 F.

Supp. 1153 (E.D. Va. 1995), aff'd, 95 F.3d 41 (4th Cir. 1996).

The Virginia Unfair Insurance Practices Act does not establish a private cause of action. A & E Supply Co. v. Nationwide Mut. Fire Ins. Co., 798 F.2d 669 (4th Cir. 1986), cert. denied, 479 U.S. 1091, 107 S. Ct. 1302, 94 L. Ed. 2d 158 (1987).

An award of punitive damages may not rest on a jury finding that defendant violated the Unfair Insurance Practices Act. A & E Supply Co. v. Nationwide Mut. Fire Ins. Co., 798 F.2d 669 (4th Cir. 1986), cert. denied, 479 U.S. 1091, 107 S. Ct. 1302, 94 L. Ed. 2d 158 (1987).

Bad faith of insurer. — An insured may be awarded attorney's fees generated in a suit against its insurer for a determination of coverage under the policy if it shows that the insurer, not acting in good faith, denied coverage or failed or refused to make payment to the insured under the policy, or an insured may seek the imposition of penalties for insurer's violations of the Unfair Insurance Practices Act. Ryder Truck Rental, Inc. v. UTF Carriers, Inc., 790 F. Supp. 637 (W.D. Va. 1992).

Liability for bad faith conduct as matter of contract rather than tort. — In a first-party Virginia insurance relationship, liability for bad faith conduct is a matter of contract rather than tort law. The obligation arises from the agreement and extends only to situations connected with the agreement. A & E Supply Co. v. Nationwide Mut. Fire Ins. Co., 798 F.2d 669 (4th Cir. 1986), cert. denied, 479 U.S. 1091, 107 S. Ct. 1302, 94 L. Ed 2d 158 (1987).

An insured does not state a tort claim by charging that an insurer was actuated by bad faith in breaching the contract of insurance. A & E Supply Co. v. Nationwide Mut. Fire Ins. Co., 798 F.2d 669 (4th Cir. 1986), cert. denied, 479 U.S. 1091, 107 S. Ct. 1302, 94 L. Ed. 2d 158 (1987).

Punitive damages not authorized. — The Virginia legislature has provided for punishment and deterrence without authorizing punitive damages against errant insurance companies. Bettius & Sanderson v. National Union Fire Ins. Co., 839 F.2d 1009 (4th Cir. 1988).

Subdivision A 6 of this section applies only when the failure to make good faith attempts to settle claims occurs with such frequency as to indicate a general business practice on the part of an insurer. Allstate Ins. Co. v. United Servs. Auto. Ass'n, 249 Va. 9, 452 S.E.2d 859 (1995).

Isolated incidents are insufficient to make insurer's conduct "a general business practice." Allstate Ins. Co. v. United Servs. Auto. Ass'n, 249 Va. 9, 452 S.E.2d 859 (1995).

§ 38.2-511. Failure to maintain record of complaints.

— No person other than agents or brokers, shall fail to maintain a complete record of all the complaints that it has received since the date of its last examination under § 38.2-1317, provided that the records of complaints of a health carrier subject to Chapter 58 (§ 38.2-5800 et seq.) of this title shall be retained for no less than five years. The record shall indicate the total number of complaints, their classification by line of insurance, the nature of each complaint, the disposition of these complaints, and the time it took to process each complaint.

As used in this section, *"complaint"* shall mean any written communication from a policyholder, subscriber or claimant primarily expressing a grievance. (Code 1950, § 38.1-52; 1952, c. 317, § 38.1-52.10; 1977, c. 529; 1978, c. 441; 1979, c. 324; 1980, c. 404; 1986, c. 562; 1998, c. 891.)

The **1998 amendment,** in the first paragraph, in the first sentence, substituted "provided that the records of complaints of a health carrier subject to Chapter 58 (§ 38.2-5800 et seq.) of this title shall be retained for no less than five years" for "or during the last three years, whichever is the more recent time period."

§ 38.2-512. Misrepresentation in insurance documents or communications.

— A. No person shall make or cause or allow to be made false or fraudulent statements or representations on or relative to an application or any document or communication relating to the business of insurance for the purpose of obtaining a fee, commission, money, or other benefit from any insurer, agent, broker, premium finance company, or individual.

B. No person shall, with respect to any document pertaining to the business of insurance, including payments made to an insurer or by an insurer, affix or cause or allow to be affixed the signature of any other person to such document without the written authorization of the person whose signature appears on such document.

C. No person shall, with respect to any document pertaining to the business of insurance, obtain or cause or allow to be obtained by false pretense the signature of another person or utilize such signature for the purpose of altering, changing or effecting the benefits, advantages, terms or conditions of any insurance contract or document related thereto, including payments made to an insurer or by an insurer. (Code 1950, § 38.1-52; 1952, c. 317, § 38.1-52.11; 1977, c. 529; 1978, c. 441; 1979, c. 324; 1980, c. 404; 1986, c. 562; 1998, c. 12.)

The 1998 amendment rewrote subsection A
and added subsections B and C.

§ 38.2-513. Favored agent or insurer; coercion of debtors. — A. No
person shall:

1. Require, as a condition precedent to the extension of credit, or any subsequent renewal thereof, that the borrower purchase an insurance policy through a particular insurer, agent or broker.

2. a. Unreasonably disapprove the insurance policy provided by a borrower or debtor for the protection of the property securing the credit or lien or unreasonably disapprove the insurance policy provided by a borrower or debtor on his own life to protect the loan. A disapproval shall be deemed unreasonable if it is not based solely on reasonable standards uniformly applied, relating to the extent of coverage required and the financial soundness and the services of an insurer. Such standards shall not discriminate against any particular type of insurer, nor shall such standards call for disapproval of an insurance policy because the policy contains coverage in addition to those required by the creditor. Use of the ratings of a nationally recognized rating service shall not be deemed unreasonable provided such ratings are based on reasonable standards uniformly applied. If an insurer, duly licensed in Virginia, does not possess the required rating of a nationally recognized rating service, no person who lends money or extends credit shall refuse to accept from the insurer a certificate of 100 percent reinsurance issued by another insurer pursuant to § 38.2-136, which does possess the required rating.

b. Every person who lends money or extends credit and who solicits insurance on real or personal property shall explain to the borrower in writing that the insurance related to such credit extensions may be purchased from an insurer or agent of the borrower's choice.

3. Require directly or indirectly that any debtor, borrower, mortgagor, purchaser, insurer, broker, or agent (i) pay a separate charge or consideration of any kind in connection with the handling of any insurance policy required as security for a loan or real estate, or (ii) pay a separate charge or consideration of any kind for substituting the insurance policy of one insurer for that of another. However, this does not include the interest which may be charged on premium loans or premium advancements in accordance with the security instrument.

4. Use or disclose information including, but not limited to, policy information and policy expiration dates on policies insuring any kind of real property being conveyed or used as collateral security to a loan and required by a borrower, mortgagor or purchaser (i) when such information is to the advantage of the mortgagee, vendor, or lender, or any subsidiary of the mortgagee, vendor, or lender, or (ii) when the information is to the detriment of the borrower, mortgagor, purchaser, insurer, agent or broker complying with this requirement, except as required by local, state or federal law or regulation.

B. The Commission may investigate the affairs of any person to whom this section applies to determine whether that person has violated this section. If a violation of this section is found, the person in violation shall be subject to the same procedures and penalties as are applicable to other provisions of this chapter.

C. No person who lends money or extends credit shall solicit insurance on real or personal property, after a person indicates interest in securing a first mortgage credit extension, until the person has received a commitment in writing from the lender as to a loan or credit extension.

D. No lending institution, bank holding company, savings institution holding company or subsidiary or affiliate of either the lending institution or holding company, including any officer or employee thereof, licensed as an insurance agency or insurance agent in this Commonwealth shall obtain or utilize in any manner or for any purpose related to the sale of insurance any information, including policy expiration dates, contained in any insurance contract covering a customer of the institution, subsidiary, or affiliate or the customer's property, if the contract was sold to the customer by a broker or agent not affiliated with the institution, subsidiary, or affiliate, and if the contract or information was obtained by the institution, subsidiary, or affiliate from the customer in connection with a request for an extension of credit.

E. Notwithstanding the provisions of this section, life insurance and accident and sickness insurance shall continue to be governed by §§ 38.2-3301, 38.2-3342, 38.2-3502, 38.2-3604, and 38.2-3724 as to the right of rescission and refund of premium. Any lending institution, bank holding company, savings institution holding company or subsidiary or affiliate licensed to sell insurance shall provide an individual who purchases insurance the right to cancel the purchase of such insurance and receive a refund or credit on a pro rata basis until midnight of the tenth day following the consummation of the insurance purchase transaction or the effective date of the coverage, whichever is later. The individual shall effect such cancellation by notifying in writing the lending institution, bank holding company, savings institution holding company or subsidiary or affiliate that made the insurance sale of the intent to cancel. The lending institution, bank holding company, savings institution holding company or subsidiary or affiliate shall (i) clearly and conspicuously disclose to any individual the rights of the individual under this section and (ii) provide appropriate forms for the exercise by the individual of his right to cancel any insurance subject to this section. Such forms shall contain a clear and specific statement setting forth:

1. The cost of the insurance;

2. That the individual may choose the person through which insurance can be obtained and that the availability of an account or loan relationship and the interest rates paid or charged for a loan or an extension of credit may not be made contingent upon the purchase of insurance;

3. The individual's right to use the cancellation period to obtain price quotations for insurance from other sources;

4. The actions necessary for the individual to cancel the insurance; and

5. The individual's right to receive a refund or a credit of the unearned pro rata portion of the insurance premium after cancellation.

F. All premiums as a result of an insurance transaction pursuant to this section shall be accounted for in accordance with § 38.2-1813. (Code 1950, § 38.1-52; 1952, c. 317, § 38.1-52.12; 1962, c. 507, § 38.1-31.3; 1977, c. 529; 1978, c. 441; 1979, c. 324; 1980, c. 404; 1986, c. 562; 1988, c. 330; 1991, c. 620.)

§ 38.2-514. Failure to make disclosure. — A. No person shall solicit or effect the sale of an annuity, a life insurance policy or an accident and sickness insurance policy without furnishing the disclosure information required by any rules and regulations of the Commission.

B. Any lending institution, bank holding company, savings institution holding company or subsidiary or affiliate of either the lending institution or holding company, including any officer or employee thereof, licensed as an insurance agency or insurance agent in this Commonwealth shall, prior to the sale of any policy of life insurance in which there is or will be an accumulation of cash value during the term of the policy, make a written disclosure to the purchaser of the policy's "interest adjusted net cost index" in compliance with regulations or forms approved by the Commission.

C. No person shall provide to an insured, claimant, subscriber or enrollee under an accident and sickness insurance policy, subscription contract, or health maintenance organization contract, an explanation of benefits which does not clearly and accurately disclose the method of benefit calculation and the actual amount which has been or will be paid to the provider of services. (Code 1950, § 38.1-52; 1952, c. 317, § 38.1-52.13; 1977, c. 529; 1978, c. 441; 1979, c. 324; 1980, c. 404; 1986, c. 562; 1991, c. 620; 1992, c. 7; 1994, c. 320.)

§ 38.2-514.1. Disclosure required. — A. Any agent soliciting, negotiating, procuring, or effecting a contract of insurance in conjunction with any automobile club service agreement or in conjunction with any accidental death and dismemberment policy shall provide to the applicant, at the time of application, a written disclosure which shall contain:

1. The name or type of each policy or contract of insurance and automobile club service agreement for which application has been made;

2. The premium quotation associated with each policy or contract of insurance and the cost of any dues, assessments or periodic payments of money associated with each automobile club service agreement for which application has been made; and

3. A statement that the applicant has elected to purchase such policies, contracts, or automobile club service agreements.

B. The disclosure required by this section shall be signed and dated by the agent and the applicant. A copy of the signed disclosure shall be given to the applicant at the time of application. If the application is made by telephonic or electronic request, a copy of the disclosure shall be signed and dated by the agent and shall be mailed to the applicant within ten days of the application.

C. The provisions of this section shall apply only to the original issuance of policies or contracts of insurance and automobile club service agreements covering personal, family, or household needs rather than business or professional needs. As used in this section, an automobile club service agreement is an agreement issued by an automobile club as defined in § 13.1-400.1.

D. Notwithstanding subsections A, B and C, this section shall not apply to the sale of group insurance. (1996, c. 473.)

§ 38.2-514.2. Disclosures required of motor vehicle rental contract insurance agents and enrollers. — No insurance may be solicited, negotiated, procured, or effected by a motor vehicle rental contract insurance agent or enroller unless a conspicuous written disclosure is provided to the prospective renter that (i) summarizes clearly and correctly the material terms of coverage offered, including the identity of the insurer or insurers, (ii) advises that the coverage offered may duplicate coverage already provided by the renter's personal motor vehicle insurance policy, homeowner's insurance policy, personal liability insurance policy, or other source of coverage, and (iii) states that the purchase of the coverages offered is not required in order to rent a motor vehicle. (1998, c. 47; 1999, c. 493.)

The **1999 amendment** added "or enroller" following "insurance agent."

§ 38.2-515. Power of Commission. — A. The Commission shall have power to examine and investigate the affairs of each person subject to this chapter to determine whether such person has been or is engaged in any unfair method of competition or in any unfair or deceptive act or practice prohibited by §§ 38.2-502 through 38.2-514.

B. The Commission is further empowered to gather information from any person subject to this chapter relative to trade practices and whether such practices adequately and fairly serve the public interest.

C. Any person who refuses or fails to provide information in a timely manner to the Commission as provided in this section shall be subject to the enforcement and penalty provisions set forth in Chapter 2 (§ 38.2-200 et seq.) of this title. (1952, c. 317, § 38.1-53; 1977, c. 529; 1980, c. 404; 1986, c. 562; 1991, c. 356.)

Law Review. — For survey of Virginia law on insurance for the year 1976-77, see 63 Va. L. Rev. 1448 (1977).

§ 38.2-516. Prohibited compensation for intra-company replacement.

— No insurer shall pay a commission or other compensation to an appointed agent who has replaced an existing individual accident and sickness policy with a policy issued by the same insurer when such new policy provides benefits substantially similar to the benefits under the replaced policy, except that an insurer may pay to such agent a commission or other compensation to the extent that the commission or other compensation does not exceed the renewal commission that would have been paid to the agent had the replaced policy continued in force. (1990, c. 265.)

§ 38.2-517. Unfair settlement practices; replacement and repair; penalty.

— A. No person shall:
1. Require an insured or claimant to utilize designated replacement or repair facilities or services, or the products of designated manufacturers, as a prerequisite to settling or paying any claim arising under a policy or policies of insurance; or
2. Engage in any act of coercion or intimidation causing or intended to cause an insured or claimant to utilize designated replacement or repair facilities or services, or the products of designated manufacturers, in connection with settling or paying any claim arising under a policy or policies of insurance.

B. Any person violating this section shall be subject to the injunctive, penalty, and enforcement provisions of Chapter 2 (§ 38.2-200 et seq.) of this title. The Commission shall investigate, with the written authorization of the insured or the claimant, any written complaints received pursuant to this section, regardless of whether such written complaints are submitted by an individual or a repair facility. For the purpose of this subsection, any insurance company utilizing a third party shall be held accountable for any violation of this section by such third party. (1992, cc. 870, 882; 1999, c. 129.)

The 1999 amendment added the last two sentences of subsection B.

CHAPTER 6.

INSURANCE INFORMATION AND PRIVACY PROTECTION.

§ 38.2-600. Purposes. — The purposes of this chapter are to:

1. Establish standards for the collection, use, and disclosure of information gathered in connection with insurance transactions by insurance institutions, agents or insurance-support organizations;

2. Maintain a balance between the need for information by those conducting the business of insurance and the public's need for fairness in insurance information practices, including the need to minimize intrusiveness;

3. Establish a regulatory mechanism to enable natural persons to ascertain what information is being or has been collected about them in connection with insurance transactions and to have access to such information for the purpose of verifying or disputing its accuracy;

4. Limit the disclosure of information collected in connection with insurance transactions; and

5. Enable insurance applicants and policyholders to obtain the reasons for any adverse underwriting decision. (1981, c. 389, § 38.1-57.3; 1986, c. 562.)

§ 38.2-601. Application of chapter. — A. The obligations imposed by this chapter shall apply to those insurance institutions, agents or insurance-support organizations that:

1. In the case of life or accident and sickness insurance:

a. Collect, receive or maintain information in connection with insurance transactions that pertains to natural persons who are residents of this Commonwealth; or

b. Engage in insurance transactions with applicants, individuals, or policyholders who are residents of this Commonwealth; and

2. In the case of property or casualty insurance:

a. Collect, receive or maintain information in connection with insurance transactions involving policies, contracts or certificates of insurance delivered, issued for delivery or renewed in this Commonwealth; or

b. Engage in insurance transactions involving policies, contracts or certificates of insurance delivered, issued for delivery or renewed in this Commonwealth.

B. The rights granted by this chapter shall extend to:

1. In the case of life or accident and sickness insurance, the following persons who are residents of this Commonwealth:

a. Natural persons who are the subject of information collected, received or maintained in connection with insurance transactions; and

b. Applicants, individuals or policyholders who engage in or seek to engage in insurance transactions; and

2. In the case of property or casualty insurance, the following persons:

a. Natural persons who are the subject of information collected, received or maintained in connection with insurance transactions involving policies, contracts or certificates of insurance delivered, issued for delivery or renewed in this Commonwealth; and

b. Applicants, individuals, or policyholders who engage in or seek to engage in insurance transactions involving policies, contracts or certificates of insurance delivered, issued for delivery or renewed in this Commonwealth.

C. For purposes of this section, a person shall be considered a resident of this Commonwealth if the person's last known mailing address, as shown in the records of the insurance institution, agent or insurance-support organization, is located in this Commonwealth.

D. Notwithstanding subsections A and B of this section, this chapter shall not apply to information collected from the public records of a governmental authority and maintained by an insurance institution or its representatives for the purpose of insuring the title to real property located in this Commonwealth. (1981, c. 389, § 38.1-57.4; 1986, c. 562.)

§ **38.2-602. Definitions.** — As used in this chapter:

"Adverse underwriting decision" means:

1. Any of the following actions with respect to insurance transactions involving insurance coverage that is individually underwritten:

  a. A declination of insurance coverage;

  b. A termination of insurance coverage;

  c. Failure of an agent to apply for insurance coverage with a specific insurance institution that an agent represents and that is requested by an applicant;

  d. In the case of a property or casualty insurance coverage:

  (1) Placement by an insurance institution or agent of a risk with a residual market mechanism or an unlicensed insurer; or

  (2) The charging of a higher rate on the basis of information that differs from that which the applicant or policyholder furnished; or

  e. In the case of a life or accident and sickness insurance coverage, an offer to insure at higher than standard rates, or with limitations, exceptions or benefits other than those applied for.

2. Notwithstanding subdivision 1 of this definition, the following actions shall not be considered adverse underwriting decisions, but the insurance institution or agent responsible for their occurrence shall provide the applicant or policyholder with the specific reason or reasons for their occurrence:

  a. The termination of an individual policy form on a class or statewide basis;

  b. A declination of insurance coverage solely because such coverage is not available on a class or statewide basis;

  c. The rescission of a policy.

"Affiliate" or *"affiliated"* means a person that directly, or indirectly through one or more intermediaries, controls, is controlled by, or is under common control with another person.

"Agent" shall have the meaning as set forth in § 38.2-1800 and shall include surplus lines brokers.

"Applicant" means any person who seeks to contract for insurance coverage other than a person seeking group insurance that is not individually underwritten.

"Consumer report" means any written, oral, or other communication of information bearing on a natural person's credit worthiness, credit standing, credit capacity, character, general reputation, personal characteristics or mode of living that is used or expected to be used in connection with an insurance transaction.

"Consumer reporting agency" means any person who:

1. Regularly engages, in whole or in part, in the practice of assembling or preparing consumer reports for a monetary fee;

2. Obtains information primarily from sources other than insurance institutions; and

3. Furnishes consumer reports to other persons.

"Control," including the terms *"controlled by"* or *"under common control with,"* means the possession, direct or indirect, of the power to direct or cause

the direction of the management and policies of a person, whether through the ownership of voting securities, by contract other than a commercial contract for goods or nonmanagement services, or otherwise, unless the power is the result of an official position with or corporate office held by the person.

"Declination of insurance coverage" means a denial, in whole or in part, by an insurance institution or agent of requested insurance coverage.

"Individual" means any natural person who:

1. In the case of property or casualty insurance, is a past, present, or proposed named insured or certificate holder;

2. In the case of life or accident and sickness insurance, is a past, present, or proposed principal insured or certificate holder;

3. Is a past, present or proposed policyowner;

4. Is a past or present applicant;

5. Is a past or present claimant; or

6. Derived, derives, or is proposed to derive insurance coverage under an insurance policy or certificate subject to this chapter.

"Institutional source" means any person or governmental entity that provides information about an individual to an agent, insurance institution or insurance-support organization, other than:

1. An agent;

2. The individual who is the subject of the information; or

3. A natural person acting in a personal capacity rather than in a business or professional capacity.

"Insurance institution" means any corporation, association, partnership, reciprocal exchange, inter-insurer, Lloyd's type of organization, fraternal benefit society, or other person engaged in the business of insurance, including health maintenance organizations, and health, legal, dental, and optometric service plans. "Insurance institution" shall not include agents or insurance-support organizations.

"Insurance-support organization" means any person who regularly engages, in whole or in part, in the practice of assembling or collecting information about natural persons for the primary purpose of providing the information to an insurance institution or agent for insurance transactions, including (i) the furnishing of consumer reports or investigative consumer reports to an insurance institution or agent for use in connection with an insurance transaction or (ii) the collection of personal information from insurance institutions, agents or other insurance-support organizations for the purpose of detecting or preventing fraud, material misrepresentation or material nondisclosure in connection with insurance underwriting or insurance claim activity. However, the following persons shall not be considered "insurance-support organizations" for purposes of this chapter: agents, governmental institutions, insurance institutions, medical-care institutions and medical professionals.

"Insurance transaction" means any transaction involving insurance primarily for personal, family, or household needs rather than business or professional needs that entails:

1. The determination of an individual's eligibility for an insurance coverage, benefit or payment; or

2. The servicing of an insurance application, policy, contract, or certificate.

"Investigative consumer report" means a consumer report or a portion thereof in which information about a natural person's character, general reputation, personal characteristics, or mode of living is obtained through personal interviews with the person's neighbors, friends, associates, acquaintances, or others who may have knowledge concerning such items of information.

"Life insurance" includes annuities.

"Medical-care institution" means any facility or institution that is licensed to provide health care services to natural persons, including but not limited to,

hospitals, skilled nursing facilities, home-health agencies, medical clinics, rehabilitation agencies, and public-health agencies or health-maintenance organizations.

"*Medical professional*" means any person licensed or certified to provide health care services to natural persons, including but not limited to, a physician, dentist, nurse, chiropractor, optometrist, physical or occupational therapist, psychiatric social worker, clinical dietitian, clinical psychologist, pharmacist, or speech therapist.

"*Medical-record information*" means personal information that:

1. Relates to an individual's physical or mental condition, medical history, or medical treatment; and

2. Is obtained from a medical professional or medical-care institution, from the individual, or from the individual's spouse, parent, or legal guardian.

"*Personal information*" means any individually identifiable information gathered in connection with an insurance transaction from which judgments can be made about an individual's character, habits, avocations, finances, occupation, general reputation, credit, health, or any other personal characteristics. "Personal information" includes an individual's name and address and medical-record information, but does not include privileged information.

"*Policyholder*" means any person who:

1. In the case of individual property or casualty insurance, is a present named insured;

2. In the case of individual life or accident and sickness insurance, is a present policyowner; or

3. In the case of group insurance that is individually underwritten, is a present group certificate holder.

"*Pretext interview*" means an interview whereby a person, in an attempt to obtain information about a natural person, performs one or more of the following acts:

1. Pretends to be someone he or she is not;

2. Pretends to represent a person he or she is not in fact representing;

3. Misrepresents the true purpose of the interview; or

4. Refuses to identify himself or herself upon request.

"*Privileged information*" means any individually identifiable information that (i) relates to a claim for insurance benefits or a civil or criminal proceeding involving an individual, and (ii) is collected in connection with or in reasonable anticipation of a claim for insurance benefits or civil or criminal proceeding involving an individual. However, information otherwise meeting the requirements of this subsection shall nevertheless be considered personal information under this chapter if it is disclosed in violation of § 38.2-613 of this chapter.

"*Residual market mechanism*" means an association, organization, or other entity defined, described, or provided for in the Virginia Automobile Insurance Plan as set forth in § 38.2-2015, or in the Virginia Property Insurance Association as set forth in Chapter 27 (§ 38.2-2700 et seq.) of this title.

"*Termination of insurance coverage*" or "*termination of an insurance policy*" means either a cancellation or nonrenewal of an insurance policy other than by the policyholder's request, in whole or in part, for any reason other than the failure to pay a premium as required by the policy.

"*Unlicensed insurer*" means an insurance institution that has not been granted a license by the Commission to transact the business of insurance in Virginia. (1981, c. 389, § 38.1-57.5; 1986, c. 562.)

§ 38.2-603. Pretext interviews. — No insurance institution, agent, or insurance-support organization shall use or authorize the use of pretext interviews to obtain information in connection with an insurance transaction. However, a pretext interview may be undertaken to obtain information from a person or institution that does not have a generally or statutorily recognized privileged relationship with the person about whom the information relates for the purpose of investigating a claim where, based upon specific information available for review by the Commission, there is a reasonable basis for suspecting criminal activity, fraud, material misrepresentation, or material nondisclosure in connection with the claim. (1981, c. 389, § 38.1-57.6; 1986, c. 562.)

§ 38.2-604. Notice of insurance information practices. — A. An insurance institution or agent shall provide a notice of insurance information practices to all applicants or policyholders in connection with insurance transactions as provided in this section:

1. In the case of an application for insurance a notice shall be provided no later than:

a. At the time of the delivery of the insurance policy or certificate when personal information is collected only from the applicant or from public records; or

b. At the time the collection of personal information is initiated when personal information is collected from a source other than the applicant or public records;

2. In the case of a policy renewal, a notice shall be provided no later than the policy renewal date, except that no notice shall be required in connection with a policy renewal if:

a. Personal information is collected only from the policyholder or from public records; or

b. A notice meeting the requirements of this section has been given within the previous twenty-four months; or

3. In the case of a policy reinstatement or change in insurance benefits, a notice shall be provided no later than the time a request for a policy reinstatement or change in insurance benefits is received by the insurance institution, except that no notice shall be required if personal information is collected only from the policyholder or from public records.

B. The notice required by subsection A of this section shall be in writing and shall state:

1. Whether personal information may be collected from persons other than an individual proposed for coverage;

2. The types of personal information that may be collected and the types of sources and investigative techniques that may be used to collect such information;

3. The types of disclosures identified in subdivisions 2, 3, 4, 5, 6, 9, 11, 12, and 14 of § 38.2-613 and the circumstances under which such disclosures may be made without prior authorization. However, only those circumstances need be described that occur with such frequency as to indicate a general business practice;

4. A description of the rights established under §§ 38.2-608 and 38.2-609 and the manner in which those rights may be exercised; and

5. That information obtained from a report prepared by an insurance-support organization may be retained by the insurance-support organization and disclosed to other persons.

C. Instead of the notice prescribed in subsection B of this section, the insurance institution or agent may provide an abbreviated notice informing the applicant or policyholder that:

1. Personal information may be collected from persons other than an individual proposed for coverage;

2. The information, as well as other personal or privileged information subsequently collected by the insurance institution or agent, in certain circumstances, may be disclosed to third parties without authorization;

3. A right of access and correction exists with respect to all personal information collected; and

4. The notice prescribed in subsection B of this section will be furnished to the applicant or policyholder upon request.

D. The obligations imposed by this section upon an insurance institution or agent may be satisfied by another insurance institution or agent authorized to act on its behalf. (1981, c. 389, § 38.1-57.7; 1986, c. 562.)

Editor's note. — In 1996, an amendment to § 38.2-613 inserted an "A" designation at the beginning of the section and added a subsection B. Therefore, the references in subdivision B 3 of this section (which was last amended in 1986) to "subdivisions 2, 3, 4, 5, 6, 9, 11, 12, and 14 of § 38-2-613" refer to what are now, in light of the 1996 amendment, subdivisions A 2, A 3, A 4, A 5, A 6, A 9, A 11, A 12, and A 14 of § 38.2-613.

§ 38.2-605. Marketing and research surveys. — An insurance institution or agent shall clearly specify those questions designed to obtain information solely for marketing or research purposes from an individual in connection with an insurance transaction. (1981, c. 389, § 38.1-57.8; 1986, c. 562.)

§ 38.2-606. Content of disclosure authorization forms. — Notwithstanding any other provision of law of this Commonwealth, no insurance institution, agent, or insurance-support organization shall utilize as its disclosure authorization form in connection with insurance transactions involving insurance policies or contracts issued after January 1, 1982, a form or statement that authorizes the disclosure of personal or privileged information about an individual to the insurance institution, agent, or insurance-support organization unless the form or statement:

1. Is written in plain language;

2. Is dated;

3. Specifies the types of persons authorized to disclose information about the individual;

4. Specifies the nature of the information authorized to be disclosed;

5. Names the insurance institution or agent and identifies by generic reference representatives of the insurance institution to whom the individual is authorizing information to be disclosed;

6. Specifies the purposes for which the information is collected;

7. Specifies the length of time such authorization shall remain valid, which shall be no longer than:

a. In the case of authorizations signed for the purpose of collecting information in connection with an application for an insurance policy, a policy reinstatement, or a request for change in policy benefits:

(1) Thirty months from the date the authorization is signed if the application or request involves life, accident and sickness, or disability insurance; or

(2) One year from the date the authorization is signed if the application or request involves property or casualty insurance;

b. In the case of authorizations signed for the purpose of collecting information in connection with a claim for benefits under an insurance policy:

(1) The term of coverage of the policy if the claim is for an accident and sickness insurance benefit; or

(2) The duration of the claim if the claim is not for an accident and sickness insurance benefit; and

8. Advises the individual or a person authorized to act on behalf of the individual that the individual or the individual's authorized representative is entitled to receive a copy of the authorization form. (1981, c. 389, § 38.1-57.9; 1986, c. 562.)

§ 38.2-607. Investigative consumer reports. — A. No insurance institution, agent, or insurance-support organization may prepare or request an investigative consumer report about an individual in connection with an insurance transaction involving an application for insurance, a policy renewal, a policy reinstatement or a change in insurance benefits unless the insurance institution or agent informs the individual:

1. That he may request to be interviewed in connection with the preparation of the investigative consumer report; and

2. That upon a request pursuant to § 38.2-608, he is entitled to receive a copy of the investigative consumer report.

B. If an investigative consumer report is to be prepared by an insurance institution or agent, the insurance institution or agent shall institute reasonable procedures to conduct a personal interview requested by an individual.

C. If an investigative consumer report is to be prepared by an insurance-support organization, the insurance institution or agent desiring the report shall inform the insurance-support organization whether a personal interview has been requested by the individual. The insurance-support organization shall institute reasonable procedures to conduct such interviews, if requested. (1981, c. 389, § 38.1-57.10; 1986, c. 562.)

§ 38.2-608. Access to recorded personal information. — A. If any individual, after proper identification, submits a written request to an insurance institution, agent, or insurance-support organization for access to recorded personal information about the individual that is reasonably described by the individual and reasonably able to be located and retrieved by the insurance institution, agent, or insurance-support organization, the insurance institution, agent, or insurance-support organization shall within thirty business days from the date the request is received:

1. Inform the individual of the nature and substance of the recorded personal information in writing, by telephone, or by other oral communication, whichever the insurance institution, agent, or insurance-support organization prefers;

2. Permit the individual to see and copy, in person, the recorded personal information pertaining to him or to obtain a copy of the recorded personal information by mail, whichever the individual prefers, unless the recorded personal information is in coded form, in which case an accurate translation in plain language shall be provided in writing;

3. Disclose to the individual the identity, if recorded, of those persons to whom the insurance institution, agent, or insurance-support organization has disclosed the personal information within two years prior to such request, and if the identity is not recorded, the names of those insurance institutions, agents, insurance-support organizations or other persons to whom such information is normally disclosed; and

4. Provide the individual with a summary of the procedures by which he may request correction, amendment, or deletion of recorded personal information.

B. Any personal information provided pursuant to subsection A of this section shall identify the source of the information if it is an institutional source.

C. Medical-record information supplied by a medical-care institution or medical professional and requested under subsection A of this section, together with the identity of the medical professional or medical care institution that provided the information, shall be supplied either directly to the individual or to a medical professional designated by the individual and licensed to provide medical care with respect to the condition to which the information relates, whichever the insurance institution, agent or insurance-support organization prefers. If it elects to disclose the information to a medical professional designated by the individual, the insurance institution, agent or insurance-support organization shall notify the individual, at the time of the disclosure, that it has provided the information to the medical professional.

D. Except for personal information provided under § 38.2-610, an insurance institution, agent, or insurance-support organization may charge a reasonable fee to cover the costs incurred in providing a copy of recorded personal information to individuals.

E. The obligations imposed by this section upon an insurance institution or agent may be satisfied by another insurance institution or agent authorized to act on its behalf. With respect to the copying and disclosure of recorded personal information pursuant to a request under subsection A of this section, an insurance institution, agent, or insurance-support organization may make arrangements with an insurance-support organization or a consumer reporting agency to copy and disclose recorded personal information on its behalf.

F. The rights granted to individuals in this section shall extend to all natural persons to the extent information about them is collected and maintained by an insurance institution, agent or insurance-support organization in connection with an insurance transaction. The rights granted to all natural persons by this subsection shall not extend to information about them that relates to and is collected in connection with or in reasonable anticipation of a claim or civil or criminal proceeding involving them.

G. For purposes of this section, the term "insurance-support organization" does not include "consumer reporting agency." (1981, c. 389, § 38.1-57.11; 1986, c. 562.)

§ **38.2-609. Correction, amendment, or deletion of recorded personal information.** — A. Within thirty business days from the date of receipt of a written request from an individual to correct, amend, or delete any recorded personal information about the individual within its possession, an insurance institution, agent, or insurance-support organization shall either:

1. Correct, amend, or delete the portion of the recorded personal information in dispute; or

2. Notify the individual of:

a. Its refusal to make the correction, amendment, or deletion;

b. The reasons for the refusal; and

c. The individual's right to file a statement as provided in subsection C of this section.

B. If the insurance institution, agent, or insurance-support organization corrects, amends, or deletes recorded personal information in accordance with subdivision 1 of subsection A of this section, the insurance institution, agent, or insurance-support organization shall so notify the individual in writing and furnish the correction, amendment, or fact of deletion to:

1. Any person specifically designated by the individual who, within the preceding two years, may have received the recorded personal information;

2. Any insurance-support organization whose primary source of personal information is insurance institutions if the insurance-support organization has systematically received the recorded personal information from the insurance institution within the preceding seven years. The correction, amendment, or fact of deletion need not be furnished if the insurance-support organization no longer maintains recorded personal information about the individual; and

3. Any insurance-support organization that furnished the personal information that has been corrected, amended, or deleted.

C. Whenever an individual disagrees with an insurance institution's, agent's, or insurance-support organization's refusal to correct, amend, or delete recorded personal information, the individual shall be permitted to file with the insurance institution, agent, or insurance-support organization:

1. A concise statement setting forth what the individual thinks is the correct, relevant, or fair information; and

2. A concise statement of the reasons why the individual disagrees with the insurance institution's, agent's, or insurance-support organization's refusal to correct, amend, or delete recorded personal information.

D. In the event an individual files either statement as described in subsection C of this section, the insurance institution, agent, or support organization shall:

1. File the statement with the disputed personal information and provide a means by which anyone reviewing the disputed personal information will be made aware of the individual's statement and have access to it; and

2. In any subsequent disclosure by the insurance institution, agent, or support organization of the recorded personal information that is the subject of disagreement, clearly identify the matter or matters in dispute and provide the individual's statement along with the recorded personal information being disclosed; and

3. Furnish the statement to the persons and in the manner specified in subsection B of this section.

E. The rights granted to individuals in this section shall extend to all natural persons to the extent information about them is collected and maintained by an insurance institution, agent, or insurance-support organization in connection with an insurance transaction. The rights granted to all natural persons by this subsection shall not extend to information about them that relates to and is collected in connection with or in reasonable anticipation of a claim or civil or criminal proceeding involving them.

F. For purposes of this section, the term "insurance-support organization" does not include "consumer reporting agency." (1981, c. 389, § 38.1-57.12; 1986, c. 562.)

§ 38.2-610. Notice of adverse underwriting decision; furnishing reasons for decisions and sources of information. — A. In the event of an adverse underwriting decision, including those that involve policies referred to in subdivision 1 of subsection E of § 38.2-2114 and in subdivision 3 of subsection F of § 38.2-2212, the insurance institution or agent responsible for the decision shall give a written notice in a form approved by the Commission that:

1. Either provides the applicant, policyholder, or individual proposed for coverage with the specific reason or reasons for the adverse underwriting decision in writing or advises such person that upon written request he may receive the specific reason or reasons in writing; and

2. Provides the applicant, policyholder, or individual proposed for coverage with a summary of the rights established under subsection B of this section and §§ 38.2-608 and 38.2-609.

B. Upon receipt of a written request within ninety business days from the date of the mailing of notice or other communication of an adverse underwriting decision to an applicant, policyholder or individual proposed for coverage, the insurance institution or agent shall furnish to such person within twenty-one business days from the date of receipt of the written request:

1. The specific reason or reasons for the adverse underwriting decision, in writing, if that information was not initially furnished in writing pursuant to subdivision 1 of subsection A of this section;

2. The specific items of personal and privileged information that support those reasons, however:

a. The insurance institution or agent shall not be required to furnish specific items of privileged information if it has a reasonable suspicion, based upon specific information available for review by the Commission, that the applicant, policyholder, or individual proposed for coverage has engaged in criminal activity, fraud, material misrepresentation, or material nondisclosure; and

b. Specific items of medical-record information supplied by a medical-care institution or medical professional shall be disclosed either directly to the individual about whom the information relates or to a medical professional designated by the individual and licensed to provide medical care with respect to the condition to which the information relates, whichever the insurance institution or agent prefers; and

3. The names and addresses of the institutional sources that supplied the specific items of information given pursuant to subdivision 2 of subsection B of this section. However, the identity of any medical professional or medical-care institution shall be disclosed either directly to the individual or to the designated medical professional, whichever the insurance institution or agent prefers.

C. The obligations imposed by this section upon an insurance institution or agent may be satisfied by another insurance institution or agent authorized to act on its behalf. However, the insurance institution or agent making an adverse underwriting decision shall remain responsible for compliance with the obligations imposed by this section.

D. When an adverse underwriting decision results solely from an oral request or inquiry, the explanation of reasons and summary of rights required by subsection A of this section may be given orally. (1981, c. 389, § 38.1-57.13; 1986, c. 562.)

§ **38.2-611. Information concerning previous adverse underwriting decisions.** — No insurance institution, agent, or insurance-support organization may seek information in connection with an insurance transaction concerning: (i) any previous adverse underwriting decision experienced by an individual, or (ii) any previous insurance coverage obtained by an individual through a residual market mechanism, unless the inquiry also requests the reasons for any previous adverse underwriting decision or the reasons why insurance coverage was previously obtained through a residual market mechanism. (1981, c. 389, § 38.1-57.14; 1986, c. 562.)

§ **38.2-612. Bases for adverse underwriting decisions.** — No insurance institution or agent may base an adverse underwriting decision in whole or in part:

1. On the fact of a previous adverse underwriting decision or on the fact that an individual previously obtained insurance coverage through a residual market mechanism. However, an insurance institution or agent may base an adverse underwriting decision on further information obtained from an insurance institution or agent responsible for a previous adverse underwriting decision;

2. On personal information received from an insurance-support organization whose primary source of information is insurance institutions. However, an insurance institution or agent may base an adverse underwriting decision on further personal information obtained as the result of information received from an insurance-support organization; or

3. On the fact that an individual previously obtained insurance coverage from a particular insurance institution or agent. (1981, c. 389, § 38.1-57.15; 1986, c. 562; 1990, c. 524.)

§ **38.2-613. Disclosure limitations and conditions.** — A. An insurance institution, agent, or insurance-support organization shall not disclose any personal or privileged information about an individual collected or received in connection with an insurance transaction unless the disclosure is:

1. With the written authorization of the individual, provided:

a. If the authorization is submitted by another insurance institution, agent, or insurance-support organization, the authorization meets the requirements of § 38.2-606; or

b. If the authorization is submitted by a person other than an insurance institution, agent, or insurance-support organization, the authorization is:

(1) Dated,

(2) Signed by the individual, and

(3) Obtained one year or less prior to the date a disclosure is sought pursuant to this subdivision; or

2. To a person other than an insurance institution, agent, or insurance-support organization, provided the disclosure is reasonably necessary:

a. To enable that person to perform a business, professional or insurance function for the disclosing insurance institution, agent, or insurance-support organization and that person agrees not to disclose the information further without the individual's written authorization unless the further disclosure:

(1) Would otherwise be permitted by this section if made by an insurance institution, agent, or insurance-support organization; or

(2) Is reasonably necessary for that person to perform its function for the disclosing insurance institution, agent, or insurance-support organization; or

b. To enable that person to provide information to the disclosing insurance institution, agent, or insurance-support organization for the purpose of:

(1) Determining an individual's eligibility for an insurance benefit or payment; or

(2) Detecting or preventing criminal activity, fraud, material misrepresentation, or material nondisclosure in connection with an insurance transaction; or

3. To an insurance institution, agent, or insurance-support organization, or self-insurer, provided the information disclosed is limited to that which is reasonably necessary:

a. To detect or prevent criminal activity, fraud, material misrepresentation, or material nondisclosure in connection with insurance transactions; or

b. For either the disclosing or receiving insurance institution, agent or insurance-support organization to perform its function in connection with an insurance transaction involving the individual; or

4. To a medical-care institution or medical professional for the purpose of (i) verifying insurance coverage or benefits, (ii) informing an individual of a medical problem of which the individual may not be aware or (iii) conducting an operations or services audit, provided only that information is disclosed as is reasonably necessary to accomplish the foregoing purposes; or

5. To an insurance regulatory authority; or

6. To a law-enforcement or other government authority:

a. To protect the interests of the insurance institution, agent or insurance-support organization in preventing or prosecuting the perpetration of fraud upon it; or

b. If the insurance institution, agent, or insurance-support organization reasonably believes that illegal activities have been conducted by the individual; or

c. Upon written request of any law-enforcement agency, for all insured or claimant information in the possession of an insurance institution, agent, or insurance-support organization which relates an ongoing criminal investigation. Such insurance institution, agent, or insurance-support organization shall release such information, including, but not limited to, policy information, premium payment records, record of prior claims by the insured or by another claimant, and information collected in connection with an insurance company's investigation of an application or claim. Any information released to a law-enforcement agency pursuant to such request shall be treated as confidential criminal investigation information and not be disclosed further except as provided by law. Notwithstanding any provision in this chapter, no insurance institution, agent, or insurance-support organization shall notify any insured or claimant that information has been requested or supplied pursuant to this section prior to notification from the requesting law-enforcement agency that its criminal investigation is completed. Within ninety days following the completion of any such criminal investigation, the law-enforcement agency making such a request for information shall notify any insurance institution, agent, or insurance-support organization from whom information was requested that the criminal investigation has been completed.

7. Otherwise permitted or required by law; or

8. In response to a facially valid administrative or judicial order, including a search warrant or subpoena; or

9. Made for the purpose of conducting actuarial or research studies, provided:

a. No individual may be identified in any actuarial or research report, and

b. Materials allowing the individual to be identified are returned or destroyed as soon as they are no longer needed, and

c. The actuarial or research organization agrees not to disclose the information unless the disclosure would otherwise be permitted by this section if made by an insurance institution, agent, or insurance-support organization; or

10. To a party or a representative of a party to a proposed or consummated sale, transfer, merger, or consolidation of all or part of the business of the insurance institution, agent, or insurance-support organization, provided:

a. Prior to the consummation of the sale, transfer, merger, or consolidation only such information is disclosed as is reasonably necessary to enable the recipient to make business decisions about the purchase, transfer, merger, or consolidation, and

b. The recipient agrees not to disclose the information unless the disclosure would otherwise be permitted by this section if made by an insurance institution, agent, or insurance-support organization; or

11. To a person whose only use of such information will be in connection with the marketing of a product or service, provided:

a. No medical-record information, privileged information, or personal information relating to an individual's character, personal habits, mode of living, or general reputation is disclosed, and no classification derived from the information is disclosed,

b. The individual has been given an opportunity to indicate that he does not want personal information disclosed for marketing purposes and has given no indication that he does not want the information disclosed, and

c. The person receiving such information agrees not to use it except in connection with the marketing of a product or service; or

12. To an affiliate whose only use of the information will be in connection with an audit of the insurance institution or agent or the marketing of an insurance product or service, provided the affiliate agrees not to disclose the information for any other purpose or to unaffiliated persons; or

13. By a consumer reporting agency, provided the disclosure is to a person other than an insurance institution or agent; or

14. To a group policyholder for the purpose of reporting claims experience or conducting an audit of the insurance institution's or agent's operations or services, provided the information disclosed is reasonably necessary for the group policyholder to conduct the review or audit; or

15. To a professional peer review organization for the purpose of reviewing the service or conduct of a medical-care institution or medical professional; or

16. To a governmental authority for the purpose of determining the individual's eligibility for health benefits for which the governmental authority may be liable; or

17. To a certificate holder or policyholder for the purpose of providing information regarding the status of an insurance transaction; or

18. To a lienholder, mortgagee, assignee, lessor or other person shown on the records of an insurance institution or agent as having a legal or beneficial interest in a policy of insurance, provided that:

a. No medical record information is disclosed unless the disclosure would be permitted by this section; and

b. The information disclosed is limited to that which is reasonably necessary to permit such person to protect his interest in the policy.

B. 1. No person proposing to issue, re-issue, or renew any policy, contract, or plan of accident and sickness insurance defined in § 38.2-109, but excluding disability income insurance, issued by any (i) insurer providing hospital, medical and surgical or major medical coverage on an expense incurred basis, (ii) corporation providing a health services plan, or (iii) health maintenance organization providing a health care plan for health care services shall disclose any genetic information about an individual or a member of such individual's family collected or received in connection with any insurance transaction unless the disclosure is made with the written authorization of the individual.

2. For the purpose of this subsection, *"genetic information"* means information about genes, gene products, or inherited characteristics that may derive from an individual or a family member.

3. Agents and insurance support organizations shall be subject to the provisions of this subsection to the extent of their participation in the issue, re-issue, or renewal of any policy, contract, or plan of accident and sickness insurance defined in § 38.2-109, but excluding disability income insurance. (1981, c. 389, § 38.1-57.16; 1986, c. 562; 1987, c. 325; 1996, c. 704.)

§ **38.2-613.01. Commission to promulgate regulations on disclosure of certain medical test results to insurance applicants.** — Pursuant to the authority granted by §§ 38.2-223 and 38.2-3100.1, the Commission shall promulgate such regulations as may be necessary or appropriate to ensure that applicants for life or accident and sickness insurance coverage or for modifications to existing coverage are notified of test results whenever insurers require such applicants to submit to testing for human immunodeficiency viruses (HIV). (1997, c. 290.)

§ **38.2-613.1. Disclosure of agent's moratorium required.** — If a duly appointed agent of an insurer proposes to place a policy of motor vehicle insurance as defined in § 38.2-2212 with another insurer or proposes to submit an application to the Virginia Automobile Insurance Plan solely because of a moratorium on such agent's soliciting, negotiating, procuring, or effecting new motor vehicle insurance that would otherwise be acceptable to such insurer and such placement or submission would result in the applicant's being charged a higher rate, the agent shall disclose to the applicant the existence of the moratorium prior to such placement or submission. (1991, c. 269.)

§ **38.2-614. Powers of Commission.** — A. The Commission shall have the power to examine and investigate the affairs of any insurance institution or agent doing business in this Commonwealth to determine whether the insurance institution or agent has been or is engaged in any conduct in violation of this chapter.

B. The Commission shall have the power to examine and investigate the affairs of any insurance-support organization that acts on behalf of an insurance institution or agent and that either (i) transacts business in this Commonwealth, or (ii) transacts business outside this Commonwealth and has an effect on a person residing in this Commonwealth, in order to determine whether the insurance-support organization has been or is engaged in any conduct in violation of this chapter. (1981, c. 389, § 38.1-57.17; 1986, c. 562.)

§ **38.2-615. Hearings and procedures.** — A. Whenever the Commission has reason to believe that an insurance institution, agent or insurance-support organization has been or is engaged in conduct in this Commonwealth that violates this chapter, or whenever the Commission has reason to believe that an insurance-support organization has been or is engaged in conduct outside this Commonwealth that has an effect on a person residing in this Commonwealth and that violates this chapter, the Commission may issue and serve upon the insurance institution, agent, or insurance-support organization a statement of charges and notice of hearing to be held at a time and place fixed in the notice. The date for such hearing shall be at least ten days after the date of service.

B. At the time and place fixed for the hearing, the insurance institution, agent, or insurance-support organization charged shall have an opportunity to answer the charges against it and present evidence on its behalf. Upon good cause shown, the Commission shall permit any adversely affected person to intervene, appear, and be heard at the hearing by counsel or in person.

C. In all matters in connection with such investigation, charge, or hearing the Commission shall have the jurisdiction, power and authority granted or conferred upon it by Title 12.1. (1981, c. 389, § 38.1-57.18; 1986, c. 562.)

§ **38.2-616. Service of process on insurance-support organizations.** — For the purpose of this chapter, an insurance-support organization transacting business outside this Commonwealth that has an effect on a person residing in this Commonwealth and which is alleged to violate this chapter shall be deemed to have appointed the clerk of the Commission to accept service of process on its behalf. Service on the clerk shall be made in accordance with § 12.1-19.1. (1981, c. 389, § 38.1-57.19; 1986, c. 562; 1991, c. 672.)

§ **38.2-617. Individual remedies.** — A. If any insurance institution, agent, or insurance-support organization fails to comply with §§ 38.2-608, 38.2-609, or § 38.2-610, any person whose rights granted under those sections are violated may apply to a court of competent jurisdiction for appropriate equitable relief.

B. An insurance institution, agent, or insurance-support organization that discloses information in violation of § 38.2-613 shall be liable for damages sustained by the individual to whom the information relates. No individual, however, shall be entitled to a monetary award that exceeds the actual damages sustained by the individual as a result of a violation of § 38.2-613.

C. In any action brought pursuant to this section, the court may award the cost of the action and reasonable attorney's fees to the prevailing party.

D. An action under this section must be brought within two years from the date the alleged violation is or should have been discovered.

E. Except as specifically provided in this section, there shall be no remedy or recovery available to individuals, in law or in equity, for occurrences constituting a violation of any provision of this chapter. (1981, c. 389, § 38.1-57.24; 1986, c. 562.)

§ 38.2-618. Immunity of persons disclosing information. — No cause of action in the nature of defamation, invasion of privacy, or negligence shall arise against any person for disclosing personal or privileged information in accordance with this chapter, nor shall such a cause of action arise against any person for furnishing personal or privileged information to an insurance institution, agent, or insurance-support organization. However, this section shall provide no immunity for disclosing or furnishing false information with malice or willful intent to injure any person. (1981, c. 389, § 38.1-57.25; 1986, c. 562.)

§ 38.2-619. Obtaining information under false pretenses. — Any person who knowingly and willfully obtains information about an individual from an insurance institution, agent or insurance-support organization under false pretenses shall be fined not more than $10,000 or punished by confinement in jail for not more than 12 months, or both. (1981, c. 389, § 38.1-57.26; 1986, c. 562.)

§ 38.2-620. Effective date. — The rights granted under §§ 38.2-608, 38.2-609 and 38.2-613 of this chapter shall take effect on January 1, 1982, regardless of the date of the collection or receipt of the information that is the subject of those sections. (1981, c. 389, § 38.1-57.28; 1986, c. 562.)

CHAPTER 7.

ANTITRUST PROVISIONS.

§ 38.2-700. When domestic insurer may hold stock of another insurer. — Subject to Article 6 (§ 38.2-1335 et seq.) of Chapter 13 and Chapter 14 (§ 38.2-1400 et seq.) of this title, any domestic insurer may retain, invest in or acquire the whole or any part of the capital stock of any other insurer, unless the effect of such action (i) substantially lessens competition generally or (ii) tends to create a monopoly, in the business of insurance. (1952, c. 317, § 38.1-58; 1983, c. 457; 1986, c. 562.)

§ 38.2-701. When director of a domestic insurer may be a director of another insurer. — Any domestic insurer may have a director who is also a director of another domestic, foreign or alien insurer, unless the effect thereof (i) substantially lessens competition generally or (ii) tends to create a monopoly, in the business of insurance. (1952, c. 317, § 38.1-59; 1986, c. 562.)

§ 38.2-702. Violations; procedure; cease and desist orders. — If the Commission has reason to believe that there is a violation of either § 38.2-700 or § 38.2-701, it shall issue and serve upon the insurer or the director concerned a statement of the charges and a notice of a hearing to be held at a time and place fixed in the notice, which shall not be less than thirty days after notice is served. The notice shall require the insurer or director to show cause why an order should not be issued directing the alleged offender to cease and desist from the violation. At such hearing, the insurer or director shall have an opportunity to be heard and to show cause why an order should not be issued requiring the insurer or director to cease and desist from the violation. In all matters in connection with such charges or hearing, the Commission shall have the jurisdiction, power, and authority granted or conferred upon it by Title 12.1, and, except as otherwise provided in this chapter, the procedure shall conform to and the right of appeal shall be the same as that provided in that title. (1952, c. 317, § 38.1-60; 1971, Ex. Sess., c. 1; 1986, c. 562.)

§ 38.2-703. Cease and desist orders may be entered. — If, after a hearing, the Commission finds that there has been a violation of § 38.2-700 or § 38.2-701, it may issue an order reciting its findings and directing the insurer or director to cease and desist from the violation. (1952, c. 317, § 38.1-61; 1986, c. 562.)

§ 38.2-704. Penalties. — A. Any person who violates a cease and desist order entered under § 38.2-703 shall be subject to the provisions of § 38.2-218.

B. Any person convicted of violating this chapter may, in addition, be punished under the provisions of Chapter 1.1 (§ 59.1-9.1 et seq.) of Title 59.1. (1952, c. 317, § 38.1-62; 1986, c. 562.)

§ 38.2-705. Antitrust provision. — Conduct subject to regulation, review or examination pursuant to this title shall, in addition, be subject to the provisions of the Virginia Antitrust Act (§ 59.1-9.1 et seq.). (1986, c. 562.)

CHAPTER 8.

SERVICE OF PROCESS.

ARTICLE 1.

Unlicensed Insurers Process.

§ 38.2-800. Definition. — For the purposes of this article, *"insurer"* includes health services plans, health maintenance organizations, legal services plans, and dental or optometric services plans as respectively provided for in Chapters 42, 43, 44 and 45 of this title. (1986, c. 562.)

Elements required to invoke regulatory statutes. — A small element of insurance should not be construed to bring a transaction within the reach of the insurance regulatory laws unless the transaction involves one or more of the evils at which the regulatory statutes were aimed and the elements of risk transfer and distribution give the transaction its distinctive character. GAF Corp. v. County Sch. Bd., 629 F.2d 981 (4th Cir. 1980).

Warranty not insurance contract. — Where supplier of roofing materials guaranteed to repair leaks caused by defects in its products and, incidentally, to repair leaks caused by faulty workmanship, the workmanship guarantee is incidental to the warranty against defects in the products sold, and thus the warranty is not a contract of insurance and the supplier is not an unauthorized insurer and is not amenable to service under the Unauthorized Insurers Process Act. GAF Corp. v. County Sch. Bd., 629 F.2d 981 (4th Cir. 1980).

§ 38.2-801. What constitutes appointment of agent for service of process. — A. The clerk of the Commission shall be deemed to be appointed by any insurer unlicensed in this Commonwealth as its agent for the service of process in accordance with § 13.1-758 if any of the following acts are effected by mail or otherwise in this Commonwealth:

1. The issuance or delivery of insurance contracts to residents of this Commonwealth or to corporations authorized to do business in this Commonwealth;

2. The solicitation of applications for these insurance contracts;

3. The collection of premiums, membership fees, assessments or other considerations for these insurance contracts; or

4. The transaction of any other insurance business in connection with these insurance contracts. (1952, c. 317, § 38.1-64; 1956, c. 431; 1958, c. 597; 1986, c. 562.)

Purpose of this section is different from that of the long arm statute. August v. HBA Life Ins. Co., 734 F.2d 168 (4th Cir. 1984).

Where a contractor guaranteed to repair leaks caused by defects in its products and, incidentally, to repair leaks caused by faulty workmanship, the workmanship guarantee was incidental to the warranty against defects in the products sold and viewed as a whole, the warranty was not a contract of insurance. The contractor is, therefore, not an unauthorized insurer and is not amenable to service under the Unauthorized Insurers Process Act. GAF Corp. v. County Sch. Bd., 629 F.2d 981 (4th Cir. 1980).

§ 38.2-802. How process served. — Service of process or notice upon any unlicensed insurer in any suit, action or proceeding arising out of or in connection with the acts listed in § 38.2-801 in this Commonwealth shall be made in the manner prescribed in § 13.1-758. (1952, c. 317, § 38.1-65; 1956, c. 431; 1958, c. 597; 1986, c. 562.)

§ 38.2-803. Alternate method of service. — A. Service of process or notice in any action, suit or proceeding shall be valid if:

1. Served upon any person within this Commonwealth who, in this Commonwealth on behalf of the unlicensed insurer, is (i) soliciting insurance, (ii) making, issuing, or delivering any insurance contract, or (iii) collecting or receiving any premium, membership fee, assessment or other consideration for insurance; and

2. A copy of the process or notice is sent within ten days thereafter by registered mail to the unlicensed insurer at its last known principal place of business.

B. A post-office receipt showing the sender's name, and the unlicensed insurer's name and address, and the plaintiff's or plaintiff's attorney's affidavit of compliance with the procedures set out in subsection A of this section shall be filed with the clerk of the court in which the proceeding is pending on or before the date the unlicensed insurer is required to appear, or within such further time as the court allows. (1952, c. 317, § 38.1-66; 1986, c. 562.)

§ 38.2-804. Other legal service not limited. — Nothing in this article shall limit the right to serve any process or notice upon any licensed insurer in any other manner permitted by law. (1952, c. 317, § 38.1-67; 1986, c. 562.)

Purpose of this section is different from that of the long arm statute. August v. HBA Life Ins. Co., 734 F.2d 168 (4th Cir. 1984).

§ 38.2-805. When judgment may be entered. — No judgment based on default of appearance shall be entered against any defendant served pursuant to § 38.2-803 until the expiration of thirty days from the date that the affidavit of compliance is filed. (1952, c. 317, § 38.1-68; 1986, c. 562.)

§ 38.2-806. Defense of action by unlicensed insurer. — A. Before any unlicensed insurer files or causes to be filed any pleading in any action, suit or proceeding instituted against it, that insurer shall either:

1. Deposit cash or securities with the clerk of the court in which the action, suit or proceeding is pending, or file with the clerk a bond in an amount to be fixed by the court which shall be sufficient to secure the payment of any final judgment; or

2. Procure a certificate of authority and a license to transact the business of insurance in this Commonwealth.

B. The court may order a postponement in any action, suit or proceeding in which service is made in the manner provided in § 38.2-802 or § 38.2-803 to afford the unlicensed insurer reasonable opportunity to comply with the provisions of subsection A of this section and to defend the action.

C. Nothing in subsection A of this section shall be construed to prevent any unlicensed insurer from appearing specially in the suit or other proceeding in which service was made in the manner provided in this article on the ground either that (i) the insurer has not done any of the acts listed in § 38.2-801, or (ii) the person on whom service was made pursuant to § 38.2-803 was not doing any of the acts listed in § 38.2-803. (1952, c. 317, § 38.1-69; 1986, c. 562.)

§ 38.2-807. Attorney fees. — A. In any action against an unlicensed insurer upon an insurance contract issued or delivered in this Commonwealth to a resident of this Commonwealth or to a corporation authorized to do business in this Commonwealth, the court may allow the plaintiff a reasonable attorney fee if (i) the insurer has failed to make payment in accordance with the terms of the contract for thirty days after demand prior to the commencement of the action and (ii) the court concludes that the refusal was vexatious and without reasonable cause. The fee shall not exceed $12^{1}/_{2}$ percent of the amount that the court or jury finds the plaintiff is entitled to recover against the insurer, but shall be at least $100.

B. Failure of the insurer to defend the action shall be deemed prima facie evidence that its failure to make payment was vexatious and without reasonable cause. (1952, c. 317, § 38.1-70; 1986, c. 562.)

ARTICLE 2.

Unlicensed Nonresident Brokers and Agents Process.

§ 38.2-808. Definition. — For the purposes of this article, *"agent"* shall have the meaning as set forth in § 38.2-1800 which shall include a legal services agent, a health agent and a dental or optometric services agent. (1986, c. 562.)

§ **38.2-809. What constitutes appointment of agent for service of process.** — The clerk of the Commission shall be deemed to be appointed by any unlicensed nonresident broker or agent as its agent for the service of process pursuant to § 13.1-758 if any of the following acts are effected by mail or otherwise in this Commonwealth by such unlicensed nonresident broker or agent: (i) the issuance or delivery of insurance contracts to residents of this Commonwealth or to corporations authorized to do business in this Commonwealth, (ii) the solicitation of applications for such contracts, (iii) the collection of premiums, membership fees, assessments or other considerations for such contracts, or (iv) the transaction of any other insurance business in connection with such contracts. (1958, c. 180, § 38.1-70.2; 1986, c. 562.)

§ **38.2-810. How process or notice served.** — Service of process or notice upon any unlicensed nonresident broker or agent in any suit, action or proceeding arising out of or in connection with the acts enumerated in § 38.2-809 in this Commonwealth shall be made in the manner prescribed in § 13.1-758. (1958, c. 180, § 38.1-70.3; 1986, c. 562.)

§ **38.2-811. Other legal service not limited.** — Nothing in this article shall limit the right to serve any process or notice upon any unlicensed nonresident broker or agent in any other manner permitted by law. (1958, c. 180, § 38.1-70.4; 1986, c. 562.)

CHAPTER 9.

Transition Provisions.

§ **38.2-900. Workers' compensation.** — All acts and parts of acts inconsistent with the provisions of this title are hereby repealed to the extent of the inconsistency. However, the provisions of this title shall not amend or repeal any provisions of Title 65.2 relating to workers' compensation. (1952, c. 317, § 38.1-43.1; 1986, c. 562.)

The General Assembly did not intend to exclude motor vehicle accidents from the workers' compensation scheme. Had the General Assembly intended to exclude motor vehicle accidents from the coverage of the Workers' Compensation Act, it would have done so directly in the Act itself, rather than indirectly through a provision in Title 38.2. Smith v. Horn, 232 Va. 302, 351 S.E.2d 14 (1986).

§ **38.2-901. References to former sections of Title 38 or Title 38.1.** — Wherever any of the conditions, requirements, provisions or contents of any section of Title 38 as such title existed prior to July 1, 1952, or Title 38.1, as that title existed before July 1, 1986, are transferred to a new or different section, and wherever any such old section is given a new section number in this title, all references to the former section of Title 38 or Title 38.1 appearing elsewhere in this Code than in this title shall be construed to apply to the new or renumbered section containing the conditions, requirements, provisions or contents. (1952, c. 317, § 38.1-43.2; 1986, c. 562.)

§ 38.2-902. Existing licenses. — Each license of an insurer, agent, surplus lines broker, or other person, issued and in force immediately before July 1, 1986, shall continue in force until its date of expiration or until terminated as provided in this title. (1952, c. 317, § 38.1-43.3; 1986, c. 562.)

§ 38.2-903. Existing form of policy, contract, certificate, application, rider or endorsement. — If any form does not comply with the provisions of this title but did comply with the provisions of any regulation or statute repealed by this Act of Assembly, it may continue to be used for a period of twelve months following July 1, 1986, unless the Commission prescribes otherwise pursuant to authority conferred by law. (1952, c. 317, § 38.1-43.4; 1986, c. 562.)

§ 38.2-904. Existing rates. — Every rate filed and presently in effect is continued and made effective until new rates are filed and become effective in accordance with the provisions of this title. (1952, c. 317, § 38.1-43.5; 1972, c. 836; 1973, c. 504; 1986, c. 562.)

CHAPTER 10.

Organization, Admission and Licensing of Insurers.

ARTICLE 1.

Organization of Domestic Insurers.

§ 38.2-1000. Incorporation of domestic stock insurers. — Domestic stock insurers shall be incorporated under the provisions of Article 3 (§ 13.1-618 et seq.) of Chapter 9 of Title 13.1. A foreign insurer may become a domestic insurer under the provisions of Article 11 (§ 13.1-705 et seq.) or Article 12 (§ 13.1-716 et seq.) of Chapter 9 of Title 13.1. Except as otherwise provided in this title, domestic stock insurers shall be subject to all the general restrictions and shall have all the general powers imposed and conferred by law. (Code 1950, §§ 38-27, 38-28; 1952, c. 317, § 38.1-71; 1956, c. 431; 1986, c. 562; 1995, c. 69.)

§ 38.2-1001. Incorporation of domestic mutual insurers. — Domestic mutual insurers shall be incorporated under the provisions of Article 3 (§ 13.1-818 et seq.) of Chapter 10 of Title 13.1. A foreign insurer may become a domestic insurer under the provisions of Article 10 (§ 13.1-884 et seq.) or Article 11 (§ 13.1-894 et seq.) of Chapter 10 of Title 13.1. Except as otherwise provided in this title, domestic mutual insurers shall be subject to all the general restrictions and shall have all the general powers imposed and conferred by law. (Code 1950, §§ 38-27, 38-497, 38-498, 38-500, 38-501, 38-502; 1952, c. 317, § 38.1-74; 1956, c. 431; 1986, c. 562; 1995, c. 69.)

Cross references. — For constitutional provisions concerning corporations, see Va. Const., Art. IX.

§ 38.2-1002. Additional requirements of articles of incorporation; name. — The articles of incorporation for a domestic mutual insurer shall be signed by at least twenty natural persons, a majority of whom are legal residents of this Commonwealth. The articles shall, in addition to complying with the requirements of Article 3 (§ 13.1-818 et seq.) of Chapter 10 of Title 13.1, set forth the classes of insurance the insurer proposes to write. (Code 1950, §§ 38-28, 38-497, 38-498, 38-499; 1952, c. 317, § 38.1-75; 1956, c. 431; 1958, c. 596; 1986, c. 562.)

§ 38.2-1003. When corporate status attained; bylaws filed with Commission. — A domestic mutual insurer shall have legal existence as soon as the charter has been recorded with the Commission, after which the board of directors named in the charter may adopt bylaws and accept applications for insurance. However, no insurance shall be put in force until the insurer has been licensed to transact the business of insurance as provided by this chapter. The bylaws and any amendments shall be filed with the Commission within thirty days after adoption. (Code 1950, § 38-503; 1952, c. 317, § 38.1-76; 1986, c. 562.)

§ 38.2-1004. Voting. — Each member of a domestic mutual insurer shall have one vote, or a number of votes based upon the insurance in force, the number of policies held, or the amount of premiums paid, as provided in the bylaws of the insurer. (Code 1950, § 38-507; 1952, c. 317, § 38.1-77; 1986, c. 562.)

§ 38.2-1005. Certain mutual companies and societies not to become stock companies without approval of State Corporation Commission. — No mutual insurance company, cooperative nonprofit life benefit company, mutual assessment life, accident and sickness company, burial society, or fraternal benefit society shall be converted into a stock corporation unless such conversion and the plan for conversion are approved by the Commission. The insurer shall comply with § 38.2-1028 before approval for conversion is granted by the Commission unless the Commission finds that the insurer will have the required capital and surplus within a reasonable time after conversion. (1952, c. 317, § 38.1-79; 1970, c. 636; 1986, c. 562.)

§ 38.2-1005.1. Conversion of a domestic mutual insurer to a domestic stock insurer. — A. Any domestic mutual insurer may convert to a domestic stock insurer pursuant to a plan of conversion approved by the Commission.

B. The Commission shall approve any such plan of conversion if, after giving notice and an opportunity to be heard to the policyholders of the domestic mutual insurer, the Commission determines that:

1. The terms and conditions of the plan are fair and equitable to the policyholders of the domestic mutual insurer;

2. The plan is subject to approval by a vote of more than two-thirds of all votes cast on the plan at a meeting of the members of the domestic mutual insurer called for that purpose at which a quorum is present;

3. Except as otherwise provided in subdivision 4 of this subsection, the plan allocates and directs that the entire stock ownership interests and other consideration to be distributed pursuant to the plan of conversion be distributed to the policyholders of the domestic mutual insurer;

4. In the case of a domestic mutual insurer that converted from a health services plan that was in existence prior to December 31, 1987, the plan of conversion allocates and distributes to the State Treasurer, in addition to any shares of stock that the Commonwealth may be entitled to receive as a policyholder, shares of stock or cash or both with a value equal to the surplus, computed in accordance with generally accepted accounting principles, of such health services plan on December 31, 1987, plus ten million dollars; and

5. Immediately after the conversion, the insurer will have the fully paid capital stock and surplus required by applicable law.

C. A plan of conversion that utilizes a statutory merger in order to effect a conversion may be approved under this section, and the provisions of § 38.2-1018 shall not be applicable to such plan of conversion. (1996, cc. 801, 831.)

Editor's note. — Acts 1996, cc. 801 and 831, cls. 2, provide: "[t]hat the provisions of this act shall be applicable to all plans of conversion acted on by the State Corporation Commission after the effective date of this act [July 1, 1996]."

Acts 1996, cc. 801 and 831, cls. 3, provide: "[t]hat, on the effective date of this act [July 1, 1996], any plan of conversion then pending before the State Corporation Commission shall not be approved by the Commission unless such plan provides for, or is amended to provide for, the appointment to the initial board of directors of the insurer's parent company, for a term of three years each, one director from a list of three nominees submitted by the Joint Rules Committee, as defined in § 51.1-124.3, and one director from a list of three nominees submitted by the Attorney General. Such nominees shall be citizens who do not hold public office and have no direct or indirect financial interest, except as a consumer, in the insurer."

ARTICLE 2.

Conversion of Domestic Stock Insurer to Mutual Insurer.

§ **38.2-1006. Conversion of a domestic stock insurer to a mutual insurer.** — A. Any domestic stock life insurer may become a mutual life insurer, and to that end may carry out a plan for the acquisition of shares of its capital stock by purchase, gift or bequest, if the plan:

1. Has been adopted by a vote of a majority of the directors of the insurer;

2. Has been approved by a vote of the holders of at least two-thirds of the stock outstanding at a meeting called for that purpose;

3. Has been submitted to and approved by the Commission; and

4. Has been approved by a majority vote of the policyholders voting at a meeting called for that purpose. Only those policyholders whose insurance is then in force and has been in force for at least one year before the meeting shall be entitled to vote.

B. For the purpose of this article, *"policyholder"* shall include the employer, or the president, secretary or other executive officer of any corporation or association, to which a master group policy has been issued, but shall exclude the holders of certificates or policies issued under or in connection with a master group policy. (Code 1950, §§ 38-420, 38-424; 1952, c. 317, §§ 38.1-489, 38.1-493; 1986, c. 562.)

§ 38.2-1007. Notice to policyholders of meeting to approve conversion. — At least thirty days before the meeting of policyholders required by § 38.2-1006, the insurer shall mail notice of the meeting to each policyholder at the last known address or shall deliver the notice in person to the policyholder. (Code 1950, § 38-421; 1952, c. 317, § 38.1-490; 1986, c. 562.)

§ 38.2-1008. Conduct of and voting at meeting. — The meeting required by § 38.2-1006 shall be conducted in the manner provided in the plan, subject to the following requirements:

1. Policyholders may vote in person, by proxy, or by mail, but all votes shall be cast by ballot; and

2. A representative of the Commission shall supervise the procedure of the meeting and shall appoint an adequate number of inspectors to oversee the voting at the meeting. The inspectors, acting under any rules and regulations prescribed by the Commission, shall have power to determine all questions concerning the verification and validity of the ballots, the qualifications of the voters, and the canvass of the vote. The inspectors shall certify the results of the voting to the representative of the Commission and to the insurer.

All necessary expenses incurred by the Commission or its representative in connection with the meeting shall be paid by the insurer. (Code 1950, § 38-422; 1952, c. 317, § 38.1-491; 1986, c. 562.)

§ 38.2-1009. Payment for shares pursuant to conversion plan. — Every payment for the acquisition of any shares of the capital stock of the insurer, the purchase price of which is not fixed by the plan, shall be subject to the approval of the Commission. Neither the plan, nor any payment under the plan, nor any payment not fixed by the plan, shall be approved by the Commission if the making of the payment reduces the surplus to policyholders to an amount less than that required at that time for the licensure of domestic mutual insurers. (Code 1950, § 38-423; 1952, c. 317, § 38.1-492; 1986, c. 562.)

§ 38.2-1010. How acquired shares held. — Until all shares are acquired, the acquired shares shall be held in trust for the policyholders of the insurer as provided in this article and shall be assigned and transferred on the books of the insurer to not less than three nor more than five trustees and shall be held by them in trust. Shares transferred to the trustees shall be voted by them at all corporate meetings at which stockholders have the right to vote until all of the capital stock of the insurer is acquired. The trustees shall be appointed and vacancies in the office of trustee shall be filled as provided in the plan adopted under § 38.2-1006. The trustees shall file with the insurer and with the Commission a verified acceptance of their appointment and a declaration that they will faithfully discharge their duties as such trustees. (Code 1950, § 38-425; 1952, c. 317, § 38.1-494; 1986, c. 562.)

§ 38.2-1011. Disposition of dividends after payments provided in conversion plan. — After the payment of stockholder dividends as provided in the plan adopted under § 38.2-1006, and after paying the necessary expenses of executing the trust all dividends and other sums received by the trustees on the shares of acquired stock, shall be immediately repaid to the insurer for the benefit of those who are or may become policyholders of the insurer and entitled to participate in the profits of the insurer. These payments shall be added to and become a part of the earned surplus of the insurer. (Code 1950, § 38-426; 1952, c. 317, § 38.1-495; 1986, c. 562.)

§ 38.2-1012. Jurisdiction to compel completion of mutualization. — Whenever (i) a plan of mutualization approved in accordance with the laws of this Commonwealth has been in effect for more than five years, and (ii) the insurer has acquired in the name of its trustees under the plan at least ninety percent of its outstanding stock, and (iii) the plan itself contains no provision for the compulsory completion of mutualization inconsistent with the terms of this article, circuit courts shall have jurisdiction to compel completion of the mutualization of the insurer upon the petition of either the insurer or any stockholder of the insurer. (1954, c. 20, § 38.1-495.1; 1986, c. 562.)

§ 38.2-1013. Venue of proceedings. — The petition may be filed in the circuit court of record with general equity jurisdiction in the county or city in which the principal office of the insurer is located. (1954, c. 20, § 38.1-495.2; 1986, c. 562.)

§ 38.2-1014. Parties and process. — Necessary parties to the proceeding shall be (i) the insurer, (ii) the registered holders of all its stock still outstanding in the hands of the public, and (iii) its policyholders as a class. Process may be served on the policyholders as a class by publication but any policyholder may, on motion, be admitted as an individual party. The court shall appoint an attorney to represent all other policyholders. (1954, c. 20, § 38.1-495.3; 1986, c. 562.)

§ 38.2-1015. Determining value of stock outstanding; dismissal of petition or entry of decree requiring payment for and transfer of stock. — The court shall determine the per share fair cash value as of the date of the filing of the petition of the stock remaining in the hands of the public. If the court finds that on that basis, completion of mutualization may not be effected without jeopardizing the solvency of the insurer or the security of its policyholders, the petition shall be dismissed. Otherwise, the court shall enter an appropriate decree to require (i) the payment into court by the insurer of the aggregate amount due the remaining stockholders, with any interest and costs, which may include attorneys' fees that the court may require, and (ii) the transfer and delivery to the insurer of all stock certificates still outstanding in the hands of the public. Upon payment by the insurer, the trustees under the plan of mutualization shall be considered, for all purposes of the plan of mutualization, to have acquired all of its outstanding stock. The holders of the stock shall possess no further right with respect to the stock, except to receive its fair cash value as determined by the court. The court shall retain jurisdiction over the distribution of the funds. (1954, c. 20, § 38.1-495.4; 1986, c. 562.)

§ 38.2-1016. Amendment of charter and bylaws; change of name; retirement and cancellation of stock; when mutualization effective; assets and liabilities; officers and directors; general restrictions and powers. — A. Upon acquisition by the trustees of all of the capital stock of the insurer pursuant to the provisions of this article, the charter of the insurer shall be amended to reflect its mutualization. The charter may be amended in any other respect considered necessary by the board of directors and trustees of the insurer in accordance with the provisions of this article and Article 11 (§ 13.1-705 et seq.) of Chapter 9 of Title 13.1. Upon the amendment of the charter of the insurer, the board of directors named in the amendment shall adopt any changes in the bylaws considered necessary, and the bylaws and any amendments to them shall be filed with the Commission within thirty days after adoption.

B. As soon as the charter of the insurer has been amended as provided in this section, the capital stock of the insurer held by the trustees shall be assigned to the insurer and shall be retired and cancelled. Certification of that action by the proper officers of the insurer shall be made to the Commission, and the trustees acting under the plan shall be discharged. The insurer shall then immediately become a mutual insurer owning all the assets of the converted stock insurer and subject to all its liabilities.

C. The officers and directors of the insurer named in the amended charter shall continue as the officers and directors of the mutual insurer until their successors are duly elected in accordance with the provisions of the amended charter and the bylaws adopted under it.

D. The converted mutual insurer, except as otherwise provided in this title, shall be subject to all the general restrictions and have all the general powers imposed and conferred upon nonstock corporations by law. (1954, c. 20, § 38.1-495.5; 1956, c. 431; 1986, c. 562.)

ARTICLE 3.

Mergers.

§ 38.2-1017. Applicability of Title 13.1. — Except as otherwise provided in this title, Article 12 (§ 13.1-716 et seq.) of Chapter 9 of Title 13.1 shall apply to mergers involving a domestic stock insurer and Article 11 (§ 13.1-894 et seq.) of Chapter 10 of Title 13.1 shall apply to mergers involving a domestic mutual insurer. (1952, c. 317, § 38.1-80; 1956, c. 431; 1986, c. 562.)

§ 38.2-1018. Plan of merger to be approved by Commission. — Before any joint agreement for the merger of domestic insurers is submitted to the stockholders or members, it shall first be submitted to and approved by the Commission. The Commission shall not approve the agreement unless, after a hearing, it finds that the plan of merger is fair, equitable, consistent with law, and that no reasonable objection to the plan exists. If the Commission fails to approve the plan it shall state the reasons in its order. (1952, c. 317, § 38.1-81; 1956, c. 431; 1986, c. 562.)

ARTICLE 4.

Redomestication of Insurers.

§ 38.2-1019. Change of status from foreign to domestic insurer. — A. Any foreign insurer licensed to transact the business of insurance in this Commonwealth may become a domestic insurer upon (i) complying with the requirements for formation of a domestic insurer under Article 1 (§ 38.2-1000 et seq.) of this chapter at the date of redomestication, and (ii) promptly filing any necessary amendments to its articles of incorporation, charters, bylaws and other corporate documents. When those requirements have been met, the Commission may issue a license dated as of the date of redomestication in accordance with the provisions of Article 5 (§ 38.2-1024 et seq.) of this chapter to permit the company to transact the business of insurance in the Commonwealth as a domestic insurer. The license shall state the date and domicile of the original incorporation of the insurer, and shall indicate its redomestication into this Commonwealth under the provisions of this chapter.

B. An insurer that changes its status from foreign to domestic in accordance with subsection A of this section has all the rights, titles and interests in the assets of the original corporation, as well as all of its liabilities and obligations. (1983, c. 441, § 38.1-949; 1986, c. 562.)

§ 38.2-1020. Transfer of domicile from Virginia to another state. — Any domestic insurer, upon the approval of the Commission, may transfer its domicile from this Commonwealth to any other state in which it is licensed to transact the business of insurance. The Commission may approve the proposed transfer of domicile if it determines that the transfer is in the best interests of the insurer's policyholders and this Commonwealth. If the Commission does not approve the transfer, it shall give the insurer written notice of the refusal and the reasons for it within thirty days after the date the request for transfer was made. If the request for transfer is granted and the insurer is otherwise qualified, it may transact the business of insurance in this Commonwealth as a foreign insurer without interruption in licensing. (1983, c. 441, § 38.1-950; 1986, c. 562.)

§ 38.2-1021. Change of domicile of foreign insurer to another foreign state. — Any foreign insurer licensed to transact the business of insurance in this Commonwealth, upon proper notice to the Commission, may change its domicile to another foreign state without interruption in licensing and without reapplying as a foreign insurer if:

1. For a foreign stock insurer, the change in domicile does not result in a reduction in its capital and surplus to policyholders below the capital and surplus requirements for licensure specified in § 38.2-1028;

2. For a foreign mutual insurer, the change in domicile does not result in a reduction in its surplus below the surplus requirements for licensure specified in § 38.2-1029;

3. There is no substantial change in the lines of insurance to be written by the insurer;

4. There is no substantial change in the nature of the insurer or its method of operations and there is no deterioration in its financial condition; and

5. The change in domicile has been approved by the supervising regulatory officials of both the former and new state of domicile. (1983, c. 441, § 38.1-951; 1986, c. 562.)

§ 38.2-1022. Commission to be notified of proposed transfer of domicile. — Each insurer licensed to transact the business of insurance in this Commonwealth that transfers its domicile to any other state shall notify the Commission of the proposed transfer and shall file promptly with it any necessary amendments to articles of incorporation, charters, bylaws, and other corporate documents. (1983, c. 441, § 38.1-952; 1986, c. 562.)

§ 38.2-1023. Effect of transfer of domicile on certificate of authority, agents' appointments and licenses, etc. — When any insurer licensed to transact the business of insurance in this Commonwealth transfers its domicile to this or any other state, its certificate of authority, agents' appointments and licenses, policy forms, rates, authorizations, and other filings and approvals that existed at the time of the transfer shall remain in effect after the transfer of domicile occurs. (1983, c. 441, § 38.1-953; 1986, c. 562.)

ARTICLE 5.

Licensing of Insurers.

§ 38.2-1024. License required to transact the business of insurance; application fee requirements for license. — A. No insurer unless authorized pursuant to Chapter 48 (§ 38.2-4800 et seq.) of this title shall transact the business of insurance in this Commonwealth until it has obtained a license from the Commission. For a foreign or alien insurer, this license shall be in addition to the certificate of authority required by § 38.2-1027. Each application for a license to transact the business of insurance in this Commonwealth shall be accompanied by a nonrefundable license application fee of $500. The fee shall be collected by the Commission and paid directly into the state treasury and credited to the Bureau of Insurance's maintenance fund as provided in subsection B of § 38.2-400. The license shall be signed by a member or other duly authorized agent of the Commission and shall expire on the next June 30 after the date on which it becomes effective, subject to renewal pursuant to § 38.2-1025.

B. The Commission shall not grant a license to do the business of insurance in this Commonwealth to any insurer until it is satisfied that, from the evidence it requires under uniform procedures suitable to and applied equally to all classes of insurers, the insurer:

1. Has paid all fees, taxes, and charges required by law;

2. Has made any deposit required by this title;

3. Has the minimum capital and surplus if a stock insurer, the minimum surplus if a mutual or a reciprocal insurer, and the minimum trusteed surplus if an alien insurer, prescribed in this title for insurers transacting the same class of insurance;

4. Has filed a financial statement or statements and any reports, certificates or other documents the Commission considers necessary to secure a full and accurate knowledge of its affairs and financial condition;

5. Is solvent and its financial condition, method of operation, and manner of doing business are such as to satisfy the Commission that it can meet its obligations to all policyholders; and

6. Has otherwise complied with all the requirements of law. (Code 1950, §§ 38-31 to 38-33, 38-505, 38-514; 1952, c. 317, §§ 38.1-85, 38.1-86; 1978, cc. 4, 20; 1981, c. 605; 1986, c. 562; 1994, c. 316.)

Title Option Plus does not constitute insurance. — Where Title Option Plus (TOP) is a "process" by which company determines the record status of title to real property in order to decide whether to make a mortgage loan, TOP does not involve a shifting of the risk of title defects, and therefore, does not constitute insurance subject to Commission regulation. Lawyers Title Ins. Corp. v. Norwest Corp., 254 Va. 388, 493 S.E.2d 114 (1997).

General contractor's liability. — Where subcontractor was uninsured in Virginia for purposes of the Virginia Workers' Compensation Act, the statutory employer, the general contractor, was liable for claimant's benefits. Falls Church Constr. Corp. v. Valle, 21 Va. App. 351, 464 S.E.2d 517 (1995).

§ 38.2-1025. Annual renewal of license. — Each insurer licensed to transact the business of insurance in this Commonwealth shall obtain an annual renewal of its license from the Commission. The Commission may refuse to renew the license of any insurer or may renew the license, subject to any restrictions considered appropriate by the Commission, if it finds an impairment of required capital and surplus or if it finds that the insurer has not satisfied all the conditions set forth in subsection B of § 38.2-1024. The Commission shall not fail to renew the license of any insurer to transact the business of insurance without giving the insurer ten days' notice and giving it an opportunity to be heard. The hearing may be informal, and the required notice may be waived by the Commission and the insurer. (Code 1950, § 38-57; 1952, c. 317, § 38.1-98; 1986, c. 562.)

Applied in Eastern Life & Cas. Co. v. Commonwealth, 205 Va. 287, 136 S.E.2d 838 (1964).

§ 38.2-1026. Retaliatory provisions as to taxes, fees, deposits and other requirements. — A. When a domestic insurer or its agents are subject to regulatory costs in another state that are greater than those imposed in this Commonwealth upon insurers domiciled in that state or their agents, then the regulatory costs imposed by this Commonwealth on those foreign insurers or their agents shall be increased to equal the regulatory costs imposed by the other state on the domestic insurer or its agents. For the purpose of this section, regulatory cost includes (i) any deposits of securities, (ii) payment of taxes, fines, penalties or fees exacted for the privilege of doing business or (iii) any restitutions, obligations or conditions necessary for doing business.

B. For the purposes of this section an alien insurance company shall be considered domiciled in the state wherein it has the largest amount of its assets held in trust and on deposit for the benefit of its policyholders, or of its policyholders and creditors in the United States. An insurance company incorporated in Canada shall be considered domiciled in Canada.

C. Any foreign or alien insurance company subject to this section shall annually, on or before March 1, file a report with the Commission which compares the regulatory costs imposed on such insurer by this Commonwealth during the preceding calendar year to the regulatory costs that would have been imposed on a similar insurer domiciled in this Commonwealth by such insurer's state of domicile during the preceding calendar year. This report shall be filed on a form and in such detail as prescribed by the Commission. Amounts owed due to the equalization of the regulatory costs imposed on such insurer by this Commonwealth and the regulatory costs of such insurer's state of domicile shall be remitted to the Commission on or before March 1 of each year. Upon the failure of any insurance company to pay amounts due under this section before the date herein prescribed, the Commission shall impose a penalty of ten percent of the amount due and interest shall be charged at a rate established pursuant to § 58.1-15 for the period between the due date and the date of full payment. (Code 1950, §§ 38-12, 38-13; 1952, c. 317, § 38.1-87; 1986, c. 562; 1998, c. 60.)

The **1998 amendment** added the subsection A and B designations and added subsection C.

This section is a retaliatory statute. Its ultimate object is to secure reciprocity, but its immediate object is to retaliate on the companies of a given state disfavors shown to Virginia companies in the same state. Equitable Fire & Marine Ins. Co. v. Commonwealth, 195 Va. 752, 80 S.E.2d 549 (1954).

And is to be strictly construed. — This section being a retaliatory statute it is to be strictly construed, executed with care and applied only to cases that clearly come within its terms. Equitable Fire & Marine Ins. Co. v. Commonwealth, 195 Va. 752, 80 S.E.2d 549 (1954).

Test of similarity is kind of business engaged in. — Under this section the test of whether companies are "similar" is the kind of business they engage in, not their financial structure or condition. Equitable Fire & Marine

Ins. Co. v. Commonwealth, 195 Va. 752, 80 S.E.2d 549 (1954).

If greater burden is imposed on Virginia companies for any purpose, section applies. — If the insurance companies are similar and any other state imposes a greater burden on Virginia companies "for the protection of policyholders or for any other purpose," i.e., for any purpose, then the retaliatory provision of this section becomes applicable. Equitable Fire & Marine Ins. Co. v. Commonwealth, 195 Va. 752, 80 S.E.2d 549 (1954).

Whether or not such burden is justified by facts. — The question is not whether the requirement made of a Virginia corporation in a foreign state was justified by the facts but simply whether it was authorized by the law of that state. Equitable Fire & Marine Ins. Co. v. Commonwealth, 195 Va. 752, 80 S.E.2d 549 (1954).

§ **38.2-1027. Admission of foreign and alien insurers.** — Before transacting any insurance business in this Commonwealth, each foreign or alien insurer shall obtain a certificate of authority and shall comply with the applicable provisions of Article 17 (§ 13.1-757 et seq.) of Chapter 9 of Title 13.1 in the case of a stock insurer and of Article 14 (§ 13.1-919 et seq.) of Chapter 10 of Title 13.1 in the case of a mutual insurer. The certificate shall be in addition to the license to transact the business of insurance required by § 38.2-1024. (Code 1950, §§ 38-32, 38-34; 1952, c. 317, § 38.1-83; 1956, c. 431; 1986, c. 562.)

Law Review. — For article, "Insurance and Antitrust Law: The McCarran-Ferguson Act and Beyond," see 25 Wm. & Mary L. Rev. 81 (1983).

The General Assembly of Virginia has authority to forbid foreign corporations engaging in any pursuit within the State; and of consequence to grant permission to engage therein only upon terms. Slaughter v. Commonwealth, 54 Va. (13 Gratt.) 767 (1856); Manhattan Life Ins. Co. v. Warwick, 61 Va. (20 Gratt.) 614, 3 Am. R. 218 (1871); Cowardin v. Universal Life Ins. Co., 73 Va. (32 Gratt.) 445 (1879).

The act providing for service of process against foreign surety companies, relates to business transacted in this State, and the general provision as to service of process cannot be construed to apply to proceedings in another state. Hopkins v. Commonwealth, 129 Va. 137, 105 S.E. 673 (1921).

General contractor's liability. — Where subcontractor was uninsured in Virginia for purposes of the Virginia Workers' Compensation Act, the statutory employer, the general contractor, was liable for claimant's benefits. Falls Church Constr. Corp. v. Valle, 21 Va. App. 351, 464 S.E.2d 517 (1995).

§ 38.2-1028. Additional licensing requirements for stock insurers. — No stock insurer shall be licensed to transact the business of insurance in this Commonwealth unless it has fully paid in capital stock of at least one million dollars and surplus of at least three million dollars. (Code 1950, §§ 38-29, 38-33, 38-36, 38-330; 1952, c. 317, §§ 38.1-88, 38.1-89; 1966, c. 580; 1977, c. 322; 1978, c. 20; 1986, c. 562; 1991, c. 261.)

§ 38.2-1029. Additional licensing requirements for mutual insurers. — No mutual insurer shall be licensed to transact the business of insurance in this Commonwealth unless it has a surplus of at least $1,600,000. (Code 1950, § 38-514; 1952, c. 317, § 38.1-94; 1966, c. 580; 1978, c. 20; 1986, c. 562; 1991, c. 261.)

§ 38.2-1030. Surplus requirements for issuing policies without contingent liability. — No domestic or foreign mutual insurer shall issue policies without contingent liability unless, at the time of issue, the insurer has at least four million dollars of surplus. In the case of an alien insurer, policies without contingent liability shall not be issued unless, at the time of issue, the insurer has at least four million dollars of trusteed surplus.

However, any mutual insurer that on June 30, 1991, was authorized to issue and was engaged in issuing policies without contingent liability may continue to do so, until July 1, 1994, by maintaining at all times the minimum surplus if a domestic or foreign insurer, and the minimum trusteed surplus if an alien insurer, required at the time of authorization. (Code 1950, § 38-508; 1952, c. 317, § 38.1-95.1; 1966, c. 580; 1977, c. 322; 1986, c. 562; 1987, c. 520; 1991, c. 261.)

§ 38.2-1031. Additional requirements, alien insurers. — A. No alien insurer shall be licensed to transact the business of insurance in this Commonwealth unless it (i) has a "trusteed surplus," as defined in subsection B of this section, of at least four million dollars and (ii) has filed with the Commission a certificate from the supervising insurance official of the state of entry certifying that it is authorized to write the classes of insurance it proposes to write in this Commonwealth or it has filed with the Commission a certificate of the supervising insurance official of its domiciliary country that it is authorized there to transact the kind of insurance business it proposes to transact in this Commonwealth.

B. *"Trusteed surplus"* of an alien insurer means the excess of the aggregate value of the assets set forth in subsection C of this section over the aggregate net amount of all of its liabilities in the United States.

C. 1. General state deposits are all of the alien insurer's assets within the United States on deposit with officers of any state for the benefit and security of all of its policyholders and creditors in the United States.

2. Special state deposits are all of the alien insurer's assets in the United States, other than general state deposits, which are on deposit with officers of any state for the benefit and security of its policyholders and creditors in the state of deposit, or for the benefit and security of certain classes of its policyholders and creditors either in the state of deposit or in the United States. The value of special state deposits shall in no event exceed the value of the liability secured by the special state deposits.

3. Trusteed assets are all of its assets in the United States, other than general state deposits and special state deposits, held by any trustee for the benefit and security of all of its policyholders and creditors in the United States.

4. Interest receivable includes any interest collectable by the state or trustee that is receivable, due and accrued on the general state deposits, the special state deposits, and the trusteed assets of the alien insurer.

D. An alien insurer's liabilities in the United States are all of the reserves and other liabilities incurred by the alien insurer in the United States, from which may be deducted:

1. An amount equal to the reinsurance credits allowed by § 38.2-1316;

2. From the amount of such liabilities for unearned premiums, the unearned portion of premiums receivable by an alien insurer from its agents or policyholders under policies issued by it in the United States and not more than ninety days past due on the date of such statement;

3. Those liabilities in the United States pertaining to any asset in the United States of the alien insurer other than the assets described in subsection C of this section. This deduction shall be allowed only to the extent considered appropriate by the Commission and shall in no case exceed that portion of the value of the asset that is applicable to the liability pertaining to the asset; and

4. The amount of the unpaid principal and interest of any loan made by the alien insurer to the holder of, and solely on the security of, any life insurance policy or annuity contract issued or assumed by it on the life of or to any person in the United States. This amount shall in no case exceed the amount of the reserve it is required to maintain on the policy or annuity contract. (Code 1950, §§ 38-38, 38-514; 1952, c. 317, § 38.1-95; 1966, c. 580; 1977, c. 322; 1978, c. 20; 1985, c. 243; 1986, c. 562; 1991, c. 261.)

Editor's note. — Section 38.2-1316, referred to in subdivision 1 of subsection D, was repealed by Acts 1991, c. 264. For present reinsurance provisions, see § 38.2-1316.1 et seq.

§ 38.2-1032. Additional licensing requirements for domestic insurers.

— No domestic insurer shall be licensed to transact the business of insurance in this Commonwealth until it has furnished the Commission with a statement under the seal of the insurer, verified by the president or treasurer or two of its directors, showing (i) the amount of surplus, (ii) the amount of capital stock fully paid in, (iii) the amount of actual cash in its treasury, (iv) the amount invested with a list of the investments and their cash value, and (v) any other information the Commission requires. In its discretion the Commission may make or direct to be made an examination of the insurer to ascertain if it is entitled to the license. (Code 1950, § 38-505; 1952, c. 317, § 38.1-91; 1960, c. 289; 1966, c. 580; 1986, c. 562.)

§ 38.2-1033. Additional licensing requirements for foreign insurers. — No foreign insurer shall be licensed to transact the business of insurance in this Commonwealth until it has filed with the Commission a certificate from the supervising insurance official of the state in which it is incorporated certifying that it is authorized to write the classes of insurance it proposes to write in this Commonwealth. (Code 1950, §§ 38-36, 38-330; 1952, c. 317, § 38.1-89; 1966, c. 580; 1977, c. 322; 1978, c. 20; 1986, c. 562.)

§ 38.2-1034. How domestic mutual insurers may acquire initial surplus. — Any domestic mutual insurer or mutual assessment property and casualty insurer may, without pledging any of its assets, provide a guaranty fund sufficient to defray the expenses of its organization and its initial minimum surplus required to obtain a license to do the business of insurance. The fund may be increased with the prior approval of the Commission by receiving advances or by borrowing funds upon an agreement that the funds, including interest at a rate not exceeding the one-year treasury bill interest rate plus three percentage points at the time the loan is made or renewed, shall be repaid only if the insurer has sufficient earned surplus. The agreement shall provide that the insurer may repay the advances or loans or any part of them whenever it is able to do so in accordance with the requirements of this article. No commission or brokerage shall be paid in acquiring the funds. No repayments of principal, either in whole or in part, and no payments of interest, shall be made without the prior written approval of the Commission. Neither the principal advanced or borrowed nor any interest accrued thereon under this provision shall form a part of the legal liabilities of the insurer until the Commission approves the repayment of such principal or the payment of interest thereon. However, all statements published or filed by the insurer shall show accrued interest and the amount of principal remaining unpaid. All claims under the instrument shall be subordinated to policyholder, claimant and beneficiary claims as well as debts owed to all other classes of creditors. (Code 1950, § 38-512; 1952, c. 317, § 38.1-92; 1960, c. 291, § 38.1-92.1; 1970, c. 595; 1980, c. 187; 1986, c. 562; 1994, c. 503.)

§ 38.2-1035. Domestic insurers to maintain minimum capital and surplus; proceedings by Commission if impairment found. — A. Each domestic insurer shall maintain at all times the minimum surplus if a mutual insurer, and the minimum capital and surplus if a stock insurer, required by §§ 38.2-1028, 38.2-1029 or § 38.2-1030. If the Commission finds that (i) the minimum capital and surplus of a domestic stock insurer is impaired or (ii) the minimum surplus of a domestic mutual insurer is impaired, the Commission shall issue an order requiring the insurer to eliminate the impairment within a period not exceeding ninety days. The Commission may by order served upon the insurer prohibit the insurer from issuing any new policies while the impairment exists.

B. Any domestic mutual insurer may make an assessment upon its assessable members for an amount that will provide funds to cover all or any part of the impairment. However, no member shall be liable for an assessment exceeding the limit specified in his policy, and no assessment shall be made upon any member under a nonassessable policy. The assessment shall be made upon each assessable member in proportion to the liability as expressed in the policy. With the prior approval of the Commission, the deficiency may be made up from advances or borrowed funds and subject to the restrictions provided in § 38.2-1034 for obtaining guaranty funds.

C. If at the expiration of the designated period the insurer has not satisfied the Commission that the impairment has been eliminated, an order for the rehabilitation or liquidation of the insurer may be entered as provided in

Chapter 15 (§ 38.2-1500 et seq.) of this title. (Code 1950, § 38-511; 1952, c. 317, §§ 38.1-90, 38.1-93; 1966, c. 580; 1977, c. 322; 1986, c. 562.)

§ 38.2-1036. Impairment of capital and surplus of foreign and alien company ground for suspension or revocation of license. — Each foreign and each alien insurer shall maintain at all times the minimum surplus, capital and surplus, or trusteed surplus required by §§ 38.2-1028, 38.2-1029, 38.2-1030 or § 38.2-1031. If the Commission finds an impairment of (i) the required minimum capital and surplus of any foreign stock insurer, (ii) the required minimum surplus of any foreign mutual insurer, or (iii) the required minimum trusteed surplus of any alien insurer, the Commission may order the insurer to eliminate the impairment and restore the minimum capital and surplus, minimum surplus or minimum trusteed surplus, to the amount required by law. The Commission may, by order served upon the insurer, prohibit the insurer from issuing any new policies while the impairment exists. If the insurer fails to comply with the Commission's order within a period of not more than ninety days, the Commission may, in the manner set out in Article 6 (§ 38.2-1040 et seq.) of this chapter, suspend or revoke the license of the insurer to transact the business of insurance in this Commonwealth. (Code 1950, § 38-511; 1952, c. 317, § 38.1-96; 1978, c. 20; 1986, c. 562.)

§ 38.2-1037. Exceptions for licensed and operating insurers. — A. Notwithstanding the other provisions of this chapter with respect to minimum required capital and surplus, any insurer which, on June 30, 1991, was licensed to write and was writing any class of insurance in this Commonwealth may continue to write that class of insurance under the appropriate license from the Commission, until July 1, 1994, if it maintains at all times (i) the minimum capital and surplus if a stock insurer, (ii) the minimum surplus if a mutual insurer, and (iii) the minimum trusteed surplus if an alien insurer, required of the insurer as of June 30, 1991.

B. Any insurer not licensed to write a class of insurance in this Commonwealth on June 30, 1991, shall meet all the capital surplus and trusteed surplus requirements of this article before it obtains a license to write that class of insurance. (1952, c. 317, § 38.1-97; 1966, c. 580; 1977, c. 322; 1978, c. 20; 1986, c. 562; 1987, c. 520; 1991, c. 261.)

§ 38.2-1038. Authority of Commission to issue orders covering insurers in hazardous financial condition. — If, after reviewing an insurer's financial condition, method of operation, or manner of doing business, the Commission finds that (i) the insurer cannot, or there is a reasonable expectation that the insurer will not be able to, meet its obligations to all policyholders or (ii) the insurer's continued operation in this Commonwealth is hazardous to policyholders, creditors and the public in this Commonwealth the Commission may order the insurer to take appropriate action to remedy the Commission's concerns. The insurer shall be given ten days' notice prior to issuing the order and shall be given the opportunity to be heard and introduce evidence on its behalf. The hearing may be informal, and the required notice may be waived by the Commission and the insurer. If the insurer fails to comply with the Commission's order within the prescribed time, the Commission may suspend or revoke the license of the insurer to transact the business of insurance in this Commonwealth as set forth in Article 6 (§ 38.2-1040 et seq.) of this chapter. (1978, c. 20, § 38.1-97.2; 1986, c. 562; 1991, c. 261.)

§ 38.2-1039. Enjoining unlicensed foreign or alien insurers from transacting the business of insurance in Commonwealth. — A. For the purposes of issuing a temporary or permanent injunction under § 38.2-220 to restrain unlicensed foreign or alien insurers from transacting the business of insurance in this Commonwealth, the following acts, effected by mail or otherwise, shall constitute transacting the business of insurance in this Commonwealth:

1. The issuance or delivery of insurance contracts to residents of this Commonwealth or to corporations authorized to do business in this Commonwealth;

2. The solicitation of applications for such contracts;

3. The collection of premiums, membership fees, assessments or other considerations for such contracts; or

4. The transaction of any other insurance business in connection with such contracts.

B. Process may be served in accordance with § 13.1-758 or in any other manner prescribed by law.

C. This section shall not apply to any nonprofit life insurance or annuity company which is organized and operated for the purpose of issuing insurance and annuity contracts, exclusively to or for the benefit of nonprofit educational or scientific institutions and individuals engaged in the service of those institutions. The clerk of the Commission shall be considered the attorney for service of process in this Commonwealth for all of such insurer's policy and contract holders in this Commonwealth. The appointment shall (i) be irrevocable, (ii) bind the insurer and any successors in interest, and (iii) remain in effect as long as there is in force in this Commonwealth any contract made by the insurer or any obligation arising from the contract.

D. This section shall not apply to the following acts:

1. The procuring of a policy of insurance upon a risk within this Commonwealth in compliance with Chapter 48 of this title;

2. Issuance of contracts of reinsurance;

3. Acts in this Commonwealth involving a policy lawfully solicited, written and delivered outside this Commonwealth covering only subjects of insurance not resident, located, or to be performed in this Commonwealth at the time of issuance of the policy;

4. Acts in this Commonwealth involving a group or blanket insurance policy or a group annuity lawfully issued and delivered in a state where the insurer was licensed to transact the business of insurance;

5. The procuring of insurance contracts issued to an "industrial insured." For the purposes of this section, an *industrial insured* is an insured (i) who procures the insurance of any risk by use of the services of a full-time employee acting as an insurance manager or buyer, (ii) whose aggregate annual premiums for insurance on all risks total at least $25,000, and (iii) who has at least 25 full-time employees.

E. Nothing in this section shall apply to nonprofit Railroad Brotherhood or other similar fraternal organizations. (1968, c. 266, § 38.1-98.1; 1986, c. 562.)

Purpose of this section is different from that of the long arm statute. August v. HBA Life Ins. Co., 734 F.2d 168 (4th Cir. 1984).

§ **38.2-1039.1. Risk retention groups.** — Except in the case of a risk retention group all of whose members are insurers, no risk retention group, as defined in Chapter 51 of this title, shall be licensed in this Commonwealth if an insurer is directly or indirectly a member or owner of such risk retention group. (1987, c. 585.)

ARTICLE 6.

Refusal, Suspension or Revocation of Insurer's License.

§ 38.2-1040. Refusal, suspension or revocation of license. — A. The Commission may refuse to issue a license to any domestic, foreign or alien insurer to transact the business of insurance in this Commonwealth, and may suspend or revoke the license of any licensee, whenever it finds that the applicant or licensee:

1. Has refused to submit its books, papers, accounts, or affairs to the reasonable inspection of the Commission or its representative;

2. Has refused, or its officers or agents have refused, to furnish satisfactory evidence of its financial and business standing or solvency;

3. Is insolvent, or is in a condition that any further transaction of business in this Commonwealth is hazardous to its policyholders, creditors and public in this Commonwealth;

4. Has failed to pay a final judgment against it within sixty days after (i) the judgment became final, (ii) the time for making an appeal has expired, or (iii) the dismissal of an appeal before final determination, whichever date is the latest;

5. Has violated any law of this Commonwealth, or has in this Commonwealth violated its charter or exceeded its corporate powers;

6. Has failed to pay any fees, taxes or charges imposed in this Commonwealth within sixty days after they are due and payable, or within sixty days after final disposition of any legal contest with respect to liability for the fees, taxes or charges;

7. Has had its corporate existence dissolved or its certificate of authority revoked in the state in which it was organized or in this Commonwealth;

8. Has been found insolvent by a court of any other state, or by the Commission or other proper officer or agency of any other state, and has been prohibited from doing business in that state;

9. Has had all its risks reinsured in their entirety in another insurer; or

10. Has notified the insured in writing or by any other means that any policy of insurance covering the ownership or operation of a motor vehicle issued by the insurer will be cancelled if the insured institutes any legal action against the insurer to pursue any rights of the insured under the policy.

B. The grounds for suspension or revocation of licenses in subsection A of this section are in addition to those provided for elsewhere in this title. (Code 1950, §§ 38-68, 38-132, 38-133, 38-134, 38-169, 38-370; 1952, c. 317, § 38.1-99; 1966, c. 457; 1986, c. 562; 1987, c. 431.)

Former statute. — For case applying former § 38-130 dealing with misrepresentation by insurance companies, see Sterling Ins. Co. v. Commonwealth, 195 Va. 422, 78 S.E.2d 691 (1953).

§ 38.2-1041. Notice to company of proposed suspension or revocation. — The Commission shall not revoke or suspend the license of any insurer to do the business of insurance in this Commonwealth upon any of the grounds set out in § 38.2-1040 until it has given the insurer ten days' notice of the reasons for the proposed revocation or suspension and has given the insurer an opportunity to introduce evidence and be heard. However, the Commission may immediately suspend the license on any of the grounds specified in subdivisions 7 and 8 of subsection A of § 38.2-1040 without prior notice to the insurer. The suspension shall remain in force until the hearing is held. Any hearing authorized by this section may be informal, and the required notice may be waived by the Commission and the insurer. (Code 1950, §§ 38-132, 38-169, 38-370; 1952, c. 317, § 38.1-100; 1986, c. 562.)

§ 38.2-1042. Agent's authority likewise suspended or revoked. —
Upon the suspension or revocation of the license of any insurer, the Commission shall suspend or revoke the authority of the insurer's agents in this Commonwealth to act for the insurer. (1952, c. 317, § 38.1-101; 1986, c. 562.)

§ 38.2-1043. Suspension or revocation published. — Unless an appeal is taken within thirty days, the Commission shall have published in one or more newspapers having general circulation in this Commonwealth a notice of any final order that suspends or revokes the license of an insurer. (Code 1950, §§ 38-68, 38-133, 38-169; 1952, c. 317, § 38.1-102; 1986, c. 562.)

§ 38.2-1044. New business prohibited. — No new business shall be done by any insurer or its agents on behalf of that insurer while its license to do business is suspended or revoked. (Code 1950, §§ 38-68, 38-135; 1952, c. 317, § 38.1-103; 1986, c. 562.)

ARTICLE 7.

Deposits.

§ 38.2-1045. Deposits required of insurers generally. — A. Except as otherwise provided in this title, before the Commission issues a license to transact the business of insurance in this Commonwealth to any insurer, that insurer shall deposit with the State Treasurer securities that (i) are legal investments under the laws of this Commonwealth for public sinking funds or for other public funds, (ii) are not in default as to principal or interest, (iii) have a current market value of not less than $50,000 nor more than $500,000, and (iv) are issued pursuant to a system of book-entry evidencing ownership interests of the securities with transfers of ownership interests effected on the records of a depository and its participants pursuant to rules and procedures established by the depository.

B. The Commission may require a reasonable amount of additional deposits in securities that meet the requirements of clauses (i), (ii) and (iv) of subsection A of this section, whenever the Commission determines that the insurer's financial condition, method of operation, or manner of doing business is such that the Commission is not satisfied that it can meet its obligations to all policyholders.

C. Neither the deposit referred to in this section nor the alternate deposit permitted by § 38.2-1049 shall be required of (i) any mutual assessment property and casualty insurance company, (ii) any fraternal benefit society, or (iii) any insurer transacting exclusively an ocean marine business in this Commonwealth.

D. Any insurer which on June 30, 1991, instead of the deposit of securities required by subsection A, has entered into a bond with surety, approved by the Commission, with any conditions the Commission requires, shall have until the next renewal, anniversary, or expiration date of such bond, or until June 30, 1992, whichever comes first, to comply with the deposit provisions of subsection A. The surety shall be licensed in this Commonwealth to transact the business of suretyship and shall not be directly or indirectly under the same ownership or management as the principal on the bond.

E. Every insurer subject to the provisions of this section having physical securities deposited with the State Treasurer on or before June 30, 1992, shall comply with the provisions of clause (iv) in subsection A not later than January 1, 1993. (Code 1950, § 38-39; 1952, c. 317, § 38.1-108; 1956, c. 234; 1960, c. 558; 1964, c. 605; 1973, c. 178; 1975, c. 556; 1986, c. 562; 1991, c. 261; 1992, c. 14.)

Cross references. — As to captive insurance companies, see §§ 38.2-1105 and 38.2-1106.

Law Review. — For survey of Virginia law on insurance for the year 1974-1975, see 61 Va. L. Rev. 1759 (1975).

§ 38.2-1046. Purpose of deposits; enforcement of lien. — A.

An insurer's deposits required by § 38.2-1045 shall be held as a special fund in trust for the insurer's liabilities which are incurred or which may be incurred as a result of a loss sustained by (i) this Commonwealth or any of its political subdivisions, (ii) any citizen or inhabitant of this Commonwealth, or (iii) any other person owning property in this Commonwealth, when the insurer fails to meet its obligations incurred in this Commonwealth. Policyholders, without preference, shall have a lien on the deposits for the amounts due or which may become due as a result of any failure of the insurer to meet its obligations. General creditors, without preference, shall be entitled to have a similar lien on the deposits which shall be subordinate to the claims of the policyholders.

B. Whenever any such insurer becomes insolvent or bankrupt, or makes an assignment for the benefit of its creditors, any person given a lien by this section may file a bill in the Circuit Court of the City of Richmond for the benefit of himself and all others given a lien by this section to subject such securities as may be on deposit with the State Treasurer or its agent to the payment of the liens thereon. The State Treasurer shall be made a party to such suit and a copy of such bill shall be served upon the Commissioner of Insurance as if he were a party to such suit. The funds shall be distributed by the court. (Code 1950, § 38-50; 1952, c. 317, § 38.1-110; 1981, c. 208; 1986, c. 562; 1988, c. 298; 1992, c. 20; 1995, c. 60.)

Purpose of deposit is not to protect reinsurers. — The deposit required is for the protection of property owners in their fire insurance contracts, and not to protect other insurance companies on their contracts of reinsurance. Shepherd v. Virginia State Ins. Co., 120 Va. 383, 91 S.E. 140 (1917).

Agent entitled to lien. — The general agent of an insurance company, to whom policyholders have assigned their policies, stands on the plane with all other holders of Virginia policies canceled by the insolvency of the company, and is entitled to share with them the benefits of his statutory lien on the securities held by the treasurer. Johnson v. Button, 120 Va. 339, 91 S.E. 151 (1917).

Fact that money recovered by policyholder may go to nonresident. — In a proceeding to enforce the claim of a resident policyholder against the statutory deposit made by an insurance company later becoming insolvent, it is beside the point that in discharging the insurance company's obligation to the resident policyholder the money required to satisfy a judgment may go to a nonresident. Andrews v. Cahoon, 196 Va. 790, 86 S.E.2d 173 (1955).

§ 38.2-1047. How deposits applied to payment of claims; deficit to be made good. — A.

This section shall apply only where:

1. The insurer has failed to pay any of its liabilities after the liabilities have been ascertained (i) by any agreement of the parties binding the insurer, or (ii) by judgment, order or decree of a court of competent jurisdiction which has not been appealed, superseded or stayed; and

2. The provisions of subsection B of § 38.2-1046 are not applicable.

B. Upon application of the person to whom the debt or money is due and after giving notice as provided in subsection C of this section, the State Treasurer shall (i) sell an amount of securities with accrued interest that provides sufficient funds to pay the sums due and the expenses of the sale and (ii) pay the sums due and expenses out of the available funds. This shall be subject to the approval of the Commission.

C. The State Treasurer shall give the insurer or its agent ten days' notice, either by mail or personally, of the time and place of the sale. The sale shall be advertised daily for ten days in a newspaper of general circulation published in the City of Richmond.

D. The insurer shall immediately make good any deficit in its deposit resulting from a sale. The State Treasurer shall report to the Commission in writing (i) the amount and kind of securities sold in accordance with the provisions of this section and (ii) the amount and kind of securities deposited to make good the deficit. (Code 1950, § 38-49; 1950, p. 996; 1952, c. 317, § 38.1-111; 1986, c. 562; 1988, c. 298.)

§ **38.2-1048. Return of deposits.** — A. The Commission, at its discretion, may direct the State Treasurer to return to any insurer all or a part of the deposit made by it under § 38.2-1045 if the insurer (i) has complied with § 38.2-1049, or (ii) has ceased to transact business in this Commonwealth. In the case of the latter, the fixed or contingent liabilities secured by the deposit shall have been satisfied or terminated or shall have been assumed by another insurer licensed to transact the business of insurance in this Commonwealth. If the Commission finds that any voluntary deposit of any insurer made under § 38.2-1050 no longer is required in whole or in part to comply with the laws of this or any other state, it may to such extent direct the return of that deposit. The Commission, before directing the return of any deposit, may require evidence it considers satisfactory that the insurer is entitled to the return of all or part of the deposit.

B. Notwithstanding the provisions in § 38.2-1046 and subsection A of this section, if an insurer domiciled in this Commonwealth is placed in receivership, and a receiver is appointed, pursuant to the provisions of Chapter 15 (§ 38.2-1500 et seq.) of this title, the Commission shall direct the State Treasurer to return any deposit made with it by the insurer to such receiver for distribution, disbursement, or other application in accordance with provisions set forth in Chapter 15 (§ 38.2-1500 et seq.) of this title and any applicable order of liquidation, conservation or rehabilitation. (Code 1950, § 38-52; 1952, c. 317, § 38.1-112; 1986, c. 562; 1988, c. 298; 1995, c. 60.)

Reinsuring company directly liable to policyholders. — A bonding company applied to the State Corporation Commission of Virginia, under this section, for leave to withdraw its assets from the State and reinsure its risk in another company. The statute specifically requires the reinsuring company to assume the risks of the retiring company. It was held that as both companies have invoked and received the advantages of the statute, they must be presumed to have assumed the burdens thereby imposed, and to have contracted with reference to the statute, and the contract comes within the reason of the cases which hold the reinsuring company directly liable to the assured, and is not a mere reinsurance contract. American Bonding Co. v. American Sur. Co., 127 Va. 209, 103 S.E. 599 (1920).

Assumption of policy obligations by reinsuring company presumed from withdrawal. — Unless the circumstances are so exceptional as to take the case out of the general rule applicable in such cases, the securities deposited with the State Treasurer by an insurance company cannot be legally withdrawn by another company taking over the business of the depositing company under the provisions of this section unless it is made to appear that the obligations of the depositing company's policies have been in fact assumed by the company withdrawing the deposit, and not merely agreed to be assumed upon certain conditions not contained in the policies. Actual assumption of the policy obligation is the burden that this section requires to be taken upon itself by the corporation withdrawing such deposit; and, notwithstanding that contract between insurance companies does not contain appropriate language to evidence such an assumption, the actual assumption will, in general, be presumed, where such a deposit has been withdrawn under such statute. Lucas v. Pittsburgh Life & Trust Co., 137 Va. 255, 119 S.E. 109 (1923).

Establishing liability against issuing company will support decree against reinsuring company. — A bonding company abandoned its business in Virginia and reinsured its risks in another company. A decree on one of its bonds was against both companies. The second company contended that there was no privity of contract between it and the complainant. It was held that as the suit was in equity, the beneficiary could not be required after establishing the liability of the first company, to pursue the second company in another suit, as under its contract and this section, the second company was ultimately responsible for the liability, the

court rightly decreed against it. American
Bonding Co. v. American Sur. Co., 127 Va. 209,
103 S.E. 599 (1920).

§ **38.2-1049. Alternate deposit requirements.** — A. The insurer, at the
discretion of the Commission, may be relieved of making the deposit required
by § 38.2-1045 if the insurer makes deposits according to the following
provisions:

1. Acceptable securities as defined in subsection B of this section are
deposited with the State Treasurer in the form prescribed in clause (iv) of
subsection A of § 38.2-1045 or with the insurance commissioner, treasurer or
other officer or official body of any other state first for the protection of the
insurer's policyholders.

2. The securities are not to be in default as to principal and interest.

3. The securities have a market value of at least $500,000.

4. A certificate is furnished to the Commission and authenticated by the
appropriate state official holding the deposit that the requirements of this
subsection have been met.

B. For the purpose of this section, acceptable securities are defined as bonds
of the United States, or of any state, or of any city, county or town of any state,
or bonds or notes secured by mortgages or deeds of trust on otherwise
unencumbered real estate of a market value in each case of not less than
double the amount loaned, or other securities approved by the Commission.
(Code 1950, §§ 38-37, 38-40, 37-175, 38-516; 1952, c. 317, § 38.1-113; 1964, c.
605; 1975, c. 556; 1986, c. 562; 1992, c. 14.)

§ **38.2-1050. Voluntary deposit in excess of amount required.** — Any
domestic insurer, in order to comply with the laws of any other state or of the
United States, may make a voluntary deposit with the State Treasurer in
excess of the amount required by § 38.2-1045. This excess deposit shall be
subject to all other applicable provisions of the laws of this Commonwealth
relating to the deposits of insurers. However, this excess deposit shall be for
the protection of all the insurer's policyholders and general creditors, notwithstanding the provisions of § 38.2-1046. (Code 1950, § 38-41; 1952, c. 317,
§ 38.1-114; 1966, c. 263; 1986, c. 562.)

§ **38.2-1051:** Repealed by Acts 1992, c. 14.

§ **38.2-1052. Exchange of securities.** — A depositing insurer may from
time to time exchange for any of the deposited securities other securities
eligible for deposit under this article if in the opinion of the Commission the
aggregate value of the deposit will not be reduced below the amount required
by law. (1952, c. 317, § 38.1-116; 1986, c. 562.)

§ **38.2-1053. Interest on deposits; to whom paid.** — The State Treasurer, at the time of receiving any securities deposited under this title, shall
give the insurer authority to collect the interest for its own use as the interest
is paid. This authority shall continue in force until the insurer fails to pay any
of its liabilities for which the deposit is security. In that case, the party paying
interest shall be notified of the failure, and thereafter the interest shall be
payable to the State Treasurer, and shall be applied, if necessary, to the
payment of the liabilities. (Code 1950, § 38-48; 1952, c. 317, § 38.1-117; 1986,
c. 562.)

§ **38.2-1054. Duty of State Treasurer when securities deposited are
paid.** — When the principal of any securities deposited under this title is paid

to the State Treasurer, the money received shall be paid to the insurer. However, if the securities were required to be deposited under § 38.2-1045, the payment shall not be made until the insurer deposits an equal amount of other securities of the character required for similar deposits. If the insurer fails to deliver to the State Treasurer, within thirty days after receiving notice of this requirement, the securities necessary to maintain its required deposit, the State Treasurer with the approval in writing of the Commission, may use the money to purchase and hold other securities of the required character. (Code 1950, § 38-51; 1952, c. 317, § 38.1-118; 1986, c. 562.)

§ 38.2-1055. Annual report of State Treasurer to Commission. — Each January the State Treasurer shall certify to the Commission the kind and face value of all securities, bonds, notes, mortgages or deeds of trust deposited under this title and held at the end of the preceding calendar year. (Code 1950, § 38-45; 1952, c. 317, § 38.1-119; 1986, c. 562.)

§ 38.2-1056. Treasurer to receipt for deposits; responsibility of Commonwealth; taxation of deposited bonds. — The State Treasurer shall provide receipts to the insurer for all securities deposited with him under the provisions of this title. The Commonwealth shall be responsible for the safekeeping of the securities. If some or all of the securities are lost, destroyed or misappropriated, the Commonwealth shall pay or satisfy the loss to the insurer making the deposit. Securities deposited with the State Treasurer shall not be subject to taxation. (Code 1950, §§ 38-42, 38-46; 1952, c. 317, § 38.1-120; 1986, c. 562.)

§ 38.2-1057. Assessment for expense of holding deposits. — For the purpose of defraying the expense of the State Treasurer's office in the safekeeping and handling of the securities or surety bonds deposited under the provisions of this title, the State Treasurer shall levy annually against each insurer an assessment of not more than one tenth of one percent of the par or face value of the securities or surety bonds deposited to its account. The assessment shall be collected every January. No part of the amount collected shall be used to increase the compensation of any person connected with the office of the State Treasurer. Whatever remains of the assessment after the payment of the expense described above shall be paid into the general fund of the state treasury. (Code 1950, § 38-43; 1952, c. 317, § 38.1-121; 1973, c. 173; 1986, c. 562.)

§ 38.2-1058. Felony for State Treasurer to dispose of securities illegally. — If the State Treasurer disposes of any securities deposited with him under this title, other than as provided in this title, he shall be guilty of a Class 3 felony, and, upon conviction, shall be punished by a fine double the amount of the disposed securities. (Code 1950, § 38-53; 1952, c. 317, § 38.1-122; 1986, c. 562.)

Cross references. — As to punishment for Class 3 felonies, see § 18.2-10.

CHAPTER 11.

CAPTIVE INSURERS.

§ 38.2-1100. Scope of chapter. — The provisions of this chapter shall apply solely to captive insurers or association captive insurers domiciled in this Commonwealth. (1980, c. 665, § 38.1-916; 1986, c. 562.)

§ 38.2-1101. Definitions. — As used in this chapter:

"Affiliated company" means (i) any company that directly or indirectly owns, controls, or holds, with power to vote, ten percent or more of the outstanding voting securities of a pure captive insurer, or (ii) any company of which ten percent or more of the voting securities are directly or indirectly owned, controlled, or held, with power to vote, by a parent, subsidiary, or associated company.

"Associated company" means any company in the same corporate system with a pure captive insurer.

"Association captive insurer" means any domestic insurer transacting the business of insurance and reinsurance only on risks, hazards, and liabilities of the members of an insurance association.

"Captive insurer" means any pure captive insurer or any association captive insurer.

"Insurance association" means any group of individuals, corporations, partnerships, associations, or governmental units or agencies whose members collectively own, control, or hold with power to vote all of the outstanding voting securities of an association captive insurer.

"Parent" means a corporation, partnership, governmental unit or agency, or individual who directly or indirectly owns, controls or holds, with power to vote, more than fifty percent of the outstanding voting securities of a pure captive insurer.

"Pure captive insurer" means any domestic insurer transacting the business of insurance and reinsurance only on risks, hazards, and liabilities of its parent, subsidiary companies of its parent, and associated and affiliated companies.

"Subsidiary company" means any corporation of which fifty percent or more of the outstanding voting securities are directly or indirectly owned, controlled, or held, with power to vote, by a parent or by a company that is a subsidiary of the parent. (1980, c. 665, § 38.1-917; 1981, c. 494; 1986, c. 562.)

§ 38.2-1102. Application for license; limitations on authority. — A. No captive insurer shall transact any insurance business in this Commonwealth unless (i) it is permitted to do so by its articles of incorporation or charter and (ii) it procures a license to transact the business of insurance from the Commission in accordance with Article 5 (§ 38.2-1024 et seq.) of Chapter 10 of this title. The license shall be renewed in accordance with § 38.2-1025. A captive insurer may only be licensed to write the classes of insurance described in §§ 38.2-110 through 38.2-120, 38.2-124, 38.2-126 and reinsure in accordance with § 38.2-136.

B. 1. The Commission shall not issue a license to transact the business of insurance in this Commonwealth to any pure captive insurer until it is satisfied that the total insurance coverage necessary to insure all risks, hazards, and liabilities would develop, in the aggregate, gross annual premiums of at least $500,000.

2. The Commission shall not issue a license to transact the business of insurance in this Commonwealth to any association captive insurer until it is satisfied (i) that the total insurance coverage necessary to insure all risks, hazards, and liabilities would develop, in the aggregate, gross annual premiums of at least one million dollars and (ii) that its insurance association has been in existence for at least one year. The Commission may waive the requirement that the insurance association be in existence for at least 1 year if the association captive insurer satisfies the Commission that each member of the insurance association would have a gross annual premium in excess of $100,000.

C. No captive insurer may write classes of personal insurance coverage for individuals unless the individual is a parent.

D. No captive insurer may write insurance or reinsurance on personally owned motor vehicles or homeowners' insurance or any component of them. (1980, c. 665, § 38.1-918; 1986, c. 562.)

§ 38.2-1103. Name. — A captive insurer shall not adopt the name of any existing company transacting a similar business or any name so familiar that it may mislead the public. (1980, c. 665, § 38.1-919; 1986, c. 562.)

§ 38.2-1104. Formation; licensure after examination; amendment of articles; principal and home office. — A. Captive insurers with shares of capital stock shall be incorporated under Article 3 (§ 13.1-618 et seq.) of Chapter 9 of Title 13.1 as modified by this title and, except as provided in this title, shall be subject to all the general restrictions and shall have all the general powers imposed and conferred upon such corporations by law.

B. Captive insurers without shares of capital stock shall be incorporated under Article 3 (§ 13.1-818 et seq.) of Chapter 10 of Title 13.1, as modified by this title and, except as provided in this title, shall be subject to all the general restrictions and shall have all the general powers imposed and conferred upon such corporations by law.

C. 1. No charter shall be granted to any captive insurer until the Commission receives a certificate from the State Treasurer showing that (i) cash, bonds or other securities in the amount required by § 38.2-1105 have been deposited or (ii) an irrevocable letter of credit in that amount has been deposited and is to be held under the provisions, terms and conditions set forth in § 38.2-1105.

2. When the certificate has been presented to the Commission, the Commission may make or direct to be made an examination of the captive insurer.

3. The Commission shall issue a license if the captive insurer complies with this chapter.

D. Any amendment of the articles of incorporation of a captive insurer shall be pursuant to Article 11 (§ 13.1-705 et seq.) of Chapter 9 or of Article 10 (§ 13.1-884 et seq.) of Chapter 10 of Title 13.1.

E. The principal and home office of every captive insurer shall be in this Commonwealth. (1980, c. 665, § 38.1-920; 1986, c. 562.)

§ 38.2-1105. Deposit of minimum capital; letter of credit instead of deposit. — A. No captive insurer shall be issued a license to transact the business of insurance in this Commonwealth until it has met the requirements of Article 5 (§ 38.2-1024 et seq.) of Chapter 10 of this title.

B. The captive insurer shall deposit with the State Treasurer cash, bonds, or securities equal to the minimum capital or, if a mutual insurer, fifty percent of the minimum surplus, as required by Article 5 (§ 38.2-1024 et seq.) of Chapter 10 of this title. The State Treasurer shall accept an irrevocable letter of credit, in a form acceptable to the Commission, on behalf of a captive insurer instead of requiring the above-mentioned deposit. The letter of credit shall be issued by a national or state bank and approved by the Commission.

C. The deposit or letter of credit shall be held by the State Treasurer for the benefit of all policyholders and creditors wherever located and shall be administered as provided in Article 7 (§ 38.2-1045 et seq.) of Chapter 10 of this title.

D. The State Treasurer shall furnish to the captive insurer a certificate certifying that the State Treasurer holds the securities or letters of credit in trust for the benefit of the policyholders and creditors of the captive insurer. (1980, c. 665, § 38.1-921; 1986, c. 562.)

§ **38.2-1106. Minimum surplus in form of letter of credit.** — A. Any licensed captive insurer may, subject to the approval of the Commission, hold all or a portion of (i) the minimum surplus as set forth in Article 5 (§ 38.2-1024 et seq.) of Chapter 10 in the form of an irrevocable letter of credit, if a stock insurer, or (ii) fifty percent of minimum surplus not subject to subsection B of § 38.2-1105, if a mutual insurer. The letter of credit shall be issued by a national or state bank and approved by the Commission.

B. Any letter of credit permitted pursuant to this section shall be held by the State Treasurer for the benefit of all policyholders and creditors and shall be administered as provided in Article 7 (§ 38.2-1045 et seq.) of Chapter 10 of this title. (1980, c. 665, § 38.1-922; 1986, c. 562.)

§ **38.2-1107. Membership in rating organizations.** — No captive insurer shall be required to join a rating organization. (1980, c. 665, § 38.1-926; 1986, c. 562.)

§ **38.2-1108. Tax on premiums collected.** — All captive insurers transacting business in this Commonwealth shall pay taxes as provided for in Chapter 25 of Title 58.1, except that taxes shall be paid on risks and property situated in any state in which the captive insurer is not licensed and upon which no premium tax is otherwise paid or payable. (1980, c. 665, § 38.1-928; 1986, c. 562.)

§ **38.2-1109. Applicability of other provisions of title.** — Except as otherwise provided, all laws of this title that apply to insurers writing the same classes of insurance that captive insurers are permitted to write, shall apply in every respect to captive insurers. (1980, c. 665, § 38.1-930; 1986, c. 562.)

CHAPTER 12.

RECIPROCAL INSURANCE.

ARTICLE 1.

General Provisions.

§ 38.2-1200. Scope of chapter. — This chapter applies to all reciprocals and reciprocal insurance as defined in § 38.2-1201. (1952, c. 317, § 38.1-688; 1986, c. 562.)

§ 38.2-1201. Definitions. — A. As used in this title:

"Reciprocal" means the aggregation of subscribers under a common name.

"Reciprocal insurance" means insurance resulting from the mutual exchange of insurance contracts among persons in an unincorporated association under a common name through an attorney-in-fact having authority to obligate each person both as insured and insurer.

B. As used in this chapter:

"Attorney" means the person designated and authorized by subscribers as the attorney-in-fact having authority to obligate them on reciprocal insurance contracts.

"Subscriber" means a person obligated under a reciprocal insurance agreement. (1952, c. 317, § 38.1-689; 1986, c. 562.)

§ 38.2-1202. Insuring power of reciprocals. — A reciprocal licensed to transact the business of insurance in this Commonwealth may write the classes of insurance enumerated in Article 2 (§ 38.2-101 et seq.) of Chapter 1 of this title, except life insurance, annuities, and title insurance. (Code 1950, § 38-543; 1952, c. 317, § 38.1-690; 1986, c. 562.)

§ 38.2-1203. What laws applicable to reciprocals; compliance with § 38.2-208. — A. Except as otherwise provided, all the provisions of this title relating to insurers generally, and those relating to insurers writing the same classes of insurance that reciprocals are permitted to write, are applicable to reciprocals.

B. A reciprocal shall be deemed to have complied with § 38.2-208 if:

1. It issues policies containing a contingent assessment liability as provided for in § 38.2-1212; and

2. It has and maintains reinsurance in an amount that the Commission considers adequate to reasonably limit the reciprocal's aggregate losses to the lesser of:

a. Ten percent of the surplus to policyholders of the reciprocal multiplied by the number of subscribers;

b. The surplus to policyholders of the reciprocal multiplied by three; or

c. Five million dollars. (Code 1950, § 38-543; 1952, c. 317, § 38.1-691; 1977, c. 58; 1986, c. 562.)

§ 38.2-1204. Power to enter into reciprocal insurance contracts. — A. Persons of this Commonwealth may enter into reciprocal insurance contracts with each other and with persons of other states and countries. For the purposes of this chapter, the definition of *"person"* shall also include any county, city, or town, school board, Transportation District Commission, or any other local governmental authority or local agency or public service corporation owned, operated or controlled by a locality or local government authority, with power to enter into contractual undertakings within or without the Commonwealth.

B. For any corporation now existing or hereafter organized under the laws of this Commonwealth, the power and authority to enter into reciprocal insurance contracts shall be in addition to the powers conferred upon it in its certificate of incorporation, and shall be incidental to the purposes for which the corporation is organized. (Code 1950, §§ 38-543, 38-550; 1952, c. 317, §§ 38.1-692, 38.1-693; 1986, c. 562.)

§ 38.2-1205. Name. — Every reciprocal shall have and use a business name that includes the word "reciprocal," "interinsurer," "interinsurance," "exchange," "underwriters," or "underwriting." (Code 1950, § 38-546; 1952, c. 317, § 38.1-694; 1986, c. 562.)

§ 38.2-1206. License required of reciprocals; surplus. — A. No reciprocal shall engage in any insurance transaction in this Commonwealth until it has obtained a license to do so in accordance with the applicable provisions of Articles 5 (§ 38.2-1024 et seq.) and 7 (§ 38.2-1045 et seq.) of Chapter 10 of this title.

B. No domestic or foreign reciprocal shall be licensed to transact the business of insurance in this Commonwealth unless it has a surplus to policyholders of at least $1,600,000, and no alien reciprocal shall be so licensed unless it has a trusteed surplus, as defined in § 38.2-1031, of at least $1,600,000. (Code 1950, § 38-549; 1952, c. 317, § 38.1-695; 1977, c. 322; 1986, c. 562; 1991, c. 261.)

§ 38.2-1207. Exceptions as to reciprocals licensed and operating. — A. Notwithstanding other provisions of this chapter regarding minimum required surplus, any reciprocal that was licensed to write and was writing any class of insurance in this Commonwealth on June 30, 1991, may continue to write that class of insurance under the appropriate license from the Commission until July 1, 1994. The reciprocal shall maintain at all times the minimum surplus, and the minimum trusteed surplus if an alien reciprocal, required on June 30, 1991.

B. Before any reciprocal obtains a license to write in this Commonwealth any class of insurance that it was not writing and licensed to write in this Commonwealth on June 30, 1991, it shall comply with all the requirements of this article regarding surplus. (1977, c. 322, § 38.1-695.1; 1986, c. 562; 1991, c. 261.)

§ 38.2-1208. Additional requirements, foreign and alien reciprocals.
— No foreign reciprocal shall be licensed to transact the business of insurance
in this Commonwealth unless it has filed with the Commission a certificate of
the supervising insurance official of the state in which it is organized. The
certificate shall show that the foreign reciprocal is licensed to write and is
writing actively in that state the class of insurance it proposes to write in this
Commonwealth. No alien reciprocal shall be licensed to transact the business
of insurance until it has filed with the Commission a certificate of the
supervising insurance official of (i) the state through which it entered the
United States or (ii) the alien reciprocal's domiciliary country. The certificate
shall show that the alien reciprocal is licensed to write and is writing actively
in that state or country the class of insurance it proposes to write in this
Commonwealth. (1952, c. 317, § 38.1-696; 1986, c. 562.)

**§ 38.2-1209. Residence and office of attorney of foreign and alien
reciprocals.** — Nothing in this title regarding the admission and licensing of
foreign and alien insurers requires that the attorney of a foreign or alien
reciprocal be resident or domiciled in this Commonwealth, or that the principal
office of the attorney be maintained in this Commonwealth. The office or offices
of the attorney shall be determined by the subscribers through the power of
attorney. (Code 1950, § 38-545; 1952, c. 317, § 38.1-698; 1986, c. 562.)

§ 38.2-1210. Contracts executed by attorney. — Reciprocal insurance
contracts shall be executed by the attorney of the reciprocal. (Code 1950,
§ 38-545; 1952, c. 317, § 38.1-699; 1986, c. 562.)

§ 38.2-1211. License required of agent. — No person shall act in this
Commonwealth as an agent of a reciprocal in the solicitation or procurement
of applications for insurance, subscriber's agreements and powers of attorney,
or in the collection of premiums in connection with the reciprocal insurer,
without first procuring a license from the Commission pursuant to the
requirements in Chapter 18 of this title. An agent shall be appointed by each
reciprocal the agent represents. (1977, c. 313, § 38.1-700.1; 1986, c. 562.)

§ 38.2-1212. Subscribers' liability. — A. Each subscriber insured under
an assessable policy shall have a contingent assessment liability for payment
of actual losses and expenses incurred while his policy was in force. This shall
be in the amount provided for in the power of attorney or subscriber's
agreement.
   B. The contingent assessment liability on any one policy in any one calendar
year shall equal the premiums earned, as defined in § 38.2-1226, on the policy
for that year multiplied by not less than one nor more than ten.
   C. The contingent assessment liability shall not be joint, but shall be
individual and several.
   D. Each assessable policy issued by the insurer shall plainly set forth a
statement of the contingent assessment liability on the front of the policy in
capital letters in no less than ten point type. (1952, c. 317, §§ 38.1-702,
38.1-716; 1986, c. 562.)

§ 38.2-1213. Nonassessable policies. — A. The Commission may issue a
certificate authorizing the reciprocal to reduce or extinguish the contingent
assessment liability of subscribers under its policies then in force in this
Commonwealth, and to omit provisions imposing contingent assessment
liability in all policies delivered or issued for delivery in this Commonwealth
for as long as all such surplus to policyholders remains unimpaired. The

certificate may be issued if, in the case of a domestic or foreign reciprocal, the reciprocal has surplus to policyholders of at least four million dollars, or, if in the case of an alien reciprocal, the reciprocal has a trusteed surplus, as defined in § 38.2-1031, of at least four million dollars. No certificate may be issued until an application of the attorney has been approved by the subscribers' advisory committee.

However, any reciprocal that on June 30, 1991, was authorized to issue and was engaged in issuing policies without contingent liability may continue to do so until July 1, 1994, by maintaining at all times the minimum surplus to policyholders if a domestic or foreign reciprocal, and the minimum trusteed surplus if an alien reciprocal, required at the time of authorization.

B. The Commission shall issue this certificate if it determines that the reciprocal's surplus to policyholders is reasonable in relation to the reciprocal's outstanding liabilities and adequate to meet its financial needs. In making that determination the following factors, among others, shall be considered:

1. The size of the reciprocal as measured by its assets, capital and surplus, reserves, premium writings, insurance in force and other appropriate criteria;

2. The extent to which the reciprocal's business is diversified among different classes of insurance;

3. The number and size of risks insured in each class of insurance;

4. The extent of the geographical dispersion of the reciprocal's insured risks;

5. The nature and extent of the reciprocal's reinsurance program;

6. The quality, diversification, and liquidity of the reciprocal's investment portfolio;

7. The recent past and trend in the size of the reciprocal's surplus to policyholders;

8. The surplus to policyholders maintained by other comparable insurers; and

9. The adequacy of the reciprocal's reserves.

C. Upon impairment of the surplus to policyholders, the Commission shall revoke the certificate. After revocation, the reciprocal shall not issue or renew any policy without providing for the contingent assessment liability of subscribers.

D. The Commission shall not authorize a domestic reciprocal to extinguish the contingent assessment liability of any of its subscribers or in any of its policies to be issued, unless it has the required surplus to policyholders and extinguishes the contingent assessment liability of all of its subscribers and in all policies to be issued for all classes of insurance written by it. However, if required by the laws of another state in which the domestic reciprocal is transacting the business of insurance as a licensed insurer, it may issue policies providing for the contingent assessment liability of its subscribers acquiring policies in that state and need not extinguish the contingent assessment liability applicable to policies already in force in that state. (1952, c. 317, § 38.1-703; 1977, cc. 58, 322; 1986, c. 562; 1991, c. 261.)

§ 38.2-1214. Savings returned to subscribers. — A reciprocal may return to its subscribers any savings or credits accruing to their accounts. Any such distribution shall not unfairly discriminate between classes of risks or policies, or between subscribers. However, the distribution may vary for classes of subscribers based upon the experience of those classes. (1952, c. 317, § 38.1-704; 1986, c. 562.)

§ 38.2-1215. Reserves. — Each reciprocal shall maintain the same unearned premium and loss or claim reserves required for stock and mutual companies writing the same classes of insurance. (Code 1950, §§ 38-558, 38-559; 1952, c. 317, § 38.1-705; 1986, c. 562.)

§ **38.2-1216. Clerk of Commission to be appointed agent for service of process; procedure thereafter.** — A. Each attorney of a domestic reciprocal who files the declaration required by § 38.2-1219, and each attorney of a foreign or alien reciprocal who applies for a license to transact the business of insurance in this Commonwealth shall file with the Commission a written power of attorney executed in duplicate by the attorney appointing the clerk of the Commission as agent of the reciprocal. Upon the appointment, the clerk of the Commission (i) may be served all lawful process against or notice to such reciprocal, and (ii) shall be authorized to enter an appearance in behalf of the reciprocal. A copy of the power of attorney, duly certified by the Commission, shall be received in evidence in all courts of this Commonwealth. Any domestic, foreign or alien reciprocal that, on July 1, 1986, has appointed the Secretary of the Commonwealth as its agent for service of process shall comply with the requirements of this section within six months of July 1, 1986.

B. Whenever any such process or notice is served upon the clerk of the Commission, a copy of the process or notice shall be mailed to the attorney at the address shown on the power of attorney. Nothing in this section shall limit the right to serve any process or notice upon any reciprocal in any other manner permitted by law. (Code 1950, § 38-547; 1952, c. 317, § 38.1-706; 1968, c. 125; 1976, c. 559; 1986, c. 562.)

§ **38.2-1217. Reciprocal may be sued as such; where action or suit may be brought; upon whom service of process had.** — A. Any reciprocal doing business in this Commonwealth may sue or be sued in the name or designation under which its insurance contracts are effected.

B. Any action or suit against a reciprocal may be brought in any county or city (i) where its principal office is located, or (ii) where the cause of action or any part of the cause of action arose. If the action or suit is to recover a loss under a policy of insurance, it may also be brought in the county or city where the property insured was situated at the date of the policy. Any action or suit against a foreign or alien reciprocal may also be brought in any county or city of this Commonwealth in which it has any debts owed to it.

C. In an action or suit against a reciprocal, process against or notice to the reciprocal may be served upon the clerk of the Commission. If the defendant in the action or suit is a domestic reciprocal, process against or notice to that domestic reciprocal shall be served upon the attorney for that domestic reciprocal unless service upon that attorney is not feasible. (Code 1950, § 38-547; 1952, c. 317, § 38.1-707; 1986, c. 562.)

§ **38.2-1218. Effect of judgment against reciprocal.** — Any judgment against a reciprocal based upon legal process duly served as provided in this chapter shall be binding upon the reciprocal and upon each of the reciprocal's subscribers as their respective interests may appear, in an amount not exceeding their respective contingent assessment liabilities. (1952, c. 317, § 38.1-708; 1986, c. 562.)

ARTICLE 2.

Domestic Reciprocals.

§ **38.2-1219. Organization of reciprocals; what declaration to contain.** — A. Twenty-five or more persons domiciled in this Commonwealth and designated as subscribers may organize a domestic reciprocal and apply to the Commission for a license to transact the business of insurance. The original

§ 38.2-1224. Modification of power of attorney and subscriber's agreement. — Modification of the terms of the power of attorney and subscriber's agreement of a domestic reciprocal shall be made jointly by the attorney and the subscribers' advisory committee. Any such modification shall be filed with the attorney and the Commission and such filing shall by operation of law bind all subscribers the same as if each subscriber individually adopted and executed the modified, altered, or amended subscriber's agreement and power of attorney, and a copy of such agreement and power of attorney shall be provided to each subscriber within ninety days of such modifications, alterations, or amendments. No modification shall be effective retroactively, nor shall it affect any insurance contract issued prior to the modification. (1952, c. 317, § 38.1-701; 1986, c. 562; 1990, c. 10.)

§ 38.2-1225. Contributions. — The attorney or other interested persons may advance to a domestic reciprocal any funds required in its operations. No repayment of the principal, or any payment of interest thereon, in whole or in part, shall be made without the approval of the Commission. The principal advanced and any interest accrued thereon shall not be treated as a liability of the reciprocal until the repayment of principal or payment of interest is approved by the Commission; nonetheless, all statements published or filed shall show accrued interest and the amount of principal remaining unpaid. In the event of a liquidation or dissolution, all claims under the instrument shall be subordinated to subscriber, claimant and beneficiary claims as well as debts owed to all other classes of creditors. The principal advanced shall not be withdrawn or repaid and no payments of interest thereon shall be made unless the reciprocal has sufficient earned surplus in excess of its minimum required surplus. No commission or brokerage shall be paid in acquiring the funds. Interest on the principal advanced shall be at a rate not exceeding the one-year treasury bill interest rate plus three percentage points at the time the loan is made or renewed. (1952, c. 317, § 38.1-713; 1986, c. 562; 1994, c. 503.)

§ 38.2-1226. Assessments. — A. Assessments may be levied upon the subscribers of a domestic reciprocal by the attorney in accordance with § 38.2-1212. The assessments shall be approved in advance by the subscribers' advisory committee and the Commission.

B. Each domestic reciprocal subscriber's share of a deficiency for which an assessment is made shall be computed by multiplying the premiums earned on the subscriber's policies during the period to be covered by the assessment by the ratio of the total deficiency to the total premiums earned during the period upon all policies subject to the assessment. However, no assessment shall exceed the aggregate contingent assessment liability computed in accordance with § 38.2-1212. For the purposes of this section, the premiums earned on the subscriber's policies are the gross premiums charged by the reciprocal for the policies minus any charges not recurring upon the renewal or extension of the policies. No subscriber shall have an offset against any assessment for which he is liable on account of any claim for unearned premium or losses payable. (1952, c. 317, § 38.1-714; 1986, c. 562.)

§ 38.2-1227. Time limit for assessment. — Every subscriber of a domestic reciprocal having contingent assessment liability shall be liable for and shall pay his share of any assessment computed in accordance with this article if, while the policy is in force or within one year after its termination, the subscriber is notified (i) by the attorney of his intention to levy the assessment or (ii) that delinquency proceedings have been commenced against the reciprocal under the provisions of Chapter 15 of this title, and the Commission or receiver intends to levy an assessment. (1952, c. 317, § 38.1-715; 1986, c. 562.)

§ 38.2-1228. Subscribers' share in assets. — Upon the liquidation of a domestic reciprocal, the assets remaining after discharge of its (i) indebtedness and policy obligations, (ii) the return of any contributions of the attorney or other person made as provided in § 38.2-1225, and (iii) the return of any unused deposits, savings or credits, shall be distributed. The distribution shall be according to a formula approved by the Commission or the court to the persons who were its subscribers within the twelve months prior to the final termination of its license. (1952, c. 317, § 38.1-717; 1986, c. 562.)

§ 38.2-1229. Impaired reciprocals. — A. If (i) the assets of a domestic reciprocal are at any time insufficient to settle the sum of its liabilities, except those on account of funds contributed by the attorney or other parties, and its required surplus to policyholders, and (ii) the deficiency is not cured from other sources, its attorney shall levy an assessment upon subscribers made subject to assessment by the terms of their policies for the amount needed to make up the deficiency. However, the assessment shall be subject to § 38.2-1212.

B. If the attorney fails to make the assessment within thirty days after the Commission orders him to to so, or if the deficiency is not fully made up within sixty days after the date the assessment was made, delinquency proceedings may be instituted and conducted against the insurer as provided in Chapter 15 of this title.

C. If liquidation of the reciprocal is ordered, an assessment shall be levied upon the subscribers for the amount the Commission or the court, as the case may be, determines to be necessary to discharge all liabilities of the reciprocal. This assessment shall exclude any funds contributed by the attorney or other persons, but shall include the reasonable cost of the liquidation. However, the assessment shall be subject to § 38.2-1212. (1952, c. 317, § 38.1-718; 1986, c. 562.)

§ 38.2-1230. Material transactions. — A. Prior written approval of the Commission shall be required for a material transaction between a domestic reciprocal, or an affiliate of the reciprocal, and any one or more of the following: the attorney of the reciprocal; an affiliate of the attorney of the reciprocal; an insurer or other reciprocal managed by the attorney of the reciprocal or by an affiliate of the attorney of the reciprocal; or any other person who, directly or indirectly, by contract or otherwise, acts on behalf of, or at the direction of, the attorney of the reciprocal or any affiliate of the attorney of the reciprocal, when the material transaction involves more than five percent of the domestic reciprocal's admitted assets as reported in its most recent statutory statement filed with the Commission. All other material transactions between such parties involving more than 0.5 percent of the domestic reciprocal's admitted assets as reported in its most recent statutory statement filed with the Commission shall be reported to the Commission within fifteen days after the end of the month in which the transaction occurs. In addition, all transactions shall meet the following standards:

1. The terms shall be fair and equitable;
2. Charges or fees for services performed shall be reasonable;
3. Expenses incurred and payments received shall be allocated to the reciprocal on an equitable basis in conformity with statutory insurance accounting practices consistently applied; and
4. The books, accounts, and records of each party shall disclose clearly and accurately the precise nature and details of the transaction.

B. The Commission, in reviewing a material transaction under this section, shall consider whether the material transaction complies with the standards set forth in subsection A and also whether the transaction may adversely affect the interests of the subscribers or the solvency of the reciprocal.

C. Within sixty days after written notification of any transaction requiring approval pursuant to this section, the Commission shall notify the insurer of its approval or disapproval, and, in the event of disapproval, its reason thereof. Failure of the Commission to act within sixty days of notification by the insurer shall constitute approval of the transaction.

D. For the purposes of this section:

1. *"Affiliate"* of a specific person means a person that directly or indirectly through one or more intermediaries, owns, is owned by or is under common ownership with the person specified. An affiliate relationship shall be presumed to exist if any person, directly or indirectly, owns or holds with the power to vote, or holds proxies representing collectively ten percent or more of the voting securities of the person specified.

2. *"Material transaction"* means a transaction, other than a claim payment, a premium payment or a reinsurance payment made pursuant to a reinsurance contract which reinsurance contract complies with the requirements of this section, occurring on or after July 1, 1996, that exceeds any minimum limits set forth in subsection A of this section. Any series of transactions occurring within a twelve-month period that are sufficiently similar in nature as to be reasonably construed as a single transaction and that in the aggregate exceed any minimum limits set forth in subsection A of this section shall be deemed a material transaction.

E. Any report or other information filed pursuant to this section shall not be open to public inspection and shall receive confidential treatment by the Commission. (1996, c. 304.)

§ 38.2-1231. Attorney's financial statement. — A. The subscribers' advisory committee of a domestic reciprocal shall annually obtain from its attorney an audited financial report of the attorney's financial position and the results of its operations as related to its management of the reciprocal. A copy of the report shall be filed with the Commission.

B. Unless the Commission provides otherwise in writing, the report required by this section shall be due within 120 days after the end of the attorney's fiscal year, shall be prepared in conformity with generally accepted accounting practices, and shall be audited by an independent certified public accountant.

C. If the attorney obtains an independent audit on a consolidated basis, the audited consolidated financial statements shall satisfy the requirements of this section provided the attorney's financial position and results of its operation as related to its management of the reciprocal are separately disclosed.

D. The report filed pursuant to this section and any information provided in connection with the preparation of such report shall not be open to public inspection and shall receive confidential treatment by the Commission. (1996, c. 304.)

CHAPTER 13.

Reports, Reserves and Examinations, Insurance Holding Companies.

ARTICLE 1.

Annual Statements and Other Reports.

§ 38.2-1300. Annual statements. — A. Each insurer licensed to transact the business of insurance in this Commonwealth shall file with the Commission annually, on or before March 1, an annual statement showing its financial condition on December 31 of the previous year. The annual statement shall be considered filed on the date the statement was sent by mail as shown by the postmark. The annual statement shall contain a detailed report of the insurer's assets and liabilities, the investment of its assets, its income and disbursements during the previous year, and all other information which the Commission considers necessary to secure a full and accurate knowledge of the affairs and condition of the insurer. The annual statement of every domestic or foreign insurer shall be signed by at least two of its principal officers subject to § 38.2-1304. No publication of the annual statement shall be required.

B. The annual statement of an alien insurer shall relate only to its transactions and affairs in the United States unless the Commission requires otherwise. The annual statement shall be verified by the alien insurer's United States manager, assistant manager, or by any of its duly authorized officers.

C. The Commission may prescribe the form of the annual statement and supplemental schedules and exhibits to include additional copies in machine-readable format, and may vary the form for different types of insurers. However, as far as practicable, the form for annual statements, supplementary schedules, and exhibits shall be the same as other such forms in general use in the United States. Unless otherwise prescribed by the Commission, such annual statements shall be prepared using an annual statement convention blank developed by the National Association of Insurance Commissioners (NAIC). The annual statement, and supplementary schedules and exhibits required by this section, shall be prepared in accordance with the appropriate annual statement instructions and the accounting practices and procedures manuals adopted by the NAIC, or any other successor publications.

D. Each domestic, foreign and alien insurer that is authorized to transact insurance in this Commonwealth shall annually on or before March 1 of each year, file with the NAIC a copy of its annual statement convention blank, along with such additional filings as prescribed by the Commission for the preceding year. The information filed with the NAIC shall be in the same format and scope as that required by the Commission and shall include the signed jurat page and any actuarial certification required by the Commission. Any amendments and addenda to the annual statement filing subsequently filed with the Commission shall also be filed with the NAIC. However, an insurer may apply to the Commission for an exemption from this subsection.

E. Foreign insurers that are domiciled in a state, which has a law substantially similar to subsection D of this section, shall be deemed to be in compliance with subsection D of this section. (Code 1950, §§ 38-122, 38-516; 1952, c. 317, § 38.1-159; 1986, c. 562; 1990, c. 240; 1991, c. 312; 1992, c. 588; 1994, c. 308.)

Oral contracts. — This section and §§ 38.2-1040, 38.2-1041, 38.2-1312, and 38.2-1318 are predicated upon the assumption that insurance contracts will be in writing and that accurate records will be kept thereof; and it is essential to their due execution that the companies shall not make and that their agents shall not be authorized to make oral contracts to any greater extent or for any greater length of time than is reasonably required by the exigencies of the business and for the orderly conduct of their business with reasonable convenience to the public. Eastern Shore Fire Ins. Co. v. Kellam, 159 Va. 93, 165 S.E. 637 (1932).

§ 38.2-1301. Additional reports. — A. In addition to the annual statement, the Commission may require a licensed insurer to file additional reports, exhibits or statements considered necessary to secure complete information concerning the condition, solvency, experience, transactions or affairs of the insurer. The Commission shall establish deadlines for filing these additional reports, exhibits or statements and may require verification by any officers of the insurer designated by the Commission.

B. The Commission may require a domestic, foreign or alien insurer that is authorized to transact insurance in this Commonwealth to file with the National Association of Insurance Commissioners (NAIC) a copy of the insurer's financial statement required to be filed pursuant to § 38.2-1301, on a quarterly basis. Unless otherwise prescribed by the Commission, all such financial statements, whether filed with the Commission or the NAIC, shall be prepared in accordance with applicable provisions of the annual statement instructions and the accounting practices and procedures manuals adopted by the NAIC, or any successor publications. The Commission may prescribe that additional copies of financial statements and other reports be filed in machine-readable format. (Code 1950, § 38-122; 1952, c. 317, § 38.1-160; 1986, c. 562; 1991, c. 312; 1992, c. 588; 1994, c. 308.)

§ 38.2-1301.1. Material transaction disclosures. — A. Every insurer domiciled in this Commonwealth shall file a report with the Commission disclosing material acquisitions and dispositions of assets or material nonrenewals, cancellations or revisions of ceded reinsurance agreements unless such acquisitions and dispositions of assets or material nonrenewals, cancellations or revisions of ceded reinsurance agreements have been submitted to the Commission for review, approval or information purposes pursuant to other provisions of Title 38.2 or the rules and regulations of the Commission.

1. The report required by this subsection is due within fifteen days after the end of the calendar month in which any of the foregoing transactions occur.

2. One complete copy of the report, including any exhibits or other attachments filed as part thereof, shall be filed with the National Association of Insurance Commissioners unless the insurer has applied for and has been granted an exemption from this requirement by the Commission.

B. All reports obtained by or disclosed to the Commission pursuant to this section, shall be given confidential treatment, shall not be subject to subpoena, and shall not be made public by the Commission, the National Association of Insurance Commissioners, or any other person, except to insurance departments of other states, without the prior written consent of the insurer to which it pertains unless the Commission, after giving the insurer which would be affected thereby, notice and an opportunity to be heard, determines that the interest of policyholders, shareholders, or the public will be served by the publication thereof, in which event the Commission may publish all or any part thereof in such manner as it may deem appropriate.

C. No acquisitions or dispositions of assets need be reported pursuant to subsection A if the acquisitions or dispositions are not material. For purposes of this section, a material acquisition, or the aggregate of any series of related acquisitions during any thirty-day period, or disposition, or the aggregate of any series of related dispositions during any thirty-day period, is one that is nonrecurring and not in the ordinary course of business and involves more than five percent of the reporting insurer's total admitted assets as reported in its most recent statutory statement filed with the Commission.

1. Asset acquisitions subject to this section include every purchase, lease, exchange, merger, consolidation, succession, or other acquisition other than the construction or development of real property by or for the reporting insurer or the acquisition of materials for such purpose.

2. Asset dispositions subject to this section include every sale, lease, exchange, merger, consolidation, mortgage, pledge or hypothecation, assignment, whether for the benefit of creditors or otherwise, abandonment, destruction, or other disposition.

3. The following information is required to be disclosed in any report of a material acquisition or disposition of assets:

a. Date of the transaction;

b. Manner of acquisition or disposition;

c. Description of the assets involved;

d. Nature and amount of the consideration given or received;

e. Purpose of, or reason for, the transaction;

f. Manner by which the amount of consideration was determined;

g. Gain or loss recognized or realized as a result of the transaction; and

h. Name of all persons from whom the assets were acquired or to whom they were disposed.

4. Insurers are required to report material acquisitions and dispositions on a nonconsolidated basis unless the insurer is part of a consolidated group of insurers which utilizes a pooling arrangement or 100 percent reinsurance agreement that affects the solvency and integrity of the insurer's reserves and such insurer ceded substantially all of its direct and assumed business to the pool. An insurer is deemed to have ceded substantially all of its direct and assumed business to a pool if the insurer has less than one million dollars total direct plus assumed written premiums during a calendar year that are not subject to a pooling arrangement and the net income of the business not subject to the pooling arrangement represents less than five percent of the insurer's capital and surplus.

D. No nonrenewals, cancellations or revisions of ceded reinsurance agreements need be reported pursuant to this section if the nonrenewals, cancellations or revisions are not material. For purposes of this section, a material nonrenewal, cancellation or revision is one that affects for property and casualty business, including accident and health business when written as such, more than fifty percent of an insurer's ceded written premium, or for life, annuity and accident and health business, more than fifty percent of the total reserve credit taken for business ceded, on an annualized basis as indicated in the insurer's most recently filed statutory statement; however, no filing is required if the insurer's ceded written premium or the total reserve credit taken for business ceded represents, on an annualized basis, less than ten percent of direct plus assumed written premium or ten percent of the statutory reserve requirement prior to any cession, respectively.

1. Subject to the foregoing criteria, a report is to be filed without regard to which party has initiated the nonrenewal, cancellation or revision of ceded reinsurance whenever one or more of the following conditions exist:

a. The entire cession has been cancelled, nonrenewed or revised and ceded indemnity and loss adjustment expense reserves after any nonrenewal, cancellation or revision represent less than fifty percent of the comparable reserves that would have been ceded had the nonrenewal, cancellation or revision not occurred;

b. An authorized or accredited reinsurer has been replaced on an existing cession by an unauthorizing reinsurer; or

c. Collateral requirements previously established for unauthorized reinsurers have been reduced; e.g., the requirement to collateralize incurred but not reported (IBNR) claim reserves has been waived with respect to one or more unauthorized reinsurers newly participating in an existing cession.

Subject to the materiality criteria, for purposes of the foregoing subdivisions b and c, a report shall be filed if the result of the revision affects more than ten percent of the cession.

2. The following information is required to be disclosed in any report of a material nonrenewal, cancellation or revision of ceded reinsurance agreements:

a. Effective date of the nonrenewal, cancellation or revision;

b. The description of the transaction with an identification of the initiator thereof;

c. Purpose of, or reason for, the transaction; and

d. If applicable, the identity of the replacement reinsurers.

3. Insurers are required to report all material nonrenewals, cancellations or revisions of ceded reinsurance agreements on a nonconsolidated basis unless the insurer is part of a consolidated group of insurers which utilizes a pooling arrangement or 100 percent reinsurance agreement that affects the solvency and integrity of the insurer's reserves and such insurer ceded substantially all of its direct and assumed business to the pool. An insurer is deemed to have ceded substantially all of its direct and assumed business to a pool if the insurer has less than one million dollars total direct plus assumed written premiums during a calendar year that are not subject to a pooling arrangement and the net income of the business not subject to the pooling arrangement represents less than five percent of the insurer's capital and surplus. (1994, c. 308.)

§ **38.2-1302. Extension of filing time.** — The Commission may extend an insurer's deadline for filing annual statements, other reports or exhibits provided the deadline for annual statements is not extended beyond April 30. (Code 1950, § 38-126; 1952, c. 317, § 38.1-161; 1986, c. 562.)

§ **38.2-1303. Printed forms to be filed by insurers; certificates to domestic insurers.** — A. The Commission shall be responsible for prescribing the type of blank or may prepare and distribute printed forms or blanks to licensed insurers for statements, reports, schedules or exhibits required by law or order.

B. The Commission shall furnish without charge to domestic insurers any certificates required to entitle them to do business in other states or countries. (Code 1950, § 38-129; 1952, c. 317, § 38.1-162; 1986, c. 562; 1994, c. 316.)

§ **38.2-1304. False statements, reports, etc., deemed a Class 5 felony.** — Any officer, manager, attorney, agent or employee of any insurer or surplus lines broker who is responsible for making or filing any annual or other statement, report, exhibit or other instrument required by this title and who knowingly or willfully makes or files any false or fraudulent statement, report or other instrument shall be charged with a Class 5 felony. If convicted, such person shall be guilty of a Class 5 felony. (Code 1950, § 38-123; 1952, c. 317, § 38.1-163; 1986, c. 562.)

Cross references. — For general statutory provisions as to perjury, see §§ 18.2-434 through 18.2-437. As to punishment for Class 5 felonies, see § 18.2-10.

§ **38.2-1305. Voluntary reports.** — Any insurer may elect to file with the Commission, in addition to the annual statement required by § 38.2-1300, a statement in condensed form of its financial condition as of the end of any calendar year or as of any other date. Any statement shall be signed by at least two of the principal officers of the insurer subject to § 38.2-1304. No insurer nor anyone on its behalf shall publish in any manner in this Commonwealth a statement purporting to show its financial condition if that statement does not correspond in substance with the verified statement last filed with the

Commission by the insurer pursuant to §§ 38.2-1300, 38.2-1301, or this section. (Code 1950, § 38-23; 1952, c. 317, § 38.1-164; 1986, c. 562.)

§ 38.2-1306. Reports to be open to public inspection. — The Commission shall keep on file for at least three years all reports required by law and all special reports required by it to be filed by insurers. The Commission shall keep copies of the annual statement convention blanks and the quarterly financial statements filed with the Commission and, pursuant to subsection D of § 38.2-1300 and subsection B of § 38.2-1301 respectively, with the National Association of Insurance Commissioners (NAIC), available for inspection by interested persons at any reasonable time.

For companies not required to file with the NAIC, the Commission shall make available for inspection copies of such comparable financial statements of financial condition as those companies may be required to file routinely with the Commission pursuant to the provisions of this title. Except as provided otherwise by statute, or by order, rule or regulation promulgated by the Commission, no special report shall be open to public inspection. (Code 1950, § 38-124; 1952, c. 317, § 38.1-165; 1986, c. 562; 1994, c. 308.)

§ 38.2-1306.1. Insurance companies' analyses confidential. — A. All regulatory or financial analyses, ratios and examination synopses concerning insurance companies that are submitted to the Commission by the National Association of Insurance Commissioners (NAIC), including information generated by any NAIC databases developed for use by regulators, are not open to public inspection and shall receive confidential treatment by the Commission.

B. Financial analyses and test ratios generated by the Commission, pursuant to the NAIC's Insurance Regulatory Information System (IRIS) or Financial Analysis and Solvency Tracking (FAST) System, any successor program, or any similar program developed by the Commission, are not public records, and shall receive confidential treatment.

C. Notwithstanding other provisions to the contrary, nothing contained in this chapter shall prevent or be construed as prohibiting the Commission from disclosing otherwise confidential information, administrative or judicial orders, or the content of any analysis or any matter related thereto, to the insurance regulatory officials of any state or country, directly or indirectly through officials at NAIC, or to law-enforcement officials of this or any other state or agency of the federal government at any time provided that those officials are required under their law to maintain its confidentiality.

D. Documents or information received from the insurance regulatory officials of any state or country which are confidential in those jurisdictions are not open to public inspection and shall receive confidential treatment by the Commission. (1987, c. 691; 1994, c. 308; 1996, c. 32.)

ARTICLE 2.

Valuation and Admissibility of Assets.

§ 38.2-1306.2. Valuation of investments and other assets. — A. The value of assets, other than those not admitted pursuant to § 38.2-1310.1, shall be determined in accordance with valuations or valuation standards announced by the National Association of Insurance Commissioners (NAIC).

B. Investments as to which the NAIC has not announced valuations or valuation standards shall be valued in a manner consistent with the provisions of this article. Any other assets as to which the NAIC has not announced valuation standards shall be valued in a manner consistent with the provisions of this chapter.

Any asset valued pursuant to this subsection shall be identified and its valuation method disclosed to the Commission simultaneously with the filing of any annual statement required by § 38.2-1300 or any quarterly supplement required under § 38.2-1301.

C. If the Commission finds that the valuation or valuation method announced by the NAIC does not reflect economic or financial circumstances relevant to a true and current value of the asset, it may approve an alternative method of valuation provided the alternative valuation method (i) produces values no greater than those which might have been produced under NAIC standards and (ii) is otherwise consistent with the provisions of this article. (1992, c. 588; 1993, c. 158.)

§ **38.2-1307. Valuation of bonds.** — A. Except to the extent otherwise provided in subsection A of § 38.2-1306.2, bonds or other evidences of indebtedness having a fixed term and rate of interest and held by any insurer licensed to transact business in this Commonwealth, if amply secured and not in default as to principal or interest, may be valued as follows:

1. If purchased at par, at the par value; or
2. If purchased above or below par, (i) on the basis of the purchase price adjusted so as to bring the value to par at the maturity date or the first callable date at par, whichever is earlier, in order to annually yield the effective rate of interest at which the purchase was made or, (ii) at the discretion of the Commission, on the basis of the method commonly known as the pro rata or straight line method.

However, in applying this rule, the purchase price shall not be taken at a higher amount than the actual market value at the time of acquisition.

B. Except to the extent otherwise provided in subsection A of § 38.2-1306.2, all bonds or other evidences of indebtedness that in the judgment of the Commission are not amply secured or that are in default as to principal or interest shall be valued as provided in § 38.2-1308. (Code 1950, § 38-5; 1952, c. 317, § 38.1-166; 1986, c. 562; 1992, c. 588; 1993, c. 158.)

§ **38.2-1308. Valuation of stocks and other securities.** — A. All stocks and all bonds or other evidences of indebtedness, except as otherwise provided in this article, owned by an insurer licensed to transact business in this Commonwealth, shall be valued at an amount not to exceed their market value as determined by current sales or stock market quotations or, in the absence of current market and current sales data, at an amount not to exceed prices determined by the Commission as representing their fair market value.

B. Such stock, if preferred or guaranteed and if paying full dividends, at the discretion of the Commission, may be carried at a fixed value instead of market value or in accordance with any method of valuation the Commission approves.

C. Such stock, if the stock of a subsidiary of an insurer, shall be valued, at the discretion of the insurer, at not more than book value, market value, or acquisition cost. Market value may be used only if the stock is listed on a national securities exchange or entered in the NASDAQ system. For other than market valuation, the value of the stock shall include only the assets that would constitute admitted assets of the insurer if held directly by the insurer. The Commission, upon notice and informal hearing, can specify the manner in which the stock of a subsidiary will be valued. (1952, ch. 317, § 38.1-167; 1954, c. 232; 1978, c. 156; 1986, c. 562; 1992, c. 588; 1993, c. 158.)

§ **38.2-1309. Valuation of real estate, leaseholds, and purchase money mortgages.** — A. Interests in real estate which cannot be valued pursuant to the provisions of subsection A of § 38.2-1306.2 shall be subject to the following. In the absence of a recent appraisal which the Commission considers reliable, real estate acquired by foreclosure or by deed instead of foreclosure by any insurer licensed to transact business in this Commonwealth shall be valued at an amount not to exceed the acquisition cost. This amount shall not be greater than the sum of (i) the unpaid principal of the defaulted loan at the date of the foreclosure or deed, (ii) any taxes and expenses paid or incurred at the time of and in connection with the acquisition, excluding any unpaid interest on the defaulted loan, (iii) the cost of additions or improvements made after acquisition, and (iv) any amounts paid after acquisition on any assessments levied for improvements in connection with the property.

B. Any real estate referred to in subsection A of this section that is subject to a contract of sale shall be valued in an amount not exceeding the lesser of the acquisition cost or the contract sale price decreased in either case by any amounts paid under the contract.

C. The value of the real estate or any interest in the real estate acquired or held as an investment for the production of income or acquired to be improved and developed for investment purposes according to a development plan shall be adjusted by an amount that includes a write-down of that part of the insurer's cost of its interest in the property which is allocable to any improvements. The write-down will be at a rate that will average not less than two percent annually of the cost for each year or fraction of that year that the property has been held.

D. Any leasehold shall be valued at not more than the cost of its acquisition and its improvement and shall be amortized within a period not exceeding the lesser of (i) eight-tenths of the unexpired term of the leasehold following the acquisition or improvement, or (ii) within a period of forty years thereafter.

E. Real estate held by an insurer for which no method of valuation has been provided in this section shall be valued in an amount not exceeding the acquisition cost which shall include a write-down of that part of the insurer's cost of its interest in the property which is allocable to any improvements; such write-down will be at a rate that will average not less than two percent annually of the cost for each year or fraction of that year that the property has been held. However, the Commission may allow such real estate to be valued at an amount up to but not in excess of the fair market value determined by appraisals the Commission considers reliable.

F. Purchase money mortgages shall be valued at an amount not exceeding the lesser of (i) the acquisition cost of the real estate encumbered by the mortgage or (ii) ninety percent of the fair market value of the real estate. (1952, c. 317, § 38.1-168; 1973, c. 121; 1983, c. 457; 1986, c. 562; 1990, c. 348; 1993, c. 158.)

§ **38.2-1310:** Repealed by Acts 1993, c. 158.

Cross references. — As to present provisions relating to valuation of investments, see § 38.2-1306.2 et seq.

§ **38.2-1310.1. Assets not admitted.** — Notwithstanding any other provisions in this article, for purposes of determining the financial condition of an insurer the following assets shall not be admitted:

1. Goodwill, trade names, and other intangible assets;

2. Advances to officers, whether secured or not, unless authorized pursuant to subsection B of § 38.2-212;

3. Advances to employees, agents, and other persons on personal security only;

4. Stock of the insurer, owned by the insurer, or any equity in the insurer or loans secured by the insurer, or any proportionate interest in the stock through

the ownership by the insurer of an interest in another firm, corporation, or business unit;

5. Furniture, fixtures, furnishings, safes, vehicles, libraries, stationery, literature and supplies except that an insurer may have as admitted assets electronic data processing equipment constituting a data processing and accounting system provided (i) the cost of the system is at least $25,000, (ii) the cost is amortized in full over a period not to exceed five years, and (iii) the amortized cost thereof does not exceed two percent of the insurer's admitted assets; title insurers may have as admitted assets such materials and plants as the insurer is expressly authorized to invest in under Chapter 46 (§ 38.2-4600 et seq.) of this title. Any domestic insurer may have as admitted assets such personal property which is acquired through foreclosure of chattel mortgages acquired pursuant to § 38.2-1439 or which is reasonably necessary to the maintenance and operation of real estate lawfully acquired and held by the insurer, other than real estate used by it for home office, branch office and similar purposes;

6. The amount, if any, by which the aggregate book value of the insurer's investments exceeds the aggregate value thereof as determined under this title;

7. Bonds, notes, or other evidence of indebtedness which are secured by mortgages or deeds of trust which are in default to the extent they exceed current market value;

8. Prepaid and deferred expenses except prepaid property taxes;

9. Federal, state or municipal tax refunds when such refund is not assured; and

10. All assets determined by the Commission to be of doubtful value or character. (1991, c. 312; 1992, c. 588.)

ARTICLE 3.

Reserves.

§ **38.2-1311. Valuation reserves.** — A. Every insurer licensed to transact the kinds of insurance specified in §§ 38.2-102, 38.2-106 and 38.2-109 and subject to the applicable provisions of this title, shall maintain:

1. Reserves on all of its life insurance policies or certificates and annuity contracts in force, computed according to the applicable tables of mortality and interest rates prescribed in this title;

2. Reserves for both reported and unreported (i) disability benefits, including reserves for disabled lives, and (ii) accidental death benefits; and

3. Any additional reserves prescribed by the Commission as necessary on account of the insurer's policies, certificates and contracts.

B. For all accident and sickness insurance policies the insurer shall maintain an active life reserve that shall (i) place a reasonable value on its liabilities under the policies, (ii) be not less than the reserve according to appropriate standards set forth in any regulations issued by the Commission and, (iii) be not less in the aggregate than the pro rata gross unearned premiums for those policies. (1952, c. 317, § 38.1-170; 1962, c. 562; 1986, c. 562.)

§ **38.2-1312. Unearned premium reserves.** — A. Except for risks or policies for which reserves are required under §§ 38.2-1311 and 38.2-4610.1, each insurer licensed to transact business in this Commonwealth, subject to the applicable provisions of this title, shall maintain reserves equal to the unearned portions of the gross premiums charged on unexpired or unterminated risks and policies.

B. Premiums charged for bulk assumption reinsurance assumed from other insurers shall be included in gross premiums charged on the basis of the original premiums and the original terms of the policies of the ceding insurer.

C. No deduction shall be made from the gross unearned premiums except for premiums paid or credited for risks reinsured as provided in § 38.2-1316.

D. The reserve for unearned premiums shall be computed, at the insurer's option, on the annual, monthly or daily pro rata fraction basis. However, the Commission, at its discretion, may (i) prescribe the basis to be used, (ii) require that the reserve be computed on each respective risk from the date of issuance of the policy, or (iii) prescribe special rules for computing the reserve for premiums covering indefinite terms. For marine insurance, premiums on unterminated trip risks shall be considered unearned, and the reserve to be carried on unterminated risks at the end of any month shall equal 100% of the premiums on trip risks written during the month unless the Commission prescribes otherwise. The reserve for premium deposits on perpetual fire insurance risks shall equal not less than ninety percent of the gross amount of those deposits. (Code 1950, § 38-228; 1952, c. 317, § 38.1-171; 1982, c. 430; 1986, c. 562.)

Editor's note. — Section 38.2-1316, referred to in subsection C, was repealed by Acts 1991, c. 264. For present reinsurance provisions, see § 38.2-1316.1 et seq.

This section was enacted for the purpose of testing the solvency of insurance companies, and has nothing to do with a determination of profits as a basis for ratemaking. Aetna Ins. Co. v. Commonwealth ex rel. SCC, 160 Va. 698, 169 S.E. 859 (1933).

Oral contracts. — This section and §§ 38.2-1040, 38.2-1041, 38.2-1300, and 38.2-1318 are predicated upon the assumption that insurance contracts will be in writing and that accurate records will be kept thereof; and it is essential to their due execution that the companies shall not make, and that their agents shall not be authorized to make, oral contracts to any greater extent or for any greater length of time than is reasonably required by the exigencies of the business and for the orderly conduct of their business with reasonable convenience to the public. Eastern Shore Fire Ins. Co. v. Kellam, 159 Va. 93, 165 S.E. 637 (1932).

§ 38.2-1313. Loss records. — Each insurer licensed to transact business in this Commonwealth shall, except for accident and sickness insurance as defined in § 38.2-109, maintain a complete and itemized record showing all losses and claims for which notice has been given. When necessary, the insurers shall maintain a record of all notices received of the occurrence of any event that may result in a loss. (1952, c. 317, § 38.1-172; 1986, c. 562.)

§ 38.2-1314. Loss or claim reserves. — Except as provided in §§ 38.2-1311 and 38.2-4609, each insurer licensed to transact the business of insurance in this Commonwealth shall maintain reserves:

1. In an amount estimated in the aggregate as being sufficient to provide for reported and unreported unpaid losses or claims arising on or prior to the date of any annual or other statement for which the insurer may be liable;

2. In an amount estimated to provide for loss adjustment expenses; and

3. For those classes of insurance specified by the Commission, any additional reserves for unpaid losses, policy obligations, or deficiencies in the unearned premium reserve as required by the Commission. Each insurer authorized to write these classes of insurance shall file with its annual statement, schedules of its experience for such insurance in the form the Commission requires and shall calculate the reserves required by this paragraph in the manner prescribed by the Commission. (Code 1950, §§ 38-229 through 38-232; 1952, c. 317, § 38.1-173; 1982, c. 430; 1986, c. 562; 1994, c. 503.)

§ 38.2-1315. Mortgage guaranty insurance contingency reserve. — A. To protect against the effect of adverse economic cycles, each insurer transacting the business of mortgage guaranty insurance in this Commonwealth shall establish and maintain a contingency reserve equal to fifty percent of its earned premium.

B. Allocations to the contingency reserve shall be maintained for 120 months. That portion of the contingency reserve that has been maintained for more than 120 months shall be released and shall no longer constitute part of the contingency reserve and shall be allocated to surplus to policyholders.

C. Upon notification to the Commission, the contingency reserve shall be available for loss payments only when the incurred losses in any one twelve-month period, less any amounts already released from the contingency reserve during that period, exceed thirty-five percent of the corresponding earned premium.

D. In the event of release of the contingency reserve for payment of losses, the contributions required by subsection A of this section shall be treated on a first-in-first-out basis.

E. Whenever the laws of any other state require a greater unearned premium reserve than that set forth in § 38.2-1312, the mortgage guaranty insurance contingency reserve of mortgage guaranty insurers organized under the laws of that state may be an amount that, when added to such unearned premium reserve, will result in a reserve equal to the sum of the unearned premium reserve required by § 38.2-1312 and the contingency reserve required by this section.

F. The authority of the Commission under § 38.2-223 to issue rules and regulations includes the authority to require that a greater reserve be established for mortgage guaranty insurance on liens other than first liens. (1973, c. 250, §§ 38.1-173.1, 38.1-173.2; 1981, c. 209; 1986, c. 562; 1989, c. 236.)

§ **38.2-1316:** Repealed by Acts 1991, c. 264.

Cross references. — For present provisions relating to reinsurance, see § 38.2-1316.1 et seq.

ARTICLE 3.1.

Reinsurance.

§ **38.2-1316.1. Definitions.** — As used in this article:

"Accredited reinsurer" means an assuming insurer accredited pursuant to the provisions of subdivision 2 of subsection A of § 38.2-1316.2.

"Credit" includes any credit for reinsurance (i) allowed as an admitted asset or as a deduction from liability and (ii) used to compute the valuation reserves required by § 38.2-1311, unearned premium reserves required by § 38.2-1312 or § 38.2-4610.1, or loss or claim reserves required by § 38.2-1314 or § 38.2-4609.

"Qualified United States financial institution," as used in subdivision 2 c of § 38.2-1316.4, means an institution that:

1. Is organized or, in the case of a United States office of a foreign banking organization, is licensed, under the laws of the United States or any state thereof;

2. Is regulated, supervised, and examined by the United States federal or state authorities having regulatory authority over banks and trust companies; and

3. Has been determined by either the Commission or the Securities Valuation Office of the National Association of Insurance Commissioners to meet such standards of financial condition and standing as are considered necessary and appropriate to regulate the quality of financial institutions whose letters of credit will be acceptable to the Commission.

"Qualified United States financial institution" means, for purposes of those provisions of this article specifying those institutions that are eligible to act as a fiduciary of a trust, an institution that:

1. Is organized or, in the case of a United States branch or agency office of a foreign banking organization, is licensed, under the laws of the United States or any state thereof and has been granted authority to operate with fiduciary powers; and

2. Is regulated, supervised and examined by federal or state authorities having regulatory authority over banks and trust companies. (1991, c. 264.)

§ 38.2-1316.2. Credit allowed a domestic ceding insurer. — A. Except as provided in § 38.2-1316.4, credit shall be allowed a domestic ceding insurer for reinsurance ceded only when the assuming insurer meets one of the following criteria:

1. Credit shall be allowed when the assuming insurer is licensed to transact insurance in this Commonwealth.

2. Credit shall be allowed when the assuming insurer is accredited as a reinsurer in this Commonwealth. An accredited reinsurer is one which:

a. Files with the Commission evidence of its submission to the Commission's jurisdiction;

b. Submits to the Commission's authority to examine its books and records;

c. Is licensed to transact insurance or reinsurance in at least one state or, in the case of a United States branch of an alien assuming insurer, is entered through and licensed to transact insurance or reinsurance in at least one state; and

d. Files annually with the Commission a copy of its annual statement filed with the insurance department of its state of domicile or entry and a copy of its most recent audited financial statement, and either (i) maintains a surplus to policyholders or, in the case of an alien insurer, a trusteed surplus, in an amount which is not less than $20 million and whose accreditation has not been denied by the Commission within ninety days of its initial submission; or (ii) maintains a surplus to policyholders or, in the case of an alien insurer, a trusteed surplus, in an amount less than $20 million and whose accreditation has been approved by the Commission.

However, no credit shall be allowed for reinsurance ceded to an accredited reinsurer if the assuming insurer's standing as an accredited reinsurer has been denied or revoked by the Commission. Such standing shall not be revoked by the Commission until after the assuming insurer has been given ten days' notice of the reasons for the proposed revocation and an opportunity to introduce evidence and be heard. Any hearing authorized by this subsection may be informal, and the required notice may be waived by the Commission and the insurer. Furthermore, the Commission may require additional reports, exhibits or statements as it determines necessary to secure complete information concerning the condition and affairs of any accredited reinsurer.

3. Credit shall be allowed when the assuming insurer is domiciled and licensed in or, in the case of a United States branch of an alien insurer, is entered through, a state which employs standards regarding credit for reinsurance substantially similar to those applicable under this statute and the assuming insurer or United States branch of an alien assuming insurer:

a. Submits to the authority of the Commission to examine its books and records; and

b. Maintains a surplus to policyholders in an amount not less than $20 million. However, unless specifically required by the Commission, this surplus requirement shall be deemed waived when reinsurance is ceded and assumed pursuant to pooling arrangements among insurers in the same holding company system.

4. Credit shall be allowed when the assuming insurer maintains a trust fund in a qualified United States financial institution for the payment of the valid claims of its United States policyholders and ceding insurers, their assigns and successors in interest. The assuming insurer shall report annually to the Commission information substantially the same as that required to be reported on the National Association of Insurance Commissioners (NAIC) Annual Statement form by licensed insurers to enable the Commission to determine the sufficiency of the trust fund.

a. In the case of a single assuming insurer, the trust shall consist of a trusteed account representing the assuming insurer's liabilities attributable to business written in the United States, and in addition, the assuming insurer shall maintain a trusteed surplus amount not less than $20 million.

b. In the case of a group, including incorporated and individual unincorporated underwriters, the trust shall consist of a trusteed account representing the group's liabilities attributable to business written in the United States and in addition, the group shall maintain a trusteed surplus of which $100 million shall be held jointly for the benefit of United States ceding insurers of any member of the group, the incorporated members of which shall not be engaged in any business other than underwriting as a member of the group and shall be subject to the same level of solvency regulation and control by the group's domiciliary regulator as are the unincorporated members; and the group shall make available to the Commission an annual certification of the solvency of each underwriter by the group's domiciliary regulator and its independent public accountants.

c. In the case of a group of incorporated insurers under common administration which complies with the filing requirements contained in the previous paragraph, and which has continuously transacted an insurance business outside the United States for at least three years, and submits to the Commission's authority to examine its books and records and bears the expense of the examination, and which has aggregate policyholders' surplus of $10 billion; the trust shall be in an amount equal to the group's several liabilities attributable to business ceded by United States ceding insurers to any member of the group pursuant to reinsurance contracts issued in the name of such group. In addition, the group shall maintain a joint trusteed surplus of which $100 million shall be held jointly for the benefit of United States ceding insurers of any member of the group as additional security for any such liabilities, and each member of the group shall make available to the Commission an annual certification of the member's solvency by the member's domiciliary regulator and its independent public accountant.

B. The trusts described in subdivision 4 of subsection A shall be established in a form acceptable to the Commission.

1. The trust instrument shall provide that contested claims shall be valid and enforceable upon the final order of any court of competent jurisdiction in the United States.

2. The trust shall vest legal title to its assets in the trustees of the trust for its United States policyholders and ceding insurers, their assigns and successors in interest.

3. The trust and the assuming insurer shall be subject to examination as determined by the Commission.

4. The trust described herein must remain in effect for as long as the assuming insurer shall have outstanding obligations due under the reinsurance agreements subject to the trust.

5. No later than February 28 of each year the trustees of the trust shall report to the Commission in writing setting forth the balance of the trust and listing the trust's investments at the preceding year end and shall certify the date of termination of the trust, if so planned, or certify that the trust shall not expire prior to the next following December 31. (1991, c. 264; 1994, c. 647.)

§ 38.2-1316.3. Credit allowed a foreign or alien ceding insurer. —
A. Except as provided in § 38.2-1316.4, credit shall be allowed a foreign or alien ceding insurer only when the assuming insurer meets one of the following criteria:

1. Credit shall be allowed when the assuming insurer is licensed or accredited in this Commonwealth.

2. Credit shall be allowed when the assuming insurer is licensed in another state and maintains a surplus to policyholders in an amount not less than $20 million.

3. Credit shall be allowed when the assuming insurer maintains trust funds for the payment of the valid claims of its United States policyholders and ceding insurers, their assigns and successors in interest in amounts equal to those prescribed in subdivision 4 of subsection A of § 38.2-1316.2, provided the assuming insurer and all requisite trusts substantially comply with the provisions of subdivision 4 of subsection A and subsection B of § 38.2-1316.2.

B. Credit allowed pursuant to the provisions of this section shall not exceed the amount of credit allowed by the ceding insurer's state of domicile or entry. Furthermore, when credit is allowed pursuant to the provisions of subdivision 2 or 3 of subsection A of this section, the Commission may require the assuming insurer, either directly or through the ceding insurer, to submit to it the most recent annual statement and any other additional reports of the assuming insurer as the Commission deems necessary to determine the financial condition of the assuming insurer. (1991, c. 264.)

§ 38.2-1316.4. Credit allowed any ceding insurer. — Credit shall be allowed any ceding insurer under the following conditions:

1. Credit shall be allowed when reinsurance is ceded to an assuming insurer not meeting the requirements of § 38.2-1316.2 or § 38.2-1316.3 but only with respect to the insurance of risks located in jurisdictions where such reinsurance is required by applicable law or regulation of that jurisdiction.

2. Credit, in the form of a reduction from liability for reinsurance ceded to an assuming insurer not meeting the requirements of § 38.2-1316.2 or § 38.2-1316.3, shall be allowed in an amount not exceeding the liabilities carried by the ceding insurer and attributable to the reinsurance, provided such reduction does not exceed the amount of funds held by or on behalf of the ceding insurer, including funds held in trust for the ceding insurer, under a reinsurance contract with such assuming insurer as security for the payment of obligations thereunder, if (i) such security is held in the United States subject to withdrawal solely by, and under the exclusive control of, the ceding insurer; or (ii) in the case of a trust, held in a qualified United States financial institution. The required security may be in the form of:

a. Cash.

b. Securities listed by the Securities Valuation Office of the National Association of Insurance Commissioners and qualifying as admitted assets with adequate liquidity and readily determinable market value.

c. Clean, irrevocable, unconditional letters of credit issued or confirmed by a qualified United States financial institution, as defined in this article, no later than December 31 in respect of the year for which filing is being made, and in the possession of the ceding company on or before the filing date of its annual statement. Letters of credit meeting applicable standards of insurer acceptability as of the dates of their issuance (or confirmation) shall, notwithstanding the issuing (or confirming) institution's subsequent failure to meet applicable standards of insurer acceptability, continue to be acceptable as security until their expiration, extension, renewal, modification or amendment, whichever first occurs.

d. Any other form of security acceptable to the Commission. (1991, c. 264.)

§ **38.2-1316.5. Terms of agreements.** — A. The reinsurance agreement for which credit is allowed under this article shall contain the following provisions:

1. A provision making the reinsurance payable by the assuming insurer on the basis of the liability of the ceding insurer under the contract or contracts reinsured without diminution because of the insolvency of the ceding insurer;

2. A provision making the reinsurance payable directly to the ceding insurer or to its domiciliary liquidator or receiver except (i) where the contract specifically provides another payee of the reinsurance in the event of the insolvency of the ceding insurer or (ii) where the assuming insurer with the consent of the direct insured has assumed the policy obligations of the ceding insurer as direct obligations of the assuming insurer to the payees under the policies and in substitution for the obligations of the ceding insurer to the payees;

3. A provision that the receiver, liquidator or statutory successor of an insolvent ceding insurer shall give written notice to the assuming insurer of any impending claim on the policy or bond reinsured; and

4. If the ceding insurer is a domestic insurer and the assuming insurer is not licensed or accredited in this Commonwealth, provisions in which the assuming insurer:

a. Agrees that in the event of the failure of the assuming insurer to perform its obligations under the terms of the reinsurance agreement, the assuming insurer, at the request of the ceding insurer, shall submit to the jurisdiction of any court of competent jurisdiction in any state of the United States, will comply with all requirements necessary to give such court jurisdiction, and will abide by the final decision of such court or of any appellate court in the event of an appeal; and

b. Designate the Commission or a designated attorney as its true and lawful attorney upon whom may be served any lawful process in any action, suit or proceeding instituted by or on behalf of the ceding company.

B. The notice required by subdivision 3 of subsection A shall be given within a reasonable time after the claim is filed in the insolvency proceeding. While waiting for the settlement of the claim, any assuming insurer at its own expense may investigate the claim and interpose in the proceeding in which the claim is to be adjudicated, any defense it considers available to the ceding insurer or its receiver, liquidator or statutory successor. The expense incurred by the assuming insurer shall be chargeable, subject to the approval of the court, against the insolvent ceding insurer as part of the expense of liquidation. The expense shall be chargeable to the extent of the proportionate share of any benefit that accrues to the ceding insurer solely as a result of the defense undertaken by the assuming insurer. Where two or more assuming insurers are involved in the same claim and a majority of interest elect to interpose a defense to the claim, the expense shall be apportioned according to the terms of the reinsurance agreement as though the expense had been incurred by the ceding insurer.

C. The requirements of this section shall not apply when credit is allowed pursuant to the provisions of subdivision 1 of § 38.2-1316.4. (1991, c. 264.)

§ **38.2-1316.6. Purpose, calculation and effect of reinsurance credits.** — A. For the purpose of determining the financial condition of a ceding insurer, the ceding insurer shall receive credit for any reinsurance for which credit is allowed under this article, calculated as follows:

1. For reinsurance of the whole or any part of any risk other than those risks specified in subdivision 2 of this subsection, the ceding insurer shall receive credit for the reinsurance by way of deduction from its:

a. Unearned premium liability specified in §§ 38.2-1312 and 38.2-1315 or § 38.2-4610.1, as the case may be; and

144

b. Loss and expense reserve liability specified in § 38.2-1314 or § 38.2-4609, as the case may be, except in the case of reinsurance covering a loss paid by the ceding insurer for which payment is owed but has not been made by the assuming insurer, the ceding insurer shall receive credit as an admitted asset for the amount owed by the assuming insurer until the payment is made. Reinsurance ceded to an assuming insurer may be deducted on the basis of the original premiums and original terms except that excess loss or catastrophe reinsurance may be deducted only on the basis of actual reinsurance premiums and actual reinsurance terms.

2. For reinsurance of the whole or any part of any life insurance, annuity or accident and sickness insurance risk, the ceding insurer shall receive credit by way of deduction from its reserve liability, specified in § 38.2-1311. The credit shall not exceed the amount which the ceding insurer would have reserved on the reinsured portion of the risk if there had been no reinsurance.

B. For the purpose of determining the financial condition of any reinsurer, the reinsurer shall establish a reserve liability at least equal to the amount that it would be required to maintain in accordance with this title if it were the direct insurer of the assumed risks as specified in the reinsurance agreement. The reinsurer shall establish unearned premium liability equal to the amount of the deduction specified in subdivision 1 of subsection A of this section.

C. The Commission shall disallow any credit for any reinsurance found by it to have been arranged for the purpose principally of deception or financial statement distortion as to any insurer's financial condition as of the date of any financial statement of the insurer. Without limiting the general purport of this provision, reinsurance of any substantial part of the ceding insurer's outstanding risks contracted for in fact within four months prior to the date of any such financial statement and canceled in fact within four months after the date of such statement, or reinsurance under which the assuming insurer bears no substantial insurance risk of net loss to itself, shall prima facie be deemed to have been arranged for the purpose principally of deception or financial statement distortion within the intent of this provision. (1991, c. 264.)

§ 38.2-1316.7. Rules and regulations. — The Commission may adopt rules and regulations implementing the provisions of this article. (1991, c. 264.)

§ 38.2-1316.8. Reinsurance agreements affected. — A. The provisions of this article shall apply to all cessions after the effective date of this article under reinsurance agreements which have had an inception, anniversary or renewal date not less than six months after July 1, 1991.

B. Credits for cessions under reinsurance agreements in force on July 1, 1991, or commenced within six months thereafter shall be governed by the requirements for such credits in effect on June 30, 1991, until the first occurring anniversary or renewal date after December 31, 1991. (1991, c. 264.)

ARTICLE 4.

Examinations.

§ 38.2-1317. Examinations; when authorized or required. — A. Whenever the Commission considers it expedient for the protection of the interests of the people of this Commonwealth, it may make or direct to be made an examination into the affairs of any person licensed to transact any insurance business in this Commonwealth or any other person subject to the jurisdiction of the Commission pursuant to provisions of this title. The

Commission may also make or direct to be made, whenever necessary or advisable an examination into the affairs of:

1. Any person having a contract under which he has the exclusive or dominant right to manage or control any licensed insurer,

2. Any person holding the shares of capital stock or policyholder proxies of any domestic insurer amounting to control as defined in § 38.2-1322 either as voting trustee or otherwise,

3. Any person engaged or assisting in, or proposing or claiming to engage or assist in the promotion or formation of a domestic insurer, or

4. Any person seeking a license to transact any insurance business in this Commonwealth.

B. The Commission shall examine or cause to be examined every domestic insurer at least once in every five years; however, on or after January 1, 1993, the Commission shall examine every insurer licensed in this Commonwealth at least once in every five years.

C. The examination of any foreign or alien insurer or any other foreign or alien person subject to examination shall be made to the extent practicable in cooperation with the insurance departments of other states.

D. Instead of making its own examination, the Commission may accept a full report of the examination of a foreign or alien person, duly authenticated by the insurance supervisory official of the state of domicile or of entry until January 1, 1994. Thereafter, such reports may only be accepted if:

1. The insurance department was at the time of the examination accredited under the National Association of Insurance Commissioners' (NAIC) Financial Regulation Standards and Accreditation Program;

2. The examination is performed under the supervision of such an accredited insurance department or with the participation of one or more examiners who are employed by an accredited insurance department and who, after a review of the examination work papers and report, state under oath that the examination was performed in a manner consistent with the standards and procedures required by their insurance department; or

3. The Commission determines, in its sole discretion, that the examination was performed in a manner consistent with standards and procedures employed by the Commission in the examination of domestic insurers, and the report of examination is duly authenticated by the insurance supervisory official of the insurer's state of domicile or entry. (Code 1950, §§ 38-125, 38-126, 38-216, 38-253.40, 38-253.86, 38-516; 1952, c. 317, § 38.1-174; 1972, c. 836; 1973, c. 504; 1977, c. 321; 1986, c. 562; 1992, c. 588; 1996, c. 47.)

Law Review. — For survey of Virginia law on insurance for the year 1972-1973, see 59 Va. L. Rev. 1535 (1973).

§ 38.2-1317.1. Examinations; nature and scope. — A. In scheduling and determining the nature, scope and frequency of examinations, the Commission shall consider such matters as the conduct of business in the marketplace, results of financial statement analyses and ratios, changes in management or ownership, actuarial opinions, reports of independent certified public accountants and other criteria as set forth in any Examiners' Handbook, or any successor publications, adopted by the NAIC and in effect when the Commission exercises discretion under this article.

Procedures for examinations concerning the conduct of business in the marketplace shall be exclusively subject to the provisions of §§ 38.2-218 through 38.2-222 and §§ 38.2-1318 and 38.2-1319.

B. For purposes of completing an examination of any company under this article, the Commission may examine or investigate any person, or the business of any person, in so far as such examination or investigation is, in the sole discretion of the Commission, necessary or material to the examination of the company.

C. The examination of any alien insurer or person shall be limited to its insurance transactions in the United States unless the Commission considers a complete examination of the alien insurer or person to be necessary.

D. As used in this article:

"Company" means any person engaging in or proposing or attempting to engage in any transaction or kind of insurance or surety business and any person or group of persons who, pursuant to the provisions of this title, Title 58.1, or any rule or regulation promulgated by the Commission, may otherwise be subject to the administrative or regulatory authority of the Commission as set forth in the provisions of this title.

"Insurance department" means the supervising regulatory officials of a given state who are responsible for administering the insurance laws of said state.

"Insurer" means an insurance institution as defined by § 38.2-602.

"Person" means any association, aggregate of individuals, business, company, corporation, individual, joint-stock company, Lloyds type of organization, organization, partnership, receiver, reciprocal or interinsurance exchange, trustee or society, or any affiliate thereof. (1992, c. 588.)

§ 38.2-1318. Examinations; how conducted. — A. Whenever the Commission examines the affairs of any person, as set forth in § 38.2-1317, it may appoint as examiners one or more competent persons.

1. To the extent practicable, the examiners shall be regular employees of the Commission.

2. No examiner may be appointed by the Commission if such examiner, either directly or indirectly, has a conflict of interest or is affiliated with the management of or owns a pecuniary interest in any person subject to examination under this article; however, this section shall not be construed to automatically preclude an examiner from being:

a. A policyholder or claimant under an insurance policy;

b. A grantor of a mortgage or similar instrument on the examiner's residence to a regulated entity if done under customary terms and in the ordinary course of business;

c. An investment owner in shares of regulated diversified investment companies; or

d. A settlor or beneficiary of a "blind trust" into which any otherwise impermissible holdings have been placed.

3. Notwithstanding the requirements of this subsection, the Commission may retain from time to time, on an individual basis, qualified actuaries, certified public accountants, or other similar individuals or firms who are independently practicing their professions, even though said persons may from time to time be similarly employed or retained by persons subject to examination under this article.

B. The examiners shall be instructed as to the scope of the examination, and, in conducting the examination, the examiner shall observe, to the extent practicable, those guidelines and procedures set forth in the Examiners' Handbook, or any successor publications, adopted by the NAIC and such other guidelines or procedures as the Commission may deem appropriate.

C. Every company or person from whom information is sought, its officers, directors, and agents shall provide the examiners convenient access at all reasonable hours to its books, records, files, securities, accounts, papers, documents, and any or all computer or other recordings relating to the property, assets, business and affairs of the company being examined or those of any person, including any affiliates or subsidiaries of the person examined, that are relevant to the examination.

1. The officers, directors, employees and agents of the company or person shall facilitate the examination and aid in the examination so far as it is in their power to do so.

2. The refusal of any company, by its officers, directors, employees or agents, to submit to examination or to comply with any reasonable written request of the examiners shall be grounds for suspension or refusal of, or nonrenewal of, any license or authority held by the company to engage in an insurance or other business subject to the Commission's jurisdiction. Any such proceedings for suspension, revocation or refusal of any license or authority shall be conducted pursuant to § 38.2-1040.

D. For the purpose of any investigation or proceeding under this article, the Commission or any individual designated by it may administer oaths and affirmations, subpoena witnesses, compel their attendance, take evidence and require the production of any books, papers, correspondence, memoranda, agreements or other documents or records which the Commission determines are relevant to the examination.

E. In connection with any examination, the Commission may retain attorneys, appraisers, independent actuaries, independent certified public accountants, security analysts or other professionals and specialists as examiners; the cost of which shall be borne by the company which is the subject of the examination.

F. Nothing contained in this article shall be construed to limit the Commission's authority to terminate or suspend any examination in order to pursue other legal or regulatory action pursuant to the provisions of this title.

G. Nothing contained in this article shall be construed to limit the Commission's authority to use and, if appropriate, to make public any final or preliminary examination report, any examiner or company workpapers or other documents, or any other information discovered or developed during the course of any examination in the furtherance of any legal or regulatory action which the Commission may deem appropriate. (Code 1950, §§ 38-69, 38-125; 1952, c. 317, § 38.1-175; 1986, c. 562; 1992, c. 588.)

Oral contracts. — This section and §§ 38.2-1040, 38.2-1041, 38.2-1300, and 38.2-1312 are predicated upon the assumption that insurance contracts will be in writing and that accurate records will be kept thereof; and it is essential to their due execution that the companies shall not make, and that their agents shall not be authorized to make, oral contracts to any greater extent or for any greater length of time than is reasonably required by the exigencies of the business and for the orderly conduct of their business with reasonable convenience to the public. Eastern Shore Fire Ins. Co. v. Kellam, 159 Va. 93, 165 S.E. 637 (1932).

§ 38.2-1319. Expense of examination. — A. Any person examined shall be liable for the necessary traveling and other expenses reasonably attributable to the examiners or incurred by the Commission on account of its examination. The Commission may require the person to pay either a reasonable living expense allowance or the actual living expenses of an examiner, whichever the Commission determines to be more appropriate. Where the examiner is other than a full-time employee of the Commission, the person may, in addition, be required to pay to the Commission's examiners, upon presentation of an itemized statement, consulting fees or a per diem compensation at a reasonable rate approved by the Commission.

B. Where the examination concerns a person domiciled or having its home office in this Commonwealth, the Commission may, at its discretion and for good cause, waive payment of expenses.

C. If the Commission finds the accounts to be inadequate, or inadequately kept or posted, it may employ experts to rewrite, post or balance them at the expense of the person examined if that person has failed to complete or correct the accounts after notice and reasonable opportunity has been given by the

Commission. (Code 1950, §§ 38-70, 38-125; 1952, c. 317, § 38.1-176; 1986, c. 562; 1992, c. 588.)

§ 38.2-1320. Examination reports; general description. — The Commission's examiners shall make a true report of every examination. The report shall include only facts appearing upon the books, records or other documents of the person examined or as ascertained from the sworn testimony of its directors, officers, employees, agents or other persons examined concerning its affairs and any conclusions and recommendations reasonably warranted from such facts. Findings of fact and conclusions made pursuant to any examination, and reported in any filed examination report for which the period for appeal has expired, shall be prima facie evidence in any subsequent legal or regulatory action. (Code 1950, §§ 38-127, 38-216; 1952, c. 317, § 38.1-177; 1986, c. 562; 1992, c. 588.)

§ 38.2-1320.1. Submission of examination report. — No later than ninety days following completion of any examination, the Commission shall furnish two copies of the report to the person examined and shall notify the person that he may, within thirty days, make a written submission with respect to any facts, conclusions or recommendations contained in the examination report.

1. If the report contains any recommendation for corrective action by or on behalf of the person examined, the person shall make a written submission explaining what procedures have been implemented or are anticipated with respect to each recommendation of corrective action.

2. Any person seeking to take issue with any matter contained in the examination report shall do so by including in its written submission a request for a hearing before the Commission. (1992, c. 588; 1994, c. 308.)

§ 38.2-1320.2. Filing of report on examination. — Within thirty days of the end of the period allowed for the receipt of written submissions, the Commission shall fully consider and review the report, together with any written submissions and any relevant portions of the examiner's workpapers and act upon the report by:

1. Certifying that the examination report as initially provided to the person examined, or with modifications or corrections, is the Commission's true examination report and filing such report in the offices of the Commission;

2. Rejecting the examination report with notice to the person examined that the Commission's examiners are being directed to reopen the examination for purposes of obtaining additional data, documentation or information, and resubmission pursuant to § 38.2-1320.1; or

3. Calling for an investigatory hearing before the Commission with no less than ten days' notice to the company for purposes of obtaining additional documentation, data, information and testimony. (1992, c. 588.)

§ 38.2-1320.3. Examination reports; orders and procedures. — A. A certified copy of the examination report filed pursuant to subdivision 1 of § 38.2-1320.2 shall be served upon the company by certified mail. Within thirty days of the filing of the report, the company shall file affidavits executed by each of its directors stating under oath that they have received a copy of the filed report and any related orders.

B. If the examination report reveals that the company is operating in violation of any law, regulation or prior order of the Commission, the Commission may order the company to take any action the Commission considers necessary and appropriate to cure such violation.

C. Any hearing conducted by the Commission under subdivision 2 of § 38.2-1320.1 or subdivision 3 of § 38.2-1320.2 shall be conducted as a nonadversarial confidential investigatory proceeding as necessary for the resolution of any inconsistencies, discrepancies or disputed issues apparent upon the face of the examination report or raised by or as a result of the Commission's review of relevant workpapers or by the written submission of the company. (1992, c. 588.)

§ 38.2-1320.4. Publication and use of examination reports. — A. Upon the filing of the examination report under subdivision 1 of § 38.2-1320.2, the Commission shall continue to hold the content of the examination report as private and confidential information for a period of ten days except to the extent provided in § 38.2-1320.3. Thereafter, the Commission may open the report for public inspection so long as no court of competent jurisdiction has stayed its publication.

B. Nothing contained in this Code shall prevent or be construed as prohibiting the Commission from disclosing the content of an examination report, preliminary examination report or results, or any matter relating thereto, to the insurance department of any state or country, or to law-enforcement officials of this or any other state or agency of the federal government at any time, so long as such agency or office receiving the report or matters relating thereto agrees in writing to hold it confidential and in a manner consistent with this article.

C. In the event the Commission determines that regulatory action is appropriate as a result of any examination, it may initiate any proceedings or actions as provided by law. (1992, c. 588.)

§ 38.2-1320.5. Confidentiality of ancillary information. — All working papers, recorded information, documents and copies thereof produced by, obtained by or disclosed to the Commission or any other person in the course of an examination made under this article shall be given confidential treatment, are not subject to subpoena, and may not be made public by the Commission or any other person, except to the extent provided in § 38.2-1320.4. Access may also be granted to the NAIC. Any parties receiving such papers must agree in writing prior to receiving the information to provide to it the same confidential treatment as required by this section, unless the prior written consent of the company to which it pertains has been obtained. (1992, c. 588.)

§ 38.2-1321. Records of examination preserved. — The Commission shall keep and preserve in permanent form the reports of all its official examinations, including all records, orders, exhibits or schedules filed in connection with these reports. (Code 1950, § 38-124; 1952, c. 317, § 38.1-178; 1986, c. 562; 1992, c. 588.)

§ 38.2-1321.1. Immunity from liability. — A. No cause of action shall arise nor shall any liability be imposed against the Commission, the Commission's authorized representatives or any examiner appointed by the Commission for any statements made or conduct performed in good faith while carrying out the provisions of this article.

B. No cause of action shall arise, nor shall any liability be imposed against any person for the act of communicating or delivering information or data to the Commission or the Commission's authorized representative or examiner pursuant to an examination made under this article, if such act of communication or delivery was performed in good faith and without fraudulent intent or the intent to deceive.

C. This section does not abrogate or modify in any way any common law or statutory privilege or immunity heretofore enjoyed by any person identified in subsection A of this section. (1992, c. 588.)

ARTICLE 5.

Insurance Holding Companies.

§ 38.2-1322. Definitions. — As used in this article:

"Acquiring person" means any person by whom or on whose behalf acquisition of control of any domestic insurer is to be effected.

"Affiliate" of a specific person or a person "affiliated" with a specific person means a person that directly or indirectly through one or more intermediaries, controls, is controlled by or is under common control with the person specified.

"Control," including the terms *"controlling," "controlled by"* and *"under common control with,"* means direct or indirect possession of the power to direct or cause the direction of the management and policies of a person, through (i) the ownership of voting securities, (ii) by contract other than a commercial contract for goods or nonmanagement services, or (iii) otherwise, unless the power is the result of an official position with or corporate office held by the person. Control shall be presumed to exist if any person directly or indirectly owns, controls, holds with the power to vote, or holds proxies representing collectively ten percent or more of the voting securities of any other person. This presumption may be rebutted by a showing made in the manner provided by subsection I of § 38.2-1329 that control does not exist. After giving all interested persons notice and opportunity to be heard and making specific findings to support its determination, the Commission may determine that control exists, notwithstanding the absence of a presumption to that effect.

"Insurance holding company system" means two or more affiliated persons, one or more of which is a person licensed pursuant to this title.

"Insurer" means an insurance company as defined in § 38.2-100 and means also a health maintenance organization licensed under Chapter 43 (§ 38.2-4300 et seq.) of this title.

"Material transaction" means (i) any sale, purchase, exchange, loan or extension of credit, or investment; (ii) any dividend or distribution; (iii) any reinsurance treaty or risk-sharing arrangement; (iv) any management contract, service contract or cost-sharing arrangement; (v) any merger with or acquisition of control of any corporation; or (vi) any other transaction or agreement that the Commission by order, rule or regulation determines to be material. Any series of transactions occurring within a twelve-month period that are sufficiently similar in nature as to be reasonably construed as a single transaction and that in the aggregate exceed any minimum limits shall be deemed a material transaction.

"Subsidiary" of a specified person means an affiliate directly or indirectly controlled by that person through one or more intermediaries.

"Voting security" means any security that enables the owner to vote for the election of directors. Voting security includes any security convertible into or evidencing a right to acquire a voting security. (1973, c. 505, § 38.1-178.1; 1977, c. 414, § 38.1-178.1:2; 1986, c. 562; 1992, c. 588; 1993, c. 158; 1998, c. 42.)

The 1998 amendment added the paragraph defining "Insurer."

Law Review. — For survey of Virginia law on insurance for the year 1972-1973, see 59 Va. L. Rev. 1535 (1973). For survey of Virginia law on business associations for the year 1976-77, see 63 Va. L. Rev. 1369 (1977).

§ 38.2-1323. Acquisition of control of insurers. — A. No person shall acquire or attempt to acquire, through merger or otherwise, control of any domestic insurer, or any person controlling a domestic insurer, unless the person has previously filed with the Commission and has sent to the insurer an application for approval of acquisition of control of the insurer, and the Commission has issued an order approving the application. No such merger or other acquisition of control shall be effective until a statement containing the information required by this article has been filed with the Commission, all other provisions of this section have been complied with, and the merger or acquisition of control has been approved by the Commission pursuant to this article.

B. If the merger or acquisition of an insurer not covered by subsection A of this section causes or tends to cause a substantial lessening of competition in any line of insurance and such lessening of competition is detrimental to policyholders or the public in general, then the Commission may suspend such insurer's license after giving the insurer ten days' notice and the opportunity to be heard.

C. Any notice issued pursuant to the provisions of subsection B shall be accompanied by a request for such information as required by § 38.2-1324. Any hearing held pursuant to the provisions of this section shall begin, unless waived by the insurer, within forty days of the receipt by the Commission of all material required by this subsection. (1977, c. 414, § 38.1-178.1:1; 1986, c. 562; 1992, c. 588; 1993, c. 158.)

Law Review. — For survey of Virginia law on business associations for the year 1976-77, see 63 Va. L. Rev. 1369 (1977).

§ 38.2-1324. Contents of application. — A. The application filed with the Commission under § 38.2-1323 shall be made under oath or affirmation and shall contain the following information:

1. The name and address of each acquiring person including:

a. If the acquiring person is a natural person, his principal occupation, all offices and positions held during the past five years, and any conviction of crimes other than minor traffic violations during the past ten years; and

b. If the acquiring person is not a natural person, (i) a report of the nature of its business operations during the existence of the acquiring person and any of its predecessors, not to exceed five years; (ii) an informative description of the business intended to be done by the person and the person's subsidiaries; and (iii) a list of all individuals who are or who have been selected to become directors or executive officers of the person or who perform or will perform functions appropriate to those positions. The report shall include the information required by subdivision 1 a of this subsection.

2. The source, nature, and amount of the consideration used or to be used in effecting the acquisition of control, a description of any transaction in which funds were or are to be obtained for that purpose, and the identity of persons furnishing the consideration. However, where a source of the consideration is a loan made in the lender's ordinary course of business, the identity of the lender shall remain confidential if requested by the person filing the application;

3. Fully audited financial information regarding the earnings and financial condition of each acquiring person during the existence of the acquiring person or the predecessors, not to exceed five years, and similar unaudited information as of a date not earlier than ninety days prior to the filing of the application;

4. Any plans or proposals that each acquiring person may have to liquidate the insurer, to sell its assets or merge or consolidate it with any person, or to

make any other material change in its business or corporate structure or management;

5. The number of shares of any security of the insurer that each acquiring person proposes to acquire and the terms of the acquisition;

6. The amount of each class of any such security that each acquiring person beneficially owns or has a right to acquire beneficial ownership of;

7. A full description of any contracts, arrangements or understandings with respect to any security in which an acquiring person is involved, including but not limited to transfer of any of the securities, joint ventures, loan or option arrangements, puts or calls, guarantees of loans, guarantees against loss or guarantees of profits, division of losses or profits, or the giving or withholding of proxies. The description shall identify the persons with whom the contracts, arrangements or understandings have been made;

8. A description of any acquiring person's purchase of any such security during the twelve calendar months preceding the filing of the application, including the dates of purchases, names of the purchasers, and consideration paid or agreed to be paid for the security;

9. A description of any recommendations to purchase any such security made by any acquiring person or by any person based upon interviews or at the suggestion of any acquiring person during the twelve calendar months preceding the filing of the application;

10. Copies of all tender offers, requests or invitations for tenders of exchange offers and agreements to acquire or exchange any such security and of additional related soliciting material which has been distributed;

11. The terms of any agreement, contract or understanding made with any broker-dealer as to solicitation of these securities for tender and the amount of any associated fees, commissions or other compensation to be paid to broker-dealers; and

12. Any additional information the Commission may prescribe as necessary or appropriate for the protection of the policyholders or the public.

B. If the person required to file the application referred to in § 38.2-1323 is a partnership, limited partnership, syndicate or other group, the Commission may require that the information called for by subsection A of this section be given with respect to (i) each partner of the partnership or limited partnership, (ii) each member of the syndicate or group, and (iii) each person who controls any partner or member. If any partner, member or person is a corporation, or if the person required to file the application referred to in § 38.2-1323 is a corporation, the Commission may require that information be given for the corporation, each officer, and director of the corporation, and each person who is directly or indirectly the beneficial owner of more than ten percent of the outstanding voting securities of the corporation as required by subsection A of this section.

C. If any material change occurs in the facts set forth in the application filed with the Commission and sent to an insurer pursuant to § 38.2-1323, an amendment setting forth the change, together with copies of all documents and other material relevant to the change, shall be filed with the Commission and sent to the insurer within two business days after the person filing the application learns of the change. (1977, c. 414, § 38.1-178.1:2; 1986, c. 562.)

Law Review. — For survey of Virginia law on business associations for the year 1976-77, see 63 Va. L. Rev. 1369 (1977).

§ 38.2-1325. Alternate filing materials. — If any acquisition referred to in § 38.2-1323 is proposed to be made by means of a registration statement under the Securities Act of 1933 or in circumstances requiring the disclosure of similar information under the Securities Exchange Act of 1934, or under the Take-Over-Bid Disclosure Act (§ 13.1-528 et seq.), the person required by § 38.2-1323 to file an application may use these documents in furnishing the required information. (1977, c. 414, § 38.1-178.1:3; 1986, c. 562.)

Editor's note. — Section 13.1-528 et seq., referred to in this section, was repealed by Acts 1989, c. 408.

§ **38.2-1326. Approval by Commission.** — The Commission shall approve the application required by § 38.2-1323 unless, after giving notice and opportunity to be heard, it determines that:

1. After the change of control, the insurer would not be able to satisfy the requirements for the issuance of a license to write the classes of insurance for which it is presently licensed;

2. The acquisition of control would lessen competition substantially or tend to create a monopoly in insurance in this Commonwealth;

3. The financial condition of any acquiring person might jeopardize the financial stability of the insurer, or prejudice the interest of its policyholders;

4. Any plans or proposals of the acquiring party to liquidate the insurer, sell its assets or consolidate or merge it with any person, or to make any other material change in its business or corporate structure or management, are unfair and unreasonable to policyholders of the insurer and not in the public interest;

5. The competence, experience, and integrity of those persons who would control the operation of the insurer are such that it would not be in the interest of policyholders of the insurer and of the public to permit the acquisition of control; or

6. After the change of control, the insurer's surplus to policyholders would not be reasonable in relation to its outstanding liabilities or adequate to its financial needs. (1977, c. 414, § 38.1-178.1:4; 1986, c. 562.)

Law Review. — For survey of Virginia law on business associations for the year 1976-77, see 63 Va. L. Rev. 1369 (1977).

§ **38.2-1327. Time for hearing; order of Commission.** — Any hearing held pursuant to § 38.2-1326 shall begin within forty days of the date the application is filed with the Commission. In approving any application filed pursuant to § 38.2-1323, the Commission may include in its order any conditions, stipulations, or provisions which the Commission determines to be necessary to protect the interests of the policyholders of the insurer and the public. (1977, c. 414, § 38.1-178.1:6; 1986, c. 562.)

§ **38.2-1328. Exemption.** — The provisions of §§ 38.2-1323 through 38.2-1327 shall not apply to any acquisition that the Commission, by order, exempts from those sections. Acquisitions granted exemption shall include those which (i) have not been made or entered into for the purpose of and do not have the effect of changing or influencing the control of a domestic insurer, or (ii) otherwise are not comprehended within these sections. (1977, c. 414, § 38.1-178.1:7; 1986, c. 562.)

§ **38.2-1329. Registration of insurers that are members of holding company system.** — A. Each insurer licensed to do business in this Commonwealth that is a member of an insurance holding company system shall register with the Commission. Any insurer subject to registration under this section shall register within fifteen days after it becomes subject to registration, unless the Commission extends the time for registration for good cause shown.

B. 1. This section shall not apply to:

a. Any foreign insurer subject to disclosure requirements and standards adopted by statute or regulation in the jurisdiction of its domicile that are substantially similar to those contained in this section; or

b. Any insurer, information, or transaction if and to the extent that the Commission exempts the same from this section.

2. Any licensed insurer that is a member of a holding company system but not subject to registration under this section may be required by the Commission to furnish a copy of the registration statement, or other information filed by the insurer, with the insurance regulatory authority of its domiciliary jurisdiction.

C. Each insurer subject to registration under this section shall file a registration statement on a form provided by the Commission. Such statement shall contain current information on:

1. The capital structure, general financial condition, ownership, and management of the insurer and any person controlling the insurer;

2. The identity of every member of the insurance holding company system;

3. The following agreements in force, continuing relationships and transactions currently outstanding between the insurer and its affiliates:

a. Loans, other investments, or purchases, sales or exchanges of securities of the affiliates by the insurer or of the insurer by its affiliates;

b. Purchases, sales, or exchanges of assets;

c. Transactions not in the ordinary course of business;

d. Guarantees or undertakings for the benefit of an affiliate that result in an actual contingent exposure of the insurer's assets to liability, other than insurance contracts entered into in the ordinary course of the insurer's business;

e. All management and service contracts and all cost-sharing arrangements, other than cost allocation arrangements based upon generally accepted accounting principles; and

f. Reinsurance agreements or other risk-sharing arrangements; and

4. Other matters relating to transactions between registered insurers and any affiliates which may be included from time to time in any registration forms adopted or approved by the Commission.

D. If information is not material for the purposes of this section, it need not be disclosed on the registration statement filed pursuant to subsection B of this section. Unless the Commission prescribes otherwise, information about transactions that are not material transactions shall not be deemed material for purposes of this section.

E. Each registered insurer shall report all additional material transactions with affiliates and any material changes in previously reported material transactions with affiliates on amendment forms provided by the Commission. Each insurer shall make its report within fifteen days after the end of the month in which it learns of each additional material transaction or material change in material transaction. Each insurer shall report to the Commission all dividends and other distributions to shareholders within two business days following their declaration. Each registered insurer shall also keep current the information required by subsection C of this section by filing an amendment to its registration statement within 120 days after the end of each fiscal year of the ultimate controlling person of the insurance holding company system.

F. The Commission shall terminate the registration of any insurer that demonstrates it no longer is a member of an insurance holding company system.

G. The Commission may require or allow two or more affiliated insurers subject to registration under this section to file a consolidated registration statement or consolidated reports amending their consolidated registration statement or their individual registration statements.

H. The Commission may allow an insurer which is authorized to do business in this Commonwealth and which is part of an insurance holding company system, to register on behalf of any affiliated insurer required to register under subsection A of this section and to file all information and material required to be filed under this section.

I. Any person may file with the Commission a disclaimer of affiliation with any authorized insurer. The disclaimer shall fully disclose all material relationships and bases for affiliation between the person and the insurer as well as the basis for disclaiming the affiliation. After a disclaimer has been filed, the insurer shall be relieved of any registering or reporting requirements under this section that may arise out of the insurer's relationship with the person unless and until the Commission disallows the disclaimer. The Commission shall disallow the disclaimer only after giving all interested parties notice and opportunity to be heard. Any disallowance shall be supported by specific findings of fact. (1973, c. 505, § 38.1-178.2; 1977, c. 414; 1986, c. 562; 1992, c. 588.)

Law Review. — For survey of Virginia law on business associations for the year 1976-77, see 63 Va. L. Rev. 1369 (1977).

§ **38.2-1330. Standards for transactions with affiliates; adequacy of surplus; dividends and other distributions.** — A. Material transactions by registered insurers with their affiliates shall be subject to the following standards:

1. The terms shall be fair and reasonable;

2. Charges or fees for services performed shall be reasonable;

3. Expenses incurred and payments received shall be allocated to the insurer in conformity with customary insurance accounting practices consistently applied;

4. The books, accounts, and records of each party shall disclose clearly and accurately the precise nature and details of the transactions; and

5. The insurer's surplus to policyholders following any dividends or distributions to shareholder affiliates shall be reasonable in relation to the insurer's outstanding liabilities and adequate to its financial needs.

B. For purposes of this article, in determining whether an insurer's surplus to policyholders is reasonable in relation to the insurer's outstanding liabilities and adequate to its financial needs, the following factors, among others, shall be considered:

1. The size of the insurer as measured by its assets, capital and surplus, reserves, premium writings, insurance in force, and other appropriate criteria;

2. The extent to which the insurer's business is diversified among different classes of insurance;

3. The number and size of risks insured in each class of business;

4. The extent of the geographical dispersion of the insurer's insured risk;

5. The nature and extent of the insurer's reinsurance program;

6. The quality, diversification, and liquidity of the insurer's investment portfolio;

7. The recent past and projected future trend in the size of the insurer's surplus to policyholders;

8. The surplus to policyholders maintained by other comparable insurers;

9. The adequacy of the insurer's reserves; and

10. The quality and liquidity of investments in subsidiaries. The Commission in its judgment may classify any investment as a nonadmitted asset for the purpose of determining the adequacy of surplus to policyholders.

C. No insurer subject to registration under § 38.2-1329 shall pay any extraordinary dividend or make any other extraordinary distribution to its shareholders or confer any rights on its shareholders regarding the dividend or distribution until approved by the Commission. The Commission must approve or disapprove the distribution within thirty days after receiving notice of the declaration of distribution. If the Commission does not disapprove the distribution within the thirty-day period, the distribution shall be considered approved.

D. For purposes of this section, an extraordinary dividend or distribution includes any dividend or distribution of cash or other property, whose fair market value together with that of other dividends or distributions made within the preceding twelve months exceeds the lesser of either (i) ten percent of the insurer's surplus to policyholders as of the immediately preceding December 31, or (ii) the net gain from operations of the insurer, if the insurer is a life insurer, or the net income, if the insurer is not a life insurer, not including realized capital gains, for the twelve-month period ending the immediately preceding December 31, but shall not include pro rata distributions of any class of the insurer's own securities. In determining whether a dividend or distribution is extraordinary, an insurer other than a life insurer may carry forward net income from the second and third preceding calendar years, not including realized capital gains, less dividends paid in the second and immediately preceding calendar years. (1973, c. 505, § 38.1-178.3; 1986, c. 562; 1987, c. 417; 1992, c. 588.)

§ 38.2-1331. Commission approval required for certain transactions.

— A. Prior written approval of the Commission shall be required for:

1. Any material transaction between a domestic insurer and any of its affiliates involving (i) more than either three percent of the insurer's admitted assets or twenty-five percent of the insurer's surplus, whichever is less, as of the immediately preceding December 31 and/or (ii) any reinsurance treaty or risk-sharing arrangement, or modifications thereto, in which the reinsurance premium or anticipated change in the insurer's liabilities equals or exceeds five percent of the insurer's surplus to policyholders reported on the immediately preceding December 31; and/or

2. Any investment in affiliated companies if on the date of investment, the sum of the insurer's investments in affiliated companies exceeds or will exceed one or more of the following: fifty percent of the surplus to policyholders reported on the immediately preceding December 31, ten percent of admitted assets reported on the immediately preceding December 31, or fifty percent of the surplus to policyholders at the time application is made to the Commission for approval of the transaction.

For the purpose of this section, an insurer's investment in affiliated companies is the sum of (i) the assets held by the insurer that represent securities issued by or, if not in security form, equity or debt interests in companies of the affiliate system; (ii) loans or extensions of credit to any person who is not an affiliate, where the insurer makes such loans or extensions of credit with the agreement or understanding that the proceeds of such transactions, in whole or substantial part, are to be used to make loans or extensions of credit to, to purchase assets of, or to make investments in, any affiliate of the insurer making such loans or such extensions of credit; (iii) the assets of the insurer that are pledged on behalf of companies in the holding company system; and (iv) the aggregate guarantees for loans or extensions of credit made to affiliates which result in an actual contingent exposure of the insurer's assets to liability. To the extent not already provided in this paragraph, the sum shall include for all affiliated companies other than domestic and foreign insurance company subsidiaries and health maintenance organization subsidiaries (i) total net moneys or other considerations expended and obligations assumed in the acquisition or formation of a subsidiary, including all organizational expenses and contributions to capital and surplus of such subsidiary whether or not represented by the purchase of capital stock or issuance of other securities and (ii) all amounts expended in acquiring additional common stock, preferred stock, debt obligations, and other securities and all contributions to the capital or surplus of a subsidiary subsequent to its acquisition or formation.

For the purposes of this section, a "transaction between a domestic insurer and any of its affiliates" includes any transaction between a domestic insurer and a nonaffiliate if such transaction involves (i) any loan or extension of credit where the insurer makes such loan or extension of credit with the agreement or understanding that the proceeds of such transaction, in whole or substantial part, are to be used to make any loan or extension of credit to, to purchase assets of, or to make investments in any affiliate of the insurer or (ii) a reinsurance agreement or risk-sharing arrangement, or modifications thereto, which requires as consideration the transfer of assets from an insurer to a nonaffiliate, if an agreement or understanding exists between the insurer and the nonaffiliate that any portion of such assets will be transferred to one or more affiliates of the insurer.

Failure of the Commission to act within sixty days after notification by the insurer shall constitute approval of the transaction.

B. Nothing contained in this section shall authorize or permit any transaction that would be otherwise contrary to law.

C. The Commission, in reviewing any material transaction under this section, shall consider whether the material transaction complies with the standards set forth in § 38.2-1330 and whether it may adversely affect the interest of policyholders. The Commission shall set forth the specific reasons for the disapproval of any material transactions.

D. The approval of any material transaction under this section shall be deemed an amendment under subsection E of § 38.2-1329 to an insurer's registration statement without further filing.

E. This section shall not apply to a material transaction that is a dividend or distribution. (1977, c. 414, § 38.1-178.3:1; 1986, c. 562; 1989, c. 606; 1992, c. 588; 1993, c. 158; 1994, c. 308.)

Law Review. — For survey of Virginia law on business associations for the year 1976-77, see 63 Va. L. Rev. 1369 (1977).

§ 38.2-1332. Examinations. — A. In addition to the powers the Commission has under Article 4 (§ 38.2-1317 et seq.) of this chapter, the Commission shall also have the power to order any insurer registered under § 38.2-1329 to produce any records, books, or other information papers in the possession of the insurer or its affiliates necessary to determine the financial condition or legality of conduct of the insurer. If the insurer fails to comply with the order, the Commission shall have the power to examine its affiliates to obtain the information.

B. The Commission shall exercise its power under subsection A of this section only if the examination of the insurer under Article 4 of this chapter is inadequate or the interests of the policyholders of the insurer may be adversely affected.

C. The Commission may retain at the registered insurer's expense any attorneys, actuaries, accountants and other experts reasonably necessary to assist in the conduct of the examination under subsection A of this section. Any persons so retained shall be under the direction and control of the Commission and shall act in a purely advisory capacity.

D. Each insurer producing books and papers for examination records pursuant to subsection A of this section shall be liable for and shall pay the expense of the examination in accordance with the provisions of Article 4 of this chapter.

E. The Commission may retain at the acquiring person's expense any attorneys, actuaries, accountants and other experts reasonably necessary to assist in the review of the contents of any application filed pursuant to § 38.2-1323. (1973, c. 505, § 38.1-178.4; 1986, c. 562; 1992, c. 588.)

§ 38.2-1333. Confidential treatment of information and documents.
— All information, documents, and copies obtained by or disclosed to the Commission or any other person in the course of an examination or investigation made pursuant to § 38.2-1332, and all information reported pursuant to § 38.2-1329, shall be confidential and shall not be made public by the Commission or any other person without the prior written consent of the insurer to which they pertain. However, this provision shall not apply to information given to insurance departments in other states. After an insurer and its affiliates have been given notice and opportunity to be heard, the Commission may publish all or any part of the information and materials referred to in this section in any manner it considers appropriate, if it determines that the interests of policyholders or the public will be served by the publication. (1973, c. 505, § 38.1-178.5; 1986, c. 562.)

§ 38.2-1334. Revocation, suspension, or nonrenewal of insurer's license.
— Whenever it appears to the Commission that any person has committed a violation of this article that makes the continued operation of an insurer contrary to the interests of policyholders or the public, the Commission after giving notice and an opportunity to be heard, may suspend, revoke or refuse to renew the insurer's license to transact business in this Commonwealth for whatever period it finds is required for the protection of policyholders or the public. Any such action shall be supported by specific findings of fact and conclusions of law. (1973, c. 505, § 38.1-178.9; 1986, c. 562.)

§ 38.2-1334.1. Voting of securities, injunctions and sequestration of voting securities.
— A. No security which is the subject of any agreement or arrangement regarding acquisition, or which is acquired or to be acquired, in contravention of the provisions of this article or of any rule, regulation or order issued by the Commission hereunder, may be voted at any shareholders' meeting, or may be counted for quorum purposes, and any action of shareholders requiring the affirmative vote of a percentage of shares may be taken as though such securities were not issued and outstanding. However, no action taken at any such meeting shall be invalidated by the voting of such securities, unless the action would materially affect control of an insurer subject to any provision of this article or unless the Commission or other court of this Commonwealth has so ordered. If the insurer has reason to believe that any security of the insurer has been or is about to be acquired in contravention of the provisions of this article or of any rule, regulation or order issued by the Commission hereunder, the insurer may apply to the Commission to enter an order (i) enjoining any offer or agreement of merger made in contravention of § 38.2-1331; (ii) enjoining any offer, request, invitation, agreement or acquisition made in contravention of § 38.2-1323; (iii) enforcing any rule, regulation

or order issued by the Commission under the foregoing sections to enjoin the voting of any security so acquired; or (iv) voiding any vote of such security already cast at any meeting of shareholders or providing for such other equitable relief as the nature of the case and the interest of the insurer's policyholders, creditors and shareholders or the public may require.

B. Whenever it appears to the Commission that any person has committed or is about to commit a violation of this article, the Commission may enter an order enjoining such person from violating or continuing to violate this article or any such rule or order, and for such other equitable relief as the nature of the case and the interests of the domestic insurer's policyholders or the public may require.

C. In any case where a person has acquired or is proposing to acquire any voting securities in violation of this article or any rule, regulation or order issued by the Commission hereunder, the Commission may, after reasonable notice, upon application of the insurer or application of the Commissioner of Insurance, seize or sequester any voting securities of the insurer owned directly or indirectly by the person, and issue the order with respect thereto as may be appropriate to effectuate the provisions of this article.

Notwithstanding any other provisions of law, for the purposes of this article, the situs of the ownership of the securities of domestic insurers shall be deemed to be in this Commonwealth.

D. The actions authorized by this section are in addition to any remedies provided for by other sections of this title and may be imposed, in addition to or in lieu of any other penalties or actions provided for by law, whenever such actions involve a person that is neither domiciled nor licensed in this Commonwealth. (1993, c. 158.)

§ **38.2-1334.2. Recovery.** — A. If an order for liquidation or rehabilitation of a domestic insurer has been entered, the receiver appointed under such order shall have a right to recover on behalf of the insurer (i) from any parent corporation or holding company or person or affiliate who otherwise controlled the insurer, the amount of distributions (other than distributions of shares of the same class of stock) paid by the insurer on its capital stock or (ii) any payment in the form of a bonus, termination settlement or extraordinary lump sum salary adjustment made by the insurer or its subsidiary or subsidiaries to a director, officer or employee, where the distribution or payment pursuant to (i) or (ii) is made at any time during the one year preceding the petition for liquidation, conservation or rehabilitation, as the case may be, subject to the limitations of subsections B, C and D of this section.

B. No such distribution shall be recoverable if the parent or affiliate shows that, when paid, such distribution was lawful and reasonable and that the insurer did not know and could not reasonably have known that such distribution might adversely affect the ability of the insurer to fulfill its contractual obligations.

C. Any person who was a parent corporation or holding company or a person who otherwise controlled the insurer or affiliate at the time such distributions were paid shall be liable up to the amount of distributions or payments under subsection A of this section. Any person who otherwise controlled the insurer at the time such distributions were declared shall be liable up to the amount of distributions he would have received if they had been paid immediately. If two or more persons are liable with respect to the same distributions, they shall be jointly and severally liable.

D. The maximum amount recoverable under this section shall be the amount needed in excess of all other available assets of the impaired or insolvent insurer to pay its obligations and to reimburse any guaranty funds.

E. To the extent that any person liable under subsection C of this section is insolvent or otherwise fails to pay claims due from it pursuant to such subsection, its parent corporation, holding company, or person who otherwise controlled it at the time the distribution was paid shall be jointly and severally liable for any resulting deficiency in the amount recovered from such parent corporation, holding company, or person who otherwise controlled it. (1993, c. 158.)

ARTICLE 6.

Subsidiaries of Insurance Companies.

§ 38.2-1335. Definitions. — The terms defined in § 38.2-1322 shall have the same meaning in this article. (1977, c. 414, § 38.1-178.11; 1986, c. 562.)

§ 38.2-1336. Subsidiaries of insurers. — Notwithstanding the provisions of any other law, a domestic insurer shall not organize, acquire, or obtain control of any subsidiary, either by itself or in cooperation with one or more persons, unless the subsidiary is engaged in the following kinds of business:

1. Transacting any kind of insurance business authorized by the jurisdiction in which the subsidiary is incorporated;

2. Acting as an insurance broker or as an insurance agent for its parent or for any of its parent's insurer subsidiaries;

3. Investing, reinvesting or trading in securities for its own account, that of its parent, any subsidiary of its parent, or any affiliate or subsidiary;

4. Managing any investment company subject to or registered pursuant to the Investment Company Act of 1940, as amended, including related sales and services;

5. Acting as a broker-dealer subject to or registered pursuant to the Securities Exchange Act of 1934, as amended;

6. Rendering investment advice to governments, governmental agencies, corporations or other organizations or groups;

7. Rendering other services related to the operations of an insurance business including, but not limited to, actuarial, loss prevention, safety engineering, data processing, accounting, claims, appraisal and collection services;

8. Owning and managing assets that the domestic insurer could itself own or manage;

9. Acting as administrative agent for a governmental instrumentality that is performing an insurance function;

10. Financing of insurance premiums or agents;

11. Engaging in any other business activity the Commission determines to be reasonably ancillary to an insurance business; or

12. Owning a corporation or corporations engaged or organized to engage exclusively in one or more of the businesses specified in this section. (1977, c. 414, § 38.1-178.12; 1986, c. 562.)

Law Review. — For survey of Virginia law on business associations for the year 1976-77, see 63 Va. L. Rev. 1369 (1977).

§ 38.2-1337. Disclaimer of control. — 1. A domestic insurer may acquire voting securities of any company in an amount sufficient to presume control without the company's being considered a subsidiary if the domestic insurer files a disclaimer of affiliation with the Commission. The disclaimer shall disclose fully (i) the nature and purpose of the investment, (ii) all material transactions and relationships between the domestic insurer and the company, and (iii) the basis for the disclaimer. The Commission may disallow the disclaimer only after giving the domestic insurer and the company notice and an opportunity to be heard. Any disallowance shall be supported by specific findings of fact.

2. If the Commission disallows the disclaimer, the domestic insurer shall immediately take action sufficient to satisfy the Commission that the domestic insurer does not control the company. (1977, c. 414, § 38.1-178.13; 1986, c. 562.)

Law Review. — For survey of Virginia law on business associations for the year 1976-77, see 63 Va. L. Rev. 1369 (1977).

§ **38.2-1338. Applicability.** — This article shall not apply to any investment or subsidiary relationship that was in effect prior to June 1, 1977, between a domestic insurer and another company. However, no domestic insurer may increase its investment or ownership of voting securities or otherwise materially increase its control over the affairs of the company without prior approval of the Commission. (1977, c. 414, § 38.1-178.14; 1986, c. 562.)

§ **38.2-1339. Exemptions.** — Nothing in this article shall exempt any domestic insurer from the provisions of Article 5 (§ 38.2-1322 et seq.) of this chapter. (1977, c. 414, § 38.1-178.15; 1986, c. 562.)

§ **38.2-1340. Revocation, suspension, or nonrenewal of insurer's license.** — Whenever it appears to the Commission that any person has committed a violation of this article that makes the continued operation of a domestic insurer contrary to the interests of policyholders or the public, the Commission may, after giving notice and an opportunity to be heard, suspend, revoke or refuse to renew the insurer's license to do business in this Commonwealth for whatever period it finds is required for the protection of policyholders or the public. Any such action shall be supported by specific findings of fact and conclusions of law. (1977, c. 414, § 38.1-178.19; 1986, c. 562.)

ARTICLE 7.

Business Transacted with Producer-Controlled Property and Casualty Insurer Act.

§ **38.2-1341. Definitions.** — As used in this article:

"Accredited state" means a state in which the insurance department or regulatory agency responsible for administering the insurance laws of said state has qualified as meeting the minimum financial regulatory standards promulgated and established from time to time by the National Association of Insurance Commissioners' (NAIC) Financial Regulation Standards and Accreditation Program.

"Control" or *"controlled"* has the meaning ascribed in § 38.2-1322.

"Controlled insurer" means a licensed insurer which is controlled, directly or indirectly, by a producer.

"Controlling producer" means a producer who, directly or indirectly, controls an insurer.

"Foreign insurer" means any foreign or alien insurer licensed to transact the business of insurance in this Commonwealth pursuant to § 38.2-1024.

"Licensed insurer," "insurer" or *"property and casualty insurer"* means any person, firm, association or corporation duly licensed under this title to write policies or agreements providing any form of insurance as defined in §§ 38.2-

110 through 38.2-134. The following, inter alia, are not licensed insurers for the purposes of this article:

1. All risk retention groups as defined in the Superfund Amendments Reauthorization Act of 1986, Pub. L. No. 99-499, 100 Stat. 1613 (1986) and the Risk Retention Act, 15 U.S.C. Section 3901 et seq. (1982 & Supp. 1986) and § 38.2-5101 of this title;

2. All residual market pools and joint underwriting authorities or associations; and

3. Any insurer licensed as a captive insurer under Chapter 11 (§ 38.2-1100 et seq.) and any foreign insurer which is either (i) an association captive or (ii) a pure captive. An *"association captive"* is an insurer whose exclusive purpose is transacting the business of insurance and reinsurance only on risks, hazards and liabilities of the members of an insurance association comprised of any group of individuals, corporations, partnerships, associations, or governmental units or agencies whose members collectively own, control, or hold with power to vote, all of the outstanding voting securities of the association insurer. A *"pure captive"* is an insurer whose exclusive purpose is transacting the business of insurance and reinsurance only on risks, hazards, and liabilities of its parent, subsidiary companies of its parent, and associated and affiliated companies.

"Producer" means:

1. Any insurance agent, managing general agent or reinsurance intermediary subject to licensure pursuant to the provisions of Chapter 18 (§ 38.2-1800 et seq.); or

2. Any person subject to substantially similar licensure provisions of another state when, for any compensation, commission or other thing of value, such agent, intermediary or person acts on behalf of an insured other than the agent, intermediary or person, or aids in any manner, in soliciting, negotiating, procuring or effecting the making of any contract of insurance in which the insured, owner and beneficiary are other than the agent, intermediary or person. (1993, c. 158.)

§ 38.2-1342. Applicability. — A. All provisions of this article shall apply to domestic insurers.

B. Effective January 1, 1994, any foreign insurer not domiciled and licensed in an accredited state shall confirm, at least once every five years, as a condition of licensing and licensing renewal, its compliance with the provisions of this article or those of a substantially similar law enacted by an accredited state in which the insurer is licensed. The method of confirmation shall be determined by the Commission and may include examination of such foreign insurer and its controlling producer pursuant to Article 4 (§ 38.2-1317 et seq.) of Chapter 13. Any foreign insurer that is unable to confirm substantial compliance in a manner satisfactory to the Commission shall be subject to all of the provisions of this title.

C. All provisions of Article 5 (§ 38.2-1322 et seq.) of this chapter and Article 2 (§ 38.2-4230 et seq.) of Chapter 42, to the extent they are not superseded by the provisions of this article, shall continue to apply to all parties within holding company systems subject to this article. (1993, c. 158.)

§ 38.2-1343. Minimum standards. — A. The provisions of this section shall apply if, in any calendar year, the aggregate amount of gross written premium on business placed with a controlled insurer by a controlling producer is equal to or greater than five percent of the admitted assets of the controlled insurer, as reported in the controlled insurer's quarterly statement filed as of September 30 of the prior year.

B. Notwithstanding the provisions of subsection A of this section, the provisions of subsections A, C, D and E of this section shall not apply if:

1. The controlling producer (i) places insurance only with the controlled insurer, or only with the controlled insurer and a member or members of the controlled insurer's holding company system, or the controlled insurer's parent, affiliate or subsidiary and receives no compensation based upon the amount of premiums written in connection with such insurance and (ii) accepts insurance placements only from nonaffiliated subproducers and not directly from insureds; and

2. The controlled insurer, except for insurance business written through a residual market facility such as the Virginia Automobile Insurance Plan, as set forth in § 38.2-2015, or the Virginia Property Insurance Association, as set forth in Chapter 27 (§ 38.2-2700 et seq.), accepts insurance business only from a controlling producer, a producer controlled by the controlled insurer, or a producer that is a subsidiary of the controlled insurer.

C. A controlled insurer shall not accept business from a controlling producer and a controlling producer shall not place business with a controlled insurer unless there is a written contract between them specifying the responsibilities of each party, which contract has been approved by the board of directors of the insurer and contains the following minimum provisions:

1. The controlled insurer may terminate the contract for cause, upon written notice to the controlling producer. The controlled insurer shall suspend the authority of the controlling producer to write business during the pendency of any dispute regarding the cause for the termination;

2. The controlling producer shall render accounts to the controlled insurer detailing all material transactions, including information necessary to support all commissions, charges and other fees received by, or owing to, the controlling producer;

3. The controlling producer shall remit all funds due under the terms of the contract to the controlled insurer on at least a monthly basis. The due date shall be fixed so that premiums or installments thereof collected shall be remitted no later than ninety days after the effective date of any policy placed with the controlled insurer under this contract;

4. All funds collected for the controlled insurer's account shall be held by the controlling producer in a fiduciary capacity, in one or more appropriately identified bank accounts in banks that are members of the Federal Reserve System, in accordance with the provisions of the insurance law as applicable. However, funds of a controlling producer not required to be licensed in this Commonwealth shall be maintained in compliance with the requirements of the controlling producer's domiciliary jurisdiction;

5. The controlling producer shall maintain separately identifiable records of business written for the controlled insurer;

6. The contract shall not be assigned in whole or in part by the controlling producer;

7. The controlled insurer shall provide the controlling producer with its underwriting standards, rules and procedures, manuals setting forth the rates to be charged, and the conditions for the acceptance or rejection of risks. The controlling producer shall adhere to the standards, rules, procedures, rates and conditions. The standards, rules, procedures, rates and conditions shall be the same as those applicable to comparable business placed with the controlled insurer by a producer other than the controlling producer;

8. The rates and terms of the controlling producer's commissions, charges or other fees and the purposes for those charges or fees shall be specified. The rates of the commissions, charges and other fees shall be no greater than those applicable to comparable business placed with the controlled insurer by producers other than controlling producers. For purposes of this subdivison

and subdivision 7 of this subsection, examples of "comparable business" include the same lines of insurance, same kinds of insurance, same kinds of risks, similar policy limits, and similar quality of business;

9. If the contract provides that the controlling producer, on insurance business placed with the insurer, is to be compensated contingent upon the insurer's profits on that business, then such compensation shall not be determined and paid until at least five years after the premiums on liability insurance are earned and at least one year after the premiums are earned on any other insurance. In no event shall the commissions be paid until the adequacy of the controlled insurer's reserves on remaining claims has been independently verified pursuant to subdivision 1 of subsection E of this section;

10. The contract shall place a limit on the controlling producer's writings in relation to the controlled insurer's surplus and total writings. The insurer may establish a different limit for each line or sub-line of business. The controlled insurer shall notify the controlling producer when the applicable limit is approached and shall not accept business from the controlling producer if the limit is reached. The controlling producer shall not place business with the controlled insurer if it has been notified by the controlled insurer that the limit has been reached; and

11. The controlling producer may negotiate but shall not bind reinsurance on behalf of the controlled insurer on business the controlling producer places with the controlled insurer, except that the controlling producer may bind facultative reinsurance contracts pursuant to obligatory facultative agreements if the contract with the controlled insurer contains underwriting guidelines including, for both reinsurance assumed and ceded, a list of reinsurers with which such automatic agreements are in effect, the coverages and amounts or percentages that may be reinsured and commission schedules.

D. Every controlled insurer shall have an Audit Committee of the Board of Directors composed of independent directors. The Audit Committee shall annually meet with management, the insurer's independent certified public accountants, and an independent casualty actuary or other independent loss reserve specialist acceptable to the Commission to review the adequacy of the insurer's loss reserves.

E. The controlled insurer shall obtain annually prior to March 1 of each year the following data and reports:

1. In addition to any other required loss reserve certification, an opinion of an independent casualty actuary reporting loss ratios for each line of business written and attesting to the adequacy of loss reserves established for losses incurred and outstanding as of year's end (including incurred but not reported) on business placed by the producer; and

2. The controlled insurer shall annually report to the Commission the amount of commissions paid to the producer during the preceding calendar year, the percentage such amount represents of the net premiums written and comparable amounts and percentage paid to noncontrolling producers for placements of the same kinds of insurance.

The data and reports required by this subsection shall be retained by the insurer for a period of not less than five years and shall be filed with the Commission upon request. (1993, c. 158.)

§ **38.2-1344. Disclosure.** — The producer, prior to the effective date of the policy, shall deliver written notice to the prospective insured disclosing the relationship between the producer and the controlled insurer. However, if the business is placed through a subproducer who is not a controlling producer, the controlling producer shall retain in his records a signed commitment from the subproducer that the subproducer is aware of the relationship between the insurer and the producer and that the subproducer has or will notify the insured. (1993, c. 158.)

§ 38.2-1345. Penalties. — A. If the Commission finds, after providing an opportunity to be heard, that the controlling producer or any other person has not materially complied with the provisions of this article, or any regulation or order promulgated hereunder, the Commission may order the controlling producer to cease placing business with the controlled insurer.

B. If it is found that because of such material noncompliance that the controlled insurer or any policyholder thereof has suffered any loss or damage, the Commission may order the controlling producer or any other party licensed under this title to make restitution to the controlled insurer or its statutory successor, including any rehabilitator, liquidator or receiver of the insurer, for the net losses or damages incurred by the insurer or its policyholders.

C. Nothing contained in this section shall affect the right of the Commission to impose any other penalties provided for in this title.

D. Nothing contained in this section is intended to or shall in any manner alter or affect the rights of policyholders, claimants, creditors or other third parties. (1993, c. 158.)

§ 38.2-1346. Licensure. — A. No person shall act in this Commonwealth as a producer, and no resident of this Commonwealth shall act as a producer, unless such person or resident is licensed as an insurance agent, reinsurance intermediary or managing general agent pursuant to the provisions of Chapter 18 (§ 38.2-1800 et seq.) of this title.

B. As used in this section, the terms "resident" and "insurance agent" have the meanings prescribed in § 38.2-1800, and the terms "managing general agent," and "reinsurance intermediary" have the meanings set forth in §§ 38.2-1846 and 38.2-1858. (1993, c. 158.)

CHAPTER 14.

INVESTMENTS.

ARTICLE 1.

General Provisions.

§ **38.2-1400. Scope and purpose of chapter.** — This chapter applies to and regulates the investments of all domestic insurers as defined in this chapter. Upon petition to, and approval by, the Commission, any one or more provisions of this chapter shall not apply to a domestic insurer in receivership in this Commonwealth pursuant to Chapter 15 (§ 38.2-1500 et seq.) of this title. A foreign or alien insurer may invest its funds and assets in any investments that are permitted by the laws of its state or country of domicile and are of the same general character and quality as those authorized under this chapter. A foreign or alien insurer whose domiciliary jurisdiction does not regulate the investments of its insurers shall be subject to the provisions of this chapter. (1983, c. 457, § 38.1-217.1; 1986, c. 562; 1990, c. 893; 1992, c. 588; 1993, c. 55.)

§ **38.2-1401. Definitions.** — As used in this chapter:

"Admitted assets" means, for purposes of the limitations and standards imposed by Articles 1 and 2 of this chapter, the amount thereof as permitted to be reported on the statutory financial statement of the insurer most recently required to be filed with the Commission pursuant to §§ 38.2-1300 and 38.2-1301 or other similar provisions within this title, but excluding the assets allocated to separate accounts established pursuant to Article 3 (§ 38.2-1443 et seq.) of this chapter.

"Business entity" means a corporation, association, partnership, joint venture, trust, church, or religious body.

"Category 1 investment" means any investment complying with Article 1 (§ 38.2-1400 et seq.) and either Article 2 (§ 38.2-1412 et seq.) or 3 (§ 38.2-1443 et seq.), or both Articles 2 and 3, of this chapter.

"Category 2 investment" means any investment complying with Article 1, but with neither Article 2 nor Article 3, of this chapter.

"Claimants" means any owners, beneficiaries, assignees, certificate holders, or third-party beneficiaries of any insurance benefit or right arising out of and within the coverage of an insurance policy, annuity contract, benefit contract, or subscription contract.

"Date of investment" means the date on which funds are disbursed for an investment.

"Domestic governmental entity" means the United States, any state, or any municipality or district in any such state, or any political subdivision, civil division, agency or instrumentality of one or more of the foregoing.

"Fair market value" means the price that property will bring when (i) offered for sale by one who desires, but who is not obligated, to sell it; (ii) bought by one who is under no necessity of having it; and (iii) sufficient time has elapsed to allow interested buyers the opportunity to become informed of the offer for sale.

"Fixed charges" means actual interest incurred in each year on funded and unfunded debt, excluding interest on bank deposit accounts, and annual apportionment of debt discount or premium. Where interest is partially or entirely contingent upon earnings, "fixed charges" includes contingent interest payments.

"High grade obligations" means obligations which (i) are rated one or two by the Securities Valuation Office of the National Association of Insurance Commissioners or (ii) if not rated by the Securities Valuation Office, are rated in an equivalent grade by a national rating agency recognized by the Commission.

"Insurer" means a company licensed pursuant to Chapter 10 (§ 38.2-1000 et seq.), 11 (§ 38.2-1100 et seq.), 12 (§ 38.2-1200 et seq.), 25 (§ 38.2-2500 et seq.), 26 (§ 38.2-2600 et seq.), 38 (§ 38.2-3800 et seq.), 39 (§ 38.2-3900 et seq.), 40 (§ 38.2-4000 et seq.), 41 (§ 38.2-4100 et seq.), 42 (§ 38.2-4200 et seq.), 43 (§ 38.2-4300 et seq.), 45 (§ 38.2-4500 et seq.), 46 (§ 38.2-4600 et seq.) or 51 (§ 38.2-5100 et seq.) of this title.

"Life insurer" means any insurer authorized to transact life insurance or to grant annuities as defined in §§ 38.2-102 through 38.2-107 or authorized pursuant to the provisions of Chapter 38, 39, 40 or 41, or any other chapter of this title, to provide any one of the following contractual benefits in any form: death benefits, endowment benefits, annuity benefits or monument or tombstone benefits.

"Lower grade obligations" means obligations which (i) are rated four, five, or six by the Securities Valuation Office of the National Association of Insurance Commissioners or (ii) if not rated by the Securities Valuation Office, are rated in an equivalent grade by a national rating agency recognized by the Commission.

"Medium grade obligations" means obligations which (i) are rated three by the Securities Valuation Office of the National Association of Insurance Commissioners or (ii) if not rated by the Securities Valuation office, are rated in an equivalent grade by a national rating agency recognized by the Commission.

"Minimum capital and surplus" means the minimum surplus to policyholders, or minimum net worth, a particular insurer must have to obtain and maintain its license to transact business in this Commonwealth pursuant to the applicable provisions of this title. In no case shall an insurer's minimum capital and surplus be less than zero.

"Net earnings available for fixed charges" means income minus operating expenses, maintenance expenses, taxes other than income taxes, depreciation, and depletion. Extraordinary nonrecurring income and expense items are excluded from the calculation of "net earnings available for fixed charges."

"Obligation" means a bond, debenture, note or other evidence of indebtedness.

"Prohibited investment" means any investment prohibited by § 38.2-1407.

"Reserve liabilities" means those liabilities which are required to be established by an insurer for all of its outstanding insurance policies, annuity contracts, benefit contracts and subscription contracts, in accordance with this title, as amended or as hereafter amended.

"Wrap-around mortgage" means a loan made by an insurer to a borrower, secured by a mortgage or deed of trust on real property encumbered by a first mortgage or first deed of trust, where the total amount of the obligation of the borrower to the insurer under the loan is not less than the sum of (i) the principal amount initially disbursed by the insurer on account of the loan and (ii) the unpaid principal balance of the obligation secured by the preexisting mortgage or deed of trust. (1983, c. 457, § 38.1-217.2; 1986, c. 562; 1992, c. 588; 1994, c. 503; 1998, c. 42.)

The 1998 amendment, in the paragraph defining "Insurer," inserted "43 (§ 38.2-4300 et seq.)" and in the paragraph defining "Minimum capital and surplus," in the first sentence, inserted "or minimum net worth."

§ 38.2-1402. Authority to invest; classification of investments by category.

— A. A domestic insurer may invest its funds and assets in accordance with this chapter. All investments of a domestic insurer shall be classified as (i) Category 1 investments, (ii) Category 2 investments, or (iii) prohibited investments.

B. The Commission, upon application by an insurer, may classify any investments made or proposed to be made and not otherwise specifically classified in Articles 1 (§ 38.2-1400 et seq.) and 2 (§ 38.2-1412 et seq.) of this chapter as a Category 1 investment. (1983, c. 457, § 38.1-217.3; 1986, c. 562.)

§ 38.2-1403. Category 2 investments limits.

— The value of Category 2 investments shall be excluded from the value of admitted assets to the extent the value of Category 2 investments exceeds seventy-five percent of the amount by which an insurer's surplus to policyholders exceeds its minimum capital and surplus. (1983, c. 457, § 38.1-217.4; 1986, c. 562; 1992, c. 588; 1998, c. 414.)

The 1998 amendment substituted "seventy-five" for "fifty."

§ 38.2-1404. Classification of existing investments.

— Any investment held on July 1, 1983, that was permitted at the time it was made under former § 38.1-181 or former §§ 38.1-183 through 38.1-217, shall be classified as a Category 1 investment. (1983, c. 457, § 38.1-217.5; 1986, c. 562.)

§ 38.2-1405. Dates of determination.

— A. The classification by investment category of each investment, based on type of investment as set forth in §§ 38.2-1415 through 38.2-1442, inclusive, shall be determined as of the date of investment.

B. In applying any percentage limitations based on the insurer's total admitted assets or surplus to policyholders, there shall be used as a base, without regard to percentage limitations, those assets or surplus to policyholders as shown by the insurer's most recent annual or quarterly statement on file with the Commission pursuant to §§ 38.2-1300 and 38.2-1301. (1983, c. 457, § 38.1-217.6; 1986, c. 562; 1992, c. 588.)

§ 38.2-1406. Investment conversions. — Investments converted to a new form and resulting in a different investment classification under § 38.2-1402, at the election of the insurer, shall retain their previous investment classification for a period not exceeding three years unless the Commission prescribes in writing that a longer period is reasonable. Any prohibited investments shall be divested within that period. The investment conversions shall include those resulting (i) from investments acquired in satisfaction of or on account of loans, mortgages, liens, judgments, or other debts previously owing to the insurer in the course of its business, or (ii) from investments acquired through lawful distributions of assets, lawful plans of reorganization, or lawful and bona fide agreements of bulk reinsurance or of consolidation. (1983, c. 457, § 38.1-217.7; 1986, c. 562.)

§ 38.2-1407. Prohibited investments. — A. No domestic insurer shall invest in or loan funds secured by:
1. Issued shares of its own capital stock without the Commission's approval. This approval shall be based on an evaluation that indicates the investment does not adversely affect the insurer or its policyholders. The insurer shall not invest in or own more than twenty percent of its outstanding issued stock, except for the purpose of mutualization;
2. Securities of an insolvent entity;
3. Securities that, by their terms, will subject the insurer to any assessment other than for taxes or for wages;
4. Investments that, as determined by the Commission, are designed to evade any prohibition of this title; or
5. Any obligation or investment prohibited by § 38.2-1411.2.
B. Notwithstanding the provisions of this chapter, the Commission may order a domestic insurer to limit or withdraw from certain investments, or discontinue certain investment practices, to the extent the Commission finds that such investment or investment practice endangers the solvency of the insurer or is otherwise hazardous to policyholders, creditors or the public in this Commonwealth. (1983, c. 457, § 38.1-217.8; 1986, c. 562; 1992, c. 588.)

Offering of insurance "package" through subsidiary violated this section. — Ownership and operation of Blue Cross of a wholly owned subsidiary which was created to provide Blue Cross with the capability of offering its subscribers a "package" of insurance coverage including not only group health and hospitalization coverage but life and disability coverage as well, where the subsidiary's agents were all Blue Cross market representatives who worked on Blue Cross's time, used Blue Cross's computer list of customers, and discussed the sale of life insurance at Blue Cross's sales meetings, constituted activity by Blue Cross that violated §§ 38.2-4225 (now repealed) through 38.2-4227 and this section. Blue Cross v. Commonwealth ex rel. Virginia Ass'n of Life Underwriters, 230 Va. 521, 338 S.E.2d 849 (1986).

§ 38.2-1408. Authorization of investments. — No domestic insurer shall make any loan, investment, or any sale or exchange of a loan or investment, except policy loans of an insurer issuing life insurance policies or annuities, unless authorized or approved. Authorization or approval shall be made by (i) its board of directors, or other governing body, or (ii) a committee authorized by the governing body or bylaws, to make investments, loans, sales or exchanges. The minutes of the committee shall be recorded, and reports of the investments, loans, sales or exchanges authorized or approved shall be submitted to the board or other governing body at its next meeting. (1983, c. 457, § 38.1-217.9; 1986, c. 562.)

§ 38.2-1409. Powers with respect to property. — Subject to any applicable limitations and restrictions in this chapter, a domestic insurer may own, hold, maintain, manage, operate, lease, sell, convey, and collect and receive income from any property acquired as permitted in this chapter. (1983, c. 457, § 38.1-217.10; 1986, c. 562.)

§ 38.2-1410. Items not deemed to be prior liens or encumbrances. — In construing and applying this title, the following shall not be deemed prior liens or encumbrances: easements; rights-of-way; joint driveways; party wall agreements; current taxes and assessments not delinquent; restrictions as to building, use and occupancy unless there is a right of reentry or forfeiture for violation; instruments reserving mineral, oil, or timber rights; title matters for which the insurer is insured against loss by a title insurer; and leases under which rents are reserved to the owner of the real estate. (1983, c. 457, § 38.1-217.11; 1986, c. 562.)

§ 38.2-1411: Repealed by Acts 1992, c. 588.

§ 38.2-1411.1. Investment limits generally. — A. Any securities described in 15 U.S.C. § 77r-1 shall be subject to all the limitations prescribed by this chapter for investments not guaranteed by the full faith and credit of the United States. However, upon prior written application by an insurer, the Commission may, until July 1, 1992, at its discretion, allow such insurer to increase its investments in § 77r-1 securities to an amount not to exceed ten percent of the insurer's total admitted assets.

B. On and after July 1, 1992, investments made in any securities described in 15 U.S.C. § 77r-1 shall be subject to the percentage limitations and requirements set forth in this chapter. (1991, c. 283; 1992, c. 588.)

§ 38.2-1411.2. Investment limits in medium grade and lower grade obligations. — A. No domestic insurer shall acquire, directly or indirectly, any medium grade or lower grade obligations of any business entity if, after giving effect to any such acquisition, the aggregate amount of all medium grade and lower grade obligations then held by the domestic insurer would exceed twenty percent of its admitted assets, provided that:

1. No more than ten percent of its admitted assets consists of lower grade obligations;

2. No more than three percent of its admitted assets consists of lower grade obligations rated five or six by the Securities Valuation Office of the National Association of Insurance Commissioners; and

3. No more than one percent of its admitted assets consists of lower grade obligations rated six by the Securities Valuation Office of the National Association of Insurance Commissioners.

Attaining or exceeding the limit of any one category shall not preclude an insurer from acquiring obligations in other categories subject to the specific and multi-category limits.

B. No domestic insurer may invest more than an aggregate of one percent of its admitted assets in medium grade obligations issued, guaranteed or insured by any one institution nor may it invest more than one-half of one percent of its admitted assets in lower grade obligations issued, guaranteed or insured by any one business entity. In no event may a domestic insurer invest more than one percent of its admitted assets in any medium or lower grade obligations issued, guaranteed or insured by any one business entity.

C. Nothing contained in this section shall prohibit a domestic insurer from acquiring any obligation which it has committed to acquire if the insurer would have been permitted to acquire that obligation pursuant to the provisions of this chapter on the date on which such insurer committed to purchase that obligation.

D. Notwithstanding the foregoing, a domestic insurer may acquire any obligation of a business entity in which the insurer already has one or more obligations, if the obligation is acquired in order to protect an investment previously made in the obligations of the business entity; however, all such acquired obligations shall not exceed one-half of one percent of the insured's admitted assets.

E. Nothing contained in this section shall prohibit a domestic insurer from acquiring any obligation as a result of a restructuring of any obligation already held.

F. Nothing contained in this section shall require a domestic insurer to sell or otherwise dispose of any obligations legally acquired prior to July 1, 1992.

G. The Board of Directors of any domestic insurer which acquires or invests, directly or indirectly, more than two percent of its admitted assets in medium grade or lower grade obligations of any individual business entity, shall adopt a written plan for the making of such investments. The plan shall contain, in addition to guidelines with respect to the quality of the issues invested in, diversification standards including, but not limited to, standards for issuer, industry, duration, liquidity and geographic location.

H. If the Commission finds that economic or other conditions render any rating of any obligation by the Securities Valuation Office of the National Association of Insurance Commissioners obsolete or unreflective of a diminished creditworthiness of the business entity issuing such obligations, the Commission may assign the obligations to a lower grade based on the findings of a national rating agency recognized by the Commission. (1992, c. 588.)

ARTICLE 2.

Category 1 Investments.

§ **38.2-1412. Scope of article.** — This article sets forth requirements for qualifying as a Category 1 investment. If an investment or portion thereof does not comply either with this article or Article 3 (§ 38.2-1443 et seq.) of this chapter, then that investment or portion of it shall be classified as a Category 2 investment or a prohibited investment, as provided in this chapter. (1983, c. 457, § 38.1-217.15; 1986, c. 562.)

§ **38.2-1413. Investment limits for one obligor, one issue or one loan.** — A. No domestic insurer shall have at any one time any combination of investments in or loans upon the security of the property and securities of any one obligor or issuer aggregating an amount exceeding the lesser of five percent of the insurer's total admitted assets or twenty percent of the insurer's surplus to policyholders. The limitations prescribed by this section shall not apply to the following:

1. Investments in or loans upon the security of general obligations of the United States;

2. Investments in foreign securities made eligible by subsection A of § 38.2-1433;

3. Investments in mortgage pass-through securities made eligible by § 38.2-1437.1;

4. Deposits in institutions insured by a federal deposit insuring agency to the extent of coverage by such deposit insuring agency;

5. Investments in subsidiaries made eligible by § 38.2-1427.3; or

6. Investments in obligations of an agency or instrumentality of the United States made eligible by subsection B of § 38.2-1415; provided that at no time shall the insurer invest pursuant to subsection B of § 38.2-1415 in excess of ten percent of its total admitted assets in any one obligor or issuer of such obligations.

B. No domestic insurer shall invest in excess of one percent of its total admitted assets in any one issue of any obligations made eligible for investment under § 38.2-1423 or § 38.2-1424.

C. No domestic insurer shall invest in excess of one-half of one percent of its total admitted assets in any one loan made eligible by subdivision 3 of § 38.2-1434.

D. The principal loan amount disbursed, excluding advances made to enforce or protect the security for the loan, by a domestic insurer under any single wrap-around mortgage made pursuant to § 38.2-1435 shall not exceed one percent of its total admitted assets.

E. The amount loaned under § 38.2-1430 shall be subject to the limitations of this section applicable to the kinds of securities or obligations pledged in connection with the loan. (1983, c. 457, § 38.1-217.16; 1986, c. 562; 1990, c. 893; 1992, c. 588; 1995, c. 60; 1998, c. 414.)

The 1998 amendment, in subsection A, in subdivision 2, inserted "subsection A of," in subdivision 4, at the end of the sentence, deleted "or," in subdivision 5, inserted "or" and added subdivision 6.

§ **38.2-1414. Limits by type of investment.** — A. The portion of a domestic insurer's total admitted assets in the following types of investments shall not exceed:

1. Ten percent for the aggregate of investments made eligible by §§ 38.2-1416 and 38.2-1417;

2. Five percent for the investments in each agency made eligible by § 38.2-1418, and ten percent for the aggregate of investments made eligible by § 38.2-1418;

3. Ten percent for the investments made eligible by § 38.2-1419;

4. Ten percent for the investments made eligible by § 38.2-1420;

5. For the aggregate of investments made eligible under §§ 38.2-1421 and 38.2-1422, (i) ninety percent for any life insurer and (ii) forty percent for all other insurers;

6. Ten percent for the investments made eligible by subsection B of § 38.2-1421; and two percent for the investments made eligible by subsection C of § 38.2-1421;

7. Twenty percent for the investments made eligible by § 38.2-1422;

8. Ten percent for the investments made eligible by § 38.2-1423;

9. Five percent for the investments made eligible by § 38.2-1424;

10. Five percent for the investments made eligible by § 38.2-1425;

11. The lesser of fifteen percent or the amount by which an insurer's surplus to policyholders exceeds its minimum capital and surplus for the aggregate of investments made eligible by §§ 38.2-1427, 38.2-1427.1 and 38.2-1427.2, of which no more than five percent of the total admitted assets shall be in investments made eligible by § 38.2-1427.1;

12. For the aggregate of investments made eligible by § 38.2-1427.3, when combined with the insurer's total investment in affiliates, the lesser of ten percent of the insurer's admitted assets or fifty percent of the insurer's surplus to policyholders in excess of its minimum capital and surplus, provided that total investments in affiliates do not include investments made by the insurer in money market mutual funds made eligible by § 38.2-1432;

13. Ten percent for investments made eligible by subsection B of § 38.2-1433, and an amount equal to its deposit and reserve obligations incurred in a foreign country for the investments made eligible by subsection A of § 38.2-1433;

14. Two percent for the investments made eligible (including those that the

insurer is obligated to make as well as those made) by subdivision 3 of § 38.2-1434;

15. Two percent for the investments made eligible by § 38.2-1435;

16. Ten percent for the investments made eligible by § 38.2-1436;

17. For the aggregate of investments made eligible by § 38.2-1437.1, when combined with the insurer's investments in mortgages under §§ 38.2-1434 through 38.2-1436 and § 38.2-1439, (i) sixty percent for any life insurer and (ii) thirty percent for all other insurers;

18. Two percent for the investments made eligible by § 38.2-1440; and

19. Twenty-five percent for the total of investments made eligible by § 38.2-1441, of which no more than five percent of the total admitted assets shall be in investments in real property to be used primarily for hotel purposes.

B. The amount loaned under § 38.2-1430 shall be subject to the limitations of this section applicable to the kinds of securities or obligations pledged in connection with the loan. (1983, c. 457, § 38.1-217.17; 1986, c. 562; 1992, c. 588; 1993, c. 47; 1995, c. 60; 1998, c. 414.)

The 1998 amendment, in subsection A, in subdivision 6, inserted "and two percent for the investments made eligible by subsection C of § 38.2-1421," and in subdivision 13, substi- tuted "Ten percent for investments made eligible by subsection B of § 38.2-1433, and an" for "An" and inserted "subsection A of."

§ 38.2-1415. Obligations of domestic governmental entities. —

A. United States obligations. A domestic insurer may invest in any bonds, notes, warrants, and other evidences of indebtedness which are direct obligations of the United States or for which the full faith and credit of the United States are pledged for the payment of principal and interest.

B. United States agencies obligations. A domestic insurer may invest in any bonds, notes, warrants and other evidence of indebtedness which are direct obligations for the payment of money, issued by an agency or instrumentality of the United States, or obligations for the payment of money to the extent guaranteed or insured as to the payment of principal and interest by an agency or instrumentality of the United States.

C. State government obligations. A domestic insurer may invest in direct, general obligations of any state of the United States for the payment of money, or obligations for the payment of money to the extent guaranteed or insured as to the payment of principal and interest by any state of the United States, on the following conditions:

1. The state has the power to levy taxes for the prompt payment of the principal and interest of its obligations;

2. The state is not in default in the payment of principal or interest on any of its direct, guaranteed or insured obligations as of the date of investment;

3. An insurer shall not invest under this subsection more than five percent of its admitted assets in obligations issued or guaranteed by any one state; and

4. An insurer shall not invest under this subsection more than thirty percent of its admitted assets.

D. Local government obligations. A domestic insurer may invest in direct, general obligations of any political subdivision, of any state of the United States, for the payment of money, or obligations for the payment of money, to the extent guaranteed as to the payment of principal and interest, by any such political subdivision, on the following conditions:

1. The obligations are payable or guaranteed from ad valorem taxes;

2. Such political subdivision is not in default in the payment of principal or interest on any of its direct or guaranteed obligations;

3. No investment shall be made under this subsection in obligations which are secured only by special assessments for local improvements;

4. An insurer shall not invest more than five percent of its admitted assets in obligations issued or guaranteed by any one such political subdivision; and

5. An insurer shall not invest more than thirty percent of its admitted assets under this subsection.

E. Anticipation obligations. An insurer may invest in the anticipation obligations of any political subdivision of any state, all within the United States, including but not limited to bond anticipation notes, tax anticipation notes, preliminary loan anticipation notes, revenue anticipation notes and construction anticipation notes, for the payment of money within twelve months from the issuance of the obligation, on the following conditions:

1. The anticipation notes must be a direct obligation of the issuer under conditions set forth in subsection D of § 38.2-1415;

2. The political subdivision is not in default in the payment of the principal or interest on any of its direct general obligations or any obligation guaranteed by such political subdivision;

3. The anticipation funds shall be specifically pledged to secure the obligation;

4. An insurer shall not invest more than two percent of its admitted assets in the anticipation obligations issued by any one such political subdivision; and

5. An insurer shall not invest more than ten percent of its admitted assets under this subsection.

F. State or municipal revenue obligations. A domestic insurer may invest in obligations of any state of the United States, a political subdivision thereof, or a public instrumentality of any one or more of the foregoing, for the payment of money, on the following conditions:

1. The obligations are payable from revenues or earnings of a public utility of such state, political subdivision, or public instrumentality which are specifically pledged therefor;

2. The law under which the obligations are issued requires that rates for service shall be charged and collected at all times such that they will produce sufficient revenue or earnings which, together with any other revenues or moneys pledged, are sufficient to pay all operating and maintenance charges of the public utility and all principal and interest on such obligations;

3. No prior or parity obligations payable from the revenues or earnings of that public utility are in default as of the date of the investment;

4. An insurer shall not invest under this subsection more than two percent of its admitted assets in the revenue obligations issued in connection with any one facility;

5. An insurer shall not invest under this subsection more than two percent of its admitted assets in revenue obligations payable from revenue or earning sources which are the contractual responsibility of any one single credit risk; and

6. An insurer shall not invest under this subsection more than twenty-five percent of its admitted assets.

G. Other revenue obligations of state and local governments. A domestic insurer may invest in other state and local government revenue obligations of any state of the United States, a political subdivision thereof, or a public instrumentality of any of the foregoing, for the payment of money, on the following conditions:

1. The obligations are payable from revenues or earnings, excluding revenues or earnings from public utilities, specifically pledged therefor by such state, political subdivision, or public instrumentality;

2. An insurer shall not invest under this subsection more than two percent of its admitted assets in the revenue obligations issued in connection with any one facility;

3. No prior or parity obligation of the same issuer payable from revenues or earnings from the same source has been in default as to principal or interest

during the five years next preceding the date of such investment, but the issuer need not have been in existence for that period, and obligations acquired under this subsection may have been newly issued;

4. An insurer shall not invest under this subsection more than two percent of its admitted assets in revenue obligations payable from sources which are the contractual responsibility of any one single credit risk; and

5. An insurer shall not invest under this subsection more than twenty-five percent of its admitted assets. (1983, c. 457, § 38.1-217.18; 1986, c. 562; 1992, c. 588; 1998, c. 414.)

The 1998 amendment, in subsection D, in subdivision 4, substituted "five" for "two" and in subdivision 5, substituted "thirty" for "twenty."

§ **38.2-1416. Canadian governmental obligations.** — A. *Obligations of Canada.* — A domestic insurer may invest in bonds, notes, warrants, and other evidences of indebtedness which are direct obligations of the government of Canada or for which the full faith and credit of the government of Canada are pledged for the payment of principal and interest.

B. No domestic insurer shall invest in any obligation under this section unless the obligation is payable both as to principal and interest in lawful money of the United States or of Canada.

C. *Obligations of provinces.* — A domestic insurer may invest in direct, general obligations of any province of Canada for the payment of money, or obligations for the payment of money to the extent guaranteed or insured as to the payment of principal and interest by any province of Canada, on the following conditions:

1. The province has the power to levy taxes for the prompt payment of the principal and interest of its obligations;

2. The province is not in default in the payment of principal or interest on any of its direct, guaranteed or insured obligations as of the date of investment; and

3. An insurer shall not invest under this subsection more than five percent of its admitted assets in obligations issued or guaranteed by any one province.

D. *Local government obligations.* — A domestic insurer may invest in direct, general obligations of any political subdivision of any province of Canada for the payment of money, or obligation for the payment of money, to the extent guaranteed as to the payment of principal and interest, by any such political subdivision, on the following conditions:

1. The obligations are payable or guaranteed from ad valorem taxes;

2. Such political subdivision is not in default in the payment of principal or interest on any of its direct or guaranteed obligations;

3. No investment shall be made under this subsection in obligations which are secured only by special assessments for local improvements; and

4. An insurer shall not invest more than two percent of its admitted assets in obligations issued or guaranteed by any one such political subdivision. (1983, c. 457, § 38.1-217.19; 1986, c. 562; 1992, c. 588.)

§ **38.2-1417. Canadian corpoꞏate obligations.** — A domestic insurer may invest in obligations issued, assumed or guaranteed by any solvent corporation created or existing under the laws of Canada, or any province of Canada. However, those obligations shall meet the standards specified in § 38.2-1421 for obligations of any business entity created or existing under the laws of the United States or any state. (1983, c. 457, § 38.1-217.20; 1986, c. 562; 1992, c. 588.)

§ 38.2-1418. Obligations of certain international agencies. — A domestic insurer may invest in valid and legally authorized high grade obligations issued, assumed or guaranteed by an international development bank of which the United States is a member. (1983, c. 457, § 38.1-217.21; 1985, c. 370; 1986, c. 562; 1992, c. 588.)

§ 38.2-1419. Railroad terminal and other securities. — A domestic insurer may invest in obligations secured by first mortgages, first deeds of trust or other similar liens upon terminal, depot or tunnel property, including lands, buildings and appurtenances, used in the service of transportation by one or more railroad corporations whose obligations are eligible as investments under § 38.2-1421. However, these obligations shall be (i) the direct obligation of the corporation or corporations, or (ii) guaranteed by endorsement by, or guaranteed by endorsement assumed by the corporation for the payment of principal and interest of those obligations. If the guarantee or assumption of guarantee is by two or more of the corporations, it shall be joint and several as to each. No such investment shall be made if there has been any default in the payment of principal or interest since the issuance of the obligations but not to exceed five years from the date of investment. (1983, c. 457, § 38.1-217.22; 1986, c. 562.)

§ 38.2-1420. Transportation equipment trust certificates. — A domestic insurer may invest in adequately secured equipment trust certificates or other adequately secured instruments evidencing (i) an interest in transportation equipment wholly or partly within the United States and (ii) a right to receive determined portions of rental, purchase or other fixed obligatory payments for the use or purchase of the transportation equipment. (1983, c. 457, § 38.1-217.23; 1986, c. 562.)

§ 38.2-1421. Business entity obligations. — A. High grade. A domestic insurer may invest in any high grade obligations issued, assumed or guaranteed by any solvent business entity that is not in default as to principal or interest on the date of investment and which is created or existing under the laws of the United States or any state.

B. Medium grade. A domestic issuer may invest in medium grade obligations issued, assumed or guaranteed by any solvent business entity that is not in default as to principal or interest on the date of investment and which is created or existing under the laws of the United States or any state.

C. Lower grade. A domestic insurer may invest in lower grade obligations rated 4 by the Securities Valuation Office of the National Association of Insurance Commissioners or, if not rated by the Securities Valuation Office, rated in an equivalent grade by a national rating agency recognized by the Commission that are issued, assumed or guaranteed by any solvent business entity that is not in default as to principal or interest on the date of investment and which is created or existing under the laws of the United States or any state.

D. As used in this section, "business entity obligations" shall not include any mortgage pass-through securities described in § 38.2-1437.1. (1983, c. 457, § 38.1-217.24; 1986, c. 562; 1992, c. 588; 1998, c. 414.)

The 1998 amendment, in subsection A, added "or any state"; added present subsection C and redesignated former subsection C as present subsection D.

§ 38.2-1422. Obligations secured by certain leases. — A. A domestic insurer may invest in obligations of any solvent company other than companies referred to in § 38.2-1419, incorporated under the laws of the United States or of any state if:

1. The obligations are secured by an assignment to the insurer of a lease, and the rents payable under the lease, of real or personal property or both to (i) a domestic governmental entity; (ii) Canada, or any province of Canada; or (iii) one or more companies incorporated under the laws of the United States, any state, Canada or any province of Canada;

2. The rentals assigned are sufficient to repay the indebtedness within the unexpired term of the lease, excluding any term that may be provided by an enforceable option of renewal;

3. The lessee on any lease securing an obligation under this section, or the guarantor of the lease, is an entity whose obligations would be eligible for investment by an insurer in accordance with §§ 38.2-1415, 38.2-1421 or § 38.2-1425;

4. The lessee or guarantor has not defaulted in payment of interest or principal on any of its obligations during the five fiscal years immediately preceding the date of investment; and

5. A first lien on the interest of the lessor in the unencumbered leased property is obtained as additional security for any obligation acquired pursuant to this section.

B. No domestic insurer shall invest under this section more than two percent of the insurer's admitted assets in the obligations of any one business entity or in the obligations secured by leases to any one business entity. (1983, c. 457, § 38.1-217.25; 1986, c. 562; 1992, c. 588.)

§ 38.2-1423. Preferred stocks. — A domestic insurer may invest in preferred stocks of any company incorporated under the laws of the United States or any state if:

1. a. The preferred stock under consideration is not in arrears as to dividends if cumulative, or

b. Full dividends on the preferred stock under consideration have been paid in the last three years, or since issue if issued less than three years before the date of investment, if noncumulative;

2. Required sinking fund payments are on a current basis; and

3. The preferred stock is rated P1, P2, P3, PSF1, PSF2 or PSF3 by the Securities Valuation Office of the National Association of Insurance Commissioners, or if not rated by the Securities Valuation Office, is rated in an equivalent grade by a national rating agency recognized by the Commission. (1983, c. 457, § 38.1-217.26; 1986, c. 562; 1998, c. 414.)

The 1998 amendment rewrote subdivision 3.

§ 38.2-1424. Guaranteed stocks. — A domestic insurer may invest in stocks guaranteed by a solvent company incorporated under the laws of the United States or of any state if for the past three years the guarantor's net earnings available for meeting fixed charges is at least $1^1/_4$ times the sum of (i) the fixed charges of the guarantor and (ii) the dividends on the guaranteed stock. (1983, c. 457, § 38.1-217.27; 1986, c. 562.)

§ 38.2-1425. Stock or obligations of banks or trust companies. — A. A domestic insurer may invest in the capital stock, notes or debentures of any bank or trust company that is a member of the Federal Deposit Insurance Corporation and that has earned a rate of return on its net worth of at least five percent for each of the preceding three years.

B. No domestic insurer shall invest in more than ten percent of the actually issued and outstanding common capital stock of any one such bank or trust company.

C. For the purpose of this section, the term "bank" includes a registered bank holding company as defined by the Federal Bank Holding Act of 1956, as amended, and a registered bank holding company shall be considered a member of the Federal Deposit Insurance Corporation if all its subsidiary banks are members of the Federal Deposit Insurance Corporation. (1983, c. 457, § 38.1-217.28; 1986, c. 562.)

§ 38.2-1426. Application of earnings tests. — If the issuing, assuming or guaranteeing business entity has not been in operation for the entire period for which earnings are being applied pursuant to §§ 38.2-1423 through 38.2-1425, the earnings tests shall be based upon pro forma statements incorporating statements of any predecessor or constituent business entity for that portion of the earnings tests period that the current business entity was not in operation, if:

1. The current business entity was formed as a consolidation or a merger of two or more business entities, at least one of which was in operation at the beginning of the period; or

2. The current business entity has acquired all of the assets of a business entity or any division or other unit of a business entity that was in operation at the beginning of the test period. (1983, c. 457, § 38.1-217.29; 1986, c. 562; 1992, c. 588.)

§ 38.2-1427. Common stock; covered call options. — A. A domestic insurer may invest in the common capital stock of any company incorporated under the laws of the United States or any state, if the common capital stock of the corporation is traded on a securities exchange or on an over-the-counter market regulated under the Securities Exchange Act of 1934, as amended.

B. A domestic insurer also may write exchange-traded, covered call options on shares of common capital stock it owns.

C. No domestic insurer shall invest, pursuant to this section, in more than ten percent of the issued and outstanding common capital stock of any one corporation or issuer. (1983, c. 457, § 38.1-217.30; 1986, c. 562; 1992, c. 588.)

§ 38.2-1427.1. Limited partnerships. — A domestic insurer may become a limited partner in a partnership organized and governed under the laws of the United States or any state for the purpose of making or participating in investments otherwise permissible for domestic insurers under the provisions of this chapter. (1992, c. 588.)

§ 38.2-1427.2. Investment company shares and units of beneficial interest. — A domestic insurer may invest in shares of common stock or units of beneficial interest issued by any solvent business corporation or trust incorporated or organized under the laws of the United States, or of any state of the United States, under the following conditions:

1. If the issuing corporation or trust is advised by an investment advisor which is the insurer or an affiliate of the insurer, the issuing corporation or trust shall have assets of $100,000 or more (which may be provided by the insurer or affiliate), or if the issuing corporation or trust has an unaffiliated investment advisor, the issuing corporation or trust shall have net assets of ten million dollars or more, and

2. The issuing corporation or trust is registered as an investment company with the Federal Securities and Exchange Commission under the Investment Act of 1940, as amended. (1992, c. 588.)

§ **38.2-1427.3. Investment authority; subsidiary corporations.** — A domestic insurer may invest in common stock, preferred stock, debt obligations, and other securities of a subsidiary.

For investments in subsidiary corporations made prior to July 1, 1995, July 1, 1995, may be deemed the date of investment. (1992, c. 588; 1993, c. 47; 1995, c. 60.)

§ **38.2-1428. Hedging transactions.** — A domestic insurer may effect or maintain bona fide hedging transactions pertaining to securities otherwise eligible for investment under §§ 38.2-1415 through 38.2-1427 including, but not limited to: (i) financial futures contracts, warrants, options, calls and other rights to purchase, and (ii) puts and other rights to require another person to purchase such securities. The contracts, options, calls, puts, and rights shall be traded on a commodity exchange regulated under the Commodity Exchange Act, as amended, or on a securities exchange or on an over-the-counter market regulated under the Securities Exchange Act of 1934, as amended. For purposes of this section, a *"bona fide hedging transaction"* means a purchase or sale of a contract, warrant, option, call, put or right entered into for the purpose of (a) minimizing interest rate risks in respect of interest obligations on insurance policies or contracts supported by securities held by the insurer or (b) offsetting changes in the market values or yield rates of securities held by the insurer. (1983, c. 457, § 38.1-217.31; 1985, c. 36; 1986, c. 562.)

§ **38.2-1429. Lending of securities.** — A. A domestic insurer may lend securities held by it pursuant to §§ 38.2-1415 through 38.2-1427.2 if:

1. Simultaneously with the delivery of the securities, the insurer receives collateral from the borrower consisting of cash or consisting of securities issued, assumed or guaranteed by the United States, an agency of the United States or any state. The securities shall have a present market value of at least 102 percent of the market value of the securities loaned;

2. The securities are loaned only for the purpose of making delivery of securities in the case of short sales, in the case of failure to receive securities requested for delivery or in other similar cases;

3. Prior to the loan, the borrower furnishes the insurer with the most recent statement of the borrower's financial condition and a representation by the borrower that there has been no material adverse change in its financial condition since the date of that statement;

4. The insurer receives a reasonable fee related to the value of the borrowed securities and to the duration of the loan;

5. The loan is made pursuant to a written loan agreement; and

6. The borrower is required to furnish by the close of each business day during the term of the loan a report of the market value of all collateral and the market value of all borrowed securities as of the close of trading on the previous business day. If at the close of any business day the market value of the collateral is less than 102 percent of the market value of the securities loaned, then the borrower shall deliver by the close of the next business day an additional amount of cash or securities. The market value of these additional securities, together with the market value of all previously delivered collateral, shall equal at least 102 percent of the market value of the securities loaned.

B. For the purposes of this section, "market value" includes accrued interest. (1983, c. 457, § 38.1-217.32; 1986, c. 562; 1992, c. 588.)

§ **38.2-1430. Collateral loans.** — A domestic insurer may make loans secured by securities eligible for investment under this article. At the date of investment, the loan shall not exceed eighty percent of the market value of the collateral pledged. However, if the collateral consists of obligations issued, assumed or guaranteed by the United States, the loan may equal the market value of the collateral pledged. (1983, c. 457, § 38.1-217.33; 1986, c. 562.)

§ 38.2-1431. Policy loans. — A domestic insurer issuing life insurance policies or annuities may loan any sum not exceeding the cash surrender value specified in the policy to its policyholder upon the pledge of the policy as collateral. (1983, c. 457, § 38.1-217.34; 1986, c. 562.)

§ 38.2-1432. Savings, certificates, etc. — A domestic insurer may invest in any of the following:

1. Interest-bearing checking or savings accounts, certificates of deposit, or other short-term investments made available or issued by any solvent bank or trust company that is a member of the Federal Deposit Insurance Corporation;

2. Interest-bearing savings or share accounts, certificates of deposit or any other short-term investments made available or issued by any solvent building and loan or savings institution insured by the Federal Deposit Insurance Corporation or other federal insurance agency;

3. Bankers acceptances of the kinds and maturities made eligible by law for rediscount with Federal Reserve Banks, provided that these securities are accepted by a bank or trust company that is a member of the Federal Reserve System;

4. Money market mutual funds, provided that the Commission has granted prior written approval to the insurer with respect to its investment in any money market mutual fund sponsored by affiliates of the insurer and that such money market fund sponsored by affiliates meets the requirements set forth in subdivisions 1 and 2 of § 38.2-1427.2; or

5. United States government bond mutual funds. (1983, c. 457, § 38.1-217.35; 1986, c. 562; 1990, c. 3; 1995, c. 60; 1996, c. 77.)

§ 38.2-1433. Foreign securities. — A. A domestic insurer transacting the business of insurance in a foreign country may invest in securities of or issued in that country of substantially the same kinds, classes, and investment grades as the insurer may acquire in the United States.

B. A domestic insurer may invest in securities of or issued in a foreign country of substantially the same kinds, classes and investment grades as the insurer may acquire in the United States, provided (i) all such securities are rated medium grade or higher by the Securities Valuation Office of the National Association of Insurance Commissioners or by a national rating agency recognized by the Commission and no more than one percent of the insurer's admitted assets are invested in such securities which are rated medium grade, and (ii) the aggregate amount of foreign investment held by the insurer under this section for a single foreign jurisdiction does not exceed three percent of the insurer's admitted assets.

C. These investments shall be payable in lawful currency of the United States, except where payment in other lawful currencies is required to match obligations denominated in such other lawful currencies. (1983, c. 457, § 38.1-217.36; 1986, c. 562; 1998, c. 414.)

The **1998 amendment** added present sub-section B and redesignated former subsection B as present subsection C.

§ 38.2-1434. Mortgage loans. — Subject to the provisions of § 38.2-1437, a domestic insurer may invest in:

1. Obligations secured by first mortgages or first deeds of trust on improved unencumbered real property located in the United States;

2. Obligations secured by first mortgages or first deeds of trust upon leasehold estates on improved and otherwise unencumbered real property where:

a. The leasehold interest lasts for a term of not less than ten years beyond the maturity of the loan as made or as extended; and

b. The mortgagee is subrogated to all the rights of the lessee on foreclosure or on taking a deed in lieu of foreclosure; or

3. Obligations secured by first mortgages or first deeds of trust on unimproved and unencumbered real property in the United States for the purpose of financing the construction of a building or other improvements on the real property subject to the mortgage or deed of trust, if:

a. These obligations mature not more than sixty months from the effective date of the mortgage or deed of trust and are the unlimited and unconditional liability of the obligor;

b. The obligor provides the insurer with a completion bond for the building or improvements at the time of making the loan; and

c. The insurer at or prior to the making of the loan (i) enters into an agreement with another party to provide permanent financing or (ii) agrees to provide permanent financing upon completion of the building or other improvement. (1983, c. 457, § 38.1-217.37; 1986, c. 562.)

§ 38.2-1435. Second mortgages; wrap-around mortgages. — A domestic insurer may invest in obligations secured by second mortgages or second deeds of trust on real property encumbered only by a first mortgage or first deed of trust complying with §§ 38.2-1434 and 38.2-1437, subject to either of the following conditions:

1. The insurer also owns the obligation secured by the first mortgage or first deed of trust, and the aggregate value of both loans does not exceed the applicable loan-to-value ratio specified in § 38.2-1437; or

2. The obligation is secured by a wrap-around mortgage where:

a. Only one preexisting mortgage or deed of trust encumbers the real property;

b. The mortgage or deed of trust securing the loan is (i) recorded and (ii) insured for at least the total amount of the obligation of the borrower to the insurer by title insurance; and

c. The insurer agrees to make the payments due under the first mortgage or first deed of trust upon receipt of payments due from the borrower under the wrap-around mortgage. (1983, c. 457, § 38.1-217.38; 1986, c. 562.)

§ 38.2-1436. Mortgage participations. — Notwithstanding the provisions of §§ 13.1-627 and 13.1-826, a domestic insurer may acquire or sell participation interests in any loans secured by a mortgage or deed of trust qualifying under § 38.2-1434 if the insurer has all or substantially all the rights of a first mortgagee. (1983, c. 457, § 38.1-217.39; 1986, c. 562.)

§ 38.2-1437. Limitations on mortgages. — A. The amount of any loan secured by a mortgage or deed of trust referred to in §§ 38.2-1434 through 38.2-1436 shall not exceed the following percentages of the fair market value of the real estate:

1. Seventy-five percent for a leasehold loan made pursuant to subdivision 2 of § 38.2-1434;

2. Ninety percent for a loan made to an employee of the insurer, other than a director or trustee thereof, whether such loan be made in connection with the initial employment of the employee or in connection with the transfer of the place of employment of the employee; or

3. Eighty percent for all other loans.

However, the percentage limits specified in this subsection may be exceeded if the excess is (i) insured or guaranteed or is to be insured or guaranteed by the United States, any state or any agency of either or (ii) insured by an insurer licensed to insure mortgage guaranty risks in this Commonwealth.

B. Any loan made pursuant to §§ 38.2-1434 through 38.2-1436 not in compliance with the requirements of subsection A of this section shall be classified as a Category 2 investment in its entirety.

C. The fair market value of the real estate interest mortgaged shall be determined by a written appraisal of at least one competent real estate appraiser as of the date of the initial loan commitment, which appraiser shall not be an employee of the insurer nor an employee of any company controlled by or under common control with the insurer. If the loan commitment is revised to reflect a change in the value of the real estate, the fair market value shall be determined as of the date of that revision.

D. Buildings and other improvements on the mortgaged premises shall be insured against fire loss for the benefit of the mortgagee in an amount not less than the lesser of their insurable value or the unpaid principal balance of the obligation.

E. The maximum term of any mortgage or deed of trust referred to in §§ 38.2-1434 through 38.2-1436 secured by real property primarily improved by a single-family residence shall not exceed thirty years.

F. A domestic insurer shall not invest, under §§ 38.2-1434 through 38.2-1436, more than two percent of its admitted assets, directly or indirectly, in mortgages covering any one secured location, nor more than four percent in the mortgages of any one obligor. (1983, c. 457, § 38.1-217.40; 1986, c. 562; 1992, c. 588.)

§ 38.2-1437.1. Mortgage pass-through securities. — A domestic insurer may invest in mortgage pass-through securities backed by a pool of mortgages of the kind, class and investment quality as those eligible for investment under §§ 38.2-1434 through 38.2-1437, under the following conditions:

1. The servicer of the pool of mortgages shall be a business entity created under the laws of the United States or any state;

2. The pool of mortgages is assigned to a business entity, other than a sole proprietorship, having a net worth of at least five million dollars, as trustee for the benefit of the holders of the securities;

3. A domestic insurer shall not invest under this section more than two percent of its admitted assets in securities backed by any single mortgage pass-through pool;

4. All mortgage pass-through securities acquired by a domestic insurer under this section shall provide for flow-through of both principal and interest payments payable on the underlying mortgage loan assets; mortgage pass-through securities promising principal-only, interest-only or residual interests-only in the underlying mortgage assets shall not be acquired; and

5. The securities on the date of investment shall be high grade obligations. (1992, c. 588; 1999, c. 483.)

The 1999 amendment substituted "net worth" for "new worth" in subdivision 2.

§ 38.2-1438. Renewals and extensions when value of property decreases. — Nothing in this chapter shall prohibit a domestic insurer from renewing or extending, or consenting to the renewal or extension of, evidences of indebtedness secured by real property or leasehold estates for the original or a lesser amount when a decrease in value of the property or estate causes the indebtedness to exceed the applicable loan-to-value ratio specified by § 38.2-

1437. Nothing in this chapter shall prohibit a domestic insurer from accepting as part payment for any real property or leasehold estate sold by it, a mortgage or other lien on the real property or leasehold estate securing a loan that exceeds the applicable loan-to-value ratio specified in § 38.2-1437. (1983, c. 457, § 38.1-217.41; 1986, c. 562.)

§ **38.2-1439. Chattel mortgages.** — A. In connection with a mortgage loan on the security of real property designed and used primarily for residential purposes and acquired pursuant to § 38.2-1434, a domestic insurer may make a loan on the security of a chattel mortgage, deed of trust or other appropriate lien. The chattel mortgage or other lien may be created separately or in combination with the mortgage loan on the real estate. It shall not exceed five years and shall constitute a first and prior lien, except for taxes not then delinquent, on personal property comprised of durable equipment owned by the mortgagor and kept and used on the mortgaged premises.

B. The term *"durable equipment"* includes only mechanical refrigerators, mechanical laundering machines, heating and cooking stoves and ranges, mechanical kitchen aids, vacuum cleaners, and fire extinguishing devices; and, for apartment houses and hotels, may also include room furniture and furnishings.

C. Before any loan or investment is made under this section, the items of property included in the security shall be separately appraised by a competent appraiser and the fair market value of the items determined. No loan made under this section shall exceed the lesser of (i) an amount obtained by multiplying the loan to the value ratio applicable to the companion loan on the real property by the fair market value of the personal property or (ii) an amount equal to twenty percent of the amount secured by the lien on the real property. (1983, c. 457, § 38.1-217.42; 1986, c. 562.)

§ **38.2-1440. Investment in personal property.** — A. A domestic insurer may invest in interests in tangible personal property for the production of income, evidenced by trust certificates or other instruments.

B. The investments shall be accompanied by (i) a right to receive rental, charter hire, purchase or other payments for the use or purchase of the personal property, (ii) a valid, binding and enforceable contract or lease for the purchase or use of the tangible personal property, and (iii) a provision for contractual payments to be made that will return the cost of the property and provide earnings on the investments within the anticipated useful life of the property which shall be at least three years.

C. The payments must be made payable or guaranteed by one or more domestic governmental entities or business entities whose obligations would qualify for investment under § 38.2-1421.

D. The unit cost of such property shall not be less than $25,000, and the cost of all property covered by any single contract or lease shall not be less than $100,000.

E. The tangible personal property shall not include furniture or fixtures. (1983, c. 457, § 38.1-217.43; 1986, c. 562; 1992, c. 588.)

§ **38.2-1441. Real estate.** — A. A domestic insurer may invest in real estate, as set forth in subsections B, C and D of this section, unless the property is to be used primarily for agricultural, horticultural, ranch, recreational, amusement or club purposes. The term *"real estate"* as used in this section shall include a leasehold of real estate having an unexpired term of not less than twenty years.

B. A domestic insurer may invest in dwellings, offices and other properties (including leasehold estates) for the production of income, other than real estate which is the subject of subsection C, situated in the United States, and the construction thereon of improvements, under the following conditions:

1. The insurer shall either directly or through a land trust own the entire property, except that it may share ownership with one or more insurers authorized to do business in this state, or other business entities, excluding sole proprietorships, having a net worth of at least five million dollars under agreements that will assume concerted action in management and control of the property in case of the insolvency of any participating company, provided that each investment made pursuant to this subsection by the insurer and by each participant shall not be less than $100,000;

2. The insurer alone or in conjunction with participants qualified under subdivision B 1 may let contracts for construction and pay costs of construction and leasing, hold, maintain, lease, and manage the property, collect rents and other income therefrom, and sell the property in whole or in part;

3. The property may be encumbered by lease to tenants and by rights-of-way, easements, mineral reservations, building restrictions, and restrictive covenants, provided none of them can interfere substantially with the use of the property or result in a forfeiture of the property, unless a policy of title insurance, issued by a responsible title insurer qualified to do business in the state wherein the property is located, insures the insurer against loss or damage arising from such encumbrances or reversionary rights; and

4. An insurer shall not invest under this subsection more than four percent of its admitted assets in any one property or in any one grouping of contiguous properties.

C. A domestic insurer may invest in real estate, including leasehold estates, for the convenient accommodation of the insurer's business operations, including home office, branch office and field office operations, under the following conditions:

1. Any parcel of real estate acquired under this subsection may include excess space for rent to others if it is reasonably anticipated that the excess will be required by the insurer for expansion or if the excess is reasonably required in order to have one or more buildings that will function as an economic unit;

2. The real estate may be subject to a mortgage;

3. An insurer shall not invest under this subsection more than ten percent of the insurer's admitted assets, except with the permission of the Commission if it is found that such percentage of the insurer's admitted assets is insufficient to provide convenient accommodation for the insurer's business; and

4. The permission of the Commission shall be obtained by an insurer prior to the purchase of any real estate under this subsection if the insurer has been authorized in this Commonwealth for a period of less than five years.

D. Real property serving as the residence of an employee of any domestic insurer, other than a director or trustee of the insurer, may be acquired only in connection with the (i) relocation by the insurer of the place of employment of the employee, or (ii) any relocation in connection with the initial employment of the employee. The purchase price shall not exceed the fair market value of the property as determined by written appraisals of at least two competent independent real estate appraisers for the purpose of the acquisition. The employee shall have made reasonable efforts otherwise to dispose of the property for a period of not less than one month immediately prior to the acquisition. (1983, c. 457, § 38.1-217.44; 1986, c. 562; 1992, c. 588.)

§ 38.2-1442. Guaranty association obligations. — A domestic insurer may invest in any obligation not in default of the Virginia Life, Accident and Sickness Insurance Guaranty Association issued pursuant to subdivision 3 of subsection J of § 38.2-1704 or the Virginia Property and Casualty Insurance

Guaranty Association issued pursuant to subdivision 2 of subsection B of § 38.2-1606. (1986, c. 562.)

ARTICLE 3.

Separate Accounts.

§ 38.2-1443. Investment of amounts allocated to separate accounts for variable life insurance and variable annuities. — The amounts allocated to separate accounts for variable life insurance and variable annuities, pursuant to the provisions of § 38.2-3113, and accumulations on them, may be invested and reinvested by a domestic insurer in any type of Category 1 investment. Any percentage limitations based on the insurer's total admitted assets or surplus to policyholders shall not apply to investments made pursuant to this section. (1983, c. 457, § 38.1-217.45; 1986, c. 562; 1992, c. 588.)

§ 38.2-1443.1. Investment of amounts allocated to separate accounts for modified guaranteed life insurance and modified guaranteed annuities. — A. Unless otherwise provided by regulation, the amounts allocated to separate accounts for modified guaranteed life insurance and modified guaranteed annuities, pursuant to the provisions of § 38.2-3113.1, and accumulations on them, may be invested and reinvested by a domestic insurer in any type of Category 1 investment.

B. Investments made pursuant to this section shall be taken into account in applying the investment limitations of §§ 38.2-1413 and 38.2-1414 to investments made by the insurer, by combining the investments under this section with all other investments subject to such limitations. In addition to the general account meeting these investment limitations, both the separate account and the general account together shall meet these investment limitations. The limitations of §§ 38.2-1413 and 38.2-1414 shall not otherwise apply to investments made pursuant to this section. (1992, c. 210.)

§ 38.2-1444. Establishment of separate accounts for pension, retirement or profit-sharing plans; investment of funds in such accounts. — A. A domestic insurer, after adoption of a resolution by its board of directors and certification of that adoption to the Commission, may allocate to one or more separate accounts, in accordance with the terms of a written agreement, any amounts paid to or held by the insurer in connection with a pension, retirement or profit-sharing plan. The plan may provide (i) retirement benefits pursuant to the terms of the agreement or under the insurer's policies or contracts and (ii) other benefits incidental to the agreement or policies. The retirement benefits may vary according to the terms of the agreement, policies or contracts and any standards incorporated in them. Any income and any realized or unrealized gain or loss on each account shall be credited to or charged against that account in accordance with the agreement, without regard to the other income, gains or losses of the insurer.

B. Notwithstanding any other provision in this title, the amounts allocated to the accounts and accumulations on them may be invested and reinvested in any kinds of investment specified in the agreement other than those prohibited by § 38.2-1407. The investments shall not be taken into account in applying the investment limitations of this chapter to investments made by the insurer.

C. Amounts allocated by an insurer to separate accounts pursuant to this section shall be owned by the insurer, and the insurer shall not be, nor hold itself out to be, a trustee for the amounts. The insurer's liability under the accounts shall be limited to the amount of funds in the account. (1983, c. 457, § 38.1-217.46; 1986, c. 562.)

§ 38.2-1445. Separate accounts deemed Category 1 investments. — All investments made in compliance with this article shall be deemed Category 1 investments except that nothing contained in this section shall be construed to affect or apply to any insurer licensed pursuant to the provisions of Chapter 42 (§ 38.2-4200 et seq.) or 45 (§ 38.2-4500 et seq.) of this title. (1983, c. 457, § 38.1-217.47; 1986, c. 562; 1992, c. 588.)

ARTICLE 4.

Asset Protection Act.

§ 38.2-1446. Prohibition of hypothecation. — A. Every domestic insurer subject to the provisions of this chapter shall at all times have and maintain free and unencumbered admitted assets in an amount equal to the sum total of its reserve liabilities and minimum capital and surplus, and no such insurer shall pledge, hypothecate, or otherwise encumber its assets in an amount in excess of the amount of its surplus to policyholders; nor shall such insurer pledge, hypothecate or otherwise encumber more than five percent of its admitted assets. However, the Commission, upon written application, may approve the hypothecation or encumbrance of any of the assets of such an insurer in any amount upon a determination that such hypothecation or encumbrance will not adversely affect the solvency of such insurer.

B. Any such insurer which pledges, hypothecates, or otherwise encumbers any of its assets shall within ten days thereafter report in writing to the Commission the amount and identity of the assets so pledged, hypothecated, or encumbered and the terms and conditions of such transaction. In addition, each such insurer shall annually, or more often if required by the Commission, file with the Commission a statement sworn to by a chief executive officer of the insurer that (i) title to assets in an amount equal to the reserve liability and minimum capital and surplus of the insurer which are not pledged, hypothecated or otherwise encumbered is vested in the insurer, (ii) the only assets of the insurer which are pledged, hypothecated or otherwise encumbered are as identified and reported in the sworn statement and no other assets of the insurer are pledged, hypothecated or otherwise encumbered, and (iii) the terms and limitations of any such transaction of pledge, hypothecation or encumbrance are as reported in the sworn statement.

C. Any person which accepts a pledge, hypothecation or encumbrance of any asset of a domestic insurer as security for a debt or other obligation of such insurer not in accordance with the terms and limitations of this article shall be deemed to have accepted such asset subject to a superior, preferential and automatically perfected lien in favor of claimants; however, such superior, preferential and automatically perfected lien in favor of claimants shall not apply to assets of a company in receivership pursuant to Chapter 15 (§ 38.2-1500 et seq.) of this title, if the receiver approves the pledge, hypothecation or encumbrance of such assets.

D. In the event of involuntary or voluntary liquidation of any domestic insurer subject to this chapter, claimants of such insurer shall have a prior and preferential claim against all assets of the insurer except those which have been pledged, hypothecated or encumbered in accordance with the terms and limitations of this article. All claimants shall have equal status and their prior and preferential claim shall be superior to any claim or cause of action against the insurer by any person, corporation, association or legal entity. (1992, c. 588.)

187

§ **38.2-1447. Exception.** — A. This article shall not apply to those assets of any insurer that are held, deposited, pledged, hypothecated or otherwise encumbered as provided herein to secure, offset, protect, or meet those reserve liabilities of such insurer which are established, incurred, or required under the provisions of a reinsurance agreement whereby such insurer has reinsured the insurance policy liabilities of a ceding insurer, provided:

1. The ceding insurer and the reinsurer are both licensed to transact business in this Commonwealth; and

2. Pursuant to a written agreement between the ceding insurer and the reinsurer, reserve assets substantially equal to the reserve liabilities required to be established by the ceding insurer on the reinsured business are either (i) deposited by or are withheld from the reinsurer and are in the custody of the ceding insurer as security for the payment of the reinsurer's obligations under the reinsurance agreement, and such assets are held subject to withdrawal by and under control of the ceding insurer or (ii) are deposited and held in a trust account for such purpose and under such conditions with a qualified United States financial institution defined as eligible to act as a fiduciary of a trust by § 38.2-1316.1.

B. The Commission shall have the right to examine any such assets, reinsurance agreements, or deposit arrangements at any time in accordance with its authority to make examinations of insurers as conferred by other provisions of this title. (1992, c. 588.)

CHAPTER 15.

REHABILITATION AND LIQUIDATION OF INSURERS.

§ **38.2-1500. Scope of chapter.** — This chapter shall, except as otherwise stated, apply to every insurer transacting, attempting to transact, or representing itself as transacting an insurance business in this Commonwealth, or which is in the process of organization as an insurer. (1952, c. 317, § 38.1-126; 1986, c. 562.)

McCarran-Ferguson Act applies to rehabilitation proceeding statutes. — The creation by statute of a single, exclusive forum for insurance company rehabilitation proceedings is regulation of the "business of insurance" for purposes of the McCarran-Ferguson Act. Eden Fin. Group, Inc. v. Fidelity Bankers Life Ins. Co., 778 F. Supp. 278 (E.D. Va. 1991).

The exclusive regulatory jurisdiction of the states over insurance companies applies only to the "business of insurance," not to the regulation of the "business of insurers." Eden Fin. Group, Inc. v. Fidelity Bankers Life Ins. Co., 778 F. Supp. 278 (E.D. Va. 1991).

While fixing claim priorities in the liquidation context may be the business of insurers, rehabilitation proceedings necessarily are the business of insurance, as that term has been defined under Union Labor Life Ins. Co. v. Pireno, 458 U.S. 119, 102 S. Ct. 3002, 73 L. Ed. 2d 647 (1982). Eden Fin. Group, Inc. v. Fidelity Bankers Life Ins. Co., 778 F. Supp. 278 (E.D. Va. 1991).

Insurance company in state rehabilitation proceedings is exempt from Federal Arbitration Act. — The McCarran-Ferguson Act bars interference with state laws regulating the business of insurance, unless such laws specifically relate to insurance; because the Federal Arbitration Act does not specifically relate to the business of insurance, an insurance company in state rehabilitation and conservation proceedings is excepted from the provisions of the Federal Arbitration Act where a party attempts to invoke arbitration against the company or its receiver. Eden Fin. Group, Inc. v. Fidelity Bankers Life Ins. Co., 778 F. Supp. 278 (E.D. Va. 1991).

Under the McCarran-Ferguson Act, federal courts must defer to the exclusive jurisdiction of state proceedings over the rehabilitation of insurance companies. Eden Fin. Group, Inc. v. Fidelity Bankers Life Ins. Co., 778 F. Supp. 278 (E.D. Va. 1991).

When demands for arbitration are stayed along with all other types of claims and causes of action in an insurance rehabilitation proceeding, the provisions of the Federal Arbitration Act must give way to the mandates and policy of the McCarran-Ferguson Act and accompanying state regulations. Eden Fin. Group, Inc. v. Fidelity Bankers Life Ins. Co., 778 F. Supp. 278 (E.D. Va. 1991).

There are three factors for determining whether a practice is the "business of insurance" for purposes of the McCarran-Ferguson Act: [F]irst, whether the practice has the effect of transferring or spreading a policyholder's risk; second, whether the practice is an integral part of the policy relationship between the insurer and the insured; and third, whether the practice is limited to entities within the insurance industry. Eden Fin. Group, Inc. v. Fidelity Bankers Life Ins. Co., 778 F. Supp. 278 (E.D. Va. 1991).

§ 38.2-1501. Definitions. — As used in this chapter:

"Association" means the Virginia Property and Casualty Insurance Guaranty Association created by Chapter 16 of this title or the Virginia Life, Accident and Sickness Insurance Guaranty Association created by Chapter 17 of this title or any person performing a similar function in another state.

"Delinquency proceeding" means any proceeding commenced against an insurance company for the purpose of liquidating, rehabilitating, reorganizing or conserving an insurer.

"Insolvent" means (i) the condition of an insurer that has liabilities in excess of assets or (ii) the inability of an insurer to pay its obligations as they become due in the usual course of business.

"Receiver" means the Commission or any person appointed to manage delinquency proceedings. (1952, c. 317, § 38.1-127; 1986, c. 562.)

§ 38.2-1502. Jurisdiction and procedure. — The jurisdiction of delinquency proceedings shall be determined by general law, except that if the Commission files a delinquency proceeding application, it shall be filed with the Circuit Court of the City of Richmond. Unless otherwise provided, all delinquency proceedings shall be conducted as a suit in equity. (1952, c. 317, § 38.1-128; 1986, c. 562.)

§ 38.2-1503. Grounds for delinquency proceedings commenced by Commission against domestic insurer. — Delinquency proceedings may be commenced by the Commission against any domestic insurer whenever the insurer:

1. Has been determined to be insolvent by the Commission;

2. Has refused to submit its books, papers, accounts, records, or affairs to the reasonable inspection of the Commission or its representative;

3. Has refused or failed to comply with any order of the Commission to make good within the time prescribed by law (i) any impairment of its minimum capital and surplus if the insurer is a stock insurer, (ii) any impairment of its minimum surplus if the insurer is other than a stock insurer, or (iii) membership requirements as set forth in § 38.2-2515 if the insurer is a mutual assessment property and casualty insurer and has had its license revoked;

4. Has transferred or attempted to transfer substantially its entire property, or has entered into any transaction which merges substantially its entire property or business, into the property or business of any other company without prior written approval of the Commission;

5. Has removed, attempted to remove, or is about to remove from this Commonwealth any material part of its property or business necessary for the continued conduct of its business if it endangers the interests of its policyholders, stockholders or members;

6. Has reinsured all or substantially all of its risks without prior written approval of the Commission;

7. Is found, after an examination, to be in a condition where any further transaction of business will be hazardous to its policyholders, creditors, members, subscribers, stockholders, or to the public;

8. Has willfully violated its charter or any law of this Commonwealth;

9. Has an officer, director or manager who has refused to be examined under oath concerning its affairs;

10. Has had any material part of its entire property sequestered in any other state or country;

11. Has not organized or completed its organization and obtained a license to transact the business of insurance in this Commonwealth within the period of time set by law; or

12. Has failed to pay a final judgment rendered against it in any state upon any insurance contract issued or assumed by it (i) within sixty days after the judgment has become final, (ii) within sixty days after time for taking an appeal has expired, or (iii) within sixty days after dismissal of an appeal before final determination, whichever date is the latest. (Code 1950, § 38-138; 1952, c. 317, § 38.1-129; 1986, c. 562.)

§ 38.2-1504. Requirements when proceedings instituted by any person other than Commission. — A. No circuit court in this Commonwealth shall appoint a receiver for any domestic insurer on application of any person other than the Commission until:

1. The applicant has presented to the Commission a copy of a bill in equity for receivership and has given reasonable notice to the affected insurer that a copy of the bill has been presented to the Commission.

2. The affected insurer has been given ten days after the service of this notice to present to the Commission a copy of the answer that it proposes to file.

3. The Commission has investigated the merits of the application for receivership and has held a hearing on the results of the investigation. The Commission shall act within a reasonable period of time.

4. Within a reasonable time after completing its investigation, the Commission shall make a recommendation to the proper court regarding the appointment of the proposed receiver.

B. The court shall appoint or refuse to appoint the proposed receiver after considering the merits of the application for a receiver. (1952, c. 317, § 38.1-130; 1986, c. 562.)

§ 38.2-1505. Commission may apply for receiver and for other relief; what orders court may enter.

— A. Whenever the Commission finds that any of the grounds for rehabilitation or liquidation of a domestic insurer set out in § 38.2-1503 exist, it may apply to the Circuit Court of the City of Richmond for an order directing the insurer to show cause on or before a designated date (i) why a receiver other than the Commission should not be appointed for the insurer, (ii) why an order should not be entered authorizing the Commission, as a receiver, to proceed with the rehabilitation or liquidation of the insurer or (iii) why other appropriate steps authorized by this chapter should not be taken. The application and order may include any other relief as the nature of the case and the interests of the policyholders, creditors, stockholders, members of the insurer and of the public may require. A copy of the application and the order to show cause shall be served upon the insurer and shall constitute legal process. The State Treasurer shall be made a party to the proceeding.

B. On or after the return of the order to show cause, and after a full hearing, the court shall either deny the application, appoint a receiver for the insurer, authorize the Commission to proceed with the rehabilitation or liquidation of the insurer or to take any other appropriate proceedings as the Commission considers advisable. (Code 1950, §§ 38-138, 38-139; 1952, c. 317, § 38.1-131; 1986, c. 562.)

McCarran-Ferguson Act applies to rehabilitation proceeding statutes. — The creation by statute of a single, exclusive forum for insurance company rehabilitation proceedings is regulation of the "business of insurance" for purposes of the McCarran-Ferguson Act. Eden Fin. Group, Inc. v. Fidelity Bankers Life Ins. Co., 778 F. Supp. 278 (E.D. Va. 1991).

The exclusive regulatory jurisdiction of the states over insurance companies applies only to the "business of insurance," not to the regulation of the "business of insurers." Eden Fin. Group, Inc. v. Fidelity Bankers Life Ins. Co., 778 F. Supp. 278 (E.D. Va. 1991).

Insurance company in state rehabilitation proceedings is exempt from Federal Arbitration Act. — The McCarran-Ferguson Act bars interference with state laws regulating the business of insurance, unless such laws specifically relate to insurance; because the Federal Arbitration Act does not specifically relate to the business of insurance, an insurance company in state rehabilitation and conservation proceedings is excepted from the provisions of the Federal Arbitration Act where a party attempts to invoke arbitration against the company or its receiver. Eden Fin. Group, Inc. v. Fidelity Bankers Life Ins. Co., 778 F. Supp. 278 (E.D. Va. 1991).

Under the McCarran-Ferguson Act, federal courts must defer to the exclusive jurisdiction of state proceedings over the rehabilitation of insurance companies. Eden Fin. Group, Inc. v. Fidelity Bankers Life Ins. Co., 778 F. Supp. 278 (E.D. Va. 1991).

When demands for arbitration are stayed along with all other types of claims and causes of action in an insurance rehabilitation proceeding, the provisions of the Federal Arbitration Act must give way to the mandates and policy of the McCarran-Ferguson Act and accompanying state regulations. Eden Fin. Group, Inc. v. Fidelity Bankers Life Ins. Co., 778 F. Supp. 278 (E.D. Va. 1991).

§ 38.2-1506. Requirements when receiver appointed; disbursement of available assets to association, etc.

— A. Whenever a receiver, other than the Commission, is appointed pursuant to § 38.2-1504 for any domestic insurer other than an insurer writing exclusively title, fidelity and surety, credit or ocean marine insurance, the receiver shall petition the court for approval of a plan to disburse the assets. This shall be completed within 120 days of a final determination by the Commission that the insurer is insolvent. After the application of an association for an insolvent insurer's available assets has been granted, the insolvent insurer's assets will be disbursed to any association entitled to them as they become available.

B. The plan shall include provisions for the receiver to take all the actions required by subsections B and C of § 38.2-1509.

C. Notice of the petition by the receiver to the court for approval of a plan to disburse an insurer's assets shall be given to the associations and the commissioners of insurance of the other states. This notice shall be deemed given when sent by certified mail at least thirty days before submission of the petition to the court. Action on the petition may be taken by the court or a judge of the court if the required notice has been given and the plan of the receiver contains the provisions set forth in this section. (1978, c. 696, § 38.1-131.1; 1986, c. 562.)

§ 38.2-1507. Further procedure; injunction may be issued. — The court may issue an injunction restraining the insurer and its officers, directors, stockholders, members, trustees, agents, employees and all other persons from transacting any business of the insurer, and from transferring, removing or disposing of its property or business until a further order of the court. The injunction may be issued on or after the institution of any delinquency proceeding, except where the rehabilitation or liquidation of the insurer has been referred to the Commission. If the Commission is authorized to proceed with the rehabilitation or liquidation, it may issue injunctions or enter any other appropriate order for the protection of the insurer's policyholders and creditors and the preservation of its property. (Code 1950, § 38-139; 1952, c. 317, § 38.1-132; 1986, c. 562.)

§ 38.2-1508. Powers of Commission when authorized to rehabilitate or liquidate companies. — Whenever the Commission is authorized to act as a receiver to rehabilitate or liquidate an insurer or to take any other authorized steps that it considers advisable in connection with the affairs of the insurer, it shall have all the power and authority of a court of record as provided in Article IX, Section 3 of the Constitution of Virginia. All further proceedings in connection with the rehabilitation or liquidation shall be conducted by the Commission without any control or supervision by the court to which the application was made. For the violation of any injunction or order issued under this chapter, the Commission shall have the same power to punish for contempt as a court. The Commission may deal with the property and affairs of the insurer in its own name or in the name of the insurer. The Commission shall be vested by law with the title to all of the property, contracts and rights of action of the insurer as of the date shown by the order of the court referred to in § 38.2-1507. The filing or recording of the order in any clerk's office in this Commonwealth shall give the same notice that a deed, bill of sale or other evidence of properly filed or recorded title have given. (Code 1950, § 38-140; 1952, c. 317, § 38.1-133; 1971, Ex. Sess., c. 1; 1986, c. 562; 1992, c. 468.)

McCarran-Ferguson Act applies to rehabilitation proceeding statutes. — The creation by statute of a single, exclusive forum for insurance company rehabilitation proceedings is regulation of the "business of insurance" for purposes of the McCarran-Ferguson Act. Eden Fin. Group, Inc. v. Fidelity Bankers Life Ins. Co., 778 F. Supp. 278 (E.D. Va. 1991).

The exclusive regulatory jurisdiction of the states over insurance companies applies only to the "business of insurance," not to the regulation of the "business of insurers." Eden Fin. Group, Inc. v. Fidelity Bankers Life Ins. Co.,

778 F. Supp. 278 (E.D. Va. 1991).

While fixing claim priorities in the liquidation context may be the business of insurers, rehabilitation proceedings necessarily are the business of insurance, as that term has been defined under Union Labor Life Ins. Co. v. Pireno, 458 U.S. 119, 102 S. Ct. 3002, 73 L. Ed. 2d 647 (1982). Eden Fin. Group, Inc. v. Fidelity Bankers Life Ins. Co., 778 F. Supp. 278 (E.D. Va. 1991).

Insurance company in state rehabilitation proceedings is exempt from Federal Arbitration Act. — The McCarran-Ferguson

Act bars interference with state laws regulating the business of insurance, unless such laws specifically relate to insurance; because the Federal Arbitration Act does not specifically relate to the business of insurance, an insurance company in state rehabilitation and conservation proceedings is excepted from the provisions of the Federal Arbitration Act where a party attempts to invoke arbitration against the company or its receiver. Eden Fin. Group, Inc. v. Fidelity Bankers Life Ins. Co., 778 F. Supp. 278 (E.D. Va. 1991).

Under the McCarran-Ferguson Act, federal courts must defer to the exclusive jurisdiction of state proceedings over the rehabilitation of insurance companies. Eden Fin. Group, Inc. v. Fidelity Bankers Life Ins. Co., 778 F. Supp. 278 (E.D. Va. 1991).

When demands for arbitration are stayed along with all other types of claims and causes of action in an insurance rehabilitation proceeding, the provisions of the Federal Arbitration Act must give way to the mandates and policy of the McCarran-Ferguson Act and accompanying state regulations. Eden Fin. Group, Inc. v. Fidelity Bankers Life Ins. Co., 778 F. Supp. 278 (E.D. Va. 1991).

§ 38.2-1509. Powers of Commission when authorized to rehabilitate or liquidate insurers by court order; disbursement of available assets to an association, etc. — A. Whenever the Commission is authorized by order of the Circuit Court of the City of Richmond to rehabilitate or liquidate any domestic insurer other than an insurer writing exclusively title, fidelity and surety, credit or ocean marine insurance, the Commission shall disburse the assets as they become available to an association. Disbursal shall not be made until an application has been filed with the Commission by an association for an insolvent insurer's available assets.

B. The Commission shall disburse the assets of an insolvent insurer as they become available in the following manner:

1. Pay, after reserving for the payment of the costs and expenses of administration, according to the following priorities: (i) claims of secured creditors with a perfected security interest not voidable under § 38.2-1513 to the extent of the value of their security, (ii) claims of the associations for "covered claims" and "contractual obligations" as defined in §§ 38.2-1603 and 38.2-1701 and claims of other policyholders arising out of insurance contracts apportioned without preference, (iii) taxes owed to the United States and other debts owed to any person, including the United States, which by the laws of the United States are entitled to priority, (iv) wages entitled to priority as provided in § 38.2-1514, and (v) other creditors; and

2. Equitably allocate disbursements to each of the entitled associations; and

3. Secure an agreement from each of the entitled associations requiring the return to the Commission of any assets previously disbursed to the association required to pay claims entitled to priority in subdivision 1 of this subsection. No bond shall be required of any entitled association; and

4. Require a full report to be made by the association to the Commission accounting for all assets disbursed to the association, all disbursements made from these assets, any interest earned on these assets and any other matter as the Commission may require.

C. The Commission shall provide for disbursements to the association in an amount estimated at least equal to the claim payments made or to be made by the association for which the association could assert a claim against the Commission. In addition, the Commission shall provide that if the assets available for disbursement do not equal or exceed the amount of claim payments made or to be made by the associations, then disbursements shall be in the amount of available assets.

D. The Commission shall notify the affected associations and the commissioners of insurance in the other states of any disbursement made according to this section. The notice shall be deemed given when sent by certified mail at least thirty days prior to disbursement. (1978, c. 696, § 38.1-133.1; 1979, c. 385; 1986, c. 562; 1996, c. 81.)

This section does not permit a reinsurer for an insurance company in receivership to obtain administrative priority over other creditors in recovering amounts owed it under an ongoing treaty of reinsurance with the insolvent company. Swiss Re Life Co. Am. v. Gross, 479 S.E.2d 857 (1997).

Virginia law prohibits creditors of an insolvent estate from earning interest on their claims. Swiss Re Life Co. Am. v. Gross, 479 S.E.2d 857 (1997).

§ 38.2-1510. Commission may appoint assistants in connection with rehabilitation or liquidation.

— The Commission shall have power to appoint one or more special deputies as its agent and to employ the counsel, clerks, and assistants considered necessary to efficiently conduct the rehabilitation or liquidation. The Commission may delegate to its agent any of its powers which are necessary to carry out the rehabilitation or liquidation. The compensation of the special deputy commissioners, counsel, clerks and assistants, and all expenses relating to the rehabilitation or liquidation of any insurer shall be set by the Commission and upon certification by the Commission be paid out of the insurer's assets. (Code 1950, § 38-141; 1952, c. 317, § 38.1-134; 1986, c. 562.)

§ 38.2-1511. Borrowing on pledge of assets.

— For the purpose of facilitating the delinquency proceeding of an insurer, the Commission, or a receiver other than the Commission with the approval of the court, may borrow money and execute, acknowledge, and deliver notes or other evidences of indebtedness and secure the repayment by mortgage, pledge, assignment, transfer in trust, or hypothecation of any or all of the property, real, personal or mixed, of the insurer. The Commission, or a receiver other than the Commission with the approval of the court, shall have power to take any action necessary and proper to consummate any loans and to provide for repayment. No note or other evidence of indebtedness made or executed by the receiver shall impose upon the receiver any liability except with respect to the assets and other property of the insurer. (1952, c. 317, § 38.1-135; 1986, c. 562.)

§ 38.2-1512. Rights and liabilities fixed upon liquidation.

— The rights and liabilities of an insurer and of its creditors, policyholders, stockholders, members, and all other persons interested in the property and assets of the insurer, shall be fixed as of the date of the entry of the order directing the liquidation of the insurer unless otherwise provided by law. The rights of claimants holding contingent claims on that date shall be determined by this chapter. (1952, c. 317, § 38.1-136; 1986, c. 562.)

§ 38.2-1513. Voidable transfers.

— A. Any transfer of or lien upon the property of an insurer that is made or created within four months before the institution of delinquency proceedings under this chapter shall be voidable if (i) done with the intent of giving or enabling any creditor to obtain a greater percentage of payment of the debt than any other creditor of the same class and (ii) the creditor accepting the transfer has reasonable cause to believe that a preference will occur.

B. Every director, officer, employee, stockholder, member, subscriber, and other person acting on behalf of an insurer who is involved in any act described in subsection A of this section, and every person receiving property of an insurer as a result of this act, shall be personally liable and held accountable to the receiver.

C. A receiver in any proceeding under this chapter may avoid any transfer of or lien upon the property of an insurer that any creditor, stockholder, subscriber or member of the insurer might have avoided. The receiver may also recover the transferred property unless the person was a valid holder for value before the date of the institution of delinquency proceedings under this chapter. The property or its value may be recovered from anyone who has received it except as a valid holder for value as specified in this subsection. (1952, c. 317, § 38.1-137; 1986, c. 562.)

§ 38.2-1514. Priority of claims for wages. — Before the payment of any other debt or claim, other than those for which a higher priority is established in § 38.2-1509, compensation shall be paid to employees other than officers of an insurer for services rendered within three months before the commencement of the delinquency proceedings. The payment shall not exceed $1,000 for each employee. At the discretion of the Commission, or a receiver other than the Commission with the approval of the court, payment may be made as soon as practicable. This priority shall be superior to any other similar priority authorized by law regarding wages or compensation of the employees.

Nothing in this section shall prohibit a receiver from allocating sufficient funds to cover the expenses of administration. (1952, c. 317, § 38.1-138; 1986, c. 562; 1996, c. 81.)

§ 38.2-1515. Mutual debts or credits, how treated. — A. In all cases of mutual debts or mutual credits between the insurer and another person in connection with any action or proceeding under this chapter, the credits and debts shall be set off and the balance only shall be allowed or paid, except as provided in subsection B of this section.

B. No offset shall be allowed in favor of any person where:

1. The obligation of the insurer to the person would not entitle him at the date of the entry of any rehabilitation or liquidation order to share as a claimant in the assets of the insurer;

2. The obligation of the insurer to the person was purchased by or transferred to the person with a view of its being used as an offset; or

3. The obligation of the person is to pay (i) an assessment levied against the members of a mutual insurer or the subscribers of a reciprocal insurer, or (ii) a balance upon a subscription to the capital stock of a stock insurer. (1952, c. 317, § 38.1-139; 1986, c. 562.)

Debts owed by an insurer cannot be acquired for the purpose of obtaining a set off. Swiss Re Life Co. Am. v. Gross, 479 S.E.2d 857 (1997).

§ 38.2-1516. Receivers to file reports, etc., with Commission. — Each receiver appointed in delinquency proceedings shall file with the Commission annually a report of the affairs of the insurer in the form prescribed by the Commission. Each receiver shall file with the Commission copies of all reports, petitions, court orders, and other pertinent papers dealing with the delinquency proceeding. (Code 1950, § 38-142; 1952, c. 317, § 38.1-140; 1986, c. 562.)

§ 38.2-1517. What included in annual report of Commission. — The Commission shall include in its annual report the names of all insurers against which delinquency proceedings are pending under this chapter, and the names and addresses of any receivers of the insurers. The report shall show whether or not the insurers have resumed business or have been liquidated, and shall contain any other matter that will inform the policyholders, creditors, stockholders, members and the public of the current status of the proceeding regarding each insurer. (Code 1950, § 38-142; 1952, c. 317, § 38.1-141; 1986, c. 562.)

§ 38.2-1518. Rehabilitation or mutualization of companies. — If at any time the Commission acting as the receiver finds that it is in the best interests of the policyholders and creditors of a delinquent insurer that it be rehabilitated or mutualized, the Commission shall prepare a plan of rehabilitation or mutualization. If at any time a receiver, other than the Commission, of a delinquent insurer reports to the court that it is in the best interests of the policyholders and creditors of the insurer that it be rehabilitated or mutualized, the receiver shall submit a plan of rehabilitation or mutualization to the court for its approval. The plan may include a provision imposing liens upon the net equities of policyholders of the insurer, and in the case of life insurers, a provision imposing a moratorium upon the loan or cash surrender values of the policies for whatever period of time is necessary. A hearing on the plan shall be held and notice of the hearing given in a manner prescribed by either the Commission or the court. After the hearing, the plan may be approved, disapproved, or modified by the Commission or the court. (Code 1950, § 38-139; 1952, c. 317, § 38.1-142; 1986, c. 562.)

§ 38.2-1519. Termination of rehabilitation; when liquidation may be entered. — A. If either the Commission or the court determines that the purposes of the rehabilitation proceeding have been accomplished and that the insurer can safely and properly resume possession of its property and the conduct of its business, an order may be entered terminating the rehabilitation proceeding and permitting the insurer to resume possession of its property and the management and conduct of its affairs. The order shall not be entered until a full hearing is held, subject to proper notice given in the manner prescribed by the Commission or the court.

B. If at any time it appears to either the Commission or the court that further efforts to rehabilitate the insurer would be useless, an order of liquidation may be entered. (Code 1950, § 38-139; 1952, c. 317, § 38.1-143; 1986, c. 562.)

§ 38.2-1520. Liquidation of alien insurers. — Proceedings in liquidation of the business of the United States branch of an alien insurer having trusteed assets in this Commonwealth may be instituted and conducted in the manner prescribed in this chapter for domestic insurers. However, only the assets of the business of the United States branch shall be included in the proceedings. (1952, c. 317, § 38.1-144; 1986, c. 562.)

§ 38.2-1521. Conservation of assets of foreign or alien insurer; when liquidation may be entered. — A. Proceedings against a foreign or alien insurer for the conservation of the insurer's assets within this Commonwealth may be instituted and conducted in the manner prescribed in this chapter for delinquency proceedings against a domestic insurer on any one or more of the applicable grounds specified in § 38.2-1503. The order of conservation shall direct the receiver to take possession of the assets of the insurer within this Commonwealth and conserve the assets for the benefit of its policyholders and for any other purpose as the nature of the cause and the interests of its policyholders, creditors, members, stockholders or the public require.

B. If the laws of any other state or country provide for the conservation, liquidation and distribution of a foreign or alien insurer's assets to creditors, policyholders, and other entitled persons, then the receiver appointed in this Commonwealth to conserve the foreign or alien insurer's assets within this Commonwealth may proceed to liquidate the business of the insurer in this Commonwealth and distribute the assets to those entitled to them. In all other cases the rights, powers, and duties of the Commission or the receiver with respect to the assets of a foreign or alien insurer shall be ancillary to the rights, powers, and duties imposed upon any receiver or other person in charge of the property, business, and affairs of the insurer in its domiciliary state or country. (1952, c. 317, § 38.1-145; 1986, c. 562.)

CHAPTER 16.

VIRGINIA PROPERTY AND CASUALTY INSURANCE GUARANTY ASSOCIATION.

ARTICLE 1.

Establishment and Operation of the Association.

§ **38.2-1600. Purpose.** — The purpose of this chapter is to establish an association that shall provide prompt payment of covered claims to reduce financial loss to claimants or policyholders resulting from the insolvency of an insurer. This association shall assist in the detection and prevention of insurer insolvencies and shall apportion the cost of this protection among insurers. (1970, c. 766, § 38.1-757; 1986, c. 562.)

Legislative intent. — The Virginia Insurance Guaranty Association Act, considered as a whole, clearly indicates that the General Assembly did not intend that the association merely step into the shoes of the insolvent insurer, since establishment of the association affords a mechanism for the timely payment of appropriate claims to avoid financial loss to certain classes of people, not merely a solvent substitute for an insolvent insurance company.

Virginia Property & Cas. Ins. Guar. Ass'n v. International Ins. Co., 238 Va. 702, 385 S.E.2d 614 (1989) (decided under former § 38.1-757).

No right of subrogation against association where insureds suffered no loss. — Where the insurer of a driver of a truck which collided with insureds became insolvent and an uninsured motorist insurer paid the insured the full amount of their claims, the uninsured motorist insurer did not then have any rights of subrogation against the Property and Casualty Insurance Guarantee Association because the insureds never suffered any financial loss due to the insolvency of driver's insurer. Northland Ins. Co. v. Virginia Property & Cas. Ins. Guar. Ass'n, 240 Va. 115, 392 S.E.2d 682 (1990).

§ 38.2-1601. Application. — This chapter shall apply to all classes of direct insurance written by member insurers but shall not be applicable to the following:

1. Life, annuity, health or disability insurance;
2. Mortgage guaranty, financial guaranty or other forms of insurance offering protection against investment risks;
3. Fidelity or surety bonds, or any other bonding obligations;
4. Credit insurance and credit involuntary unemployment insurance;
5. Insurance of warranties or service contracts;
6. Title insurance;
7. Insurance of vessels or craft used primarily in a trade or business, their cargoes, and marine builders' risk and marine protection and indemnity;
8. Any transaction or combination of transactions between a person, including affiliates of such person, and an insurer, including affiliates of such insurer, which involves the transfer of investment or credit risk unaccompanied by transfer of insurance risk; or
9. Any class of insurance written by cooperative nonprofit life benefit companies, mutual assessment life, accident and sickness insurers, burial societies, fraternal benefit societies, captive insurers, risk retention groups, and home protection companies. (1970, c. 766, § 38.1-758; 1986, c. 562; 1987, c. 529; 1993, cc. 77, 774; 1998, c. 230.)

The 1998 amendment, in subdivision 9, inserted "risk retention groups."

§ 38.2-1602. Liberal construction. — This chapter shall be liberally construed to effect the purpose under § 38.2-1600, which shall constitute an aid and guide to interpretation. (1970, c. 766, § 38.1-759; 1986, c. 562.)

§ 38.2-1603. Definitions. — As used in this chapter:

"Account" means any one of the three accounts created by § 38.2-1604.

"Affiliate" means a person who directly, or indirectly, through one or more intermediaries, controls, is controlled by, or is under common control with an insolvent insurer on December 31 of the year next preceding the date the insurer becomes an insolvent insurer.

"Association" means the Virginia Property and Casualty Insurance Guaranty Association created under § 38.2-1604.

"Claimant" means any insured making a first party claim or any person instituting a liability claim; provided that no person who is an affiliate of the insolvent insurer may be a claimant.

"Control" means the possession, direct or indirect, of the power to direct or cause the direction of the management and policies of a person, whether through the ownership of voting securities, by contract other than a commercial contract for goods or nonmanagement services, or otherwise, unless the power is the result of an official position with or corporate office held by the person. Control shall be presumed to exist if any person, directly or indirectly, owns, controls, holds with the power to vote, or holds proxies representing, ten percent or more of the voting securities of any other person. This presumption may be rebutted by a showing that control does not exist in fact.

"Covered claim" means an unpaid claim, including one for unearned premiums, submitted by a claimant, which arises out of and is within the coverage and is subject to the applicable limits of a policy covered by this chapter and

issued by an insurer who has been declared to be an insolvent insurer. The claimant or insured shall be a resident of this Commonwealth at the time of the insured loss, provided that for entities other than an individual, the residence of a claimant or insured is the state in which its principal place of business is located at the time of the insured loss or the property from which the claim arises shall be permanently located in this Commonwealth. "Covered claim" shall not include any amount awarded as punitive or exemplary damages or sought as a return of premium under any retrospective rating plan.

"*Insolvent insurer*" means an insurer that is (i) licensed to transact the business of insurance in this Commonwealth either at the time the policy was issued or when the insured loss occurred and (ii) against whom an order of liquidation with a finding of insolvency has been entered after July 1, 1987, by a court of competent jurisdiction in the insurer's state of domicile or of this Commonwealth under the provisions of Chapter 15 (§ 38.2-1500 et seq.) of this title, and which order of liquidation has not been stayed or been the subject of a writ of supersedeas or other comparable order.

"*Member insurer*" means any person who (i) writes any class of insurance to which this chapter applies under § 38.2-1601, including reciprocal insurance contracts, and (ii) is licensed to transact the business of insurance in this Commonwealth but shall not include persons listed in subdivision 9 of § 38.2-1601.

"*Net direct written premiums*" means direct gross premiums written in this Commonwealth on insurance policies applicable to this chapter, less return premiums and dividends paid or credited to policyholders on direct business. "Net direct written premiums" does not include premiums on contracts between insurers or reinsurers. (1970, c. 766, § 38.1-760; 1986, c. 562; 1987, c. 529; 1998, c. 230.)

The 1998 amendment, in the paragraph defining "Member insurer," inserted "but shall not include persons listed in subdivision 9 of § 38.2-1601."

Legislative intent. — The Virginia Insurance Guaranty Association Act, considered as a whole, clearly indicates that the General Assembly did not intend that the association merely step into the shoes of the insolvent insurer, since establishment of the association affords a mechanism for the timely payment of appropriate claims to avoid financial loss to certain classes of people, not merely a solvent substitute for an insolvent insurance company. Virginia Property & Cas. Ins. Guar. Ass'n v. International Ins. Co., 238 Va. 702, 385 S.E.2d 614 (1989) (decided under former § 38.1-760).

§ 38.2-1604. Association created; members; divided into three accounts.

— The nonprofit unincorporated legal entity known as the Virginia Property and Casualty Insurance Guaranty Association, created by former § 38.1-761, shall continue in existence. All insurers defined as "member insurers" under § 38.2-1603 shall be and remain members of the Association as a condition of their license to transact the business of insurance in this Commonwealth. The Association shall perform its functions under a plan of operation established and approved under § 38.2-1607 and shall exercise its powers through a board of directors established under § 38.2-1605. For purposes of administration and assessment, the Association shall have three separate accounts: (i) the workers' compensation insurance account; (ii) the automobile insurance account; and (iii) the account for all other insurance to which this chapter applies. These accounts shall be in addition to and separate from the safety fund authorized by § 38.2-1619. (1970, c. 766, § 38.1-761; 1986, c. 562; 1998, c. 230.)

The **1998 amendment** added the last sentence.
Applied in International Ins. Co. v. Virginia

Ins. Guar. Ass'n, 649 F. Supp. 58 (E.D. Va. 1986).

§ 38.2-1605. Board of directors. — A. The board of directors of the Association shall consist of at least five but no more than nine persons serving terms specified in the plan of operation. The members of the board shall be elected by member insurers, giving consideration among other things to whether all types of member insurers are fairly represented. Vacancies on the board shall be filled for the remaining period of the term in the same manner as initial appointments.

B. Members of the board may be reimbursed from the assets of the Association for expenses incurred by them as members of the board of directors. (1970, c. 766, § 38.1-762; 1986, c. 562.)

§ 38.2-1606. Duties and powers of Association. — A. The Association shall:

1. Be obligated to pay covered claims that existed prior to the determination of insolvency and which arose before the earliest of (i) ninety-one days after the determination of insolvency, (ii) the policy expiration date, or (iii) the date the insured replaces or cancels the policy.

a. Such obligation shall be satisfied by paying to the claimant an amount as follows:

(i) The full amount of a covered claim for benefits under a workers' compensation insurance coverage; or

(ii) An amount not exceeding $300,000 per claimant for all other covered claims.

b. In no event shall the Association be obligated to pay a claimant for an amount in excess of the insolvent insurer's obligation for a covered claim. Notwithstanding any other provision of this chapter, a covered claim shall not include any claim filed with the Guaranty Association after the final date set by the court for the filing of claims against the liquidator or receiver of an insolvent insurer. The Association shall pay only that amount of each unearned premium which is in excess of fifty dollars. A covered claim shall not include any claim filed with the Association after the final date set by the court for the filing of claims against the liquidator or receiver of an insolvent insurer.

2. Be deemed the insurer to the extent of the insolvent insurer's obligation on the covered claims and to that extent shall have all the rights, duties, and obligations of the insolvent insurer as if the insurer had not become insolvent.

3. Allocate claims paid and expenses incurred among the three accounts and assess member insurers separately for each account (i) the amounts necessary to pay the obligations of the Association under subdivision 1 of this subsection subsequent to an insolvency, (ii) the expenses of handling covered claims subsequent to an insolvency, and (iii) other expenses authorized by this chapter. The assessment of each member insurer shall be based on the ratio of the net direct written premiums of the member insurer to the net direct written premiums of all member insurers. This ratio shall be determined using the premiums for the calendar year preceding the assessment on the classes of insurance in the account. Each member insurer shall be notified of the assessment at least thirty days before it is due. No member insurer may be assessed in any year on any account an amount greater than two percent of that member insurer's net direct written premiums for the calendar year preceding the assessment on the classes of insurance in the account. If the sum of the maximum assessment and the assets of the account does not provide in any one year an amount sufficient to make all necessary payments from that account, the funds available shall be prorated and the unpaid portion shall be

paid as soon as funds become available. The Association shall pay claims in any order which it may deem reasonable, including the payment of claims as such are received from the claimants or in groups or categories of claims. The Association may exempt or defer, in whole or in part, the assessment of any member insurer if payment of the assessment would cause the member insurer's financial statement to reflect an impairment of the insurer's minimum capital and surplus in any jurisdiction in which the member insurer is authorized to transact insurance; provided, that during the period of deferment, no dividends shall be paid to shareholders or policyholders. Deferred assessments shall be paid when the payments shall not cause an impairment of minimum capital and surplus. These payments shall be refunded to those members receiving larger assessments by virtue of the deferment, or at the election of any such company, credited against future assessments. Each member insurer may set off against any assessment, payments authorized by the Association and made on covered claims and expenses incurred in the payment of those claims. The offset shall be allowed only if the payments are chargeable to the account for which the assessment is made.

3a. The Association shall issue to each insurer paying an assessment under this chapter, other than assessments paid pursuant to subdivision 3 (iii) of this subsection, a certificate of contribution in a form prescribed by the Commission, for the amount of the assessment paid, excluding interest penalties. All outstanding certificates shall be of equal priority without reference to amounts or dates of issue. A certificate of contribution may be shown by the insurer on its financial statement as an asset. This shall be shown in a form, in an amount, and for a period of time approved by the Commission.

4. Investigate claims brought against the Association and adjust, compromise, settle, and pay covered claims to the extent of the Association's obligation and deny all other claims. The Association may review settlements, releases and judgments to which the insolvent insurer or its insureds were parties to determine the extent to which the settlements, releases and judgments may be properly contested.

5. Notify those persons as the Commission directs under subdivision 8 of this subsection.

6. Handle claims through its employees or through one or more insurers or other persons designated as servicing facilities. Designation of a servicing facility is subject to (i) the approval of the Commission and (ii) acceptance by the designated insurer.

7. Reimburse each servicing facility for the Association's obligations paid by the facility and for expenses incurred by the facility while handling claims on behalf of the Association. The Association shall pay the other expenses authorized by this chapter.

8. Notify the insureds of the insolvent insurer and any other interested parties of the determination of insolvency and of their rights under this chapter. Notification shall be sent by mail to the insureds' last known address. If the Association is unable to obtain the information required to mail the notice in a timely manner, the Association shall publish the notice in newspapers of general circulation likely to cover geographical areas occupied by the policyholders.

B. The Association may:

1. Employ or retain persons necessary to perform the duties of the Association.

2. Borrow funds necessary to effect the purposes of this chapter in accord with the plan of operation.

3. Sue or be sued.

4. Negotiate and become a party to those contracts necessary to carry out the purpose of this chapter.

5. Perform any other acts necessary or proper to achieve the purpose of this chapter.

6. Pay refunds to the member insurers in proportion to their contributions made to each account during the five years immediately preceding the date of the refund. The total refund shall be the amount by which the assets of the account are expected to exceed the liabilities for the coming year as determined by the board of directors.

7. Obtain commitments or lines of credit, and in the event a natural disaster such as an earthquake, windstorm or fire results in covered claims, with the approval of its board of directors and the Commission, secure indebtedness for borrowed money to be used for the purpose set forth in subsection A of § 38.2-1622 in an amount not to exceed the amount reasonably estimated by its board of directors and the Commission as the aggregate amount of assessments which the Association will be authorized to make during the succeeding calendar year, by pledge, assignment, transfer in trust or hypothecation of any or all of the assessments to be made against its member insurers. (1970, c. 766, §§ 38.1-763, 38.1-765; 1971, Ex. Sess., c. 1; 1982, c. 353; 1983, c. 486; 1986, c. 562; 1987, cc. 529, 565, 655; 1998, c. 230.)

The 1998 amendment, in subsection A, in subdivision 1, added the subdivisions a and b designations; and in subsection B, added subdivision 7.

Legislative intent. — The Virginia Insurance Guaranty Association Act, considered as a whole, clearly indicates that the General Assembly did not intend that the association merely step into the shoes of the insolvent insurer, since establishment of the association affords a mechanism for the timely payment of appropriate claims to avoid financial loss to certain classes of people, not merely a solvent substitute for an insolvent insurance company. Virginia Property & Cas. Ins. Guar. Ass'n v. International Ins. Co., 238 Va. 702, 385 S.E.2d 614 (1989) (decided under former § 38.1-763).

The legislation that created the Association, considered as a whole, clearly indicates the General Assembly did not intend the Association to be merely a solvent substitute for an insolvent insurance company. Uninsured Employer's Fund v. Mounts, 24 Va. App. 550, 484 S.E.2d 140 (1997), aff'd, 255 Va. 254, 497 S.E.2d 464 (1998).

No right of subrogation against association where insureds suffered no loss. — Where the insurer of a driver of a truck collided with insureds became insolvent and an uninsured motorist insurer paid the insured the full amount of their claims, the uninsured motorist insurer did not then have any rights of subrogation against the Property and Casualty Insurance Guarantee Association because the insureds never suffered any financial loss due to the insolvency of driver's insurer. Northland Ins. Co. v. Virginia Property & Cas. Ins. Guar. Ass'n, 240 Va. 115, 392 S.E.2d 682 (1990).

Applied in International Ins. Co. v. Virginia Ins. Guar. Ass'n, 649 F. Supp. 58 (E.D Va. 1986).

§ 38.2-1607. Plan of operation. — A. 1. The plan of operation and any amendments to it shall be submitted to the Commission by the Association and shall not become effective until approved by the Commission in writing. The Commission shall approve the plan or amendment to the plan if it complies with this chapter and assures the fair, reasonable, and equitable administration of the Association.

2. The plan of operation approved under former § 38.1-764 shall remain in effect until modified in accordance with subdivision 3 of this subsection.

3. If the Association fails to submit suitable amendments to the plan, the Commission shall, after notice and hearing, adopt and promulgate any reasonable rules that are necessary or advisable to effect this chapter. Those rules shall continue in force until modified by the Commission or superseded by a plan or amendments submitted by the Association and approved by the Commission.

B. All member insurers shall comply with the plan of operation.

C. The plan of operation shall:

1. Establish the procedures for exercising the powers and duties of the Association under § 38.2-1606.

2. Establish procedures for handling assets of the Association.

3. Establish the amount and method of reimbursing members of the board of directors under § 38.2-1605.

4. Establish procedures by which claims may be filed with the Association and establish acceptable forms of proof of covered claims. Notice of claims to the receiver or liquidator of the insolvent insurer shall be deemed notice to the Association or its agent and a list of those claims shall be periodically submitted to the Association or similar organizations in another state by the receiver or liquidator.

5. Establish regular places and times for meetings of the board of directors.

6. Establish procedures for records to be kept of all financial transactions of the Association, its agents, and the board of directors.

7. Provide that any member insurer aggrieved by any final action or decision of the Association may appeal to the Commission within thirty days after the action or decision.

8. Establish the procedures for submitting to the Commission the names of elected members of the board of directors.

9. Contain additional provisions necessary or proper for the execution of the powers and duties of the Association.

D. The plan of operation may provide that any or all powers and duties of the Association, except those under subdivision 3 of subsection A of § 38.2-1606 and subdivision 2 of subsection B of § 38.2-1606, shall be delegated to a corporation, association, or other organization that performs or will perform functions similar to those of this Association, or its equivalent, in two or more states. The corporation, association or organization shall be compensated for providing those and any other permissible services. A delegation under this subsection shall take effect only with the approval of both the board of directors and the Commission. The delegation may be made only to a corporation, association, or organization that extends protection which is substantially no less favorable or effective than that provided by this chapter. (1970, c. 766, § 38.1-764; 1986, c. 562.)

§ 38.2-1608. Duties and powers of Commission; judicial review. —

A. The Commission shall:

1. Notify the Association of the existence of an insolvent insurer within three days after it receives notice of the determination of the insolvency. The Association shall be entitled to a copy of any complaint seeking an order of liquidation with a finding of insolvency against a member company at the same time that such complaint is filed with a court of competent jurisdiction.

2. Upon request of the board of directors, provide the Association with a statement of the net direct written premiums of each member insurer.

B. The Commission may:

1. Suspend or revoke, after notice and hearing, the license to transact the business of insurance in this Commonwealth of any member insurer which fails to pay an assessment when due or fails to comply with the plan of operation. As an alternative, the Commission may levy a fine on any member insurer that fails to pay an assessment when due. The fine shall not exceed five percent of the unpaid assessment per month, except that no fine shall be less than $100 per month.

2. Revoke the designation of any servicing facility if it finds that claims are being handled unsatisfactorily. (1970, c. 766, § 38.1-765; 1971, Ex. Sess., c. 1; 1986, c. 562; 1987, c. 529.)

Legislative intent. — The Virginia Insurance Guaranty Association Act, considered as a whole, clearly indicates that the General Assembly did not intend that the association merely step into the shoes of the insolvent insurer, since establishment of the association affords a mechanism for the timely payment of appropriate claims to avoid financial loss to certain classes of people, not merely a solvent substitute for an insolvent insurance company. Virginia Property & Cas. Ins. Guar. Ass'n v. International Ins. Co., 238 Va. 702, 385 S.E.2d 614 (1989) (decided under former § 38.1-767).

The exhaustion requirement applies in instances where the claim: (1) meets the defi-

nition of "covered claim" under the Virginia Insurance Guaranty Association Act; and (2) can validly be asserted against a solvent insurer under an insurance policy. Virginia Property & Cas. Ins. Guar. Ass'n v. International Ins. Co., 238 Va. 702, 385 S.E.2d 614 (1989) (decided under former § 38.1-767).

§ 38.2-1609. Insured's rights and liabilities; settlements binding on receiver or liquidator; priority of claims; statements to be filed with receiver or liquidator. — A. 1. Any person recovering under this chapter shall be deemed to have assigned his rights under the policy to the Association to the extent of his recovery from the Association. Each insured or claimant seeking the protection of this chapter shall cooperate with the Association to the same extent as the person would have been required to cooperate with the insolvent insurer. The Association shall have no cause of action against the insured of the insolvent insurer for any sums it has paid out except the causes of action the insolvent insurer would have had if those sums had been paid by the insolvent insurer and except as provided in subdivision 2 of this subsection. In the case of an insolvent insurer operating on an assessment plan, payments of claims by the Association shall not reduce the liability of insureds to the receiver, liquidator, or statutory successor for unpaid assessments previously made. However, the receiver, liquidator, or statutory successor shall under no circumstances levy an additional assessment against the insured, regardless of the terms of the policy.

2. The Association shall have the right to recover from the following persons the amount of any "covered claim" paid on behalf of such persons pursuant to this chapter:

a. Any insured whose net worth on December 31 of the year next preceding the date the insurer becomes an insolvent insurer exceeds fifty million dollars and whose liability obligations to other persons are satisfied in whole or in part by payments made under this chapter; and

b. Any person who is an affiliate of the insolvent insurer and whose liability obligations to other persons are satisfied in whole or in part by payments made under this chapter.

B. The receiver, liquidator, or statutory successor of an insolvent insurer shall be bound by settlements of covered claims by the Association or a similar organization in another state. The court having jurisdiction shall grant those claims priority equal to that which the claimant would have been entitled in the absence of this chapter against the assets of the insolvent insurer. The expenses of the Association or a similar organization incurred in handling claims shall be accorded the same priority as the liquidator's expenses.

C. The Association shall preserve its rights to the insolvent insurer by periodically filing with the receiver or liquidator statements of the covered claims paid by the Association and estimates of anticipated claims on the Association. (1970, c. 766, § 38.1-766; 1986, c. 562; 1987, c. 529.)

Applied in International Ins. Co. v. Virginia Ins. Guar. Ass'n, 649 F. Supp. 58 (E.D. Va. 1986).

§ 38.2-1610. Exhaustion of remedies under policy; claims recoverable from more than one association. — A. Any person having a claim against an insurer under any provision in an insurance policy, other than a policy of an insolvent insurer under which the claim is also covered, shall be required to first seek recovery under the policy covered by the insurer which is not insolvent. Any amount payable on a covered claim under this chapter shall be reduced by the amount of any recovery under the insurance policy.

A1. Any person having a claim or legal right of recovery under any governmental insurance or guaranty program which is also a covered claim, shall be required to exhaust first his right under such program. Any amount payable on a covered claim under this chapter shall be reduced by the amount of any recovery under such program.

B. Any person having a claim that may be recovered under more than one insurance guaranty association or its equivalent shall seek recovery first from the association of the state where the insured resides. However, if it is a first party claim for damage to property with a permanent location, the insured shall seek recovery first from the association of the state where the property is located. For a workers' compensation claim recovery shall first be sought from the association of the state where the claimant resides. Any recovery under this chapter shall be reduced by the amount of the recovery from any other insurance guaranty association or its equivalent. (1970, c. 766, § 38.1-767; 1986, c. 562; 1987, c. 529.)

Legislative intent. — The Virginia Insurance Guaranty Association Act, considered as a whole, clearly indicates that the General Assembly did not intend that the association merely step into the shoes of the insolvent insurer, since establishment of the association affords a mechanism for the timely payment of appropriate claims to avoid financial loss to certain classes of people, not merely a solvent substitute for an insolvent insurance company. Virginia Property & Cas. Ins. Guar. Ass'n v. International Ins. Co., 238 Va. 702, 385 S.E.2d 614 (1989) (decided under former § 38.1-767).

The exhaustion requirement applies in instances where the claim: (1) meets the definition of "covered claim" under the Virginia Insurance Guaranty Association Act; and (2) can validly be asserted against a solvent insurer under an insurance policy. Virginia Prop-

erty & Cas. Ins. Guar. Ass'n v. International Ins. Co., 238 Va. 702, 385 S.E.2d 614 (1989) (decided under former § 38.1-767).

Uninsured Employer's Fund liable for benefits without apportionment. — Workers' Compensation Commission properly ruled that award of lifetime benefits to coal worker should be paid by the Uninsured Employer's Fund rather than being apportioned between the Fund and the Virginia Property and Casualty Insurance Guaranty Association. The Fund exhibits the indicia of a governmental insurance or guaranty program and therefore falls within the statutory purview of those entities from which recovery must be exhausted before the Guaranty Association is required to make payments. Uninsured Employer's Fund v. Flanary, 27 Va. App. 201, 497 S.E.2d 912 (1998).

§ 38.2-1611. Aids in detection and prevention of insurer insolvencies. — To aid in the detection and prevention of insurer insolvencies:

1. The Association's board of directors has the duty, upon a majority vote, (i) to make recommendations to the Commission for the detection and prevention of insurer insolvencies, and (ii) to respond to requests by the Commission to discuss and make recommendations regarding the status of any member insurer whose financial condition may be hazardous to the policyholders or the public.

2 through 5. [Repealed.]

6. At the request of the Commission and at the conclusion of any insurer's insolvency in which the Association was obligated to pay covered claims, the board of directors may prepare a report on the history and causes of the insolvency based on the information available to the Association. The report shall be submitted to the Commission. (1970, c. 766, § 38.1-768; 1986, c. 562; 1987, c. 529.)

§ 38.2-1611.1. Tax write-offs of certificates of contribution. — A. A member insurer shall have at its option the right to show a certificate of contribution as an asset in the form approved by the Commission pursuant to

subdivision 3a of subsection A of § 38.2-1606 at the original face amount for the calendar year of issuance. Such amount may be amortized as follows:

1. Certificates of contribution issued prior to January 1, 1998, shall be amortized in each succeeding calendar year through December 31, 1997, at an amount not to exceed 0.05 of one percent of the member's direct gross premium income for the classes of insurance in the account for which the member insurer is assessed. As used herein, the definition of direct gross premium income shall be the same as that specified in § 58.1-2500. If the amount of the certificate has not been fully amortized by the contributing insurer by December 31, 1997, the unamortized balance of the certificate amount shall be amortized, at the option of the contributing insurer, either (i) in the same manner as the certificate was amortized prior to January 1, 1998; however, if not amortized in full prior to calendar year 2010, the unamortized balance of the certificate shall be amortized in full during calendar year 2010, or (ii) over the ten successive calendar years commencing January 1, 1998, in amounts each equal to ten percent of such unamortized balance. A contributing insurer whose certificate has not been fully amortized by December 31, 1997, shall notify the Commission in writing of the amortization schedule option it has selected on or before March 1, 1998; however, if a contributing insurer fails to notify the Commission by such date, the insurer shall be deemed to have selected the option described in clause (i) of the preceding sentence.

2. Certificates of contribution issued on or after January 1, 1998, shall be amortized over the ten calendar years following the year the contribution was paid in amounts each equal to ten percent of the amount of the contribution.

B. The insurer may offset the amount of the certificate amortized in a calendar year as provided in subsection A. This amount shall be deducted from the premium tax liability incurred on business transacted in this Commonwealth for that year. However, the Association shall diligently pursue all rights available to it to recover its expenditures made in the fulfillment of its responsibilities under this chapter. In the event the Commission determines after a hearing that the Association is not diligently pursuing available measures of recovery, participating insurers will not be able to offset amounts amortized during the period that the Commission determines that the Association has not been diligently pursuing available measures of recovery.

C. Any sums that have been (i) amortized by contributing insurers and offset against premium taxes as provided in subsection B and (ii) subsequently refunded pursuant to subdivision 3 of subsection A of § 38.2-1606 or subdivision 6 of subsection B of § 38.2-1606 shall be paid to the Commission and deposited with the State Treasurer for credit to the general fund of this Commonwealth.

D. The amount of any credit against premium taxes provided for in this section for an insurer shall be reduced by the amount of reduction in federal income taxes for any deduction claimed by the insurer for an assessment paid pursuant to this chapter. (1987, cc. 565, 655; 1991, c. 371; 1997, c. 160.)

§ 38.2-1612. Examination and regulation of Association by Commission; annual financial report. — The Association shall be subject to examination and regulation by the Commission. The board of directors shall submit, not later than May 1 of each year, a financial report for the preceding calendar year in a form approved by the Commission. (1970, c. 766, § 38.1-769; 1986, c. 562; 1996, c. 245.)

§ 38.2-1613. Exemption from payment of fees and taxes. — The Association shall be exempt from payment of all fees and all taxes levied by this Commonwealth or any of its subdivisions except taxes levied on real or personal property. (1970, c. 766, § 38.1-770; 1986, c. 562.)

§ 38.2-1614: Repealed by Acts 1993, c. 679.

§ 38.2-1615. No liability for action taken in good faith. — There shall be no liability on the part of and no cause of action shall arise against any member insurer, the Association or its agents or employees, the board of directors, or the Commission or its representatives for any action taken or statement made by them in good faith in the performance of their powers and duties under this chapter. The Association's board of directors shall not incur any civil liability for any statements made in good faith under this provision. (1970, c. 766, § 38.1-772; 1986, c. 562.)

§ 38.2-1616. Stay of proceedings against insolvent insurer; setting aside judgment, etc.; access to records. — A. All proceedings in which the insolvent insurer is a party or is obligated to defend a party in any court in this Commonwealth shall be stayed for up to six months and such additional time thereafter as may be determined by the court from the date the insolvency is determined or an ancillary proceeding is instituted in the Commonwealth, whichever is later, to permit proper defense by the Association of all pending causes of action. For any covered claims arising from a judgment under any decision, verdict or finding based on the default of the insolvent insurer or its failure to defend an insured, the Association either on its own behalf or on behalf of the insured may apply to have the judgment, order, decision, verdict or finding set aside by the same court or administrator that made the judgment, order, decision, verdict or finding and shall be permitted to defend against the claim on the merits.

B. The liquidator, receiver, or statutory successor of an insolvent insurer covered by this chapter shall permit access by the board or its authorized representatives to such of the insolvent insurer's records which are necessary for the board in carrying out its functions under this chapter with regard to covered claims. In addition, the liquidator, receiver or statutory successor shall provide the board or its representative with copies of such records upon the request by the board and at the expense of the board. (1970, c. 766, § 38.1-773; 1986, c. 562; 1987, c. 529.)

§ 38.2-1617. Termination of operation of Association; expiration of chapter. — A. The Commission shall by order terminate the operation of the Association for any class of insurance covered by this chapter with respect to which it has found, after hearing, that there is in effect a statutory or voluntary plan which:

1. Is a permanent plan that is adequately funded or for which adequate funding is provided; and

2. Extends or will extend to the policyholders and residents of this Commonwealth protection and benefits with respect to insolvent insurers not substantially less favorable and effective to those policyholders and residents than the protection and benefits provided with respect to the classes of insurance under this chapter.

B. The Commission shall, by the same order, authorize discontinuance of future payments by insurers to the Association regarding the same classes of insurance. However, the assessments and payments shall continue, as necessary, to pay (i) covered claims of insurers determined to be insolvent prior to the order and (ii) the related expenses not covered by any other plan.

C. In the event the operation of the Association is terminated for all other classes of insurance within its scope, the Association shall, as soon as possible, distribute the balance of moneys and assets remaining. Distribution shall be made after the Association has settled all prior insurer insolvencies not covered by any other plan, including their related expenses. The distribution shall be made to the insurers that are then writing in this Commonwealth policies of the classes of insurance covered by this chapter and that had made payments to the Association. Distribution shall be made using a pro rata method based upon the aggregate of the payments made by the respective insurers during the five years immediately preceding the date of the order. Upon completion of the distribution for all of the classes of insurance covered by this chapter, this chapter shall be deemed to have expired. (1970, c. 766, § 38.1-774; 1986, c. 562.)

ARTICLE 2.

Additional Funds Paid to Association.

§ 38.2-1618. Purpose and applicability of article. — The purpose of this article is to provide directions and guidelines for the control and use of funds provided pursuant to § 38.2-225, obtained through secured borrowings made pursuant to subdivision B 7 of § 38.2-1606, or obtained from sources of funds not specified in Article 1 (§ 38.2-1600 et seq.) of this chapter. (1986, c. 562; 1998, c. 230.)

The 1998 amendment inserted "obtained through secured borrowings made pursuant to subdivision B 7 of § 38.2-1606" and substituted "obtained from sources" for "any other sources."

§ 38.2-1619. Safety fund. — The Association shall maintain a separate asset account to be known as the safety fund. The safety fund shall be used to assist the Association in meeting the objectives specified in § 38.2-1600. (1986, c. 562.)

§ 38.2-1620. Financing the safety fund, maximum amount, distribution of excess. — A. The safety fund, at the discretion of the Commission, shall receive penalty payments levied against member insurers made pursuant to subsection B of § 38.2-225 or any other payments approved by the Commission. Such payments shall include funds borrowed under the provisions of subdivision B 7 of § 38.2-1606 in the event of a natural disaster in order to provide for the prompt payment of covered claims and expenses related thereto.

B. The Commission may approve the payment of funds to the Association provided the balance in the safety fund account does not exceed two percent of the total of all member insurers' net direct written premiums for classes of insurance covered by the accounts specified in § 38.2-1604.

C. Except as provided in subsection D of this section, investment income earned on assets held in the safety fund shall be credited to the safety fund.

D. In the event the safety fund balance exceeds three percent of the net written premium for all classes of insurance covered by the accounts specified in § 38.2-1604, at the discretion of the Commission the difference shall be paid to the state treasury to the credit of the Literary Fund or shall be subject to subsection F of § 38.2-1622.

E. In the event the fund is dissolved, remaining assets in the safety fund will be distributed to the state treasury to the credit of the Literary Fund. (1986, c. 562; 1998, c. 230.)

The 1998 amendment, in subsection A, added the second sentence; and in subsection B, substituted "insurers'" for "insurer's."

§ 38.2-1621. Investment of safety fund. — The assets held in the safety fund may be invested in securities set forth in § 38.2-1415. (1986, c. 562; 1998, c. 230.)

The 1998 amendment substituted "held in the safety fund" for "of the safety fund."

§ 38.2-1622. Use of safety fund, repayment, etc. — A. The purpose of the safety fund is to provide for the payment of covered claims in the event the assessment limit specified in subdivision A 3 of § 38.2-1606 is reached.

B. In the event the assets in the safety fund are needed to pay covered claims, these assets shall be loaned to the respective account specified in § 38.2-1604. This loan shall be the general obligation of the Association

C. Assets in the safety fund derived from borrowed moneys obtained under the provisions of subdivision B 7 of § 38.2-1606 shall be lent to an account at the rate of interest the Association is paying the lender providing such moneys. Interest on any other loan shall be compounded quarterly and be based upon the average ninety-day treasury bill rate for the most recently completed calendar quarter as published in the Federal Reserve Bulletin. This rate will be updated quarterly in order to conform with the market rates of interest.

D. Loans shall be repaid by levying assessments pursuant to subdivision A 3 of § 38.2-1606 against the members for the account on whose behalf the loan was negotiated. Unless otherwise approved by the Commission, the loan shall be repaid within six months of its issuance. This assessment in conjunction with any other assessments levied, shall not exceed the limit specified in subdivision A 3 of § 38.2-1606.

E. Subject to the approval of the Commission, assets in the safety fund may be loaned to any account specified in § 38.2-1604 even though the maximum assessment in subdivision A 3 of § 38.2-1606 has not been levied if the directors of the Association determine that this action will minimize the cost to the Association in paying covered claims.

F. Excess assets in the safety fund set forth in subsection D of § 38.2-1620 may be used to pay the Association's covered claims without the members incurring a liability to repay the safety fund. (1986, c. 562; 1998, c. 230.)

The 1998 amendment inserted "A" preceding "3 of § 38.2-1606" throughout this section; in subsection B, in the first sentence, substituted "in the safety fund" for "of the safety fund," and in the second sentence, deleted "members and shall be evidenced by an agreement approved by the Commission" following "Association"; in subsection C, added the present first sentence and in the present second sentence, substituted "any other" for "this"; in subsection D, in the first sentence substituted "Loans" for "This loan"; in subsection E, substituted "in the safety fund" for "of the safety fund"; and in subsection F, substituted "assets in the safety fund" for "safety fund assets."

§ 38.2-1623. Association as a fiduciary. — In handling the assets of the safety fund, the Association shall be deemed a fiduciary for the Commonwealth. (1986, c. 562.)

CHAPTER 17.

VIRGINIA LIFE, ACCIDENT AND SICKNESS INSURANCE GUARANTY ASSOCIATION.

ARTICLE 1.

Establishment and Operation of the Association.

§ 38.2-1700. Purpose and applicability of chapter. — A. The purpose of this chapter is to protect, subject to certain limitations, policyowners, insureds, beneficiaries, annuitants, payees, and assignees of life insurance policies, accident and sickness insurance policies, annuity contracts, and supplemental contracts against failure to fulfill contractual obligations due to the impairment or insolvency of the insurers issuing those policies or contracts. To provide this protection, (i) an association of insurers is created to enable the guaranty of payment of benefits and of continuation of coverages, (ii) members of the Association are subject to assessments to provide funds to carry out the purpose of this chapter, and (iii) the Association is authorized to assist the Commission, in the prescribed manner, in the detection and prevention of insurer impairments or insolvencies.

B. This chapter shall apply to direct life insurance policies, accident and sickness insurance policies, annuity contracts, and contracts supplemental to life, accident and sickness insurance policies and annuity contracts issued by insurers licensed to transact insurance in this Commonwealth at any time.

C. This chapter shall not apply to:

1. That portion or part of a variable life insurance or variable annuity contract not guaranteed by an insurer;

2. That portion or part of any policy or contract under which the risk is borne by the policyholder;

3. Any policy or contract, or part of a policy or contract assumed by the impaired or insolvent insurer under a contract of reinsurance, other than reinsurance for which assumption certificates have been issued;

4. Any policy or contract issued by cooperative nonprofit life benefit companies, mutual assessment life, accident and sickness insurance companies, burial societies, fraternal benefit societies, dental and optometric services plans and health services plans not subject to § 38.2-4213; or

5. Any contract or certificate which is not issued to and owned by an individual, except to the extent of (i) any annuity benefits guaranteed to an individual by an insurer under such contract or certificate, (ii) any annuity benefits payable for the benefit of an individual by an insurer under an annuity contract issued to fund a structured settlement agreement on account of personal injury or sickness, or (iii) any life insurance benefits and accident and sickness insurance benefits guaranteed payable to any person by an insurer.

D. This chapter shall provide coverage for the policies and contracts specified in subsection B:

1. To persons who, regardless of where they reside (except for nonresident certificate holders under group policies or contracts), are the beneficiaries, assignees or payees of the persons covered under subdivision 2, and

2. To persons who are owners of or certificate holders under such policies or contracts, and who

a. are residents, or

b. are not residents, but only under all of the following conditions: (i) the insurers which issued such policies or contracts are domiciled in this state; (ii) such insurers at the time of issuance of such policies or contracts did not hold a license or certificate of authority in the states in which such persons reside; and (iii) such persons are not eligible for coverage by an association of another state where such association is similar to the association created by this chapter.

E. Any member insurer which has been declared insolvent and is placed under a final order of liquidation, rehabilitation, or conservation by a court of competent jurisdiction prior to July 1, 1991, shall be subject to the provisions of Chapter 17 as this chapter existed prior to July 1, 1991. (1976, c. 330, § 38.1-482.18; 1986, c. 562; 1988, c. 178; 1991, c. 340; 1992, c. 299.)

Inapplicable to beneficial or equitable owners. — This section excludes from coverage any contract or certificate which is not both issued and owned by an individual and nothing in the statutory language permits an interpretation that a mere beneficial or equitable owner can satisfy the "issued to" and the "owned by" requirements. Bennet v. Virginia Life, Accident & Sickness Ins. Guar. Ass'n, 251 Va. 382, 468 S.E.2d 910 (1996).

§ **38.2-1701. Definitions.** — As used in this chapter:

"Account" means any one of the three accounts created under § 38.2-1702.

"Association" means the Virginia Life, Accident and Sickness Insurance Guaranty Association created under § 38.2-1702.

"Contractual obligation" means any obligation under covered policies.

"Covered policy" means any policy or contract within the scope of this chapter under § 38.2-1700.

"Impaired insurer" means a solvent member insurer considered by the Commission to be potentially unable to fulfill its contractual obligations.

"Insolvent insurer" means a member insurer that becomes insolvent and is placed under a final order of liquidation, rehabilitation, or conservation by a court of competent jurisdiction.

"Member insurer" means any person licensed to write in this Commonwealth any class of insurance to which this chapter applies under § 38.2-1700.

"Premiums" means direct gross insurance premiums and annuity considerations received on covered policies, less any return of premiums, and considerations on covered policies, and dividends paid or credited to policyholders on this business. "Premiums" do not include premiums and considerations on contracts between insurers and reinsurers.

"Resident" means any person who resides in this Commonwealth at the time a member with contractual obligations is determined to be impaired or insolvent. (1976, c. 330, § 38.1-482.19; 1980, c. 186; 1986, c. 562.)

Law Review. — For survey of Virginia insurance law for the year 1975-1976, see 62 Va. L. Rev. 1446 (1976).

§ **38.2-1702. Association; creation; memberships; accounts; supervision.** — A. The nonprofit legal entity to be known as the Virginia Life,

Accident and Sickness Insurance Guaranty Association, created by former § 38.1-482.20, shall continue in existence. All member insurers shall continue to be members of the Association as a condition of their license to transact the business of insurance in this Commonwealth. The Association shall perform its functions under the plan of operation established and approved under § 38.2-1706 and shall exercise its powers through a board of directors established under § 38.2-1703. For purposes of administration and assessment, the Association shall maintain three accounts: (i) the accident and sickness insurance account; (ii) the life insurance account; and (iii) the annuity account.

B. The Association shall come under the immediate supervision of the Commission and shall be subject to the applicable provisions of the insurance laws of this Commonwealth. (1976, c. 330, § 38.1-482.20; 1980, c. 186; 1986, c. 562.)

§ 38.2-1703. Board of directors of Association. — A. The board of directors of the Association shall consist of not less than five nor more than nine member insurers serving terms as established in the plan of operation. The members of the board shall be selected by member insurers subject to the approval of the Commission. Vacancies on the board shall be filled for the remainder of the term by a majority vote of the remaining board members, subject to the approval of the Commission.

B. In approving selections or in appointing members to the board the Commission shall consider, among other things, whether all domestic and foreign member insurers are fairly represented.

C. Members of the board may be reimbursed from the assets of the Association for expenses incurred by them as members of the board of directors but members of the board shall not be otherwise compensated by the Association for their services. (1976, c. 330, § 38.1-482.21; 1986, c. 562.)

Law Review. — For survey of Virginia insurance law for the year 1975-1976, see 62 Va. L. Rev. 1446 (1976).

§ 38.2-1704. Powers and duties of Association. — In addition to the powers and duties enumerated in other sections of this chapter:

A. In the case of an impaired domestic insurer and subject to (i) conditions imposed by the Association other than those that impair the contractual obligations of the impaired insurer, (ii) approval by the impaired insurer and (iii) approval by the Commission, the Association may:

1. Guarantee or reinsure, or cause to be guaranteed, assumed, or reinsured, any or all of the covered policies of the impaired insurer;

2. Provide moneys, pledges, notes, guarantees or other means required for compliance with subdivision 1 of this subsection and assure payment of the contractual obligations of the impaired insurer pending action under that subdivision; and

3. Loan money to the impaired insurer.

B. In the case of an insolvent insurer, the Association shall, subject to the approval of the Commission:

1. Guarantee, assume, or reinsure or cause to be guaranteed, assumed, or reinsured the covered policies of the insolvent insurer;

2. Assure payment of the contractual obligations of the insolvent insurer; and

3. Provide moneys, pledges, notes, guarantees, or other means reasonably necessary to discharge its duties.

C. Subsection B shall not apply in the case of a foreign or alien insurer where the Commission has determined that the foreign or alien insurer's domiciliary jurisdiction or state of entry provides protection by statute or regulation for residents of this Commonwealth.

D. 1. In carrying out its duties under subsection B of this section, the Association may request that permanent policy liens or contract liens be imposed in connection with any guarantee, assumption, or reinsurance agreement, and those liens may be imposed if the court:

a. Finds that the amounts which can be assessed under this chapter are less than the amounts needed to assure full and prompt performance of the insolvent insurer's contractual obligations, or that economic or financial conditions are sufficiently adverse so that policy or contract liens are in the public interest; and

b. Approves the specific policy or contract liens to be used.

2. Before being obligated under subsection B of this section, the Association may request that temporary moratoriums or liens be imposed on payments of cash values and policy loans in addition to any contractual provisions for deferral of cash or policy loan values, and the temporary moratoriums and liens may be imposed if they are approved by the court.

E. If the Association fails to act as provided in subsection B of this section within a reasonable period of time, the Commission, on behalf of the Association, shall exercise the powers and duties of the Association under this chapter with respect to insolvent insurers.

F. Upon request, the Association may provide assistance and advice to the Commission concerning rehabilitation, payment of claims, continuation of coverage, or the performance of other contractual obligations of an impaired or insolvent insurer.

G. The Association shall have standing to appear before any court in this Commonwealth regarding all matters germane to the powers and duties of the Association, including, but not limited to, proposals for reinsuring or guaranteeing the covered policies of the insolvent insurer and the determination of the covered policies and contractual obligations.

H. Any person receiving benefits under this chapter shall be deemed to have assigned the rights under the covered policy to the Association to the extent of the benefits received because of this chapter whether the benefits are payments of contractual obligations or continuation of coverage. The Association shall require an assignment to it of those rights by any payee, policy or contract owner, beneficiary, insured or annuitant as a condition prior to the receipt of any rights or benefits conferred by this chapter upon that person. The Association shall be subrogated to those rights against the assets of any insolvent insurer. The subrogation rights of the Association under this subsection shall have the same priority against the assets of the insolvent insurer as that possessed by the person entitled to receive benefits under this chapter.

I. The contractual obligations for which the Association may become liable shall in no event exceed the lesser of:

1. The contractual obligations for which the insurer is liable or would have been liable if it were not an impaired or insolvent insurer; or

2. With respect to any one life, regardless of the number of policies or contracts:

a. $300,000 in life insurance death benefits, but not more than $100,000 in net cash surrender and net cash withdrawal values for life insurance;

b. $300,000 in health insurance benefits, including any net cash surrender and net cash withdrawal values;

c. $100,000 in the present value of annuity benefits, including net cash surrender and net cash withdrawal values.

However, in no event shall the Association be liable to expend more than $300,000 in the aggregate with respect to any one individual.

J. The Association may:

1. Enter into contracts necessary or proper to fulfill the provisions and purposes of this chapter.

2. Sue or be sued, including taking any legal actions necessary or proper for recovery of any unpaid assessments under § 38.2-1705.

3. Borrow money to effect the purposes of this chapter. Any notes or other evidence of indebtedness of the Association not in default shall be Category 1 investments, as defined in § 38.2-1401, for domestic insurers.

4. Employ or retain persons necessary to handle the financial transactions of the Association, and to perform other functions required by this chapter.

5. Negotiate and contract with any liquidator, rehabilitator, conservator, or ancillary receiver to carry out the powers and duties of the Association.

6. Take legal action required to avoid payment of improper claims.

7. Exercise, for the purposes of this chapter and to the extent approved by the Commission, the powers of a domestic life or accident and sickness insurer, but in no case shall the Association issue insurance policies or annuity contracts other than those issued to perform the contractual obligations of the impaired or insolvent insurer. (1976, c. 330, § 38.1-482.22; 1986, c. 562; 1991, c. 340; 1993, c. 142.)

Law Review. — For survey of Virginia insurance law for the year 1975-1976, see 62 Va. L. Rev. 1446 (1976).

§ 38.2-1705. Assessments. — A. For the purpose of providing the funds necessary to carry out the powers and duties of the Association, the board of directors shall assess the member insurers, separately for each account, at any time and for any amounts as the board finds necessary. Assessments shall be due not less than thirty days after written notice has been given to the member insurers. Interest shall be compounded quarterly and be based upon the average ninety day treasury bill rate for the most recently completed calendar quarter as published in the Federal Reserve Bulletin. Interest will accrue on and after the due date.

B. There shall be two classes of assessments, as follows:

1. Class A assessments shall be made for the purpose of meeting administrative and legal costs and other expenses, including the cost of examinations conducted under the authority of § 38.2-1708 E. Class A assessments may be made whether or not related to a particular impaired or insolvent insurer.

2. Class B assessments shall be made to the extent necessary to carry out the powers and duties of the Association under § 38.2-1704 with regard to an impaired or an insolvent insurer.

C. 1. The amount of any Class A assessment shall be determined by the board and may be made on a pro-rata or nonpro-rata basis. If pro rata, the board may provide that it be credited against future Class B assessments. A nonpro-rata assessment shall not exceed $200 per member insurer in any one calendar year. With respect to any insurer that became impaired or insolvent after January 1, 1991, the amount of any Class B assessment shall be allocated for assessment purposes among the accounts pursuant to an allocation formula which may be based on the premiums or reserves of the impaired or insolvent insurer or any other standard deemed by the board in its sole discretion as being fair and reasonable under the circumstances.

2. Class B assessments against member insurers for each account shall be in the proportion that the premiums received on business in this Commonwealth by each assessed member insurer on policies or contracts covered by each account for the three most recent calendar years for which information is available preceding the year in which the insurer became impaired or insolvent bear to such premiums received on business in this Commonwealth for such calendar years by all assessed member insurers.

3. Assessments for funds to meet the requirements of the Association with respect to an impaired or insolvent insurer shall not be made until necessary

to implement the purposes of this chapter. Classification of assessments under subsection B of this section and computation of assessments under this subsection shall be made with a reasonable degree of accuracy, recognizing that exact determinations may not always be possible.

D. The Association may abate or defer, in whole or in part, the assessment of a member insurer if, in the opinion of the board, payment of the assessment would endanger the ability of the member insurer to fulfill its contractual obligations. In the event an assessment against a member insurer is abated or deferred in whole or in part, the amount by which the assessment is abated or deferred may be assessed against the other member insurers in a manner consistent with the basis for assessments set forth in this section.

E. The total of all assessments upon a member insurer for each account shall not in any one calendar year exceed two percent of the member insurer's premiums received on the policies covered by the account in this Commonwealth during the calendar year preceding the assessment. If the maximum assessment, together with the other assets of the Association in any account, does not provide in any one year in any account an amount sufficient to carry out the responsibilities of the Association, the necessary additional funds shall be assessed as soon as permitted by this chapter.

F. The board may refund to member insurers, in proportion to the contribution of each insurer to that account, the amount the assets of the account exceed the amount the board finds necessary to fulfill the Association's obligations during the coming year. In determining the refunds, assets accruing from net realized gains and income from investments shall be included. A reasonable amount may be retained in any account to provide funds for the continuing expenses of the Association and for future losses if refunds are impractical.

G. It shall be proper for any member insurer to consider the amount reasonably necessary to meet its Class A assessment obligations in determining its premium rates and policyowner dividends for any class of insurance covered by this chapter.

H. The Association shall issue to each insurer paying an assessment under this chapter, other than a Class A assessment, a certificate of contribution in a form prescribed by the Commission, for the amount of the assessment paid, excluding interest penalties. All outstanding certificates shall be of equal priority without reference to amounts or dates of issue. A certificate of contribution may be shown by the insurer on its financial statement as an asset. This shall be shown in a form, in an amount, and for a period of time approved by the Commission. (1976, c. 330, § 38.1-482.23; 1980, c. 186; 1986, c. 562; 1992, c. 299.)

§ **38.2-1706. Plan of operation.** — A. 1. Neither the plan of operation nor any amendment to it shall become effective until submitted to and approved by the Commission. The Commission shall approve the plan or any amendment to it if it assures the fair, reasonable, and equitable administration of the Association.

2. The plan of operation approved under former § 38.1-482.24 shall remain in effect until modified in accordance with subdivision 3 of this subsection.

3. If the Association fails to submit suitable amendments to the plan, the Commission shall, after notice and hearing, adopt and promulgate reasonable rules that are necessary or advisable to effect this chapter. These rules shall continue in force until modified by the Commission or superseded by a plan or amendment submitted by the Association and approved by the Commission.

B. All member insurers shall comply with the plan of operation.

C. The plan of operation shall, in addition to requirements enumerated elsewhere in this chapter:

1. Establish procedures for handling assets of the Association.

2. Establish the amount and method of reimbursing members of the board of directors under § 38.2-1703.

3. Establish regular places and times for meetings of the board of directors.

4. Establish procedures to keep records of all financial transactions of the Association, its agents, and the board of directors.

5. Establish the procedures for submitting to the Commission selections for the board of directors.

6. Establish any additional procedures for assessments under § 38.2-1705.

7. Establish a plan for equitable distribution of refunds to members.

8. Contain additional provisions necessary or proper for the execution of the powers and duties of the Association.

D. Except as provided by subdivision 3 of subsection A of § 38.2-1704 and § 38.2-1705, the plan of operation may provide that any or all powers and duties of the Association may be delegated to the corporation, association, or other organization which performs or will perform functions similar to those of this Association, or its equivalent, in two or more states. The corporation, association, or organization shall be reimbursed for any payments made on behalf of the Association and shall be paid for its performance of any function of the Association. A delegation under this subsection shall take effect only with the approval of both the board of directors and the Commission, and may be made only to a corporation, association, or organization that extends protection not substantially less favorable and effective than that provided by this chapter. (1976, c. 330, § 38.1-482.24; 1986, c. 562.)

§ **38.2-1707. Duties and powers of the Commission.** — A. In addition to the duties and powers enumerated elsewhere in this chapter, the Commission shall:

1. Upon request of the board of directors, provide the Association with a statement of the premiums in the appropriate states for each member insurer.

2. When an impairment is declared and the amount of the impairment is determined, serve a demand upon the impaired insurer to make good the impairment within a reasonable time. Notice to the impaired insurer shall constitute notice to its shareholders, if any. The failure of the insurer to promptly comply with this demand shall not excuse the Association from the performance of its powers and duties under this chapter.

3. Be appointed as the liquidator or rehabilitator in any liquidation or rehabilitation proceeding involving a domestic insurer. If a foreign or alien member insurer is subject to a liquidation proceeding in its domiciliary jurisdiction or state of entry, the Commission shall be appointed conservator.

B. The Commission may suspend or revoke, after notice and hearing, the license to transact the business of insurance in this Commonwealth of any member insurer that fails to pay an assessment when due or fails to comply with the plan of operation. As an alternative the Commission may levy a forfeiture on any member insurer that fails to pay an assessment when due. The forfeiture shall not exceed five percent of the unpaid assessment per month, but no forfeiture shall be less than $100 per month.

C. Any action of the board of directors or the Association may be appealed to the Commission by any member insurer if the appeal is taken within thirty days of the action being appealed. Any final action or order of the Commission shall be subject to judicial review in accordance with the provisions of §§ 12.1-39 through 12.1-41.

D. The liquidator, rehabilitator, or conservator of any impaired insurer may notify all interested persons of the effect of this chapter. (1976, c. 330, § 38.1-482.25; 1986, c. 562.)

§ 38.2-1708. Detection and prevention of insolvencies. — A. To aid in the detection and prevention of insurer insolvencies, the Commission shall have the duty to:

1. Notify the insurance departments of all of the other states within thirty days of taking any of the following actions against a member insurer:

a. Revocation of license;

b. Suspension of license;

c. Making any formal order that requires the insurer to (i) restrict its premium writing, (ii) obtain additional contributions to surplus, (iii) withdraw from the Commonwealth, (iv) reinsure all or any part of its business, or (v) increase its capital, surplus, or any other account for the security of policyholders or creditors.

2. Report to the board of directors when (i) any actions set forth in subdivision 1 of this subsection have been taken or (ii) a report has been received from any other insurance department indicating that an action has been taken in another state. The report to the board of directors shall contain (i) all significant details of the action taken or (ii) the report from the other insurance department.

3. Report to the board of directors when it has reasonable cause to believe that an insurer may be insolvent or in a financial condition hazardous to the policyholders or the public. The report may be based on a member insurer's financial examination, whether completed or in progress.

B. The Commission may seek the advice and recommendations of the board of directors concerning any matter affecting its duties and responsibilities regarding the financial condition of member insurers and insurers seeking admission to transact the business of insurance in this Commonwealth.

C. The board of directors may, upon majority vote, make reports and recommendations to the Commission upon any matter germane to the solvency, liquidation, rehabilitation or conservation of any member insurer or to the solvency of any insurer seeking to transact the business of insurance in this Commonwealth. These reports and recommendations shall not be considered public documents.

D. The board of directors shall have the duty, upon majority vote, to notify the Commission of any information indicating that a member insurer may be insolvent or in a financial condition hazardous to the policyholders or the public.

E. The board of directors, upon majority vote, may request that the Commission order an examination of any member insurer that the board, in good faith, believes may be in a financial condition hazardous to the policyholders or the public. Within thirty days of the receipt of the request, the Commission shall begin the examination. The examination may be conducted as the National Association of Insurance Commissioners examination or may be conducted by persons the Commission designates. The cost of the examination shall be paid by the Association, and the examination report shall be treated like other examination reports. In no event shall the examination report be released to the board of directors prior to its release to the public, but this shall not preclude the Commission from complying with subsection A of this section. The Commission shall notify the board of directors when the examination is completed. The request for an examination shall be kept on file by the Commission but it shall not be open to public inspection prior to the release of the examination report to the public.

F. The board of directors may, upon majority vote, make recommendations to the Commission for the detection and prevention of insurer insolvencies.

G. The board of directors shall, at the conclusion of any insurer insolvency in which the Association was obligated to pay covered claims, prepare a report to the Commission containing all information it has in its possession relating to the history and causes of the insolvency.

H. The board shall cooperate with the board of directors of guaranty associations in other states in preparing a report on the history and causes for a member's insolvency, and may adopt by reference any report prepared by other associations. (1976, c. 330, § 38.1-482.26; 1986, c. 562.)

§ **38.2-1709. Tax write-offs of certificates of contributions.** — A. A member insurer shall have at its option the right to show a certificate of contribution as an asset in the form approved by the Commission pursuant to subsection H of § 38.2-1705 at the original face amount for the calendar year of issuance. Such amount may be amortized as follows:

1. Certificates of contribution issued prior to January 1, 1998, shall be amortized in each succeeding calendar year through December 31, 1997, at an amount not to exceed 0.05 of one percent of the member's direct gross premium income for the classes of insurance in the account for which the member insurer is assessed. As used herein, the definition of direct gross premium income shall be the same as that specified in § 58.1-2500. If the amount of the certificate has not been fully amortized by the contributing insurer by December 31, 1997, the unamortized balance of the certificate amount shall be amortized, at the option of the contributing insurer, either (i) in the same manner as the certificate was amortized prior to January 1, 1998; however, if not amortized in full prior to calendar year 2010, the unamortized balance of the certificate shall be amortized in full during calendar year 2010, or (ii) over the ten successive calendar years commencing January 1, 1998, in amounts each equal to ten percent of such unamortized balance. A contributing insurer whose certificate has not been fully amortized by December 31, 1997, shall notify the Commission in writing of the amortization schedule option it has selected on or before March 1, 1998; however, if a contributing insurer fails to notify the Commission by such date, the insurer shall be deemed to have selected the option described in clause (i) of the preceding sentence.

2. Certificates of contribution issued on or after January 1, 1998, shall be amortized over the ten calendar years following the year the contribution was paid in amounts each equal to ten percent of the amount of the contribution.

B. The insurer may offset the amount of the certificate amortized in a calendar year as provided in subsection A. This amount shall be deducted from the premium tax liability incurred on business transacted in this Commonwealth for that year. However, the Association shall diligently pursue all rights available to it to recover its expenditures made in the fulfillment of its responsibilities under this chapter. In the event the Commission determines after a hearing that the Association is not diligently pursuing available measures of recovery, participating insurers will not be able to offset amounts amortized during the period that the Commission determines that the Association has not been diligently pursuing available measures of recovery.

C. Any sums that have been (i) amortized by contributing insurers and offset against premium taxes as provided in subsection B and (ii) subsequently refunded pursuant to subsection F of § 38.2-1705 shall be paid to the Commission and deposited with the State Treasurer for credit to the general fund of this Commonwealth.

D. The amount of any credit against premium taxes provided for in this section for an insurer shall be reduced by the amount of reduction in federal income taxes for any deduction claimed by the insurer for an assessment paid pursuant to this chapter. (1976, c. 330, § 38.1-482.27; 1986, c. 562; 1987, cc. 565, 655; 1991, c. 371; 1997, c. 160.)

§ **38.2-1710. Miscellaneous provisions.** — A. Nothing in this chapter shall be construed to reduce the liability for unpaid assessments of the insureds on an impaired or insolvent insurer operating under a plan with assessment liability.

218

B. Records shall be kept of all negotiations and meetings in which the Association or its representatives are involved in carrying out its powers and duties under § 38.2-1704. Records of these negotiations or meetings shall be made public only upon (i) the termination of a liquidation, rehabilitation, or conservation proceeding involving the impaired or insolvent insurer, (ii) the termination of the impairment or insolvency of the insurer, or (iii) the order of a court of competent jurisdiction. Nothing in this subsection shall limit the duty of the Association to render a report of its activities under § 38.2-1711.

C. For the purpose of carrying out its obligations under this chapter, the Association shall be deemed to be a creditor of the impaired or insolvent insurer to the extent of assets attributable to covered policies reduced by any amounts to which the Association is entitled as subrogee pursuant to subsection H of § 38.2-1704. All assets of the impaired or insolvent insurer attributable to covered policies shall be used to continue all covered policies and pay all contractual obligations of the impaired or insolvent insurer as required by this chapter. For the purpose of this subsection, assets attributable to covered policies is that proportion of the assets which the reserves, that should have been established for these policies, bear to the reserves that should have been established for all insurance policies written by the impaired or insolvent insurer.

D. 1. Prior to the termination of any liquidation, rehabilitation, or conservation proceeding, the court, in making an equitable distribution of the ownership rights of the insolvent insurer, may take into consideration the contributions of the respective parties, including the Association, the shareholders and policyowners of the insolvent insurer, and any other party with a legitimate interest. In this determination, consideration shall be given to the welfare of the policyholders of the continuing or successor insurer.

2. No distribution to any stockholders of an impaired or insolvent insurer shall be made until the total amount of valid claims have been fully recovered by the Association for funds expended in carrying out its powers and duties under § 38.2-1704.

E. 1. If an order for liquidation of an insurer domiciled in this Commonwealth has been entered, the receiver appointed under that order shall have a right to recover from any controlling affiliate on behalf of the insurer distributions, other than stock dividends, made at any time during the five years preceding the petition for liquidation or rehabilitation. This shall be subject to the limitations of subdivisions 2 through 4 of this subsection.

2. No dividend shall be recoverable if the insurer shows that the distribution was lawful and reasonable at the time of payment, and that the insurer did not know and could not reasonably have known that the distribution might adversely affect the ability of the insurer to fulfill its contractual obligations.

3. Any person who was an affiliate that controlled the insurer at the time the distributions were paid shall be liable up to the amount of distributions he received. Any person who was an affiliate that controlled the insurer at the time the distributions were declared shall be liable up to the amount of distributions he would have received if they had been paid immediately. If two persons are liable with respect to the same distributions, they shall be jointly and severally liable.

4. The maximum amount recoverable under this subsection shall be the amount in excess of all other available assets of the insolvent insurer needed to pay (i) the contractual obligations of the insolvent insurer and (ii) the reasonable expenses of the Association incurred in connection with the performance of its duties for the insolvent insurer.

5. If any person liable under subdivision 3 of this subsection is insolvent, all its affiliates that controlled it at the time the dividend was paid shall be jointly and severally liable for any resulting deficiency in the amount recovered from the insolvent affiliate. (1976, c. 330, § 38.1-482.28; 1986, c. 562.)

§ 38.2-1711. Examination of the Association; annual report. — The Association shall be subject to examination and regulation by the Commission. The board of directors shall submit to the Commission, not later than each May 1, a financial report for the preceding calendar year in a form approved by the Commission and a report of its activities during the preceding calendar year. (1976, c. 330, § 38.1-482.29; 1986, c. 562.)

§ 38.2-1712. Tax exemptions. — The Association shall be exempt from the payment of all fees and all taxes levied by this Commonwealth or any of its subdivisions, except taxes levied on real and personal property. (1976, c. 330, § 38.1-482.30; 1986, c. 562.)

§ 38.2-1713. Immunity. — There shall be no liability on the part of, and no cause of action of any nature shall arise against, any member insurer or its agents or employees, the Association or its agents or employees, members of the board of directors, or the Commission or its representatives, for any action taken by them in the performance of their powers and duties under this chapter. (1976, c. 330, § 38.1-482.31; 1986, c. 562.)

§ 38.2-1714. Stay of proceedings; reopening default judgments. — All proceedings in which the insolvent insurer is a party in any court in this Commonwealth shall be stayed sixty days from the date an order of liquidation, rehabilitation, or conservation is final. This will allow time for proper legal action by the Association on all matters germane to its powers and duties. The Association may apply to have the judgment under any decision, order, verdict, or finding based on default set aside by the same court that made the judgment and shall be permitted to defend against the suit on the merits. (1976, c. 330, § 38.1-482.32; 1986, c. 562.)

§ 38.2-1715. Prohibition against advertising guaranty funds. — No person, including an insurer, agent, or affiliate of an insurer shall make, publish, disseminate, circulate, or place before the public, or cause, directly or indirectly, to be made, published, disseminated, circulated or placed before the public, in any newspaper, magazine or other publication, or in the form of a notice, circular, pamphlet, letter or poster, or over any radio station or television station, or in any other way, any advertisement, announcement or statement which uses the existence of the Association of this Commonwealth for the purpose of sales, solicitation, or inducement to purchase any form of insurance covered by this chapter. (1976, c. 330, § 38.1-482.33; 1986, c. 562.)

ARTICLE 2.

Additional Funds Paid to the Association.

§ 38.2-1716. Purpose and applicability of article. — The purpose of this article is to provide directions and guidelines for the control and use of funds provided pursuant to § 38.2-225 or any other sources of funds not specified in Article 1 (§ 38.2-1700 et seq.) of this chapter. (1986, c. 562.)

§ 38.2-1717. Safety fund. — The Association shall maintain a separate asset account to be known as the safety fund for the purpose of meeting the Association's objectives as specified in § 38.2-1700. (1986, c. 562.)

§ 38.2-1718. Financing the safety fund, maximum amount, distribution of excess. — A. The safety fund, at the discretion of the Commission, shall receive penalty payments levied against member insurers made pursuant to subsection B of § 38.2-225 or any other payments approved by the Commission.

B. The Commission may approve the payment of funds to the Association provided the balance in the safety fund account does not exceed two percent of the total of all member insurer's premium received in this Commonwealth for classes of insurance covered by the accounts specified in subsection A of § 38.2-1702.

C. Investment income earned on assets held in the safety fund shall be credited to the safety fund provided the balance of the safety fund does not exceed three percent of the total of all member insurer's premium received in this Commonwealth for classes of insurance covered by the accounts specified in subsection A of § 38.2-1702 unless otherwise determined by the Commission.

D. In the event the safety fund balance exceeds the amount specified in subsection C of this section, at the discretion of the Commission the difference shall be paid to the state treasury to the credit of the Literary Fund or shall be subject to subsection F of § 38.2-1720.

E. In the event the fund is dissolved, remaining assets in the safety fund will be distributed to the state treasury to the credit of the Literary Fund. (1986, c. 562.)

§ **38.2-1719. Investment of safety fund.** — The assets of the safety fund may be invested in securities set forth in § 38.2-1415. (1986, c. 562.)

§ **38.2-1720. Use of safety fund, repayment, etc.** — A. The purpose of the safety fund is to provide for the payment of covered claims in the event the assessment limit specified in subsection E of § 38.2-1705 is reached.

B. In the event the assets of the safety fund are needed to pay covered claims, these assets shall be loaned to the respective account listed in subsection A of § 38.2-1702. This loan shall be the general obligation of the Association members and shall be evidenced by an agreement approved by the Commission.

C. Interest on this loan shall be compounded quarterly and be based upon the average ninety-day treasury bill rate for the most recently completed calendar quarter as published in the Federal Reserve Bulletin. This rate will be updated quarterly in order to conform with market rates of interest.

D. This loan shall be repaid by levying assessments against the members for the account on whose behalf the loan was negotiated. Unless otherwise approved by the Commission, the loan shall be repaid within six months of its issuance. This assessment in conjunction with any other assessments levied, shall not exceed the limit specified in subsection E of § 38.2-1705.

E. Subject to the approval of the Commission assets of the safety fund may be loaned to any account in subsection A of § 38.2-1702 even though the maximum assessment in subsection E of § 38.2-1705 has not been levied if the directors of the Association determine that this action will minimize the cost to the Association in paying covered claims.

F. Excess safety fund assets set forth in subsection D of § 38.2-1718 may be used to pay the Association's covered claims without the members incurring a liability to repay the safety fund. (1986, c. 562.)

§ **38.2-1721. Association as a fiduciary.** — In handling the assets of the safety fund, the Association shall be deemed a fiduciary for the Commonwealth. (1986, c. 562.)

CHAPTER 18.

INSURANCE AGENTS.

ARTICLE 1.

Definitions and General Provisions.

§ **38.2-1800. Definitions.** — As used in this chapter:

"Agent" or *"insurance agent,"* when used without qualification, means an individual, partnership, limited liability company, or corporation that solicits, negotiates, procures or effects contracts of insurance or annuity in this Commonwealth.

"Appointed agent" or *"appointed insurance agent,"* when used without qualification, means an individual, partnership, limited liability company, or corporation licensed in this Commonwealth to solicit, negotiate, procure, or effect contracts of insurance or annuity of the classes authorized within the scope of such license and who is appointed by a company licensed in this Commonwealth to solicit, negotiate, procure, or effect in its behalf contracts of insurance of the classes authorized within the scope of such license and, if authorized by the company, may collect premiums on those contracts.

"Automobile club agent" means an agent licensed in this Commonwealth to solicit, negotiate, procure, or effect automobile club contracts on behalf of automobile clubs licensed under Chapter 3.1 (§ 13.1-400.1 et seq.) of Title 13.1.

"Burial insurance agent" means an agent licensed in this Commonwealth to solicit, negotiate, procure, or effect burial insurance on behalf of insurers licensed under Chapter 40 (§ 38.2-4000 et seq.) of this title.

"Cooperative nonprofit life benefit insurance agent" means an agent licensed in this Commonwealth to solicit, negotiate, procure, or effect life insurance, accident and sickness insurance or annuities on behalf of insurers licensed under Chapter 38 (§ 38.2-3800 et seq.) of this title.

"Credit life and health insurance agent" means an agent licensed in this Commonwealth exclusively to solicit, negotiate, procure, or effect credit life insurance and credit accident and sickness insurance on behalf of insurers licensed in this Commonwealth, but only to the extent authorized in Chapter 37.1 (§ 38.2-3717 et seq.) of this title.

"Credit property and involuntary unemployment insurance agent" means an agent licensed in this Commonwealth to solicit, negotiate, procure, or effect insurance as defined in § 38.2-122.1 or insurance against direct physical damage to personal household property used as security for a loan or other credit transaction. Such insurance may insure the creditor as sole beneficiary or may insure both the creditor and the debtor with the creditor as primary beneficiary and the debtor as beneficiary of proceeds not paid to the creditor. As used in this definition, "personal household property" does not include motor vehicles, mobile homes, or watercraft.

"Dental services agent" means an agent licensed in this Commonwealth to solicit, negotiate, procure, or effect dental services plan contracts on behalf of dental services plans licensed under Chapter 45 (§ 38.2-4500 et seq.) of this title.

"Filed" means received by the Commission.

"Legal services agent" means an agent licensed in this Commonwealth to solicit, negotiate, procure, or effect legal services plan contracts on behalf of legal services plans licensed under Chapter 44 (§ 38.2-4400 et seq.) of this title.

"Licensed agent" or *"licensed insurance agent,"* when used without qualification, means an individual, partnership, limited liability company, or corporation licensed in this Commonwealth to solicit, negotiate, procure or effect contracts of insurance or annuity of the classes authorized within the scope of such license.

"Life and health insurance agent" means an agent licensed in this Commonwealth to solicit, negotiate, procure, or effect life insurance, annuity contracts, and accident and sickness insurance as defined in §§ 38.2-102, 38.2-103, 38.2-104, 38.2-106, 38.2-108 and 38.2-109, respectively, and variable contracts as defined in §§ 38.2-105 and 38.2-107, if so qualified, on behalf of insurers licensed in this Commonwealth. Except as otherwise provided, limitations or restrictions as to methods of compensation imposed by this title on agents shall not apply to life and health insurance agents.

"Mortgage accident and sickness insurance agent" means an agent licensed in this Commonwealth to solicit, negotiate, procure, or effect mortgage accident and sickness insurance on behalf of insurers licensed in this Commonwealth.

"Mortgage guaranty insurance agent" means an agent licensed in this Commonwealth to solicit, negotiate, procure, or effect mortgage guaranty insurance on behalf of insurers licensed in this Commonwealth.

"Mortgage redemption insurance agent" means an employee of a lending institution, whether or not the institution accepts deposits from the public, licensed in this Commonwealth to solicit, negotiate, procure, or effect mortgage redemption insurance and mortgage accident and sickness insurance. *"Mortgage redemption insurance"* means a nonrenewable, nonconvertible, decreasing term life insurance policy written in connection with a mortgage transac-

tion for a period of time coinciding with the term of the mortgage. The initial sum shall not exceed the amount of the indebtedness outstanding at the time the insurance becomes effective, rounded up to the next $1,000.

"Motor vehicle rental contract enroller" means an unlicensed hourly or salaried employee of a motor vehicle rental company that is in the business of providing primarily private motor vehicles to the public under a rental agreement for a period of less than six months, and receives no direct or indirect commission from the insurer, the renter or the vehicle rental company.

"Motor vehicle rental contract insurance agent" means a person who (i) is a selling agent of a motor vehicle rental company that is in the business of providing primarily private passenger motor vehicles to the public under a rental agreement for a period of less than six months and (ii) is licensed in the Commonwealth as an agent to solicit, negotiate, procure, or effect the following insurance coverages solely in connection with and incidental to the rental contract:

1. Personal accident insurance which provides benefits in the event of accidental death or injury occurring during the rental period;

2. Liability coverage sold to the renter in excess of the rental company's obligations under §§ 38.2-2204, 38.2-2205, or Title 46.2, as applicable;

3. Personal effects insurance which provides coverages for the loss of or damage to the personal effects of the renter and other vehicle occupants while such personal effects are in or upon the rental vehicle during the rental period;

4. Roadside assistance and emergency sickness protection programs; and

5. Other travel-related or vehicle-related insurance coverage that a motor vehicle rental company offers in connection with and incidental to the rental of vehicles.

The term "motor vehicle rental contract insurance agent" does not include motor vehicle rental contract enrollers.

"Mutual assessment life and health insurance agent" means an agent licensed in this Commonwealth to solicit, negotiate, procure, or effect mutual assessment life and accident and sickness insurance on behalf of insurers licensed under Chapter 39 (§ 38.2-3900 et seq.) of this title.

"Mutual assessment property and casualty insurance agent" means an agent licensed in this Commonwealth to solicit, negotiate, procure, or effect mutual assessment property and casualty insurance on behalf of insurers licensed under Chapter 25 (§ 38.2-2500 et seq.) of this title.

"Ocean marine insurance agent" means an agent licensed in this Commonwealth to solicit, negotiate, procure, or effect those classes of insurance classified in § 38.2-126, except those kinds specifically classified as inland marine insurance, on behalf of insurers licensed in this Commonwealth.

"Optometric services agent" means an agent licensed in this Commonwealth to solicit, negotiate, procure, or effect optometric services plan contracts on behalf of optometric services plans licensed under Chapter 45 (§ 38.2-4500 et seq.) of this title.

"Pet accident, sickness and hospitalization insurance agent" means an agent licensed in this Commonwealth to solicit, negotiate, procure or effect pet accident, sickness and hospitalization insurance on behalf of insurers licensed in this Commonwealth.

"Property and casualty insurance agent" means an agent licensed in this Commonwealth to solicit, negotiate, procure, or effect insurance as defined in §§ 38.2-110 through 38.2-122.1, and §§ 38.2-124 through 38.2-134 on behalf of insurers licensed in this Commonwealth.

"Resident" means (i) an individual domiciled and residing in Virginia; (ii) a partnership duly formed and recorded in Virginia; (iii) a corporation incorporated and existing under the laws of Virginia; or (iv) a limited liability company organized and existing under the laws of Virginia.

"Single interest insurance agent" means an agent licensed in this Commonwealth to solicit, negotiate, procure, or effect single interest insurance on behalf of insurers licensed in this Commonwealth.

"Solicit, negotiate, procure, or effect" means and includes the selling or attempted selling, placing or attempted placing of insurance or coverage, whether directly or indirectly, in this Commonwealth, and for which action the agent receives, or would receive, direct or indirect compensation in the form of commissions, fees, or other inducements or benefits.

"Title insurance agent" means an agent licensed in this Commonwealth to solicit, negotiate, procure, or effect title insurance on behalf of title insurance companies licensed under Chapter 46 (§ 38.2-4600 et seq.) of this title.

"Travel accident insurance agent" means an individual at transportation terminal buildings, or a ticket-selling agent of a railroad, steamship company, air carrier, or public bus carrier, who is licensed in this Commonwealth solely to act as an agent in the sale of travel accident insurance to individuals.

"Travel baggage insurance agent" means the ticket-selling agent of a railroad or steamship company, air carrier, or public bus carrier who is licensed in this Commonwealth solely to act as an agent in the sale of travel baggage insurance to individuals.

"Variable contract agent" means an agent licensed in this Commonwealth to solicit, negotiate, procure, or effect variable contracts on behalf of insurers licensed in this Commonwealth. (1979, c. 513, § 38.1-327.1; 1981, c. 604; 1983, c. 480; 1984, c. 719; 1986, c. 562; 1987, cc. 520, 521; 1992, c. 586; 1994, cc. 106, 316; 1995, c. 167; 1998, cc. 16, 47, 164; 1999, cc. 86, 490, 493, 586.)

The 1998 amendments. — The 1998 amendment by c. 16 added the paragraph defining "Automobile club agent," and arranged the remaining paragraphs in alphabetical order.

The 1998 amendment by c. 47 added the paragraph defining "Motor vehicle rental contract insurance agent."

The 1998 amendment by c. 164 added the paragraph defining "Pet accident, sickness and hospitalization insurance agent."

The 1999 amendments. — The 1999 amendment by c. 86 deleted the paragraph defining "Health agent" which read: "Health agent" means an agent licensed in this Commonwealth to solicit, negotiate, procure, or effect applications and coverage on behalf of corporations licensed in this Commonwealth under Chapter 42 (§ 38.2-4200 et seq.) of this title or for health maintenance organizations licensed in this Commonwealth under Chapter 43 (§ 38.2-4300 et seq.) of this title. Nothing in this chapter prohibits any person licensed in this Commonwealth as a life and health agent from also acting as a health agent."

The 1999 amendment by c. 490 deleted the former paragraph defining "Bail bond agent" which read: "Bail bond agent" means an agent licensed in this Commonwealth for the sole purpose of writing appearance bonds as surety, as defined in subdivision 3 of § 38.2-121."

The 1999 amendment by c. 493 added the paragraph defining "Motor vehicle rental contract enroller," and added the concluding paragraph of the definition for "Motor vehicle rental contract insurance agent."

The 1999 amendment by c. 586 in the paragraph defining "Credit property and involuntary unemployment insurance agent," inserted "and involuntary unemployment" following "Credit property," inserted "as defined in § 38.2-122.1 or insurance," and substituted "personal household" for "household personal" in the last sentence.

Authority of life insurance agent and fire or casualty agent distinguished. — The authority of a life insurance agent is very different from that of a fire or casualty insurance agent. As is generally known, the latter may, and universally does, make binding contracts of insurance for his principal; on the contrary, a life insurance agent may only take applications for life insurance and is never authorized to actually make contracts. This distinction is recognized in this section. Botts v. Shenandoah Life Ins. Co., 134 F. Supp. 893 (W.D. Va. 1954) (decided under former § 38.1-280).

§ 38.2-1800.1. Proof of residency.

— For purposes of this chapter, an individual shall be deemed to be a resident of this Commonwealth provided such individual (i) maintains his principal place of residence within this Commonwealth; (ii) declares himself to be a Virginia resident on his federal tax return; and (iii) declares himself to be a Virginia resident for purposes of paying Virginia income tax and personal property taxes; and provided that such individual is able to document the above to the satisfaction of the Commission. The Commission may also consider other documentation furnished by the individual, such as a valid current Virginia driver's license or voter registration card, as additional proof of residency. An individual applying for or holding a license issued pursuant to this chapter who is unable to document his residency as set forth above shall be deemed not to be a resident of Virginia for purposes of this chapter. (1997, c. 583.)

§ 38.2-1801. Person soliciting insurance deemed agent of insurer; prohibition against misrepresenting agency relationship. — A. A licensed agent shall be held to be the agent of the insurer that issued the insurance solicited by or applied for through such agent in any controversy between the insured or his beneficiary and the insurer. No licensed agent or any other person shall claim to be a representative of, authorized agent of, agent of, or other term implying an appointed relationship with a particular insurer unless such agent has become an appointed agent of that insurer. For the purpose of notice of claim or suit, the agent or producer of record shall be deemed to be the agent of the insurer. In the case of policies of life insurance, accident and sickness insurance, annuities and variable annuities, such notice shall be given to the insurer at its home office as shown in the policy of insurance.

B. A premium payment made by an insured to an agent, whether appointed by an insurer or not, or to a surplus lines broker, where the insurer or its appointed agent acknowledged specific insurance for a specific policy period by the issuance of a policy, written binder, or other contract of temporary insurance, whether new or renewal, shall be considered payment to the insurer, and such insurer shall be liable to the insured for (i) any covered losses under the insurance and (ii) the return to the insured of any unearned premium amount due the insured except as provided in subsection D of § 38.2-1806.

C. Except as provided in subsection D of § 38.2-1806, where premiums for the issuance of a policy or endorsement have been financed by an insurance premium finance company and payment and evidence of financing for such policy or endorsement have been received by the insurer or its appointed agent, the insurer shall be liable for the return to the insurance premium finance company of any unearned premium due the insurance premium finance company. (Code 1950, § 38.1-292; 1952, c. 317; 1979, c. 513, § 38.1-327.2; 1986, c. 562; 1987, c. 521; 1988, c. 229; 1989, c. 543; 1993, c. 145.)

Agency held conclusively established. — Where the insurance agency for which the agent worked and which he partly owned, solicited insurance for a mutual insurance company, under this section, this solicitation conclusively established agency. Hitt v. Cox, 737 F.2d 421 (4th Cir. 1984).

Narrow federal interpretation. — This section is contrary to common law principles of agency which hold that agency relationships are questions of fact; as such, the federal district court would presume no change in the common law beyond that which is expressly stated. Agency Servs. v. Canal Ins. Co., 943 F. Supp. 592 (1993).

§ 38.2-1802. Acting as agent for unlicensed insurer prohibited; penalties. — A. No person other than a licensed surplus lines broker shall solicit, negotiate, procure, or effect contracts of insurance in this Commonwealth on behalf of any insurer which is not licensed to transact the business of insurance in this Commonwealth. Nothing in this section shall prohibit any person from obtaining insurance upon his own life or property from an unlicensed insurer.

B. Any person violating the provisions of this section shall be guilty upon conviction of a Class 1 misdemeanor and punished for each offense. In addition, any person violating this section shall be (i) liable on any claim against any unlicensed insurer that arises out of a contract or policy solicited, negotiated, procured, or effected by the person or which the person assisted in soliciting, negotiating, procuring, or effecting, or (ii) punished as provided in §§ 38.2-218 and 38.2-1831, or (iii) subject to both (i) and (ii).

C. Nothing in this section shall apply to the solicitation, negotiation, procuring, or effecting of contracts of insurance on:

1. Vessels or craft, their cargo, freight, marine builder's risk, maritime protection and indemnity, ship repairer's legal liability, tower's liability or other risks commonly insured under ocean marine insurance policies as distinguished from inland marine insurance policies, provided that a property and casualty or ocean marine insurance agent licensed in this Commonwealth solicits, negotiates, procures, or effects these classes of insurance on behalf of any insurer not licensed to transact the business of insurance in this Commonwealth; or

2. The rolling stock and operating properties of railroads used in interstate commerce or of any liability or other risks incidental to their ownership, maintenance or operation. (Code 1950, § 38.1-281; 1952, c. 317; 1956, c. 173; 1979, c. 513, § 38.1-327.3; 1982, c. 264; 1983, c. 480; 1986, c. 562; 1987, cc. 519, 521.)

Cross references. — As to punishment for Class 1 misdemeanors, see § 18.2-11.

Record not showing where policy solicited. — In a suit by the liquidator of a foreign insurance company to recover assessments on automobile liability policies issued to defendant, it was admitted that there had been no compliance with the requirements of statutes providing for the domestication of foreign insurance companies. However, the record failed to show how or where the policies issued to defendant were solicited, whether by agents of the insurance company operating in this State or by correspondence or otherwise. Therefore it could not be said that the policies were procured in violation of predecessor statute and were, consequently, unenforceable. Isaac Fass, Inc. v. Pink, 178 Va. 357, 17 S.E.2d 379 (1941). But see §§ 38.2-1024, 38.2-1027.

§ 38.2-1803. Countersignature not required; splitting commissions. — There shall be no requirement that a licensed agent who is a resident of this Commonwealth sign or countersign a policy of insurance covering a subject of insurance resident, located, or to be performed in this Commonwealth. However, if the laws or regulations of another state require a signature or countersignature by an agent resident in that state on a policy written by a nonresident agent or nonresident broker of that state, then any policy written by an agent resident of that state licensed as a nonresident agent in this Commonwealth covering a subject of insurance resident, located, or to be performed in this Commonwealth shall be signed or countersigned in writing by an appointed agent resident in this Commonwealth. No policy shall be deemed invalid due to the absence of the required signature or countersignature. If the laws or regulations of another state require an agent or broker resident in that state, who so requests, to retain a portion of the commission paid on a like policy of insurance written, countersigned or delivered by the agent or broker in that state, then an equal pro rata portion of any commission on the policy of insurance shall be retained by the appointed agent resident in this Commonwealth who signed or countersigned a policy of insurance written by a resident of that state licensed as a nonresident agent in this Commonwealth covering a subject of insurance resident, located, or to be performed in this Commonwealth. (1979, c. 513, § 38.1-327.4; 1986, c. 562; 1987, c. 521.)

§ 38.2-1804. Blank contracts. — No agent shall sign or allow an applicant to sign any incomplete or blank form pertaining to insurance in this Commonwealth. (Code 1950, § 38.1-288; 1952, c. 317; 1979, c. 513, § 38.1-327.5; 1986, c. 562.)

§ 38.2-1805. Acceptance by life and health insurance agents of premiums in arrears; how advance premiums recorded. — A. No agent of a combination or home service insurer shall accept, and no insurer or licensed agent shall knowingly permit an agent to accept, payment of premiums in arrears on any policy of life insurance or accident and sickness insurance on which the premiums are collected at least monthly that has lapsed and that the insured seeks to reinstate, unless the payment (i) at least equals the total of all premiums in arrears and (ii) entitles the policyholder to make immediate application for reinstatement of the policy.

B. Every advance premium paid to an agent on a life insurance policy or accident and sickness insurance policy on which the premiums are collected at least monthly shall be recorded in the receipt book of the insured and in the record book of the agent in exactly the same manner as current premiums are recorded. However, the failure to do so shall not invalidate the policy. (Code 1950, § 38.1-293; 1952, c. 317; 1979, c. 513, § 38.1-327.6; 1986, c. 562; 1987, c. 521; 1990, c. 464.)

§ 38.2-1806. Interest with respect to credit extended or money lent for premiums on certain policies. — A. Any property and casualty insurance agent, mutual assessment property and casualty insurance agent, or ocean marine insurance agent licensed in this Commonwealth may charge interest on credit extended by the agent to the holder of any fire, casualty, surety or marine insurance policy, written or being serviced by or through such agent, for the premium due on such policy. The rate of interest shall not exceed 1½ percent per month of the unpaid balance. However, the extension of credit or the making of the loan shall not be in conflict with the contract between the agent and the insurer that issues the policy.

B. A licensed insurance agent extending credit as authorized in this section shall not be required to comply with the provisions of Chapter 47 (§ 38.2-4700 et seq.) of this title with respect to the licensing of premium finance companies.

C. Notwithstanding the provisions of §§ 38.2-2114 and 38.2-2212, if any insured fails to discharge any of his obligations to a licensed insurance agent when due in connection with the payment of any premium for a policy of insurance, that agent may request in writing that the insurer cancel such policy for nonpayment of premium. Within ten work days of the receipt of such written request, which shall also state the amount owed the agent by the policyholder, the insurer shall deliver or mail a written notice of cancellation to the named insured at the address shown in the policy and to any mortgagee or lienholder. This notice shall state the date on which the cancellation shall become effective. That date shall be established by giving at least the number of days notice prior to cancellation that are required by statute or the terms of the policy. Except for statutory requirements and contractual obligations, there shall be no liability on the part of the insurer for improper cancellation under this section if the insurer (i) in good faith relies upon the request of the agent and (ii) gives notice of cancellation in compliance with the provisions of this section.

D. The insurance agent shall have a lien on any return premium for the policy to the extent of the amount owed by the policyholder. Within thirty days of the mailing of the notice of cancellation, the insurer shall forward that amount to the agent and shall forward the remainder, if any, of the return premium to the policyholder. (Code 1950, § 38.1-293.1; 1970, c. 370; 1979, c. 513, § 38.1-327.7; 1980, c. 581; 1985, c. 33; 1986, c. 562; 1987, c. 521.)

Law Review. — For article, "Uniform Consumer Credit Code — A Prospect for Consumer Credit Reform in Virginia," see 28 Wash. & Lee L. Rev. 75 (1971).

§ 38.2-1807. Sale of accident airtrip insurance by means of vending machines. — Any insurer qualified to transact business in this Commonwealth and to write accident airtrip insurance may solicit applications for and issue policies of accident airtrip insurance by means of mechanical vending machines in public airports. The machines shall be under the supervision of an appointed agent and the insurer shall comply with all the requirements prescribed by the Commission for the conduct of the business. (1958, c. 453, § 38.1-356.1; 1986, c. 562; 1987, c. 521.)

§ 38.2-1808. All agreements to be expressed in contract. — No agent shall make any contract of insurance or agreement with respect to the insurance that is not plainly expressed in the policy or contract issued. (Code 1950, § 38.1-294; 1952, c. 317; 1979, c. 513, § 38.1-327.8; 1986, c. 562; 1987, c. 521.)

Not applicable to agreement for cancellation. — The prohibition of former statute that no agent of any insurance corporation should make any contract for insurance or agreement as to such contract other than that which was plainly expressed in the policy was directed against the alteration of the terms of the policy and did not refer to an agreement of cancellation. Prillaman v. Century Indem. Co., 138 F.2d 821 (4th Cir. 1943).

§ 38.2-1809. Power of Commission to investigate affairs of persons engaged in insurance business; penalties for refusal to permit investigation. — A. The Commission shall have power to examine and investigate the business affairs of any person engaged or alleged to be engaged in the business of insurance in this Commonwealth, including all agents, to determine whether the person has engaged or is engaging in any violation of this title. The Commission shall have the right to examine all records relating to the writing or alleged writing of insurance by any such person in this Commonwealth to determine whether the person is now or has been violating any of the provisions of this title. Any licensed agent, licensed insurance consultant, or any person purporting to be a licensed agent or a licensed insurance consultant, or any person whose actions have led any person to believe that he is a licensed agent or insurance consultant, who refuses to permit the Commission or any of its employees or agents, including employees of the Bureau of Insurance, to make an examination or who fails or refuses to comply with the provisions of this section may, after notice and an opportunity to be heard, be subject to any of the penalties relating to agents or insurance consultants licensed by the Commission provided in this title, including the suspension or revocation of his license.

B. Except as otherwise provided in this title, every licensed agent and insurance consultant shall retain all of the agent's or consultant's records relative to insurance transactions for the three previous calendar years except that records of premium quotations which are not accepted by the insured or prospective insured need not be kept. These records shall be made available promptly upon request for examination by the Commission or its employees without notice during normal business hours. (Code 1950, § 38.1-295.1; 1968, c. 238; 1979, c. 513, § 38.1-327.9; 1985, c. 3; 1986, c. 562; 1987, c. 521; 1990, c. 464; 1991, c. 417.)

§ 38.2-1810. Report of acts deemed larceny under § 18.2-111; privileged communications; attorney for the Commonwealth to be informed. — A. Whenever any insurer licensed to transact the business of insurance in this Commonwealth knows or has reasonable cause to believe that any insurance agent or surplus lines broker has committed any act of larceny as prescribed in § 18.2-111 with respect to any money, bill, note, check, order, draft or other property either belonging to the insurer or received by the agent or surplus lines broker on behalf of the insurer, it shall be the duty of the insurer within sixty days after acquiring the knowledge to file with the Commission a complete statement of the relevant facts and circumstances. Each statement shall be a privileged communication, and when made and filed shall not subject the insurer, or any individual representative of it that is making or filing the statement, to any liability whatsoever.

B. The Commission shall inform the attorney for the Commonwealth of the appropriate county or city of each statement filed pursuant to subsection A of this section. (1962, c. 263, § 38.1-165.1; 1986, c. 562; 1987, c. 521.)

§ 38.2-1811: Repealed by Acts 1991, c. 620.

§ 38.2-1812. Payment and sharing of commissions. — A. No insurer shall pay directly or indirectly any commission or other valuable consideration to any person for services as an agent or a surplus lines broker within this Commonwealth unless the person is then a duly appointed agent of such insurer and, at the time of the transaction out of which arose the right to such commission or other valuable consideration, held a valid license as an agent, or valid license as surplus lines broker, for the class of insurance involved. No person other than a duly licensed and appointed agent or a surplus lines broker may accept any such commission or other valuable consideration unless such person, at the time of the transaction out of which arose the right to such commission or other valuable consideration, held a valid license as an agent or surplus lines broker for the class of insurance involved. An agent of a combination insurer who is assigned a debit may receive, and the insurer may pay, commissions on business written on the debit prior to the agent's becoming licensed and appointed, provided that the agent is duly licensed and, if appropriate, appointed on the day such commissions are paid to and received by him. This provision shall not prevent the payment or receipt of renewal or other deferred commissions or compensation to or by any person if the person was so duly licensed and appointed, where the appointment was necessary, at the time of the transactions out of which arose the right to such renewals or deferred commissions or compensation. This provision shall not prevent the payment of commissions to a trade name which has been filed with the Bureau of Insurance pursuant to subsection E of § 38.2-1822.

B. No agent or surplus lines broker shall directly or indirectly share his commissions or other compensation received or to be received by him on account of a transaction under his license with any person not also then licensed under this chapter or Chapter 48 of this title, for the class of insurance involved in the transactions. No agent or surplus lines broker not then licensed and qualified for the same class of insurance shall receive any commission or other compensation. This provision shall not affect payment of the regular salaries due employees of the licensee. (1979, c. 513, § 38.1-327.11; 1986, c. 562; 1987, c. 521; 1999, c. 97.)

The 1999 amendment inserted the last
sentence in subsection A.

§ 38.2-1812.1. Placement of insurance for public bodies.

— No insurance agent may provide or offer to provide, directly or indirectly, insurance products to a public body while concurrently and on its behalf (i) evaluating proposals from other insurance agents and (ii) recommending the placement of insurance. (1996, c. 989.)

§ 38.2-1812.2. Administrative charges in excess of premium prohibited; exceptions.

— A. Notwithstanding the provisions of § 38.2-310 and Article 4 (§ 38.2-1837 et seq.) of this chapter, no agent shall charge, or demand or receive from, an applicant for insurance or a policyholder any consideration in return for rendering services associated with a contract of insurance, when the consideration is in addition to the premium for such contract, unless:

1. The applicant or policyholder consents in writing before any services are rendered. Consent shall be provided on a form that includes the applicant's or policyholder's signature, the duration of services and amount of fees to be charged, the services for which the fees are charged, and a statement that the agent is entitled to receive a commission from the insurer for soliciting, negotiating, procuring or effecting the insurance; and

2. A schedule of fees and documentation for services rendered is maintained in the agent's office and is made available to applicants or policyholders upon request.

B. This section shall not apply to charges for services described in subsection C of § 38.2-4608 when provided by title insurance agents.

C. This section shall apply to new and renewal policies issued or renewed on or after July 1, 1999. (1999, c. 2.)

§ 38.2-1813. Reporting and accounting for premiums.

— A. All premiums, return premiums, or other funds received in any manner by an agent or a surplus lines broker shall be held in a fiduciary capacity and shall be accounted for by such agent or broker. The agent or surplus lines broker shall, in the ordinary course of business, pay the funds to the insured or his assignee, insurer, insurance premium finance company or agent entitled to the payment.

B. With the exception of premium funds made payable to insurers or insureds for remittance and funds referred to in subsection D of this section, on and after January 1, 1993, all funds referred to in subsection A of this section shall be maintained in a fiduciary account separate from all other business and personal funds. Funds deposited into the separate fiduciary account may not be commingled or combined with other funds except for the purpose of advancing premiums, establishing reserves for the payment of return premiums, or establishing funds to maintain a minimum balance or to guarantee the adequacy of the account. The agent or surplus lines broker shall maintain an accurate record and itemization of the funds deposited into this account. The commission portion of any premiums deposited to this separate account may be withdrawn at the discretion of the agent or surplus lines broker.

C. For the purposes of this section, the separate fiduciary account of a licensed corporation shall be considered the fiduciary account of an individual agent or surplus lines broker acting on behalf of the corporation.

D. This section shall not require any agent who is a duly appointed agent of an insurer and who has a written contractual relationship with such insurer which includes provisions regarding remittance of funds to maintain a separate fiduciary account for the funds. Such funds shall be held separately from any personal or nonbusiness funds and shall be reasonably ascertainable from the books of accounts and records of the agent. (1979, c. 513, § 38.1-327.12; 1986, c. 562; 1992, c. 49; 1993, c. 145.)

Legislative intent. — This section is a gratuitous effort to legislate the status of a business relationship between an insurance company and its agents. National Agents Serv. Co. v. Duiser, 8 Bankr. 397 (Bankr. W.D. Va.), rehearing denied, 12 Bankr. 538 (Bankr. W.D. Va. 1981).

Applicability. — This section was drafted to apply to the debtor-creditor relationship of insurance company and agent and not to the debtor-creditor relationship of an insurance finance company and an insurance agent. National Agents Serv. Co. v. Duiser, 8 Bankr. 397 (Bankr. W.D. Va.), rehearing denied, 12 Bankr. 538 (Bankr. W.D. Va. 1981).

Insureds, or their assignees, can appoint agents to receive return premiums on their behalf. Agency Servs. v. Canal Ins. Co., 943 F. Supp. 592 (1993).

In order to prove embezzlement, existence of a formal fiduciary relationship is not necessary. Rather, the Commonwealth must prove that the defendant was entrusted with the property of another. In this case, victim entrusted defendant as his insurance agent, with $1,400 to pay over to insurance company. The court found irrespective of this section that these facts established the required entrustment to sustain defendant's conviction. Chiang v. Commonwealth, 6 Va. App. 13, 365 S.E.2d 778 (1988).

Applied in Cosby v. Commonwealth ex rel. State Corp. Comm'n, 248 Va. 551, 450 S.E.2d 121 (1994).

ARTICLE 2.

Qualification of Property and Casualty Insurance Agents, Life and Health Insurance Agents and Health Agents.

§ 38.2-1814. License required of resident property and casualty insurance agent. — No individual who is a resident of this Commonwealth shall obtain a license as a property and casualty insurance agent from the Commission unless he has passed a written examination prescribed by the Commission. However, any individual may obtain a license as an automobile club agent, credit property and involuntary unemployment insurance agent, mortgage guaranty insurance agent, motor vehicle rental contract insurance agent, ocean marine insurance agent, pet accident, sickness and hospitalization insurance agent or travel baggage insurance agent without taking a written examination. Mutual assessment property and casualty insurance agents shall be licensed without examination only within the limitations of § 38.2-2525. (1979, c. 513, § 38.1-327.15; 1985, c. 616; 1986, cc. 364, 562; 1987, c. 521; 1989, c. 435; 1994, c. 106; 1995, c. 167; 1998, cc. 16, 47, 164; 1999, cc. 490, 586.)

Editor's note. — Pursuant to § 9-77.11, effect has been given in this section, as set out above, to Acts 1986, c. 364, which amended former § 38.1-327.15, the comparable provision in former Title 38.1.

The 1998 amendments. — The 1998 amendment by c. 16, in the second sentence, deleted "a" following "license as" and inserted "an automobile club agent."

The 1998 amendment by c. 47, in the second sentence, inserted "motor vehicle rental contract insurance agent."

The 1998 amendment by c. 164, in the second sentence, inserted "pet accident, sickness and hospitalization insurance agent."

The 1999 amendments. — The 1999 amendment by c. 490 deleted "bail bond agent" preceding "credit property" in the second sentence.

The 1999 amendment by c. 586 inserted "and involuntary unemployment" in the second sentence.

§ 38.2-1814.1. What agent may transact title insurance. — A. No individual who is a resident of this Commonwealth shall obtain a license as a title insurance agent from the Commission unless he has passed a written examination prescribed by the Commission.

B. [Repealed.]

C. Officers or employees who are not agents of a title insurance company shall be exempt from the provisions of this section.

D. Agents who, as of January 1, 1987, are authorized agents of title insurance companies licensed to transact title insurance in this Commonwealth shall be exempt from the examination requirements of subsection A of this section. (1986, c. 364, § 38.1-327.15:1; 1987, c. 521; 1988, c. 187; 1989, c. 435.)

Editor's note. — This section was enacted as § 38.1-327.15:1 by Acts 1986, c. 364, effective Jan. 1, 1987. Pursuant to § 9-77.11, this section has been incorporated into Title 38.2 as § 38.2-1814.1.

§ **38.2-1815. License required of resident life and health insurance agents and health agents.** — No individual who is a resident of this Commonwealth shall obtain a license as a life and health insurance agent from the Commission unless he has passed a written examination prescribed by the Commission. However, any individual may obtain a license as a travel accident insurance agent, a motor vehicle rental contract insurance agent, a mortgage redemption insurance agent, a credit life and health insurance agent, a dental services agent, an optometric services agent, or a legal services agent, without taking a written examination. Agents of an association referred to in § 38.2-3318.1 who will be limited to soliciting members of that association for burial association group life insurance certificates in amounts of $5,000 or less may also obtain a license without taking a written examination. Agents of burial societies as defined in Chapter 40 (§ 38.2-4000 et seq.) of this title who will be limited to soliciting members for such societies, and where the certificates of membership will not exceed $5,000 on any individual, may also obtain a license without taking written examination. Mutual assessment life and health insurance agents shall be licensed without examination only within the limitations of § 38.2-3919. (1979, c. 513, § 38.1-327.24; 1982, c. 223; 1983, cc. 160, 185; 1985, c. 616; 1986, c. 562; 1987, c. 521; 1993, c. 695; 1998, c. 47; 1999, c. 86.)

The 1998 amendment, in the second sentence, inserted "a motor vehicle rental contract insurance agent."

The 1999 amendment deleted "or health agent" following "insurance agent" in the first sentence.

§ **38.2-1816. Study course required; exception based upon employment experience.** — A. Before registering to take an examination for a license, each applicant shall have completed an insurance study course of forty-five hours of classroom instruction or equivalent distance learning, or any combination thereof, in accordance with an examination content outline approved by the Commission and shall submit proof of such completion in a form acceptable to the Commission.

1. The term "classroom instruction," as used in this section, shall mean actual hours in a classroom environment with an instructor. Instructors shall have the right to consider an applicant to have met the classroom-hour requirement if the applicant was present for no less than ninety-five percent of the required hours. The term "distance learning," as used in this section, means instruction delivered under the general supervision of an instructor through a medium other than a classroom setting.

2. The proof of study course completion referred to in this section shall be signed by the applicant and sworn to before a notary public, indicating that the applicant completed a course for which the requisite number of classroom hours, or equivalent distance learning, were completed. Any applicant who submits a materially false proof of course completion shall, in addition to any applicable civil or criminal penalties for perjury, be deemed to have committed a knowing and willful violation of this section, and shall be punished as set forth in § 38.2-218. Upon receipt of acceptable proof that an applicant

submitted a materially false proof of course completion, the Commission may administratively terminate any license issued based upon such submission.

3. The proof of study course completion referred to in this section shall be certified by the individual who acted as instructor for the course, and such individual shall be required to certify that the requisite number of classroom hours, or equivalent distance learning, were completed by the applicant. An instructor who is found to have submitted a materially false certification that an applicant completed the requisite number of classroom hours, or equivalent distance learning, shall be deemed to have committed a knowing and willful violation of this section, and shall be punished as set forth in § 38.2-218. If such instructor is also a licensed insurance agent or insurance consultant, the additional penalties set forth in §§ 38.2-1831 and 38.2-1843, respectively, may also be imposed by the Commission.

B. An applicant shall register to take an examination for a license and shall attain a passing grade on such examination within one year after meeting the education requirement in subsection A of this section. The Commission, however, may waive this time limit in individual circumstances in accordance with such criteria as may be prescribed.

C. An applicant may apply to the Commission to take the examination for a license without taking the required study course if the applicant submits proof in a form acceptable to the Commission that he has attained equivalent knowledge through employment experience as determined by the Commission. The employment experience shall include no less than one year of full-time experience as an employee of an insurer, an insurance department, an insurance agency, or equivalent employment as determined by the Commission. The employment experience shall have involved the performance of responsible insurance duties in connection with the kind of insurance for which the applicant has applied for a license. The applicant shall register for and attain a passing grade on such examination within one year of completion of the required employment experience. (1979, c. 513, § 38.1-327.16; 1983, c. 185; 1985, c. 616; 1986, c. 562; 1987, c. 521; 1989, c. 435; 1990, c. 464; 1997, cc. 513, 583; 1999, c. 86.)

The 1999 amendment deleted the former second sentence of subsection A, which read: "However, applicants for a health agent license shall complete an insurance study course of twenty-five hours of classroom instruction or equivalent distance learning, or any combination thereof, in accordance with an examination content outline approved by the Commission."

§ 38.2-1817. Examination for license; fee required; when fee forfeited. — A. 1. Examinations for licenses shall be conducted at least monthly at the times and places the Commission prescribes. Each applicant shall pass a written examination prescribed by the Commission unless otherwise exempted.

2. If an applicant fails three times to pass the examination, the applicant must take or retake the study course required in § 38.2-1816 before the applicant may retake the examination.

B. An applicant who has been awarded the designation of Chartered Property and Casualty Underwriter shall be exempt from the education and examination requirements of this article for a property and casualty insurance license. An applicant who has been awarded the designation of Chartered Life Underwriter shall be exempt from the education and examination requirements for a life and health insurance license. However, no applicant shall be exempt from the requirement to submit the application and pay the fee required by § 38.2-1819.

C. No individual shall obtain a license for variable life insurance and variable annuity contracts unless he currently holds a life and health insurance agent's license and has passed the National Association of Security Dealers examination or other examination prescribed by the Commission.

D. Each applicant for an examination shall make a written application in the form and containing the information the Commission prescribes.

E. Each applicant shall, at the time of applying to take the examination, pay such fee as may be prescribed by the Commission and in a manner prescribed by the Commission. The prescribed examination fee shall not be less than $20 nor more than $100. The examination fee shall be nonrefundable.

F. [Repealed.]

G. If the applicant fails to take the examination within three months from the date his registration for the examination is accepted, the examination fee shall be forfeited and the registration shall be considered withdrawn.

H. If the applicant fails to apply to the Commission for a license within six months from the date he passes the examination, the examination grade shall be considered invalid and the examination fee and application processing fee shall be forfeited. Such applicant shall be required to reapply for the examination and to satisfy any appropriate prelicensing requirements. (1979, c. 513, § 38.1-327.17; 1985, c. 616; 1986, c. 562; 1987, c. 521; 1989, c. 435; 1990, c. 464; 1999, c. 86.)

The **1999 amendment** deleted "or a health license" following "health insurance license" at the end of the second sentence of subsection B.

§ **38.2-1818. Individual moving from another state or Canadian province.** — An applicant who has moved into this Commonwealth from another state or a province of Canada shall meet any applicable education and examination requirements as set forth in §§ 38.2-1816 and 38.2-1817, and shall submit the application and pay the license fee required by § 38.2-1819. Agents with active nonresident Virginia agent licenses may continue to operate under their nonresident licenses for up to sixty days while satisfying the requirements for and applying for resident Virginia agent's licenses. Appointments made under such nonresident licenses shall remain in effect during the sixty-day period, unless terminated for other reasons. Appointments held by an agent under a nonresident agent license shall automatically be converted to resident agent appointments if the agent obtains an equivalent resident Virginia agent license during the sixty-day period. If an agent fails to obtain such resident license by the end of the sixty-day period, the equivalent nonresident license and all associated appointments under that license shall terminate at the end of the sixty-day period. (1979, c. 513, § 38.1-327.19; 1980, c. 743; 1986, c. 562; 1987, c. 521; 1997, c. 583.)

§ **38.2-1819. Application for license; fee required.** — A. Each applicant for a license shall make a written application to the Commission, in the form and containing the information the Commission prescribes. Each applicant shall, at the time of applying for a license, pay a nonrefundable application processing fee in an amount and in a manner prescribed by the Commission. The prescribed application processing fee shall not be less than fifteen dollars nor more than thirty dollars. The fee shall be collected by the Commission and paid directly into the state treasury and credited to the fund for the maintenance of the Bureau of Insurance as provided in subsection B of § 38.2-400.

B. Each applicant shall submit his written application no later than one year from the date he satisfies the prelicensing education or experience requirements set forth in § 38.2-1816. Applications submitted beyond the one-year period shall be rejected and applicants shall be required to satisfy all prelicensing requirements again. (1979, c. 513, § 38.1-327.20; 1986, c. 562; 1987, c. 521; 1989, c. 435; 1994, c. 316.)

§ 38.2-1820. Issue of license. — Each applicant who is at least eighteen years of age and who has satisfied the Commission that he is of good character, has a good reputation for honesty, and has complied with the other requirements of this article is entitled to and shall receive a license in the form the Commission prescribes. (1979, c. 513, § 38.1-327.21; 1985, c. 616; 1986, c. 562.)

§ 38.2-1821. Revocation, etc., of license revokes appointment. — If the Commission refuses to grant or revokes or suspends a license, any appointment of such licensee shall likewise be revoked or suspended. No individual whose license is revoked shall be issued another license without first complying with all requirements of this article. (1979, c. 513, § 38.1-327.22; 1985, c. 616; 1986, c. 562; 1987, c. 521.)

ARTICLE 3.

Licensing of Agents.

§ 38.2-1822. License required of agents; individual acting for partnership, limited liability company, or corporate licensee. — A. No person shall act, and no insurer or licensed agent shall knowingly permit a person to act, in this Commonwealth as an agent of an insurer licensed to transact the business of insurance in this Commonwealth without first obtaining a license in a manner and in a form prescribed by the Commission. As used in this section, "act as an agent" means soliciting, negotiating, procuring, or effecting contracts of insurance or annuity on behalf of an insurer licensed in this Commonwealth or receiving or sharing, directly or indirectly, any commission or other valuable consideration arising therefrom. No person shall submit business to any joint underwriting association or any plan established under this title for the equitable distribution of risks among insurers unless the person holds a valid license to transact the class of insurance involved.

B. No individual shall act as an agent on behalf of either a partnership, limited liability company, or a corporation in the transaction of insurance unless he is licensed as an agent and appointed, if appointment is required by statute.

C. No partnership, limited liability company, or corporation may act as an agent in this Commonwealth unless licensed and appointed, if appointment is required by statute. The existence of the partnership, limited liability company, or corporation shall be recorded pursuant to law, and the authority of the corporation to act as an insurance agent or agency shall be specifically set forth in its charter. The Commission may require proof of the foregoing before issuing a license to the partnership, limited liability company, or corporation.

D. For a nonresident partnership, a nonresident limited liability company, or a nonresident corporation, a certification by the insurance department of the nonresident's state of domicile satisfying the requirements of subsection A of § 38.2-1836 shall be deemed to satisfy the foregoing requirements.

E. In addition to the requirements of §§ 59.1-69 and 59.1-70, any person, partnership, limited liability company, or corporation conducting the business of insurance in this Commonwealth under an assumed or fictitious name shall notify the Bureau of Insurance, in writing, either at the time the application for a license to do business is filed or the assumed or fictitious name is adopted, setting forth the name under which such business is to be conducted.

F. When the business of insurance is no longer conducted under an assumed or fictitious name, written notification to the Bureau of Insurance is required as soon as practicable.

G. Notwithstanding any other provision in this chapter, no license shall be required of a person whose employment responsibilities include enrolling individuals under a group insurance policy, provided that such person receives no commission or other valuable consideration for such enrollments, and that such compensation is in no manner contingent upon the number of individuals enrolled or the amount of premium generated by such enrollments. As used in this subsection "enrolling individuals" means the process of informing individuals of the availability of coverages, calculating the insurance charge, assisting with completion of the enrollment application, preparing and delivering the certificate of insurance, answering questions regarding the coverages, and assisting the individual in making an informed decision whether or not enrollment under the group insurance plan is to be elected. (Code 1950, § 38.1-302; 1952, c. 317; 1956, c. 172; 1979, c. 513, § 38.1-327.33; 1980, c. 581; 1981, c. 604; 1985, c. 616; 1986, c. 562; 1987, c. 521; 1989, c. 435; 1991, c. 88; 1994, c. 316; 1997, c. 583; 1999, c. 586.)

The 1999 amendment added subsection G.

Conduct proscribed. — The plain language of the second sentence of subsection A of this section covers two different situations. First, the sentence proscribes solicitation or procurement of insurance business, regardless of whether the unlicensed person was compensated for doing so. Second, it proscribes the sharing of commissions, directly or indirectly, regardless of whether the unlicensed person participated in securing the insurance business. Cosby v. Commonwealth ex rel. State Corp. Comm'n, 248 Va. 551, 450 S.E.2d 121 (1994).

§ **38.2-1823. Penalty for acting for insurer, joint underwriting association, etc., when not licensed.** — Any person submitting business, in violation of § 38.2-1822, while the person is not a holder of a valid agent's license to transact the class of insurance involved shall be penalized a sum equal to the first year commission for the placement of that business and in addition shall be subject to the penalties prescribed in §§ 38.2-218 and 38.2-1831. (1979, c. 513, § 38.1-327.34; 1981, c. 604; 1985, c. 616; 1986, c. 562; 1987, c. 521.)

§ **38.2-1824. Kinds of agents' licenses and appointments issued.** — A. The Commission shall issue the following kinds of agents' licenses and appointments: life and health insurance, property and casualty insurance, automobile club, cooperative nonprofit life benefit insurance, burial insurance, credit life and health insurance, credit property and involuntary unemployment insurance, dental services insurance, legal services insurance, mortgage accident and sickness insurance, mortgage guaranty insurance, mortgage redemption insurance, motor vehicle rental contract insurance, mutual assessment property and casualty insurance, mutual assessment life and health insurance, ocean marine insurance, optometric services insurance, pet accident, sickness and hospitalization insurance, title insurance, travel accident insurance, travel baggage insurance, and variable contract insurance.

B. All individuals and agencies who on July 1, 1987, held limited licenses to write accident and sickness insurance, or automobile insurance, or casualty insurance, or fidelity and surety bonds, or fire insurance, or life insurance and annuities, may remain licensed under such limited licenses, but no such license which has lapsed or been revoked shall be reinstated, and no new or additional licenses for any of the categories enumerated above shall be issued.

C. All individuals who, on July 1, 1999, held a health insurance agent license may retain such license until June 30, 2000, at which time such license shall terminate. No such license which has lapsed or been revoked shall be reinstated, and no new health insurance agent license shall be issued on or after July 1, 1999. Agents holding a health insurance agent license who wish to continue to be authorized to solicit, negotiate, procure or effect the types of insurance authorized under such license on or after July 1, 2000, shall be required to obtain a life and health insurance agent license by June 30, 2000.

D. All individuals and agencies who on July 1, 1999, held limited licenses to write bail (appearance) bonds may remain licensed under such limited licenses, but no such license which has lapsed or been revoked shall be reinstated, and no new or additional licenses of such type shall be issued. (Code 1950, § 38.1-306; 1952, c. 317; 1979, c. 513, § 38.1-327.35; 1986, c. 562; 1987, c. 521; 1988, c. 32; 1991, c. 620; 1994, c. 106; 1995, c. 167; 1998, cc. 16, 47, 164; 1999, cc. 86, 490, 586.)

The 1998 amendments. — The 1998 amendment by c. 16, in subsection A, inserted "automobile club."

The 1998 amendment by c. 47, in subsection A, inserted "motor vehicle rental contract insurance."

The 1998 amendment by c. 164, in subsection A, inserted "pet accident, sickness and hospitalization insurance."

The 1999 amendments. — The 1999 amendment by c. 86 deleted "health insurance" following "dental service insurance" in subsection A; and added subsection C.

The 1999 amendment by c. 490 deleted "bail (appearance) bonds" preceding "burial insurance" in subsection A; and added subsection D.

The 1999 amendment by c. 586 inserted "and involuntary unemployment" in subsection A.

§ 38.2-1825. Duration and termination of licenses and appointments. — A. A license issued to:

1. An individual agent shall authorize him to act as an agent until his license is otherwise terminated, suspended or revoked.

2. A partnership, limited liability company, or corporation shall authorize such partnership, limited liability company, or corporation to act as an agent until such license is otherwise terminated, suspended, or revoked. The dissolution or discontinuance of a partnership, whether by intent or by operation by law, shall automatically terminate all licenses issued to such partnership. The Bureau shall automatically terminate all insurance licenses within ninety days of receiving notification from the clerk of the Commission that the charter of a domestic limited liability company or corporation, whether by intent or by operation of law, has been terminated or that the certificate of authority of a foreign limited liability company or corporation has been revoked.

A1. An agent's license shall automatically terminate after a period of six months during which no appointment of such agent under such license was in effect except for good cause shown to the Commission and payment of the prescribed fee.

B. An appointment issued to an agent by an insurer, unless terminated, suspended or revoked, shall authorize the appointee to act as an agent for that insurer and to be compensated therefor notwithstanding the provisions of §§ 38.2-1812 and 38.2-1823.

C. Upon the suspension or revocation of a license, the agent, or any person having possession of that license, shall immediately return it to the Commission. (Code 1950, § 38.1-305; 1952, c. 317; 1978, c. 4; 1979, c. 513, § 38.1-327.36; 1981, c. 604; 1984, c. 549; 1985, c. 616; 1986, c. 562; 1987, c. 521; 1997, c. 583.)

§ 38.2-1826. Requirement to report to Commission. — A. Each licensed agent shall report within thirty days to the Commission, and to every insurer for which he is appointed any change in his residence or name. Any licensed agent who has moved his residence from this Commonwealth shall have all licenses immediately terminated by the Commission.

B. Each licensed agent convicted of a felony shall report within thirty days to the Commission the facts and circumstances regarding the criminal conviction. (1979, c. 513, § 38.1-327.37; 1986, c. 562; 1987, c. 521; 1999, c. 59.)

The 1999 amendment inserted the subsection A designator, and added subsection B.

§ 38.2-1827. License may include one or more classes of insurance.
— Except as otherwise provided in this title, an appointment of a licensed
agent authorizes that person, if qualified, to solicit, negotiate, procure, or effect
any one or more of the classes of insurance (i) for which the agent is licensed
in this Commonwealth and (ii) for which the appointing insurer is also licensed
in this Commonwealth. (Code 1950, § 38.1-303; 1952, c. 317; 1979, c. 513,
§ 38.1-327.38; 1986, c. 562; 1987, c. 521.)

§ 38.2-1828. Selling accident and sickness insurance. — Any individual who desires to solicit, negotiate, procure, or effect accident and sickness
insurance as defined in § 38.2-109 shall obtain a life and health insurance
agent's license. However, this requirement does not apply to individuals
eligible for limited licenses pursuant to § 38.2-1815, or those agents selling
medical, hospital, surgical, funeral or weekly indemnity benefits as a part of a
policy of motor vehicle or aircraft insurance. (1979, c. 513, § 38.1-327.39; 1985,
c. 616; 1986, c. 562; 1987, c. 521.)

§ 38.2-1829. Additional requirement to hold insurance license. —
Each licensed agent shall "engage actively in the insurance business." This
means that during any given year the agent will write or place insurance for
others having a total premium volume greater than the combined total
premium volume of similar insurance written or placed by the agent upon his
or its own property risks, whether in an individual or in a fiduciary capacity,
and if the agent is an individual, upon property or risks in connection with the
business of his employer. For the purpose of this section, persons placing
property for sale or rent with real estate agents shall not be deemed employers
of the real estate agents, nor shall any public transportation company be
deemed the employer of any ticket-selling agent who acts as an insurance
agent only in the issuance of accident or travel baggage insurance policies
primarily for the purpose of covering risks of travel. (Code 1950, § 38.1-308;
1952, c. 317; 1979, c. 513, § 38.1-327.40; 1986, c. 562; 1987, c. 521.)

§ 38.2-1830. Temporary licenses and appointments; when issued. —
A. Temporary licenses and appointments for life and health insurance agents
or property and casualty insurance agents shall be issued by the Commission
in the following circumstances:
   1. Upon the death of an agent, to his personal representative, surviving
spouse, employee, child or next of kin;
   2. Upon the inability of an agent to act because of sickness, injury or mental
incapacity, to his spouse, child, next of kin, employee or legal representative;
   3. Upon the sale of the agent's business, to any person employed in the
business. In the event no person is available and suitable for licensing and
appointment, the Commission may license and appoint any other suitable
person; or
   4. To an applicant who is to be an appointed agent of a combination insurer,
and who will be assigned a debit and will actually collect the premiums on
insurance contracts during the period of such temporary license. A "combination insurer" means an insurer selling industrial or ordinary life insurance or
accident and sickness insurance on a debit, where the premiums are payable
at least monthly directly by the owner of the policy or a person representing
the owner to a representative of the insurer.
   B. Before any temporary license is issued, the applicant shall file with the
Commission a written application in the form and containing the information

the Commission prescribes. No written examination shall be required of the applicant; however, no license shall be issued until the Commission is satisfied that the applicant is trustworthy and competent to be licensed. Only one temporary license of each type shall be issued to any individual during his lifetime and that license shall be valid for ninety days. Appointments made by insurers of agents holding temporary licenses shall expire upon the expiration of the temporary license, unless the agent has obtained prior to expiration of the temporary license, a permanent license of the same type, in which event the appointment shall remain in effect subject to the provisions of § 38.2-1825. An individual holding a temporary license shall not be prevented from securing a license by meeting the applicable requirements for the license, nor shall a temporary license be required before an individual may obtain a license. The Commission, in its sole discretion and for good cause shown, may renew licenses granted under this section. (Code 1950, § 38.1-310; 1952, c. 317; 1979, c. 513, § 38.1-327.42; 1986, c. 562; 1987, c. 521; 1989, c. 435.)

§ 38.2-1831. Refusal, revocation, or suspension of license. — The Commission may refuse to issue an agent's license to any person and, in addition to or in lieu of a penalty imposed under § 38.2-218, may suspend or revoke the license of any licensee whenever it finds that the applicant or licensee:

1. Has misappropriated any insurance premium;

2. Has failed to apply any premium as directed by the holder or prospective holder of the contract of insurance;

3. Has violated any provisions of any law of this Commonwealth applicable to insurance and insurance agents;

4. Has been guilty of rebating;

5. Has been guilty of twisting the contracts of other insurers, where "twisting" means misrepresenting a policy for the purpose of inducing a policyholder to terminate an existing policy to take a new policy;

6. Has been guilty of misrepresenting the provisions of the contract he is selling, or the contracts of other insurers;

7. Has been guilty of fraudulent or dishonest practices;

8. If not exempted from the requirement of § 38.2-1829, has not been "actively engaged" in the insurance business during the preceding year as required by that section;

9. Has been convicted of a felony;

10. Is not trustworthy or competent to solicit, negotiate, procure, or effect the classes of insurance for which a license is applied for or held; or

11. Has failed or refused to obey any order of the Commission entered against such applicant or licensee. (Code 1950, § 38.1-311; 1952, c. 317; 1970, c. 656; 1979, c. 513, § 38.1-327.43; 1986, c. 562; 1987, c. 521; 1996, c. 10.)

Purpose. — Predecessor statute was designed to compel a faithful discharge of that duty which an agent owes to his principal. Commonwealth v. Sharp, 155 Va. 714, 156 S.E. 570 (1931); National Sur. Co. v. Page, 59 F.2d 370 (4th Cir. 1932).

Meaning of "misappropriate". — In predecessor statute providing for the revocation of a certificate of an insurance agent, the use of the word "misappropriate" was general in its scope. Its meaning was not limited to that appropriation of money which approaches the crime of embezzlement but extended to a willful withholding of money due by the agent to his principal. Commonwealth v. Sharp, 155 Va. 714, 156 S.E. 570 (1931).

The contention of complainant was that a trust relationship existed between plaintiff and defendant, and when it appeared that defendant had written a policy of insurance and by reason thereof had become indebted to the insurer and failed to account for the premium, he then and there was technically guilty of misappropriation of funds. It was held that the statute contemplated more than a mere failure to pay money due by the insurance agent. Commonwealth v. Sharp, 155 Va. 714, 156 S.E. 570 (1931).

For case applying former § 38-84, relating to misrepresentation and "twisting" by agents, see Sterling Ins. Co. v. Commonwealth, 195 Va. 422, 78 S.E.2d 691 (1953).

§ 38.2-1832. Refusal to issue and revocation of license; hearing; new application.

— If the Commission believes that any applicant for a license is not of good character or does not have a good reputation for honesty, it may refuse to issue the license, subject to the right of the applicant to demand a hearing on the application. Except as provided in § 38.2-1042, the Commission shall not revoke or suspend an existing license until the licensee is given an opportunity to be heard before the Commission. If the Commission refuses to issue a new license or proposes to revoke or suspend an existing license, it shall give the applicant or licensee at least ten days' notice in writing of the time and place of the hearing if a hearing is requested. The notice shall contain a statement of the objections to the issuance of the license, or the reason for its proposed revocation or suspension, as the case may be. The notice may be given to the applicant or licensee by registered or certified mail, sent to the last known address of record pursuant to § 38.2-1826, or the last known business address if the address of record is incorrect, or in any other lawful manner the Commission prescribes. The Commission may summon witnesses to testify with respect to the applicant or licensee, and the applicant or licensee may introduce evidence in his or its behalf. No applicant to whom a license is refused after a hearing, nor any licensee whose license is revoked, shall again apply for a license until after the time, not exceeding two years, the Commission prescribes in its order. (Code 1950, § 38.1-312; 1952, c. 317; 1979, c. 513, § 38.1-327.44; 1981, c. 604; 1985, c. 616; 1986, c. 562; 1987, c. 521.)

An action for malicious prosecution may be based upon a proceeding to revoke an insurance agent's license. National Sur. Co. v. Page, 58 F.2d 145 (4th Cir. 1932).

Probable cause. — An agent who refuses to pay over premiums which he has collected for his principal, and as to which there is no dispute, except upon condition that the principal accept the undisputed amount as payment in full and release the agent from a liability which is disputed, is certainly not discharging faithfully the duty which he owes his principal; and a proceeding to have his license revoked because of such breach of duty cannot be said to be without probable cause. National Sur. Co. v. Page, 59 F.2d 370 (4th Cir. 1932).

Sufficient evidence to support order of Commission. — On an appeal from an order of the State Corporation Commission revoking the certificate of registration of an insurance agent because of conduct alleged to violate the obligations imposed by a predecessor statute, the order was affirmed where there was sufficient evidence to support it. Story v. Commonwealth, 175 Va. 615, 9 S.E.2d 344 (1940).

§ 38.2-1833. Appointments of agents.

— A. Subject to the requirement of § 38.2-1801, every licensed agent may solicit applications for insurance for any one or more of the classes of insurance for which he is licensed on behalf of an insurer (i) also licensed in this Commonwealth for those classes of insurance and (ii) by which the licensed agent has not yet been validly appointed, subject to the following requirements:

1. The insurer shall, within thirty days of the date of execution of the first insurance application submitted by a licensed but not yet appointed agent, either reject such application or file with the Commission a written notice of appointment on a form acceptable to the Commission.

2. The insurer shall mail to the licensed agent, within the same thirty-day period, a copy of the notice of appointment form filed with the Commission.

3. Upon receipt of the notice of appointment form, the Commission shall verify that the agent holds a valid license and that the form has been properly completed. If the Commission determines that the appointment is invalid, it shall notify the appointing insurer within five days of its receipt of the

appointment form. If the appointment is valid, the Commission shall issue an acknowledgement of appointment to the agent within five days of its receipt of the appointment form, and shall simultaneously notify the appointing insurer of the issuance of such acknowledgement of appointment.

4. If the licensed agent does not receive from the Commission an acknowledgement of his appointment within forty-five days from the date of execution of the first insurance application submitted to the insurer, then the agent shall immediately discontinue any soliciting of insurance on behalf of that insurer until such acknowledgement is received. Any such further solicitation after forty-five days but prior to receipt of such acknowledgement shall constitute a violation of this section and shall be subject to penalties as prescribed in §§ 38.2-218 and 38.2-1831.

B. Each licensed agent's appointment record shall be public information and shall be available for public inspection during normal business hours of the Commission. The Commission may charge a reasonable fee to cover the costs incurred in providing this information.

C. Each insurer shall pay an appointment fee, in an amount prescribed by the Commission, for each agent appointed by the insurer. The prescribed appointment fee shall not be less than seven dollars nor more than fifteen dollars. Such fees shall be billed to the insurer by the Commission on a quarterly basis and shall be due and payable immediately upon receipt by the insurer. Such quarterly billing shall include all agents appointed by the insurer during the immediately preceding quarter, regardless of the current status of any such appointees. All appointment fees collected by the Commission shall be paid directly into the state treasury and placed to the credit of the fund for the maintenance of the Bureau of Insurance as provided in subsection B of § 38.2-400. (1985, c. 616, § 38.1-327.44:1; 1986, c. 562; 1987, c. 521; 1988, c. 302; 1994, c. 316.)

§ 38.2-1834. Duration of appointment; annual renewal of agent's appointment. — A. A valid appointment of an agent shall authorize the agent to act for the insurer during the time for which the appointing insurer is licensed to do business in this Commonwealth, unless such appointment is otherwise terminated, suspended, or revoked. Upon the termination, suspension or revocation of such appointment, the agent, or any other person having possession of the appointment, shall immediately return it to the Commission.

B. Prior to August 1 of each year, every insurer shall remit in a manner prescribed by the Commission a renewal appointment fee in an amount prescribed by the Commission, which shall be collected by the Commission and paid directly into the state treasury and credited to the fund for the maintenance of the Bureau of Insurance as provided in subsection B of § 38.2-400.

C. Upon the termination of an agent by an insurer, the insurer shall notify the agent of such termination within five days and the Commission within thirty days in a manner acceptable to the Commission, whereupon termination of the agent's appointment to represent the insurer shall be recorded by the Commission.

D. Any license in effect on January 1, 1986, shall be deemed to be an appointment for the unexpired term of that license. Certificates of qualifications issued prior to January 1, 1986, shall be deemed to be the license required by this chapter.

E. [Repealed.]

F. An appointment of an agent holding a restricted or limited license shall authorize such agent to solicit, negotiate, procure or effect only those classes of insurance specifically included in such agent's license authority. (1985, c. 616, § 38.1-327.44:2; 1986, c. 562; 1987, c. 521; 1988, c. 32; 1994, c. 316.)

§ **38.2-1835. Failure to appoint.** — Any insurer that accepts applications from an unlicensed agent or does not appoint a licensed agent pursuant to the provisions of § 38.2-1833 shall be penalized as provided in §§ 38.2-218 and 38.2-1040. (1985, c. 616, § 38.1-327.44:3; 1986, c. 562; 1987, c. 521.)

§ **38.2-1836. Licensing nonresidents; clerk of the Commission to be appointed agent for service of process; reciprocal agreements with other states and Canadian provinces.** — A. A person who is not a resident as defined in § 38.2-1800, but who is a resident of another state or a province of Canada, may obtain a license as set forth in Article 2 (§ 38.2-1814 et seq.) of this chapter if the applicant first files with the Commission a certification from the insurance department of the applicant's state or province of domicile setting forth that the applicant is licensed or otherwise authorized in that state or province to solicit, negotiate, procure or effect the classes of insurance for which the license is being sought in this Commonwealth. An applicant for a nonresident license shall be exempt from the education and examination requirements set forth in §§ 38.2-1816 and 38.2-1817, provided all requirements set forth in this section and § 38.2-1819 are met.

B. For the purposes of this chapter, any person whose place of residence and place of business are in a city or town located partly within the Commonwealth and partly within another state may be considered as meeting the requirements as a resident of this Commonwealth, provided the other state has established by law or regulation similar requirements as to residence of these persons.

C. No agent's license shall be issued to any nonresident of this Commonwealth unless the nonresident executes a power of attorney appointing the clerk of the Commission as the agent for service of process on the applicant in any action or proceeding arising in this Commonwealth out of or in connection with the exercise of the license. The appointment of an agent for service of process shall be irrevocable during the period within which a cause of action against the nonresident may arise out of nonresident transactions with respect to subjects of insurance in this Commonwealth. Service of process on the clerk of the Commission shall conform to the provisions of Chapter 8 (§ 38.2-800 et seq.) of this title.

D. The Commission may enter into a reciprocal agreement with an appropriate official of any other state or province of Canada if such an agreement is required in order for a Virginia resident to be similarly licensed as a nonresident in that state or province. No applicant for a nonresident agent license shall be permitted to obtain such a license unless such agent's state of domicile will grant a similar license to a resident of the Commonwealth.

E. Any licenses and appointments issued to nonresidents pursuant to this section shall be terminated at any time that the nonresident's equivalent authority in his state or province of domicile is terminated, suspended, or revoked. (Code 1950, § 38.1-301.9; 1956, c. 541; 1979, c. 513, § 38.1-327.45; 1980, c. 743; 1981, c. 604; 1986, c. 562; 1987, c. 521; 1988, c. 335; 1989, c. 435; 1990, c. 464.)

ARTICLE 4.

Licensing of Insurance Consultants.

§ **38.2-1837. Definitions.** — As used in this article:

"Insurance consultant" means any individual, partnership, limited liability company or corporation who acts as an independent contractor in relation to his client and for a fee or compensation, other than from an insurer or agent or surplus lines broker, advises or offers or purports to advise, as to life and

health or property and casualty insurance, any person actively or prospectively insured. "Insurance consultant" shall not include:

1. Any licensed attorney acting in his professional capacity;

2. [Repealed.]

3. A trust officer of a bank acting in the normal course of his employment;

4. Any actuary or certified public accountant who consults during the normal course of his business; and

5. Any person employed as a risk manager and who consults for his employer only.

"Life and health insurance consultant" means an insurance consultant whose services are limited to insurance as defined in §§ 38.2-102 through 38.2-109 or health services as provided for in Chapters 42 (§ 38.2-4200 et seq.) and 43 (§ 38.2-4300 et seq.) of this title.

"Property and casualty insurance consultant" means an insurance consultant whose services are limited to insurance as defined in §§ 38.2-110 through 38.2-122 and 38.2-124 through 38.2-134. (1985, c. 3, § 38.1-327.62; 1986, c. 562; 1987, cc. 521, 678; 1992, c. 574.)

§ 38.2-1838. License required of consultants. — A. Any person not licensed as a life and health or property and casualty insurance consultant who, in the Commonwealth, holds himself out to be an insurance advisor, consultant, planner or counselor or any person who uses any other designation or title likely to mislead the public, that he has particular insurance qualifications other than those for which he may otherwise be licensed or qualified shall be punished as provided in § 38.2-218 in addition to any other penalties specifically provided for in this chapter. As used in this section, "hold himself out to be an insurance advisor, consultant, planner or counselor" shall mean:

1. Representing that one's business is insurance consulting; or

2. Receiving, directly or indirectly, special and specific compensation for insurance advice, other than commissions received by a licensed insurance agent or surplus lines broker resulting from soliciting, negotiating, procuring, or effecting insurance or health care services as allowed by his license.

B. Each applicant for an insurance consultant's license shall apply to the Commission in a form acceptable to the Commission, and shall provide satisfactory evidence of having met the following requirements:

1. To be licensed as a property and casualty insurance consultant the applicant must (i) successfully complete a forty-five-hour property and casualty study course as required in § 38.2-1816 and (ii) pass, within six months prior to the date of application for such license, the property and casualty examination as required in § 38.2-1817, except that an applicant who, at the time of such application holds an active property and casualty insurance agent license, shall be exempt from the study course and examination requirements;

2. To be licensed as a life and health insurance consultant, the applicant must (i) successfully complete a forty-five-hour life and health study course as required in § 38.2-1816 and (ii) pass, within six months prior to the date of application for such license, the life and health examination as required in § 38.2-1817, except that an applicant who, at the time of such application holds an active life and health insurance agent license, shall be exempt from the study course and examination requirements.

B1. [Repealed.]

C. Any individual who acts as an insurance consultant for a partnership, limited liability company or corporation shall be licensed as an insurance consultant. (1985, c. 3, § 38.1-327.63; 1986, c. 562; 1987, c. 678; 1992, c. 574; 1997, c. 583.)

§ 38.2-1839. Contract required; placement of insurance for public bodies. — A. Any insurance consultant shall enter into a written contract with his client prior to any act as a consultant in this Commonwealth. The contract shall include, without limitation, the amount and basis of any consulting fee and the duration of employment. If the insurance consultant may also receive commissions for soliciting, negotiating, procuring, or effecting insurance as a part of his services in addition to a consulting fee, unless otherwise prohibited, such information shall be disclosed in the contract.

B. No insurance consultant may provide or offer to provide, directly or indirectly, insurance products to a public body while concurrently and on its behalf (i) evaluating proposals from other insurance agents and (ii) recommending the placement of insurance. (1985, c. 3, § 38.1-327.64; 1986, c. 562; 1987, cc. 521, 678; 1996, c. 989.)

§ **38.2-1840. Annual license fee.** — The nonrefundable application processing fee and the annual nonrefundable renewal processing fee for each insurance consultant's license shall be fifty dollars, which shall be paid in a manner prescribed by the Commission. Prior to August 1 of each year thereafter, every consultant shall renew his license in the manner prescribed by the Commission. All fees shall be collected by the Commission and paid into the state treasury and placed to the credit of the fund for the maintenance of the Bureau of Insurance as provided in subsection B of § 38.2-400. (1985, c. 3, § 38.1-327.65; 1986, c. 562; 1987, cc. 521, 678; 1994, c. 316; 1999, c. 44.)

The 1999 amendment in the first sentence, inserted "nonrefundable application processing" prior to "fee," inserted "and the" preceding "annual," and inserted "nonrefundable renewal processing fee" preceding "for each insurance consultant."

§ **38.2-1841. Renewal of license; termination, suspension or revocation of license.** — A. A license issued to an individual insurance consultant shall authorize him to act as an insurance consultant until his license is otherwise terminated, suspended, or revoked.

B. A license issued to a partnership, limited liability company or corporation shall authorize such partnership, limited liability company, or corporation to act as an insurance consultant until such license is otherwise terminated, suspended, or revoked. The dissolution or discontinuance of a partnership, whether by intent or by operation of law, shall automatically terminate the insurance consultant's license issued to such partnership. The Bureau shall automatically terminate all insurance consultant licenses within ninety days of receiving notification from the clerk of the Commission that the charter of a domestic limited liability company or corporation, whether by intent or by operation of law, has been terminated or that the certificate of authority of a foreign limited liability company or corporation has been revoked.

C. Upon the termination, suspension or revocation of an insurance consultant's license, the insurance consultant or the person having possession of the license shall immediately return it to the Commission.

D. Before August 1 of each year, each insurance consultant shall remit the nonrefundable renewal application processing fee prescribed in § 38.2-1840 for the renewal of the license, unless the license has been terminated, suspended or revoked on or before July 31 of that year. Any consultant license for which the required renewal form and nonrefundable renewal application processing fee has been received by the Commission on or before July 31 shall be renewed for a one-year period ending on the following July 31. Any consultant license for which the required renewal form and nonrefundable renewal application processing fee has not been received by the Commission by July 31 shall not be renewed effective on that date.

E. The termination of an insurance agent's license pursuant to subsection A of § 38.2-1825 shall not result in the termination of the agent's consultant license provided the annual nonrefundable renewal application processing fee prescribed in § 38.2-1840 continues to be paid and the consultant license continues to be renewed as otherwise required by this section. (1985, c. 3, § 38.1-327.66; 1986, c. 562; 1987, cc. 521, 678; 1992, c. 574; 1997, c. 583; 1999, c. 44.)

The 1999 amendment, in subsection D, inserted "nonrefundable renewal application processing" in the first sentence, in the second sentence, inserted "nonrefundable" preceding "renewal," inserted "application processing" preceding "fee," in the third sentence, inserted "nonrefundable" preceding "renewal" inserted "application processing" preceding "fee"; and in subsection E, substituted "consultant" for "consultant's," and substituted "nonrefundable renewal application processing" for "license."

§ 38.2-1842. Requirement to report to Commission. — A. Each insurance consultant shall report within thirty days to the Commission any change in his residence or name. Any insurance consultant who has moved his residence from this Commonwealth shall have his license immediately terminated by the Commission.

B. Each insurance consultant convicted of a felony shall report within thirty days to the Commission the facts and circumstances regarding the criminal conviction. (1985, c. 3, § 38.1-327.67; 1986, c. 562; 1987, cc. 521, 678; 1999, c. 59.)

The 1999 amendment inserted the subsection A designator, and added subsection B.

§ 38.2-1843. Refusal or revocation of license. — The Commission may refuse to issue an insurance consultant's license and, in addition to or in lieu of a penalty under § 38.2-218, may suspend or revoke the license of any licensee whenever it finds such applicant or licensee:

1. Has violated any provisions of any law of this Commonwealth applicable to insurance;

2. Has misappropriated any funds held in a fiduciary capacity;

3. Has shared fees with persons not licensed as a consultant or exempted under this statute;

4. Has misrepresented the provisions of any insurance contract;

5. Has been guilty of twisting the contracts of other insurers where *"twisting"* means misrepresenting a policy for the purpose of inducing a policyholder to terminate an existing policy to take a new policy;

6. Has been guilty of rebating. For the purposes of this section, "rebating" shall include reducing the fee or compensation provided for in § 38.2-1837 for the purpose of inducing a client or potential client to purchase a policy;

7. Has committed fraudulent or dishonest practices;

8. Is not trustworthy or is not competent to transact the insurance business for which a license is applied for or held;

9. Has been convicted of a felony; or

10. Has failed or refused to obey any order of the Commission entered against such applicant or licensee. (1985, c. 3, § 38.1-327.68; 1986, c. 562; 1987, cc. 521, 678; 1996, c. 10.)

§ 38.2-1844. Refusal to issue and revocation of license; hearing; appeal; new application. — If the Commission is of the opinion that any applicant for an insurance consultant's license is not of good character or does not have a good reputation for honesty, it may refuse to issue the license, subject to the right of the applicant to demand a hearing on the application. The Commission shall not revoke or suspend an existing license until the

licensee is given an opportunity to be heard before the Commission. If the Commission refuses to issue a new license or proposes to revoke or suspend an existing license, it shall give the applicant or licensee at least ten days' notice in writing of the time and place of the hearing, if a hearing is requested. The notice shall contain a statement of the objections to the issuance of the license, or the reason for its proposed revocation or suspension as the case may be. The notice may be given to the applicant or licensee by registered or certified mail, sent to the last known address of record pursuant to § 38.2-1842, or the last known business address if the address of record is incorrect, or in any other lawful manner the Commission prescribes. The Commission may summon witnesses to testify with respect to the applicant or licensee, and the applicant or licensee may introduce evidence in his or its behalf. No applicant to whom a license is refused after a hearing, nor any licensee whose license is revoked, shall again apply for a license until after the time, not exceeding two years, the Commission prescribes in its order. (1985, c. 3, § 38.1-327.69; 1986, c. 562; 1987, cc. 521, 678.)

§ **38.2-1845. Licensing nonresidents.** — A person who is not a resident as defined in § 38.2-1800, but who is a resident of another state or a province of Canada, may obtain a license as set forth in this article provided that the applicant first files with the Commission a certification from the insurance department of the applicant's state or province of domicile setting forth that the applicant is licensed or otherwise authorized in that state or province as an insurance consultant.

No applicant for a nonresident consultant license shall be permitted to obtain such a license unless such agent's state of domicile will grant a similar license to a resident of this Commonwealth. (1985, c. 3, § 38.1-327.70; 1986, c. 562; 1987, cc. 521, 678; 1988, c. 335.)

ARTICLE 5.

Licensing of Reinsurance Intermediaries.

§ **38.2-1846. Definitions.** — As used in this article:
"Actuary" means a person who is a member in good standing of the American Academy of Actuaries.

"Controlling" shall have the same meaning as set forth in § 38.2-1322 of this title.

"Insurer" means any person duly licensed in this Commonwealth pursuant to Chapters 10, 11, 12, 25, 26, 38 through 46, and 51 of this title.

"Licensed reinsurance intermediary" means an agent, broker or reinsurance intermediary licensed to act as a reinsurance intermediary pursuant to the applicable provision of this article.

"Qualified United States financial institution" means an institution that:

1. Is organized or (in the case of a U.S. office of a foreign banking organization) licensed, under the laws of the United States or any state thereof;

2. Is regulated, supervised and examined by U.S. federal or state authorities having regulatory authority over banks and trust companies; and

3. Has been determined by either the Commission, or the Securities Valuation Office of the National Association of Insurance Commissioners, to meet such standards of financial condition and standing as are considered necessary and appropriate to regulate the quality of financial institutions whose letters of credit will be acceptable to the Commission.

"Reinsurance intermediary" means a reinsurance intermediary broker or a reinsurance intermediary manager as these terms are defined in this article.

"Reinsurance intermediary broker" means any person, other than an officer or employee of the ceding insurer, who, without the power to bind the ceding insurer, solicits, negotiates or places reinsurance cessions or retrocessions on behalf of a ceding insurer or otherwise negotiates with a ceding insurer concerning reinsurance cessions or retrocessions.

"Reinsurance intermediary manager" means any person who has (i) authority to bind reinsurance risks or (ii) manages all or part of the assumed reinsurance business of a reinsurer, including the management of a separate division, department or underwriting office, and acts as an agent for such reinsurer whether known as a reinsurance intermediary manager or other similar term. Notwithstanding the foregoing, the following persons shall not be considered a reinsurance intermediary manager, for the purposes of this article, provided such person is acting in the capacity of employee or agent, as described herein, and properly discharging the duties of such employment or agency:

1. An employee of the reinsurer;

2. A U.S. manager of the United States branch of an alien reinsurer;

3. An underwriting manager which, pursuant to contract, manages all or part of the reinsurance operations of the reinsurer, is under common control with the reinsurer, subject to Article 5 (§ 38.2-1322 et seq.) of Chapter 13 or Article 2 (§ 38.2-4230 et seq.) of Chapter 42 of this title, and whose compensation is not based on the volume of premiums written;

4. The manager of a group, association, pool or organization of insurers which engages in joint underwriting or joint reinsurance and which is subject to examination by the supervising insurance official of the state, as defined in § 38.2-100, in which the manager's principal business office is located; or

5. A licensed managing general agent which binds facultative reinsurance contracts by placing individual risks pursuant to obligatory facultative agreements and subdivision 10 of § 38.2-1860.

"Reinsurer" means any insurer licensed in this Commonwealth with the authority to cede or accept from any insurer reinsurance pursuant to § 38.2-136. (1992, c. 588; 1994, c. 308.)

§ 38.2-1847. License requirements. — A. No insurer shall permit a person to act, and no person shall act, as a reinsurance intermediary broker in this Commonwealth if the reinsurance intermediary broker maintains an office either directly or as a member or employee of a firm or association, or an officer, director or employee of a corporation:

1. In this Commonwealth, unless such reinsurance intermediary broker is a licensed reinsurance intermediary in this Commonwealth; or

2. In another state, unless such reinsurance intermediary broker is a licensed reinsurance intermediary in this Commonwealth or in another state having a law substantially similar to this law.

B. No insurer shall permit a person to act, and no person shall act, as a reinsurance intermediary manager:

1. For a reinsurer domiciled in this Commonwealth, unless such reinsurance intermediary manager is a licensed reinsurance intermediary in this Commonwealth;

2. In this Commonwealth, if the reinsurance intermediary manager maintains an office either directly or as a member or employee of a firm or association, or an officer, director or employee of a corporation in this Commonwealth, unless such reinsurance intermediary manager is a licensed reinsurance intermediary in this Commonwealth; or

3. In another state for an insurer not domiciled in this Commonwealth, unless such reinsurance intermediary manager is a licensed reinsurance intermediary in this Commonwealth or in another state having a law substantially similar to this law.

C. The Commission may require a reinsurance intermediary manager to:

1. Be bonded in a manner acceptable to the Commission for the protection of the reinsurer; and

2. Maintain an errors and omissions policy in an amount acceptable to the Commission.

D. 1. The Commission may issue a reinsurance intermediary license to any person who has complied with the requirements of this article. Any such license issued to a partnership or corporation will authorize all the members of such partnership or corporation and any designated officers, directors or employees to act as reinsurance intermediaries under the license, and all such persons shall be named in the application and any supplements thereto.

2. If the applicant for a reinsurance intermediary license is a nonresident, such applicant, as a condition precedent to receiving or holding a license, shall designate the clerk of the Commission as agent for service of process in the manner, and with the same legal effect, provided for by this title for designation of service of process upon unauthorized insurers; and also shall furnish the clerk of the Commission with the name and address of a resident of this Commonwealth upon whom notices or orders of the Commission or process affecting such nonresident reinsurance intermediary may be served. Such licensee shall promptly notify the clerk of the Commission in writing of every change in its designated agent for service of process, and such change shall not become effective until acknowledged by the Commission.

E. The Commission may refuse to issue a reinsurance intermediary license, subject to the right of the applicant to demand a hearing on the application, if the Commission believes the applicant, any person named on the application, or any member, principal, officer or director of the applicant, is not trustworthy; that any controlling person of such applicant is not trustworthy to act as a reinsurance intermediary; or that any of the foregoing has given cause for revocation or suspension of such license or has failed to comply with any prerequisite for the issuance of such license.

F. Residents of Virginia who are members of the Virginia State Bar when acting in their professional capacity as such shall be exempt from the requirements of this section.

G. Any person seeking to be licensed as a reinsurance intermediary in this Commonwealth shall apply for such license in a form acceptable to the Commission, and shall pay to the Commission a nonrefundable application fee in an amount prescribed by the Commission. Such fee shall be not less than $500 and not more than $1,000. Every licensed reinsurance intermediary shall pay to the Commission a nonrefundable biennial renewal fee in an amount prescribed by the Commission. Such fee shall be not less than $500 and not more than $1,000. Each license shall expire on June 30 of the appropriate year. Prior to April 1 of the renewal year, each licensed reinsurance intermediary shall submit to the Commission a renewal application form and fee in the manner and form prescribed by the Commission. All fees shall be collected by the Commission and paid into the state treasury and placed to the credit of the fund for the maintenance of the Bureau of Insurance as provided in subsection B of § 38.2-400.

H. Any person seeking to be licensed as a reinsurance intermediary in this Commonwealth shall observe and abide by the laws of this Commonwealth and submit with its license application the following:

1. A statement identifying its principal place of business, organizational structure, and other such information as the Commission may require to verify that the reinsurance intermediary is qualified under the definition of this article;

2. A copy of its plan of operations;

3. A statement of registration which designates the clerk of the Commission as its agent for the purpose of receiving service of legal documents or process;

4. A copy of its current financial statement, which shall be certified by an independent public accountant and in a form acceptable to the Commission; and

5. Such information or reports as may be required to verify its continuing qualification as a reinsurance intermediary. (1992, c. 588; 1999, c. 44.)

The 1999 amendment added the last sentence in subsection G.

§ 38.2-1848. Required contract provisions; reinsurance intermediary brokers.

— Transactions between a reinsurance intermediary broker and the insurer it represents in such capacity shall only be entered into pursuant to a written authorization, specifying the responsibilities of each party. The authorization shall, at a minimum, provide that:

1. The insurer may terminate the reinsurance intermediary broker's authority at any time;

2. The reinsurance intermediary broker will render accounts to the insurer accurately detailing all material transactions, including information necessary to support all commissions, charges and other fees received by, or owing, to the reinsurance intermediary broker, and remit all funds due to the insurer within thirty days of receipt;

3. All funds collected for the insurer's account will be held by the reinsurance intermediary broker in a fiduciary capacity in a bank which is a qualified United States financial institution as defined in this article;

4. The reinsurance intermediary broker will comply with § 38.2-1849;

5. The reinsurance intermediary broker will comply with the written standards established by the insurer for the cession or retrocession of all risks; and

6. The reinsurance intermediary broker will disclose to the insurer any relationship with any reinsurer to which business will be ceded or retroceded. (1992, c. 588.)

§ 38.2-1849. Books and records; reinsurance intermediary brokers.

— A. For at least ten years after expiration of each contract of reinsurance transacted by the reinsurance intermediary broker, the reinsurance intermediary broker will keep a complete record for each transaction showing:

1. The type of contract, limits, underwriting restrictions, classes or risks and territory;

2. Period of coverage, including effective and expiration dates, cancellation provisions and notice required of cancellation;

3. Reporting and settlement requirements of balances;

4. Rate used to compute the reinsurance premium;

5. Names and addresses of assuming reinsurers;

6. Rates of all reinsurance commissions, including the commissions on any retrocessions handled by the reinsurance intermediary broker;

7. Related correspondence and memoranda;

8. Proof of placement;

9. Details regarding retrocessions handled by the reinsurance intermediary broker including the identity of retrocessionaires and percentage of each contract assumed or ceded;

10. Financial records, including but not limited to, premium and loss accounts; and

11. When the reinsurance intermediary broker procures a reinsurance contract on behalf of a licensed ceding insurer:

a. Directly from any assuming reinsurer, written evidence that the assuming reinsurer has agreed to assume the risk; or

b. If placed through a representative of the assuming reinsurer, other than an employee, written evidence that such reinsurer has delegated binding authority to the representative.

B. The insurer will have reasonable access to and the right to copy and audit all accounts and records maintained by the reinsurance intermediary broker related to its business in a form usable by the Commission. (1992, c. 588.)

§ 38.2-1850. Duties of insurers utilizing the services of a reinsurance intermediary broker. — A. An insurer shall not engage the services of any person, firm, association or corporation to act as a reinsurance intermediary broker on its behalf unless such person is licensed as required by § 38.2-1847.

B. An insurer may not employ an individual who is employed by a reinsurance intermediary broker with which it transacts business, unless such reinsurance intermediary broker is under common control with the insurer and subject to Article 5 (§ 38.2-1322 et seq.) of Chapter 13 or Article 2 (§ 38.2-4230 et seq.) of Chapter 42 of this title.

C. The insurer shall annually obtain a copy of the current financial statement of each reinsurance intermediary broker with which it transacts business. Such statement shall be certified by an independent public accountant and in a form acceptable to the Commission. (1992, c. 588.)

§ 38.2-1851. Required contract provisions; reinsurance intermediary managers. — Transactions between a reinsurance intermediary manager and the reinsurer it represents in such capacity shall only be entered into pursuant to a written contract, specifying the responsibilities of each party, which shall be approved by the reinsurer's Board of Directors. At least thirty days before such reinsurer assumes or cedes business through such reinsurance intermediary manager, a true copy of the approved contract shall be filed with the Commission for approval. The contract shall, at a minimum, provide that:

1. The reinsurer may terminate the contract for cause upon written notice to the reinsurance intermediary manager. The reinsurer may immediately suspend the authority of the reinsurance intermediary manager to assume or cede business during the pendency of any dispute regarding the cause for termination.

2. The reinsurance intermediary manager will render timely accounts to the reinsurer accurately detailing all material transactions, including information necessary to support all commissions, charges and other fees received by, or owing to the reinsurance intermediary manager, and remit all funds due under the contract to the reinsurer on not less than a monthly basis.

3. All funds collected for the reinsurer's account will be held by the reinsurance intermediary manager in a fiduciary capacity in a bank which is a qualified United States financial institution as defined in § 38.2-1846. The reinsurance intermediary manager may retain no more than three months' estimated claims payments and allocated loss adjustment expenses. The reinsurance intermediary manager shall maintain a separate bank account for each reinsurer that it represents.

4. For at least ten years after expiration of each contract of reinsurance transacted by the reinsurance intermediary manager, the reinsurance intermediary manager will keep a complete record for each transaction showing:

a. The type of contract, limits, underwriting restrictions, classes or risks and territory;

b. Period of coverage, including effective and expiration dates, cancellation provisions and notice required of cancellation, and disposition of outstanding reserves on covered risks;

c. Reporting and settlement requirements of balances;

d. Rate used to compute the reinsurance premium;

e. Names and addresses of assuming reinsurers;

f. Rates of all reinsurance commissions, including the commissions on any retrocessions handled by the reinsurance manager;

g. Related correspondence and memoranda;

h. Proof of placement;

i. Details regarding retrocessions handled by the reinsurance intermediary manager, as permitted by subsection D of § 38.2-1853, including the identity of retrocessionaires and percentage of each contract assumed or ceded;

j. Financial records, including but not limited to, premium and loss accounts; and

k. When the reinsurance intermediary manager places a reinsurance contract on behalf of a ceding insurer:

(1) Directly from any assuming reinsurer, written evidence that the assuming reinsurer has agreed to assume the risk; or

(2) If placed through a representative of the assuming reinsurer, other than an employee, written evidence that such reinsurer has delegated binding authority to the representative.

5. The reinsurer will have reasonable access to and the right to copy all accounts and records maintained by the reinsurance intermediary manager related to its business in a form usable by the reinsurer.

6. The contract cannot be assigned in whole or in part by the reinsurance intermediary manager.

7. The reinsurance intermediary manager will comply with the written underwriting and rating standards established by the insurer for the acceptance, rejection or cession of all risks.

8. Sets forth the rates, terms and purposes of commissions, charges and other fees which the reinsurance intermediary manager may levy against the reinsurer.

9. If the contract permits the reinsurance intermediary manager to settle claims on behalf of the reinsurer:

a. All claims will be reported to the reinsurer in a timely manner;

b. A copy of the claim file will be sent to the reinsurer at its request or as soon as it becomes known that the claim:

(1) Has the potential to exceed one percent of the insurer's surplus to policyholders as of December 31 of the last completed calendar year, an amount set by the reinsurer, or any other amount deemed appropriate by the Commission, whichever is less;

(2) Involves a coverage dispute;

(3) May exceed the reinsurance intermediary manager's claims settlement authority;

(4) Is open for more than six months; or

(5) Is closed by payment of an amount exceeding one percent of the insurer's surplus to policyholders as of December 31 of the last completed calendar year, an amount set by the reinsurer, or any other amount deemed appropriate by the Commission, whichever is less;

c. All claim files will be the joint property of the reinsurer and reinsurance intermediary manager. However, upon entry of order of liquidation or the appointment of a receiver for the liquidation of the reinsurer, such files shall become the sole property of the reinsurer or its estate; the reinsurance intermediary manager shall have reasonable access to and the right to copy the files on a timely basis;

d. Any settlement authority granted to the reinsurance intermediary manager may be terminated for cause upon the reinsurer's written notice to the reinsurance intermediary manager or upon the termination of the contract.

The reinsurer may suspend the settlement authority during the pendency of the dispute regarding the cause of termination.

10. Where electronic claims files are in existence, the contract must address the timely transmission of the data.

11. If the contract provides for a sharing of interim profits by the reinsurance intermediary manager, such interim profits will not be paid until one year after the end of each underwriting period for property business and five years after the end of each underwriting period for casualty business, or a later period set by the Commission for specified lines of insurance, and not until the adequacy of reserves on remaining claims has been verified pursuant to subsection C of § 38.2-1853.

12. The reinsurance intermediary manager will annually provide the reinsurer with a current financial statement prepared by an independent certified accountant in a form acceptable to the Commission.

13. The reinsurer shall, at least semi-annually, conduct an on-site review of the underwriting and claims processing operations of the reinsurance intermediary manager.

14. The reinsurance intermediary manager will disclose to the reinsurer any relationship it has with any insurer prior to negotiating any business with such insurer pursuant to this contract.

15. Within the scope of its actual or apparent authority, the acts of the reinsurance intermediary manager shall be deemed to be the acts of the reinsurer on whose behalf it is acting. (1992, c. 588.)

§ **38.2-1852. Prohibited acts.** — No insurer shall authorize its reinsurance intermediary manager to, and no reinsurance intermediary manager shall:

1. Cede retrocessions on behalf of the reinsurer, except that the reinsurance intermediary manager may cede facultative retrocessions pursuant to obligatory facultative agreements if the contract between the reinsurance intermediary manager and the reinsurer contains reinsurance underwriting guidelines for such retrocessions. Such guidelines shall include a list of reinsurers with which such automatic agreements are in effect, and for each such reinsurer, the coverages and amounts or percentages that may be reinsured, and commission schedules.

2. Commit the reinsurer to participate in reinsurance syndicates.

3. Permit any agent or reinsurance intermediary to represent the reinsurer without assuring that the agent or reinsurance intermediary is lawfully licensed.

4. Without prior approval of the reinsurer, pay or commit the reinsurer to pay a claim, net of retrocessions, that exceeds the lesser of an amount specified by the reinsurer or one percent of the reinsurer's surplus to policyholders as of December 31 of the last completed calendar year.

5. Collect any payment from a retrocessionaire or commit the reinsurer to any claim settlement with a retrocessionaire, without prior approval of the reinsurer. If prior approval is given, a report must be promptly forwarded to the reinsurer.

6. Jointly employ an individual who is employed by the reinsurer unless such reinsurance manager is under common control with the reinsurer subject to Article 5 (§ 38.2-1322 et seq.) of Chapter 13 or Article 2 (§ 38.2-4230 et seq.) of Chapter 42 of this title.

7. Appoint a sub-reinsurance intermediary manager. (1992, c. 588.)

§ **38.2-1853. Duties of reinsurers utilizing the services of a reinsurance intermediary manager.** — A. A reinsurer shall not engage the services of any person to act as a reinsurance intermediary manager on its behalf unless such person is licensed as required by § 38.2-1847.

B. The reinsurer shall annually obtain a copy of the current financial statement of each reinsurance intermediary manager which such reinsurer has engaged. Such statements shall be prepared by an independent certified accountant in a form acceptable to the Commission.

C. If a reinsurance intermediary manager establishes loss reserves, the reinsurer shall annually obtain the opinion of an actuary attesting to the adequacy of loss reserves established for losses incurred and outstanding on business produced by the reinsurance intermediary manager. This opinion shall be in addition to any other required loss reserve certification.

D. Binding authority for all retrocessional contracts or participation in reinsurance syndicates shall rest with an officer of the reinsurer who shall not be affiliated with the reinsurance intermediary manager.

E. Within thirty days of termination of a contract with a reinsurance intermediary manager, the reinsurer shall provide written notification of such termination in a form acceptable to the Commission.

F. A reinsurer shall not appoint to its board of directors, any officer, director, employee, controlling shareholder or subproducer of its reinsurance intermediary manager. This subsection shall not apply to relationships governed by Article 5 (§ 38.2-1322 et seq.) of Chapter 13 or Article 2 (§ 38.2-4230 et seq.) of Chapter 42 of this title.

G. An insurer shall not delegate to any person, other than one of its officers, the authority to enter into or bind any reinsurance agreement by which the insurer agrees to cede or retrocede any risk to a reinsurer, except that an insurer may delegate the specific authority to bind facultative reinsurance contracts by placing individual risks pursuant to the provisions of subdivision 1 of § 38.2-1852 or subdivision 10 of § 38.2-1860.

1. The officer shall be a regular salaried employee of such insurer and shall not be affiliated with the reinsurance intermediary.

2. The insurer is not prohibited by the provisions of this subsection from delegating the authority to enter into or bind an agreement to assume a risk to a licensed reinsurance intermediary manager pursuant to the provisions of this article, provided the authority to cede and assume a given risk is not simultaneously vested in the same intermediary. (1992, c. 588.)

§ **38.2-1854. Examination authority.** — A. A reinsurance intermediary shall be subject to examination by the Commission. The Commission shall have reasonable access to all books, bank accounts and records of the reinsurance intermediary in a form usable to the Commission.

B. In addition to examination pursuant to § 38.2-1809, a reinsurance intermediary manager may be examined, pursuant to Article 4 (§ 38.2-1317 et seq.) of Chapter 13 of this title, as if it were the reinsurer. (1992, c. 588.)

§ **38.2-1855. Penalties and liabilities; refusal or revocation of license.** — A. If the Commission finds, after providing an opportunity to be heard that any person has violated any provisions of this article, the Commission may in addition to any other remedies authorized by this title, order the reinsurance intermediary to make restitution to the insurer, reinsurer, rehabilitator or liquidator or receiver of the insurer or reinsurer for the net losses incurred by the insurer or reinsurer attributable to such violation.

B. The Commission may refuse to issue a reinsurance intermediary's license and, in addition to or in lieu of a penalty under § 38.2-218 of this title, may suspend or revoke the license of any licensed reinsurance intermediary whenever it finds such applicant or licensed reinsurance intermediary:

1. Has violated any provisions of any law of this Commonwealth applicable to insurance or reinsurance;

2. Has misappropriated any funds held in a fiduciary capacity;

3. Has misrepresented the provisions of any insurance or reinsurance contract;

4. Has engaged in fraudulent or dishonest practices;

5. Is not trustworthy or is not competent to transact business for which a license is applied for or held;

6. Has been convicted of a felony; or

7. Has failed or refused to obey any order of the Commission entered against such applicant or licensed reinsurance intermediary.

C. If the Commission is of the opinion that any applicant for licensing pursuant to this article is not of good character or does not have a good reputation for honesty, it may refuse to issue the license, subject to the right of the applicant to demand a hearing on the application. The Commission shall not revoke or suspend an existing license until the licensee is given an opportunity to be heard before the Commission. If the Commission refuses to issue a new license or proposes to revoke or suspend an existing license, it shall give the applicant or licensee at least ten days' notice in writing of the time and place of the hearing, if a hearing is requested. The notice shall contain a statement of the objections to the issuance of the license, or the reason for its proposed revocation or suspension as the case may be. The notice may be given to the applicant or licensee by registered or certified mail, sent to the last known address of record pursuant to § 38.2-1857, or the last known business address if the address of record is incorrect, or in any other lawful manner the Commission prescribes. The Commission may summon witnesses to testify with respect to the applicant or licensee, and the applicant or licensee may introduce evidence in his or its behalf. No applicant to whom a license is refused after a hearing, nor any licensee whose license is revoked, shall again apply for a license until after the time, not exceeding two years, the Commission prescribes in its order.

D. Nothing contained in this article is intended to or shall in any manner limit or restrict the rights of policyholders, claimants, creditors or other third parties or confer any rights to such persons.

E. If an order of rehabilitation or liquidation of the insurer has been entered pursuant to Chapter 15 (§ 38.2-1500 et seq.) of this title or the rehabilitation and liquidation statutes of a reciprocal state, and the receiver appointed under that order determines that the reinsurance intermediary or any other person has not materially complied with the provisions of this article, or any rule, regulation or order promulgated thereunder, and the insurer suffered any loss or damage therefrom, the receiver may maintain a civil action for recovery of damages or other appropriate sanctions for the benefit of the insurer. (1992, c. 588; 1994, c. 308; 1996, c. 10.)

§ 38.2-1856. Requirement to report to Commission. — A. Each licensed reinsurance intermediary shall report any change in business or residence address or name within thirty days to the Commission and to any contracted insurer.

B. Each licensed reinsurance intermediary convicted of a felony shall report within thirty days to the Commission the facts and circumstances regarding the criminal conviction. (1992, c. 588; 1999, c. 59.)

The 1999 amendment inserted the subsection A designator, and added subsection B.

§ 38.2-1857. Effective date. — This article shall take effect on July 1, 1992. No insurer or reinsurer may continue to utilize the services of a reinsurance intermediary on and after October 1, 1992, unless utilization is in compliance with this article. (1992, c. 588.)

ARTICLE 6.

Licensing of Managing General Agents.

§ 38.2-1858. Definitions. — As used in this article:

"Actuary" means a person who is a member in good standing of the American Academy of Actuaries.

"Insurer" means any person, duly licensed in the Commonwealth pursuant to Chapters 10, 11, 12, 25, 26, and 38 through 46, and 51 of this title.

"Managing general agent" means any person who (1) manages all or part of the insurance business of an insurer, including the management of a separate division, department or underwriting office; and (2) acts as an agent for such insurer whether known as a managing general agent, manager or other similar term, who, with or without the authority, either separately or together with affiliates, produces, directly or indirectly, and underwrites an amount of gross direct written premium equal to or exceeding five percent of the surplus to policyholders of the insurer as reported in the last annual statement of the insurer in any one quarter or year together with one or more of the following: (i) adjusts or pays claims in excess of an amount determined by the Commission or (ii) negotiates reinsurance on behalf of the insurer.

Notwithstanding the above, the following persons shall not be considered as managing general agents for the purposes of this article:

1. An employee of the insurer;

2. A U.S. manager of the United States branch of an alien insurer;

3. An underwriting manager which, pursuant to contract, manages all or part of the insurance operations of the insurer, is under common control with the insurer, subject to Article 5 (§ 38.2-1322 et seq.) of Chapter 13 or Article 2 (§ 38.2-4230 et seq.) of Chapter 42 of this title, and whose compensation is not based on the volume of premiums written;

4. The attorney-in-fact authorized by and acting for the subscribers of a reciprocal insurer.

"Qualified United States financial institutions" means an institution that:

1. Is organized or, in the case of a United States office of a foreign banking organization, licensed, under the laws of the United States or any state thereof;

2. Is regulated, supervised and examined by United States federal or state authorities having regulatory authority over banks and trust companies; and

3. Has been determined by either the Commission, or the Securities Valuation Office of the National Association of Insurance Commissioners, to meet such standards of financial condition and standing as are considered necessary and appropriate to regulate the quality of financial institutions whose letters of credit will be acceptable to the Commission.

"Underwrite" means the authority to accept or reject risk on behalf of the insurer. (1992, c. 588; 1994, c. 308.)

§ 38.2-1859. Licensure. — A. No domestic insurer shall permit a person to act, and no person shall act, in the capacity of a managing general agent for an insurer domiciled in this Commonwealth unless such person is licensed in this Commonwealth to act as a managing general agent.

B. No foreign or alien insurer shall permit a person to act, and no person shall act, in the capacity of a managing general agent representing such an insurer unless such person is licensed (i) in this Commonwealth to act as a managing general agent or (ii) in another state under laws which are substantially similar to the provisions of this article.

C. The Commission may license as a managing general agent any person who has complied with the requirements of this article and any regulations concerning licensure which may be promulgated by the Commission. The Commission may refuse to issue a license, subject to the right of the applicant to demand a hearing on the application, if the Commission believes the applicant, any person named on the application, or any member, principal, officer or director of the applicant is not trustworthy to act as a managing general agent, or that any of the foregoing has given cause for revocation or suspension of such license, or has failed to comply with any prerequisite for issuance of such license.

D. Any person seeking a license pursuant to subsection A or B (i) of this section shall apply for such license in a form acceptable to the Commission, and shall pay to the Commission a nonrefundable application fee in an amount prescribed by the Commission. Such fee shall be not less than $500 and not more than $1,000. Every licensed managing general agent shall pay to the Commission a nonrefundable biennial renewal fee in an amount prescribed by the Commission. Such fee shall be not less than $500 and not more than $1,000. Each license shall expire on June 30 of the appropriate year. Prior to April 1 of the renewal year, each licensed managing general agent shall submit to the Commission a renewal application form and fee in the manner and form prescribed by the Commission. All fees shall be collected by the Commission, paid into the state treasury, and placed to the credit of the fund for maintenance of the Bureau of Insurance as provided in subsection B of § 38.2-400.

E. The Commission may require that the managing general agent be bonded in a manner acceptable to the Commission for the protection of the insurer.

F. The Commission may require a managing general agent to maintain an errors and omissions policy. (1992, c. 588; 1999, c. 44.)

The 1999 amendment added the last sentence in subsection D.

§ **38.2-1860. Required contract provisions.** — No insurer shall retain or act through a managing general agent unless there is in force a written contract between said insurer and its managing general agent which sets forth the responsibilities of each party and where both parties share responsibility for a particular function, specifies the division of such responsibilities, and which contains the following minimum provisions:

1. The insurer may terminate the contract for cause upon written notice to the managing general agent. The insurer may suspend the underwriting authority of the managing general agent during the pendency of any dispute regarding the cause for termination.

2. The managing general agent will render accounts to the insurer detailing all transactions and remit all funds due under the contract to the insurer on not less than a monthly basis.

3. All funds collected for the account of an insurer will be held by the managing general agent in a fiduciary capacity in a bank which is a qualified U.S. financial institution. This account shall be used for all payments on behalf of the insurer. The managing general agent may retain no more than three months' estimated claims payments and allocated loss adjustment expenses. The managing general agent shall maintain a separate bank account for each insurer it represents.

4. Separate records of business written by the managing general agent will be maintained. The insurer shall have reasonable access to and the right to copy all accounts and records related to its business in a form usable by the insurer, and the Commission shall have access to all books, bank accounts and records of the managing general agent in a form usable by the Commission. Such records shall be retained in order to accomplish the purpose of subdivision 9 of this section but in no case for a period of less than five years.

5. The contract may not be assigned in whole or part by the managing general agent.

6. Appropriate underwriting guidelines including:

a. The maximum annual premium volume;

b. The basis of the rates to be charged;

c. The types of risks which may be written;

d. Maximum limits of liability;

e. Applicable exclusions;

f. Territorial limitations;

g. Policy cancellation provisions; and

h. The maximum policy period.

The insurer shall have the right to cancel or nonrenew any policy of insurance subject to the applicable laws and regulations.

7. If the contract permits the managing general agent to settle claims on behalf of the insurer:

a. All claims must be reported to the insurer in a timely manner.

b. A copy of the claim file will be sent to the insurer at its request or as soon as it becomes known that the claim:

1. Has the potential to exceed one percent of the insurer's surplus to policyholders as of December 31 of the last completed calendar year, an amount set by the company, or any other amount deemed appropriate by the Commission, whichever is less;

2. Involves a coverage dispute;

3. May exceed the managing general agent's claims settlement authority;

4. Is open for more than six months; or

5. Is closed by payment of an amount exceeding one percent of the insurer's surplus to policyholders as of December 31 of the last completed calendar year, an amount set by the company, or any other amount deemed appropriate by the Commission, whichever is less.

c. All claim files will be the joint property of the insurer and the managing general agent. However, upon entry of an order of liquidation or the appointment of a receiver for the liquidation of an insurer, such files shall become the sole property of the insurer or its estate; the managing general agent shall have reasonable access to and the right to copy the files on a timely basis.

d. Any settlement authority granted to the managing general agent may be terminated for cause upon the insurer's written notice to the managing general agent or upon the termination of the contract. The insurer may suspend the settlement authority during the pendency of any dispute regarding the cause for termination.

8. Where electronic claims files are in existence, the contract must address the timely transmission of the data.

9. If the contract provides for a sharing of interim profits by the managing general agent, and the managing general agent has the authority to determine the amount of the interim profits by establishing loss reserves or controlling claim payments, or in any other manner, interim profits will not be paid to the managing general agent until the profits have been verified pursuant to subsection B of § 38.2-1861 of this article (i) one year after they are earned for property insurance business and health insurance business and (ii) five years after they are earned on casualty insurance business.

10. The managing general agent shall not:

a. Bind reinsurance contracts or similar risk sharing arrangements, except that a managing general agent which acts on behalf of a ceding insurer may bind facultative reinsurance contracts by placing individual risks pursuant to obligatory facultative agreements provided that the contract between the insurer and the managing general agent contains reinsurance underwriting guidelines including, for both reinsurance assumed and ceded, a list of reinsurers with which such automatic agreements are in effect, the coverages and amounts or percentages that may be reinsured and commission schedules;

b. Commit the insurer to participate in insurance or reinsurance syndicates;

c. Appoint any agent unless (i) the agent is lawfully licensed to transact the type of insurance for which he is appointed and (ii) the insurer has notified the Commission, in writing, of the managing general agent's authorization to appoint agents on its behalf;

d. Without prior approval of the insurer, pay or commit the insurer to pay a claim over a specified amount, net of reinsurance, which amount shall not exceed one percent of the insurer's surplus to policyholders as of December 31 of the last completed calendar year;

e. Collect any payment from a reinsurer or commit the insurer to any claim settlement with a reinsurer, without prior approval of the insurer. If prior approval is given, a report must be promptly forwarded to the insurer;

f. Permit any agent appointed by the managing general agent to serve on the insurer's board of directors;

g. Jointly employ an individual who is employed with the insurer; or

h. Utilize or engage a submanaging general agent. (1992, c. 588.)

§ 38.2-1861. Duties of insurers utilizing managing general agents. —
A. The insurer shall annually obtain a copy of the current financial statement, which shall be certified by an independent public accountant and in a form acceptable to the Commission, of each managing general agent with which it transacts business.

B. If the managing general agent establishes loss reserves, the insurer shall annually obtain the opinion of an actuary attesting to the adequacy of loss reserves established for losses incurred and outstanding on business produced by the managing general agent. This is in addition to any other required loss reserve certification.

C. The insurer shall conduct, at least semiannually, an on-site review of the underwriting and claims processing operations of the managing general agent.

D. Binding authority for participation in insurance syndicates or reinsurance syndicates shall rest with an officer of the insurer, who shall not be affiliated with the managing general agent.

E. Within thirty days of entering into or termination of a contract with a managing general agent, the insurer shall provide, in a form acceptable to the Commission, written notification of such appointment or termination to the Commission. The notice of appointment of a managing general agent shall include a statement of duties which the applicant is expected to perform on behalf of the insurer, the lines of insurance for which the applicant is to be authorized to act, and any other information the Commission may request.

F. An insurer shall review its books and records each quarter to determine if any agent as defined by § 38.2-1800 has become a managing general agent as defined in § 38.2-1858. If the insurer determines that an agent has become a managing general agent pursuant to the above, the insurer shall promptly notify the agent and the Commission of such determination, and the insurer and agent must fully comply with the provisions of this article within thirty days.

G. An insurer shall not appoint to its board of directors an officer, director, employee, agent or controlling shareholder of its managing general agent. This subsection shall not apply to relationships governed by Article 5 (§ 38.2-1322 et seq.) of Chapter 13 or Article 2 (§ 38.2-4230 et seq.) of Chapter 42 of this title.

H. The insurer shall not delegate to any person, other than one of its officers, the authority to enter into or bind any reinsurance agreement by which the insurer agrees to cede any risk to a reinsurer, except that an insurer may delegate the specific authority to bind facultative reinsurance contracts by placing individual risks pursuant to the provisions of subdivision 1 of § 38.2-1852 or subdivision 10 of § 38.2-1860.

1. The officer shall be a regular salaried employee of the insurer and shall not be affiliated with the managing general agent.

2. The insurer is not prohibited by the provisions of this subsection from delegating to its managing general agent the authority to enter into or bind an agreement to assume a risk provided the managing general agent is licensed to act as a reinsurance intermediary manager under the provisions of Article 5 (§ 38.2-1846 et seq.) of this chapter and the authority to both cede and assume a given risk is not simultaneously vested in the same intermediary. (1992, c. 588.)

§ **38.2-1862. Examination authority.** — The acts of a managing general agent are considered to be the acts of the insurer on whose behalf it is acting. In addition to examination pursuant to § 38.2-1809, a managing general agent may be examined pursuant to Article 4 (§ 38.2-1317 et seq.) of Chapter 13 of this title as if it were the insurer. (1992, c. 588.)

§ **38.2-1863. Penalties and liabilities; refusal or revocation of license.** — A. If the Commission finds, after providing an opportunity to be heard, that any person under its jurisdiction has violated any provision of this article, the Commission may, in addition to any other remedies authorized by this title, order the managing general agent to reimburse the insurer, the rehabilitator or liquidator, or the receiver of the insurer for any losses incurred by the insurer caused by a violation of this article committed by the managing general agent.

B. The Commission may refuse to issue a managing general agent's license and, in addition to or in lieu of a penalty under § 38.2-218, may suspend or revoke the license of any licensee under its jurisdiction whenever it finds such applicant or licensee:

1. Has violated any provisions of any law of this Commonwealth applicable to insurance;

2. Has misappropriated any funds held in a fiduciary capacity;

3. Has misrepresented the provisions of any insurance contract;

4. Has been guilty of twisting the contracts of other insurers where "twisting" means misrepresenting a policy for the purpose of inducing a policyholder to terminate an existing policy to take a new policy;

5. Has been guilty of rebating. For the purposes of this section, "rebating" shall include reducing the fee or compensation provided for in § 38.2-1837 for the purpose of inducing a client or potential client to purchase a policy;

6. Has engaged in fraudulent or dishonest practices;

7. Is not trustworthy or is not competent to transact the insurance business for which a license is applied for or held;

8. Has been convicted of a felony; or

9. Has failed or refused to obey any order of the Commission entered against such applicant or licensee.

C. If the Commission is of the opinion that any applicant for a managing general agent's license is not of good character or does not have a good reputation for honesty, it may refuse to issue the license, subject to the right of the applicant to demand a hearing on the application. The Commission shall not revoke or suspend an existing license until the licensee is given an opportunity to be heard before the Commission. If the Commission refuses to issue a new license or proposes to revoke or suspend an existing license, it shall give the applicant or licensee at least ten days' notice in writing of the time and place of the hearing, if a hearing is requested. The notice shall contain a statement of the objections to the issuance of the license, or the reason for its proposed revocation or suspension as the case may be. The notice may be given to the applicant or licensee by registered or certified mail, sent to the last known address of record pursuant to § 38.2-1864, or the last known business address if the address of record is incorrect, or in any other lawful manner the Commission prescribes. The Commission may summon witnesses to testify with respect to the applicant or licensee, and the applicant or licensee may introduce evidence in his or its behalf. No applicant to whom a license is refused after a hearing, nor any licensee whose license is revoked, shall again apply for a license until after the time, not exceeding two years, the Commission prescribes in its order.

D. Nothing contained in this article is intended to or shall in any manner limit or restrict the rights of policyholders, claimants and auditors.

E. If an order of rehabilitation or liquidation of the insurer has been entered pursuant to Chapter 15 (§ 38.2-1500 et seq.) of this title or the rehabilitation and liquidation statutes of a reciprocal state, and the receiver appointed under that order determines that the managing general agent or any other person has not materially complied with the provisions of this article, or any rule, regulation or order promulgated thereunder, and the insurer suffered any loss or damage therefrom, the receiver may maintain a civil action for recovery of damages or other appropriate sanctions for the benefit of the insurer. (1992, c. 588; 1994, c. 308; 1996, c. 10.)

§ 38.2-1864. Requirement to report to Commission. — A. Each licensed managing general agent shall report within thirty days to the Commission and to any contracted insurer any change in business or residence address or name.

B. Each licensed managing general agent convicted of a felony shall report within thirty days to the Commission the facts and circumstances regarding the criminal conviction. (1992, c. 588; 1999, c. 59.)

The **1999 amendment** inserted the subsection A designator, and added subsection B.

§ 38.2-1865. Effective date. — This article shall take effect on July 1, 1992. No insurer may continue to utilize the services of a managing general agent on and after October 1, 1992, unless such utilization is in compliance with this article. (1992, c. 588.)

ARTICLE 7.

Continuing Education.

§ 38.2-1866. (Effective until January 1, 2000) Continuing education requirements. — A. Every resident and nonresident (i) insurance consultant, (ii) health insurance agent, (iii) life and health insurance agent, (iv) property and casualty insurance agent, and (v) title insurance agent shall, on a biennial basis, furnish evidence as set forth in this article that the continuing education requirements of this article have been satisfied. As used in this article, the term "agent" shall be construed to refer to any of the licensees referred to above.

B. Any agent who holds one type of license subject to this section shall complete sixteen hours of continuing education credits. Any agent who holds more than one type of license subject to this section shall complete twenty-four hours of continuing education credits with a minimum of eight credit hours in each license type. Of the total required credits for each biennium, two credit hours shall be in insurance law and regulations applicable in Virginia. Agents may receive no more than seventy-five percent of their required credits from courses provided by insurance companies or agencies. The Board, in its sole discretion, shall, at the time of course approval, determine whether any particular course shall be considered to be insurance company or agency sponsored, and shall require all course sponsors to provide this information clearly and conspicuously to all those enrolling in that course. (1992, c. 570; 1994, c. 175; 1996, c. 159; 1998, c. 46.)

Section set out twice. — The section above is effective until January 1, 2000. For the version of this section effective January 1, 2000, see the following section, also numbered 38.2-1866.

The numbers of §§ 38.2-1866 through 38.2-1874 were assigned by the Virginia Code Commission, the numbers in the 1992 act hav-

ing been 38.2-1846 through 38.2-1854.

The 1998 amendment, effective March 11, 1998, in subsection A, added the second sentence; in subsection B, in the fourth sentence, substituted "courses provided by insurance companies or agencies" for "insurance company or agency sponsored courses" and added the last sentence.

§ 38.2-1866. (Effective January 1, 2000) Continuing education requirements. — A. Every resident and nonresident (i) insurance consultant, (ii) life and health insurance agent, (iii) property and casualty insurance agent, and (iv) title insurance agent shall, on a biennial basis, furnish evidence as set forth in this article that the continuing education requirements of this article have been satisfied. As used in this article, the term "agent" shall be construed to refer to any of the licensees referred to above.

B. Any agent who holds one type of license subject to this section shall complete sixteen hours of continuing education credits. Any agent who holds more than one type of license subject to this section shall complete twenty-four hours of continuing education credits with a minimum of eight credit hours in each license type. Of the total required credits for each biennium, two credit hours shall be in insurance law and regulations applicable in Virginia. Agents may receive no more than seventy-five percent of their required credits from courses provided by insurance companies or agencies. The Board, in its sole discretion, shall, at the time of course approval, determine whether any particular course shall be considered to be insurance company or agency sponsored, and shall require all course sponsors to provide this information clearly and conspicuously to all those enrolling in that course. (1992, c. 570; 1994, c. 175; 1996, c. 159; 1998, c. 46; 1999, c. 86.)

Section set out twice. — The section above is effective January 1, 2000. For this section as in effect until January 1, 2000, see the preceding section, also numbered 38.2-1866.

The 1999 amendment, effective January 1,

2000, in subsection A, deleted former clause (ii), which read: "health insurance agent," and redesignated former clauses (iii) through (v) as present clauses (ii) through (iv).

§ 38.2-1867. Insurance continuing education board; approval of credits. — A. An insurance continuing education board, hereinafter called the Board, appointed by the Commission, shall approve all continuing education instructors, continuing education courses and programs of instruction. The Board shall establish and monitor standards for the education of insurance agents, approve courses including evaluating credit hours for all courses or programs offered, and set minimum requirements for course instructors. The Board shall have the authority to disapprove or withdraw approval of course sponsors, courses or course instructors when the established standards are not satisfied.

1. The number of credits for each self-study course, correspondence course, or program of classroom instruction shall be determined in a manner pre-

scribed by the Board. However, for an approved classroom course, a credit hour shall be equivalent to a classroom hour providing at least fifty minutes of continuous instruction or participation. No credits shall be granted for approved classroom courses unless notice to the Board is accompanied by proof of attendance by the course provider. No credits shall be granted for any correspondence or self-study course that does not include a written test of the subject matter which shall be successfully completed by each agent requesting credit. The Board shall have the right to review and approve or disapprove the proposed test as part of the course approval process.

2. An instructor of an approved continuing education course shall be eligible to receive the same number of credits as a person enrolled in the course for the purpose of meeting the requirements. However, agents and instructors may apply credits for attending or teaching the same course only once during any biennium.

3. Excess credit hours accumulated during any biennium may be carried forward to the next biennium only.

B. Members of the Board shall be appointed as follows:

1. One representative from the Independent Insurance Agents of Virginia;

2. One representative from the Professional Insurance Agents of Virginia and the District of Columbia;

3. Two representatives from the Virginia Association of Life Underwriters;

4. One representative of a licensed property and casualty insurance company writing business in this Commonwealth that operates through an exclusive agency force;

5. One representative of a licensed life and health insurance company writing business in the Commonwealth that operates through an exclusive agency force;

6. One representative of a licensed property and casualty insurance company domiciled and writing business in this Commonwealth;

7. One representative of a licensed life and health insurance company domiciled and writing business in this Commonwealth;

8. One representative of a licensed life and health insurance company writing business in this Commonwealth;

9. One representative of a licensed property and casualty insurance company writing business in this Commonwealth;

10. One representative from the Virginia Land Title Association; and

11. One representative from the adult education or higher education field.

C. On and after July 1, 1996, no person shall be appointed to serve as a member of the Board if, in the opinion of the Commission, other than as an incidental part of or unrelated to such person's employment, such person prepares, submits for approval, or teaches insurance continuing education courses in Virginia or in any other jurisdiction.

D. No meeting of the Board or any subcommittee of the Board shall be held unless timely notice of such meeting has been provided to the Commission's Bureau of Insurance. At any such meeting of the Board or any subcommittee of the Board, one or more representatives from the Bureau of Insurance shall be permitted to attend and to participate in such meeting, except that such Bureau of Insurance representative or representatives shall not have the right to vote on any matters before the Board.

E. Actions of the Board shall be exempt from the application of the Administrative Process Act (§ 9-6.14:1 et seq.). (1992, c. 570; 1996, c. 159.)

§ **38.2-1868:** Repealed by Acts 1996, c. 159.

§ **38.2-1868.1. Proof of compliance; late filing penalty, exemption or waiver.** — A. As used in this article:

"Proof of compliance" shall mean all documents, forms and fees specified by

the Board for (i) filing proof of completion of Board-approved continuing education courses for the appropriate number of hours and for the appropriate content or (ii) filing proof of meeting the exemption requirements set forth in subsection B of § 38.2-1871.

"Received by the Board or its administrator" shall mean delivered into the possession of the Board or its administrator at the business address of the Board's administrator.

B. Each agent holding one or more licenses subject to the continuing education requirements of this article shall complete all continuing education course, exemption, or waiver requirements by no later than December 31 of each even-numbered year, and shall submit to the Board or its administrator proof of compliance with or exemption from the continuing education requirements in the form and manner required by the Board.

1. Such proof of compliance must be received by the Board or its administrator by the close of business on February 28 of the following year, or the next working day thereafter if February 28 falls on a weekend.

2. Agents shall be permitted to submit proof of compliance for an additional period of time, until the close of business on March 31, or the next working day thereafter if March 31 falls on a weekend, of such year subject to payment by the agent, in addition to any filing fee imposed by the Board for timely filing of proof of compliance, of a late filing penalty of $250, payable to the Board in such manner as may be prescribed by the Board. No agent whose proof of compliance is received during the extension provided by this subdivision shall be considered in compliance with the continuing education requirements unless the filing fee and the late filing penalty described herein have been paid by the close of business on March 31, or the next working day thereafter if March 31 falls on a weekend.

3. Failure of an agent to furnish proof of compliance by such date shall result in the imposition of the penalties set forth in § 38.2-1869.

C. Agents seeking a waiver of continuing education requirements for a biennium pursuant to § 38.2-1870 shall submit all documentation, forms and fees specified by the Board so as to be received by the Board or its administrator as set forth in § 38.2-1870.

D. Any agent holding one or more licenses subject to this article who fails to submit complete documentation showing proof of compliance with continuing education requirements, as well as all specified forms and fees, so as to be received by the Board or its administrator by the close of business on the date specified in subsection B or C of this section shall be deemed to be in noncompliance with the requirements of this article. (1996, c. 159; 1998, c. 46.)

The **1998 amendment,** effective March 11, 1998, in subsection B, in the introductory language, inserted "complete all continuing education course, exemption, or waiver requirements by no later than December 31 of each even-numbered year, and shall," and inserted "or exemption from," rewrote subdivision 1, and added subdivisions 2 and 3; and in subsection D, substituted "the close of business" for "midnight."

§ 38.2-1869. Failure to satisfy requirements; termination of license.

— A. Failure of an agent to satisfy the requirements of this article by the last day of each even-numbered year beginning December 31, 1994, either by obtaining the continuing education credits required and furnishing evidence of same to the Board or its administrator as required by this article, or by furnishing to the Board acceptable evidence of exemption from the requirements of this article, or by obtaining, in a manner prescribed by the Board pursuant to this article, a waiver of the requirements for that biennium, shall result, subsequent to notification by the Board to the Commission, in the administrative termination of each license held by the agent for which the requirement was not satisfied. An agent whose license is terminated pursuant to this section shall have the right to appeal such termination in the manner set forth by the Board pursuant to subdivision A 7 of § 38.2-1874. However, failure of an agent to provide written notice of such appeal in the form and manner required by the Board within sixty days following the date of termination of such license shall be deemed a waiver by such agent of the right to appeal such license termination.

1. The Board shall, on or about a date six months prior to the end of each biennium, provide a status report to each agent who has not yet fully satisfied the requirements of this article for such biennium. Such report shall inform the agent of his current compliance status for each license held that is subject to this article, and the consequences associated with noncompliance, and shall be sent by first-class mail to such agent at his last-known residence address as shown in the Commission's records. Failure of an agent to receive such notification shall not be grounds for contesting license termination.

2. The Board shall, on or about a date forty-five days prior to the end of each biennium, provide a status report to each agent who has not yet fully satisfied the requirements of this article for such biennium. Such report shall inform the agent of his current compliance status for each license held that is subject to this article, and the consequences associated with noncompliance, and shall be sent by first class mail to such agent at his last known residence address as shown in the Commission's records. Failure of an agent to receive such notification shall not be grounds for contesting license termination.

3. No such administrative termination shall become effective until the Commission has provided thirty days' written notice of such impending termination to the agent by first-class mail sent to the agent at the agent's last known residence address as shown in the Commission's records. The thirty-day notice period shall commence on the date that the written notice is deposited in the United States mail. Failure of an agent to receive such notification shall not be grounds for contesting a license termination. Neither the Board, nor its administrator, nor the Commission shall have the power to grant an agent additional time for completing the continuing education credits required by subsection B of § 38.2-1866 or the time for seeking waivers or exemption pursuant to § 38.2-1870 or § 38.2-1871. The sole purpose of such thirty-day period shall be for the agent to demonstrate to the satisfaction of the Board that the agent had, in fact, submitted and the Board or its administrator had received proof of compliance on or before the filing deadlines set forth in subsection A or B of § 38.2-1868.1. The Board shall not be obligated to review or respond to any other submissions during such thirty-day period except submissions indicating that the Board's records of compliance for such agent were incorrect. No more than fifteen days after the end of such thirty-day period, the Board shall provide to the Commission a final updated record of those agents who complied with the requirements of this article, whereupon the Commission shall administratively terminate the licenses of those agents required to submit proof of compliance and by whom proof of compliance was not submitted in a proper or timely manner.

4. Pursuant to the requirements of subsection C of § 38.2-1817, an agent holding a license for variable life insurance and variable annuities whose life and health insurance agent license is administratively terminated for failure to satisfy the requirements of this article shall also have such variable life insurance and variable annuities license administratively terminated by the Commission. Such license may be applied for again after the agent has obtained a new life and health insurance agent's license.

B. 1. Except as provided in subdivision 2 of this subsection, no resident or nonresident agent whose license has been terminated under the terms of this section shall be permitted to make application for a new license prior to the expiration of a period of ninety days from the date of termination of such license. No resident or nonresident agent applying for a license after termination of a previous license pursuant to this section shall be issued a license unless the agent has successfully completed, subsequent to the biennium, any study course required by § 38.2-1816 and the examination required by § 38.2-1817. In such an event, these study course and examination requirements shall not be subject to waiver under any circumstances, including those set forth in §§ 38.2-1816, 38.2-1817, 38.2-1836, and 38.2-1845.

2. A resident or nonresident agent whose license has been terminated under the terms of this section shall be permitted to make application for a new license prior to the expiration of the ninety-day period provided in this subsection, provided that such agent (i) pays to the Commission, in addition to any license processing fees, an administrative penalty of $1,000, which shall be paid into the state treasury and credited to the fund for the maintenance of the Bureau of Insurance and (ii) has successfully completed, subsequent to the end of the biennium, any study course required by § 38.2-1816 and the examination required by § 38.2-1817. In such an event, the study course and examination requirements shall not be subject to waiver under any circumstances, including those set forth in §§ 38.2-1816, 38.2-1817, 38.2-1836, and 38.2-1845.

C. A resident or nonresident agent who voluntarily surrenders his license without prejudice during a biennium or within 120 days after the end of a biennium, and who has not provided proof of compliance for such biennium, shall not be permitted to apply for a new license of the same type until such agent has complied with the requirements of subsection B of this section. Further, if such agent chooses not to apply for a new license under the terms of subdivision B 2 of this section, such agent shall not be permitted to obtain a new license of the same type until the expiration of the same ninety-day period applicable to agents whose licenses are terminated pursuant to subsection A of this section.

D. A resident agent whose license terminates because, within 180 days prior to or within 120 days after the end of a biennium, such agent moves his residence to another state, and who had not, prior to such relocation, provided proof of compliance for such biennium shall not be permitted to apply for a new license of the same type until such agent has complied with the requirements of subdivisions B 1 and B 2 of this section. Further, if the agent chooses not to apply for a new license under the terms of subdivision B 2 of this section, such agent shall not be permitted to obtain a new license of the same type until the expiration of the same ninety-day period applicable to agents whose licenses are terminated pursuant to subsection A of this section.

E. An insurance consultant who fails to renew his consultant license by the date specified in § 38.2-1840, but who obtains a new insurance consultant license within twelve months following such renewal date shall be treated, for purposes of determining exemption from continuing education requirements pursuant to § 38.2-1871, as if such insurance consultant license had been renewed in a timely manner. (1992, c. 570; 1994, c. 175; 1995, c. 554; 1996, c. 159; 1997, c. 583; 1998, c. 46.)

Editor's note. — Acts 1996, c. 159, cl. 3, provides: "That the provisions of subdivision A 1 of § 38.2-1869 of this act shall become effective on January 1, 1997."

The 1996 amendment, in subsection A, substituted "Failure" for "With the exception of the extension of time granted in § 38.2-1868 for completing and filing proof of having completed Board-approved courses for the biennium ending December 31, 1994, failure" and inserted "subsequent to notification by the Board to the Commission" following "shall result"; added subdivisions A 1, A 2, and A 4; inserted the 3 designation at the beginning of the fourth paragraph; in present subdivision A 3, substituted "first-class mail" for "regular mail" in the first sentence, deleted the former third sentence which read: "During such thirty-day period, the agent may provide proof of compliance with the requirements of this article, in a manner and form acceptable to the Commission," and added the present third, fourth, fifth, sixth, and seventh sentences; substituted "no earlier than the date of the thirty-day written notice required by subdivision A 3 of this section" for "subsequent to such license termination" in the second sentence of subsection B; and added subsections C and D. For the effective date of subdivision A 1, see the Editor's note at the beginning of this section.

The 1998 amendment, effective March 11, 1998, in subsection A, in the introductory language, added the second and last sentences, in subdivision 2, in the first sentence, substituted "on or about a date forty-five days" for "by a date thirty days," and in subdivision 3, in the fifth sentence, substituted "filing deadlines set forth in subsection A or B of § 38.2-1868.1" for

"last day of the biennium," and in the last sentence, substituted "No more than fifteen days after" for "At"; in subsection B, added the subdivision 1 designation, in the first sentence, added "Except as provided in subdivision 2 of this subsection," and in the second sentence, substituted "subsequent to the biennium" for "no earlier than the date of the thirty-day written notice required by subdivision A 3 of this section," and added subdivision 2; in subsection C, in the second sentence, inserted "if such agent chooses not to apply for a new license under the terms of subdivision B 2 of this section"; and in subsection D, in the first sentence, inserted the language beginning "to apply for a new license of the same type" and in the second sentence, added the language beginning "Further" and ending "permitted."

§ **38.2-1870. Waiver of continuing education requirements.** — The requirements of this article may be waived by the Board for good cause shown. As used herein, "good cause" includes long-term illness or incapacity and such other emergency situations as may be determined by the Board as preventing the agent from satisfying the continuing education credit hours required by this article. Requests for waivers of continuing education requirements shall be made in a form and manner prescribed by the Board, and shall be submitted to the Board no later than ninety days prior to the end of the biennium for which such waiver is requested. In the event that the long-term illness, incapacity, or such other emergency situation referenced above manifests itself within 120 days prior to the end of the biennium, the agent shall be permitted to request a waiver by submitting such request to the Board, in the form and manner prescribed by the Board, provided such request is received by the Board no later than thirty days prior to the end of the biennium for which such waiver is requested. The Board shall approve or disapprove the waiver request within thirty days of receipt thereof, and shall provide written notice of its decision to the applicant for waiver within five days of rendering its decision. Any waiver granted pursuant to this section shall be valid only for the biennium for which waiver application was made. (1992, c. 570; 1996, c. 159.)

§ **38.2-1871. Licensees exempt from continuing education requirements of article.** — A. The following licensees are exempt from fulfilling the continuing education credit requirements set forth in this article for the biennium in which such licenses are issued:

1. Resident agents who have successfully passed the required examination for a license during a biennium pursuant to § 38.2-1817 will be exempt from meeting the continuing education requirements for that license for that biennium; and

2. Resident or nonresident agents who have been issued a license during the last twelve months of the biennium, and who are not otherwise exempt from the continuing education requirements for that license, shall have such requirements waived for that license for that biennium.

B. The following licensees are exempt from fulfilling the continuing education credit requirements set forth in this article:

1. Life and health insurance consultants who are licensed as life and health agents and who satisfy the continuing education requirements needed for continuation of their life and health agent license;

2. Property and casualty insurance consultants who are also licensed as property and casualty agents and who satisfy the continuing education

requirements needed for continuation of their property and casualty agent license;

3. Agents who will have attained at least the age of sixty-five by the end of a biennium with respect to any license that they have held continuously for at least twenty years, subject to submission of a request for permanent exemption prior to the end of a biennium during which they satisfy the exemption requirements, in the form and manner required by the Board; and

4. Nonresident agents who reside in states requiring continuing education for their resident insurance producers, and who furnish evidence in the form and manner required by the Board of their compliance with such continuing education requirements in their state of residence, provided that the insurance supervisory official of the nonresident agent's state of residence will grant similar exemptions to Virginia residents who have satisfied Virginia's continuing education requirements. (1992, c. 570; 1994, c. 175; 1996, c. 159; 1997, c. 583.)

§ 38.2-1872. Administrative duties of Board; transfer to outside administrator. — A. The Board shall have the authority to transfer all or part of its administrative duties to an outside administrator. The performance of the administrator shall be confirmed at least annually by the Board and appropriate corrective action shall be taken for any deficiencies. Such administrator shall maintain records reflecting the continuing education status of all licensed agents reporting credits to it, subject to the requirements of this article.

B. The Board or its administrator shall, on a date and in a form acceptable to the Commission but in no event later than May 30 following the end of each biennium, provide to the Commission a report of all licensees who satisfied the requirements of this article for such biennium. The Board or its administrator shall not, however, be required to include in such report those licensees exempt pursuant to subsection A of § 38.2-1871. The administrative termination of licenses, as required by subdivision A 3 of § 38.2-1869 shall be carried out by operation of law.

C. The Board or its administrator shall be provided such information from the Commission's records as the Board may reasonably require in order to carry out its duties, including, but not limited to, (i) requesting and receiving from the Commission computer-generated reports, mailing labels, or other computer-generated information containing the names, license identification numbers, license types, and residence addresses of all licensees subject to the requirements of this article; and (ii) direct on-line "inquiry only" access to such automated system data as the Commission may deem appropriate. (1992, c. 570; 1996, c. 159; 1998, c. 46.)

The 1998 amendment, effective March 11, 1998, in subsection B, in the first sentence, substituted "May 30" for "January 15," and deleted the former second sentence, which read: "However, for the biennium ending December 31, 1996, the Board shall have until January 31, 1997, to provide such report to the Commission."

§ 38.2-1873. Continuing insurance education fees. — The continuing insurance education program established by this article shall be self-supporting, and any costs incurred by the Commission, administrator, or the Board or its members, including legal fees and other legal expenses incurred during or as a result of the good faith execution of their duties, shall be borne by the continuing insurance education fees paid by agents, course sponsors, and course instructors. (1992, c. 570; 1996, c. 159.)

§ 38.2-1874. Continuing education program; plan of operation; approval by Commission. — A. The Board shall submit to the Commission a plan of operation which provides for the fair and nondiscriminatory administration of the continuing insurance education program established pursuant to this article. Such plan shall not become effective until approved by the Commission in writing. The Board may, at any time, propose amendments to the plan of operation, and such amendments shall not become effective until approved by the Commission. The plan of operation shall:

1. Establish guidelines for the Board to utilize in adopting procedures for exercising its powers and duties;

2. Establish guidelines for the Board to utilize in adopting procedures for handling the assets of the continuing insurance education program;

3. Establish guidelines for reimbursing members of the Board for the necessary expenses incurred in the performance of their official duties and for indemnifying members for all expenses and liabilities incurred as a result of their serving as members of the Board;

4. Establish guidelines for determining places and times for meetings of the Board;

5. Establish guidelines for adopting procedures for records to be kept of all financial transactions of the Board and administrator;

6. Establish procedures for the election of Board officers;

7. Establish guidelines pursuant to which the Board may adopt a reasonable means whereby any person aggrieved by an action of the Board or administrator with regard to a course or instructor submission may appeal such action to the Board, whose decision in such matters shall be final; and a reasonable means whereby any licensee aggrieved by an action of the Board or administrator having the potential to affect directly such licensee's license status may, after written request, be heard in person or by an authorized representative to review the grievance. Guidelines pertaining to licensees may include additional levels of appeal other than those set forth herein, but shall provide, at a minimum, that (i) if the Board or its administrator fails to grant or reject the grievance within thirty days after it is made, the licensee filing the grievance may proceed in the same manner as if his grievance had been rejected; (ii) any licensee adversely affected by the action of the Board or its administrator on such request may, within thirty days after written notice of the action, make a written request for informal review by the Bureau of Insurance, which shall affirm or reverse the action upon not less than ten days' written notice to the licensee and to the Board or its administrator; and (iii) any licensee adversely affected by the action of the Bureau of Insurance on such request may, within thirty days after written notice of the action, appeal to the Commission pursuant to the Commission's "Rules of Practice and Procedure." The Commission may affirm or reverse the action upon not less than ten days' written notice to the licensee and to the Board or its administrator; and

8. Contain guidelines for the Board to utilize in adopting additional provisions necessary or proper for the execution of the powers and duties of the Board including but not limited to (i) program requirements and approved programs of study; (ii) qualifications and responsibilities of course instructors; (iii) management and record-keeping responsibilities; (iv) fee schedules and filing requirements; and (v) course refund policies and procedures.

B. If the Commission disapproves all or any part of the proposed plan of operation or amendment thereto, the Board shall within fifteen days submit for review an appropriate revised plan of operation or amendment thereto. If the Board fails to do so, the Commission shall promulgate a plan of operation or an amended plan of operation. The plan of operation or amended plan of operation approved or promulgated by the Commission shall become effective and operational upon order of the Commission.

C. A regular meeting of the Board shall be held at least annually at such time, date, and place approved by the Board. Special meetings may be called at any time by the chairman. Notices of all regular and special meetings shall be sent to each person serving as a representative on the Board or a subcommittee of the Board and to the Commission. Each notice shall state the purpose of the meeting and include any proposed changes in rules or procedures. Any such meeting notices shall be given in such form as may be acceptable to the Board at least twenty days prior to the date of the meeting.

D. The books of account, records, reports and other documents of the Board and its administrator shall be open to the Commission for examination at all reasonable hours.

E. There shall be no liability on the part of and no cause of action shall arise against any member of the Board, the Board, the Board's agents or employees, or the Commission or its representatives for any action taken or statement made by them in good faith in the performance of their powers and duties under this article. (1992, c. 570; 1994, c. 175; 1996, c. 159.)

CHAPTER 19.

REGULATION OF RATES GENERALLY.

271

§ 38.2-1900. Purposes of chapter. — A. This chapter shall be liberally construed to achieve the purposes stated in subsection B of this section.

B. The purposes of this chapter are to:

1. Protect policyholders and the public against the adverse effects of excessive, inadequate or unfairly discriminatory rates;

2. Encourage independent action by insurers and reasonable price competition among insurers as the most effective way to produce rates that conform to the standards of subdivision 1;

3. Provide formal regulatory controls for use if independent action and price competition fail;

4. Authorize cooperative action among insurers in the rate making process, and regulate such cooperation in order to prevent practices that tend to create monopoly or to lessen or destroy competition;

5. Provide rates that are responsive to competitive market conditions and improve the availability of insurance in this Commonwealth; and

6. Regulate the business of insurance in a manner that will preclude application of federal antitrust laws. (1973, c. 504, § 38.1-279.29; 1986, c. 562.)

Law Review. — For survey of Virginia law on insurance for the year 1972-1973, see 59 Va. L. Rev. 1535 (1973). For an article analyzing ratemaking issues under the SCC, see 14 Wm. & Mary L. Rev. 601 (1973).

§ 38.2-1901. Definitions. — As used in this chapter:

"Classification system" or *"classification"* means the plan, system, or arrangement for grouping risks with similar characteristics or a specified class of risk by recognizing differences in exposure to hazards.

"Experience rating" means a statistical procedure utilizing past risk experience to produce a prospective premium credit, debit, or unity modification.

"Market segment" means any line or class of insurance or, if it is described in general terms, any subdivision of insurance or any class of risks or combination of classes.

"Prospective loss costs" means historical aggregate losses and loss adjustment expenses projected through development to their ultimate value and through trending to a future point in time. Prospective loss costs do not include provisions for profit or expenses other than loss adjustment expenses.

"Rate service organization" means any entity, including its affiliates or subsidiaries, which either has two or more member insurers or is controlled either directly or indirectly by two or more insurers, other than a joint underwriting association under § 38.2-1915, which assists insurers in ratemaking or filing by (i) collecting, compiling, and furnishing loss statistics; (ii) recommending, making, or filing prospective loss costs or supplementary rate information; or (iii) advising about rate questions, except as an attorney giving legal advice. Two or more insurers having a common ownership or operating in this Commonwealth under common management or control constitute a single insurer for purposes of this definition.

"Retrospective rating plan" means a rating plan that adjusts the premium for the insurance to which it applies on the basis of losses incurred during the period covered by that insurance.

"Statistical plan" means the plan, system, or arrangement used in collecting data for rate making or other purposes.

"Supplementary rate information" includes any manual or plan of rates, experience rating plan, statistical plan, classification, rating schedule, minimum premium, or minimum premium rule, policy fee, rating rule, rate-related underwriting rule, and any other information not otherwise inconsistent with the purposes of this chapter required by the Commission.

"Supporting data" includes:

1. The experience and judgment of the filer and, to the extent the filer wishes or the Commission requires, the experience and judgment of other insurers or rate service organizations;

2. The filer's interpretation of any statistical data relied upon;

3. Descriptions of the actuarial and statistical methods employed in setting the rates; and

4. Any other relevant information required by the Commission. (1973, c. 504, §§ 38.1-279.30, 38.1-279.40; 1986, c. 562; 1990, c. 596; 1993, c. 985; 1997, c. 153.)

§ 38.2-1902. Scope of chapter. — A. Except as provided in subsection B of this section, this chapter applies to the classes of insurance defined in §§ 38.2-110 through 38.2-122.1, §§ 38.2-124 through 38.2-128 and §§ 38.2-130 through 38.2-133.

B. This chapter does not apply to:

1. Insurance written through the Virginia Workers' Compensation Plan pursuant to Chapter 20 (§ 38.2-2000 et seq.) of this title;

2. Insurance on a specific risk as provided in § 38.2-1920;

3. Reinsurance, other than joint reinsurance, to the extent stated in § 38.2-1915;

4. Life insurance as defined in § 38.2-102;

5. Annuities as defined in §§ 38.2-106 and 38.2-107;

6. Accident and sickness insurance as defined in § 38.2-109;

7. Title insurance as defined in § 38.2-123;

8. Insurance of vessels or craft used primarily in a trade or business, their cargoes, marine builders' risks and marine protection and indemnity;

9. Insurance against loss of or damage to hulls of aircraft, including their accessories and equipment, or against liability, other than workers' compensation and employers' liability, arising out of the ownership, maintenance or use of aircraft;

10. Automobile bodily injury and property damage liability insurance issued to: (i) any motor carrier of property who is required to file such insurance with the Department of Motor Vehicles pursuant to § 46.2-2028 or any amendment to that section; or (ii) any motor carrier of property required by 49 U.S.C.A. § 315, or any rule or regulation prescribed by the Interstate Commerce Commission pursuant to 49 U.S.C.A. § 315, to file such insurance with the Interstate Commerce Commission;

11. Uninsured motorist coverage required by subsection A of § 38.2-2206;

12. Insurance written through the Virginia Automobile Insurance Plan. However, § 38.2-1905 shall apply to insurance written through the Plan;

13. Insurance provided pursuant to Chapter 27 (§ 38.2-2700 et seq.) of this title;

14. Home protection contracts as defined by § 38.2-2600 and their rates until such time as the Commission determines there is sufficient competition in the industry as provided by § 38.2-2608.

C. This chapter shall not apply to any class of insurance written (i) by any mutual assessment property and casualty insurance company organized and operating under the laws of this Commonwealth and doing business only in this Commonwealth, or (ii) by any mutual insurance company or association organized under the laws of this Commonwealth, conducting business only in this Commonwealth, and issuing only policies providing for perpetual insurance. (1973, c. 504, § 38.1-279.31; 1976, c. 636; 1981, c. 530; 1986, c. 562; 1987, c. 519; 1993, cc. 774, 985; 1995, cc. 744, 803.)

Law Review. — For survey of Virginia law
on insurance for the year 1972-1973, see 59 Va.
L. Rev. 1535 (1973).

§ 38.2-1903. Exemptions. — The Commission may by rule exempt any person, class of persons, or market segment from any or all of the provisions of this chapter to the extent that it finds their application unnecessary to achieve the purposes of this chapter. Retrospective rating plans and large deductible plans for use in writing workers' compensation insurance for large risks shall be exempt from the filing requirements of Chapter 19 (§ 38.2-1900 et seq.). For purposes of this section, large risks are risks which generate total estimated standard premium for workers' compensation insurance of at least $250,000 annually (or less or in combination with other lines if approved by the Commission). Large deductible plans shall be defined for the purposes of this section as workers' compensation rating plans that include a per claim deductible of at least $100,000. Workers' compensation insurance for large risks may be retrospectively rated, or rated under a large deductible rating plan, as mutually agreed upon by the insurer and the insured in writing. A copy of any large risk retrospective rating plan and large deductible plan shall be made available to the Commission upon request. Notwithstanding these exemptions for retrospective rating plans and large deductible plans for large risks, insurers' experience attributable to large risks shall be filed with the Commission in accordance with § 38.2-1919. (1973, c. 504, § 38.1-279.32; 1986, c. 562; 1997, c. 153; 1999, c. 491.)

The **1999 amendment** substituted "and large deductible plans for use in writing workers' compensation insurance for large risks shall be exempt from the filing requirements" for "for large risks shall be exempt from the provisions" in the second sentence; in the third sentence, added "For purposes of this section," and substituted "insurance of at least $250,000" for "of at least $500,000," inserted the present fourth sentence; redesignated the former fourth sentence as the present fifth sentence and rewrote the sentence, which formerly read: "Large risks may be retrospectively rated as mutually agreed upon by the insurer and the insured in writing"; in the present sixth sentence, substituted "retrospective rating plan and large deductible plan" for "rating plan"; and substituted "these exemptions for retrospective rating plans and large deductible plans" for "the exemptions for retrospective rating plans" in the last sentence.

§ 38.2-1904. Rate standards. — A. Rates for the classes of insurance to which this chapter applies shall not be excessive, inadequate or unfairly discriminatory. All rates and all changes and amendments to rates to which this chapter applies for use in this Commonwealth shall consider loss experience and other factors within Virginia if relevant and actuarially sound; provided, other data, including countrywide, regional or other state data, may be considered where such data is relevant and where a sound actuarial basis exists for considering data other than Virginia-specific data.

1. No rate shall be held to be excessive unless it is unreasonably high for the insurance provided and a reasonable degree of competition does not exist in the area with respect to the classification to which the rate applies.

2. No rate shall be held inadequate unless it is unreasonably low for the insurance provided and (i) continued use of it would endanger solvency of the insurer or (ii) use of the rate by the insurer has or, if continued, will have the effect of destroying competition or creating a monopoly.

3. No rate shall be unfairly discriminatory if a different rate is charged for the same coverage and the rate differential (i) is based on sound actuarial principles or (ii) is related to actual or reasonably anticipated experience.

B. 1. In determining whether rates comply with the standards of subsection A of this section, separate consideration shall be given to (i) past and prospective loss experience within and outside this Commonwealth, (ii) conflagration or catastrophe hazards, (iii) a reasonable margin for underwriting profit and contingencies, (iv) dividends, savings or unabsorbed premium deposits allowed or returned by insurers to their policyholders, members or subscribers, (v) past and prospective expenses both countrywide and those specifically applicable to this Commonwealth, (vi) the loss reserving practices, standards and procedures utilized by the insurer, (vii) investment income earned or realized by insurers from their unearned premium and loss reserve and the Commission may give separate consideration to investment income earned on surplus funds, and (viii) all other relevant factors within and outside this Commonwealth. When actual experience or data does not exist, the Commission may consider estimates.

2. In the case of fire insurance rates, consideration shall be given to the experience of the fire insurance business during a period of not less than the most recent five-year period for which such experience is available.

3. In the case of workers' compensation insurance rates for volunteer firefighters or volunteer lifesaving or volunteer rescue squad members, the rates shall be calculated based upon the combined experience of both volunteer firefighters or volunteer lifesaving or volunteer rescue squad members and paid firefighters or paid lifesaving or paid rescue squad members, so that the resulting rate is the same for both volunteer and paid members, but in no event shall resulting premiums be less than forty dollars per year for any volunteer firefighter or rescue squad member.

C. For the classes of insurance to which this chapter applies, including insurance against contingent, consequential and indirect losses as defined in § 38.2-133 (i) the systems of expense provisions included in the rates for use by any insurer or group of insurers may differ from those of other insurers or groups of insurers to reflect the requirements of the operating methods of any such insurer or group for any class of insurance, or with respect to any subdivision or combination of insurance for which separate expense provisions are applicable, and (ii) risks may be grouped by classifications for the establishment of rates and minimum premiums. Classification rates may be modified to produce rates for individual risks in accordance with rating plans that establish standards for measuring variations in hazards, expense provisions, or both. The standards may measure any difference between risks that can be demonstrated to have a probable effect upon losses or expenses. Notwithstanding any other provision of this subsection, except as permitted by § 38.2-1908, each member of a rate service organization shall use the uniform classification system, uniform experience rating plan, and uniform statistical plan of its designated rate service organization in the provision of insurance defined in § 38.2-119.

D. No insurer shall use any information pertaining to any motor vehicle conviction or accident to produce increased or surcharged rates above their filed manual rates for individual risks for a period longer than thirty-six months. This period shall begin no later than twelve months after the date of the conviction or accident.

E. Each authorized insurer subject to the provisions of this chapter may file with the Commission an expense reduction plan that permits variations in expense provisions. Such filing may contain provisions permitting agents to reduce their commission resulting in an appropriate reduction in premium. Nothing in this section shall be construed to require an agent to reduce a commission, nor may an insurer unreasonably refuse to reduce a premium due to a commission reduction as permitted by its filed expense reduction plan. (1973, c. 504, § 38.1-279.33; 1975, c. 155; 1977, c. 415; 1981, c. 243; 1982, c. 226; 1986, c. 562; 1987, c. 697; 1991, c. 104; 1993, c. 985; 1996, c. 250.)

Editor's note. — Acts 1993, c. 985, in cl. 3 provides: "That the provisions of this act shall become effective on January 1, 1994; provided however that prior to the effective date a rate service organization or an insurer may file prospective loss costs and supplementary rate information and the Commission may approve such information for rates to be effective on or after January 1, 1994."

The 1993 amendment, effective January 1, 1994, added the last sentence in subsection C.

Law Review. — For survey of Virginia law on insurance for the year 1974-1975, see 61 Va. L. Rev. 1759 (1975).

§ 38.2-1905. Motor vehicle insurer not to charge points or increase premiums in certain instances. — A.

No insurer may increase its insured's premium or may charge points under a safe driver insurance plan to its insured as a result of a motor vehicle accident unless the accident was caused either wholly or partially by the named insured, a resident of the same household, or other customary operator. No insurer may increase its insured's premium or may charge points to its insured where the operator causing the accident is a principal operator insured under a separate policy. Any insurer increasing a premium or charging points as a result of a motor vehicle accident shall notify the named insured in writing and in the same notification shall inform the named insured that he may appeal the decision of the insurer to the Commissioner if he feels his premium has increased or he has been charged points as a result of a motor vehicle accident without just cause.

B. An appeal of a premium increase or of a point charge by the named insured shall be requested in writing within sixty days of receipt of the notice of any premium adjustment or of any point charge resulting from a motor vehicle accident. Upon receipt of the request, the Commissioner shall promptly initiate a review to determine whether the premium increase or the point charge is justified. The premium increase or the point charge shall remain in full force and effect until the Commissioner rules that the premium be adjusted or the point charge be removed because it is not justified, or because the point charge was not assigned in accord with the insurer's filed rating plan, and so notifies the insurer and the insured. Upon receipt of the ruling, the insurer shall promptly refund any premiums paid as a direct result of the premium increase or the point charge, and shall adjust future billings to reflect the Commissioner's ruling.

C. On and after January 1, 1991, no insurer shall assign points under a safe-driver insurance policy to any vehicle other than the vehicle customarily driven by the operator responsible for incurring points.

D. If an insured is a law-enforcement officer, as defined in subdivision 9 of § 9-169, no insurer may increase such insured's personal insurance premium or may charge points under a safe driver insurance plan to such insured as a result of an accident which occurred in the course of the insured's employment as a law-enforcement officer while the insured was driving a motor vehicle provided by the employing law-enforcement agency and was engaged in a law-enforcement activity at the time of such accident. (1981, c. 243, § 38.1-279.33:1; 1986, c. 562; 1990, cc. 275, 960; 1994, c. 925.)

§§ 38.2-1905.1, 38.2-1905.2: Repealed by Acts 1997, c. 199.

§ 38.2-1906. Filing and use of rates. — A.

Each authorized insurer subject to the provisions of this chapter shall file with the Commission all rates and supplementary rate information and all changes and amendments to the rates and supplementary rate information made by it for use in this Commonwealth on or before the date they become effective.

In cases where the Commission has made a determination pursuant to § 38.2-1912 that competition is not an effective regulator of rates for a line or subclassification of insurance, such rates, supplementary rate information, changes and amendments to rates and supplementary rate information for that line or subclassification shall be filed in accordance with and shall be subject to the provisions of § 38.2-1912.

B. Each rate service organization licensed under § 38.2-1914 that has been designated by an insurer for the filing of prospective loss costs or supplementary rate information under § 38.2-1908 shall file with the Commission all prospective loss costs or supplementary rate information and all changes and amendments to the prospective loss costs or supplementary rate information made by it for use in this Commonwealth on or before the date they become effective. Prospective loss costs and supplementary rate information for insurance defined in § 38.2-119 must comply with the provisions of § 38.2-1912.1 prior to being used by an insurer in a filing establishing or changing its rate.

C. Prospective loss costs filings and supplementary rate information filed by rate service organizations shall not contain final rates, minimum premiums, or minimum premium rules.

D. No insurer shall make or issue an insurance contract or policy of a class to which this chapter applies, except in accordance with the rate and supplementary rate information filings that are in effect for the insurer.

E. For insurance as defined in § 38.2-119 any authorized insurer that does not rely on prospective loss costs or supplementary rate information filed by a rate service organization shall comply with the filing provisions of § 38.2-1912 as if competition was not an effective regulator of rates. (1973, c. 504, § 38.1-279.34; 1976, c. 278; 1986, c. 562; 1987, c. 697; 1990, cc. 596, 597; 1993, c. 985; 1997, c. 199.)

Editor's note. — Acts 1993, c. 985, which amended this section, in cl. 3 provides: "That the provisions of this act shall become effective on January 1, 1994; provided, however, that prior to the effective date a rate service organization or an insurer may file prospective loss costs and supplementary rate information and the Commission may approve such information for rates to be effective on or after January 1, 1994."

The 1993 amendment, effective January 1, 1994, added the present next-to-last sentence in the introductory paragraph of subsection A; and added subsection D.

Federal district court lacks jurisdiction to change rates set by Commission. — Under subsection B, an insurer must charge the rates set by the State Corporation Commission (SCC). For a federal district court to award plaintiffs any relief, it must, in effect, rule that the insurer cannot charge the rates set by the SCC. Such a ruling would conflict with the mandate of subsection B and would amount to a judicial rollback of the insurer's rates. Only the SCC or the Virginia Supreme Court is empowered to take such action. Gahres v. Phico Ins. Co., 672 F. Supp. 249 (E.D. Va. 1987).

§ 38.2-1906.1. Misquote of premium.

§ **38.2-1906.1. Misquote of premium.** — Notwithstanding any other provision of this chapter, if an insurer or its agent provides a written quotation for insurance to an insured or applicant for insurance and the rate filing in effect for the insurer results in a premium increase of ten percent or more over the quoted premium, the insured or applicant may, within fifteen days of written notification of the increase by the insurer or its agent, request cancellation of the contract or policy. The insurer shall, upon receipt of such request, cancel the contract or policy calculating the earned premium pro rata using the premium originally quoted by the insurer or its agent. Nothing in this section shall apply to any increase in premium which is the result of incorrect information furnished by the insured or applicant or information omitted by the insured or applicant. (1990, c. 503.)

§ **38.2-1907. Filings open to inspection.** — Each filing and all supplementary rate information filed under this chapter shall be open to public inspection. Copies may be obtained by any person on request and upon payment of a reasonable charge for the copies. Where feasible, the Commission shall compile and make available to the public the lists of rates charged by insurers for or in connection with the insurance contracts or policies to which this chapter applies so as to inform the public of price competition among insurers. (1973, c. 504, § 38.1-279.35; 1986, c. 562.)

Law Review. — For survey of Virginia law on insurance for the year 1972-1973, see 59 Va. L. Rev. 1535 (1973).

§ 38.2-1908. Rate making and delegation of filing obligation. — A. An insurer shall establish rates and supplementary rate information for any market segment based on the factors in § 38.2-1904. A rate service organization shall establish prospective loss costs and supplementary rate information for any market segment based on the factors in § 38.2-1904. An insurer may use supplementary rate information prepared by a rate service organization and may use prospective loss costs determined by the rate service organization with modification for its own expense and profit. The insurer may modify the prospective loss costs based on its own loss experience as the credibility of that loss experience allows.

B. An insurer may discharge its obligation to file supplementary rate information under subsection A of § 38.2-1906 by giving notice to the Commission that it uses supplementary rate information prepared and filed with the Commission by a designated rate service organization of which it is a member, subscriber, or service purchaser. The Commission may by order require an insurer to provide information in addition to that filed by the rate service organization. The insurer's supplementary rate information shall be that filed from time to time by the rate service organization, including any amendments to the supplementary rate information, subject to modifications filed by the insurer.

C. Every insurer shall adhere to the uniform classification system, uniform experience rating plan, and uniform statistical plan approved by the Commission in the provision of insurance defined in § 38.2-119. An insurer may develop subclassifications of the uniform classification system upon which rates for insurance defined in § 38.2-119 may be made; however, such subclassification must first be filed with and approved by the Commission. An insurer filing such subclassifications must certify to the Commission that the data it produces can be reported in a manner consistent with the uniform statistical plan and uniform classification system of its designated rate service organization. (1973, c. 504, § 38.1-279.36; 1976, c. 275; 1982, c. 201; 1986, c. 562; 1987, c. 697; 1990, c. 596; 1993, c. 985.)

Editor's note. — Acts 1993, c. 985, which amended this section, in cl. 3 provides: "That the provisions of this act shall become effective on January 1, 1994; provided, however, that prior to the effective date a rate service organization or an insurer may file prospective loss costs and supplementary rate information and the Commission may approve such information for rates to be effective on or after January 1, 1994."

The 1993 amendment, effective January 1, 1994, added subsection C.

§ 38.2-1909. Review of rates by Commission. — The Commission may investigate and determine, (i) upon its own motion, (ii) at the request of any citizen or any interested party in this Commonwealth, or (iii) at the request of any insurer subject to this chapter, whether rates in this Commonwealth for the classes of insurance to which this chapter applies are excessive, inadequate or unfairly discriminatory or whether loss experience and other factors within the Commonwealth are being properly used to determine the rates. In any such investigation and determination the Commission shall give separate consideration to those factors in the manner specified in § 38.2-1904. (1973, c. 504, § 38.1-279.37; 1986, c. 562; 1987, c. 697.)

Insureds' remedy where insurer allegedly obtained rate increase by fraud on the State Corporation Commission (SCC) was to request that the SCC investigate insurer's rates and, if successful, seek a rollback of rates and a refund of excessive premiums. Gahres v. Phico Ins. Co., 672 F. Supp. 249 (E.D. Va. 1987).

§ 38.2-1910. Disapproval of rates. — A. If the Commission finds, after providing notice and opportunity to be heard, that a rate is not in compliance with § 38.2-1904, or is in violation of § 38.2-1916, the Commission shall order that use of the rate be discontinued for any policy issued or renewed after a date specified in the order. The order may provide for rate modifications. The order may also provide for refund of the excessive portion of premiums collected (i) during a period not exceeding one year prior to the date of any request or motion for review made pursuant to § 38.2-1909 and (ii) during all periods subsequent to any such request or motion until the date of the order. If a refund is ordered, the order may provide for the payment of interest thereon at a rate set by the Commission. Except as provided in subsection B of this section, the order shall be issued within thirty days after the close of the hearing or within another reasonable time extension fixed by the Commission.

B. Pending a hearing, the Commission may order the suspension prospectively of a rate filed by an insurer and reimpose the last previous rate in effect if the Commission has reasonable cause to believe that: (i) a reasonable degree of competition does not exist in the area with respect to the classification to which the rate applies, (ii) the filed rate will have the effect of destroying competition or creating a monopoly, (iii) use of the rate will endanger the solvency of the insurer, or (iv) Virginia loss experience and other factors specifically applicable to the Commonwealth have not been properly used to determine the rates. If the Commission suspends a rate under this provision, it shall hold a hearing within fifteen business days after issuing the order suspending the rate unless the right to a hearing is waived by the insurer. In addition, the Commission shall make its determination and issue its order as to whether the rate shall be disapproved within fifteen business days after the close of the hearing.

C. At any hearing held under the provisions of subsection A or B of this section, the insurer shall have the burden of justifying the rate in question. All determinations of the Commission shall be on the basis of findings of fact and conclusions of law. If the Commission disapproves a rate, the disapproval shall take effect not less than fifteen days after its order and the last previous rate in effect for the insurer shall be reimposed for a period of one year unless the Commission approves a substitute or interim rate under the provisions of subsection D or E of this section.

D. For one year after the effective date of a disapproval order, no rate promulgated to replace a rate disapproved under the order may be used until it has been filed with the Commission and not disapproved within sixty days after filing.

E. Whenever an insurer has no legally effective rates as a result of the Commission's disapproval of rates or other act, the Commission shall, on the insurer's request, specify interim rates for the insurer that are high enough to protect the interests of all parties. The Commission may order that a specified portion of the premiums be placed in an escrow account approved by it. When new rates become legally effective, the Commission shall order the escrowed funds or any overcharge in the interim rates to be distributed appropriately, except that refunds to policyholders that are de minimis shall not be required. (1973, c. 504, § 38.1-279.38; 1976, c. 276; 1986, c. 562; 1987, c. 697; 1990, cc. 290, 597.)

Insureds' remedy where insurer allegedly obtained rate increase by fraud on the State Corporation Commission (SCC) was to request that the SCC investigate insurer's rates and, if successful, seek a rollback of rates and a refund of excessive premiums. Gahres v. Phico Ins. Co., 672 F. Supp. 249 (E.D. Va. 1987).

§ 38.2-1911. Special restrictions on individual insurers.

— A. The Commission may by order require that a particular insurer file any or all of its rates and supplementary rate information thirty days prior to their effective date, if the Commission finds, after providing notice and opportunity to be heard, that the protection of the interests of the insurer's policyholders and the public in this Commonwealth requires closer supervision of the insurer's rates because of the insurer's financial condition or repetitive filing of rates that are not in compliance with § 38.2-1904. The Commission may extend the waiting period of any filing for thirty additional days by written notice to the insurer before the first thirty-day period expires.

B. The filing shall be approved or disapproved during the waiting period or during its extension. If the filing is not disapproved before the expiration of the waiting period or of its extension, the filing shall be deemed to meet the requirements of this chapter, subject to the possibility of subsequent disapproval under § 38.2-1910.

C. Any insurer affected by an order entered under subsection A of this section may request a rehearing by the Commission after the expiration of twelve months from the date of the Commission's former order. (1973, c. 504, § 38.1-279.39; 1986, c. 562.)

§ 38.2-1912. Delayed effect of rates; certification of reinsurance with affiliated company.

— A. If the Commission finds in any class, line, or subdivision of insurance, or in any rating class or rating territory or for insurance as defined in § 38.2-119 that (i) competition is not an effective regulator of the rates charged, (ii) Virginia loss experience and other factors specifically applicable to the Commonwealth have not been properly used to determine the rate, (iii) a substantial number of insurers are competing irresponsibly through the rates charged, or (iv) there are widespread violations of this chapter, it shall promulgate a rule requiring that any subsequent changes in the rates or supplementary rate information for that class, line, subdivision, rating class or rating territory shall be filed with the Commission at least sixty days before they become effective. The Commission may extend the waiting period for thirty additional days by written notice to the filer before the first sixty-day period expires. Upon filing any rate to which this section is applicable, the insurer shall give notice to the Division of Consumer Counsel of the Office of the Attorney General that such rate has been filed with the Commission and such insurer shall so certify to the Commission in its rate filing.

B. By this rule, the Commission may require the filing of supporting data for any classes, lines or subdivisions of insurance, or classes of risks or combinations thereof it deems necessary for the proper functioning of the rate monitoring and regulating process.

C. A rule promulgated under this section shall expire no later than twenty-seven months after issue. The Commission may renew the rule after a hearing and appropriate findings under this section.

D. If a filing is not accompanied by the information the Commission has required under subsection B of this section, the Commission shall within thirty days of the initial filing inform the insurer that the filing is not complete, and the filing shall be deemed to be made when the information is furnished.

E. If an insurer files for a rate reduction pursuant to a rule promulgated under this section, the Commission may order the provisional use of the requested rate reduction for such period as the Commission may require to evaluate the insurer's rate filing and supplementary rate information. The implementation of such a provisional rate reduction shall not relieve an insurer of its obligation to submit such information as deemed necessary by the Commission for its consideration of the rate filing, nor shall it interfere with the Commission's authority to suspend use of the provisional rate, reimpose the previous rate, consider and approve a revised rate request, or otherwise exercise its authority under § 38.2-1910.

F. Each insurer shall so certify in a rate filing if coverage to which the rate filing applies is reinsured by another company (i) under common management, (ii) under common controlling ownership, or (iii) under other common effective legal control as defined in § 38.2-1322. (1973, c. 504, § 38.1-279.40; 1986, c. 562; 1987, c. 697; 1990, cc. 487, 597; 1993, c. 985.)

Editor's note. — Acts 1993, c. 985, which amended this section, in cl. 3 provides: "That the provisions of this act shall become effective on January 1, 1994; provided, however, that prior to the effective date a rate service organization or an insurer may file prospective loss costs and supplementary rate information and the Commission may approve such information for rates to be effective on or after January 1, 1994."

The 1993 amendment, effective January 1, 1994, inserted "or for insurance as defined in § 38.2-119" in the first sentence of subsection A.

§ 38.2-1912.1. Approval of prospective loss costs and supplementary rate information; § 38.2-119 rate filings.

— A. No prospective loss costs or supplementary rate information for insurance as defined in § 38.2-119 shall be applied or be used in this Commonwealth until it has been approved by the Commission.

B. Prospective loss costs and supplementary rate information filed under this section shall be deemed to meet the requirements of this chapter and may be applied or used unless disapproved by the Commission within sixty days of the time that the filing was made. The Commission may extend the waiting period for an additional thirty days by written notice to the filer before the sixty-day period expires.

C. If a filing is not accompanied by the information necessary for the Commission to determine if the requirements of § 38.2-1904 are satisfied, the Commission shall so inform the filer within sixty days of the initial filing, and the filing shall be deemed to be made when the necessary information is furnished.

D. The provisions of subsection B of this section shall be suspended when the Commission has ordered a hearing to be held. The provisions of § 38.2-2007 pertaining to public notice, hearings, and approvals shall apply to filings made under this section.

E. Upon making a filing under this section, the filer shall give notice to the Division of Consumer Counsel of the Office of Attorney General that such a filing has been made and shall certify to the Commission that such a notice has been given.

F. Once a filing has been approved under this section, an insurer may use the information in such filing pursuant to the provisions of §§ 38.2-1906 and 38.2-1908. (1993, c. 985.)

Editor's note. — Acts 1993, c. 985, which enacted this section, in cl. 3 provides: "That the provisions of this act shall become effective on January 1, 1994; provided, however, that prior to the effective date a rate service organization or an insurer may file prospective loss costs and supplementary rate information and the Commission may approve such information for rates to be effective on or after January 1, 1994."

§ 38.2-1913. Operation and control of rate service organizations. —

A. No rate service organization shall provide any service relating to the rates of any insurance subject to this chapter, and no insurer shall use the service of a rate service organization for such purposes unless the rate service organization has obtained a license under § 38.2-1914.

B. No rate service organization shall refuse to supply any services for which it is licensed in this Commonwealth to any insurer authorized to do business in this Commonwealth and offering to pay the fair and usual compensation for the services.

C. Any rate service organization subject to this chapter may provide for the examination of policies, daily reports, binders, renewal certificates, endorsements, other evidences of insurance, or evidences of the cancellation of insurance, and may make reasonable rules governing their submission and the correction of any errors or omissions in them. This provision applies to the classes of insurance for which the rate service organization is licensed pursuant to § 38.2-1914.

D. A rate service organization may develop a uniform policy and uniform (i) statistical plans, (ii) experience rating plans, and (iii) classification systems for use by its members in the provision of insurance defined in § 38.2-119 and the reporting of the experience of this line of insurance. Each rate service organization may also develop manual rules for the recording and reporting of experience data of members pursuant to its uniform plans and systems. Such uniform plans, systems, and rules shall be filed with the Commission by the rate service organization and be approved prior to their use by members of the rate service organization.

E. No insurer shall be required to become a member or subscriber to any rate service organization. (1973, c. 504, § 38.1-279.41; 1986, c. 562; 1990, c. 596; 1993, c. 985.)

Editor's note. — Acts 1993, c. 985, which amended this section, in cl. 3 provides: "That the provisions of this act shall become effective on January 1, 1994; provided, however, that prior to the effective date a rate service organization or an insurer may file prospective loss costs and supplementary rate information and the Commission may approve such information for rates to be effective on or after January 1, 1994."

The 1993 amendment, effective January 1, 1994, added subsections D and E.

§ 38.2-1914. Licensing of rate service organizations. — A. A rate

service organization applying for a license as required by § 38.2-1913 shall include with its application:

1. A copy of its constitution, charter, articles of organization, agreement, association or incorporation, and a copy of its bylaws, plan of operation and any other rules or regulations governing the conduct of its business;

2. A list of its members and subscribers;

3. The name and address of one or more residents of this Commonwealth upon whom notices, process affecting it or orders of the Commission may be served;

4. A statement showing its technical qualifications for acting in the capacity for which it seeks a license; and

5. Any other relevant information and documents that the Commission may require.

B. Each organization which has applied for a license under subsection A of this section shall promptly notify the Commission of every material change in the facts or in the documents on which its application was based.

C. If the Commission finds that the applicant and the natural persons through whom it acts are competent, trustworthy, and technically qualified to provide the services proposed, and that all requirements of law have been met, the Commission shall issue a license specifying the authorized activity of the applicant.

D. Licenses issued under subsection C of this section shall remain in effect until the licensee withdraws from the Commonwealth or until the license is suspended or revoked.

E. Any amendment to a document filed under subdivision 1 of subsection A of this section shall be filed promptly after it becomes effective. Failure to comply with this subsection shall be a ground for revocation of the license granted under subsection C of this section. (1973, c. 504, § 38.1-279.42; 1986, c. 562.)

§ 38.2-1915. Joint underwriting or joint reinsurance organizations. — A. Each group, association or other organization of insurers that engages in joint underwriting or joint reinsurance for a class of insurance to which this chapter applies shall file with the Commission (i) a copy of its constitution, articles of incorporation, agreement or association, and of its bylaws, rules and regulations governing its activities, all duly certified by the custodian of the originals of the copies, (ii) a list of its members, and (iii) the name and address of a resident of this Commonwealth upon whom notices or orders of the Commission or process may be served.

B. Each such organization of insurers shall notify the Commission promptly of every change in the information required to be filed by subsection A of this section.

C. Each group, association or other organization of insurers that engages in joint underwriting for a class of insurance to which this chapter applies shall be subject to this chapter. Each such organization of insurers that engages in joint reinsurance for a class of insurance to which this chapter applies shall be subject to §§ 38.2-1926, 38.2-1927, and 38.2-1928.

D. If, after providing notice and opportunity to be heard, the Commission finds that any activity or practice of any such organization of insurers is unfair, unreasonable or otherwise inconsistent with this chapter, it shall issue a written order (i) specifying in what respect the activity or practice is unfair, unreasonable or otherwise inconsistent with this chapter, and (ii) requiring the discontinuance of the activity or practice. (1973, c. 504, § 38.1-279.43; 1986, c. 562.)

§ 38.2-1916. Certain conduct by insurers and rate service organizations prohibited. — A. As used in this section, the word *"insurer"* includes two or more insurers (i) under common management, (ii) under common controlling ownership or (iii) under other common effective legal control and in fact engaged in joint or cooperative underwriting, investment management, marketing, servicing or administration of their business and affairs as insurers.

B. No insurer or rate service organization shall:

1. Combine or conspire with any other person to monopolize or attempt to monopolize the business of insurance or any kind, subdivision or class of insurance;

2. Agree with any other insurer or rate service organization to charge or adhere to any rate, although insurers and rate service organizations may continue to exchange statistical information;

3. Make any agreement with any other insurer, rate service organization or other person to restrain trade unreasonably;

4. Make any agreement with any other insurer, rate service organization or other person that may substantially lessen competition in any kind, subdivision or class of insurance; or

5. Make any agreement with any other insurer or rate service organization to refuse to deal with any person in connection with the sale of insurance.

C. No insurer may acquire or retain any capital stock or assets of, or have any common management with, any other insurer if such acquisition, retention or common management substantially lessens competition in the business of insurance or any kind, subdivision or class thereof.

D. No rate service organization, or any of its members or subscribers, shall interfere with the right of any insurer to make its rates independently of the rate service organization.

E. No rate service organization shall have or adopt any rule, exact any agreement, or engage in any program that would require any member, subscriber or other insurer to utilize some or all of its services, or to adhere to its rates, rating plans, rating systems, underwriting rules, or policy forms, or to prevent any insurer from acting independently. Notwithstanding the foregoing, with respect to insurance defined in § 38.2-119, a rate service organization may develop uniform (i) policies, (ii) classification systems, (iii) statistical plans, (iv) experience rating plans, and (v) manual rules which shall be adhered to by its members. (1976, c. 279, § 38.1-279.44:1; 1986, c. 562; 1990, c. 596; 1993, c. 985.)

Editor's note. — Acts 1993, c. 985, which amended this section, in cl. 3 provides: "That the provisions of this act shall become effective on January 1, 1994; provided, however, that prior to the effective date a rate service organization or an insurer may file prospective loss costs and supplementary rate information and the Commission may approve such information for rates to be effective on or after January 1, 1994."

The 1993 amendment, effective January 1, 1994, in subsection A, in the introductory paragraph, deleted "or" following "management," and inserted the clause (iii) designation; and added the second sentence in subsection E.

§ **38.2-1916.1. Investigation by Attorney General of suspected violations; investigative demand to witnesses; access to business records, etc.; penalties.** — A. 1. Whenever it appears to the Attorney General, either upon complaint or otherwise, that any person has engaged in, or is engaging in, or is about to engage in any act or practice prohibited by § 38.2-1916, the Attorney General may, consistent with his powers and duties to enforce the laws of the Commonwealth prohibiting conduct that unreasonably restrains trade, after notice to the Commission:

a. Either require or permit such person to file with him a statement in writing or otherwise, under oath, as to all facts and circumstances concerning the subject matter;

b. Require such other data and information as he may deem relevant to the subject matter of an investigation of a possible violation of § 38.2-1916; and

c. Issue an investigative demand to witnesses by which he may (i) compel the attendance of such witnesses; (ii) examine such witnesses under oath before himself or the Commission; (iii) subject to subsection B of this section, require the production of any documents or things that he deems relevant or material to the inquiry; and (iv) issue written interrogatories to be answered by the witness served or, if the witness served is a public or private corporation or a partnership or association or governmental agency, by any officer or agent, who shall furnish such information as is available to the witness.

2. The investigative powers authorized shall not abate or terminate by reason of any action or proceeding brought by the Attorney General or the Commission under this title. When a document or thing is demanded by an investigative demand, that demand shall not (i) contain any requirement that would be unreasonable or improper if contained in a subpoena duces tecum issued by a court of this Commonwealth; or (ii) require the disclosure of any document or thing that would be privileged, or production of which for any other reason would not be required by a subpoena duces tecum issued by a court of this Commonwealth.

B. Where the information requested pursuant to an investigative demand may be derived or ascertained from the business records of the party upon whom the interrogatory has been served or from an examination, audit, or inspection of such business records, or from a compilation, abstract, or summary based therein, and the burden of deriving or ascertaining the answer is substantially the same for the Attorney General as for the party from whom such information is requested, it shall be sufficient for that party to specify the records from which the answer may be derived or ascertained and to afford the Attorney General, or other individuals properly designated by the Attorney General, reasonable opportunity to examine, audit, or inspect such records and to make copies, compilations, abstracts, or summaries. The Attorney General is authorized, and may so elect, to require the production pursuant to this section, of documents or things before or after the taking of any testimony of the person summoned pursuant to an investigative demand, in which event, those documents or things shall be made available for inspection and copying during normal business hours at the principal place of business of the person served, or at such other time and place as may be agreed upon by the person served and the Attorney General.

C. Any investigative demand issued by the Attorney General under this section shall contain (i) a citation to this statute and section, (ii) a citation to the statute and section pertaining to the alleged violation under investigation, (iii) the subject matter of the investigation, and (iv) the date, place, and time the person is required to appear to produce testimony or documentary material in his possession, custody or control. Such date shall not be less than twenty days from the date of the investigative demand. Where documentary material is required to be produced, it shall be described by class so as to clearly indicate the material demanded.

D. Service of an investigative demand as provided in this section may be made by:

1. Delivery of a duly executed copy thereof to the person served or, if a person is not a natural person, to the principal place of business of the person to be served; or

2. Mailing by certified mail, return receipt requested, a duly executed copy thereof addressed to the person to be served at his principal place of business in this Commonwealth, or if that person has no place of business in this Commonwealth, to his principal office.

E. Within twenty days after the service of any such demand upon any person or enterprise, or at any time before the return date specified in the demand, whichever period is shorter, such party may file with the Commission and serve upon the Attorney General a petition for an order of the Commission modifying or setting aside such demand. The time allowed for compliance with the demand, in whole or in part as deemed proper and ordered by the Commission, shall not run during the pendency of such petition in the Commission. Such petition shall specify each ground upon which the petitioner relies in seeking such relief, and may be based upon any failure of such demand to comply with the provisions of this section or upon any constitutional or other legal right or privilege of such party. The provisions of this subsection shall be the exclusive means for a witness summoned pursuant to an investigative demand under this section to challenge an investigative demand issued pursuant to subsection A of this section.

F. The examination of all witnesses under this section shall be conducted by the Attorney General, or his designee, before an officer authorized to administer oaths in this Commonwealth. The testimony shall be taken stenographically or by a sound-recording device and shall be transcribed.

G. Any person required to testify or to submit documentary evidence shall be entitled, on payment of lawfully prescribed cost, to procure a copy of any document produced by such person and of his own testimony as stenographically reported or, in the case of depositions, as reduced to writing by or under the direction of a person taking the deposition. Any party compelled to testify or to produce documents or things may be accompanied and advised by counsel, but counsel may not, as a matter of right, otherwise participate in the investigation.

H. All persons served with an investigative demand by the Attorney General under this section, other than any person or persons whose conduct or practices are being investigated or any officer, director, or person in the employ of such person under investigation, shall be paid the same fees and mileage as paid witnesses in the courts of this Commonwealth. No person shall be excused from attending such inquiry pursuant to the mandate of an investigative demand, from producing a document or thing, or from being examined or required to answer questions, on the ground of failure to tender or pay a witness fee or mileage, unless a demand therefor is made at the time testimony is about to be taken and is made as a condition precedent to offering such production or testimony and unless payment is not made.

I. Any natural person who neglects or refuses (i) to attend and testify, (ii) to answer any lawful inquiry, or (iii) to produce documents or things, if in his power to do so, in obedience of an investigative demand or lawful request of the Attorney General or those properly authorized by the Attorney General, pursuant to this section, shall be subject to the penalty provisions of § 38.2-218. Any natural person who commits perjury, false swearing, or contempt in answering or failing to answer, or in producing a document or thing or failing to do so in accordance with an investigative demand or lawful request by the Attorney General, pursuant to this section, shall be guilty of a misdemeanor and upon conviction therefor by a court of competent jurisdiction shall be punished by a fine of not more than $5,000 or by imprisonment in jail for not more than one year, or both.

J. In any investigation brought by the Attorney General pursuant to this chapter, no individual shall be excused from attending, testifying or producing documentary material, objects, or intangible things in obedience to an investigative demand or under order of the Commission on the ground that the testimony, document, or thing required of him may tend to incriminate him or subject him to any penalty. No testimony or other information compelled either by the Attorney General or under order of the Commission or a court or any information directly or indirectly derived from such testimony or other information may be used against the individual or witness in any criminal case. However, he may be prosecuted or subjected to penalty or forfeiture for any perjury, false swearing, or contempt committed in answering or failing to answer, or in producing any document or thing or failing to do so in accordance with the demand of the Attorney General or the Commission. If an individual refuses to testify or produce any document or thing after being granted immunity from criminal prosecution and after being ordered to testify or produce any document or thing as authorized by this section, he may be found to be in civil contempt by a court of competent jurisdiction and incarcerated until such time as he purges himself of contempt by testifying, producing such document or thing, or presenting a written statement as ordered. Such finding of contempt shall not prevent the Attorney General from instituting other appropriate contempt proceedings against any person who violates any of the provisions of this section.

K. It shall be the duty of all public state and local officials, their employees, and all other persons to render and furnish to the Attorney General or his designee, when so requested, all information and assistance in their possession or within their power. Any officer participating in such inquiry and any person examined as a witness upon such inquiry who discloses to any person other than the Attorney General the name of any witness examined or any other information obtained upon such inquiry, except as so directed by the Attorney General, shall be guilty of a misdemeanor and subject to the sanctions prescribed in subsection I of this section. Such inquiry may upon written authorization by the Attorney General be made public.

L. The Attorney General may recommend rules and regulations to implement and carry out the provisions of this section. All such rules and regulations shall be subject to the approval of the Commission.

M. It shall be the duty of the Attorney General, or his designees, to maintain the secrecy of all evidence, testimony, documents, or other results of such investigations until formal proceedings are instituted. Violation of this subsection shall be punishable pursuant to § 38.2-218. Nothing contained in this section shall be construed to prevent the disclosure of any such investigative evidence by the Attorney General in his discretion to the Commissioner of Insurance, the State Corporation Commission, or to any federal or state law-enforcement authority that has restrictions governing confidentiality similar to those contained in this subsection. (1990, c. 596.)

§ 38.2-1916.2. Penalties; injunctive relief; restitution. — A. Notwithstanding the provisions of § 38.2-218, any insurer, rate service organization or other person who knowingly or willfully violates any provision of § 38.2-1916 shall be punished for each such violation by a penalty of not more than $100,000 and may be subject to suspension or revocation of any license issued by the Commission.

B. Any person threatened with injury or damage to his business or property by reason of a violation of § 38.2-1916 may petition the Commission for injunctive relief pursuant to § 38.2-220.

C. The Commission may require an insurer, rate service organization, or other person to make restitution in the amount of the direct actual financial loss, including any costs associated with bringing such a matter before the Commission and reasonable attorney's fees, to (i) the Commonwealth, a political subdivision thereof, or any public agency injured in its business or property or (ii) any person injured in his business or property by reason of a violation of § 38.2-1916. If the Commission finds that the violation is willful or flagrant, it may increase the restitution payment to an amount not in excess of three times the actual damages sustained. (1990, c. 596.)

§ 38.2-1917. Injunctive relief. — Any person injured in his business or property by reason of any violation of § 38.2-1916 may maintain an action to enjoin the violation. (1976, c. 279, § 38.1-279.44:3; 1986, c. 562.)

§ 38.2-1918. Agreements for equitable apportionment of insurance. — A. Nothing in this chapter shall prohibit the making of agreements among insurers for the equitable apportionment among them of insurance which may be afforded applicants who are in good faith entitled to but who are unable to procure it through ordinary methods. Insurers may agree among themselves on the use of reasonable rate modifications for such insurance. These agreements and rate modifications shall be subject to the approval of the Commission.

B. The Commission may approve policy forms and endorsements for use by such insurers with respect to insurance afforded such applicants. (1973, c. 504, § 38.1-279.45; 1986, c. 562.)

§ 38.2-1919. Collection of experience data; uniformity; compilations available to insurers and rate service organizations. — A. The Commission may promulgate reasonable rules and statistical plans for each of the rating systems on file with it, which may be modified from time to time. These rules and plans shall be used by each insurer in the recording and reporting of its loss and countrywide expense experience, so that the experience of all insurers may be made available, at least annually, in the form and detail necessary to aid the Commission in determining whether rating systems comply with the standards set forth in § 38.2-1904. The rules and plans may also provide for the recording and reporting of expense experience items that are specially applicable to this Commonwealth and cannot be determined by prorating the countrywide experience.

B. In promulgating the rules and plans the Commission shall give due consideration (i) to the rating systems on file with it and (ii) to the rules and to the form of the plans used for rating systems in other states so that the rules and plans may be as uniform as is practicable among the several states.

C. The Commission may designate one or more rate service organizations or other agencies to assist it in gathering the experience data and making compilations of it. These compilations shall be made available, subject to reasonable rules promulgated by the Commission, to insurers and rate service organizations. Any rate service organization designated by the Commission shall retain the experience data and compilations of the experience data in the format and detail required by the applicable statistical plan and shall submit this information to the Commission upon request.

D. Every rate service organization that has uniform (i) statistical plans, (ii) classification systems, (iii) experience rating plans, and (iv) manual rules filed and approved in accordance with the provisions of § 38.2-1913 D shall gather and compile the experience data of its members for insurance as defined in § 38.2-119. Each member insurer shall adhere to such uniform plans, systems, and rules of its designated rate service organization in the recording of its experience and the reporting of such information to the rate service organization. Each rate service organization that gathers and compiles information pursuant to this subsection shall be subject to the provisions of subsection C as to the availability, retention, and filing of the experience data of its members. (1973, c. 504, § 38.1-279.46; 1976, c. 329; 1986, c. 562; 1993, c. 985.)

Editor's note. — Acts 1993, c. 985, which amended this section, in cl. 3 provides: "That the provisions of this act shall become effective on January 1, 1994; provided, however, that prior to the effective date a rate service organization or an insurer may file prospective loss costs and supplementary rate information and the Commission may approve such information for rates to be effective on or after January 1, 1994."

The 1993 amendment, effective January 1, 1994, added subsection D.

§ 38.2-1919.1. Interchange of rating data and information. — To promote uniform administration of rate regulatory laws, the Commission and each insurer and each rate service organization subject to this chapter may (i) exchange information and experience data with insurance supervisory officials, insurers, and rate service organizations in other states and (ii) consult with them regarding rate making and the application of rating schedules and rating plans. Reasonable rules and plans may be promulgated by the Commission for the interchange of data necessary for the application of rating plans. (1993, c. 985.)

Editor's note. — Acts 1993, c. 985, which enacted this section, in cl. 3, provides: "That the provisions of this act shall become effective on January 1, 1994; provided, however, that prior to the effective date a rate service organization or an insurer may file prospective loss costs and supplementary rate information and the Commission may approve such information for rates to be effective on or after January 1, 1994."

§ 38.2-1920. Excess rate for a specific risk. — Subject to the Commission's approval, a rate in excess of that provided by an applicable filing may be used for a specific risk upon the filing of (i) written application of the insurer stating its reasons for the increased rate and (ii) the written consent of the insured or prospective insured. (1973, c. 504, § 38.1-279.47; 1986, c. 562.)

§ 38.2-1921. Combination policies. — The Commission may approve for use in this Commonwealth policies or forms for writing at divisible or indivisible rates and premiums any combination of the classes of insurance set forth in subsection A of § 38.2-1902, except insurance on or with respect to operating properties of railroads. The rates and premiums for combination policies, whether divisible or indivisible, shall be subject to this chapter. (1973, c. 504, § 38.1-279.49; 1986, c. 562.)

Law Review. — For survey of Virginia law on insurance for the year 1972-1973, see 59 Va. L. Rev. 1535 (1973).

§ 38.2-1922. No rule prohibiting or regulating payment of dividends, etc., to be adopted. — No rate service organization subject to this chapter shall adopt any rule prohibiting or regulating the payment of dividends, savings or unabsorbed premium deposits allowed or returned by insurers to their policyholders, members or subscribers. (1973, c. 504, § 38.1-279.50; 1986, c. 562.)

§ 38.2-1923. Person aggrieved by application of rating system to be heard; appeal to Commission. — Each rate service organization and each insurer subject to this chapter shall provide within this Commonwealth reasonable means for any person aggrieved by the application of its rating system to be heard in person or by an authorized representative on his written request. Any person who makes the written request shall be entitled to review the manner in which the rating system has been applied to the insurance afforded him. If the rate service organization or insurer fails to grant or reject the request within thirty days after it is made, the applicant may proceed in the same manner as if his application had been rejected. Any person affected by the action of the rate service organization or the insurer on the request may, within thirty days after written notice of the action, appeal to the Commission. The Commission may affirm or reverse the action after a hearing held upon not less than ten days' written notice to the applicant and to the rate service organization or insurer. (1973, c. 504, § 38.1-279.51; 1986, c. 562; 1990, c. 596.)

§ 38.2-1924. Cooperation among rate service organizations, or among rate service organizations and insurers, authorized; review by Commission. — Cooperation among rate service organizations or among rate service organizations and insurers in rate making or in other matters within the scope of this chapter is hereby authorized if the filings resulting from such cooperation are subject to all the provisions of this chapter applying to filings generally. The Commission may review such cooperative activities and practices. If, after providing notice and opportunity to be heard, it finds that any cooperative activity or practice is unfair, unreasonable or otherwise inconsistent with this chapter, the Commission shall issue a written order (i) specifying in what respects the cooperative activity or practice is unfair, unreasonable or otherwise inconsistent with this chapter, and (ii) requiring the discontinuance of the cooperative activity or practice. (1973, c. 504, § 38.1-279.52; 1986, c. 562.)

§ 38.2-1925. Examination of rate service organizations and joint underwriting and joint reinsurance organizations. — A. Whenever the Commission considers it necessary to be informed about any matter related to the enforcement of the insurance laws, it may examine the affairs and condition of any rate service organization under subsection A of § 38.2-1913 and of any joint underwriting or joint reinsurance organization under § 38.2-1915.

B. So far as reasonably necessary for any examination under subsection A of this section, the Commission may examine the accounts, records, documents or evidence of transactions, so far as they relate to the examinee, of any (i) officer, (ii) manager, (iii) general agent, (iv) employee, (v) person who has executive authority over or is in charge of any segment of the examinee's affairs, (vi) person controlling or having a contract under which he has the right to control the examinee whether exclusively or with others, (vii) person who is under the control of the examinee, or (viii) person who is under the control of a person who controls or has a right to control the examinee whether exclusively or with others.

C. On demand every examinee under subsection A of this section shall make available to the Commission for examination any of its own accounts, records, documents or evidences of transactions and any of those of the persons listed in subsection B of this section.

D. The Commission may examine every licensed rate service organization at intervals established by the Commission.

E. 1. Instead of all or part of an examination under subsections A and B of this section, or in addition to it, the Commission may order an independent audit by certified public accountants or actuarial evaluation by actuaries approved by it of any person subject to the examination requirement. Any accountant or actuary selected shall be subject to standards respecting conflicts of interest used by the Commission. Any audit or evaluation under this subsection shall be subject to subsections H through O of this section, so far as appropriate.

2. Instead of all or part of an examination under this section, the Commission may accept the report of an audit already made by certified public accountants or actuarial evaluation by actuaries approved by it, or the report of an examination made by the insurance department of another state.

F. [Reserved.]

G. An examination may cover comprehensively all aspects of the examinee's affairs and condition. The Commission shall determine the exact nature and scope of each examination, and in doing so shall take into account all relevant factors, including but not limited to (i) the length of time the examinee has been operating, (ii) the length of time it has been licensed in this Commonwealth, (iii) the nature of the services provided, (iv) the nature of the accounting records available and (v) the nature of examinations performed elsewhere.

H. For each examination under this section, the Commission shall issue an order stating the scope of the examination and designating the examiner in charge. On demand a copy of the order shall be exhibited to the examinee.

I. Any examiner authorized by the Commission shall, so far as necessary for the purposes of the examination, have access at all reasonable hours to the premises and to any books, records, files, securities, documents or property of the examinee and to those of persons under subsection B of this section so far as they relate to the affairs of the examinee.

J. The officers, employees and agents of the examinee and of persons under subsection B of this section shall comply with every reasonable request of the examiners for assistance in any matter relating to the examination. No person shall obstruct or interfere with the examination in any way other than by legal process.

K. If the Commission finds the accounts or records to be inadequate for proper examination of the condition and affairs of the examinee or improperly kept or posted, it may employ experts to rewrite, post or balance them at the expense of the examinee.

L. The examiner in charge of an examination shall make a proposed report of the examination that shall include the information and analysis as is ordered in subsection H of this section, together with the examiner's recommendations. At the discretion of the examiner in charge, preparation of the proposed report may include conferences with the examinee or its representatives. The proposed report shall remain confidential until filed under subsection M of this section.

M. The Commission shall serve a copy of the proposed report upon the examinee. Within twenty days after service, the examinee may serve upon the Commission a written demand for a hearing on the contents of the report. If a hearing is demanded the Commission shall give notice and hold a hearing, and on demand by the examinee the hearing shall be informal and private. The Commission shall adopt the report with any necessary modifications and file it for public inspection, or it may order a new examination within either (i) sixty days after the hearing or (ii) if no hearing is demanded, sixty days after the last day on which the examinee might have demanded a hearing.

N. The Commission shall forward a copy of the examination report to the examinee immediately upon adoption, except that if the proposed report is adopted without change, the Commission need only so notify the examinee.

O. The examinee shall furnish copies of the adopted report to each member of its board of directors or other governing board.

P. The Commission may furnish, without cost or at a price to be determined by it, a copy of the adopted report to the insurance commissioner of any jurisdiction in which the examinee is licensed and to any other interested person in this Commonwealth or elsewhere.

Q. In any proceeding by or against the examinee or any officer or agent of the examinee, the examination report as adopted by the Commission shall be admissible as evidence of the facts stated in the examination report. In any proceeding by or against the examinee the facts asserted in any report properly admitted in evidence shall be presumed to be true in the absence of contrary evidence.

R. The reasonable costs of an examination under this section shall be paid by the examinee except as provided in subsection U of this section. The costs shall include the salary and expenses of each examiner and any other expenses directly apportioned to the examination.

S. The amount payable under subsection R of this section shall become due ten days after the examinee has been served a detailed account of the costs.

T. The Commission may require any examinee, before or during an examination, to deposit with the State Treasurer any deposits the Commission considers necessary to pay the cost of the examination. Any deposit and any payment made under subsections R and S of this section shall be credited to the special fund of the Bureau of Insurance.

U. On the examinee's request or on its own motion, the Commission may pay all or part of the costs of an examination whenever it finds that, because of the frequency of examinations or other factors, imposition of the costs would place an unreasonable burden on the examinee. The Commission shall include in its annual report information about any instance in which it applied this subsection.

V. Deposits and payments under subsections R through U of this section shall not be considered to be a tax or license fee within the meaning of any law. If any other state charges a per diem fee for examination of examinees domiciled in this Commonwealth, any examinee domiciled in that other state shall pay the same fee when examined by the Commission. (1973, c. 504, § 38.1-279.53; 1986, c. 562.)

§ 38.2-1926. Action of Commission upon request for hearing on order or decision made without a hearing. — A. Any person aggrieved by an order or a decision of the Commission made under this chapter without a hearing may, within thirty days after notice of the order or decision, make a written request to the Commission for a hearing on that order or decision. Within a reasonable time after the request the Commission, after having given not less than ten days' written notice of the time and place of hearing, shall hear the person aggrieved by the order or decision. Within a reasonable time after the hearing the Commission shall affirm, reverse or modify its previous action, specifying its reasons for the affirmation, reversal or modification.

B. Pending the hearing and decision on its previous action, the Commission may suspend or postpone the effective date of the order or decision to which the hearing relates. (1973, c. 504, § 38.1-279.54; 1986, c. 562.)

§ 38.2-1927. Withholding information; giving false or misleading information. — No person shall willfully withhold information from or knowingly give false or misleading information to (i) the Commission, (ii) any statistical agency designated by the Commission, (iii) any rate service organization or (iv) any insurer, if that information will affect the rates or premiums subject to this chapter. (1973, c. 504, § 38.1-279.55; 1986, c. 562.)

Insureds' remedy where insurer allegedly obtained rate increase by fraud on the State Corporation Commission (SCC) was to request that the SCC investigate insurer's rates and, if successful, seek a rollback of rates and a refund of excessive premiums. Gahres v. Phico Ins. Co., 672 F. Supp. 249 (E.D. Va. 1987).

§ 38.2-1928. Violations of chapter. — The issuance, procurement or negotiation of a single policy of insurance shall be deemed a separate violation. (1973, c. 504, § 38.1-279.56; 1976, c. 279; 1986, c. 562.)

CHAPTER 20.

REGULATION OF RATES FOR CERTAIN TYPES OF INSURANCE.

ARTICLE 1.

General Provisions.

§ **38.2-2000. Purposes of chapter.** — A. The purposes of this chapter are to protect policyholders and the public against the adverse effects of excessive, inadequate, or unfairly discriminatory insurance rates, and to authorize and regulate cooperative action among insurers in rate making and in other matters within the scope of this chapter. Nothing in this chapter is intended to (i) prohibit or discourage reasonable competition, or (ii) prohibit or encourage uniformity in insurance rates, rating systems and rating plans or practices, except to the extent necessary to accomplish the purposes mentioned above.

B. This chapter shall be liberally interpreted to effect the purposes of this chapter. (1952, c. 317, § 38.1-218; 1986, c. 562.)

Law Review. — For article analyzing ratemaking issues under the SCC, see 14 Wm. & Mary L. Rev. 601 (1973). For survey of Virginia law on insurance for the year 1973-1974, see 60 Va. L. Rev. 1553 (1974).

§ **38.2-2000.1. Definitions.** — As used in this chapter:

"Pool" means an arrangement, either voluntary or mandated by law, established on an on-going basis, pursuant to which two or more insurers participate in the sharing of risks on a predetermined basis, which arrangement may operate through an association, syndicate, or other pool arrangement.

"Residual market mechanism" means an arrangement, either voluntary or mandated by law, involving participation by insurers in equitable apportionment among themselves of insurance which may be afforded applicants who are unable to obtain insurance through ordinary methods including any filed and approved plans.

"Virginia Auto Insurance Plan" means that organization established for assigned risks pursuant to the provisions of § 46.2-464.

"Virginia Property Insurance Association" means that organization established pursuant to Chapter 27 (§ 38.2-2700 et seq.) of this title.

"Virginia Workers' Compensation Insurance Plan" means that organization established for assigned risks pursuant to the provisions of § 65.2-820. (1993, c. 985.)

§ 38.2-2001. Insurance to which chapter applies. — This chapter applies only to (i) insurance written through the Virginia Workers' Compensation Insurance Plan, (ii) the coverages provided in the Virginia Automobile Insurance Plan, (iii) the coverages provided pursuant to Chapter 27 (§ 38.2-2700 et seq.) of this title, (iv) uninsured motorist coverage as required by subsection A of § 38.2-2206, and (v) home protection contracts as defined by § 38.2-2600. (Code 1950, §§ 38-195, 38-247, 38-253.43; 1950, p. 1033; 1952, c. 317, § 38.1-220; 1972, c. 836; 1973, c. 504; 1981, c. 530; 1986, c. 562; 1993, c. 985.)

Law Review. — For survey of Virginia law on insurance for the year 1972-1973, see 59 Va. L. Rev. 1535 (1973).

§ 38.2-2002. Joint underwriting and joint reinsurance. — A. 1. Each group, association or other organization of insurers that engages in joint underwriting or joint reinsurance for the insurance to which this chapter applies shall file with the Commission (i) a copy of its constitution, its articles of incorporation, agreement or association, and a copy of its bylaws, rules and regulations governing its activities, all duly certified by the custodian of the originals of the copies, (ii) a list of its members, and (iii) the name and address of a resident of this Commonwealth upon whom notices or orders of the Commission or process may be served.

2. Each such organization of insurers shall notify the Commission promptly of every change in the information required to be filed by this subsection.

3. This subsection shall not apply to the Virginia Automobile Insurance Plan, the Virginia Property Insurance Association and the Virginia Workers' Compensation Insurance Plan.

B. Each group, association or other organization of insurers that engages in joint underwriting for the insurance to which this chapter applies shall be subject to this chapter. Each such organization of insurers that engages in joint reinsurance for the insurance to which this chapter applies shall be subject to § 38.2-2026.

C. If, after providing notice and opportunity to be heard, the Commission finds any activity or practice of any such organization of insurers to be unfair, unreasonable or otherwise inconsistent with this chapter, it shall issue a written order (i) specifying in what respect the activity or practice is unfair, unreasonable or otherwise inconsistent with this chapter, and (ii) requiring the discontinuance of the activity or practice. (Code 1950, §§ 38-218.2, 38-249, 38-253.46; 1952, c. 317, § 38.1-224; 1973, c. 504, § 38.1-279.43; 1986, c. 562; 1993, c. 985.)

§ 38.2-2002.1. Residual market mechanism; reinsurance pool. — Notwithstanding any other provision of law, insurers and rate service organizations participating in joint reinsurance pools organized for the purpose of establishing a residual market mechanism may, in connection with such purpose, act in cooperation with each other in the making of rates, rating systems, policy forms, underwriting rules, surveys, inspections, investigations, the furnishing of statistical or other information on losses and expenses, or the conduct of research. (1993, c. 985.)

ARTICLE 2.

Rate Filings and Making of Rates.

§ 38.2-2003. Rate filings by insurer; supporting information. —
A. Each insurer writing in this Commonwealth a class of insurance to which this chapter applies shall file with the Commission every manual of classifications, minimum rate, class rate, rating schedule, rating plan, rating rule, and every modification of any of the foregoing that it proposes to use. Every filing shall indicate the character and extent of coverage contemplated. When a filing is not accompanied by the information upon which the insurer supports the filing, and the Commission does not have sufficient information to determine whether the filing meets the requirements of this chapter, the Commission may require the insurer to furnish the information upon which it supports the filing. A filing and any supporting information shall be a public record. Upon filing any rate to which this chapter is applicable, the insurer shall give notice to the Division of Consumer Counsel of the Office of the Attorney General that such rate has been filed with the Commission and such insurer shall so certify to the Commission in its rate filing. For the purposes of this section, a group or fleet of insurers operating under the same general management may be considered an insurer.

B. Each insurer shall submit with each rate filing so much of the following information as deemed appropriate by the Commission:

1. Number of exposures;
2. Direct premiums written;
3. Direct premiums earned;
4. Direct losses paid identified by such period as the Commission may require;
5. Number of claims paid;
6. Direct losses incurred during the year, direct losses incurred during the year which occurred and were paid during the year, and direct losses incurred during the year which were reported during the year but were not yet paid;
7. Any loss development factor used and supporting data thereon;
8. Number of claims unpaid;
9. Loss adjustment expenses paid identified by such period as the Commission may require;
10. Loss adjustment expenses incurred during the year, loss adjustment expenses incurred during the year for losses which occurred and were paid during the year, and loss adjustment expenses incurred during the year for losses which were reported during the year but were not yet paid;
11. Other expenses incurred, separately by category of expense, excluding loss adjustment expenses;
12. Investment income on assets related to reserve and allocated surplus accounts;
13. Total return on allocated surplus;
14. Any loss trend factor used and supporting data thereon;
15. Any expense trend factor used and supporting data thereon; and
16. Such other information as may be required by rule of the Commission, including statewide rate information presented separately for Virginia and each state wherein the insurer writes the line, subline or rating classification for which the rate filing is made and which the Commission deems necessary for its consideration.

C. Where actual experience does not exist or is not credible, the Commission may allow the use of estimates for the information required by subdivisions 1 through 15 of subsection B of this section and may require the insurer to submit such information as the Commission deems necessary to support such estimates.

D. The Commission shall develop uniform statements or formats specifying the information categories specified in this section. Such statements or formats shall be utilized by all insurers in all rate filings. (Code 1950, §§ 38-253.26, 38-253.72; 1950, p. 381; 1952, c. 317, § 38.1-241; 1972, c. 836; 1973, c. 504; 1986, c. 562; 1987, c. 697; 1988, c. 189.)

§ 38.2-2004. Filings by rate service organization. — An insurer may satisfy its obligation to make the rate filings required in § 38.2-2003 by becoming a member of or a subscriber to a rate service organization that makes such filings and that is licensed pursuant to § 38.2-1914, and by authorizing the Commission to accept the filings on its behalf. Filings made by rate service organizations shall meet the requirements of § 38.2-2003. No insurer shall be required to become a member of or a subscriber to any rate service organization. (Code 1950, §§ 38-253.27, 38-253.73; 1952, c. 317, § 38.1-242; 1972, c. 836; 1973, c. 504; 1986, c. 562.)

Applied in Commonwealth v. National Council on Comp. Ins., 238 Va. 513, 385 S.E.2d 568 (1989).

§ 38.2-2005. Provisions governing making of rates. — A. Rates for the classes of insurance to which this chapter applies shall not be excessive, inadequate or unfairly discriminatory. All rates and all changes and amendments to rates to which this chapter applies for use in this Commonwealth shall consider loss experience and other factors within Virginia if relevant and actuarially sound; however, other data, including countrywide, regional or other state data, may be considered where such data is relevant and where a sound actuarial basis exists for considering data other than Virginia-specific data.

B. 1. In making rates for the classes of insurance to which this chapter applies, separate consideration shall be given to (i) past and prospective loss experience within and outside this Commonwealth, (ii) conflagration or catastrophe hazards, (iii) a reasonable margin for underwriting profit and contingencies, (iv) dividends, savings or unabsorbed premium deposits allowed or returned by insurers to their policyholders, members or subscribers, (v) past and prospective expenses both countrywide and those specifically applicable to this Commonwealth, (vi) investment income earned or realized by insurers from their unearned premium and loss reserve and the Commission may give separate consideration to investment income earned on surplus funds, (vii) the loss reserving practices, standards and procedures utilized by the insurer, and (viii) all other relevant factors within and outside this Commonwealth. When actual experience or data does not exist, the Commission may consider estimates.

2. In the case of fire insurance rates, consideration shall be given to the experience of the fire insurance business during a period of not less than the most recent five-year period for which such experience is available.

3. In the case of uninsured motorist coverage required by subsection A of § 38.2-2206, consideration shall be given to all sums distributed by the Commission from the Uninsured Motorists Fund in accordance with the provisions of Chapter 30 of this title.

In the case of workers' compensation insurance rates for volunteer firefighters or volunteer lifesaving or volunteer rescue squad members written through the Virginia Worker's Compensation Insurance Plan, the rates shall be calculated based upon the combined experience of both volunteer firefighters or volunteer lifesaving or volunteer rescue squad members and paid firefighters or paid lifesaving or paid rescue squad members, so that the resulting rate is the same for both volunteer and paid members, but in no event shall resulting premiums be less than forty dollars per year for any volunteer firefighter or rescue squad member.

C. For the classes of insurance to which this chapter applies (i) the systems of expense provisions included in the rates for use by any insurer or group of insurers may differ from those of other insurers or groups of insurers to reflect the requirements of the operating methods of any such insurer or group for any class of insurance, or for any subdivision or combination of insurance for which separate expense provisions apply, and (ii) risks may be grouped by classifications for the establishment of rates and minimum premiums. Classification rates may be modified to produce rates for individual risks in accordance with rating plans that establish standards for measuring variations in hazards, expense provisions, or both. The standards may measure any difference among risks that can be demonstrated to have a probable effect upon losses or expenses.

D. All rates, rating schedules or rating plans and every manual of classifications, rules and rates, including every modification thereof, approved by the Commission under this chapter, shall be used until a change is approved by the Commission. (Code 1950, §§ 38-208, 38-253.21, 38-253.68; 1950, p. 403; 1952, c. 317, § 38.1-252; 1962, c. 253; 1970, c. 186; 1972, c. 836; 1973, c. 504; 1986, c. 562; 1987, c. 697; 1996, c. 250.)

Law Review. — For article analyzing ratemaking issues under the SCC, see 14 Wm. & Mary L. Rev. 601 (1973).

Duty of Commission. — The Commission has not only the duty to protect the insurance-purchasing public against excessive or unfairly discriminatory rates, but also the duty to protect the policyholders, and investors in the insurance business, against inadequate rates. American Druggists' Ins. Co. v. Commonwealth, 201 Va. 275, 110 S.E.2d 509 (1959).

Uniformity of rates and classification. — There is no express statutory requirement for uniformity of rates or classification. Moreover, the very process of permitting deviations authorized under former § 38.1-258 contemplated that there might be differences of classifications within the limitations therein specified. But the fact that the Bureau was required to make certain filings (former § 38.1-226) that they were deemed to be filed on behalf of all of its members (former § 38.1-232), and that all members had to except for permitted deviations adhere to such filings (former § 38.1-258), contemplated that generally speaking the classifications would be uniform. Allstate Ins. Co. v. Commonwealth, 199 Va. 434, 100 S.E.2d 31 (1957).

The establishment of a base in rate making is inextricably related to the fixing of the rate. Virginia Mfrs. Ass'n v. Workmen's Comp. Inspection Rating Bureau, 205 Va. 535, 138 S.E.2d 12 (1964).

The manual rates apply equally to stock and mutual companies. There is not one manual rate for stock companies and a lower manual rate for mutual companies on the theory that mutual companies do not need to make profits. Harford Mut. Ins. Co. v. Commonwealth, 201 Va. 491, 112 S.E.2d 142 (1960).

Rates must be neither too high nor too low. — The statutory requirement for fixing rates is that they must not be too high nor too low. It is extremely important that they be high enough to keep the companies solvent. American Druggists' Ins. Co. v. Commonwealth, 201 Va. 275, 110 S.E.2d 509 (1959).

Uniform rates for all companies are based on the statistics applicable to all companies as a group, and not on the experience of some one company. American Druggists' Ins. Co. v. Commonwealth, 201 Va. 275, 110 S.E.2d 509 (1959).

The formula for establishing fire insurance rates which the Commission has used to determine whether fire insurance rates are excessive, inadequate or unfairly discriminatory, gives consideration to the elements which this section says shall be considered in making and establishing insurance rates. American Druggists' Ins. Co. v. Commonwealth, 201 Va. 275, 110 S.E.2d 509 (1959).

Purpose of premium. — A premium is designed to pay casualty losses and to provide for operating expenses and underwriting profit. Virginia State AFL-CIO v. Commonwealth, 209 Va. 776, 167 S.E.2d 322 (1969).

Premium income does not become stockholders' profit by the mere passage of time, without any charge for the payment of casualty losses. Virginia State AFL-CIO v. Commonwealth, 209 Va. 776, 167 S.E.2d 322 (1969).

Subdivision B 1 requires the production of data reflecting Virginia acquisition expenses. Without such data the Commission cannot know whether Virginia expenses are lower than the national average, necessitating a compensating adjustment in Virginia rates to prevent Virginia motorists from paying in part for policies written in other states. Virginia State AFL-CIO v. Commonwealth, 209 Va. 776, 167 S.E.2d 322 (1969).

"Underwriting profit" excludes all investment income. — Since "underwriting profit" is usually defined as "the sum arrived at by deducting from earned premiums all incurred losses and incurred expenses," that term excludes all investment income. Virginia State AFL-CIO v. Commonwealth, 209 Va. 776, 167 S.E.2d 322 (1969).

Income derived from investment of the unearned premium reserve is a "relevant factor" in fixing rates. Virginia State AFL-CIO v. Commonwealth, 209 Va. 776, 167 S.E.2d 322 (1969).

Income derived from the investment of the loss reserve, as well as the unearned premium reserve, should be considered in fix-

ing rates for fire insurance coverage. Virginia State AFL-CIO v. Commonwealth, 209 Va. 776, 167 S.E.2d 322 (1969).

Loss reserve. — The loss reserve represents the part of the premiums paid by the policyholders that, it is expected, will be devoted to the payment of losses. So premiums paid by policyholders, rather than assets contributed by stockholders, "go into" the loss reserve. Virginia State AFL-CIO v. Commonwealth, 209 Va. 776, 167 S.E.2d 322 (1969).

Judicial review. — In reviewing the action of the Commission in fixing insurance rates, the Supreme Court will not disturb its action unless it appears that it has exceeded its authority, or has acted unreasonably in exercising its authority, or that it has made a mistake of law, or that its finding is contrary to the evidence or without evidence to support it, or that it is fixed so low as to amount to confiscation. Virginia Mfrs. Ass'n v. Workmen's Comp. Inspection Rating Bureau, 205 Va. 535, 138 S.E.2d 12 (1964).

§ 38.2-2006. Approval by Commission prerequisite to use of filing. — A. Except as provided in § 38.2-2010, no filing shall become effective, be applied, or be used in this Commonwealth until it has been approved by the Commission. However, a rate produced in accordance with a rating schedule or rating plan, previously approved by the Commission, may be used pending the approval.

B. A filing shall be deemed to meet the requirements of this chapter and to become effective unless disapproved by the Commission within sixty days of the time that the filing was made. However, the Commission may extend the waiting period for thirty additional days by written notice to the filer before the sixty-day period expires.

C. If a filing is not accompanied by the information necessary for the Commission to determine if the requirements of § 38.2-2005 are satisfied, the Commission shall so inform the filer within sixty days of the initial filing. The filing shall be deemed to be made when the necessary information is furnished.

D. The provisions of subsection B of this section shall be suspended when the Commission has ordered a hearing to be held under the provisions of § 38.2-2007. (Code 1950, §§ 38-210, 38-253.29, 38-253.75; 1952, c. 317, § 38.1-253; 1986, c. 562; 1987, c. 697.)

Law Review. — For article analyzing ratemaking issues under the SCC, see 14 Wm. & Mary L. Rev. 601 (1973).

§ 38.2-2007. Commission to determine if notice of filing to be published; hearing; approval or disapproval. — A. When a filing has been made with the Commission, the Commission shall determine whether publication of notice of the filing is necessary. If the Commission determines that such publication is required, the notice shall be published in the form and for the time prescribed by the Commission, not to exceed once a week for four consecutive weeks, in a newspaper or newspapers of general circulation published in the Commonwealth.

B. Prior to publication or upon completion of publication, the Commission shall determine whether a hearing should be held before acting upon the filing. If the Commission determines that a hearing should be held, it shall order one to be held within a reasonable time, but not less than ten days after issuing the order setting the hearing. The Commission shall notify the person making the filing and any other person it deems interested in the filing of the hearing.

C. Upon determination that publication of notice of a filing is unnecessary, upon completion of any required publication when no hearing is ordered, or upon completion of a hearing, the Commission shall (i) approve the filing as submitted or with any modifications deemed appropriate by the Commission, or (ii) disapprove the filing. If a filing is approved with modifications, or is disapproved, the order of such approval or disapproval shall state the reasons for the decision. (Code 1950, §§ 38-209, 38-253.28, 38-253.74; 1952, c. 317, § 38.1-254; 1986, c. 562.)

Law Review. — For article analyzing ratemaking issues under the SCC, see 14 Wm. & Mary L. Rev. 601 (1973).

§ 38.2-2008. Review of rates by Commission. — The Commission may investigate and determine, (i) upon its own motion, (ii) at the request of any citizen of this Commonwealth, or (iii) at the request of any insurer subject to this chapter, whether rates in this Commonwealth for the insurance to which this chapter applies are excessive, inadequate or unfairly discriminatory. In accordance with its findings, the Commission may order changes in the rates that are fair and equitable to all interested parties. In any investigation and determination, the Commission shall give due consideration to those factors specified in subsection B of § 38.2-2005. (Code 1950, §§ 38-212, 38-253.23, 38-253.69; 1952, c. 317, § 38.1-255; 1986, c. 562.)

§ 38.2-2009: Repealed by Acts 1993, c. 985, effective January 1, 1994.

§ 38.2-2010. Suspension or modification of requirement for filing. — The Commission, by order, may suspend or modify the filing requirement of this chapter for any kind of insurance or subdivision or combination of insurance, or for classes of risks, where the rates for the insurance cannot practicably be filed before they are used. The order shall be made known to insurers and rate service organizations affected by it. The Commission may make any examination it deems advisable to determine whether any rates affected by the order meet the standards set out in subsection A of § 38.2-2005. (Code 1950, §§ 38-253.31, 38-253.77; 1952, c. 317, § 38.1-259; 1986, c. 562.)

§ 38.2-2011. Interchange of rating data and information. — To promote uniform administration of rate regulatory laws, the Commission and each insurer and each rate service organization subject to this chapter may (i) exchange information and experience data with insurance supervisory officials, insurers, and rate service organizations in other states, and (ii) consult with them regarding rate making and the application of rating schedules and rating plans. Reasonable rules and plans may be promulgated by the Commission for the interchange of data necessary for the application of rating plans. (Code 1950, §§ 38-218, 38-253.37, 38-253.38, 38-253.83, 38-253.84; 1952, c. 317, § 38.1-260; 1986, c. 562.)

§ 38.2-2012. Collection of experience data; uniformity; compilations available to insurers and rate service organizations. — A. The Commission may promulgate reasonable rules and statistical plans for each of the rating systems on file with it, which may be modified from time to time. These rules and plans shall be used by each insurer in the recording and reporting of its loss and countrywide expense experience, so that the experience of all insurers may be made available, at least annually, in the form and detail as may be necessary to aid the Commission in determining whether rating systems comply with the standards set forth in subsection A of § 38.2-2005. The rules and plans may also provide for the recording and reporting of expense experience items that are specially applicable to this Commonwealth and cannot be determined by prorating the countrywide expense experience.

B. In promulgating the rules and plans, the Commission shall give due consideration to (i) the rating systems on file with it and (ii) the rules and the form of the plans used for rating systems in other states so that the rules and plans may be as uniform as practicable among the several states. No insurer shall be required to record or report its loss experience on a classification basis that is inconsistent with the rating system filed by it or on its behalf.

C. The Commission may designate one or more rate service organizations or other agencies to assist it in gathering the experience data and making compilations of it. The compilations shall be made available, subject to reasonable rules promulgated by the Commission, to insurers and rate service organizations. (Code 1950, §§ 38-253.36, 38-253.82; 1952, c. 317, § 38.1-261; 1986, c. 562.)

§ **38.2-2013. Excess rate for specific risk.** — Subject to the Commission's approval, a rate in excess of that provided by an applicable filing may be used for a specific risk upon the filing of (i) written application of an insurer stating its reasons for the increased rate, accompanied by (ii) the written consent of the insured or prospective insured. (Code 1950, §§ 38-211, 38-253.32, 38-253.78; 1952, c. 317, § 38.1-262; 1986, c. 562.)

Law Review. — For article analyzing ratemaking issues under the SCC, see 14 Wm. & Mary L. Rev. 601 (1973).

§ **38.2-2014. Contract or policy to accord with filings.** — No insurer shall make or issue an insurance policy or contract to which this chapter applies, except in accordance with the filings that are in effect for that insurer, or in accordance with an applicable provision in § 38.2-2010 or § 38.2-2013. (Code 1950, §§ 38-253.33, 38-253.79; 1950, p. 381; 1952, c. 317, § 38.1-263; 1986, c. 562; 1993, c. 985.)

§ **38.2-2015. Agreements for equitable apportionment of insurance; reasonable performance standards; Virginia Workers' Compensation Insurance Plan.** — A. Agreements among insurers may be made for the equitable apportionment among them of insurance that may be afforded applicants who are in good faith entitled to insurance but who are unable to procure it through ordinary methods. Insurers may agree among themselves on the use of reasonable rate modifications for the insurance. The agreements and rate modifications shall be subject to the approval of the Commission.

B. The Commission may require that the agreements contain reasonable performance standards for insurers or agents, or both, with respect to insurance afforded such applicants. The performance standards may contain, but shall not be limited to: (i) original applications, (ii) premium payments, (iii) policy issuance, (iv) policy changes, (v) return premium, (vi) return commission and (vii) administrative procedures for monitoring compliance with the standards.

C. The Commission may approve policy forms and endorsements for use by such insurers with respect to insurance afforded such applicants.

D. All licensed insurers writing workers' compensation insurance in the Commonwealth shall participate in the Virginia Workers' Compensation Insurance Plan, which shall provide for the equitable apportionment among the participants of insurance that may be afforded applicants who are in good faith entitled to but who are unable to procure such insurance through ordinary methods. Notwithstanding any other provision of law, insurers and rate service organizations participating in the Virginia Workers' Compensation Insurance Plan may, in connection with such participation, act in cooperation with each other in the making of rates, rating systems, policy forms, underwriting rules, surveys, inspections, investigations, the furnishing of statistical or other information on losses and expenses, or the conduct of research. The rates and supplementary rate information to be used by such plan shall be approved by the Commission. Such rates shall reflect residual market experience to the extent actuarially appropriate and shall be set so that the amount received in premiums, together with reasonable investment income earned on those premiums, is reasonably expected to be sufficient to pay claims and losses incurred and reasonable operating expenses of the servicing insurers. (Code 1950, § 38-250; 1952, c. 317, § 38.1-264; 1964, c. 596; 1966, c. 299; 1980, c. 112; 1986, c. 562; 1993, c. 985.)

Law Review. — For article analyzing ratemaking issues under the SCC, see 14 Wm. & Mary L. Rev. 601 (1973).

Assigned risk policies distinguished from Safety Responsibility Act policies. — Policies issued pursuant to the Virginia Automobile Assigned Risk Plan, adopted by authority of this section, are to be distinguished from so-called "certified" policies issued under § 46.1-497 et seq. (now § 46.2-464). The latter are subject to certain special statutory restrictions. See § 46.2-479. Virginia Farm Bureau Mut. Ins. Co. v. Saccio, 204 Va. 769, 133 S.E.2d 268 (1963). See also Buckeye Union Cas. Co. v. Robertson, 206 Va. 863, 147 S.E.2d 94 (1966).

Insured not guilty of misrepresentation of fact material to risk. — Where insured answered the questions in the application in good faith and did not willfully make an incorrect or misleading statement in order to become eligible for a policy of insurance under the Voluntary Assigned Risk Plan, and, if there was any concealment under the facts and circumstances, he was not responsible for it, he was not guilty of misrepresentation of a fact which was material to the risk. Buckeye Union Cas. Co. v. Robertson, 206 Va. 863, 147 S.E.2d 94 (1966).

§ 38.2-2016. Information regarding rates to be furnished insured. —

Each rate service organization and each insurer subject to this chapter that makes its own rates shall furnish to any insured affected by those rates, or to the authorized representative of the insured, all pertinent information regarding the rate within a reasonable time after receiving a written request for the information. (Code 1950, §§ 38-215, 38-251, 38-253.47; 1952, c. 317, § 38.1-266; 1986, c. 562.)

§ 38.2-2017. No rule prohibiting or regulating payment of dividends, etc., to be adopted. —

No rate service organization subject to this chapter shall adopt any rule prohibiting or regulating the payment of dividends, savings or unabsorbed premium deposits allowed or returned by insurers to their policyholders, members or subscribers. (Code 1950, §§ 38-253.12, 38-253.58; 1952, c. 317, § 38.1-267; 1986, c. 562.)

§ 38.2-2018. Person aggrieved by application of rating system to be heard; appeal to Commission. —

Each rate service organization and each insurer subject to this chapter that makes its own rates shall provide within this Commonwealth reasonable means whereby any person aggrieved by the application of its rating system may, after written request, be heard in person or by an authorized representative to review the manner in which the rating system has been applied to the insurance afforded him. If the rate service organization or insurer fails to grant or reject the request within thirty days after it is made, the applicant may proceed in the same manner as if his application had been rejected. Any person affected by the action of the rate service organization or the insurer on such request may, within thirty days after written notice of the action, appeal to the Commission. The Commission may affirm or reverse the action after a hearing held upon not less than ten days' written notice to the applicant and to the rate service organization or insurer. (Code 1950, §§ 38-252, 38-253.48; 1952, c. 317, § 38.1-268; 1986, c. 562.)

§ 38.2-2019. Cooperation among rate service organizations, or among rate service organizations and insurers, authorized; review by Commission. — Cooperation among rate service organizations or among rate service organizations and insurers in rate making or in other matters within the scope of this chapter is authorized if the filings resulting from the cooperation are subject to all the provisions of this chapter that are applicable to filings generally. The Commission may review cooperative activities and practices. If, after providing notice and opportunity to be heard, it finds that any activity or practice is unfair, unreasonable or otherwise inconsistent with this chapter, it shall issue an order (i) specifying in what respects the activity or practice is unfair, unreasonable or otherwise inconsistent with this chapter, and (ii) requiring the discontinuance of the activity or practice. (Code 1950, §§ 38-253.13, 38-253.59; 1952, c. 317, § 38.1-269; 1986, c. 562.)

Law Review. — For article analyzing ratemaking issues under the SCC, see 14 Wm. & Mary L. Rev. 601 (1973).

§ 38.2-2020. Rate service organization may procure actuarial, technical or other services. — Any rate service organization subject to this chapter may subscribe for or purchase actuarial, technical or other services if these services are available without discrimination to all members of and subscribers to the rate service organization. (Code 1950, §§ 38-204, 38-253.14, 38-253.61; 1952, c. 317, § 38.1-270; 1986, c. 562.)

§ 38.2-2021. Examination of policies or other evidences of insurance. — Any rate service organization subject to this chapter for the classes of insurance for which it files rates may provide for the examination of policies, daily reports, binders, renewal certificates, endorsements or other evidences of insurance, or evidences of the cancellation of insurance, and may make reasonable rules governing their submission and the correction of any errors or omissions in them. (Code 1950, §§ 38-205, 38-253.15, 38-253.60; 1952, c. 317, § 38.1-271; 1986, c. 562.)

ARTICLE 3.

Advisory Organizations.

§ 38.2-2022. Advisory organizations defined. — For the purpose of this article, *"advisory organization"* means any group, association or other organization of insurers, located within or outside this Commonwealth, that assists insurers who make their own filings or rate service organizations in rate making, by the collection and furnishing of loss or expense statistics or by the submission of recommendations, but that does not make filings under this chapter for the kind of insurance involved. (Code 1950, §§ 38-218.1, 38-253.16, 38-253.63; 1952, c. 317, § 38.1-272; 1986, c. 562.)

§ 38.2-2023. What to be filed with Commission by advisory organization. — Each advisory organization shall file with the Commission:

1. A copy of its constitution, its articles of agreement or association or its certificate of incorporation, and of its bylaws, rules and regulations governing its activities;

2. A list of its members; and

3. The name and address of a resident of this Commonwealth upon whom may be served notices or orders of the Commission or process issued at its direction. (Code 1950, §§ 38-218.1, 38-253.17, 38-253.64; 1952, c. 317, § 38.1-273; 1986, c. 562.)

§ 38.2-2024. Unfair acts or practices of advisory organization. — If after a hearing the Commission finds that the furnishing of information or assistance by any advisory organization involves any act or practice that is unfair, unreasonable or otherwise inconsistent with this chapter, the Commission may issue a written order (i) specifying in what respects the act or practice is unfair, unreasonable or otherwise inconsistent with this chapter, and (ii) requiring the discontinuance of the act or practice. (Code 1950, §§ 38-218.1, 38-253.18, 38-253.65; 1952, c. 317, § 38.1-274; 1986, c. 562.)

§ 38.2-2025. Statistics or recommendations by advisory organization not complying with this article or order of Commission. — No insurer that makes its own filings nor any rate service organization shall support its filings by statistics or adopt rate making recommendations furnished to it by an advisory organization that has not complied with (i) the provisions of this article or (ii) any order of the Commission entered under § 38.2-2024, involving such statistics or recommendations. If the Commission finds any insurer or rate service organization to be in violation of this section it may issue an order requiring the discontinuance of the violation. (Code 1950, §§ 38-253.19, 38-253.66; 1952, c. 317, § 38.1-275; 1986, c. 562.)

ARTICLE 4.

Hearings, Offenses and Penalties.

§ 38.2-2026. Action of Commission upon request for hearing on order or decision made without a hearing. — A. Any person aggrieved by an order or a decision of the Commission made under this chapter without a hearing may, within thirty days after notice of the order or decision, make a written request to the Commission for a hearing on the order or decision. Within a reasonable time after the request the Commission, after having given at least ten days' written notice of the time and place of hearing, shall hear the person aggrieved by the order or decision. Within a reasonable time after the hearing the Commission shall affirm, reverse or modify its previous action, specifying its reasons for the affirmation, reversal or modification.

B. Pending the hearing and decision on its previous action, the Commission may suspend or postpone the effective date of the order or decision to which the hearing relates. (Code 1950, §§ 38-218.11, 38-253, 38-253.49; 1952, c. 317, § 38.1-276; 1986, c. 562.)

§ 38.2-2027. Withholding information; giving false or misleading information. — No person shall willfully withhold information from or knowingly give false or misleading information to (i) the Commission, (ii) any statistical agency designated by the Commission, (iii) any rate service organization or (iv) any insurer that will affect the rates or premiums subject to this chapter. (Code 1950, §§ 38-218.6, 38-253.41, 38-253.87; 1952, c. 317, § 38.1-277; 1986, c. 562.)

CHAPTER 21.

FIRE INSURANCE POLICIES.

§ **38.2-2100. Application of chapter.** — This chapter applies only to contracts or policies of fire insurance, and contracts or policies of fire insurance in combination with other insurance coverages. (1986, c. 562.)

§ **38.2-2101. Policies shall conform to provisions of this chapter.** — No insurance policy or contract on any property in this Commonwealth shall be issued or delivered in this Commonwealth unless the policy or contract meets the requirements of this chapter. (Code 1950, § 38-177; 1952, c. 317, § 38.1-363; 1986, c. 562.)

Purpose of provisions prescribing form of policy. — The purpose of the General Assembly in passing § 38.2-2100 et seq. was to assure in all cases a fair and equitable contract of insurance between the parties, and not to cut off estoppels designed to prevent fraud or imposition, which had theretofore been enforced by the courts in cases in which the policy in question contained the same provisions as those which are contained in the standard policy prescribed by the act. North River Ins. Co. v. Belcher, 155 Va. 588, 155 S.E. 699 (1930); Spicer v. Hartford Fire Ins. Co., 171 Va. 428, 199 S.E. 499 (1938).

Principle of estoppel not abrogated. — Section 38.2-2100 et seq. have not abrogated the principle of estoppel, where before the issuance of the policy the insurance company, or its agent, has knowledge of facts which under the express terms of the policy render it void or unenforceable from its inception. North River Ins. Co. v. Belcher, 155 Va. 588, 155 S.E. 699 (1930).

The right to rely upon estoppel of a fire insurance company to claim that a policy issued by it was void because of the existence of certain facts of which the company had knowledge at the time of issuance has not been abrogated by §§ 38.1-363 through 38.1-372 (now §§ 38.2-2101 through 38.2-2116). Franklin Fire Ins. Co. v. Bolling, 173 Va. 228, 3 S.E.2d 182 (1939).

§ 38.2-2102. Excluding loss or damage caused by nuclear reaction, nuclear radiation, or radioactive contamination.

— The standard policy of fire insurance prescribed by this chapter shall not cover loss or damage caused by nuclear reaction, nuclear radiation, or radioactive contamination, whether resulting directly or indirectly from a peril insured under the policy. Insurers issuing the standard policy of fire insurance are authorized to affix to the policy or include therein a written statement that the policy does not cover loss or damage caused by nuclear reaction, nuclear radiation, or radioactive contamination, whether resulting directly or indirectly from a peril insured under the policy. However, an endorsement or endorsements specifically assuming coverage for loss or damage caused by nuclear reaction, nuclear radiation, or radioactive contamination may be attached to the standard policy of fire insurance. (1960, c. 117, § 38.1-363.1; 1986, c. 562.)

§ 38.2-2103. Information to be printed on policy.

— There shall be prominently printed on every policy issued on property in this Commonwealth (i) the name of the insurer issuing the policy, (ii) the location of the home office of the insurer, and (iii) a statement specifying whether the insurer is a stock company, a mutual company, a reciprocal insurer, or other form of insurer. If the policy is jointly issued by more than one insurer, the information shall be included for each insurer. (Code 1950, § 38-178; 1950, p. 993; 1952, c. 317, § 38.1-364; 1986, c. 562.)

§ 38.2-2104. Standard insuring agreement for fire insurance policies.

— A. Each policy shall provide space for listing amounts of insurance, rates, and premiums for the coverages provided in the policy and endorsements attached to the policy, and shall show the location of the agency and the name and location of the insurer issuing the policy. Except as provided in § 38.2-2107, each policy shall contain the following insuring agreement:

In consideration of the provisions and stipulations herein or added hereto and of the premium above specified, this Company for the term of .... At 12:01 A.M. .... At 12:01 A.M. from ....(Standard Time) to .... (Standard Time) at location of property involved, to an amount not exceeding the amount(s) above specified, does insure .... and legal representatives, to the extent of the actual cash value of the property at the time of loss, but not exceeding the amount which it would cost to repair or replace the property with material of like kind and quality within a reasonable time after such loss, without allowance for any increased cost of repair or reconstruction by reason of any ordinance or law regulating construction or repair, and without compensation for loss resulting from interruption of business or manufacture, nor in any event for more than the interest of the insured, against all direct loss by fire, lightning and by removal from premises endangered by the perils insured against in this policy, except as hereinafter provided, to the property described hereinafter while located or contained as described in this policy, or pro rata for five days at each proper place to which any of the property shall necessarily be removed for preservation from the perils insured against in this policy, but not elsewhere.

Assignment of this policy shall not be valid except with the written consent of this Company.

This policy is made and accepted subject to the foregoing provisions and stipulations and those hereinafter stated, which are hereby made a part of this policy, together with such other provisions, stipulations and agreements as may be added hereto, as provided in this policy.

B. No change shall be made in the sequence of the words and paragraphs of the insuring agreement except that additional matter relating to the coverage provided under the policy and supplemental contracts or extended coverage endorsements may be inserted following any paragraph. The additional matter shall not be inconsistent or in conflict with the standard provisions for policies set out in this chapter, and shall conform with other applicable laws relating to the regulation of fire insurance.

C. For the purpose of more accurate identification of the subject matter or more accurate reference to other provisions, substitutions may be made in the standard insuring agreement for the words "above specified," "hereinafter," or other similar terms; but no substitution shall be made if the purpose and intent of the contract is changed by the substitution. (Code 1950, §§ 38-186, 38-190; 1950, pp. 994, 995; 1952, c. 317, §§ 38.1-365, 38.1-367; 1986, c. 562.)

Liability limited to cost of repair. — A frame apartment house building was insured under standard fire insurance policies which conformed to the provisions of former § 38-188 and provided for payment in event of loss "not exceeding the amount which it would cost to repair or replace the property with material of like kind and quality." Loss having occurred by fire, liability was limited to the cost of repair, and insured was not entitled to recover the full value of the building in spite of the fact that because of zoning regulations the building could not be repaired for use as an apartment house, and according to insured's contention it was of no value for other purposes. Weinstein v. Commerce Ins. Co., 196 Va. 106, 82 S.E.2d 477 (1954).

§ 38.2-2105. Standard provisions, conditions, stipulations and agreements for such policies. — A. Except as provided in § 38.2-2107, each policy shall contain the following provisions, conditions, stipulations, and agreements:

1 **Concealment,**   This entire policy shall be void, if whether
2 **fraud.**   before or after a loss, the insured has wil-
3   fully concealed or misrepresented any ma-
4 terial fact or circumstance concerning this insurance or the
5 subject thereof, or the interest of the insured therein, or in case
6 of any fraud or false swearing by the insured relating thereto.
7 **Uninsurable**   This policy shall not cover accounts, bills,
8 **and**   currency, deeds, evidences of debt, money or
9 **excepted property.** securities; nor, unless specifically named
10   hereon in writing, bullion or manuscripts.
11 **Perils not**   This Company shall not be liable for loss by
12 **included.**   fire or other perils insured against in this
13   policy caused, directly or indirectly, by: (a)
14 enemy attack by armed forces, including action taken by mili-
15 tary, naval or air forces in resisting in actual or immediately
16 impending enemy attack; (b) invasion; (c) insurrection; (d)
17 rebellion; (e) revolution; (f) civil war; (g) usurped power;
18 (h) order of any civil authority except acts of destruction at the time
19 of and for the purpose of preventing the spread of fire, provided
20 that such fire did not originate from any of the perils excluded

21 by this policy; (i) neglect of the insured to use all reasonable
22 means to save and preserve the property at and after a loss, or
23 when the property is endangered by fire in neighboring prem-
24 ises; (j) nor shall this Company be liable for loss by theft.
25 **Other Insurance.**   Other insurance may be prohibited or the
26   amount of insurance may be limited by en-
27   dorsement attached hereto.
28 **Conditions suspending or restricting insurance.** Unless other-
29 wise provided in writing added hereto this Company shall not
30 be liable for loss occurring
31 (a) While the hazard is increased by any means within the
32 control or knowledge of the insured; or
33 (b) while a described building, whether intended for occupancy
34 by owner or tenant, is vacant or unoccupied beyond a period of
35 sixty consecutive days; or
36 (c) as a result of explosion or riot, unless fire ensue, and in
37 that event for loss by fire only.
38 **Other perils**   Any other peril to be insured against or sub-
39 **or subjects.**   ject of insurance to be covered in this policy
40   shall be by endorsement by writing hereon or
41 added hereto.
42 **Added provisions.** The extent of the application of insurance
43   under this policy and of the contribution to
44 be made by this Company in case of loss, and any other pro-
45 vision or agreement not inconsistent with the provisions of this
46 policy, may be provided for in writing added hereto, but no pro-
47 vision may be waived except such as by the terms of this policy
48 is subject to change.
49 **Waiver**   No permission affecting this insurance shall
50 **provisions.**   exist, or waiver of any provision be valid,
51   unless granted herein or expressed in writing
52 added hereto. No provision, stipulation or forfeiture shall be
53 held to be waived by any requirement or proceeding on the part
54 of this Company relating to appraisal or to any examination
55 provided for herein.
56 **Cancellation**   This policy shall be cancelled at any time
57 **of policy.**   at the request of insured, in which case
58   this Company shall, upon demand and sur-
59 render of this policy, refund the excess of paid premium above
60 the customary short rates for the expired time. This pol-
61 icy may be cancelled at any time by this Company by giving
62 to the insured a five days' written notice of cancellation with
63 or without tender of the excess of paid premium above the pro
64 rata premium for the expired time, which excess, if not ten-
65 dered, shall be refunded on demand. Notice of cancellation shall
66 state that said excess premium (if not tendered) will be
67 refunded on demand.
68 **Mortgagee**   If loss hereunder is made payable in whole
69 **interests and**   or in part, to a designated mortgagee not
70 **obligations.**   named herein as the insured, such interest in
71   this policy may be cancelled by giving to such
72   mortgagee a ten days' written notice of can-
73 cellation.
74 If the insured fails to render proof of loss such mortgagee, upon
75 notice, shall render proof of loss in the form herein specified
76 within sixty (60) days thereafter and shall be subject to the pro-

77 visions hereof relating to appraisal and time of payment and of
78 bringing suit. If this Company shall claim that no liability ex-
79 isted as to the mortgagor or owner, it shall, to the extent of pay-
80 ment of loss to the mortgagee, be subrogated to all mort-
81 gagee's rights of recovery, but without impairing mortgagee's
82 right to sue; or it may pay off the mortgage debt and require
83 an assignment thereof and of the mortgage. Other provisions
84 relating to the interest and obligations of such mortgagee may
85 be added hereto by agreement in writing.
86 **Pro rata liability.**   This Company shall not be liable for a greater
87   proportion of any loss than the amount
88 hereby insured shall bear to the whole insurance covering the
89 property against the peril involved, whether collectible or not.
90 **Requirements in**   The insured shall give immediate written
91 **case loss occurs.**   notice to this Company of any loss, protect
92   the property from further damage, forthwith
93 separate the damaged and undamaged personal property, put
94 it in the best possible order, and furnish a complete inventory
95 of the destroyed or damaged property setting forth for each item,
96 or by category if itemization is not reasonably practicable,
97 the amount of loss claimed. The Company may, in addition,
98 require the insured to furnish a complete inventory of
99 the destroyed, damaged and undamaged property, showing in
100 detail quantities, costs, actual cash value and amount of loss
101 claimed; and within sixty days after the loss, unless such time
102 is extended in writing by this Company, the insured shall render
103 to this Company a proof of loss, signed and sworn to by the
104 insured, stating the knowledge and belief of the insured as to
105 the following: the time and origin of the loss, the interest of the
106 insured and of all others in the property, the actual cash value of
107 each item thereof and the amount of loss thereto, all encum-
108 brances thereon, all other contracts of insurance, whether valid
109 or not, covering any of said property, any changes in the title,
110 use, occupation, location, possession or exposures of said prop-
111 erty since the issuing of this policy, by whom and for what
112 purpose any building herein described and the several parts
113 thereof were occupied at the time of loss and whether or not it
114 then stood on leased ground, and shall furnish a copy of all the
115 descriptions and schedules in all policies and, if required, verified
116 plans and specifications of any building, fixtures or machinery
117 destroyed or damaged. The insured, as often as may be reason-
118 ably required, shall exhibit to any person designated by this
119 Company all that remains of any property herein described, and
120 submit to examinations under oath by any person named by this
121 Company, and subscribe the same; and, as often as may be
122 reasonably required, shall produce for examination all books of
123 account, bills, invoices and other vouchers, or certified copies
124 thereof if originals be lost, at such reasonable time and place as
125 may be designated by this Company or its representative, and
126 shall permit extracts and copies thereof to be made.
127 **Appraisal.**   In case the insured and this Company shall
128   fail to agree as to the actual cash value or
129 the amount of loss, then, on the written demand of either, each
130 shall select a competent and disinterested appraiser and notify
131 the other of the appraiser selected within twenty days of such
132 demand. The appraisers shall first select a competent and dis-

133 interested umpire; and failing for fifteen days to agree upon
134 such umpire, then, on request of the insured or this Company,
135 such umpire shall be selected by a judge of a court of record in
136 the state in which the property covered is located. The ap-
137 praisers shall then appraise the loss, stating separately actual
138 cash value and loss to each item; and, failing to agree, shall
139 submit their differences, only, to the umpire. An award in writ-
140 ing, so itemized, of any two when filed with this Company shall
141 determine the amount of actual cash value and loss. Each
142 appraiser shall be paid by the party selecting him and the ex-
143 penses of appraisal and umpire shall be paid by the parties
144 equally; provided, however, if the written demand is made by this
145 Company, then the insured shall be reimbursed by this Company for
146 the reasonable cost of the insured's appraiser and the insured's
147 portion of the cost of the umpire.
148 **Company's**   It shall be optional with this Company to
149 **options.**   take all, or any part, of the property at the
150   agreed or appraised value, and also to re-
151 pair, rebuild or replace the property destroyed or damaged with
152 other of like kind and quality within a reasonable time, on giv-
153 ing notice of its intention so to do within thirty days after the
154 receipt of the proof of loss herein required.
155 **Abandonment.**   There can be no abandonment to this Com-
156   pany of any property.
157 **When loss**   The amount of loss for which this Company
158 **payable.**   may be liable shall be payable sixty days
159   after proof of loss, as herein provided, is
160 received by this Company and ascertainment of the loss is made
161 either by agreement between the insured and this Company ex-
162 pressed in writing or by the filing with this Company of an
163 award as herein provided.
164 **Suit.**   No suit or action on this policy for the recov-
165   ery of any claim shall be sustainable in any
166 court of law or equity unless all the requirements of this policy
167 shall have been complied with, and unless commenced within
168 two years next after inception of the loss.
169 **Subrogation.**   This Company may require from the insured
170   an assignment of all right of recovery against
171 any party for loss to the extent that payment therefor is made
172 by this Company.

B. No change shall be made in the sequence of the words and paragraphs of the standard provisions, conditions, stipulations and agreements prescribed by this section, or in the arrangement of the words into lines. The numbers given the lines in the standard form and the catch words placed at the beginning of the paragraphs shall be retained. (Code 1950, § 38-186; 1950, p. 994; 1952, c. 317, § 38.1-366; 1972, c. 115; 1979, c. 458; 1986, c. 562.)

Law Review. — For note on waiver, election and estoppel in Virginia insurance litigation, see 48 Va. L. Rev. 416 (1962). For survey of Virginia law on insurance for the year 1971-1972, see 58 Va. L. Rev. 1291 (1972). For survey of Virginia law on insurance for the year 1972-1973, see 59 Va. L. Rev. 1535 (1973). For comment, "Spouse's Fraud as a Bar to Insurance Recovery," see 21 Wm. & Mary L. Rev. 543 (1979). For survey of Virginia law on insurance for the year 1978-1979, see 66 Va. L. Rev. 321 (1980).

Purpose. — While requiring claimants to prove loss is one of the intents behind this section, it is also clear that one of the purposes for requiring examinations under oath and the production of documents is to protect the insurance company against false claims. Powell v.

United States Fid. & Guar. Co., 855 F. Supp. 858 (E.D. Va. 1994), aff'd, 88 F. 3d 271 (4th Cir. 1996).

Under Virginia law, an insurer must include in its policy all standard fire-insurance-policy provisions provided for in the Code, or any deviation therefrom that is in no respect less favorable to the insured than the standard policy form and is approved by the Insurance Commission prior to issue. Powell v. United States Fid. & Guar. Co., 88 F.3d 271 (4th Cir. 1996).

A misrepresentation made in an application for insurance will render any policy issued thereon void ab initio if such misrepresentation is material to the risk when assumed. The same rule of law is also applicable to policies issued under the Virginia assigned risk plan. Utica Mut. Ins. Co. v. Stegall, 293 F. Supp. 199 (W.D. Va. 1968).

The privilege against self-incrimination does not protect insureds from having to disclose financial information. Powell v. United States Fid. & Guar. Co., 855 F. Supp. 858 (E.D. Va. 1994), aff'd, 88 F. 3d 271 (4th Cir. 1996).

Increase in hazard. — Where a policy described the insured building as an "owner-occupied dwelling" the use being made of the premises at the time of the fire for selling cigarettes, soft drinks, etc., was such as to bring into operation the condition of the policy suspending coverage "while the hazard is increased by any means within the control or knowledge of the insured ...." American Ins. Co. v. Peyton, 272 F.2d 58 (4th Cir. 1959).

Limitation begins to run at time of loss. — The limitation period contained in a policy conforming with this section begins to run at the time of the loss, and is unaffected by the provision that the amount of loss is not payable until 60 days after proof of loss. Ramsey v. Home Ins. Co., 203 Va. 502, 125 S.E.2d 201 (1962).

Trustee in bankruptcy takes policies subject to limitation periods. — Trustee in bankruptcy, because he only acquires the debtor's interest in insurance policies, takes such policies subject to their limitation periods. United States Fid. & Guar. Co. v. Houska, 184 Bankr. 494 (E.D. Va. 1995), modified, American Bankers Ins. Co. v. Maness, 101 F.3d 358 (4th Cir. 1994).

Contractual limitation tolled. — If by reason of mistake in the execution of the policy it is necessary to have it reformed in equity, and the necessity of such reformation is not discovered until after the bringing of an action at law, the action in equity may be regarded as ancillary to, or a continuation of, the first action and will not be barred if the first action was brought in time. Weinstein v. Glens Falls Ins. Co., 202 Va. 722, 119 S.E.2d 497 (1961).

Proof of loss must be filed before suit is brought. — A policy requirement that the insured should file a proof of loss within 60 days after the fire should be construed to require that it shall, unless waived, be filed before suit is brought. Eden Corp. v. Utica Mut. Ins. Co., 350 F. Supp. 637 (W.D. Va. 1972).

Filing proof of loss within sixty days of expiration of period of limitation. — If the policy provides that the company cannot be required to settle until 60 days after proof of loss filed, and that no suit shall be brought unless brought in the period of limitation, then, unless the company has waived filing of proof of loss, a failure to file proof of loss until within 60 days of the expiration of the period will bar an action on the policy. Eden Corp. v. Utica Mut. Ins. Co., 350 F. Supp. 637 (W.D. Va. 1972).

Requirement of proof of loss may be waived by insurer. — The provisions on a policy of fire insurance pertaining to the requirement of preliminary proof of loss are for the benefit of the insurer and may be waived by it or by its duly authorized agent. Eden Corp. v. Utica Mut. Ins. Co., 350 F. Supp. 637 (W.D. Va. 1972).

What constitutes waiver. — Everything said or done by the insurer or his proper agents upon which the insured may reasonably rely, which might fairly induce him to conclude that such proof of loss has in his case been dispensed with or excused, and he is thereby influenced to act in good faith in accordance with such conduct, may amount to a waiver of such formal stipulation. Eden Corp. v. Utica Mut. Ins. Co., 350 F. Supp. 637 (W.D. Va. 1972).

The examination under oath clause in the Virginia Standard Insurance Policy encompasses investigation into possible motives for suspected fraud, including arson. Powell v. United States Fid. & Guar. Co., 88 F.3d 271 (4th Cir. 1996).

Acceptance of unsworn statement of loss may operate as waiver. — When a fire insurance company calls for and accepts from an insured, without objection, an unsworn statement of a loss, and so conducts itself with the insured when investigating the loss as to induce his reasonable belief that it is satisfied with the statement and does not desire formal proof of the loss, such formality will be treated as waived. Eden Corp. v. Utica Mut. Ins. Co., 350 F. Supp. 637 (W.D. Va. 1972).

As may recognition of liability by insurer. — A recognition of liability by the insurance company of its duly authorized agent may operate as a waiver of the policy provisions relative to proof of loss. Eden Corp. v. Utica Mut. Ins. Co., 350 F. Supp. 637 (W.D. Va. 1972).

Or negotiations for settlement. — Negotiations with the insured by an authorized agent of the insurer for settlement of the loss may constitute a waiver of proof of loss. Eden Corp. v. Utica Mut. Ins. Co., 350 F. Supp. 637 (W.D. Va. 1972).

Or denial of all liability. — Denial of all liability for a loss claimed under a policy operates as a waiver of the policy requirement of proof of loss. Eden Corp. v. Utica Mut. Ins. Co., 350 F. Supp. 637 (W.D. Va. 1972).

The "appraisal" provision of this section does not unconstitutionally deprive the insured of the intervention of a jury to determine its damages. The "appraisal" provision merely provides for a fair method of determining the amount of loss, and failing that, the insured may bring suit on the policy for recovery of the amount he feels he deserves. Eden Corp. v. Utica Mut. Ins. Co., 350 F. Supp. 637 (W.D. Va. 1972).

When insured absolved from compliance with appraisal provision. — If the failure to submit the loss to an appraisal was through some fault of the insurer, and the insured was free from fault, then the insured would be absolved from compliance with the appraisal provision of this section. Eden Corp. v. Utica Mut. Ins. Co., 350 F. Supp. 637 (W.D. Va. 1972).

The award is a necessary element of the plaintiff's cause of action, if demanded at a time when the company has a right to demand it, and when it can be made. Eden Corp. v. Utica Mut. Ins. Co., 350 F. Supp. 637 (W.D. Va. 1972).

But may be waived. — The filing of an award may be waived by an insurance company. Eden Corp. v. Utica Mut. Ins. Co., 350 F. Supp. 637 (W.D. Va. 1972).

Burden of proof on insured. — The burden of proving compliance with the necessary requirements of an insurance policy as to proofs of loss, or the waiver of such compliance on the part of the company, is on the insured; and, if he fails to establish the same by a preponderance of evidence, his action must fail. Eden Corp. v. Utica Mut. Ins. Co., 350 F. Supp. 637 (W.D. Va. 1972).

Father's statement that he was the sole owner of vehicle constituted a misrepresentation, but the insurer was, nevertheless, liable on the contract of insurance because it had not proved that the misrepresentation was material to the risk. Utica Mut. Ins. Co. v. Stegall, 293 F. Supp. 199 (W.D. Va. 1968).

Failure to comply with policy disclosure requirements found. — The weight of authority as decided in both state and federal courts is to allow for full disclosure within reasonable bounds, and that the financial condition of the claimants is material when the insurance company suspects fraud. While the plaintiffs in this case did not refuse to answer every question about their finances, they did refuse, on the basis of materiality, to provide a substantial amount of requested information which related to their financial condition at the time of the fire and was relevant to this case. Thus, the plaintiffs failed to cooperate as required by the policy. Powell v. United States Fid. & Guar. Co., 855 F. Supp. 858 (E.D. Va. 1994), aff'd, 88 F. 3d 271 (4th Cir. 1996).

Applied in Whitmer v. Graphic Arts Mut. Ins. Co., 242 Va. 349, 410 S.E.2d 642 (1991).

§ 38.2-2106. Standard form for execution of policies. — Except as provided in § 38.2-2107, each policy shall contain the following clause, which shall be used in executing and attesting the policy:

IN WITNESS WHEREOF, this Company has executed and attested these presents

Immediately following the execution clause a space shall be left for the signature of the officer or officers of the company authorized to sign the policy. (Code 1950, § 38-186; 1950, p. 994; 1952, c. 317, § 38.1-367; 1986, c. 562.)

§ 38.2-2107. Commission may establish guidelines for filing readable fire insurance policy forms. — The Commission may establish guidelines for the filing of simplified and readable policies of insurance. An insurer may issue a simplified and readable policy of insurance that deviates in language from the standard policy form provided for in §§ 38.2-2104, 38.2-2105 and 38.2-2106 if the deviating policy form is (i) in no respect less favorable to the insured than the standard policy form, and is (ii) approved by the Commission prior to issuance. (1977, c. 255, § 38.1-367.1; 1979, c. 176; 1986, c. 562.)

Under Virginia law, an insurer must include in its policy all standard fire-insurance-policy provisions provided for in the Code, or any deviation therefrom that is in no respect less favorable to the insured than the standard policy form and is approved by the

Insurance Commission prior to issue. Powell v. United States Fid. & Guar. Co., 88 F.3d 271 (4th Cir. 1996).

Applied in Whitmer v. Graphic Arts Mut. Ins. Co., 242 Va. 349, 410 S.E.2d 642 (1991).

§ 38.2-2108. Standards for content of fire insurance policies. —

A. The Commission may establish standards for the content of any policy or any rider, endorsement or other supplemental agreement or provision for use in connection with any policy written to insure owner-occupied dwellings which is to be issued or delivered in this Commonwealth.

B. Following adoption of the standards of content and notwithstanding the provisions of §§ 38.2-2104, 38.2-2105 and 38.2-2106, no insurer shall issue or renew any policy or any rider, endorsement, or other supplemental agreement or provision for use in connection with any policy written to insure owner-occupied dwellings unless the policy form has been filed with the Commission. The Commission shall determine whether the policy form meets the standards of content and is in compliance with any other statutory requirements.

C. Nothing in this section prevents an insurer from issuing policies with coverages, terms and conditions which are broader and more favorable to the insured than the standards established by the Commission. The language, style and format of the coverages, terms and conditions shall be consistent with the language, style and format of the entire policy form. (1979, c. 457, § 38.1-367.2; 1986, c. 562.)

Law Review. — For survey of Virginia law on insurance for the year 1978-1979, see 66 Va. L. Rev. 321 (1980).

§ 38.2-2109. Execution of policies. —

The policy shall be executed by the proper officers of the insurer or insurers, whose signatures on the policy may be in facsimile. (Code 1950, § 38-179; 1950, p. 993; 1952, c. 317, § 38.1-368; 1977, c. 313; 1986, c. 562.)

§ 38.2-2110. Other matter permitted in the policy. —

The policy may contain information on the insurer, its officers and agents, the agent issuing the policy, the amount of insurance for each peril covered, the premium for each peril, and any other relevant matter not inconsistent or in conflict with the standard provisions for policies prescribed by this chapter. (Code 1950, §§ 38-184, 38-185, 38-190; 1950, pp. 994, 995; 1952, c. 317, § 38.1-369; 1986, c. 562.)

§ 38.2-2111. Special regulations to be added to policy. —

If the policy is issued by any insurer having special regulations for the payment of assessments by the insured, the regulations shall be printed upon and made a part of the policy. If the policy is issued by an insurer having other regulations appropriate to or required by its form of organization, those other regulations shall be either (i) written or printed upon the policy or (ii) attached to the policy by endorsement. (Code 1950, §§ 38-180, 38-513; 1952, c. 317, § 38.1-370; 1986, c. 562.)

§ 38.2-2112. Temporary insurance contracts; duration; what deemed to include. —

A. Oral or written binders or other temporary insurance contracts may be made and used for a period not exceeding sixty days pending the issuance of the policy, and shall be deemed to include all agreements and provisions set out in §§ 38.2-2104 and 38.2-2105 and all applicable endorsements designated in the temporary insurance contract. Unless otherwise expressly provided, the contract shall be deemed to include the usual provisions, stipulations and agreements which are commonly used in this Commonwealth in effecting the insurance.

B. No temporary insurance contract shall include any provision or agreement which is inconsistent with or waives any provision, stipulation, agreement or condition required by § 38.2-2104 or § 38.2-2105. However, the cancellation provision and the provision fixing the hour of inception may be superseded by the express terms of the temporary insurance contract. (Code 1950, § 38-181; 1952, c. 317, § 38.1-371; 1986, c. 562.)

Cross references. — As to acceptance of temporary written contracts of insurance by lenders engaged in making or servicing real estate mortgage or deed of trust loans on one to four family residences, see § 38.2-205.1.

Oral contracts other than for temporary insurance invalid. — The provisions of §§ 38.2-2101 through 38.2-2116, when read in the light of the statutes providing for the supervision and regulation of fire insurance companies, provide by implication that all oral contracts of insurance shall be void and unenforceable, except such as fall within the provisions of this section. Eastern Shore Fire Ins. Co. v. Kellam, 159 Va. 93, 165 S.E. 637 (1932).

§ 38.2-2113. Mailing of notice of cancellation or refusal to renew. — A. No written notice of cancellation or refusal to renew a policy written to insure owner-occupied dwellings shall be effective when mailed by an insurer unless:

1. a. It is sent by registered or certified mail, or

b. At the time of mailing the insurer obtains a written receipt from the United States Postal Service showing the name and address of the insured stated in the policy; and

2. The insurer retains a copy of the notice of cancellation or refusal to renew.

3. [Repealed.]

B. This section shall not apply to policies written through the Virginia Property Insurance Association or any other residual market facility established pursuant to Chapter 27 (§ 38.2-2700 et seq.) of this title.

C. If the terms of the policy require the notice of cancellation or refusal to renew to be given to any lienholder, then the insurer shall mail such notice and retain a copy of the notice in the manner required by subsection A of this section. If the notices sent to the insured and the lienholder are part of the same form, the insurer may retain a single copy of the notice. The registered, certified or regular mail postal receipt and copy of the notices required by this section shall be retained by the insurer for at least one year from the date of termination.

D. Copy, as used in this section, shall include photographs, microphotographs, photostats, microfilm, microcard, printouts or other reproductions of electronically stored data or copies from optical disks, electronically transmitted facsimiles, or any other reproduction of an original from a process which forms a durable medium for its recording, storing, and reproducing. (1972, c. 110, § 38.1-371.1; 1983, c. 371; 1986, c. 562; 1992, c. 160.)

Law Review. — For survey of Virginia law on insurance for the year 1971-1972, see 58 Va. L. Rev. 1291 (1972).

§ 38.2-2114. Grounds and procedure for termination of policy; contents of notice; review by Commissioner; exceptions; immunity from liability. — A. Notwithstanding the provisions of § 38.2-2105, no policy or contract written to insure owner-occupied dwellings shall be canceled by an insurer unless written notice is mailed or delivered to the named insured at the

address stated in the policy, and cancellation is for one of the following reasons:
1. Failure to pay the premium when due;
2. Conviction of a crime arising out of acts increasing the probability that a peril insured against will occur;
3. Discovery of fraud or material misrepresentation;
4. Willful or reckless acts or omissions increasing the probability that a peril insured against will occur as determined from a physical inspection of the insured premises; or
5. Physical changes in the property which result in the property becoming uninsurable as determined from a physical inspection of the insured premises.

B. No policy or contract written to insure owner-occupied dwellings shall be terminated by an insurer by refusal to renew except at the expiration of the stated policy period or term and unless the insurer or its agent acting on behalf of the insurer mails or delivers to the named insured, at the address stated in the policy, written notice of the insurer's refusal to renew the policy or contract.

C. A written notice of cancellation of or refusal to renew a policy or contract written to insure owner-occupied dwellings shall:
1. State the date that the insurer proposes to terminate the policy or contract, which shall be at least thirty days after mailing or delivering to the named insured the notice of cancellation or refusal to renew. However, when the policy is being terminated for the reason set forth in subdivision 1 of subsection A of this section, the date that the insurer proposes to terminate the policy may be less than thirty days but at least ten days from the date of mailing or delivery;
2. State the specific reason for terminating the policy or contract and provide for the notification required by the provisions of §§ 38.2-608 and 38.2-609 and subsection B of § 38.2-610. However, those notification requirements shall not apply when the policy is being canceled or not renewed for the reason set forth in subdivision 1 of subsection A of this section;
3. Advise the insured that within ten days of receipt of the notice of termination he may request in writing that the Commissioner review the action of the insurer in terminating the policy or contract;
4. Advise the insured of his possible eligibility for fire insurance coverage through the Virginia Property Insurance Association; and
5. Be in a type size authorized by § 38.2-311.

D. Within ten days of receipt of the notice of termination any insured or his attorney shall be entitled to request in writing to the Commissioner that he review the action of the insurer in terminating a policy or contract written to insure owner-occupied dwellings. Upon receipt of the request, the Commissioner shall promptly initiate a review to determine whether the insurer's cancellation or refusal to renew complies with the requirements of this section and of § 38.2-2113, if sent by mail. The policy shall remain in full force and effect during the pendency of the review by the Commissioner except where the cancellation or refusal to renew is for reason of nonpayment of premium, in which case the policy shall terminate as of the date stated in the notice. Where the Commissioner finds from the review that the cancellation or refusal to renew has not complied with the requirements of this section or of § 38.2-2113, if sent by mail, he shall immediately notify the insurer, the insured, and any other person to whom notice of cancellation or refusal to renew was required to be given by the terms of the policy that the cancellation or refusal to renew is not effective. Nothing in this section authorizes the Commissioner to substitute his judgment as to underwriting for that of the insurer.

E. Nothing in this section shall apply:
1. To any policy written to insure owner-occupied dwellings that has been in effect for less than ninety days when the notice of termination is mailed or delivered to the insured, unless it is a renewal policy;
2. If the insurer or its agent acting on behalf of the insurer has manifested its willingness to renew by issuing or offering to issue a renewal policy,

certificate or other evidence of renewal, or has otherwise manifested its willingness to renew in writing to the insured. The written manifestation shall include the name of a proposed insurer, the expiration date of the policy, the type of insurance coverage and information regarding the estimated renewal premium;

3. If the named insured or his duly constituted attorney-in-fact has notified the insurer or its agent orally, or in writing, if the insurer requires such notification to be in writing, that he wishes the policy to be canceled, or that he does not wish the policy to be renewed, or if, prior to the date of expiration, he fails to accept the offer of the insurer to renew the policy; or

4. To any contract or policy written through the Virginia Property Insurance Association or any residual market facility established pursuant to Chapter 27 (§ 38.2-2700 et seq.) of this title.

F. Each insurer shall maintain, for at least one year, records of cancellation and refusal to renew and copies of every notice or statement referred to in subsection E of this section that it sends to any of its insureds.

G. There shall be no liability on the part of and no cause of action of any nature shall arise against the Commissioner or his subordinates; any insurer, its authorized representative, its agents, or its employees; or any firm, person or corporation furnishing to the insurer information as to reasons for cancellation or refusal to renew, for any statement made by any of them in complying with this section or for providing information pertaining to the cancellation or refusal to renew.

H. Nothing in this section requires an insurer to renew a policy written to insure owner-occupied dwellings, if the insured does not conform to the occupational or membership requirements of an insurer who limits its writings to an occupation or membership of an organization.

I. No insurer or agent shall refuse to renew a policy written to insure an owner-occupied dwelling, solely because of any one or more of the following factors:

1. Age;
2. Sex;
3. Residence;
4. Race;
5. Color;
6. Creed;
7. National origin;
8. Ancestry;
9. Marital status;
10. Lawful occupation, including the military service; however, nothing in this subsection shall require any insurer to renew a policy for an insured where the insured's occupation has changed so as to increase materially the risk;
11. Credit information contained in a "consumer report," as defined in the federal Fair Credit Reporting Act, 15 U.S.C. § 1681 et seq., bearing on a natural person's creditworthiness, credit standing or credit capacity, unless, in addition to any other requirements that may apply, the insurer includes in the notice required by this section the following statement or a statement substantially similar to it: "This nonrenewal is based on information contained in a consumer report relating to you and/or someone else who resides in your household." The notice shall also contain: (i) the name and address of an institutional source from whom the insurer obtained the credit information and (ii) a statement advising the insured that, if the insured wishes to inquire further about the credit information on which the nonrenewal is based and obtain a free copy of the "consumer report," the insured may do so by mailing a written request to the insurer, or such other party as the insurer shall identify in the notice, no more than ten days after the date on which the notice

of nonrenewal was mailed to the insured. If the insured submits such written notification, the nonrenewal shall not become effective until thirty days after the accuracy of the credit information, which the insured has questioned and on which the nonrenewal was based, has been verified and communicated to the insured. Such verification shall be deemed to have been made upon completion of the investigation of the credit information which the insured has questioned and on which the nonrenewal was based. The insured must cooperate in the investigation of the credit information, including responding to any communication submitted by, or on behalf of, the insurer no more than ten days after the date on which such communication was mailed to the insured. If the insured fails to cooperate in the investigation of the credit information, the insurer may, after providing fifteen days' written notice to the insured, terminate such investigation and nonrenew the policy. An insurer may require that an insured submit written documentation authorizing the insurer, or such other party as the insurer shall identify, to perform the investigation of the credit information. The insured shall be obligated to pay any pro rata premium due for insurance provided during the period in which the investigation of the credit information is pending up to the date on which the policy nonrenewal becomes effective. Although the obligations imposed upon an insurer by this subdivision may be satisfied by a third party who agrees, and is authorized, to act on behalf of the insurer, the insurer shall remain responsible for compliance with the obligations imposed by this subdivision; or

12. Any claim resulting primarily from natural causes.

Nothing in this section prohibits any insurer from setting rates in accordance with relevant actuarial data.

J. No insurer shall cancel or refuse to renew a policy written to insure an owner-occupied dwelling because an insured under the policy is a foster parent and foster children reside at the insured dwelling. (1972, c. 110, § 38.1-371.2; 1975, c. 350; 1978, c. 441; 1983, c. 371; 1986, c. 562; 1990, c. 293; 1995, c. 3; 1996, c. 237; 1998, c. 142.)

The **1998 amendment,** in subdivision E 3, inserted "orally, or" and inserted "if the insurer requires such notification to be in writing."

Law Review. — For survey of Virginia law on insurance for the year 1971-1972, see 58 Va. L. Rev. 1291 (1972). For survey of Virginia law on insurance for the year 1974-1975, see 61 Va. L. Rev. 1759 (1975).

§ 38.2-2114.1. Powers of Commission; replacement policies. — Upon the verified petition of an insurer, where the petitioning insurer proposes to replace all or substantially all of its polices in another insurer, the Commission may relieve the insurer of the requirements of subsections B and C of § 38.2-2114 and of the mailing requirements of § 38.2-2113; provided the insurer demonstrates to the satisfaction of the Commission that (i) the replacement policy is underwritten by an affiliate insurer under common control with the petitioning insurer; (ii) the replacement policy is substantially similar to the existing policy with the petitioning insurer; (iii) the premium charged for the replacement policy is no greater than that charged by the petitioning insurer for the existing policy; and (iv) the replacement insurer is duly licensed to transact the business of insurance in the Commonwealth of Virginia. The replacement insurer shall retain a copy of any offer of replacement for a period of one year from the expiration of any existing policy that is not replaced. The Commission may further condition any such relief to protect the best interests of the policyholder. (1991, c. 292.)

§ 38.2-2115. Discrimination in issuance of fire insurance. — No insurer or agent shall refuse to issue a policy solely because of any one or more of the following factors: the age, sex, residence, race, color, creed, national origin, ancestry, marital status or lawful occupation, including the military service, of the person seeking insurance. Nothing in this section prohibits any insurer from limiting the issuance of policies to those who are residents of this Commonwealth, nor does it prohibit any insurer from limiting the issuance of policies only to persons engaging in or who have engaged in a particular profession or occupation, or who are members of a particular religious sect. Nothing in this section prohibits any insurer from setting rates in accordance with relevant actuarial data. (1986, c. 562.)

§ 38.2-2116. Policies issued by two or more insurers. — A. With the consent of the Commission, two or more licensed insurers may jointly issue a policy, using a distinctive title that is prominently printed on the policy followed by the names and the home office addresses of the insurers obligated under the policy. The policy shall be executed by the proper officers of each insurer. Before issuance, the form and any terms of the policy that are in addition to the standard provisions set out in §§ 38.2-2104 and 38.2-2105 shall be approved by the Commission. The terms of the policy shall not be inconsistent with the standard provisions, and shall be placed under a separate title headed as follows: "Provisions specially applicable to this jointly issued policy." The special provisions shall contain in substance that:

1. The insurers executing the policy are severally liable for the full amount of any loss or damage according to the terms of the policy or for specified percentages or amounts of any loss or damage aggregating the full amount of insurance under the policy; and

2. Service of process upon, or notice of proof of loss required by the policy and given to any of the insurers executing the policy, shall be deemed to be service upon or notice to all such insurers.

B. The unearned premium reserve on each policy shall be allocated to each insurer on the basis of each insurer's pro rata share of the face amount of the policy, except to the extent that the risk is transferred under a valid contract of reinsurance. (Code 1950, § 38-183; 1952, c. 317, § 38.1-372; 1986, c. 562.)

Actions of Commission are ministerial. — Since the substance of all the provisions that may be contained in a combination fire insurance policy under this section is expressly set out in the Code, the required consent to the issuance of the policy and the approval of its provisions by the Commission are merely ministerial duties comparable to that performed by it in ascertaining whether articles of incorporation or charter amendment comply with the law. Commonwealth ex rel. Goddin, Goodridge & Robertson v. James T. Phelps & Co., 198 Va. 9, 92 S.E.2d 283 (1956).

And insurer may assume that proper policy will be approved. — Insofar as this section is concerned, a person who offers the insurance authorized may proceed with assurance that, if the provisions of his proposed policy comply with the statutory requirements, it will receive the necessary consent and approval of the Commission. Commonwealth ex rel. Goddin, Goodridge & Robertson v. James T. Phelps & Co., 198 Va. 9, 92 S.E.2d 283 (1956).

Consent for policy not required prior to bid. — This section does not require the Commission's consent and approval of a combination fire insurance policy prior to the submission of a bid offering the insurance therein authorized, nor can such a requirement be implied from the language employed by it. The failure of the legislature to make such a requirement part of the statute will result in no public harm. On the contrary, it will be more likely to benefit the public by encouraging competitive bidding, a factor that cannot be effectively obtained if every bidder can learn from the public records the bid to be submitted by his competitor. Commonwealth ex rel. Goddin, Goodridge & Robertson v. James T. Phelps & Co., 198 Va. 9, 92 S.E.2d 283 (1956).

This section provides for the issuance of policies of fire insurance by two or more companies and nowhere refers to a bid on or offer of insurance. Commonwealth ex rel. Goddin, Goodridge & Robertson v. James T. Phelps & Co., 198 Va. 9, 92 S.E.2d 283 (1956).

§ 38.2-2117. Approval of forms or provisions for additional coverage. — The Commission may approve and authorize the use of appropriate forms or provisions contained in supplemental contracts or extended coverage endorsements used in connection with policies on property in this Commonwealth to provide coverage for one or more perils in addition to the perils covered by the standard insuring agreement and standard provisions prescribed in this chapter. (Code 1950, § 38-190; 1950, p. 995; 1952, c. 317, § 38.1-373; 1986, c. 562.)

§ 38.2-2118. Required statement on insurance policies for owner-occupied dwellings. — Each insurer writing insurance on owner-occupied dwellings and appurtenant structures with a replacement cost provision under the provisions of Chapter 19 (§ 38.2-1900 et seq.) of this title shall give each applicant for insurance a statement summarizing: (i) any minimum coverage requirement necessary for the replacement cost provision to be fully effective, and (ii) the effect on claim payment of not meeting the minimum coverage requirement. (1977, c. 530, § 38.1-279.49:1; 1986, c. 562.)

Law Review. — For survey of Virginia law on insurance for the year 1976-77, see 63 Va. L. Rev. 1448 (1977).

Applied in Whitmer v. Graphic Arts Mut. Ins. Co., 242 Va. 349, 410 S.E.2d 642 (1991).

§ 38.2-2119. Approval of forms or provisions for certain risks. — A. The Commission may approve and authorize the use of appropriate forms or provisions for supplemental contracts or extended coverage endorsements where the insured may be indemnified for (i) the difference between the actual cash value of the property at the time of loss and the cost of repair or replacement of the property on the same site with new materials of like kind and quality, within a reasonable time after the loss, and without deduction for depreciation, (ii) additional cost or loss by reason of any ordinance or law in force at the time of loss which necessitates the demolition of any portion of the insured property, (iii) any increased cost of repair or replacement by reason of any ordinance or law regulating construction or repair of the insured building, and (iv) loss from interruption of business, untenantability, or termination of leasehold interest because of damage to or destruction of the property described in the policy. These forms or provisions shall apply to coverage provided to an insured having any interest in an insured building or structure which is a part of the building described in the policy, including service equipment for the building.

B. Where any policy of insurance issued or delivered in this Commonwealth pursuant to this chapter provides for the payment of the full replacement cost of property insured thereunder, the policy shall permit the insured to assert a claim for the actual cash value of the property without prejudice to his right to thereafter assert a claim for the difference between the actual cash value and the full replacement cost unless a claim for full replacement cost has been previously resolved. Any claim for such difference must be made within six months of (i) the last date on which the insured received a payment for actual cash value or (ii) date of entry of a final order of a court of competent jurisdiction declaratory of the right of the insured to full replacement cost, whichever shall last occur.

C. Notwithstanding the provisions of § 38.2-2104, insurers may offer, as an option, coverage limited to the amount necessary to repair or replace damaged property with functionally equivalent property at a lower cost than would be required to repair or replace the damaged property with material of like kind and quality. Such policies may also permit, at the option of the insured, settlement based on the market value of the damaged property at the time of loss. No new policy or original premium notice of insurance covering property insured on a functional replacement cost basis shall be issued or delivered unless it contains the following statement printed in boldface type, or unless the statement is attached to the front of or is enclosed with the policy or premium notice:

Important Notice

The coverage under this policy applies on a functional replacement cost basis which means that, under certain conditions, claims may be settled for less than the actual cash value of the property insured. (Code 1950, § 38-190; 1950, p. 995; 1952, c. 317, § 38.1-374; 1986, c. 562; 1992, c. 762; 1996, c. 373.)

Policies not specifically approved. — This section does not, by inference, allow depreciation on the cost of new materials in losses under policies which have not been specifically approved. Harper v. Penn Mut. Fire Ins. Co., 199 F. Supp. 663 (E.D. Va. 1961).

Replacement costs. — Insurance company was not required to pay insured replacement costs before property had actually been replaced. Whitmer v. Graphic Arts Mut. Ins. Co., 242 Va. 349, 410 S.E.2d 642 (1991).

§ 38.2-2120. Optional coverage to be offered with homeowner's policy.
— Any insurer who issues or delivers a homeowner's insurance policy in this Commonwealth shall offer as an option a provision insuring against loss caused or resulting from water which backs up through sewers or drains. (1974, c. 564, § 38.1-335.2; 1986, c. 562.)

§ 38.2-2121. When courts may appoint umpires.
— Whenever appraisers selected under the standard provisions for fire insurance policies set out in § 38.2-2105 fail for fifteen days to agree upon a person to serve as umpire, the insured or the insurer may apply in writing, for the appointment of an umpire, to the judge of the circuit court of the county or city in which the damaged or destroyed property was located at the time of loss. If the application is filed by the insured, a copy of the application shall first be delivered to a registered agent of the insurer. If the application is filed by the insurer, a copy of the application shall first be delivered to the insured. Upon showing, by affidavit or otherwise, the failure or neglect of the appraisers to agree upon and select an umpire within the time specified in the policy, the judge shall upon twenty-one days' notice to all parties appoint a competent and disinterested person to serve as umpire in determining the amount of loss or damage sustained. (Code 1950, § 38-172; 1952, c. 317, § 38.1-375; 1986, c. 562; 1992, c. 470.)

§ 38.2-2122. Appraisers and umpire to be citizens of Virginia; oath to be taken.
— Whenever any appraisal is to be made under the standard provisions of a policy for loss or damage to property, the appraisers and the umpire shall be citizens and actual residents of this Commonwealth unless otherwise agreed to in writing by the insured and the insurer. Each appraiser and umpire shall, before acting as such, take an oath that he is not directly or indirectly in the employment of the insured, the insurer or any other insurer, that he is not related to the insured or any officer of the insurer, and that he will faithfully discharge the duties imposed upon him. (Code 1950, §§ 38-173, 38-174; 1952, c. 317, § 38.1-376; 1986, c. 562.)

Compensation. — Under this section neither the insured nor the insurance company should select as their arbitrators men on their payroll. It is fundamental to the conception of such an appraisement, which is in effect an arbitration, that the person selected to make it should be free from the control and direction of the respective parties whose interests have been confided to them, and should act independently and upon their own judgment. But this

319

does not mean that the arbitrator is not to be paid by the party who retains him. Hurst v. Hope, 152 Va. 405, 147 S.E. 222 (1929); Equitable Fire & Marine Ins. Co. v. Stieffens, 154 Va. 281, 153 S.E. 731 (1930).

§ 38.2-2123. Chapter not applicable to certain mutual insurers. — This chapter shall not apply to mutual assessment property and casualty insurers, or to mutual insurers and associations organized under the laws of this Commonwealth, conducting business only in this Commonwealth, and issuing only policies providing for perpetual insurance. (Code 1950, §§ 38-182, 38-183, 38-193; 1952, c. 317, § 38.1-378; 1960, c. 293; 1986, c. 562.)

§ 38.2-2124. Optional coverage to be offered with fire insurance policy. — Any insurer that issues or delivers in this Commonwealth a new or renewal contract or policy of fire insurance, or a new or renewal contract or policy of fire insurance in combination with other insurance coverages, shall offer in writing as an option a provision that property will be repaired or replaced in accordance with applicable ordinances or laws that regulate construction, repair or demolition. (1993, c. 156.)

CHAPTER 22.

LIABILITY INSURANCE POLICIES.

§ 38.2-2200. Required provisions as to insolvency or bankruptcy, and as to when action maintained against insurer.

— No policy or contract insuring or indemnifying against liability for injury to or the death of any person, or for injury to or destruction of property, shall be issued or delivered in this Commonwealth unless it contains in substance the following provisions or other provisions that are at least equally favorable to the insured and to judgment creditors:

1. That the insolvency or bankruptcy of the insured, or the insolvency of the insured's estate, shall not relieve the insurer of any of its obligations under the policy or contract.

2. That if execution on a judgment against the insured or his personal representative is returned unsatisfied in an action brought to recover damages for injury sustained or for loss or damage incurred during the life of the policy or contract, then an action may be maintained against the insurer under the terms of the policy or contract for the amount of the judgment not exceeding the amount of the applicable limit of coverage under the policy or contract. (Code 1950, § 38-238; 1952, c. 317, § 38.1-380; 1986, c. 562.)

Law Review. — For note on automobile liability insurance and the voluntary-certified policy dichotomy, see 29 Wash. & Lee L. Rev. 426 (1972).

Section is for benefit of those who suffer damage. — This section and §§ 38.2-2204 through 38.2-2207 are, by force of their provisions, made a part of the policy and were enacted for the benefit of those who suffer damage from the negligent use of the car by one operating it with the permission of the owner, express or implied. Storm v. Nationwide Mut. Ins. Co., 199 Va. 130, 97 S.E.2d 759 (1957); General Accident Fire & Life Assurance Corp. v. Aetna Cas. & Sur. Co., 208 Va. 467, 158 S.E.2d 750 (1968).

This section applies to any policy insuring or indemnifying against liability for personal injuries, death, or property damage. Vermont Mut. Ins. Co. v. Everette, 875 F. Supp. 1181 (E.D. Va. 1995).

And is liberally construed. — This section having been enacted for the benefit of the injured parties, it is to be liberally construed so that the purpose intended may be accomplished. Storm v. Nationwide Mut. Ins. Co., 199 Va. 130, 97 S.E.2d 759 (1957).

This section and §§ 38.2-2204 through 38.2-2207 were enacted for the benefit of the injured party and are to be liberally construed. Davis v. National Grange Ins. Co., 281 F. Supp. 998 (E.D. Va. 1968).

The prohibitory provision of this section is general, and is applicable to both ownership and nonownership policies. Clarke v. Harleysville Mut. Cas. Co., 123 F.2d 499 (4th Cir. 1941).

Beneficiary is anyone injured. — In Virginia anyone injured by the negligence of the insured under the policy is a beneficiary of the policy. Davis v. National Grange Ins. Co., 281 F. Supp. 998 (E.D. Va. 1968).

Injured party may maintain action in his own name. — Since the injured party was a beneficiary under the policy, and it was made for his benefit, it would seem the injured party is intended by the language of § 55-22 as one entitled to maintain an action in his own name. Davis v. National Grange Ins. Co., 281 F. Supp. 998 (E.D. Va. 1968). But see Rowe v. United States Fid. & Guar. Co., 421 F.2d 937 (4th Cir. 1970).

Action by injured party is on contract. — Where an injured party has obtained judgment against the assured on an indemnity policy, which judgment remains unsatisfied because of the insolvency of insured, and the injured party brings his action against the insurance company for the amount of the judgment against assured, the action is plainly upon the insurance contract and not upon the judgment against the assured, and is therefore subject to any proper defense by the company under the terms of the contract. Whether the right of the plaintiff to maintain his action is rested upon this section, or upon the stipulation in the policy, or upon § 55-22, he is seeking only to enforce compliance on the part of the company with the terms of its contract, and therefore the company can make any defense available to it in a suit by the assured. Indemnity Ins. Co. of N. Am. v. Davis' Adm'r, 150 Va. 778, 143 S.E. 328 (1928).

Policy of insurance is not solely one of indemnity. — Under this legislation a policy of insurance is not solely one of indemnity for loss by the named insured, but it is a contract of liability and is extended to cover anyone operating the vehicle with the permission of the named insured. Storm v. Nationwide Mut. Ins. Co., 199 Va. 130, 97 S.E.2d 759 (1957); General Accident Fire & Life Assurance Corp. v. Aetna Cas. & Sur. Co., 208 Va. 467, 158 S.E.2d 750 (1968).

Insurer's liability not enlarged. — It is usually held that provisions that give the injured person the right to sue the insurer do not enlarge or extend the insurer's liability but only permit the injured person to exercise or succeed to the insured's rights against the insurer. Storm v. Nationwide Mut. Ins. Co., 199 Va. 130, 97 S.E.2d 759 (1957); General Accident Fire & Life Assurance Corp. v. Aetna Cas. & Sur. Co., 208 Va. 467, 158 S.E.2d 750 (1968).

Injured party may bring action where execution returned unsatisfied. — The injured party's cause of action on the contract arises when and where the execution is returned unsatisfied. Thus venue may be laid at such place. Virginia Farm Bureau Mut. Ins. Co. v. Saccio, 204 Va. 769, 133 S.E.2d 268 (1963).

Judgment fixes liability of insurer. — Under this section, whenever it is made to appear that a judgment has been recovered against a party who clearly comes within the provisions of the policy fixing the status of an assured, then the liability of the insurer is definitely fixed, unless, of course, fraud or collusion is shown in the procurement of the judgment. Union Indem. Co. v. Small, 154 Va. 458, 153 S.E. 685 (1930), followed in Employers' Liab. Assurance Corp. v. Taylor, 164 Va. 103, 178 S.E. 772 (1935).

In an action to compel defendant to pay a judgment obtained against the operator of an automobile owned by one who was insured in defendant company and who was a brother of the operator of the car, liability was denied on the ground, among others, that there was no privity of contract between plaintiff and defendant. It was held that under this section whenever it is made to appear that a judgment has been recovered against a party who comes within the provisions of the policy, then the liability of the insurer is definitely fixed. State Farm Mut. Auto. Ins. Co. v. Justis, 168 Va. 158, 190 S.E. 163 (1937).

Defenses that may be asserted by the insurer against the insured are usually good against the injured person, if they do not arise from agreement after the accident and are not made as a result of collusion between the insurer and the insured. Storm v. Nationwide Mut. Ins. Co., 199 Va. 130, 97 S.E.2d 759 (1957).

The right of the injured person to maintain the action against the insurer rises no higher than the right of the insured against the insurer. The injured person stands in the same shoes as the insured, and the same defenses that would be available to the insurer in an action brought by the insured are available to the insurer in the action brought by the injured person. Ampy v. Metro. Cas. Ins. Co., 200 Va. 396, 105 S.E.2d 839 (1958); General Accident Fire & Life Assurance Corp. v. Aetna Cas. & Sur. Co., 208 Va. 467, 158 S.E.2d 750 (1968).

Res judicata. — The driver of an automobile involved in an accident sued a liability insurer for reimbursement for a sum which he had had to pay for property damages arising out of the accident. The insurer successfully defended on the ground that the driver had bought the car from the named insured the day before the accident and therefore was not an additional insured but the owner and was not covered by the policy. It was held that the judgment in this action was not res judicata in a subsequent action brought against the insurer by a person injured in the accident, since the injured person's rights arose when she was injured, and could not thereafter be determined in an action to which she was not a party. Storm v. Nationwide Mut. Ins. Co., 199 Va. 130, 97 S.E.2d 759 (1957).

Subrogation to rights of insured. — A person injured by a party carrying indemnity insurance is subrogated to insured's rights. He has no greater rights against the company than the insured possessed. Farm Bureau Mut. Auto. Ins. Co. v. Hammer, 177 F.2d 793 (4th Cir. 1949), cert. denied, 339 U.S. 914, 70 S. Ct. 575, 94 L. Ed. 1339 (1950).

When a policy excludes unlawful acts of insured the insurer is released from defending the insured in actions for injuries caused by such acts, is not bound by the judgments obtained, and is entitled to its day in court to show, if it can, that its policy did not cover the injurious acts which the insured committed. Farm Bureau Mut. Auto. Ins. Co. v. Hammer, 177 F.2d 793 (4th Cir. 1949), cert. denied, 339 U.S. 914, 70 S. Ct. 575, 94 L. Ed. 1339 (1950).

Breach of policy provision for cooperation by insured. — The test is not whether failure to fulfill the condition precedent prejudiced the insurer, but whether the condition precedent was unfulfilled by insured. To constitute a breach of a cooperation clause by the insured there must be a lack of cooperation in some substantial and material respect. State Farm Mut. Auto. Ins. Co. v. Arghyris, 189 Va. 913, 55 S.E.2d 16 (1949).

Action for breach of contract. — If the injured party is a beneficiary under the contract of insurance and the policy is made for his benefit, then he should be entitled to maintain an action in his own name for a breach of that contract. Davis v. National Grange Ins. Co., 281 F. Supp. 998 (E.D. Va. 1968). But see Rowe v.

United States Fid. & Guar. Co., 421 F.2d 937 (4th Cir. 1970).

Action for bad faith conduct. — This section does not prohibit the insured from maintaining an action against the company for bad faith conduct. Davis v. National Grange Ins. Co., 281 F. Supp. 998 (E.D. Va. 1968). But see Rowe v. United States Fid. & Guar. Co., 421 F.2d 937 (4th Cir. 1970).

Assignment of right to sue. — An action for damages in excess of the policy limits based on an insurer's wrongful failure to settle is assignable, whether considered as sounding in tort or in contract, and the insured may assign his right to sue to the injured party. Davis v. National Grange Ins. Co., 281 F. Supp. 998 (E.D. Va. 1968). But see Rowe v. United States Fid. & Guar. Co., 421 F.2d 937 (4th Cir. 1970).

Timeliness of notice of accident required by automobile liability policy. See State Farm Mut. Auto. Ins. Co. v. Douglas, 207 Va. 265, 148 S.E.2d 775 (1966).

§ 38.2-2201. Provisions for payment of medical expense and loss of income benefits.

— A. Upon request of an insured, each insurer licensed in this Commonwealth issuing or delivering any policy or contract of bodily injury or property damage liability insurance covering liability arising from the ownership, maintenance or use of any motor vehicle shall provide on payment of the premium, as a minimum coverage (i) to persons occupying the insured motor vehicle; and (ii) to the named insured and, while resident of the named insured's household, the spouse and relatives of the named insured while in or upon, entering or alighting from or through being struck by a motor vehicle while not occupying a motor vehicle, the following health care and disability benefits for each accident:

1. All reasonable and necessary expenses for medical, chiropractic, hospital, dental, surgical, ambulance, prosthetic and rehabilitation services, and funeral expenses, resulting from the accident and incurred within three years after the date of the accident, up to $2,000 per person; however, if the insured does not elect to purchase such limit the insurer and insured may agree to any other limit;

2. If the person is usually engaged in a remunerative occupation, an amount equal to the loss of income incurred after the date of the accident resulting from injuries received in the accident up to $100 per week during the period from the first workday lost as a result of the accident up to the date the person is able to return to his usual occupation. However, the period shall not extend beyond one year from the date of the accident; and

3. An expense described in subdivision 1 shall be deemed to have been incurred:

a. If the insured is directly responsible for payment of the expense;

b. If the expense is paid by (i) a health care insurer pursuant to a negotiated contract with the health care provider or (ii) Medicaid or Medicare, where the actual payment with reference to the medical bill rendered by the provider is less than or equal to the provider's usual and customary fee, in the amount of the actual payment; however, if the insured is required to make a payment in addition to the actual payment by the health care insurer or Medicaid or Medicare, the amount shall be increased by the payment made by the insured;

c. If no medical bill is rendered or specific charge made by a health care provider to the insured, an insurer, or any other person, in the amount of the usual and customary fee charged in that community for the service rendered.

B. The insured has the option of purchasing either or both of the coverages set forth in subdivisions 1 and 2 of subsection A of this section. Either or both of the coverages, as well as any other medical expense or loss of income coverage under any policy of automobile liability insurance, shall be payable to the covered injured person notwithstanding the failure or refusal of the named insured or other person entitled to the coverage to give notice to the insurer of an accident as soon as practicable under the terms of the policy, except where the failure or refusal prejudices the insurer in establishing the validity of the claim.

C. In any policy of personal automobile insurance in which the insured has purchased coverage under subsection A of this section, every insurer providing such coverage arising from the ownership, maintenance or use of no more than four motor vehicles shall be liable to pay up to the maximum policy limit available on every motor vehicle insured under that coverage if the health care or disability expenses and costs mentioned in subsection A of this section exceed the limits of coverage for any one motor vehicle so insured. (1972, c. 859, § 38.1-380.1; 1973, c. 294; 1977, c. 112; 1982, c. 450; 1983, cc. 197, 370; 1986, c. 562; 1987, c. 429; 1989, c. 243; 1991, c. 4; 1996, c. 276; 1997, c. 503.)

Editor's note. — Acts 1989, c. 243, cl. 2 provides that the provisions of the act become effective Jan. 1, 1990, and that all original or renewed policies issued or delivered on or after Jan. 1, 1990, shall contain the new notice provision provided by the act.

Law Review. — For 1995 survey of insurance law, see 29 U. Rich. L. Rev. 1089 (1995).

Subdivision A 1 formerly did not require the coverage of chiropractic treatment. Rogers v. Nationwide Mut. Ins. Co., 222 Va. 345, 281 S.E.2d 817 (1981) (decided prior to 1982 amendment).

But insurer may include chiropractic care. — Because subdivision A 1 of this section sets only minimum coverage standards, an insurer is free to include coverage for chiropractic care in a medical payments clause of a motor vehicle insurance policy if it chooses to do so. Rogers v. Nationwide Mut. Ins. Co., 222 Va. 345, 281 S.E.2d 817 (1981) (decided prior to 1982 amendment).

Coverage for injuries from being "struck by an automobile" also covers injuries from motorcycles. — The medical payments provision of an automobile policy, the terms of which provide the insured and his relatives are covered when "struck by an automobile," also covers injuries resulting from being struck by a motorcycle. This section requires such coverage, upon request and payment of premium, as to injuries resulting from being struck by a "motor vehicle." "Motor vehicle" carries a statutory definition, in § 46.2-100, sufficiently broad to include a motorcycle. Further, under § 38.2-318, a policy otherwise invalid for failure to comply with this title shall be construed and applied as if it were in compliance. USAA Cas. Ins. Co. v. Yaconiello, 226 Va. 423, 309 S.E.2d 324 (1983).

Specific request for optional coverage required. — The elaborate method set out in § 38.2-2202 for notifying an insured of the availability of medical payments for injuries sustained in a nonowned motor vehicle indicates that a specific request for coverage under this section is required. State Farm Mut. Auto. Ins. Co. v. Seay, 236 Va. 275, 373 S.E.2d 910 (1988).

Effect of failure to request coverage. — Where insured received notice of optional coverage pursuant to § 38.2-2202, but failed to specifically request coverage for injuries sustained while occupying a nonowned motor vehicle, this section would not apply to supersede the provisions in his existing policy. State Farm Mut. Auto. Ins. Co. v. Seay, 236 Va. 275, 373 S.E.2d 910 (1988).

Exclusion from coverage absent statutory authorization. — Although this section required the insurer to provide medical benefits as a result of bodily injury caused by accident and arising out of the use of a motor vehicle, insurer was permitted to exclude from coverage those benefits payable under a workers' compensation statute. Baker v. State Farm Mut. Auto. Ins. Co., 242 Va. 74, 405 S.E.2d 624 (1991); Scarbrow v. State Farm Mut. Auto. Ins. Co., 256 Va. 357, 504 S.E.2d 860 (1998).

While this section mandates medical expense coverage for the resident relatives of the named insured while in or upon any motor vehicle, where a policy provision excludes coverage for that "which is not an insured motor vehicle," and where nothing in the statute prohibits such exclusion, the exclusion is clear and unambiguous, such exclusion of substantial risks that are unknown to the carrier and for which it receives no premium are clearly reasonable. Cotchan v. State Farm Fire & Cas. Co., 250 Va. 232, 462 S.E.2d 78 (1995).

§ 38.2-2202. Required notice of optional coverage available. — A. No original premium notice for insurance covering liability arising out of the ownership, maintenance, or use of any motor vehicle shall be issued or delivered unless it contains on the front of the premium notice or unless there is enclosed with the premium notice, in boldface type, the following statement:

IMPORTANT NOTICE

IN ADDITION TO THE MINIMUM INSURANCE REQUIRED BY LAW, YOU MAY PURCHASE ADDITIONAL INSURANCE COVERAGE FOR THE NAMED INSURED AND FOR HIS RELATIVES WHO ARE MEMBERS OF HIS HOUSEHOLD WHILE IN OR UPON, ENTERING OR ALIGHTING FROM A MOTOR VEHICLE, OR THROUGH BEING STRUCK BY A MOTOR VEHICLE WHILE NOT OCCUPYING A MOTOR VEHICLE, AND FOR OCCUPANTS OF THE INSURED MOTOR VEHICLE. THE FOLLOWING HEALTH CARE AND DISABILITY BENEFITS ARE AVAILABLE FOR EACH ACCIDENT:
1. PAYMENT OF UP TO $2,000 PER PERSON FOR ALL REASONABLE AND NECESSARY EXPENSES FOR MEDICAL, CHIROPRACTIC, HOSPITAL, DENTAL, SURGICAL, AMBULANCE, PROSTHETIC AND REHABILITATION SERVICES, AND FUNERAL EXPENSES RESULTING FROM THE ACCIDENT AND INCURRED WITHIN THREE YEARS AFTER THE DATE OF THE ACCIDENT. HOWEVER, IF YOU DO NOT PURCHASE THE $2,000 LIMIT OF COVERAGE, YOU AND THE COMPANY MAY AGREE TO ANY OTHER LIMIT; AND
2. AN AMOUNT EQUAL TO THE LOSS OF INCOME UP TO $100 PER WEEK IF THE INJURED PERSON IS ENGAGED IN AN OCCUPATION FOR WHICH HE RECEIVES COMPENSATION, FROM THE FIRST WORKDAY LOST AS A RESULT OF THE ACCIDENT UP TO THE DATE THE PERSON IS ABLE TO RETURN TO HIS USUAL OCCUPATION. SUCH PAYMENTS ARE LIMITED TO A PERIOD EXTENDING ONE YEAR FROM THE DATE OF THE ACCIDENT.
IF YOU DESIRE TO PURCHASE EITHER OR BOTH OF THESE COVERAGES AT AN ADDITIONAL PREMIUM, YOU MAY DO SO BY CONTACTING THE AGENT OR COMPANY THAT ISSUED YOUR POLICY.
The insurer issuing the premium notice shall inform the insured by any reasonable means of communication of the approximate premium for the additional coverage.

B. No new policy or original premium notice of insurance covering liability arising out of the ownership, maintenance, or use of any motor vehicle shall be issued or delivered unless it contains the following statement printed in boldface type, or unless the statement is attached to the front of or is enclosed with the policy or premium notice:

IMPORTANT NOTICE

IN ADDITION TO THE INSURANCE COVERAGE REQUIRED BY LAW TO PROTECT YOU AGAINST A LOSS CAUSED BY AN UNINSURED MOTORIST,
IF YOU HAVE PURCHASED LIABILITY INSURANCE COVERAGE THAT IS HIGHER THAN THAT REQUIRED BY LAW TO PROTECT YOU AGAINST LIABILITY ARISING OUT OF THE OWNERSHIP, MAINTENANCE, OR USE OF THE MOTOR VEHICLES COVERED BY THIS POLICY, AND YOU HAVE NOT ALREADY PURCHASED UNINSURED MOTORIST INSURANCE COVERAGE EQUAL TO YOUR LIABILITY INSURANCE COVERAGE;

1. YOUR UNINSURED AND UNDERINSURED MOTORIST INSUR-
ANCE COVERAGE HAS INCREASED TO THE LIMITS OF YOUR LIABIL-
ITY COVERAGE AND THIS INCREASE WILL COST YOU AN EXTRA
PREMIUM CHARGE; AND
2. YOUR TOTAL PREMIUM CHARGE FOR YOUR MOTOR VEHICLE
INSURANCE COVERAGE WILL INCREASE IF YOU DO NOT NOTIFY
YOUR AGENT OR INSURER OF YOUR DESIRE TO REDUCE COVERAGE
WITHIN 20 DAYS OF THE MAILING OF THE POLICY OR THE PREMIUM
NOTICE, AS THE CASE MAY BE.
3. IF THIS IS A NEW POLICY AND YOU HAVE ALREADY SIGNED A
WRITTEN REJECTION OF SUCH HIGHER LIMITS IN CONNECTION
WITH IT, PARAGRAPHS 1 AND 2 OF THIS NOTICE DO NOT APPLY.

After twenty days, the insurer shall be relieved of the obligation imposed by
this subsection to attach or imprint the foregoing statement to any subsequently delivered renewal policy, extension certificate, other written statement
of coverage continuance, or to any subsequently mailed premium notice. (1974,
c. 607, § 38.1-380.2; 1977, c. 112; 1981, c. 245; 1982, cc. 450, 642; 1986, c. 562;
1987, c. 429; 1989, c. 243; 1992, c. 230.)

Editor's note. — Acts 1989, c. 243, which amended this section, in cl. 2 provides that the provisions of the 1989 act become effective Jan. 1, 1990, and that all original or renewed policies issued or delivered on or after Jan. 1, 1990, shall contain the new notice provision provided by the act.

Law Review. — For survey of Virginia law on insurance for the year 1973-1974, see 60 Va. L. Rev. 1553 (1974). For 1995 survey of insurance law, see 29 U. Rich. L. Rev. 1089 (1995).

How violation of section is redressable. — Violation of this section is redressable by the State Corporation Commission in its regulatory capacity and not through extension of coverage, at least where the insured seeks no coverage whatever and additional coverage is not in issue. Dairyland Ins. Co. v. Collier, 453 F. Supp. 883 (W.D. Va. 1978).

Specific request for optional coverage required. — The elaborate method set out in this section for notifying an insured of the availability of medical payments for injuries sustained in a non-owned motor vehicle indi- cates that a specific request for coverage under § 38.2-2201 is required. State Farm Mut. Auto. Ins. Co. v. Seay, 236 Va. 275, 373 S.E.2d 910 (1988).

Effect of failure to request coverage. — Where insured received notice of optional cov- erage pursuant to this section, but failed to specifically request coverage for injuries sus- tained while occupying a non-owned motor ve- hicle, § 38.2-2201 would not apply to supersede the provisions in his existing policy. State Farm Mut. Auto. Ins. Co. v. Seay, 236 Va. 275, 373 S.E.2d 910 (1988).

Rejection requirement. — This section's explicit rejection requirement is consistent with its purpose of affording adequate protec- tion to those injured by underinsured motor- ists. White v. National Union Fire Ins. Co., 913 F.2d 165 (4th Cir. 1990).

Information that supports an inference by the insurer that the insured intends to reject a default level of coverage does not suffice, under this section, as an actual "rejection" of that coverage. White v. National Union Fire Ins. Co., 913 F.2d 165 (4th Cir. 1990).

When insurance company did not need to send selection form. — Where the in- sured's policy was a renewal policy not requir- ing the insurance company to send the insured an "uninsured motorist coverage selection form" under subsection B, insurance company that did send the form could not avoid the lack of a statutorily required rejection of default coverage by pointing to a prior one where a subsequent, albeit inadequate, rejection was furnished. White v. National Union Fire Ins. Co., 913 F.2d 165 (4th Cir. 1990).

Waiver of higher coverage remaining in effect. — Where in 1984, insured executed and returned a waiver form to insurer by which he requested $25,000 uninsured motorist (UM) coverage and rejected the higher level of cover- age, which would have been $100,000, and where in 1990, insurer mailed insured a re- newal policy for the 1991 period covering the date of the accident; however, insured did not return this waiver form to insurer, the mere fact that insurer sent insured a waiver form was not sufficient to negate earlier decision to reject the higher limits of UM coverage. Thus, the 1984 waiver of higher UM coverage re- mained in effect through later policy renewals, so that insured's UM coverage at the time of the accident was $25,000. USAA Cas. Ins. Co. v. Alexander, 248 Va. 185, 445 S.E.2d 145 (1994).

§ 38.2-2203. Policy providing for reimbursement for services that may be performed by certain practitioners other than physicians. — Notwithstanding any provision of any policy or contract of bodily injury liability insurance, when the policy or contract provides for reimbursement for any service that may be legally performed by a person licensed in this Commonwealth for the practice of chiropractic, reimbursement under the policy shall not be denied because the service is rendered by a licensed chiropractor. (1984, c. 441, § 38.1-380.3; 1986, c. 562.)

§ 38.2-2204. Liability insurance on motor vehicles, aircraft and watercraft; standard provisions; "omnibus clause." — A. No policy or contract of bodily injury or property damage liability insurance, covering liability arising from the ownership, maintenance, or use of any motor vehicle, aircraft, or private pleasure watercraft, shall be issued or delivered in this Commonwealth to the owner of such vehicle, aircraft or watercraft, or shall be issued or delivered by any insurer licensed in this Commonwealth upon any motor vehicle, aircraft, or private pleasure watercraft that is principally garaged, docked, or used in this Commonwealth, unless the policy contains a provision insuring the named insured, and any other person using or responsible for the use of the motor vehicle, aircraft, or private pleasure watercraft with the expressed or implied consent of the named insured, against liability for death or injury sustained, or loss or damage incurred within the coverage of the policy or contract as a result of negligence in the operation or use of such vehicle, aircraft, or watercraft by the named insured or by any such person; however, nothing contained in this section shall be deemed to prohibit an insurer from limiting its liability under any one policy for bodily injury or property damage resulting from any one accident or occurrence to the liability limits for such coverage set forth in the policy for any such accident or occurrence regardless of the number of insureds under that policy. Each such policy or contract of liability insurance, or endorsement to the policy or contract, insuring private passenger automobiles, aircraft, or private pleasure watercraft principally garaged, docked, or used in this Commonwealth, that has as the named insured an individual or husband and wife and that includes, with respect to any liability insurance provided by the policy, contract or endorsement for use of a nonowned automobile, aircraft or private pleasure watercraft, any provision requiring permission or consent of the owner of such automobile, aircraft, or private pleasure watercraft for the insurance to apply, shall be construed to include permission or consent of the custodian in the provision requiring permission or consent of the owner.

B. For aircraft liability insurance, such policy or contract may contain the exclusions listed in § 38.2-2227. Notwithstanding the provisions of this section or any other provisions of law, no policy or contract shall require pilot experience greater than that prescribed by the Federal Aviation Administration, except for pilots operating air taxis, or pilots operating aircraft applying chemicals, seed, or fertilizer.

C. No policy or contract of bodily injury or property damage liability insurance relating to the ownership, maintenance, or use of a motor vehicle shall be issued or delivered in this Commonwealth to the owner of such vehicle or shall be issued or delivered by an insurer licensed in this Commonwealth upon any motor vehicle principally garaged or used in this Commonwealth without an endorsement or provision insuring the named insured, and any other person using or responsible for the use of the motor vehicle with the expressed or implied consent of the named insured, against liability for death or injury sustained, or loss or damage incurred within the coverage of the policy or contract as a result of negligence in the operation or use of the motor vehicle by the named insured or by any other such person; however, nothing contained in this section shall be deemed to prohibit an insurer from limiting its liability under any one policy for bodily injury or property damage resulting from any one accident or occurrence to the liability limits for such coverage set forth in the policy for any such accident or occurrence regardless of the number of insureds under that policy. This provision shall apply notwithstanding the failure or refusal of the named insured or such other person to cooperate with the insurer under the terms of the policy. If the failure or refusal to cooperate prejudices the insurer in the defense of an action for damages arising from the operation or use of such insured motor vehicle, then the endorsement or provision shall be void. If an insurer has actual notice of a motion for judgment or complaint having been served on an insured, the mere failure of the insured to turn the motion or complaint over to the insurer shall not be a defense to the insurer, nor void the endorsement or provision, nor in any way relieve the insurer of its obligations to the insured, provided the insured otherwise cooperates and in no way prejudices the insurer.

Where the insurer has elected to provide a defense to its insured under such circumstances and files responsive pleadings in the name of its insured, the insured shall not be subject to sanctions for failure to comply with discovery pursuant to Part Four of the Rules of the Supreme Court of Virginia unless it can be shown that the suit papers actually reached the insured, and that the insurer has failed after exercising due diligence to locate its insured, and as long as the insurer provides such information in response to discovery as it can without the assistance of the insured.

D. Any endorsement, provision or rider attached to or included in any such policy of insurance which purports or seeks to limit or reduce the coverage afforded by the provisions required by this section shall be void, except an insurer may exclude such coverage as is afforded by this section, where such coverage would inure to the benefit of the United States Government or any agency or subdivision thereof under the provisions of the Federal Tort Claims Act, the Federal Drivers Act and Public Law 86-654 District of Columbia Employee Non-Liability Act, or to the benefit of the Commonwealth under the provisions of the Virginia Tort Claims Act (§ 8.01-195.1 et seq.) and the self-insurance plan established by the Department of General Services pursuant to § 2.1-526.8 for any state employee who, in the regular course of his employment, transports patients in his own personal vehicle. (Code 1950, § 38-238; 1952, c. 317, § 38.1-381; 1958, c. 282; 1959, Ex. Sess., cc. 42, 70; 1970, c. 462; 1962, c. 457; 1964, c. 477; 1966, cc. 182, 459; 1968, cc. 199, 721; 1970, c. 494; 1971, Ex. Sess., c. 216; 1973, cc. 225, 390; 1974, c. 87; 1976, cc. 121, 122; 1977, c. 78; 1979, c. 113; 1980, cc. 326, 331; 1981, Sp. Sess., c. 6; 1982, cc. 638, 642; 1984, c. 541; 1985, cc. 39, 325; 1986, cc. 544, 562; 1992, c. 140; 1995, c. 652; 1999, c. 4.)

Cross references. — As to the issuance of a certificate of self-insurance when the Commissioner is reasonably satisfied, inter alia that such certificate provides for protection against the uninsured motorist to the extent required by this section of certain policies of insurance, provided that such protection shall be secondary coverage, see § 46.2-368. As to application of liability insurance policy to vehicle carrying plates from insured vehicle, see § 46.2-721.

Editor's note. — Pursuant to § 9-77.11, effect has been given in this section, as set out above, to Acts 1986, c. 544, which amended former § 38.1-381, the comparable provision in former Title 38.1.

The 1999 amendment inserted the language beginning "however, nothing contained" and ending "insureds under that policy" at the end of the first sentence in subsections A and C.

Law Review. — For comment on admissibility of evidence of insurance in automobile negligence actions, see 19 Wash. & Lee L. Rev. 146 (1962). For discussion of changes made by 1966 General Assembly, see 53 Va. L. Rev. 190 (1967). For survey of Virginia law on insurance for the year 1969-1970, see 56 Va. L. Rev. 1356 (1970). For survey of Virginia law on insurance for the year 1970-1971, see 57 Va. L. Rev. 1608 (1971). For survey of Virginia law on insurance for the year 1971-1972, see 58 Va. L. Rev. 1291 (1972). For survey of Virginia law on practice and pleading for the year 1971-1972, see 58 Va.

L. Rev. 1309 (1972). For note on automobile liability insurance and the voluntary-certified policy dichotomy, see 29 Wash. & Lee L. Rev. 426 (1972). For survey of Virginia law on evidence for the year 1972-1973, see 59 Va. L. Rev. 1526 (1973). For survey of Virginia law on insurance for the year 1972-1973, see 59 Va. L. Rev. 1535 (1973). For survey of Virginia law on torts for the year 1972-1973, see 59 Va. L. Rev. 1590 (1973). For survey of Virginia law on insurance for the year 1973-1974, see 60 Va. L. Rev. 1553 (1974). For survey of Virginia law on insurance for the year 1974-1975, see 61 Va. L.

Rev. 1759 (1975). For survey of Virginia insurance law for the year 1975-1976, see 62 Va. L. Rev. 1446 (1976). For survey of Virginia insurance law for the year 1977-1978, see 64 Va. L. Rev. 1477 (1978). For comment on the application of lex loci delicti in light of McMillan v. McMillan, 219 Va. 1127, 253 S.E.2d 662 (1979), see 4 Geo. Mason L. Rev. 151 (1981). For article on the law governing airplane accidents, see 39 Wash. & Lee L. Rev. 1303 (1982). For article, "The Duty to Settle," see 76 Va. L. Rev. 1113 (1990).

I. General Consideration.
II. Liability Covered.
III. Consent of Insured.

I. GENERAL CONSIDERATION.

This section does not violate Va. Const., Art. IV, § 12 requiring laws to deal with only one object expressed in the title. Doe v. Brown, 203 Va. 508, 125 S.E.2d 159 (1962).

Statutory purpose. — The literal reading of the statutory language is completely consonant with the statutory purpose of expanding coverage under liability insurance policies. Gordon v. Liberty Mut. Ins. Co., 675 F. Supp. 321 (E.D. Va. 1987).

The General Assembly has decided, as a matter of public policy, to extend the benefits of uninsured motorist coverage only to those injured by a motor vehicle which is uninsured, and not to those injured by a motor vehicle which, though fully insured under the statute, is only partly insured as to claims presented. Billings v. State Farm Mut. Auto. Ins. Co., 680 F. Supp. 778 (E.D. Va. 1988).

"Custodian." — Under a literal reading of the statute, the "custodian" of an automobile is any person who has possession of the automobile who in fact safeguards or intends to safeguard the automobile from damage. Gordon v. Liberty Mut. Ins. Co., 675 F. Supp. 321 (E.D. Va. 1987).

Any person who is in possession of and intends to safeguard an automobile is a custodian of said automobile within the meaning of subsection A of this section. Gordon v. Liberty Mut. Ins. Co., 675 F. Supp. 321 (E.D. Va. 1987).

Plaintiff, as lessee of automobile, qualified as custodian under statute and if a driver reasonably believed that he had the permission of the rental car's custodian, he would be covered by the insurance policy. Gordon v. Liberty Mut. Ins. Co., 675 F. Supp. 321 (E.D. Va. 1987).

"Omnibus clause." — The "omnibus clause" statute is to be construed liberally to effectuate the clearly manifested legislative purpose to broaden automobile liability insurance cover-

age. Gordon v. Liberty Mut. Ins. Co., 675 F. Supp. 321 (E.D. Va. 1987).

"Include." — The word "include" in this section allows that permission of an automobile's custodian alone suffices to provide coverage under insurance company's non-owned vehicle provision. Gordon v. Liberty Mut. Ins. Co., 675 F. Supp. 321 (E.D. Va. 1987).

Section is not retroactive. — This section relates only to a policy issued subsequent to its passage, and is in no sense retroactive in its effect. Ellis v. New Amsterdam Cas. Co., 169 Va. 620, 194 S.E. 687 (1938).

The court must look to the words used in this section to determine its meaning, and only the meaning of the section as determined should be given effect. Grange Mut. Cas. Co. v. Criterion Ins. Co., 212 Va. 753, 188 S.E.2d 91 (1972).

This section is applied with an eye to the attainment of its purpose; protection of the public. Bernstein v. Nationwide Mut. Ins. Co., 458 F.2d 506 (4th Cir.), cert. denied, 409 U.S. 812, 93 S. Ct. 70, 34 L. Ed. 2d 68 (1972), aff'g by an equally divided court, the decision in Nationwide Mut. Ins. Co. v. Stephens, 313 F. Supp. 890 (W.D. Va. 1970), declaring a policy void ab initio for material misrepresentations in the application.

Liberal interpretation. — The "omnibus clause" statute, as remedial legislation, must be liberally interpreted to subserve the clear public policy reflected in the statute, to broaden the coverage of automobile-liability policies. Jordan v. Shelby Mut. Plate Glass & Cas. Co., 142 F.2d 52 (4th Cir. 1944).

This section and § 46.1-504 (now § 46.2-472) are to be liberally construed to subserve the policy manifest therein. American Auto. Ins. Co. v. Fulcher, 201 F.2d 751 (4th Cir. 1953), construing former § 38-238. See Fidelity & Cas. Co. v. Harlow, 191 Va. 64, 59 S.E.2d 872 (1950); Utica Mut. Ins. Co. v. Rollason, 246 F 2d 105 (4th Cir. 1957).

The permission requirement should be liberally interpreted to effectuate the public policy of giving coverage to the injured party. United States Fid. & Guar. Co. v. Trussell, 208 F. Supp. 154 (W.D. Va. 1962).

This section is to be liberally construed to accomplish its intended purpose. Rose v. Travelers Indem. Co., 209 Va. 755, 167 S.E.2d 339 (1969).

This section and § 38.2-2200 were enacted for the benefit of the injured party and are to be liberally construed. Davis v. National Grange Ins. Co., 281 F. Supp. 998 (E.D. Va. 1968).

The standard omnibus clause is required in Virginia and is to be liberally construed. Nationwide Mut. Ins. Co. v. Allstate Ins. Co., 304 F. Supp. 343 (W.D. Va. 1969).

The Virginia omnibus statute is remedial in purpose and is to be liberally construed in order to broaden coverage. Emick v. Dairyland Ins. Co., 519 F.2d 1317 (4th Cir. 1975).

This section is remedial and must be liberally interpreted to subserve the clear public policy reflected in it, which is to broaden the coverage of automobile liability policies. Liberty Mut. Ins. Co. v. Mueller, 432 F. Supp. 325 (W.D. Va. 1977), aff'd, 570 F.2d 508 (4th Cir. 1978).

The statute is to be liberally construed to effectuate insurance coverage to permissive users. City of Norfolk v. Ingram, 235 Va. 433, 367 S.E.2d 725 (1988).

Since this section is remedial, it must be interpreted liberally in construing clauses such as clause in automobile insurance policy which provides coverage for a person who is using a motor vehicle with the expressed or implied consent of the named insured. Hartford Fire Ins. Co. v. Davis, 246 Va. 495, 436 S.E.2d 429 (1993).

Construction of section by federal court. — That certain provisions of this section had not been construed by any Virginia court did not mean that a federal court should decline from passing on the question. State Farm Mut. Auto. Ins. Co. v. Drewry, 191 F. Supp. 852 (W.D. Va. 1960), aff'd, 316 F.2d 716 (4th Cir. 1963).

Section does not authorize the restriction of manner of operation. — Nowhere in this section is there any authority to restrict the manner of operation. If the omnibus coverage to operate a motor vehicle could be conditioned upon a restriction against driving it while intoxicated, there is no rational reason why such coverage could not be limited by the owner's prohibition of the user's operation of the loaned vehicle in violation of law. Such a rule would essentially undercut the legislative policies of protecting a permissive user against liability to others and creating a means of recovery to any party injured when struck by a vehicle operated by a permissive user. City of Norfolk v. Ingram, 235 Va. 433, 367 S.E.2d 725 (1988).

This section is for the benefit of a party who has suffered damage by the negligent use of the insured's car when operated by another with the permission of the owner. Every automobile liability policy issued in Virginia will be considered to contain an omnibus clause extending the said coverage to one legally operating the car with the owner's permission, express or implied. Liberty Mut. Ins. Co. v. Tiller, 189 Va. 544, 53 S.E.2d 814 (1949); Liberty Mut. Ins. Co. v. Venable, 194 Va. 357, 73 S.E.2d 366 (1952), construing former § 38-238. See Coureas v. Allstate Ins. Co., 198 Va. 77, 92 S.E.2d 378 (1956); Aetna Cas. & Sur. Co. v. Anderson, 200 Va. 385, 105 S.E.2d 869 (1958), construing former § 38-238.

This section and § 38.2-2200 are by force of their provisions, made a part of the policy and were enacted for the benefit of those who suffer damage from the negligent use of the car by one operating it with the permission of the owner, express or implied. Storm v. Nationwide Mut. Ins. Co., 199 Va. 130, 97 S.E.2d 759 (1957).

It is applicable only to policies issued to the owner of an automobile. Clarke v. Harleysville Mut. Cas. Co., 123 F.2d 499 (4th Cir. 1941); Byrd v. American Guarantee & Liab. Ins. Co., 89 F. Supp. 158 (E.D. Va. 1949), aff'd, 180 F.2d 246 (4th Cir. 1950).

It does not make the owner of an automobile liable for the negligence of another simply because such negligent party was operating the car with his permission. Lumbermens Mut. Cas. Co. v. Indemnity Ins. Co. of N. Am., 186 Va. 204, 42 S.E.2d 298 (1947).

Rule of parental immunity anachronistic. — The very high incidence of liability insurance covering Virginia-based motor vehicles, together with the mandatory uninsured motorist endorsements to insurance policies, has made the rule of parental immunity anachronistic when applied to automobile accident litigation. In such litigation, the rule can be no longer supported as generally calculated to promote the peace and tranquility of the home and the advantageous disposal of the parents' exchequer. Smith v. Kauffman, 212 Va. 181, 183 S.E.2d 190 (1971).

Omnibus clause not applicable to personal liability policy. — A contract of insurance known as a "personal and farm liability policy" was not a policy issued upon a motor vehicle to cover liability arising from its ownership, maintenance or use. The policy was not written upon any items of equipment or rolling stock. It was a personal liability policy, and the "omnibus clause" is not applicable to such a policy. Commercial Union Ins. Co. v. St. Paul Fire & Marine Ins. Co., 211 Va. 373, 177 S.E.2d 625 (1970).

The provisions of this section become a part of the contract of insurance, irrespective of any inconsistent provisions therein contained. Prillaman v. Century Indem. Co., 49 F. Supp. 197 (W.D. Va.), aff'd, 138 F.2d 821 (4th Cir. 1943); Newton v. Employers Liab. Assurance Corp., 107 F.2d 164 (4th Cir. 1939), cert. denied, 309 U.S. 673, 60 S. Ct. 616, 84 L. Ed. 1018 (1940); Maxey v. American Cas. Co., 180 Va. 285, 23 S.E.2d 221 (1942); Jordan v. Shelby Mut. Plate Glass & Cas. Co., 51 F. Supp. 240 (W.D. Va. 1943), aff'd, 142 F.2d 52 (4th Cir. 1944); Jenkins v. Morano, 74 F. Supp. 234 (E.D. Va. 1947).

The controlling instrument is the statute and provisions in the insurance policy that conflict with the requirements of the statute, either by adding to or taking from its requirements, are void and ineffective. Bryant v. State Farm Mut. Auto. Ins. Co., 205 Va. 897, 140 S.E.2d 817 (1965); State Farm Mut. Auto. Ins. Co. v. United Serv. Auto. Ass'n, 211 Va. 133, 176 S.E.2d 327 (1970).

This section is by force of its provisions made a part of a liability policy. Rose v. Travelers Indem. Co., 209 Va. 755, 167 S.E.2d 339 (1969).

This section is by force of its provisions made a part of a liability policy, and is to be liberally construed to accomplish its intended purpose. Grange Mut. Cas. Co. v. Criterion Ins. Co., 212 Va. 753, 188 S.E.2d 91 (1972).

By the force of its provisions, this section is made a part of each motor vehicle liability policy to which it applies. Nationwide Mut. Ins. Co. v. Government Employees Ins. Co., 215 Va. 676, 212 S.E.2d 297 (1975).

Construction of insurance contract. — In the case of an ambiguity, the rule is that where the language of an insurance contract is susceptible of two constructions, it is to be construed strictly against the insurer and liberally in favor of the insured. American Fid. Fire Ins. Co. v. Allstate Ins. Co., 212 Va. 302, 184 S.E.2d 11 (1971).

Prompt notice and investigation important under medical payments clause. — The insurer's undertaking, under the typical medical payments clause, is similar to a carrier's obligation in a personal accident policy and does not depend on the insured's negligence. Nonetheless, prompt notice to the insurer and the need for swift investigation of the claim is just as important in the medical payment context as in the liability context. Lord v. State Farm Mut. Auto. Ins. Co., 224 Va. 283, 295 S.E.2d 796 (1982).

There is no significant difference in the need for prompt investigation of a medical payments claim vis-a-vis a liability claim. This is especially true when the insurance policy expressly provides that the notice clause applies with equal force to all coverages under the policy. Thus, the requirement of notice in the medical payment context is no less stringent. Lord v. State Farm Mut. Auto. Ins. Co., 224 Va. 283, 295 S.E.2d 796 (1982).

Necessity of causal connection. — The Supreme Court of Virginia has made clear that there must be a causal connection between the injury and the use of the vehicle as a vehicle. Doe v. State Farm Fire & Cas. Co., 878 F. Supp. 862 (E.D. Va. 1995).

Notice of claim is condition precedent. — Performance of a provision requiring the insured to provide the insurer notice of the claim as soon as possible is a condition precedent to coverage under the insurance contract, requiring substantial compliance by the insured. Lord v. State Farm Mut. Auto. Ins. Co., 224 Va. 283, 295 S.E.2d 796 (1982).

Failure to give notice of accident or suit. — The giving of notice of an accident, the giving of notice of suit, and the forwarding of suit papers are conditions precedent to coverage under an insurance policy where such action by the insured is required by terms of the policy and failure to comply relieves the insurer of any obligations under the policy, regardless of whether the insurer was prejudiced by such conduct of the insured. State Farm Mut. Auto. Ins. Co. v. Porter, 221 Va. 592, 272 S.E.2d 196 (1980); Erie Ins. Exch. v. Meeks, 223 Va. 287, 288 S.E.2d 454 (1982).

Question of timely notice is usually for the fact finder to determine and the insurer need not establish it was prejudiced by violation of the notice provision. Lord v. State Farm Mut. Auto. Ins. Co., 224 Va. 283, 295 S.E.2d 796 (1982).

The mandate of this section may not be avoided and the statutory coverage of the policy narrowed by the method followed in the assessment and collection of premiums. That the Bureau of Insurance may have followed a practice not in conformity with the requirements of the statute cannot change its plain meaning. Newton v. Employers Liab. Assurance Corp., 107 F.2d 164 (4th Cir. 1939), cert. denied, 309 U.S. 673, 60 S. Ct. 616, 84 L. Ed. 1018 (1940).

An automobile insurance policy is not a private one solely between the insurer and the policyholder, vitiable at any time by the act or omission of either. Bernstein v. Nationwide Mut. Ins. Co., 458 F.2d 506 (4th Cir.), appeal dismissed and cert. denied, 409 U.S. 812, 93 S. Ct. 70, 34 L. Ed. 2d 68 (1972), aff'g by an equally divided court, the decision in Nationwide Mut. Ins. Co. v. Stephens, 313 F. Supp. 890 (W.D. Va. 1970), declaring a policy void ab initio for material misrepresentations in the application.

General public is third-party beneficiary of contract. — This section renders the insurer chargeable for money damages awarded against the owner or driver in an action brought by anyone who was injured through the negligent operation of the vehicle. Thus the general public is a third-party beneficiary to the contract of insurance. Bernstein v. Nationwide Mut. Ins. Co., 458 F.2d 506 (4th Cir.), appeal dismissed and cert. denied, 409 U.S. 812, 93 S. Ct. 70, 34 L. Ed. 2d 68 (1972), aff'g by an equally divided court, the decision in Nationwide Mut. Ins. Co. v. Stephens, 313 F. Supp. 890 (W.D. Va. 1970), declaring a policy void ab initio for material misrepresentations in the application.

Insurer cannot exact representations which exceed scope of statutes. — The insurer cannot exact representations from the applicant which exceed the scope of the state's statutes. Bernstein v. Nationwide Mut. Ins. Co., 458 F.2d 506 (4th Cir.), appeal dismissed and cert. denied, 409 U.S. 812, 93 S. Ct. 70, 34 L. Ed. 2d 68 (1972), aff'g by an equally divided court, the decision in Nationwide Mut. Ins. Co. v. Stephens, 313 F. Supp. 890 (W.D. Va. 1970), declaring a policy void ab initio for material misrepresentations in the application.

Insurer's right of rescission. — Even if the insurer may for fraud in its procurement rescind a policy ab initio and withdraw its protection of the named insured alone, this power ought not to exist indefinitely as against the public's right of protection. Bernstein v. Nationwide Mut. Ins. Co., 458 F.2d 506 (4th Cir.), appeal dismissed and cert. denied, 409 U.S. 812, 93 S. Ct. 70, 34 L. Ed. 2d 68 (1972), aff'g by an equally divided court, the decision in Nationwide Mut. Ins. Co. v. Stephens, 313 F. Supp. 890 (W.D. Va. 1970), declaring a policy void ab initio for material misrepresentations in the application.

A rule which would permit an automobile liability insurer indefinitely to postpone determination of the validity of a liability policy and to retain its right to rescind the policy defeats not only the public service obligations of the insurer but also the basic policy of this section, which aims to make owners of motor vehicles financially responsible to those injured by them in the operation of such vehicles. Bernstein v. Nationwide Mut. Ins. Co., 458 F.2d 506 (4th Cir.), appeal dismissed and cert. denied, 409 U.S. 812, 93 S. Ct. 70, 34 L. Ed. 2d 68 (1972), aff'g by an equally divided court, the decision in Nationwide Mut. Ins. Co. v. Stephens, 313 F. Supp. 890 (W.D. Va. 1970), declaring a policy void ab initio for material misrepresentations in the application.

If the insurer is always possessed of the potential of rescission ab initio, the result is to cloud the protection which the State intends for the public. Bernstein v. Nationwide Mut. Ins. Co., 458 F.2d 506 (4th Cir.), appeal dismissed and cert. denied, 409 U.S. 812, 93 S. Ct. 70, 34 L. Ed. 2d 68 (1972), aff'g by an equally divided court, the decision in Nationwide Mut. Ins. Co. v. Stephens, 313 F. Supp. 890 (W.D. Va. 1970), declaring a policy void ab initio for material misrepresentations in the application.

Insurer's remedy for fraud. — When a policy applicant has defrauded the insurance carrier, then the latter's recourse is against the cheater for damages for the imposture but the company should not be permitted to pass any such loss on to the public. Bernstein v. Nationwide Mut. Ins. Co., 458 F.2d 506 (4th Cir.), appeal dismissed and cert. denied, 409 U.S. 812, 93 S. Ct. 70, 34 L. Ed. 2d 68 (1972), aff'g by an equally divided court, the decision in Nationwide Mut. Ins. Co. v. Stephens, 313 F. Supp. 890 (W.D. Va. 1970), declaring a policy void ab initio for material misrepresentations in the application.

Burden of showing prejudice. — The 1966 amendment to subsection (a1) of former § 38.1-381 (see now subsection C of this section) apparently requires prejudice to be shown from the lack of cooperation. Lumbermens Mut. Cas. Co. v. Harleysville Mut. Cas. Co., 287 F. Supp. 932 (W.D. Va. 1968), aff'd, 406 F.2d 836 (4th Cir. 1969).

The insurer must show prejudice when relying on a breach of the "cooperation clause" as a defense. Safeway Moving & Storage Corp. v. Aetna Ins. Co., 317 F. Supp. 238 (E.D. Va. 1970), modified, 452 F.2d 79 (4th Cir. 1971).

The 1966 amendment, which added subsection (a1) of former § 38.1-381 (see now subsection C of this section), in effect requires an insurer to prove prejudice before it has the right to deny coverage because of an insured's failure or refusal to cooperate with the insurer under the terms of the policy. Erie Ins. Exch. v. Meeks, 223 Va. 287, 288 S.E.2d 454 (1982).

Insurer has the burden of proving prejudice under subsection C. State Farm Mut. Auto. Ins. Co. v. Davies, 226 Va. 310, 310 S.E.2d 167 (1983).

Application of 1966 amendment. — The General Assembly intended the 1966 amendment (Acts 1966, c. 182), which added subsection (a1) of § 38.1-381 (see now subsection C of this section), to apply only to the "cooperation" clause of the policy. Erie Ins. Exch. v. Meeks, 223 Va. 287, 288 S.E.2d 454 (1982).

Insurer must show that nonappearance deprived it of evidence to establish jury issue. — In determining whether the insured's failure to cooperate prejudiced the insurer, the Supreme Court favors neither a per se rule that would permit an insurer to show merely that its insured failed to appear at trial nor a rule that would require an insurer to show that, had its insured appeared, the result would have been in his or her favor. Instead, the proper rule lies midway between these two extremes. In an action on the policy, when the insurer shows that the insured's willful failure to appear at the original trial deprived the insurer of evidence which would have made a jury issue of the insured's liability and supported a verdict in his or her favor, the insurer has established a reasonable likelihood the result would have been favorable to the insured and has carried its burden of proving prejudice under subsection C of this section. State Farm Mut. Auto. Ins. Co. v. Davies, 226 Va. 310, 310 S.E.2d 167 (1983).

Beneficiary is anyone injured. — In Virginia anyone injured by the negligence of the insured under the policy is a beneficiary of the policy. Davis v. National Grange Ins. Co., 281 F. Supp. 998 (E.D. Va. 1968).

Delivery of policy. — When an insurer mails a contract of insurance to its agent for unconditional delivery to the insured, delivery is effected when deposited in the mail. Grange Mut. Cas. Co. v. Criterion Ins. Co., 212 Va. 753, 188 S.E.2d 91 (1972).

The General Assembly has required prejudice to be shown under certain circumstances for violation of policy provisions requiring prompt delivery of suit papers to an insurer. However, the General Assembly, obviously aware of the prejudice issue in connection with insurance policy conditions, has not taken such action with reference to consent-to-settlement clauses; thus courts will not engage in judicial legislation on the subject by requiring a showing of prejudice. Osborne v. National Union Fire Ins. Co., 251 Va. 53, 465 S.E.2d 835 (1996).

Policy purchased and delivered and covering automobile titled, licensed and located in another state. — Where an insurance policy was purchased and delivered in Ohio to cover an automobile titled, licensed and then in Ohio, which automobile was to be principally used for weekend trips between Ohio and Norfolk, where the owner was stationed in the navy, there was no requirement that the "omnibus clause" of this section should be included in the policy. Grange Mut. Cas. Co. v. Criterion Ins. Co., 212 Va. 753, 188 S.E.2d 91 (1972).

The exclusion for negligence of an employee is the type of nonstatutory exclusion the legislature sought to prevent by enacting subsection D of this section as the Supreme Court recognized in Southside Distrib. Co. v. Travelers Indem. Co., 213 Va. 38, 189 S.E.2d 681 (1972). Roberts v. Aetna Cas. & Sur. Co., 687 F. Supp. 239 (W.D. Va. 1988).

Applied in Continental Ins. Co. v. State Farm Fire & Cas. Co., 238 Va. 209, 380 S.E.2d 661 (1989).

II. LIABILITY COVERED.

Severability of interests clause shall be deemed to restrict the definition of "insured" to the person claiming coverage under the particular policy provisions. Bankers & Shippers Ins. Co. v. Watson, 216 Va. 807, 224 S.E.2d 312 (1976).

Policy must cover liability of operator even though owner is not liable. — The reasonable construction of this section is that all automobile liability policies issued within the State shall contain the widely used omnibus coverage clause, covering liability of anyone operating the car with the permission of the owner, whether the owner is liable or not. Newton v. Employers Liab. Assurance Corp., 107 F.2d 164 (4th Cir. 1939), cert. denied, 309 U.S. 673, 60 S. Ct. 616, 84 L. Ed. 1018 (1940); Maxey v. American Cas. Co., 180 Va. 285, 23 S.E.2d 221 (1942).

Under this section a policy of automobile accident public liability insurance should be construed as covering the liability of a person operating a car with the consent of the insured owner, but under such circumstances as not to impose liability on the owner, and a garage liability policy falls within the rule. Newton v. Employers Liab. Assurance Corp., 107 F.2d 164 (4th Cir. 1939), cert. denied, 309 U.S. 673, 60 S. Ct. 616, 84 L. Ed. 1018 (1940).

Non-owned vehicles excluded. — The "express or implied consent" language of subsection (B) of § 38.2-2206 modifies "the motor vehicle to which the policy applies" clause. If the Legislature, in the uninsured motorist statute, had meant to include as insureds of the second class occupants of non-owned vehicles, then the General Assembly would have used language similar to that in subsection (A) of this section, which deals with the sort of permission needed when one is operating a non-owned vehicle. Therefore, "the vehicle" referred to in subsection (B) of § 38.2-2206 includes only owned, not non-owned vehicles. Thus, there is no statutory mandate that requires the courts to ignore the insurer's policy language as written. Stone v. Liberty Mut. Ins. Co., 253 Va. 12, 478 S.E.2d 883 (1996).

Liability is not limited to acts of negligence in the operation of the motor vehicle in the business of the owner. Liberty Mut. Ins. Co. v. Tiller, 189 Va. 544, 53 S.E.2d 814 (1949); Coureas v. Allstate Ins. Co., 198 Va. 77, 92 S.E.2d 378 (1956); Aetna Cas. & Sur. Co. v. Anderson, 200 Va. 385, 105 S.E.2d 869 (1958), construing former § 38-238.

Agreements as to limitations and restrictions are permitted. — This section was not intended to change the rule regarding the right of the insurer and the insured to agree upon reasonable limitations and restrictions of coverage. Lumbermens Mut. Cas. Co. v. Indemnity Ins. Co. of N. Am., 186 Va. 204, 42 S.E.2d 298 (1947).

Omnibus coverage clause required. — Every automobile liability policy sold in Virginia is required by the statute to contain an omnibus coverage clause extending the same coverage to one operating a motor vehicle with the owner's permission as that given the named insured. Liberty Mut. Ins. Co. v. Venable, 194

Va. 357, 73 S.E.2d 366 (1952), construing former § 38-238.

A salient aim of the omnibus clause is to establish a more comprehensive provision for the public by conferring financial answerability upon any driver. Bernstein v. Nationwide Mut. Ins. Co., 458 F.2d 506 (4th Cir.), appeal dismissed and cert. denied, 409 U.S. 812, 93 S. Ct. 70, 34 L. Ed. 2d 68 (1972), aff'g by an equally divided court, the decision in Nationwide Mut. Ins. Co. v. Stephens, 313 F. Supp. 890 (W.D. Va. 1970), declaring a policy void ab initio for material misrepresentations in the application.

One of the omnibus clause's principal aims is to establish a more comprehensive provision for the public by conferring financial answerability upon any driver. Emick v. Dairyland Ins. Co., 519 F.2d 1317 (4th Cir. 1975).

The legislature did not by the enactment of the omnibus clause intend to convert a liability policy into a policy covering first-party loss. What the legislature did intend was not an expansion of coverage but a prohibition of nonstatutory exclusions within the coverage afforded. Safeco Ins. Co. of Am. v. Merrimack Mut. Fire Ins. Co., 785 F.2d 480 (4th Cir. 1986).

Burden of proof is on the party seeking to bring himself within the omnibus-coverage clause of automobile insurance policy. Hartford Fire Ins. Co. v. Davis, 246 Va. 495, 436 S.E.2d 429 (1993).

The purpose of subsection D is to prohibit the issuance of policies containing exclusions permitted under the Supreme Court's previous interpretation of the "omnibus clause." Southside Distrib. Co. v. Travelers Indem. Co., 213 Va. 38, 189 S.E.2d 681 (1972); United States v. GEICO, 409 F. Supp. 986 (E.D. Va. 1976).

Subsection D insulates the insured from limitations placed on his insurance coverage in the form of nonstatutory exclusions from the omnibus clause of the insurance contract. United States v. GEICO, 409 F. Supp. 986 (E.D. Va. 1976).

Subsection D does not permit a nonstatutory omnibus clause exclusion into its automobile liability policies and, in the absence of federal preemption of the Virginia statute, the Virginia insurance law governs the contract between the insured and the insurer. United States v. GEICO, 409 F. Supp. 986 (E.D. Va. 1976).

The United States is an insured within the provisions of subsection A. United States v. GEICO, 409 F. Supp. 986 (E.D. Va. 1976).

Subsection D and 28 U.S.C. § 2679(b)-(e) share a common purpose of affording maximum protection to the operator of a motor vehicle. United States v. GEICO, 409 F. Supp. 986 (E.D. Va. 1976).

The concurrent operation of 28 U.S.C. § 2679(b)-(e) and subsection D has the result of making a federal employee's automobile liability insurance carrier an indemnitor of the United States for the negligence of its employees. United States v. GEICO, 409 F. Supp. 986 (E.D. Va. 1976).

Under the Virginia insurance scheme, a federal employee has the protection of both private insurance coverage and the Federal Drivers Act if he so chooses. United States v. GEICO, 409 F. Supp. 986 (E.D. Va. 1976).

A conflict does not exist in the operation of 28 U.S.C. § 2679(b) and subsection D. United States v. GEICO, 409 F. Supp. 986 (E.D. Va. 1976).

Postjudgment interest extra-contractual obligation. — Although the insurer's duty to pay damages is a contractual liability, enforced by the insurance statutes, the duty to pay postjudgment interest is an extra-contractual obligation that is imposed as a statutory penalty for failure to pay a liquidated debt when due. Dairyland Ins. Co. v. Douthat, 248 Va. 627, 449 S.E.2d 799 (1994).

No prejudgment interest duty fund. — Because no such obligation is imposed by § 8.01-382 or any other statute, an insurer has no duty to pay prejudgment interest in excess of its policy limits, absent a contractual provision to the contrary. Dairyland Ins. Co. v. Douthat, 248 Va. 627, 449 S.E.2d 799 (1994).

Exclusions not expressly authorized are prohibited. — The "omnibus clause," as amended by subsection D, prohibits any exclusions from policy coverage except those expressly provided for by statute. Southside Distrib. Co. v. Travelers Indem. Co., 213 Va. 38, 189 S.E.2d 681 (1972); United States v. GEICO, 409 F. Supp. 986 (E.D. Va. 1976).

The phrase "by statute" employed by the court in Southside Distrib. Co. v. Travelers Indem. Co., 213 Va. 38, 189 S.E.2d 681 (1972), makes reference to Virginia statutory exclusions only and not to exclusions permitted by the Federal Drivers Act, 28 U.S.C. § 2679(b)-(e). United States v. GEICO, 409 F. Supp. 986 (E.D. Va. 1976).

Subsection D prohibits any exclusions other than those expressly allowed by a Virginia statute. United States v. GEICO, 409 F. Supp. 986 (E.D. Va. 1976).

The exclusions permitted under subsection D do not include those permitted by the Federal Drivers Act, 28 U.S.C. § 2679(b)-(e). United States v. GEICO, 409 F. Supp. 986 (E.D. Va. 1976).

Provision in boat owner's insurance policy that policy did not apply to bodily injury to named insured or any relative if resident of same household did not violate this section. Safeco Ins. Co. of Am. v. Merrimack Mut. Fire Ins. Co., 785 F.2d 480 (4th Cir. 1986).

When subsection A applicable. — Subsection A is applicable when a policy covering liability for bodily injury arising out of the ownership or use of a motor vehicle is (1) "issued or delivered in this State to the owner of such vehicle," or (2) when "issued or delivered by any insurer licensed in this State upon any motor vehicle ... then principally garaged ... or principally used in this State." Rose v. Travelers Indem. Co., 209 Va. 755, 167 S.E.2d 339 (1969).

The key word "then" in subsection A refers to the place where the car is principally garaged or principally used at the time the policy is issued, and not where it is principally garaged or principally used at a subsequent time. Rose v. Travelers Indem. Co., 209 Va. 755, 167 S.E.2d 339 (1969).

Permissive user furnished same coverage as named insured. — Subsection A requires each policy of automobile liability insurance to furnish a permissive user the same coverage as is afforded the named insured. American Motorists Ins. Co. v. Kaplan, 209 Va. 53, 161 S.E.2d 675 (1968); Hardware Mut. Cas. Co. v. Celina Mut. Ins. Co., 209 Va. 60, 161 S.E.2d 680 (1968); Hardware Mut. Cas. Co. v. General Accident Fire & Life Assurance Corp., 212 Va. 780, 188 S.E.2d 218 (1972).

A restriction which denies any protection to a permissive user under the policy who has other valid and collectible automobile liability insurance available to him is void. American Motorists Ins. Co. v. Kaplan, 209 Va. 53, 161 S.E.2d 675 (1968); Hardware Mut. Cas. Co. v. Celina Mut. Ins. Co, 209 Va. 60, 161 S.E.2d 680 (1968).

Coverage for permissive user of nonowned vehicle not required. — The omnibus statute, subsection A, does not require that coverage be afforded a permissive user of a nonowned vehicle. It only requires that the owner's policy extend coverage to a permissive user for liability "resulting in the operation or use of such [owner's] vehicle ...." American Motorists Ins. Co. v. Kaplan, 209 Va. 53, 161 S.E.2d 675 (1968); Hardware Mut. Cas. Co. v. Celina Mut. Ins. Co., 209 Va. 60, 161 S.E.2d 680 (1968).

Coverage for insured although insurer paid limits on permissive user's behalf. — This section required an insurance company, which had issued an automobile liability insurance policy, to provide full and separate coverage to its named insured who was allegedly guilty of negligent entrustment of a vehicle, even though the insurer had already paid the insurance policy limits on behalf of a permissive user who negligently operated the insured vehicle. Haislip v. Southern Heritage Ins. Co., 254 Va. 265, 492 S.E.2d 135 (1997).

Policy may not be conditioned on representations as to persons who may use car. — To allow an insurance carrier to condition the policy on representations as to persons other than the owner, or members of his household who might use the car, would impermissibly confine effectuation of this section's objective. Bernstein v. Nationwide Mut. Ins. Co., 458 F.2d 506 (4th Cir.), appeal dismissed and cert. denied, 409 U.S. 812, 93 S. Ct. 70, 34 L. Ed. 2d 68 (1972), aff'g by an equally divided court, the decision in Nationwide Mut. Ins. Co. v. Stephens, 313 F. Supp. 890 (W.D. Va. 1970), declaring a policy void ab initio for material misrepresentations in the application.

Carrier must honor coverage of any permissive user. — With the policy once issued, the carrier is bound by law to honor, for the benefit of the public, its coverage of any permissive user of the car. Hence, no matter the record of any driver, besides the applicant for the policy or members of his household, this section guarantees the driver's solvency. Bernstein v. Nationwide Mut. Ins. Co., 458 F.2d 506 (4th Cir.), appeal dismissed and cert. denied, 409 U.S. 812, 93 S. Ct. 70, 34 L. Ed. 2d 68 (1972), aff'g by an equally divided court, the decision in Nationwide Mut. Ins. Co. v. Stephens, 313 F. Supp. 890 (W.D. Va. 1970), declaring a policy void ab initio for material misrepresentations in the application.

Injuries to insured may be excepted. — An automobile liability policy had provisions precluding coverage for bodily injuries sustained by the insured while the automobile was being operated by another with his permission. These provisions were not void as being in conflict with this section requiring automobile liability policies to contain a clause covering liability of anyone operating an automobile with the owner's permission. Jenkins v. Morano, 74 F. Supp. 234 (E.D. Va. 1947).

Member of household. — One may be held a member of a household within a provision extending coverage though not for purposes of policy exclusion. White v. Nationwide Mut. Ins. Co., 245 F. Supp. 1 (W.D. Va. 1965), aff'd, 361 F.2d 785 (4th Cir. 1966).

When a plaintiff went to stay with her parents and remained with them until her husband rejoined her, during which time plaintiff ate, slept, and lived at the home of her parents, her relationship to her family being the same as before she was married, it was held that plaintiff was a member of the household of her father. White v. Nationwide Mut. Ins. Co., 245 F. Supp. 1 (W.D. Va. 1965), aff'd, 361 F.2d 785 (4th Cir. 1966).

A named insured could not recover from his liability insurance carrier for damage to his own property when the policy excluded from coverage property owned by "the insured" where the term "the insured" necessarily referred to and embraced the named insured. Transit Cas. Co. v. Hartman's, Inc., 218 Va. 703, 239 S.E.2d 894 (1978).

Accidental discharge of firearm in vehicle held not covered. — Injury caused by the discharge (the cause of which was unknown) of a shotgun mounted on a rack in a stopped pickup truck was not covered under an automobile liability insurance policy, since it did not arise out of the ownership, maintenance, or use of the vehicle, within the meaning of the insurance contract. State Farm Mut. Auto. Ins. Co. v. Powell, 227 Va. 492, 318 S.E.2d 393 (1984).

Sexual assault in vehicle not covered. — Standard uninsured motorist provision of a Virginia automobile insurance policy did not provide coverage for incident in which insured was abducted in a stolen vehicle, transported to an isolated location, and sexually assaulted within the automobile. Doe v. State Farm Fire & Cas. Co., 878 F. Supp. 862 (E.D. Va. 1995).

III. CONSENT OF INSURED.

The issue under this section is not one of agency but one of permission — a pointedly different thing. When an owner entrusts his vehicle to another, to use it for the bailee's own purposes, the owner is not liable for the bailee's negligence, because there is no relation of agency between them. The bailee, however, is covered under the omnibus clause of the insurance policy because it does not require the existence of an agency, but merely that the bailee shall have acted with the permission of the insured owner. Utica Mut. Ins. Co. v. Rollason, 246 F.2d 105 (4th Cir. 1957).

The issue under this section is not one of agency but one of permission. Aetna Cas. & Sur. Co. v. Anderson, 200 Va. 385, 105 S.E.2d 869 (1958), construing former § 38-238.

The permission, "express or implied," must be either an express permission or a permission reasonably to be implied from the circumstances of the case. This means the express or implied permission to use or operate the motor vehicle either in the business of the owner or for any other purpose for which express permission was given or as to which it may be implied that permission was given. Permission to do a specific thing is not permission to do all things. Sordelett v. Mercer, 185 Va. 823, 40 S.E.2d 289 (1946); State Farm Mut. Auto. Ins. Co. v. Cook, 186 Va. 658, 43 S.E.2d 863 (1947); Liberty Mut. Ins. Co. v. Tiller, 189 Va. 544, 53 S.E.2d 814 (1949); Fidelity & Cas. Co. v. Harlow, 191 Va. 64, 59 S.E.2d 872 (1950). But see Jones v. New York Cas. Co., 23 F. Supp. 932 (E.D. Va. 1938); Liberty Mut. Ins. Co. v. Venable, 194 Va. 357, 73 S.E.2d 366 (1952), construing former § 38-238.

An implied permission to drive an automobile, within the meaning of this section, is not confined to affirmative action. It involves an inference arising from a course of conduct or relationship between the parties, in which there is mutual acquiescence or lack of objec-

tion under circumstances signifying assent. The permission, to be express, must be of an affirmative character, directly and distinctly stated, clear and outspoken, and not merely implied or left to inference. Hinton v. Indemnity Ins. Co. of N. Am., 175 Va. 205, 8 S.E.2d 279 (1940); Aetna Cas. & Sur. Co. v. Anderson, 200 Va. 385, 105 S.E.2d 869 (1958), construing former § 38-238.

Implied permission may arise from a course of conduct between the parties and such permission has a negative rather than an affirmative implication; that is, a permitted act may be one not specifically prohibited as contrasted to an act affirmatively and specifically authorized. Coureas v. Allstate Ins. Co., 198 Va. 77, 92 S.E.2d 378 (1956); Liberty Mut. Ins. Co. v. Mueller, 432 F. Supp. 325 (W.D. Va. 1977), aff'd, 570 F.2d 508 (4th Cir. 1978); Hartford Fire Ins. Co. v. Davis, 246 Va. 495, 436 S.E.2d 429 (1993).

Implied permission arises from either a course of conduct involving a mutual acquiescence in, or a lack of objection to, a continued use of the automobile, signifying consent. Liberty Mut. Ins. Co. v. Mueller, 432 F. Supp. 325 (W.D. Va. 1977), aff'd, 570 F.2d 508 (4th Cir. 1978).

When "implied permission" interpreted more liberally. — The more liberal interpretation of "implied permission" should result when the original permission was granted in furtherance of personal or social purposes. Liberty Mut. Ins. Co. v. Mueller, 432 F. Supp. 325 (W.D. Va. 1977), aff'd, 570 F.2d 508 (4th Cir. 1978).

And when interpreted more strictly. — A stricter interpretation of "implied permission" should result when the original permission of the named insured was given in furtherance of his own business purposes. Liberty Mut. Ins. Co. v. Mueller, 432 F. Supp. 325 (W.D. Va. 1977), aff'd, 570 F.2d 508 (4th Cir. 1978).

Assumption of permission. — A general permission, or a comprehensive permission, is much more readily to be assumed where the use of the car is for social or nonbusiness purposes. Emick v. Dairyland Ins. Co., 519 F.2d 1317 (4th Cir. 1975).

Owner need not know identity of operator. — To support liability predicated upon implied permission, it is not necessary that the owner of the automobile be aware of the identity of the person operating it or know of the particular use being made of it at the time of the accident. American Auto. Ins. Co. v. Fulcher, 201 F.2d 751 (4th Cir. 1953); Bernstein v. Nationwide Mut. Ins. Co., 458 F.2d 506 (4th Cir.), appeal dismissed and cert. denied, 409 U.S. 812, 93 S. Ct. 70, 34 L. Ed. 2d 68 (1972), aff'g by an equally divided court, the decision in Nationwide Mut. Ins. Co. v. Stephens, 313 F. Supp. 890 (W.D. Va. 1970), declaring a policy void ab initio for material misrepresentations in the application.

In order for coverage to apply, it is not necessary that the owner know the identity of the person operating the car with his implied permission. United States Fid. & Guar. Co. v. Trussell, 208 F. Supp. 154 (W.D. Va. 1962).

Automobile driven by guest of person to whom it was lent. — The owner of an insured automobile delivered it to another to use over the weekend, with option to purchase. Such user permitted one of his guests to drive the automobile while he and others rode therein, and a fatal accident resulted. It was held that at the time of the accident the prospective purchaser was using the automobile within the terms of this section, and that the general permission given by the owner was sufficient to include this type of use. Prillaman v. Century Indem. Co., 49 F. Supp. 197 (W.D. Va.), aff'd, 138 F.2d 821 (4th Cir. 1943).

Leaving automobile with one who permits its use by another. — If an insured automobile is left by the owner with someone for general use and he in turn permits its use by another, the use is deemed to be with the permission of the owner. Utica Mut. Ins. Co. v. Rollason, 246 F.2d 105 (4th Cir. 1957).

The evidence was sufficient to support the finding that an automobile furnished by the named insured, a motor service company, to its service manager, was furnished with permission to make general use of the automobile including use for personal purposes; that the service manager had implied permission to lend the automobile to his son for personal use; and that the use of the vehicle by the son, for the purpose in which he was engaged at the time of the accident, was with his father's unrestricted permission and hence, in legal contemplation, with the permission of the named insured. Utica Mut. Ins. Co. v. Rollason, 246 F.2d 105 (4th Cir. 1957).

When a finance company, after repossession, placed a car on the lot of a car dealer, it gave permission to the dealer to use the car to promote sale and implied permission to anyone with whom the dealer placed it in efforts to effectuate the sale, thus a prospective purchaser had implied permission to drive the car within the meaning of the finance company's liability insurance issued in conformance with this section. United States Fid. & Guar. Co. v. Trussell, 208 F. Supp. 154 (W.D. Va. 1962).

One with whom the named insured has left a vehicle for general use may permit its use by another, who will be deemed to have the permission of the named insured. Virginia Farm Bureau Mut. Ins. Co. v. APCO, 228 Va. 72, 321 S.E.2d 84 (1984).

Only if the named insured had given another general use of the vehicle could the one to whom use had been given bring a third person within the policy coverage by granting him permissive use. Virginia Farm Bureau Mut. Ins. Co. v. APCO, 228 Va. 72, 321 S.E.2d 84 (1984).

Permission may be withdrawn. — Even if a vehicle is left with another for general use, the permission for general use may be withdrawn. Virginia Farm Bureau Mut. Ins. Co. v. APCO, 228 Va. 72, 321 S.E.2d 84 (1984).

Permission for general use is question of fact. — Whether there is permission to use a car is generally a question of fact. If the evidence is not conflicting, of course, the question of implied permission to use a car is not for the jury. Virginia Farm Bureau Mut. Ins. Co. v. APCO, 228 Va. 72, 321 S.E.2d 84 (1984).

Deviation from permitted use. — In addition to whether permission has been given a person using a motor vehicle at the time of an accident, there is the question in respect to the coverage under the omnibus clause where there has been a deviation from the permitted use. Permission will not be implied from employer to employee where the employee goes off on an independent venture which is totally unrelated to the employer's business. Aetna Cas. & Sur. Co. v. Anderson, 200 Va. 385, 105 S.E.2d 869 (1958), construing former § 38-238.

Employee driving car contrary to instructions of employer was not operating it with his permission within the meaning of this section, and such employee was not additional insured under the omnibus clause of the employer's public liability insurance policy. Jordan v. Shelby Mut. Plate Glass & Cas. Co., 142 F.2d 52 (4th Cir. 1944).

An employee drove his employer's car to town on a business purpose and, contrary to the instructions of his employer, took a friend with him. Upon being instructed by his employer to spend the night in town, the employee drove the car back for the purpose of returning the friend. It was held that the employee was not at that time operating the car with the permission of his employer. Jordan v. Shelby Mut. Plate Glass & Cas. Co., 51 F. Supp. 240 (W.D. Va. 1943), aff'd, 142 F.2d 52 (4th Cir. 1944).

Where the driver of a tractor-trailer, who detached the tractor from the trailer and used it on a personal pleasure trip, not only was never given permission to use the tractor at any time except on the business of the owner, but had been given express instructions forbidding him to use it for his personal benefit, and had been told that in case of a violation of the instructions he would be summarily dismissed, such driver was not an additional insured under an omnibus clause in an insurance policy. Fidelity & Cas. Co. v. Harlow, 191 Va. 64, 59 S.E.2d 872 (1950).

An employee on the night of the accident had been told to drive a fellow employee to his home in the employer's truck and there unload fertilizer. Under a plant rule, which he admittedly understood, he was then to take the vehicle to his own home and park it for the night. Personal use by him was expressly prohibited. Instead, he detoured by a store and to a different house, where he and his passenger drank beer. The accident occurred on the way from this house. There being no real conflict in the evidence on these points, it appeared as a matter of law that the employee had no permission to use the truck at the time of the collision and the trial court should not have let the case go to the jury. Aetna Cas. & Sur. Co. v. Anderson, 200 Va. 385, 105 S.E.2d 869 (1958), construing former § 38-238.

Where employee had permission to use employer's car but was specifically prohibited from lending it to anyone else, another employee who was driving the automobile at the time of the accident was not driving it with the implied permission of the insured. Hopson v. Shelby Mut. Cas. Co., 203 F.2d 434 (4th Cir. 1953), construing former § 38-238.

If permission is procured by fraud, then it is not a true permission contemplated by the omnibus clause in the liability policy. There would be no meeting of the minds under the circumstances and therefore no consent. Fraud perpetrated by a permittee vitiates the alleged assent itself and he becomes a converter of the vehicle the moment he takes possession of it. Hodge v. Lumbermens Mut. Cas. Co., 203 Va. 275, 123 S.E.2d 372 (1962).

Issue of fraudulently procured permission for jury. — The entire evidence upon which defendant relied was not sufficient to hold that there was fraud in the procurement of permission, as a matter of law, and this issue was one for the jury to decide. Hodge v. Lumbermens Mut. Cas. Co., 203 Va. 275, 123 S.E.2d 372 (1962).

Emergency circumstances exception. — Generally, coverage under the omnibus clause would not extend beyond the first permittee when the named insured has expressly prohibited operation of the vehicle by another; an exception to this general rule is based on circumstances that require the first permittee to transfer operation of the vehicle to another; under emergency circumstances such an exception is appropriate and should support a finding of implied consent by the named insured, thereby qualifying the substitute driver for insurance coverage as a permissive user under the omnibus clause. State Farm Mut. Auto. Ins. Co. v. GEICO Indem. Co., 241 Va. 326, 402 S.E.2d 21 (1991).

The elements which must be shown to support the emergency circumstances exception includes the definition of emergency as an unforeseen combination of circumstances or the resulting state that calls for immediate action; there is no requirement that the "combination of circumstances" be a life threatening event, but mere convenience will not activate the exception. State Farm Mut. Auto. Ins. Co. v. GEICO Indem. Co., 241 Va. 326, 402 S.E.2d 21 (1991).

The facts of each case must be examined to determine whether the reason for the incapacity of the permittee was unforeseen and a substitution of drivers was required. State Farm Mut. Auto. Ins. Co. v. GEICO Indem. Co., 241 Va. 326, 402 S.E.2d 21 (1991).

The driver's evaluation of his or her own ability to drive, while not demonstrative, is probative of the need for a replacement driver; the ultimate issue, however, is whether the driver acted as a reasonable person under the circumstances. State Farm Mut. Auto. Ins. Co. v. GEICO Indem. Co., 241 Va. 326, 402 S.E.2d 21 (1991).

The nature of the emergency will dictate the second permittee's subsequent operation of the vehicle. Not all emergencies require a trip to a medical facility or to a destination other than that originally intended; continuing the trip as the first permittee originally intended may be reasonable as well as beneficial to such permittee. State Farm Mut. Auto. Ins. Co. v. GEICO Indem. Co., 241 Va. 326, 402 S.E.2d 21 (1991).

The subsequent use or destination of the vehicle may be probative evidence as to whether the first permittee was faced with circumstances requiring a change of drivers. State Farm Mut. Auto. Ins. Co. v. GEICO Indem. Co., 241 Va. 326, 402 S.E.2d 21 (1991).

The implied permission given the second permittee to operate the vehicle terminates when the emergency subsides. State Farm Mut. Auto. Ins. Co. v. GEICO Indem. Co., 241 Va. 326, 402 S.E.2d 21 (1991).

Burden of proof. — Where plaintiff obtained judgment against insured's employee for injuries sustained in accident while riding in insured's truck driven by employee and seeks to recover against insurance company under "omnibus clause" of automobile policy issued to insured, plaintiff had burden of proving that employee was, at time of the accident, driving the truck with permission express or implied of the insured. Liberty Mut. Ins. Co. v. Venable, 194 Va. 357, 73 S.E.2d 366 (1952), construing former § 38-238. See Hopson v. Shelby Mut. Cas. Co., 203 F.2d 434 (4th Cir. 1953).

The plaintiff has the burden of proof on the issue of permissive use. Emick v. Dairyland Ins. Co., 519 F.2d 1317 (4th Cir. 1975).

The burden of proof is on the party alleging express or implied permission given by a named insured for another driver to operate an automobile. Liberty Mut. Ins. Co. v. Mueller, 432 F. Supp. 325 (W.D. Va. 1977), aff'd, 570 F.2d 508 (4th Cir. 1978).

Grant and withdrawal of permission are jury questions. — It is for the jury to determine whether permission for general use was given, and, if so, whether it was withdrawn. Virginia Farm Bureau Mut. Ins. Co. v. APCO, 228 Va. 72, 321 S.E.2d 84 (1984).

Issue of implied permission for jury. — Where a bailor gives express permission to a bailee, within a social context, to operate an automobile, and does not give specific limiting instructions, the jury is empowered to decide whether, under all the circumstances, the bailee also has implied permission to use the automobile for a personal errand or other social purposes not utterly inconsistent with the purposes of the bailor. Emick v. Dairyland Ins. Co., 519 F.2d 1317 (4th Cir. 1975).

The question of whether a named insured gave implied permission to another driver to operate an automobile is a jury question. Liberty Mut. Ins. Co. v. Mueller, 432 F. Supp. 325 (W.D. Va. 1977), aff'd, 570 F.2d 508 (4th Cir. 1978).

Evidence held sufficient for submission to jury of question whether employee was using car with the permission, express or implied, of his employer. Travelers Indem. Co. v. Neal, 176 F.2d 380 (4th Cir. 1949).

Evidence held to show implied consent of owner of car for its use by his brother. American Auto. Ins. Co. v. Fulcher, 201 F.2d 751

(4th Cir. 1953), construing former § 38-238.

Where the evidence shows that a contract of personal injury or property damage liability insurance containing an omnibus clause has been issued, and that the insured and his wife are living together as husband and wife prior to, at the time of and subsequent to a collision in which the wife was driving the insured vehicle, the jury is entitled to find, absent proof to the contrary, that, at the time of the accident, the wife was driving with her husband's implied consent. Coureas v. Allstate Ins. Co., 198 Va. 77, 92 S.E.2d 378 (1956).

Where insured lessee had knowledge of and acquiesced in use of tractor by lessor, and where primary purpose of such use was to maintain the tractor in good repair, a duty imposed upon lessor by the terms of the lease, the court found that lessor used the tractor with the implied permission of the lessee. Bankers & Shippers Ins. Co. v. Watson, 216 Va. 807, 224 S.E.2d 312 (1976).

Review of jury's verdict. — Because the issue of permissive use is one of fact, the jury's verdict will not be disturbed unless it is "contrary to the evidence, without evidence to support it, or a 'plain deviation from right and justice.'" Emick v. Dairyland Ins. Co., 519 F.2d 1317 (4th Cir. 1975).

§ 38.2-2205. Liability insurance on motor vehicles; standard provisions; applicability of other valid and collectible insurance. — A. 1. Each policy or contract of bodily injury or property damage liability insurance which provides insurance to a named insured in connection with the business of selling, leasing, repairing, servicing, storing or parking motor vehicles, against liability arising from the ownership, maintenance, or use of any motor vehicle incident thereto shall contain a provision that the insurance coverage applicable to those motor vehicles shall not be applicable to a person other than the named insured and his employees in the course of their employment if there is any other valid and collectible insurance applicable to the same loss covering the other person under a policy with limits at least equal to the financial responsibility requirements specified in § 46.2-472. Such provision shall apply to motor vehicles which are either for the purpose of demonstrating to the other person as a prospective purchaser, or which are loaned or leased to the other person as a convenience during the repairing or servicing of a motor vehicle for the other person, or leased to the other person for a period of six months or more. This provision shall apply whether such repair or service is performed by the owner of the vehicle being loaned or leased or by some other person or business.

2. If the other valid and collectible insurance has limits less than the financial responsibility requirements specified in § 46.2-472, then the coverage afforded a person other than the named insured and his employees in the course of their employment shall be applicable to the extent necessary to equal the financial responsibility requirements specified in § 46.2-472.

3. If there is no other valid and collectible insurance available, the coverage under such policy afforded a person, other than the named insured and his employees in the course of their employment, shall be applicable, but the amount recoverable in such case shall not exceed the financial responsibility requirements specified in § 46.2-472. If there is no other valid and collectible

collision or upset insurance available and if such policy provides insurance to the named insured for collision or upset, it shall include any such other person as an additional insured, unless in the case of a leased vehicle such other person receives a conspicuous written disclosure at the commencement of the lease, warning such person that he is not an additional insured under the owner's policy for collision or upset coverage.

B. 1. Any policy or contract of bodily injury or property damage liability insurance relating to the ownership, maintenance, or use of a motor vehicle shall exclude coverage to persons other than (i) the named insured, or (ii) directors, stockholders, partners, agents, or employees of the named insured, or (iii) residents of the household of either (i) or (ii), while those persons are employed or otherwise engaged in the business of selling, repairing, servicing, storing, or parking motor vehicles if there is any other valid or collectible insurance applicable to the same loss covering the persons under a policy with limits at least equal to the financial responsibility requirements specified in § 46.2-472.

2. If the other valid and collectible insurance has limits less than the financial responsibility requirements specified in § 46.2-472, then the coverage afforded a person other than the named insured while that person is employed or otherwise engaged in the business of selling, repairing, servicing, storing, or parking motor vehicles shall be applicable to the extent necessary to equal the financial responsibility requirements specified in § 46.2-472.

3. If there is no other valid and collectible insurance available, the coverage afforded a person other than the named insured while that person is employed or otherwise engaged in the business of selling, repairing, servicing, storing, or parking motor vehicles shall apply, but the amount recoverable shall not exceed the financial responsibility requirements specified in § 46.2-472. (Code 1950, § 38-238; 1952, c. 317, § 38.1-381; 1958, c. 282; 1959, Ex. Sess., cc. 42, 70; 1970, c. 462; 1962, c. 457; 1964, c. 477; 1966, cc. 182, 459; 1968, cc. 199, 721; 1970, c. 494; 1971, Ex. Sess., c. 216; 1973, cc. 225, 390; 1974, c. 87; 1976, cc. 121, 122; 1977, c. 78; 1979, c. 113; 1980, cc. 326, 331; 1981, Sp. Sess., c. 6; 1982, cc. 638, 642; 1984, c. 541; 1985, cc. 39, 325; 1986, c. 562; 1987, c. 685; 1992, c. 474.)

Law Review. — For comment on "other insurance" clauses in garage liability policies, see 26 Wash. & Lee L. Rev. 47 (1969). For comment discussing primary liability under excess insurance clauses, see 13 U. Rich. L. Rev. 165 (1978).

Editor's note. — See also the case annotations under the heading "I. General Consideration" under § 38.2-2204.

Subdivision A 1 is as much a part of policy as if incorporated therein. — The statutory provisions of subdivision A 1 of this section are as much a part of a liability policy issued to a long-term lessor as if incorporated therein. Aetna Cas. & Sur. Co. v. National Union Fire Ins., 233 Va. 49, 353 S.E.2d 894 (1987).

Subdivision A 1 inapplicable to uninsured motorist coverage. — The language of subdivision A 1, defining an exception to coverage afforded a permissive user under a garage liability policy, is inapplicable to uninsured motorist coverage. GEICO v. Universal Underwriters Ins. Co., 232 Va. 326, 350 S.E.2d 612 (1986).

Where "other insurance" clauses of two policies **are of identical effect** in that they operate mutually to reduce or eliminate the amount of collectible insurance available, neither provides primary coverage and pro rata distribution as ordered by the trial court is appropriate. Aetna Cas. & Sur. Co. v. National Union Fire Ins., 233 Va. 49, 353 S.E.2d 894 (1987).

"Business of leasing." — Where a finance company provided the blank lease documents for use by dealerships, approved the leases before the dealership entered into them, purchased the vehicles, took assignments of the leases, assumed all of the duties and rights of ownership of the leased vehicles, and performed administrative duties during the term of the leases, it was found to be "in the business of leasing" within the meaning of the statute. Jaynes v. Becker, 256 Va. 187, 501 S.E.2d 402 (1998).

Finance company's acknowledgment that it was "in the business of financing" was not factually inconsistent with its contention that it was a "named insured" in an insurance policy issued "in connection with the business of leasing." Jaynes v. Becker, 256 Va. 187, 501 S.E.2d 402 (1998).

Where a finance company was found to be in the "business of leasing" within the meaning of this section, and the lessee/driver was person- ally uninsured, the limitation of liability cover- age under the policy in which the finance com- pany was the named insured, applied. Jaynes v. Becker, 256 Va. 187, 501 S.E.2d 402 (1998).

§ 38.2-2205.1. Suspension of liability coverage at insured's request.

— A. Each insurer issuing or delivering a policy or contract of motor vehicle insurance that includes coverage for bodily injury or property damage liability arising from the ownership, maintenance or use of any motor vehicle as provided in this chapter, shall suspend any coverage for any motor vehicle at the request of a named insured ordered to military duty outside this Common- wealth, or his personal representative, during any period that the motor vehicle is impounded in a motor vehicle impound lot on a military base of the United States Armed Forces, the Reserves of the United States Armed Forces or the National Guard. However, an insurer may decline to suspend such coverage (i) unless satisfactory evidence of such impoundment is furnished to it, or (ii) if the period for which coverage suspension is requested is less than thirty days. The suspended coverage shall be reinstated upon request of the named insured, or his personal representative, effective not earlier than the receipt of such request by the insurer or any of its authorized representatives.

B. Any insurer suspending coverage pursuant to this section shall refund any unearned premium to the named insured, or his personal representative, on a pro rata basis.

C. The provisions of this section shall not alter or limit the insured's obligations under Article 8 (§ 46.2-705 et seq.) of Chapter 6 of Title 46.2. (1991, c. 699.)

§ 38.2-2206. Uninsured motorist insurance coverage.

— A. Except as provided in subsection J of this section, no policy or contract of bodily injury or property damage liability insurance relating to the ownership, maintenance, or use of a motor vehicle shall be issued or delivered in this Commonwealth to the owner of such vehicle or shall be issued or delivered by any insurer licensed in this Commonwealth upon any motor vehicle principally garaged or used in this Commonwealth unless it contains an endorsement or provisions under- taking to pay the insured all sums that he is legally entitled to recover as damages from the owner or operator of an uninsured motor vehicle, within limits not less than the requirements of § 46.2-472. Those limits shall equal but not exceed the limits of the liability insurance provided by the policy, unless any one named insured rejects the additional uninsured motorist insurance coverage by notifying the insurer as provided in subsection B of § 38.2-2202. This rejection of the additional uninsured motorist insurance coverage by any one named insured shall be binding upon all insureds under such policy as defined in subsection B of this section. The endorsement or provisions shall also obligate the insurer to make payment for bodily injury or property damage caused by the operation or use of an underinsured motor vehicle to the extent the vehicle is underinsured, as defined in subsection B of this section. The endorsement or provisions shall also provide for at least $20,000 coverage for damage or destruction of the property of the insured in any one accident but may provide an exclusion of the first $200 of the loss or damage where the loss or damage is a result of any one accident involving an unidentifiable owner or operator of an uninsured motor vehicle.

B. As used in this section, the term "bodily injury" includes death resulting from bodily injury.

"Insured" as used in subsections A, D, G, and H of this section means the named insured and, while resident of the same household, the spouse of the

named insured, and relatives, wards or foster children of either, while in a motor vehicle or otherwise, and any person who uses the motor vehicle to which the policy applies, with the expressed or implied consent of the named insured, and a guest in the motor vehicle to which the policy applies or the personal representative of any of the above.

"*Uninsured motor vehicle*" means a motor vehicle for which (i) there is no bodily injury liability insurance and property damage liability insurance in the amounts specified by § 46.2-472, (ii) there is such insurance but the insurer writing the insurance denies coverage for any reason whatsoever, including failure or refusal of the insured to cooperate with the insurer, (iii) there is no bond or deposit of money or securities in lieu of such insurance, (iv) the owner of the motor vehicle has not qualified as a self-insurer under the provisions of § 46.2-368, or (v) the owner or operator of the motor vehicle is immune from liability for negligence under the laws of the Commonwealth or the United States, in which case the provisions of subsection F shall apply and the action shall continue against the insurer. A motor vehicle shall be deemed uninsured if its owner or operator is unknown.

A motor vehicle is "*underinsured*" when, and to the extent that, the total amount of bodily injury and property damage coverage applicable to the operation or use of the motor vehicle and available for payment for such bodily injury or property damage, including all bonds or deposits of money or securities made pursuant to Article 15 (§ 46.2-435 et seq.) of Chapter 3 of Title 46.2, is less than the total amount of uninsured motorist coverage afforded any person injured as a result of the operation or use of the vehicle.

"*Available for payment*" means the amount of liability insurance coverage applicable to the claim of the injured person for bodily injury or property damage reduced by the payment of any other claims arising out of the same occurrence.

If an injured person is entitled to underinsured motorist coverage under more than one policy, the following order of priority of policies applies and any amount available for payment shall be credited against such policies in the following order of priority:

1. The policy covering a motor vehicle occupied by the injured person at the time of the accident;

2. The policy covering a motor vehicle not involved in the accident under which the injured person is a named insured;

3. The policy covering a motor vehicle not involved in the accident under which the injured person is an insured other than a named insured.

Where there is more than one insurer providing coverage under one of the payment priorities set forth, their liability shall be proportioned as to their respective underinsured motorist coverages.

Recovery under the endorsement or provisions shall be subject to the conditions set forth in this section.

C. There shall be a rebuttable presumption that a motor vehicle is uninsured if the Commissioner of the Department of Motor Vehicles certifies that, from the records of the Department of Motor Vehicles, it appears that: (i) there is no bodily injury liability insurance and property damage liability insurance in the amounts specified by § 46.2-472 covering the owner or operator of the motor vehicle; or (ii) no bond has been given or cash or securities delivered in lieu of the insurance; or (iii) the owner or operator of the motor vehicle has not qualified as a self-insurer in accordance with the provisions of § 46.2-368.

D. If the owner or operator of any motor vehicle that causes bodily injury or property damage to the insured is unknown, and if the damage or injury results from an accident where there has been no contact between that motor vehicle and the motor vehicle occupied by the insured, or where there has been no contact with the person of the insured if the insured was not occupying a motor vehicle, then for the insured to recover under the endorsement required by subsection A of this section, the accident shall be reported promptly to either (i) the insurer or (ii) a law-enforcement officer having jurisdiction in the county or city in which the accident occurred. If it is not reasonably practicable to make the report promptly, the report shall be made as soon as reasonably practicable under the circumstances.

E. If the owner or operator of any vehicle causing injury or damages is unknown, an action may be instituted against the unknown defendant as "John Doe" and service of process may be made by delivering a copy of the motion for judgment or other pleadings to the clerk of the court in which the action is brought. Service upon the insurer issuing the policy shall be made as prescribed by law as though the insurer were a party defendant. The provisions of § 8.01-288 shall not be applicable to the service of process required in this subsection. The insurer shall have the right to file pleadings and take other action allowable by law in the name of John Doe.

F. If any action is instituted against the owner or operator of an uninsured or underinsured motor vehicle by any insured intending to rely on the uninsured or underinsured coverage provision or endorsement of this policy under which the insured is making a claim, then the insured shall serve a copy of the process upon this insurer in the manner prescribed by law, as though the insurer were a party defendant. The provisions of § 8.01-288 shall not be applicable to the service of process required in this subsection. The insurer shall then have the right to file pleadings and take other action allowable by law in the name of the owner or operator of the uninsured or underinsured motor vehicle or in its own name. Notwithstanding the provisions of subsection A, the immunity from liability for negligence of the owner or operator of a motor vehicle shall not be a bar to the insured obtaining a judgment enforceable against the insurer for the negligence of the immune owner or operator, and shall not be a defense available to the insurer to the action brought by the insured, which shall proceed against the named defendant although any judgment obtained would be enforceable against the insurer and any other nonimmune defendant. Nothing in this subsection shall prevent the owner or operator of the uninsured motor vehicle from employing counsel of his own choice and taking any action in his own interest in connection with the proceeding.

G. Any insurer paying a claim under the endorsement or provisions required by subsection A of this section shall be subrogated to the rights of the insured to whom the claim was paid against the person causing the injury, death, or damage and that person's insurer, although it may deny coverage for any reason, to the extent that payment was made. The bringing of an action against the unknown owner or operator as John Doe or the conclusion of such an action shall not bar the insured from bringing an action against the owner or operator proceeded against as John Doe, or against the owner's or operator's insurer denying coverage for any reason, if the identity of the owner or operator who caused the injury or damages becomes known. The bringing of an action against an unknown owner or operator as John Doe shall toll the statute of limitations for purposes of bringing an action against the owner or operator who caused the injury or damages until his identity becomes known. In no event shall an action be brought against an owner or operator who caused the injury or damages, previously filed against as John Doe, more than three years from the commencement of the action against the unknown owner or operator as John Doe in a court of competent jurisdiction. Any recovery against the owner or operator, or the insurer of the owner or operator shall be paid to the insurer of the injured party to the extent that the insurer paid the named insured in the action brought against the owner or operator as John Doe. However, the insurer shall pay its proportionate part of all reasonable costs and expenses incurred in connection with the action, including reasonable attorney's fees. Nothing in an endorsement or provisions made under this subsection nor any other provision of law shall prevent the joining in an action against John Doe of the owner or operator of the motor vehicle causing the injury as a party defendant, and the joinder is hereby specifically authorized.

H. No endorsement or provisions providing the coverage required by subsection A of this section shall require arbitration of any claim arising under the endorsement or provisions, nor may anything be required of the insured except the establishment of legal liability, nor shall the insured be restricted or prevented in any manner from employing legal counsel or instituting legal proceedings.

I. Except as provided in § 65.2-309.1, the provisions of subsections A and B of § 38.2-2204 and the provisions of subsection A of this section shall not apply to any policy of insurance to the extent that it covers the liability of an employer under any workers' compensation law, or to the extent that it covers liability to which the Federal Tort Claims Act applies. No provision or application of this section shall limit the liability of an insurer of motor vehicles to an employee or other insured under this section who is injured by an uninsured motor vehicle; provided that in the event an employee of a self-insured employer receives a workers' compensation award for injuries resulting from an accident with an uninsured motor vehicle, such award shall be set off against any judgment for damages awarded pursuant to this section for personal injuries resulting from such accident.

J. Policies of insurance whose primary purpose is to provide coverage in excess of other valid and collectible insurance or qualified self-insurance may include uninsured motorist coverage as provided in subsection A of this section. Insurers issuing or providing liability policies that are of an excess or umbrella type or which provide liability coverage incidental to a policy and not related to a specifically insured motor vehicle, shall not be required to offer, provide or make available to those policies uninsured or underinsured motor vehicle coverage as defined in subsection A of this section.

K. A liability insurance carrier providing coverage under a policy issued or renewed on or after July 1, 1988, may pay the entire amount of its available coverage without obtaining a release of a claim if the claimant has underinsured insurance coverage in excess of the amount so paid. Any liability insurer making a payment pursuant to this section shall promptly give notice to its insured and to the insurer which provides the underinsured coverage that it has paid the full amount of its available coverage. (Code 1950, § 38-238; 1952, c. 317, § 38.1-381; 1958, c. 282; 1959, Ex. Sess., cc. 42, 70; 1960, c. 462; 1962, c. 457; 1964, c. 477; 1966, cc. 182, 459; 1968, cc. 199, 721; 1970, c. 494; 1971, Ex. Sess., c. 216; 1973, cc. 225, 390; 1974, c. 87; 1976, cc. 121, 122; 1977, c. 78; 1979, c. 113; 1980, cc. 326, 331; 1981, Sp. Sess., c. 6; 1982, cc. 638, 642; 1984, c. 541; 1985, cc. 39, 325; 1986, c. 562; 1987, c. 519; 1988, cc. 565, 578, 585, 586, 594; 1989, c. 621; 1993, c. 381; 1995, cc. 189, 267, 476; 1997, cc. 170, 191; 1999, c. 992.)

Editor's note. — Acts 1989, c. 621, cl. 2, provides that the provisions of the 1989 act shall be applicable to all original or renewed policies issued or delivered on or after July 1, 1989.

Acts 1995, c. 476, cl. 2, provides: "That the provisions of this act shall be applicable to all motor vehicles policies issued, renewed or issued for delivery on or after July 1, 1995."

The 1995 amendments. — The 1995 amendment by c. 476, in subsection B, inserted

"wards or foster children", following "relatives" in the paragraph defining "Insured."

The 1999 amendment inserted the third and fourth sentences of subsection G.

Law Review. — For note, "Uninsured Motorist Coverage in Virginia: The Scope of Protection and the New Underinsurance Provisions," see 69 Va. L. Rev. 355 (1983). For article, "Stacking of Uninsured and Underinsured Motor Vehicle Coverages," see 24 U. Rich. L. Rev. 87 (1989). For article, "An Overview of Automobile Liability Insurance in Virginia," see 28 U. Rich. L. Rev. 863 (1994). For 1995 survey of

insurance law, see 29 U. Rich. L. Rev. 1089 (1995).

I. GENERAL CONSIDERATION.

Editor's note. — See also the case annotations under the heading "I. General Consideration" under § 38.2-2204.

Legislative purpose of 1982 amendment to former § 38.1-381(c) (now subsection B of this section) was to increase total protection afforded by insurance to claimants injured or damaged by negligent motorists. In paraphrase, the statute as amended provides that the uninsured motorist endorsement obligates the insurer to pay a claimant damages caused by the operation of an underinsured motor vehicle to the extent such vehicle is underinsured, and that, definitionally, a motor vehicle is underinsured to the extent that liability coverage on such vehicle is less than the uninsured motorist coverage available to the claimant on account of the operation of such vehicle. If the General Assembly had intended the obligation under an underinsurance endorsement to be offset by the aggregate of obligations due a claimant under multiple liability policies insuring multiple vehicles, it would have included the plural as well as the singular form in its definition of the term "underinsured." Nationwide Mut. Ins. Co. v. Scott, 234 Va. 573, 363 S.E.2d 703 (1988).

Application of 1988 amendment. — The 1988 statutory amendment, subsequent to the issuance of the policies and the insured's injury, did not alter the contractual provisions of the primary insurer's and the secondary insurer's insurance policies, which otherwise fixed the order for payment of an agreed liability. Virginia Farm Bureau Ins. Co. v. Travelers Indem. Co., 242 Va. 203, 408 S.E.2d 898 (1991).

There are two reasons why the 1988 statutory amendment would not affect preexisting contractual rights: First, there is a presumption that a statute is intended to be prospective and not retrospective in operation. Second, a legislative change in the contractually agreed order of priority of liability would impair the obligation of the insurance contracts in violation of U.S. Const., Art. I, § 10, and Va. Const., Art. I, § 11. Virginia Farm Bureau Ins. Co. v.

Travelers Indem. Co., 242 Va. 203, 408 S.E.2d 898 (1991).

Construction with § 46.2-368. — Language of § 46.2-368 specifying that uninsured or underinsured motorist benefits provided by a self-insured entity shall be secondary coverage to other valid and collectible insurance does not alter or reverse the credit priorities, as opposed to the payment priorities, set forth in this section. Catron v. State Farm Mut. Auto. Ins. Co., 255 Va. 31, 496 S.E.2d 436 (1998).

In order to recover under uninsured motorist policy issued in conformity with this Code, it is necessary for the insured motorist to establish the liability of the uninsured motorist by judgment. Wimmer v. Mann, 58 Bankr. 953 (Bankr. W.D. Va. 1986).

Plaintiff may seek recovery from own carrier for unknown tortfeasor, before exhausting known tortfeasor's insurance. — An individual plaintiff, within the coverage of the Virginia uninsured motorist law who obtains a joint judgment against both a known and an unknown tortfeasor can seek satisfaction from his own insurance carrier under the uninsured motorist provision for the unknown tortfeasor's liability before exhausting the known tortfeasor's liability insurance. Harleysville Mut. Ins. Co. v. Nationwide Mut. Ins. Co., 789 F.2d 272 (4th Cir. 1986).

Legislative intent. — The legislature, in enacting the uninsured motorist statute, intended to create two classes of insured persons, with different benefits accruing to each class. Nationwide Mut. Ins. Co. v. Shelton, 225 Va. 316, 302 S.E.2d 36 (1983).

The public policy in favor of settlement of tort suits, which is contained in § 8.01-35.1, has no bearing on the question of whether an insured must comply with policy provisions in order to collect insurance money in lieu of damages from a tortfeasor. Virginia Farm Bureau Mut. Ins. Co. v. Gibson, 236 Va. 433, 374 S.E.2d 58 (1988).

For discussion of purpose of uninsured motorist protection, generally, see Virginia Farm Bureau Mut. Ins. Co. v. Gibson, 236 Va. 433, 374 S.E.2d 58 (1988).

A consent-to-settlement clause protects the insurer's power to preserve potential sources of recovery; therefore, the clause prevents an uninsured motorist carrier from paying a claim when another source of funds should pay, and may be properly included in a policy. Virginia Farm Bureau Mut. Ins. Co. v. Gibson, 236 Va. 433, 374 S.E.2d 58 (1988).

A provision in the uninsured motorist portion of a Virginia insurance policy which required the insured to secure the insurer's consent prior to settlement with any person or organization "who may be legally liable" for causing bodily injury or property damage was valid. Virginia Farm Bureau Mut. Ins. Co. v. Gibson, 236 Va. 433, 374 S.E.2d 58 (1988).

The uninsured motorist legislation is remedial in nature and is to be liberally construed so that the purpose intended may be accomplished. State Farm Mut. Auto. Ins. Co. v. Brower, 204 Va. 887, 134 S.E.2d 277 (1964); Nationwide Mut. Ins. Co. v. Sours, 205 Va. 602, 139 S.E.2d 51 (1964); McDaniel v. State Farm Mut. Auto. Ins. Co., 205 Va. 815, 139 S.E.2d 806 (1965).

Liberal construction has been accorded the Uninsured Motorist Law. White v. Nationwide Mut. Ins. Co., 245 F. Supp. 1 (W.D. Va. 1965), aff'd, 361 F.2d 785 (4th Cir. 1966).

The Uninsured Motorist Law was enacted for the benefit of injured persons and it is to be liberally construed so that the purpose intended may be accomplished. Bryant v. State Farm Mut. Auto. Ins. Co., 205 Va. 897, 140 S.E.2d 817 (1965); Grossman v. Glens Falls Ins. Co., 211 Va. 195, 176 S.E.2d 318 (1970).

The uninsured motorist statutes are remedial in nature and are to be construed liberally in favor of insurance protection for qualified claimants. Tudor v. Allstate Ins. Co., 216 Va. 918, 224 S.E.2d 156 (1976).

The uninsured motorist statute should be liberally construed. Wood v. State Farm Mut. Auto. Ins. Co., 432 F. Supp. 41 (W.D. Va. 1977).

In resolving issues of uninsured motorist coverage, Supreme Court will apply the well-established principles that the legislation mandating uninsured motorist coverage is remedial in nature, is to be liberally construed, and that, in the case of conflict between the provisions of the insurance policy and the statutory requirements, the statute controls. Nationwide Mut. Ins. Co. v. Hill, 247 Va. 78, 439 S.E.2d 335 (1994).

However, the court must look to the words used in the statute to determine its meaning, and only the meaning of the statute as determined should be given effect. Wood v. State Farm Mut. Auto. Ins. Co., 432 F. Supp. 41 (W.D. Va. 1977).

The effect of the Uninsured Motorist Law is not to provide insurance coverage upon each and every uninsured vehicle, but is to provide coverage to the insured motorist, his family, and permissive users of his vehicle, against the peril of injury by the uninsured motorist. Assuming this view of the purpose and effect of the law to be sound, there is no reason why the insurer may not limit its coverage, the limit of course to be not less than that required by § 46.1-1 (8) (now § 46.2-100). The very fact that the Uninsured Motorist Law requires minimum limits seems to support this view. State Farm Mut. Auto. Ins. Co. v. Drewry, 191 F. Supp. 852 (W.D. Va. 1960), aff'd, 316 F.2d 716 (4th Cir. 1963).

The intent of the General Assembly in enacting the "Uninsured Motorist Act," was to provide benefits and protection against peril of injury by an uninsured motorist to an insured motorist, his family and permissive users of his vehicle. It was not enacted to provide insurance coverage upon each and every uninsured vehicle to everyone. Travelers Indem. Co. v. Wells, 209 F. Supp. 784 (W.D. Va. 1962), rev'd on other grounds, 316 F.2d 770 (4th Cir. 1963); Hobbs v. Buckeye Union Cas. Co., 212 F. Supp. 349 (W.D. Va. 1962). But see Harleysville Mut. Ins. Co. v. Nationwide Mut. Ins. Co., 789 F.2d 272 (4th Cir. 1986).

It is not the purpose of the Uninsured Motorist Law to provide coverage for the uninsured vehicle; its object is to afford the insured additional protection in event of an accident. Travelers Indem. Co. v. Wells, 209 F. Supp. 784 (W.D. Va. 1962), rev'd on other grounds, 316 F.2d 770 (4th Cir. 1963); Hobbs v. Buckeye Union Cas. Co., 212 F. Supp. 349 (W.D. Va. 1962). But see Harleysville Mut. Ins. Co. v. Nationwide Mut. Ins. Co., 789 F.2d 272 (4th Cir. 1986); United States Fid. & Guar. Co. v. Byrum, 206 Va. 815, 146 S.E.2d 246 (1966); General Accident Fire & Life Assurance Corp. v. Aetna Cas. & Sur. Co., 208 Va. 467, 158 S.E.2d 750 (1968); Midwest Mut. Ins. Co. v. Aetna Cas. & Sur. Co., 216 Va. 926, 223 S.E.2d 901 (1976).

The Uninsured Motorist Law is primarily concerned with providing adequate compensation for injured insureds when other sources are lacking. Hobbs v. Buckeye Union Cas. Co., 212 F. Supp. 349 (W.D. Va. 1962). But see Harleysville Mut. Ins. Co. v. Nationwide Mut. Ins. Co., 789 F.2d 272 (4th Cir. 1986); Southern v. Lumbermens Mut. Cas. Co., 236 F. Supp. 370 (W.D. Va. 1964); Pulley v. Allstate Ins. Co., 242 F. Supp. 330 (E.D. Va. 1965); Grossman v. Glens Falls Ins. Co., 211 Va. 195, 176 S.E.2d 318 (1970).

An uninsured motorist provision does not create insurance for the uninsured motorist or the uninsured automobile. Pulley v. Allstate Ins. Co., 242 F. Supp. 330 (E.D. Va. 1965).

The purpose of the Uninsured Motorist Law is to benefit injured parties. White v. Nationwide Mut. Ins. Co., 245 F. Supp. 1 (W.D. Va. 1965), aff'd, 361 F.2d 785 (4th Cir. 1966).

Virginia's Uninsured Motorist Law does not create insurance for uninsured motorists. Southern v. Lumbermens Mut. Cas. Co., 236 F. Supp. 370 (W.D. Va. 1964).

This section requires that all automobile liability insurance policies issued in the State shall contain an endorsement indemnifying the insured for injury caused by an uninsured motor vehicle. Nationwide Mut. Ins. Co. v. Akers, 340 F.2d 150 (4th Cir. 1965).

The uninsured motorist provision or endorsement does not afford coverage to the uninsured motor vehicle or the operator of the uninsured automobile, whether known or unknown. It is protection afforded an injured (or killed) insured by reason of a contractual agreement after the liability of the uninsured motorist, known or unknown, has been established by a court of competent jurisdiction. Johnson v. GMC, 242 F. Supp. 778 (E.D. Va. 1965).

The reason for requiring compulsory uninsured motorist coverage was to give needed relief to injured parties through insurance paid for by the insured and assessments from uninsured motorists. No benefit was intended to accrue to the uninsured motorist, since full subrogation rights in favor of the insurer are preserved in the law. Travelers Indem. Co. v. Wells, 209 F. Supp. 784 (W.D. Va. 1962), rev'd on other grounds, 316 F.2d 770 (4th Cir. 1963).

As the court stated in Horne v. Superior Life Ins. Co., 203 Va. 282, 123 S.E.2d 401 (1962): "... It is not the purpose of the Uninsured Motorist Law to provide coverage for the uninsured vehicle, but its object is to afford the insured additional protection in event of an accident. Here, [the uninsured motorist carrier] does not stand in the shoes of ... the uninsured motorist. Its policy does not insure [the uninsured motorist] against liability. It insures [the insured] ... against inadequate compensation." Bobbitt v. Shelby Mut. Ins. Co., 209 Va. 37, 161 S.E.2d 671 (1968).

A motorist pays an additional premium on his liability policy in order that he might be afforded "coverage" or "protection" in event of an accident with an automobile that is uninsured. Grossman v. Glens Falls Ins. Co., 211 Va. 195, 176 S.E.2d 318 (1970).

Uninsured motorist coverage is meant only to indemnify the insured rather than to provide liability coverage for an uninsured motorist. Maxey v. Doe, 217 Va. 22, 225 S.E.2d 359 (1976).

The General Assembly has decided, as a matter of public policy, to extend the benefits of uninsured motorist coverage only to those injured by a motor vehicle which is uninsured, and not to those injured by a motor vehicle which, though fully insured under the statute, is only partly insured as to claims presented. Tudor v. Allstate Ins. Co., 216 Va. 918, 224 S.E.2d 156 (1976).

Uninsured motorist coverage is meant to protect an insured motorist, his family, and permissive users of his vehicle against the peril of injury by an uninsured wrongdoer, not to provide insurance coverage upon each and every uninsured vehicle to everyone. Bayer v. Travelers Indem. Co., 221 Va. 5, 267 S.E.2d 91 (1980).

When coverage exists. — Uninsured motorist coverage exists pursuant to this section if (1) a liability policy is issued or delivered in this State insuring a motor vehicle or (2) an insurer, licensed in this State, issues or delivers a liability policy insuring a motor vehicle then principally garaged or docked or principally used in this State. Wood v. State Farm Mut. Auto. Ins. Co., 432 F. Supp. 41 (W.D. Va. 1977).

There was no uninsured motorist coverage of a truck where, at the time the insurance policy was issued to the insured, the truck was principally garaged and docked outside of Virginia and was not principally used in Virginia, even though subsequent to the issuance of the policy the truck was brought to Virginia as a replacement truck where it was docked until the time of the accident. Wood v. State Farm Mut. Auto. Ins. Co., 432 F. Supp. 41 (W.D. Va. 1977).

The scope of subsection H of this section is unambiguous. By its plain language, it limits the conditions that an insurer can place on the uninsured motorist coverage mandated by subsection A of this section. Since this language is unambiguous, it is not subject to judicial construction and must be applied as written. Thus, the language contained in subsection H applies only to uninsured motorist coverage and has no relevance to medical payments coverage. Allstate Insurance Co. v. Eaton, 248 Va. 426, 448 S.E.2d 652 (1994).

Coverage as used in the Uninsured Motorist Law means more than the mere ownership and possession of a contract of automobile liability insurance. The statute contemplates a contract of insurance with a company that is in a financial position, not just to pay a lawyer's fee and defend an action against a policyholder, but to pay any recovery that is had within its policy limits. Grossman v. Glens Falls Ins. Co., 211 Va. 195, 176 S.E.2d 318 (1970).

A named insured generally cannot give permission to use a vehicle that the named insured does not own. Stone v. Liberty Mut. Ins. Co., 253 Va. 12, 478 S.E.2d 883 (1996).

Rejection of higher coverage. — This section requires that each named insured under an automobile insurance policy reject the higher coverage. State Farm Mut. Auto. Ins. Co. v. Weisman, 247 Va. 199, 441 S.E.2d 16 (1994).

Underinsurance must be provided. — In requiring a self-insurer to prove uninsured motorist insurance coverage, § 46.2-368(B), when read with this section, also required a self-insurer to provide underinsurance coverage. Hackett v. Arlington County, 247 Va. 41, 439 S.E.2d 348 (1994).

Policy coverage is not in issue in action against uninsured motorist. — In the action against the uninsured motorist the issue of the coverage afforded by the insurance policy has no place. That issue may be decided in an action ex contractu brought on the policy by the interested judgment plaintiff, or in a declaratory judgment proceeding. Rodgers v. Danko, 204 Va. 140, 129 S.E.2d 828 (1963).

Liability and uninsured insurance do not need to be in equal amounts. — In Virginia, one must carry both liability and uninsured/underinsured (UM) insurance coverage, though not necessarily in equal amounts. One may arrange for minimum UM coverage of $25,000 yet purchase liability coverage at a greater amount. Insurance Co. of N. Am. v. MacMillan, 945 F.2d 729 (4th Cir. 1991).

Rejection of equal coverage need not be supplied if rejection already signed. — The written rejection of uninsured/underinsured (UM) coverage equal to liability coverage, in the case of a new policy, need not be supplied to the insured by the insurer if a written rejection has already been signed. After 20 days, the insurer is relieved of its obligation imposed by the statute to attach to any subsequently delivered renewal policy the notice statement required by that statute. Insurance Co. of N. Am. v. MacMillan, 945 F.2d 729 (4th Cir. 1991).

In Virginia, the limits of each liability policy must at least equal Virginia's financial responsibility limits for bodily injury at $25,000 each person and $50,000 each accident. The policy also must provide uninsured and underinsured coverage with at least those limits. If an insured purchases liability coverage with greater limits, his uninsured and underinsured coverage limits will automatically increase to the increased liability limits unless he rejects those higher limits within 20 days. Moody v. Federated Mut. Ins. Co., 886 F. Supp. 5 (W.D. Va. 1994), aff'd, 48 F.3d 1216 (4th Cir. 1995).

An uninsured motorist is one who operates an uninsured motor vehicle. McDaniel v. State Farm Mut. Auto. Ins. Co., 205 Va. 815, 139 S.E.2d 806 (1965).

Action brought against uninsured motorist is purely ex delicto. — An action brought by an insured against an uninsured motorist, although perhaps primarily for the purpose of establishing the insurer's contractual liability, is purely an action ex delicto. Orlikowski v. Mearns, 212 F. Supp. 37 (E.D. Va. 1962).

And plaintiff's right is given not by policy endorsement but by statute. — The right of plaintiff to bring an action to establish legal liability on the uninsured motorist and to recover damages is not given by the policy endorsement but by the statute. Doe v. Brown, 203 Va. 508, 125 S.E.2d 159 (1962); Bryant v. State Farm Mut. Auto. Ins. Co., 205 Va. 897, 140 S.E.2d 817 (1965).

The insurer's liability under the uninsured motorist provision is contractual in nature. White v. Nationwide Mut. Ins. Co., 245 F. Supp. 1 (W.D. Va. 1965), aff'd, 361 F.2d 785 (4th Cir. 1966); General Accident Fire & Life Assurance Corp. v. Aetna Cas. & Sur. Co., 208 Va. 467, 158 S.E.2d 750 (1968).

Necessity of causal connection. — The Supreme Court of Virginia has made clear that there must be a causal connection between the injury and the use of the vehicle as a vehicle. Doe v. State Farm Fire & Cas. Co., 878 F. Supp. 862 (E.D. Va. 1995).

Necessity of stacking before comparing. — The clear and unambiguous language of subsection B of this section requires that all the uninsured motorist coverage available to injured motorists be stacked before the total amount of this coverage is compared with the total amount of liability coverage available to tortfeasor motorist. USAA Cas. Ins. Co. v. Alexander, 248 Va. 185, 445 S.E.2d 145 (1994).

The insurer maintains all his rights against the uninsured motorist after payment to the insured. White v. Nationwide Mut. Ins. Co., 245 F. Supp. 1 (W.D. Va. 1965), aff'd, 361 F.2d 785 (4th Cir. 1966).

No recovery by collision insurer from liability insurer. — A collision insurer, having paid a claim for a risk which it had assumed and having been paid a premium to assume such risk, did not show itself entitled, either under the Virginia Uninsured Motorist Act or under equitable principles of subrogation, to have its loss reimbursed by insured's liability insurer. Bobbitt v. Shelby Mut. Ins. Co., 209 Va. 37, 161 S.E.2d 671 (1968).

An automobile collision insurance carrier, which has paid a loss sustained by its insured and caused by the negligence of an uninsured motorist, cannot recover the amount so paid from its insured's automobile liability insurance carrier under the uninsured motorist endorsement in the latter's policy. Bobbitt v. Shelby Mut. Ins. Co., 209 Va. 37, 161 S.E.2d 671 (1968).

Judgment is the event which determines legal entitlement to recovery. Midwest Mut. Ins. Co. v. Aetna Cas. & Sur. Co., 216 Va. 926, 223 S.E.2d 901 (1976).

The obligation of the uninsured motorist insurer arises only if it is determined that the insured is "legally entitled to recover" damages from the owner or operator of an uninsured motor vehicle. Midwest Mut. Ins. Co. v. Aetna Cas. & Sur. Co., 216 Va. 926, 223 S.E.2d 901 (1976).

Pursuant to an uninsured motorist policy issued in conformity with this section, it is necessary for the insured motorist to establish "legally" the liability of the uninsured motorist by judgment. Elliott v. Hardison, 25 Bankr. 305 (E.D. Va. 1982).

Subsections E and F do not affect requirements of A. — The requirement that a judgment be obtained to determine legal entitlement to recovery, expressed in subsection A, is not eliminated by the so-called "permissive" provisions of subsections E and F, when the insured elects to enforce his coverage by settlement. Midwest Mut. Ins. Co. v. Aetna Cas. & Sur. Co., 216 Va. 926, 223 S.E.2d 901 (1976).

Where one insurer which pays a settlement to its insured seeks contribution from coinsurer, use of "may" and "if" in subsections E and F has no substantive effect and does not manifest a legislative intent that legal liability can be fixed, without judgment, against a nonsettling coinsurer. Midwest Mut. Ins. Co. v. Aetna Cas. & Sur. Co., 216 Va. 926, 223 S.E.2d 901 (1976).

Right of tortfeasor's nonsettling insurer to demand insured's compliance with law. — The uninsured motorist carrier may settle its contractual obligation with its insured rather than requiring its insured to obtain a judgment under subsection H against the tortfeasor; but while the uninsured motorist carrier may waive for itself the requirement that the insured establish liability of the tortfeasor, it cannot by its unilateral act waive the right of the tortfeasor's nonsettling liability carrier which can demand full compliance by the insured with the uninsured motorist law. United Servs. Auto. Ass'n v. Nationwide Mut. Ins. Co., 218 Va. 861, 241 S.E.2d 784 (1978).

Read together, subsection A and § 46.1-1(8) (now § 46.2-100) define the quantum and quality of the coverage liability imposed upon an insurer. The latter section fixes the minimum monetary coverage; the former section restricts coverage to "damages." Nationwide Mut. Ins. Co. v. Finley, 215 Va. 700, 214 S.E.2d 129 (1975).

Policy provides to named insured broad reservoir of coverage. — A policy issued pursuant to the uninsured motorist statute, subsection A, provides to a person who is the named insured a broad reservoir of coverage. Lipscombe v. Security Ins. Co., 213 Va. 81, 189 S.E.2d 320 (1972).

Uninsured motorist insurance provides the named insured with two kinds of coverage: while he is in his insured automobile, and wherever else he may happen to be when he suffers bodily injury due to an uninsured motorist. This latter constitutes a broad reservoir of coverage. Cunningham v. Insurance Co. of N. Am., 213 Va. 72, 189 S.E.2d 832 (1972).

And he may "stack" coverages in policy separately listing two or more automobiles. — The named insured is permitted to "stack" the coverages provided by the uninsured motorist provisions of a policy separately listing three automobiles owned by the insured. Lipscombe v. Security Ins. Co., 213 Va. 81, 189 S.E.2d 320 (1972).

Where a single policy insures the owner of two listed automobiles against loss from damages caused by an uninsured motorist and a separate, equal premium is charged for each vehicle, an ambiguity is created in the absence of "plain, unmistakable language" restricting the coverage to that applicable to a single vehicle. And the ambiguity is to be construed against the insurance company, with the result that the insured is entitled to double coverage for the double premium paid. Lipscombe v. Security Ins. Co., 213 Va. 81, 189 S.E.2d 320 (1972).

Where an insurance company chose to issue coverage on two separate automobiles and to accept a premium for each, the coverage intended by payment of an equal premium for a second automobile also includes the broad reservoir of coverage secured under the first premium for the first automobile. Cunningham v. Insurance Co. of N. Am., 213 Va. 72, 189 S.E.2d 832 (1972).

It is now the rule in Virginia that the stacking of uninsured motorist coverage will be permitted unless clear and unambiguous language exists on the face of the policy to prevent such multiple coverage, and any ambiguity contained within a policy will be construed against the insurer. Goodville Mut. Cas. Co. v. Borror, 221 Va. 967, 275 S.E.2d 625 (1981).

The language of an insurance company's policy which read "regardless of the number of motor vehicles to which this insurance applies," was clear and unambiguous and required the construction that stacking to provide double the minimum coverage for a single accident was not permissible; thus the policy plainly limited the insurance company's uninsured motorist liability for damages to any one person as a result of any one accident to $25,000, and the mere fact that two vehicles were insured and two separate premiums were charged was of no consequence in light of the express language of the policy. Goodville Mut. Cas. Co. v. Borror, 221 Va. 967, 275 S.E.2d 625 (1981).

A decedent's estate can accumulate three uninsured motorist coverages under a policy held by the decedent, who was the named insured therein. Cunningham v. Insurance Co. of N. Am., 213 Va. 72, 189 S.E.2d 832 (1972).

Determining extent to which tortfeasor's vehicle underinsured. — In applying subsection (B), a passenger injured in a single vehicle accident is not entitled to include the uninsured/underinsured motorist coverage contained in the tortfeasor's automobile liability insurance policy when determining the extent to which the tortfeasor's vehicle was underinsured. Trisvan v. Agway Ins. Co., 254 Va. 416, 492 S.E.2d 628 (1997).

The limit of the recovery of a plaintiff under any or all insurance policies carrying the uninsured motorist provision would be the amount of the insured's judgment against the uninsured motorist. Bryant v. State Farm Mut. Auto. Ins. Co., 205 Va. 897, 140 S.E.2d 817 (1965); White v. Nationwide Mut. Ins. Co., 245 F. Supp. 1 (W.D. Va. 1965), aff'd, 361 F.2d 785 (4th Cir. 1966).

Payment obligation of insurer. — When an injured person has purchased only "minimum limit" uninsured motorist (UM) coverage, but has a "total amount of uninsured motorist coverage afforded" that is greater than the statutory minimum, an insurer shall be deemed obligated to make payment "to the extent the vehicle is underinsured," as defined in subsection B of this section. USAA Cas. Ins. Co. v. Alexander, 248 Va. 185, 445 S.E.2d 145 (1994) (decided under prior law).

Changes in the mandatory form of the uninsured motorist endorsement adopted by the State Corporation Commission, so as to specifically restrict coverage to only those automobiles to which the liability provisions of the policy applies, did not establish that any liability policy which contained the old form of endorsement would provide coverage of automobiles not covered by the original policy. Nationwide Mut. Ins. Co. v. Akers, 340 F.2d 150 (4th Cir. 1965).

Coverage includes punitive damages. — It is true that the uninsured motorist statute does not mention punitive damages as such, but the uninsured motorist statute, subsection A, does provide that all automobile insurance policies issued in this State must contain "provisions undertaking to pay the insured all sums which he shall be legally entitled to recover as damages from the owner or operator of an uninsured motor vehicle." This language was intended to include punitive damages. Lipscombe v. Security Ins. Co., 213 Va. 81, 189 S.E.2d 320 (1972).

The insurance company may pursue and place upon the uninsured motorist the burden of the punitive damages. Lipscombe v. Security Ins. Co., 213 Va. 81, 189 S.E.2d 320 (1972).

An insurance provision which places a limitation upon the requirement of subsection A and conflicts with the plain terms of this section is illegal and of no effect. State Farm Mut. Auto. Ins. Co. v. United Serv. Auto. Ass'n, 211 Va. 133, 176 S.E.2d 327 (1970).

"Other insurance" clause invalid. — An "other insurance" clause in a policy that limits the insured's coverage to the amount by which the policy's applicable limit exceeds the sum of the applicable limits of other insurance available to him is invalid because it conflicts with subsection A, which requires that every policy contain an endorsement binding the insurer to pay, within the statutory limit, all sums which the insured shall be legally entitled to recover from the owner or operator of the uninsured vehicle. Cunningham v. Insurance Co. of N. Am., 213 Va. 72, 189 S.E.2d 832 (1972).

Other insurance provision of a policy was invalid because in conflict with the requirement of subsection A of this section. Bryant v. State Farm Mut. Auto. Ins. Co., 205 Va. 897, 140 S.E.2d 817 (1965).

As is clause absolving insurer where any other insurance is present. — An outright "escape" clause, absolving an insurer from any liability where any other insurance is present, would be patently invalid under subsection I of this section. Travelers Indem. Co. v. Wells, 209 F. Supp. 784 (W.D. Va. 1962), rev'd on other grounds, 316 F.2d 770 (4th Cir. 1963).

Insurer's endorsement attempting to limit the "insured" to one who has no other valid and collectible automobile liability insurance is invalid as being contrary to this section. Pulley v. Allstate Ins. Co., 242 F. Supp. 330 (E.D. Va. 1965).

A clause in an automobile liability policy limiting coverage of permissive drivers by providing that they would be covered only when they did not have other collectible and valid insurance, is void because it violates this section. Maryland Cas. Co. v. Burley, 345 F.2d 138 (4th Cir. 1965).

But coverage may be limited to excess over other similar insurance available to insured. — The provisions of subsection I of this section did not prohibit limitation of coverage under an uninsured motorist endorsement for injuries received by insured in another's automobile to excess over any other similar insurance available to the insured. Travelers Indem. Co. v. Wells, 316 F.2d 770 (4th Cir. 1963). But see Bryant v. State Farm Mut. Auto. Ins. Co., 205 Va. 897, 140 S.E.2d 817 (1965).

An underinsured motorist carrier has the right to file pleadings and take other actions allowable by law for injuries when the tortfeasor confesses judgment in an amount exceeding the applicable liability coverage. State Farm Mut. Auto. Ins. Co. v. Beng, 249 Va. 165, 455 S.E.2d 2 (1995).

Protection not to be expanded beyond limits fixed in law. — Unless policy expressly stipulates higher limits, protection of a person or persons injured by an uninsured automobile driver is not to be expanded beyond the limits fixed in the law. Travelers Indem. Co. v. Wells, 316 F.2d 770 (4th Cir. 1963).

An excess coverage clause does not conflict with subsection A and is valid when it merely provides an orderly process for determining the distribution of liability among several insurance carriers and only requires the exhaustion of the primary coverage before the excess coverage comes into play. State Farm Mut. Auto. Ins. Co. v. United Serv. Auto. Ass'n, 211 Va. 133, 176 S.E.2d 327 (1970).

This section did not propose to provide an injured guest with uninsured protection beyond the statutory amounts through a combination of the host's insurance and that owned by the guest for himself. Travelers Indem. Co. v. Wells, 316 F.2d 770 (4th Cir. 1963). But see Bryant v. State Farm Mut. Auto. Ins. Co., 205 Va. 897, 140 S.E.2d 817 (1965).

And a guest injured by an uninsured driver may not also recover upon his own uninsured policy if his claim cannot be satisfied in full by his host's uninsured insurance. Travelers Indem. Co. v. Wells, 316 F.2d 770 (4th Cir. 1963). But see Bryant v. State Farm Mut. Auto. Ins. Co., 205 Va. 897, 140 S.E.2d 817 (1965).

When accident occurred in a state without compatible uninsured motorist law. — The liability under the statutory endorsement exists even though the accident happened in a state which has no uninsured motorist law like that of Virginia. Buchanan v. Doe, 246 Va. 67, 431 S.E.2d 289 (1993).

Endorsement applies to injuries sustained outside State. — An uninsured motor vehicle endorsement contained in a policy issued pursuant to this section applied to injuries sustained by a Virginia insured outside of the State. Travelers Indem. Co. v. Wells, 316 F.2d 770 (4th Cir. 1963).

The endorsement required by subsection A has no territorial limitation, but binds the insurance company to pay the insured all sums which he shall be legally entitled to recover as damages from the owner or operator of an uninsured motor vehicle even though the accident happened in a state which has no uninsured motorist law like that of Virginia. Hodgson v. Doe, 203 Va. 938, 128 S.E.2d 444 (1962); Bryant v. State Farm Mut. Auto. Ins. Co., 205 Va. 897, 140 S.E.2d 817 (1965).

To limit the coverage of the endorsement to accidents happening in Virginia would be to create a limitation which the statute does not contain. Bryant v. State Farm Mut. Auto. Ins. Co., 205 Va. 897, 140 S.E.2d 817 (1965).

Insurer's obligation to pay irrespective of procedural defects. — In considering the purpose of the legislature in enacting the Uninsured Motorist Law, the intent of the legislature would point to a positive obligation to pay irrespective of procedural defects. Travelers Indem. Co. v. Wells, 209 F. Supp. 784 (W.D. Va. 1962), rev'd on other grounds, 316 F.2d 770 (4th Cir. 1963).

The language of the last sentence in subsection G is not "plain." Baker v. Doe,

211 Va. 158, 176 S.E.2d 436 (1970).

Insurer not party to tort action. — Subsection F, in compliance with due process, provides notice and a means of protection to one who ultimately may be held contractually liable pursuant to its contract of insurance. It does not make the uninsured motorist insurer a party to the tort action. Zurenda v. Holloman, 616 F. Supp. 212 (E.D. Va. 1985).

Uninsured motorist carrier is not a party defendant within 28 U.S.C. § 1441, the federal removal statute, in the initial action based on the automobile accident. Zurenda v. Holloman, 616 F. Supp. 212 (E.D. Va. 1985).

Joinder of defendants in the alternative is not allowed by the last sentence in subsection G. Baker v. Doe, 211 Va. 158, 176 S.E.2d 436 (1970).

Insurer filing pleadings in own name becomes "adverse party." — While action by an insurance company in filing pleadings in its own name under this section does not, in itself, subject the insurance carrier to the payment of a judgment rendered against the named defendant, it would appear that the insurance company by answering the complaint, comes within the framework of Rule 33 of the Federal Rules of Civil Procedure and is an "adverse party." Ivory v. Nichols, 34 F.R.D. 128 (E.D. Va. 1963).

After the uninsured motorist claim is asserted, insurer and insured assume an adversary relationship. In such a posture, the insurer is under no duty to inform the insured that, should their dealings and negotiations fail to resolve the claim, it will rely on insured's failure to file the SR-300 report as required by subsection D. Maxey v. Doe, 217 Va. 22, 225 S.E.2d 359 (1976).

And discovery provisions of Federal Rules of Civil Procedure apply to it. — Rule 33 of the Federal Rules of Civil Procedure, relating to interrogatories, should be available to an insurance company filing pleadings in its own name under the Virginia Uninsured Motorist Law. Like provisions with respect to production of documents under Rule 34, the physical or mental examination of a party under Rule 35, and request for admission of facts and genuineness of documents under Rule 36, should be equally available to a plaintiff and the insurance company pleading in its own name under this section. Ivory v. Nichols, 34 F.R.D. 128 (E.D. Va. 1963).

A reasonable interpretation of the Virginia Uninsured Motorist Law compels the insurer to answer certain interrogatories propounded to it wherever the insurance company elects to "file pleadings and take other action allowable by law ... in its own name" as provided by this section. To hold otherwise would foreclose the right of the insurance company — filing pleadings and taking other action allowable by law in its own name — to resort to many of the

Federal Rules of Civil Procedure. Ivory v. Nichols, 34 F.R.D. 128 (E.D. Va. 1963).

Failure to forward process and like papers need not be accompanied by prejudice but it must be of such substantial and material nature as to justify the voiding of the insurance contract. The question of substantiality and materiality is for the trier of fact. Lack of prejudice, if it appears, is to be considered as going to the question of the materiality of the information which the insured failed to give. Dairyland Ins. Co. v. Hughes, 317 F. Supp. 928 (W.D. Va. 1970).

Insurer, uninsured motorist, may not control actions of each other. — Both the uninsured motorist and the insurer may, for example, employ counsel, file pleadings, participate in discovery, make and argue motions, examine and cross-examine witnesses, engage in argument at trial, admit liability, or pursue appeals. And each is entitled to control his or its own actions but not the actions of the other. State Farm Mut. Auto. Ins. Co. v. Cuffee, 248 Va. 11, 444 S.E.2d 720 (1994).

No presumption where uninsured motorist fails to testify. — The presumptions which might normally arise upon the failure of a party to testify or produce evidence controlled by him have no application to a factual situation where there are two defendants one of whom is an uninsured motorist who does not appear for trial. This is so because to apply such presumptions would create an undue advantage for the appearing defendant while denying the insurance carriers, the real parties in interest, an opportunity to explain the uninsured motorist's absence. Facchina v. Richardson, 213 Va. 440, 192 S.E.2d 791 (1972).

Court costs incurred by insured. — Absent a commitment in the policy to the contrary, an insurer providing uninsured motorist coverage insurance is not liable for court costs incurred by its insured in recovering judgment against an uninsured tort-feasor. Nationwide Mut. Ins. Co. v. Finley, 215 Va. 700, 214 S.E.2d 129 (1975).

Statutory obligation to pay interest. — The fact that an uninsured motorist insurer is not a party to the tort action gives it no exemption from the statutory obligation to pay interest. Nationwide Mut. Ins. Co. v. Finley, 215 Va. 700, 214 S.E.2d 129 (1975).

Accumulated interest may increase insurer's obligation beyond coverage fixed in contract. — Subsection A imposes upon the insurer a contract liability which makes the insurer, although not a party to tort action, an obligor on that portion of the judgment which becomes a liquidated debt as does not exceed the policy coverage. Statutory interest accumulates on that portion until the insurer pays its obligation (unless the judgment be set aside), and it is irrelevant that the accumulated interest may increase the total obligation to a sum greater than the limit of coverage fixed in the insurance contract. Nationwide Mut. Ins. Co. v. Finley, 215 Va. 700, 214 S.E.2d 129 (1975).

Where the policy but not the uninsured motorist endorsement, contained a provision for arbitration of claims by the insured under the uninsured motorist clause, subsection H of this section nullified the effectiveness of the arbitration provisions of the policy. Matthews v. Allstate Ins. Co., 194 F. Supp. 459 (E.D. Va. 1961).

Conduct not essential. — The claimant in the present case was not engaged in a transaction essential to the use of the pickup truck when she was injured and, therefore she was not covered by this section. United States Fire Ins. Co. v. Parker, 250 Va. 374, 463 S.E.2d 464 (1995).

Applied in Arnold v. Liberty Mut. Ins. Co., 866 F. Supp. 955 (W.D. Va. 1994); Osborne v. National Union Fire Ins. Co., 251 Va. 53, 465 S.E.2d 835 (1996).

II. WHO IS COVERED.

Carrier held not entitled to attorney's fees from primary insurer. — An uninsured motorist carrier owed no duty to defend a party who had been denied coverage by his primary insurer, and its subrogation rights did not include entitlement to attorney's fees from the primary insurer. State Farm Fire & Cas. Co. v. Scott, 236 Va. 116, 372 S.E.2d 383 (1988).

Uninsured motorist coverage is designed to protect not vehicles, but persons, i.e., the innocent victims of negligent uninsured motorists. Lipscombe v. Security Ins. Co., 213 Va. 81, 189 S.E.2d 320 (1972).

The emphasis of the uninsured motorist statute is upon the status of an insured when injured, rather than upon vehicles, in determining whether coverage applies. Lipscombe v. Security Ins. Co., 213 Va. 81, 189 S.E.2d 320 (1972).

And statute creates two classes of insured persons. — The legislature, in enacting the uninsured motorist statute, intended to create two classes of insured persons with different benefits accruing to each class. Cunningham v. Insurance Co. of N. Am., 213 Va. 72, 189 S.E.2d 832 (1972).

Subsection B recognizes the distinction between a named insured and an insured. Cunningham v. Insurance Co. of N. Am., 213 Va. 72, 189 S.E.2d 832 (1972).

Protection of named insured and insured distinguished. — The named insured is protected while occupying any insured vehicle or otherwise, but an insured who is not the named insured is protected only while occupying an insured vehicle. Lipscombe v. Security Ins. Co., 213 Va. 81, 189 S.E.2d 320 (1972).

The named insured in an uninsured motorist policy receives coverage, and a contract benefit, for which he has paid a consideration. He seeks indemnity based on the payment of that premium and where he has paid separate premiums he is entitled to the additional coverages. This argument and reasoning do not apply to a permissive user of a vehicle, who pays no premium and does not receive the broader uninsured motorist coverage of a named insured. Cunningham v. Insurance Co. of N. Am., 213 Va. 72, 189 S.E.2d 832 (1972).

Benefits extended to named insured while operating vehicle not covered by policy. — Benefits under an uninsured motorist provision in a liability policy issued to a named insured on one motor vehicle owned by him extend to the named insured while he is operating another motor vehicle owned by him and not covered in such liability policy. Allstate Ins. Co. v. Meeks, 207 Va. 897, 153 S.E.2d 222 (1967).

Named insured, spouse and relatives protected while in vehicle or otherwise. — Subsection B creates two classes of insured persons with different benefits accruing to each class. The first class includes the named insured and, while resident of the same household, the spouse of any such named insured and relatives of either. A member of this class is protected, "while in a motor vehicle or otherwise." The second class of insured persons contemplated by the statute, is those "who use," with the consent, expressed or implied, of the named insured, the vehicle to which the policy applies and those who are guests in such vehicle. Insurance Co. of N. Am. v. Perry, 204 Va. 833, 134 S.E.2d 418 (1964); Allstate Ins. Co. v. Meeks, 207 Va. 897, 153 S.E.2d 222 (1967).

But user with permission is covered only while using vehicle. — One who uses the vehicle with the permission of the named insured is not covered by the uninsured motorist endorsement except while using the vehicle. Insurance Co. of N. Am. v. Perry, 204 Va. 833, 134 S.E.2d 418 (1964).

Guest in vehicle driven without permission of owner is not covered. — A guest in a vehicle being driven by one without the permission of the owner was not entitled to the coverage of the uninsured motorist endorsement contained in the policy issued to the owner. Such a "guest" is not included within the definition set forth in subsection B. Nationwide Mut. Ins. Co. v. Harleysville Mut. Cas. Co., 203 Va. 600, 125 S.E.2d 840 (1962).

Uninsured owner-passenger not covered by driver's policy. — A claimant injured while a passenger in his own uninsured automobile during a collision with another uninsured vehicle may not recover under the uninsured motorist endorsement of a liability policy written on other vehicles owned by the driver of the claimant's automobile. Bayer v. Travelers Indem. Co., 221 Va. 5, 267 S.E.2d 91 (1980).

Worker "operating or using" truck. — Highway worker killed while placing lane-closure signs on highway was "operating or using" employer's truck for purposes of uninsured/underinsured motorists coverage where he kept the truck's yellow warning light flashing, remained at an appropriate distance from the truck, and otherwise was using the truck's specialized equipment in a manner for which it was specifically designed or equipped. Randall v. Liberty Mut. Ins. Co., 255 Va. 62, 496 S.E.2d 54 (1998).

In determining whether person was "using" insured vehicle at time he was injured within the meaning of this section, the relevant inquiry was whether there was a causal relationship between the accident and the use of the insured vehicle as a vehicle. Edwards v. Government Employees Ins. Co., 256 Va. 128, 500 S.E.2d 819 (1998).

Where person changing flat tire was using insured vehicle's equipment at the time of the accident, with the immediate intent to drive the vehicle after replacing the tire, there was a causal relationship between the accident and person's use of the vehicle as a vehicle. Edwards v. Government Employees Ins. Co., 256 Va. 128, 500 S.E.2d 819 (1998).

Person "occupying" vehicle. — One who was leaning over the front of a disabled car to check the wiring was not "occupying" the car within the meaning of a policy which defined "occupying" as "in or upon or entering into or alighting from." Pennsylvania Nat'l Mut. Cas. Ins. Co. v. Bristow, 207 Va. 381, 150 S.E.2d 125 (1966).

Person attempting to replace the tire on the insured vehicle was not "occupying" the vehicle within the meaning of a policy which defined "occupying" as "in or upon or entering into or alighting from" the motor vehicle. Edwards v. Government Employees Ins. Co., 256 Va. 128, 500 S.E.2d 819 (1998).

Person "using" vehicle. — In determining whether, at the time he or she was injured, a person was actually "using" an insured motor vehicle within the meaning of this section, which requires coverage for any person who "uses" the insured vehicle, the relevant inquiry is whether there was a causal relationship between the accident and the use of the insured vehicle as a vehicle. Newman v. Erie Ins. Exch., 256 Va. 501, 507 S.E.2d 348 (1998).

Student "using" school bus while crossing street. — A child was "using" a school bus at the time he was injured when the child was struck while crossing the lane opposite the lane in which the bus had stopped, after activating its warning lights and "stop" arm, to enter the bus; the child was using the bus as a vehicle at the time he was injured, based on his use of the bus' specialized safety equipment and his immediate intent to become a passenger in the bus and these facts established the required causal relationship between the vehicle and the child's use of the bus as a vehicle. Newman v. Erie Ins. Exch., 256 Va. 501, 507 S.E.2d 348 (1998).

Actual use of a vehicle for purposes of UM/UIM coverage mandated by this section is not restricted to the transportation function of a vehicle and, if the injured person is using the insured vehicle as a vehicle and as an integral part of his or her mission when he or she is injured, the injured person is entitled to UM/UIM coverage under this section; in this context, the use of a vehicle "as a vehicle" requires that at the time of the injury, the vehicle was being used in a manner for which it was specifically designed and equipped. Newman v. Erie Ins. Exch., 256 Va. 501, 507 S.E.2d 348 (1998).

Passenger as "insured." — As defendant-customer was operating an automobile owned by an automobile agency with the permission of the latter, and since the plaintiff-passenger was an "other person while occupying an insured automobile," plaintiff became an "insured" under the uninsured motorist provision of the defendant's policy. Pulley v. Allstate Ins. Co., 242 F. Supp. 330 (E.D. Va. 1965).

Paying passenger. — Although it is true that subsection B of this section uses the words "guest in such motor vehicle to which the policy applies," which might be construed to preclude coverage of paying passengers, where a driver's liability policy did not employ such limiting language and merely defined an insured in that class as "any other person while occupying an insured automobile," the fact that a passenger was a paying passenger made no difference in determining, under the driver's policy, the uninsured motorist coverage regarding the passenger. Hobbs v. Buckeye Union Cas. Co., 212 F. Supp. 349 (W.D. Va. 1962). But see Harleysville Mut. Ins. Co. v. Nationwide Mut. Ins. Co., 789 F.2d 272 (4th Cir. 1986).

The word "alighting" is not ambiguous; it merely varies from case to case. Because of the limitations of the other tests, the court would consider all the facts and circumstances in light of this section to determine whether plaintiff was alighting from the vehicle when struck by drunk driver. Roberts v. GEICO, 686 F. Supp. 135 (W.D. Va. 1988).

Passenger alighting from vehicle. — Under all the facts and circumstances and in view of the purpose of this section, the court concluded that plaintiff was still in the act of alighting when struck by drunk driver and was therefore occupying the vehicle he had just gotten out of, where the driver of the vehicle knew or should have known the danger of engaging plaintiff in conversation in the road,

and he assumed the obligation of taking plaintiff home, opened the door for him and prevented him from leaving the street to go home. Roberts v. GEICO, 686 F. Supp. 135 (W.D. Va. 1988).

Transfer of policy to insured's wife's name. — Whether driver of a vehicle involved in an accident with an unknown driver had transferred a liability policy, containing an uninsured motorist provision, to his wife's name prior to the accident made no difference with respect to coverage under the provision. Hobbs v. Buckeye Union Cas. Co., 212 F. Supp. 349 (W.D. Va. 1962). But see Harleysville Mut. Ins. Co. v. Nationwide Mut. Ins. Co., 789 F.2d 272 (4th Cir. 1986).

Employee injured by stranger to employment may recover under employer's policy. — An employee may recover under the uninsured motorist provisions of an insurance policy issued to his employer where he is injured by an uninsured motorist who is a stranger to the employment. Fidelity & Cas. Co. v. Futrell, 211 Va. 751, 180 S.E.2d 502 (1971).

A policy excluding an employee of the named insured from the benefit of the policy is not in conflict with the uninsured motorist statute, but is a permissible exclusion and operates to exclude the employee from the coverage of the policy. Aetna Cas. & Sur. Co. v. Kellam, 207 Va. 736, 152 S.E.2d 287 (1967), commented on in 53 Va. L. Rev. 1763 (1967).

The decision in Aetna Cas. & Sur. Co. v. Kellam, 207 Va. 736, 152 S.E.2d 287 (1967), cited above, should have been, and is now, limited to the situation where an employee is injured by a co-employee during the course of their employment by the named insured. Fidelity & Cas. Co. v. Futrell, 211 Va. 751, 180 S.E.2d 502 (1971).

Where defendant drove a private automobile that was not insured on business for his employer, and plaintiff had issued a liability policy insuring employer against the negligent acts of its employees, the vehicle was not an uninsured vehicle within the intent of subsection B. United States Fid. & Guar. Co. v. Byrum, 206 Va. 815, 146 S.E.2d 246 (1966).

Moped was covered where policy failed to exclude. — While insurer, in selecting language of policy, saw fit to exclude from definition of "motor vehicle" farm tractors, and vehicles operated on rails or crawler treads, and where insurer might also have excluded mopeds from coverage without offending minimum requirements imposed by statutory scheme, it nevertheless failed to do so, although moped is not included within statutory definition of "uninsured motor vehicle" for which § 38.2-2206 mandates coverage, ambiguity in insurer's policy was construed against insurer and in favor of coverage and thus policy's definition of "motor vehicle" included moped. Hill v. State Farm Mut. Auto. Ins. Co., 237 Va. 148, 375 S.E.2d 727 (1989).

Coverage not subject to this section. — Neither the Virginia Municipal Liability Pool's (VMLP) admission that its governing body made the decision to provide uninsured motorists coverage or a renewal letter sent by VMLP's administrator stating that, by offering uninsured motorists coverage, VMLP was required to comply with this section, were a resolution qualifying under former § 15.1-503.4:4 (now § 15.2-2704), therefore the trial court erred in holding that the uninsured motorists coverage offered by VMLP was subject to the provisions of this section. Virginia Municipal Liab. Pool v. Kennon, 247 Va. 254, 441 S.E.2d 8 (1994).

Fire department captain, who was approximately 20 to 25 feet away from his fire truck when he was struck and killed by a speeding hit-and-run driver, was an insured for purpose of the mandatory uninsured motorist coverage. Great Am. Ins. Co. v. Cassell, 239 Va. 421, 389 S.E.2d 476 (1990).

III. DENIAL OF COVERAGE.

Denial of coverage need not be express to constitute vehicle as "uninsured." — The denial of coverage referred to in subsection B (ii), with respect to what constitutes an "uninsured motor vehicle," need not be an express denial. It was enough that the insurance company, which was being liquidated in an insolvency proceeding in Delaware, had neither defended the action against its policyholder nor paid any part of the judgment against him. State Farm Mut. Auto. Ins. Co. v. Brower, 204 Va. 887, 134 S.E.2d 277 (1964).

Subsection B (ii) does not say that the denial must be express. It says only that the automobile is an uninsured vehicle if the insurance company "denies coverage." There is nothing in the letter of the statute nor in the spirit and purpose of the statute, that requires the denial to be expressed. Grossman v. Glens Falls Ins. Co., 211 Va. 195, 176 S.E.2d 318 (1970).

A denial of coverage can be by conduct as well as in writing or verbally. Grossman v. Glens Falls Ins. Co., 211 Va. 195, 176 S.E.2d 318 (1970).

To deny means to withhold, to refuse to grant. Grossman v. Glens Falls Ins. Co., 211 Va. 195, 176 S.E.2d 318 (1970).

There is no apparent reason why the words in the phrase "denies coverage" should not be given their natural and commonly understood meaning in the context in which they are used. Grossman v. Glens Falls Ins. Co., 211 Va. 195, 176 S.E.2d 318 (1970).

"Coverage" in the field of insurance means protection by insurance policy; in-clusion within the scope of a protective or beneficial plan (coverage against liability claims). Grossman v. Glens Falls Ins. Co., 211 Va. 195, 176 S.E.2d 318 (1970).

An insurer denies coverage to its insured when it fails or refuses to accord protection it contracted to give. Grossman v. Glens Falls Ins. Co., 211 Va. 195, 176 S.E.2d 318 (1970).

Failure of insurer to appear, defend, and pay as denial of coverage. — Where insurer failed to give insured protection against the damages he had "become legally obligated to pay" which insurer specifically promised to pay for him, its failure to appear, to defend and to pay was a denial of coverage within the meaning of subsection B (ii), and insured's car was therefore "an uninsured motor vehicle." Grossman v. Glens Falls Ins. Co., 211 Va. 195, 176 S.E.2d 318 (1970).

Rejection requirement. — Section 38.2-2202's explicit rejection requirement is consistent with its purpose of affording adequate protection to those injured by underinsured motorists. White v. National Union Fire Ins. Co., 913 F.2d 165 (4th Cir. 1990).

Information that supports an inference by the insurer that the insured intends to reject a default level of coverage does not suffice, under § 38.2-2202, as an actual "rejection" of that coverage. White v. National Union Fire Ins. Co., 913 F.2d 165 (4th Cir. 1990).

When insurance company did not need to send selection form. — Where the insured's policy was a renewal policy not requiring the insurance company to send the insured an "uninsured motorist coverage selection form" under § 38.2-2202 B, insurance company that did send the form could not avoid the lack of a statutorily required rejection of default coverage by pointing to a prior one where a subsequent, albeit inadequate, rejection was furnished. White v. National Union Fire Ins. Co., 913 F.2d 165 (4th Cir. 1990).

Husband not wife's agent in rejecting coverage. — Where husband and wife were the named insureds that statute required both to reject the higher coverage and where wife did not execute any rejection form, husband acted for himself and not as wife's agent when he signed the rejection form. State Farm Mut. Auto. Ins. Co. v. Weisman, 247 Va. 199, 441 S.E.2d 16 (1994).

An insurer who becomes insolvent "denies coverage." Grossman v. Glens Falls Ins. Co., 211 Va. 195, 176 S.E.2d 318 (1970).

Most assuredly a person with an automobile liability insurance policy in an insolvent company is neither covered nor protected, for his company is unable to pay on his behalf "all sums which the insured shall become legally obligated to pay as damages because of bodily injury sustained by any person caused by accident and arising out of the ownership, maintenance and use of the automobile by the insured." Such a person is an uninsured motorist within the meaning and intent of the statute. Grossman v. Glens Falls Ins. Co., 211 Va. 195, 176 S.E.2d 318 (1970).

An insurance company that is insolvent and unable to pay an amount which it has obligated itself to pay, by contract with an insured, has thereby denied, withheld and refused payment, and has failed to accord its insured protection and coverage. Grossman v. Glens Falls Ins. Co., 211 Va. 195, 176 S.E.2d 318 (1970).

IV. NOTICE OF ACCIDENT.

Subsection D refers to an action which arises ex contractu, for its requirements are qualified by the words "in order for the insured to recover under the endorsement." Nationwide Mut. Ins. Co. v. Clark, 213 Va. 666, 194 S.E.2d 699 (1973), decided prior to the 1974 amendment.

The language employed in subsection D is mandatory and establishes a condition precedent to the benefits of the statute, unless waived by the insurance company. Nationwide Mut. Ins. Co. v. Clark, 213 Va. 666, 194 S.E.2d 699 (1973), decided prior to the 1974 amendment.

Satisfaction of the requirement of subsection D is a prerequisite to a recovery under uninsured motorist coverage. The language of this section leaves no doubt as to its intent and purpose. Nationwide Mut. Ins. Co. v. Clark, 213 Va. 666, 194 S.E.2d 699 (1973), decided prior to the 1974 amendment.

The language of subsection D of this section is clear and unequivocal. Nationwide Mut. Ins. Co. v. Clark, 213 Va. 666, 194 S.E.2d 699 (1973), decided prior to the 1974 amendment.

The importance of reporting an accident involving bodily injuries and property damages, caused by the owner of a vehicle who is unknown, is obvious. Delay in reporting the accident and in alerting those entitled to know the details thereof, the injuries involved and damages done could cause a delay in the investigation. This could result in a failure to discover the identity of the unknown motorist and the imposition of liability where it does not primarily belong. Nationwide Mut. Ins. Co. v. Clark, 213 Va. 666, 194 S.E.2d 699 (1973), decided prior to the 1974 amendment.

Filing of report by policy insured satisfies subsection D. — The filing of the accident report by the insured named in the policy satisfies the purposes and requirements of subsection D. Nationwide Mut. Ins. Co. v. Clark, 213 Va. 666, 194 S.E.2d 699 (1973), decided prior to the 1974 amendment.

Notice required by subsection D is not prerequisite to action against John Doe. — The notice provision in subsection D is not a requirement in an action against John Doe, for the action against John Doe is not an action on the policy, but a tort action raising the issue of the legal liability of the unknown motorist. Doe v. Brown, 203 Va. 508, 125 S.E.2d 159 (1962).

The notice to the Division (now Department) of Motor Vehicles required by subsection D is not a prerequisite to an action against John Doe. Hodgson v. Doe, 203 Va. 938, 128 S.E.2d 444 (1962).

Subsection D of this section and § 46.1-400 (now § 46.2-372), requiring the filing of accident reports, are police regulations intended for the collection of data which may be useful in preventing other accidents; they are not designed to affect the rights of a party in an action to recover for injuries sustained in an automobile accident. Nationwide Mut. Ins. Co. v. Sours, 205 Va. 602, 139 S.E.2d 51 (1964).

This section is silent on the requirement of contact and notice to the insurance company; hence, it is not necessary to allege contact and notice in the motion for judgment. Bryant v. State Farm Mut. Auto. Ins. Co., 205 Va. 897, 140 S.E.2d 817 (1965).

Policy endorsements requiring such notice and contact between vehicles do not affect action. — In an action against John Doe, it was not necessary to allege or prove that notice had been given to the Division (now Department) of Motor Vehicles and the insurance company or that there was contact between the insured automobile and that of the unknown driver. Endorsements on the policy which established these requirements did not affect the John Doe action. Doe v. Brown, 203 Va. 508, 125 S.E.2d 159 (1962).

A provision of a policy which required report of an accident to the company in hit-and-run cases, defined to mean cases where the vehicle causing injury makes physical contact with the insured or with the insured vehicle, was invalid because it imposed on the insured a condition not contained in this section, which establishes the exclusive terms and obligation of uninsured motorist coverage. Nationwide Mut. Ins. Co. v. Sours, 205 Va. 602, 139 S.E.2d 51 (1964).

A failure to give notice as soon as practicable under the terms of a policy need not be accompanied by prejudice to allow the insurer to avoid coverage. It is regarded as a condition precedent to coverage. Dairyland Ins. Co. v. Hughes, 317 F. Supp. 928 (W.D. Va. 1970).

"As soon as practicable" means a reasonable time. What is a reasonable time is for the trier of fact under all the circumstances of the case. Dairyland Ins. Co. v. Hughes, 317 F. Supp. 928 (W.D. Va. 1970).

V. SERVICE OF PROCESS.

The provision for service of process on John Doe does not deny him due process

of law. John Doe is a fictitious person created under the provisions of the statute to stand in the place of the unknown motorist. John Doe is not a person, but for the purpose of this proceeding speaks through the insurance company. The insurance company, which is the party ultimately liable under the provisions of its policy for payment of a judgment obtained against John Doe, speaks and defends the action through and in the name of John Doe. Since John Doe is afforded the opportunity to defend the action through the insurance company, he has not been denied due process of law. Doe v. Brown, 203 Va. 508, 125 S.E.2d 159 (1962).

Subsection F applies to causes of action arising after its effective date, even though the insurance policy involved was issued prior to that date. Creteau v. Phoenix Assurance Co., 202 Va. 641, 119 S.E.2d 336 (1961).

The language employed in subsection F is mandatory and establishes as a condition precedent to the benefits of the statute that a copy of the process be served upon the insurance company. Creteau v. Phoenix Assurance Co., 202 Va. 641, 119 S.E.2d 336 (1961); State Farm Mut. Auto. Ins. Co. v. Duncan, 203 Va. 440, 125 S.E.2d 154 (1962).

The language employed in subsection F is mandatory and establishes a condition precedent to the benefits of the statute unless waived by the insurance company. Roenke v. Virginia Farm Bureau Mut. Ins. Co., 209 Va. 128, 161 S.E.2d 704 (1968).

Copy of the process must be served on the insurance company before it may be held liable under the Uninsured Motorist Act. The language employed is mandatory and establishes a condition precedent to the benefits of the statute unless waived by the insurance company. Midwest Mut. Ins. Co. v. Aetna Cas. & Sur. Co., 216 Va. 926, 223 S.E.2d 901 (1976).

The General Assembly could have provided other and different methods of notification, but it did not do so. By this statute it required formal service on the company, the same as if it were a defendant, and provided that a copy of the process must be served before the company could be held liable under the Uninsured Motorist Act. It used language which is exacting and established such service as a condition precedent to entitlement to the benefits of the statute. Roenke v. Virginia Farm Bureau Mut. Ins. Co., 209 Va. 128, 161 S.E.2d 704 (1968).

The provisions of subsection F of this section are clear and unequivocal, and the statute is mandatory. It says in plain language that any insured who intends to rely on the uninsured motorist coverage shall, if action is instituted against the owner or operator of an uninsured motor vehicle, serve a copy of the process upon the insurance company issuing the policy in the manner prescribed by law as though such in-

surance company were a party defendant. Roenke v. Virginia Farm Bureau Mut. Ins. Co., 209 Va. 128, 161 S.E.2d 704 (1968).

The notice required to be given an insurance company can be given in only one way, and that is by the service of a copy of the process in the manner prescribed by law. Roenke v. Virginia Farm Bureau Mut. Ins. Co., 209 Va. 128, 161 S.E.2d 704 (1968).

As to causes of action arising subsequent to April 27, 1959, the mandatory provisions of subsection F of this section are applicable, and if an insured intends to rely on the coverage provided by the uninsured motorist endorsement, it is incumbent upon the insured to serve a copy of the process upon the insurance company issuing the policy "as though such insurance company were a party defendant." Matthews v. Allstate Ins. Co., 194 F. Supp. 459 (E.D. Va. 1961).

Service under subsection F is mandatory and a condition precedent to the benefits of the statute unless waived by the insurance company. McDaniel v. State Farm Mut. Auto. Ins. Co., 205 Va. 815, 139 S.E.2d 806 (1965).

And is part of policy. — The requirement of subsection F is a part of the policy even though not mentioned therein. State Farm Mut. Auto. Ins. Co. v. Duncan, 203 Va. 440, 125 S.E.2d 154 (1962).

Even service of a copy of the process does not make the insurance company a defendant to the cause of action. The statute simply prescribes a precise and formal method of notification of the commencement or filing of a legal action to a party that is, or may be, interested in the action. Thereafter, the insurance company is given the right to file pleadings, and to take such other action allowable by law in the name of the owner or operator of the uninsured motor vehicle or in its own name. Roenke v. Virginia Farm Bureau Mut. Ins. Co., 209 Va. 128, 161 S.E.2d 704 (1968).

Service of process not waived. — That the insurance company had actual notice of the time, date and place of trial well in advance of it and had a legal representative present at the trial who did not participate therein was not enough to constitute a waiver of the service of process required by subsection F. Creteau v. Phoenix Assurance Co., 202 Va. 641, 119 S.E.2d 336 (1961).

The requirement for service on the company under subsection F was not waived by including in the policy a "Notice of Legal Action" clause providing merely that the company be supplied a copy of any process served in action by the insured against any party responsible for the use of an automobile involved in the accident. The notice provision of the policy served a different purpose than does the statutory requirement of service. Hence the inclusion of the notice provision indicated no intentional relinquishment by the company of its rights under the provisions of the statute. State Farm Mut. Auto. Ins. Co. v. Duncan, 203 Va. 440, 125 S.E.2d 154 (1962).

There was no merit in the contention that when the representatives of the defendant insurance company dealt with the representatives of the plaintiff in an effort to settle the dispute between them, it became the duty of the representatives of the insurance company to advise the plaintiff that it was relying upon the provisions of the statute regarding service rather than the terms and provisions of the policy. State Farm Mut. Auto. Ins. Co. v. Duncan, 203 Va. 440, 125 S.E.2d 154 (1962).

There was no merit to insurer's contention that plaintiff was required to state in his motion for judgment the grounds for serving it on his own insurance carrier. Such requirement is not contained in the statute and would be impracticable. McDaniel v. State Farm Mut. Auto. Ins. Co., 205 Va. 815, 139 S.E.2d 806 (1965).

Where the most that the evidence showed was that the insurer, with knowledge of the accident and pending action in Tennessee, corresponded and had some contact with insured's counsel, and intimated an interest in effecting a settlement of the case against an uninsured motorist, if it could be settled for a nominal amount, this was not enough to constitute a waiver of service of process or to estop the insurer from relying on the provisions of this statute. Roenke v. Virginia Farm Bureau Mut. Ins. Co., 209 Va. 128, 161 S.E.2d 704 (1968).

The insurer was under no legal obligation to notify the insured that it was his responsibility and obligation to follow this statute in serving the insurer with process. Roenke v. Virginia Farm Bureau Mut. Ins. Co., 209 Va. 128, 161 S.E.2d 704 (1968).

Time limitation period not same as filing action against tortfeasor. — This section, which requires an insured who intends to rely upon the uninsured motorist's coverage provision of his policy to serve a copy of the process upon the insurance company, does not require that such service be accomplished within the limitation period for filing an action against a tortfeasor. Glens Falls Ins. Co. v. Stephenson, 235 Va. 420, 367 S.E.2d 722 (1988).

Timely service held not shown. — Where the only evidence of the time of receipt of process offered by plaintiffs, other than an undated return receipt, was the testimony of their own counsel that an employee of defendant insurer had telephoned him "two days before the return day," even if counsel's testimony had been admitted into evidence, it would not have proved that the letter was received in the time required by §§ 8.01-288 and 16.1-82. Davis v. American Interinsurance Exch., 228 Va. 1, 319 S.E.2d 723 (1984).

Right of insurer to defend action against uninsured motorist before enactment of subsection F. — See Matthews v. Allstate Ins. Co., 194 F. Supp. 459 (E.D. Va. 1961).

VI. JOHN DOE ACTIONS.

Under the Virginia Uninsured Motorist Act, John Doe is a fictitious person who speaks through the uninsured motorist carrier, which is the party ultimately liable. Truman v. Spivey, 225 Va. 274, 302 S.E.2d 517 (1983).

Plaintiff must prove that there was a vehicle driven by an unknown person. — To support an action against John Doe under the uninsured motorist statute, a plaintiff must prove not only that John Doe existed — that is, that there was a vehicle, but also that the operator is unknown. Haymore v. Brizendine, 210 Va. 578, 172 S.E.2d 774 (1970).

Defendant must show that John Doe was known. — Where the plaintiff has introduced evidence that there was a vehicle driven by an unknown person, it is incumbent on the defendant to bring forth evidence that John Doe was known. Haymore v. Brizendine, 210 Va. 578, 172 S.E.2d 774 (1970).

There is no limitation on the commonly accepted meaning of the word "unknown" in this section. Bryant v. State Farm Mut. Auto. Ins. Co., 205 Va. 897, 140 S.E.2d 817 (1965).

Plaintiff must establish that John Doe is liable to him and to what extent as a prerequisite to asserting any claim against his insurer. Johnson v. GMC, 242 F. Supp. 778 (E.D. Va. 1965).

No judgment can be entered against plaintiff's insurer and its name cannot be mentioned in the presence of the jury until John Doe's liability is established. Johnson v. GMC, 242 F. Supp. 778 (E.D. Va. 1965).

Under Virginia law, an insurer would not be subject to an action in contract on its uninsured motorist endorsement until judgment in tort had been entered against the unknown defendant as "John Doe." Willard v. Aetna Cas. & Sur. Co., 213 Va. 481, 193 S.E.2d 776 (1973).

Insured is not required to exercise due diligence to identify unknown motorist. — The uninsured motorist statute does not say that if an insured fails to exercise due care or diligence to ascertain the identity of an unknown motorist causing him bodily injury or property damage he cannot maintain an action to establish legal liability against an unknown party. The statute simply states that if the owner or operator be "unknown" he shall be deemed to be uninsured. There is no limitation in the statute on the commonly accepted meaning of the word "unknown." To say that an insured has the duty to exercise due diligence to ascertain the identity of an unknown motorist would be reading into the statute language which does not there appear. Mangus v. Doe, 203 Va. 518, 125 S.E.2d 166 (1962).

For the Supreme Court to say that an insured had the duty to exercise due diligence to ascertain the identity of an unknown motorist would be reading into the statute language which does not there appear. Bryant v. State Farm Mut. Auto. Ins. Co., 205 Va. 897, 140 S.E.2d 817 (1965).

Issue is whether owner or operator was unknown to plaintiff. — Under subsection E the issue is not whether the plaintiff "was unable to identify the owner or operator" of the other vehicle involved in an accident, but whether the "owner or operator" was "unknown" to the plaintiff. Doe v. Simmers, 207 Va. 956, 154 S.E.2d 146 (1967).

John Doe, through the insurance carrier, can make any defense that the real defendant could make. Truman v. Spivey, 225 Va. 274, 302 S.E.2d 517 (1983).

A John Doe action under the Virginia Uninsured Motorist Act is not on the insurance contract but is an action in tort. Truman v. Spivey, 225 Va. 274, 302 S.E.2d 517 (1983).

Venue for a John Doe action is to be determined under the general venue statutes as if the action against John Doe were against the insurance company itself. Hodgson v. Doe, 203 Va. 938, 128 S.E.2d 444 (1962); Truman v. Spivey, 225 Va. 274, 302 S.E.2d 517 (1983).

Insurer is not party to John Doe action. — The insurance company is not a named party defendant in the action against the uninsured motorist even though the insurance company must be served. No judgment may be entered against the insurance company in such action, and the only issues presented are the establishment of the legal liability of the uninsured motorist. Rodgers v. Danko, 204 Va. 140, 129 S.E.2d 828 (1963).

While it may be true that if John Doe is determined to be a party liable to plaintiff in a wrongful death accident, plaintiff's insurer may then be called upon to pay the plaintiff to the extent of its uninsured motorist liability, this does not mean that it is the real party in interest. Johnson v. GMC, 242 F. Supp. 778 (E.D. Va. 1965).

"John Doe" practice is unwarranted in diversity cases, and the action is subject to dismissal unless the John Does are eliminated or their citizenship affirmatively alleged. Johnson v. GMC, 242 F. Supp. 778 (E.D. Va. 1965).

The unidentified person need not be joined in a removal petition if a cause of action is not stated in the complaint filed against a John Doe defendant. Johnson v. GMC, 242 F. Supp. 778 (E.D. Va. 1965).

It is necessary for a removing defendant to show that a John Doe codefendant was a nonresident, absent clear proof of bad faith in joinder, at the time of the institution of the action, unless, of course, a separable controversy appears from the complaint. Johnson v. GMC, 242 F. Supp. 778 (E.D. Va. 1965).

There was no requirement that plaintiff's testimony in a John Doe action must be corroborated in accord with former § 8-286 [now § 8.01-397]. That section was inapplicable. John Doe v. Faulkner, 203 Va. 522, 125 S.E.2d 169 (1962).

Trial courts should not permit the motion for judgment to be seen by the jury or carried to their room where the jury may thus learn that the defendant, John Doe, is covered by insurance. Doe v. Brown, 203 Va. 508, 125 S.E.2d 159 (1962).

Amendment of motion for judgment subsequent to expiration of limitation period. — Where a motorist brought a John Doe action within the two-year limitation period, but amended his motion for judgment to include the name of the previously unknown motorist after the statute of limitations had run, his action against the other motorist was not time-barred. Any surprise arising from the claim against the other motorist was on the motorist bringing the action, not his insurance carrier, since he first learned of the other motorist's identity from the carrier's responsive pleadings. Any problems in gathering evidence resulting from the amendment would likewise fall on the motorist bringing the action. Further, the interests of the other motorist would be protected by the incentive for the carrier to undertake defensive action on behalf of the uninsured motorist. Truman v. Spivey, 225 Va. 274, 302 S.E.2d 517 (1983).

VII. CONTRIBUTION.

Insurer of one tort-feasor is not entitled to contribution from insurer of injured party for any part of the judgment rendered against the insured tort-feasor and an uninsured tort-feasor. Southern v. Lumbermens Mut. Cas. Co., 236 F. Supp. 370 (W.D. Va. 1964).

A liability insurer of one tort-feasor can go against the other tort-feasor, or against the other tort-feasor's insurer, but not against the insurer of the injured party, since Virginia law does not create insurance for uninsured motorists. Southern v. Lumbermens Mut. Cas. Co., 236 F. Supp. 370 (W.D. Va. 1964).

Insurer, which paid, under uninsured motorist coverage, judgment obtained by passenger in insured's car against an unknown motorist and the insured, as joint tort-feasors, was not entitled to any contribution from the insurer of the passenger. Hobbs v. Buckeye Union Cas. Co., 212 F. Supp. 349 (W.D. Va. 1962). But see Harleysville Mut. Ins. Co. v. Nationwide Mut. Ins. Co., 789 F.2d 272 (4th Cir. 1986).

Subsection G grants to an insurer a presently protectable right to preserve subrogation, even though the right to be paid in subrogation cannot be enforced until some time in the future. Virginia Farm Bureau Mut. Ins. Co. v. Gibson, 236 Va. 433, 374 S.E.2d 58 (1988).

VIII. SUBROGATION.

Subsection G is the only provision in the Uninsured Motorist Law which permits subrogation. United States Fid. & Guar. Co. v. Byrum, 206 Va. 815, 146 S.E.2d 246 (1966); General Accident Fire & Life Assurance Corp. v. Aetna Cas. & Sur. Co., 208 Va. 467, 158 S.E.2d 750 (1968); United Servs. Auto. Ass'n v. Nationwide Mut. Ins. Co., 218 Va. 861, 241 S.E.2d 784 (1978).

Employer or compensation carrier has no right of subrogation against employee's insurer. — There is nothing in subsection I which gives an employer or its workmen's compensation carrier a right of subrogation against an insurer of the employee under the uninsured motorist provision of a liability policy contracted for by the employee or someone for his benefit. Horne v. Superior Life Ins. Co., 203 Va. 282, 123 S.E.2d 401 (1962).

But employer's right of subrogation against third party is superior to that of insurer. — An employer's right of subrogation against a negligent third party under the Workers' Compensation Act, former § 65.1-41 (now § 65.2-309), is superior to that of the insurer under subsection G. Horne v. Superior Life Ins. Co., 203 Va. 282, 123 S.E.2d 401 (1962).

When subrogation action can be maintained against tort-feasor's insurer. — Since in Virginia an injured person must reduce her claim to judgment before bringing an action against the tort-feasor's liability insurer, and § 8.01-5 prohibits joinder of an insurance company on the account of issuance of an insurance policy to or for the benefit of any party to any cause, where subrogation is the vehicle by which relief is sought, neither the insured nor the uninsured motorist carrier, as her subrogee, can maintain an action against the tort-feasor's liability insurer unless a judgment has first been obtained against the tort-feasor. United Servs. Auto. Ass'n v. Nationwide Mut. Ins. Co., 218 Va. 861, 241 S.E.2d 784 (1978).

No subrogation against Property and Casualty Insurance Guarantee Association. — Where the insurer of a driver of a truck which collided with insureds became insolvent and an uninsured motorist insurer paid the insured the full amount of their claims, the uninsured motorist insurer did not then have any rights of subrogation against the Property and Casualty Insurance Guarantee Association because the insureds never suffered any finan-

cial loss due to the insolvency of driver's insurer. Northland Ins. Co. v. Virginia Property & Cas. Ins. Guar. Ass'n, 240 Va. 115, 392 S.E.2d 682 (1990).

IX. WORKERS' COMPENSATION POLICIES.

Primary effect of subsection I. — Subsection I of this section deals primarily, and seemingly exclusively, with incidents of workers' compensation laws. Travelers Indem. Co. v. Wells, 316 F.2d 770 (4th Cir. 1963).

The intent of the General Assembly in enacting subsection I was to make it clear that policy coverage required by this section did not apply to workers' compensation policies, and that the benefits of the section would not accrue to an employer who became liable for workers' compensation benefits to an employee injured by an uninsured motorist while in a motor vehicle owned by the employer. Aetna Cas. & Sur. Co. v. Kellam, 207 Va. 736, 152 S.E.2d 287 (1967), commented on in 53 Va. L. Rev. 1763 (1967).

The 1960 addition to subsection (h) of former § 38.1-381 (see now subsection I of this section) was apparently for the purpose of making clear that the subsection was not designed to affect the liability of an insurer to an insured employee or other person injured by an uninsured motor vehicle. It was not intended to give to an employee a protection not otherwise given by this section. Aetna Cas. & Sur. Co. v. Kellam, 207 Va. 736, 152 S.E.2d 287 (1967), commented on in 53 Va. L. Rev. 1763 (1967).

Virginia law does not permit recovery by an insured's estate under the uninsured motorist provision of the insured's policy (paid for by the insured), where the insured was killed in a work-related motor vehicle accident and where the employer/vehicle owner and co-employee/vehicle operator both had insurance, but where the exclusive remedy clause of the Virginia Workers' Compensation Act bars recovery under those other policies. Aetna Cas. & Sur. Co. v. Dodson, 235 Va. 346, 367 S.E.2d 505 (1988).

Timing of recovery not controlling of set-off right. — The timing of a third-party recovery cannot be allowed to control the extent of a self-insured employer's right to set-off or credit pursuant to subsection I of this section. Dale v. City of Newport News Pub. Utils., 18 Va. App. 800, 447 S.E.2d 878 (1994).

Extent of set-off. — Subsection I of this section grants a self-insured employer a set-off against continuing and future workers' compensation liability. Dale v. City of Newport News Pub. Utils., 18 Va. App. 800, 447 S.E.2d 878 (1994).

Employee's recovery not limited to worker's compensation benefits where

360

employer self-insures its motor vehicles. The employee of an employer which self-insures its motor vehicles is entitled to recovery under the uninsured motorist protection statute, and the employee's recovery was not limited to worker's compensation benefits by the exclusivity provision in former § 65.1-40 (now § 65.2-307). William v. City of Newport News, 240 Va. 425, 397 S.E.2d 813 (1990).

Where the employee of an employer which self-insured its motor vehicles was entitled to recovery under the uninsured motorist statute, this application of the Workers' Compensation Act, former § 65.1-40 (now § 65.2-307), the uninsured motorist protection provision, this section, and the motor vehicle code, § 46.2-368, as they relate to an employee, was consistent with the language of the statutes and the intent of the General Assembly in enacting uninsured motorist protection provisions. William v. City of Newport News, 240 Va. 425, 397 S.E.2d 813 (1990).

Decision in Aetna Cas. & Sur. Co. v. Kellam is limited. — The decision in Aetna Cas. & Sur. Co. v. Kellam, 207 Va. 736, 152 S.E.2d 287 (1967), cited above, should have been, and is now, limited to the situation where an employee is injured by a co-employee during the course of their employment by the named insured. Fidelity & Cas. Co. v. Futrell, 211 Va. 751, 180 S.E.2d 502 (1971).

Policy provision not in conflict with subsection I. — The provision of a policy that it was not to inure to the benefit of any workers' compensation carrier or self-insurer was not in conflict with subsection I. Horne v. Superior Life Ins. Co., 203 Va. 282, 123 S.E.2d 401 (1962).

X. ILLUSTRATIVE CASES.

Refusal to pay punitive damages did not deny coverage where such coverage not provided for. — Where the defendant's car was fully insured under this section, and the insurers did not contract to provide coverage for punitive damages, the insurers of the car, in refusing to pay punitive damages, did not deny any coverage which they had contracted to supply. Rossman v. State Farm Mut. Auto. Ins. Co., 832 F.2d 282 (4th Cir. 1987).

Where garage liability policy expressly excluded coverage of a garage customer whenever he was insured by other valid and collectible insurance "whether primary, excess or contingent" and the insurance available to a garage customer under customer's policy was excess insurance, its existence was an event which triggered the garage liability policy's escape clause, and the customer's insurer had primary coverage. GEICO v. Universal Underwriters Ins. Co., 232 Va. 326, 350 S.E.2d 612 (1986).

Because employer pizza delivery company did not own plaintiff's car, it could not grant him permission to use his automobile for purposes of coverage under its policy with defendant; therefore, plaintiff was not covered under the policy when he made deliveries, including the trip during which the claimed accident occurred, and defendant could not be held liable. Stone v. Liberty Mut. Ins. Co., 105 F.3d 188 (4th Cir. 1997).

Primary, not secondary, carrier entitled to subsection B credit. — Primary and not secondary underinsured motorist carrier was entitled to subsection B credit for the tortfeasor's liability coverage payment although secondary carrier contended that because motorcyclist was not "entitled to underinsured motorist coverage under more than one policy," the statutory priority provisions did not apply in the case; under secondary carriers' theory, the credit was first deducted from motorcyclist's entitlement to underinsured motorist coverage, reducing that entitlement to $25,000, the coverage of only one policy—that of the primary carrier. There was a flaw in this reasoning. The emphasis of the disputed portion of the statute was upon an injured person's entitlement to multiple underinsured motorist coverage. After a determination of such an entitlement, the statute then fixed the multiple carriers' order of liability and finally designates the priority of each carrier in the credit. Dairyland Ins. Co. v. Sylva, 242 Va. 191, 409 S.E.2d 127 (1991).

Reading provisions to give credit to primary carrier did not create conflict in provisions. — Where provisions of the statute were read to give primary carrier priority in credit over secondary carrier, such reading did not create a conflict in its provisions and thus result in an absurdity; a conflict arises in a document only when it deals inconsistently with the same subject matter; here, the statutory allocation of liability among the members of the group is one matter and the allocation of a credit against that liability arising from an outside source is a different matter. Dairyland Ins. Co. v. Sylva, 242 Va. 191, 409 S.E.2d 127 (1991).

Although credit to primary carrier illogical, court applied statute as written. — Although secondary carrier argued that because of primary carrier's basic liability to pay motorcyclist's underinsured motorist claim, an award of the credit to primary carrier would be illogical, since the disputed provisions of a statute are plain and unambiguous, the court was not concerned with the logic or wisdom of the legislature and applied the statute as written. Dairyland Ins. Co. v. Sylva, 242 Va. 191, 409 S.E.2d 127 (1991).

Waiver of higher coverage remaining in effect. — Where in 1984, insured executed and returned a waiver form to insurer by which he requested $25,000 uninsured motorist (UM) coverage and rejected the higher level of coverage, which would have been $100,000, and where in 1990, insurer mailed insured a renewal policy for the 1991 period covering the date of the accident; however, insured did not return this waiver form to insurer, the mere fact that insurer sent insured a waiver form was not sufficient to negate earlier decision to reject the higher limits of UM coverage. Thus, the 1984 waiver of higher UM coverage remained in effect through later policy renewals, so that insured's UM coverage at the time of the accident was $25,000. USAA Cas. Ins. Co. v. Alexander, 248 Va. 185, 445 S.E.2d 145 (1994).

Limitation void. — Since the limitation on uninsured motorist coverage in policy conflicted with the statute, it was void. Moody v. Federated Mut. Ins. Co., 886 F. Supp. 5 (W.D. Va. 1994), aff'd, 48 F.3d 1216 (4th Cir. 1995).

"Operator" status not lost by merely leaving vehicle. — Driver of an uninsured vehicle was an "operator" where the evidence showed that he was driving an uninsured motor vehicle along the Interstate when he had a tire blow-out and alighted from the vehicle, went to the trunk of the car to use the spare tire, found it had insufficient air pressure, and walked away from the vehicle carrying the spare, intending to find a service station so the tire could be fully inflated, and after walking approximately 200 feet from the disabled vehicle, driver climbed an embankment and near the top of the embankment he slipped, fell, and dropped the tire and it rolled down the embankment striking the windshield of a bus since the term "operator," according to the plain language of the policy, identifies the person from whom recovery may be had for injury or damage, and one's status as "operator" is not relinquished or lost by merely leaving the vehicle. Colonial Ins. Co. v. Rainey, 237 Va. 270, 377 S.E.2d 393 (1989).

Insured struck simultaneously by two uninsured vehicles entitled to recover only for single accident. — Insurer of a policy containing uninsured motorist endorsement was only liable to the insured up to the policy limit for a single accident where insured's automobile was struck virtually simultaneously by two uninsured vehicles. State Farm Mut. Auto. Ins. Co. v. Drewry, 316 F.2d 716 (4th Cir. 1963).

And only up to policy limit. — Where plaintiffs' automobile was struck almost simultaneously by two uninsured motorists, plaintiffs' contention that subsection A provided each uninsured motorist with coverage up to the statutory limit was without merit. The policy provision limiting liability to $15,000 as to any one person and $30,000 as a result of any one accident was in compliance with the statute and was therefore controlling. Drewry v. State Farm Mut. Auto. Ins. Co., 204 Va. 231, 129 S.E.2d 681 (1963). See State Farm Mut. Auto. Ins. Co. v. Drewry, 191 F. Supp. 852 (W.D. Va. 1960), aff'd, 316 F.2d 716 (4th Cir. 1963).

Applicability of Virginia law. — Although automobile in question was principally garaged in Tennessee, not in Virginia, at the time of the accident Virginia dealer license plates were affixed to the vehicle and it had been left for repair in Virginia. Accordingly, the Virginia uninsured motorists statute was applicable. Moody v. Federated Mut. Ins. Co., 886 F. Supp. 5 (W.D. Va. 1994), aff'd, 48 F.3d 1216 (4th Cir. 1995).

Sexual assault in vehicle not covered. — Standard uninsured motorist provision of a Virginia automobile insurance policy did not provide coverage for incident in which insured is abducted in a stolen vehicle, transported to an isolated location, and sexually assaulted within the automobile. Doe v. State Farm Fire & Cas. Co., 878 F. Supp. 862 (E.D. Va. 1995).

The attorney for the insurer should have been allowed to tell the jury, without identifying himself as insurance counsel, only that he was present in court to assist the uninsured motorist in his defense. Travelers Ins. Co. v. Lobello, 212 Va. 534, 186 S.E.2d 80 (1972).

Injection of insurance into case was prejudicial error. — In an action for damages against several motorists, of whom one was uninsured, it was error, prejudicial to the other defendant, to permit the injection of insurance into the case, because to tell the jury that one defendant was uninsured was to permit it to infer that the other was insured, and where two or more defendants may be jointly and severally liable, to say that one defendant has "insurance backing" is to create a situation permitting the return of a possibly inflated verdict binding upon all defendants so liable. Travelers Ins. Co. v. Lobello, 212 Va. 534, 186 S.E.2d 80 (1972).

§ 38.2-2207. No policy to exclude coverage to employee. — No policy or contract of bodily injury or property damage liability insurance relating to the ownership, maintenance, or use of a motor vehicle, aircraft or watercraft shall exclude coverage to an employee of the insured in any controversy arising between employees even though one employee shall be awarded compensation as provided in Title 65.2. (Code 1950, § 38-238; 1952, c. 317, § 38.1-381; 1958, c. 282; 1959, Ex. Sess., cc. 42, 70; 1970, c. 462; 1962, c. 457; 1964, c. 477; 1966, cc. 182, 459; 1968, cc. 199, 721; 1970, c. 494; 1971, Ex. Sess., c. 216; 1973, cc.

225, 390; 1974, c. 87; 1976, cc. 121, 122; 1977, c. 78; 1979, c. 113; 1980, cc. 326, 331; 1981, Sp. Sess., c. 6; 1982, cc. 638, 642; 1984, c. 541; 1985, cc. 39, 325; 1986, c. 562; 1987, c. 519.)

Editor's note. — See also the case annotations under the heading "I. General Consideration" under § 38.2-2204.

The General Assembly did not intend to exclude motor vehicle accidents from the workers' compensation scheme. Had the General Assembly intended to exclude motor vehicle accidents from the coverage of the Workers' Compensation Act, it would have done so directly in the Act itself, rather than indirectly through a provision in Title 38.2. Smith v. Horn, 232 Va. 302, 351 S.E.2d 14 (1986).

§ 38.2-2208. Notices of cancellation of or refusal to renew motor vehicle insurance policies. — A. No written notice of cancellation or refusal to renew that is mailed by an insurer to an insured in accordance with the provisions of a motor vehicle insurance policy shall be effective unless:

1. a. It is sent by registered or certified mail, or

b. At the time of mailing the insurer obtains a written receipt from the United States Postal Service showing the name and address of the insured stated in the policy; and

2. The insurer retains a copy of the notice of cancellation or refusal to renew.

3. [Repealed.]

B. If the terms of the policy require the notice of cancellation or refusal to renew to be given to any lienholder, then the insurer shall mail such notice and retain a copy of the notice in the manner required by subsection A of this section. If the notices sent to the insured and the lienholder are part of the same form, the insurer may retain a single copy of the notice. The registered, certified or regular mail postal receipt and the copy of the notices required by this section shall be retained by the insurer for at least one year from the date of termination.

C. Copy, as used in this section, shall include photographs, microphotographs, photostats, microfilm, microcard, printouts or other reproductions of electronically stored data, or copies from optical disks, electronically transmitted facsimiles, or any other reproduction of an original from a process which forms a durable medium for its recording, storing, and reproducing. (1954, c. 263, § 38.1-381.1; 1960, c. 127; 1975, c. 164; 1983, c. 371; 1986, c. 562; 1992, c. 160.)

Law Review. — For survey of Virginia law on insurance for the year 1974-1975, see 61 Va. L. Rev. 1759 (1975).

The cancellation of an automobile liability insurance policy is a matter of importance, not only to the insured thereunder but to third parties whose rights are affected thereby. Gregory v. Providence Wash. Ins. Co., 214 Va. 134, 198 S.E.2d 616 (1973).

This section becomes a part of the insurance policy contract by force of its language and either party seeking to cancel the policy has to comply with it. Ampy v. Metro. Cas. Ins. Co., 200 Va. 396, 105 S.E.2d 839 (1958); Harleysville Mut. Ins. Co. v. Dollins, 201 Va. 73, 109 S.E.2d 405 (1959).

This section becomes a part of an insurance policy contract by virtue of its language and a party seeking to cancel a policy has to comply strictly with its provisions. Gregory v. Providence Wash. Ins. Co., 214 Va. 134, 198 S.E.2d 616 (1973).

Insurers must comply strictly with conditions relating to cancellation. — Under the law of Virginia, insurers, who depend upon such mailings to cancel their coverages, are properly required to comply strictly with the conditions stipulated in the policy when they exercise the right of cancellation. Riddick v. State Capital Ins. Co., 271 F.2d 641 (4th Cir. 1959).

But cancellation may be effective whether or not notice was actually received. — Cancellation complying with requirements of this section and of policy effective whether or not assured actually received notice thereof. Riddick v. State Capital Ins. Co., 271 F.2d 641 (4th Cir. 1959).

It is not necessary to prove actual receipt of the cancellation notice. If the notice is mailed in accordance with the terms of the policy and the provisions of this section the notice of cancellation is effective. Ampy v. Metro. Cas. Ins. Co., 200 Va. 396, 105 S.E.2d 839 (1958).

And mailing of notice, properly addressed, may be sufficient. — Where cancellation notice complied in all respects with the requirements of the policy and was properly addressed, its mailing effectively cancelled the insurance coverage as of the date specified in the notice. Riddick v. State Capital Ins. Co., 271 F.2d 641 (4th Cir. 1959).

Notice of cancellation by an insurer may be sent the insured by mail in accordance with the provisions of the policy. Gregory v. Providence Wash. Ins. Co., 214 Va. 134, 198 S.E.2d 616 (1973).

An address is complete and proper without reference to the county in which the post office is located. Riddick v. State Capital Ins. Co., 271 F.2d 641 (4th Cir. 1959).

An unsigned or blank certificate does not comply with this section. Gregory v. Providence Wash. Ins. Co., 214 Va. 134, 198 S.E.2d 616 (1973).

Authority of agency to issue a policy does not carry with it the power to cancel it. National Union Fire Ins. Co. v. Dixon, 206 Va. 568, 145 S.E.2d 187 (1965).

Burden. — The defendant, having interposed the cancellation of the policy as its sole defense, had the burden of proving the effective cancellation thereof. National Union Fire Ins. Co. v. Dixon, 206 Va. 568, 145 S.E.2d 187 (1965).

The insurance company having interposed and relied upon the cancellation of the policy as its defense had the burden of proving the effective cancellation thereof in compliance with this section. Gregory v. Providence Wash. Ins. Co., 214 Va. 134, 198 S.E.2d 616 (1973).

Compliance with policy is question of law. — The question of whether the mailing of a cancellation notice complied with the requirements of the policy was one of law which should have been decided by the court, rather than a jury. Riddick v. State Capital Ins. Co., 271 F.2d 641 (4th Cir. 1959).

Section does not preclude witness from explaining insurance company procedures. — Nothing in this section precludes a witness from explaining procedures that an insurance company utilizes to generate documents that must be sent to an insured. Motley v. Regal Ins. Co., 245 Va. 97, 425 S.E.2d 506 (1993).

§ 38.2-2209. Motor vehicle liability medical benefit insurer not to retain right of subrogation to recover from third party. — No policy or contract of bodily injury or property damage liability insurance that contains any representation by an insurer to pay all reasonable medical expenses incurred for bodily injury caused by accident to the insured or any relative or other person coming within the provisions of the policy, shall be issued or delivered by any insurer licensed in this Commonwealth upon any motor vehicle then principally garaged or principally used in this Commonwealth, if the insurer retains the right of subrogation to recover amounts paid on behalf of an injured person under the provision of the policy from any third party. (1964, c. 612, § 38.1-381.2; 1986, c. 562.)

The legislature has expressly prohibited the inclusion of subrogation provisions for medical payments in automobile liability policies. Collins v. Blue Cross, 213 Va. 540, 193 S.E.2d 782 (1973).

§ 38.2-2210. Warning concerning cancellation to appear on application for motor vehicle liability insurance; reason for cancellation or nonrenewal required on application. — A. Any application for the original issuance of a policy of insurance covering liability arising out of the ownership, maintenance, or use of any motor vehicle as defined in § 38.2-2212 shall have the following statement printed on or attached to the first page of the application form, in boldface type: READ YOUR POLICY. THE POLICY OF INSURANCE FOR WHICH THIS APPLICATION IS BEING MADE, IF ISSUED, MAY BE CANCELLED WITHOUT CAUSE AT THE OPTION OF THE INSURER AT ANY TIME IN THE FIRST 60 DAYS DURING WHICH IT IS IN EFFECT AND AT ANY TIME THEREAFTER FOR REASONS STATED IN THE POLICY.

B. Any application for the original issuance of a policy of insurance covering liability arising out of the ownership, maintenance, or use of any motor vehicle defined in § 38.2-2212 that requires the insured to disclose information as to any previous cancellation or refusal to renew shall also permit the insured to offer or provide a full explanation of the reason for the cancellation or refusal to renew.

C. The notice required by this section shall be given by the insurer to any applicant within ten days of the application in the event the applicant is not provided a written copy of the application and the coverage has been bound by such insurer.

D. This section shall not apply to the renewal of any policy of insurance. (1966, c. 523, § 38.1-381.3; 1986, c. 562; 1988, cc. 655, 665.)

§ 38.2-2211. Motor vehicle liability insurer not to receive credit for other medical expense insurance. — No policy or contract of bodily injury or property damage liability insurance that contains any representation by an insurer to pay all reasonable medical expenses incurred for bodily injury caused by accident to the insured, relative or any other person coming within the provisions of the policy, shall be issued or delivered by any insurer licensed in this Commonwealth upon any motor vehicle then principally garaged or principally used in this Commonwealth, if the policy provides for credit against the medical expense coverage for any other medical expense insurance to which the injured person may be entitled. Nothing in this section allows the injured person to collect more than his actual medical expenses as a result of an accident from any one or any combination of all policies providing motor vehicle medical payment coverage applicable to the accident. (1968, c. 759, § 38.1-381.4; 1986, c. 562.)

Law Review. — For survey of Virginia law on insurance for the year 1969-1970, see 56 Va. L. Rev. 1356 (1970).

§ 38.2-2212. Grounds and procedure for cancellation of or refusal to renew motor vehicle insurance policies; review by Commissioner. — A. The following definitions shall apply to this section:

"Cancellation" or *"to cancel"* means a termination of a policy during the policy period.

"Insurer" means any insurance company, association, or exchange licensed to transact motor vehicle insurance in this Commonwealth.

"Policy of motor vehicle insurance" or *"policy"* means a policy or contract for bodily injury or property damage liability insurance issued or delivered in this Commonwealth covering liability arising from the ownership, maintenance, or use of any motor vehicle, insuring as the named insured one individual or husband and wife who are residents of the same household, and under which the insured vehicle designated in the policy is either:

a. A motor vehicle of a private passenger, station wagon, or motorcycle type that is not used commercially, rented to others, or used as a public or livery conveyance where the term "public or livery conveyance" does not include car pools, or

b. Any other four-wheel motor vehicle which is not used in the occupation, profession, or business, other than farming, of the insured, or as a public or livery conveyance, or rented to others. The term "policy of motor vehicle insurance" or "policy" does not include (i) any policy issued through the Virginia Automobile Insurance Plan, (ii) any policy covering the operation of a garage, sales agency, repair shop, service station, or public parking place, (iii) any policy providing insurance only on an excess basis, or (iv) any other contract providing insurance to the named insured even though the contract may incidentally provide insurance on motor vehicles.

"Renewal" or *"to renew"* means (i) the issuance and delivery by an insurer of a policy superseding at the end of the policy period a policy previously issued

and delivered by the same insurer, providing types and limits of coverage at least equal to those contained in the policy being superseded, or (ii) the issuance and delivery of a certificate or notice extending the term of a policy beyond its policy period or term with types and limits of coverage at least equal to those contained in the policy. Each renewal shall conform with the requirements of the manual rules and rating program currently filed by the insurer with the Commission. Except as provided in subsection K of this section, any policy with a policy period or term of less than twelve months or any policy with no fixed expiration date shall for the purpose of this section be considered as if written for successive policy periods or terms of six months from the original effective date.

B. This section shall apply only to that portion of a policy of motor vehicle insurance providing the coverage required by §§ 38.2-2204, 38.2-2205 and 38.2-2206.

C. 1. No insurer shall refuse to renew a motor vehicle insurance policy solely because of any one or more of the following factors:

a. Age;

b. Sex;

c. Residence;

d. Race;

e. Color;

f. Creed;

g. National origin;

h. Ancestry;

i. Marital status;

j. Lawful occupation, including the military service;

k. Lack of driving experience, or number of years driving experience;

l. Lack of supporting business or lack of the potential for acquiring such business;

m. One or more accidents or violations that occurred more than forty-eight months immediately preceding the upcoming anniversary date;

n. One or more claims submitted under the uninsured motorists coverage of the policy where the uninsured motorist is known or there is physical evidence of contact;

o. A single claim by a single insured submitted under the medical expense coverage due to an accident for which the insured was neither wholly nor partially at fault;

p. One or more claims submitted under the comprehensive or towing coverages. However, nothing in this section shall prohibit an insurer from modifying or refusing to renew the comprehensive or towing coverages at the time of renewal of the policy on the basis of one or more claims submitted by an insured under those coverages, provided that the insurer shall mail or deliver to the insured at the address shown in the policy written notice of any such change in coverage at least forty-five days prior to the renewal;

q. Two or fewer motor vehicle accidents within a three-year period unless the accident was caused either wholly or partially by the named insured, a resident of the same household, or other customary operator; or

r. Credit information contained in a "consumer report," as defined in the federal Fair Credit Reporting Act, 15 U.S.C. § 1681 et seq., bearing on a natural person's creditworthiness, credit standing or credit capacity, unless, in addition to any other requirements that may apply, the insurer includes in the notice required by this section the following statement or a statement substantially similar to it: "This nonrenewal is based on information contained in a consumer report relating to you and/or someone else who resides in your household." The notice shall also contain: (i) the name and address of an institutional source from whom the insurer obtained the credit information and (ii) a statement advising the insured that, if the insured wishes to inquire further about the credit information on which the nonrenewal is based and obtain a free copy of the "consumer report," the insured may do so by mailing a written request to the insurer, or such other party as the insurer shall identify in the notice, no more than ten days after the date on which the notice of nonrenewal was mailed to the insured. If the insured submits such written notification, the nonrenewal shall not become effective until forty-five days after the accuracy of the credit information, which the insured has questioned and on which the nonrenewal was based, has been verified and communicated to the insured. Such verification shall be deemed to have been made upon completion of the investigation of the credit information which the insured has questioned and on which the nonrenewal was based. The insured must cooperate in the investigation of the credit information, including responding to any communication submitted by, or on behalf of, the insurer no more than ten days after the date on which such communication was mailed to the insured. If the insured fails to cooperate in the investigation of the credit information, the insurer may, after providing fifteen days' written notice to the insured, terminate such investigation and nonrenew the policy. An insurer may require that an insured submit written documentation authorizing the insurer, or such other party as the insurer shall identify, to perform the investigation of the credit information. The insured shall be obligated to pay any pro rata premium due for insurance provided during the period in which the investigation of the credit information is pending up to the date on which the policy nonrenewal becomes effective. Although the obligations imposed upon an insurer by this subdivision may be satisfied by a third party who agrees, and is authorized, to act on behalf of the insurer, the insurer shall remain responsible for compliance with the obligations imposed by this subdivision.

2. Nothing in this section shall require any insurer to renew a policy for an insured where the insured's occupation has changed so as to materially increase the risk. Nothing contained in subdivisions C 1 n, 1 o and 1 p of this subsection shall prohibit an insurer from refusing to renew a policy where a claim is false or fraudulent. Nothing in this section prohibits any insurer from setting rates in accordance with relevant actuarial data.

D. No insurer shall cancel a policy except for one or more of the following reasons:

1. The named insured or any other operator who either resides in the same household or customarily operates a motor vehicle insured under the policy has had his driver's license suspended or revoked during the policy period or, if the policy is a renewal, during its policy period or the ninety days immediately preceding the last effective date.

2. The named insured fails to pay the premium for the policy or any installment of the premium, whether payable to the insurer or its agent either directly or indirectly under any premium finance plan or extension of credit.

3. The named insured or his duly constituted attorney-in-fact has notified the insurer of a change in the insured's legal residence to a state other than Virginia and the insured vehicle will be principally garaged in the new state of legal residence.

E. No cancellation or refusal to renew by an insurer of a policy of motor vehicle insurance shall be effective unless the insurer delivers or mails to the named insured at the address shown in the policy a written notice of the cancellation or refusal to renew. The notice shall:

1. Be in a type size authorized under § 38.2-311.

2. State the effective date of the cancellation or refusal to renew. The effective date of cancellation or refusal to renew shall be at least forty-five days after mailing or delivering to the insured the notice of cancellation or notice of

refusal to renew. However, when the policy is being canceled or not renewed for the reason set forth in subdivision 2 of subsection D of this section the effective date may be less than forty-five days but at least fifteen days from the date of mailing or delivery.

3. State the specific reason of the insurer for cancellation or refusal to renew and provide for the notification required by §§ 38.2-608, 38.2-609, and subsection B of § 38.2-610. However, those notification requirements shall not apply when the policy is being canceled or not renewed for the reason set forth in subdivision 2 of subsection D of this section.

4. Inform the insured of his right to request in writing within fifteen days of the receipt of the notice that the Commissioner review the action of the insurer.

The notice of cancellation or refusal to renew shall contain the following statement to inform the insured of such right:

IMPORTANT NOTICE

Within fifteen days of receiving this notice, you or your attorney may request in writing that the Commissioner of Insurance review this action to determine whether the insurer has complied with Virginia laws in canceling or nonrenewing your policy. If this insurer has failed to comply with the cancellation or nonrenewal laws, the Commissioner may require that your policy be reinstated. However, the Commissioner is prohibited from making underwriting judgments. If this insurer has complied with the cancellation or nonrenewal laws, the Commissioner does not have the authority to overturn this action.

5. Inform the insured of the possible availability of other insurance which may be obtained through his agent, through another insurer, or through the Virginia Automobile Insurance Plan.

6. If sent by mail, comply with the provisions of § 38.2-2208.

Nothing in this subsection prohibits any insurer or agent from including in the notice of cancellation or refusal to renew, any additional disclosure statements required by state or federal laws, or any additional information relating to the availability of other insurance.

F. Nothing in this section shall apply:

1. If the insurer or its agent acting on behalf of the insurer has manifested its willingness to renew by issuing or offering to issue a renewal policy, certificate, or other evidence of renewal, or has manifested its willingness to renew in writing to the insured. The written manifestation shall include the name of a proposed insurer, the expiration date of the policy, the type of insurance coverage, and information regarding the estimated renewal premium. The insurer shall retain a copy of each written manifestation for a period of at least one year from the expiration date of any policy that is not renewed;

2. If the named insured, or his duly constituted attorney-in-fact, has notified the insurer or its agent orally, or in writing, if the insurer requires such notification to be in writing, that he wishes the policy to be canceled or that he does not wish the policy to be renewed, or if prior to the date of expiration he fails to accept the offer of the insurer to renew the policy; or

3. To any motor vehicle insurance policy which has been in effect less than sixty days when the termination notice is mailed or delivered to the insured, unless it is a renewal policy.

G. There shall be no liability on the part of and no cause of action of any nature shall arise against the Commissioner or his subordinates; any insurer, its authorized representatives, its agents, or its employees; or any person furnishing to the insurer information as to reasons for cancellation or refusal to renew, for any statement made by any of them in complying with this section or for providing information pertaining to the cancellation or refusal to renew. For the purposes of this section, no insurer shall be required to furnish a notice of cancellation or refusal to renew to anyone other than the named insured, any person designated by the named insured, or any other person to whom such notice is required to be given by the terms of the policy and the Commissioner.

H. Within fifteen days of receipt of the notice of cancellation or refusal to renew, any insured or his attorney shall be entitled to request in writing to the Commissioner that he review the action of the insurer in canceling or refusing to renew the policy of the insured. Upon receipt of the request, the Commissioner shall promptly begin a review to determine whether the insurer's cancellation or refusal to renew complies with the requirements of this section and of § 38.2-2208 if the notice was sent by mail. The policy shall remain in full force and effect during the pendency of the review by the Commissioner except where the cancellation or refusal to renew is for the reason set forth in subdivision 2 of subsection D of this section, in which case the policy shall terminate as of the effective date stated in the notice. Where the Commissioner finds from the review that the cancellation or refusal to renew has not complied with the requirements of this section or of § 38.2-2208, he shall immediately notify the insurer, the insured and any other person to whom such notice was required to be given by the terms of the policy that the cancellation or refusal to renew is not effective. Nothing in this section authorizes the Commissioner to substitute his judgment as to underwriting for that of the insurer. Where the Commissioner finds in favor of the insured, the Commission in its discretion may award the insured reasonable attorneys' fees.

I. Each insurer shall maintain for at least one year, records of cancellation and refusal to renew and copies of every notice or statement referred to in subsection E of this section that it sends to any of its insureds.

J. The provisions of this section shall not apply to any insurer that limits the issuance of policies of motor vehicle liability insurance to one class or group of persons engaged in any one particular profession, trade, occupation, or business. Nothing in this section requires an insurer to renew a policy of motor vehicle insurance if the insured does not conform to the occupational or membership requirements of an insurer who limits its writings to an occupation or membership of an organization. No insurer is required to renew a policy if the insured becomes a nonresident of Virginia.

K. Notwithstanding any other provision of this section, a motor vehicle insurance policy with a policy period or term of five months or less may expire at its expiration date when the insurer has manifested in writing its willingness to renew the policy for at least thirty days and has mailed the written manifestation to the insured at least fifteen days before the expiration date of the policy. The written manifestation shall include the name of the proposed insurer, the expiration date of the policy, the type of insurance coverage, and the estimated renewal premium. The insurer shall retain a copy of the written manifestation for at least one year from the expiration date of any policy that is not renewed. (1970, c. 564, § 38.1-381.5; 1972, c. 273; 1975, cc. 63, 319; 1978, c. 441; 1982, c. 482; 1983, cc. 125, 371; 1984, c. 340; 1986, c. 562; 1988, c. 655; 1990, c. 960; 1991, c. 116; 1995, c. 3; 1996, cc. 206, 239; 1998, cc. 141, 142.)

Cross references. — As to notice required when an insurance policy certified under the provisions of Chapter 3 of Title 46.2 is cancelled or terminated, see § 46.2-482.

The 1998 amendments. — The 1998 amendment by c. 141, in subdivision C 1 o, deleted "medical payments coverage or" preceding "medical expense coverage"; and in subdivision D 1, deleted "anniversary of the" preceding "effective date."

The 1998 amendment by c. 142, in subdivision F 2, deleted "in writing" following "has notified," and inserted "orally, or in writing, if the insurer requires such notification to be in writing."

Law Review. — For survey of recent legislation on insurance — cancellation and renewals of automobile liability insurance, see 5 U. Rich. L. Rev. 197 (1970). For survey of Virginia law on insurance for the year 1969-1970, see 56 Va. L. Rev. 1356 (1970). For survey of Virginia law on insurance for the year 1974-1975, see 61 Va. L. Rev. 1759 (1975).

Legislative intent. — The legislature intended under this section to provide specified procedural safeguards to an insured when his insurance policy is terminated against his wishes. American Interinsurance Exch. v. Lucy, 222 Va. 530, 281 S.E.2d 895 (1981) (decided prior to 1984 amendment to subdivision F 2).

Subsection E ensures right to challenge any involuntary cancellation. — The requirements of subsection E of this section make certain the insured is informed of his right to challenge involuntary cancellation in order that he may take the necessary steps to procure continuous insurance coverage when an insurer has cancelled the insured's policy against his wishes. The policy reasons for granting these rights are applicable whenever an insurance policy is being terminated involuntarily, whether the insurance company at its own initiative or at the request of a premium finance company. American Interinsurance Exch. v. Lucy, 222 Va. 530, 281 S.E.2d 895 (1981) (decided prior to 1984 amendment to subdivision F 2, which inserted "or his duly constituted attorney-in-fact.").

Including cancellation at request of premium finance company. — An insurer's cancellation at the request of a premium finance company is a form of involuntary termination triggering the procedural safeguards provided in subsection E of this section. American Interinsurance Exch. v. Lucy, 222 Va. 530, 281 S.E.2d 895 (1981) (decided prior to 1984 amendment to subdivision F 2, which inserted "or his duly constituted attorney-in-fact.").

The General Assembly intended to view an insurer's cancellation of policy coverage at the request of a premium finance company to be a cancellation against the insured's wishes. American Interinsurance Exch. v. Lucy, 222 Va. 530, 281 S.E.2d 895 (1981) (decided prior to 1984 amendment to subdivision F 2, which inserted "or his duly constituted attorney-in-fact.").

Insurance company not required to comply with subsection E. — Where the insurance company mailed a notice of cancellation to the insured 55 days after his policy was issued, the insurance company was not required to comply with the requirements of subsection E even though the notice of cancellation would be effective 10 days thereafter. Virginia Mut. Ins. Co. v. Liberty Mut. Ins. Co., 218 Va. 807, 241 S.E.2d 754 (1978).

There is nothing in subsection F requiring that the effective date of the cancella-

tion must be within 60 days. Virginia Mut. Ins. Co. v. Liberty Mut. Ins. Co., 218 Va. 807, 241 S.E.2d 754 (1978).

It is to the mailing of the cancellation notice within 60 days that the statute speaks. Virginia Mut. Ins. Co. v. Liberty Mut. Ins. Co., 218 Va. 807, 241 S.E.2d 754 (1978).

Purpose of subdivision F 2. — The exemption provided in subdivision F 2 of this section was merely an acknowledgment that the procedural safeguards of this section serve absolutely no purpose where an insured has voluntarily cancelled his policy, has indicated he does not wish to renew the policy, or has failed to accept the insurer's renewal offer. American Interinsurance Exch. v. Lucy, 222 Va. 530, 281 S.E.2d 895 (1981) (decided prior to 1984 amendment to subdivision F 2, which inserted "or his duly constituted attorney-in-fact.").

Request by premium finance company not covered by subdivision F 2. — When the General Assembly adopted subdivision F 2 of this section, the legislature did not intend to include within that subdivision a premium finance company's request for termination of an insurance policy when the insured has given that company a power of attorney to request the policy's cancellation in the event of a default in payment of the premium. American Interinsurance Exch. v. Lucy, 222 Va. 530, 281 S.E.2d 895 (1981) (decided prior to 1984 amendment to subdivision F 2, which inserted "or his duly constituted attorney-in-fact.").

Even when company has power of attorney. — When the General Assembly exempted from the safeguards of subsection E instances where "the named insured" has notified the insurer "that he wishes the policy to be cancelled," the legislature did not intend to exempt cancellation requests by a premium finance company, even when the insured had previously given the company a power of attorney to request such cancellation in the event of a premium payment default. American Interinsurance Exch. v. Lucy, 222 Va. 530, 281 S.E.2d 895 (1981) (decided prior to 1984 amendment to subdivision F 2, which inserted "or his duly constituted attorney-in-fact.").

Estoppel not raised by mere handling of delinquent payment. — Mere computer posting and subsequent negotiation of a money order representing the amount of a delinquent premium payment, without more, does not give rise to an estoppel to deny coverage when the sum is refunded within a reasonable time. Notice of cancellation, when furnished under the terms of the policy and the applicable statute, terminates the policy ipso facto, and the obligation to return the unearned premium merely creates a debtor-creditor relationship. Harris v. Criterion Ins. Co., 222 Va. 496, 281 S.E.2d 878 (1981).

§ 38.2-2212.1. Powers of Commission; replacement policies. — Upon the verified petition of an insurer, where the petitioning insurer proposes to replace all or substantially all of its policies in another insurer, the Commission may relieve the insurer of the requirements of subsection E of § 38.2-2212 and of the mailing requirements of § 38.2-2208, provided the insurer demonstrates to the satisfaction of the Commission that (i) the replacement policy is underwritten by an affiliate insurer under common control with the petitioning insurer; (ii) the replacement policy is substantially similar to the existing policy with the petitioning insurer; (iii) the premium charged for the replacement policy is no greater than that charged by the petitioning insurer for the existing policy; and (iv) the replacement insurer is duly licensed to transact the business of insurance in the Commonwealth of Virginia. The replacement insurer shall retain a copy of any offer of replacement for a period of one year from the expiration of any existing policy that is not replaced. The Commission may further condition any such relief to protect the best interests of the policyholder. (1991, c. 215.)

§ 38.2-2213. Discrimination in issuance of motor vehicle insurance. — No insurer or agent shall refuse to issue a motor vehicle insurance policy as defined in § 38.2-2212 solely because of any one or more of the following factors: the age, sex, residence, race, color, creed, national origin, ancestry, marital status, or lawful occupation, including the military service, of the person seeking the coverage. Nothing in this section prohibits any insurer from limiting the issuance of motor vehicle insurance policies to those who are residents of this Commonwealth nor does this section prohibit any insurer from limiting the issuance of motor vehicle insurance policies only to persons engaging in or who have engaged in a particular profession or occupation, or who are members of a particular religious sect. Nothing in this section prohibits any insurer from setting rates in accordance with relevant actuarial data. (1976, c. 495, § 38.1-381.6; 1977, c. 181; 1983, c. 61; 1986, c. 562.)

§ 38.2-2214. Statement defining rate classifications to be provided by insurer to insured. — Any insurer issuing motor vehicle insurance policies as defined in § 38.2-2212, including those policies assigned to any insurer by the Virginia Automobile Insurance Plan, shall provide the named insured with a statement defining his rate classifications. This statement shall be provided at the time of issuance or at the time of renewal if there has been a change in the named insured's rate classification. The statement shall not be considered a part of the policy and shall not be deemed a warranty or representation by the insurer to the insured.

The Commission shall approve the form of the statement prior to its use. (1977, c. 188, § 38.1-381.7; 1979, c. 4; 1986, c. 562.)

§ 38.2-2215. Failure to issue or failure to renew motor vehicle liability insurance on the basis of a motor vehicle's age prohibited. — No insurer or agent shall refuse to issue or fail to renew a policy of motor vehicle liability insurance solely because of the age of the motor vehicle to be insured, provided the motor vehicle is licensed. (1978, c. 56, § 38.1-381.8; 1983, c. 61; 1986, c. 562.)

§ 38.2-2216. Medical benefit offset against liability or uninsured motorist coverage prohibited. — No policy or contract of bodily injury liability insurance which contains any representation by an insurer to pay medical expenses incurred for bodily injuries caused by an accident to the insured or any relative or any other person coming under the provisions of the

371

policy, shall be issued or delivered by any insurer licensed in this Commonwealth upon any motor vehicle then principally garaged or principally used in this Commonwealth, if the policy contains any provision reducing the amount of damages covered under the liability or uninsured motorist coverages of the policy by the amount of payments made by the insurer under the medical expense or other medical payments coverage of the policy. (1984, c. 383, § 38.1-381.9; 1986, c. 562.)

§ 38.2-2217. Reduction in rates for certain persons who attend motor vehicle accident prevention courses and driver improvement clinics. — A. Any schedule of rates, rate classifications or rating plans for motor vehicle insurance as defined in § 38.2-2212 filed with the Commission shall provide for an appropriate reduction in premium charges for those insured persons who are fifty-five years of age and older and who qualify as provided in this subsection. Only those insured persons who have successfully completed a motor vehicle accident prevention course approved by the Department of Motor Vehicles shall qualify for a three-year period after the completion of the course for the reduction in rates. No reduction in premiums shall be allowed for a self-instructed course or for any course that does not provide actual classroom instruction for a minimum number of hours as determined by the Department of Motor Vehicles.

B. Any schedule of rates, rate classifications or rating plans for motor vehicle insurance as defined in § 38.2-2212 filed with the Commission may provide for an appropriate reduction in premium charges for a two-year period for those insured persons who are fifty-four years of age or younger and who have satisfactorily completed a driver improvement clinic approved by the Department of Motor Vehicles, as set forth in Article 19 (§ 46.2-489 et seq.) of Chapter 3 of Title 46.2. No person assigned by the courts or notified by the Department of Motor Vehicles to attend a driver improvement clinic shall be eligible for such reduction in premium charges.

C. The Commission and the Department of Motor Vehicles may promulgate rules and regulations which will assist them in carrying out the provisions of this section.

D. All insurers writing motor vehicle insurance in Virginia as defined in § 38.2-2212 shall allow an appropriate reduction in premium charges to all eligible persons subject to the provisions of subsection A.

E. Upon successfully completing the approved course, the course's sponsor shall issue to each participant a certificate approved by the Department of Motor Vehicles which shall be evidence of satisfactory completion of either a motor vehicle accident prevention course or a driver improvement clinic for the reduction in premium charges. Participants shall be required to provide satisfactory evidence to the insurance provider that the course or clinic was completed in accordance with this section.

F. Each participant in a motor vehicle accident prevention course shall take an approved course every three years in order to continue to be eligible for the reduction in premium charges. Each voluntary participant in a driver improvement clinic shall take an approved course every two years in order to continue to be eligible for the reduction in premium charges, if any.

G. Nothing in this section prevents an insurer from offering appropriately reduced rates based solely on age. (1984, c. 686, § 38.1-381.10; 1986, c. 562; 1995, c. 226.)

§ 38.2-2217.1. Insurers required to renew motor vehicle liability coverage for vanpools; exceptions. — A. As used in this section, *"vanpooling"* means the type of joint arrangement described in subdivision 6 of § 46.2-2000.1 where such motor vehicles are used to transport commuters to and from their places of employment on a regular basis. *"Motor vehicle"* as used in this section shall mean any motor vehicle designed to transport not less than ten nor more than fifteen passengers in fixed seats.

B. No insurer as defined in § 38.2-2212 shall cancel or refuse to renew a policy of liability insurance coverage for motor vehicles used in vanpooling as defined in subsection A of this section for a period of one year following July 1, 1986, except for one or both of the following specified reasons:

1. The named insured fails to discharge when due any payment of the premium for the policy or any installment thereof; or

2. The driving record of the named insured or any regular driver is such that it substantially increases the risk.

C. Notwithstanding any provision of this section, on and after July 1, 1986, no insurer who issues or renews a policy of motor vehicle liability insurance to an insured who intends to use a vehicle for vanpooling which was not so used at the time the policy was issued or last renewed shall be subject to the provisions of this section unless the insurer has received by certified mail thirty days' written notice that the insured intends to use the vehicle for vanpooling. (1986, c. 612, § 38.1-381.11; 1995, cc. 744, 803.)

Editor's note. — This section was enacted as § 38.1-381.11 by Acts 1986, c. 612. Pursuant to § 9-77.11, this section has been incorporated into Title 38.2 as § 38.2-2217.1.

§ 38.2-2218. Adoption of standard forms for motor vehicle insurance.

— The Commission shall prepare a standard form whenever it believes that any form of policy or any form of rider, endorsement, or other supplemental agreement or provision, for use in connection with any contract of motor vehicle insurance to be issued or delivered upon any motor vehicle principally garaged or principally used in this Commonwealth, is so extensively used that a standard form is desirable. The Commission shall file a copy of the standard form in its office and shall provide by order that, at least thirty days after the order, the form shall become a standard form for use by all insurers unless objection to the proposed form is filed with the Commission within twenty days after the entry of the order. The Commission shall mail a copy of its order to all insurers licensed to transact the class of insurance to which the form is applicable, and to all rate service and advisory organizations representing those insurers. (Code 1950, §§ 38-240, 38-551; 1952, c. 317, § 38.1-382; 1986, c. 562.)

Law Review. — For article, "Insurer's Liability in Excess of Policy Limits," see 44 Va. L. Rev. 267 (1958).

This section does not permit the Commission to interpret Virginia insurance law nor does it require adherence to contract forms which violate statutory provisions. United States v. GEICO, 409 F. Supp. 986 (E.D. Va. 1976).

Conflict between form and statute. — The Commission does not have any right to require adherence to contract forms which violate statutory provisions, and wherever such a conflict between form and statute is found to exist, the statute is controlling and the Com-

mission's conflicting form provision is null and void. Travelers Indem. Co. v. Wells, 209 F. Supp. 784 (W.D. Va. 1962), rev'd on other grounds, 316 F.2d 770 (4th Cir. 1963).

Where there is a conflict between form and statute, the statute is controlling and the conflicting form is null and void. United States v. GEICO, 409 F. Supp. 986 (E.D. Va. 1976).

Individual named insured endorsement need not be appended to all policies. — This section does not require that the individual named insured endorsement be appended to all business auto policies. Greenbaum v. Travelers Ins. Co., 705 F. Supp. 1138 (E.D. Va. 1989).

§ 38.2-2219. Hearing on objections to the form.

— If any insurer or rate service organization affected by an order entered pursuant to § 38.2-2218 files objections to a proposed standard form within the time prescribed in the

Commission's order, the Commission shall rescind the order and shall notify all insurers and rate service organizations affected by the order that on a day specified in the notice, which shall be at least thirty days from the date on which the objections are received, it will hold a public hearing on the adoption of the proposed form, and that at the hearing any person interested may appear and be heard. After the hearing the Commission may by order confirm or amend the proposed form and set a day, at least thirty days after the entry of the order, when the approved form shall become a standard form for use by all insurers. The Commission may by like order refuse to adopt the proposed form. (Code 1950, §§ 38-241, 38-552; 1952, c. 317, § 38.1-383; 1986, c. 562.)

§ 38.2-2220. Use of form after adoption. — Except as provided in § 38.2-2223, after any standard form is adopted by the Commission, no insurer shall use any form covering substantially the same provisions contained in the standard form unless it is in the precise language of the form filed and adopted by the Commission. (Code 1950, §§ 38-240, 38-551; 1952, c. 317, § 38.1-384; 1981, c. 172; 1986, c. 562.)

§ 38.2-2221. Amendment of standard form. — The Commission may amend the provisions of any standard form in the manner provided in this chapter for the adoption of a new standard form. (Code 1950, §§ 38-242, 38-553; 1952, c. 317, § 38.1-385; 1986, c. 562.)

§ 38.2-2222. Withdrawal of form. — Whenever the Commission believes there is no further necessity for requiring the use of any standard form adopted under the provisions of this chapter, it may, by order entered of record, withdraw the form, and thereafter its use shall not be required. (Code 1950, §§ 38-243, 38-554; 1952, c. 317, § 38.1-386; 1986, c. 562.)

§ 38.2-2223. Variations of, or additions to, form. — For the word "company" appearing in any standard form, there may be substituted a more accurate descriptive term for the type of insurer. Additional provisions, other than those in the standard form, or coverages more favorable than those in the standard form, may be used with a standard form by any insurer with the approval of the Commission. However, the Commission shall first determine that the more favorable coverage or the additional provisions are not in conflict or inconsistent with the standard form, the laws of this Commonwealth or any rules and regulations adopted by the Commission. (Code 1950, §§ 38-244, 38-555; 1952, c. 317, § 38.1-387; 1981, c. 172; 1986, c. 562; 1994, c. 316.)

§ 38.2-2224. Commission to establish guidelines for filing readable motor vehicle insurance policy forms. — The Commission may establish guidelines for the filing of simplified and readable motor vehicle insurance policy forms that are acceptable for issuance. Notwithstanding the provisions of §§ 38.2-2218 through 38.2-2223, an insurer may issue a motor vehicle insurance policy that deviates in language, but not in substance or coverage, from the standard policy form provided for in §§ 38.2-2218 through 38.2-2223, if the deviating policy form is (i) in no respect less favorable to the insured than the standard form, and (ii) approved by the Commission prior to issuance. (1977, c. 255, § 38.1-387.1; 1981, c. 172; 1986, c. 562.)

§ 38.2-2225. Sending copies of orders to companies affected. — A copy of each order entered by the Commission in accordance with the provisions of this chapter shall be sent to every insurer and rate service organization affected by the order. (Code 1950, §§ 38-245, 38-556; 1952, c. 317, § 38.1-388; 1986, c. 562.)

§ 38.2-2226. Insurer to give notice to claimant of intention to rely on certain defenses and of execution of nonwaiver of rights agreement. —

Whenever any insurer on a policy of liability insurance discovers a breach of the terms or conditions of the insurance contract by the insured, the insurer shall notify the claimant or the claimant's counsel of the breach. Notification shall be given within forty-five days after discovery by the insurer of the breach or of the claim, whichever is later. Whenever, on account of such breach, a nonwaiver of rights agreement is executed by the insurer and the insured, or a reservation of rights letter is sent by the insurer to the insured, notice of such action shall be given to the claimant or the claimant's counsel within forty-five days after that agreement is executed or the letter is sent, or after notice of the claim is received, whichever is later. Failure to give the notice within forty-five days will result in a waiver of the defense based on such breach to the extent of the claim by operation of law. (1968, c. 410, § 38.1-389.1; 1986, c. 562; 1997, c. 377.)

Law Review. — For survey of Virginia law on insurance for the year 1971-1972, see 58 Va. L. Rev. 1291 (1972).

Purpose of section. — The obvious purpose of this section is to require a liability insurer which intends to rely on a breach of the terms and conditions of the policy contract, in defense of any claim under the policy, to furnish prompt notice of such intention to the claimant or his attorney, so that steps may be taken by the claimant, a stranger to the insurance contract, to protect his rights. Liberty Mut. Ins. Co. v. Safeco Ins. Co. of Am., 223 Va. 317, 288 S.E.2d 469 (1982); Dan River, Inc. v. Commercial Union Ins. Co., 227 Va. 485, 317 S.E.2d 485 (1984).

This statute was designed to inform injured claimant against alleged insured of a breach of policy terms which might cause the insured to become an uninsured motorist. Thus, the claimant would have knowledge in order that he might be able to comply with the demands of the uninsured motorist law. Gordon v. Liberty Mut. Ins. Co., 675 F. Supp. 321 (E.D. Va. 1987).

Legitimate interest manifested through section. — Virginia, through this section, has manifested a legitimate interest in safeguarding the rights of persons injured within her boundaries. Federal Ins. Co. v. Nationwide Mut. Ins. Co., 448 F. Supp. 723 (W.D. Va. 1978).

The public policy of Virginia as set forth in this section is procedural for choice of law purposes since it does not affect the contractual relation between the insured and the insurer, but rather requires the insurer to give notice to the claimant when coverage is denied for breach of contract. Federal Ins. Co. v. Nationwide Mut. Ins. Co., 448 F. Supp. 723 (W.D. Va. 1978).

Section has no effect upon contractual relations between insured and insurer. Dan River, Inc. v. Commercial Union Ins. Co., 227 Va. 485, 317 S.E.2d 485 (1984).

This section has no application to a noncoverage situation. Berry v. State Farm Mut. Auto. Ins. Co., 340 F. Supp. 228 (E.D. Va. 1972).

And it does not apply to the provisions of the uninsured motorist statute or policy endorsement. Maxey v. Doe, 217 Va. 22, 225 S.E.2d 359 (1976).

If there has been a breach of an insurance contract, this section specifically requires notice only to a claimant or his counsel. Maxey v. Doe, 217 Va. 22, 225 S.E.2d 359 (1976).

Waiver occurs only where the rights of a claimant who is a stranger to the insurance contract may be prejudiced. Maxey v. Doe, 217 Va. 22, 225 S.E.2d 359 (1976).

This section does not operate as a waiver of insurer's right to rely upon plaintiff's failure to file the SR-300 accident report. Maxey v. Doe, 217 Va. 22, 225 S.E.2d 359 (1976).

Insurance company satisfied this section by sending "reservation of rights" letters to defendant and by then forwarding copies of these letters to victim's attorney. Vermont Mut. Ins. Co. v. Everette, 875 F. Supp. 1181 (E.D. Va. 1995).

§ 38.2-2227. Aircraft liability policy not to deny coverage for violation of federal or civil regulations, etc.; permitted exclusions or conditions. —

No insurance policy issued or delivered in this Commonwealth covering loss, expense, or liability arising out of the loss, maintenance, or use of an aircraft shall act to exclude or deny coverage because the aircraft is operated in violation of federal or civil regulations or any state or local ordinance. This section does not prohibit the use of specific exclusions or conditions in any policy that relates to any of the following:

1. Certification of an aircraft in a stated category by the Federal Aviation Administration;
2. Certification of a pilot in a stated category by the Federal Aviation Administration;
3. Establishing requirements for pilot experience; or
4. Restricting the use of the aircraft to the purposes stated in the policy. (1970, c. 227, § 38.1-389.2; 1986, c. 562.)

Law Review. — For survey of Virginia law on insurance for the year 1969-1970, see 56 Va. L. Rev. 1356 (1970). For survey of Virginia law on insurance for the year 1970-1971, see 57 Va. L. Rev. 1608 (1971).

§§ 38.2-2228, 38.2-2228.1: Repealed by Acts 1996, c. 31.

§ 38.2-2229. Claims-made liability insurance. — Pursuant to the authority granted in § 38.2-223, the Commission may issue regulations regarding claims-made liability insurance policies. These regulations may include, but are not limited to, (i) the pricing of extended reporting period coverage, (ii) provisions for installment payment of premiums for such coverage, and (iii) the providing of such coverage in the event of the death, disability, or retirement of the insured. (1990, c. 241.)

§ 38.2-2230. Mandatory offer of rental reimbursement coverage. — Every insurer issuing a new or renewal policy of motor vehicle insurance, as defined in § 38.2-2212, which provides comprehensive or collision coverage, shall offer in writing to the named insured the option of purchasing rental reimbursement coverage. (1994, c. 9.)

§ 38.2-2231. Physical damage arbitration between insurers; alternate forums. — A. Except as otherwise provided hereafter, insurers shall arbitrate and settle all disputed claims made for automobile physical damage between them in accordance with the terms of the Nationwide Intercompany Arbitration Agreement, or any successor thereto, as adopted and from time to time amended by its members, and the rules promulgated pursuant to the Agreement, unless the parties mutually agree, on a per case basis, to use another forum, which forum may include a court of competent jurisdiction, in which case the claim shall be arbitrated or tried in that alternate forum. Mandatory arbitration of disputed claims shall be limited solely to the issues of liability and damages.

B. Every automobile liability or physical damage insurer doing business in the Commonwealth shall be a member of the Nationwide Intercompany Arbitration Agreement, or any successor thereto, sponsored by the Committee on Insurance Arbitration. However, if any such insurer is unable to furnish proof of its membership in such agreement, an action may be asserted in a court of competent jurisdiction. (1994, c. 346; 1999, c. 514.)

The number of this section was assigned by the Virginia Code Commission, the number in the 1994 act having been 38.2-2230.

The 1999 amendment, in the first paragraph, added the subsection A designator, added "Except as otherwise provided hereafter" at the beginning of the paragraph, inserted "or any successor thereto" following "Arbitration Agreement," substituted "forum, which forum may include a court of competent jurisdiction" for "arbitration forum," and inserted "or tried" following "be arbitrated"; in the second paragraph, added the B designator, in the first sentence, inserted "or any successor thereto" following "Arbitration Agreement," and added the last sentence.

§ 38.2-2232. Liability insurance on private pleasure watercraft; optional coverage.

— A. Every insurer issuing a new or renewal policy or contract covering liability arising from the ownership, maintenance or use of a private pleasure watercraft shall offer, in writing, to the named insured the option of purchasing coverage for damages which the insured is legally entitled to recover from the owner or operator of an uninsured private pleasure watercraft arising out of the ownership, maintenance, or use of such uninsured watercraft. Such insurer shall be required to offer limits of liability for uninsured private pleasure watercraft coverage equal to the limits of the liability insurance provided by the policy. However, no insurer shall be required to pay damages for uninsured private pleasure watercraft coverage in excess of the limits of uninsured private pleasure watercraft coverage provided by the policy. Uninsured private pleasure watercraft coverage shall include coverage for bodily injury and property damage liability; provided, however, that such property damage liability coverage shall be excess over any other valid and collectible insurance of any kind applicable to the property. Insurers issuing or providing liability policies that are of an excess or umbrella type or which provide liability coverage incidental to a policy not related to a specifically insured private pleasure watercraft shall not be required to offer, provide or make available to those policies uninsured private pleasure watercraft coverage.

For purposes of this section, a "new or renewal policy or contract covering liability arising from the ownership, maintenance or use of a private pleasure watercraft" shall mean and include only a policy or contract of marine protection and indemnity insurance, as defined in subsection B of § 38.2-126, written as a separate policy, which is not in combination with any other class of insurance defined in Article 2 (§ 38.2-101 et seq.) of Chapter 1 of this title, to insure a private pleasure watercraft.

For purposes of this section, "uninsured private pleasure watercraft" means a private pleasure watercraft for which there is no valid insurance policy or contract covering liability arising from the ownership, maintenance, or use of such private pleasure watercraft in effect at the time liability is incurred. Such term does not, however, include any watercraft owned by, furnished to, or available for the regular use of any insured, or owned by any governmental unit or agency.

B. If any action is instituted against an owner or operator of an uninsured private pleasure watercraft by any insured intending to rely on the coverage required by this section, then the insured shall serve a copy of the process upon the insurer in the manner prescribed by law, as though the insurer were a party defendant, but the provisions of § 8.01-288 shall not be applicable to service of process under this section. The insurer shall then have the right to file pleadings and take other actions allowable by law in the name of the owner or operator of the uninsured private pleasure watercraft or in its own name.

Any insurer paying a claim under coverage required by this section shall be subrogated to the rights of the insured to the extent of any payment on such claim. (1998, c. 726; 1999, c. 918.)

The 1999 amendment added the subsection A designator, in the first sentence, substituted "for damages which the insured is legally entitled to recover" for "undertaking to pay all sums the insured is legally entitled to recover as damages," inserted the second and third sentences, added the second paragraph, substituted "valid insurance policy or contract covering liability arising from the ownership, main-tenance, or use of such private pleasure watercraft in effect at the time liability is incurred. Such term does not, however, include any watercraft owned by, furnished to, or available for the regular use of any insured, or owned by any governmental unit or agency" for "liability insurance" in the third paragraph, and added subsection B.

CHAPTER 23.

LEGAL SERVICES INSURANCE.

Sec.
38.2-2300. Conditions; permitted contracts;
            approval.

§ 38.2-2300. Conditions; permitted contracts; approval. — A. Legal services insurance may be offered in this Commonwealth subject to the following conditions:

1. Premium rates shall be made in accordance with Chapter 19 (§ 38.2-1900 et seq.) of this title.

2. No policy of legal services insurance may be delivered or issued for delivery in this Commonwealth unless it contains a provision that the insurer shall issue to the person in whose name the policy is issued, for delivery to each insured, a certificate summarizing the essential features of the insurance coverage and to whom benefits under the policy are payable. If dependents are included in the coverage, only one certificate need be issued for each family unit.

B. An insurer authorized to transact legal services insurance in this Commonwealth may, in connection with the implementation and operation of any legal services insurance program, contract with any person that offers and manages a group legal services insurance plan, including a state, city, county, or circuit bar association; or any person permitted to practice law in this Commonwealth.

C. The Commission shall not approve any legal services insurance contract if, after providing notice and opportunity to be heard, the Commission finds that the contract violates any law of this Commonwealth. (1976, c. 636, § 38.1-389.4; 1986, c. 562.)

Cross references. — For definitions of legal services insurance, see § 38.2-127. As to contracts and plans for future legal services, see § 38.2-4400 et seq.

Law Review. — For survey of Virginia insurance law for the year 1975-1976, see 62 Va. L. Rev. 1446 (1976).

CHAPTER 24.

FIDELITY AND SURETY INSURANCE.

ARTICLE 1.

General Provisions.

§ 38.2-2400. Class of insurance to which chapter applies. — This chapter applies to fidelity and surety insurance as defined in §§ 38.2-120 and 38.2-121. (1952, c. 317, § 38.1-639; 1986, c. 562.)

§ 38.2-2401. Fidelity and surety insurer defined. — The term *"fidelity and surety insurer"* means any company licensed to transact fidelity or surety insurance in this Commonwealth, and includes any company elsewhere designated or referred to in this Code as a guaranty, indemnity, fidelity, surety or security company. (1952, c. 317, § 38.1-640; 1986, c. 562.)

§ 38.2-2402. Fidelity and surety insurer not to transact insurance without appropriate license. — No fidelity and surety insurer shall transact the business of fidelity insurance or surety insurance without first obtaining a license from the Commission to transact that class of insurance. (1986, c. 562.)

§ 38.2-2403. Limitation of liability on risks. — In applying the limitation specified in § 38.2-208 to fidelity and surety risks, the net amount of exposure on any single risk shall be considered to be within the prescribed limit if the fidelity and surety insurer is protected against losses in excess of the limit by:

1. Reinsurance with a fidelity and surety insurer that enables the obligee or beneficiary to maintain an action on the contract against the insurer jointly with the reinsurer;

2. The cosuretyship of any other fidelity and surety insurer;

3. A deposit of property with it in pledge, or conveyance of property to it in trust for its protection;

4. A conveyance or mortgage of property for its protection;

5. A deposit or other disposition of a portion of any property held in trust so that no future sale, mortgage, pledge or other disposition can be made of that portion of the property except with the consent of the fidelity and surety insurer or by decree or order of a competent court whenever the obligation is entered into on behalf or on account of a person holding property in a fiduciary capacity; or

6. A guarantee by the Small Business Administrator that the surety shall not suffer loss as set forth in the Small Business Investment Act of 1958. (Code 1950, §§ 38-343, 38-344; 1952, c. 317, § 38.1-641; 1986, c. 562; 1988, cc. 529, 548.)

§ 38.2-2404. Limit when penalty of bond exceeds actual exposure to risk. — When the penalty of a suretyship obligation exceeds (i) the amount of a judgment described on the obligation as appealed from and secured by the obligation, (ii) the amount of the subject matter in controversy, or (iii) the amount of the estate held in trust by the person acting in a fiduciary capacity, the bond may be executed by any fidelity and surety insurer if the actual amount of the judgment or the subject matter in controversy or estate not subject to supervision or control of the surety is not in excess of the limitation specified in § 38.2-208. When the penalty of a suretyship obligation executed for the performance of a contract exceeds the contract price, the contract price shall be taken as the basis for estimating the limit of risk specified in § 38.2-208. (1952, c. 317, § 38.1-642; 1986, c. 562.)

§ **38.2-2405. When insurer accepted as surety.** — Any fidelity and surety insurer shall be accepted as surety upon any bond required by the laws of this Commonwealth or by any court, judge, public officer, board, or organization upon presentation of evidence satisfactory to the court, judge, or other officer authorized to approve the bond that the insurer is licensed to transact surety insurance. (Code 1950, § 38-332; 1952, c. 317, § 38.1-643; 1986, c. 562.)

§ **38.2-2406. Requirements deemed met by insurer.** — Whenever a bond, undertaking, recognizance, guaranty, or similar obligation is required, permitted, authorized or allowed by any law of this Commonwealth, or whenever the performance of any act, duty or obligation, or the refraining from any act, is required, permitted, authorized or allowed to be secured or guaranteed by any law of this Commonwealth, the bond or similar obligation, or the security or guaranty, may be executed by any fidelity and surety insurer licensed to execute such instruments. The execution by any fidelity and surety insurer of a bond, undertaking, recognizance, guaranty or similar obligation by its officer, attorney-in-fact, or other authorized representative shall be accepted as fully complying with every law or other requirement, now or hereafter in force, requiring that the bond, undertaking, recognizance, guaranty or similar obligation be given or accepted or that it be executed by one or more sureties, or that the surety or sureties be residents, householders or freeholders, or possess any other qualifications. (1952, c. 317, § 38.1-644; 1986, c. 562.)

§ **38.2-2407. Sureties with respect to guaranteed arrest bond certificates of automobile clubs and associations.** — A. Any domestic or foreign fidelity and surety insurer licensed to transact surety business in this Commonwealth may become surety in any year for any guaranteed arrest bond certificates issued in that year by an automobile club or association by filing with the Commission an undertaking to become surety. The insurer shall file the undertaking on or before the date it is to become effective.

B. The undertaking shall be in a form prescribed by the Commission and shall state the following:

1. The name and address of the automobile club or automobile association issuing the guaranteed arrest bond certificates for which the fidelity and surety insurer undertakes to be surety.

2. The unqualified obligation of the fidelity and surety insurer to pay the fine or forfeiture of any person who, after posting a guaranteed arrest bond certificate for which the fidelity and surety insurer has undertaken to be surety, fails to make the appearance guaranteed by the arrest bond certificate.

C. The term *"guaranteed arrest bond certificate"* as used in this chapter means any printed card or other certificate (i) issued by an automobile club or association to any of its members, (ii) signed by the member and (iii) containing a printed statement that the automobile club or association and a fidelity and surety insurer guarantee the appearance of the person whose signature appears on the card or certificate and that they will pay any fine or forfeiture imposed on that person in the event that the person fails to appear in court at the time of trial. (1952, c. 186; 1952, c. 317, § 38.1-644.1; 1982, c. 63; 1986, c. 562; 1987, c. 519.)

§ 38.2-2408. Guaranteed arrest bond certificate to be accepted in lieu of cash bail in event of violation of motor vehicle laws. — Any guaranteed arrest bond certificate for which a fidelity and surety insurer has become surety as provided in § 38.2-2407 shall be accepted as a bail bond in lieu of cash bail when posted by the person whose signature appears on it. The guaranteed arrest bond certificate shall be accepted as a guarantee of the person's appearance in any court, including general district courts, in this Commonwealth at the court appointed time. The bond may be posted for any person arrested for violation of any motor vehicle law of this Commonwealth or ordinance of any municipality in this Commonwealth committed prior to the date of expiration shown on the guaranteed arrest bond certificate. However, the bond may not be posted for the offense of driving while intoxicated or for any felony. Any guaranteed arrest bond certificate posted as a bail bond in any court in this Commonwealth shall be subject to the forfeiture and enforcement provisions for bail bonds posted in criminal cases as set forth in Chapter 9 (§ 19.2-119 et seq.) of Title 19.2. Any guaranteed arrest bond certificate posted as a bail bond in any general district court in this Commonwealth shall be subject to the forfeiture and enforcement provisions of this chapter or ordinance of the particular municipality pertaining to bail bonds posted. (1952, c. 186; 1952, c. 317, § 38.1-644.2; 1986, c. 562.)

§ 38.2-2409. Agreement for joint control of money and assets. — Any person required to execute a bond, undertaking or other obligation may agree with his surety to deposit any or all assets for which he and his surety may be held responsible. The deposit shall be with a bank, savings bank, safe deposit company, or trust company authorized by law to do business as such, or with any other depository approved by the court or a judge of the court, if the deposit is otherwise proper. Assets shall be deposited for safekeeping and held in a manner that prevents the withdrawal of the whole or any part of the deposit without the written consent of the surety, or without an order of a court or a judge, made on any notice to the surety which the court or judge directs. The agreement shall not in any manner release or change the liability of the principal or sureties as established by the terms of the bond. (Code 1950, § 38-345; 1952, c. 317, § 38.1-645; 1986, c. 562.)

§ 38.2-2410. Expense of securing bond to be allowed in settlements; exceptions. — Any court, judge or other officer whose duty it is to approve the account of any person required to execute a bond with surety shall, whenever a fidelity and surety insurer has become surety on the bond, allow a sum for the expense of obtaining the surety in the settlement of the account. The sum allowed shall accord with the applicable rate filing in effect for the insurer under the provisions of this title. The allowance shall not be made to any state, county or municipal officer. (Code 1950, § 38-347; 1952, c. 317, § 38.1-646; 1986, c. 562.)

§ 38.2-2411. Furnishing court clerks with information as to licensed insurers. — In April of each year the Commission shall furnish the Clerk of the Supreme Court of Virginia and the clerk of every circuit court in this Commonwealth a list of the names of all fidelity and surety insurers in this

Commonwealth, together with a statement of the assets and liabilities of each of the insurers. Each clerk shall file the list in his office. (Code 1950, § 38-334; 1952, c. 317, § 38.1-647; 1986, c. 562.)

§ 38.2-2412. Notice to clerks of revocation of an insurer's license. — Whenever the Commission revokes the license of any fidelity and surety insurer, it shall immediately give notice of the revocation to the Clerk of the Supreme Court of Virginia and each circuit court in this Commonwealth. (Code 1950, § 38-335; 1952, c. 317, § 38.1-648; 1986, c. 562.)

§ 38.2-2413. Release of insurers from liability; rights and remedies. — Any fidelity and surety insurer shall be released from its liability on the same terms and conditions as are prescribed by law for the release of individuals. Any fidelity and surety insurer shall have all the rights, remedies and relief to which an individual guarantor, indemnitor, or surety is entitled. (Code 1950, § 38-333; 1952, c. 317, § 38.1-649; 1986, c. 562.)

§ 38.2-2414. Insurer estopped to deny power to assume liability. — Any fidelity and surety insurer that executes any bond as surety under the provisions of this chapter shall be estopped, in any proceedings to enforce the liability it has assumed, to deny its power to execute the bond or assume the liability. (Code 1950, § 38-348; 1952, c. 317, § 38.1-650; 1986, c. 562.)

§ 38.2-2415. Where civil proceedings may be instituted. — Any suit or other civil proceeding may be instituted against any fidelity and surety insurer (i) at the place where it became surety or assumed any duty or obligation that may be the subject of suit or other civil proceeding; or (ii) at the place where the principal obligor for whom it has become surety may be sued. When the Commonwealth is a party, plaintiff or defendant, the suit or proceeding shall be in the Circuit Court of the City of Richmond. (Code 1950, § 38-346; 1952, c. 317, § 38.1-651; 1986, c. 562.)

Section gives no authority for suits in other states. — This section contemplates judgments recovered against the surety company upon suits instituted and prosecuted within Virginia, and does not intend to provide authority for suits against surety companies in any state in the Union where the principal obligor for whom the company had become surety might be sued. Hopkins v. Common-wealth, 129 Va. 137, 105 S.E. 673 (1921).

Under this section a Virginia material-man who has furnished a United States contractor with materials for a post office in North Carolina has no right of action in Virginia against the surety on the contractor's bond executed in Washington. Hopkins v. Commonwealth, 129 Va. 137, 105 S.E. 673 (1921).

ARTICLE 2.

Power of Attorney to Execute Bonds.

§ 38.2-2416. Power of attorney to be recorded. — Each power of attorney from a fidelity and surety insurer to an agent making the agent an attorney-in-fact to execute any bond or other obligation in the name and on behalf of the insurer as surety, shall, unless the power of attorney is special and limited to one transaction or to definitely stated transactions, be duly acknowledged for recordation and recorded in the deed book in the clerk's office of each county or corporation in which the powers delegated by it are to be exercised. (Code 1950, § 38-339; 1952, c. 317, § 38.1-653; 1986, c. 562.)

§ 38.2-2417. Continuance of power; revocation. — The power of an attorney-in-fact to bind the fidelity and surety insurer as surety within the authority conferred by a power of attorney shall, unless the power of attorney is otherwise limited, continue for the agency until the expiration of the power of attorney or until the power is revoked by the insurer's sealed written instrument duly acknowledged for recordation and admitted to record in the county or corporation in which the power of attorney is recorded. (Code 1950, § 38-340; 1952, c. 317, § 38.1-654; 1986, c. 562.)

§ 38.2-2418. Recordation of instrument of revocation. — Any instrument of revocation shall be recorded in the deed book in the office of the clerk in which the power of attorney was recorded, upon the acknowledgment prescribed by law for the acknowledgment of deeds for recordation. The admission to record the instrument of revocation shall constitute notice to all concerned of the revocation of the power previously conferred. (Code 1950, § 38-341; 1952, c. 317, § 38.1-655; 1986, c. 562.)

§ 38.2-2419. Marginal notation of revocation; indexing. — When the power of attorney has been revoked, the clerk in whose office the power of attorney is recorded shall note its revocation on the margin of the page of the deed book where the power of attorney is recorded, together with a reference to the book and page where the instrument of revocation is recorded. The clerk shall index the instrument of revocation both in the name of the fidelity and surety insurer and of its attorney-in-fact. (Code 1950, § 38-342; 1952, c. 317, § 38.1-656; 1986, c. 562.)

§ 38.2-2420. Bonds executed under power of attorney binding on insurer. — Any bond or obligation executed in the name and on behalf of the insurer as surety under the authority of the power of attorney shall have the same force, effect and validity, and shall be as binding upon the insurer in the name and on behalf of which it is executed as if it were properly executed by the insurer itself through its officers under its common seal. For the purpose of this section, the seal of the insurer or the seal of the attorney-in-fact shall not be required to be affixed to the bond or obligation. (Code 1950, § 38-338; 1952, c. 317, § 38.1-657; 1986, c. 562.)

CHAPTER 25.

MUTUAL ASSESSMENT PROPERTY AND CASUALTY INSURERS.

ARTICLE 1.

General Provisions.

§ 38.2-2500. Scope of chapter. — This chapter applies to mutual assessment property and casualty insurers as defined in this chapter, and to insurance written by those insurers. (1952, c. 317, § 38.1-658; 1986, c. 562.)

§ 38.2-2501. Definitions. — As used in this chapter:

"Mutual assessment insurance" means property and casualty insurance written by an insurer which has a right to assess its members for contributions and which is licensed pursuant to this chapter.

"Mutual assessment property and casualty insurer" means a company without capital stock that writes only mutual assessment insurance insuring property located in or protecting against losses of members who are residents of this Commonwealth. (Code 1950, §§ 38-523, 38-526, 38-529; 1952, c. 317, § 38.1-659; 1954, c. 161; 1960, c. 292; 1962, c. 172; 1974, c. 244; 1986, c. 562.)

Law Review. — For survey of Virginia law on insurance for the year 1973-1974, see 60 Va. L. Rev. 1553 (1974).

§ 38.2-2502. Mutual assessment insurance authorized. — Mutual assessment property and casualty insurers licensed pursuant to this chapter may write mutual assessment insurance. (1952, c. 317, § 38.1-660; 1986, c. 562.)

§ 38.2-2503. Classes of insurance that may be written by mutual assessment property and casualty insurers; minimum surplus to policyholders required. — A. Any mutual assessment property and casualty insurer with surplus to policyholders of at least $25,000 may write the following classes:

1. Fire insurance as defined in § 38.2-110;
2. Miscellaneous property damage insurance as defined in § 38.2-111; and
3. Animal insurance as defined in § 38.2-116.

B. Any mutual assessment property and casualty insurer with surplus to policyholders of at least $100,000 may write the following classes of insurance, in addition to those classes enumerated in subsection A of this section:

1. Water damage insurance as defined in § 38.2-112;
2. Burglary and theft insurance as defined in § 38.2-113;
3. Glass insurance as defined in § 38.2-114;
4. Boiler and machinery insurance as defined in § 38.2-115;
5. Personal injury liability insurance as defined in § 38.2-117;
6. Property damage liability insurance as defined in § 38.2-118;
7. Marine insurance as defined in § 38.2-126;
8. Home protection insurance as defined in § 38.2-129;
9. Homeowners insurance as defined in § 38.2-130;
10. Farmowners insurance as defined in § 38.2-131;
11. Commercial multi-peril insurance as defined in § 38.2-132; and
12. Contingent and consequential losses insurance as defined in § 38.2-133. The liability coverages specified in this subsection may be written only by insurers having a surplus to policyholders of at least $300,000 unless the coverages are fully reinsured.

C. Any mutual assessment property and casualty insurer with surplus to policyholders of at least $800,000 may write the following classes of insurance, in addition to those classes enumerated in subsections A and B of this section:

1. Workers' compensation and employers' liability insurance as defined in § 38.2-119;
2. Fidelity insurance as defined in § 38.2-120;
3. Surety insurance as defined in § 38.2-121;
4. Credit insurance as defined in § 38.2-122;
5. Motor vehicle insurance as defined in § 38.2-124;
6. Aircraft insurance as defined in § 38.2-125;
7. Legal services insurance as defined in § 38.2-127; and
8. Mortgage guaranty insurance as defined in § 38.2-128. (Code 1950, §§ 38-523, 38-526, 38-529; 1952, c. 317, § 38.1-659; 1954, c. 161; 1960, c. 292; 1962, c. 172; 1974, c. 244; 1986, c. 562.)

§ 38.2-2504. Property beyond authorized territory. — A mutual assessment property and casualty insurer shall not insure real property outside the limits of the territory for which it is authorized to write insurance as specified in its charter or bylaws. However, members may be provided liability or other insurance on risks other than real property insurable under this chapter, wherever located. When members own real property near the border of the territory which extends in a contiguous manner beyond the territory, all of the property may be insured if otherwise insurable under this chapter, whether the property is within or without the territory. (Code 1950, §§ 38-526, 38-529; 1952, c. 317, § 38.1-661; 1986, c. 562.)

§ 38.2-2505. Risks limited to those specified in this chapter; personal liability for loss. — No mutual assessment property and casualty insurer shall insure against any losses except as specified in this chapter. Any officer or agent who knowingly or willfully violates or who causes the insurer to violate this provision shall be fined in accordance with § 38.2-218. (Code 1950, § 38-541; 1952, c. 317, § 38.1-687; 1986, c. 562.)

§ 38.2-2506. What laws applicable. — Except as otherwise provided in this chapter, and except when the context otherwise requires, all the provisions of this title relating to insurers generally, and those relating to insurers writing the same class of insurance that mutual assessment property and casualty insurers are authorized to write under this chapter, are applicable to these insurers.

The provisions of §§ 38.2-1032 and 38.2-1035 shall not apply to mutual assessment property and casualty insurers. (Code 1950, §§ 38-505, 38-525; 1952, c. 317, §§ 38.1-91, 38.1-662; 1960, c. 289; 1966, c. 580; 1986, c. 562.)

§ 38.2-2507. Conversion of mutual assessment property and casualty insurers. — A. Any mutual assessment property and casualty insurer desiring to remove itself from the provisions of this chapter and desiring to become an insurer under the provisions of Chapter 10 (§ 38.2-1000 et seq.) of this title may do so by meeting the requirements of Chapter 10. The mutual assessment property and casualty insurer shall submit an application to the Commission showing that each requirement of Chapter 10 has been met. If the applicant does not meet the requirements of Chapter 10, the applicant may submit a plan that includes a schedule for meeting the requirements of Chapter 10. The schedule shall provide for compliance with those requirements within ten years of the approval of the application. For good cause shown, the Commission may grant, after informal hearing, an additional period in order to achieve compliance with the requirements of Chapter 10.

B. If the Commission approves the application, the insurer shall have all the rights, privileges and responsibilities of an insurer licensed under the provisions of Chapter 10 of this title.

C. Upon failure of the applicant to comply with the terms of the approved schedule, the Commission may require the applicant to adhere to the provisions of this chapter. (1986, c. 562.)

ARTICLE 2.

Organization and Licensing of Insurers.

§ 38.2-2508. Incorporation of insurers. — Mutual assessment property and casualty insurers formed after July 1, 1986, shall be incorporated under the provisions of Article 3 (§ 13.1-818 et seq.) of Chapter 10 of Title 13.1, as modified by the provisions of this title. Except as otherwise provided in this title, mutual assessment property and casualty insurers shall be subject to all the general restrictions and have all the general powers imposed and conferred upon those corporations by law. Mutual assessment property and casualty insurers formed prior to July 1, 1986, may continue to operate as organized. (Code 1950, § 38-523; 1952, c. 317, § 38.1-666; 1956, c. 431; 1986, c. 562.)

§ 38.2-2509. Directors; terms; annual meetings; voting; executive committee. — As provided in the certificate or articles of incorporation and the bylaws, the management of any mutual assessment property and casualty insurer shall be vested in a board of at least five directors, each of whom shall be a member of the insurer. Each director shall hold office for one year or for a longer term if specified in the bylaws, and thereafter until his successor is elected and has qualified. Vacancies in the board may be filled for the unexpired term by the remaining directors. The annual meeting of the members of the insurer shall be held as provided by the certificate or articles of incorporation or the bylaws. A quorum shall consist of (i) ten members or (ii) the number of members specified by either the certificate or articles of incorporation or the bylaws, whichever number is larger. In all meetings of members, each member of the insurer shall be entitled to one vote, or a number of votes based upon insurance in force, the number of policies held or the amount of premiums paid as provided by the bylaws of the insurer. Votes by proxy may be received in accordance with the certificate or articles of incorporation or the bylaws. The date of the annual meeting shall be stated in the policy, or notice of the date and location of the annual meeting shall be provided annually. Notwithstanding the provisions of the charter of any insurer, upon a resolution adopted by the board of directors and approved by a majority of its members present in person or by proxy, the directors may be divided into classes and a portion only elected each year. Pursuant to the provisions of § 13.1-869, the directors may appoint an executive committee to exercise the powers and perform the duties set out in that section. (1952, c. 317, § 38.1-667; 1956, c. 431; 1986, c. 562.)

§ 38.2-2510. Officers. — Unless the certificate or articles of incorporation provides otherwise, the directors shall elect from their number a president. The directors shall also elect a secretary, treasurer, and any additional officers they consider necessary, who may or may not be members. The offices of secretary and treasurer may be held by one person. Unless otherwise provided in the certificate or articles of incorporation, the term of those officers shall be not less than one year nor more than three years or until their successors are elected or selected and qualified. (1952, c. 317, § 38.1-667.1; 1986, c. 562.)

§ 38.2-2511. How license obtained. — The applicant insurer shall file with and have approved by the Commission its application for the license required by § 38.2-1024 prior to transacting the business of insurance in this Commonwealth. The Commission shall not grant a license to any insurer until it is satisfied that the insurer has complied with the requirements of § 38.2-1024 and has filed with the Commission a statement signed by its president and secretary or two of its directors subject to § 38.2-1304, setting forth:

1. That the corporation holds bona fide applications for insurance of the classes proposed to be issued from 100 or more persons who own property insurable by the insurer under the provisions of this chapter and who desire to become members of the insurer;

2. The names of the proposed members and the amount of insurance subscribed for by each;

3. A statement that the insurer has received from each proposed member the initial fees and assessments required for the insurance requested;

4. The names and addresses of the officers and directors of the insurer;

5. The location of the insurer's principal office in this Commonwealth;

6. The classes of insurance proposed to be written; and

7. The territory within which the insurer proposes to transact insurance. (Code 1950, § 38-524; 1952, c. 317, § 38.1-668; 1986, c. 562.)

ARTICLE 3.

Members.

§ 38.2-2512. Who may become members. — Any person having a risk insurable under this chapter who resides in the territory in which the insurer operates or who owns property located in the territory may become a member of a mutual assessment property and casualty insurer and shall be entitled to all the rights and privileges pertaining to membership. Any officer, trustee, board member or legal representative of a corporation, board, estate or association may be recognized as acting for or on its behalf for the purpose of the membership, but shall not be personally liable under the contract of insurance by reason of acting in such representative capacity. (1952, c. 317, § 38.1-669; 1986, c. 562.)

§ 38.2-2513. Withdrawal and exclusion of members. — A. Any member of a mutual assessment property and casualty insurer may withdraw as a member at any time by giving at least thirty days' written notice to the insurer and paying his share of all losses against the insurer that have occurred prior to the member's withdrawal and which have not been fully reserved or for which surplus is inadequate. Upon this withdrawal the member shall be paid by the insurer any unearned premium, unearned fee or unearned assessment paid in advance.

B. Any member who neglects or refuses to pay an assessment or premium when due may be excluded from membership for that or any other reason satisfactory to a majority of the directors or the executive committee, or as the bylaws prescribe. The member shall remain liable for the payment of any assessments made for losses that have occurred prior to his exclusion, and also for the amounts provided for in § 38.2-2522, if action is instituted within twelve months after the time the assessments become due. (Code 1950, §§ 38-527, 38-537; 1952, c. 317, §§ 38.1-669.1, 38.1-670; 1986, c. 562.)

§ **38.2-2514. Procedure upon exclusion of member.** — If any member is excluded from the insurer as provided in this article, the insurer shall note upon its records the exclusion of the member, the cancellation of his insurance policies, and the date of the exclusion. The insurer shall notify the member by mail of the exclusion and cancellation, and after at least five days have elapsed from the mailing of the notice, the policy shall no longer be effective and all further liability of the insurer under the policy shall cease. Proper notification shall be deemed to have been effected if the notice is deposited with the United States Postal Service and mailed to the member at his address as shown on the records of the insurer. If the bylaws or the policy provide that a member's policy shall be void without any notice if the member neglects or refuses to pay any assessment, that provision shall be valid and the notice required in this section need not be given. Upon the cancellation of the insurance or upon the policy becoming void, the member shall be entitled to receive from the insurer a repayment of an equitable portion of any premium, fee or assessment which was paid in advance. (Code 1950, §§ 38-537, 38-538; 1952, c. 317, § 38.1-671; 1986, c. 562.)

§ **38.2-2515. Insurers to maintain membership of 100 or more; license suspended or revoked if membership not maintained; rehabilitation or liquidation.** — Every mutual assessment property and casualty insurer shall maintain a membership of at least 100 persons at all times. Whenever the number of members falls below 100, the insurer shall notify the Commission immediately of that fact. Upon receipt of that notice, or upon information from any source that the membership of the insurer is less than 100, the Commission may revoke the insurer's license, or may issue an order requiring the insurer to increase its membership to at least 100 within a designated period not exceeding 90 days.

If at the expiration of the designated period the membership has not been increased to at least 100, the Commission shall revoke the insurer's license. Upon the revocation of its license as authorized in this section, delinquency proceedings against the insurer may be instituted and conducted as provided in Chapter 15 of this title. (1952, c. 317, § 38.1-672; 1986, c. 562.)

ARTICLE 4.

Insurance Transactions.

§ **38.2-2516. Issuance of policies; bylaws as part of contract.** — The directors of every mutual assessment property and casualty insurer shall issue insurance policies requiring the insurer to pay all losses or damages caused by the risk insured against during the time the policy is in force. Payment shall not exceed the amount insured. There shall be attached to or included in each of those policies the portion of the bylaws that constitute a part of the policy contract. Bylaws or their amendments that are not a part of the policy contract shall not affect the policy contract unless they are included as a suitable endorsement mailed or delivered to the policyholder. (Code 1950, § 38-529; 1952, c. 317, § 38.1-673; 1954, c. 161; 1986, c. 562.)

§ 38.2-2517. Policy forms to be filed. — Every mutual assessment property and casualty insurer shall file with the Commission a copy of all policy forms and standard endorsements which the insurer intends to use in the transaction of its business. Mutual assessment property and casualty insurers shall be exempt from the filing requirements of Chapter 3 (§ 38.2-300 et seq.) of this title except for those classes of insurance enumerated in subsection C of § 38.2-2503, where full compliance with Chapter 3 shall be required. (1986, c. 562.)

§ 38.2-2518. Assessment contract. — Each person insured by a mutual assessment property and casualty insurer shall be issued a contract prescribed by the insurer, that shall be uniform among members of the respective classes of insurance written by the insurer. Each member shall agree to pay his pro rata share of all losses or damages sustained, expenses of operation of the insurer, and the maintenance of an adequate surplus to policyholders as determined by the board of directors. Periodic assessments may be collected as advance premiums or post assessments or by both methods. The amount of assessments shall be established by the directors of the insurer. (Code 1950, § 38-530; 1952, c. 317, § 38.1-677; 1954, c. 161; 1986, c. 562.)

§ 38.2-2519. Classification of risks; rates. — Any insurer writing mutual assessment property and casualty insurance may classify the property or risk insured in accordance with the risk or hazard to which the property is subject, and fix the rate of assessment or premium for that insurance in accordance with the classification. (Code 1950, § 38-531; 1952, c. 317, § 38.1-676; 1974, c. 244; 1986, c. 562.)

Law Review. — For survey of Virginia law on insurance for the year 1973-1974, see 60 Va. L. Rev. 1553 (1974).

§ 38.2-2520. Right to limit assessment liability. — Any mutual assessment property and casualty insurer having a surplus to policyholders equal to at least 3 times the average annual losses and expenses of the insurer during the last 5-year period or a surplus to policyholders of at least $800,000 may limit the assessment liability of members. The liability of members for assessment may be limited during any one year to an amount not less than one additional current annual assessment. (1952, c. 317, § 38.1-683.1; 1986, c. 562.)

§ 38.2-2521. Notice of assessment; how given. — After an assessment is made, the insurer shall give every member subject to the assessment written notice stating the amount of the member's assessment and the date when payment is due. Except where the provisions of the bylaws or the policy provide otherwise, the time of payment shall be at least thirty days and no more than sixty days from the service of the notice. That notice may be served personally or by mail. If mailed, the notice shall be deposited with the United States Postal Service and addressed to the member at his residence or place of business as shown on the company records. (Code 1950, § 38-535; 1952, c. 317, § 38.1-684; 1986, c. 562.)

§ 38.2-2522. Action to recover assessments; penalty. — Within twelve months after an assessment becomes due, a mutual assessment property and casualty insurer may institute suit against any member to recover any assessment that the member fails to pay. The insurer shall be entitled to recover (i) the amount shown to be due, (ii) lawful interest, and (iii) fifty percent of the principal amount as liquidated damages for neglect or refusal to pay within the time required. (Code 1950, § 38-536; 1952, c. 317, § 38.1-685; 1986, c. 562.)

§ 38.2-2523. Notice of loss and adjustment. — Each policyholder after sustaining loss or damage from any cause specified in the policy shall notify the mutual assessment property and casualty insurer within the time prescribed in the policy. The insurer shall promptly proceed to ascertain and adjust the loss or damage in the manner provided by the policy, law and bylaws of the company. (Code 1950, § 38-530; 1952, c. 317, § 38.1-678; 1986, c. 562.)

§ 38.2-2524. Proceeding when loss or damage exceeds cash on hand. — If at any time any loss or damage to property insured by a mutual assessment property and casualty insurer exceeds the insurer's cash available to pay the loss or damage, the insurer may borrow money in an amount sufficient to pay the loss or damage. This shall be approved by the board of directors or the executive committee. The board of directors or the executive committee may levy an assessment sufficient to repay the loan or to pay the loss or damage, or any portion that is in excess of the cash on hand. (Code 1950, § 38-532; 1952, c. 317, § 38.1-681; 1986, c. 562.)

§ 38.2-2525. Agents licenses required. — Agents representing a mutual assessment property and casualty insurer shall be licensed by the Commission and appointed by the insurer in accordance with Chapter 18 of this title. However, agents whose licenses are limited to those classes of insurance referred to in subsections A and B of § 38.2-2503 shall not be required to take a written examination from the Commission in accordance with § 38.2-1814. (1986, c. 562.)

ARTICLE 5.

Financial Provisions.

§ 38.2-2526. Surplus to policyholders. — A. Surplus to policyholders in addition to the required surplus specified in subsections A and B of § 38.2-2503 may be accumulated in amounts as determined by the board of directors. The surplus may be used for the payment of losses and operating expenses of the insurer.

B. Income earned on any surplus to policyholders may be used to pay losses, operating expenses, or added to surplus.

C. The provisions of this section shall become effective July 1, 1986.

D. Any mutual assessment property and casualty insurer already licensed on July 1, 1986, shall comply with the minimum surplus requirements of § 38.2-2503 by July 1, 1991. Any mutual assessment property and casualty insurer that does not meet the surplus requirements of this section as of July 1, 1986, and is not writing any of the classes authorized in subsections B and C of § 38.2-2503 on July 1, 1986, shall not write any of those classes until the specified surplus requirement is met. (1986, c. 562.)

§ 38.2-2527. Limitation on single risk to be assumed. — A. No single risk shall be assumed by a mutual assessment property and casualty insurer in an amount exceeding ten percent of its surplus to policyholders. Any risk or portion of any risk which has been reinsured in accordance with § 38.2-2528 shall be deducted in determining the limitation of risk prescribed by this section. For the purposes of this section the amount of surplus to policyholders shall be determined on the basis of the last financial statement of the insurer, or the last report of examination filed with the Commission, whichever is more recent, at the time the risk is assumed. Mutual assessment property and casualty insurers licensed on or before July 1, 1986, shall conform to this limitation by July 1, 1991.

B. Until July 1, 1991, the following single risk limits after deducting for reinsurance will apply:

1. No insurer having less than $2 million insurance in force shall insure any 1 risk for more than $10,000;

2. No insurer having more than $2 million but less than $5 million insurance in force shall insure any 1 risk for more than $12,000;

3. No insurer having more than $5 million but less than $10 million insurance in force shall insure any 1 risk for more than $20,000;

4. No insurer having more than $10 million insurance in force shall insure any 1 risk for a sum in excess of 15¢ for each $100 insurance it has in force; and

5. An insurer may insure any one risk in larger sums than prescribed in this section if (i) the excess over such prescribed maximum is reinsured as authorized in this chapter or (ii) the excess may be increased by the extent of twenty-five percent of the surplus of the insurer as of the time the insurance is written. (1986, c. 562.)

§ 38.2-2528. Reinsurance. — Any mutual assessment property and casualty insurer may reinsure the whole or any part of its risks with any solvent insurer licensed in this Commonwealth or licensed or approved in any other state and meeting standards of solvency at least equal to those required in this Commonwealth if the reinsurance is ceded without contingent liability on the part of the reinsured insurer. Any mutual assessment property and casualty insurer having a surplus in excess of $800,000 may accept or assume reinsurance from any licensed property and casualty insurer. Any of those companies may accept or assume reinsurance on risks located within or without the territory in which it is authorized to transact insurance.

Nothing in this section shall be construed to prohibit the participation of a mutual assessment property and casualty insurer in a pool or other plan among similar companies approved by the Commission for the purpose of spreading losses or providing reinsurance or catastrophe coverage for participants. The acceptance of reinsurance by any insurer outside the territory in which it is authorized to transact the business of insurance shall not be construed to enlarge its territory so as to affect any tax exemption to which it may be entitled. (1952, c. 317, § 38.1-675; 1986, c. 562.)

§ 38.2-2529. Unearned premium reserves required. — A. Advance assessments received by mutual assessment property and casualty insurers shall be considered premiums and, except as provided in subsection B of this section, shall be subject to the requirement of an unearned premium reserve computed in accordance with § 38.2-1312. The reserves may be reduced for applicable reinsurance in accordance with the provisions of Article 3.1 (§ 38.2-1316.1 et seq.) of Chapter 13 of this title.

B. The amount each insurer shall maintain in reserves for unearned premium reserves shall be as follows:

1. For calendar year 1987, at least ten percent of the unearned premium reserve as calculated in subsection A of this section; and

2. For each subsequent year, at least an additional ten percent as calculated in subsection A for that subsequent year in order that the full amount of unearned premium reserves shall be established by December 31, 1996. (1986, c. 562; 1994, c. 316.)

CHAPTER 26.

HOME PROTECTION COMPANIES.

§ **38.2-2600. Definitions.** — As used in this chapter:

"Fronting company" means a licensed insurer or licensed home protection company which generally transfers to one or more unlicensed insurers or unlicensed home protection companies by reinsurance or otherwise all or substantially all of the risk of loss under all of the home protection contracts written by it in this Commonwealth.

"Home protection company" means any person who performs, or arranges to perform, services pursuant to a home protection insurance contract.

"Home protection insurance contract" or *"contract"* means any insurance contract or agreement whereby a person undertakes for a specified period of time and for a predetermined fee to furnish, arrange for or indemnify for service, repair, or replacement of any and all of the structural components, parts, appliances, or systems of any covered residential dwelling necessitated by wear and tear, deterioration, inherent defect, or by the failure of an inspection to detect the likelihood of failure.

The contract shall provide for a system to effect repair or replacement if the contract undertakes to provide for repair or replacement services. The contract shall not include protection against consequential damage from the failure of any structural component, part, appliance or system.

"Structural component" means the roof, foundation, basement, walls, ceilings, or floors of a home. (1981, c. 530, §§ 38.1-932, 38.1-944; 1982, c. 132; 1986, c. 562.)

§ **38.2-2601. Exemptions.** — This chapter shall not apply to:

1. Performance guarantees given by either (i) the builder of a home or (ii) the manufacturer, seller, or lessor of the property that is the subject of the contract if no identifiable charge is made for the guarantee.

2. Any service contract, guarantee, or warranty intending to guarantee or warrant the repairs or service of a home appliance, component, part, or system

that is issued (i) by a person who has sold, serviced, repaired, or provided replacement of the appliance, component, part, or system at the time of or prior to issuance of the service contract, guarantee or warranty if such person does not engage in the business of a home protection company or (ii) by a home protection company which sells such service contracts, guarantees or warranties in the Commonwealth of Virginia and which has net worth in excess of $100 million. (1981, c. 530, § 38.1-933; 1986, c. 562; 1992, c. 21.)

§ 38.2-2602. Limited applicability to certain insurers.

— A property and casualty insurer may be licensed to transact home protection insurance as defined in § 38.2-129. An insurer licensed in this Commonwealth to transact the class of insurance defined by § 38.2-111 on July 1, 1986, may also transact home protection insurance without additional authority. No other provision of this chapter, except § 38.2-2606 and §§ 38.2-2608 through 38.2-2614, shall be applicable to the insurers, their businesses, or their home protection contracts. (1981, c. 530, §§ 38.1-933, 38.1-945; 1986, c. 562.)

§ 38.2-2603. License required; application; fee.

— Except as provided in § 38.2-2602, no home protection company shall issue or offer to issue home protection contracts in this Commonwealth until a home protection company license has been granted by the Commission. Application for a license shall be made in writing, in the form prescribed by the Commission, and shall be accompanied by a nonrefundable application fee of $500. (1981, c. 530, § 38.1-933; 1986, c. 562.)

§ 38.2-2604. Qualification for license; net worth; deposit of securities with State Treasurer.

— A. No license shall be issued to any home protection company unless the applicant:

1. Is a Virginia corporation formed under the provisions of Article 3 (§ 13.1-618 et seq.) of Chapter 9 of Title 13.1, or Article 3 (§ 13.1-818 et seq.) of Chapter 10 of Title 13.1; or

2. Is a foreign corporation subject to regulation and licensing under the laws of its domiciliary jurisdiction which are substantially similar to those provided in this chapter, and has obtained a certificate of authority to transact business in this Commonwealth;

3. Furnishes the Commission with evidence satisfactory to it that the management of the home protection company is competent and trustworthy, and can be reasonably expected to successfully manage the company's affairs in compliance with law;

4. Establishes to the satisfaction of the Commission that it (i) maintains employees or has contractual arrangements sufficient to provide the services or indemnity undertaken by it, and (ii) agrees to accept requests for heating, electrical and plumbing services contracted for twenty-four hours per day, seven days per week;

5. Makes the deposit of bonds or other securities required by this section;

6. Is otherwise in compliance with this chapter;

7. Has filed the required application and paid the required fee;

8. Has paid all fees, taxes, and charges required by law;

9. Has the minimum net worth prescribed by this section;

10. Has filed any financial statement and any reports, certificates, or other documents as the Commission deems necessary to secure a full and accurate knowledge of its affairs and financial condition; and

11. Keeps adequate, correct and complete books and records of accounts and maintains proper accounting controls.

B. The Commission shall not issue a license to or renew the license of a home protection company unless it is satisfied that the financial condition, the method of operation, and the manner of doing business enable the home protection company to meet its obligations to all contract holders and that the home protection company has otherwise complied with all the requirements of law.

C. A home protection company shall maintain a net worth in an amount not less than 20% of the premiums charged on its contracts currently in force; however, the minimum required net worth shall be not less than $100,000, and the maximum required net worth shall be that amount required of insurers under the provisions of Article 5 (§ 38.2-1024 et seq.) of Chapter 10 of this title.

D. No license shall be granted to any home protection company until it presents to the Commission a certificate of the State Treasurer that bonds or other securities have been deposited with him to be held in accordance with the provisions of and upon the terms and conditions and in the amount as provided in Article 7 (§ 38.2-1045 et seq.) of Chapter 10 of this title. (1981, c. 530, § 38.1-934; 1982, c. 132; 1984, c. 640; 1986, c. 562.)

§ 38.2-2605. Expiration and renewal of license. — Every home protection company licensed under this chapter shall obtain a renewal of its license annually from the Commission. Every license issued under this chapter shall expire at midnight on June 30 immediately following the date of issuance. No renewal license shall be issued unless the home protection company has paid all taxes, fees, assessments and other charges imposed upon it, and has complied with all the other requirements of law. The Commission shall not fail or refuse to renew the license of any home protection company without giving the home protection company ten days' notice of the failure or refusal to renew and providing it an opportunity to be heard and to introduce evidence in its behalf. Any such hearing may be informal, and the required notice may be waived by the Commission and the home protection company. (1981, c. 530, § 38.1-935; 1986, c. 562.)

§ 38.2-2606. Reserves required. — A home protection company licensed in this Commonwealth shall maintain reserves in an amount sufficient to provide for its liability to furnish appropriate indemnity, repairs, and replacement services under its issued and outstanding contracts. The reserve account shall be calculated according to sound actuarial principles, but shall equal at a minimum fifty percent of the premiums received from all contracts in force in this Commonwealth, net of applicable reinsurance and any amounts paid on account of liabilities incurred under the contracts. To receive credit for reinsurance on home protection contracts, the reinsurance contract or policy shall be issued by a solvent insurer licensed in this Commonwealth or any other state having standards of solvency at least equal to those required in this Commonwealth. (1981, c. 530, § 38.1-936; 1986, c. 562.)

§ 38.2-2607. Annual statements. — On or before March 1 of each year, each home protection company shall file with the Commission its annual statement pursuant to the provisions of § 38.2-1300, in the form prescribed by the Commission. The annual statement may be based on accounting principles common to the home protection business, provided that they enable the Commission to ascertain whether the reserves required by § 38.2-2606 have been established. However, the Commission may prescribe a uniform accounting system to be used by home protection companies. The Commission may also require the uniform reporting of statistical information under a plan prescribed or approved by the Commission. (1981, c. 530, § 38.1-937; 1986, c. 562.)

§ 38.2-2608. Home protection contracts; filing; form and contents; application or agreement to purchase; regulation of rates and

charges. — A. No home protection contract shall be issued or used in this Commonwealth unless it has been filed with and approved by the Commission.

B. No home protection contract shall be issued in this Commonwealth unless it:

1. Is written in simple and readable words with common meanings and is understandable without special insurance knowledge or training;

2. Specifically sets forth:

a. The services to be performed by the home protection company and the terms and conditions of the performance;

b. Any service fee or deductible amount applicable per claim or per occurrence;

c. Each of the systems, appliances, and structural components covered by the contract;

d. All exclusions and limitations respecting the extent of coverage;

e. The period during which the contract will remain in effect and the cancellation provision;

f. All limitations regarding the performance of services, including any restrictions as to the time periods when services will be performed;

3. Provides for the initiation of covered services contracted for upon telephonic request without first requiring the filing of written claim forms or written applications; and

4. Provides for the initiation of covered services contracted for by or under the direction of the home protection company within seventy-two hours of the request for the service by the contract holder, and provides for the completion of the services as soon as reasonably possible. For malfunctions of furnace or heating systems during the winter months, the contract must provide for the initiation of services immediately.

C. Every application for or agreement to purchase a home protection contract shall include a statement that the purchase of the contract is not mandatory and may be waived, and shall include a statement of the premium.

D. 1. Chapter 20 (§ 38.2-2000 et seq.) of this title shall apply to the rates charged by home protection companies until such time as the Commission determines, after proper notice and hearing, that sufficient competition exists in the home protection industry to justify its regulation under Chapter 19 (§ 38.2-1900 et seq.) of this title. Upon this determination, Chapter 19 of this title shall apply to the rates charged by home protection companies.

2. No home protection company shall make or issue a contract except in accordance with the filings that are in effect for that company. No home protection company or any of its representatives shall charge or receive any fee, compensation or consideration for the contract that is not included in the rate in effect for that company.

3. The rates charged shall be based on sound actuarial principles and shall not be excessive, inadequate, or unfairly discriminatory as defined in § 38.2-1904. (1981, c. 530, § 38.1-938; 1984, c. 640; 1986, c. 562.)

§ 38.2-2609. Qualifications of agents. — No person shall recommend, solicit, negotiate, or sell home protection contracts in this Commonwealth unless (i) he has a valid license to transact property and casualty insurance in this Commonwealth, (ii) he has a valid license to sell real estate in this Commonwealth, issued pursuant to Chapter 21 (§ 54.1-2100 et seq.) of Title 54.1, or (iii) he is the builder of the home or one of his authorized agents. (1981, c. 530, § 38.1-939; 1984, c. 640; 1986, c. 562.)

§ 38.2-2610. Cancellation of home protection contracts. — A. No home protection contract shall be cancellable by the home protection company during the initial term for which it is issued, except for:

1. Nonpayment of premium;

2. Fraud or misrepresentation of facts material to the issuance of the contract; or

3. Contracts providing coverage prior to the time the residential property is purchased, provided that purchase of the property does not occur.

B. Nothing in this section establishes the right of a contract holder to renew any contract. (1981, c. 530, § 38.1-940; 1986, c. 562.)

§ 38.2-2611. **Unfair discrimination.** — No person shall make or permit any unfair discrimination between individuals in the rates or fees charged for any contract, in the performance of services or payments for services, or in any other terms or conditions of the contract. (1981, c. 530, § 38.1-941; 1986, c. 562.)

§ 38.2-2612. **Unfair trade practices.** — In addition to the provisions of Chapter 5 (§ 38.2-500) of this title, the Commission may order any home protection company or its representatives to cease and desist from engaging in the following unfair trade practices:

1. The making of any false or misleading statements, either oral or written, in connection with the sale, offer to sell, or advertisement of a home protection contract;

2. The omission of any material statement in connection with the sale, offer to sell, or advertisement of a contract that under the circumstances should have been made in order to make the statements that were made not misleading;

3. The making of any statement that the purchase of a home protection contract is mandatory;

4. The making of any false or misleading statements, either oral or written, about the benefits or services available under the contract;

5. The failure to perform the services promised under the contract in a timely, competent, or workmanlike manner; or

6. Any statement or practice which has the effect of creating or maintaining a fraud. (1981, c. 530, § 38.1-942; 1986, c. 562.)

§ 38.2-2613. **Application of insurance laws.** — Except as otherwise specifically provided in this chapter or where the context requires otherwise, all of the provisions of this title that apply to property and casualty insurers shall apply in every respect to home protection companies licensed under this chapter. In addition, Article 1 (§ 58.1-2500 et seq.) and Article 2 (§ 58.1-2520 et seq.) of Chapter 25 of Title 58.1 shall apply to the operation of a home protection company. (1981, c. 530, § 38.1-943; 1986, c. 562.)

§ 38.2-2614. **Fronting not permitted.** — No licensed insurer or licensed home protection company shall act as a fronting company for any unlicensed insurer or unlicensed home protection company. (1981, c. 530, § 38.1-944; 1986, c. 562.)

§ 38.2-2615. **Other insurance transactions prohibited.** — A. A home protection company that engages in any business other than the business of a home protection company is not eligible for the issuance or renewal of a license in this Commonwealth.

B. Nothing in this chapter shall be deemed to authorize any home protection company to transact any business other than that of a home protection company or to transact any other business of insurance, unless the company is authorized by a license issued by the Commission. (1981, c. 530, § 38.1-945; 1986, c. 562.)

CHAPTER 27.

BASIC PROPERTY INSURANCE RESIDUAL MARKET FACILITY AND JOINT UNDERWRITING ASSOCIATION.

§ 38.2-2700. Purposes of chapter. — The purposes of this chapter are:

1. To assure stability in the property insurance market of this Commonwealth;

2. To assure the availability of basic property insurance for qualified property;

3. To encourage maximum use of the voluntary insurance market provided by licensed insurers in obtaining basic property insurance; and

4. To provide for the equitable distribution among licensed insurers of the responsibility for insuring qualified property for which basic property insurance cannot be obtained through the voluntary insurance market. (1968, c. 559, § 38.1-746; 1986, c. 562.)

§ 38.2-2701. Definitions. — As used in this chapter:

"Basic property insurance" means insurance against direct loss to any property caused by perils defined and limited in the standard fire policy prescribed in §§ 38.2-2101 through 38.2-2112, and in the extended coverage endorsement approved by the Commission pursuant to § 38.2-2117 and such additional lines of insurance and forms of coverage as may be recommended by the governing body of the residual market facility and approved by the Commission.

"Inspection service" means any organization designated or approved by the Commission to determine the insurability and conditions of the properties for which basic property insurance is sought.

"Net direct premiums written" means gross direct premiums written in this Commonwealth on all policies of basic property insurance and the basic property insurance component of multi-peril policies less (i) all return premiums on those policies, (ii) dividends paid or credited to policyholders, and (iii) the unused or unabsorbed portions of premium deposits.

"Qualified property" means all real property and all tangible personal property at a fixed location in this Commonwealth, whether or not the property is subject to exposure from an external hazard located on property that is

neither owned nor controlled by the prospective insured, and whether or not the property is subject to exposure from riot hazard, where the property:

1. Is not used for manufacturing purposes;

2. Complies with applicable state laws and regulations and local building codes and ordinances;

3. Is not commonly owned or controlled, or combinable for rating purposes, with property insured for similar coverages elsewhere; and

4. Has characteristics of ownership, condition or occupancy that do not violate any public policy.

"*Residual market facility*" means any organization approved by the Commission to equitably distribute the responsibility to provide basic property insurance on qualified property among insurers licensed to write basic property insurance or other insurance containing a basic property insurance component. (1968, c. 559, § 38.1-747; 1980, c. 156; 1982, c. 664; 1986, c. 562; 1987, c. 520; 1995, c. 119.)

§ 38.2-2702. Establishment of residual market facility. — A. A residual market facility shall be established and maintained by all insurers licensed to write basic property insurance or other insurance containing a basic property insurance component. The plan of operation of the residual market facility shall be subject to approval by the Commission.

B. The residual market facility shall be governed by a board of fifteen directors. Four directors shall be appointed by the Commissioner, two of whom shall be property and casualty insurance agents and two of whom shall be from the general public.

C. The residual market facility shall have the power to:

1. Employ or retain persons necessary to perform the duties of the residual market facility;

2. Acquire, hold, and dispose of real and personal property, or any interest in real and personal property;

3. Borrow funds necessary to effect the purposes of this chapter in accord with the plan of operation;

4. Negotiate and become a party to those contracts necessary to carry out the purposes of this chapter;

5. Indemnify any director or member of its governing body, officer, employee, or agent in the manner permitted by and subject to the limitations contained in Article 9 (§ 13.1-875 et seq.) of Chapter 10 of Title 13.1; and provide any other or further indemnity to any such person that may be authorized by the plan of operation except an indemnity against his gross negligence or willful misconduct, and purchase and maintain insurance in the manner permitted by § 13.1-882; and

6. Perform any other acts necessary or proper to carry out the purposes of this chapter.

D. The residual market facility shall not be deemed to be an insurer within the provisions of § 38.2-100. (1968, c. 559, § 38.1-748; 1973, c. 451, § 38.1-748.1; 1980, c. 156; 1982, c. 664; 1986, c. 562.)

§ 38.2-2703. Rules, rates, policy forms and endorsements subject to the approval of Commission. — The rules, rates, policy forms, and endorsements of the residual market facility shall be subject to the Commission's approval prior to use. (1986, c. 562.)

§ 38.2-2704. Inspection of property. — Any person having an insurable interest in real property and tangible personal property at a fixed location in this Commonwealth is entitled, upon request, to an inspection of the property by representatives of the residual market facility to determine whether the property is within the definition of qualified property. A copy of the inspection report shall be made available upon request to the applicant, his agent, or the insurer. (1968, c. 559, § 38.1-748; 1980, c. 156; 1982, c. 664; 1986, c. 562.)

§ **38.2-2705. Operation of inspection service.** — A. The residual market facility may employ other organizations to perform inspection services to determine whether property is within the definition of qualified property.

B. The plan of operation regarding the inspection service, the experience and qualifications of the organization proposed to conduct the inspection service, the manner and scope of the inspection, and the form of the inspection report shall be set forth by the residual market facility in a written report made to the Commission and shall be subject to approval by the Commission. (1968, c. 559, § 38.1-748; 1980, c. 156; 1982, c. 664; 1986, c. 562.)

§ **38.2-2706. Service of process.** — Service of any notice, proof of loss, legal process or other communication relating to the policy or any notice or order of the Commission shall be made upon the residual market facility by service upon the residual market facility's manager, or any duly appointed assistant manager. (1973, c. 451, § 38.1-748.1; 1986, c. 562.)

§ **38.2-2707. When Commission may order implementation of §§ 38.2-2708 and 38.2-2709.** — If the Commission finds, after a reasonable period of time, that the residual market facility established by § 38.2-2702 is not creating a market that meets the purposes of this chapter, the Commission may order the implementation of §§ 38.2-2708 and 38.2-2709. (1968, c. 559, § 38.1-749; 1973, c. 451; 1986, c. 562.)

§ **38.2-2708. Creation and plan of operation of joint underwriting association.** — A. After providing notice and opportunity to be heard and upon promulgation of an order by the Commission pursuant to § 38.2-2707, a joint underwriting association shall be created consisting of all insurers licensed to write basic property insurance or other insurance that contains a basic property insurance component in this Commonwealth, but excluding insurers exempted from rate regulation by subsection C of § 38.2-1902. Each insurer that is required to be a member of the joint underwriting association shall remain a member as a condition of its license to write basic property insurance and other insurance that contains a basic property insurance component in this Commonwealth.

B. The joint underwriting association shall, pursuant to this chapter and the plan of operation, have the power to (i) cause its members to issue policies of basic property insurance on qualified property to applicants; (ii) assume reinsurance on qualified property from members; and (iii) cede reinsurance.

C. 1. Within ninety days following the effective date of the order of the Commission, the joint underwriting association shall submit to the Commission for its review a proposed plan of operation consistent with this chapter. The plan of operation shall provide for economical, fair and nondiscriminatory administration and for the prompt and efficient provision of basic property insurance to promote orderly community development. The plan of operation shall include, but not be limited to, (i) preliminary assessment of all members for initial expenses necessary to commence operations, (ii) establishment of necessary facilities, (iii) management of the joint underwriting association, (iv) assessment of members to defray losses and expenses, (v) commission arrangements, (vi) reasonable underwriting standards and limits of liability, (vii) acceptance and cession of reinsurance, and (viii) procedures for determining amounts of insurance to be provided.

2. The plan of operation shall be subject to approval by the Commission after consultation with affected individuals and organizations, and shall take effect ten days after its approval. If the Commission disapproves all or any part of the proposed plan of operation, the joint underwriting association shall within thirty days submit for review an appropriately revised plan of operation. If the joint underwriting association fails to submit a revised plan, or if the revised plan is unacceptable, the Commission shall promulgate whatever plan of operation it deems necessary to carry out the purposes of this chapter.

3. The joint underwriting association may, on its own initiative or at the request of the Commission, amend the plan of operation. Any amendment to the plan of operation shall be subject to the Commission's approval. (1968, c. 559, § 38.1-750; 1973, c. 504; 1986, c. 562.)

§ 38.2-2709. Ceding basic property insurance to association; participation of members; governing body. — A. Any member of the joint underwriting association may cede to the association basic property insurance written on qualified property, to the extent and on the terms and conditions set forth in the plan of operation.

B. All members of the joint underwriting association shall participate in its writings, expenses, profits and losses, or in any categories thereof that may be separately established by the joint underwriting association, in the proportion that the net direct premiums written by each member during the preceding calendar year bear to the aggregate net direct premiums written in this Commonwealth by all members of the joint underwriting association during the preceding calendar year, but excluding (i) premiums on property used for manufacturing purposes, and (ii) that portion of premiums attributable to the operation of the joint underwriting association.

C. The joint underwriting association shall be governed by a board of fifteen directors. Four directors shall be appointed by the Commissioner, two of whom shall be property and casualty insurance agents and two of whom shall be from the general public. The remaining eleven directors shall be elected annually by a cumulative vote of the joint underwriting association's members, whose votes shall be weighted in accordance with each member's premiums written during the preceding calendar year. The first board shall be elected at a meeting of the members or their authorized representatives, which shall be held within thirty days after approval of the plan of operation as provided in § 38.2-2708. (1968, c. 559, § 38.1-751; 1982, c. 665; 1986, c. 562.)

§ 38.2-2710. Supervision and regulation by Commission. — The residual market facility, any inspection service, and any joint underwriting association shall at all times be subject to the supervision and regulation of the Commission. The Commission, or any person designated by it, shall have the power:

1. To visit and examine the operations of the residual market facility, any inspection service, and any joint underwriting association;

2. To examine directors, officers, agents, employees, or any other person having knowledge of those operations;

3. To summon and qualify witnesses under oath and, pursuant to these powers, to have free access to all books, records, files, papers and documents that relate to those operations; and

4. To require that the association file annually a financial report that is approved by the board of directors and prepared in a form prescribed by the Commission. Unless the Commission provides otherwise, the report shall be filed within 120 days after the end of each fiscal year and shall be for the preceding twelve months. (1968, c. 559, § 38.1-752; 1986, c. 562; 1995, c. 60.)

§ 38.2-2711. Immunity from liability; reports, etc., not public documents.

— A. There shall be no liability on the part of, and no cause of action shall arise against any insurer, any inspection service, the residual market facility, the joint underwriting association, or their directors, governing committee members, officers, agents or employees, or the Commission or its authorized representatives, for any action taken by them in good faith in the performance of their powers and duties under this chapter, nor for any inspections undertaken or statements made by them (i) in any reports and communications concerning the property insured or to be insured, (ii) at the time of the hearings conducted in connection with the property insured or to be insured, or (iii) in the findings required by this chapter.

B. The reports and communications of an inspection bureau service, the residual market facility, and the joint underwriting association shall not be public documents. (1968, c. 559, § 38.1-753; 1985, c. 401; 1986, c. 562.)

§ 38.2-2712. Appeal from decision of inspection service, residual market facility or joint underwriting association.

— Any person aggrieved by any action or decision of an inspection service, the residual market facility, or the joint underwriting association may appeal to the Commission within thirty days from the action or the decision. The Commission shall provide the aggrieved person and the inspection service, the residual market facility, or the joint underwriting association an opportunity to be heard on not less than ten days' written notice. The Commission shall then issue an order (i) approving the action or decision, (ii) disapproving the action or decision, or (iii) directing the inspection service, the residual market facility or the joint underwriting association to reinspect the property, or place the application or cause it to be placed pursuant to its plan of operation, whichever is appropriate. (1968, c. 559, § 38.1-754; 1986, c. 562.)

§ 38.2-2713. Obligations not to be impaired in event of repeal of chapter.

— If the General Assembly repeals this chapter, (i) the obligations incurred by the residual market facility and the joint underwriting association and policies issued by either organization or by their members shall not be impaired by the repeal, and (ii) the residual market facility and joint underwriting association shall be continued until they have fully performed their respective outstanding obligations. (1970, c. 45, § 38.1-755.1; 1986, c. 562.)

CHAPTER 28.

MEDICAL MALPRACTICE JOINT UNDERWRITING ASSOCIATION.

§ 38.2-2800. Definitions. — As used in this chapter:

"Association" means the joint underwriting association established pursuant to the provisions of this chapter.

"Incidental coverage" means any other type of liability insurance covering activities directly related to the continued and efficient delivery of health care that: (i) cannot be obtained in the voluntary market because medical malpractice insurance is being provided pursuant to this chapter; and (ii) cannot be obtained through other involuntary market mechanisms.

"Liability insurance" includes the classes of insurance defined in §§ 38.2-117 through 38.2-119 and the liability portions of the insurance defined in §§ 38.2-124, 38.2-125, and 38.2-130 through 38.2-132.

"Medical malpractice insurance" means insurance coverage against the legal liability of the insured and against loss, damage, or expense incident to a claim arising out of the death or injury of any person as the result of negligence in rendering or failing to render professional service by any provider of health care.

"Net direct premiums written" means gross direct premiums written in this Commonwealth on all policies of liability insurance less, (i) all return premiums on the policy, (ii) dividends paid or credited to policyholders, and (iii) the unused or unabsorbed portions of premium deposits on liability insurance.

"Provider of health care" means any of the following deemed by the Commission to be necessary for the delivery of health care: (i) a physician and any other individual licensed or certified pursuant to Chapter 29 (§ 54.1-2900 et seq.) of Title 54.1; (ii) a nurse, dentist, or pharmacist licensed pursuant to Title 54.1; (iii) any health facility licensed or eligible for licensure pursuant to Chapter 5 (§ 32.1-123 et seq.) of Title 32.1 or Chapter 8 (§ 37.1-179 et seq.) of Title 37.1; and (iv) any other group, type, or category of individual or health-related facility that the Commission finds to be necessary for the continued delivery of health care after providing notice and opportunity to be heard. (1976, c. 85, § 38.1-775; 1986, c. 562.)

Law Review. — For survey of Virginia insurance law for the year 1975-1976, see 62 Va. L. Rev. 1446 (1976). For survey of Virginia tort law for the year 1975-1976, see 62 Va. L. Rev. 1489 (1976). For comment on Virginia's Birth-Related Neurological Injury Compensation Act, see 22 U. Rich. L. Rev. 431 (1988).

§ 38.2-2801. Association activation; members; purpose; determinations by Commission; powers of association. — A. After investigation, notice, and hearing, the Commission shall be empowered to activate a joint underwriting association if it finds that medical malpractice insurance cannot be made reasonably available in the voluntary market for a significant number of any class, type, or group of providers of health care. The association shall consist of all insurers licensed to write and engaged in writing liability insurance within this Commonwealth on a direct basis except those exempted from rate regulation by subsection C of § 38.2-1902. Each such insurer shall be a member of the association as a condition of its license to write liability insurance in this Commonwealth.

B. The purpose of the association shall be to provide a market for medical malpractice insurance on a self-supporting basis without subsidy from its members.

C. 1. The association shall not commence underwriting operations for any class, type or group of providers of health care until it is activated by the Commission. At the direction of the Commission, the association shall commence operations in accordance with the provisions of this chapter.

2. If the Commission determines at any time that medical malpractice insurance can be made reasonably available in the voluntary market for any class, type or group of providers of health care, the association shall, at the

direction of the Commission, cease its underwriting operations for that class, type or group of providers of health care.

D. The Commission shall also determine after investigation and a hearing whether the association shall be the exclusive source of medical malpractice insurance for any class, type or group of providers of health care and the type of policy or policies that shall be issued to any class, type or group of providers of health care. If the Commission determines that a claims-made policy will be issued to any class, type or group of providers of health care, the Commission shall also provide for the guaranteed availability of insurance that covers claims that (i) result from incidents occurring during periods when the basic claims-made policies are in force, and (ii) are reported after the expiration of the basic claims-made policies. The Commission may from time to time after an investigation and hearing reexamine and reconsider any determination made pursuant to this subsection.

E. Pursuant to this chapter and the plan of operation required by § 38.2-2804, the association shall have the power on behalf of its members to: (i) issue, or cause to be issued, policies of medical malpractice insurance to applicants, including incidental coverages, subject to limits as specified in the plan of operation but not to exceed one million dollars for each claimant under any one policy and three million dollars for all claimants under one policy in any one year; (ii) underwrite the insurance and adjust and pay losses on the insurance; (iii) appoint a service company or companies to perform the functions enumerated in this subsection; (iv) assume reinsurance from its members; and (v) reinsure its risks in whole or in part. (1976, c. 85, § 38.1-776; 1980, c. 286, § 38.1-776.2; 1986, c. 562.)

§ 38.2-2802. Dissolution. — A. When the association has ceased all of its underwriting operations by order of the Commission under subsection C of § 38.2-2801, it shall be subject during its continued existence to the following:

1. The association shall remain in existence for the sole purpose of completing its orderly dissolution;

2. The association shall refund to all of its members all preliminary assessments contributions and other funds paid to the association that have not been reimbursed prior to dissolution; and

3. The board of the association shall satisfy and discharge its obligations and, subject to the approval of the Commission, shall have authority to do all other acts required to conclude its business affairs, including but not limited to, transfer of policies in force to approved carriers.

B. When the Commission finds the association has met its obligations incident to termination of its business affairs, the Commission shall by order issue a certificate of dissolution and the existence of the association shall cease. (1980, c. 286, § 38.1-776.1; 1986, c. 562; 1987, c. 554.)

Editor's note. — Acts 1987, c. 554, cl. 2 provides that any insurance carrier licensed to write liability insurance in the Commonwealth upon the effective date (July 1, 1987) of the act who subsequently withdraws or fails to renew such licensure within the two years immediately following such enactment shall be barred from writing such insurance in the Commonwealth for a period of five years from the date of such withdrawal or failure to renew.

§ 38.2-2803. Directors. — A. The association shall be governed by a board of fourteen directors. Two directors shall be appointed by each of the following three insurance industry trade associations: (i) the American Insurance Association; (ii) the Alliance of American Insurers; and (iii) the National Association of Independent Insurers. The Commission shall appoint two directors to represent insurers not affiliated with the insurance industry trade associations listed above. One director shall be appointed by each of the following two agent trade associations: (a) the Independent Insurance Agents of Virginia; and (b) the Professional Insurance Agents Association of Virginia and the District of Columbia. Two directors shall be appointed by the Medical Society of Virginia and two directors shall be appointed by the Virginia Hospital Association.

B. If any of the foregoing associations fail to appoint a director or directors within a reasonable period of time, the Commission shall have the power to make the appointments. (1976, c. 85, § 38.1-777; 1986, c. 562.)

§ **38.2-2804. Plan of operation.** — A. Within forty-five days of the date the Commission makes a determination to activate a joint underwriting association pursuant to subsection A of § 38.2-2801, the directors of the association shall submit to the Commission for review a proposed plan of operation consistent with this chapter.

B. The plan of operation shall provide for economic, fair and nondiscriminatory administration and for the prompt and efficient provision of medical malpractice insurance. The plan shall contain other provisions including (i) preliminary assessment of all members for initial expenses necessary to commence operations, (ii) establishment of necessary facilities, (iii) management of the association, (iv) assessment of members to defray losses and expenses, (v) reasonable and objective minimum underwriting standards developed in consultation with the medical and hospital advisory committees provided for in § 38.2-2805, (vi) acceptance and cession of reinsurance, (vii) appointment of servicing carriers or other servicing arrangements, (viii) the establishment of premium payment plans, (ix) procedures for determining amounts of insurance to be provided by the association, (x) procedures for the recoupment of preliminary assessments and other assessments of members as authorized by this chapter, and (xi) any other matters necessary for the efficient and equitable operation and termination of the association.

C. The plan of operation shall be subject to approval by the Commission after consultation with the members of the association and representatives of interested individuals and organizations. If the Commission disapproves all or any part of the proposed plan of operation, the directors shall within fifteen days submit for review an appropriate revised plan of operation. If the directors fail to do so, the Commission shall promulgate a plan of operation. The plan of operation approved or promulgated by the Commission shall become effective and operational upon order of the Commission.

D. Amendments to the plan of operation may be made by the directors of the association, subject to the approval of the Commission. (1976, c. 85, § 38.1-778; 1980, c. 286; 1986, c. 562; 1987, c. 554; 1988, c. 341.)

Editor's note. — Acts 1987, c. 554, cl. 2 provides that any insurance carrier licensed to write liability insurance in the Commonwealth upon the effective date (July 1, 1987) of the act who subsequently withdraws or fails to renew such licensure within the two years immediately following such enactment shall be barred from writing such insurance in the Commonwealth for a period of five years from the date of such withdrawal or failure to renew.

Law Review. — For survey of Virginia insurance law for the year 1975-1976, see 62 Va. L. Rev. 1446 (1976).

§ **38.2-2805. Medical and hospital advisory committees.** — The Commission shall appoint a medical advisory committee to the association composed of five physicians licensed to practice medicine in this Commonwealth and a hospital advisory committee composed of five representatives of hospitals licensed in this Commonwealth. (1976, c. 85, § 38.1-779; 1986, c. 562.)

§ 38.2-2806. Policy forms; applicants to be issued policies; cancellation of policies; rates; examination of business of association. — A. All policies issued by the association shall be subject to the group retrospective premium adjustment and to the stabilization reserve fund required by § 38.2-2807. No policy form shall be used by the association unless it has been filed with the Commission and either (i) the Commission has approved it or (ii) thirty days have elapsed and the Commission has not disapproved the form or endorsement for one or more of the reasons enumerated in subsection A of § 38.2-317.

B. Policies shall be issued by the association, after receipt of the premium or portion of the premium prescribed by the plan of operation, to applicants that (i) meet the minimum underwriting standards, and (ii) have no unpaid or uncontested premium due as evidenced by the applicant having failed to make written objection to premium charges within thirty days after billing.

C. Any policy issued by the association may be cancelled for any one of the following reasons: (i) nonpayment of premium or portion of the premium; (ii) suspension or revocation of the insured's license; (iii) failure of the insured to meet the minimum underwriting standards; (iv) failure of the insured to meet other minimum standards prescribed by the plan of operation; and (v) nonpayment of any stabilization reserve fund charge.

D. The rates, rating plans, rating rules, rating classifications, premium payment plans and territories applicable to the insurance written by the association, and related statistics shall be subject to the provisions of Chapter 20 (§ 38.2-2000 et seq.) of this title. Due consideration shall be given to the past and prospective loss and expense experience for medical malpractice insurance written and to be written in this Commonwealth, trends in the frequency and severity of losses, the investment income of the association, and other information the Commission requires. All rates shall be on an actuarially sound basis, giving due consideration to the stabilization reserve fund, and shall be calculated to be self-supporting. The Commission shall take all appropriate steps to make available to the association the loss and expense experience of insurers writing or having written medical malpractice insurance in this Commonwealth.

E. All policies issued by the association shall be subject to a nonprofit group retrospective premium adjustment to be approved by the Commission under which the final premium for all policyholders of the association, as a group, will be calculated based upon the experience of all policyholders. The experience of all policyholders shall be calculated following the end of each fiscal period and shall be based upon earned premiums, administrative expenses, loss and loss adjustment expenses, and taxes, plus a reasonable allowance for contingencies and servicing. Policyholders shall be given full credit for all investment income, net of expenses and a reasonable management fee on policyholder supplied funds. Any final premium resulting from a retrospective premium adjustment will be collected from the stabilization fund set forth in § 38.2-2807. The maximum premium for all policyholders as a group shall be limited as provided in § 38.2-2807.

F. 1. The association shall certify to the Commission the estimated amount of any deficit remaining after the stabilization reserve fund has been exhausted in payment of the maximum final premium for all policyholders of the association. Within sixty days after such certification, the Commission shall authorize the association to recover from the members their respective share of the deficit.

2. Members shall be permitted to recover any assessment made by the association under subdivision 1 by deducting the members' share of the deficit from future premium taxes due the Commonwealth. The amount of premium tax deduction for each member's share of the deficit shall be apportioned by the

Commission so that the amount of each member's premium tax deduction in each of the ten calendar years following the payment of the member's assessment is equal to ten percent of the assessment paid by the member.

G. In the event that sufficient funds are not available for the sound financial operation of the association, subject to recoupment as provided in this chapter and the plan of operation, all members shall, on a temporary basis, contribute to the financial requirements of the association in the manner provided in this chapter. The contribution shall be reimbursed to the members by the procedure set forth in subdivision F 2.

H. The Commission shall examine the business of the association as often as it deems appropriate to make certain that the group retrospective premium adjustments are being calculated and applied in a manner consistent with this section. If the Commission finds that they are not being calculated and applied in a manner consistent with this section, it shall issue an order to the association, specifying (i) how the calculation and application are not consistent and (ii) stating what corrective action shall be taken. (1976, c. 85, § 38.1-780; 1986, c. 562; 1987, cc. 520, 554; 1988, c. 341; 1997, c. 160.)

Editor's note. — Acts 1987, c. 554, cl. 2 provides that any insurance carrier licensed to write liability insurance in the Commonwealth upon the effective date (July 1, 1987) of the act who subsequently withdraws or fails to renew such licensure within the two years immediately following such enactment shall be barred from writing such insurance in the Commonwealth for a period of five years from the date of such withdrawal or failure to renew.

Law Review. — For survey of Virginia insurance law for the year 1975-1976, see 62 Va. L. Rev. 1446 (1976).

§ **38.2-2807. Stabilization reserve fund.** — A. When an association is activated under § 38.2-2801, a stabilization reserve fund shall be created. The fund shall be administered by five directors appointed by the Commission, one of whom shall be a representative of the Commission, two of whom shall be representatives of the association, and two of whom shall be representatives of the association's policyholders.

B. The directors shall act by majority vote with three directors constituting a quorum for the transaction of any business or the exercise of any power of the fund. The directors shall serve without salary, but each director shall be reimbursed for actual and necessary expenses incurred in the performance of his official duties as a director of the fund. The directors shall not be subject to any personal liability with respect to the administration of the fund.

C. Each policyholder shall pay to the association a stabilization reserve fund charge equal to one-third of the annual premium due for medical malpractice insurance through the association until the fund reaches a level deemed appropriate by the Commission. The means of payment shall be set forth in the plan of operation and shall be separately stated in the policy. The association shall cancel the policy of any policyholder who fails to pay the stabilization reserve fund charge. Upon the termination of any policy during the term of the policy, payments made to the stabilization reserve fund shall be returned to the policyholder on a pro rata basis identical to that applied in computing that portion of the premium which is returned to the policyholder.

D. All moneys received by the fund shall be held in a separate restricted cash account under the sole control of an independent fund manager to be selected by the directors. The fund manager may invest the moneys held, subject to the approval of the directors. All investment income shall be credited to the fund. All expenses of administration of the fund shall be charged against the fund. The moneys held shall be used solely for the following purposes: (i) to reimburse the association for any and all expenses, taxes, licenses and fees paid by the association which are properly chargeable or allocable to the stabilization reserve fund; or (ii) to pay any retrospective premium adjustment charge levied by the association. Payment of retrospective premium adjustment charges and other authorized payments shall be made by the directors upon certification to them by the association of the amount due. If all moneys accruing to the fund are exhausted in payment of retrospective premium adjustment charges, all liability and obligations of the association's policyholders with respect to the payment of retrospective premium adjustment charges shall terminate and shall be conclusively presumed to have been discharged.

E. The association shall promptly pay the fund manager of the fund all stabilization reserve fund charges that it collects from its policyholders.

F. Upon dissolution of the association, all assets remaining in the fund shall be distributed equitably to the policyholders who have contributed to the fund under procedures authorized by the directors. Distribution of assets remaining in the fund shall be made after final disposition of all claims, expenses, and liabilities against the fund, including reimbursement of preliminary organizational assessments made pursuant to subsection B of § 38.2-2804. (1976, c. 85, § 38.1-781; 1977, c. 154; 1986, c. 562; 1987, cc. 526, 554; 1988, c. 341.)

Editor's note. — Acts 1987, c. 554, cl. 2 provides that any insurance carrier licensed to write liability insurance in the Commonwealth upon the effective date (July 1, 1987) of the act who subsequently withdraws or fails to renew such licensure within the two years immediately following such enactment shall be barred from writing such insurance in the Commonwealth for a period of five years from the date of such withdrawal or failure to renew.

§ 38.2-2808. Participation in association by insurers. — Each insurer that is a member of the association shall participate in the temporary contributions to finance the operation of the association in the proportion that the net direct premiums written by each member during the preceding calendar year bears to the aggregate net direct premiums written in this Commonwealth by all members of the association. However, the net direct premiums written by each member shall exclude that portion of premiums attributable to the operation of the association. Each insurer's participation in the association shall be determined annually on the basis of such premiums written during the preceding calendar year in the manner set forth in the plan of operation. (1976, c. 85, § 38.1-782; 1986, c. 562.)

§ 38.2-2809. Review of actions or decisions of association. — Any insurer, applicant or other person aggrieved by any action or decision of the association or of any insurer as a result of its participation in the association, may appeal to the board of directors of the association. The decision of the board of directors may be appealed to the Commission within thirty days from the date the aggrieved person received notice of the board's action. (1976, c. 85, § 38.1-783; 1986, c. 562.)

§ 38.2-2810. Annual statements. — The association shall file an annual statement with the Commission within three months of the close of each fiscal year. The annual statement shall contain information on its transactions, condition, operations and affairs during the preceding fiscal year. The form and content of the annual statement shall be subject to the Commission's approval. The Commission may at any time require the association to furnish additional information on its transactions, condition or any matter connected with the association considered to be material and of assistance in evaluating the scope, operation and experience of the association. (1976, c. 85, § 38.1-784; 1986, c. 562.)

§ 38.2-2811. Examination into affairs of association. — The Commission shall examine the affairs of the association pursuant to § 38.2-1317. The examination shall be performed in the manner prescribed in §§ 38.2-1317 through 38.2-1321.1. (1976, c. 85, § 38.1-785; 1986, c. 562; 1999, c. 61.)

The **1999 amendment** substituted "pursuant to § 38.2-1317" for "at least annually" in the first sentence, in the second sentence, substituted "performed" for "conducted and the report of the examination filed" and substituted "38.2-1321.1" for "38.2-1321," and deleted the former third sentence, which read: "The expenses of each examination shall be borne and paid by the association."

§ 38.2-2812. Public officers or employees. — No member of the board of directors of the stabilization reserve fund who is a public officer or employee shall forfeit his office or employment, or incur any loss or diminution in the rights and privileges associated with his office or employment, because of membership on the board. (1976, c. 85, § 38.1-786; 1986, c. 562.)

§ 38.2-2813. Commissions for placing and servicing risk with association. — For any medical malpractice insurance or incidental coverage policy issued by the association, the commission payable to the person that places the risk with the joint underwriting association or services the risk shall be limited to 5 percent of the annual premium for the policy or $1,000, whichever is less. (1976, c. 85, § 38.1-787; 1986, c. 562.)

§ 38.2-2814. Liability. — There shall be no liability imposed on the part of and no civil cause of action of any nature shall arise against the association or the stabilization reserve fund, their board of directors, their agents, their employees, any service carrier, any participating insurer or its employees, any licensed producer, the Commission or its authorized representatives, the medical and hospital advisory committees, or their members or employees for any statements or actions made by them in good faith in carrying out the provisions of this chapter. (1976, c. 85, § 38.1-788; 1986, c. 562; 1987, c. 519.)

———

CHAPTER 29.

COMMERCIAL LIABILITY INSURANCE JOINT UNDERWRITING ASSOCIATION.

§ 38.2-2900. Definitions. — As used in this chapter:

"Association" means the joint underwriting association established pursuant to the provisions of this chapter.

"Commercial liability insurance" means the commercial classes of insurance defined in §§ 38.2-117 and 38.2-118, but for the purposes of this chapter, does not include medical malpractice insurance as defined in § 38.2-2800, nuclear

liability or any risks, lines, or subclassifications that are determined by the Commission to be uninsurable; provided, no such determination shall be based solely upon evidence that no insurers are then insuring such risk, line, or subclassification. The Commission may exclude from this definition any other line, subclassification or type of commercial liability insurance as it deems appropriate.

"Incidental coverage" means any other type of liability insurance covering activities directly related to the continued and efficient delivery of business and professional services that: (i) cannot be separately obtained in the voluntary market because commercial liability insurance is being provided pursuant this chapter; and (ii) cannot be separately obtained through other involuntary market mechanisms.

"Market assistance plan" means a voluntary association of insurers and insurance agents licensed to do business in the Commonwealth that is formed, pursuant to a plan of operation filed with and approved by the Commission, to assist with the individual placement of commercial liability insurance coverage that is not reasonably available on the voluntary market.

"Net direct premiums written" means gross direct premiums written in this Commonwealth on all policies of liability insurance less (i) all return premiums on the policy, (ii) dividends paid or credited to policyholders, and (iii) the unused or unabsorbed portions of premium deposits on liability insurance. For the purposes of this chapter, *"liability insurance"* means the classes of insurance defined in §§ 38.2-117 through 38.2-119, and the liability portions of the insurance defined in §§ 38.2-124, 38.2-125 and 38.2-130 through 38.2-132. (1988, cc. 769, 783.)

§ **38.2-2900.1. Market assistance plan.** — The Commission may authorize the formation of a voluntary market assistance plan to assist in the individual placement of coverage for any lines, subclassifications, or types of commercial liability insurance. Such plan shall not be an insurer capable of assuming insurance risks. (1988, cc. 769, 783.)

§ **38.2-2901. Association activation; members; purpose; determinations by Commission; powers of Association.** — A. After investigation, notice, and hearing, the Commission shall be empowered to activate a Joint Underwriting Association with respect to any line, subclassification or type of commercial liability insurance coverage if it finds that such line, subclassification, or type of commercial liability insurance coverage is not reasonably available for a significant number of any class, type, or group of such risks in the voluntary market or through a market assistance plan. The Association shall consist of all insurers licensed to write and engaged in writing the classes of insurance defined in §§ 38.2-117 through 38.2-119, and the liability portions of the insurance defined in §§ 38.2-124, 38.2-125 and 38.2-130 through 38.2-132 within this Commonwealth on a direct basis except those exempted from rate regulation by subsection C of § 38.2-1902. Each such insurer shall be a member of the Association as a condition of its license to write such insurance in this Commonwealth.

B. The purpose of the Association shall be to provide markets for commercial liability insurance for persons with eligible risks who are unable to obtain commercial liability insurance coverage, including incidental coverage, through the voluntary market. It shall also be the purpose of the Association to do so on a self-supporting basis without subsidy from its members.

C. 1. The Association shall not commence underwriting operations for any line, subclassification or type of commercial liability insurance coverage until so ordered by the Commission. At the direction of the Commission, the Association shall commence operations in accordance with the provisions of this chapter.

2. If the Commission determines at any time that a line, subclassification or type of commercial liability insurance coverage is reasonably available at adequate levels in the voluntary market, the Association shall, at the direction of the Commission, cease its underwriting operations for that line, subclassification, or type of commercial liability insurance coverage.

D. The Commission shall also determine after investigation and a hearing whether the Association shall be the exclusive source of any line, subclassification or type of commercial liability insurance which it finds not to be reasonably available pursuant to subsection A of this section and the type of policy or policies that shall be issued for any line, subclassification or type of commercial liability insurance. If the Commission determines that a claims-made policy will be issued for any line, subclassification or type of coverage, the Commission shall also provide for the guaranteed availability of insurance that covers claims which (i) result from incidents occurring during periods when the basic claims-made policies are in force; and (ii) are reported after the expiration of the basic claims-made policies. The Commission may from time to time after an investigation and hearing reexamine and reconsider any determination made pursuant to this subsection.

E. Pursuant to this chapter and the plan of operation required by § 38.2-2904, the Association shall have the power on behalf of its members to:

1. Issue, or cause to be issued, policies of commercial liability insurance to eligible applicants, including incidental coverages, subject to limits specified in the plan of operation but not to exceed one million dollars for each claimant under any one policy and three million dollars for all claimants under one policy in any one year;

2. Provide a means for establishing eligibility of a risk for obtaining insurance through the plan;

3. Underwrite the insurance and adjust and pay losses on the insurance;

4. Appoint a service company or companies to perform functions enumerated in this subsection;

5. Provide a means for the equitable apportionment of profits or losses and expenses among participating insurers;

6. Develop rules for the classification of risks and rates which reflect the past and prospective loss experience and a rating plan which reasonably reflects the prior claims experience of the insureds;

7. Assume reinsurance from its members;

8. Reinsure its risks in whole or in part; and

9. Take such other action as is necessary for the efficient and equitable operation and termination of the Association. (1988, cc. 769, 783.)

§ 38.2-2902. Dissolution. — A. When the Association has ceased all of its underwriting operations by order of the Commission under subdivision 2 of subsection C of § 38.2-2901, it shall be subject during its continued existence to the following:

1. The Association shall remain in existence for the sole purpose of completing its orderly dissolution.

2. The Association shall refund to all of its members all preliminary assessments, contributions and other funds paid to the Association that have not been reimbursed prior to dissolution.

3. The board of the Association shall satisfy and discharge its obligations and, subject to the approval of the Commission, shall have authority to do all other acts required to conclude its business affairs, including but not limited to, transfer of policies in force to approved carriers.

B. When the Commission finds the Association has met its obligations incident to termination of its business affairs, the Commission shall by order issue a certificate of dissolution and the existence of the Association shall cease. (1988, cc. 769, 783.)

§ **38.2-2903. Directors.** — A. The Association shall be governed by a board of eleven directors, including one who shall be elected chairman. Two directors shall be appointed by each of the following three insurance industry trade associations: (i) the American Insurance Association; (ii) the Alliance of American Insurers; and (iii) the National Association of Independent Insurers. One director shall be appointed by each of the following two insurance agents' trade associations: (i) the Independent Insurance Agents of Virginia and (ii) the Professional Insurance Agents Association of Virginia and the District of Columbia. The Commission shall appoint three directors not affiliated with the aforementioned trade associations. If, for any reason, any of the trade associations fail to appoint a director or directors within a reasonable period of time, the Commission shall have the power to make the appointment.

B. All board members, including the chairman, shall be appointed to serve for two-year terms beginning on a date designated by the plan.

C. Six directors shall constitute a quorum for the transaction of any business or exercise of any power of the Association. The directors of the Association shall act by vote of a majority of those present. The directors shall serve without salary, but each director shall be reimbursed for actual and necessary expenses incurred in the performance of his or her official duties as a director of the Association. (1988, cc. 769, 783.)

§ **38.2-2904. Plan of operation.** — A. Within forty-five days after appointment of the members of the board, the directors of the Association shall submit to the Commission for review a proposed plan of operation consistent with this chapter.

B. The plan of operation shall provide for economic, fair and nondiscriminatory administration and for the prompt and efficient provision of commercial liability insurance. The plan shall contain other provisions governing:

1. Preliminary assessment of all members for initial expenses necessary to commence operations;

2. Establishment of necessary facilities;

3. Management of the Association;

4. Assessment of members to defray losses and expenses;

5. Reasonable and objective minimum underwriting standards;

6. Acceptance and cession of reinsurance;

7. Appointment of servicing carriers or other servicing arrangements;

8. The establishment of premium payment plans;

9. Procedures for determining amounts of insurance to be provided by the Association;

10. Procedures for the recoupment of preliminary assessments and other assessments of members as authorized by this chapter; and

11. Any other matters necessary for the efficient and equitable operation and termination of the Association.

C. The plan of operation shall be subject to approval by the Commission after consultation with the members of the Association and representatives of interested individuals and organizations. If the Commission disapproves all or any part of the proposed plan of operation, the directors shall within fifteen days submit for review an appropriate revised plan of operation. If the directors fail to do so, the Commission shall promulgate a plan of operation. The plan of operation approved or promulgated by the Commission shall become effective and operational upon order of the Commission.

D. At any time after the Association is activated, and after investigation, notice, and hearing, the Commission may order the submission of a supplemental plan of operation if it finds that any line, subclassification or type of commercial liability insurance not covered by the existing plan of operation is not reasonably available according to the terms of subsection A of § 38.2-2901.

Such supplemental plan of operation shall be submitted within forty-five days of the Commission's order and shall be subject to all other provisions of this chapter governing the plan of operation.

E. Amendments to the plan of operation may be made by the directors of the Association, subject to the approval of the Commission. (1988, cc. 769, 783.)

§ 38.2-2905. Policy forms; applicants to be issued policies; cancellation of policies; rates; group retrospective rating plan; examination of business of Association. — A. All policies issued by the Association shall be subject to the group retrospective premium adjustment and to the stabilization reserve fund required by § 38.2-2906. No policy form shall be used by the Association unless it has been filed with the Commission and either (i) the Commission has approved it or (ii) thirty days have elapsed and the Commission has not disapproved the form or endorsement for one or more of the reasons enumerated in subsection A of § 38.2-317.

B. Policies shall be issued by the Association, after receipt of the premium or portion of the premium prescribed by the plan of operation, to applicants that (i) meet the minimum underwriting standards of the Association, and (ii) have no unpaid or uncontested premium due as evidenced by the applicant having failed to make written objection to premium charges within thirty days after billing.

C. Any policy issued by the Association may be cancelled for any one of the following reasons:

1. Nonpayment of premium or portion of the premium;
2. Suspension or revocation of the insured's license to conduct business;
3. Failure of the insured to meet the minimum underwriting standards;
4. Failure of the insured to meet other minimum standards prescribed by the plan of operation; or
5. Nonpayment of any stabilization reserve fund charge.

D. The rates, rating plans, rating rules, rating classifications, premium payment plans and territories applicable to the insurance written by the Association, and related supplementary rate information shall be subject to the provisions of Chapter 20 (§ 38.2-2000 et seq.) of this title. Due consideration shall be given to the past and prospective loss and expense experience for the line, subclassification or type of commercial liability insurance written in this Commonwealth, trends in the frequency and severity of losses, the investment income of the Association, and other information the Commission requires. All rates shall be on an actuarially sound basis, giving due consideration to the stabilization reserve fund, and shall be calculated to be self-supporting. The Commission shall take all appropriate steps to make available to the Association the loss and expense experience of insurers writing or having written the same line, subclassification or type of commercial liability insurance in this Commonwealth.

E. All policies issued by the Association shall be subject to a nonprofit group retrospective premium adjustment to be approved by the Commission under which the final total premium for all policyholders for each line, subclassification or type of commercial liability insurance issued each year by the Association, as a group, will be calculated based upon the experience of all such policyholders. The experience of all such policyholders shall be calculated following the end of each year and shall be based upon earned premiums, administrative expenses, loss and loss adjustment expenses, and taxes, plus a reasonable allowance for contingencies and servicing, for each line, subclassification or type of commercial liability insurance. Policyholders shall be given full credit for all investment income, net of expenses and a reasonable management fee on policyholder supplied funds. Any final premium resulting from a retrospective premium adjustment will be collected from those moneys in the stabilization reserve fund set forth in § 38.2-2906 that are attributable to the policies written for the particular line, subclassification or type of commercial liability insurance or group of such risks for which activation occurred pursuant to § 38.2-2901. The maximum premium for all policyholders as a group shall be limited as provided in § 38.2-2906.

F. 1. If the stabilization reserve fund account for one or more lines, subclassifications or types of commercial liability insurance is exhausted in the payment of the maximum final premium for all such policies issued during the year for which a deficit exists, the Association shall certify to the Commission the estimated amount of any remaining deficit for any year's policies. Within sixty days after such certification, the Commission shall authorize the Association to recover from the members their respective share of such deficit. No member insurer may be assessed in any year an amount greater than two percent of the member's direct gross premium income as defined in § 58.1-2500 from liability insurance for the calendar year preceding the assessment. If an assessment in any year is not sufficient to eliminate such deficit, a like assessment may be made the ensuing year but not thereafter.

2. A member shall be permitted to recover any assessment made by the Association under subdivision 1 of this subsection by deducting the member's share of the deficit from future premium taxes due the Commonwealth. The amount of premium tax deduction for each member's share of the deficit shall be apportioned by the Commission so that in the aggregate, the total premium tax deduction permitted for all members in any one taxable year shall not exceed 0.05 of one percent of the direct gross premium income for the liability insurance written by member insurers defined in subsection A of § 38.2-2901. To the extent that the said 0.05 of one percent is reached in any one taxable year, any amount not so offset may be carried over to a subsequent year or years.

G. In the event that sufficient funds are not available for the sound financial operation of the Association, subject to recoupment as provided in this chapter and the plan of operation, all members shall, on a temporary basis, contribute to the financial requirements of the Association in the manner provided in this chapter. The contribution shall be reimbursed to the members by the procedure set forth in subdivision 2 of subsection F of this section.

H. The Commission shall examine the business of the Association as often as it deems appropriate to make certain that the group retrospective premium adjustments are being calculated and applied in a manner consistent with this section. If the Commission finds that the group retrospective premium adjustments are not being made in a manner consistent with this section, it shall issue an order to the Association, specifying (i) how such calculation and application are not consistent and (ii) stating what corrective action shall be taken. (1988, cc. 769, 783.)

§ **38.2-2906. Stabilization reserve fund.** — A. When an Association is activated under this chapter, a stabilization reserve fund shall be created for the lines, subclassifications and types of commercial liability insurance for which such activation occurred. The fund shall be administered by five directors appointed by the Commission, one of whom shall be a representative of the Commission, two of whom shall be representatives of the Association, and two of whom shall be representatives of the Association's policyholders.

B. The directors of the fund shall act by majority vote of those present with three directors constituting a quorum for the transaction of any business or the exercise of any power of the fund. The directors shall serve without salary, but each director shall be reimbursed for actual and necessary expenses incurred in the performance of his or her official duties as a director of the fund. The directors shall not be subject to any personal liability with respect to the administration of the fund.

C. Each policyholder shall pay to the Association a stabilization reserve fund charge equal to one-third of the annual premium due for commercial liability insurance obtained through the Association. The means of payment shall be set forth in the plan of operation and shall be separately stated in the policy. The Association shall cancel the policy of any policyholder who fails to pay the stabilization reserve fund charge. Upon the termination of any policy during the term of the policy, payments made to the stabilization reserve fund shall be returned to the policyholder on a pro rata basis identical to that applied in computing that portion of the premium which is returned to the policyholder.

D. All moneys received by the fund shall be held in a separate restricted cash account or accounts under the sole control of an independent fund manager to be selected by the directors of the fund. The fund manager shall account separately for the moneys paid to the fund for each year's policies written for a given line, subclassification or type of commercial liability insurance. The fund manager may invest the moneys held, subject to the approval of the directors. All investment income shall be credited to the fund. All expenses of administration of the fund shall be charged against the fund. The moneys held shall be used solely for the following purposes: (i) to reimburse the Association for any and all expenses, taxes, licenses and fees paid by the Association which are properly chargeable or allocable to the stabilization reserve fund, and (ii) to pay any retrospective premium adjustment charge levied by the Association. Payment of retrospective premium adjustment charges and other authorized payments shall be made by the directors of the fund upon certification to them by the Association of the amount due. If all moneys accruing to the fund for a particular year's policies for a given line, subclassification or type of commercial liability insurance are exhausted in payment of retrospective premium adjustment charges for the particular year, all liability and obligations of the holders of said policies with respect to the payment of retrospective premium adjustment charges shall terminate and shall be conclusively presumed to have been discharged.

E. The Association shall promptly pay the fund manager all stabilization reserve fund charges that it collects from its policyholders under subsection C of this section.

F. Upon dissolution of the Association, all assets remaining in the fund shall be distributed equitably to the policyholders who have contributed to the fund under procedures authorized by the directors. Distribution of assets remaining in the fund shall be made after final disposition of all claims, expenses, and liabilities against the fund, including reimbursement of preliminary organizational assessments made pursuant to subsection B of § 38.2-2904. (1988, cc. 769, 783.)

§ **38.2-2907. Participation in Association by insurers.** — Each insurer that is a member of the Association shall participate in the contributions to finance the operation of the Association in the proportion that the net direct premiums written by each member during the preceding calendar year bears to the aggregate net direct premiums written in this Commonwealth by all members of the Association. However, the net direct premiums written by each member shall exclude that portion of premiums attributable to the operation of the Association. Each insurer's participation in the Association shall be determined annually on the basis of such premiums written during the preceding calendar year in the manner set forth in the plan of operation. (1988, cc. 769, 783.)

§ **38.2-2908. Review of actions or decisions of Association.** — Any insurer, applicant or other person aggrieved by any action or decision of the

Association or of any insurer as a result of its participation in the Association, may appeal to the board of directors of the Association. The decision of the board of directors may be appealed to the Commission within thirty days from the date the aggrieved person received notice of the board's action. (1988, cc. 769, 783.)

§ **38.2-2909. Annual statements.** — The Association shall file an annual statement with the Commission within three months of the close of each fiscal year. The annual statement shall contain information on its transactions, conditions, operations and affairs during the preceding fiscal year. The form and content of the annual statement shall be subject to the Commission's approval. The Commission may at any time require the Association to furnish additional information on its transactions, condition or any matter connected with the Association considered to be material and of assistance in evaluating the scope, operation and experience of the Association. (1988, cc. 769, 783.)

§ **38.2-2910. Annual examination into affairs of Association.** — The Commission shall examine the affairs of the Association at least annually. The examination shall be conducted and the report of the examination filed in the manner prescribed in §§ 38.2-1317 through 38.2-1321. The expenses of each examination shall be borne and paid by the Association. (1988, cc. 769, 783.)

§ **38.2-2911. Public officers or employees.** — No member of the board of directors of the Association or of the board of directors of the stabilization reserve fund who is a public officer or employee shall forfeit his office or employment, or incur any loss or diminution in the rights and privileges associated with his office or employment, because of membership on either board. (1988, cc. 769, 783.)

§ **38.2-2912. Commissions for placing and servicing risk with Association.** — For any policy issued by the Association, the commission payable to the person that places the risk with the Joint Underwriting Association or services the risk shall be limited to five percent of the annual premium for the policy or $1,000, whichever is less. (1988, cc. 769, 783.)

§ **38.2-2913. Liability.** — There shall be no liability imposed on the part of, and no civil cause of action of any nature shall arise against, the Association or the stabilization reserve fund, their boards of directors, agents, and employees; any service carrier or its employees; any participating insurer or its employees; any licensed producer; the Commission, its authorized representatives, members or employees; or any committee established by the Association's board of directors or its members or employees for any statements or actions made in good faith in carrying out the provisions of this chapter. (1988, cc. 769, 783.)

CHAPTER 30.

Uninsured Motorists Fund.

§ 38.2-3000. Supervision and control of Fund by Commission; payments from Fund. — The Uninsured Motorists Fund, referred to in this chapter as the Fund, shall be under the supervision and control of the Commission. Payments from the Fund shall be made on warrants of the Comptroller issued on vouchers signed by a person designated by the Commission. The purpose of the Fund is to reduce the cost of the insurance required by subsection A of § 38.2-2206. (Code 1950, § 12-65; 1958, c. 455, § 38.1-379.1; 1962, c. 253; 1971, Ex. Sess., c. 44; 1986, c. 562.)

Uninsured motor vehicle assessment creates fund that benefits general public. — The uninsured motor vehicle assessment, which may substitute for insurance coverage, creates a fund that benefits the general public by reducing the overall cost of uninsured motorist insurance coverage and is an involuntary exaction rather than a payment to receive permission to engage in a voluntary activity. Wil-

liams v. Motley, 925 F.2d 741 (4th Cir. 1991).

Uninsured motor vehicle assessment is an involuntary pecuniary burden levied upon uninsured motorists for a proper governmental purpose and is an excise tax for purposes of 11 U.S.C. § 507 (a) (7) (E) and thus is nondischargeable in bankruptcy. Williams v. Motley, 925 F.2d 741 (4th Cir. 1991).

§ 38.2-3001. Distribution to insurers; records of loss experience as prerequisite to payment. — The Commission shall distribute moneys annually from the Fund among the several insurers writing motor vehicle bodily injury and property damage liability insurance on motor vehicles registered in this Commonwealth. Moneys shall be distributed in the proportion that each insurer's premium income for the basic uninsured motorists limits coverage bears to the total premium income for basic uninsured motorists limits coverage written in this Commonwealth during the preceding year. Premium income shall be gross premiums less cancellation and return premiums for coverage required by subsection A of § 38.2-2206. Only insurers that maintain records satisfactory to the Commission shall receive any payment from the Fund. Records shall be considered satisfactory if they adequately disclose the loss experience for the coverage required by subsection A of § 38.2-2206. (Code 1950, § 12-66; 1958, c. 455, § 38.1-379.2; 1962, c. 253; 1971, Ex. Sess., c. 44; 1986, c. 562.)

Law Review. — For survey of Virginia law on insurance for the year 1970-1971, see 57 Va. L. Rev. 1608 (1971).

Uninsured motor vehicle assessment creates fund that benefits general public. — The uninsured motor vehicle assessment, which may substitute for insurance coverage, creates a fund that benefits the general public by reducing the overall cost of uninsured motorist insurance coverage and is an involuntary

exaction rather than a payment to receive permission to engage in a voluntary activity. Williams v. Motley, 925 F.2d 741 (4th Cir. 1991).

Uninsured motor vehicle assessment is an involuntary pecuniary burden levied upon uninsured motorists for a proper governmental purpose and is an excise tax for purposes of 11 U.S.C. § 507 (a) (7) (E) and thus is nondischargeable in bankruptcy. Williams v. Motley, 925 F.2d 741 (4th Cir. 1991).

CHAPTER 31.

LIFE INSURANCE.

ARTICLE 1.

General Provisions.

§ 38.2-3100. Scope of chapter. — Except as otherwise provided, this chapter applies to insurers transacting life insurance and the granting of annuities, and to life insurance and annuities as defined in §§ 38.2-102 through 38.2-107.1. (1952, c. 317, § 38.1-431; 1986, c. 562; 1994, c. 316.)

Law Review. — For article, "The 1952 Revision of the Virginia Life Insurance Laws," see 39 Va. L. Rev. 547 (1953).

§ 38.2-3100.1. Forms of insurance authorized. — A. Life insurance and annuities shall be issued only in the following forms:
1. Individual life insurance and annuities; or
2. Group life insurance and annuities.

B. Pursuant to the authority granted by § 38.2-223, the Commission may promulgate such regulations as may be necessary or appropriate to govern insurers' practices with regard to Acquired Immunodeficiency Syndrome (AIDS) or presence of the Human Immunodeficiency Virus (HIV), including advertising practices, underwriting practices, policy provisions, claim practices, or other practices with regard to individual or group life insurance and annuities, delivered or issued for delivery in the Commonwealth of Virginia and certificates or evidences of coverage, issued under any contract delivered or issued for delivery in the Commonwealth of Virginia. (1989, c. 653.)

§ 38.2-3101. Legal reserve insurers. — Any life insurer, association or society whose policies or certificates are required to contain any provision that a person insured shall, upon surrender of the policy during his lifetime, receive a surrender value, either in cash, paid-up insurance, or extended insurance, shall be regarded as a "legal reserve insurer," and shall maintain a reserve calculated in accordance with the provisions of Article 3 (§ 38.2-3126 et seq.) of this chapter. Nothing in this section shall be construed to apply to any insurer in the transaction of industrial sick benefit insurance as defined in § 38.2-3544, nor to fraternal benefit societies. (Code 1950, § 38-389; 1952, c. 317, § 38.1-432; 1986, c. 562.)

§ 38.2-3102. Domestic insurers prohibited from insuring lives and persons of residents of "reciprocal states." — A. As used in this section, *"reciprocal state"* means a state whose laws prohibit its domestic insurers from insuring the lives or persons of residents of this Commonwealth unless the insurer is licensed in this Commonwealth. The prohibition may be subject to exceptions similar to those set forth in subsection C of this section.

B. Subject to the exceptions set forth in subsection C of this section, a domestic insurer shall not enter into an insurance contract upon the life or person of a resident of a reciprocal state unless the insurer is licensed in that state.

C. The following are exceptions to the provisions of subsection B of this section:
1. Contracts entered into when the person insured, or proposed to be insured, is, at the time he signs the application, personally present in a state where the insurer is licensed;
2. Certificates issued under any lawfully issued group life or group accident and sickness policy, when the group policy is entered into in a state where the insurer is licensed;
3. Contracts made pursuant to a pension or retirement plan of an employer, when the contracts are applied for in a state where the employer is personally present or doing business and where the insurer is also licensed; or
4. Contracts renewed, reinstated, converted, or continued in force, with or without modification, that are otherwise lawful and that were not originally executed in violation of this section. (Code 1950, § 38-364; 1952, c. 317, § 38.1-433; 1986, c. 562.)

§ 38.2-3103. Fraudulent procurement of policy; penalty. — A. No person shall knowingly secure, attempt to secure or cause to be secured a life insurance policy on any person who is not in an insurable condition by means of misrepresentations or false or fraudulent statements.

B. An insurance agent who violates this section shall be subject to penalties under § 38.2-1831 in addition to the penalties of § 38.2-218. (Code 1950, § 38-369; 1952, c. 317, § 38.1-434; 1986, c. 562.)

§ 38.2-3104. No policy to be issued purporting to take effect more than six months before application made; conversion permitted. — A. No life insurance policy delivered or issued for delivery in this Commonwealth shall be backdated more than six months from the date the written application for the insurance was made if the premium on the policy is less than the premium that would be payable on the policy, as determined by the nearest birthday of the insured when the application was made.

B. Neither the provisions of subsection A of this section nor any other provision of general law shall prohibit the conversion or exchange to some form of life insurance dated back to become effective at an age not less than the insured's age at his nearest birthday on the date of issue of the existing contract for:

1. A policy insuring one person for a policy insuring another person dated not earlier than the original policy exchanged;

2. The conversion of any existing life insurance policy; or

3. Any deferred annuity contract purchased by a consideration payable in annual or more frequent installments, and under which no annuity payments have yet been made.

The exchanged or converted form of life insurance shall not exceed the greater of (i) the amount of insurance under the existing policy or (ii) the amount of insurance that the premium or consideration paid for the existing policy or contract would have purchased at the insured's age on his nearest birthday at the date of issue of the existing policy or contract. (Code 1950, § 38-363; 1952, c. 317, § 38.1-435; 1956, c. 417; 1980, c. 205; 1986, c. 562.)

§ 38.2-3105. What contracts with respect to life insurance may be made by minors. — A. A minor who is at least fifteen years of age:

1. Shall be competent to contract for life insurance upon his own life for his own benefit or for the benefit of his ascending or descending kindred, spouse, brothers or sisters;

2. May exercise every right, privilege and benefit provided by any life insurance policy on his own life, subject to the foregoing limitations as to designation of beneficiary; and

3. Shall not be permitted to recover any premiums paid on the policy solely because he is a minor.

B. If the minor resides with at least one of his parents, the application for the policy shall be approved in writing by the parent with whom he resides. No promissory note or other evidence of debt given by a minor in payment of any first year premium on a policy shall be validated by this section.

C. Any such minor shall be competent to give a valid discharge for any benefit accruing or money payable under the policy, and to create liens on the policy in favor of the insurer issuing the policy for money borrowed or for unpaid premiums and interest on the policy. However, any beneficiary or beneficiaries named in the policy who are then at least fifteen years of age shall unite in the discharge or in the instrument creating the lien. (Code 1950, § 38-10; 1952, c. 317, § 38.1-436; 1960, c. 31; 1986, c. 562.)

§ 38.2-3106. Suicide and execution not grounds of defense; exception. — A. Except as provided in subsection B of this section, the fact that an insured committed suicide, or was executed under law, shall not be a defense in any action, motion or other proceeding on a life insurance policy that (i) was issued to any person residing in this Commonwealth at the time of issuance, or (ii) is otherwise subject to the laws of this Commonwealth, to recover for the death of that person.

B. An express provision in the body of the policy limiting the liability of the insurer to an insured who, whether sane or insane, dies by his own act within two years from the date of the policy shall be valid but the insurer shall be obligated to return or pay at the least the amount of the premium paid for the policy. (Code 1950, § 38-365; 1952, c. 317, § 38.1-437; 1986, c. 562.)

Liberal construction. — The proviso of this section relating to suicide, the purpose of which was to preserve the common-law rule for the limited period of two years where provision to that effect is contained in the policy, should be given a liberal and not a strained construction. New England Mut. Life Ins. Co. v. Mitchell, 118 F.2d 414 (4th Cir.), cert. denied, 314 U.S. 629, 62 S. Ct. 60, 86 L. Ed. 505 (1941).

Provision limiting liability. — Any language showing that liability of the insurer under the policy shall not extend to death from suicide and that, in such event, the premiums paid on the policy shall be returned, is a sufficient compliance with the requirements of this section. New England Mut. Life Ins. Co. v. Mitchell, 118 F.2d 414 (4th Cir.), cert. denied, 314 U.S. 629, 62 S. Ct. 60, 86 L. Ed. 505 (1941).

Effect of suicide clause. — The suicide clause, whether it provides that the policy shall be void in case of suicide or that suicide is not a risk covered, is necessarily a limitation on coverage. Its effect is to except death by suicide from the promise to pay the amount of the policy in case of death. New England Mut. Life Ins. Co. v. Mitchell, 118 F.2d 414 (4th Cir.), cert. denied, 314 U.S. 629, 62 S. Ct. 60, 86 L. Ed. 505 (1941).

Policy taken out upon termination of coverage under group policy. — A policy of group life insurance provided for termination of coverage upon termination of employment but gave the employee the right to take out a policy without medical examination within 31 days after termination of employment, said policy to become effective at the end of this 31-day period. Insured's employment was terminated on October 2, 1954; he applied for and obtained a policy whose stated effective date was November 2, 1954; and committed suicide in April, 1955. The policy limited the company's liability to return of premiums if suicide occurred within two years from its effective date. Under the circumstances and the terms of the policy it was held that the new policy was not a continuation of the group insurance but a new and different policy and its provisions as to suicide would be given effect. Provident Life & Accident Ins. Co. v. Kegley, 199 Va. 273, 99 S.E.2d 601 (1957).

The defense of suicide, to avail, must exclude every hypothesis of accidental death. The party making the defense has the burden of proof. It will not be presumed. The mere fact that the body of an insured is found with a pistol in his hand and a bullet in his head is not sufficient to prove suicide. Cosmopolitan Life Ins. Co. v. Koegel, 104 Va. 619, 52 S.E. 166 (1905); Metropolitan Life Ins. Co. v. DeVault's Adm'x, 109 Va. 392, 63 S.E. 982 (1909); South Atl. Life Ins. Co. v. Hurt, 115 Va. 398, 79 S.E. 401 (1913). See also Life Ins. Co. v. Hairston, 108 Va. 832, 62 S.E. 1057 (1908).

§ 38.2-3107. Incontestability of certain policies. — A. No life insurance policy shall be contestable after it has been in force during the lifetime of the insured for two years from its date, except for nonpayment of premiums.

B. Provisions relating to benefits in event of disability, and provisions granting additional insurance specifically against death by accident or accidental means may be exempted in an incontestability provision. (Code 1950, § 38-366; 1952, c. 317, § 38.1-438; 1962, c. 139; 1986, c. 562.)

Purpose of section. — This section and kindred laws are wise statutes of limitation. Insurance companies should not be permitted with shut eyes to receive in silence the profits of their contracts, and to grow articulate only when called upon to pay. The authorities are full-handed to show that such provisions are valid when a reasonable time is given the company in which to make inquiry, and are liberally construed in favor of the assured. Harrison v. Provident Relief Ass'n, 141 Va. 659, 126 S.E. 696 (1925).

Incontestable provision does not affect coverage. — The incontestable provision nowhere undertakes to define risks not assumed, and has nothing at all to do with coverage. It does apply, however, to conditions broken. United Sec. Life Ins. & Trust Co. v. Massey, 159 Va. 850, 167 S.E. 248 (1933).

For this section does not deal with rights of litigants, but is one of limitation, wisely conceived and to be liberally construed. If such section did not apply to false warranties and to conditions broken, it would be of little value. United Sec. Life Ins. & Trust Co. v. Massey, 159 Va. 850, 167 S.E. 248 (1933).

Incontestable clause construed in favor as assured. — It is agreed that as a rule the contract including the incontestable clauses should be liberally construed in favor of the assured and against the party who prepared the contract; that is, against the assurer. Harrison v. Provident Relief Ass'n, 141 Va. 659, 126 S.E. 696 (1925).

It is for the benefit of the beneficiary. — While the contract is with the insured and not with the beneficiary, nevertheless, it is for the use of the beneficiary and there is no reason to say that the incontestable clause is not meant for his benefit as well as for the benefit of the insured. Harrison v. Provident Relief Ass'n, 141 Va. 659, 126 S.E. 696 (1925).

The incontestable statute is a short statute of limitation, applied when the validity of the policy is contested. It is not a limitation upon the amount of the coverage, nor of the risk assumed. It does not limit the right of the insurance carrier to refuse the payment of a larger sum than is made payable by the terms of the policy, nor limit the right to contend that the terms of the policy exclude certain risks. Darden v. North Am. Benefit Ass'n, 170 Va. 479, 197 S.E. 413 (1938).

Effect of incontestability clause on material misrepresentation. — An insurer must contest a contract's validity for false or fraudulent statements within the period prescribed in the policy, thus, an incontestability clause forecloses untimely challenges based on material misrepresentations in insurance applications. Nyonteh v. Peoples Sec. Life Ins. Co., 958 F.2d 42 (4th Cir. 1992).

Which is a limitation for questioning truthfulness of answers. — Under this section the validity of the contract of life insurance as such, the truthfulness of the answers to the questions propounded to the applicant, and such like things, cannot be questioned by the insurer as a defense against the policy, after the expiration of what some of the courts have termed "a short statute of limitations." United Sec. Life Ins. & Trust Co. v. Massey, 159 Va. 832, 164 S.E. 529 (1932), rev'd on other grounds, 159 Va. 850, 167 S.E. 248 (1933).

Under the incontestable clause, the insurer may not contest the validity of the contract for false or fraudulent statements made by the insured to secure the policy, for questions involved in the inception of the policy, nor for breach of covenants and conditions subsequent by the insured, after liability has become fixed. But the statute does not deny to the insurance carrier the right to question the genuineness of the claim, controvert the amount of its liability, or to contend that the risk involved was not assumed in the coverage. Darden v. North Am. Benefit Ass'n, 170 Va. 479, 197 S.E. 413 (1938).

Commencement of contestability period. — Where plaintiff asserted that policy became incontestable two years after the date on which plaintiff's husband signed the application form and paid the first premium in advance, the clear language of subsection (A) and § 38.2-3305, and the clear language of the policy, precluded use of plaintiff's starting point for the commencement of the contestability period. The contestability period in husband's policy began to run on the date on the receipt which was part of the policy. Parkerson v. Federal Home Life Ins. Co., 797 F. Supp. 1308 (E.D. Va. 1992).

What constitutes a "contest." — An insurance company is not liable for a loss not covered by its policy, and a denial of liability for a loss not covered by the policy will not constitute a contest. But if liability were denied because of some condition subsequently broken, that would be a contest within the purview of this section. United Sec. Life Ins. & Trust Co. v. Massey, 159 Va. 850, 167 S.E. 248 (1933).

Contest relating to coverage. — In an action on an insurance policy, the policy stated that the beneficiary should be entitled to only one fifth of the amount otherwise due, should the assured die of heart disease having its incipiency within two years from the date of the policy. Assured died of heart disease which had its inception within the two-year period, but plaintiff contended that this section (as it stood prior to the 1962 amendment) made the policy incontestable after one year from its date. It was held that the contest related to the coverage, and not to the validity of the policy, and hence this section had no application. Darden v. North Am. Benefit Ass'n, 170 Va. 479, 197 S.E. 413 (1938).

This section does not apply where premiums have not been paid and it does not apply to losses not covered by the policy. Collins v. Metropolitan Life Ins. Co., 163 Va. 833, 178 S.E. 40 (1935).

Recovery allowed on policy covering life convict. — In view of this section, in regard to incontestable policies, it is not against public policy to permit a recovery upon a policy on the life of a life convict. Harrison v. Provident Relief Ass'n, 141 Va. 659, 126 S.E. 696 (1925).

§ 38.2-3108. Misstatement of age. — Each life insurance policy shall contain a provision that, if at any time before final settlement under the policy the age of the insured, or the age of any other person if considered in determining the premium, is found to have been misstated, the amount payable under the policy shall be the amount that the premium would have purchased at the correct age at the time the policy was issued. (Code 1950, § 38-366; 1952, c. 317, § 38.1-439; 1986, c. 562.)

§ 38.2-3109. Contestability of reinstated policy. — Reinstatement of a life insurance policy shall not affect the running of the contestable period except as provided in this section. A life insurance policy reinstated after July 1, 1986, regardless of whether the original policy was issued before or after July 1, 1986, shall be contestable on account of fraud or misrepresentation of any material fact pertaining to the reinstatement contained in a written application for reinstatement, or in any written statement supplemental to the application for reinstatement, only for the same period after reinstatement as the policy provides for contestability after original issue. (Code 1950, § 38-366.1; 1950, p. 181; 1952, c. 317, § 38.1-440; 1986, c. 562.)

Writing required. — This section does not introduce a general requirement that all reinstatement applications be in writing; rather, it limits charges of misrepresentation to those based on written statements. Nyonteh v. Peoples Sec. Life Ins. Co., 958 F.2d 42 (4th Cir. 1992).

Contestable misrepresentations not limited to applicant's. — While this section limits challenges based on material misrepresentations to those based on written statements, it is not only applicable to written statements made by the applicant. Thus, beneficiary's signing of reinstatement application which did not acknowledge his leukemia diagnosis could be classified as a misrepresentation under this section. Nyonteh v. Peoples Sec. Life Ins. Co., 958 F.2d 42 (4th Cir. 1992).

The insurer might not contest for fraud incident to each reinstatement where it had failed to comply with a definite legislative enactment (contained in repealed § 38-371 prior to its amendment by Acts 1950, p. 179) requiring a recital in the policy by the insurer that such contestable period was applicable to the reinstatement. Ambrose v. Acacia Mut. Life Ins. Co., 190 Va. 189, 56 S.E.2d 372 (1949). See note to § 38.2-3315.

§ 38.2-3110. Incontestability not applicable to excluded or restricted coverage. — Any life insurance policy provision stating that the policy shall be incontestable after a specified period shall preclude only a contest of the validity of the policy, and shall not preclude the assertion at any time of defenses based upon provisions in the policy that exclude or restrict coverages, whether or not those restrictions or exclusions are excepted in the incontestability provision. (1952, c. 317, § 38.1-441; 1986, c. 562.)

§ 38.2-3111. Assignment of life insurance policies. — No life insurance policy shall be taken out by the insured or by a person having an insurable interest in the insured's life for the mere purpose of assignment. A policy may be assigned whether or not the assignee has an insurable interest in the life insured unless the policy provides otherwise. (Code 1950, § 38-367; 1952, c. 317, § 38.1-442; 1962, c. 590; 1986, c. 562.)

This section explicitly authorizes the assignment of life insurance policies. Dennis v. Aetna Life Ins. & Annuity Co., 873 F. Supp. 1000 (E.D. Va. 1995).

The assignment may be made by delivery of policy, with intent to assign it, notwithstanding the requirements of the insurance company for writing lodged with the company and signed by the insured. New York Life Ins. Co. v. Farthing's Adm'r, 1 Va. L. Reg. (n.s.) 587 (1915).

§ 38.2-3112. Designation of testamentary trustee as beneficiary. —

A. A life insurance policy may designate as beneficiary a trustee or trustees named or to be named by will if the designation is made in accordance with the provisions of the policy and the requirements of the insurer issuing the policy.

B. A trustee may qualify immediately after probate of the will. Upon appointment and qualification of a trustee, the proceeds of the insurance shall be paid to the trustee to be held and disposed of under the terms of the will. If there is no valid will appointing a trustee or if the trust provided by the will is invalid for any other cause, the designation of a trustee as beneficiary of the policy shall be void. If no qualified trustee makes claim to the proceeds from the insurer within one year after the death of the insured, or if satisfactory evidence is furnished to the insurer within the one-year period showing that no trustee can qualify to receive the proceeds, payment shall be made by the insurer to the executors, administrators or assigns of the insured, unless otherwise provided for by the owner of the policy, if the owner is other than the insured, or by the insured by agreement with the insurer.

C. The proceeds of the insurance as collected by a trustee shall not be subject to debts of the insured nor to estate taxes to any greater extent than if the proceeds were payable to any other named beneficiary other than the estate of the insured.

D. For purposes of trust administration, the proceeds shall be subject to the court's jurisdiction over the trust as in any other testamentary trust, but the proceeds shall not be considered as payable to the estate of the insured.

E. This section does not authorize payment of policy proceeds to any testamentary trustee who is not otherwise qualified to act as a testamentary trustee. A qualified substitute trustee may be appointed to perform the trust provided by the will.

F. Enactment of this section shall not be construed as casting any doubt upon the validity of any previous life insurance policy beneficiary designations naming trustees of a trust established or to be established by will.

G. As used in this section, *"life insurance policy"* shall include other types of contracts under which proceeds become payable on the death of the testator to the end that interests other than those described as "life insurance" may be made payable or transferred to a trustee named or to be named in a will in the same manner and to the same extent they could be made payable to or transferable to any other person. (1968, c. 524, § 38.1-408.1; 1968, c. 553, § 38.1-442.1; 1986, c. 562.)

§ 38.2-3113. Variable life insurance and variable annuities; separate accounts to be established; authority to issue; reports; special voting rights and procedures for owners. —

A. Each domestic insurer that issues life insurance or annuities providing for payments that vary directly according to investment experience shall establish one or more separate accounts in connection with these types of life insurance or annuities. All amounts received by the insurer that are required by contract to be applied to provide for variable payments shall be added to the appropriate separate account. The assets of any such separate account shall not be chargeable with liabilities arising out of any other business the insurer may conduct. Any surplus or deficit that may arise in any separate account by virtue of mortality experience shall be adjusted by withdrawals from or additions to the account so that the assets of the account shall always at least equal the assets required to satisfy the insurer's obligations for the variable payments.

B. A foreign or alien insurer licensed to do business in this Commonwealth may be licensed to deliver or issue for delivery life insurance or annuity contracts in this Commonwealth providing for payments which vary directly according to investment experience only if authorized to issue such life insurance or annuity contracts under the laws of its domicile.

C. No domestic, foreign, or alien insurer shall be licensed to deliver or issue for delivery variable life insurance or variable annuity contracts in this Commonwealth, until the insurer has satisfied the Commission that its condition and methods of operation in connection with the issuance of variable life insurance or variable annuity contracts will not render its operation hazardous to the public or to its policyholders in this Commonwealth. In determining the qualification of an insurer to deliver or issue for delivery such variable life insurance or variable annuity contracts in this Commonwealth, the Commission shall consider, but shall not be limited to considering, the following: (i) the history and financial condition of the insurer; (ii) the character, responsibility, and general fitness of the officers and directors of the insurer; and, (iii) in the case of a foreign or alien insurer, whether the regulation provided by the laws of its domicile provides a degree of protection to policyholders and the public substantially equal to that provided by this section and any rules and regulations issued by the Commission.

D. Each insurer that delivers or issues for delivery variable life insurance or variable annuity contracts in this Commonwealth shall file with the Commission, in addition to the annual statement required by § 38.2-1300, any other periodic or special reports the Commission prescribes.

E. The provisions of this section shall not apply to any contracts or policies which do not provide for payments which vary directly according to investment experience.

F. Any domestic life insurer that establishes one or more separate accounts pursuant to this section may amend its charter to provide for special voting rights and procedures for the owners of variable life insurance or variable annuity contracts relating to investment policy, investment advisory services and selection of certified public accountants, in relation to the administration of the assets in any such separate account. This subsection shall not in any way affect existing laws pertaining to the voting rights of the insurer's policyholders. (1966, c. 289, § 38.1-443; 1976, c. 562; 1986, c. 562.)

§ **38.2-3113.1. Modified guaranteed life insurance and modified guaranteed annuities; separate accounts; authority to issue; statements required; regulations to be issued; approval expenses.** — A. For purposes of this section, *"modified guaranteed contracts"* means modified guaranteed life insurance or modified guaranteed annuity contracts. The provisions of this section apply only to such contracts.

B. A domestic insurer that issues modified guaranteed contracts may establish one or more separate accounts in connection with these types of contracts. All amounts received by the insurer to provide benefits under contracts for which separate accounts have been established shall be added to the appropriate separate account. Unless provided otherwise in the contract and approved by the Commission in its discretion, the assets of any such separate account shall be chargeable with liabilities arising out of any other business the insurer may conduct.

C. A foreign or alien insurer licensed to do business in this Commonwealth may be licensed to deliver or issue for delivery modified guaranteed contracts in this Commonwealth only if authorized to issue such contracts under the laws of its domicile.

D. No domestic, foreign, or alien insurer shall be licensed to deliver or issue for delivery modified guaranteed contracts in this Commonwealth, until the insurer has satisfied the Commission that its condition and methods of operation in connection with the issuance of modified guaranteed contracts will not render its operation hazardous to the public or to its policyholders in this Commonwealth. In determining the qualifications of an insurer to deliver or issue for delivery such modified guaranteed contracts in this Commonwealth, the Commission shall consider, but shall not be limited to considering, the following: (i) the history and financial condition of the insurer; (ii) the character, responsibility, and general fitness of the officers and directors of the insurer; and (iii) in the case of a foreign or alien insurer, whether the regulation provided by the laws of its domicile provides a degree of protection to policyholders and the public substantially equal to that provided by this section and any rules and regulations issued by the Commission.

E. Each insurer that has established any separate accounts in connection with modified guaranteed contracts, and delivers or issues for delivery modified guaranteed contracts in this Commonwealth shall file with the Commission, in addition to the annual statement required by § 38.2-1300, any other periodic or special reports the Commission prescribes.

F. Any modified guaranteed contract delivered or issued for delivery in this Commonwealth, and any certificate evidencing nonforfeiture benefits that vary according to a market-value adjustment formula issued pursuant to any life insurance or annuity contract issued on a group basis shall (i) contain, on its first page, a prominent statement that the nonforfeiture values may increase or decrease, based on the market-value adjustment formula in the contract, and (ii) for modified guaranteed life insurance only, be accompanied by a written disclosure to the purchaser of the policy's "interest adjusted net cost index" in compliance with regulations or forms approved by the Commission.

G. The Commission may promulgate reasonable regulations applicable to modified guaranteed contracts and to any separate accounts that may be established in connection with such contracts.

H. Reasonable actuarial expenses incurred in connection with approval of a modified contract shall be paid by the person seeking approval of such a contract. (1992, c. 210.)

§ 38.2-3113.2. Qualified charitable gift annuities; issuance not business of insurance; disclosures to donors; unfair trade practices provisions not applicable. — A. The issuance of a qualified charitable gift annuity does not constitute engaging in the business of insurance in this Commonwealth. A charitable gift annuity issued before the effective date of this section is a qualified charitable gift annuity for purposes of this title if it meets the requirements of § 501 (m) (5) of the Internal Revenue Code of 1986 (26 U.S.C. § 501 (m) (5)) and § 514 (c) (5) of the Internal Revenue Code of 1986 (26 U.S.C. § 514 (c) (5)), and the issuance of that charitable gift annuity does not constitute engaging in the business of insurance in this Commonwealth.

B. When entering into an agreement for a qualified charitable gift annuity, the charitable organization shall disclose to the donor in writing in the annuity agreement that a qualified charitable gift annuity is not insurance under the laws of this Commonwealth and is neither subject to regulation by the Commission nor protected by the Virginia Life, Accident and Sickness Insurance Guaranty Association. The notice provisions required by this subsection shall be in a separate paragraph in a print size no smaller than that employed in the annuity agreement generally.

C. The solicitation or issuance of a qualified charitable gift annuity does not constitute a violation of the unfair trade practices provisions of Chapter 5 (§ 38.2-500 et seq.) of this title. (1996, c. 425.)

Editor's note. — Acts 1996, c. 425, cl. 2, provides: "[t]hat the provisions of this act amending § 38.2-106, the definition of 'charitable gift annuity' as added by this act in § 38.2-106.1, and subsections A and C in § 38.2-3113.2 as added by this act are declarative of existing law."

§ 38.2-3114. Statements required in variable life insurance and variable annuity contracts and certificates issued pursuant to group variable life insurance and group variable annuity contracts. — Any variable life insurance or variable annuity contract delivered or issued for delivery in this Commonwealth, and any certificate evidencing variable benefits issued pursuant to any life insurance or annuity contract issued on a group basis shall:

1. State the essential features of the procedure to be followed by the insurer in determining the value of benefits or other contractual payments under the contract;

2. State clearly that the benefits may decrease or increase according to the procedure; and

3. State clearly on its first page that the benefits or other contractual payments are on a variable basis. (1966, c. 289, § 38.1-408; 1976, c. 562; 1986, c. 562.)

§ 38.2-3115. Interest on life insurance proceeds. — A. If an action to recover the proceeds due under a life insurance policy or annuity contract results in a judgment against the insurer, interest on the judgment at the legal rate of interest shall be paid from (i) the date of presentation to the insurer of proof of death on a life insurance policy or annuity contract or (ii) the date of maturity of an endowment policy to the date judgment is entered.

B. If no action is brought, interest upon the principal sum paid to the beneficiary or policyowner shall be computed daily at an annual rate of $2\frac{1}{2}$ percent or at the annual rate currently paid by the insurer on proceeds left under the interest settlement option, whichever is greater, commencing from the date of death on a life insurance policy or annuity contract claim and from the date of maturity of an endowment contract to the date of payment. The interest shall be added to and become a part of the total sum payable.

C. No insurer shall be required to pay interest computed under this section if the total interest is less than five dollars.

D. This section shall not apply to (i) credit life insurance for which the premium is paid wholly from funds of the creditor with no specific identifiable charge being made to insureds for the insurance and upon which post-death interest on the indebtedness is waived by the creditor in an amount at least equal to the amount of interest that would otherwise be payable under this section; or (ii) policies or contracts issued prior to July 1, 1977, but shall apply to any renewals or reissues of group life insurance policies or contracts occurring after that date. (1977, c. 264, § 38.1-443.1; 1986, c. 562; 1991, c. 368.)

§ 38.2-3116. Commission to establish standards for simplified and readable life insurance and annuity policies. — A. Pursuant to the authority granted under § 38.2-223, the Commission may issue rules and regulations establishing standards for simplified and readable life insurance policies and annuity contracts. The standards shall apply to all policy forms for annuities as defined in §§ 38.2-106 and 38.2-107 and life insurance as defined in §§ 38.2-102 through 38.2-105.

B. As used in this section, *"policy form"* means:

1. Any individual life insurance policy, plan or agreement, and any annuity contract delivered or issued for delivery in this Commonwealth;

2. Any policy, certificate or contract, including any riders, endorsements or amendments providing death benefits, delivered or issued for delivery in this Commonwealth by a fraternal benefit society;

3. Any group life insurance policy, contract, plan or agreement, including any riders, endorsements or amendments, delivered or issued for delivery in this Commonwealth, to a group with ten or fewer members; or

4. Any certificate, including any riders, endorsements or amendments, issued under a group life insurance policy delivered or issued for delivery in this Commonwealth.

C. No insurer shall issue a life insurance policy that has been filed with the Commission unless the Commission has determined that the policy form satisfies the readability standards established by the rules and regulations and complies with other statutory requirements. (1986, c. 562.)

§ 38.2-3117. Standards for certain policies; prohibited policies. — A. Pursuant to the authority granted under § 38.2-223, the Commission may issue rules and regulations that may include but shall not be limited to policy provisions, definitions, standards for full and fair disclosure and standards for minimum benefits, for variable life insurance policies, universal life insurance policies or other nontraditional types of life insurance policies, annuities and variable annuities.

B. The Commission may prescribe the method of identification of policies and contracts based upon coverage provided.

C. The Commission may issue rules and regulations that specify prohibited policies or policy provisions not otherwise specifically authorized by statute which in the opinion of the Commission are unjust, unfair or unfairly discriminatory to the policyholder, beneficiary, owner, or any other person insured under the policy. (1986, c. 562.)

ARTICLE 2.

Proceeds of Certain Policies.

§ 38.2-3118. Spendthrift trusts created under life insurance policies. — If, under the terms of any life insurance policy or of any written agreement supplemental to a life insurance policy, the proceeds are retained by the insurer at maturity or otherwise, no person entitled to any part of the proceeds, or to any installment of interest due or becoming due, may commute, anticipate, encumber, alienate or assign the proceeds or any part of the proceeds or interest if permission is expressly withheld by the terms of the policy or supplemental agreement. If the life insurance policy or supplemental agreement provides, no payments of interest or principal shall be in any way subject to the person's debts, contracts or engagements, nor to any judicial process to levy upon or attach the interest or principal for payment of those debts, contracts, or engagements. (Code 1950, § 38-115; 1952, c. 317, § 38.1-444; 1986, c. 562.)

§ 38.2-3119. Limitation on § 38.2-3118. — A. The provisions of § 38.2-3118 shall not apply to any proportionate part of the proceeds of any such policy or supplemental contract mentioned in § 38.2-3118 arising or resulting from premiums paid by the beneficiary. The proportionate part of the proceeds shall be determined by comparing the total premiums paid for the policy, without interest, with the premiums for the policy, without interest, paid by the beneficiary.

B. Notwithstanding the other provisions of this section, an insurer who (i) has no written notice of any claim that premiums have been paid by the beneficiary and (ii) has no written notice of an adverse claim of any other character under this section, shall be protected in making or withholding payments pursuant to the terms of a policy or supplemental agreement.

C. Notwithstanding the other provisions of this section, upon an insurer's acceptance of proof that premiums have been paid by the beneficiary and the insurer's payment of the corresponding proportionate part of the proceeds of the policy or supplemental agreement, the insurer's payment shall constitute full release of the insurer from all liability with respect to the proportionate part of the proceeds of the policy or supplemental agreement. (Code 1950, § 38-116; 1952, c. 317, § 38.1-445; 1986, c. 562.)

§ **38.2-3120. Application of exemptions; protection of insurer; applicability of § 55-19.** — The exemption from the debts of the beneficiary provided under §§ 38.2-3118 and 38.2-3119 and any similar exemption available to any beneficiary under the provisions of § 55-19 shall not exceed in the aggregate the amount prescribed in § 55-19. The beneficiary shall make an election as to the manner in which the exemptions shall be applied as between the proceeds of life insurance policies and estates in trust, and the election of the beneficiary shall be binding on all creditors. In the absence of notice of an adverse claim under this section, an insurer shall be protected in making or withholding payments pursuant to the terms of a policy or supplemental agreement referred to in §§ 38.2-3118 and 38.2-3119. (Code 1950, § 38-117; 1952, c. 317, § 38.1-446; 1986, c. 562.)

§ **38.2-3121. Segregation of proceeds not required.** — No insurer holding the proceeds of any policy mentioned in § 38.2-3118 shall be required to segregate the proceeds but may hold them as a part of its general corporate funds. (Code 1950, § 38-118; 1952, c. 317, § 38.1-447; 1986, c. 562.)

§ **38.2-3122. Proceeds of policies payable to others free of claims against insured.** — The assignee or lawful beneficiary of an insurance policy shall be entitled to its proceeds against any claims of the creditors or representatives of the insured or the person effecting the policy, except in cases of transfer with intent to defraud creditors, subject to the following conditions:

1. The policy shall have been effected by a person on his own life or on another life, in favor of a person other than himself;

2. The assignee of the policy, or the payee, if the policy is otherwise made payable to another, shall not be the insured, nor the person effecting the policy, nor the executors or administrators;

3. The right to change the beneficiary may or may not have been reserved or permitted;

4. The policy may be payable to the person whose life is insured if the beneficiary or assignee predeceases the insured; and

5. Subject to the statute of limitations, the amount of any premiums for such policy paid with the intent to defraud creditors, or paid under such circumstances as to be void under § 55-81, with the interest thereon, shall be to the benefit of the creditors from the proceeds of the policy. (Code 1950, § 38-119; 1952, c. 317, § 38.1-448; 1986, c. 562.)

Law Review. — For article, "Exemption of the Debtors' Life Insurance in Virginia," see 42 Va. L. Rev. 239 (1956). For discussion of debtors' life insurance exemptions, see 17 Wash. & Lee L. Rev. 19 (1960). For article on the need for reform of and a proposed revision of Virginia's exemption statutes, see 37 Wash. & Lee L. Rev. 127 (1980). For article, "How Bankruptcy Exemptions Work: Virginia as an Illustration of Why the 'Opt Out' Clause Was a Bad Idea," see 8 Geo. Mason L. Rev. 1 (1985). For survey on creditors' rights in Virginia for 1989, see 23 U. Rich. L. Rev. 561 (1989).

For interpretation of life insurance exemption statutes, see In re Manicure, 29 Bankr. 248 (Bankr. W.D. Va. 1983).

Debtors in bankruptcy may use Virginia's life insurance exemptions. In re Redmon, 31 Bankr. 756 (Bankr. E.D. Va. 1983).

Where defendant had an absolute right to disclaim the proceeds of her husband's life insurance policy, plaintiff's unjust enrichment claim against defendant-children was barred by this section. Abbott v. Willey, 479 S.E.2d 528 (1997).

Life insurance exemptions found in this section and § 38.2-3123 are independent from homestead exemption found in Title

34 and are not limited by the provisions of § 34-21. In re Redmon, 31 Bankr. 756 (Bankr. E.D. Va. 1983).

Section 34-21 does not limit debtors' rights to

exempt the cash surrender value of their life insurance policies pursuant to this section and § 38.2-3123. In re Redmon, 31 Bankr. 756 (Bankr. E.D. Va. 1983).

§ 38.2-3123. Amount of proceeds limited in certain cases. — In the case of policies under the terms of which the right to change the beneficiary is reserved and as to which the cash surrender or loan value of the policy is claimed by the creditors, the insurance shall not be entitled to the protection afforded by § 38.2-3122. (Code 1950, § 38-120; 1952, c. 317, § 38.1-449; 1986, c. 562; 1990, c. 942.)

Law Review. — For article on the need for reform of and a proposed revision of Virginia's exemption statutes, see 37 Wash. & Lee L. Rev. 127 (1980). For article, "How Bankruptcy Exemptions Work: Virginia as an Illustration of Why the 'Opt Out' Clause Was a Bad Idea," see 8 Geo. Mason L. Rev. 1 (1985).

For interpretation of life insurance exemption statutes, see In re Manicure, 29 Bankr. 248 (Bankr. W.D. Va. 1983).

Up to $10,000 of cash surrender value, rather than face value, is exempted by this section. Smith v. Giles, 35 Bankr. 377 (W.D. Va. 1983).

Section 34-21 does not limit debtors' rights to exempt the cash surrender value of their life insurance policies pursuant to § 38.2-3122 and this section. In re Redmon, 31 Bankr. 756 (Bankr. E.D. Va. 1983).

In light of the liberality that must be afforded debtors in construing Virginia's exemption laws and in light of the clear meaning of § 34-21, it must be concluded that the life insurance exemptions found in § 38.2-3122 and this section are separate and independent from the homestead exemption found in Title 34 and are not limited by the provisions of § 34-21. In re Redmon, 31 Bankr. 756 (Bankr. E.D. Va. 1983).

§ 38.2-3124. Protection of insurers from creditor's claims. — Notwithstanding §§ 38.2-3122 and 38.2-3123 any insurer issuing any insurance policy shall be discharged of all liability on that policy by payment of its proceeds in accordance with its terms, unless before payment the insurer receives written notice by or on behalf of a creditor of a claim, stating the amount claimed and the nature of the claim. (Code 1950, § 38-121; 1952, c. 317, § 38.1-450; 1986, c. 562.)

§ 38.2-3125. Other rights of beneficiaries and assignees protected. — Since the purpose of §§ 38.2-3122 and 38.2-3123 is to confer additional rights, privileges and benefits upon beneficiaries and assignees of policies, no beneficiary or assignee shall by reason of these sections be divested or deprived of or prohibited from exercising or enjoying any right, privilege or benefit that he would have or could exercise or enjoy had §§ 38.2-3122 and 38.2-3123 not been enacted. (Code 1950, § 38-119; 1952, c. 317, § 38.1-451; 1986, c. 562.)

ARTICLE 3.

Reserves.

§ 38.2-3126. Annual valuation of reserves. — A. The Commission shall annually value or have valued the reserve liabilities, referred to in this article as "reserves," for all outstanding life insurance policies and annuity and pure endowment contracts of each life insurer doing business in this Commonwealth. For an alien insurer the valuation shall be limited to its United States business. The Commission may certify the amount of the reserves, specifying the mortality table, interest rates and net level premium or other methods to be used in calculating the reserves. In calculating the reserves, the Commission may use group methods and approximate averages for suitable periods. The Commission may accept a certificate of valuation from the insurer for the reserve liability for the disability provision incorporated in life insurance policies if the Commission is satisfied, by using general averages and percentages, that the reserve has been computed in accordance with this article.

B. On or before the last day of February of each year, every domestic incorporated life insurer shall furnish the Commission the necessary data for determining the valuation of all of its policies outstanding on the last preceding December 31. For good cause shown, the Commission may extend an insurer's deadline for submitting this data. (Code 1950, § 38-390; 1952, c. 317, § 38.1-452; 1986, c. 562; 1990, c. 333.)

§ 38.2-3127. Acceptance of valuation of another state. — A. Instead of the valuation of the reserves required of any foreign or alien insurer under § 38.2-3126, the Commission may accept any valuation made, or caused to be made, by the insurance supervisory official of any state or other jurisdiction if (i) the valuation complies with the minimum standards of this article and (ii) the official of the jurisdiction accepts, as sufficient and valid for all legal purposes, the certificate of valuation of the Commission when that certificate states the valuation to have been made in a specified manner according to which the aggregate reserves would be at least as large as if they had been computed in the manner prescribed by the law of that state or jurisdiction.

B. Each foreign or alien insurer shall annually furnish to the Commission a certificate from the insurance supervisory official of its state of domicile or entry into the United States that he has made a valuation of the insurer's policies in force on December 31, and that he finds the value of the policies to be as reported in the insurer's annual statement. Any insurer failing to furnish this certificate shall have its policies valued by the Commission as provided in § 38.2-3126. (Code 1950, § 38-391; 1952, c. 317, § 38.1-453; 1986, c. 562; 1990, c. 333.)

§ 38.2-3127.1. Actuarial opinion of reserves. — A. Effective December 31, 1992, every life insurer doing business in this Commonwealth shall annually submit an actuarial opinion that complies with the provisions of this section. Such an opinion shall be rendered by a qualified actuary and shall state whether the reserves and related actuarial items held in support of designated policies and contracts, are computed appropriately, are based on assumptions which satisfy contractual provisions, are consistent with prior reported amounts and comply with applicable laws of this Commonwealth. The Commission shall specify by regulation the types of reserves and related actuarial items on which the opinion is to be expressed.

1. The Commission by regulation shall define the specifics of this opinion and add any other items deemed to be necessary to its scope.

2. The opinion shall be submitted with the annual statement filed pursuant to § 38.2-1300 and shall reflect the valuation of such reserve liabilities for each year ending on or after December 31, 1992.

3. The opinion shall apply to all business in force, including individual and group health insurance plans, in a form and substance acceptable to the Commission as specified by regulation.

4. The opinion shall be based on standards adopted from time to time by the Actuarial Standards Board and on such additional standards as the Commission may by regulation prescribe.

5. In the case of an opinion required to be submitted by a foreign or alien insurer, the Commission may accept the opinion filed by that insurer with the insurance supervisory official of another state if the Commission determines that the opinion reasonably meets the requirements applicable to a insurer domiciled in this Commonwealth.

6. For the purposes of this section, *"qualified actuary"* means a member in good standing of the American Academy of Actuaries who meets the requirements set forth in regulations promulgated by the Commission.

7. Except in cases of fraud or willful misconduct, the qualified actuary shall not be liable for damages to any person, other than the insurer and the Commission, for any act, error, omission, decision or conduct with respect to the actuary's opinion.

B 1. Effective December 31, 1992, every life insurer, except as exempted by or pursuant to regulation, shall also annually include in the opinion required by subsection A of this section, an opinion of the same qualified actuary as to whether the reserves and related actuarial items held in support of the policies and contracts, when considered in light of the assets held by the insurer with respect to the reserves and related actuarial items, including but not limited to the investment earnings on the assets and the considerations anticipated to be received and retained under the policies and contracts, make adequate provision for the insurer's obligations under the policies and contracts, including but not limited to the benefits under and expenses associated with the policies and contracts. The Commission shall specify by regulation the types of reserves and related actuarial items on which the opinion is to be expressed.

2. The Commission may provide by regulation for a transition period for establishing any higher reserves which the qualified actuary may deem necessary in order to render the opinion required by this section.

3. A memorandum, in form and substance acceptable to the Commission as specified by regulation, shall be prepared to support each actuarial opinion.

4. If the insurer fails to provide a supporting memorandum at the request of the Commission within a period specified by regulation or the Commission determines that the supporting memorandum provided by the insurer fails to meet the standards prescribed by the regulations or is otherwise unacceptable to the Commission, the Commission may engage a qualified actuary at the expense of the insurer to review the opinion and the basis for the opinion and prepare such supporting memorandum as is required by the Commission.

5. Any supporting memorandum, and any other material provided by the insurer to the Commission in connection therewith, shall be kept confidential by the Commission and shall not be made public and shall not be subject to subpoena. However, the memorandum or other material may otherwise be released by the Commission (i) with the written consent of the insurer or (ii) to the American Academy of Actuaries upon the Academy's written request stating that the memorandum or other material is required for professional disciplinary proceedings and that the American Academy of Actuaries will observe procedures satisfactory to the Commission to preserve the confidentiality of the memorandum or other material. Once any portion of the confidential memorandum is cited by the insurer in its marketing efforts or is cited before any governmental agency other than a state insurance department or is released by the insurer to the news media, all portions of the memorandum shall be no longer confidential. (1992, c. 588.)

§ 38.2-3128. Decrease of standards higher than minimum. — Each insurer that has adopted a standard of valuation producing greater aggregate reserves than those calculated according to the minimum standard provided in this article may, with the approval of the Commission, adopt any lower standard of valuation that equals or exceeds the minimum provided in this article. However, for purposes of this section, the holding of additional reserves previously determined by a qualified actuary to be necessary to render the opinion required by § 38.2-3127.1 shall not be deemed to be the adoption of a higher standard of valuation. (Code 1950, § 38-392; 1952, c. 317, § 38.1-454; 1986, c. 562; 1992, c. 588.)

§ 38.2-3129. Minimum valuation standard for policies issued prior to certain dates. — This section shall apply only to those policies and contracts issued prior to the operative date stated in § 38.2-3214.

1. The legal minimum standard for the valuation of life insurance contracts issued prior to January 1, 1937, shall be on the basis of the American Experience Table of Mortality, with interest at four percent per year, and strictly in accordance with the terms and conditions of such contracts, and for life insurance contracts issued on and after that date shall be the one-year preliminary term method of valuation, as hereinafter modified, on the basis of the American Experience Table of Mortality or at the option of the insurer, the American Men Ultimate Table of Mortality with interest at $3^{1}/_{2}$ percent per year.

2. If the net renewal premium under a limited payment life preliminary term policy providing for the payment of less than twenty annual premiums under the policy, or under an endowment preliminary term policy, exceeds that under a twenty payment life preliminary term policy, the reserve for that policy at the end of any year, including the first, shall be at least the reserve on a twenty payment life preliminary term policy issued in the same year and at the same age, together with an amount equivalent to the accumulation of a net level premium sufficient to provide for a pure endowment maturing one year after the date on which the last annual premium is due, or at the end of twenty years if the policy provides for the payment of premiums for more than twenty years, equal to the difference between the value on the maturity date of a twenty payment life preliminary term policy and the full net level premium reserve at such time of such a limited payment life or endowment policy. Policies valued by the above method shall contain a clause specifying either that the reserve of the policies shall be computed in accordance with the twenty payment life modification of the preliminary term method of valuation, or that the first year's insurance is term insurance.

3. Except as otherwise provided in § 38.2-3131 for group annuity and pure endowment contracts, the legal minimum standard for the valuation of annuities issued on and after January 1, 1937, shall be the Combined Annuity Table, with interest at four percent per year, but annuities deferred ten or more years and written in connection with life insurance shall be valued on the same basis as that used in computing the consideration or premium for the life insurance, or upon any higher standard, at the insurer's option.

4. The legal minimum standard for the calculation of the reserve liability for insurance against disability incorporated in life insurance policies issued on and after January 1, 1937, shall be on the basis of any table adopted by the insurer and approved by the Commission, with interest at $3^{1}/_{2}$ percent per year. However, in no case shall such liability be less than one-half of the net annual premium for the disability benefit computed by the table.

5. The legal standard for the valuation of group insurance written as yearly renewable term insurance issued on and after January 1, 1937, shall be on the basis of the American Men Ultimate Table of Mortality with interest at $3^{1}/_{2}$ percent per year.

6. The legal minimum standard for the valuation of industrial policies issued on and after January 1, 1937, shall be the American Experience Table of Mortality, with interest at $3^{1}/_{2}$ percent per year; however, any insurer may voluntarily value its industrial policies on the basis of the standard industrial mortality table or the substandard industrial mortality table, and by the level net premium method or in accordance with their terms by the modified preliminary term method as described in subdivision 2 of this section, or the full preliminary term method.

All industrial policies issued on and after January 1, 1937, shall be valued under the rules set forth in this section, whether or not the policies provide for surrender values, either in cash, paid-up insurance, or extended insurance.

7. The Commission may vary the standards of interest and mortality in the case of alien insurers as to contracts issued by those insurers in countries other than the United States, and in particular cases of invalid lives and other extra hazards.

8. If the actual annual premium charged for insurance is less than the net annual premium for the insurance, computed as specified in this section, the insurer shall set up an additional reserve equal to the value of an annuity of the difference between the actual premium charged and the net premium required by this section, and the term of which at the date of the valuation shall equal the period during which future premium payments are to become due on the insurance. The annuity shall be valued according to the table of mortality with the rate of interest at which the net annual premium is calculated.

9. Reserves for all of these policies and contracts, or all of any class of these policies and contracts, may be calculated, at the insurer's option, according to any standards which produce greater aggregate reserves for all the policies and contracts, or all of the class of the policies and contracts so valued, than the minimum reserves required by this section; and in each case the insurer shall report to the Commission in its annual statement the standards it used in making the valuation. (Code 1950, § 38-393; 1952, c. 317, § 38.1-455; 1975, c. 215; 1979, c. 437; 1986, c. 562.)

§ 38.2-3130. Minimum valuation standard of policies subsequently issued. — This section shall apply only to those policies and contracts issued on or after the operative date stated in § 38.2-3214, except as provided in this article and except as otherwise provided in §§ 38.2-3131 through 38.2-3136 for group annuity and pure endowment contracts issued before the operative date.

Except as otherwise provided in §§ 38.2-3131 through 38.2-3136, the minimum standard for the valuation of all such policies and contracts shall be the Commissioners reserve valuation methods defined in §§ 38.2-3137, 38.2-3138 and 38.2-3141, $3^1/_2$ percent interest, or for policies and contracts other than annuity and pure endowment contracts issued on or after July 1, 1975, four percent interest for such policies issued before July 1, 1979, $5^1/_2$ percent interest for single premium life insurance policies and $4^1/_2$ percent interest for all other policies issued on or after July 1, 1979, and the following tables:

1. For all ordinary policies of life insurance issued on the standard basis, excluding any disability and accidental death benefits in those policies, the Commissioners 1941 Standard Ordinary Mortality Table for those policies issued before the operative date of § 38.2-3215, and the Commissioners 1958 Standard Ordinary Mortality Table for those policies issued on or after the operative date of § 38.2-3215 and before the operative date of § 38.2-3209. For any category of those policies issued on female risks, all modified net premiums and present values referred to in this section may be calculated according to an age not more than six years younger than the actual age of the insured. For policies issued on or after the operative date of § 38.2-3209 (i) the Commissioners 1980 Standard Ordinary Mortality Table, or (ii) at the election of the insurer for any one or more specified plans of life insurance, the Commissioners 1980 Standard Ordinary Mortality Table with Ten-Year Select Mortality Factors, or (iii) any ordinary mortality table adopted after 1980 by the National Association of Insurance Commissioners and approved by regulation promulgated by the Commission for use in determining the minimum standard of valuation for those policies.

2. For all industrial life insurance policies issued on the standard basis, excluding any disability and accidental death benefits in those policies, the 1941 Standard Industrial Mortality Table for those policies issued before the operative date of § 38.2-3216, and for those policies issued on or after that

operative date the Commissioners 1961 Standard Industrial Mortality Table or any industrial mortality table adopted after 1980 by the National Association of Insurance Commissioners and approved by regulation promulgated by the Commission for use in determining the minimum standard of valuation for those policies.

3. For individual annuity and pure endowment contracts, excluding any disability and accidental death benefits in those contracts — the 1937 Standard Annuity Mortality Table or, at the insurer's option, the Annuity Mortality Table for 1949 Ultimate, or any modification of those tables approved by the Commission.

4. For group annuity and pure endowment contracts, excluding any disability and accidental death benefits in those contracts — the Group Annuity Mortality Table for 1951, any modification of that table approved by the Commission, or, at the insurer's option, any of the tables or modifications of tables specified for individual annuity and pure endowment contracts.

5. For total and permanent disability benefits in or supplementary to ordinary policies or contracts — for policies or contracts issued on or after January 1, 1966, the tables of Period 2 disablement rates and the 1930 to 1950 termination rates of the 1952 Disability Study of the Society of Actuaries, with due regard to the type of benefit or any tables of disablement rates and termination rates adopted after 1980 by the National Association of Insurance Commissioners and approved by regulation promulgated by the Commission for use in determining the minimum standard of valuation for those policies; for policies or contracts issued on or after January 1, 1961, and prior to January 1, 1966, either those tables or, at the insurer's option, the Class (3) Disability Table (1926); and for policies issued before January 1, 1961, the Class (3) Disability Table (1926). Any such table shall, for active lives, be combined with a mortality table permitted for calculating the reserves for life insurance policies.

6. For accidental death benefits in or supplementary to policies — for policies issued on or after January 1, 1966, the 1959 Accidental Death Benefits Table or any accidental death benefits table adopted after 1980 by the National Association of Insurance Commissioners and approved by regulation promulgated by the Commission for use in determining the minimum standard of valuation for those policies; for policies issued on or after January 1, 1961, and before January 1, 1966, either that table or, at the insurer's option, the Inter-Company Double Indemnity Mortality Table; and for policies issued before January 1, 1961, the Inter-Company Double Indemnity Mortality Table. Either table shall be combined with a mortality table permitted for calculating the reserves for life insurance policies.

7. For group life insurance, life insurance issued on the substandard basis and other special benefits, any table approved by the Commission. (Code 1950, § 38-394; 1952, c. 317, § 38.1-456; 1959, Ex. Sess., c. 43; 1962, c. 562; 1975, c. 215; 1979, c. 437; 1982, c. 227; 1986, c. 562.)

§ 38.2-3131. Minimum valuation standard for annuities subsequently issued. — A. Except as provided in §§ 38.2-3132 through 38.2-3136, the minimum standard for the valuation of all individual annuity and pure endowment contracts issued on or after the operative date of this section as defined herein, and for all annuities and pure endowments purchased on or after that date under group annuity and pure endowment contracts, shall be the Commissioners reserve valuation methods defined in §§ 38.2-3137 and 38.2-3138 and the following tables and interest rates:

1. For individual annuity and pure endowment contracts issued before July 1, 1979, excluding any disability and accidental death benefits in those contracts — the 1971 Individual Annuity Mortality Table, or any modification

of that table approved by the Commission, and six percent interest for single premium immediate annuity contracts, and four percent interest for all other individual annuity and pure endowment contracts.

2. For individual single premium immediate annuity contracts issued on or after July 1, 1979, excluding any disability and accidental death benefits in those contracts — the 1971 Individual Annuity Mortality Table or any individual annuity mortality table adopted after 1980 by the National Association of Insurance Commissioners and approved by regulation promulgated by the Commission for use in determining the minimum standard of valuation for those contracts, or any modification of those tables approved by the Commission, and $7^1/_2$ percent interest.

3. For individual annuity and pure endowment contracts issued on or after July 1, 1979, other than single premium immediate annuity contracts, excluding any disability and accidental death benefits in those individual annuity and pure endowment contracts — the 1971 Individual Annuity Mortality Table or any individual annuity mortality table adopted after 1980 by the National Association of Insurance Commissioners and approved by regulation promulgated by the Commission for use in determining the minimum standard of valuation for those contracts, or any modification of those tables approved by the Commission, and $5^1/_2$ percent interest for single premium deferred annuity and pure endowment contracts and $4^1/_2$ percent interest for all other individual annuity and pure endowment contracts.

4. For all annuities and pure endowments purchased before July 1, 1979, under group annuity and pure endowment contracts, excluding any disability and accidental death benefits purchased under those contracts — the 1971 Group Annuity Mortality Table, or any modification of that table approved by the Commission, and six percent interest.

5. For all annuities and pure endowments purchased on or after July 1, 1979, under group annuity and pure endowment contracts, excluding any disability and accidental death benefits purchased under those contracts — the 1971 Group Annuity Mortality Table or any group annuity mortality table adopted after 1980 by the National Association of Insurance Commissioners and approved by regulation promulgated by the Commission for use in determining the minimum standard of valuation for those annuities and pure endowments, or any modification of those tables approved by the Commission, and $7^1/_2$ percent interest.

B. After July 1, 1975, any insurer may file with the Commission a written notice of its election to comply with the provisions of this section after a specified date before January 1, 1979, which shall be the operative date of this section for that insurer; however, an insurer may elect a different operative date for individual annuity and pure endowment contracts from that elected for group annuity and pure endowment contracts. If an insurer makes no such election, the operative date of this section for that insurer shall be January 1, 1979. (Code 1950, § 38-394; 1952, c. 317, § 38.1-456; 1959, Ex. Sess., c. 43; 1962, c. 562; 1975, c. 215; 1979, c. 437; 1982, c. 227; 1986, c. 562.)

§ **38.2-3132. Computation of minimum valuation standard of policies subsequently issued.** — The interest rates used in determining the minimum standard for the valuation of the following items shall be the calendar year statutory valuation interest rates as defined in §§ 38.2-3130 through 38.2-3136:

1. All life insurance policies issued in a particular calendar year, on or after the operative date of § 38.2-3209;

2. All individual annuity and pure endowment contracts issued in a particular calendar year on or after January 1, 1983, except that an insurer may elect for this to apply to all individual annuity and pure endowment contracts issued after July 1, 1982;

3. All annuities and pure endowments purchased in a particular calendar

year on or after January 1, 1983, under group annuity and pure endowment contracts; and

4. Any net increase in a particular calendar year after January 1, 1983, in amounts held under guaranteed interest contracts. (Code 1950, § 38-394; 1952, c. 317, § 38.1-456; 1959, Ex. Sess., c. 43; 1962, c. 562; 1975, c. 215; 1979, c. 437; 1982, c. 227; 1986, c. 562.)

§ 38.2-3133. Calendar year statutory valuation interest rates. — A. The calendar year statutory valuation interest rates, referred to in this section as "I," shall be determined as follows and the results rounded to the nearest one-quarter of one percent:

1. For life insurance,

$$I = .03 + W (R1-.03) + (W/2) (R2-.09)$$

where

R1 is the lesser of R and .09,

R2 is the greater of R and .09,

R is the reference interest rate defined in § 38.2-3135, and

W is the weighting factor defined in § 38.2-3134;

2. For single premium immediate annuities, and for annuity benefits involving life contingencies arising from other annuities with cash settlement options, and from guaranteed interest contracts with cash settlement options,

$$I = .03 + W (R-.03)$$

where

R is the reference interest rate defined in § 38.2-3135, and

W is the weighting factor defined in § 38.2-3134;

3. For other annuities with cash settlement options and guaranteed interest contracts with cash settlement options, valued on an issue year basis, except as stated in subdivision 2 of this subsection, the formula for life insurance stated in subdivision 1 of this subsection shall apply to annuities and guaranteed interest contracts with guarantee durations in excess of ten years. The formula for single premium immediate annuities stated in subdivision 2 of this subsection shall apply to annuities and guaranteed interest contracts with guarantee duration of ten years or less;

4. For other annuities with no cash settlement options and for guaranteed interest contracts with no cash settlement options, the formula for single premium immediate annuities stated in subdivision 2 of this subsection shall apply;

5. For other annuities with cash settlement options and guaranteed interest contracts with cash settlement options, valued on a change in fund basis, the formula for single premium immediate annuities stated in subdivision 2 of this subsection shall apply.

B. However, if the calendar year statutory valuation interest rate for any life insurance policies issued in any calendar year determined without reference to this sentence differs from the corresponding actual rate for similar policies issued in the immediately preceding calendar year by less than one-half of one percent, the calendar year statutory valuation interest rate for life insurance policies shall equal the corresponding actual rate for the immediately preceding calendar year. For purposes of applying the immediately preceding sentence, the calendar year statutory valuation interest rate for life insurance policies issued in a calendar year shall be determined for 1980, using the reference interest rate defined for 1979, and shall be determined for each later calendar year regardless of when § 38.2-3209 becomes operative. (Code 1950, § 38-394; 1952, c. 317, § 38.1-456; 1959, Ex. Sess., c. 43; 1962, c. 562; 1975, c. 215; 1979, c. 437; 1982, c. 227; 1986, c. 562.)

§ 38.2-3134. Weighting factors. — The weighting factors referred to in the formulas in § 38.2-3133 are given in the following tables:

1. Weighting Factors for Life Insurance:

Guarantee Duration (Years)	Weighting Factors
10 or less	.50
More than 10, but not more than 20	.45
More than 20	.35

For life insurance, the guarantee duration is the maximum number of years the life insurance can remain in force on a basis guaranteed in the policy or under options to convert to plans of life insurance with premium rates or nonforfeiture values or both that are guaranteed in the original policy.

2. Weighting factor for single premium immediate annuities and for annuity benefits involving life contingencies arising from other annuities with cash settlement options and guaranteed interest contract with cash settlement options:

.80

3. Weighting factors for other annuities and for guaranteed interest contracts, except as stated in subdivision 2 of this section, shall be as specified in tables a, b, and c below, according to the rules and definitions in subdivisions 4, 5 and 6 of this section:

a. For annuities and guaranteed interest contracts valued on an issue year basis:

Guarantee Duration (Years)	Weighting Factor For Plan Type		
	A	B	C
5 or less:	.80	.60	.50
More than 5, but not more than 10:	.75	.60	.50
More than 10, but not more than 20:	.65	.50	.45
More than 20:	.45	.35	.35

	Plan Type		
	A	B	C
b. For annuities and guaranteed interest contracts valued on a change in fund basis, the factors shown in table a increased by:	.15	.25	.05

	Plan Type		
	A	B	C
c. For annuities and guaranteed interest contracts valued on an issue year basis, other than those with no cash settlement options, that do not guarantee interest on considerations received more than one year after issue or purchase and for annuities and guaranteed interest contracts valued on a change in fund basis that do not guarantee interest rates on considerations received more than twelve months beyond the valuation date, the factors			

	Plan Type		
shown in table a or derived	A	B	C
in table b increased by:	.05	.05	.05

4. For other annuities with cash settlement options and guaranteed interest contracts with cash settlement options, the guarantee duration is the number of years for which the contract guarantees interest rates in excess of the calendar year statutory valuation interest rates for life insurance policies with guarantee duration in excess of twenty years. For other annuities with no cash settlement options and for guaranteed interest contracts with no cash settlement options, the guarantee duration is the number of years from the date of issue or date of purchase to the date annuity benefits are scheduled to begin.

5. Plan type as used in the above tables is defined as follows:

Plan Type A: At any time policyholders may withdraw funds only (i) with an adjustment to reflect changes in interest rates or asset values since receipt of the funds by the insurer, (ii) without that adjustment but in installments over five years or more, (iii) as an immediate life annuity, or (iv) no withdrawal permitted.

Plan Type B: Before expiration of the interest rate guarantee, the policyholder may withdraw funds only (i) with an adjustment to reflect changes in interest rates or asset values since receipt of the funds by the insurer, (ii) without that adjustment but in installments over five years or more, or (iii) no withdrawal permitted. At the end of the interest rate guarantee, funds may be withdrawn without the adjustment in a single sum or in installments over less than five years.

Plan Type C: The policyholder may withdraw funds before expiration of the interest rate guarantee in a single sum or in installments over less than five years either (i) without adjustment to reflect changes in interest rate or asset values since receipt of the funds by the insurer, or (ii) subject only to a fixed surrender charge stipulated in the contract as a percentage of the fund.

6. An insurer may elect to value guaranteed interest contracts with cash settlement options and annuities with cash settlement options on either an issue-year basis or on a change-in-fund basis. Guaranteed interest contracts with no cash settlement options and other annuities with no cash settlement options must be valued on an issue-year basis. As used in §§ 38.2-3132 through 38.2-3136, an issue-year basis of valuation refers to a valuation basis under which the interest rate used to determine the minimum valuation standard for the entire duration of the annuity or guaranteed interest contract is the calendar year valuation interest rate for the year of issue or year of purchase of the annuity or guaranteed interest contract. As used in §§ 38.2-3132 through 38.2-3136, the change-in-fund basis of valuation refers to a valuation basis under which the interest rate used to determine the minimum valuation standard applicable to each change in the fund held under the annuity or guaranteed interest contract is the calendar year valuation interest rate for the year of the change in the fund. (Code 1950, § 38-394; 1952, c. 317, § 38.1-456; 1959, Ex. Sess., c. 43; 1962, c. 562; 1975, c. 215; 1979, c. 437; 1982, c. 227; 1986, c. 562.)

§ 38.2-3135. Reference interest rate. — The reference interest rate referred to in § 38.2-3133 means:

1. For all life insurance, the lesser of the average over a period of thirty-six months and the average over a period of twelve months, ending on June 30 of the calendar year next preceding the year of issue, of Moody's Corporate Bond Yield Average — Monthly Average Corporates, as published by Moody's Investors Service, Inc.

2. For single premium immediate annuities and for annuity benefits involving life contingencies arising from other annuities with cash settlement options and guaranteed interest contracts with cash settlement options, the average over a period of twelve months, ending on June 30 of the calendar year of issue or year of purchase, of Moody's Corporate Bond Yield Average — Monthly Average Corporates, as published by Moody's Investors Service, Inc.

3. For other annuities with cash settlement options and guaranteed interest contracts with cash settlement options, valued on a year-of-issue basis, except as stated in subdivision 2 of this section, with guarantee duration in excess of ten years, the lesser of the average over a period of thirty-six months and the average over a period of twelve months, ending on June 30 of the calendar year of issue or purchase, of Moody's Corporate Bond Yield Average — Monthly Average Corporates, as published by Moody's Investors Service, Inc.

4. For other annuities with cash settlement options and guaranteed interest contracts with cash settlement options, valued on a year-of-issue basis, except as stated in subdivision 2 of this section, with guarantee duration of ten years or less, the average over a period of twelve months, ending on June 30 of the calendar year of issue or purchase, of Moody's Corporate Bond Yield Average — Monthly Average Corporates, as published by Moody's Investors Service, Inc.

5. For other annuities with no cash settlement options and for guaranteed interest contracts with no cash settlement options, the average over a period of twelve months, ending on June 30 of the calendar year of issue or purchase, of Moody's Corporate Bond Yield Average — Monthly Average Corporates, as published by Moody's Investors Service, Inc.

6. For other annuities with cash settlement options and guaranteed interest contracts with cash settlement options, valued on a change-in-fund basis, except as stated in subdivision 2 of this section, the average over a period of twelve months, ending on June 30 of the calendar year of the change in the fund, of Moody's Corporate Bond Yield Average — Monthly Average Corporates, as published by Moody's Investors Service, Inc. (Code 1950, § 38-394; 1952, c. 317, § 38.1-456; 1959, Ex. Sess., c. 43; 1962, c. 562; 1975, c. 215; 1979, c. 437; 1982, c. 227; 1986, c. 562.)

§ 38.2-3136. Alternative method for determining reference interest rates. — If Moody's Corporate Bond Yield Average — Monthly Average Corporates is no longer published by Moody's Investors Service, Inc., or if the National Association of Insurance Commissioners determines that Moody's Corporate Bond Yield Average — Monthly Average Corporates as published by Moody's Investors Service, Inc. is no longer appropriate for the determination of the reference interest rate as defined in § 38.2-3135, then an alternative method for determination of the reference interest rate may be substituted if it is adopted by the National Association of Insurance Commissioners and approved by the Commission. (Code 1950, § 38-394; 1952, c. 317, § 38.1-456; 1959, Ex. Sess., c. 43; 1962, c. 562; 1975, c. 215; 1979, c. 437; 1982, c. 227; 1986, c. 562.)

§ 38.2-3137. Reserve valuation method — Life insurance and endowment benefits. — A. Except as otherwise provided in §§ 38.2-3138 and 38.2-3141, reserves according to the Commissioners reserve valuation method, for the life insurance and endowment benefits of policies providing for a uniform amount of insurance and requiring the payment of uniform premiums shall be any excess of the present value at the date of valuation of any future guaranteed benefits provided for by those policies, over the then present value of any future modified net premiums for those policies. The modified net premiums for any such policy shall be a uniform percentage of the respective contract premiums for those benefits, excluding any extra premiums charged because of impairments or special hazards, so that the present value at the date of issue of the policy of all the modified net premiums shall be equal to the sum of the then present value of those benefits provided for by the policy and the excess of 1 over 2, as follows:

1. A net level annual premium equal to the present value at the date of issue of those benefits provided for after the first policy year, divided by the present value at the date of issue of an annuity of one dollar per year payable on the first and each following anniversary of the policy on which a premium falls due. However, the net level annual premium shall not exceed the net level annual premium on the nineteen-year premium whole life plan for insurance of the same amount at an age one year higher than the age at issue of the policy.

2. A net one-year term premium for the benefits provided for in the first policy year.

B. For any life insurance policy issued on or after January 1, 1986, (i) for which the contract premium in the first policy year exceeds that of the second year, (ii) for which no comparable additional benefit is provided in the first year for that excess first year premium and (iii) that provides an endowment benefit or a cash surrender value or a combination of both in an amount greater than the excess first year premium, the reserve according to the Commissioners reserve valuation method as of any policy anniversary occurring on or before the assumed ending date, defined to be the first policy anniversary on which the sum of any endowment benefit and any cash surrender value then available is greater than the excess premium, shall, except as otherwise provided in § 38.2-3141, be the greater of the reserve as of the policy anniversary calculated as described in subsection A of this section and the reserve as of the policy anniversary calculated as described in that subsection, but with (a) the value defined in subdivision 1 of that subsection being reduced by fifteen percent of the amount of the excess first year premium, (b) all present values of benefits and premiums being determined without reference to premiums or benefits provided for by the policy after the assumed ending date, (c) the policy being assumed to mature on the annual ending date as an endowment, and (d) the cash surrender value provided on the annual ending date being considered as an endowment benefit. In making the above comparison the mortality and interest bases stated in §§ 38.2-3130 through 38.2-3136 shall be used.

C. Reserves according to the Commissioners reserve valuation method for (i) life insurance policies providing for a varying amount of insurance or requiring the payment of varying premiums, (ii) group annuity and pure endowment contracts purchased under a retirement plan or plan of deferred compensation, established or maintained by an employer, including a partnership or sole proprietorship, or by an employee organization, or by both, other than a plan providing individual retirement accounts or individual retirement annuities under § 408 of the Internal Revenue Code, as amended, (iii) disability and accidental death benefits in all policies and contracts, and (iv) all other benefits, except life insurance and endowment benefits in life insurance policies and benefits provided by all other annuity and pure endowment contracts, shall be calculated by a method consistent with the principles of this section. (Code 1950, § 38-394; 1952, c. 317, § 38.1-456; 1959, Ex. Sess., c. 43; 1962, c. 562; 1975, c. 215; 1979, c. 437; 1982, c. 227; 1986, c. 562.)

§ 38.2-3138. Same — Annuity and pure endowment benefits. — A. This section shall apply to annuity and pure endowment contracts, other than group annuity and pure endowment contracts purchased under a retirement plan or plan of deferred compensation, established or maintained by an employer, including a partnership or sole proprietorship, or by an employee organization, or by both, other than a plan providing individual retirement accounts or individual retirement annuities under § 408 of the Internal Revenue Code, as amended.

B. Reserves according to the Commissioners annuity reserve method for benefits under annuity or pure endowment contracts, excluding any disability and accidental death benefits in those contracts, shall be the greatest of the respective excesses of the present values, at the date of valuation, of the future guaranteed benefits, including guaranteed nonforfeiture benefits, provided for by those contracts at the end of each respective contract year, over the present value at the date of valuation of any future valuation considerations derived from future gross considerations required by the terms of the contract that become payable before the end of the respective contract year. The future guaranteed benefits shall be determined by using the mortality table, if any, and the interest rate or rates specified in those contracts for determining guaranteed benefits. The valuation considerations are the portions of the respective gross considerations applied under the terms of those contracts to determine nonforfeiture values. (Code 1950, § 38-394; 1952, c. 317, § 38.1-456; 1959, Ex. Sess., c. 43; 1962, c. 562; 1975, c. 215; 1979, c. 437; 1982, c. 227; 1986, c. 562.)

§ **38.2-3139. Minimum reserves.** — A. In no event shall an insurer's aggregate reserves for all life insurance policies, excluding disability and accidental death benefits, be less than the aggregate reserves calculated in accordance with the methods set forth in §§ 38.2-3137, 38.2-3138, 38.2-3141 and 38.2-3142 and the mortality table or tables and rate or rates of interest used in calculating nonforfeiture benefits for those policies.

B. In no event shall the aggregate reserves for all policies, contracts and benefits be less than the aggregate reserves determined by the qualified actuary to be necessary to render the opinion required by § 38.2-3127.1. (Code 1950, § 38-394; 1952, c. 317, § 38.1-456; 1959, Ex. Sess., c. 43; 1962, c. 562; 1975, c. 215; 1979, c. 437; 1982, c. 227; 1986, c. 562; 1992, c. 588.)

§ **38.2-3140. Optional reserve calculation.** — Reserves for any category of policies, contracts or benefits as established by the Commission may be calculated, at the insurer's option, according to any standards that produce greater aggregate reserves for the category than those calculated according to the minimum standard provided in this article, but the rate or rates of interest used for policies and contracts other than annuity and pure endowment contracts shall not be higher than the corresponding rate or rates of interest used in calculating any nonforfeiture benefits provided for in those policies and contracts. However, for purposes of this section, the holding of additional reserves previously determined by a qualified actuary to be necessary to render the opinion required by § 38.2-3127.1 shall not be deemed to be the adoption of a higher standard of valuation. (Code 1950, § 38-394; 1952, c. 317, § 38.1-456; 1959, Ex. Sess., c. 43; 1962, c. 562; 1975, c. 215; 1979, c. 437; 1982, c. 227; 1986, c. 562; 1992, c. 588.)

§ **38.2-3141. Reserve calculation — Valuation net premium exceeding the gross premium charge.** — A. If in any contract year the gross premium charged by a life insurer on any policy or contract is less than the valuation net premium for the policy or contract calculated by the method used in calculating the reserve on the policy or contract but using the minimum valuation standards of mortality and rate of interest, the minimum reserve required for the policy or contract shall be the greater of either the reserve calculated according to the mortality table, rate of interest, and method actually used for the policy or contract, or the reserve calculated by the method actually used for the policy or contract but using the minimum valuation standards of mortality and rate of interest and replacing the valuation net premium by the actual gross premium in each contract year for which the valuation net premium exceeds the actual gross premium. The minimum valuation standards of mortality and rate of interest referred to in this section are those standards stated in §§ 38.2-3130 through 38.2-3136.

B. For any life insurance policy issued on or after January 1, 1986, for which the gross premium in the first policy year exceeds that of the second year and for which no comparable additional benefit is provided in the first year for that excess and which provides an endowment benefit or a cash surrender value or a combination of both in an amount greater than the excess premium, the provisions of this section shall be applied as if the method actually used in calculating the reserve for the policy were the method described in § 38.2-3137, ignoring subsection B of § 38.2-3137. The minimum reserve at each policy anniversary of such a policy shall be the greater of the minimum reserve calculated in accordance with § 38.2-3137, and the minimum reserve calculated in accordance with this section. (Code 1950, § 38-394; 1952, c. 317, § 38.1-456; 1959, Ex. Sess., c. 43; 1962, c. 562; 1975, c. 215; 1979, c. 437; 1982, c. 227; 1986, c. 562.)

§ 38.2-3142. Same — Indeterminate premium plans. — For any plan of life insurance that provides for future premium determination, the amounts of which are to be determined by the insurer based on estimates of future experience, or for any plan of life insurance or annuity whose minimum reserves cannot be determined by the methods described in §§ 38.2-3137, 38.2-3138 and 38.2-3141, the reserves held under any such plan shall:

1. Be appropriate in relation to the benefits and the pattern of premiums for that plan; and

2. Be computed by a method consistent with the principles of this article, as determined by regulations promulgated by the Commission. (Code 1950, § 38-394; 1952, c. 317, § 38.1-456; 1959, Ex. Sess., c. 43; 1962, c. 562; 1975, c. 215; 1979, c. 437; 1982, c. 227; 1986, c. 562.)

§ 38.2-3143. Assessment against insurers whose policies are valued. — The Commission is hereby authorized to assess against every insurer whose policies are valued a sum equal to the cost of valuation, which shall be paid into the state treasury and placed by the Comptroller to the credit of the maintenance fund of the Bureau of Insurance. (Code 1950, § 38-395; 1952, c. 317, § 38.1-457; 1986, c. 562; 1992, c. 588.)

§ 38.2-3144. Article not applicable in certain cases. — Nothing in this article shall be construed to apply to any insurer in the transaction of industrial sick benefit insurance as defined in § 38.2-3544, nor to fraternal benefit societies, except for § 38.2-3127.1. (Code 1950, § 38-396; 1952, c. 317, § 38.1-458; 1986, c. 562; 1992, c. 588.)

CHAPTER 32.

STANDARD NONFORFEITURE PROVISIONS FOR LIFE INSURANCE.

§ 38.2-3200. Nonforfeiture benefits and cash surrender values in life policies issued prior to operative date stated in § 38.2-3214. — A. This section shall apply only to life insurance policies issued prior to the operative date stated in § 38.2-3214.

B. The nonforfeiture benefit referred to in § 38.2-3309 shall be available to the insured in the event of default in premium payments, after premiums have been paid for three full years. The premium paid for the insured under any policy provision shall not be considered in default. The nonforfeiture benefit shall be a stipulated form of insurance, effective from the due date of the defaulted premium, the net value of which shall at least equal the reserve at the date of default on the policy and on any dividend additions to the policy, exclusive of the reserve on account of return premium insurance and on total and permanent disability and additional accidental death benefits, less a sum not more than $2^{1}/_{2}$ percent of the amount insured by the policy and of any dividend additions to the policy and less any existing indebtedness to the insurer on or secured by the policy. The policy shall specify the mortality table and rate of interest used in computing these reserves. Instead of allowing a deduction from the reserve of a sum not more than $2^{1}/_{2}$ percent of the amount insured by the policy, and of any dividend additions to the policy, the insurer may insert in the policy a provision that one-fifth of the reserve may be deducted, or may provide in the policy that a deduction may be made of $2^{1}/_{2}$ percent of the amount insured by the policy or one-fifth of the reserve, at the insurer's option. The cash surrender value referred to in § 38.2-3309 shall be available upon surrender of the policy to the insurer within one month of the due date of the defaulted premium and shall at least equal the sum which would otherwise be available for the purchase of insurance. The insurer may defer payment for not more than three months after the application for the cash surrender value is made.

C. If more than one option is provided, the policy shall stipulate which of the options shall be effective if the insured does not elect any option on or before the expiration of the grace period allowed for the payment of the premium.

D. A provision may also be inserted in the policy that in the event of default in a premium payment before the options become available, the reserve on any dividend additions then in force may, at the insurer's option, be paid in cash or applied as a net premium to the purchase of paid-up term insurance for any amount not exceeding the face amount of the original policy.

E. This section shall apply to term insurance policies only if the term is for more than twenty years. (Code 1950, § 38-374; 1952, c. 317, § 38.1-459; 1986, c. 562.)

§ **38.2-3201. Same; for industrial life policies.** — A. This section shall apply only to industrial life insurance policies issued prior to the operative date stated in § 38.2-3214.

B. The nonforfeiture benefits referred to in § 38.2-3347 shall be available in the event of default in premium payments after premiums have been paid for five full years, without action on the part of the insured. The nonforfeiture benefit shall be a stipulated form of insurance, effective from the due date of the defaulted premium, the net value of which at least equals the reserve on the policy, excluding any reserves for provisions (i) relating to benefits for specific types of disability, (ii) granting additional insurance specifically against accidental death, and (iii) granting other benefits in addition to life insurance, at the end of the last completed policy year for which premiums have been paid, and on any dividend additions to the policy, less a specified maximum percentage, not more than $2^1/_2$ percent, of the maximum face amount insured by the policy and of any dividend additions to the policy and less any existing indebtedness to the insurer on or secured by the policy. The policy shall specify the mortality table, rate of interest and method of valuation used for computing these reserves. The policy shall also specify the percentage or other rule of calculation so as to permit determination of the values for each year for which required values are not included in the policy. Instead of allowing for the deduction from the reserve of a sum not more than $2^1/_2$ percent of the maximum face amount insured by the policy and of any dividend additions to the policy, the insurer may insert in the policy a provision that one-fifth of the reserve may be deducted, or may provide in the policy that a deduction may be made of $2^1/_2$ percent of the maximum face amount insured by the policy or one-fifth of the reserve at the insurer's option.

C. If more than one option is provided, the policy shall stipulate which of the options shall apply if the insured fails to notify the insurer of his selection of an option.

D. The cash surrender value referred to in § 38.2-3347 shall be available after premiums have been paid for ten full years upon surrender of the policy to the insurer within three months of the due date of the defaulted premium and shall be at least equal to the sum which would otherwise be available for the purchase of insurance. The insurer may defer payment for not more than three months after the application for the cash surrender value is made. This section shall not apply to term insurance policies of twenty years or less, but such term policy shall specify the mortality table, rate of interest and method of valuation adopted for computing reserves. (Code 1950, § 38-375; 1952, c. 317, § 38.1-460; 1986, c. 562.)

§ **38.2-3202. Standard nonforfeiture law; required policy provisions.** — A. On and after the operative date stated in § 38.2-3214, no life insurance policy, except as stated in § 38.2-3213, shall be delivered or issued for delivery in this Commonwealth unless it contains in substance the following provisions and statements, or corresponding provisions and statements that in the opinion of the Commission (i) are at least as favorable to the defaulting or surrendering policyholder and (ii) essentially comply with § 38.2-3212:

1. That in the event of default in any premium payment, the insurer will grant, upon proper request not later than sixty days after the due date of the premium in default, a paid-up nonforfeiture benefit on a plan stipulated in the policy, effective as of the due date, in the amount specified in this article. Instead of the stipulated paid-up nonforfeiture benefit, the insurer may

substitute, upon proper request not later than sixty days after the due date of the premium in default, an actuarially equivalent alternative paid-up nonforfeiture benefit that provides a greater amount or longer period of death benefits or, if applicable, a greater amount or earlier payment of endowment benefits.

2. That upon surrender of the policy within sixty days after the due date of any premium payment in default, after premiums have been paid for at least three full years for ordinary insurance or five full years for industrial insurance, the insurer will pay, instead of any paid-up nonforfeiture benefit, a cash surrender value in the amount specified in this chapter.

3. That a specified paid-up nonforfeiture benefit shall become effective as specified in the policy unless the person entitled to make an election selects another available option not later than sixty days after the due date of the premium in default.

4. That for a policy paid up by completion of all premium payments or continued under any paid-up nonforfeiture benefit that became effective on or after the third policy anniversary for ordinary insurance or the fifth policy anniversary for industrial insurance, the insurer will pay, upon surrender of the policy within thirty days after any policy anniversary, a cash surrender value in the amount specified in this article.

5. For policies that provide on a basis guaranteed in the policy unscheduled changes in benefits or premiums, or both, or that provide an option for changes in benefits or premiums, or both, other than a change to a new policy, a statement of the mortality table, interest rate, and method used in calculating cash surrender values and the paid-up nonforfeiture benefits available under the policy. All other policies shall include a statement of the mortality table and interest rate used in calculating the cash surrender values and the paid-up nonforfeiture benefits available under the policy, together with a table showing any cash surrender value and any paid-up nonforfeiture benefit available under the policy on each policy anniversary either during the first twenty policy years or during the term of the policy, whichever is shorter. The values and benefits referred to in this subdivision shall be calculated upon the assumption that there are no dividends or paid-up additions credited to the policy and that there is no indebtedness to the insurer on the policy.

6. A brief and general statement of the method to be used in calculating the cash surrender value and the paid-up nonforfeiture benefits available under the policy on any policy anniversary beyond the last anniversary for which the values and benefits are consecutively shown in the policy, with an explanation of how the existence of any paid-up additions credited to the policy or any indebtedness to the insurer on the policy affects the cash surrender values and the paid-up nonforfeiture benefits.

B. To the extent that any of the foregoing provisions are not applicable to the plan of insurance, they may be omitted from the policy with the approval of the Commission.

C. The insurer shall reserve the right to defer the payment of any cash surrender value for no more than six months after demand for the cash surrender value and surrender of the policy. (Code 1950, § 38-376; 1952, c. 317, § 38.1-461; 1982, c. 228; 1986, c. 562.)

§ **38.2-3203. Same; cash surrender value in case of default.** — A. Any cash surrender value available under any life insurance policy issued on or after the operative date stated in § 38.2-3214 in the event of default in a premium payment due on any policy anniversary, whether or not required by § 38.2-3202, shall at least equal any excess of the present value, on that anniversary, of the future guaranteed benefits that would have been provided for by the policy, including any existing paid-up additions had there been no default, over the sum of (i) the then present value of the adjusted premiums as defined in §§ 38.2-3205 through 38.2-3209, corresponding to premiums that would have fallen due on and after that anniversary, and (ii) the amount of any indebtedness to the insurer on the policy.

B. For any policy issued on or after the operative date of § 38.2-3209 and providing at the option of the insured supplemental life insurance or annuity benefits for an identifiable additional premium by rider or supplemental policy provision, the cash surrender value referred to in subsection A of this section shall at least equal the sum of (i) the cash surrender value defined in subsection A for an otherwise similar policy issued at the same age without the rider or supplemental policy provision and (ii) the cash surrender value defined in subsection A for a policy providing only the benefits provided by the rider or supplemental policy provision.

C. For any family policy issued on or after the operative date of § 38.2-3209, defining a primary insured and providing term insurance on the life of the spouse of the primary insured expiring before the spouse achieves the age of seventy-one, the cash surrender value referred to in subsection A of this section shall at least equal the sum of (i) the cash surrender value defined in subsection A for an otherwise similar policy issued at the same age without the term insurance on the life of the spouse and (ii) the cash surrender value defined in subsection A for a policy providing only the benefits provided by the term insurance on the life of the spouse.

D. Any cash surrender value available within thirty days after any policy anniversary under any policy paid-up by completion of all premium payments or any policy continued under any paid-up nonforfeiture benefit, whether or not required by § 38.2-3202, shall at least equal the present value, on that anniversary, of the future guaranteed benefits provided for by the policy, including any existing paid-up additions, decreased by any indebtedness to the insurer on the policy. (Code 1950, § 38-377; 1952, c. 317, § 38.1-462; 1982, c. 228; 1986, c. 562.)

§ 38.2-3204. Same; present value of paid-up nonforfeiture benefits on default. — Any paid-up nonforfeiture benefit available under a life insurance policy issued on or after the operative date stated in § 38.2-3214 in the event of default in a premium payment due on any policy anniversary shall be such that its present value as of that anniversary shall at least equal the cash surrender value then provided for by the policy or, if none is provided for, shall equal the cash surrender value that would have been required by § 38.2-3203 in the absence of the condition that premiums have been paid for a specified period. (Code 1950, § 38-378; 1952, c. 317, § 38.1-463; 1986, c. 562.)

§ 38.2-3205. Same; calculation of adjusted premiums. — A. The provisions of this section shall not apply to policies issued on or after the operative date as defined in § 38.2-3209. Except as provided in subsection C of this section, the adjusted premium for any life insurance policy issued on or after the operative date stated in § 38.2-3214 shall be calculated on an annual basis and shall be a uniform percentage of the respective premiums specified in the policy for each policy year, excluding any extra premiums charged because of impairments or special hazards, so that the present value at the date of issue of the policy of all adjusted premiums is equal to the sum of: (i) the then present value of the future guaranteed benefits provided for by the policy; (ii) two percent of the amount of insurance, if the insurance is uniform in amount, or of the equivalent uniform amount as defined in subsection B of this section if the amount of insurance varies with the duration of the policy; (iii) forty percent of the adjusted premium for the first policy year; and (iv) twenty-five percent of either the adjusted premium for the first policy year or the adjusted premium for a whole life policy of the same uniform or equivalent uniform amount with uniform premiums for the whole of life issued at the same age for the same amount of insurance, whichever is less. However, in applying the percentages specified in (iii) and (iv) of this subsection, no adjusted premium shall be deemed to exceed four percent of the amount of insurance or level amount equivalent to the amount of insurance. The date of issue of a policy for the purpose of this section shall be the date as of which the rated age of the insured is determined.

B. The equivalent uniform amount of a policy providing an amount of insurance varying with the duration of the policy is the level amount of insurance provided by an otherwise similar policy, containing the same endowment benefit or benefits, if any, issued at the same age and for the same term, the amount of which does not vary with duration and the benefits under which have the same present value at the date of issue as the benefits under the policy. However, for a policy providing a varying amount of insurance issued on the life of a child under age ten, the equivalent uniform amount may be computed as though the amount of insurance provided by the policy prior to the attainment of age ten were the amount provided by the policy at age ten.

C. The adjusted premiums for any policy providing term insurance benefits by a rider or a supplemental policy provision shall equal (i) the adjusted premiums for an otherwise similar policy issued at the same age without the term insurance benefits, increased, during the period for which premiums for the term insurance benefits are payable by (ii) the adjusted premiums for the term insurance. Items (i) and (ii) of this subsection shall be calculated separately and as specified in subsections A and B of this section. For the purposes of items (ii), (iii), and (iv) of subsection A of this section, the amount of insurance or equivalent uniform amount of insurance used in the calculation of the adjusted premiums referred to in item (ii) of this subsection shall equal the excess of the corresponding amount determined for the entire policy over the amount used in the calculation of the adjusted premiums in item (i) of this subsection. (Code 1950, § 38-379; 1952, c. 317, § 38.1-464; 1962, c. 562; 1982, c. 228; 1986, c. 562.)

§ 38.2-3206. Same; tables used for calculations. — Except as otherwise provided in §§ 38.2-3207 and 38.2-3208, all adjusted premiums and present values referred to in §§ 38.2-3202 through 38.2-3205 shall for all policies of ordinary insurance be calculated on the basis of the Commissioners 1941 Standard Ordinary Mortality Table. However, for any category of ordinary insurance issued on female risks, adjusted premiums and present values may be calculated according to an age not more than three years younger than the actual age of the insured and the calculations for all policies of industrial insurance shall be made on the basis of the 1941 Standard Industrial Mortality Table. All calculations shall be made on the basis of the rate of interest, not exceeding $3^1/_2$ percent per year, specified in the policy for calculating cash surrender values and paid-up nonforfeiture benefits. However, in calculating the present value of any paid-up term insurance with any accompanying pure endowment, if any, offered as a nonforfeiture benefit, the rates of mortality assumed may be not more than 130 percent of the rates of mortality according to the applicable table. For insurance issued on a substandard basis, the calculation of any adjusted premiums and present values may be based on any other table of mortality specified by the insurer and approved by the Commission. (Code 1950, § 38-380; 1952, c. 317, § 38.1-465; 1959, Ex. Sess., c. 43; 1962, c. 562; 1982, c. 228; 1986, c. 562.)

§ 38.2-3207. Same; use of new mortality table; ordinary policies. — The provisions of this section shall not apply to ordinary policies issued on or after the operative date as defined in § 38.2-3209. In the case of ordinary policies issued on or after the operative date of § 38.2-3215, all adjusted premiums and present values referred to in §§ 38.2-3202 through 38.2-3205 shall be calculated on the basis of the Commissioners 1958 Standard Ordinary Mortality Table and the rate of interest specified in the policy for calculating cash surrender values and paid-up nonforfeiture benefits. However, the rate of interest shall not exceed (i) $3^1/_2$ percent per year for policies issued before July 1, 1975, (ii) four percent per year for policies issued on or after July 1, 1975, and prior to July 1, 1979, and (iii) $5^1/_2$ percent per year for policies issued on or after July 1, 1979. Notwithstanding the foregoing provisions of this section, the rate of interest for any single premium whole life or endowment insurance policy issued on or after July 1, 1979, may be a rate not exceeding $6^1/_2$ percent per year. For any category of ordinary insurance issued on female risks, adjusted premiums and present values may be calculated according to an age not more than six years younger than the actual age of the insured. In calculating the present value of any paid-up term insurance with any accompanying pure endowment offered as a nonforfeiture benefit, the rates of mortality assumed may be not more than those shown in the Commissioners 1958 Extended Term Insurance Table. For insurance issued on a substandard basis the calculation of any adjusted premiums and present values may be based on any other table of mortality specified by the insurer and approved by the Commission. (1959, Ex. Sess., c. 43, § 38.1-465.1; 1975, c. 215; 1979, c. 437; 1982, c. 228; 1986, c. 562.)

§ 38.2-3208. Same; industrial policies. — The provisions of this section shall not apply to industrial policies issued on or after the operative date as defined in § 38.2-3209. For industrial policies issued on or after the operative date of § 38.2-3216, all adjusted premiums and present values referred to in §§ 38.2-3202 through 38.2-3205 shall be calculated on the basis of the Commissioners 1961 Standard Industrial Mortality Table and the rate of interest specified in the policy for calculating cash surrender values and paid-up nonforfeiture benefits. However, the rate of interest shall not exceed (i) $3^1/_2$ percent per year for policies issued before July 1, 1975, (ii) four percent per year for policies issued on or after July 1, 1975, and prior to July 1, 1979, and (iii) $5^1/_2$ percent per year for policies issued on or after July 1, 1979. Notwithstanding the foregoing provisions of this section, the rate of interest for any single premium whole life or endowment insurance policy issued on or after July 1, 1979, may be a rate not exceeding $6^1/_2$ percent per year. In calculating the present value of any paid-up term insurance with any accompanying pure endowment offered as a nonforfeiture benefit, the rates of mortality assumed may be not more than those shown in the Commissioners 1961 Industrial Extended Term Insurance Table. For insurance issued on a substandard basis, the calculations of any adjusted premiums and present values may be based on any other table of mortality specified by the insurer and approved by the Commission. (1962, c. 562, § 38.1-465.2; 1975, c. 215; 1979, c. 437; 1982, c. 228; 1986, c. 562.)

§ 38.2-3209. Same; adjusted premiums for policies. — A. This section shall apply to all policies issued on or after the operative date as defined in this section. Except as provided in subsection G of this section, the adjusted premiums for any policy shall be calculated on an annual basis and shall be a uniform percentage of the respective premiums specified in the policy for each policy year, excluding amounts payable as extra premiums to cover impairments or special hazards and also excluding any uniform annual contract charge or policy fee specified in the policy in a statement of the method to be used in calculating the cash surrender values and paid-up nonforfeiture benefits, so that the present value at the date of issue of the policy of all adjusted premiums shall equal the sum of (i) the then present value of the future guaranteed benefits provided for by the policy; (ii) 1 percent of either the amount of insurance, if the insurance is uniform in amount, or the average amount of insurance at the beginning of each of the first 10 policy years; and (iii) 125 percent of the nonforfeiture net level premium as defined in subsection B of this section. However, in applying the percentage specified in (iii) of this subsection no nonforfeiture net level premium shall be deemed to exceed four percent of either the amount of insurance, if the insurance is uniform in amount, or the average amount of insurance at the beginning of each of the first ten policy years. The date of issue of a policy for the purpose of this section shall be the date as of which the rated age of the insured is determined.

B. The nonforfeiture net level premium shall equal the present value, at the date of issue of the policy, of the guaranteed benefits provided for by the policy divided by the present value, at the date of issue of the policy, of an annual annuity of one dollar payable on the date of issue of the policy and on each anniversary of the policy on which a premium falls due.

C. For a policy that provides, on a basis guaranteed in the policy, unscheduled changes in benefits or premiums, or both, or that provides an option for changes in benefits or premiums, or both, other than a change to a new policy, the adjusted premiums and present values shall initially be calculated on the assumption that future benefits and premiums do not change from those stipulated at the date of issue of the policy. At the time of any change in the benefits or premiums, the future adjusted premiums, nonforfeiture net level premiums and present values shall be recalculated on the assumption that future benefits and premiums do not change from those stipulated by the policy immediately after the change.

D. Except as otherwise provided in subsection G of this section, the recalculated future adjusted premiums for any policy referred to in subsection C of this section shall be a uniform percentage of the respective future premiums specified in the policy for each policy year, excluding amounts payable as extra premiums to cover impairments and special hazards, and also excluding any uniform annual contract charge or policy fee specified in the policy in a statement of the method to be used in calculating the cash surrender values and paid-up nonforfeiture benefits, so that the present value at the time of change to the newly defined benefits or premiums of all future adjusted premiums shall equal the excess of (1) over (2), where (1) is (i) the then present value of the then future guaranteed benefits provided for by the policy plus (ii) any additional expense allowance and (2) is the then cash surrender value, if any, or present value of any paid-up nonforfeiture benefit under the policy.

E. The additional expense allowance, at the time of the change to the newly defined benefits or premiums, shall be the sum of (i) 1 percent of the excess, if positive, of the average amount of insurance at the beginning of each of the first 10 policy years after the change over the average amount of insurance before the change at the beginning of each of the first 10 policy years after the time of the most recent previous change, or, if there has been no previous change, the date of issue of the policy and (ii) 125 percent of the increase, if positive, in the nonforfeiture net level premium.

F. The recalculated nonforfeiture net level premium shall equal (1) divided by (2), where (1) is the sum of (i) the nonforfeiture net level premium applicable before the change times the present value of an annual annuity of one dollar payable on each anniversary of the policy on or after the date of the change on which a premium would have fallen due had the change not occurred, and (ii) the present value of the increase in future guaranteed benefits provided by the policy, and (2) is the present value of an annual annuity of one dollar payable on each anniversary of the policy on or after the date of change on which a premium falls due.

G. Notwithstanding any other provisions of this section, for a policy issued on a substandard basis that provides reduced graded amounts of insurance so that, in each policy year, the policy has the same tabular mortality cost as an otherwise similar policy issued on the standard basis that provides higher uniform amounts of insurance, adjusted premiums and present values for the substandard policy may be calculated as if it were issued to provide the higher uniform amounts of insurance on the standard basis.

H. All adjusted premiums and present values referred to in §§ 38.2-3202 through 38.2-3213 shall for all policies of ordinary insurance be calculated on the basis of (i) the Commissioners 1980 Standard Ordinary Mortality Table or (ii) at the election of the insurer for any one or more specified plans of life insurance, the Commissioners 1980 Standard Ordinary Mortality Table with Ten-Year Select Mortality Factors. The premiums and values shall for all policies of industrial insurance be calculated on the basis of the Commissioners 1961 Standard Industrial Mortality Table. The premiums and values shall for all policies issued in a particular calendar year be calculated on the basis of a rate of interest not exceeding the nonforfeiture interest rate as defined in this section for policies issued in that calendar year, provided that:

1. At the insurer's option, calculations for all policies issued in a particular calendar year may be made on the basis of a rate of interest not exceeding the nonforfeiture interest rate, as defined in this section, for policies issued in the immediately preceding calendar year;

2. Under any paid-up nonforfeiture benefit, including any paid-up dividend additions, any cash surrender value available, whether or not required by § 38.2-3202, shall be calculated on the basis of the mortality table and rate of interest used in determining the amount of the paid-up nonforfeiture benefit and any paid-up dividend additions;

3. An insurer may calculate the amount of any guaranteed paid-up nonforfeiture benefit, including any paid-up additions, under the policy on the basis of an interest rate no lower than that specified in the policy for calculating cash surrender values;

4. In calculating the present value of any paid-up term insurance with any accompanying pure endowment offered as a nonforfeiture benefit, the rates of mortality assumed may be not more than those shown in the Commissioners 1980 Extended Term Insurance Table for policies of ordinary insurance and not more than the Commissioners 1961 Industrial Extended Term Insurance Table for policies of industrial insurance;

5. For insurance issued on a substandard basis, the calculation of any adjusted premiums and present values may be based on appropriate modifications of the tables referred to in this section;

6. Any ordinary mortality tables adopted after 1980 by the National Association of Insurance Commissioners and approved by the Commission for use in determining the minimum nonforfeiture standard may be substituted for the Commissioners 1980 Standard Ordinary Mortality Table with or without Ten-Year Select Mortality Factors or for the Commissioners 1980 Extended Term Insurance Table; and

7. Any industrial mortality tables adopted after 1980 by the National Association of Insurance Commissioners and approved by the Commission for use in determining the minimum nonforfeiture standard may be substituted for the Commissioners 1961 Standard Industrial Mortality Table or the Commissioners 1961 Industrial Extended Term Insurance Table.

I. The nonforfeiture annual interest rate for any policy issued in a particular calendar year shall equal 125 percent of the calendar year statutory valuation interest rate for the policy as defined in §§ 38.2-3130 through 38.2-3142, rounded to the nearest one-quarter percent.

J. Any refiling of nonforfeiture values or their methods of computation for any previously approved policy form that involves only a change in the interest

450

rate or mortality table used to compute nonforfeiture values shall not require refiling of any other provisions of that policy form.

K. After July 1, 1982, any insurer may file with the Commission a written notice of its election to comply with the provisions of this section after a specified date before January 1, 1989, which shall be the operative date of this section for that insurer. If an insurer makes no election, the operative date of this section for that insurer shall be January 1, 1989. (1982, c. 228, § 38.1-465.3; 1986, c. 562.)

§ 38.2-3210. Same; life insurance providing future premium determination. — For any plan of life insurance providing for future premium determination, the amounts of which are to be determined by the insurer based on then estimates of future experience, or for any plan of life insurance for which minimum values cannot be determined by the methods described in §§ 38.2-3202 through 38.2-3209, then:

1. The Commission shall be satisfied that the benefits provided under the plan are substantially as favorable to policyholders and insureds as the minimum benefits otherwise required by §§ 38.2-3202 through 38.2-3209;

2. The Commission shall be satisfied that the benefits and the pattern of premiums of the plan are not misleading to prospective policyholders or insureds; and

3. The cash surrender values and paid-up nonforfeiture benefits provided by the plan shall not be less than the minimum values and benefits required for the plan computed by a method consistent with the principles of §§ 38.2-3202 through 38.2-3213, as determined by the Commission. (1982, c. 228, § 38.1-465.4; 1986, c. 562.)

§ 38.2-3211. Same; other factors in calculations. — A. Any cash surrender value and any paid-up nonforfeiture benefit available under any life insurance policy issued on or after the operative date stated in § 38.2-3214 in the event of default in a premium payment due at any time other than on the policy anniversary, shall be calculated with allowance for the lapse of time and the payment of fractional premiums beyond the last preceding policy anniversary. All values referred to in §§ 38.2-3203 through 38.2-3209 may be calculated upon the assumption that any death benefit is payable at the end of the policy year of death. The net value of any paid-up additions, other than paid-up term additions, shall at least equal the amounts used to provide these additions.

B. 1. Notwithstanding the provisions of § 38.2-3203, additional benefits payable in the following cases and premiums for them shall be disregarded in ascertaining cash surrender values and nonforfeiture benefits required by §§ 38.2-3202 through 38.2-3216:

a. Death or dismemberment by accident or accidental means;

b. Total and permanent disability;

c. Reversionary annuity or deferred reversionary annuity benefits;

d. Term insurance benefits provided by a rider or supplemental policy provision to which, if issued as a separate policy, this section would not apply;

e. Term insurance on the life of a child or on the lives of children provided in a policy on the life of a parent of the child, if the term insurance expires before the child's age is twenty-six, is uniform in amount after the child's age is one, and has not become paid-up by reason of the death of a parent of the child; and

f. Other policy benefits additional to life insurance and endowment benefits.

2. No additional benefits shall be required to be included in any paid-up

nonforfeiture benefits. (Code 1950, § 38-381; 1952, c. 317, § 38.1-466; 1959, Ex. Sess., c. 43; 1962, c. 562; 1982, c. 228; 1986, c. 562.)

§ 38.2-3212. Same; policies issued on or after January 1, 1986. — A. This section, in addition to all other applicable sections of law, shall apply to all policies issued on or after January 1, 1986. Any cash surrender value available under the policy in the event of default in a premium payment due on any policy anniversary shall not differ by more than two-tenths percent of either (i) the amount of insurance, if the insurance is uniform in amount, or (ii) the average amount of insurance at the beginning of each of the first ten policy years, from the sum of (i) the greater of zero and the basic cash value specified in this section and (ii) the present value of any existing paid-up additions less the amount of any indebtedness to the insurer under the policy.

B. The basic cash value shall equal the present value on that anniversary of the future guaranteed benefits that would have been provided for by the policy, excluding any existing paid-up additions and before deduction of any indebtedness to the insurer, if there had been no default, less the then present value of the nonforfeiture factors, as defined in this section, corresponding to premiums that would have fallen due on and after that anniversary. However, the effects on the basic cash value of supplemental life insurance or annuity benefits or of family coverage, as described in § 38.2-3203 or § 38.2-3205, whichever applies, shall be the same as the effects specified in § 38.2-3203 or § 38.2-3205, whichever applies, on the cash surrender values defined in those sections.

C. 1. The nonforfeiture factor for each policy year shall equal a percentage of the adjusted premium for the policy year, as defined in § 38.2-3205 or § 38.2-3209, whichever applies. Except as required by subdivision 2 of this subsection, such percentage:

a. Shall be the same percentage for each policy year between the second policy anniversary and the later of (i) the fifth policy anniversary and (ii) the first policy anniversary at which there is available under the policy a cash surrender value in an amount, before including any paid-up additions and before deducting any indebtedness, of at least two-tenths percent of either the amount of insurance, if the insurance is uniform in amount, or the average amount of insurance at the beginning of each of the first ten policy years; and

b. Shall be such that no percentage after the later of the two policy anniversaries specified in subdivision 1 a of this subsection may apply to fewer than five consecutive policy years.

2. No basic cash value shall be less than the value that would be obtained if the adjusted premiums for the policy, as defined in § 38.2-3205 or § 38.2-3209, whichever applies, were substituted for the nonforfeiture factors in the calculation of the basic cash value.

D. All adjusted premiums and present values referred to in this section shall for a particular policy be calculated on the same mortality and interest bases used in demonstrating the policy's compliance with the other sections of this article. The cash surrender values referred to in this section shall include any endowment benefits provided for by the policy.

E. Any cash surrender value available other than in the event of default in a premium payment due on a policy anniversary, and the amount of any paid-up nonforfeiture benefit available under the policy in the event of default in a premium payment, shall be determined by a method consistent with the methods specified for determining the analogous minimum amounts in §§ 38.2-3202 through 38.2-3204, 38.2-3209 and 38.2-3211. The amounts of any cash surrender values and of any paid-up nonforfeiture benefits granted in connection with additional benefits, such as those listed as B1 a through B1 f in § 38.2-3211, shall conform with the principles of this section. (1982, c. 228, § 38.1-466.1; 1986, c. 562.)

§ 38.2-3213. Same; exemptions from application of certain sections.
— A. Sections 38.2-3202 through 38.2-3212 shall not apply to any:
1. Certificates of fraternal benefit societies;
2. Reinsurance;
3. Group insurance;
4. Pure endowments;
5. Annuities or reversionary annuity contracts;
6. Term policies of uniform amount (i) that provide no guaranteed nonforfeiture or endowment benefits, or renewal thereof; (ii) that are of twenty years or less expiring before age seventy-one; and (iii) for which uniform premiums are payable during the entire term of the policy;
7. Term policies of decreasing amount (i) that provide no guaranteed nonforfeiture or endowment benefits; (ii) on which each adjusted premium calculated as specified in §§ 38.2-3205 through 38.2-3209 is less than the adjusted premium calculated on term policies of uniform amount, or renewal thereof; (iii) that provide no guaranteed nonforfeiture or endowment benefits; (iv) that are issued at the same age and for the same initial amounts of insurance and for terms of twenty years or less expiring before age seventy-one; and (v) for which uniform premiums are payable during the entire term of the policy;
8. Policies (i) that provide no guaranteed nonforfeiture or endowment benefits and (ii) for which any cash surrender value or present value of any paid-up nonforfeiture benefit at the beginning of any policy year, calculated as specified in §§ 38.2-3203 through 38.2-3209, does not exceed $2^1/_2\%$ of the amount of insurance at the beginning of the same policy year; or
9. Policies delivered outside this Commonwealth through an agent or other representative of the insurer issuing the policy.
B. For purposes of determining the applicability of §§ 38.2-3202 through 38.2-3216, the age at expiry for a joint term life insurance policy shall be the age at expiry of the oldest life. (Code 1950, § 38-382; 1952, c. 317, § 38.1-467; 1962, c. 562; 1982, c. 228; 1986, c. 562.)

§ 38.2-3214. Same; operative date. — After March 17, 1948, any insurer may file with the Commission a written notice of its election to comply with the provisions of §§ 38.2-3202 through 38.2-3213 after a specified date before April 1, 1948. After the filing of the notice upon the specified date, which shall be the operative date for that insurer, the sections shall become operative with respect to the policies thereafter issued by that insurer. If an insurer makes no election, the operative date for the insurer shall be April 1, 1948. The Commission, for good cause shown by any insurer, may extend the operative date for that insurer to not later than January 1, 1949. (Code 1950, § 38-383; 1952, c. 317, § 38.1-468; 1986, c. 562.)

§ 38.2-3215. Same; operative date for § 38.2-3207. — After July 1, 1959, any insurer may file with the Commission a written notice of its election to comply with the provisions of § 38.2-3207 after a specified date before January 1, 1966. After the filing of the notice, then upon the specified date, which shall be the operative date of this section for the insurer, § 38.2-3207 shall become operative with respect to the ordinary policies thereafter issued by that insurer. If an insurer makes no such election, the operative date of § 38.2-3207 for the insurer shall be January 1, 1966. (1959, Ex. Sess., c. 43, § 38.1-468.1; 1986, c. 562.)

§ 38.2-3216. Same; operative date for § 38.2-3208. — After July 1, 1962, any insurer may file with the Commission a written notice of its election to comply with the provisions of § 38.2-3208 after a specified date before January

1, 1968. After the filing of the notice, then upon the specified date, which shall be the operative date of this section for the insurer, § 38.2-3208 shall become operative with respect to the industrial policies thereafter issued by that insurer. If an insurer makes no election, the operative date of § 38.2-3208 for the insurer shall be January 1, 1968. (1962, c. 562, § 38.1-468.2; 1986, c. 562.)

§ **38.2-3217. Loan provisions in policies issued prior to operative date stated in § 38.2-3214.** — For those policies issued prior to the operative date stated in § 38.2-3214, the loan value referred to in former § 38.1-397 shall be the reserve at the end of the current policy year on the policy and on any dividend additions to the policy, exclusive of the reserve on account of return premium insurance and of total and permanent disability and additional accidental death benefits, less a sum not more than $2^1/_2$ percent of the amount insured by the policy and of any dividend additions to the policy. The policy shall specify the mortality table and rates of interest adopted for computing the reserve. The policy may further provide that the loan may be deferred for up to three months after the application for the loan is made. Instead of permitting the deduction from a loan on the policy of a sum not more than $2^1/_2$ percent of the amount insured by the policy and of any dividend additions to the policy, an insurer may insert in the policy a provision that one-fifth of the reserve may be deducted in case of a loan under the policy, or may provide in the policy that the deduction may be $2^1/_2$ percent of the amount insured by the policy or one-fifth of the reserve, at the insurer's option. (Code 1950, § 38-384; 1952, c. 317, § 38.1-469; 1986, c. 562.)

§ **38.2-3218. Same; in policies subsequently issued.** — For policies issued on or after the operative date stated in § 38.2-3214, the loan value referred to in former § 38.1-397 or § 38.2-3308, whichever applies, shall be the cash surrender value at the end of the current policy year required by § 38.2-3202. The insurer shall have the right to defer for up to six months after application for the loan is made a loan on the policy, except when made to pay premiums to the insurer. (Code 1950, § 38-385; 1952, c. 317, § 38.1-470; 1986, c. 562.)

§ **38.2-3219. Applicability.** — Sections 38.2-3220 through 38.2-3229 shall not apply to any (i) reinsurance; (ii) group annuity purchased under a retirement plan or plan of deferred compensation established or maintained by an employer, including a partnership or sole proprietorship, or by an employee organization, or by both, other than a plan providing individual retirement accounts or individual retirement annuities under § 408 of the Internal Revenue Code, as amended; (iii) premium deposit fund; (iv) variable annuity; (v) investment annuity; (vi) immediate annuity; (vii) deferred annuity contract after annuity payments have commenced; (viii) reversionary annuity; (ix) modified guaranteed annuity; or (x) contract delivered outside this Commonwealth through an agent or other representative of the insurer issuing the contract. (1979, c. 437, § 38.1-470.1; 1986, c. 562; 1992, c. 210.)

§ **38.2-3220. Nonforfeiture requirements.** — A. For contracts issued on or after the operative date as defined in § 38.2-3229, no contract of annuity, except as stated in § 38.2-3219, shall be delivered or issued for delivery in this Commonwealth unless it contains in substance the following provisions and statements, or corresponding provisions and statements that in the opinion of the Commission are at least as favorable to the contract holder, upon cessation of payment of consideration under the contract:
1. That upon cessation of payment of considerations under a contract, the insurer will grant a paid-up annuity benefit on a plan stipulated in the contract of the value specified in §§ 38.2-3222 through 38.2-3225 and 38.2-3227.

2. If a contract provides for a lump sum settlement at maturity or at any other time, a provision that upon surrender of the contract at or before the beginning of any annuity payments, the insurer will pay instead of any paid-up annuity benefits a cash surrender benefit of the amount specified in §§ 38.2-3222, 38.2-3223, 38.2-3225 and 38.2-3227. The insurer shall reserve the right to defer the payment of the cash surrender benefit for up to six months after demand for payment with surrender of the contract.

3. A statement of the mortality table and interest rates used in calculating any minimum paid-up annuity, cash surrender or death benefits that are guaranteed under the contract, together with sufficient information to determine the amounts of those benefits.

4. That any paid-up annuity, cash surrender or death benefits that may be available under the contract are not less than the minimum benefits required by any statute of the state in which the contract is delivered and an explanation of how the existence of any additional amounts credited by the insurer to the contract, any indebtedness to the insurer on the contract or any prior withdrawals from or partial surrenders of the contract affects the benefits.

B. Notwithstanding the requirements of this subsection, any deferred annuity contract may provide that if no considerations have been received under a contract for a period of two full years and the portion of the paid-up annuity benefit at maturity on the plan stipulated in the contract arising from considerations paid prior to that period would be less than twenty dollars monthly, the insurer may at its option terminate the contract by payment in cash of the then present value of the portion of the paid-up annuity benefit, calculated on the basis of the mortality table, if any, and interest rate specified in the contract for determining the paid-up annuity benefit. This payment shall relieve the insurer of any further obligation under the contract. (1979, c. 437, § 38.1-470.1; 1986, c. 562.)

§ **38.2-3221. Minimum values.** — The minimum values specified in §§ 38.2-3222 through 38.2-3225 and 38.2-3227 of any paid-up annuity, cash surrender or death benefits available under an annuity contract shall be based upon the minimum nonforfeiture amounts defined in this section.

A. 1. For contracts providing for flexible considerations, the minimum nonforfeiture amount at or any time before the beginning of any annuity payments shall equal an accumulation up to that time at an annual rate of interest of three percent of percentages of the net considerations as defined in this section, paid prior to that time, increased by an existing additional amount credited by the insurer to the contract and decreased by the sum of:

a. Any prior withdrawals from or partial surrenders of the contract accumulated at a rate of interest of three percent per year; and

b. The amount of any indebtedness to the insurer on the contract, including interest due and accrued.

2. The net considerations for a given contract year used to define the minimum nonforfeiture amount shall be not less than zero and shall equal the corresponding gross considerations credited to the contract during that contract year less an annual contract charge of thirty dollars and less a collection charge of one dollar and twenty-five cents per consideration credited to the contract during that contract year. The percentages of net considerations shall be sixty-five percent of the net consideration for the first contract year and $87^1/_2$ percent of the net considerations for the second and later contract years. Notwithstanding the provisions of the preceding sentence, the percentage shall be sixty-five percent of the portion of the total net consideration for any renewal contract year that exceeds by not more than two times the sum of those portions of the net considerations in all prior contract years for which the percentage was sixty-five percent.

B. For contracts providing for fixed scheduled considerations, minimum nonforfeiture amounts shall be calculated on the assumption that considerations are paid annually in advance and shall be the same as for contracts with flexible considerations that are paid annually with two exceptions:

1. The portion of the net consideration for the first contract year to be accumulated shall be the sum of sixty-five percent of the net consideration for the first contract year plus $22^1/_2$ percent of the excess of the net consideration for the first contract year over the lesser of the net considerations for the second and third contract years.

2. The annual contract charge shall be the lesser of (i) thirty dollars or (ii) ten percent of the gross annual consideration.

C. For contracts providing for a single consideration, minimum nonforfeiture amounts shall be the same as for contracts with flexible considerations except that the percentage of net consideration used to determine the minimum nonforfeiture amount shall equal ninety percent, and the net consideration shall be the gross consideration less a contract charge of seventy-five dollars. (1979, c. 437, § 38.1-470.1; 1986, c. 562.)

§ **38.2-3222. Computation of present value.** — Any paid-up annuity benefit available under a contract shall be such that its present value on the date annuity payments are to commence at least equals the minimum nonforfeiture amount on that date. The present value shall be computed using the mortality table, if any, and the interest rate specified in the contract for determining the minimum paid-up annuity benefits guaranteed in the contract. (1979, c. 437, § 38.1-470.1; 1986, c. 562.)

§ **38.2-3223. Calculation of cash surrender values.** — For contracts that provide cash surrender benefits, the cash surrender benefits available before maturity shall not be less than the present value as of the date of surrender of that portion of the maturity value of the paid-up annuity benefit that would be provided under the contract at maturity arising from considerations paid before the time of cash surrender, reduced by the amount appropriate to reflect any prior withdrawals from or partial surrenders of the contract. The present value shall be calculated on the basis of an interest rate not more than one percent higher than the interest rate specified in the contract for accumulating the net considerations to determine the maturity value, decreased by the amount of any indebtedness to the insurer on the contract, including interest due and accrued, and increased by any existing additional amounts credited by the insurer to the contract. In no event shall any cash surrender benefit be less than the minimum nonforfeiture amount at that time. The death benefit under such contracts shall at least equal the cash surrender benefit. (1979, c. 437, § 38.1-470.1; 1986, c. 562.)

§ **38.2-3224. Calculation of paid-up annuity benefits.** — For contracts that do not provide cash surrender benefits, the present value of any paid-up annuity benefit available as a nonforfeiture option at any time prior to maturity shall not be less than the present value of that portion of the maturity value of the paid-up annuity benefit provided under the contract arising from considerations paid before the time the contract is surrendered in exchange for, or changed to, a deferred paid-up annuity. The present value shall be calculated for the period before the maturity date on the basis of the interest rate specified in the contract for accumulating the net considerations to determine the maturity value, and increased by any existing additional amounts credited by the insurer to the contract. For contracts that do not provide any death benefits before the beginning of any annuity payments, the present values shall be calculated on the basis of the interest rate and the mortality table specified in the contract for determining the maturity value of the paid-up annuity benefit. In no event shall the present value of a paid-up annuity benefit be less than the minimum nonforfeiture amount at that time. (1979, c. 437, § 38.1-470.1; 1986, c. 562.)

§ 38.2-3225. Maturity date. — For the purpose of determining the benefits calculated under §§ 38.2-3223 and 38.2-3224 for annuity contracts under which an election may be made to have annuity payments commence at optional maturity dates, the maturity date shall be deemed to be the latest date for which election is permitted by the contract, but shall not be deemed to be later than the anniversary of the contract next following the annuitant's seventieth birthday or the tenth anniversary of the contract, whichever is later. (1979, c. 437, § 38.1-470.1; 1986, c. 562.)

§ 38.2-3226. Disclosure of limited death benefits. — Any contract that does not provide cash surrender benefits or does not provide death benefits at least equal to the minimum nonforfeiture amount before the beginning of any annuity payments shall include a statement in a prominent place in the contract that those benefits are not provided. (1979, c. 437, § 38.1-470.1; 1986, c. 562.)

§ 38.2-3227. Inclusion of lapse of time considerations. — Any paid-up annuity, cash surrender or death benefits available at any time, other than on the contract anniversary under any contract with fixed scheduled considerations, shall be calculated with allowance for a lapse of time and the payment of any scheduled considerations beyond the beginning of the contract year in which cessation of payment of considerations under the contract occurs. (1979, c. 437, § 38.1-470.1; 1986, c. 562.)

§ 38.2-3228. Proration of values; additional benefits. — For any contract that provides, within the same contract by rider or supplemental contract provision, both annuity benefits and life insurance benefits that are in excess of the greater of cash surrender benefits or a return of the gross considerations with interest, the minimum nonforfeiture benefits shall equal the sum of the minimum nonforfeiture benefits for the annuity portion and any minimum nonforfeiture benefits for the life insurance portion computed as if each portion were a separate contract. Notwithstanding the provisions of §§ 38.2-3222 through 38.2-3225 and 38.2-3227, additional benefits payable (i) in the event of total and permanent disability, (ii) as reversionary annuity or deferred reversionary annuity benefits, or (iii) as other policy benefits additional to life insurance, endowment and annuity benefits, and considerations for all the additional benefits, shall be disregarded in ascertaining the minimum nonforfeiture amounts, paid-up annuity, cash surrender and death benefits that may be required by this article. The inclusion of these additional benefits shall not be required in any paid-up benefits, unless the additional benefits separately would require minimum nonforfeiture amounts, paid-up annuity, cash surrender and death benefits. (1979, c. 437, § 38.1-470.1; 1986, c. 562.)

§ 38.2-3229. Effective date. — After July 1, 1979, any insurer may file with the Commission a written notice of its election to comply with the provisions of §§ 38.2-3219 through 38.2-3229 after a specified date before July 1, 1981. The date specified in the notice shall be the operative date for that insurer in complying with the requirements of §§ 38.2-3219 through 38.2-3229 which shall apply to annuity contracts thereafter issued by that insurer. The operative date for insurers making no election shall be July 1, 1981. (1979, c. 437, § 38.1-470.1; 1986, c. 562.)

CHAPTER 33.

LIFE INSURANCE POLICIES.

ARTICLE 1.

Life Insurance Policies; Annuities.

§ 38.2-3300. Requirements; exceptions. — A. No individual life insurance policy shall be delivered or issued for delivery in this Commonwealth unless it contains in substance all of the requirements prescribed in §§ 38.2-3301 through 38.2-3315 of this article.

B. As used in this article, *"individual life insurance"* means any life insurance other than group life insurance, industrial life insurance, annuities, credit life insurance, and pure endowments, with or without return of premiums or of premiums and interest. However, for the purposes of § 38.2-3308, *"policy"* includes annuity contracts that provide for policy loans and certificates issued by a fraternal benefit society.

C. The requirements of §§ 38.2-3300 through 38.2-3315 shall not apply to policies of reinsurance or to policies issued or granted in exchange for lapsed or surrendered policies. (Code 1950, §§ 38-371, 38-373; 1952, c. 317, §§ 38.1-390, 38.1-405; 1977, c. 174; 1986, c. 562.)

Law Review. — For survey of Virginia law on insurance for the year 1969-1970, see 56 Va. L. Rev. 1356 (1970).

§ 38.2-3301. Ten-day right to examine policy. — No individual life insurance policy shall be delivered or issued for delivery in this Commonwealth unless it has printed on it a notice stating in substance that if, during a ten-day period from the date the policy is delivered to the policyowner, the policy is surrendered to the insurer or its agent with a written request for cancellation, the policy shall be void from the beginning and the insurer shall refund any premium paid for the policy. Nothing in this section shall prohibit an insurer from extending the right to examine period to more than ten days if the period is specified in the policy. (1977, c. 174, § 38.1-390.1; 1986, c. 562.)

Defining delivery and issuance to be distinct events in no way interferes with the requirement of this section that an insured be given at least ten days to rescind the policy after its delivery. Anderson v. Primerica Life Ins., Co., 934 F. Supp. 188 (W.D. Va. 1996).

§ 38.2-3302. How premiums payable. — Each individual life insurance policy shall have a provision that all premiums after the first premium shall be payable in advance. (Code 1950, § 38-371(1); 1950, p. 179; 1952, c. 317, § 38.1-391; 1986, c. 562.)

§ 38.2-3303. Grace period. — A. Each individual life insurance policy shall contain a provision that the insured is entitled to a grace period of not less than thirty-one days within which the payment of any premium after the first premium may be made, subject at the insurer's option to an interest charge that is not to exceed six percent per year for the number of days of grace elapsing before the payment of the premium.

B. The provision shall also state that during the grace period the policy shall continue in full force, but if a claim arises under the policy during the grace period before the overdue premium or any overdue premium installment is paid, the amount of any earned overdue premium or installment through the policy month of death with interest may be deducted from any amount payable under the policy in settlement. The grace period shall start on the premium payment due date. (Code 1950, § 38-371(2); 1950, p. 179; 1952, c. 317, § 38.1-392; 1986, c. 562.)

§ 38.2-3304. Policy constitutes entire contract; statements deemed representations. — A. Each individual life insurance policy shall contain a provision that the policy, or the policy and the application for the policy if a copy of the application is endorsed upon or attached to the policy when issued or delivered, shall constitute the entire contract between the parties.

B. The provision shall also state that:

1. All statements made by the insured shall, in the absence of fraud, be deemed representations and not warranties; and

2. No statement shall be used in defense of a claim under the policy unless it is contained in a written application that is endorsed upon or attached to the policy when issued or delivered.

C. As used in this section, *"policy"* shall include any riders, endorsements or amendments. (Code 1950, § 38-371(3); 1950, p. 179; 1952, c. 317, § 38.1-393; 1986, c. 562; 1990, c. 223.)

Law Review. — For comment on fraud as a defense to insurance contracts, see 18 Wash. & Lee L. Rev. 172 (1961). For survey of Virginia law on insurance for the year 1969-1970, see 56 Va. L. Rev. 1356 (1970).

This section does not apply to false statements made by the beneficiary. Southland Life Ins. Co. v. Donati, 201 Va. 855, 114 S.E.2d 595 (1960).

Statements relied on to show fraud must

be endorsed on or attached to policy. — The defense of fraud in the procurement of the policy is not available to the insurance company if it omitted to endorse upon or attach to the policy when issued a copy of the statement or statements contained in the application made by the insured and relied upon by the insurer to establish the alleged fraud. Southland Life Ins. Co. v. Donati, 201 Va. 855, 114 S.E.2d 595 (1960).

§ 38.2-3305. Incontestability. — A. Each individual life insurance policy shall contain a provision that the policy shall be incontestable after it has been in force during the lifetime of the insured for two years from its date of issue except for nonpayment of premiums.

B. Provisions relating to benefits in event of disability, and provisions granting additional insurance specifically against death by accident or accidental means, may be excepted in the incontestability provision. (Code 1950, § 38-371(3); 1950, p. 179; 1952, c. 317, § 38.1-394; 1986, c. 562.)

Commencement of contestability period. — Where plaintiff asserted that policy became incontestable two years after the date on which her husband signed the application form and paid the first premium in advance, the clear language of this section and § 38.2-3107(A), and the clear language of the policy,

precluded use of plaintiff's starting point for the commencement of the contestability period. The contestability period in husband's policy began to run on the date on the receipt which was part of the policy. Parkerson v. Federal Home Life Ins. Co., 797 F. Supp. 1308 (E.D. Va. 1992).

§ 38.2-3306. Misstatement of age. — Each individual life insurance policy shall contain a provision that if, at any time before final settlement under the policy, the age of the insured, or the age of any other person if considered in determining the premium, is found to have been misstated, the amount payable under the policy shall equal the amount that the premium would have purchased at the insured's or other person's correct age at the time the policy was issued. (Code 1950, § 38-371(4); 1950, p. 179; 1952, c. 317, § 38.1-395; 1986, c. 562.)

§ 38.2-3307. Participation in surplus. — A. Each participating individual life insurance policy shall contain a provision that the policy shall participate in the surplus of the insurer. Any policy containing a provision for participation at the end of the first policy year, and annually thereafter, may also provide that each dividend shall be paid subject to the payment of the premiums for the next ensuing year. The policyowner under any annual dividend policy shall have the right each year to have the dividend arising from the participation paid in cash. If the policy provides other dividend options, it shall also state which of the options shall be effective if the insured does not elect any option on or before the expiration of the grace period allowed for the payment of the premium.

B. This section shall not apply to any form of paid-up insurance, temporary insurance, or pure endowment insurance, issued or granted in exchange for lapsed or surrendered policies. (Code 1950, § 38-371 (5); 1950, p. 180; 1952, c. 317, § 38.1-396; 1986, c. 562.)

§ **38.2-3308. Policy loans.** — A. Each individual life insurance policy shall contain a provision that after the policy has been in force three policy years the insurer shall at any time, while the policy is in force other than as extended term insurance, advance, on proper assignment or pledge of the policy and on the sole security of the policy, a sum equal to or, at the option of the policyowner, less than the amount required by § 38.2-3218, under the conditions specified by that section.

B. Each individual life insurance policy issued after July 1, 1975, and prior to July 1, 1981, shall contain only one of the following policy loan interest rate provisions:

1. A provision that a policy loan shall bear interest at a specified rate not exceeding eight percent per year; or

2. A provision that all loans under the policy, including outstanding loans, shall bear interest at a variable rate not exceeding eight percent per year, specified from time to time by the insurer. The effective date of any increase in the variable rate shall be not less than one year after the effective date of the establishment of the previous rate. If the interest rate is increased, the amount of the increase shall not exceed one percent per year. The variable rate may be decreased without restriction as to amount or frequency. With respect to policies providing for a variable rate, the insurer shall give notice of:

a. The variable rate currently effective when a loan is made and when notification of interest due is furnished;

b. Any increase in the variable rate at least thirty days before the effective date for any loans outstanding forty days before that date; and

c. The increase at the time a loan is made for any loans made during the forty days before the effective date of the increase. The notice shall be given as directed by the policyowner and any assignee as shown on the records of the insurer at its home office.

C. 1. Each individual life insurance policy issued after July 1, 1981, shall contain a policy loan interest rate provision permitting either:

a. A maximum fixed interest rate of not more than eight percent per year; or

b. An adjustable maximum interest rate established from time to time by the insurer as permitted by law.

2. The interest rate charged on a policy loan made under subdivision 1 b of this subsection shall not exceed the greater of:

a. The Published Monthly Average for the calendar month ending two months before the date on which the rate is determined; or

b. The rate used to compute the cash surrender values under the policy during the applicable period plus one percent per year.

3. For the purposes of this subsection, the "Published Monthly Average" means:

a. Moody's Corporate Bond Yield Average — Monthly Average Corporates as published by Moody's Investors Service, Inc., or any successor thereto; or

b. If the Moody's Corporate Bond Yield Average — Monthly Average Corporates is no longer published, a substantially similar average, established by regulation issued by the Commission.

4. If the maximum interest rate is determined pursuant to subdivision 1 b of this subsection, the policy shall contain a provision setting forth the frequency at which the rate is to be determined for that policy.

5. The maximum interest rate for each policy shall be determined at regular intervals at least once every twelve months, but not more frequently than once every three months. At the intervals specified in the policy:

a. The rate being charged may be increased whenever the increase as determined under subdivision 2 of this subsection would increase that rate by one-half percent or more per year;

b. The rate being charged shall be reduced whenever the reduction as determined under subdivision 2 of this subsection would decrease that rate by one-half percent or more per year.

6. The insurer shall:

a. Notify the policyowner at the time a cash loan is made of the initial interest rate;

b. Notify the policyowner of the initial interest rates on a premium loan as soon as it is reasonably practical to do so after making the loan. Notice need not be given to the policyowner when a further premium loan is added, except as provided in subdivision 6 c below;

c. Send reasonable advance notice of any increase in the rates to policyowners with loans; and

d. Include the substance of the pertinent provisions of subdivisions 1 and 4 of this subsection in the notices required above.

7. No policy shall terminate in a policy year as the sole result of a change in the interest rate during that policy year, and the insurer shall maintain coverage during that policy year until the time at which it would otherwise have terminated if there had been no change during that policy year.

8. The substance of the pertinent provisions of subdivisions 1 and 4 of this subsection shall be set forth in the policies to which they apply.

9. For the purposes of this section:

a. The interest rate on policy loans permitted under this section includes the interest rate charged on reinstatement of policy loans for the period during and after any lapse of a policy.

b. The term "policy loan" includes any premium loan made under a policy to pay one or more premiums that were not paid to the insurer as they fell due.

c. The term "policy" includes certificates issued by a fraternal benefit society and annuity contracts that provide for policy loans.

10. No other provision of law, including Chapter 7.3 (§ 6.1-330.49 et seq.) of Title 6.1, shall apply to policy loan interest rates unless made specifically applicable to the rates.

D. The insurer may deduct from the loan value any indebtedness not already deducted in determining the value of any unpaid balance of the premium for the current policy year and any interest that may be allowable on the loan to the end of the current policy year. The policy may further provide that if the interest on the loan is not paid when due, it shall be added to the existing loan and shall bear interest at the same rate.

E. A policy loan provision shall not be required in term insurance policies. (1981, c. 46, § 38.1-397.1; 1986, c. 562.)

§ 38.2-3309. Nonforfeiture benefits and cash surrender values. — A. Each individual life insurance policy shall contain a provision for nonforfeiture benefits. The provision shall specify the options to which the policyowner is entitled, in accordance with the requirements of § 38.2-3202.

B. Each individual life insurance policy shall have a provision for cash surrender values in accordance with the requirements of § 38.2-3203. (Code 1950, § 38-371(7), (8); 1950, p. 180; 1952, c. 317, § 38.1-398; 1986, c. 562.)

§ 38.2-3310. Table of values and options. — Each individual life insurance policy shall contain a table showing the loan values in figures, line by line. The table shall also show any options available under the policy each year upon default in premium payments, during at least the first twenty years of the policy or during the premium-paying period if it is less than twenty years. (Code 1950, § 38-371(9); 1950, p. 180; 1952, c. 317, § 38.1-399; 1986, c. 562.)

§ 38.2-3311. Reinstatement. — Each individual life insurance policy shall have a provision that in the event of default in premium payments, if (i) the value of the policy has been applied automatically to the purchase of other insurance as provided for in this article, (ii) the insurance is in force, and (iii) the original policy has not been surrendered to the insurer and cancelled, the policy may be reinstated within three years from default, upon:
1. Evidence of insurability satisfactory to the insurer;
2. Payment of premiums in arrears with interest at a rate not exceeding six percent per year payable annually; and
3. The payment or reinstatement of any other indebtedness to the insurer upon the policy, with interest at the rate set forth in the policy for the indebtedness. (Code 1950, § 38-371(10); 1950, p. 180; 1952, c. 317, § 38.1-400; 1986, c. 562.)

§ 38.2-3312. Settlement. — Each individual life insurance policy shall contain a provision that when a death claim arises under the policy, settlement shall be made upon receipt of due proof of death. (Code 1950, § 38-371(11); 1950, p. 181; 1952, c. 317, § 38.1-401; 1986, c. 562.)

§ 38.2-3313. Table of installments. — If an individual life insurance policy provides that the proceeds may be payable in installments that are determinable prior to the maturity of the policy, the policy shall have a table showing the guaranteed installments. (Code 1950, § 38-371(12); 1950, p. 181; 1952, c. 317, § 38.1-402; 1986, c. 562.)

§ 38.2-3314. Title. — Each individual life insurance policy shall have a title on its face that shall briefly and accurately describe the nature and form of the policy. (Code 1950, § 38-371(13); 1950, p. 181; 1952, c. 317, § 38.1-403; 1986, c. 562.)

The obvious purpose of this section is to require an insurance company to display on the face and on the back of a policy a description of its nature and form in order that a prospective purchaser may know what type of insurance he is purchasing. Such requirement is for the benefit of the prospective purchaser and he is entitled to rely on it. While it may not be strictly accurate to say that such an endorsement is a part of the contract of insurance, in construing the contract the policy must be considered as a whole and the endorsement read in connection with the remainder thereof, as an aid in arriving at the intention of the parties. Suggs v. Life Ins. Co., 207 Va. 7, 147 S.E.2d 707 (1966).

§ 38.2-3315. Variations for certain forms of policies; providing more favorable terms. — A. Any of the requirements of §§ 38.2-3300 through 38.2-3314 not applicable to single premium, nonparticipating, term, variable, or flexible premium life insurance policies shall to that extent, as approved by the Commission, be appropriately modified or not be incorporated in these policies.

B. Any individual life insurance policy that, in the opinion of the Commission, contains provisions more favorable to the policyholder than those required by §§ 38.2-3300 through 38.2-3314, may be delivered or issued for delivery in this Commonwealth after approval by the Commission. (Code 1950, § 38-372; 1952, c. 317, § 38.1-404; 1976, c. 562; 1986, c. 562.)

Omission of statutory provision. — An insurer issuing a policy without a provision reserving the right to contest for fraud incident to reinstatement, which provision was, at the time of the issuance of the policy, prescribed by statute, could not be heard to say that the provisions of the policy in that respect were not in the opinion of the State Corporation Commission more favorable than required by statute. Ambrose v. Acacia Mut. Life Ins. Co., 190 Va. 189, 56 S.E.2d 372 (1949).

§ 38.2-3316. Provisions prohibited. — No individual life insurance policy shall be delivered or issued for delivery in this Commonwealth if it contains any provision:

1. Limiting the time within which any action at law or in equity may be commenced to less than one year after the cause of action accrues;

2. For any mode of settlement at maturity, of less value than the amount insured on the face of the policy plus any dividend additions, less any indebtedness to the insurer on or secured by the policy, and less any premium or portion of any premium, that may by the terms of the policy be deducted. This paragraph shall not apply to any nonforfeiture provision that employs the cash value less any indebtedness to purchase paid-up or extended insurance, and shall not prohibit the issuance of policies providing for a limitation in the amount payable under certain specified conditions;

3. For forfeiture of the policy for failure to repay any loan on the policy, or to pay interest on any policy loan, while the total indebtedness on the policy, including interest, is less than the loan value of the policy; or

4. To the effect that the agent soliciting the insurance is the agent of the person insured under the policy, or making the acts or representations of the agent binding upon the person insured under the policy. (Code 1950, § 38-386; 1952, c. 317, § 38.1-406; 1956, c. 417; 1986, c. 562.)

§ 38.2-3317. Provisions required by other jurisdictions. — Individual life insurance policies issued by any foreign or alien insurer for delivery in this Commonwealth may contain any provision that is prescribed by the laws of its domiciliary jurisdiction and that is not in conflict with the laws of this Commonwealth. Policies issued by any domestic insurer for delivery in any other jurisdiction may contain any provision required by the laws of that jurisdiction. (Code 1950, § 38-387; 1952, c. 317, § 38.1-407; 1986, c. 562.)

ARTICLE 2.

Group Life Insurance Policies.

§ 38.2-3318: Repealed by Acts 1998, c. 154.

§ 38.2-3318.1. Group life insurance requirements. — Except as provided in § 38.2-3319.1, no policy of group life insurance shall be delivered in this Commonwealth unless it conforms to one of the following descriptions:

A. A policy issued to an employer, or to the trustees of a fund established by an employer, which employer or trustees shall be deemed the policyholder, to insure employees of the employer for the benefit of persons other than the employer, subject to the following requirements:

1. The employees eligible for insurance under the policy shall be all of the employees of the employer, or all of any class or classes thereof. The policy may provide that the term "employees" include:

a. The employees of one or more subsidiary corporations, and the employees, individual proprietors, and partners of one or more affiliated corporations, proprietorships or partnerships if the business of the employer and of such affiliated corporations, proprietorships, or partnerships is under common control;

b. The individual proprietor or partners if the employer is an individual proprietorship or partnership;

c. Retired employees, former employees and directors of a corporate employer; or

d. If the policy is issued to insure the employees of a public body, elected or appointed officials.

2. The premium for the policy shall be paid either from the employer's funds or from funds contributed by the insured employees, or from both. Except as provided in subdivision 3 of this subsection, a policy on which no part of the premium is to be derived from funds contributed by the insured employees must insure all eligible employees, except those who reject such coverage in writing.

3. An insurer may exclude or limit the coverage on any person as to whom evidence of individual insurability is not satisfactory to the insurer.

B. A policy which is:

1. Not subject to Chapter 37.1 (§ 38.2-3727 et seq.) of this title, and

2. Issued to a creditor or its parent holding company or to a trustee or trustees or agent designated by two or more creditors, which creditor, holding company, affiliate, trustee, trustees or agent shall be deemed the policyholder, to insure debtors of the creditor, or creditors, subject to the following requirements:

a. The debtors eligible for insurance under the policy shall be all of the debtors of the creditor or creditors, or all of any class or classes thereof. The policy may provide that the term "debtors" includes:

(1) Borrowers of money or purchasers or lessees of goods, services, or property for which payment is arranged through a credit transaction;

(2) The debtors of one or more subsidiary corporations; and

(3) The debtors of one or more affiliated corporations, proprietorships, or partnerships if the business of the policyholder and of such affiliated corporations, proprietorships, or partnerships is under common control.

b. The premium for the policy shall be paid either from the creditor's funds, or from charges collected from the insured debtors, or from both. Except as provided in subdivision 3 of this subsection, a policy on which no part of the premium is to be derived from the funds contributed by insured debtors specifically for their insurance must insure all eligible debtors.

3. An insurer may exclude any debtors as to whom evidence of individual insurability is not satisfactory to the insurer.

4. The amount of the insurance on the life of any debtor shall at no time exceed the greater of the scheduled or actual amount of unpaid indebtedness to the creditor.

5. The insurance may be payable to the creditor or any successor to the right, title, and interest of the creditor. Such payment shall reduce or extinguish the unpaid indebtedness of the debtor to the extent of such payment and any excess of the insurance shall be payable to the estate of the insured.

6. Notwithstanding the provisions of the above subsections, insurance on agricultural credit transaction commitments may be written up to the amount of the loan commitment on a nondecreasing or level term plan. Insurance on educational credit transaction commitments may be written up to the amount of the loan commitment less the amount of any repayments made on the loan.

C. A policy issued to a labor union, or similar employee organization, which shall be deemed to be the policyholder, to insure members of such union or organization for the benefit of persons other than the union or organization or any of its officials, representatives, or agents, subject to the following requirements:

1. The members eligible for insurance under the policy shall be all of the members of the union or organization, or all of any class or classes thereof.

2. The premium for the policy shall be paid either from funds of the union or organization, or from funds contributed by the insured members specifically for their insurance, or from both. Except as provided in subdivision 3 of this subsection, a policy on which no part of the premium is to be derived from funds contributed by the insured members specifically for their insurance must insure all eligible members, except those who reject such coverage in writing.

3. An insurer may exclude or limit the coverage on any person as to whom evidence of individual insurability is not satisfactory to the insurer.

D. A policy issued to or for (i) a multiple employer welfare arrangement, a rural electric cooperative, or a rural electric telephone cooperative as these terms are defined in 29 U.S.C. § 1002, or (ii) a trust or to the trustees of a fund established or adopted by two or more employers, or by one or more labor unions or similar employee organizations, or by one or more employers and one or more labor unions or similar employee organizations, which trust or trustees shall be deemed the policyholder, to insure employees of the employers or members of the unions or organizations for the benefit of persons other than the employees or the unions or organizations, subject to the following requirements:

1. The persons eligible for insurance shall be all of the employees of the employers or all of the members of the unions or organizations, or all of any class or classes thereof. The policy may provide that the term employees includes:

a. The employees of one or more subsidiary corporations, and the employees, individual proprietors, and partners of one or more affiliated corporations, proprietorships or partnerships if the business of the employer and of such affiliated corporations, proprietorships or partnerships is under common control;

b. The individual proprietor or partners if the employer is an individual proprietorship or partnership;

c. Retired employees, former employees and directors of a corporate employer; or

d. The trustees or their employees, or both, if their duties are principally connected with such trusteeship.

2. The premium for the policy shall be paid from funds contributed by the employer or employers of the insured persons, or by the union or unions or similar employee organizations, or by both, or from funds contributed by the insured persons or from both the insured persons and the employers or unions or similar employee organizations. Except as provided in subdivision 3 of this subsection, a policy on which no part of the premium is to be derived from funds contributed by the insured persons specifically for their insurance must insure all eligible persons, except those who reject such coverage in writing.

3. An insurer may exclude or limit the coverage on any person as to whom evidence of individual insurability is not satisfactory to the insurer.

E. 1. A policy issued to an association or to a trust or to the trustees of a fund established, created, or maintained for the benefit of members of one or more associations. The association or associations shall:

a. Have at the outset a minimum of 100 persons;

b. Have been organized and maintained in good faith for purposes other than that of obtaining insurance;

c. Have been in active existence for at least five years; and

d. Have a constitution and bylaws which provide that: (i) the association or associations hold regular meetings not less than annually to further purposes

466

of the members, (ii) except for credit unions, the association or associations collect dues or solicit contributions from members, and (iii) the members have voting privileges and representation on the governing board and committees.

2. The policy shall be subject to the following requirements:

a. The policy may insure members of such association or associations, employees thereof or employees of members, or one or more of the preceding or all of any class or classes thereof for the benefit of persons other than the employee's employer.

b. The premium for the policy shall be paid from funds contributed by the association or associations, or by employer members, or by both, or from funds contributed by the covered persons or from both the covered persons and the association, associations, or employer members.

c. Except as provided in clause d of this subdivision, a policy on which no part of the premium is to be derived from funds contributed by the covered persons specifically for the insurance must insure all eligible persons, except those who reject such coverage in writing.

d. An insurer may exclude or limit the coverage on any person as to whom evidence of individual insurability is not satisfactory to the insurer.

F. A policy issued to a credit union or to a trustee or trustees or agent designated by two or more credit unions, which credit union, trustee, trustees, or agent shall be deemed policyholder, to insure members of such credit union or credit unions for the benefit of persons other than the credit union or credit unions, trustee or trustees, or agent or any of their officials, subject to the following requirements:

1. The members eligible for insurance shall be all of the members of the credit union or credit unions, or all of any class or classes thereof.

2. The premium for the policy shall be paid by the policyholder from the credit union's funds and, except as provided in subdivision 3 of this subsection, must insure all eligible members.

3. An insurer may exclude or limit the coverage on any member as to whom evidence of individual insurability is not satisfactory to the insurer.

G. A policy issued to an incorporated association as described in § 38.2-4000, whose principal purpose is to assist its members in (i) financial planning for their funerals and burials and (ii) obtaining insurance for the payment, in whole or in part, for funeral, burial and other expenses. The association shall be deemed the policyholder, to insure the members of the association for the benefit of persons other than the association. The policy shall be subject to the following requirements:

1. A policy may not be issued to an association in which membership is conditioned upon the member's designation at any time of a specific funeral director or cemetery as the beneficiary under the insurance, so as to deprive the representatives or family of the deceased member from, or in any way control them in, obtaining funeral supplies and services in an open competitive market.

2. The policy shall insure members of such association.

3. The premium for the policy shall be paid from funds contributed by the association, or from funds contributed by the covered persons, or both.

4. Except as provided in subdivision 5 of this subsection, a policy on which no part of the premium is to be derived from funds contributed by the covered persons specifically for the insurance must insure all eligible persons except those who reject the coverage in writing.

5. An insurer may exclude or limit the coverage on any person as to whom evidence of individual insurability is not satisfactory to the insurer. (1998, c. 154.)

§ **38.2-3319:** Repealed by Acts 1998, c. 154.

§ **38.2-3319.1. Limits of group life insurance.** — Group life insurance offered to a resident of this Commonwealth under a group life insurance policy issued to a group other than one described in § 38.2-3318.1 shall be subject to the following requirements:

A. No such group life insurance policy shall be delivered in this Commonwealth unless the Commission finds that:

1. The issuance of such group policy is not contrary to Virginia's public policy and is in the best interest of the citizens of this Commonwealth;

2. The issuance of the group policy would result in economies of acquisition or administration; and

3. The benefits are reasonable in relation to the premiums charged.

Insurers filing policy forms seeking approval under the provisions of this subsection shall accompany the forms with a certification, signed by the officer of the company with the responsibility for forms compliance, in which the company certifies that each such policy form will be issued only where the requirements set forth in subdivisions 1 through 3 of this subsection have been met.

B. No such group life insurance coverage may be offered in this Commonwealth by an insurer under a policy issued in another state unless this Commonwealth or another state having requirements substantially similar to those contained in subdivisions 1, 2 and 3 of subsection A has made a determination that such requirements have been met.

An insurer offering group life insurance coverage in this Commonwealth under this subsection shall file a certification, signed by the officer of the company having responsibility for forms compliance in which the company certifies that all group insurance coverage marketed to residents of this Commonwealth under policies which have not been approved by this Commonwealth will comply with the provisions of § 38.2-3318.1 or have met the requirements set forth in subdivisions A 1 through A 3 of this section, and which clearly demonstrates that the substantially similar requirements of the state in which the contract will be issued have been met. The certification shall be accompanied by documentation from such state evidencing the determination that such requirements have been met.

C. The premium for the policy shall be paid either from the policyholder's funds or from funds contributed by the covered persons, or from both.

D. An insurer may exclude or limit the coverage on any person as to whom evidence of individual insurability is not satisfactory to the insurer. (1998, c. 154.)

§ **38.2-3319.2. Review of records.** — The Commission may review the records of any insurer to determine that the insurer's policies have been issued in compliance with the requirements set forth in this article. Insurers issuing coverage not complying with the provisions of § 38.2-3318.1 and not complying with the requirements of § 38.2-3319.1 shall be deemed to have committed a knowing and willful violation of this article, and shall be punished as set forth in subsection A of § 38.2-218. (1998, c. 154.)

§ **38.2-3320:** Repealed by Acts 1998, c. 154.

§ **38.2-3320.1. Policies issued outside of the Commonwealth of Virginia.** — A group life insurance policy issued outside of this Commonwealth, providing coverage to residents of this Commonwealth, that does not qualify under § 38.2-3318.1 or does not comply with § 38.2-3319.1 shall be subject to the statutory requirements of this title and may subject the insurer issuing such policy to the penalties available under this title for violation of such requirements. (1998, c. 154.)

§ **38.2-3321:** Repealed by Acts 1998, c. 154.

§ 38.2-3321.1. Requirements for those marketing group life insurance. — Insurance marketed to certificate holders of a group that does not qualify pursuant to § 38.2-3318.1 must be marketed by a person holding a valid life and health insurance agent license as required by Chapter 18 (§ 38.2-1800 et seq.) of this title. (1998, c. 154.)

§ 38.2-3322: Repealed by Acts 1998, c. 154.

§ 38.2-3322.1. Regulations. — The Commission may issue regulations to establish standards for group life insurance pursuant to the authority provided in § 38.2-223. (1998, c. 154.)

§ 38.2-3322.2. Lives covered. — A group life insurance policy shall cover at least two persons, other than spouses or minor children, at the issue date and at each policy anniversary date. (1998, c. 154.)

§ 38.2-3323. Group life insurance coverages of spouses and minor dependent children; dependent handicapped children. — A. Coverage under a group life insurance policy, except a policy issued pursuant to § 38.2-3318.1 B, may be extended to insure the spouse and any child who is under the age of nineteen years or who is a dependent and a full-time student under twenty-five years of age, or any class of spouses and dependent children, of each insured group member who so elects. The amount of insurance on the life of a spouse or child shall not exceed the amount of insurance on the life of the insured group member.

B. A spouse insured under this section shall have the same conversion right to the insurance on his or her life as the insured group member.

C. Notwithstanding the provisions of § 38.2-3331, one certificate may be issued for each family unit if a statement concerning any spouse's or dependent child's coverage is included in the certificate.

D. In addition to the coverages afforded by the provisions of this section, any such plan for group life insurance which includes coverage for children shall afford coverage to any child who is both (i) incapable of self-sustaining employment by reason of mental retardation or physical handicap and (ii) chiefly dependent upon the employee for support and maintenance. Upon request of the insurer, proof of incapacity and dependency shall be furnished to the insurer by the policyowner within thirty-one days of the child's attainment of the specified age. Subsequent proof may be required by the insurer but not more frequently than annually after the two-year period following the child's attainment of the specified age. The insurer shall be allowed to charge a premium at the insurer's then customary rate applicable to such group policy for such extended coverage.

E. 1. Upon termination of such group coverage of a child, the child shall be entitled to have issued to him by the insurer, without evidence of insurability, an individual life insurance policy without disability or other supplementary benefits, if:

a. An application for the individual policy is made, and the first premium paid to the insurer, within thirty-one days after such termination; and

b. The individual policy, at the option of such person, is on any one of the forms then customarily issued by the insurer at the age and for the amount applied for, except that the group policy may exclude the option to elect term insurance;

c. The individual policy is in an amount not in excess of the amount of life insurance which ceases because of such termination, less the amount of any life insurance for which such person becomes eligible under the same or any other group policy within thirty-one days after such termination, provided that any amount of insurance which has matured on or before the date of such termination as an endowment payable to the person insured, whether in one sum or in installments or in the form of an annuity, shall not, for the purposes of this provision, be included in the amount which is considered to cease because of such termination; and

d. The premium on the individual policy is at the insurer's then customary rate applicable to the form and amount of the individual policy, to the class of risk to which such person then belongs, and to the individual age attained on the effective date of the individual policy.

2. Subject to the same conditions set forth above, the conversion privilege shall be available (i) to a surviving dependent, if any, at the death of the group member, with respect to the coverage under the group policy which terminates by reason of such death, and (ii) to the dependent of the group member upon termination of coverage of the dependent, while the group member remains insured under the group policy, by reason of the dependent ceasing to be a qualified family member under the group policy. (1960, c. 272, § 38.1-472.1; 1976, c. 111; 1980, c. 110; 1984, c. 364; 1985, c. 28; 1986, c. 562; 1995, c. 259; 1998, c. 154.)

The **1998 amendment**, in the first sentence of subsection A, substituted "policy issued pursuant to § 38.2-3318.1 B" for "group credit life insurance policy."

§ **38.2-3324. Standard provisions required; exceptions.** — A. No group life insurance policy shall be delivered or issued for delivery in this Commonwealth unless it contains in substance the standard provisions prescribed in this article. The standard provisions required for individual life insurance policies shall not apply to group life insurance policies.

B. If a group life insurance policy is not term insurance, it shall contain a nonforfeiture provision that in the opinion of the Commission is equitable to the insured persons and to the policyholder. This subsection shall not be construed to require that group life insurance policies contain the same nonforfeiture provisions as are required for individual life insurance policies.

C. The provisions of § 38.2-3330, subsection A of § 38.2-3331, and §§ 38.2-3332 through 38.2-3334 shall not apply to policies issued pursuant to § 38.2-3318.1 B or group life insurance contracts in which the insurable interest is as described in subdivision 3 of subsection B of § 38.2-301. (Code 1950, §§ 38-429, 38-431; 1952, c. 317, § 38.1-424; 1960, c. 273; 1968, c. 282; 1970, c. 145; 1986, c. 562; 1993, c. 105; 1998, c. 154.)

The **1998 amendment**, in subsection C, substituted "policies issued pursuant to § 38.2-3318.1 B" for "group credit life insurance policies."

§ **38.2-3325. Grace period.** — Each group life insurance policy shall contain a provision that the policyowner is entitled to a grace period of not less than thirty-one days for the payment of any premium due except the first. The provision shall also state that during the grace period the death benefit coverage shall continue in force, unless the policyowner has given the insurer written notice of discontinuance in accordance with the terms of the policy and in advance of the date of discontinuance. The policy may provide that the policyowner shall be liable to the insurer for the payment of a pro rata premium for the time the policy was in force during the grace period. (1960, c. 273, § 38.1-424.1; 1986, c. 562.)

§ **38.2-3326. Incontestability.** — A. Each group life insurance policy shall contain a provision that the validity of the policy shall not be contested, except for nonpayment of premiums, after it has been in force for two years from its date of issue.

B. The provision shall also state that no statement made by any person insured under the policy relating to his insurability or the insurability of his insured dependents shall be used in contesting the validity of the insurance with respect to which such statement was made:

1. After the insurance has been in force prior to the contest for a period of two years during the lifetime of the person about whom the statement was made; and

2. Unless the statement is contained in a written instrument signed by him. (Code 1950, § 38-429(1); 1952, c. 317, § 38.1-425; 1986, c. 562.)

§ **38.2-3327. Entire contract; statements deemed representations.** — A. Each group life insurance policy shall contain a provision that the policy and any application of the policyowner, and any individual applications of the persons insured shall constitute the entire contract between the parties.

B. The provision shall also state that:

1. A copy of any application of the policyowner shall be attached to the policy when issued;

2. All statements made by the policyowner or by the persons insured shall be deemed representations and not warranties; and

3. No written statement made by any person insured shall be used in any contest unless a copy of the statement has been furnished to the person, his beneficiary or his personal representative. (Code 1950, § 38-429(2); 1952, c. 317, § 38.1-426; 1960, c. 273; 1986, c. 562.)

Certificate of insurance not part of contract. — As a matter of statute in Virginia, a certificate of insurance furnished to an insured pursuant to § 38.2-3331 was not part of his contract of insurance. Shenandoah Life Ins. Co. v. French, 236 Va. 427, 373 S.E.2d 718 (1988).

A widow was not entitled to insurance benefits as shown in her insurance certificate, issued pursuant to § 38.2-3331, since this section states that in each policy there shall be a provision that the policy shall constitute the entire contract and does not mention the certificate of insurance as part of the contract, and also since § 38.2-3331 treats certificates as notices, has no penalty for violation, and confers no rights to the certificate. Shenandoah Life Ins. Co. v. French, 236 Va. 427, 373 S.E.2d 718 (1988).

§ **38.2-3328. Evidence of individual insurability.** — Each group life insurance policy shall contain a provision setting forth any conditions under which the insurer reserves the right to require a person eligible for insurance to furnish evidence of individual insurability satisfactory to the insurer as a condition to part or all of his coverage. (1960, c. 273, § 38.1-426.1; 1986, c. 562.)

§ **38.2-3329. Misstatement of age.** — Each group life insurance policy shall contain a provision that an equitable adjustment of premiums, benefits, or both shall be made if the age of a person insured has been misstated. The provision shall contain a clear statement of the method of adjustment to be used. (Code 1950, § 38-429(3); 1952, c. 317, § 38.1-427; 1960, c. 273; 1986, c. 562.)

§ **38.2-3330. Payment of benefits.** — Each group life insurance policy shall contain a provision that any sum payable because of the death of the person insured shall be payable to the beneficiary or beneficiaries designated by the person insured, subject to:

1. The provisions of the policy as to all or any part of such sum if there is no designated beneficiary living at the time of death of the person insured; and

2. Any right reserved by the insurer in the policy and set forth in the certificate to pay a part of the sum, not exceeding $2,000, to any person

appearing to the insurer to be equitably entitled thereto because of having incurred funeral or other expenses incident to the death or last illness of the person insured. (1960, c. 273, § 38.1-427.1; 1986, c. 562.)

§ 38.2-3331. Individual certificates. — A. Each group life insurance policy shall contain a provision that the insurer will issue to the policyholder, for delivery to each person insured, an individual certificate setting forth:

1. The insured person's insurance protection, including any limitations, reductions and exclusions applicable to the coverage provided;

2. To whom the insurance benefits are payable; and

3. The rights and conditions set forth in §§ 38.2-3332, 38.2-3333 and 38.2-3334.

B. Each policy issued pursuant to § 38.2-3318.1 B, where any part of the premium is paid by the debtors or by the creditor from identifiable charges collected from the insured debtors not required of an uninsured debtor, shall contain a provision that the insurer will furnish to the policyholder for delivery to each debtor insured under the policy a form that will contain a statement that the life of the debtor is insured under the policy and that any death benefit paid under the policy by reason of his death shall be applied to reduce or extinguish the indebtedness. (Code 1950, § 38-429(4); 1952, c. 317, § 38.1-428; 1960, c. 273, § 38.1-428.4; 1986, c. 562; 1998, c. 154.)

The **1998 amendment** substituted "policy issued pursuant to § 38.2-3318.1 B" for "group credit life insurance policy" near the beginning of subsection B.

Certificate of insurance not part of contract. — As a matter of statute in Virginia, a certificate of insurance furnished to an insured pursuant to this section was not part of his contract of insurance. Shenandoah Life Ins. Co. v. French, 236 Va. 427, 373 S.E.2d 718 (1988).

A widow was not entitled to insurance benefits as shown in her insurance certificate, issued pursuant to this section, since § 38.2-3327 states that in each policy there shall be a provision that the policy shall constitute the entire contract and does not mention the certificate of insurance as part of the contract, and also since this section treats certificates as notices, has no penalty for violation, and confers no rights to the certificate. Shenandoah Life Ins. Co. v. French, 236 Va. 427, 373 S.E.2d 718 (1988).

§ 38.2-3332. Right to individual policy upon termination of employment or membership. — Each group life insurance policy shall contain a provision that if the insurance, or any portion of it, on a person covered under the policy, other than a minor child insured pursuant to § 38.2-3323, ceases because of termination of employment or of membership in the class or classes eligible for coverage under the policy, the person shall be entitled to have the insurer issue him without evidence of insurability an individual policy of life insurance, without disability or other supplementary benefits, subject to the following:

1. Application for the individual policy shall be made, and the first monthly or other mutually agreeable modal premium paid to the insurer, within thirty-one days after the termination;

2. The individual policy shall at the option of the person be on any one of the forms, except term insurance, then customarily issued by the insurer, subject to the insurer's customary age and amount requirements for the forms;

3. The amount of the individual policy shall not exceed the amount of terminated group life insurance less the amount of any group life insurance that the person is or becomes eligible for within thirty-one days after the termination. Any amount of insurance maturing on or before the date of the termination as an endowment payable to the person insured, whether in one sum, installments or in the form of an annuity, shall not be included in the amount of terminated group life insurance; and

4. The premium on the individual policy shall be at the insurer's then current rate applicable to the form and amount of the individual policy, to the class of risk to which the person then belongs, and to the person's age on the effective date of the individual policy. (1960, c. 273, § 38.1-428.1; 1986, c. 562.)

Decedent was not entitled to exercise the privilege, provided insureds in his group life insurance policy, of converting his policy to an individual policy, and his beneficiary was not entitled to proceeds under the conversion policy issued to the decedent, where the decedent was not in "active service" of his employer as required under the group policy in order to be eligible for benefits under the group policy, and therefore could not have been eligible to exercise the conversion privilege. North Am. Life & Cas. Co. v. Tyree, 220 Va. 397, 258 S.E.2d 110 (1979).

The classification of an insurance policy as life or accident was a legal question to be resolved by the court. Gudnason v. Life Ins. Co. of N. Am., 231 Va. 197, 343 S.E.2d 54 (1986).

§ 38.2-3333. Right to individual policy upon termination of group policy or elimination of class of insured persons.

— Each group life insurance policy shall contain a provision that if the group policy terminates or is amended so as to terminate the insurance of any class of insured persons, every person, other than a minor child insured pursuant to § 38.2-3323, whose insurance terminates and who has been insured for at least five years prior to the termination date shall be entitled to have the insurer issue him an individual life insurance policy. The individual life policy shall be subject to the conditions and limitations set forth in § 38.2-3332. However, the group policy may contain a provision that the amount of the individual policy shall not exceed the smaller of (i) the amount of the person's life insurance protection ceasing because of the termination or amendment of the group policy, less the amount of any life insurance for which he is or becomes eligible under any group policy issued or reinstated by the same or another insurer within 31 days after the termination, or (ii) $10,000. (1960, c. 273, § 38.1-428.2; 1986, c. 562.)

§ 38.2-3334. Death after termination of group insurance and before issuance of individual policy.

— Each group life insurance policy shall contain a provision that if a person insured under the group policy dies during the period within which he is entitled to have an individual policy issued to him in accordance with § 38.2-3332 or § 38.2-3333 and before the individual policy has become effective, the amount of life insurance that he would have been entitled to have issued to him under an individual policy shall be payable as a claim under the group policy, whether or not application for the individual policy or the payment of the first premium was made. (1960, c. 273, § 38.1-428.3; 1986, c. 562.)

The classification of an insurance policy as life or accident was a legal question to be resolved by the court. Gudnason v. Life Ins. Co. of N. Am., 231 Va. 197, 343 S.E.2d 54 (1986).

§ 38.2-3335. Additional persons becoming eligible.

— Each group life insurance policy shall contain a provision that any person who subsequently becomes a member of a group or class that is covered under the policy shall be eligible for group life insurance in accordance with the same requirements as any other member of the group or class. (Code 1950, § 38-429(5); 1952, c. 317, § 38.1-429; 1986, c. 562.)

§ 38.2-3336. Provisions required by other jurisdictions.

— Group life insurance policies issued by any foreign or alien insurer for delivery in this

Commonwealth may contain any provision that is prescribed by the laws of its domiciliary jurisdiction and that is not in conflict with the laws of this Commonwealth. Policies issued by any domestic insurer for delivery in any other jurisdiction may contain any provision required by the laws of that jurisdiction. (Code 1950, § 38-430; 1952, c. 317, § 38.1-430; 1986, c. 562.)

§ 38.2-3337. Assignment. — With mutual agreement among the insured, the policyholder, and the insurer, any person insured under a group life insurance policy may make an irrevocable assignment of the rights and benefits conferred on him by any provision of the policy or by this article. The assignment may be made to any person other than the insured's employer. (Code 1950, §§ 38-429, 38-431; 1952, c. 317, § 38.1-424; 1960, c. 273; 1968, c. 282; 1970, c. 145; 1986, c. 562.)

§ 38.2-3338. Provisions prohibited. — No group life insurance policy shall be delivered or issued for delivery in this Commonwealth if it contains any provision:
1. Limiting the time within which any action at law or in equity may be commenced to less than one year after the cause of action accrues; or
2. To the effect that the agent soliciting the insurance is the agent of the person insured under the policy, or making the acts or representations of the agent binding upon the person insured under the policy. (Code 1950, § 38-386; 1952, c. 317, § 38.1-406; 1956, c. 417; 1986, c. 562.)

§ 38.2-3339. Exemption of group life insurance policies from legal process. — No group life insurance policy, nor its proceeds, shall be liable to attachment, garnishment, or other process, or to be seized, taken, appropriated, or applied by any legal or equitable process or operation of law, to pay any debt or liability of any person insured under the policy, or his beneficiary, or any other person who has a right under the policy, either before or after payment. If the proceeds of a group life insurance policy are not made payable to a named beneficiary, the proceeds shall not constitute a part of the insured person's estate for the payment of his debts. (Code 1950, § 38-432; 1952, c. 317, § 38.1-482; 1986, c. 562.)

Law Review. — For discussion of debtors' exemptions, see 17 Wash. & Lee L. Rev. 19 (1960). For article on the need for reform of and a proposed revision of Virginia's exemption statutes, see 37 Wash. & Lee L. Rev. 127 (1980).

The purpose of this section is to protect the dependents of the insured. John Hancock Mut. Life Ins. Co. v. Sykes, 106 F. Supp. 116 (E.D. Va. 1952), construing former § 38-432.

ARTICLE 3.

Industrial Life Insurance Policies.

§ 38.2-3340. Definition of industrial life insurance. — *"Industrial life insurance"* means life insurance provided by an individual insurance contract (i) under which premiums are payable monthly or more frequently, and (ii) with the words "industrial policy" printed upon the policy as a part of the descriptive matter. (Code 1950, § 38-433; 1952, c. 317, § 38.1-482; 1986, c. 562.)

§ 38.2-3341. Standard provisions required. — No industrial life insurance policy shall be delivered or issued for delivery in this Commonwealth, unless it contains in substance the provisions prescribed in this article or provisions that are, in the Commission's opinion, more favorable to policyowners. (Code 1950, §§ 38-434, 38-435; 1952, c. 317, § 38.1-410; 1986, c. 562.)

§ **38.2-3342. Ten-day right to examine policy.** — No industrial life insurance policy shall be delivered or issued for delivery in this Commonwealth unless it has printed on it a notice stating in substance that if during a ten-day period from the date the policy is delivered to the policyowner, the policy is surrendered to the insurer or its agent with a written request for cancellation, the policy shall be void from the beginning and the insurer shall refund any premium paid for the policy. Nothing in this section shall prohibit an insurer from extending the right to examine period to more than ten days if the period is specified in the policy. (1977, c. 174, § 38.1-410.1; 1986, c. 562.)

§ **38.2-3343. Grace period.** — A. Each industrial life insurance policy shall contain a provision that the insured is entitled to a grace period of twenty-eight days within which the payment of any premium after the first may be made. This grace period shall terminate at noon on the twenty-eighth day after the due date of the defaulted premium. However, for monthly payment policies the insured shall be entitled to a grace period of not less than thirty-one days.

B. Each policy shall also contain a provision that during the grace period the policy shall continue in full force, but if a claim arises under the policy during the grace period and before the overdue premiums are paid, the amount of overdue premiums may be deducted in any settlement under the policy. (Code 1950, § 38-434(1); 1952, c. 317, § 38.1-411; 1986, c. 562.)

§ **38.2-3344. Policy and application to constitute entire contract; statements deemed representations.** — A. Each industrial life insurance policy shall contain a provision that the policy, or the policy and the application for the policy, if a copy of the application is endorsed upon or attached to the policy when issued, shall constitute the entire contract between the parties.

B. The provision shall also state that:

1. All statements made by the insured shall, in the absence of fraud, be deemed representations and not warranties; and

2. No such statement shall be used in defense of a claim under the policy unless it is contained in a written application that is endorsed upon or attached to the policy when issued. (Code 1950, § 38-434(2); 1952, c. 317, § 38.1-412; 1986, c. 562.)

§ **38.2-3345. Incontestability.** — Each industrial life insurance policy shall contain a provision that the policy shall be incontestable after it has been in force for two years from the date of issue during the lifetime of the insured, except for nonpayment of premiums, and except as to provisions and conditions (i) relating to benefits in the event of certain specific types of disability and (ii) granting additional insurance specifically against death by accident or accidental means. (Code 1950, § 38-434(3); 1952, c. 317, § 38.1-413; 1986, c. 562.)

§ **38.2-3346. Misstatement of age.** — Each industrial life insurance policy shall contain a provision that if, before final settlement of the policy, the age of the insured or the age of any other person if considered in determining the premium is found to have been misstated, the amount payable under the policy shall equal the amount that the premium would have purchased at the insured's or other person's correct age, at the time the policy was issued. (Code 1950, § 38-434(4); 1952, c. 317, § 38.1-414; 1986, c. 562.)

§ 38.2-3347. Nonforfeiture benefits and cash surrender values. — Each industrial life insurance policy shall contain a provision for nonforfeiture benefits in accordance with the requirements of §§ 38.2-3202 and 38.2-3208, and a provision for cash surrender values in accordance with the requirements of §§ 38.2-3203 and 38.2-3209. (Code 1950, § 38-434(5), (6); 1952, c. 317, § 38.1-415; 1986, c. 562.)

§ 38.2-3348. Reinstatement. — Each industrial life insurance policy shall contain a provision that the policy, if not surrendered for its cash value or if the period of extended term insurance has not expired, may be reinstated within one year from the date of default in payment of premiums upon:
1. Payment of all overdue premiums and, at the insurer's option, interest on the overdue premiums at an annual rate not exceeding six percent; and
2. Presentation of evidence satisfactory to the insurer of the insurability of the insured. (Code 1950, § 38-434(7); 1952, c. 317, § 38.1-416; 1986, c. 562.)

§ 38.2-3349. Table of nonforfeiture options. — Each industrial life insurance policy shall contain a table showing the nonforfeiture options available under the policy each year upon default in the payment of premiums during at least the first twenty years of the policy, or during the premium-paying period if less than twenty years. There shall also be a provision that the insurer will furnish, upon request, an extension of the table beyond the years shown in the policy. (Code 1950, § 38-434(8); 1952, c. 317, § 38.1-417; 1986, c. 562.)

§ 38.2-3350. Settlement. — Each industrial life insurance policy shall contain a provision that when a death claim arises under the policy, settlement shall be made within two months after receipt of due proof of death. (Code 1950, § 38-434(9); 1952, c. 317, § 38.1-418; 1986, c. 562.)

§ 38.2-3351. Title. — Each industrial life insurance policy shall have a title on its face that briefly and accurately describes the nature and form of the policy. (Code 1950, § 38-434(10); 1952, c. 317, § 38.1-419; 1986, c. 562.)

§ 38.2-3352. Provisions not required in certain policies. — The provisions of this article do not apply to policies issued or granted in exercise of the nonforfeiture provisions of § 38.2-3347. (Code 1950, § 38-438; 1952, c. 317, § 38.1-420; 1986, c. 562.)

§ 38.2-3353. Provisions required by other jurisdictions. — Industrial life insurance policies issued by any foreign or alien insurer for delivery in this Commonwealth may contain any provision that is prescribed by the laws of its domiciliary jurisdiction and is not in conflict with the laws of this Commonwealth. Policies issued by any domestic insurer for delivery in any other jurisdiction may contain any provision required by the laws of that jurisdiction. (Code 1950, § 38-436; 1952, c. 317, § 38.1-421; 1986, c. 562.)

§ 38.2-3354. Prohibited provisions. — No industrial life insurance policy shall be delivered or issued for delivery in this Commonwealth if it contains any of the following provisions:
1. Limiting the time within which any action at law or in equity may be commenced to less than one year after the cause of action accrues;
2. For any mode of settlement at maturity of less value than the amount insured by the policy plus any dividend additions to the policy, less (i) any indebtedness to the insurer on or secured by the policy and (ii) any premium

that may by the terms of the policy be deducted. This subdivision shall not apply to any nonforfeiture provision that employs the cash value less any indebtedness, to purchase paid up or extended insurance, and shall not prohibit the issuance of policies providing for a limitation in the amount payable under certain specified conditions; or

3. To the effect that the agent soliciting the insurance is the agent of the person insured under the policy, or making the acts or representations of the agent binding upon the person insured under the policy. (Code 1950, § 38-437; 1952, c. 317, § 38.1-422; 1986, c. 562.)

CHAPTER 34.

PROVISIONS RELATING TO ACCIDENT AND SICKNESS INSURANCE.

Article 4.

Limited Mandated Benefit Accident and Sickness Insurance Policies and Subscription Contracts.

Article 4.1.

Individual Health Insurance Coverage.

Article 5.

Group Market Reforms and Individual Coverage Offered to Employees of Small Employers.

Article 3.

Jurisdiction Over Providers of Health Care Services.

ARTICLE 1.

General Provisions.

§ 38.2-3400. Application of chapter. — A. This chapter and Chapter 35 (§ 38.2-3500 et seq.) of this title apply to insurance policies or contracts of the

class described in § 38.2-109 delivered or issued for delivery in this Commonwealth except as provided in subsection B of this section.

B. Nothing in this chapter shall apply to or affect:

1. Any workers' compensation insurance policy;

2. Any liability insurance policy with or without supplementary expense
coverage, including any motor vehicle liability insurance policy, providing
weekly indemnity or other specific benefits to persons who are injured and
specific death benefits to dependents, beneficiaries or personal representatives
of persons who are killed, irrespective of the legal liability of the insured or any
other person;

3. Any policy or contract of reinsurance;

4. Life insurance or annuities;

5. Any industrial sick benefit insurance; or

6. Any credit accident and sickness insurance policy. (Code 1950, § 38-225;
1950, p. 1016; 1952, c. 317, §§ 38.1-347, 38.1-360; 1956, c. 678; 1974, c. 95;
1975, c. 281; 1976, c. 355; 1977, c. 606; 1978, c. 496; 1979, cc. 13, 97; 1980, c.
719; 1986, c. 562.)

Accident defined. — An accident is an event that takes place without one's foresight or expectation, an undesigned, sudden, and unexpected event; further, it is generally held that if the insured voluntarily provokes or is the aggressor in an encounter, and knows, or under the circumstances should reasonably anticipate, that he will be in danger of death or great bodily harm as the natural or probable consequence of his act or course of action, his death or injury is not caused by an accident within the meaning of such a policy. Harris v. Bankers Life & Cas. Co., 222 Va. 45, 278 S.E.2d 809 (1981).

Issue of accident improperly decided by court. — In an action claiming that defendant insurance company breached a contract insuring plaintiff's husband against accidental death or dismemberment, where evidence showed that the husband was stabbed to death by another woman with whom he lived after the husband had disciplined the woman's child and pushed the woman, the trial court erred in deciding as a matter of law that the husband's death was not an accident, since whether the husband should have anticipated that his disciplining the child or his pushing the woman would lead to a violent reaction presented a factual issue dependent on the relationship of the parties and the circumstances of the incident. Harris v. Bankers Life & Cas. Co., 222 Va. 45, 278 S.E.2d 809 (1981).

§ 38.2-3401. Forms of insurance authorized. — A. Accident and sickness insurance shall be issued only in the following forms:

1. Individual accident and sickness policies; or

2. Group accident and sickness policies.

B. Pursuant to the authority granted by § 38.2-223, the Commission may
promulgate such regulations as may be necessary or appropriate to govern
insurers' practices with regard to Acquired Immunodeficiency Syndrome
(AIDS) or the presence of the Human Immunodeficiency Virus (HIV), including
advertising practices, underwriting practices, policy provisions, claim practices, or other practices with regard to individual or group accident and
sickness insurance policies delivered or issued for delivery in the Commonwealth of Virginia and certificates or evidences of coverage, issued under any
contract delivered or issued for delivery in the Commonwealth of Virginia.
(1986, c. 562; 1989, c. 653.)

§ 38.2-3402. Certification to accompany application. — A. Each ap-
plication for an individual accident and sickness insurance policy shall contain
a certification, signed by both the applicant and the agent soliciting the
insurance, to the effect that: "The undersigned applicant and agent certify that
the applicant has read, or had read to him, the completed application and that
the applicant realizes that any false statement or misrepresentation in the
application may result in loss of coverage under the policy." If the application

is to be used in a solicitation where no agent is involved, the certification may delete the reference to and signature of the agent soliciting the insurance.

B. Subsection A of this section shall also apply to an application by an individual for coverage under a group policy where individual underwriting is done.

C. If the certification is wholly or partially inapplicable to a particular form of policy, the insurer may modify or omit the certification with the approval of the Commission. (1966, c. 342, § 38.1-348.2; 1986, c. 562.)

§ 38.2-3403. Fraudulent procurement of policy. — A. No person shall knowingly secure, attempt to secure or cause to be secured an individual accident and sickness insurance policy on any person not in an insurable condition by means of misrepresentations or false or fraudulent statements.

B. An insurance agent who violates this section shall be subject to the penalties under § 38.2-1831 in addition to the penalties of § 38.2-218. (1966, c. 342, § 38.1-348.3; 1986, c. 562.)

§ 38.2-3404. Commission may establish rules and regulations for simplified and readable accident and sickness insurance policies. — A. Pursuant to the authority granted in § 38.2-223, the Commission may issue rules and regulations establishing standards for simplified and readable accident and sickness insurance policy forms. Any such rules and regulations shall apply to any policy forms of accident and sickness insurance as defined in § 38.2-109, except credit accident and sickness insurance, issued on a nongroup basis or to groups with ten or fewer members.

B. The rules and regulations issued hereunder may permit an insurer to issue policies containing policy provisions that deviate in language from the policy provisions required by §§ 38.2-3500 through 38.2-3506 where applicable, provided the provisions in each instance are not less favorable to the insured or the beneficiary.

C. No insurer shall deliver or issue for delivery an accident and sickness insurance policy in this Commonwealth unless the Commission has determined that the policy form satisfies the readability standards established by the rules and regulations and is in compliance with other statutory requirements. (1979, c. 47, § 38.1-354.1; 1986, c. 562.)

Law Review. — For survey of Virginia law on insurance for the year 1978-1979, see 66 Va. L. Rev. 321 (1980).

§ 38.2-3405. Certain subrogation provisions and limitations upon recovery in hospital, medical, etc., policies forbidden. — A. No insurance contract providing hospital, medical, surgical and similar or related benefits, and no subscription contract or health services plan delivered or issued for delivery or providing for payment of benefits to or on behalf of persons residing in or employed in this Commonwealth shall contain any provision providing for subrogation of any person's right to recovery for personal injuries from a third person.

B. No such contract, subscription contract or health services plan shall contain any provision requiring the beneficiary of any such contract or plan to sign any agreement to pay back to any company issuing such a contract or creating a health services plan any benefits paid pursuant to the terms of such contract or plan from the proceeds of a recovery by such a beneficiary from any other source; provided, that this provision shall not prohibit an exclusion of benefits paid or payable under workers' compensation laws or federal or state programs, nor shall this provision prohibit coordination of benefits provisions when there are two or more such accident and sickness insurance contracts or plans providing for the payment of the same benefits. Coordination of benefits provisions may not operate to reduce benefits because of any benefits paid, payable, or provided by any liability insurance contract or any benefits paid, payable, or provided by any medical expense or medical payments insurance provided in conjunction with liability coverage.

C. Whenever benefits paid or payable under workers' compensation are excluded from coverage under the terms of any such contract, subscription contract or health services plan, the issuer thereof shall not exclude coverage for any medical condition pursuant to such exclusion if (i) an award of the Workers' Compensation Commission pursuant to § 65.2-704 denies compensation benefits relating to such medical condition and no request for review of such award is made pursuant to and within the time prescribed by § 65.2-705 or (ii) an award of the Workers' Compensation Commission, after review by the full Commission pursuant to § 65.2-705, denies compensation benefits relating to such medical condition. Following the entry of a workers' compensation award pursuant to clause (i) or (ii) having the effect of prohibiting the application of any such exclusion, the issuer shall immediately provide coverage for such medical condition to the extent otherwise covered under the contract, subscription contract or health services plan. If, upon appeal to the Court of Appeals or the Supreme Court, such medical condition is held to be compensable under the Virginia Workers' Compensation Act (Title 65.2), the issuer may recover from the applicable employer or workers' compensation insurance carrier the costs of coverage for medical conditions found to be compensable under the Act. (1973, c. 28, § 38.1-342.2; 1979, c. 341; 1986, c. 562; 1988, c. 840; 1989, c. 487; 1994, c. 609; 1995, c. 68.)

Law Review. — For survey of Virginia law on insurance for the year 1972-1973, see 59 Va. L. Rev. 1535 (1973). For survey of Virginia insurance law for the year 1977-1978, see 64 Va. L. Rev. 1477 (1978). For survey of Virginia law on insurance for the year 1978-1979, see 66 Va. L. Rev. 321 (1980).

Purpose of section. — This section was enacted by the General Assembly to reverse the holding in Collins v. Blue Cross, 213 Va. 540, 193 S.E.2d 782 (1973), that a conventional subrogation provision in a hospital indemnity contract was not invalid as contrary to public policy. Reynolds Metals Co. v. Smith, 218 Va. 881, 241 S.E.2d 794 (1978).

This section proscribes a subrogation provision in the policy. Reynolds Metals Co. v. Smith, 218 Va. 881, 241 S.E.2d 794 (1978).

"Responsible" explicitly refers to responsibility for the injuries themselves, not to responsibility for their treatment or for other financial loss occasioned thereby. Hines v. Blue Cross Blue Shield, 788 F.2d 1016 (4th Cir. 1986).

"Responsible" means "causally responsible." Hines v. Blue Cross Blue Shield, 788 F.2d 1016 (4th Cir. 1986).

The ordinary meaning of a "person responsible for such injuries" is the person who caused the injuries, who did the damage. The Virginia Supreme Court has used "responsible" in this way as well. Hines v. Blue Cross

Blue Shield, 788 F.2d 1016 (4th Cir. 1986).

Workers' compensation as other insurance. — If this section is to be consistent with § 38.2-3509, "other insurance," including workers' compensation, must be differentiated from recovery from a tortfeasor. A contract may eliminate duplication of benefits when the benefits come from workers' compensation and the injured party's insurer, but not when they are derived from a health insurance carrier and a tortfeasor. Workers' compensation is regarded as "other insurance" for the purposes of § 38.2-3509. For the purposes of this section, workers' compensation should be regarded as akin to other insurance rather than to recovery from a tortfeasor. Hines v. Blue Cross Blue Shield, 788 F.2d 1016 (4th Cir. 1986).

This section does not operate to prohibit provisions that exclude coverage when there has already been recovery under workers' compensation law. Hines v. Blue Cross Blue Shield, 788 F.2d 1016 (4th Cir. 1986).

Section was inapplicable. — In case in which insurer sought to recover moneys advanced to plan participant after she was injured in an auto accident, this section was not applicable, as the case concerned a dispute over the terms of the insurance contract itself, and the contract did not provide for subrogation against a third party. All insurer sought was the money it paid out to the insured; it did not seek to step into her shoes. Provident Life &

Accident Ins. Co. v. Waller, 906 F.2d 985 (4th Cir.), cert. denied, 498 U.S. 982, 111 S. Ct. 512, 112 L. Ed. 2d 524 (1990) (declining to consider the issue of preemption by federal ERISA provisions).

A county government's health benefit plan which paid benefits through an agent was an insurance agreement covered by the anti-subrogation statute (formerly § 38.1-342.2), and therefore the agent could not recover amounts paid to a beneficiary when that beneficiary obtained judgment against a third-party tortfeasor. Group Hospitalization Medical Serv., Inc. v. Smith, 236 Va. 228, 372 S.E.2d 159 (1988).

§ **38.2-3405.1. Commonwealth's right to certain accident and sickness benefits.** — A. The Department of Medical Assistance Services shall be entitled to direct reimbursement under any accident and sickness insurance policy, health services plan, or health maintenance organization contract for covered services or items to the extent that payment has been made by the Department of Medical Assistance Services on behalf of an individual covered under such policy, plan, or contract for such services or items.

B. No insurer, health services plan, or health maintenance organization shall impose upon the Department of Medical Assistance Services or any state agency, which has been assigned or has otherwise acquired the rights of an individual eligible for medical assistance ("Medicaid") and covered for health benefits by the insurance policy, health services plan, or health maintenance organization contract, any requirements that are different from requirements applicable to an agent or assignee of any other individual so covered. (1994, c. 213.)

§ **38.2-3406. Accident and sickness benefits not subject to legal process.** — The installment payments to the holder of any accident and sickness insurance policy or certificate shall not be subject to the lien of any attachment, garnishment proceeding, writ of fieri facias, or to levy or distress in any manner for any debt due by the holder of the policy or certificate. (Code 1950, § 38-227; 1952, c. 317, § 38.1-346; 1986, c. 562.)

Purpose of section. — The legislative intent was to except such payments or benefits to one entitled thereto from all claims of creditors. The legislative purpose of this statute was to protect from the claims of creditors such a policyholder who might be overtaken by accident or sickness and who has become entitled to benefit payments and thus likely prevent him and his family from becoming an object of public charity. Atlantic Life Ins. Co. v. Ring, 167 Va. 121, 187 S.E. 449 (1936).

Exemption from setoff. — While this section does not in express terms mention "setoff" along with "the lien of a judgment," etc., yet it must be remembered that such statutes being remedial they should have a liberal construction in order that the legislative intent and purpose may be accomplished. The exemption of such payments from setoff finds strong support in the textbooks and in decided cases. There are few cases to the contrary. Atlantic Life Ins. Co. v. Ring, 167 Va. 121, 187 S.E. 449 (1936); Norfolk S. Ry. v. Lassiter, 193 Va. 360, 68 S.E.2d 641 (1952).

§ **38.2-3407. Health benefit programs.** — A. One or more insurers may offer or administer a health benefit program under which the insurer or insurers may offer preferred provider policies or contracts that limit the numbers and types of providers of health care services eligible for payment as preferred providers.

B. Any such insurer shall establish terms and conditions that shall be met by a hospital, physician or type of provider listed in § 38.2-3408 in order to qualify for payment as a preferred provider under the policies or contracts. These terms and conditions shall not discriminate unreasonably against or among such health care providers. No hospital, physician or type of provider listed in § 38.2-3408 willing to meet the terms and conditions offered to it or him shall be excluded. Neither differences in prices among hospitals or other institutional providers produced by a process of individual negotiations with providers or based on market conditions, or price differences among providers in different geographical areas, shall be deemed unreasonable discrimination. The Commission shall have no jurisdiction to adjudicate controversies growing out of this subsection.

C. Mandated types of providers set forth in § 38.2-3408, and types of providers whose services are required to be made available and that have been specifically contracted for by the holder of any such policy or contract shall, to the extent required by § 38.2-3408, have the same opportunity to qualify for payment as a preferred provider as do doctors of medicine.

D. Preferred provider policies or contracts shall provide for payment for services rendered by nonpreferred providers, but the payments need not be the same as for preferred providers.

E. For the purposes of this section, *"preferred provider policies or contracts"* are insurance policies or contracts that specify how services are to be covered when rendered by preferred and nonpreferred classifications of providers. (1983, c. 464, § 38.1-347.2; 1986, c. 562.)

Legislative distinction. — The application of this section to insured preferred provider organizations (PPOs), and not to uninsured PPOs, is a distinction created by the Virginia legislature. Richter v. Capp Care, Inc., 868 F. Supp. 163 (E.D. Va. 1994), aff'd, 77 F.3d 470 (4th Cir. 1996).

Statute preempted by ERISA. — This statute at the very least indirectly bears upon, and therefore relates to, employee benefit plans covered by ERISA, and is preempted by ERISA as prescribed by Congress. Furthermore, because the statute does not regulate insurance, or the business of insurance, the statute is not thereby saved from preemption. HCA Health Servs. of Va., Inc. v. Aetna Life Ins. Co., 803 F. Supp. 1132 (E.D. Va. 1992).

Though Virginia statute regulates the relationship between the insurer and insured through the formation of the insurer's preferred provider organization (PPO), it is nonetheless a law regulating the business of insurance, for statute satisfied the three criteria of transferring or spreading policyholder's risk, is an integral part of the policy relationship between insurer and insured, and it is expressly limited to entities within the insurance industry and thus, ERISA's insurance savings clause exempts the Virginia statute from application of preemption clause. Stuart Circle Hosp. Corp. v. Aetna Health Mgt., 995 F.2d 500 (4th Cir. 1993), cert. denied, 510 U.S. 1003, 114 S. Ct. 579, 126 L. Ed. 2d 478 (1993).

The any willing provider provisions only apply to insurance preferred provider organizations (PPOs) within the insurance industry, and regulates the relationship between insurer and insured and the type of policy which could be issued. Richter v. Capp Care, Inc., 868 F. Supp. 163 (E.D. Va. 1994), aff'd, 77 F.3d 470 (4th Cir. 1996).

Insurer has considerable latitude in determining manner in which it selects preferred provider. — The language of this section suggests that an insurer has considerable latitude in determining the manner in which it selects a preferred provider for its preferred provider organization (PPO). This section does not define "terms and conditions" but rather implies that such terms are variable and dependent upon the specific context in which a PPO is established. HCA Health Servs. of Va., Inc. v. Metropolitan Life Ins. Co., 752 F. Supp. 202 (E.D. Va. 1990).

Communication of selection criteria to all providers. — Health insurance company fulfilled its legal duty by establishing and communicating to all providers with which it negotiated the selection criteria used to devise a short list of eligible providers. HCA Health Servs. of Va., Inc. v. Metropolitan Life Ins. Co., 752 F. Supp. 202 (E.D. Va. 1990).

Proposal of targeted lower per diem rate is a valid negotiating technique. — Health insurance company's proposal at the onset of negotiations of a targeted per diem rate that is lower than the prices charged by the hospitals is a valid negotiating technique. HCA Health Servs. of Va., Inc. v. Metropolitan Life Ins. Co., 752 F. Supp. 202 (E.D. Va. 1990).

Selection criteria functional equivalent of statutorily required terms and conditions. — Selection criteria used by health insurance company to devise a short list of eligible providers with which the company would engage in price negotiations were the functional equivalent of statutorily required terms and conditions. HCA Health Servs. of Va., Inc. v. Metropolitan Life Ins. Co., 752 F. Supp. 202 (E.D. Va. 1990).

Statute prohibits unreasonable discrimination. — This section does not mandate nondiscriminatory terms and conditions; rather, it prohibits unreasonable discrimination against or among providers. Reasonable discrimination between providers is necessary to establish a limited network that can effectively reduce costs by inducing hospitals to lower prices in exchange for a greater market share. HCA Health Servs. of Va., Inc. v. Metropolitan Life Ins. Co., 752 F. Supp. 202 (E.D. Va. 1990).

Exclusion of certain providers did not unreasonably discriminate among providers. — Neither the exclusion of institutional providers that deliver specialized rather than general acute care services nor the exclusion of providers whose services have not been heavily utilized in the past by the insurer's beneficiaries unreasonably discriminates among providers for the purpose of establishing a preferred provider organization. HCA Health Servs. of Va., Inc. v. Metropolitan Life Ins. Co., 752 F. Supp. 202 (E.D. Va. 1990).

Division of territory into areas reflecting usage of providers does not discriminate among providers. — The division of a territory into service areas that reflect the population usage of providers does not inherently unreasonably discriminate against or among providers. HCA Health Servs. of Va., Inc. v. Metropolitan Life Ins. Co., 752 F. Supp. 202 (E.D. Va. 1990).

Discrimination in credentialing not found. — Preferred provider organization's credentialing policy to deny the applications of physicians who have been disciplined for professional misconduct did not discriminate unreasonably against plaintiff. There was no evidence to show that defendant accepted the applications of other similarly situated physicians who were disciplined by the Virginia Board of Medicine or that defendant's consideration, in its credentialing, of plaintiff's reprimand by the Virginia Board of Medicine for professional misconduct was an unreasonable criterion. Richter v. Capp Care, Inc., 868 F. Supp. 163 (E.D. Va. 1994), aff'd, 77 F.3d 470 (4th Cir. 1996).

Preemption claim should be first addressed. — In dispute between hospitals and insurer brought under this section, district court erred in interpreting the state statute before deciding if the hospital's state law claims were preempted by the Employee Retirement Income Security Act of 1974 (ERISA). If ERISA preempts a state law, that is the end of the matter. HCA Health Servs. v. Metropolitan Life Ins. Co., 957 F.2d 120 (4th Cir. 1992).

§ 38.2-3407.1. Interest on accident and sickness claim proceeds. — A. If an action to recover the claim proceeds due under an individual or group accident and sickness policy results in a judgment against an insurer, interest on the judgment at the legal rate of interest shall be paid from the date of presentation to the insurer of proof of loss to the date judgment is entered.

B. If no action is brought, interest upon the claim proceeds paid to the policyholder, insured, claimant, or assignee entitled thereto shall be computed daily at the legal rate of interest from the date of fifteen working days from the insurer's receipt of proof of loss to the date of claim payment.

C. This section shall not apply to individual policies issued prior to July 1, 1990, but shall apply to any renewals or reissues of group accident and sickness policies occurring after that date.

D. This section shall not apply to claims for which payment has been or will be made directly to health care providers pursuant to a negotiated reimbursement arrangement requiring uniform or periodic interim payments to be applied against the insurer's obligation on such claims.

E. For purposes of this section, *"proof of loss"* means all necessary documentation reasonably required by the insurer to make a determination of benefit coverage. (1990, c. 531; 1992, c. 23; 1996, c. 75.)

§ 38.2-3407.2. Coverage for medical child support. — A. No insurer, health services plan, or health maintenance organization shall refuse to enroll a child under a parent's coverage because (i) the child was born out of wedlock; (ii) the child is not claimed as a dependent on the parent's federal income tax return; or (iii) the child does not reside with the parent or in the insurer's, health services plan's, or health maintenance organization's service area.

B. Upon receipt of proof that a parent eligible for family coverage under an accident and sickness policy, health services plan, or health maintenance organization contract has been required by a court or administrative order to provide health coverage for a child, the insurer, health services plan, or health maintenance organization shall:

1. Permit such parent to enroll under such family coverage any such child who is otherwise eligible for such coverage, without regard to any enrollment season restrictions;

2. If such parent is enrolled but fails to make application to obtain coverage for such child, enroll such child upon application by the child's other parent or by the Department of Social Services; and

3. Not disenroll or otherwise eliminate coverage of such child unless the insurer, health services plan, or health maintenance organization is provided satisfactory written evidence that:

a. Such court or administrative order is no longer in effect;

b. Such child is or will be enrolled in comparable health coverage through another insurer, health services plan, or health maintenance organization which will take effect not later than the effective date of termination of the child's coverage under the policy or contract issued by the insurer, health services plan, or health maintenance organization; or

c. Family health coverage has been eliminated under the insurance policy, health services plan, or health maintenance organization contract.

C. Any insurer, health services plan, or health maintenance organization providing coverage to the child of a noncustodial parent shall (i) provide to the custodial parent, upon request, any information that is necessary to obtain benefits for such child under such coverage; (ii) permit the custodial parent, or the provider of health services if approved by the custodial parent, to submit claims for services without the approval of the noncustodial parent; and (iii) make payment on claims submitted pursuant to clause (ii) directly to such custodial parent, provider, or the Department of Medical Assistance Services. (1994, c. 213.)

§ 38.2-3407.3. Calculation of cost-sharing provisions. — A. An insurer, health services plan or health maintenance organization that issues an accident and sickness insurance policy or contract pursuant to which the insured, subscriber or enrollee is required to pay a specified percentage of the cost of covered services, shall calculate such amount payable based upon an amount not to exceed the total amount actually paid or payable to the provider of such services for the services provided to the insured, subscriber or enrollee. When an insured, subscriber or enrollee receives covered services outside the insurer's, health services plan's or health maintenance organization's provider network, and such entity utilizes another insurer's, health services plan's or health maintenance organization's provider network located outside the Commonwealth, such entity may satisfy the obligation of this section by using the cost of services as reported by the out-of-state insurer, health services plan or health maintenance organization when calculating the insured's, subscriber's or enrollee's percentage of the cost of covered services.

B. Any insurer, health services plan or health maintenance organization failing to administer its contracts as set forth herein shall be deemed to have committed a knowing and willful violation of this section, and shall be punished as set forth in subsection A of § 38.2-218. Each claim payment found to have been calculated in noncompliance with this section shall be deemed a separate and distinct violation, and shall further be deemed a violation subject to subdivision D 1 c of § 38.2-218, permitting the Commission to require restitution in addition to any other penalties. (1994, c. 320; 1997, c. 56; 1998, c. 49.)

The 1998 amendment added the second sentence in subsection A.

§ 38.2-3407.3:1. Premium payment arrearages; order of crediting payments. — Each (i) insurer proposing to issue individual or group accident and sickness insurance policies providing hospital, medical and surgical or major medical coverage on an expense-incurred basis, (ii) corporation providing individual or group accident and sickness subscription contracts, and (iii) health maintenance organization providing a health care plan for health care services, shall when accepting premium payments in arrears, credit any such payments first to the longest-outstanding arrearage, and then in succession to the most recent arrearage or payment due. (1999, c. 321.)

§ 38.2-3407.4. Explanation of benefits. — A. Each insurer issuing an accident and sickness insurance policy, a corporation issuing subscription contracts, and each health maintenance organization shall file for approval explanation of benefits forms. These explanation of benefit forms shall be subject to the requirements of § 38.2-316 or § 38.2-4306 as applicable.

B. The explanation of benefits shall accurately and clearly set forth the benefits payable under the contract.

C. The Commission may issue regulations to establish standards for the accuracy and clarity of the information presented in an explanation of benefits.

D. The term "explanation of benefits" as used in this section shall include any form provided by an insurer, health services plan or health maintenance organization which explains the amounts covered under a policy or plan or shows the amounts payable by a covered person to a health care provider. (1994, c. 320.)

The number of this section was assigned by the Virginia Code Commission, the number in the 1994 act having been 38.2-3407.2.

§ 38.2-3407.4:1. Uniform referral form. — The State Corporation Commission shall adopt a uniform referral form for any health care entity defined as a utilization management organization by the Health Care Financing Administration for its Electronic Data Interchange (EDI). In developing the form, the Commission shall incorporate only the data elements adopted by the Health Care Financing Administration for its EDI standards. Any such entity which requires its insureds, subscribers or enrollees to obtain a referral in writing to receive consultation services shall use the uniform referral form adopted by the Commission as the only instrument for referrals for consultation services. Such entity may not impose, as a condition of coverage, any requirement to modify the uniform referral form or submit additional referral forms. (1998, c. 148.)

§ 38.2-3407.5. Denial of benefits for certain prescription drugs prohibited. — A. Each (i) insurer proposing to issue individual or group accident and sickness insurance policies providing hospital, medical and surgical or major medical coverage on an expense incurred basis, (ii) corporation providing individual or group accident and sickness subscription contracts, and (iii) health maintenance organization providing a health care plan for health care services, whose policy, contract or plan, including any certificate or evidence of coverage issued in connection with such policy, contract or plan, includes coverage for prescription drugs, whether on an inpatient basis, outpatient basis, or both, shall provide in each such policy, contract, plan, certificate, and evidence of coverage that such benefits will not be denied for any drug approved by the United States Food and Drug Administration for use in the treatment of cancer on the basis that the drug has not been approved by the United States Food and Drug Administration for the treatment of the specific type of cancer for which the drug has been prescribed, provided the drug has been recognized as safe and effective for treatment of that specific type of cancer in any of the standard reference compendia.

B. Each (i) insurer proposing to issue individual or group accident and sickness insurance policies providing hospital, medical and surgical or major medical coverage on an expense-incurred basis, (ii) corporation providing individual or group accident and sickness subscription contracts, and (iii) health maintenance organization providing a health care plan for health care services, whose policy, contract or plan, including any certificate or evidence of coverage issued in connection with such policy, contract or plan, includes coverage for prescription drugs, whether on an inpatient basis, outpatient basis, or both, shall provide in each such policy, contract, plan, certificate, and evidence of coverage that such benefits will not be denied for any drug prescribed to treat a covered indication so long as the drug has been approved by the United States Food and Drug Administration for at least one indication and the drug is recognized for treatment of the covered indication in one of the standard reference compendia or in substantially accepted peer-reviewed medical literature.

C. For the purposes of subsections A and B:

"Peer-reviewed medical literature" means a scientific study published only after having been critically reviewed for scientific accuracy, validity, and reliability by unbiased independent experts in a journal that has been determined by the International Committee of Medical Journal Editors to have met the Uniform Requirements for Manuscripts submitted to biomedical journals. Peer-reviewed medical literature does not include publications or supplements to publications that are sponsored to a significant extent by a pharmaceutical manufacturing company or health carrier.

"Standard reference compendia" means the American Medical Association Drug Evaluations, the American Hospital Formulary Service Drug Information, or the United States Pharmacopoeia Dispensing Information.

D. Coverage, as described in subsections A and B, includes medically necessary services associated with the administration of the drug.

E. Subsections A and B shall not be construed to do any of the following:

1. Require coverage for any drug if the United States Food and Drug Administration has determined its use to be contraindicated for the treatment of the specific type of cancer or indication for which the drug has been prescribed;

2. Require coverage for experimental drugs not otherwise approved for any indication by the United States Food and Drug Administration;

3. Alter any law with regard to provisions limiting the coverage of drugs that have not been approved by the United States Food and Drug Administration;

4. Create, impair, alter, limit, modify, enlarge, abrogate, or prohibit reimbursement for drugs used in the treatment of any other disease or condition; or

5. Require coverage for prescription drugs in any contract, policy or plan that does not otherwise provide such coverage.

F. The provisions of this section shall not apply to short-term travel, or accident-only policies, or to short-term nonrenewable policies of not more than six months' duration.

G. The provisions of subsection A are applicable to contracts, policies or plans delivered, issued for delivery or renewed in this Commonwealth on and after July 1, 1994, and the provisions of subsection B are applicable to contracts, policies or plans delivered, issued for delivery or renewed in this Commonwealth on and after July 1, 1997. (1994, c. 374; 1997, c. 656.)

The number of this section was assigned
by the Virginia Code Commission, the number
in the 1994 act having been 38.2-3407.2.

§ 38.2-3407.5:1. Coverage for prescription contraceptives. — A. Each
(i) insurer proposing to issue individual or group accident and sickness
insurance policies providing hospital, medical and surgical or major medical
coverage on an expense incurred basis; (ii) corporation providing individual or
group accident and sickness subscription contracts; and (iii) health maintenance organization providing a health care plan for health care services, whose
policy, contract or plan, including any certificate or evidence of coverage issued
in connection with such policy, contract or plan, includes coverage for prescription drugs on an outpatient basis, shall offer and make available coverage
thereunder for any prescribed drug or device approved by the United States
Food and Drug Administration for use as a contraceptive.

B. No insurer, corporation or health maintenance organization shall impose
upon any person receiving prescription contraceptive benefits pursuant to this
section any (i) copayment, coinsurance payment or fee that is not equally
imposed upon all individuals in the same benefit category, class, coinsurance
level or copayment level receiving benefits for prescription drugs, or (ii)
reduction in allowable reimbursement for prescription drug benefits.

C. The provisions of subsection A shall not be construed to:

1. Require coverage for prescription coverage benefits in any contract, policy
or plan that does not otherwise provide coverage for prescription drugs;

2. Preclude the use of closed formularies, provided, however, that such
formularies shall include oral, implant and injectable contraceptive drugs,
intrauterine devices and prescription barrier methods; or

3. Require coverage for experimental contraceptive drugs not approved by
the United States Food and Drug Administration.

D. The provisions of this section shall not apply to short-term travel,
accident-only, limited or specified disease policies, or contracts designed for
issuance to persons eligible for coverage under Title XVIII of the Social
Security Act, known as Medicare, or any other similar coverage under state or
federal governmental plans, or to short-term nonrenewable policies of not more
than six months' duration.

E. The provisions of this section shall be applicable to contracts, policies or
plans delivered, issued for delivery or renewed in this Commonwealth on and
after July 1, 1997. (1997, c. 748.)

§ 38.2-3407.6. Exclusion of podiatrist not permitted under certain
circumstances. — No podiatrist shall be excluded from participating in any
preferred provider plan pursuant to this chapter or Chapter 42 (§ 38.2-4200 et
seq.) of this title or health maintenance organization pursuant to Chapter 43
(§ 38.2-4300 et seq.) of this title solely because such preferred provider plan or
health maintenance organization requires that participating health care
providers have active medical staff privileges or admitting medical staff
privileges at specified hospitals, provided that the podiatrist has a delineation
of privileges that enables such podiatrist to perform the type of services that
are covered by the preferred provider plan or health maintenance organization
at the designated hospital or hospitals. The Commission shall have no
jurisdiction to adjudicate controversies arising out of this section. (1994, c.
522.)

The number of this section was assigned
by the Virginia Code Commission, the number
in the 1994 act having been 38.2-3407.2.

§ 38.2-3407.6:1. Denial of benefits for certain prescription drugs prohibited. — A. Each (i) insurer proposing to issue individual or group accident and sickness insurance policies providing hospital, medical and surgical or major medical coverage on an expense-incurred basis, (ii) corporation providing individual or group accident and sickness subscription contracts, and (iii) health maintenance organization providing a health care plan for health care services, whose policy, contract or plan, including any certificate or evidence of coverage issued in connection with such policy, contract or plan, includes coverage for prescription drugs, whether on an inpatient basis, an outpatient basis, or both, shall provide in each such policy, contract, plan, certificate, and evidence of coverage that such benefits shall not be denied for any drug approved by the United States Food and Drug Administration for use in the treatment of cancer pain on the basis that the dosage is in excess of the recommended dosage of the pain-relieving agent, if the prescription in excess of the recommended dosage has been prescribed in compliance with §§ 54.1-2971.01, 54.1-3303 and 54.1-3408.1 for a patient with intractable cancer pain.

B. The provisions of this section shall not apply to short-term travel, or accident-only policies, or to short-term nonrenewable policies of not more than six months' duration.

C. The provisions of this section are applicable to contracts, policies or plans delivered, issued for delivery or renewed in this Commonwealth on and after July 1, 1999. (1999, c. 857.)

§ 38.2-3407.7. Pharmacies; freedom of choice. — A. Notwithstanding any provision of § 38.2-3407 to the contrary, no insurer proposing to issue preferred provider policies or contracts shall prohibit any person receiving pharmacy benefits furnished thereunder from selecting, without limitation, the pharmacy of his choice to furnish such benefits. This right of selection extends to and includes pharmacies that are nonpreferred providers and that have previously notified the insurer, by facsimile or otherwise, of their agreement to accept reimbursement for their services at rates applicable to pharmacies that are preferred providers, including any copayment consistently imposed by the insurer, as payment in full. Each insurer shall permit prompt electronic or telephonic transmittal of the reimbursement agreement by the pharmacy and ensure prompt verification to the pharmacy of the terms of reimbursement. In no event shall any person receiving a covered pharmacy benefit from a nonpreferred provider which has submitted a reimbursement agreement be responsible for amounts that may be charged by the nonpreferred provider in excess of the copayment and the insurer's reimbursement applicable to all of its preferred pharmacy providers.

B. No such insurer shall impose upon any person receiving pharmaceutical benefits furnished under any such policy or contract:

1. Any copayment, fee or condition that is not equally imposed upon all individuals in the same benefit category, class or copayment level, whether or not such benefits are furnished by pharmacists who are nonpreferred providers;

2. Any monetary penalty that would affect or influence any such person's choice of pharmacy; or

3. Any reduction in allowable reimbursement for pharmacy services related to utilization of pharmacists who are nonpreferred providers.

C. For purposes of this section, a prohibited condition or penalty shall include, without limitation: (i) denying immediate access to electronic claims filing to a pharmacy which is a nonpreferred provider and which has complied with subsection D below or (ii) requiring a person receiving pharmacy benefits to make payment at point of service, except to the extent such conditions and penalties are similarly imposed on preferred providers.

D. Any pharmacy which wishes to be covered by this section shall, if requested to do so in writing by an insurer, within thirty days of the pharmacy's receipt of the request, execute and deliver to the insurer the direct service agreement or preferred provider agreement which the insurer requires all of its preferred providers of pharmacy benefits to execute. Any pharmacy which fails to timely execute and deliver such agreement shall not be covered by this section with respect to that insurer unless and until the pharmacy executes and delivers the agreement.

E. The Commission shall have no jurisdiction to adjudicate controversies arising out of this section. (1994, c. 963; 1995, c. 467.)

The number of this section was assigned by the Virginia Code Commission, the number in the 1994 act having been 38.2-3407.2.

§ **38.2-3407.8:** Repealed by Acts 1995, c. 467.

§ **38.2-3407.9. Reimbursement for ambulance services.** — A. If an accident and sickness insurance policy provides coverage for ambulance services, any person providing such services to a person covered under such policy shall receive reimbursement for such services directly from the issuer of such policy, when the issuer of such policy is presented with an assignment of benefits by the person providing such services.

B. For the purposes of this section, "ambulance services" means the transportation of any person requiring resuscitation or emergency relief or where human life is endangered, by means of any ambulance, rescue or life-saving vehicle designed or used principally for such purposes. Such term includes emergency medical services ambulances and mobile intensive care units. (1995, c. 420.)

§ **38.2-3407.9:01. Prescription drug formularies.** — A. Each (i) insurer proposing to issue individual or group accident and sickness insurance policies providing hospital, medical and surgical or major medical coverage on an expense-incurred basis, (ii) corporation providing individual or group accident and sickness subscription contracts, and (iii) health maintenance organization providing a health care plan for health care services, whose policy, contract or plan, including any certificate or evidence of coverage issued in connection with such policy, contract or plan, includes coverage for prescription drugs on an outpatient basis may apply a formulary to the prescription drug benefits provided by the insurer, corporation, or health maintenance organization if the formulary is developed, reviewed at least annually, and updated as necessary in consultation with and with the approval of a pharmacy and therapeutics committee, a majority of whose members are actively practicing licensed pharmacists, physicians and other licensed health care providers.

B. If an insurer, corporation, or health maintenance organization maintains one or more closed drug formularies, each insurer, corporation or health maintenance organization shall:

1. Make available to participating providers and pharmacists and to any nonpreferred or nonparticipating pharmacists as described in §§ 38.2-3407.7 and 38.2-4312.1, the complete, current drug formulary or formularies, or any updates thereto, maintained by the insurer, corporation, or health maintenance organization, including a list of the prescription drugs on the formulary by major therapeutic category that specifies whether a particular prescription drug is preferred over other drugs; and

2. Establish a process to allow an enrollee to obtain, without additional cost-sharing beyond that provided for formulary prescription drugs in the

enrollee's covered benefits, a specific, medically necessary nonformulary prescription drug if the formulary drug is determined by the insurer, corporation, or health maintenance organization, after reasonable investigation and consultation with the prescribing physician, to be an inappropriate therapy for the medical condition of the enrollee. The insurer, corporation or health maintenance organization shall act on such requests within one business day of receipt of the request. (1999, cc. 643, 649.)

§ 38.2-3407.10. Health care provider panels. — A. As used in this section:

"Carrier" means:

1. Any insurer proposing to issue individual or group accident and sickness insurance policies providing hospital, medical and surgical or major medical coverage on an expense incurred basis;

2. Any corporation providing individual or group accident and sickness subscription contracts;

3. Any health maintenance organization providing health care plans for health care services;

4. Any corporation offering prepaid dental or optometric services plans; or

5. Any other person or organization that provides health benefit plans subject to state regulation, and includes an entity that arranges a provider panel for compensation.

"Enrollee" means any person entitled to health care services from a carrier.

"Provider" means a hospital, physician or any type of provider licensed, certified or authorized by statute to provide a covered service under the health benefit plan.

"Provider panel" means those providers with which a carrier contracts to provide health care services to the carrier's enrollees under the carrier's health benefit plan. However, such term does not include an arrangement between a carrier and providers in which any provider may participate solely on the basis of the provider's contracting with the carrier to provide services at a discounted fee-for-service rate.

B. Any such carrier which offers a provider panel shall establish and use it in accordance with the following requirements:

1. Notice of the development of a provider panel in the Commonwealth or local service area shall be filed with the Department of Health Professions.

2. Carriers shall provide a provider application and the relevant terms and conditions to a provider upon request.

C. A carrier that uses a provider panel shall establish procedures for:

1. Notifying an enrollee of:

a. The termination from the carrier's provider panel of the enrollee's primary care provider who was furnishing health care services to the enrollee; and

b. The right of an enrollee upon request to continue to receive health care services for a period of up to ninety days from the date of the primary care provider's notice of termination from a carrier's provider panel, except when a provider is terminated for cause.

2. Notifying a provider at least ninety days prior to the date of the termination of the provider, except when a provider is terminated for cause.

3. Providing reasonable notice to primary care providers in the carrier's provider panel of the termination of a specialty referral services provider.

4. Notifying the purchaser of the health benefit plan, whether such purchaser is an individual or an employer providing a health benefit plan, in whole or in part, to its employees and enrollees of the health benefit plan of:

a. A description of all types of payment arrangements that the carrier uses to compensate providers for health care services rendered to enrollees, including, but not limited to, withholds, bonus payments, capitation and fee-for-service discounts; and

b. The terms of the plan in clear and understandable language which reasonably informs the purchaser of the practical application of such terms in the operation of the plan.

D. Whenever a provider voluntarily terminates his contract with a carrier to provide health care services to the carrier's enrollees under a health benefit plan, he shall furnish reasonable notice of such termination to his patients who are enrollees under such plan.

E. A carrier may not deny an application for participation or terminate participation on its provider panel on the basis of gender, race, age, religion or national origin.

F. 1. For a period of at least ninety days from the date of the notice of a provider's termination from the carrier's provider panel, except when a provider is terminated for cause, the provider shall be permitted by the carrier to render health care services to any of the carrier's enrollees who:

a. Were in an active course of treatment from the provider prior to the notice of termination; and

b. Request to continue receiving health care services from the provider.

2. Notwithstanding the provisions of subdivision 1, any provider shall be permitted by the carrier to continue rendering health services to any enrollee who has entered the second trimester of pregnancy at the time of a provider's termination of participation, except when a provider is terminated for cause. Such treatment shall, at the enrollee's option, continue through the provision of postpartum care directly related to the delivery.

3. Notwithstanding the provisions of subdivision 1, any provider shall be permitted by the carrier to continue rendering health services to any enrollee who is determined to be terminally ill (as defined under § 1861 (dd) (3) (A) of the Social Security Act) at the time of a provider's termination of participation, except when a provider is terminated for cause. Such treatment shall, at the enrollee's option, continue for the remainder of the enrollee's life for care directly related to the treatment of the terminal illness.

4. A carrier shall reimburse a provider under this subsection in accordance with the carrier's agreement with such provider existing immediately before the provider's termination of participation.

G. 1. A carrier shall provide to a purchaser prior to enrollment and to existing enrollees at least once a year a list of members in its provider panel, which list shall also indicate those providers who are not currently accepting new patients.

2. The information provided under subdivision 1 shall be updated at least once a year.

H. No contract between a carrier and a provider may require that the provider indemnify the carrier for the carrier's negligence, willful misconduct, or breach of contract, if any.

I. No contract between a carrier and a provider shall require a provider, as a condition of participation on the panel, to waive any right to seek legal redress against the carrier.

J. No contract between a carrier and a provider shall prohibit, impede or interfere in the discussion of medical treatment options between a patient and a provider.

K. A contract between a carrier and a provider shall permit and require the provider to discuss medical treatment options with the patient.

L. Any carrier requiring preauthorization prior to rendering medical treatment shall have personnel available to provide such authorization at all times when such preauthorization is required.

M. Carriers shall provide to their group policyholders written notice of any benefit reductions during the contract period at least sixty days before such benefit reductions become effective. Group policyholders shall, in turn, provide to their enrollees written notice of any benefit reductions during the contract period at least thirty days before such benefit reductions become effective.

N. No contract between a provider and a carrier shall include provisions which require a health care provider or health care provider group to deny covered services that such provider or group knows to be medically necessary and appropriate that are provided with respect to a specific enrollee or group of enrollees with similar medical conditions.

O. The Commission shall have no jurisdiction to adjudicate controversies arising out of this section.

P. The requirements of this section shall apply to all insurance policies, contracts, and plans delivered, issued for delivery, reissued, or extended on or after July 1, 1996. However, the ninety-day period referred to in subdivisions C 1 b and C 2 of this section, the requirements set forth in subdivisions F 2 and F 3, and the requirements set forth in subsections L, M, and N shall apply to contracts between carriers and providers that are entered into or renewed on or after July 1, 1999. (1996, c. 776; 1999, cc. 643, 649.)

The 1999 amendments. — The 1999 amendment by c. 643, in subsection C, substituted "ninety" for "sixty" in subdivisions 1 b and 2; in subsection F, substituted "ninety" for "sixty" in subdivision 1, redesignated former subdivision 2 as present subdivision 4; inserted present subdivisions 2 and 3; redesignated former subsections L and M as present subsections O and P; inserted present subsections L through N; and added the final sentence in subsection P.

The 1999 amendment by c. 649, in subsection C, substituted "ninety" for "sixty" in subdivisions 1 b and 2; in subsection F, substituted "ninety" for "sixty" in subdivision 1, redesignated former subdivision 2 as present subdivision 4, inserted present subdivisions 2 and 3, substituted "such provider existing immediately before the provider's termination of participation" for "the providers" in subdivision 4; redesignated former subsections L and M as subsections O and P, inserted present subsections L through N; in subsection P, deleted "or at any time after the effective date hereof when any term of any such policy, contract, or plan is changed or any premium adjustment is made." at the end of the first sentence, deleted the former second sentence, which read: "In addition, the requirements of this section shall apply to contracts between carriers and providers that are entered into or renewed on or after July 1, 1996" and added the present second sentence.

§ 38.2-3407.11. Access to obstetrician-gynecologists. — A. Each (i) insurer proposing to issue individual or group accident and sickness insurance policies providing hospital, medical and surgical or major medical coverage on an expense incurred basis, (ii) corporation providing individual or group accident and sickness subscription contracts, and (iii) health maintenance organization providing a health care plan for health care services, whose policies, contracts or plans, including any certificate or evidence of coverage issued in connection with such policies, contracts or plans, include coverage for obstetrical or gynecological services, shall permit any female of age thirteen or older covered thereunder direct access, as provided in subsection B, to the health care services of a participating obstetrician-gynecologist (i) authorized to provide services under such policy, contract or plan and (ii) selected by such female.

B. An annual examination, and routine health care services incident to and rendered during an annual visit, may be performed without prior authorization from the primary care physician. However, additional health care services may be provided subject to the following:

1. Consultation, which may be by telephone, with the primary care physician for follow-up care or subsequent visits;

2. Prior consultation and authorization by the primary care physician, including a visit to the primary care physician, if determined necessary by the

primary care physician before the patient may be directed to another specialty provider; and

3. Prior authorization by the insurer, corporation, or health maintenance organization for proposed inpatient hospitalization or outpatient surgical procedures.

C. For the purpose of this section, *"health care services"* means the full scope of medically necessary services provided by the obstetrician-gynecologist in the care of or related to the female reproductive system and breasts and in performing annual screening and immunization for disorders and diseases in accordance with the most current published recommendations of the American College of Obstetricians and Gynecologists. The term includes services provided by nurse practitioners, physician assistants, and certified nurse midwives in collaboration with the obstetrician-gynecologists providing care to individuals covered under any such policies, contracts or plans.

D. Nothing contained herein shall prohibit an insurer, corporation, or health maintenance organization from requiring a participating obstetrician-gynecologist to provide written notification to the covered female's primary care physician of any visit to such obstetrician-gynecologist. Such notification may include a description of the health care services rendered at the time of the visit.

E. Each insurer, corporation or health maintenance organization subject to the provisions of this section shall inform subscribers of the provisions of this section. Such notice shall be provided in writing.

F. The requirements of this section shall apply to all insurance policies, contracts, and plans delivered, issued for delivery, reissued, renewed, or extended or at any time when any term of any such policy, contract, or plan is changed or any premium adjustment is made. The provisions of this section shall not apply to short-term travel or accident-only policies, or to short-term nonrenewable policies of not more than six months' duration. (1996, c. 967; 1997, c. 806.)

The number of this section was assigned by the Virginia Code Commission, the number in the 1996 act having been 38.2-3407.10.

§ 38.2-3407.11:1. Access to specialists; standing referrals. — A. Each (i) insurer proposing to issue individual or group accident and sickness insurance policies providing hospital, medical and surgical or major medical coverage on an expense-incurred basis, (ii) corporation providing individual or group accident and sickness subscription contracts, and (iii) health maintenance organization providing a health care plan for health care services shall permit any individual covered thereunder direct access, as provided in subsection B, to the health care services of a participating specialist (i) authorized to provide services under such policy, contract or plan and (ii) selected by such individual.

B. An insurer, corporation, or health maintenance organization, in connection with the provision of health insurance coverage, shall have a procedure by which an individual who is a participant, beneficiary, or enrollee and who has an ongoing special condition may, after consultation with the primary care physician, receive a referral to a specialist for such condition who shall be responsible for and capable of providing and coordinating the individual's primary and specialty care related to the initial specialty care referral. If such an individual's care would most appropriately be coordinated by such a specialist, such plan or issuer shall refer the individual to a specialist. For the purposes of this section, "special condition" means a condition or disease that is (i) life-threatening, degenerative, or disabling and (ii) requires specialized medical care over a prolonged period of time.

C. Within the treatment period authorized by the referral, such specialist shall be permitted to treat the individual without a further referral from the individual's primary care provider and may authorize such referrals, procedures, tests, and other medical services related to the initial referral as the individual's primary care provider would otherwise be permitted to provide or authorize.

D. An insurer, corporation, or health maintenance organization, in connection with the provision of health insurance coverage, shall have a procedure by which an individual who is a participant, beneficiary, or enrollee and who has an ongoing special condition that requires ongoing care from a specialist may receive a standing referral to such specialist for the treatment of the special condition. If the plan or issuer, or if the primary care provider in consultation with the plan or issuer and the specialist, if any, determines that such a standing referral is appropriate, the plan or issuer shall make such a referral to a specialist.

E. Nothing contained herein shall prohibit an insurer, corporation, or health maintenance organization from requiring a participating specialist to provide written notification to the covered individual's primary care physician of any visit to such specialist. Such notification may include a description of the health care services rendered at the time of the visit.

F. Each insurer, corporation or health maintenance organization subject to the provisions of this section shall inform subscribers of the provisions of this section. Such notice shall be provided in writing, and included in the policy or evidence of coverage.

G. The requirements of this section shall apply to all insurance policies, contracts, and plans delivered, issued for delivery, reissued, renewed, or extended or at any time when any term of any such policy, contract, or plan is changed or any premium adjustment is made. The provisions of this section shall not apply to short-term travel or accident-only policies, to short-term nonrenewable policies of not more than six months' duration, or policies or contracts issued to persons eligible under Title XVIII of the Social Security Act, known as Medicare, or any other similar coverage under state or federal governmental plans. (1999, cc. 643, 649.)

§ **38.2-3407.11:2. Standing referral for cancer patients.** — A. Each (i) insurer proposing to issue individual or group accident and sickness insurance policies providing hospital, medical and surgical or major medical coverage on an expense incurred basis, (ii) corporation providing individual or group accident and sickness subscription contracts, and (iii) health maintenance organization providing a health care plan for health care services, whose policies, contracts or plans, including any certificate or evidence of coverage issued in connection with such policies, contracts or plans, shall have a procedure in place to permit any individual covered thereunder who has been diagnosed with cancer to have a standing referral to a board-certified physician in pain management or oncologist who is authorized to provide services under such policy, contract or plan and has been selected by the cancer patient.

B. The board-certified physician in pain management or oncologist shall consult on a regular basis, as required under the terms of the policy, contract or plan, by telephone or through written communication, with the primary care physician and any oncologist providing care to the patient concerning the plan of pain management for the patient. Further, this section shall not be construed to authorize the board-certified physician in pain management or oncologist to direct the patient to other health care services.

C. Nothing contained herein shall prohibit an insurer, corporation, or health maintenance organization from requiring a participating board-certified physician in pain management or oncologist to provide written notification to the cancer patient's primary care physician of any visit to him. Such notification may include a description of the health care services rendered at the time of the visit.

D. Each insurer, corporation or health maintenance organization subject to the provisions of this section shall inform subscribers, in writing, within the policy or evidence of coverage of the provisions of this section.

E. The requirements of this section shall apply to all insurance policies, contracts, and plans delivered, issued for delivery, reissued, renewed, or extended or at any time when any term of any such policy, contract, or plan is changed or any premium adjustment is made. The provisions of this section shall not apply to short-term travel or accident-only policies, to short-term nonrenewable policies of not more than six months' duration, or policies or contracts issued to persons eligible under Title XVIII of the Social Security Act, known as Medicare, or any other similar coverage under state or federal governmental plans. (1999, c. 856.)

The number of this section was assigned by the Virginia Code Commission, the number in the 1999 act having been § 38.2-3407.11:1.

§ 38.2-3407.12. Patient optional point-of-service benefit. — A. As used in this section:

"Affiliate" shall have the meaning set forth in § 38.2-1322.

"Allowable charge" means the amount from which the carrier's payment to a provider for any covered item or service is determined before taking into account any cost-sharing arrangement.

"Carrier" means:

1. Any insurer licensed under this title proposing to offer or issue accident and sickness insurance policies which are subject to Chapter 34 (§ 38.2-3400 et seq.) or 39 (§ 38.2-3900 et seq.) of this title;

2. Any nonstock corporation licensed under this title proposing to issue or deliver subscription contracts for one or more health services plans, medical or surgical services plans or hospital services plans which are subject to Chapter 42 (§ 38.2-4200 et seq.) of this title;

3. Any health maintenance organization licensed under this title which provides or arranges for the provision of one or more health care plans which are subject to Chapter 43 (§ 38.2-4300 et seq.) of this title;

4. Any nonstock corporation licensed under this title proposing to issue or deliver subscription contracts for one or more dental or optometric services plans which are subject to Chapter 45 (§ 38.2-4500 et seq.) of this title; and

5. Any other person licensed under this title which provides or arranges for the provision of health care coverage or benefits or health care plans or provider panels which are subject to regulation as the business of insurance under this title.

"Co-insurance" means the portion of the carrier's allowable charge for the covered item or service which is not paid by the carrier and for which the enrollee is responsible.

"Co-payment" means the out-of-pocket charge other than co-insurance or a deductible for an item or service to be paid by the enrollee to the provider towards the allowable charge as a condition of the receipt of specific health care items and services.

"Cost sharing arrangement" means any co-insurance, co-payment, deductible or similar arrangement imposed by the carrier on the enrollee as a condition to or consequence of the receipt of covered items or services.

"Deductible" means the dollar amount of a covered item or service which the enrollee is obligated to pay before benefits are payable under the carrier's policy or contract with the group contract holder.

"Enrollee" or *"member"* means any individual who is enrolled in a group health benefit plan provided or arranged by a health maintenance organization or other carrier. If a health maintenance organization arranges or contracts for the point-of-service benefit required under this section through another carrier, any enrollee selecting the point-of-service benefit shall be treated as an enrollee of that other carrier when receiving covered items or services under the point-of-service benefit.

"Group contract holder" means any contract holder of a group health benefit plan offered or arranged by a health maintenance organization or other carrier. For purposes of this section, the group contract holder shall be the person to which the group agreement or contract for the group health benefit plan is issued.

"Group health benefit plan" shall mean any health care plan, subscription contract, evidence of coverage, certificate, health services plan, medical or hospital services plan, accident and sickness insurance policy or certificate, or other similar certificate, policy, contract or arrangement, and any endorsement or rider thereto, offered, arranged or issued by a carrier to a group contract holder to cover all or a portion of the cost of enrollees (or their eligible dependents) receiving covered health care items or services. Group health benefit plan does not mean (i) health care plans, contracts or policies issued in the individual market; (ii) coverages issued pursuant to Title XVIII of the Social Security Act, 42 U.S.C. § 1395 et seq. (Medicare), Title XIX of the Social Security Act, 42 U.S.C. § 1396 et seq. or Title XX of the Social Security Act, 42 U.S.C. § 1397 et seq. (Medicaid), 5 U.S.C. § 8901 et seq. (federal employees), 10 U.S.C. § 1071 et seq. (CHAMPUS) or Chapter 2 (§ 2.1-11.1 et seq.) of Title 2.1 (state employees); (iii) accident only, credit or disability insurance, or long-term care insurance, plans providing only limited health care services under § 38.2-4300 (unless offered by endorsement or rider to a group health benefit plan), CHAMPUS supplement, Medicare supplement, or workers' compensation coverages; (iv) an employee welfare benefit plan (as defined in section 3 (1) of the Employee Retirement Income Security Act of 1974, 29 U.S.C. § 1002 (1)), which is self-insured or self-funded; or (v) the essential and standard health benefit plans developed pursuant to § 38.2-3431 C.

"Group specific administrative cost" means the direct administrative cost incurred by a carrier related to the offer of the point-of-service benefit to a particular group contract holder.

"Health care plan" shall have the meaning set forth in § 38.2-4300.

"Person" means any individual, corporation, trust, association, partnership, limited liability company, organization or other entity.

"Point-of-service benefit" means a health maintenance organization's delivery system or covered benefits, or the delivery system or covered benefits of another carrier under contract or arrangement with the health maintenance organization, which permit an enrollee (and eligible dependents) to receive covered items and services outside of the provider panel, including optometrists and clinical psychologists, of the health maintenance organization under the terms and conditions of the group contract holder's group health benefit plan with the health maintenance organization or with another carrier arranged by or under contract with the health maintenance organization and which otherwise complies with this section. Without limiting the foregoing, the benefits offered or arranged by a carrier's indemnity group accident and sickness policy under Chapter 34 (§ 38.2-3400 et seq.) of this title, health services plan under Chapter 42 (§ 38.2-4200 et seq.) of this title or preferred provider organization plan under Chapter 34 (§ 38.2-3400 et seq.) or 42 (§ 38.2-4200 et seq.) of this title which permit an enrollee (and eligible dependents) to receive the full range of covered items and services outside of a provider panel, including optometrists and clinical psychologists, and which

are otherwise in compliance with applicable law and this section shall constitute a point-of-service benefit.

"Preferred provider organization plan" means a health benefit program offered pursuant to a preferred provider policy or contract under § 38.2-3407 or covered services offered under a preferred provider subscription contract under § 38.2-4209.

"Provider" means any physician, hospital or other person, including optometrists and clinical psychologists, that is licensed or otherwise authorized in the Commonwealth to deliver or furnish health care items or services.

"Provider panel" means the participating providers or referral providers who have a contract, agreement or arrangement with a health maintenance organization or other carrier, either directly or through an intermediary, and who have agreed to provide items or services to enrollees of the health maintenance organization or other carrier.

B. To the maximum extent permitted by applicable law, every health care plan offered or proposed to be offered in this Commonwealth by a health maintenance organization licensed under this title to a group contract holder shall provide or include, or the health maintenance organization shall arrange for or contract with another carrier to provide or include, a point-of-service benefit to be provided or offered in conjunction with the health maintenance organization's health care plan as an additional benefit for the enrollee, at the enrollee's option, individually to accept or reject. In connection with its group enrollment application, every health maintenance organization shall, at no additional cost to the group contract holder, make available or arrange with a carrier to make available to the prospective group contract holder and to all prospective enrollees, in advance of initial enrollment and in advance of each reenrollment, a notice in form and substance acceptable to the Commission which accurately and completely explains to the group contract holder and prospective enrollee the point-of-service benefit and permits each enrollee to make his or her election. The form of notice provided in connection with any reenrollment may be the same as the approved form of notice used in connection with initial enrollment and may be made available to the group contract holder and prospective enrollee by the carrier in any reasonable manner.

C. To the extent permitted under applicable law, a health maintenance organization providing or arranging, or contracting with another carrier to provide, the point-of-service benefit under this section and a carrier providing the point-of-service benefit required under this section under arrangement or contract with a health maintenance organization:

1. May not impose, or permit to be imposed, a minimum enrollee participation level on the point-of-service benefit alone;

2. May not refuse to reimburse a provider of the type listed or referred to in § 38.2-3408 or § 38.2-4221 for items or services provided under the point-of-service benefit required under this section solely on the basis of the license or certification of the provider to provide such items or services if the carrier otherwise covers the items or services provided and the provision of the items or services is within the provider's lawful scope of practice or authority; and

3. Shall rate and underwrite all prospective enrollees of the group contract holder as a single group prior to any enrollee electing to accept or reject the point-of-service benefit.

D. The premium imposed by a carrier with respect to enrollees who select the point-of-service benefit may be different from that imposed by the health maintenance organization with respect to enrollees who do not select the point-of-service benefit. Unless a group contract holder determines otherwise, any enrollee who accepts the point-of-service benefit shall be responsible for the payment of any premium over the amount of the premium applicable to an enrollee who selects the coverage offered by the health maintenance organization without the point-of-service benefit and for any identifiable group specific administrative cost incurred directly by the carrier or any administrative cost incurred by the group contract holder in offering the point-of-service benefit to the enrollee. If a carrier offers the point-of-service benefit to a group contract holder where no enrollees of the group contract holder elect to accept the point-of-service benefit and incurs an identifiable group specific administrative cost directly as a consequence of the offering to that group contract holder, the carrier may reflect that group specific administrative cost in the premium charged to other enrollees selecting the point-of-service benefit under this section. Unless the group contract holder otherwise directs or authorizes the carrier in writing, the carrier shall make reasonable efforts to ensure that no portion of the cost of offering or arranging the point-of-service benefit shall be reflected in the premium charged by the carrier to the group contract holder for a group health benefit plan without the point-of-service benefit. Any premium differential and any group specific administrative cost imposed by a carrier relating to the cost of offering or arranging the point-of-service benefit must be actuarially sound and supported by a sworn certification of an officer of each carrier offering or arranging the point-of-service benefit filed with the Commission certifying that the premiums are based on sound actuarial principles and otherwise comply with this section. The certifications shall be in a form, and shall be accompanied by such supporting information in a form acceptable to the Commission.

E. Any carrier may impose different co-insurance, co-payments, deductibles and other cost-sharing arrangements for the point-of-service benefit required under this section based on whether or not the item or service is provided through the provider panel of the health maintenance organization; provided that, except to the extent otherwise prohibited by applicable law, any such cost-sharing arrangement:

1. Shall not impose on the enrollee (or his or her eligible dependents, as appropriate) any co-insurance percentage obligation which is payable by the enrollee which exceeds the greater of: (i) thirty percent of the carrier's allowable charge for the items or services provided by the provider under the point-of-service benefit or (ii) the co-insurance amount which would have been required had the covered items or services been received through the provider panel;

2. Shall not impose on an enrollee (or his or her eligible dependents, as appropriate) a co-payment or deductible which exceeds the greatest co-payment or deductible, respectively, imposed by the carrier or its affiliate under one or more other group health benefit plans providing a point-of-service benefit which are currently offered and actively marketed by the carrier or its affiliate in the Commonwealth and are subject to regulation under this title; and

3. Shall not result in annual aggregate cost-sharing payments to the enrollee (or his or her eligible dependents, as appropriate) which exceed the greatest annual aggregate cost-sharing payments which would apply had the covered items or services been received under another group health benefit plan providing a point-of-service benefit which is currently offered and actively marketed by the carrier or its affiliate in the Commonwealth and which is subject to regulation under this title.

F. Except to the extent otherwise required under applicable law, any carrier providing the point-of-service benefit required under this section may not utilize an allowable charge or basis for determining the amount to be reimbursed or paid to any provider from which covered items or services are received under the point-of-service benefit which is not at least as favorable to the provider as that used:

1. By the carrier or its affiliate in calculating the reimbursement or payment to be made to similarly situated providers under another group health benefit plan providing a point-of-service benefit which is subject to regulation under this title and which is currently offered or arranged by the carrier or its affiliate and actively marketed in the Commonwealth, if the carrier or its affiliate offers or arranges another such group health benefit plan providing a point-of-service benefit in the Commonwealth; or

2. By the health maintenance organization in calculating the reimbursement or payment to be made to similarly situated providers on its provider panel.

G. Except as expressly permitted in this section or required under applicable law, no carrier shall impose on any person receiving or providing health care items or services under the point-of-service benefit any condition or penalty designed to discourage the enrollee's selection or use of the point-of-service benefit, which is not otherwise similarly imposed either: (i) on enrollees in another group health benefit plan, if any, currently offered or arranged and actively marketed by the carrier or its affiliate in the Commonwealth or (ii) on enrollees who receive the covered items or services from the health maintenance organization's provider panel. Nothing in this section shall preclude a carrier offering or arranging a point-of-service benefit from imposing on enrollees selecting the point-of-service benefit reasonable utilization review, preadmission certification or precertification requirements or other utilization or cost control measures which are similarly imposed on enrollees participating in one or more other group health benefit plans which are subject to regulation under this title and are currently offered and actively marketed by the carrier or its affiliates in the Commonwealth or which are otherwise required under applicable law.

H. Except as expressly otherwise permitted in this section or as otherwise required under applicable law, the scope of the health care items and services which are covered under the point-of-service benefit required under this section shall at least include the same health care items and services which would be covered if provided under the health maintenance organization's health care plan, including without limitation any items or services covered under a rider or endorsement to the applicable health care plan. Carriers shall be required to disclose prominently in all group health benefit plans and in all marketing materials utilized with respect to such group health benefit plans that the scope of the benefits provided under the point-of-service option are at least as great as those provided through the HMO's health care plan for that group. Filings of point-of-service benefits submitted to the Commission shall be accompanied by a certification signed by an officer of the filing carrier certifying that the scope of the point-of-service benefits includes at a minimum the same health care items and services as are provided under the HMO's group health care plan for that group.

I. Nothing in this section shall prohibit a health maintenance organization from offering or arranging the point-of-service benefit (i) as a separate group health benefit plan or under a different name than the health maintenance organization's group health benefit plan which does not contain the point-of-service benefit or (ii) from managing a group health benefit plan under which the point-of-service benefit is offered in a manner which separates or otherwise differentiates it from the group health benefit plan which does not contain the point-of-service benefit.

J. Notwithstanding anything in this section to the contrary, to the extent permitted under applicable law, no health maintenance organization shall be required to offer or arrange a point-of-service benefit under this section with respect to any group health benefit plan offered to a group contract holder if the health maintenance organization determines in good faith that the group contract holder will be concurrently offering another group health benefit plan or a self-insured or self-funded health benefit plan which allows the enrollees to access care from their provider of choice whether or not the provider is a member of the health maintenance organization's panel.

K. This section shall apply only to group health benefit plans issued in the Commonwealth in the commercial group market by carriers regulated by this title and shall not apply to (i) health care plans, contracts or policies issued in the individual market; (ii) coverages issued pursuant to Title XVIII of the Social Security Act, 42 U.S.C. § 1395 et seq. (Medicare), Title XIX of the Social Security Act, 42 U.S.C. § 1396 et seq. or Title XX of the Social Security Act, 42 U.S.C. § 1397 et seq. (Medicaid), 5 U.S.C. § 8901 et seq. (federal employees), 10 U.S.C. § 1071 et seq. (CHAMPUS) or Chapter 2 (§ 2.1-11.1 et seq.) of Title 2.1 (state employees); (iii) accident only, credit or disability insurance, or long-term care insurance, plans providing only limited health care services under § 38.2-4300 (unless offered by endorsement or rider to a group health benefit plan), CHAMPUS supplement, Medicare supplement, or workers' compensation coverages; (iv) an employee welfare benefit plan (as defined in section 3 (1) of the Employee Retirement Income Security Act of 1974, 29 U.S.C. § 1002 (1)), which is self-insured or self-funded; or (v) the essential and standard health benefit plans developed pursuant to § 38.2-3431 C.

L. This section shall apply to group health benefit plans issued or renewed by carriers in this Commonwealth on or after July 1, 1998.

M. Nothing in this section shall operate to limit any rights or obligations arising under §§ 38.2-3407, 38.2-3407.7, 38.2-3407.10, 38.2-3407.11, 38.2-4209, 38.2-4209.1, 38.2-4312 or § 38.2-4312.1.

N. If any provision of this section or its application to any person or circumstance is held invalid for any reason in a court of competent jurisdiction, the invalidity shall not affect the other provisions or any other application of this section which shall be given effect without the invalid provision or application, and for this purpose the provisions of this section are declared severable. (1998, c. 908.)

§ 38.2-3407.13. Refusal to accept assignments prohibited; dentists and oral surgeons. — A. No insurer proposing to issue individual or group accident and sickness insurance policies providing hospital, medical and surgical or major medical coverage on an expense-incurred basis, no corporation providing individual or group accident and sickness subscription contracts, and no dental services plan offering or administering prepaid dental services shall refuse to accept or make reimbursement pursuant to an assignment of benefits made to a dentist or oral surgeon by an insured, subscriber or plan enrollee.

B. For the purpose of this section, *"assignment of benefits"* means the transfer of dental care coverage reimbursement benefits or other rights under an insurance policy, subscription contract or dental services plan by an insured, subscriber or plan enrollee to a dentist or oral surgeon. The assignment of benefits shall not be effective until the insured, subscriber or enrollee notifies the insurer, corporation or plan in writing of the assignment. (1999, cc. 643, 649.)

§ 38.2-3407.14. Notice of premium increases. — A. Each (i) insurer issuing individual or group accident and sickness insurance policies providing hospital, medical and surgical or major medical coverage on an expense-incurred basis, (ii) corporation providing individual or group accident and sickness subscription contracts, and (iii) health maintenance organization providing a health care plan for health care services, shall provide in conjunction with the proposed renewal of coverage under any such policies,

contracts or plans, prior written notice of intent to increase by more than thirty-five percent the annual premium charged for coverage thereunder.

B. Notice required by this section shall be provided in writing at least sixty days prior to the proposed renewal of coverage under any such policy, contract, or plan to the policyholder, contract holder or subscriber, as appropriate. (1999, cc. 643, 649.)

§ 38.2-3407.15. Ethics and fairness in carrier business practices. —

A. As used in this section:

"Carrier," "enrollee" and *"provider"* shall have the meanings set forth in § 38.2-3407.10; however, a "carrier" shall also include any person required to be licensed under this title which offers or operates a managed care health insurance plan subject to Chapter 58 (§ 38.2-5800 et seq.) of this title or which provides or arranges for the provision of health care services, health plans, networks or provider panels which are subject to regulation as the business of insurance under this title.

"Claim" means any bill, claim, or proof of loss made by or on behalf of an enrollee or a provider to a carrier (or its intermediary, administrator or representative) with which the provider has a provider contract for payment for health care services under any health plan; however, a "claim" shall not include a request for payment of a capitation or a withhold.

"Clean claim" means a claim (i) that has no material defect or impropriety (including any lack of any reasonably required substantiation documentation) which substantially prevents timely payment from being made on the claim or (ii) with respect to which a carrier has failed timely to notify the person submitting the claim of any such defect or impropriety in accordance with this section.

"Health care services" means items or services furnished to any individual for the purpose of preventing, alleviating, curing, or healing human illness, injury or physical disability.

"Health plan" means any individual or group health care plan, subscription contract, evidence of coverage, certificate, health services plan, medical or hospital services plan, accident and sickness insurance policy or certificate, managed care health insurance plan, or other similar certificate, policy, contract or arrangement, and any endorsement or rider thereto, to cover all or a portion of the cost of persons receiving covered health care services, which is subject to state regulation and which is required to be offered, arranged or issued in the Commonwealth by a carrier licensed under this title. Health plan does not mean (i) coverages issued pursuant to Title XVIII of the Social Security Act, 42 U.S.C. § 1395 et seq. (Medicare), Title XIX of the Social Security Act, 42 U.S.C. § 1396 et seq. or Title XX of the Social Security Act, 42 U.S.C. § 1397 et seq. (Medicaid), 5 U.S.C. § 8901 et seq. (federal employees), or 10 U.S.C. § 1071 et seq. (CHAMPUS); or (ii) accident only, credit or disability insurance, long-term care insurance, CHAMPUS supplement, Medicare supplement, or workers' compensation coverages.

"Provider contract" means any contract between a provider and a carrier (or a carrier's network, provider panel, intermediary or representative) relating to the provision of health care services.

"Retroactive denial of a previously paid claim" or *"retroactive denial of payment"* means any attempt by a carrier retroactively to collect payments already made to a provider with respect to a claim by reducing other payments currently owed to the provider, by withholding or setting off against future payments, or in any other manner reducing or affecting the future claim payments to the provider.

B. Subject to subsection H, every provider contract entered into by a carrier shall contain specific provisions which shall require the carrier to adhere to and comply with the following minimum fair business standards in the processing and payment of claims for health care services:

1. A carrier shall pay any claim within forty days of receipt of the claim except where the obligation of the carrier to pay a claim is not reasonably clear due to the existence of a reasonable basis supported by specific information available for review by the person submitting the claim that:

a. The claim is determined by the carrier not to be a clean claim due to a good faith determination or dispute regarding (i) the manner in which the claim form was completed or submitted, (ii) the eligibility of a person for coverage, (iii) the responsibility of another carrier for all or part of the claim, (iv) the amount of the claim or the amount currently due under the claim, (v) the benefits covered, or (vi) the manner in which services were accessed or provided; or

b. The claim was submitted fraudulently.

Each carrier shall maintain a written or electronic record of the date of receipt of a claim. The person submitting the claim shall be entitled to inspect such record on request and to rely on that record or on any other admissible evidence as proof of the fact of receipt of the claim, including without limitation electronic or facsimile confirmation of receipt of a claim.

2. A carrier shall, within thirty days after receipt of a claim, request electronically or in writing from the person submitting the claim the information and documentation that the carrier reasonably believes will be required to process and pay the claim or to determine if the claim is a clean claim. Upon receipt of the additional information requested under this subsection necessary to make the original claim a clean claim, a carrier shall make the payment of the claim in compliance with this section. No carrier may refuse to pay a claim for health care services rendered pursuant to a provider contract which are covered benefits if the carrier fails timely to notify or attempt to notify the person submitting the claim of the matters identified above unless such failure was caused in material part by the person submitting the claims; however, nothing herein shall preclude such a carrier from imposing a retroactive denial of payment of such a claim if permitted by the provider contract unless such retroactive denial of payment of the claim would violate subdivision B 6. Nothing in this subsection shall require a carrier to pay a claim which is not a clean claim.

3. Any interest owing or accruing on a claim under § 38.2-3407.1 or § 38.2-4306.1 of this title, under any provider contract or under any other applicable law, shall, if not sooner paid or required to be paid, be paid, without necessity of demand, at the time the claim is paid or within sixty days thereafter.

4. a. Every carrier shall establish and implement reasonable policies to permit any provider with which there is a provider contract (i) to confirm in advance during normal business hours by free telephone or electronic means if available whether the health care services to be provided are medically necessary and a covered benefit and (ii) to determine the carrier's requirements applicable to the provider (or to the type of health care services which the provider has contracted to deliver under the provider contract) for (a) pre-certification or authorization of coverage decisions, (b) retroactive reconsideration of a certification or authorization of coverage decision or retroactive denial of a previously paid claim, (c) provider-specific payment and reimbursement methodology, coding levels and methodology, downcoding, and bundling of claims, and (d) other provider-specific, applicable claims processing and payment matters necessary to meet the terms and conditions of the provider contract, including determining whether a claim is a clean claim.

b. Every carrier shall make available to such providers within ten business days of receipt of a request, copies of or reasonable electronic access to all such policies which are applicable to the particular provider or to particular health care services identified by the provider. In the event the provision of the entire policy would violate any applicable copyright law, the carrier may instead comply with this subsection by timely delivering to the provider a clear explanation of the policy as it applies to the provider and to any health care services identified by the provider.

5. Every carrier shall pay a claim if the carrier has previously authorized the health care service or has advised the provider or enrollee in advance of the provision of health care services that the health care services are medically necessary and a covered benefit, unless:

a. The documentation for the claim provided by the person submitting the claim clearly fails to support the claim as originally authorized; or

b. The carrier's refusal is because (i) another payor is responsible for the payment, (ii) the provider has already been paid for the health care services identified on the claim, (iii) the claim was submitted fraudulently or the authorization was based in whole or material part on erroneous information provided to the carrier by the provider, enrollee, or other person not related to the carrier, or (iv) the person receiving the health care services was not eligible to receive them on the date of service and the carrier did not know, and with the exercise of reasonable care could not have known, of the person's eligibility status.

6. No carrier may impose any retroactive denial of a previously paid claim unless the carrier has provided the reason for the retroactive denial and (i) the original claim was submitted fraudulently, (ii) the original claim payment was incorrect because the provider was already paid for the health care services identified on the claim or the health care services identified on the claim were not delivered by the provider, or (iii) the time which has elapsed since the date of the payment of the original challenged claim does not exceed the lesser of (a) twelve months or (b) the number of days within which the carrier requires under its provider contract that a claim be submitted by the provider following the date on which a health care service is provided. Effective July 1, 2000, a carrier shall notify a provider at least thirty days in advance of any retroactive denial of a claim.

7. No provider contract may fail to include or attach at the time it is presented to the provider for execution (i) the fee schedule, reimbursement policy or statement as to the manner in which claims will be calculated and paid which is applicable to the provider or to the range of health care services reasonably expected to be delivered by that type of provider on a routine basis and (ii) all material addenda, schedules and exhibits thereto and any policies (including those referred to in subdivision B 4) applicable to the provider or to the range of health care services reasonably expected to be delivered by that type of provider under the provider contract.

8. No amendment to any provider contract or to any addenda, schedule, exhibit or policy thereto (or new addenda, schedule, exhibit, or policy) applicable to the provider (or to the range of health care services reasonably expected to be delivered by that type of provider) shall be effective as to the provider, unless the provider has been provided with the applicable portion of the proposed amendment (or of the proposed new addenda, schedule, exhibit, or policy) and has failed to notify the carrier within fifteen business days of receipt of the documentation of the provider's intention to terminate the provider contract at the earliest date thereafter permitted under the provider contract.

9. In the event that the carrier's provision of a policy required to be provided under subdivision B 7 or B 8 would violate any applicable copyright law, the carrier may instead comply with this section by providing a clear, written explanation of the policy as it applies to the provider.

C. Without limiting the foregoing, in the processing of any payment of claims for health care services rendered by providers under provider contracts and in performing under its provider contracts, every carrier subject to regulation by this title shall adhere to and comply with the minimum fair business standards required under subsection B, and the Commission shall have the jurisdiction to determine if a carrier has violated the standards set forth in subsection B by failing to include the requisite provisions in its provider contracts and shall have jurisdiction to determine if the carrier has failed to implement the minimum fair business standards set out in subdivisions B 1 and B 2 in the performance of its provider contracts.

D. No carrier shall be in violation of this section if its failure to comply with this section is caused in material part by the person submitting the claim or if the carrier's compliance is rendered impossible due to matters beyond the carrier's reasonable control (such as an act of God, insurrection, strike, fire, or power outages) which are not caused in material part by the carrier.

E. Any provider who suffers loss as the result of a carrier's violation of this section or a carrier's breach of any provider contract provision required by this section shall be entitled to initiate an action to recover actual damages. If the trier of fact finds that the violation or breach resulted from a carrier's gross negligence and willful conduct, it may increase damages to an amount not exceeding three times the actual damages sustained. Notwithstanding any other provision of law to the contrary, in addition to any damages awarded, such provider also may be awarded reasonable attorney's fees and court costs. Each claim for payment which is paid or processed in violation of this section or with respect to which a violation of this section exists shall constitute a separate violation. The Commission shall not be deemed to be a "trier of fact" for purposes of this subsection.

F. No carrier (or its network, provider panel or intermediary) shall terminate or fail to renew the employment or other contractual relationship with a provider, or any provider contract, or otherwise penalize any provider, for invoking any of the provider's rights under this section or under the provider contract.

G. This section shall apply only to carriers subject to regulation under this title.

H. This section shall apply with respect to provider contracts entered into, amended, extended or renewed on or after July 1, 1999.

I. Pursuant to the authority granted by § 38.2-223, the Commission may promulgate such rules and regulations as it may deem necessary to implement this section.

J. If any provision of this section, or the application thereof to any person or circumstance, is held invalid or unenforceable, such determination shall not affect the provisions or applications of this section which can be given effect without the invalid or unenforceable provision or application, and to that end the provisions of this section are severable.

K. The Commission shall have no jurisdiction to adjudicate individual controversies arising out of this section. (1999 cc. 709, 739.)

The number of this section was assigned by the Virginia Code Commission, the number in the 1999 act having been § 38.2-3407.13.

§ 38.2-3407.16. Requirements for obstetrical care. — A. Each (i) insurer proposing to issue individual or group accident and sickness insurance policies providing hospital, medical and surgical or major medical coverage on an expense-incurred basis, (ii) corporation providing individual or group accident and sickness subscription contracts, and (iii) health maintenance organization providing a health care plan for health care services, whose policies, contracts, or plans, including any certificate or evidence of coverage issued in connection with such policies, contracts or plans, include coverage for obstetrical services as an inpatient in a general hospital or obstetrical services by a physician shall provide such benefits with durational limits, deductibles, coinsurance factors, and copayments that are no less favorable than for physical illness generally.

B. The requirements of this section shall apply to all insurance policies, contracts, and plans delivered, issued for delivery, reissued, renewed, or extended or at any time when any term of any such policy, contract, or plan is changed or any premium adjustment is made, on and after the effective date of this section. The provisions of this section shall not apply to short-term travel, accident only, limited or specified disease, or individual conversion policies or contracts, nor to policies or contracts designed for issuance to persons eligible for coverage under Title XVIII of the Social Security Act, known as Medicare, or any other similar coverage under state or federal governmental plans. (1999, c. 923.)

The number of this section was assigned by the Virginia Code Commission, the number in the 1999 act having been § 38.2-3407.13.

Effective date. — This section is effective March 29, 1999.

ARTICLE 2.

Mandated Benefits.

§ 38.2-3408. Policy providing for reimbursement for services that may be performed by certain practitioners other than physicians. — A. If an accident and sickness insurance policy provides reimbursement for any service that may be legally performed by a person licensed in this Commonwealth as a chiropractor, optometrist, optician, professional counselor, psychologist, clinical social worker, podiatrist, physical therapist, chiropodist, clinical nurse specialist who renders mental health services, audiologist, speech pathologist, certified nurse midwife, or licensed acupuncturist, reimbursement under the policy shall not be denied because the service is rendered by the licensed practitioner.

B. This section shall not apply to Medicaid, or any state fund. (1968, c. 588, § 38.1-347.1; 1973, c. 428; 1979, c. 13; 1986, c. 562; 1987, cc. 549, 551, 557; 1989, cc. 7, 201; 1997, c. 203; 1998, c. 146.)

Cross references. — For section prohibiting certain subrogation provisions in hospitalization, medical, etc., policies, see § 38.2-3405.

The 1998 amendment, in subsection A, deleted "or" preceding "certified nurse midwife"

and inserted "or licensed acupuncturist."

Applied in HCA Health Servs. of Va., Inc. v. Aetna Life Ins. Co., 803 F. Supp. 1132 (E.D. Va. 1992).

§ 38.2-3409. Coverage of dependent children. — A. Any group or individual accident and sickness insurance policy or subscription contract delivered or issued for delivery in this Commonwealth which provides that coverage of a dependent child shall terminate upon that child's attainment of a specified age, shall also provide in substance that attainment of the specified age shall not terminate the child's coverage during the continuance of the policy while the dependent child is and continues to be both: (i) incapable of self-sustaining employment by reason of mental retardation or physical handicap, and (ii) chiefly dependent upon the policyowner for support and maintenance.

B. Proof of incapacity and dependency shall be furnished to the insurer by the policyowner within thirty-one days of the child's attainment of the specified age. Subsequent proof may be required by the insurer but not more frequently than annually after the two-year period following the child's attainment of the specified age.

C. The insurer may charge an additional premium for any continuation of coverage beyond the specified age. The additional premium shall be determined by the insurer on the basis of the class of risks applicable to the child. (1968, c. 411, § 38.1-348.1; 1974, c. 95; 1986, c. 562.)

§ 38.2-3410. Construction of policy generally; words "physician" and "doctor" to include dentist. — Each accident and sickness insurance policy or subscription contract shall be construed according to the entirety of its terms and conditions as set forth in the policy and as amplified, extended or modified by any rider, endorsement, or application attached to and made a part of the policy. However, the word "physician" or "doctor" when used in any accident or sickness insurance policy, or subscription contract shall be construed to include a dentist performing covered services within the scope of his professional license. (1968, c. 292, § 38.1-348.5; 1986, c. 562.)

§ 38.2-3411. Coverage of newborn children required. — A. Each individual and group accident and sickness insurance policy or individual and group subscription contract providing coverage on an expense incurred basis that provides coverage for a family member of the insured or the subscriber shall, as to the family members' coverage, also provide that the accident and sickness insurance benefits applicable for children shall be payable with respect to a newly born child of the insured or subscriber from the moment of birth.

B. Coverage for newly born children shall be identical to coverage provided to the insured or subscriber, except that, regardless of whether such coverage would otherwise be provided under the terms and conditions of the insurance policy or subscription contract, coverage shall be provided for:

1. Necessary care and treatment of medically diagnosed congenital defects and birth abnormalities, with coverage limits no more restrictive than for any injury or sickness covered under the insurance policy or subscription contract; and

2. Inpatient and outpatient dental, oral surgical, and orthodontic services which are medically necessary for the treatment of medically diagnosed cleft lip, cleft palate or ectodermal dysplasia. Such coverage shall be subject to any deductible, cost-sharing, and policy or contract maximum provisions, provided they are no more restrictive for such services than for any injury or sickness covered under the insurance policy or subscription contract.

C. If payment of a specific premium or subscription fee is required to provide coverage for a child, the policy or subscription contract may require that notification of birth of a newly born child and payment of the required premium or fees shall be furnished to the insurer issuing the policy or corporation issuing the subscription contract within thirty-one days after the date of birth in order to have the coverage continue beyond the thirty-one-day period. (1975, c. 281, § 38.1-348.6; 1976, c. 342; 1986, c. 562; 1993, c. 263.)

Law Review. — For survey of Virginia law on insurance for the year 1974-1975, see 61 Va. L. Rev. 1759 (1975).

§ 38.2-3411.1. Coverage for child health supervision services. — A. Every individual or group accident and sickness insurance policy, subscription contract providing coverage under a health services plan, or evidence of coverage of a health care plan delivered or issued for delivery in the Commonwealth or renewed, reissued, or extended if already issued, shall offer and make available coverage under such policy or plan for child health supervision services to provide for the periodic examination of children covered under such policy or plan.

B. As used in this section, the term *"child health supervision services"* means the periodic review of a child's physical and emotional status by a licensed and qualified physician or pursuant to a physician's supervision. A review shall include but not be limited to a history, complete physical examination, developmental assessment, anticipatory guidance, appropriate immunizations, and laboratory tests in keeping with prevailing medical standards.

C. Each such policy or plan, offering and making available such coverage, shall, at a minimum, provide benefits for child health supervision services at approximately the following age intervals: birth, two months, four months, six months, nine months, twelve months, fifteen months, eighteen months, two years, three years, four years, five years, and six years. A policy or plan may provide that child health supervision services which are rendered during a periodic review shall only be covered to the extent that such services are provided by or under the supervision of a single physician during the course of one visit.

D. Benefits for coverage for child health supervision services shall be exempt from any copayment, coinsurance, deductible, or other dollar limit provision in the policy or plan. Such exemption shall be expressly stated on the policy, plan, rider, endorsement, or other attachment providing such coverage.

E. The premiums for such coverage shall take into consideration (i) the cost of providing such coverage, (ii) cost savings realized or likely to be realized as a consequence of such coverage, (iii) a reasonable profit for the insurer, and (iv) any other relevant information or data the Commission deems appropriate.

F. This section shall not apply to any insurer or health services plan having fewer than 1,000 covered individuals insured or covered in Virginia or less than $500,000 in premiums in Virginia as of its last annual statement nor to specified disease, hospital indemnity or other limited benefit policies issued to provide supplemental benefits to a policy providing primary care benefits. (1990, c. 901.)

§ 38.2-3411.2. Coverage of adopted children required. —
A. Notwithstanding the provisions of § 38.2-3419, each insurer proposing to issue individual or group accident and sickness insurance policies providing hospital, medical and surgical or major medical coverage on an expense incurred basis, each corporation providing individual or group accident and sickness subscription contracts, and each health maintenance organization providing a health care plan for health care services that offers coverage for a family member of the insured, subscriber, or plan enrollee, shall, as to the family members' coverage, also provide that the accident and sickness insurance benefits applicable for children shall be payable with respect to adopted children of the insured, subscriber, or plan enrollee.

B. The coverage of such policy, subscription, or plan, applicable to family members of the insured, subscriber or enrollee, shall apply in the same manner and to the same but no greater extent to adopted children of the insured, subscriber or enrollee.

C. An adopted child shall be eligible for the coverage required by this section from the date of adoptive or parental placement with an insured, subscriber or plan enrollee for the purpose of adoption; and, in addition as to a child whose adoptive or parental placement has occurred within thirty-one days of birth, such child shall be considered a newborn child of the insured, subscriber or plan enrollee as of the date of adoptive or parental placement. Once coverage is in effect, it shall continue according to the terms of the policy, subscription contract, or plan, unless the said placement is disrupted prior to final decree of adoption, and the child is removed from placement with the insured, subscriber or plan enrollee.

D. If payment of a specific premium or subscription fee is required to provide coverage for a child, the policy or subscription contract may require notification of the placement of an adoptive child and payment of the required premium or fees shall be furnished to the insurer issuing the policy or corporation issuing the subscription contract within thirty-one days after the date of parental or adoptive placement in order to have the coverage continue beyond the thirty-one-day period.

E. No insurer, health services plan or health maintenance organization shall restrict coverage for any dependent child adopted or placed for adoption solely because of a preexisting condition of such child at the time that such child would otherwise become eligible for coverage under the plan. (1991, c. 103; 1994, c. 213.)

§ **38.2-3412:** Repealed by Acts 1993, c. 132.

Cross references. — As to present provisions relating to coverage for mental health and substance abuse services, see § 38.2-3412.1.

§ **38.2-3412.1. (Effective until January 1, 2000 and after July 1, 2004) Coverage for mental health and substance abuse services.** — A. As used in this section:

"Adult" means any person who is nineteen years of age or older.

"Alcohol or drug rehabilitation facility" means a facility in which a state-approved program for the treatment of alcoholism or drug addiction is provided. The facility shall be either (i) licensed by the State Board of Health pursuant to Chapter 5 (§ 32.1-123 et seq.) of Title 32.1 or by the State Mental Health, Mental Retardation and Substance Abuse Services Board pursuant to Chapter 8 (§ 37.1-179 et seq.) of Title 37.1 or (ii) a state agency or institution.

"Child or adolescent" means any person under the age of nineteen years.

"Inpatient treatment" means mental health or substance abuse services delivered on a twenty-four-hour per day basis in a hospital, alcohol or drug rehabilitation facility, an intermediate care facility or an inpatient unit of a mental health treatment center.

"Intermediate care facility" means a licensed, residential public or private facility that is not a hospital and that is operated primarily for the purpose of providing a continuous, structured twenty-four-hour per day, state-approved program of inpatient substance abuse services.

"Medication management visit" means a visit no more than twenty minutes in length with a licensed physician or other licensed health care provider with prescriptive authority for the sole purpose of monitoring and adjusting medications prescribed for mental health or substance abuse treatment.

"Mental health services" means treatment for mental, emotional or nervous disorders.

"Mental health treatment center" means a treatment facility organized to provide care and treatment for mental illness through multiple modalities or techniques pursuant to a written plan approved and monitored by a physician, clinical psychologist, or a psychologist licensed to practice in this Commonwealth. The facility shall be (i) licensed by the Commonwealth, (ii) funded or eligible for funding under federal or state law, or (iii) affiliated with a hospital under a contractual agreement with an established system for patient referral.

"Outpatient treatment" means mental health or substance abuse treatment services rendered to a person as an individual or part of a group while not confined as an inpatient. Such treatment shall not include services delivered through a partial hospitalization or intensive outpatient program as defined herein.

"Partial hospitalization" means a licensed or approved day or evening treatment program that includes the major diagnostic, medical, psychiatric and psychosocial rehabilitation treatment modalities designed for patients with mental, emotional, or nervous disorders, and alcohol or other drug dependence who require coordinated, intensive, comprehensive and multidisciplinary treatment. Such a program shall provide treatment over a period of six or more continuous hours per day to individuals or groups of individuals who are not admitted as inpatients. Such term shall also include intensive outpatient programs for the treatment of alcohol or other drug dependence which provide treatment over a period of three or more continuous hours per day to individuals or groups of individuals who are not admitted as inpatients.

"Substance abuse services" means treatment for alcohol or other drug dependence.

"Treatment" means services including diagnostic evaluation, medical, psychiatric and psychological care, and psychotherapy for mental, emotional or nervous disorders or alcohol or other drug dependence rendered by a hospital, alcohol or drug rehabilitation facility, intermediate care facility, mental health treatment center, a physician, psychologist, clinical psychologist, licensed clinical social worker, licensed professional counselor, licensed substance abuse treatment practitioner, marriage and family therapist or clinical nurse specialist who renders mental health services. Treatment for physiological or psychological dependence on alcohol or other drugs shall also include the services of counseling and rehabilitation as well as services rendered by a state certified alcoholism, drug, or substance abuse counselor employed by a facility or program licensed to provide such treatment.

B. Each individual and group accident and sickness insurance policy or individual and group subscription contract providing coverage on an expense-incurred basis for a family member of the insured or the subscriber shall provide coverage for inpatient and partial hospitalization mental health and substance abuse services as follows:

1. Treatment for an adult as an inpatient at a hospital, inpatient unit of a mental health treatment center, alcohol or drug rehabilitation facility or intermediate care facility for a minimum period of twenty days per policy or contract year.

2. Treatment for a child or adolescent as an inpatient at a hospital, inpatient unit of a mental health treatment center, alcohol or drug rehabilitation facility or intermediate care facility for a minimum period of twenty-five days per policy or contract year.

3. Up to ten days of the inpatient benefit set forth in subdivisions 1 and 2 of this subsection may be converted when medically necessary at the option of the person or the parent, as defined in § 16.1-336, of a child or adolescent receiving such treatment to a partial hospitalization benefit applying a formula which shall be no less favorable than an exchange of 1.5 days of partial hospitalization coverage for each inpatient day of coverage. An insurance policy or subscription contract described herein which provides inpatient benefits in excess of twenty days per policy or contract year for adults or twenty-five days per policy or contract year for a child or adolescent may provide for the conversion of such excess days on the terms set forth in this subdivision.

4. The limits of the benefits set forth in this subsection shall not be more restrictive than for any other illness, except that the benefits may be limited as set out in this subsection.

5. This subsection shall not apply to short-term travel, accident only, limited or specified disease policies or contracts, nor to policies or contracts designed for issuance to persons eligible for coverage under Title XVIII of the Social Security Act, known as Medicare, or any other similar coverage under state or federal governmental plans.

C. Each individual and group accident and sickness insurance policy or individual and group subscription contract providing coverage on an expense-incurred basis for a family member of the insured or the subscriber shall also provide coverage for outpatient mental health and substance abuse services as follows:

1. A minimum of twenty visits for outpatient treatment of an adult, child or adolescent shall be provided in each policy or contract year.

2. The limits of the benefits set forth in this subsection shall be no more restrictive than the limits of benefits applicable to physical illness; however, the coinsurance factor applicable to any outpatient visit beyond the first five of such visits covered in any policy or contract year shall be at least fifty percent.

3. For the purpose of this section, medication management visits shall be covered in the same manner as a medication management visit for the treatment of physical illness and shall not be counted as an outpatient treatment visit in the calculation of the benefit set forth herein.

4. For the purpose of this subsection, if all covered expenses for a visit for outpatient mental health or substance abuse treatment apply toward any deductible required by a policy or contract, such visit shall not count toward the outpatient visit benefit maximum set forth in the policy or contract.

5. This subsection shall not apply to short-term travel, accident only, or limited or specified disease policies or contracts, nor to policies or contracts designed for issuance to persons eligible for coverage under Title XVIII of the Social Security Act, known as Medicare, or any other similar coverage under state or federal governmental plans.

D. The requirements of this section shall apply to all insurance policies and subscription contracts delivered, issued for delivery, reissued, or extended, or at any time when any term of the policy or contract is changed or any premium adjustment made. (1993, c. 132; 1995, c. 270; 1996, c. 41; 1997, c. 901.)

Section set out twice. — The section above is effective until January 1, 2000 and after July 1, 2004. For the version of this section effective January 1, 2000 until July 1, 2004, see the following section, also numbered 38.2-3412.1.

Editor's note. — Title XVIII of the Social Security Act, referred to in subdivision C 5, is found at 42 U.S.C. § 1395 et seq.

§ 38.2-3412.1. (Effective January 1, 2000 until July 1, 2004) Coverage for mental health and substance abuse services. — A. As used in this section:

"*Adult*" means any person who is nineteen years of age or older.

"*Alcohol or drug rehabilitation facility*" means a facility in which a state-approved program for the treatment of alcoholism or drug addiction is provided. The facility shall be either (i) licensed by the State Board of Health pursuant to Chapter 5 (§ 32.1-123 et seq.) of Title 32.1 or by the State Mental Health, Mental Retardation and Substance Abuse Services Board pursuant to Chapter 8 (§ 37.1-179 et seq.) of Title 37.1 or (ii) a state agency or institution.

"*Child or adolescent*" means any person under the age of nineteen years.

"*Inpatient treatment*" means mental health or substance abuse services delivered on a twenty-four-hour per day basis in a hospital, alcohol or drug rehabilitation facility, an intermediate care facility or an inpatient unit of a mental health treatment center.

"*Intermediate care facility*" means a licensed, residential public or private facility that is not a hospital and that is operated primarily for the purpose of providing a continuous, structured twenty-four-hour per day, state-approved program of inpatient substance abuse services.

"Medication management visit" means a visit no more than twenty minutes in length with a licensed physician or other licensed health care provider with prescriptive authority for the sole purpose of monitoring and adjusting medications prescribed for mental health or substance abuse treatment.

"Mental health services" means treatment for mental, emotional or nervous disorders.

"Mental health treatment center" means a treatment facility organized to provide care and treatment for mental illness through multiple modalities or techniques pursuant to a written plan approved and monitored by a physician, clinical psychologist, or a psychologist licensed to practice in this Commonwealth. The facility shall be (i) licensed by the Commonwealth, (ii) funded or eligible for funding under federal or state law, or (iii) affiliated with a hospital under a contractual agreement with an established system for patient referral.

"Outpatient treatment" means mental health or substance abuse treatment services rendered to a person as an individual or part of a group while not confined as an inpatient. Such treatment shall not include services delivered through a partial hospitalization or intensive outpatient program as defined herein.

"Partial hospitalization" means a licensed or approved day or evening treatment program that includes the major diagnostic, medical, psychiatric and psychosocial rehabilitation treatment modalities designed for patients with mental, emotional, or nervous disorders, and alcohol or other drug dependence who require coordinated, intensive, comprehensive and multidisciplinary treatment. Such a program shall provide treatment over a period of six or more continuous hours per day to individuals or groups of individuals who are not admitted as inpatients. Such term shall also include intensive outpatient programs for the treatment of alcohol or other drug dependence which provide treatment over a period of three or more continuous hours per day to individuals or groups of individuals who are not admitted as inpatients.

"Substance abuse services" means treatment for alcohol or other drug dependence.

"Treatment" means services including diagnostic evaluation, medical, psychiatric and psychological care, and psychotherapy for mental, emotional or nervous disorders or alcohol or other drug dependence rendered by a hospital, alcohol or drug rehabilitation facility, intermediate care facility, mental health treatment center, a physician, psychologist, clinical psychologist, licensed clinical social worker, licensed professional counselor, licensed substance abuse treatment practitioner, marriage and family therapist or clinical nurse specialist who renders mental health services. Treatment for physiological or psychological dependence on alcohol or other drugs shall also include the services of counseling and rehabilitation as well as services rendered by a state certified alcoholism, drug, or substance abuse counselor employed by a facility or program licensed to provide such treatment.

B. Each individual and group accident and sickness insurance policy or individual and group subscription contract providing coverage on an expense-incurred basis for a family member of the insured or the subscriber shall provide coverage for inpatient and partial hospitalization mental health and substance abuse services as follows:

1. Treatment for an adult as an inpatient at a hospital, inpatient unit of a mental health treatment center, alcohol or drug rehabilitation facility or intermediate care facility for a minimum period of twenty days per policy or contract year.

2. Treatment for a child or adolescent as an inpatient at a hospital, inpatient unit of a mental health treatment center, alcohol or drug rehabilitation facility

or intermediate care facility for a minimum period of twenty-five days per policy or contract year.

3. Up to ten days of the inpatient benefit set forth in subdivisions 1 and 2 of this subsection may be converted when medically necessary at the option of the person or the parent, as defined in § 16.1-336, of a child or adolescent receiving such treatment to a partial hospitalization benefit applying a formula which shall be no less favorable than an exchange of 1.5 days of partial hospitalization coverage for each inpatient day of coverage. An insurance policy or subscription contract described herein which provides inpatient benefits in excess of twenty days per policy or contract year for adults or twenty-five days per policy or contract year for a child or adolescent may provide for the conversion of such excess days on the terms set forth in this subdivision.

4. The limits of the benefits set forth in this subsection shall not be more restrictive than for any other illness, except that the benefits may be limited as set out in this subsection.

5. This subsection shall not apply to short-term travel, accident only, limited or specified disease policies or contracts, nor to policies or contracts designed for issuance to persons eligible for coverage under Title XVIII of the Social Security Act, known as Medicare, or any other similar coverage under state or federal governmental plans.

C. Each individual and group accident and sickness insurance policy or individual and group subscription contract providing coverage on an expense-incurred basis for a family member of the insured or the subscriber shall also provide coverage for outpatient mental health and substance abuse services as follows:

1. A minimum of twenty visits for outpatient treatment of an adult, child or adolescent shall be provided in each policy or contract year.

2. The limits of the benefits set forth in this subsection shall be no more restrictive than the limits of benefits applicable to physical illness; however, the coinsurance factor applicable to any outpatient visit beyond the first five of such visits covered in any policy or contract year shall be at least fifty percent.

3. For the purpose of this section, medication management visits shall be covered in the same manner as a medication management visit for the treatment of physical illness and shall not be counted as an outpatient treatment visit in the calculation of the benefit set forth herein.

4. For the purpose of this subsection, if all covered expenses for a visit for outpatient mental health or substance abuse treatment apply toward any deductible required by a policy or contract, such visit shall not count toward the outpatient visit benefit maximum set forth in the policy or contract.

5. This subsection shall not apply to short-term travel, accident only, or limited or specified disease policies or contracts, nor to policies or contracts designed for issuance to persons eligible for coverage under Title XVIII of the Social Security Act, known as Medicare, or any other similar coverage under state or federal governmental plans.

D. The provisions of this section shall not be applicable to "biologically based mental illnesses," as defined in § 38.2-3412.1:01, unless coverage for any such mental illness is not otherwise available pursuant to the provisions § 38.2-3412.1:01.

E. The requirements of this section shall apply to all insurance policies and subscription contracts delivered, issued for delivery, reissued, or extended, or at any time when any term of the policy or contract is changed or any premium adjustment made. (1993, c. 132; 1995, c. 270; 1996, c. 41; 1997, c. 901; 1999, c. 941.)

Section set out twice. — The section above is effective January 1, 2000 until July 1, 2004.

For this section as in effect until January 1, 2000 and after July 1, 2004, see the preceding section, also numbered 38.2-3412.1.

Editor's note. — Acts 1999, c. 941, cl. 4, provides: "That the Special Advisory Commission on Mandated Health Insurance Benefits, pursuant to its authority under Chapter 34 (§ 9-297 et seq.) of Title 9 of the Code of Virginia, shall collect such data, perform such studies, and convene such public hearings as are necessary to determine the effects, if any, of the coverage required under §§ 38.2-3412.1:01, 38.2-3412.1 and 38.2-4319 pursuant to this act on claims experience for and costs of policies,

contracts or plans, and shall submit a written report of its findings regarding the same to the Governor and the General Assembly not later than December 1, 2001; December 1, 2002; and December 1, 2003."

Acts 1999, c. 941, cl. 5, provides: "That the provisions of this act shall expire on July 1, 2004."

The 1999 amendment, effective January 1, 2000, added subsection D, and redesignated former subsection D as present subsection E. For expiration provision, see the Editor's note.

§ 38.2-3412.1:01. (Effective January 1, 2000 until July 1, 2004) Coverage for biologically based mental illness. — A. Notwithstanding the provisions of § 38.2-3419, each insurer proposing to issue individual or group accident and sickness insurance policies providing hospital, medical and surgical, or major medical coverage on an expense-incurred basis; each corporation providing individual or group accident and sickness subscription contracts; and each health maintenance organization providing a health care plan for health care services shall provide coverage for biologically based mental illnesses.

B. Benefits for biologically based mental illnesses may be different from benefits for other illnesses, conditions or disorders if such benefits meet the medical criteria necessary to achieve the same outcomes as are achieved by the benefits for any other illness, condition or disorder that is covered by such policy or contract.

C. Coverage for biologically based mental illnesses shall neither be different nor separate from coverage for any other illness, condition or disorder for purposes of determining deductibles, benefit year or lifetime durational limits, benefit year or lifetime dollar limits, lifetime episodes or treatment limits, copayment and coinsurance factors, and benefit year maximum for deductibles and copayment and coinsurance factors.

D. Nothing shall preclude the undertaking of usual and customary procedures to determine the appropriateness of, and medical necessity for, treatment of biologically based mental illnesses under this option, provided that all such appropriateness and medical necessity determinations are made in the same manner as those determinations made for the treatment of any other illness, condition or disorder covered by such policy or contract.

E. For purposes of this section, a "biologically based mental illness" is any mental or nervous condition caused by a biological disorder of the brain that results in a clinically significant syndrome that substantially limits the person's functioning; specifically, the following diagnoses are defined as biologically based mental illness as they apply to adults and children: schizophrenia, schizoaffective disorder, bipolar disorder, major depressive disorder, panic disorder, obsessive-compulsive disorder, attention deficit hyperactivity disorder, autism, and drug and alcoholism addiction.

F. The provisions of this section shall not apply to (i) short-term travel, accident only, limited or specified disease policies, (ii) short-term nonrenewable policies of not more than six months' duration, (iii) policies, contracts, or plans issued in the individual market or small group markets to employers with 25 or fewer employees, or (iv) policies or contracts designed for issuance to persons eligible for coverage under Title XVIII of the Social Security Act, known as Medicare, or any other similar coverage under state or federal governmental plans. (1999, c. 941.)

Editor's note. — Acts 1999, c. 941, cl. 4, provides: "That the Special Advisory Commission on Mandated Health Insurance Benefits, pursuant to its authority under Chapter 34 (§ 9-297 et seq.) of Title 9 of the Code of Virginia, shall collect such data, perform such studies, and convene such public hearings as are necessary to determine the effects, if any, of the coverage required under §§ 38.2-3412.1:01, 38.2-3412.1 and 38.2-4319 pursuant to this act on claims experience for and costs of policies,

contracts or plans, and shall submit a written report of its findings regarding the same to the Governor and the General Assembly not later than December 1, 2001; December 1, 2002; and December 1, 2003."

Acts 1999, c. 941, cl. 5, provides: "That the provisions of this act shall expire on July 1, 2004."

Effective date. — This section is effective January 1, 2000.

§ 38.2-3413: Repealed by Acts 1993, c. 132.

§ 38.2-3414. Optional coverage for obstetrical services. — A. Each insurer proposing to issue a group hospital policy or a group major medical policy in this Commonwealth and each corporation proposing to issue group hospital, group medical or group major medical subscription contracts shall provide coverage for obstetrical services as an option available to the group policyholder or the contract holder in the case of benefits based upon treatment as an inpatient in a general hospital. The reimbursement for obstetrical services by a physician shall be based on the charges for the services determined according to the same formula by which the charges are developed for other medical and surgical procedures. Such coverage shall have durational limits, dollar limits, deductibles and coinsurance factors that are no less favorable than for physical illness generally.

B. This section shall not apply to short-term travel, accident only, limited or specified disease, or individual conversion policies or contracts, nor to policies or contracts designed for issuance to persons eligible for coverage under Title XVIII of the Social Security Act, known as Medicare, or any other similar coverage under state or federal governmental plans. (1978, c. 375, § 38.1-348.9; 1986, c. 562.)

Editor's note. — Title XVIII of the Social Security Act, referred to in subsection B, is found at 42 U.S.C. § 1395 et seq.

§ 38.2-3414.1. Obstetrical benefits; coverage for postpartum services. — A. Each insurer proposing to issue an individual or group hospital policy or major medical policy in this Commonwealth, each corporation proposing to issue an individual or group hospital, medical or major medical subscription contract, and each health maintenance organization providing a health care plan for health care services that provides benefits for obstetrical services shall provide coverage for postpartum services as provided in this section.

B. Such coverage shall include benefits for inpatient care and a home visit or visits which shall be in accordance with the medical criteria, outlined in the most current version of or an official update to the "Guidelines for Perinatal Care" prepared by the American Academy of Pediatrics and the American College of Obstetricians and Gynecologists or the "Standards for Obstetric-Gynecologic Services" prepared by the American College of Obstetricians and Gynecologists. Such coverage shall be provided incorporating any changes in such Guidelines or Standards within six months of the publication of such Guidelines or Standards or any official amendment thereto.

C. The requirements of this section shall apply to all insurance policies, contracts and plans delivered, issued for delivery, reissued, or extended on and after July 1, 1996, or at any time thereafter when any term of the policy, contract or plan is changed or any premium adjustment is made.

D. This section shall not apply to short-term travel, accident only, limited or specified disease, or individual conversion policies or contracts, nor to policies or contracts designed for issuance to persons eligible for coverage under Title XVIII of the Social Security Act, known as Medicare, or any other similar coverage under state or federal governmental plans. (1996, cc. 155, 201.)

§ 38.2-3415. Exclusion or reduction of benefits for certain causes prohibited. — No group accident and sickness insurance policy, nor any group subscription contract, delivered or issued for delivery in this Commonwealth or renewed, reissued or extended if already issued, shall contain any provision excluding or reducing the benefits of any insured or subscriber because benefits have been paid or are payable under any individually underwritten and individually issued policy or subscription contract providing exclusively for accident and sickness benefits and for which the entire premium has been paid by the insured, a member of the insured's family, or the insured's guardian or conservator. (1978, c. 496, § 38.1-348.10; 1986, c. 562; 1997, c. 801.)

Editor's note. — Acts 1997, c. 801, cl. 2, provides: "That the provisions of this act shall become effective on January 1, 1998. The powers granted and duties imposed pursuant to this act shall apply prospectively to guardians and conservators appointed by court order entered on or after that date, or modified on or after that date if the court so directs, without regard to when the petition was filed. The procedures specified in this act governing proceedings for appointment of a guardian or conservator or termination or other modification of a guardianship shall apply on and after that date without regard to when the petition therefor was filed or the guardianship or conservatorship created."

The 1997 amendment, effective January 1, 1998, inserted "or conservator" at the end of the section.

§ 38.2-3416. Conversion on termination of eligibility; insurer required to offer conversion policy or group coverage. — A. Before an insurer who delivers or issues for delivery in this Commonwealth or who renews, reissues or extends if already issued, any group hospital, medical and surgical or group major medical policy, the insurer shall be required to be able to offer without evidence of insurability to residents of this Commonwealth who are covered under the policy, whose eligibility may terminate under the policy, and who may elect Option 1 under § 38.2-3541 a nongroup policy of accident and sickness insurance, either individual or family, whichever is appropriate, pursuant to the provisions of § 38.2-3541 unless such termination is due to termination of the group policy under circumstances in which the insured person is insurable under other replacement group coverage or health care plan without waiting periods or preexisting conditions under the replacement coverage or plan.

B. Any insurer who has in effect prior to January 1, 1985, any group policy described in subsection A of this section, may be exempted from the provisions of subsection A of this section. However, for persons affected by the termination of eligibility, the insurer shall be required to continue coverage under the existing group policy, without evidence of insurability and at the insurer's current rate applicable to the group policy, for as long as the affected persons elect or as long as the insurer is not required to offer an acceptable conversion policy. (1984, c. 300, § 38.1-348.10:1; 1986, c. 562; 1988, c. 551.)

§ 38.2-3417. Deductibles and coinsurance options required. — A. An insurer issuing accident and sickness insurance or a corporation issuing subscription contracts on an expense incurred basis shall make available in offering such coverage or contract to the potential insured or contract holder one or more of the following options under which the individual insured or group certificate holder pays for:

1. The first $100 of the cost of the services covered or benefits payable by the policy or contract during a 12-month period;

2. Twenty percent of the first $1,000 of the cost of the services covered or benefits payable by the policy or contract during a 12-month period;

3. The first $100 and 20 percent of the next $1,000 of the cost of the services covered or benefits payable by the policy or contract during a 12-month period; or

4. Any other option containing a greater deductible, coinsurance, or cost-sharing provision. However, the option shall not be inconsistent with standards established with respect to deductibles, coinsurance, or cost-sharing pursuant to § 38.2-3519.

B. As used in this section, *"make available"* means that the insurer or corporation shall disseminate information concerning the option or options and make a policy or contract containing the option or options available to potential insureds or contract holders at the same time and in the same manner as the insurer or corporation disseminates information concerning other policies or contracts and coverage options and makes other policies or contracts and coverage options available.

C. This section shall not apply to short-term travel, accident only, limited or specified disease, or individual conversion policies or contracts, nor to policies or contracts designed for issuance to persons eligible for coverage under Title XVIII of the Social Security Act, known as Medicare, or any other similar coverage under state or federal governmental plans. (1981, c. 322, § 38.1-348.12:1; 1986, c. 562.)

§ 38.2-3418. Coverage for victims of rape or incest. — Each hospital expense, medical-surgical expense, major medical expense or hospital confinement indemnity insurance policy issued by an insurer, each individual and group subscription contract providing hospital, medical, or surgical benefits issued by a corporation, and each contract issued by a health maintenance organization which provide benefits as a result of an "accident" or "accidental injury" shall be construed to include benefits for pregnancy following an act of rape of an insured or subscriber which was reported to the police within seven days following its occurrence, to the same extent as any other covered accident. The 7-day requirement shall be extended to 180 days in the case of an act of rape or incest of a female under 13 years of age. (1981, c. 42, § 38.1-348.13; 1986, c. 562.)

§ 38.2-3418.1. Coverage for mammograms. — A. 1. Notwithstanding the provisions of § 38.2-3419, each insurer proposing to issue individual or group accident and sickness insurance policies providing hospital, medical and surgical or major medical coverage on an expense incurred basis, each corporation providing individual or group accident and sickness subscription contracts and each health maintenance organization providing a health care plan for health care services shall provide coverage under such policy, contract or plan delivered, issued for delivery or renewed in this Commonwealth on and after July 1, 1996, for low-dose screening mammograms for determining the presence of occult breast cancer. Such coverage shall make available one screening mammogram to persons age thirty-five through thirty-nine, one such mammogram biennially to persons age forty through forty-nine, one such mammogram annually to persons age fifty and over and may be limited to a benefit of fifty dollars per mammogram subject to such dollar limits, deductibles and coinsurance factors as are no less favorable than for physical illness generally.

2. The term *"mammogram"* shall mean an X-ray examination of the breast using equipment dedicated specifically for mammography, including but not limited to the X-ray tube, filter, compression device, screens, film and cassettes, with an average radiation exposure of less than one rad mid-breast, two views of each breast.

B. In order to be considered a screening mammogram for which coverage shall be made available under this section:

1. The mammogram must be (i) ordered by a health care practitioner acting within the scope of his licensure and, in the case of an enrollee of a health maintenance organization, by the health maintenance organization physician, (ii) performed by a registered technologist, (iii) interpreted by a qualified radiologist, (iv) performed under the direction of a person licensed to practice medicine and surgery and certified by the American Board of Radiology or an equivalent examining body and (v) a copy of the mammogram report must be sent or delivered to the health care practitioner who ordered it;

2. The equipment used to perform the mammogram shall meet the standards set forth by the Virginia Department of Health in its radiation protection regulations; and

3. The mammography film shall be retained by the radiologic facility performing the examination in accordance with the American College of Radiology guidelines or state law.

C. The provisions of this section shall not apply to short-term travel, accident only, limited or specified disease policies, or to short-term nonrenewable policies of not more than six months' duration. (1989, c. 646; 1990, c. 284; 1996, c. 610.)

§ 38.2-3418.1:1. Coverage for bone marrow transplants. — A. Each insurer proposing to issue individual or group accident and sickness insurance policies providing hospital, medical and surgical, or major medical coverage on an expense-incurred basis, each corporation providing individual or group accident and sickness subscription contracts, and each health maintenance organization providing a health care plan for health care services shall offer and make available coverage under such policy, contract or plan delivered, issued for delivery or renewed in this Commonwealth on and after January 1, 1995, for the treatment of breast cancer by dose-intensive chemotherapy/autologous bone marrow transplants or stem cell transplants when performed pursuant to protocols approved by the institutional review board of any United States medical teaching college including, but not limited to, National Cancer Institute protocols that have been favorably reviewed and utilized by hematologists or oncologists experienced in dose-intensive chemotherapy/autologous bone marrow transplants or stem cell transplants.

B. Such coverage shall not be subject to any greater copayment than that applicable to any other coverage provided by such policies, contracts or plans, and such coverage shall be subject to the same deductible as that applicable to any other coverage; however, a deductible for such coverage in an amount different than that applicable to any other coverage may also be offered and made available.

C. The provisions of this section shall not apply to short-term travel, accident-only, limited or specified disease policies, or to short-term nonrenewable policies of not more than six months' duration. (1994, c. 699.)

§ 38.2-3418.1:2. Coverage for pap smears. — A. Notwithstanding the provisions § 38.2-3419, each insurer proposing to issue individual or group accident and sickness insurance policies providing hospital, medical and surgical or major medical coverage on an expense-incurred basis, each corporation providing individual or group accident and sickness subscription contracts and each health maintenance organization providing a health care plan for health care services shall provide coverage under such policy, contract or plan delivered, issued for delivery or renewed in this Commonwealth on and after July 1, 1996, for annual pap smears, including coverage, on and after July 1, 1999, for annual testing performed by any FDA-approved gynecologic cytology screening technologies.

B. The provisions of this section shall not apply to short-term travel, accident only, limited or specified disease policies, or to short-term nonrenewable policies of not more than six months' duration. (1996, c. 611; 1999, c. 921.)

The 1999 amendment added "including coverage, on and after July 1, 1999, for annual testing performed by any FDA-approved gyne- cologic cytology screening technologies" at the end of subsection A.

§ 38.2-3418.2. Coverage of procedures involving bones and joints. —

A. Each insurer proposing to issue individual or group accident and sickness insurance policies providing hospital, medical and surgical or major medical coverage on an expense-incurred basis, each corporation providing individual or group accident and sickness subscription contracts, and each health maintenance organization providing a health care plan for health care services that provides coverage under such policy, contract or plan for diagnostic and surgical treatment involving any bone or joint of the skeletal structure shall not, under such policy, contract or plan delivered, issued for delivery or renewed in this Commonwealth on and after July 1, 1995, exclude coverage for such diagnostic and surgical treatment involving any bone or joint of the head, neck, face or jaw or impose limits that are more restrictive than limits on coverage applicable to such treatment involving any bone or joint of the skeletal structure if the treatment is required because of a medical condition or injury which prevents normal function of the joint or bone and is deemed medically necessary to attain functional capacity of the affected part.

B. The provisions of this section shall not apply to short-term travel, accident-only, limited or specified disease policies, or to short-term nonrenewable policies of not more than six months' duration. (1995, c. 537.)

§ 38.2-3418.3. Coverage for hemophilia and congenital bleeding disorders. — A. Notwithstanding the provisions of § 38.2-3419, each insurer proposing to issue individual or group accident and sickness insurance policies providing hospital, medical and surgical, or major medical coverage on an expense-incurred basis; each corporation providing individual or group accident and sickness subscription contracts; and each health maintenance organization providing a health care plan for health care services shall provide coverage for hemophilia and congenital bleeding disorders under such policy, contract or plan delivered, issued for delivery or renewed in this Commonwealth on and after July 1, 1998.

B. For the purpose of this section:

"Blood infusion equipment" includes, but is not limited to, syringes and needles.

"Blood product" includes, but is not limited to, Factor VII, Factor VIII, Factor IX, and cryoprecipitate.

"Hemophilia" means a lifelong hereditary bleeding disorder usually affecting males that results in prolonged bleeding primarily into joints and muscles.

"Home treatment program" means a program where individuals or family members are trained to provide infusion therapy at home in order to achieve optimal health and cost effectiveness.

"State-approved hemophilia treatment center" means a hospital or clinic which receives federal or state Maternal and Child Health Bureau, and/or

Centers for Disease Control funds to conduct comprehensive care for persons with hemophilia and other congenital bleeding disorders.

C. The benefits to be provided shall include coverage for expenses incurred in connection with the treatment of routine bleeding episodes associated with hemophilia and other congenital bleeding disorders. The benefits to be provided shall include coverage for the purchase of blood products and blood infusion equipment required for home treatment of routine bleeding episodes associated with hemophilia and other congenital bleeding disorders when the home treatment program is under the supervision of the state-approved hemophilia treatment center.

D. The provisions of this section shall not apply to short-term travel, accident only, limited or specified disease policies, policies or contracts designed for issuance to persons eligible for coverage under Title XVIII of the Social Security Act, known as Medicare, or to any other similar coverage under state or federal governmental plans, or to short-term nonrenewable policies of not more than six months' duration. (1998, cc. 43, 120.)

§ **38.2-3418.4. Coverage for reconstructive breast surgery.** — A. Notwithstanding the provisions of § 38.2-3419, each insurer proposing to issue individual or group accident and sickness insurance policies providing hospital, medical and surgical, or major medical coverage on an expense-incurred basis; each corporation providing individual or group accident and sickness subscription contracts; and each health maintenance organization providing a health care plan for health care services shall provide coverage for reconstructive breast surgery under such policy, contract or plan delivered, issued for delivery or renewed in this Commonwealth on or after July 1, 1998.

B. The reimbursement for reconstructive breast surgery shall be determined according to the same formula by which charges are developed for other medical and surgical procedures. Such coverage shall have durational limits, dollar limits, deductibles and coinsurance factors that are no less favorable than for physical illness generally.

C. For purposes of this section, *"mastectomy"* means the surgical removal of all or part of the breast as a result of breast cancer and *"reconstructive breast surgery"* means surgery performed on or after July 1, 1998, (i) coincident with a mastectomy performed for breast cancer or (ii) following a mastectomy performed on or after July 1, 1998, for breast cancer to reestablish symmetry between the two breasts.

D. The provisions of this section shall not apply to short-term travel, accident only, limited or specified disease policies (except policies issued for cancer), policies or contracts designed for issuance to persons eligible for coverage under Title XVIII of the Social Security Act, known as Medicare, or any other similar coverage under state or federal governmental plans or to short-term nonrenewable policies of not more than six months' duration. (1998, c. 56.)

The number of this section was assigned by the Virginia Code Commission, the number in the 1998 act having been 38.2-3418.3.

§ **38.2-3418.5. Coverage for early intervention services.** — A. Notwithstanding the provisions of § 38.2-3419, each insurer proposing to issue individual or group accident and sickness insurance policies providing hospital, medical and surgical, or major medical coverage on an expense-incurred basis; each corporation providing individual or group accident and sickness subscription contracts; and each health maintenance organization providing a health care plan for health care services shall provide coverage for medically necessary early intervention services under such policy, contract or plan delivered, issued for delivery or renewed in this Commonwealth on and after July 1, 1998. Such coverage shall be limited to a benefit of $5,000 per insured or member per policy or calendar year and, except as set forth in subsection C, shall be subject to such dollar limits, deductibles and coinsurance factors as are no less favorable than for physical illness generally.

B. For the purpose of this section, *"early intervention services"* means medically necessary speech and language therapy, occupational therapy, physical therapy and assistive technology services and devices for dependents from birth to age three who are certified by the Department of Mental Health, Mental Retardation and Substance Abuse Services as eligible for services under Part H of the Individuals with Disabilities Education Act (20 U.S.C. § 1471 et seq.). *"Medically necessary early intervention services for the population certified by the Department of Mental Health, Mental Retardation and Substance Abuse Services"* shall mean those services designed to help an individual attain or retain the capability to function age-appropriately within his environment, and shall include services that enhance functional ability without effecting a cure.

C. The cost of early intervention services shall not be applied to any contractual provision limiting the total amount of coverage paid by the insurer, corporation or health maintenance organization to or on behalf of the insured or member during the insured's or member's lifetime.

D. *"Financial costs,"* as used in this section, shall mean any copayment, coinsurance, or deductible in the policy or plan. Financial costs may be paid through the use of federal Part H program funds, state general funds, or local government funds appropriated to implement Part H services for families who may refuse the use of their insurance to pay for early intervention services due to a financial cost.

E. The provisions of this section shall not apply to short-term travel, accident only, limited or specified disease policies, policies or contracts designed for issuance to persons eligible for coverage under Title XVIII of the Social Security Act, known as Medicare, or any other similar coverage under state or governmental plans or to short-term nonrenewable policies of not more than six months' duration. (1998, c. 625.)

The number of this section was assigned by the Virginia Code Commission, the number in the 1998 act having been 38.2-3418.3.

§ 38.2-3418.6. Minimum hospital stay for mastectomy and certain lymph node dissection patients. — A. Notwithstanding the provisions of § 38.2-3419, each insurer proposing to issue individual or group accident and sickness insurance policies providing hospital, medical and surgical, or major medical coverage on an expense-incurred basis; each corporation providing individual or group accident and sickness subscription contracts; and each health maintenance organization providing a health care plan for health care services shall provide coverage providing a minimum stay in the hospital of not less than forty-eight hours for a patient following a radical or modified radical mastectomy and not less than twenty-four hours of inpatient care following a total mastectomy or a partial mastectomy with lymph node dissection for the treatment of breast cancer. Nothing in this section shall be construed as requiring the provision of inpatient coverage where the attending physician in consultation with the patient determines that a shorter period of hospital stay is appropriate. Such provision shall be included under any policy, contract or plan delivered, issued for delivery or renewed in this Commonwealth on and after July 1, 1998.

The provisions of this section shall not apply to short-term travel, accident only, limited or specified disease policies, policies or contracts designed for issuance to persons eligible for coverage under Title XVIII of the Social Security Act, known as Medicare, or any other similar coverage under state or federal governmental plans, or to short-term nonrenewable policies of not more than six months' duration. (1998, c. 631.)

The number of this section was assigned by the Virginia Code Commission, the number in the 1998 act having been 38.2-3418.3.

§ 38.2-3418.7. Coverage for PSA testing. — A. Notwithstanding the provisions of § 38.2-3419, each insurer proposing to issue individual or group accident and sickness insurance policies providing hospital, medical and surgical, or major medical coverage on an expense-incurred basis; each corporation providing individual or group accident and sickness subscription contracts; and each health maintenance organization providing a health care plan for health care services shall provide coverage to (i) persons age fifty and over and (ii) persons age forty and over who are at high risk for prostate cancer, according to the most recent published guidelines of the American Cancer Society, for one PSA test in a twelve-month period and digital rectal examinations, all in accordance with American Cancer Society guidelines under any such policy, contract or plan delivered, issued for delivery or renewed in this Commonwealth on and after July 1, 1998.

B. For the purpose of this section, "PSA testing" means the analysis of a blood sample to determine the level of prostate specific antigen.

C. The provisions of this section shall not apply to (i) short-term travel, accident only, limited or specified disease policies other than cancer policies, (ii) short-term nonrenewable policies of not more than six months' duration, or (iii) policies or contracts designed for issuance to persons eligible for coverage under Title XVIII of the Social Security Act, known as Medicare, or any other similar coverage under state or federal governmental plans. (1998, cc. 709, 858.)

The number of this section was assigned by the Virginia Code Commission, the number in the 1998 act having been 38.2-3418.3.

§ 38.2-3418.8. Coverage for clinical trials for treatment studies on cancer. — A. Notwithstanding the provisions of § 38.2-3419, each insurer proposing to issue individual or group accident and sickness insurance policies providing hospital, medical and surgical, or major medical coverage on an expense-incurred basis; each corporation providing individual or group accident and sickness subscription contracts; and each health maintenance organization providing a health care plan for health care services shall provide coverage for patient costs incurred during participation in clinical trials for treatment studies on cancer, including ovarian cancer trials, under any such policy, contract or plan delivered, issued for delivery, or renewed in this Commonwealth on and after July 1, 1999.

B. The reimbursement for patient costs incurred during participation in clinical trials for treatment studies on cancer shall be determined in the same manner as reimbursement is determined for other medical and surgical procedures. Such coverage shall have durational limits, dollar limits, deductibles, copayments and coinsurance factors that are no less favorable than for physical illness generally.

C. For purposes of this section:

"Cooperative group" means a formal network of facilities that collaborate on research projects and have an established NIH-approved peer review program operating within the group. "Cooperative group" includes (i) the National Cancer Institute Clinical Cooperative Group and (ii) the National Cancer Institute Community Clinical Oncology Program.

"FDA" means the Federal Food and Drug Administration.

"Member" means a policyholder, subscriber, insured, or certificate holder or a covered dependent of a policyholder, subscriber, insured or certificate holder.

"Multiple project assurance contract" means a contract between an institution and the federal Department of Health and Human Services that defines the relationship of the institution to the federal Department of Health and Human Services and sets out the responsibilities of the institution and the procedures that will be used by the institution to protect human subjects.

"NCI" means the National Cancer Institute.

"NIH" means the National Institutes of Health.

"Patient cost" means the cost of a medically necessary health care service that is incurred as a result of the treatment being provided to the member for purposes of a clinical trial. "Patient cost" does not include (i) the cost of nonhealth care services that a patient may be required to receive as a result of the treatment being provided for purposes of a clinical trial, (ii) costs associated with managing the research associated with the clinical trial, or (iii) the cost of the investigational drug or device.

D. Coverage for patient costs incurred during clinical trials for treatment studies on cancer shall be provided if the treatment is being conducted in a Phase II, Phase III, or Phase IV clinical trial. Such treatment may, however, be provided on a case-by-case basis if the treatment is being provided in a Phase I clinical trial.

E. The treatment described in subsection D shall be provided by a clinical trial approved by:

1. The National Cancer Institute;

2. An NCI cooperative group or an NCI center;

3. The FDA in the form of an investigational new drug application;

4. The federal Department of Veterans Affairs; or

5. An institutional review board of an institution in the Commonwealth that has a multiple project assurance contract approved by the Office of Protection from Research Risks of the NCI.

F. The facility and personnel providing the treatment shall be capable of doing so by virtue of their experience, training, and expertise.

G. Coverage under this section shall apply only if:

1. There is no clearly superior, noninvestigational treatment alternative;

2. The available clinical or preclinical data provides a reasonable expectation that the treatment will be at least as effective as the noninvestigatonal alternative; and

3. The member and the physician or health care provider who provides services to the member under the insurance policy, subscription contract or health care plan conclude that the member's participation in the clinical trial would be appropriate, pursuant to procedures established by the insurer, corporation or health maintenance organization and as disclosed in the policy and evidence of coverage.

H. The provisions of this section shall not apply to short-term travel, accident-only, limited or specified disease policies or contracts designed for issuance to persons eligible for coverage under Title XVIII of the Social Security Act, known as Medicare, or any other similar coverage under state or governmental plans or to short-term nonrenewable policies of not more than six months' duration. (1999, cc. 643, 649.)

§ 38.2-3418.9. Minimum hospital stay for hysterectomy. —
A. Notwithstanding the provisions of § 38.2-3419, each insurer proposing to issue an individual or group hospital policy or major medical policy in this Commonwealth, each corporation proposing to issue an individual or group hospital, medical or major medical subscription contract, and each health maintenance organization providing a health care plan for health care shall provide coverage for laparoscopy-assisted vaginal hysterectomy and vaginal hysterectomy as provided in this section.

B. Such coverage shall include benefits for a minimum stay in the hospital of not less than twenty-three hours for a laparoscopy-assisted vaginal hysterectomy and forty-eight hours for a vaginal hysterectomy as outlined in Milliman & Robertson's nationally recognized guidelines. Nothing in this subsection shall be construed as requiring the provision of the total hours referenced when the attending physician, in consultation with the patient, determines that a shorter period of hospital stay is appropriate.

C. The requirements of this section shall apply to all insurance policies, contracts and plans delivered, issued for delivery, reissued, or extended on and after July 1, 1999, or at any time thereafter when any term of the policy, contract or plan is changed or any premium adjustment is made.

D. This section shall not apply to short-term travel, accident-only, limited or specified disease, or individual conversion policies or contracts, nor to policies or contracts designed for issuance to persons eligible for coverage under Title XVIII of the Social Security Act, known as Medicare, or any other similar coverage under state or federal governmental plans. (1999, cc. 643, 649.)

§ 38.2-3418.10. Coverage for diabetes. — A. Each insurer proposing to issue an individual or group hospital policy or major medical policy in this Commonwealth, each corporation proposing to issue an individual or group hospital, medical or major medical subscription contract, and each health maintenance organization providing a health care plan for health care services shall provide coverage for diabetes as provided in this section.

B. Such coverage shall include benefits for equipment, supplies and outpatient self-management training and education, including medical nutrition therapy, for the treatment of insulin-dependent diabetes, insulin-using diabetes, gestational diabetes and noninsulin-using diabetes if prescribed by a health care professional legally authorized to prescribe such items under law.

C. To qualify for coverage under this section, diabetes outpatient self-management training and education shall be provided by a certified, registered or licensed health care professional.

D. No insurer, corporation, or health maintenance organization shall impose upon any person receiving benefits pursuant to this section any copayment, fee or condition that is not equally imposed upon all individuals in the same benefit category.

E. The requirements of this section shall apply to all insurance policies, contracts and plans delivered, issued for delivery, reissued, or extended on and after July 1, 1999, or at any time thereafter when any term of the policy, contract or plan is changed or any premium adjustment is made.

F. This section shall not apply to short-term travel, accident only, limited or specified disease, or individual conversion policies or contracts, nor to policies or contracts designed for issuance to persons eligible for coverage under Title XVIII of the Social Security Act, known as Medicare, or any other similar coverage under state or federal governmental plans. (1999, c. 35.)

The number of this section was assigned by the Virginia Code Commission, the number in the 1999 act having been § 38.2-3418.8.

Editor's note. — Acts 1999, c. 35, cl. 2,

provides: "That the provisions of this act shall become effective notwithstanding the provisions of § 9-299."

§ 38.2-3418.11. Coverage for hospice care. — A. Notwithstanding the provisions of § 38.2-3419, each insurer proposing to issue individual or group accident and sickness insurance policies providing hospital, medical and surgical, or major medical coverage on an expense-incurred basis; each corporation providing individual or group accident and sickness subscription contracts; and each health maintenance organization providing a health care plan for health care services shall provide coverage for hospice services under such policy, contract or plan delivered, issued for delivery or renewed in this Commonwealth on and after July 1, 1999.

B. As used in this section:

"Hospice services" shall mean a coordinated program of home and inpatient care provided directly or under the direction of a hospice licensed under Article 7 (§ 32.1-162.1 et seq.) of Chapter 5 of Title 32.1, and shall include palliative and supportive physical, psychological, psychosocial and other health services to individuals with a terminal illness utilizing a medically directed interdisciplinary team.

"Individuals with a terminal illness" shall mean individuals whose condition has been diagnosed as terminal by a licensed physician, whose medical prognosis is death within six months, and who elect to receive palliative rather than curative care.

"Medicare" shall mean Title XVIII of the Social Security Act.

"Palliative care" shall mean treatment directed at controlling pain, relieving other symptoms, and focusing on the special needs of the patient as he experiences the stress of the dying process, rather than treatment aimed at investigation and intervention for the purpose of cure or prolongation of life.

C. For the purposes of this section, documentation requirements shall be no greater than those required for the same services under Medicare.

D. Nothing in this section shall prohibit an insurer, corporation, or health maintenance organization from offering or providing coverage for hospice services when it cannot be demonstrated that the illness is terminal or for individuals with life expectancies of longer than six months.

E. The provisions of this section shall not apply to short-term travel, accident only, short-term nonrenewable policies of not more than six months' duration, or to policies or contracts designed for issuance to persons eligible for coverage under Title XVIII of the Social Security Act, known as Medicare, or any other similar coverage under state or federal governmental plans. (1999, c. 858.)

The number of this section was assigned by the Virginia Code Commission, the number in the 1999 act having been § 38.2-3418.8.

Editor's note. — Acts 1999, c. 858, cl. 2, provides: "That the provisions of this act shall become effective notwithstanding the provisions of § 9-299."

§ 38.2-3419. Additional mandated coverage made optional to group policy or contract holder. — Any new or existing group policy or contract holder for whom coverage under an accident and sickness insurance policy is issued or renewed by an insurer or for whom coverage under a contract is issued or renewed by a corporation licensed pursuant to Chapter 42 (§ 38.2-4200 et seq.) of this title, shall be given the option to purchase any coverage, benefits or services first mandated under this chapter on or after July 1, 1982, provided that all mandated coverages as of June 30, 1982, will not be affected. (1982, c. 577, § 38.1-348.14; 1986, c. 562.)

§ 38.2-3419.1. Report of costs and utilization of mandated benefits.
— A. Beginning with the calendar year 1991, every insurer, health services plan, and health maintenance organization from which a report is deemed necessary under regulations adopted by the Commission shall report to the Commission cost and utilization information for each of the mandated benefits and providers set forth in this article. The reporting period shall be as determined by the Commission in its regulations, but not less often than biennially. Each report shall be submitted no later than the next May 1 following the reporting period. The reports shall be in detail and form as required under regulations adopted by the Commission so as to provide the information deemed necessary by the Commission to determine the financial impact of each mandated benefit and provider.

B. The Commission shall prepare a consolidation of these reports to provide to the General Assembly such information concerning the costs of mandated benefits, the utilization of services under mandated benefits, and such other information as the Commission or the General Assembly may deem appropriate. Such consolidated reports shall be submitted to the General Assembly no later than the next October 31 following the reporting period. (1990, cc. 393, 439; 1994, c. 316.)

ARTICLE 3.

Jurisdiction Over Providers of Health Care Services.

§ 38.2-3420. Authority and jurisdiction of Commission. — Any person offering or providing coverage in this Commonwealth for health care services, whether the coverage is by direct payment, reimbursement, or otherwise, shall be presumed to be subject to the jurisdiction of the Commission to the extent the person is not regulated by another agency of this Commonwealth, any subdivision of this Commonwealth, or the federal government relating to the offering or providing of coverage for health care services. (1983, c. 417, § 38.1-43.7; 1986, c. 562; 1990, c. 477.)

Jurisdiction for health care services. — As the body charged with the regulation of the business of insurance in the Commonwealth of Virginia, the SCC maintains subject matter jurisdiction over persons offering or providing coverage in the Commonwealth for health care services. Employers Resource Mgt. Co. v. Shannon, 65 F.3d 1126 (4th Cir. 1995), cert. denied, 516 U.S. 1094, 116 S. Ct. 816, 133 L. Ed. 2d 761 (1996).

§ 38.2-3421. How to show jurisdiction of other state agency or federal government. — A person may show that it is regulated by another agency of this Commonwealth, any subdivision of this Commonwealth, or the federal government by providing to the Commission the appropriate certificate, license or other document issued by the other governmental agency that permits or qualifies it to provide those services set forth in § 38.2-3420. Provided, however, in lieu of such certificate, license or other documentation, the Commission may determine that such person is not subject to the jurisdiction of the Commission if the Commission is otherwise satisfied that such person is regulated by another agency of this Commonwealth, any subdivision of this Commonwealth or the federal government relating to the offering or providing of coverage for health care services. Any person who has provided such certificate, license, or other document shall immediately notify the Commission if such person ceases to be regulated by the governmental agency as stated in the certificate, license, or other document provided to the Commission. Any other person who is otherwise determined by the Commission not to be subject to the jurisdiction of the Commission shall also notify the Commission of any change in its circumstances which may materially affect such determination of the Commission. (1983, c. 417, § 38.1-43.8; 1986, c. 562; 1990, c. 477.)

§ 38.2-3422. Examination. — Any person that fails to show that it is regulated by another agency of this Commonwealth, any subdivision of this Commonwealth, or the federal government as provided by § 38.2-3421 shall be subject to an examination by the Commission to determine the organization and solvency of the person and whether or not the person is in compliance with the applicable provisions of this title. (1983, c. 417, § 38.1-43.9; 1986, c. 562; 1990, c. 477.)

§ 38.2-3423. When subject to this title. — Any person that fails to show that it is regulated by another agency of this Commonwealth, any subdivision of this Commonwealth, or the federal government as provided by § 38.2-3421 shall be subject to all appropriate provisions of this title regarding the operation of its business. (1983, c. 417, § 38.1-43.10; 1986, c. 562; 1990, c. 477.)

§ 38.2-3424. Disclosure of extent and elements of coverage. — A. Any agent, agency, administrator, or other person that advertises, sells, transacts, or administers coverage for health care services in this Commonwealth where that coverage is provided by any person subject to the provisions of this article shall inform any purchaser, prospective purchaser, or covered person of (i) the lack of insurance or other coverage, unless that coverage is fully insured or otherwise fully covered by an admitted life insurer, accident and sickness insurer, health services plan, dental or optometric services plan, or health maintenance organization and (ii) if the coverage is fully insured or otherwise fully covered, the terms, coverages, limits, and deductibles including the amount of "stop-loss" insurance in effect.

B. No person, including an administrator, insurer, agent, or affiliate of an insurer shall make, publish, disseminate, circulate, or place before the public, or cause, directly or indirectly, to be made, published, disseminated, circulated, or placed before the public, in any newspaper, magazine or other publication, or in the form of a notice, circular, pamphlet, letter or poster, or over any radio station or television station, or in any other way, any advertisement, announcement, or statement soliciting membership, offering coverage, or evidencing coverage in any health care plan or arrangement which is subject to regulation by the Commission under this article and not otherwise regulated by this title, unless such advertisement, announcement, or statement contains the following disclosure:

Your plan of coverage is not protected under the Virginia Life, Accident and Sickness Insurance Guaranty Association Act. Therefore:

1. In the event of an insolvency of your plan, you may be unable to collect any amount you are owed for covered claims, regardless of the coverage provided under the plan;

2. The payment of premiums into your plan does not guarantee payment of claims under your plan, regardless of the coverage provided under the plan. When such disclosure is contained in print, it shall be no smaller than boldfaced ten-point type. (1983, c. 417, § 38.1-43.11; 1986, c. 562; 1990, c. 477.)

§ 38.2-3424.1. Applicability. — Nothing contained in this article shall be construed to apply to any plan for providing health insurance coverage established pursuant to § 2.1-20.1. (1990, c. 477.)

The number of this section was assigned by the Virginia Code Commission, the number in the 1990 act having been 38.2-3425.

ARTICLE 4.

Limited Mandated Benefit Accident and Sickness Insurance Policies and Subscription Contracts.

§§ 38.2-3425 through 38.2-3430: Expired.

Editor's note. — This article was enacted by Acts 1990, cc. 795, 802, and expired by its own terms on January 1, 1995 pursuant to § 38.2- 3430 as amended by Acts 1993, c. 960, and Acts 1994, c. 138.

ARTICLE 4.1.

Individual Health Insurance Coverage.

Editor's note. — Acts 1997, cc. 807 and 913, cl. 3, provide: "That the Bureau of Insurance within the State Corporation Commission, in cooperation with the Joint Commission on Health Care, monitor the impact of the provisions of this act [which, in part, enacted this article] on the Commonwealth's health insurance marketplace. In monitoring the impact of this act, the State Corporation Commission shall: (i) review the federal regulations that will be promulgated to implement P.L. 104-191 (The Health Insurance Portability and Accountability Act), and determine whether any changes to this act are required by federal regulations adopted pursuant to P.L. 104-191; (ii) monitor the impact of the guaranteed issue requirements in the individual market and evaluate any specific concerns regarding such requirements identified and documented to the satisfaction of the State Corporation Commission by health insurance issuers; and (iii) recommend to the Governor and the 1998 Session of the General Assembly any revisions, corrections or improvements to the provisions of this act that would require the enactment of additional legislation."

§ **38.2-3430.1. Application of article.** — This article applies to individual health insurance coverage offered, sold, issued, or renewed in this Commonwealth, but shall not apply to any individual health insurance coverage for any of the "excepted benefits" defined in § 38.2-3431. In the event of conflict between the provisions in this article and other provisions of this title, the provisions of this article shall be controlling. (1997, cc. 807, 913.)

§ **38.2-3430.2. Definitions.** — A. The terms defined in § 38.2-3431 that are used in this article shall have the meanings set forth in that section.

B. For purposes of this article:

"Eligible individual" means an individual:

1. (i) for whom, as of the date on which the individual seeks coverage under this section, the aggregate of the periods of creditable coverage is eighteen or more months and (ii) whose most recent prior creditable coverage was under individual health insurance coverage, a group health plan, governmental plan or church plan or health insurance coverage offered in connection with any such plan;

2. Who is not eligible for coverage under (i) a group health plan, (ii) part A or part B of Title XVIII of the Social Security Act, or (iii) a state plan under Title XIX of such Act, or any successor program, and does not have other health insurance coverage;

3. With respect to whom the most recent coverage within the coverage period described in subdivision 1 was not terminated based on a factor described in subdivision B 1 or B 2 of § 38.2-3430.7 relating to nonpayment of premiums or fraud;

4. If the individual had been offered the option of continuation coverage under a COBRA continuation provision or under a similar state program, who elected such coverage;

5. Who, if the individual elected such continuation coverage, has exhausted such continuation coverage under such provision or program; and

6. In the case where individual health insurance coverage is the most recent creditable coverage, the coverage was nonrenewed by the health insurance issuer under the conditions allowed in subdivision C 2 of § 38.2-3430.7, in which case the aggregate period of creditable coverage required is reduced to twelve months.

For the purposes of determining the aggregate of the periods of creditable coverage under subdivision B 1 (i) of this section, a period of creditable coverage shall not be counted with respect to enrollment of an individual under a health benefit plan if, after such period, there was a sixty-three-day period during all of which the individual was not covered under any creditable coverage or was not serving a waiting period for coverage under a group health plan, or for group health insurance coverage or was in an affiliation period. (1997, cc. 807, 913; 1998, c. 24; 1999, c. 1004.)

The **1998 amendment** added the last paragraph in subsection B.

The **1999 amendment** inserted "individual health insurance coverage" in subdivision B 1 (ii), deleted "and" at the end of subdivision B 4, added "and" at the end of subdivision B 5, and added subdivision B 6.

§ 38.2-3430.3. Guaranteed availability of individual health insurance coverage to certain individuals with prior group coverage. —

A. Guaranteed availability.

1. All eligible individuals shall be provided a choice of all individual health insurance coverage currently being offered by a health insurance issuer and the chosen coverage shall be issued.

2. Such coverage provided as required in subdivision A 1 shall not impose any preexisting condition exclusion with respect to such coverage.

B. Health insurance issuers are prohibited from imposing any limitations or exclusions based upon named conditions that apply to eligible individuals.

C. Health insurance issuers shall include on all applications for health insurance coverage questions which will enable the health insurance issuer to determine if an applicant is applying for coverage as an eligible individual as defined in § 38.2-3430.2. (1997, cc. 807, 913; 1999, c. 1004.)

Effective date. — This section is effective January 1, 1998.

The **1999 amendment** added subsection C.

§ 38.2-3430.3:1: Expired.

Editor's note. — This section was enacted by Acts 1998, c. 25, effective March 9, 1998, and expired by the terms of Acts 1998, c. 25, cl. 3 on January 1, 1999.

§ 38.2-3430.4. Special rules for network plans. — A health insurance issuer that offers health insurance coverage in the individual market may:

1. Limit the eligible individuals who may be enrolled under such coverage to those who live, reside, or work within the service area for such network plan;

2. Within the service area of such plan, deny such coverage to such individuals if the health insurance issuer has demonstrated to the Commission that: (i) it will not have the capacity to deliver services adequately to additional individual enrollees because of its obligations to existing group contract holders, enrollees and enrollees covered under individual contracts; and (ii) it is applying this section uniformly to individuals without regard to any health status-related factor of such individuals and without regard to whether the individuals are eligible individuals;

3. A health insurance issuer, upon denying health insurance coverage in any service area in accordance with subdivision A 2, may not offer coverage in the individual market within such service area for a period of 180 days after such coverage is denied. (1997, cc. 807, 913; 1998, c. 24.)

The 1998 amendment inserted "eligible" in subsection 1.

§ 38.2-3430.5. Application of financial capacity limits. — A. A health insurance issuer may deny health insurance coverage in the individual market to an eligible individual if the health insurance issuer has demonstrated to the satisfaction of the Commission that:

1. It does not have the financial reserves necessary to underwrite additional coverage; and

2. It is applying this section uniformly to all individuals in the individual market in the Commonwealth consistent with the laws of this Commonwealth and without regard to any health status-related factor of such individuals and without regard to whether the individuals are eligible individuals.

B. A health insurance issuer, upon denying individual health insurance coverage in any service area in accordance with subsection A, may not offer such coverage in the individual market within such service area for a period of 180 days after the date such coverage is denied or until the health insurance issuer has demonstrated to the satisfaction of the Commission that the health insurance issuer has sufficient financial reserves to underwrite additional coverage, whichever is later. (1997, cc. 807, 913.)

§ 38.2-3430.6. Market requirements. — A. The provisions of § 38.2-3430.3 shall not be construed to require that a health insurance issuer offering health insurance coverage only in connection with group health plans or through one or more bona fide associations, or both, offer such health insurance coverage in the individual market.

B. A health insurance issuer offering health insurance coverage in connection with group health plans under this title shall not be deemed to be a health insurance issuer offering individual health insurance coverage solely because such issuer offers a conversion policy. (1997, cc. 807, 913; 1998, c. 24.)

The 1998 amendment substituted "§ 38.2-3430.3" for "§ 38.2-3427" in subsection A.

§ 38.2-3430.7. Renewability of individual health insurance coverage. — A. Except as provided in this section, a health insurance issuer that provides individual health insurance coverage shall renew or continue in force such coverage at the option of the individual.

B. A health insurance issuer may nonrenew or discontinue health insurance coverage of an individual in the individual market based on one or more of the following:

1. The individual has failed to pay premiums or contributions in accordance with the terms of the health insurance coverage or the issuer has not received timely premium payments;

2. The individual has performed an act or practice that constitutes fraud or made an intentional misrepresentation of material fact under the terms of the coverage;

3. The issuer is ceasing to offer coverage in the individual market in accordance with subsection C and applicable state law;

4. In the case of a health insurance issuer that offers health insurance coverage in the individual market through a network plan, the individual no

longer resides, lives, or works in the service area, or in an area for which the health insurance issuer is authorized to do business but only if such coverage is terminated under this section uniformly without regard to any health status-related factor of covered individuals; or

5. In the case of health insurance coverage that is made available in the individual market only through one or more bona fide associations, the membership of the individual in the association (on the basis of which the coverage is provided) ceases but only if such coverage is terminated under this section uniformly without regard to any health status-related factor of covered individuals.

C. Requirements for uniform termination of coverage.

1. In any case in which a health insurance issuer decides to discontinue offering a particular type of health insurance coverage offered in the individual market, coverage of such type may be discontinued by the health insurance issuer only if:

a. The health insurance issuer provides notice to each covered individual provided coverage of this type in such market of such discontinuation at least ninety days prior to the date of the discontinuation of such coverage;

b. The health insurance issuer offers to each individual in the individual market provided coverage of this type, the option to purchase any other individual health insurance coverage currently being offered by the health insurance issuer for individuals in such market; and

c. In exercising the option to discontinue coverage of this type and in offering the option of coverage under subdivision 1 b of this subsection, the health insurance issuer acts uniformly without regard to any health status-related factor of enrolled individuals or individuals who may become eligible for such coverage.

2. Discontinuance of all coverage.

a. Subject to subdivision 1 c of this subsection, in any case in which a health insurance issuer elects to discontinue offering all health insurance coverage in the individual market in the Commonwealth, health insurance coverage may be discontinued by the health insurance issuer only if: (i) the health insurance issuer provides notice to the Commission and to each individual of such discontinuation at least 180 days prior to the date of the expiration of such coverage, and (ii) all health insurance issued or delivered for issuance in this Commonwealth in such market is discontinued and coverage under such health insurance coverage in such market is not renewed.

b. In the case of discontinuation under subdivision 2 a of this subsection in the individual market, the health insurance issuer may not provide for the issuance of any health insurance coverage in the individual market in this Commonwealth during the five-year period beginning on the date of the discontinuation of the last health insurance coverage not so renewed.

D. At the time of coverage renewal, a health insurance issuer may modify the health insurance coverage for a policy form offered to individuals in the individual market so long as such modification is consistent with the laws of this Commonwealth and effective on a uniform basis among all individuals with that policy form.

E. In applying this section in the case of health insurance coverage that is made available by health insurance issuers in the individual market to individuals only through one or more associations, a reference to an "individual" is deemed to include a reference to such an association of which the individual is a member. (1997, cc. 807, 913.)

§ **38.2-3430.8. Certification of coverage.** — The provisions of § 38.2-3432.3 shall apply to health insurance coverage offered by a health insurance issuer in the individual market in the same manner as they apply to health insurance coverage offered by a health insurance issuer in connection with a group health plan in the small or large group market. (1997, cc. 807, 913; 1999, c. 1004.)

The 1999 amendment deleted "subsections F through I of" preceding "§ 38.2-3432.3."

§ **38.2-3430.9. Regulations establishing standards.** — A. The Commission may adopt regulations to enable it to establish and administer such standards relating to the provisions of this article and Article 5 (§ 38.2-3431 et seq.) of this chapter as may be necessary to (i) implement the requirements of this article and (ii) assure that the Commonwealth's regulation of health insurance issuers is not preempted pursuant to P. L. 104-191 (The Health Insurance Portability & Accountability Act of 1996).

B. The Commission may revise or amend such regulations and may increase the scope of the regulations to the extent necessary to maintain federal approval of the Commonwealth's program for regulation of health insurance issuers pursuant to the requirements established by the United States Department of Health and Human Services.

C. The Commission shall annually advise the standing committees of the General Assembly having jurisdiction over insurance matters of revisions and amendments made pursuant to subsection B. (1997, cc. 807, 913.)

§ **38.2-3430.10. Effective date.** — The provisions of this article shall be effective on July 1, 1997, with the exception of § 38.2-3430.3 which shall be effective on January 1, 1998. (1997, cc. 807, 913.)

ARTICLE 5.

Group Market Reforms and Individual Coverage Offered to Employees of Small Employers.

§ **38.2-3431. Application of article; definitions.** — A. This article applies to group health plans and to health insurance issuers offering group health insurance coverage, and individual policies offered to employees of small employers.

Each insurer proposing to issue individual or group accident and sickness insurance policies providing hospital, medical and surgical or major medical coverage on an expense incurred basis, each corporation providing individual or group accident and sickness subscription contracts, and each health maintenance organization or multiple employer welfare arrangement providing health care plans for health care services that offers individual or group coverage to the small employer market in this Commonwealth shall be subject to the provisions of this article. Any issuer of individual coverage to employees of a small employer shall be subject to the provisions of this article if any of the following conditions are met:

1. Any portion of the premiums or benefits is paid by or on behalf of the employer;

2. The eligible employee or dependent is reimbursed, whether through wage adjustments or otherwise, by or on behalf of the employer for any portion of the premium;

3. The employer has permitted payroll deduction for the covered individual and any portion of the premium is paid by the employer, provided that the health insurance issuer providing individual coverage under such circumstances shall be registered as a health insurance issuer in the small group market under this article, and shall have offered small employer group insurance to the employer in the manner required under this article; or

4. The health benefit plan is treated by the employer or any of the covered individuals as part of a plan or program for the purpose of §§ 106, 125, or 162 of the United States Internal Revenue Code.

B. For the purposes of this article:

"*Actuarial certification*" means a written statement by a member of the American Academy of Actuaries or other individual acceptable to the Commission that a health insurance issuer is in compliance with the provisions of this article based upon the person's examination, including a review of the appropriate records and of the actuarial assumptions and methods used by the health insurance issuer in establishing premium rates for applicable insurance coverage.

"*Affiliation period*" means a period which, under the terms of the health insurance coverage offered by a health maintenance organization, must expire before the health insurance coverage becomes effective. The health maintenance organization is not required to provide health care services or benefits during such period and no premium shall be charged to the participant or beneficiary for any coverage during the period.

1. Such period shall begin on the enrollment date.

2. An affiliation period under a plan shall run concurrently with any waiting period under the plan.

"*Beneficiary*" has the meaning given such term under section 3(8) of the Employee Retirement Income Security Act of 1974 (29 U.S.C. § 1002 (8)).

"*Bona fide association*" means, with respect to health insurance coverage offered in this Commonwealth, an association which:

1. Has been actively in existence for at least five years;

2. Has been formed and maintained in good faith for purposes other than obtaining insurance;

3. Does not condition membership in the association on any health status-related factor relating to an individual (including an employee of an employer or a dependent of an employee);

4. Makes health insurance coverage offered through the association available to all members regardless of any health status-related factor relating to such members (or individuals eligible for coverage through a member);

5. Does not make health insurance coverage offered through the association available other than in connection with a member of the association; and

6. Meets such additional requirements as may be imposed under the laws of this Commonwealth.

"*Certification*" means a written certification of the period of creditable coverage of an individual under a group health plan and coverage provided by a health insurance issuer offering group health insurance coverage and the coverage if any under such COBRA continuation provision, and the waiting period if any and affiliation period if applicable imposed with respect to the individual for any coverage under such plan.

"*Church plan*" has the meaning given such term under section 3(33) of the Employee Retirement Income Security Act of 1974 (29 U.S.C. § 1002 (33)).

"*COBRA continuation provision*" means any of the following:

1. Section 4980B of the Internal Revenue Code of 1986 (26 U.S.C. § 4980B), other than subsection (f) (1) of such section insofar as it relates to pediatric vaccines;

2. Part 6 of subtitle B of Title I of the Employee Retirement Income Security Act of 1974 (29 U.S.C. § 1161 et seq.), other than section 609 of such Act; or

3. Title XXII of P.L. 104-191.

"*Community rate*" means the average rate charged for the same or similar coverage to all small employer groups with the same area, age and gender characteristics. This rate shall be based on the health insurance issuer's combined claims experience for all groups within its small employer market.

"Creditable coverage" means with respect to an individual, coverage of the individual under any of the following:

1. A group health plan;
2. Health insurance coverage;
3. Part A or B of Title XVIII of the Social Security Act (U.S.C. § 1395c or § 1395);
4. Title XIX of the Social Security Act (42 U.S.C. § 1396 et seq.), other than coverage consisting solely of benefits under section 1928;
5. Chapter 55 of Title 10, United States Code (10 U.S.C. § 1071 et seq.);
6. A medical care program of the Indian Health Service or of a tribal organization;
7. A state health benefits risk pool;
8. A health plan offered under Chapter 89 of Title 5, United States Code (5 U.S.C. § 8901 et seq.);
9. A public health plan (as defined in federal regulations);
10. A health benefit plan under section 5 (e) of the Peace Corps Act (22 U.S.C. § 2504(e)); or
11. Individual health insurance coverage.

Such term does not include coverage consisting solely of coverage of excepted benefits.

"Dependent" means the spouse or child of an eligible employee, subject to the applicable terms of the policy, contract or plan covering the eligible employee.

"Eligible employee" means an employee who works for a small group employer on a full-time basis, has a normal work week of thirty or more hours, has satisfied applicable waiting period requirements, and is not a part-time, temporary or substitute employee.

"Eligible individual" means such an individual in relation to the employer as shall be determined:

1. In accordance with the terms of such plan;
2. As provided by the health insurance issuer under rules of the health insurance issuer which are uniformly applicable to employers in the group market; and
3. In accordance with all applicable law of this Commonwealth governing such issuer and such market.

"Employee" has the meaning given such term under section 3(6) of the Employee Retirement Income Security Act of 1974 (29 U.S.C. § 1002 (6)).

"Employer" has the meaning given such term under section 3(5) of the Employee Retirement Income Security Act of 1974 (29 U.S.C. § 1002 (5)), except that such term shall include only employers of two or more employees.

"Enrollment date" means, with respect to an eligible individual covered under a group health plan or health insurance coverage, the date of enrollment of the eligible individual in the plan or coverage or, if earlier, the first day of the waiting period for such enrollment.

"Essential and standard health benefit plans" means health benefit plans developed pursuant to subsection C of this section.

"Excepted benefits" means benefits under one or more (or any combination thereof) of the following:

1. Benefits not subject to requirements of this article:
a. Coverage only for accident, or disability income insurance, or any combination thereof;
b. Coverage issued as a supplement to liability insurance;
c. Liability insurance, including general liability insurance and automobile liability insurance;
d. Workers' compensation or similar insurance;
e. Medical expense and loss of income benefits;
f. Credit-only insurance;

g. Coverage for on-site medical clinics; and

h. Other similar insurance coverage, specified in regulations, under which benefits for medical care are secondary or incidental to other insurance benefits.

2. Benefits not subject to requirements of this article if offered separately:

a. Limited scope dental or vision benefits;

b. Benefits for long-term care, nursing home care, home health care, community-based care, or any combination thereof; and

c. Such other similar, limited benefits as are specified in regulations.

3. Benefits not subject to requirements of this article if offered as independent, noncoordinated benefits:

a. Coverage only for a specified disease or illness; and

b. Hospital indemnity or other fixed indemnity insurance.

4. Benefits not subject to requirements of this article if offered as separate insurance policy:

a. Medicare supplemental health insurance (as defined under section 1882 (g) (1) of the Social Security Act (42 U.S.C. § 1395ss (g) (1));

b. Coverage supplemental to the coverage provided under Chapter 55 of Title 10, United States Code (10 U.S.C. § 1071 et seq.); and

c. Similar supplemental coverage provided to coverage under a group health plan.

"*Federal governmental plan*" means a governmental plan established or maintained for its employees by the government of the United States or by an agency or instrumentality of such government.

"*Governmental plan*" has the meaning given such term under section 3(32) of the Employee Retirement Income Security Act of 1974 (29 U.S.C. § 1002 (32)) and any federal governmental plan.

"*Group health insurance coverage*" means in connection with a group health plan, health insurance coverage offered in connection with such plan.

"*Group health plan*" means an employee welfare benefit plan (as defined in section 3 (1) of the Employee Retirement Income Security Act of 1974 (29 U.S.C. § 1002 (1)), to the extent that the plan provides medical care and including items and services paid for as medical care to employees or their dependents (as defined under the terms of the plan) directly or through insurance, reimbursement, or otherwise.

"*Health benefit plan*" means any accident and health insurance policy or certificate, health services plan contract, health maintenance organization subscriber contract, plan provided by a MEWA or plan provided by another benefit arrangement. "Health benefit plan" does not mean accident only, credit, or disability insurance; coverage of Medicare services or federal employee health plans, pursuant to contracts with the United States government; Medicare supplement or long-term care insurance; Medicaid coverage; dental only or vision only insurance; specified disease insurance; hospital confinement indemnity coverage; limited benefit health coverage; coverage issued as a supplement to liability insurance; insurance arising out of a workers' compensation or similar law; automobile medical payment insurance; medical expense and loss of income benefits; or insurance under which benefits are payable with or without regard to fault and that is statutorily required to be contained in any liability insurance policy or equivalent self-insurance.

"*Health insurance coverage*" means benefits consisting of medical care (provided directly, through insurance or reimbursement, or otherwise and including items and services paid for as medical care) under any hospital or medical service policy or certificate, hospital or medical service plan contract, or health maintenance organization contract offered by a health insurance issuer.

"*Health insurance issuer*" means an insurance company, or insurance organization (including a health maintenance organization) which is licensed to engage in the business of insurance in this Commonwealth and which is subject to the laws of this Commonwealth which regulate insurance within the meaning of section 514 (b) (2) of the Employee Retirement Income Security Act of 1974 (29 U.S.C. § 1144 (b) (2)). Such term does not include a group health plan.

"Health maintenance organization" means:

1. A federally qualified health maintenance organization;

2. An organization recognized under the laws of this Commonwealth as a health maintenance organization; or

3. A similar organization regulated under the laws of this Commonwealth for solvency in the same manner and to the same extent as such a health maintenance organization.

"Health status-related factor" means the following in relation to the individual or a dependent eligible for coverage under a group health plan or health insurance coverage offered by a health insurance issuer:

1. Health status;

2. Medical condition (including both physical and mental illnesses);

3. Claims experience;

4. Receipt of health care;

5. Medical history;

6. Genetic information;

7. Evidence of insurability (including conditions arising out of acts of domestic violence); or

8. Disability.

"Individual health insurance coverage" means health insurance coverage offered to individuals in the individual market, but does not include coverage defined as excepted benefits. Individual health insurance coverage does not include short-term limited duration coverage.

"Individual market" means the market for health insurance coverage offered to individuals other than in connection with a group health plan.

"Large employer" means, in connection with a group health plan or health insurance coverage with respect to a calendar year and a plan year, an employer who employed an average of at least fifty-one employees on business days during the preceding calendar year and who employs at least two employees on the first day of the plan year.

"Large group market" means the health insurance market under which individuals obtain health insurance coverage (directly or through any arrangement) on behalf of themselves (and their dependents) through a group health plan maintained by a large employer or through a health insurance issuer.

"Late enrollee" means, with respect to coverage under a group health plan or health insurance coverage provided by a health insurance issuer, a participant or beneficiary who enrolls under the plan other than during:

1. The first period in which the individual is eligible to enroll under the plan; or

2. A special enrollment period as required pursuant to subsections J through M of § 38.2-3432.3.

"Medical care" means amounts paid for:

1. The diagnosis, cure, mitigation, treatment, or prevention of disease, or amounts paid for the purpose of affecting any structure or function of the body;

2. Transportation primarily for and essential to medical care referred to in subdivision 1; and

3. Insurance covering medical care referred to in subdivisions 1 and 2.

"Network plan" means health insurance coverage of a health insurance issuer under which the financing and delivery of medical care (including items and services paid for as medical care) are provided, in whole or in part, through a defined set of providers under contract with the health insurance issuer.

"Nonfederal governmental plan" means a governmental plan that is not a federal governmental plan.

"Participant" has the meaning given such term under section 3(7) of the Employee Retirement Income Security Act of 1974 (29 U.S.C. § 1002 (7)).

"Placed for adoption," or *"placement"* or *"being placed"* for adoption, in connection with any placement for adoption of a child with any person, means the assumption and retention by such person of a legal obligation for total or partial support of such child in anticipation of adoption of such child. The child's placement with such person terminates upon the termination of such legal obligation.

"Plan sponsor" has the meaning given such term under section 3(16) (B) of the Employee Retirement Income Security Act of 1974 (29 U.S.C. § 1002 (16) (B)).

"Preexisting condition exclusion" means, with respect to coverage, a limitation or exclusion of benefits relating to a condition based on the fact that the condition was present before the date of enrollment for such coverage, whether or not any medical advice, diagnosis, care, or treatment was recommended or received before such date. Genetic information shall not be treated as a preexisting condition in the absence of a diagnosis of the condition related to such information.

"Premium" means all moneys paid by an employer and eligible employees as a condition of coverage from a health insurance issuer, including fees and other contributions associated with the health benefit plan.

"Rating period" means the twelve-month period for which premium rates are determined by a health insurance issuer and are assumed to be in effect.

"Service area" means a broad geographic area of the Commonwealth in which a health insurance issuer sells or has sold insurance policies on or before January 1994, or upon its subsequent authorization to do business in Virginia.

"Small employer" means in connection with a group health plan or health insurance coverage with respect to a calendar year and a plan year, an employer who employed an average of at least two but not more than fifty employees on business days during the preceding calendar year and who employs at least two employees on the first day of the plan year.

"Small group market" means the health insurance market under which individuals obtain health insurance coverage (directly or through any arrangement) on behalf of themselves (and their dependents) through a group health plan maintained by a small employer or through a health insurance issuer.

"State" means each of the several states, the District of Columbia, Puerto Rico, the Virgin Islands, Guam, American Samoa, and the Northern Mariana Islands.

"Waiting period" means, with respect to a group health plan or health insurance coverage provided by a health insurance issuer and an individual who is a potential participant or beneficiary in the plan, the period that must pass with respect to the individual before the individual is eligible to be covered for benefits under the terms of the plan. If an employee or dependent enrolls during a special enrollment period pursuant to subsections J through M of § 38.2-3432.3 or as a late enrollee, any period before such enrollment is not a waiting period.

C. The Commission shall adopt regulations establishing the essential and standard plans for sale in the small employer market. Such regulations shall incorporate the recommendations of the Essential Health Services Panel, established pursuant to Chapter 847 of the 1992 Acts of Assembly. The Commission shall modify such regulations as necessary to incorporate any revisions to the essential and standard plans submitted by the Special Advisory Commission on Mandated Health Insurance Benefits pursuant to § 9-298. Every health insurance issuer shall, as a condition of transacting business in Virginia with small employers, offer to small employers the essential and standard plans, subject to the provisions of § 38.2-3432.2. However, any regulation adopted by the Commission shall contain a provision requiring all health insurance issuers to offer an option permitting a small employer electing to be covered under either an essential or standard health benefit plan to choose coverage that does not provide dental benefits. The regulation shall also require a small employer electing such option, as a condition of continuing eligibility for coverage pursuant to this article, to purchase separate dental coverage for all eligible employees and eligible dependents from a dental services plan authorized pursuant to Chapter 45 of this title. All health insurance issuers shall issue the plans to every small employer that elects to be covered under either one of the plans and agrees to make the required premium payments, and shall satisfy the following provisions:

1. Such plan may include cost containment features such as, but not limited to, utilization review of health care services including review of medical necessity of hospital and physician services; case management; selective contracting with hospitals, physicians and other health care providers, subject to the limitations set forth in §§ 38.2-3407 and 38.2-4209 and Chapter 43 (§ 38.2-4300 et seq.) of this title; reasonable benefit differentials applicable to providers that participate or do not participate in arrangements using restricted network provisions; or other managed care provisions. The essential and standard plans for health maintenance organizations shall contain benefits and cost-sharing levels which are consistent with the basic method of operation and benefit plans of federally qualified health maintenance organizations, if a health maintenance organization is federally qualified, and of nonfederally qualified health maintenance organizations, if a health maintenance organization is not federally qualified. The essential and standard plans of coverage for health maintenance organizations shall be actuarial equivalents of these plans for health insurance issuers.

2. No law requiring the coverage or offering of coverage of a benefit shall apply to the essential or standard health care plan or riders thereof.

3. Every health insurance issuer offering group health insurance coverage shall, as a condition of transacting business in Virginia with small employers, offer and make available to small employers an essential and a standard health benefit plan, subject to the provisions of § 38.2-3432.2.

4. All essential and standard benefit plans issued to small employers shall use a policy form approved by the Commission providing coverage defined by the essential and standard benefit plans. Coverages providing benefits greater than and in addition to the essential and standard plans may be provided by rider, separate policy or plan provided that no rider, separate policy or plan shall reduce benefit or premium. A health insurance issuer shall submit all policy forms, including applications, enrollment forms, policies, subscription contracts, certificates, evidences of coverage, riders, amendments, endorsements and disclosure plans to the Commission for approval in the same manner as required by § 38.2-316. Each rider, separate policy or plan providing benefits greater than the essential and standard benefit plans may require a specific premium for the benefits provided in such rider, separate policy or plan. The premium for such riders shall be determined in the same manner as the premiums are determined for the essential and standard plans. The Commission at any time may, after providing notice and an opportunity for a hearing to a health insurance issuer, disapprove the continued use by the health insurance issuer of an essential or standard health benefit plan on the grounds that such plan does not meet the requirements of this article.

5. No health insurance issuer offering group health insurance coverage is required to offer coverage or accept applications pursuant to subdivisions 3 and 4 of this subsection:

a. From a small employer already covered under a health benefit plan except for coverage that is to commence on the group's anniversary date, but this subsection shall not be construed to prohibit a group from seeking coverage or a health insurance issuer offering group health insurance coverage from issuing coverage to a group prior to its anniversary date; or

b. If the Commission determines that acceptance of an application or applications would result in the health insurance issuer being declared an impaired insurer.

A health insurance issuer offering group health insurance coverage that does not offer coverage pursuant to subdivision 5 b may not offer coverage to small employers until the Commission determines that the health insurance issuer is no longer impaired.

6. Every health insurance issuer offering group health insurance coverage shall uniformly apply the provisions of subdivision C 5 of this section and shall fairly market the essential and standard health benefit plans to all small employers in their service area of the Commonwealth. A health insurance issuer offering group health insurance coverage that fails to fairly market as required by this subdivision may not offer coverage in the Commonwealth to new small employers until the later of 180 days after the unfair marketing has been identified and proven to the Commission or the date on which the health insurance issuer submits and the Commission approves a plan to fairly market to the health insurance issuer's service area.

7. No health maintenance organization is required to offer coverage or accept applications pursuant to subdivisions 3 and 4 of this subsection in the case of any of the following:

a. To small employers, where the policy would not be delivered or issued for delivery in the health maintenance organization's approved service areas;

b. To an employee, where the employee does not reside or work within the health maintenance organization's approved service areas;

c. To small employers if the health maintenance organization is a federally qualified health maintenance organization and it demonstrates to the satisfaction of the Commission that the federally qualified health maintenance organization is prevented from doing so by federal requirement; however, any such exemption under this subdivision would be limited to the essential plan; or

d. Within an area where the health maintenance organization demonstrates to the satisfaction of the Commission, that it will not have the capacity within that area and its network of providers to deliver services adequately to the enrollees of those groups because of its obligations to existing group contract holders and enrollees. A health maintenance organization that does not offer coverage pursuant to this subdivision may not offer coverage in the applicable area to new employer groups with more than fifty eligible employees until the later of 180 days after closure to new applications or the date on which the health maintenance organization notifies the Commission that it has regained capacity to deliver services to small employers. In the case of a health maintenance organization doing business in the small employer market in one service area of this Commonwealth, the rules set forth in this subdivision shall apply to the health maintenance organization's operations in the service area, unless the provisions of subdivision 6 of this subsection apply.

8. In order to ensure the broadest availability of health benefit plans to small employers, the Commission shall set market conduct and other requirements for health insurance issuers, agents and third-party administrators, including requirements relating to the following:

a. Registration by each health insurance issuer offering group health insurance coverage with the Commission of its intention to offer health insurance coverage in the small group market under this article;

b. Publication by the Commission of a list of all health insurance issuers who offer coverage in the small group market, including a potential requirement applicable to agents, third-party administrators, and health insurance issuers that no health benefit plan may be sold to a small employer by a health insurance issuer not so identified as a health insurance issuer in the small group market;

c. The availability of a broadly publicized toll-free telephone number for the Commission's Bureau of Insurance for access by small employers to information concerning this article;

d. To the extent deemed to be necessary to ensure the fair distribution of small employers among carriers, periodic reports by health insurance issuers about plans issued to small employers; provided that reporting requirements shall be limited to information concerning case characteristics and numbers of health benefit plans in various categories marketed or issued to small employers. Health insurance issuers shall maintain data relating to the essential and standard benefit plans separate from data relating to additional benefits made available by rider for the purpose of complying with the reporting requirements of this section; and

e. Methods concerning periodic demonstration by health insurance issuers offering group health insurance coverage that they are marketing and issuing health benefit plans to small employers in fulfillment of the purposes of this article.

9. All essential and standard health benefits plans contracts delivered, issued for delivery, reissued, renewed, or extended in this Commonwealth on or after July 1, 1997, shall include coverage for 365 days of inpatient hospitalization for each covered individual during a twelve-month period. If coverage under the essential or standard health benefits plan terminates while a covered person is hospitalized, the inpatient hospital benefits shall continue to be provided until the earliest of (i) the day the maximum amount of benefit has been provided or (ii) the day the covered person is no longer hospitalized as an inpatient. (1992, c. 800; 1993, cc. 148, 960; 1994, c. 303; 1996, c. 262; 1997, cc. 415, 807, 913; 1998, cc. 24, 26; 1999, cc. 789, 815, 1004.)

Editor's note. — Acts 1997, cc. 807 and 913, cl. 3, provide: "That the Bureau of Insurance within the State Corporation Commission, in cooperation with the Joint Commission on Health Care, monitor the impact of the provisions of this act on the Commonwealth's health insurance marketplace. In monitoring the impact of this act, the State Corporation Commission shall: (i) review the federal regulations that will be promulgated to implement P.L. 104-191 (The Health Insurance Portability and Accountability Act), and determine whether any changes to this act are required by federal regulations adopted pursuant to P.L. 104-191; (ii) monitor the impact of the guaranteed issue requirements in the individual market and evaluate any specific concerns regarding such requirements identified and documented to the satisfaction of the State Corporation Commission by health insurance issuers; and (iii) recommend to the Governor and the 1998 Session of the General Assembly any revisions, corrections or improvements to the provisions of this act that would require the enactment of additional legislation."
The 1998 amendments. — The 1998 amendment by c. 24, in subsection B, in the paragraph defining "Creditable coverage," in subdivision 3, substituted "Title XVIII" for "Title XVII," and in subdivision 9, inserted "federal," deleted the former paragraph defining "Established geographic service area," in the paragraph defining "Medical care," in subdivisions 2 and 3, deleted "Amounts paid for" at the beginning of each subdivision, added the paragraph defining "Service area," in the paragraph defining "Small employer," inserted "or health insurance coverage," and in the paragraph defining "Waiting period," added the second sentence; and in subsection C, in the fourth sentence of the introductory paragraph and in subdivision 3, added "subject to the provisions of § 38.2-3432.2," and in subdivision 6, deleted "established geographic" preceding "service area" in the first and second sentences.
The 1998 amendment by c. 26, deleted "primary" preceding "small" throughout this section; and in subsection B deleted the former paragraph defining "Primary small employer."
The 1999 amendments. — The 1999 amendments by cc. 789 and 815 are identical, and in subdivision A 3, substituted "and any

portion" for "or any portion," and inserted "provided that the health insurance issuer providing individual coverage under such circumstances shall be registered as a health insurance issuer in the small group market under this article, and shall have offered small employer group insurance to the employer in the manner required under this article."

The 1999 amendment by c. 1004, in subsection B, in the paragraph defining "Creditable coverage" deleted "or" at the end of subdivision 9, added "or" at the end of subdivision 10, and added subdivision 11.

§ **38.2-3432:** Repealed by Acts 1997, cc. 807 and 913.

§ **38.2-3432.1. Renewability.** — A. Every health insurance issuer that offers health insurance coverage in the group market in this Commonwealth shall renew or continue in force such coverage with respect to all insureds at the option of the employer except:

1. For nonpayment of the required premiums by the policyholder, or contract holder, or where the health insurance issuer has not received timely premium payments;

2. When the health insurance issuer is ceasing to offer coverage in the small group market in accordance with subdivisions 9 and 10;

3. For fraud or misrepresentation by the employer, with respect to their coverage;

4. With regard to coverage provided to an eligible employee, for fraud or misrepresentation by the employee with regard to his or her coverage;

5. For failure to comply with contribution and participation requirements defined by the health benefit plan;

6. For failure to comply with health benefit plan provisions that have been approved by the Commission;

7. When a health insurance issuer offers health insurance coverage in the group market through a network plan, and there is no longer an enrollee in connection with such plan who lives, resides, or works in the service area of the health insurance issuer (or in the area for which the health insurance issuer is authorized to do business) and, in the case of the group market, the health insurance issuer would deny enrollment with respect to such plan under the provisions of subdivision 9 or 10;

8. When health insurance coverage is made available in the group market only through one or more bona fide associations, the membership of an employer in the association (on the basis of which the coverage is provided) ceases but only if such coverage is terminated under this subdivision uniformly without regard to any health status related factor relating to any covered individual;

9. When a health insurance issuer decides to discontinue offering a particular type of group health insurance coverage in the group market in this Commonwealth, coverage of such type may be discontinued by the health insurance issuer in accordance with the laws of this Commonwealth in such market only if (i) the health insurance issuer provides notice to each plan sponsor provided coverage of this type in such market (and participants and beneficiaries covered under such coverage) of such discontinuation at least ninety days prior to the date of the discontinuation of such coverage; (ii) the health insurance issuer offers to each plan sponsor provided coverage of this type in such market, the option to purchase any other health insurance coverage currently being offered by the health insurance issuer to a group health plan in such market; and (iii) in exercising the option to discontinue coverage of this type and in offering the option of coverage under this subdivision, the health insurance issuer acts uniformly without regard to the claims experience of those sponsors or any health status-related factor relating to any participants or beneficiaries covered or new participants or beneficiaries who may become eligible for such coverage;

10. In any case in which a health insurance issuer elects to discontinue offering all health insurance coverage in the group market in this Commonwealth, health insurance coverage may be discontinued by the health insurance issuer only in accordance with the laws of this Commonwealth and if: (i) the health insurance issuer provides notice to the Commission and to each plan sponsor (and participants and beneficiaries covered under such coverage) of such discontinuation at least 180 days prior to the date of the discontinuation of such coverage; and (ii) all health insurance issued or delivered for issuance in this Commonwealth in such market (or markets) are discontinued and coverage under such health insurance coverage in such market (or markets) is not renewed;

11. In the case of a discontinuation under subdivision 10 of this subsection in a market, the health insurance issuer may not provide for the issuance of any health insurance coverage in the market and this Commonwealth during the five-year period beginning on the date of the discontinuation of the last health insurance coverage not so renewed;

12. At the time of coverage renewal, a health insurance issuer may modify the health insurance coverage for a product offered to a group health plan or health insurance issuer offering group health insurance coverage in the group market if, for coverage that is available in such market other than only through one or more bona fide associations, such modification is consistent with the laws of this Commonwealth and effective on a uniform basis among group health plans or health insurance issuers offering group health insurance coverage with that product;

13. In applying this section in the case of health insurance coverage that is made available by a health insurance issuer in the group market to employers only through one or more associations, a reference to "plan sponsor" is deemed, with respect to coverage provided to an employer member of the association, to include a reference to such employer; or

14. Benefits and premiums which have been added by rider to the essential or standard benefit plans issued to small employers shall be renewable at the sole option of the health insurance issuer.

B. If coverage to the small employer market pursuant to this article ceases to be written, administered or otherwise provided, such coverage shall continue to be governed by this article with respect to business conducted under this article that was transacted prior to the effective date of termination and that remains in force. (1997, cc. 807, 913; 1998, c. 24.)

Editor's note. — Acts 1997, cc. 807 and 913, cl. 3, provide: "That the Bureau of Insurance within the State Corporation Commission, in cooperation with the Joint Commission on Health Care, monitor the impact of the provisions of this act [which, in part, enacted this section] on the Commonwealth's health insurance marketplace. In monitoring the impact of this act, the State Corporation Commission shall: (i) review the federal regulations that will be promulgated to implement P.L. 104-191 (The Health Insurance Portability and Accountability Act), and determine whether any changes to this act are required by federal regulations adopted pursuant to P.L. 104-191;

(ii) monitor the impact of the guaranteed issue requirements in the individual market and evaluate any specific concerns regarding such requirements identified and documented to the satisfaction of the State Corporation Commission by health insurance issuers; and (iii) recommend to the Governor and the 1998 Session of the General Assembly any revisions, corrections or improvements to the provisions of this act that would require the enactment of additional legislation."

The 1998 amendment, in subsection A, in subdivision 11, substituted "subdivision 10" for "subdivision 9."

§ **38.2-3432.2. Availability.** — A. If coverage is offered under this article in the small employer market:

1. Such coverage shall be offered and made available to all the eligible

employees of every small employer and their dependents, including late enrollees, that apply for such coverage. No coverage may be offered only to certain eligible employees or their dependents and no employees or their dependents may be excluded or charged additional premiums because of health status; and

2. All products that are approved for sale in the small group market that the health insurance issuer is actively marketing must be offered to all small employers, and the health insurance issuer must accept any employer that applies for any of those products.

B. No coverage offered under this article shall exclude an employer based solely on the nature of the employer's business.

C. A health insurance issuer that offers health insurance coverage in a small group market through a network plan may:

1. Limit the employers that may apply for such coverage to those eligible individuals who live, work or reside in the service area for such network plan; and

2. Within the service area of such plan, deny such coverage to such employers if the health insurance issuer has demonstrated, if required, to the satisfaction of the Commission that:

a. It will not have the capacity to deliver services adequately to enrollees of any additional groups because of its obligations to existing group contract holders and enrollees; and

b. It is applying this subdivision uniformly to all employers without regard to the claims experience of those employers and their employees (and their dependents) or any health status-related factors relating to such employees and dependents.

3. A health insurance issuer upon denying health insurance coverage in any service area in accordance with subdivision D 1, may not offer coverage in the small group market within such service area for a period of 180 days after the date such coverage is denied.

D. A health insurance issuer may deny health insurance coverage in the small group market if the health insurance issuer has demonstrated, if required, to the satisfaction of the Commission that:

1. It does not have the financial reserves necessary to underwrite additional coverage; and

2. It is applying this subdivision uniformly to all employers in the small group market in the Commonwealth consistent with the laws of this Commonwealth and without regard to the claims experience of those employers and their employees (and their dependents) or any health status-related factor relating to such employees and dependents.

E. A health insurance issuer upon denying health insurance coverage in accordance with subsection D in the Commonwealth may not offer coverage in the small group market for a period of 180 days after the date such coverage is denied or until the health insurance issuer has demonstrated to the satisfaction of the Commission that the health insurance issuer has sufficient financial reserves to underwrite additional coverage, whichever is later.

F. Nothing in this article shall be construed to preclude a health insurance issuer from establishing employer contribution rules or group participation rules in connection with a health benefit plan offered in the small group market. As used in this article, the term *"employer contribution rule"* means a requirement relating to the minimum level or amount of employer contribution toward the premium for enrollment of eligible individuals and the term *"group participation rule"* means a requirement relating to the minimum number of eligible employees that must be enrolled in relation to a specified percentage or number of eligible employees. Any employer contribution rule or group participation rule shall be applied uniformly among small employers without reference to the size of the small employer group, health status of the small employer group, or other factors. (1997, cc. 807, 913; 1998, c. 24.)

Editor's note. — Acts 1997, cc. 807 and 913, cl. 3, provide: "That the Bureau of Insurance within the State Corporation Commission, in cooperation with the Joint Commission on Health Care, monitor the impact of the provisions of this act [which, in part, enacted this section] on the Commonwealth's health insurance marketplace. In monitoring the impact of this act, the State Corporation Commission shall: (i) review the federal regulations that will be promulgated to implement P.L. 104-191 (The Health Insurance Portability and Accountability Act), and determine whether any changes to this act are required by federal regulations adopted pursuant to P.L. 104-191;

(ii) monitor the impact of the guaranteed issue requirements in the individual market and evaluate any specific concerns regarding such requirements identified and documented to the satisfaction of the State Corporation Commission by health insurance issuers; and (iii) recommend to the Governor and the 1998 Session of the General Assembly any revisions, corrections or improvements to the provisions of this act that would require the enactment of additional legislation."

The 1998 amendment rewrote subsection A, and in subsection E, deleted "in connection with group health plans" following "coverage" in two places.

§ 38.2-3432.3. Limitation on preexisting condition exclusion period.
— A. Subject to subsection B, a health insurer offering health insurance coverage, may, with respect to a participant or beneficiary, impose a preexisting limitation only if:

1. For group health insurance coverage, such exclusion relates to a condition (whether physical or mental), regardless of the cause of the condition, for which medical advice, diagnosis, care, or treatment was recommended or received within the six-month period ending on the enrollment date;

2. For individual health insurance coverage, such exclusion relates to a condition that, during a twelve-month period immediately preceding the effective date of coverage, had manifested itself in such a manner as would cause an ordinarily prudent person to seek diagnosis, care, or treatment, or for which medical advice, diagnosis, care or treatment was recommended or received within twelve months immediately preceding the effective date of coverage;

3. Such exclusion extends for a period of not more than twelve months (or twelve months in the case of a late enrollee) after the enrollment date; and

4. The period of any such preexisting condition exclusion is reduced by the aggregate of the periods of creditable coverage, if any, applicable to the participant or beneficiary as of the enrollment date.

B. Exceptions:

1. Subject to subdivision 4 of this subsection, a health insurance issuer offering health insurance coverage, may not impose any preexisting condition exclusion in the case of an individual who, as of the last day of the thirty-day period beginning with the date of birth, is covered under creditable coverage;

2. Subject to subdivision 4 of this subsection, a health insurance issuer offering health insurance coverage, may not impose any preexisting condition exclusion in the case of a child who is adopted or placed for adoption before attaining eighteen years of age and who, as of the last day of the thirty-day period beginning on the date of the adoption or placement for adoption, is covered under creditable coverage. The previous sentence shall not apply to coverage before the date of such adoption or placement for adoption;

3. A health insurance issuer offering health insurance coverage, may not impose any preexisting condition exclusion relating to pregnancy as a preexisting condition, except in the case of individual health insurance coverage, where the health insurance issuer may impose a preexisting condition exclusion for a pregnancy existing on the effective date of coverage;

4. Subdivisions 1 and 2 of this subsection shall no longer apply to an individual after the end of the first sixty-three-day period during all of which the individual was not covered under any creditable coverage; and

5. Subdivision A 4 of § 38.2-3432.3 shall not apply to health insurance coverage offered in the individual market on a "guarantee issue" basis without regard to health status including open enrollment policies or contracts issued pursuant to § 38.2-4216.1 and policies, contracts, certificates or evidences of coverage issued through a bona fide association or to students through school sponsored programs at a college or university unless the person is an eligible individual as defined in § 38.2-3430.2.

C. A period of creditable coverage shall not be counted, with respect to enrollment of an individual under a health benefit plan, if, after such period and before the enrollment date, there was a sixty-three-day period during all of which the individual was not covered under any creditable coverage.

D. For purposes of subdivision B 4 and subsection C, any period that an individual is in a waiting period for any coverage under a group health plan (or for group health insurance coverage) or is in an affiliation period shall not be taken into account in determining the continuous period under subsection C.

E. Methods of crediting coverage:

1. Except as otherwise provided under subdivision 2 of this subsection, a health insurance issuer offering group health coverage shall count a period of creditable coverage without regard to the specific benefits covered during the period;

2. A health insurance issuer offering group health insurance coverage, may elect to count a period of creditable coverage based on coverage of benefits within each of several classes or categories of benefits rather than as provided under subdivision 1 of this subsection. Such election shall be made on a uniform basis for all participants and beneficiaries. Under such election a health insurance issuer shall count a period of creditable coverage with respect to any class or category of benefits if any level of benefits is covered within such class or category;

3. In the case of an election with respect to a group plan under subdivision 2 of this subsection (whether or not health insurance coverage is provided in connection with such plan), the plan shall: (i) prominently state in any disclosure statements concerning the plan, and state to each enrollee at the time of enrollment under the plan, that the plan has made such election and (ii) include in such statements a description of the effect of this election; and

4. In the case of an election under subdivision 2 of this subsection with respect to health insurance coverage offered by a health insurance issuer in the small or large group market, the health insurance issuer shall: (i) prominently state in any disclosure statements concerning the coverage, and to each employer at the time of the offer or sale of the coverage, that the health insurance issuer has made such election and (ii) include in such statements a description of the effect of such election.

F. Periods of creditable coverage with respect to an individual shall be established through presentation of certifications described in subsection G or in such other manner as may be specified in federal regulations.

G. A health insurance issuer offering group health insurance coverage, shall provide for certification of the period of creditable coverage:

1. At the time an individual ceases to be covered under the plan or otherwise becomes covered under a COBRA continuation provision;

2. In the case of an individual becoming covered under a COBRA continuation provision, at the time the individual ceases to be covered under such provision; and

3. At the request, or on behalf of, an individual made not later than twenty-four months after the date of cessation of the coverage described in

subdivision 1 or 2 of this subsection, whichever is later. The certification under subdivision 1 of this subsection may be provided, to the extent practicable, at a time consistent with notices required under any applicable COBRA continuation provision.

H. To the extent that medical care under a group health plan consists of group health insurance coverage, the plan is deemed to have satisfied the certification requirement under this section if the health insurance issuer offering the coverage provides for such certification in accordance with this section.

I. In the case of an election described in subdivision E 2 by a health insurance issuer, if the health insurance issuer enrolls an individual for coverage under the plan and the individual provides a certification of coverage of the individual under subsection F:

1. Upon request of such health insurance issuer, the entity which issued the certification provided by the individual shall promptly disclose to such requesting group insurance issuer information on coverage of classes and categories of health benefits available under such entity's plan or coverage; and

2. Such entity may charge the requesting health insurance issuer for the reasonable cost of disclosing such information.

J. A health insurance issuer offering group health insurance coverage, shall permit an employee who is eligible, but not enrolled, for coverage under the terms of the plan (or a dependent of such an employee if the dependent is eligible, but not enrolled, for coverage under such terms) to enroll for coverage under the terms of the plan if each of the following conditions is met:

1. The employee or dependent was covered under a group health plan or had health insurance coverage at the time coverage was previously offered to the employee or dependent;

2. The employee stated in writing at such time that coverage under a group health plan or health insurance coverage was the reason for declining enrollment, but only if the plan sponsor or health insurance issuer (if applicable) required such a statement at such time and provided the employee with notice of such requirement (and the consequences of such requirement) at such time;

3. The employee's or dependent's coverage described in subdivision 1 of this subsection: (i) was under a COBRA continuation provision and the coverage under such provision was exhausted or (ii) was not under such a provision and either the coverage was terminated as a result of loss of eligibility for the coverage (including as a result of legal separation, divorce, death, termination of employment, or reduction in the number of hours of employment) or employer contributions towards such coverage were terminated; and

4. Under the terms of the plan, the employee requests such enrollment not later than thirty days after the date of exhaustion of coverage described in subdivision 3 (i) of this subsection or termination of coverage or employer contribution described in subdivision 3 (ii) of this subsection.

K. If: (i) a health insurance issuer makes coverage available with respect to a dependent of an individual; (ii) the individual is a participant under the plan (or has met any waiting period applicable to becoming a participant under the plan and is eligible to be enrolled under the plan but for a failure to enroll during a previous enrollment period); and (iii) a person becomes such a dependent of the individual through marriage, birth, or adoption or placement for adoption, the health insurance issuer shall provide for a dependent special enrollment period described in subsection L of this subsection during which the person (or, if not otherwise enrolled, the individual) may also be enrolled under the plan as a dependent of the individual, and in the case of the birth or adoption of a child, the spouse of the individual may also be enrolled as a dependent of the individual if such spouse is otherwise eligible for coverage.

L. A dependent special enrollment period under this subsection shall be a period of not less than thirty days and shall begin on the later of:

1. The date dependent coverage is made available; or

2. The date of the marriage, birth, or adoption or placement for adoption (as the case may be) described in subsection K.

M. If an individual seeks to enroll a dependent during the first thirty days of such a dependent special enrollment period, the coverage of the dependent shall become effective:

1. In the case of marriage, not later than the first day of the first month beginning after the date the completed request for enrollment is received;

2. In the case of a dependent's birth, as of the date of such birth; or

3. In the case of a dependent's adoption or placement for adoption, the date of such adoption or placement for adoption.

N. A late enrollee may be excluded from coverage for up to eighteen months or may have a preexisting condition limitation apply for up to eighteen months; however, in no case shall a late enrollee be excluded from some or all coverage for more than eighteen months. An eligible employee or dependent shall not be considered a late enrollee if all of the conditions set forth below in subdivisions 1 through 4 are met or one of the conditions set forth below in subdivision 5 or 6 is met:

1. The individual was covered under a public or private health benefit plan at the time the individual was eligible to enroll.

2. The individual certified at the time of initial enrollment that coverage under another health benefit plan was the reason for declining enrollment.

3. The individual has lost coverage under a public or private health benefit plan as a result of termination of employment or employment status eligibility, the termination of the other plan's entire group coverage, death of a spouse, or divorce.

4. The individual requests enrollment within thirty days after termination of coverage provided under a public or private health benefit plan.

5. The individual is employed by a small employer that offers multiple health benefit plans and the individual elects a different plan offered by that small employer during an open enrollment period.

6. A court has ordered that coverage be provided for a spouse or minor child under a covered employee's health benefit plan, the minor is eligible for coverage and is a dependent, and the request for enrollment is made within thirty days after issuance of such court order.

However, such individual may be considered a late enrollee for benefit riders or enhanced coverage levels not covered under the enrollee's prior plan. (1997, cc. 807, 913; 1998, c. 24; 1999, c. 1004.)

Editor's note. — Acts 1997, cc. 807 and 913, cl. 3, provide: "That the Bureau of Insurance within the State Corporation Commission, in cooperation with the Joint Commission on Health Care, monitor the impact of the provisions of this act [which, in part, enacted this section] on the Commonwealth's health insurance marketplace. In monitoring the impact of this act, the State Corporation Commission shall: (i) review the federal regulations that will be promulgated to implement P.L. 104-191 (The Health Insurance Portability and Accountability Act), and determine whether any changes to this act are required by federal regulations adopted pursuant to P.L. 104-191; (ii) monitor the impact of the guaranteed issue requirements in the individual market and evaluate any specific concerns regarding such requirements identified and documented to the satisfaction of the State Corporation Commission by health insurance issuers; and (iii) recommend to the Governor and the 1998 Session of the General Assembly any revisions, corrections or improvements to the provisions of this act that would require the enactment of additional legislation."

The 1998 amendment, in subsection A, in subdivision 1, substituted "within the six-month period" for "within the 6 month period"; in subsection J, in the introductory language, deleted "as a late enrollee for coverage" following "to enroll for coverage"; in subsection K, substituted "subsection L" for "subdivision J 2"; in subsection L, in subdivision 2, substituted "subsection K" for "subdivision J 3"; in subsection M, substituted "thirty days" for "30 days" in the introductory language; and added subsection N.

The 1999 amendment, in subsection A, deleted "group" preceding "health insurance coverage" in the introductory paragraph, added "For group health insurance coverage" at the beginning of subdivsion A 1, added present subdivision A 2, redesignated former subdivi-

sions A 2 and A 3 as present subdivisions A 3 and A 4, and substituted "twelve" for "eighteen" in subdivision A 3; inserted "except in the case of individual health insurance coverage, where the health insurance issuer may impose a preexisting condition exclusion for a pregnancy existing on the effective date of coverage" in subdivision B 3, deleted "and" at the end of subdivision B 3, added "and" at the end of subdivision B 4, and added subdivision B 5.

§ 38.2-3433. Small employer market premium and disclosure provisions. — A. New or renewal premium rates for essential or standard health benefit plans issued by a health insurance issuer to a small employer not currently enrolled with that same health insurance issuer shall be based on a community rate subject to the following conditions:

1. A health insurance issuer may use the following risk classification factors in rating small groups: demographic rating, including age and gender; and geographic area rating. A health insurance issuer may not use claim experience, health status, duration or other risk classification factors in rating such groups, except as provided in subdivision 2 of this subsection.

2. The premium rates charged by a health insurance issuer may deviate from the community rate filed by the health insurance issuer by not more than twenty percent above or twenty percent below such rate for claim experience, health status and duration only during a rating period for such groups within a similar demographic risk classification for the same or similar coverage. Rates for a health benefit plan may vary based on the number of the eligible employee's enrolled dependents.

3. Health insurance issuers shall apply rating factors consistently with respect to all small employers in a similar demographic risk classification. Adjustments in rates for claims experience, health status and duration from issue may not be applied individually. Any such adjustment must be applied uniformly to the rate charged for all participants of the small employer.

B. In connection with the offering for sale of any health benefit plan to a small employer, each health insurance issuer shall make a reasonable disclosure, as part of its solicitation and sales materials, of:

1. The extent to which premium rates for a specific small employer are established or adjusted in part based upon the actual or expected variation in claims costs or actual or expected variation in health condition of the eligible employees and dependents of such small employer;

2. Provisions relating to renewability of policies and contracts; and

3. Provisions affecting any preexisting conditions provision.

C. Each health insurance issuer shall maintain at its principal place of business a complete and detailed description of its rating practices and renewal underwriting practices pertaining to its small employer business, including information and documentation that demonstrate that its rating methods and practices are based upon commonly accepted actuarial assumptions and are in accordance with sound actuarial principles.

D. Each health insurance issuer shall file with the Commission annually on or before March 15 the community rates and an actuarial certification certifying that the health insurance issuer and its rates are in compliance with this article. A copy of such certification shall be retained by the health insurance issuer at its principal place of business.

E. A health insurance issuer shall make the information and documentation described in subsection C of this section available for review by the Commission upon request. (1993, c. 960; 1994, c. 303; 1997, cc. 807, 913; 1998, c. 26.)

Editor's note. — Acts 1993, c. 960, cl. 2, as amended by Acts 1994, c. 138, cl. 2, effective March 31, 1994, provides that the provisions of Acts 1993, c. 960, shall become effective on July 1, 1994.

The 1998 amendment deleted "primary" preceding "small" throughout this section.

§ 38.2-3434. Disclosure of information. — Any health insurance issuer offering health insurance coverage to a employer shall make a reasonable disclosure of the availability of information to such an employer, as part of its solicitation and sales materials, and upon request of such an employer, information concerning: (i) the provisions of such coverage concerning the health insurance issuer's right to change premium rates and the factors that may affect changes in premium rates; (ii) the provisions of such coverage relating to renewability of coverage; (iii) the provisions of such coverage relating to any preexisting condition exclusion; and (iv) the benefits and premiums available under all health insurance coverage for which the employer is qualified.

A health insurance issuer is not required under this article to disclose any information that is proprietary and trade secret information. (1997, cc. 807, 913.)

Editor's note. — Acts 1997, cc. 807 and 913, cl. 3, provide: "That the Bureau of Insurance within the State Corporation Commission, in cooperation with the Joint Commission on Health Care, monitor the impact of the provisions of this act [which, in part, enacted this section] on the Commonwealth's health insurance marketplace. In monitoring the impact of this act, the State Corporation Commission shall: (i) review the federal regulations that will be promulgated to implement P.L. 104-191 (The Health Insurance Portability and Accountability Act), and determine whether any changes to this act are required by federal regulations adopted pursuant to P.L. 104-191; (ii) monitor the impact of the guaranteed issue requirements in the individual market and evaluate any specific concerns regarding such requirements identified and documented to the satisfaction of the State Corporation Commission by health insurance issuers; and (iii) recommend to the Governor and the 1998 Session of the General Assembly any revisions, corrections or improvements to the provisions of this act that would require the enactment of additional legislation."

§ 38.2-3435. Exclusions. — The provisions of this article shall not apply to:

1. Any health insurance issuer offering group health insurance coverage for any plan year if, on the first day of such plan year, such plan has less than two participants who are current employees; or

2. Any health insurance issuer offering group health insurance coverage for any of the excepted benefits. (1997, cc. 807, 913; 1998, c. 24.)

Editor's note. — Acts 1997, cc. 807 and 913, cl. 3, provide: "That the Bureau of Insurance within the State Corporation Commission, in cooperation with the Joint Commission on Health Care, monitor the impact of the provisions of this act [which, in part, enacted this section] on the Commonwealth's health insurance marketplace. In monitoring the impact of this act, the State Corporation Commission shall: (i) review the federal regulations that will be promulgated to implement P.L. 104-191 (The Health Insurance Portability and Accountability Act), and determine whether any changes to this act are required by federal regulations adopted pursuant to P.L. 104-191; (ii) monitor the impact of the guaranteed issue requirements in the individual market and evaluate any specific concerns regarding such requirements identified and documented to the satisfaction of the State Corporation Commission by health insurance issuers; and (iii) recommend to the Governor and the 1998 Session of the General Assembly any revisions, corrections or improvements to the provisions of this act that would require the enactment of additional legislation."

The 1998 amendment rewrote this section.

§ 38.2-3436. Eligibility to enroll. — A. A health insurance issuer offering group health insurance coverage, may not establish rules for eligibility (including continued eligibility) of any individual to enroll under the terms of the plan based on any of the health status-related factors.

B. The provisions of this section shall not be construed:

1. To require a group health insurance coverage to provide particular benefits other than those provided under the terms of such plan or coverage; or

2. To prevent a health insurance issuer offering group health insurance coverage from establishing limitations or restrictions on the amount, level, extent or nature of the benefits or coverage for similarly situated individuals enrolled in the plan or coverage rules for eligibility to enroll under a plan which includes rules defining any applicable waiting periods for such enrollment.

C. A health insurance issuer offering group health insurance coverage, may not require an individual (as a condition of enrollment or continued enrollment under the plan) to pay a premium or contribution which is greater than such premium or contribution for a similarly situated individual enrolled in the plan on the basis of any health status related factor in relation to the individual or to an individual enrolled under the plan as a dependent of the individual.

D. Nothing in subsection C shall be construed:

1. To restrict the amount that an employee may be charged for coverage under a group health plan or group health insurance coverage; or

2. To prevent a health insurance issuer offering group health insurance coverage, from establishing premium discounts or rebates or modifying otherwise applicable copayments or deductibles in return for adherence to programs of health promotion and disease prevention. (1997, cc. 807, 913.)

Editor's note. — Acts 1997, cc. 807 and 913, cl. 3, provide: "That the Bureau of Insurance within the State Corporation Commission, in cooperation with the Joint Commission on Health Care, monitor the impact of the provisions of this act [which, in part, enacted this section] on the Commonwealth's health insurance marketplace. In monitoring the impact of this act, the State Corporation Commission shall: (i) review the federal regulations that will be promulgated to implement P.L. 104-191 (The Health Insurance Portability and Accountability Act), and determine whether any changes to this act are required by federal regulations adopted pursuant to P.L. 104-191; (ii) monitor the impact of the guaranteed issue requirements in the individual market and evaluate any specific concerns regarding such requirements identified and documented to the satisfaction of the State Corporation Commission by health insurance issuers; and (iii) recommend to the Governor and the 1998 Session of the General Assembly any revisions, corrections or improvements to the provisions of this act that would require the enactment of additional legislation."

§ 38.2-3437. Rules used to determine group size. — A. All employers treated as a single employer under subsection (b), (c), (m), or (o) of § 414 of the Internal Revenue Code of 1986 (26 U.S.C. § 414) shall be treated as one employer.

B. In the case of an employer which was not in existence throughout the preceding calendar year, the determination of whether such employer is a small or large group employer shall be based on the average number of employees that it is reasonably expected such employer will employ on business days in the current calendar year.

C. Any reference in this section to an employer shall include a reference to any predecessor of such employer. (1997, cc. 807, 913.)

Editor's note. — Acts 1997, cc. 807 and 913, cl. 3, provide: "That the Bureau of Insurance within the State Corporation Commission, in cooperation with the Joint Commission on Health Care, monitor the impact of the provisions of this act [which, in part, enacted this section] on the Commonwealth's health insurance marketplace. In monitoring the impact of this act, the State Corporation Commission shall: (i) review the federal regulations that will be promulgated to implement P.L. 104-191 (The Health Insurance Portability and Accountability Act), and determine whether any changes to this act are required by federal regulations adopted pursuant to P.L. 104-191; (ii) monitor the impact of the guaranteed issue requirements in the individual market and evaluate any specific concerns regarding such requirements identified and documented to the satisfaction of the State Corporation Commission by health insurance issuers; and (iii) recommend to the Governor and the 1998 Session of the General Assembly any revisions, corrections or improvements to the provisions of this act that would require the enactment of additional legislation."

CHAPTER 35.

ACCIDENT AND SICKNESS INSURANCE POLICIES.

Article 1.

Individual Accident and Sickness Insurance Policies.

Article 2.

Individual Accident and Sickness Insurance Minimum Standards.

Article 3.

Group Accident and Sickness Insurance Policies.

ARTICLE 1.

Individual Accident and Sickness Insurance Policies.

§ 38.2-3500. Form of policy. — A. No individual accident and sickness insurance policy shall be delivered or issued for delivery to any person in this Commonwealth unless:

1. The entire consideration for the policy is expressed in the policy;

2. The time at which the insurance takes effect and terminates is expressed in the policy;

3. The policy insures only one person, except that it may insure eligible family members, originally or by subsequent amendment, upon the application of an adult member of a family who shall be deemed the policyowner;

4. The exceptions and reductions are set forth in the policy and, except those that are set forth in §§ 38.2-3503 through 38.2-3508, are printed with the benefit provisions to which they apply, or under an appropriate caption, but if an exception or reduction specifically applies only to a particular benefit of the policy, a statement of the exception or reduction shall be included with that benefit provision;

5. Each form, including riders and endorsements, is identified by a form number in the lower left-hand corner of the first page of the form;

6. It contains no provision making any portion of the charter, rules, constitution, or bylaws of the insurer a part of the policy unless that portion is set forth in the policy, except in the case of the incorporation of, or reference to, a statement of rates or classification of risks, or short-rate table filed with the Commission; and

7. It contains a statement about the provisions of subsections A and B of § 32.1-325.2 regarding the status of the Department of Medical Assistance Services as the payor of last resort.

B. If any policy is issued by an insurer domiciled in this Commonwealth for delivery to a person residing in another state, and if the insurance supervisory official of the other state advises the Commission that any such policy is not subject to approval or disapproval by such official, the Commission may by ruling require that such policy meet the standards set forth in this chapter.

C. *"Eligible family member"* means the (i) spouse, (ii) dependent children, without regard to whether such children reside in the same household as the policyowner, (iii) children under a specified age not greater than nineteen years, and (iv) any person dependent on the policyowner. (1952, c. 317, § 38.1-348; 1986, cc. 550, 562; 1993, c. 306; 1994, c. 316.)

Editor's note. — Pursuant to § 9-77.11, effect has been given in this section, as set out above, to Acts 1986, ch. 550, which amended former § 38.1-348, the comparable provision in former Title 38.1.

§ 38.2-3501. Policy forms; powers of Commission. — Individual accident and sickness insurance policy forms and the rate manuals showing rules and classification of risks applicable to individual accident and sickness insurance policy forms shall be subject to the provisions of § 38.2-316. The Commission, subject to § 38.2-316, may disapprove or withdraw approval of any such policy form if it finds that the benefits provided in the policy form are or are likely to be unreasonable in relation to the premium charged. If the Commission disapproves a policy form or withdraws approval of a form, an insurer may proceed as indicated in § 38.2-1926. (1979, c. 726, § 38.1-362.8; 1986, c. 562.)

§ 38.2-3502. Notice to be printed on policy; return of policy to insurer. — A. Any individual accident and sickness insurance policy delivered or issued for delivery in this Commonwealth shall have printed on it a notice stating substantially:
"THIS POLICY MAY NOT APPLY WHEN YOU HAVE A CLAIM! PLEASE READ! This policy was issued based on the information entered in your application, a copy of which is attached to the policy. If you know of any misstatement in your application, or if any information concerning the medical history of any insured person has been omitted, you should advise the Company immediately regarding the incorrect or omitted information; otherwise, your policy may not be a valid contract.
RIGHT TO RETURN POLICY WITHIN 10 DAYS. If for any reason you are not satisfied with your policy, you may return this policy to the Company within ten days of the date you received it and the premium you paid will be promptly refunded."
B. If a policyowner returns the policy within ten days from the date of receipt, coverage under that policy shall become void from its inception upon the mailing or delivery of the policy to the insurer or its agent.
C. If the first paragraph of the notice required in subsection A of this section is inapplicable or partially inapplicable to a particular form of policy, the insurer may modify or omit the notice with the Commission's approval.
D. Nothing in this section shall prohibit an insurer from extending the right to examine period to more than ten days if the period is stated in the policy. (1966, c. 342, § 38.1-348.4; 1986, c. 562.)

§ 38.2-3503. Required accident and sickness policy provisions. — Except as provided in § 38.2-3505, each individual accident and sickness insurance policy delivered or issued for delivery in this Commonwealth shall contain the provisions specified in this section using the same words which appear in this section. An insurer may substitute corresponding provisions of different wording approved by the Commission that are in each instance not less favorable in any respect to the insured or the beneficiary. These provisions shall be preceded individually by the caption "REQUIRED PROVISIONS" or by such appropriate individual or group captions or subcaptions as the Commission may approve.
1. Provision 1:
ENTIRE CONTRACT; CHANGES: This policy, including the endorsements and the attached papers, if any, constitutes the entire contract of insurance. No change in this policy shall be valid until approved by an executive officer of the Company and unless such approval is endorsed hereon or attached hereto. No agent has authority to change this policy or to waive any of its provisions.
2. Provision 2:
TIME LIMIT ON CERTAIN DEFENSES: (a) Misstatements in the application: After two years from the date of this policy, only fraudulent misstatements in the application may be used to void the policy or deny any claim for

loss incurred or disability (as defined in the policy) that starts after the two-year period.

Provision 2 shall not be construed to affect any legal requirement for avoidance of a policy or denial of a claim during such initial two-year period, nor to limit the application of subdivisions 1, 2, 3, 4 and 5 of § 38.2-3504 in the event of misstatement with respect to age, occupation or other insurance.

Instead of Provision 2, a policy which the insured has the right to continue in force subject to its terms by the timely payment of premium (i) until at least age fifty or, (ii) for a policy issued after age forty-four, for at least five years from its date of issue, may contain the following provision, from which the clause in parentheses may be omitted at the insurer's option:

INCONTESTABLE:

(a) Misstatements in the application: After this policy has been in force for two years during the Insured's lifetime (excluding any period during which the Insured is disabled), the Company cannot contest the statements in the application.

PREEXISTING CONDITIONS:

(b) No claim for loss incurred or disability (as defined in the policy) that starts after one year from the date of issue of this policy will be reduced or denied because a sickness or physical condition, not excluded by name or specific description before the date of loss, had existed before the effective date of coverage.

3. Provision 3:

GRACE PERIOD: This policy has a .... day grace period. This means that if a renewal premium is not paid on or before the date it is due, it may be paid during the following .... days. During the grace period the policy shall continue in force.

In Provision 3 a number not less than "7" for weekly premium policies, "10" for monthly premium policies and "31" for all other policies shall be inserted between the words "a" and "day," and between "following" and "days."

A policy that contains a cancellation provision may add, at the end of Provision 3: "subject to the right of the Company to cancel in accordance with the cancellation provision."

A policy in which the insurer reserves the right to refuse any renewal shall have, in Provision 3, the following sentence:

The grace period will not apply if, at least .... days before the premium due date, the Company has delivered or has mailed to the Insured's last address shown in the Company's records written notice of the Company's intent not to renew this policy.

In the above sentence a number not less than "7" for weekly premium policies, "10" for monthly premium policies and "31" for all other policies shall be inserted between the words "least" and "days."

4. Provision 4:

REINSTATEMENT: If the renewal premium is not paid before the grace period ends, the policy will lapse. Later acceptance of the premium by the Company or by an agent authorized to accept payment, without requiring an application for reinstatement, will reinstate the policy. If the Company or its agent requires an application for reinstatement, the Insured will be given a conditional receipt for the premium. If the application is approved the policy will be reinstated as of the approval date. Lacking such approval, the policy will be reinstated on the forty-fifth day after the date of the conditional receipt unless the Company has previously written the Insured of its disapproval. The reinstated policy will cover only loss that results from an injury sustained after the date of reinstatement and sickness that starts more than ten days after such date. In all other respects the rights of the Insured and the Company will remain the same, subject to any provisions noted or attached to the reinstated policy. Any premiums the Company accepts for a reinstatement will be applied to a period for which premiums have not been paid. No premiums will be applied to any period more than sixty days prior to the date of reinstatement.

The last sentence of Provision 4 may be omitted from any policy that the Insured has the right to continue in force subject to its terms by the timely payment of premiums (i) until at least age fifty, or (ii) for a policy issued after age forty-four, for at least five years from its effective date.

5. Provision 5:

NOTICE OF CLAIM: Written notice of claim must be given within twenty days after a covered loss starts or as soon as reasonably possible. The notice can be given to the Company at .... (insert the location of such office as the insurer may designate for the purpose), or to the Company's agent. Notice should include the name of the Insured, and Claimant if other than the Insured, and the policy number.

Optional paragraph: If the Insured has a disability for which benefits may be payable for at least two years, at least once in every six months after the Insured has given notice of claim, the Insured must give the Company notice that the disability has continued. The Insured need not do this if legally incapacitated. The first six months after any filing of proof by the Insured or any payment or denial of a claim by the Company will not be counted in applying this provision. If the Insured delays in giving this notice, the Insured's right to any benefits for the six months before the date the Insured gives notice will not be impaired.

6. Provision 6:

CLAIM FORMS: When the Company receives the notice of claim, it will send the Claimant forms for filing proof of loss. If these forms are not given to the Claimant within fifteen days after the giving of such notice, the Claimant shall meet the proof of loss requirements by giving the Company a written statement of the nature and extent of the loss within the time limit stated in the Proofs of Loss Section.

7. Provision 7:

PROOFS OF LOSS: If the policy provides for periodic payment for a continuing loss, written proof of loss must be given the Company within ninety days after the end of each period for which the Company is liable. For any other loss, written proof must be given within ninety days after such loss. If it was not reasonably possible to give written proof in the time required, the Company shall not reduce or deny the claim for this reason if the proof is filed as soon as reasonably possible. In any event, except in the absence of legal capacity, the proof required must be given no later than one year from the time specified.

8. Provision 8:

TIME OF PAYMENT OF CLAIMS: After receiving written proof of loss, the Company will pay .... (Insert period for payment which must not be less frequently than monthly) all benefits then due for .... (Insert type of loss). Benefits for any other loss covered by this policy will be paid as soon as the Company receives proper written proof.

9. Provision 9:

PAYMENT OF CLAIMS: Benefits will be paid to the Insured. Loss of life benefits are payable in accordance with the beneficiary designation in effect at the time of payment. If none is then in effect, the benefits will be paid to the Insured's estate. Any other benefits unpaid at death may be paid, at the Company's option, either to the Insured's beneficiary or the Insured's estate.

Optional paragraph: If benefits are payable to the Insured's estate or a beneficiary who cannot execute a valid release, the Company can pay benefits up to $ .... (insert an amount which shall not exceed $2,000), to someone related to the Insured or beneficiary by blood or by marriage whom the

Company considers to be entitled to the benefits. The Company will be discharged to the extent of any payment made in good faith.

Optional paragraph: The Company may pay all or a portion of any indemnities provided for health care services to the health care services provider, unless the Insured directs otherwise in writing by the time proofs of loss are filed. The Company cannot require that the services be rendered by a particular health care services provider.

10. Provision 10:

PHYSICAL EXAMINATIONS AND AUTOPSY: The Company at its own expense has the right to have the Insured examined as often as reasonably necessary while a claim is pending. It may also have an autopsy made unless prohibited by law.

11. Provision 11:

LEGAL ACTIONS: No legal action may be brought to recover on this policy within sixty days after written proof of loss has been given as required by this policy. No legal action may be brought after three years from the time written proof of loss is required to be given.

12. Provision 12:

CHANGE OF BENEFICIARY: The Insured can change the beneficiary at any time by giving the Company written notice. The beneficiary's consent is not required for this or any other change in the policy, unless the designation of the beneficiary is irrevocable. (1952, c. 317, § 38.1-349; 1958, c. 452; 1966, c. 101; 1986, c. 562; 1987, c. 520; 1995, c. 522.)

Purpose of incontestability clause, placing a time limit on challenges to the insurance application, is to give security to the policyholder, and sensibly that purpose is achieved by measuring the period of contest from the date of the issuance of the policy rather than from the date when a disability happens to occur. Sutton v. American Health & Life Ins. Co., 683 F.2d 92 (4th Cir. 1982).

Subdivision 2 construed. — Because any defense made to a claim of disability commencing within two years on account of statements made in the application must necessarily go to the validity of the policy, the first part of the statute ("After two years from the date of issue . . . .") must control the latter part ("commencing after the expiration of such two-year period"), or the latter part must control the first. The first part governs, for permitting the latter part to govern the first would run against the sense of an incontestable clause. Sutton v. American Health & Life Ins. Co., 683 F.2d 92 (4th Cir. 1982).

When a claim is denied because of misrepresentations in the application for insurance, the thesis can only be that the insurer has rescinded the contract on that account. Hence, when the provision speaks of the voiding of the contract after two years, it necessarily deals with a rescission made to defend against a claim for disability whether the disability arose within or after the two-year period. It means that after two years the insurer cannot avoid liability for a disability which commenced within the two-year period except for fraudu-

lent misstatements. Sutton v. American Health & Life Ins. Co., 683 F.2d 92 (4th Cir. 1982).

Statements in application not included in policy are not admissible. — The defendant, without objection from plaintiff, introduced in evidence plaintiff's original application for insurance, which contained a question and answer not included in a copy of the application which was attached to plaintiff's policy. It was held under former § 38-221 that notwithstanding the fact that plaintiff did not object to the introduction of the original application, it was the duty of the Supreme Court to eliminate all statements in the original application not set out in the purported copy incorporated in the policy. Mutual Benefit Health & Accident Ass'n v. Alley, 167 Va. 144, 187 S.E. 456 (1936).

Effect of contract limiting incontestability to policyholders. — Since this section requires that the insurance policy be incontestable except for fraudulent misstatements by the applicant, the statutory provision must be read into a contract which states that its incontestability clause applies only to "policyholders." Sutton v. American Health & Life Ins. Co., 683 F.2d 92 (4th Cir. 1982).

Failure to instruct jury as to fraud in misstatements. — It is error to fail to instruct the jury that any misstatements in the application which were relied upon by the defendant must have been fraudulent misstatements in accordance with this section. Sutton v. American Health & Life Ins. Co., 683 F.2d 92 (4th Cir. 1982).

§ 38.2-3504. Other provisions. — Except as provided in § 38.2-3505, no individual accident and sickness insurance policy delivered or issued for delivery in this Commonwealth shall contain provisions respecting the matters set forth below unless such provisions use the same words which appear in this section. The insurer may use a corresponding provision of different wording approved by the Commission that is not less favorable in any respect to the Insured or the beneficiary. Any such provision shall be preceded individually by the appropriate caption OTHER PROVISIONS or by such appropriate individual or group captions or subcaptions as the Commission may approve.

1. Provision 1:

CHANGE OF OCCUPATION: If the Insured is injured or contracts sickness after having changed his occupation to one classified by the Company as more hazardous than that stated in this policy or while doing for compensation anything pertaining to an occupation so classified, the Company will pay only the portion of the indemnities provided in this policy as the premium paid would have purchased at the rates and within the limits fixed by the Company for the more hazardous occupation. If the Insured changes his occupation to one classified by the Company as less hazardous than that stated in this policy, the Company, upon receipt of proof of the change of occupation, will reduce the premium rate accordingly and will return the excess pro rata unearned premium from the date of change of occupation or from the policy anniversary date immediately preceding receipt of such proof, whichever is more recent. In applying this provision, the classification of occupational risk and the premium rates shall be such as have been last filed by the Company prior to the occurrence of the loss for which the Company is liable or prior to the date of proof of change in occupation with the state insurance supervisory official in the state where the Insured resided at the time this policy was issued; but if the filing was not required, then the classification of occupational risk and the premium rates shall be those last made effective by the Company in the state prior to the occurrence of the loss or prior to the date of proof of change in occupation.

2. Provision 2:

MISSTATEMENT OF AGE: If the Insured's age has been misstated, the benefits will be those the premium paid would have purchased at the correct age.

3. Provision 3:

OTHER INSURANCE IN THIS COMPANY: If an accident or sickness or accident and sickness policy or policies previously issued by the Company to the Insured is in force concurrently herewith, making the aggregate indemnity for . . . . . . (insert type of coverage or coverages) in excess of $ . . . . . . (insert maximum limit of indemnity or indemnities) the excess insurance shall be void and all premiums paid for such excess shall be returned to the Insured or to his estate.

Instead of Provision 3, the following provision may be used:

Insurance effective at any one time on the Insured under a like policy or policies in this Company is limited to the one such policy elected by the Insured, his beneficiary or his estate, as the case may be, and the Company will return all premiums paid for all other such policies.

4. Provision 4:

INSURANCE WITH OTHER COMPANIES: If there is other valid coverage, not with this Company, providing benefits for the same loss on a provision of service basis or on an expense incurred basis and of which this Company has not been given written notice prior to the occurrence or commencement of loss, the only liability under any expense incurred coverage of this policy shall be for such proportion of the loss as the amount which would otherwise have been payable under this policy plus the total of the like amounts under all such other valid coverages for the same loss of which this Company had notice bears to the total like amounts under all valid coverages for such loss, and for the return of such portion of the premiums paid as shall exceed the pro rata portion for the amount so determined. For the purpose of applying this provision when other coverage is on a provision of service basis, the "like amount" of such other coverage shall be taken as the amount which the services rendered would have cost in the absence of such coverage.

If Provision 4 is included in a policy that also contains Provision 5, the phrase "EXPENSE INCURRED BENEFITS" shall be added to the caption of Provision 4. The insurer may include in this provision a definition of "other valid coverage," approved by the Commission. The definition shall be limited in subject matter to coverage provided by organizations subject to regulation by insurance law or by insurance authorities of this Commonwealth or any other jurisdiction of the United States or Canada, and by hospital or medical service organizations, and to any other coverage the inclusion of which may be approved by the Commission. In the absence of such definition the term shall not include group insurance, automobile medical payments insurance, or coverage provided by hospital or medical service organizations, by union welfare plans, or employer or employee benefit organizations.

For the purpose of applying Provision 4, any amount of benefit provided for such insured pursuant to any compulsory benefit statute, including any workers' compensation or employer's liability statute, whether provided by a governmental agency or otherwise, shall in all cases be deemed to be "other valid coverage" of which the company has had notice. In applying Provision 4 no third party liability coverage shall be included as "other valid coverage."

5. Provision 5:

INSURANCE WITH OTHER COMPANIES: If there is other valid coverage, not with this Company, providing benefits for the same loss on other than an expense incurred basis and of which this Company has not been given written notice prior to the occurrence or commencement of loss, the only liability for such benefits under this policy shall be for such proportion of the indemnities otherwise provided under this policy for such loss as the like indemnities of which the Company had notice, including the indemnities under this policy, bear to the total amount of all like indemnities for such loss, and for the return of such portion of the premium paid as shall exceed the pro rata portion for the indemnities thus determined.

If Provision 5 is included in a policy that also contains Provision 4, the phrase "OTHER BENEFITS" shall be added to the caption of Provision 5. The insurer may include in this provision a definition of "other valid coverage," approved by the Commission. The definition shall be limited in subject matter to coverage provided by organizations subject to regulation by insurance law or by insurance authorities of this Commonwealth or any other jurisdiction of the United States or Canada, and to any other coverage approved by the Commission. In the absence of such definition the term shall not include group insurance, or benefits provided by union welfare plans or by employer or employee benefit organizations. For the purpose of applying Provision 5, any amount of benefit provided for the insured pursuant to any compulsory benefit statute, including any workers' compensation or employer's liability statute, whether provided by a governmental agency or otherwise, shall in all cases be deemed to be "other valid coverage" of which the Company has had notice. In applying Provision 5 no third party liability coverage shall be included as "other valid coverage."

6. Provision 6:

RELATION OF EARNINGS TO INSURANCE: If the total monthly amount of loss of time benefits promised for the same loss under all valid loss of time coverage upon the Insured, whether payable on a weekly or monthly basis, shall exceed the monthly earnings of the Insured at the time disability commenced or his average monthly earnings for the period of two years immediately preceding a disability for which a claim is made, whichever is greater, the Company will be liable only for the proportionate amount of the benefits under this policy as the amount of the monthly earnings or the average monthly earnings of the Insured bears to the total amount of monthly benefits for the same loss under all the coverage upon the insured at the time the disability commences and for the return of the part of the premiums paid during such two years that exceeds the pro rata amount of the premiums for the benefits actually paid hereunder; but this shall not operate to reduce the total monthly amount of benefits payable under all the coverage upon the Insured below the sum of $200 or the sum of the monthly benefits specified in the coverages, whichever is less, nor shall it operate to reduce benefits other than those payable for loss of time.

Provision 6 may be inserted only in a policy that the insured has the right to continue in force subject to its terms by the timely payment of premiums (i) until at least age fifty or (ii) for a policy issued after age forty-four, for at least five years from its date of issue. The insurer may include in this provision a definition of "valid loss of time coverage" approved by the Commission. The definition shall be limited in subject matter to coverage provided by governmental agencies or by organizations subject to regulation by insurance law or by insurance authorities of this Commonwealth or any other jurisdiction of the United States or Canada, or to any other coverage the inclusion of which may be approved by the Commission or any combination of coverages. In the absence of such definition the term shall not include any coverage provided for the Insured pursuant to any compulsory benefit statute, including any workers' compensation or employer's liability statute, or benefits provided by union welfare plans or by employer or employee benefit organizations.

7. Provision 7:

UNPAID PREMIUM: When a claim is paid, any premium due and unpaid may be deducted from the claim payment.

8. Provision 8:

CANCELLATION: The Company may cancel this policy at any time by written notice delivered to the Insured, or mailed to his last address as shown by the records of the Company, stating when, no less than . . . . . . days thereafter, the cancellation shall be effective; and after the policy has been continued beyond its original term the Insured may cancel this policy at any time by written notice delivered or mailed to the Company effective upon receipt or on such later date as may be specified in the notice. In the event of cancellation, the Company will return promptly the unearned portion of any premium paid. If the Insured cancels, the earned premium shall be computed by the use of the short-rate table last filed with the state insurance supervisory official in the state where the Insured resided when the policy was issued. If the Company cancels, the earned premium shall be computed pro rata. Cancellation shall be without prejudice to any claim originating prior to the effective date of cancellation.

In Provision 8 a number no less than "7" for weekly premium policies, "10" for monthly premium policies and "31" for all other policies shall be inserted between the words "than" and "days."

9. Provision 9:

CONFORMITY WITH STATE STATUTES: Any provision of this policy that on its effective date is in conflict with the laws of the state in which the Insured resides on that date is hereby amended to conform to the minimum requirements of the laws.

10. Provision 10:

ILLEGAL OCCUPATION: The Company will not be liable for any loss that results from the Insured's committing or attempting to commit a felony or from the Insured's engaging in an illegal occupation.

11. Provision 11:
INTOXICANTS AND NARCOTICS: The Company will not be liable for any loss resulting from the Insured's being drunk, or under the influence of any narcotic unless taken on the advice of a physician. (1952, c. 317, § 38.1-350; 1986, c. 562.)

Assured assumes risk of receipt of cancellation notice. — A contract of accident insurance providing that the company might cancel the policy by written notice mailed to the latest address of assured appearing on the company's check for the unearned part of the premium, is a valid contract, and the company has the right to cancel in the manner provided. If the notice properly addressed was mailed to the assured at his latest address appearing on the company's record, accompanied by the company's check for the unearned premium, that was sufficient. The assured assumed the risk of the due receipt of the notice. Wolonter v. United States Cas. Co., 126 Va. 156, 101 S.E. 58 (1919).

Defective notice of cancellation. — From the standpoint of a demurrer to the evidence by the defendant, notice of a change of residence was given twice to an agent of the company who had been requested to obtain the address, and the records of the company did not show the change, and when the policy was originally taken out the address of the assured was given as "in care of Virginia Bridge and Iron Company," and this was not shown by the records of the company. It was held that a notice of cancellation not addressed to assured at his place of residence or "in care of Virginia Bridge and Iron Company" was fatally defective. Wolonter v. United States Cas. Co., 126 Va. 156, 101 S.E. 58 (1919).

In the instant case the records of the company should have shown, but for the negligence of the company or its agents, upon which it cannot rely, that the words "care of Virginia Bridge Company" were a part of the address of the assured at Roanoke, Virginia. A notice of cancellation, which did not conform to this address, but was merely addressed to the assured at Roanoke, Virginia, was insufficient. It was wholly immaterial whether the assured was still in the employment of the bridge company or not, or whether a letter addressed to him in care of that company would have reached him or not; the contract of the parties stipulated how the notice was to be sent, and it was not so sent. Wolonter v. United States Cas. Co., 126 Va. 156, 101 S.E. 58 (1919).

§ 38.2-3505. Inapplicable or inconsistent provisions.

— If any provision of this article is inapplicable to or inconsistent with the coverage provided by a particular form of policy, the insurer, with the Commission's approval, shall omit or modify the inapplicable or inconsistent provision to make that provision consistent with the coverage provided by the policy. (1952, c. 317, § 38.1-351; 1986, c. 562.)

§ 38.2-3506. Order of certain policy provisions.

— The provisions that are the subject of §§ 38.2-3503 and 38.2-3504, or any corresponding provisions that are used instead of them in accordance with these sections, shall be printed in the consecutive order of the provisions in such sections. However, any such provision may appear as a unit in any part of the policy, with other provisions to which it may be logically related, provided the resulting policy shall not be in whole or in part unintelligible, uncertain, ambiguous, abstruse, or likely to mislead a person to whom the policy is offered, delivered or issued. (1952, c. 317, § 38.1-352; 1986, c. 562.)

§ 38.2-3507. Third-party ownership.

— The word *"insured,"* as used in this article, shall not be construed to prevent a person with a proper insurable interest from applying for and owning a policy covering another person or from being entitled to any indemnities, benefits and rights provided under the policy. (1952, c. 317, § 38.1-353; 1986, c. 562.)

§ 38.2-3508. Requirements of other jurisdictions.

— A. Any individual accident and sickness insurance policy delivered or issued for delivery to any person in this Commonwealth by a foreign or alien insurer may contain any provision that is prescribed or required by the insurer's domiciliary jurisdiction and that is not less favorable than the provisions of this article to the insured or the beneficiary.

B. Any individual accident and sickness insurance policy delivered or issued for delivery by a domestic insurer in any other jurisdiction may contain any provision permitted or required by the laws of the other jurisdiction. (Code 1950, § 38-224; 1952, c. 317, § 38.1-354; 1986, c. 562.)

§ 38.2-3509. Denial or reduction of benefits because of existence of other like insurance. — A. No individual accident and sickness insurance policy, nor any subscription contract as provided for in Chapter 42 (§ 38.2-4200 et seq.) of this title, delivered or issued for delivery in this Commonwealth shall contain any provision for the denial or reduction of benefits because of the existence of other like insurance except to the extent that the aggregate benefits, with respect to the covered medical expenses incurred under the policy or plan and all other like insurance with other insurers, exceed all covered medical expenses incurred.

B. The term *"other like insurance"* may include group insurance or coverage provided by hospital or medical service organizations, union welfare plans, employer or employee benefit organizations, or workers' compensation insurance. (1970, c. 378, § 38.1-355; 1986, c. 562.)

Under this statute, the insurer cannot deny the insured benefits unless his medical expenses are fully covered by other insurance, here workers' compensation. The proviso enables the insurers to prevent the insured from receiving multiple recoveries in excess of total medical expenses. Hines v. Blue Cross Blue Shield, 788 F.2d 1016 (4th Cir. 1986).

Workers' compensation as other insurance. — If § 38.2-3405 is to be consistent with this section, "other insurance," including workers' compensation, must be differentiated from recovery from a tortfeasor. A contract may eliminate duplication of benefits when the benefits come from workers' compensation and the injured party's insurer, but not when they are derived from a health insurance carrier and a tortfeasor. Workers' compensation is regarded as "other insurance" for the purposes of this section. For the purposes of § 38.2-3405, workers' compensation should be regarded as akin to other insurance rather than to recovery from a tortfeasor. Hines v. Blue Cross Blue Shield, 788 F.2d 1016 (4th Cir. 1986).

§ 38.2-3510. Conforming to statute. — No individual accident and sickness insurance policy provision that is not subject to this article shall make an individual accident and sickness insurance policy, or any portion of the policy, less favorable in any respect to the insured or the beneficiary than the provisions that are subject to this article. (Code 1950, § 38-223; 1952, c. 317, § 38.1-356; 1986, c. 562.)

§ 38.2-3511. Application. — A. The insured shall not be bound by any statement made in an application for an individual accident and sickness policy unless a copy of the application is attached to or endorsed on the policy when issued as a part of the policy. If any such policy delivered or issued for delivery in this Commonwealth is reinstated or renewed, and the insured, beneficiary or assignee of the policy makes a written request to the insurer for a copy of the reinstatement or renewal application, if any, the insurer shall within fifteen days after the receipt of the request, deliver or mail to the person making the request, a copy of the application. If a copy is not so delivered or mailed, the insurer shall be precluded from introducing the application as evidence in any action or proceeding based upon or involving the policy or its reinstatement or renewal.

B. No alteration of any written application for any such policy shall be made by any person other than the applicant without his written consent, except that insertions may be made by the insurer, for administrative purposes only, in a manner indicating clearly that such insertions are not to be ascribed to the applicant.

C. The falsity of any statement in the application for any policy covered by this article may not bar the right to recovery under the policy unless the false statement materially affected either the acceptance of the risk or the hazard assumed by the insurer. (1952, c. 317, § 38.1-357; 1986, c. 562.)

§ **38.2-3512. Notice; waiver.** — The acknowledgment by any insurer of the receipt of notice given under any individual accident and sickness insurance policy, the furnishing of forms for filing proofs of loss, the acceptance of such proofs, or the investigation of any claim thereunder shall not operate as a waiver of any of the rights of the insurer in defense of any claim arising under the policy. (1952, c. 317, § 38.1-358; 1986, c. 562.)

§ **38.2-3513. Age limit.** — A. If any individual accident and sickness insurance policy contains a provision establishing, as an age limit or otherwise, a date after which the coverage provided by the policy will not be effective, and if the date falls within a period for which a premium is accepted by the insurer or if the insurer accepts a premium after the date, the coverage provided by the policy will continue in force subject to any right of cancellation until the end of the period for which the premium has been accepted.

B. If the age of the insured has been misstated, and if according to the correct age of the insured, the coverage provided by the policy would not have become effective or would have ceased prior to the acceptance of the premium, then the liability of the insurer shall be limited to the refund, upon request, of all premiums paid for the period not covered by the policy. (1952, c. 317, § 38.1-359; 1986, c. 562.)

§ **38.2-3514. When liability not to be denied because of preexisting disease, physical impairment or defect.** — No insurer that has delivered or issued for delivery in this Commonwealth an accident and sickness insurance policy pursuant to the provisions of this article shall deny liability on any claim otherwise covered under such policy because of the existence of a disease or physical impairment or defect, congenital or otherwise, at the time of the making of the application for such policy, unless it is shown that the applicant knew or might reasonably have been expected to know of such disease, impairment or defect. (1966, c. 184, § 38.1-361.1; 1986, c. 562.)

Law Review. — For survey of Virginia law on insurance for the year 1971-1972, see 58 Va. L. Rev. 1291 (1972).

This section permits an insurer to limit its liability to risks not specifically excluded (e.g., self-inflicted injury). Sharp v. Richmond Life Ins. Co., 212 Va. 229, 183 S.E.2d 132 (1971).

The coverage of an insurance contract may not be extended by estoppel or implied waiver to include risks expressly excluded. Sharp v. Richmond Life Ins. Co., 212 Va. 229, 183 S.E.2d 132 (1971).

The terms "good health" and "sound health" in applications for insurance policies have been construed to import apparent and reasonably sound health without any knowledge on the part of the applicant to the contrary, and this rule of construction has now been codified and expanded in this section. Sharp v. Richmond Life Ins. Co., 212 Va. 229, 183 S.E.2d 132 (1971).

No "sound health" requirement or exclusion of preexisting illness may be enforced if the applicant did not know or might not reasonably have been expected to know about the insured's condition. Sharp v. Richmond Life Ins. Co., 212 Va. 229, 183 S.E.2d 132 (1971).

§ **38.2-3514.1. Preexisting conditions provisions.** — A. In determining whether a preexisting conditions provision applies to an insured, all coverage shall credit the time the person was covered under previous individual or group policies providing hospital, medical and surgical or major medical coverage on an expense incurred basis if the previous coverage was continuous to a date not more than thirty days prior to the effective date of the new coverage, exclusive of any applicable waiting period under such coverage.

B. As used herein, a "preexisting conditions provision" means a policy provision that limits, denies, or excludes coverage for charges or expenses incurred during a twelve-month period following the insured's effective date of coverage, for a condition that, during a twelve-month period immediately preceding the effective date of coverage, had manifested itself in such a manner as would cause an ordinarily prudent person to seek diagnosis, care, or treatment, or for which medical advice, diagnosis, care, or treatment was recommended or received within twelve months immediately preceding the effective date of coverage or as to pregnancy existing on the effective date of coverage.

C. This section shall not apply to the following insurance policies or contracts:

1. Short-term travel;

2. Accident-only;

3. Limited or specified disease contracts;

4. Long-term care insurance;

5. Short-term nonrenewable policies or contracts of not more than six months' duration which are subject to no medical underwriting or minimal underwriting;

6. Policies subject to Article 4.1 (§ 38.2-3430.1 et seq.) of Chapter 34 of this title;

7. Policies or contracts designed for issuance to persons eligible for coverage under Title XVIII of the Social Security Act, known as Medicare, or any other similar coverage under state or federal government plans; and

8. Disability income. (1995, c. 522; 1997, c. 291; 1999, c. 1004.)

The 1999 amendment rewrote subdivision C 6, which formerly read: "Individual open enrollment policies or contracts issued pursuant to § 38.2-4216.1 to persons who were previously covered under a group health insurance policy or contract issued by another unaffiliated insurer, health services plan or health maintenance organization, and who, due to health status, are eligible for individual coverage only under §§ 38.2-3416 and 38.2-4216.1."

§ 38.2-3514.2. Renewability of coverage. — A. Every individual policy, subscription contract or plan delivered, issued for delivery or renewal in this Commonwealth providing benefits to or on behalf of an individual shall provide for the renewability of such coverage at the sole option of the insured, policyholder, subscriber, or enrollee. The insurer, health services plan or health maintenance organization issuing such policy, subscription contract or plan shall be permitted to refuse to renew the policy, subscription contract or plan only for one or more of the following reasons:

1. Nonpayment of the required premiums by the insured, policyholder, subscriber, or enrollee, or such individual's representative;

2. In the event that the policy, subscription contract or plan contains a provision requiring the use of network providers, a documented pattern of abuse or misuse of such provision by the insured, policyholder, subscriber, or enrollee, continuing for a period of no less than two years;

3. Subject to the time limits contained in subdivision 2 of § 38.2-3503 or in regulations adopted by the Commission governing the practices of health maintenance organizations, for fraud or material misrepresentation by the individual, with respect to his application for coverage;

4. Eligibility of an individual insured for Medicare, provided that such coverage may not terminate with respect to other individuals insured under the same policy, subscription contract or plan and who are not eligible for Medicare; and

5. The insured, subscriber, or enrollee has not maintained a legal residence in the service area of the insurer, health services plan or health maintenance organization for a period of at least six months.

B. This section shall not apply to the following insurance policies, subscription contracts or plans:

1. Short-term travel;
2. Accident-only;
3. Disability income;
4. Limited or specified disease contracts;
5. Long-term care insurance;
6. Short-term nonrenewable policies or contracts of not more than six months' duration which are subject to no medical underwriting or minimal underwriting; and
7. Individual health insurance coverage as defined in subsection B of § 38.2-3431. (1996, c. 550; 1998, c. 24.)

The 1998 amendment, in subsection B, in subdivision 5, deleted "and" following "insur- ance," in subdivision 6, added "and" and added subdivision 7.

§ 38.2-3515. Required coverage on connecting or returning planes. — In each airtrip accident policy, issued in this Commonwealth through a mechanical vending machine or otherwise, the coverage of the policy, according to its terms and provisions, shall extend to an accident on a connecting or returning plane on which the insured's initial airtrip ticket entitles him to ride, if it is shown that the insured would be entitled to recover under the policy had the accident occurred while the insured was riding on the initial plane designated on the ticket. (1952, c. 317, § 38.1-349; 1958, c. 452; 1966, c. 101; 1986, c. 562.)

ARTICLE 2.

Individual Accident and Sickness Insurance Minimum Standards.

§ 38.2-3516. Purpose. — The purpose of this article is to authorize the Commission, pursuant to the authority granted in § 38.2-223, to issue rules and regulations to:

1. Provide reasonable standardization and simplification of terms and coverages of individual accident and sickness insurance policies;
2. Facilitate public understanding and comparison;
3. Eliminate provisions contained in individual accident and sickness insurance policies which may be misleading or unreasonably confusing in connection either with the purchase of coverages or with the settlement of claims; and
4. Provide for full disclosure in the sale of individual accident and sickness policies. (1980, c. 204, § 38.1-362.11; 1986, c. 562.)

§ 38.2-3517. Definitions. — As used in this article:

"Form" means policies, contracts, riders, endorsements, and applications.

"Policy" means the entire contract between the insurer and the insured, including the policy riders, endorsements, and the application, if attached. (1980, c. 204, § 38.1-362.12; 1986, c. 562.)

§ 38.2-3518. Standards for policy provisions. — A. Pursuant to the authority granted in § 38.2-223, the Commission may issue rules and regulations to establish specific standards, including standards of full and fair disclosure, for the sale of individual accident and sickness insurance policies. These rules and regulations shall be in addition to and in accordance with

applicable laws of this Commonwealth, including Chapter 34 (§ 38.2-3400 et seq.) and Articles 1 (§ 38.2-3500 et seq.) and 2 (§ 38.2-3516 et seq.) of this chapter which may cover but shall not be limited to:
 1. Terms of renewability;
 2. Initial and subsequent conditions of eligibility;
 3. Nonduplication of coverage provisions;
 4. Coverage of dependents;
 5. Coverage of persons eligible for Medicare by reason of age;
 6. Preexisting conditions;
 7. Termination of insurance;
 8. Probationary periods;
 9. Limitations;
 10. Exceptions;
 11. Reductions;
 12. Elimination periods;
 13. Requirements for replacement;
 14. Recurrent conditions; and
 15. Definition of terms including but not limited to the following: hospital, accident, sickness, injury, physician, accidental means, total disability, partial disability, nervous disorder, guaranteed renewable, and noncancellable.
 For the purposes of this article, licensed health care practitioners, to the extent required by law, shall be deemed physicians.
 B. Pursuant to the authority granted in § 38.2-223, the Commission may issue rules and regulations that specify prohibited policies or policy provisions not otherwise specifically authorized by statute that in the opinion of the Commission are unjust, unfair, or unfairly discriminatory to the policyowner, beneficiary, or any person insured under the policy. (1980, c. 204, § 38.1-362.13; 1981, c. 575; 1986, c. 562.)

 § 38.2-3519. Minimum standards for benefits. — A. Pursuant to the authority granted in § 38.2-223, the Commission may issue rules and regulations establishing minimum standards for benefits under each of the following categories of coverage in individual policies of accident and sickness insurance:
 1. Basic hospital expense coverage;
 2. Basic medical-surgical expense coverage;
 3. Hospital confinement indemnity coverage;
 4. Major medical expense coverage;
 5. Disability income protection coverage;
 6. Accident only coverage;
 7. Specified disease or specified accident coverage;
 8. Medicare supplement coverage; and
 9. Limited benefit health coverage.
 B. Nothing in this section shall preclude the issuance of any policy that combines two or more of the categories of coverage enumerated in subdivisions 1 through 6 of subsection A of this section.
 C. No policy shall be delivered or issued for delivery in this Commonwealth that does not meet the prescribed minimum standards for the categories of coverage listed in subdivisions 1 through 9 of subsection A of this section or does not meet the requirements set forth in § 38.2-3501.
 D. The Commission may prescribe the method of identification of policies based upon coverages provided. (1980, c. 204, § 38.1-362.14; 1986, c. 562.)

 § 38.2-3520. Coverage of preexisting conditions. — Notwithstanding the provisions of § 38.2-3503, if an insurer elects to use a simplified application form, with or without a specific question as to the applicant's health, but without any detailed questions concerning the insured's health history or medical treatment history, the policy shall cover any loss occurring after twelve months from the effective date of coverage from any preexisting condition not specifically excluded from coverage by terms of the policy. Except as so provided, the policy shall not include wording that would permit a defense based upon preexisting conditions. (1980, c. 204, § 38.1-362.15; 1981, c. 575; 1986, c. 562.)

ARTICLE 3.

Group Accident and Sickness Insurance Policies.

§ **38.2-3521:** Repealed by Acts 1998, c. 154.

§ **38.2-3521.1. Group accident and sickness insurance definitions.** — Except as provided in § 38.2-3522.1, no policy of group accident and sickness insurance shall be delivered in this Commonwealth unless it conforms to one of the following descriptions:

A. A policy issued to an employer, or to the trustees of a fund established by an employer, which employer or trustees shall be deemed the policyholder, to insure employees of the employer for the benefit of persons other than the employer, subject to the following requirements:

1. The employees eligible for insurance under the policy shall be all of the employees of the employer, or all of any class or classes thereof. The policy may provide that the term "employees" shall include the employees of one or more subsidiary corporations, and the employees, individual proprietors, and partners of one or more affiliated corporations, proprietorships or partnerships if the business of the employer and of such affiliated corporations, proprietorships or partnerships is under common control. The policy may provide that the term "employees" shall include retired employees, former employees and directors of a corporate employer. A policy issued to insure the employees of a public body may provide that the term "employees" shall include elected or appointed officials.

2. The premium for the policy shall be paid either from the employer's funds or from funds contributed by the insured employees, or from both. Except as provided in subdivision 3 of this subsection, a policy on which no part of the premium is to be derived from funds contributed by the insured employees must insure all eligible employees, except those who reject such coverage in writing.

3. An insurer may exclude or limit the coverage on any person as to whom evidence of individual insurability is not satisfactory to the insurer, except as otherwise prohibited in this title.

B. A policy which is:

1. Not subject to Chapter 37.1 (§ 38.2-3727 et seq.) of this title, and

2. Issued to a creditor or its parent holding company or to a trustee or trustees or agent designated by two or more creditors, which creditor, holding company, affiliate, trustee, trustees or agent shall be deemed the policyholder, to insure debtors of the creditor or creditors with respect to their indebtedness, subject to the following requirements:

a. The debtors eligible for insurance under the policy shall be all of the debtors of the creditor or creditors, or all of any class or classes thereof. The policy may provide that the term "debtors" shall include:

(1) Borrowers of money or purchasers or lessees of goods, services, or property for which payment is arranged through a credit transaction;

(2) The debtors of one or more subsidiary corporations; and

(3) The debtors of one or more affiliated corporations, proprietorships or partnerships if the business of the policyholder and of such affiliated corporations, proprietorships or partnerships is under common control.

b. The premium for the policy shall be paid either from the creditor's funds, or from charges collected from the insured debtors, or from both. Except as provided in subdivision 3 of this subsection, a policy on which no part of the premium is to be derived from funds contributed by insured debtors specifically for their insurance must insure all eligible debtors.

3. An insurer may exclude any debtors as to whom evidence of individual insurability is not satisfactory to the insurer.

4. The total amount of insurance payable with respect to an indebtedness shall not exceed the greater of the scheduled or actual amount of unpaid indebtedness to the creditor. The insurer may exclude any payments which are delinquent on the date the debtor becomes disabled as defined in the policy.

5. The insurance may be payable to the creditor or any successor to the right, title, and interest of the creditor. Such payment or payments shall reduce or extinguish the unpaid indebtedness of the debtor to the extent of each such payment and any excess of the insurance shall be payable to the insured or the estate of the insured.

6. Notwithstanding the preceding provisions of this section, insurance on agricultural credit transaction commitments may be written up to the amount of the loan commitment. Insurance on educational credit transaction commitments may be written up to the amount of the loan commitment less the amount of any repayments made on the loan.

C. A policy issued to a labor union, or similar employee organization, which labor union or organization shall be deemed to be the policyholder, to insure members of such union or organization for the benefit of persons other than the union or organization or any of its officials, representatives, or agents, subject to the following requirements:

1. The members eligible for insurance under the policy shall be all of the members of the union or organization, or all of any class or classes thereof.

2. The premium for the policy shall be paid either from funds of the union or organization, or from funds contributed by the insured members specifically for their insurance, or from both. Except as provided in subdivision 3 of this subsection, a policy on which no part of the premium is to be derived from funds contributed by the insured members specifically for their insurance must insure all eligible members, except those who reject such coverage in writing.

3. An insurer may exclude or limit the coverage on any person as to whom evidence of individual insurability is not satisfactory to the insurer, except as otherwise prohibited in this title.

D. A policy issued (i) to or for a multiple employer welfare arrangement, a rural electric cooperative, or a rural electric telephone cooperative as these terms are defined in 29 U.S.C. § 1002, or (ii) to a trust, or to the trustees of a fund, established or adopted by or for two or more employers, or by one or more labor unions of similar employee organizations, or by one or more employers and one or more labor unions or similar employee organizations, which trust or trustees shall be deemed the policyholder, to insure employees of the employers or members of the unions or organizations for the benefit of persons other than the employers or the unions or organizations, subject to the following requirements:

1. The persons eligible for insurance shall be all of the employees of the employers or all of the members of the unions or organizations, or all of any class or classes thereof. The policy may provide that the term "employee" shall include the employees of one or more subsidiary corporations, and the employees, individual proprietors, and partners of one or more affiliated corporations, proprietorships or partnerships if the business of the employer and of such affiliated corporations, proprietorships or partnerships is under common control. The policy may provide that the term "employees" shall include retired employees, former employees and directors of a corporate

employer. The policy may provide that the term "employees" shall include the trustees or their employees, or both, if their duties are principally connected with such trusteeship.

2. The premium for the policy shall be paid from funds contributed by the employer or employers of the insured persons, or by the union or unions or similar employee organizations, or by both, or from funds contributed by the insured persons or from both the insured persons and the employers or unions or similar employee organizations. Except as provided in subdivision 3 of this subsection, a policy on which no part of the premium is to be derived from funds contributed by the insured persons specifically for their insurance must insure all eligible persons, except those who reject such coverage in writing.

3. An insurer may exclude or limit the coverage on any person as to whom evidence of individual insurability is not satisfactory to the insurer, except as otherwise prohibited in this title.

E. 1. A policy issued to an association or to a trust or to the trustees of a fund established, created, or maintained for the benefit of members of one or more associations which association or trust shall be deemed the policyholder. The association or associations shall:

a. Have at the outset a minimum of 100 persons;

b. Have been organized and maintained in good faith for purposes other than that of obtaining insurance;

c. Have been in active existence for at least five years;

d. Have a constitution and bylaws which provide that (i) the association or associations hold regular meetings not less than annually to further purposes of the members, (ii) except for credit unions, the association or associations collect dues or solicit contributions from members, and (iii) the members have voting privileges and representation on the governing board and committees;

e. Does not condition membership in the association on any health status-related factor relating to an individual (including an employee of an employer or a dependent of an employee);

f. Makes health insurance coverage offered through the association available to all members regardless of any health status-related factor relating to such members (or individuals eligible for coverage through a member);

g. Does not make health insurance coverage offered through the association available other than in connection with a member of the association; and

h. Meets such additional requirements as may be imposed under the laws of this Commonwealth.

2. The policy shall be subject to the following requirements:

a. The policy may insure members of such association or associations, employees thereof or employees of members, or one or more of the preceding or all of any class or classes thereof for the benefit of persons other than the employee's employer.

b. The premium for the policy shall be paid from funds contributed by the association or associations, or by employer members, or by both, or from funds contributed by the covered persons or from both the covered persons and the association, associations, or employer members.

3. Except as provided in subdivision 4 of this subsection, a policy on which no part of the premium is to be derived from funds contributed by the covered persons specifically for their insurance must insure all eligible persons, except those who reject such coverage in writing.

4. An insurer may exclude or limit the coverage on any person as to whom evidence of individual insurability is not satisfactory to the insurer, except as otherwise prohibited in this title.

F. A policy issued to a credit union or to a trustee or trustees or agent designated by two or more credit unions, which credit union, trustee, trustees, or agent shall be deemed the policyholder, to insure members of such credit union or credit unions for the benefit of persons other than the credit union or credit unions, trustee or trustees, or agent or any of their officials, subject to the following requirements:

1. The members eligible for insurance shall be all of the members of the credit union or credit unions, or all of any class or classes thereof.

2. The premium for the policy shall be paid by the policyholder from the credit union's funds and, except as provided in subdivision 3 of this subsection, must insure all eligible members.

3. An insurer may exclude or limit the coverage on any person as to whom evidence of individual insurability is not satisfactory to the insurer.

G. A policy issued to a health maintenance organization as provided in subsection B of § 38.2-4314. (1998, c. 154.)

§ **38.2-3522:** Repealed by Acts 1998, c. 154.

§ **38.2-3522.1. Limits of group accident and sickness insurance.** — Group accident and sickness insurance offered to a resident of this Commonwealth under a group accident and sickness insurance policy issued to a group other than one described in § 38.2-3521.1 shall be subject to the following requirements:

A. No such group accident and sickness insurance policy shall be delivered in this Commonwealth unless the Commission finds that:

1. The issuance of such group policy is not contrary to Virginia's public policy and is in the best interest of the citizens of this Commonwealth;

2. The issuance of the group policy would result in economies of acquisition or administration; and

3. The benefits are reasonable in relation to the premiums charged.

Insurers filing policy forms seeking approval under the provisions of this subsection shall accompany the forms with a certification, signed by the officer of the company with the responsibility for forms compliance, in which the company certifies that each such policy form will be issued only where the requirements set forth in subdivisions 1 through 3 of this subsection have been met.

B. No such group accident and sickness insurance coverage may be offered in this Commonwealth by an insurer under a policy issued in another state unless this Commonwealth or another state having requirements substantially similar to those contained in subdivisions 1, 2, and 3 of subsection A has made a determination that such requirements have been met.

1. An insurer offering group accident and sickness insurance coverage in this Commonwealth under this subsection shall file a certification, signed by the officer of the company having responsibility for forms compliance, in which the company certifies that all group insurance coverage marketed to residents of this Commonwealth under policies which have not been approved by this Commonwealth will comply with the provisions of § 38.2-3521.1 or have met the requirements set forth in subdivisions A 1 through A 3 of this section, and which clearly demonstrates that the substantially similar requirements of the state in which the contract will be issued have been met. The certification shall be accompanied by documentation from such state, evidencing the determination that such requirements have been met.

2. An insurer offering group accident and sickness insurance in this Commonwealth under this subsection that is unable to provide the documentation required in subdivision 1 of this subsection shall be required to file policy forms consistent with requirements in § 38.2-316 which are imposed on policies issued in Virginia. The policy shall be required to be approved as meeting all requirements of this title prior to its being offered to residents of this Commonwealth.

C. The premium for the policy shall be paid either from the policyholder's funds or from funds contributed by the covered persons, or from both.

D. An insurer may exclude or limit the coverage on any person as to whom evidence of individual insurability is not satisfactory to the insurer, except as otherwise prohibited in this title. (1998, c. 154.)

§ **38.2-3523:** Repealed by Acts 1998, c. 154.

§ **38.2-3523.1. Review of records.** — The Commission may review the records of any insurer to determine that the insurer's policies have been issued in compliance with the requirements set forth in this article. Insurers issuing coverage not complying with the provisions of § 38.2-3521.1 and not complying with the provisions of § 38.2-3522.1 shall be deemed to have committed a knowing and willful violation of this article, and shall be punished as set forth in subsection A of § 38.2-218. (1998, c. 154.)

§ **38.2-3523.2. Policies issued outside of the Commonwealth of Virginia.** — A group accident and sickness insurance policy issued outside of this Commonwealth, providing coverage to residents of this Commonwealth, that does not qualify under § 38.2-3521.1 or § 38.2-3522.1 shall be subject to the statutory requirements of this title and may subject the insurer issuing such policy to the penalties available under this title for violation of such requirements. (1998, c. 154.)

§ **38.2-3523.3. Requirements for those marketing group accident and sickness insurance.** — Insurance marketed to certificate holders of a group which does not qualify under § 38.2-3521.1 or § 38.2-3522.1 must be marketed by a person holding a valid life and health insurance agent license as required by Chapter 18 (§ 38.2-1800 et seq.) of this title. (1998, c. 154; 1999, c. 86.)

The **1999 amendment** deleted "or health agent" following "insurance agent."

§ **38.2-3523.4. Minimum number of persons covered.** — A group accident and sickness insurance policy shall on the issue date and at each policy anniversary date, cover at least two persons, other than spouses or minor children, unless such spouse or minor child is determined to be an eligible employee as defined in § 38.2-3431. (1998, c. 154.)

§ **38.2-3524:** Repealed by Acts 1998, c. 154.

§ **38.2-3525. Group accident and sickness insurance coverages of spouses or dependent children.** — A. Coverage under a group accident and sickness insurance policy, except a policy issued pursuant to § 38.2-3521.1 B, may be extended to insure the spouse and any child who is under the age of nineteen years or who is a dependent and a full-time student under twenty-five years of age, without regard to whether such child resides in the same household as the certificate holder, or any class of spouse and dependent children, of each insured group member who so elects. The amount of accident and sickness insurance for the spouse or dependent child shall not exceed the amount of accident and sickness insurance for the insured group member.

B. Notwithstanding the provisions of § 38.2-3538, one certificate may be issued for each family unit if a statement concerning any spouse's or dependent child's coverage is included in the certificate. (1986, c. 562; 1993, c. 306; 1998, c. 154.)

The **1998 amendment** substituted "policy issued pursuant to § 38.2-3521.1 B" for "group credit accident and sickness insurance policy" in the first sentence of subsection A.

§ 38.2-3526. Standard provisions required; exceptions. — A. No group accident and sickness insurance policy shall be delivered or issued for delivery in this Commonwealth unless it contains the standard provisions prescribed in this article.

B. The provisions of § 38.2-3531, subsection A of §§ 38.2-3533 and 38.2-3538 shall not apply to policies issued pursuant to § 38.2-3522.1 B. (1986, c. 562; 1998, c. 154.)

The **1998 amendment,** in subsection B, deleted "group credit accident and sickness insurance" preceding "policies" and inserted "issued pursuant to § 38.2-3522.1 B."

§ 38.2-3527. Grace period. — Each group accident and sickness insurance policy shall contain a provision that the policyowner is entitled to a grace period of not less than thirty-one days for the payment of any premium due except the first premium. The provision shall also state that during the grace period the accident and sickness coverage shall continue in force unless the policyowner has given the insurer written notice of discontinuance in accordance with the terms of the policy and in advance of the date of discontinuance. The policy may provide that the policyowner shall be liable to the insurer for the payment of a pro rata premium for the time the policy was in force during the grace period. (1986, c. 562.)

§ 38.2-3528. Incontestability. — A. Each group accident and sickness insurance policy shall contain a provision that the validity of the policy shall not be contested, except for nonpayment of premiums, after it has been in force for two years from its date of issue.

B. The provision shall also state that no statement made by any person insured under the policy relating to his insurability or the insurability of his insured dependents shall be used in contesting the validity of the insurance with respect to which such statement was made:

1. After the insurance has been in force prior to the contest for a period of two years during the lifetime of the person about whom the statement was made; and

2. Unless the statement is contained in a written instrument signed by him.

C. This provision shall not preclude the assertion at any time of defenses based on the person's ineligibility for coverage under the policy or upon other provisions in the policy. (1986, c. 562.)

§ 38.2-3529. Entire contract; statements deemed representations. — A. Each group accident and sickness insurance policy shall contain a provision that the policy, and any application of the policyowner, and any individual applications of the persons insured shall constitute the entire contract between the parties.

B. The provision shall also state that:

1. A copy of any application of the policyowner shall be attached to the policy when issued;

2. All statements made by the policyowner or by the persons insured shall be deemed representations and not warranties; and

3. No written statement made by any person insured shall be used in any contest unless a copy of the statement is furnished to the person or to his beneficiary or personal representative. (1986, c. 562.)

§ 38.2-3530. Evidence of individual insurability. — Each group accident and sickness insurance policy shall contain a provision setting forth any conditions under which the insurer reserves the right to require a person eligible for insurance to furnish evidence of individual insurability satisfactory to the insurer as a condition to part or all of his coverage. (1986, c. 562.)

§ 38.2-3531. Additional exclusions and limitations. — A. Each group accident and sickness insurance policy shall contain a provision specifying all additional exclusions or limitations applicable under the policy for any disease or physical condition of a person, not otherwise excluded from the person's coverage by name or specific description effective on the date of the person's loss, which existed prior to the effective date of the person's coverage under the policy.

B. Any such exclusion or limitation may only apply to a disease or physical condition for which medical advice or treatment was received by the person during the twelve months prior to the effective date of the person's coverage. The exclusion or limitation shall not apply to loss incurred or disability commencing after the earlier of (i) the end of a continuous period of twelve months commencing on or after the effective date of the person's coverage during which the person receives no medical advice or treatment in connection with the disease or physical condition, or (ii) the end of the two-year period commencing on the effective date of the person's coverage.

C. This section shall not apply to group accident and sickness policies providing hospital, medical and surgical or major medical coverage on an expense incurred basis to an employer's employees and their dependents. (1986, c. 562; 1998, c. 24.)

The **1998 amendment** added subsection C.

§ 38.2-3532. Misstatement of age. — Each group accident and sickness insurance policy where the premiums or benefits vary by age shall contain a provision that an equitable adjustment of premiums, benefits or both shall be made if the age of a person insured has been misstated. The provision shall contain a clear statement of the method of adjustment to be used. (1986, c. 562.)

§ 38.2-3533. Individual certificates. — A. Each group accident and sickness insurance policy shall contain a provision that the insurer will issue to the policyholder for delivery to each person insured a certificate setting forth:

1. The insured person's insurance protection, including any limitations, reductions, and exclusions applicable to the coverage provided;

2. To whom the insurance benefits are payable;

3. Any family member's or dependent's coverage; and

4. The rights and conditions set forth in § 38.2-3541.

B. Each group policy issued pursuant to § 38.2-3522.1 B, where any part of the premium is paid by debtors from identifiable charges collected from the insured debtors not required of an uninsured debtor, shall contain a provision that the insurer will furnish to the policyholder for each debtor insured under the policy a form that will contain a statement describing the debtor's coverage and that the benefits payable shall be applied to reduce or extinguish the indebtedness. (1986, c. 562; 1998, c. 154.)

The **1998 amendment,** in subsection B, deleted "credit accident and sickness" preced-ing "policy" and inserted "issued pursuant to § 38.2-3522.1 B."

§ 38.2-3534. Notice of claim. — Each group accident and sickness insurance policy shall contain a provision that written notice of a claim shall be given to the insurer within twenty days after the occurrence or commencement of any loss covered by the policy. Failure to give notice within that time shall not invalidate or reduce any claim if it can be shown that notice was given as soon as reasonably possible. (1986, c. 562.)

§ 38.2-3535. Claim forms. — Each group accident and sickness insurance policy shall contain a provision that the insurer will furnish forms for filing proof of loss to the person making a claim or to the policyholder for delivery to that person. If the forms are not furnished within fifteen days after the insurer received notice of any claim under the policy, the person making the claim shall be deemed to have complied with the requirements of the policy as to proof of loss upon submitting within the time fixed in the policy of filing proof of loss, written proof covering the occurrence, character, and extent of the loss for which a claim is made. (1986, c. 562.)

§ 38.2-3536. Proofs of loss. — A. Each group accident and sickness insurance policy shall contain a provision that written proof of the loss shall be furnished to the insurer within ninety days after the date of the loss. In the case of a claim for loss of time for disability, each group accident and sickness insurance policy shall contain a provision that written proof of the loss shall be furnished to the insurer within ninety days after the commencement of the period for which the insurer is liable. Subsequent written proof of the continuance of the disability shall be furnished to the insurer at reasonable intervals required by the insurer.

B. Failure to furnish such proof within the prescribed time shall not invalidate or reduce any claim if it was not reasonably possible to furnish the proof within that time and the proof is furnished as soon as reasonably possible. In no event, except in the absence of legal capacity of the claimant, shall such proof be furnished later than one year from the time proof is otherwise required. (1986, c. 562.)

§ 38.2-3537. Time of payment of claims. — Each group accident and sickness insurance policy shall contain a provision that all benefits payable under the policy other than benefits for loss of time shall be payable within sixty days after receipt of proof of loss. The provision shall also state that, subject to proof of loss, all accrued benefits payable under the policy for loss of time shall be paid at least monthly during the continuance of the period for which the insurer is liable, and that any balance remaining unpaid at the termination of such period will be paid as soon as possible. (1986, c. 562.)

§ 38.2-3538. Payment of benefits. — Each group accident and sickness insurance policy shall contain a provision that benefits for loss of life of the person insured shall be payable to the beneficiary designated by the person insured. However, if the policy contains conditions pertaining to family status, the beneficiary may be the family member specified by the policy terms. In either case, payment of those benefits is subject to the provisions of the policy in the event no such designated or specified beneficiary is living at the death of the person insured. The policy may also provide that if any benefit is payable to the estate of a person, or to a person who is a minor or otherwise not competent to give a valid release, the insurer may pay the benefit, up to an amount not exceeding $5,000, to any relative by blood or connection by marriage of the person who is deemed by the insurer to be equitably entitled to the benefit. The policy may also provide that all or any portion of any benefits provided for health care services may be paid to the health care services provider. All other benefits of the policy shall be payable to the person insured. (1986, c. 562; 1991, c. 87.)

§ **38.2-3539. Physical examinations and autopsy.** — Each group accident and sickness insurance policy shall contain a provision that the insurer shall have the right (i) to examine the person for whom a claim is made when and as often as it may reasonably require during the pendency of claim under the policy and (ii) to make an autopsy where it is not prohibited by law. (1986, c. 562.)

§ **38.2-3540. Legal actions.** — Each group accident and sickness insurance policy shall contain a provision that no action at law or in equity shall be brought to recover on the policy within sixty days after proof of loss has been filed in accordance with the policy requirements and that no such action shall be brought after the expiration of three years from the time that proof of loss was required to be filed. (1986, c. 562.)

One-year limitation period in group health plan contract had to be enforced as a valid contractual provision which violated no state or federal public policy. Koonan v. Blue Cross & Blue Shield, 802 F. Supp. 1424 (E.D. Va. 1992).

§ **38.2-3540.1. Claims experience.** — A. Each group accident and sickness insurance policy shall contain a provision which provides that an insurer, upon request, shall provide the policyholder with a complete record of the policyholder's claims experience incurred under the group policy. This record shall include all claims incurred for the lesser of (i) the period of time since the policy was issued or issued for delivery or (ii) the period of time since the policy was last renewed, reissued or extended, if already issued. This record shall be made available promptly to the policyholder upon request made not less than thirty days prior to the date upon which the premiums or contractual terms of the policy may be amended. Nothing in this section shall require the disclosure of personal or privileged information about an individual that is protected from disclosure under Chapter 6 (§ 38.2-600 et seq.) of this title, or under any other applicable federal or state law or regulation.

B. The requirements of this section shall apply to all policies, contracts, and plans delivered, issued for delivery, reissued or extended on and after July 1, 1999, or at any time after the effective date hereof when any term of any such policy, contract or plan is changed or any premium adjustment is made. (1992, c. 800; 1999, c. 116.)

The 1999 amendment added the subsection A designator, substituted "thirty" for "sixty" in the third sentence of subsection A, and added subsection B.

§ **38.2-3541. Conversion or continuation on termination of eligibility.** — Each group hospital policy, group medical and surgical policy or group major medical policy delivered or issued for delivery in this Commonwealth or renewed, reissued or extended if already issued, shall contain, subject to the policyholder's selection, one of the options set forth in this section. These options shall apply if the insurance on a person covered under such a policy ceases because of the termination of the person's eligibility for coverage, prior to that person becoming eligible for Medicare or Medicaid benefits unless such termination is due to termination of the group policy under circumstances in which the insured person is insurable under other replacement group coverage or health care plan without waiting periods or preexisting conditions under the replacement coverage or plan.

1. Option 1: To have the insurer issue him, without evidence of insurability, an individual accident and sickness insurance policy in the event that the insurer is not exempt under § 38.2-3416 and offers such policy, subject to the following requirements:

a. The application for the policy shall be made, and the first premium paid to the insurer within thirty-one days after the termination;

b. The premium on the policy shall be at the insurer's then customary rate applicable: (i) to such policies, (ii) to the class of risk to which the person then belongs, and (iii) to his or her age on the effective date of the policy;

c. The policy will not result in over-insurance on the basis of the insurer's underwriting standards at the time of issue;

d. The benefits under the policy shall not duplicate any benefits paid for the same injury or same sickness under the prior policy;

e. The policy shall extend coverage to the same family members that were insured under the group policy; and

f. Coverage under this option shall be effected in such a way as to result in continuous coverage during the thirty-one-day period for such insured.

2. Option 2: To have his present coverage under the policy continued for a period of ninety days immediately following the date of the termination of the person's eligibility, without evidence of insurability, subject to the following requirements:

a. The application for the extended coverage is made to the group policy-holder and the total premium for the ninety-day period is paid to the group policyholder prior to the termination;

b. The premium for continuing the group coverage shall be at the insurer's current rate applicable to the group policy; and

c. Continuation shall only be available to an employee or member who has been continuously insured under the group policy during the entire three months' period immediately preceding termination of eligibility. (1979, c. 97, § 38.1-348.11; 1982, c. 625; 1984, c. 300; 1986, c. 562; 1988, c. 551.)

§ 38.2-3542. Notice to employees upon termination of coverage; penalty for failure to remit funds. — A. Any employer who (i) assumes part or all of the cost of providing group accident and sickness insurance or a group health services plan or group health care plan for his employees under a group insurance policy or subscription contract or other evidence of coverage; (ii) provides a facility for deducting the full amount of the premium from employees' salaries and remitting such premium to the insurer, health services plan, or health maintenance organization; or (iii) provides for health and medical care or reimbursement of medical expenses for his employees as a self-insurer, shall give written notice to participating employees in the event of termination or upon the receipt of notice of termination of any such policy, contract, coverage, or self-insurance not later than fifteen days after the termination of a self-insured plan or receipt of the notice of termination required by subsection C of this section.

B. Any employer who collects from his employees or covers any part of the cost of any of the policies, contracts, or coverages specified in subsection A of this section and who knowingly fails to remit to the insurer or plan such funds required to maintain coverage in accordance with the policy or contract provisions under which the employees are covered shall be guilty of a Class 1 misdemeanor and shall be subject to civil suit for any medical expenses the employee may become liable for as a result of the employer letting such coverage be terminated.

C. In the event the coverages specified in subsection A of this section are terminated due to nonpayment of premium by the employer, no such coverages shall be terminated by an insurer, health services plan, health maintenance organization or health insurance issuer as defined in § 38.2-3431 with respect to a covered individual unless and until the employer has been provided with a written or printed notice of termination, including a specific date, not less than fifteen days from the date of such notice, by which coverage will terminate if overdue premium is not paid. Coverage shall not be permitted to terminate for at least fifteen days after such notice has been mailed. Each insurer, health services plan, or health maintenance organization shall make reimbursement on all valid claims for services incurred prior to the date coverage is terminated. (1982, c. 586, § 38.1-356.01; 1986, cc. 251, 562; 1990, c. 301; 1999, c. 276.)

Cross references. — As to punishment for Class 1 misdemeanors, see § 18.2-11.

Editor's note. — Pursuant to § 9-77.11, effect has been given in this section, as set out above, to Acts 1986, c. 251, which amended former § 38.1-356.01, the comparable provision in former Title 38.1.

The 1999 amendment, in subsection A, deleted "or" at the end of clause (i), inserted present clause (ii), redesignated former clause (ii) as present clause (iii), and substituted "termination of a self-insured plan or receipt of the notice of termination required by subsection C of this section" for "termination or receipt of the notice of termination" at the end of the subsection; in subsection B, inserted "or covers," deleted "the funds" following "fails to remit," inserted "such funds required to maintain coverage," inserted "and shall be subject to civil suit for any medical expenses the employee may become liable for as a result of the employer letting such coverage be terminated"; and added subsection C.

§ 38.2-3543. Provisions required by other jurisdictions. — A. Group accident and sickness insurance policies of a foreign or alien insurer, delivered or issued for delivery in this Commonwealth, may contain any provision that is not less favorable to the insured or the beneficiary than the provisions required by this article and that is prescribed by the laws of its domiciliary jurisdiction.

B. Any group accident and sickness insurance policy of a domestic insurer may, when delivered or issued for delivery in any other jurisdiction, contain any provision permitted or required by the laws of that jurisdiction. (1986, c. 562.)

§ 38.2-3543.1. Regulations. — The Commission may establish rules and regulations for coordination of benefits, as well as to establish standards to be met in connection with the marketing and contracting for group accident and sickness insurance in this Commonwealth. Pursuant to the authority granted by § 38.2-223, the Commission may promulgate such rules and regulations as it may deem necessary to establish standards with regard to coordination of benefits provisions. (1994, c. 316; 1998, c. 154.)

The 1998 amendment, in the first sentence, added the language beginning "as well as to establish standards."

§ 38.2-3543.2. Applicability of laws. — In the event of conflict between the provisions of this article and other provisions of this title, the provisions of this article shall be controlling. (1998, c. 154.)

ARTICLE 4.

Industrial Sick Benefit Insurance.

§ 38.2-3544. Definition of industrial sick benefit insurance. — Industrial sick benefit insurance means life insurance combined with accident and sickness insurance under which:

1. Premiums, dues or assessments are payable weekly;

2. A ten dollar maximum weekly indemnity is paid to members or policyowners in the event of sickness or accident;

3. A $250 maximum death benefit is provided, and the named beneficiary is confined to the spouse of the insured, a relative of the insured by blood, marriage or adoption, a person bound in a pledge of marriage to the insured, or any person dependent on the insured; and

4. The issuing insurer is not required by its charter, bylaws, or by statute to maintain the legal reserve for death benefits. (Code 1950, §§ 38-350, 38-351, 38-352; 1952, c. 317, § 38.1-483; 1986, c. 562.)

§ 38.2-3545. Further restrictions as to beneficiaries. — Within the permitted classes of beneficiaries prescribed in § 38.2-3544, the issuing insurer may designate the classes of beneficiaries. No change of beneficiary shall be made by assignment, will, or otherwise to any person outside the designated classes without the consent of the insurer. If no person within the classes of beneficiaries prescribed in § 38.2-3544 survives the insured, the insurer may discharge its liability by payment of the proceeds of the policy to any person appearing to the insurer to be equitably entitled to the proceeds because of having incurred expense for the maintenance, medical attention or burial of the insured. (Code 1950, § 38-352; 1952, c. 317, § 38.1-484; 1986, c. 562.)

§ 38.2-3546. Cancellation of sick benefit portion of policy. — Every policy of industrial sick benefit insurance issued in this Commonwealth after June 18, 1922, shall contain a provision that:

1. The sick benefit portion of the policy may be cancelled by either the insurer or the insured and the life portion continued by a payment of twenty percent of the original premium;

2. If the cancellation is by the insurer, it shall be without prejudice to any claim arising on account of disability commencing prior to the date on which the cancellation takes effect; and

3. Written notice of the cancellation and payment for the unearned portion of the premium shall be delivered to the insured or mailed to him at his last known address. (Code 1950, § 38-359; 1952, c. 317, § 38.1-485; 1986, c. 562.)

§ 38.2-3547. Excessive insurance; remedy. — A. Any person holding industrial sick benefit insurance policies of several insurers, that, in the aggregate, provide sick benefits in excess of 150 percent of his weekly salary, wages or earnings, shall not be permitted to recover the excess, nor shall the insurer be compelled to pay the excess, unless the existence of all previous policies was admitted by the insured in all applications for insurance in excess of such sum. If by misstatements, or by the failure to admit the existence of previous policies, the insured has obtained such excess additional policies, and has received benefits under such policies in excess of the amount specified above the excess paid may be deducted from the death benefit provided for in the policies.

B. This section shall not apply in any case where the application for the excess policy did not contain any question in regard to the amount of insurance already carried by the applicant, nor where the application blank was printed in less than ten-point type. (Code 1950, § 38-360; 1952, c. 317, § 38.1-486; 1986, c. 562.)

§ 38.2-3548. Agents subject to other insurance laws.

— Each person representing any insurer in the sale of industrial sick benefit insurance shall be subject to the laws governing agents of insurers. (Code 1950, § 38-361; 1952, c. 317, § 38.1-487; 1986, c. 562.)

Agents taxable. — While § 58.1-2501 exempts sick benefit companies and associations from all local taxation, it does not exempt the agents of such companies from such taxation. By the terms of this section they are subject to the laws governing agents of insurance compa-

nies, and the latter are plainly taxable. Such a license tax is not a tax on the companies. At least, the agents are not plainly exempt from taxation. Tabb v. City of Richmond, 116 Va. 227, 81 S.E. 34 (1914).

§ 38.2-3549. Benefits not subject to legal process.

— The payments in weekly or monthly installments to the holder of any policy of industrial sick benefit insurance shall not be subject to the lien of any attachment, garnishment proceeding, writ of fieri facias, or to levy or distress in any manner, for any debt due by the holder of the policy. (Code 1950, § 38-227; 1952, c. 317, § 38.1-488; 1986, c. 562.)

Law Review. — For article on the need for reform of and a proposed revision of Virginia's exemption statutes, see 37 Wash. & Lee L. Rev. 127 (1980).

§ 38.2-3550. Effective date.

— No industrial sick benefit insurance policy as defined in § 38.2-3544 shall be delivered or issued for delivery in this Commonwealth after June 30, 1987. (1986, c. 562.)

CHAPTER 36.

MEDICARE SUPPLEMENT POLICIES.

§ 38.2-3600. Medicare supplement policy; definition.

— *"Medicare supplement policy"* means an individual or group accident and sickness insurance policy or certificate, or a health maintenance organization subscription contract or evidence of coverage, issued or issued for delivery in this Commonwealth which is (i) designed primarily to supplement Medicare by providing benefits for payment of hospital, medical or surgical expenses, or (ii) advertised, marketed or otherwise purported to be a supplement to Medicare.

For group policies, the term does not include

a policy or contract of one or more employers or labor organizations, or of the trustees of a fund established by one or more employers or labor organizations, or a combination of employees and labor organizations, for employees, former employees, or a combination of employees and labor organizations or for members or former members, or combination thereof, of the labor organizations. (1979, c. 726, § 38.1-362.7; 1986, c. 562; 1992, c. 225; 1996, c. 11.)

§ 38.2-3601. Medicare supplement policies; minimum return for group policies generally. — Group Medicare supplement policies shall be expected to return to policyholders in the form of aggregate benefits at least seventy-five percent of the aggregate amount of premiums collected. (1981, c. 575, § 38.1-362.8:1; 1986, c. 562.)

Cross references. — For other provisions as to Medicare supplement policies, see §§ 38.2-3518, 38.2-3605, and 38.2-3607.

§ 38.2-3602: Repealed by Acts 1989, c. 151, § 2.

§ 38.2-3603. Same; minimum return for individual policies. — Medicare supplement policies sold on an individual basis shall be expected to return to policyowners in the form of aggregate benefits at least sixty-five percent of the aggregate amount of premiums collected. (1981, c. 575, § 38.1-362.8:3; 1986, c. 562; 1991, c. 120.)

Cross references. — For other provisions as to Medicare supplement policies, see §§ 38.2-3518, 38.2-3605, and 38.2-3607.

§ 38.2-3604. Free look notice required. — Notwithstanding the provisions of § 38.2-3502, Medicare supplement policies shall have printed on the policy a notice stating substantially: "RIGHT TO RETURN POLICY WITHIN THIRTY DAYS. If for any reason you are not satisfied with your policy you may return this policy to the company within thirty days of the date you received it and the premium paid will be promptly refunded."

A policy returned pursuant to the notice shall be void upon the mailing or delivery of the policy to the insurer.

Nothing in this section shall prohibit an insurer from extending the right to examine period to more than thirty days if the period is specified in the policy. (1980, c. 204, § 38.1-362.13; 1981, c. 575; 1986, c. 562; 1989, c. 151.)

§ 38.2-3605. Coverage of preexisting conditions; Medicare supplement policies. — Notwithstanding subdivision 2 (b) of § 38.2-3503 or the provisions of § 38.2-3514.1, an insurer that issues a Medicare supplement policy shall not deny a claim for losses incurred more than six months from the effective date of coverage on the grounds that a condition existed prior to the effective date of coverage regardless of the application form used. Except as so provided, the policy or contract shall not include wording that would permit a defense based upon preexisting conditions. (1980, c. 204, § 38.1-362.15; 1981, c. 575; 1986, c. 562; 1995, c. 522.)

§ 38.2-3606. Outline of coverage. — Pursuant to the authority granted in § 38.2-223, the Commission may issue rules and regulations that may (i) require that an outline of coverage for Medicare supplement policies be delivered to the insured at the time the application is made and (ii) prescribe the format and content of the outline of coverage. (1980, c. 204, § 38.1-362.16; 1986, c. 562; 1996, c. 11.)

§ 38.2-3607. Group or individual Medicare supplement policies; minimum standards. — A. The provisions of §§ 38.2-3418.1, 38.2-3604, 38.2-3605, 38.2-3606 and 38.2-3516 through 38.2-3520 shall be applicable to group Medicare supplement policies. The term "policy" as used in this article shall include a certificate issued under a group Medicare supplement policy which has been delivered or issued for delivery in this Commonwealth.

B. The provisions of § 38.2-3418.1 shall be applicable to individual Medicare supplement policies.

C. No Medicare supplement policy or certificate in force in this Commonwealth shall contain benefits that duplicate benefits provided by Medicare. (1981, c. 575, § 38.1-362.17; 1986, c. 562; 1989, c. 646; 1996, c. 11.)

Cross references. — As to the minimum percentage of premiums required to be returned as benefits under Medicare supplement policies, see §§ 38.2-3601 through 38.2-3603.

The 1996 amendment added subsection C.

§ 38.2-3608. Regulations establishing minimum standards. — A. The Commission may issue regulations to establish minimum standards for payment of claims under Medicare supplement policies and for marketing practices, compensation arrangements, requirements for loss ratio refunds or credits, Medicare select policies and certificates, and reporting practices of insurers providing such policies.

B. The Commission may revise or amend such regulations and may increase the scope of the regulations only to the extent necessary to maintain federal approval of the Commonwealth's program for regulation of Medicare supplement insurance pursuant to the requirements established by the United States Department of Health and Human Services.

C. The Commission shall annually advise the standing committees of the General Assembly having jurisdiction over insurance matters of revisions and amendments made pursuant to subsection B. (1989, c. 151; 1990, c. 268; 1992, c. 225; 1996, c. 11.)

§ 38.2-3609. Insurer to file copy of advertisement with Commission. — Every insurer, health service plan or health maintenance organization providing Medicare supplement insurance or benefits in this Commonwealth shall file with the Commission a copy of any Medicare supplement advertisement intended for use in this Commonwealth whether through written, radio or television medium. (1989, c. 151.)

CHAPTER 37.

CREDIT LIFE INSURANCE AND CREDIT ACCIDENT AND SICKNESS INSURANCE.

§§ 38.2-3700 through 38.2-3716: Repealed by Acts 1992, c. 586, effective January 1, 1993.

Cross references. — For provisions relating to credit life insurance and credit accident and sickness insurance, effective January 1, 1993, see § 38.2-3717 et seq.

CHAPTER 37.1.

CREDIT LIFE INSURANCE AND CREDIT ACCIDENT AND SICKNESS INSURANCE.

§ 38.2-3717. Scope. — All life insurance and all accident and sickness insurance issued or sold in connection with loans or other credit transactions shall be subject to the provisions of this chapter except:

1. Such insurance issued in connection with a loan or other credit transaction of more than ten years duration;

2. Such insurance written in connection with a credit transaction that is:

a. Secured by a first mortgage or deed of trust; and

b. Made to finance the purchase of real property or the construction of a dwelling thereon, or to refinance a prior credit transaction made for such a purpose;

3. Where the issuance of such insurance is an isolated transaction on the part of the insurer not related to an agreement or a plan for insuring debtors of the creditor. (1960, c. 67, § 38.1-482.1; 1972, c. 527, § 38.2-3700; 1982, c. 223; 1986, c. 562; 1990, c. 236; 1992, c. 586.)

Law Review. — For survey of Virginia law on insurance for the year 1971-1972, see 58 Va. L. Rev. 1291 (1972).

Promulgation of rule regulating reserves unauthorized. — The State Corporation Commission lacks the statutory authority to promulgate a section of the "Rules Governing Credit Life Insurance" which regulates reserves maintained by credit life insurance companies, since this section clearly stipulates that no other provisions of this title shall be applicable unless otherwise specifically provided and since nothing in this chapter specifically grants the Commission the authority to regulate reserves. American Bankers Life Assurance Co. v. Division of Consumer Counsel, 220 Va. 773, 263 S.E.2d 867 (1980).

§ 38.2-3718. Definitions. — For the purposes of this chapter:

"Commission" means the State Corporation Commission.

"Creditor" means the lender of money or vendor or lessor of goods, services, or property, rights or privileges, for which payment is arranged through a credit transaction, or any successor to the right, title or interest of any such lender, vendor, or lessor and an affiliate, associate or subsidiary of any of them or any other person in any way associated with them.

"Credit transaction" means any transaction by the terms of which the repayment of money loaned or loan commitment made, or payment for goods, services or properties sold or leased is to be made at a future date or dates.

"Critical period coverage" means a death benefit or an accident and sickness insurance benefit in which the benefit is equal to a specified number of monthly payments or the remaining payments on the loan, whichever is less.

"Debtor" means a borrower of money or a purchaser or lessee of goods, services, property, rights or privileges for which payment is arranged through a credit transaction.

"Form" means any policy, contract, rider, endorsement, amendment, certificate, application, enrollment request, or notice of proposed insurance pertaining to credit life insurance or credit accident and sickness insurance. For the purpose of administering §§ 38.2-3726, 38.2-3727 and 38.2-3730, (i) the earned premiums and incurred claims of all credit accident and sickness insurance forms issued in this Commonwealth with the same waiting period will be combined to determine the loss ratio in this Commonwealth regardless of differences in the contractual terms of each form and, (ii) the earned premiums and incurred claims of all credit life insurance forms issued in this Commonwealth will be combined to determine the loss ratio in this Commonwealth regardless of differences in the contractual terms or coverage types.

"Indebtedness" means the total amount payable by a debtor to a creditor in connection with a loan or other credit transaction.

"Open-end credit" means credit extended under an agreement in which:

1. The creditor reasonably contemplates repeated transactions;

2. The creditor imposes a finance charge from time to time on an outstanding unpaid balance; and

3. The amount of credit that may be extended to the debtor during the term of the agreement (up to any limit set by the creditor) is generally made available to the extent that any outstanding balance is repaid.

"Truncated coverage" means a credit life insurance benefit or a credit accident and sickness insurance benefit with a term of insurance coverage that is less than the term of the loan. (1960, c. 67, § 38.1-482.2; 1982, c. 223, § 38.2-3701; 1986, c. 562; 1992, c. 586.)

§ 38.2-3719. Forms of credit life insurance and credit accident and sickness insurance. — A. Credit life insurance and credit accident and sickness insurance shall be issued only in the following forms:

1. Individual policies of life insurance issued to debtors on the term plan;

2. Individual policies of accident and sickness insurance issued to debtors on a term plan or disability benefit provisions in individual policies of credit life insurance;

3. Group policies of life insurance issued to creditors providing insurance upon the lives of debtors on the term plan;

4. Group policies of accident and sickness insurance issued to creditors on a term plan insuring debtors or disability benefit provisions in group credit life insurance policies to provide such coverage.

B. A policy of group credit life insurance or group credit accident and sickness insurance may be issued to a creditor or its parent holding company or to a trustee, trustees or agent designated by two or more creditors, which creditor, holding company, affiliate, trustee, trustees or agent shall be deemed the policyholder, to insure debtors of the creditor or creditors, subject to the following requirements:

1. The debtors eligible for insurance under the policy shall be all of the debtors of the creditor or creditors, or all of any class or classes of the group. The policy may provide that the term *"debtors"* shall include (i) borrowers of money or purchasers of goods, services or property for which payment is

arranged through a credit transaction; (ii) the debtors of one or more subsidiary corporations; and (iii) the debtors of one or more affiliated corporations, proprietors or partnerships if the business of the policyholder and of such affiliated corporations, proprietors or partnerships is under common control.

2. The premium for the policy shall be paid by the policyholder, either from the creditor's funds, or from charges collected from the insured debtors, or from both. Except as provided in subdivision 3 of this subsection, a policy on which no part of the premium is to be derived from the collection of such identifiable charges must insure all eligible debtors.

3. Credit life insurance and credit accident and sickness insurance must be offered to all eligible debtors of a creditor except those for whom evidence of individual insurability is not satisfactory to the insurer. (Code 1950, § 38-428(6); 1950, p. 1001; 1952, c. 317, § 38.1-480; 1960, c. 272, § 38.2-3702; 1962, c. 154; 1975, c. 69; 1982, c. 223, § 38.1-482.3:1; 1983, c. 182; 1986, c. 562; 1987, c. 520; 1992, c. 586.)

§ 38.2-3720. Amount of credit life insurance and credit accident and sickness insurance. — A. *Credit life insurance.*

1. Where an indebtedness is repayable in substantially equal installments, the amount of credit life insurance shall at no time exceed the actual amount of unpaid indebtedness.

2. Notwithstanding the provisions of subdivision A 1, insurance on agricultural credit transaction commitments not exceeding one year in duration may be written up to the amount of the loan commitment, on a nondecreasing or level-term plan.

3. Notwithstanding the provisions of subdivision A 1 of this subsection, or any other subsection, insurance on educational credit transaction commitments may be written for the amount of the loan commitment.

B. *Credit accident and sickness insurance.* — The total amount of periodic indemnity payable by credit accident and sickness insurance in the event of disability, as defined in the policy, shall not exceed the aggregate of the periodic scheduled unpaid installments of the indebtedness; and the amount of each periodic indemnity payment shall not exceed the original indebtedness divided by the number of periodic installments.

C. *Maximum aggregate provisions.* — A provision in a credit life insurance or credit accident and sickness insurance policy or certificate issued thereunder that sets a maximum limit on total benefits payable thereunder shall apply only to that specific indebtedness for which such policy or certificate was issued.

D. The amount of credit life insurance on an indebtedness of any debtor shall not exceed $70,000 with any one insurance company. (1960, c. 67, § 38.1-482.4; 1972, c. 527, §§ 38.2-3703, 38.2-3704; 1982, c. 223; 1986, c. 562; 1992, c. 586.)

Law Review. — For survey of Virginia law on insurance for the year 1971-72, see 58 Va. L. Rev. 1291 (1972).

Insured held not to have had notice of **limitation in policy on amount of coverage.** — See General Fid. Life Ins. Co. v. Bank of Callao, 206 Va. 582, 145 S.E.2d 212 (1965) (decided under former § 38.2-3703).

§ 38.2-3721. Term of credit life insurance and credit accident and sickness insurance. — A. The term of any policy or certificate of credit life insurance or credit accident and sickness insurance shall, subject to acceptance by the insurer, commence on the date when the debtor becomes obligated to the creditor; except that where a group policy provides coverage with respect to existing obligations, the insurance on a debtor with respect to such indebtedness shall commence on the effective date of the policy. Where

evidence of insurability is required and such evidence is furnished more than thirty days after the date when the debtor becomes obligated to the creditor, the term of the insurance may commence on the date the insurance company determines the evidence to be satisfactory, and in such event there shall be an appropriate refund or adjustment of any charge to the debtor for insurance. The term of such insurance shall not extend more than fifteen days beyond the scheduled maturity date of the indebtedness except when extended without additional cost to the debtor. In all cases of termination prior to scheduled maturity, a refund shall be paid or credited as provided in § 38.2-3729.

B. *Renewal or refinancing of the indebtedness.* — If the indebtedness is discharged due to renewal or refinancing prior to the scheduled maturity date, the insurance in force shall be terminated before any new insurance may be issued in connection with the renewed or refinanced indebtedness. In all cases of such termination prior to scheduled maturity, a refund shall be paid or credited to the debtor as provided in § 38.2-3729. In any renewal or refinancing of the indebtedness, the effective date of the coverage for purposes of application of any policy provision shall be deemed to be the first date on which the debtor became insured under the policy covering the indebtedness which was renewed or refinanced at least to the extent of the remaining amount and duration of coverage in force on the indebtedness that was renewed or refinanced.

C. *Termination of group credit insurance policy.* — 1. If a debtor is covered by a group credit insurance policy providing for the payment of single premiums to the insurer, then provision shall be made by the insurer that in the event of termination of the policy for any reason, insurance coverage with respect to any debtor insured under such policy shall be continued for the entire period for which the single premium has been paid.

2. If a debtor is covered by a group credit insurance policy providing for the payment of premiums to the insurer on a monthly outstanding balance basis, then the policy shall provide that, in the event of termination of such policy for whatever reason, notice of termination thereof shall be given to the insured debtor at least thirty days prior to the effective date of termination except where replacement of the coverage by the same or another insurer in the same or greater amount takes place without lapse of coverage. The notice required in this subdivision shall be given by the insurer or, at the option of the insurer, by the creditor, in writing, mailed to the insured debtor at the insured debtor's address as shown in the records of the insurer or creditor.

D. Each credit life insurance or credit accident and sickness insurance policy or certificate shall contain a provision that the insurance may be terminated upon written request of the debtor except if the insurance was required as security for any indebtedness at the time of the credit transaction. If insurance is required, the debtor shall have the right to terminate the insurance by furnishing evidence of other insurance that is at least equal in coverage and protection to the creditor. (1960, c. 67, § 38.1-482.5; 1982, c. 223, § 38.2-3706; 1986, c. 562; 1992, c. 586.)

§ 38.2-3722. Variable interest rate indebtedness; amount; disclosure; refunds. — A. Notwithstanding the terms of § 38.2-3720, if the credit transaction provides for a variable interest rate and the insurance premiums are calculated and charged on a single premium basis, the initial amount of insurance coverage shall not exceed the scheduled amounts of unpaid indebtedness based upon the initial contract interest rate; and the death benefit shall be equal to the scheduled amount of insurance at the date of death or the amount required to liquidate the indebtedness in accordance with the terms of the contract of indebtedness, whichever is greater. If the actual interest rate charged at any time exceeds the original contract interest rate, the term of the insurance shall continue without additional charge for a period not to exceed three months. No additional premiums shall be charged for any additional coverage provided beyond that included in the single premium charge.

B. Each individual policy or group certificate of credit insurance issued in connection with credit transactions involving variable interest rates shall include a disclosure (i) that the death benefit shall in no case be less than the insured scheduled amount of coverage or the amount required to liquidate the insured indebtedness in accordance with the terms of the contract of indebtedness, whichever is greater; and (ii) that the term of insurance shall continue for a period not to exceed three months if the actual interest rate charge at any time exceeds the original contract interest rate.

C. Each individual policy or group certificate of credit insurance issued in connection with credit transactions involving variable interest rates shall provide that in the event of termination of the insurance prior to the original scheduled maturity date of the indebtedness, a refund of any amount paid by the debtor for such insurance shall be made in accordance with § 38.2-3729. Such refund shall be based on the terms of the original loan and the actual elapsed time.

For a loan with a term of more than sixty-one months, computation of such refund using the actuarial method shall be deemed to comply with the requirements hereof. For a loan with a term of sixty-one months or less, computation of such refund using the Rule of 78 shall be deemed to comply with the requirement hereof. (1984, c. 664, § 38.1-482.4:2; 1985, c. 234, § 38.2-3705; 1986, c. 562; 1992, c. 586.)

§ 38.2-3723. Reserves. — A. Each insurer licensed to write credit life insurance in this Commonwealth shall establish and maintain reserves on all such business written in this Commonwealth. At valuation date the reserves shall be not less than 130 percent of the aggregate reserves on all such business calculated by the net premium method on the basis of the Commissioners' 1958 Standard Ordinary Mortality Table or, at the option of the insurer, 100 percent of such reserves calculated on the Commissioners' 1958 Standard Ordinary Mortality Table with 130 percent mortality, with interest at five and one-half percent for single premium insurance and four and one-half percent for all other insurance annually. Reserves may be calculated on an annual or a monthly basis with a reasonable assumption, subject to statistical proof, as to average ages at issue or at expiration. Tables used in calculating reserves must be filed with and approved by the Commission.

B. Each insurer licensed to write credit accident and sickness insurance in this Commonwealth shall establish and maintain reserves on all such business written in this Commonwealth, which shall at all times be no less than the total unearned gross premiums calculated by (i) the Rule of 78 for loans with terms of sixty-one months or less or (ii) the actuarial method for loans with terms of more than sixty-one months. It may be assumed that all business written in any calendar month was written as of the fifteenth of such month. (1982, c. 223, § 38.1-482.12:1; 1986, c. 562, § 38.2-3715; 1992, c. 586.)

§ 38.2-3724. Policy provisions; disclosure to debtors; delivery of policy or certificate. — A. Credit life insurance and credit accident and sickness insurance shall be evidenced by an individual policy, or in the case of group insurance by a certificate of insurance. The policy or certificate of insurance shall: (i) be a document separate and apart from the loan or credit agreement, (ii) refer exclusively to the insurance coverage, and (iii) be delivered to the debtor.

B. Each policy or certificate of credit life insurance or credit accident and sickness insurance shall set forth:

1. The name and address of the insurer;

2. The name or names of the debtor or, in the case of a certificate, the identity by name or otherwise of the debtor;

3. The age or date of birth of the debtor(s);

4. The premium or amount payable by the debtor separately for credit life insurance and credit accident and sickness insurance;

5. A description of the coverage including the amount and term of the coverage, and any exceptions, limitations or restrictions;

6. A statement that the benefits shall be paid to the creditor to reduce or extinguish the unpaid indebtedness; and

7. A statement that if the amount of insurance exceeds the amount necessary to discharge the indebtedness, any such excess shall be payable to a beneficiary, other than the creditor, named by the debtor or to his estate.

C. A credit life or credit accident and sickness insurance policy or certificate, which provides truncated or critical period coverage or any other type of similar coverage that does not provide benefits or coverage for the entire term or amount of the indebtedness, shall be subject to the following requirements:

1. The credit life or credit accident and sickness insurance policy or certificate shall include a statement printed on the face of the policy or first page of the certificate which clearly describes the limited nature of the insurance. The statement shall be printed in capital letters and in bold twelve-point or larger type; and

2. The credit life or credit accident and sickness insurance policy or certificate shall not include any benefits or coverage other than truncated or critical period coverage or any other type of similar coverage that does not provide benefits or coverage for the entire term or amount of the indebtedness.

D. No individual or group credit life insurance or credit accident and sickness insurance policy shall be delivered or issued for delivery in this Commonwealth unless the policy complies with the following requirements:

1. Each policy shall contain a provision (i) that the policy, or the policy and any application endorsed upon or attached to the policy when issued, shall constitute the entire contract between the parties, and (ii) that all statements made by the creditor or by the individual debtors shall, in the absence of fraud, be deemed representations and not warranties;

2. Each policy shall contain a provision that the validity of the policy shall not be contested, except for nonpayment of premiums, after it has been in force for two years from its date of issue; and that no statement made by any person insured under the policy relating to his insurability shall be used in contesting the validity of the insurance with respect to which such statement was made after the insurance has been in force for a period of two years during such person's lifetime, and prior to the date on which the claim thereunder arose;

3. Each policy shall contain a provision that when a claim for the death or disability of the insured arises, settlement shall be made upon receipt of due proof of such death or disability;

4. On the face of each policy and certificate there shall be a title that briefly and accurately describes the nature and form of the policy;

5. Each policy and certificate, including any rider or endorsement, shall be identified by a form number in the lower lefthand corner of the first page of the form. The type size of the text of the policy form or certificate, including any rider and endorsement, shall not be less than ten-point type, one-point leaded;

6. Each individual policy or group certificate shall meet the readability standards established by the Commission; and

7. Each individual policy and certificate shall have printed on it a notice stating in substance that if, during a period of at least ten days from the date the policy or certificate is delivered to the policyowner or certificateholder the policy or certificate is surrendered to the insurer or its agent with a written

request for cancellation, the policy or certificate shall be void from the beginning and the insurer shall refund any premium paid for the policy or certificate.

E. An individual credit life insurance or credit accident and sickness insurance policy or certificate of insurance shall be delivered or mailed to the insured debtor at the time the indebtedness is incurred or within ten business days thereafter except as provided in subsection F of this section. For open-end credit transactions, agricultural or educational loan commitments, or where no direct charge is made to the debtor for his insurance, the individual policy or group certificate of insurance may be delivered to the insured debtor at the time he first becomes eligible for the insurance and need not be delivered again each time new indebtedness is added.

F. If the individual policy or certificate of insurance is not delivered or mailed to the debtor at the time indebtedness is incurred, or within ten business days thereafter, a notice of proposed insurance, setting forth (i) the name and address of the insurer, (ii) the name or names of the debtor, (iii) the age of the debtor, (iv) the premium or amount of payment by the debtor, if any, separately for credit life insurance and credit accident and sickness insurance, and (v) the amount, term and a brief description of the coverage provided, shall be delivered to the debtor. The notice of proposed insurance shall refer exclusively to insurance coverage and shall be separate and apart from the loan or credit transaction. Upon acceptance of the insurance by the insurer and within thirty days of the date upon which the indebtedness is incurred, the insurer shall deliver or mail the individual policy or group certificate of insurance to the debtor. The notice of proposed insurance shall state that upon acceptance by the insurer, the insurance shall become effective as provided in § 38.2-3721.

G. If the policy or certificate is issued by any insurer other than the insurer listed on the application, enrollment request, or notice of proposed insurance, the debtor shall receive a policy or certificate of insurance setting forth the name and address of the substituted insurer and the amount of the premium to be charged. If the amount of the premium is less than that set forth in the notice of proposed insurance, an appropriate refund shall be made. (1960, c. 67, § 38.1-482.6; 1982, c. 223, §§ 38.2-3707, 38.2-3709; 1986, c. 562; 1988, c. 551; 1992, c. 586.)

Editor's note. — The cases annotated below were decided under former § 38.2-3707.

Written policy required. — While oral insurance contracts are generally enforceable if the essential elements are adequately proven, this rule does not apply to an oral contract for credit insurance. The statute governing credit accident and sickness insurance requires that all credit insurance be evidenced by a written policy, certificate, or statement and sets forth the required provisions of such instruments. First Protection Life Ins. Co. v. Compton, 230 Va. 166, 335 S.E.2d 262 (1985).

Some elements may be supplied by inference. — By statute, a policy, certificate, or statement of credit accident or sickness insurance must state, among other things, "a description of the coverage including the amount and term thereof, and any exceptions, limitations, or restrictions." Although the parties normally must expressly agree on each essential element of an insurance contract, some of these elements may be supplied by inference in certain circumstances, including cases involving temporary insurance binders. First Protection Life Ins. Co. v. Compton, 230 Va. 166, 335 S.E.2d 262 (1985).

Oral binders for temporary insurance. — It is apparent that the General Assembly intended to proscribe only oral contracts of insurance never commemorated by a writing, not oral binders or contracts of temporary credit insurance pending issuance of a written policy. First Protection Life Ins. Co. v. Compton, 230 Va. 166, 335 S.E.2d 262 (1985).

§ 38.2-3725. Policy forms to be filed with Commission; approval or disapproval by Commission. — A. No form shall be delivered or issued for delivery in this Commonwealth until a copy of each form has been filed with and approved by the Commission.

B. If a group policy of credit life or credit accident and sickness insurance is delivered in another state, the insurer shall be required to file the group certificate, application or enrollment request, and notice of proposed insurance delivered or issued for delivery in this state for approval. These forms shall comply with § 38.2-3724, with the exception of subsection D and § 38.2-3737. The premium rates shall comply with those established in this chapter or it must be demonstrated to the satisfaction of the Commission that the rates are actuarially equivalent to those required by §§ 38.2-3726 and 38.2-3727 if the coverage differs from that required in Virginia. In no case shall the premiums exceed those set by the Commission in §§ 38.2-3726 and 38.2-3727, as amended by § 38.2-3730.

C. The Commission shall disapprove or withdraw approval previously given to any form if the Commission determines that:

1. It does not comply with the laws of this Commonwealth;

2. It contains any provision or has any title, heading, backing or other indication of the contents of any or all of its provisions which encourage misrepresentation or are unjust, unfair, misleading, deceptive or contrary to the public policy of this Commonwealth; or

3. The premium rates or charges are not reasonable in relation to the benefits provided.

D. The benefits provided by any credit life insurance form shall be considered reasonable in relation to the premium charged provided that the rate does not exceed the current prima facie rate set by the Commission. The prima facie rate that shall be effective January 1, 1993, shall be that set forth in § 38.2-3726. Thereafter, effective January 1, 1995, the Commission shall, on a triennial basis, set forth adjusted prima facie rates that will achieve a sixty percent loss ratio. The methodology used by the Commission in setting the prima facie rates shall be as set forth in § 38.2-3730. The prima facie rates shall be provided to insurers no later than September 1 prior to each triennium and shall be effective as to all forms issued on or after January 1 of the following triennium.

E. The benefits provided by any credit accident and sickness insurance form shall be considered reasonable in relation to the premium charged provided that the rate does not exceed the current prima facie rates set by the Commission. The Commission shall set forth adjusted prima facie rates that will achieve a fifty percent loss ratio as of January 1, 1993, and adjusted prima facie rates that will achieve a sixty percent loss ratio as of January 1, 1995. Thereafter, the Commission shall, on a triennial basis, set forth adjusted prima facie rates that will achieve a sixty percent loss ratio. The methodology used by the Commission in setting the prima facie rates shall be as set forth in § 38.2-3730. The prima facie rates shall be provided to insurers no later than September 1, 1992, for the rates to be effective January 1, 1993; September 1, 1994, for the rates to be effective January 1, 1995; and September 1 prior to each triennium thereafter, and shall be effective as to all forms issued on or after such January 1.

F. If necessary to assure availability of credit insurance, the Commission may consider other factors in order to provide a fair return to insurers. These other factors may include, but are not limited to, the following: (i) actual and expected loss experience; (ii) general and administrative expenses; (iii) loss settlement and adjustment expenses; (iv) reasonable creditor compensation; (v) investment income; (vi) the manner in which premiums are charged; (vii) other acquisition costs, reserves, taxes, regulatory license fees and fund assessments; and (viii) other relevant data consistent with generally accepted actuarial standards.

G. The Commission shall, within thirty days after the filing of any form requiring approval, notify the insurer filing the form of the form's approval or disapproval. If a form is disapproved, the Commission shall also notify the insurer of its reasons for disapproval. The Commission may extend the period within which it shall indicate its approval or disapproval of a form by thirty days. Any form received but not approved or disapproved by the Commission shall be deemed approved at the expiration of the thirty days, or sixty days if the period is extended. No insurer shall use a form deemed approved under the provisions of this section until the insurer has filed with the Commission a written notice of its intent to use the form together with a copy of the form and the original transmittal letter thereof. The notice shall be filed in the offices of the Commission at least ten days prior to the insurer's use of the form.

H. If the Commission proposes to withdraw approval previously given to any form, it shall notify the insurer in writing not less than thirty days prior to the proposed effective date of withdrawal and give its reasons for withdrawal. No insurer shall issue such forms or use them after the effective date of withdrawal, except as provided in subsection I of this section.

I. Any insurer aggrieved by the disapproval or withdrawal of approval of any form may proceed as indicated in § 38.2-1926. (1982, c. 223, § 38.1-482.7:1; 1986, c. 562, § 38.2-3710; 1992, c. 586; 1999, c. 586.)

The **1999 amendment** substituted "shall" for "must" following "premium rates" in the third sentence of subsection B, and added the last sentence in subsection F.

§ 38.2-3726. Credit life insurance rates.

— A. The benefits provided by any credit life insurance form shall be deemed reasonable in relation to the premium charged or to be charged if the rates do not exceed the rates set forth below, except as such rates are modified pursuant to the requirements of § 38.2-3730:

1. $.7519 per month per $1,000 of outstanding insured indebtedness if premiums are payable on a monthly outstanding balance basis.

2. $.48 per $100 of initial indebtedness repayable in twelve equal monthly installments. If premiums are payable on a single premium basis and the amount of the insurance decreases in equal monthly amounts, the following formula shall be used to develop single premium rates from the outstanding balance rate:

$$Sp = \frac{(n+1)}{\frac{20\,(1 + .0363\,n)}{24}}\,Op$$

where Sp is the single term premium per $100 of initial insured indebtedness, n is the credit term in months, and Op is the monthly outstanding balance rate per $1,000 of outstanding insured indebtedness.

3. If premiums are payable on a single premium basis when the benefit provided is level term, the following formula shall be used to develop single premium rates from the outstanding balance rate:

$$Sp = \frac{n}{\frac{10\,(1 + .055\,n)}{24}}\,Op$$

where Sp is the single term premium per $100 of initial insured indebtedness, n is the credit term in months, and Op is the monthly outstanding balance rate per $1,000 of outstanding insured indebtedness.

4. If the benefits provided are other than those described in the introduction to this subsection, premium rates for such benefits shall be actuarially consistent with the rates provided in the above subdivisions.

5. Joint coverage on any of the bases in this subsection shall not exceed 165 percent of the specific rate for that type of coverage.

B. The premium rates in subsection A shall apply to policies providing credit life insurance to be issued with or without evidence of insurability, to be offered to all debtors, and, except as set forth below, containing: (i) no exclusions other than suicide within six months of the incurred indebtedness; and (ii) age restrictions making ineligible for coverage debtors age seventy or over at the time the indebtedness is incurred or debtors having attained age seventy or over on the maturity date of the indebtedness.

1. Insurance written in connection with an open-end credit plan may provide for the cessation of insurance or a reduction in the amount of insurance upon attainment of an age not less than seventy.

2. On insurance written in connection with closed-end credit plans and open-end credit plans where the amount of insurance is based on or limited to the outstanding unpaid balance, no provision excluding or denying a claim for death resulting from a preexisting condition except for those conditions for which the insured debtor received medical diagnosis or treatment within six months preceding the effective date of coverage and which caused the death of the insured debtor within six months following the effective date of coverage. The effective date of coverage for each part of the insurance attributable to a different advance or charge to the plan account is the date on which the advance or charge is posted to the plan account.

3. At the option of the insurer and in lieu of a preexisting condition exclusion on insurance written in connection with open-end credit where the amount of insurance is based on or limited to the outstanding unpaid balance, a provision limiting the amount of insurance payable on death due to natural causes to the balance as it existed six months prior to the date of death if there have been one or more increases in the outstanding balance during such six-month period and if evidence of insurability has not been required in the six-month period prior to date of death. (1992, c. 586.)

§ **38.2-3727. Credit accident and sickness insurance rates.** — A. The Commission shall, based on a morbidity study, promulgate seven-, fourteen- and thirty-day retroactive and nonretroactive credit accident and sickness insurance premium rates which will reasonably be expected to produce the loss ratio as required by subsection E of § 38.2-3725. These prima facie rates will be published by the Commission no later than September 1, 1992, and will be effective on or after January 1, 1993. After this date, the premium charged in connection with any credit accident and sickness insurance policy or certificate issued in this Commonwealth may not exceed the then-published prima facie rate as set forth in this section and as may be adjusted pursuant to § 38.2-3730.

The morbidity study shall be based on policies and certificates issued in this Commonwealth for the past three years, the premiums charged for those contracts and the experience produced by those contracts. The Commission may also take into consideration the reserves held on these contracts and the methods used to produce those reserves and any other information which the Commission in its discretion may consider necessary to produce a credible morbidity study.

B. The benefits provided by any credit accident and sickness insurance form shall be deemed reasonable in relation to the premium charged or to be charged if the rates do not exceed the rates initially published by the Commission pursuant to subsection A of this section, except as such rates are modified pursuant to the requirements of § 38.2-3730.

C. If premiums are paid on the basis of a premium rate per month per $1,000 of outstanding insured indebtedness, they shall be computed according to the following formula or according to a formula approved by the Commission which produces rates actuarially equivalent to the single premium rates:

$$\text{Opn} = \frac{20 \ \text{Spn}}{n+1}$$

Where Spn = Single Premium Rate per $100 of initial insured indebtedness repayable in n equal monthly installments.

Op = Monthly Outstanding Balance Premium Rate per $1,000.

n = Original repayment period, in months.

D. A credit accident and sickness insurance form may not be issued with a waiting period, retroactive or nonretroactive, which differs from the waiting periods set forth in this section.

E. The premium rates in subsection B shall apply to policies providing credit accident and sickness insurance to be issued with or without evidence of insurability, to be offered to all eligible debtors, and containing:

1. No provision excluding or denying a claim for disability resulting from preexisting conditions except for those conditions for which the insured debtor received medical advice, diagnosis or treatment within six months preceding the effective date of the debtor's coverage and which caused loss within the six months following the effective date of coverage. The effective date of coverage for each part of the insurance attributable to a different advance or charge to an open-end credit account is the date on which the advance or charge is posted to the plan account.

2. No other provision which excludes or restricts liability in the event of disability caused in a specific manner except that it may contain provisions excluding or restricting coverage in the event of normal pregnancy and intentionally self-inflicted injuries.

3. No actively-at-work requirement more restrictive than one requiring that the debtor be actively at work at a full-time gainful occupation on the effective date of coverage. *"Full-time"* means a regular work week of not less than thirty hours. A debtor shall be deemed to be actively at work if absent from work due solely to regular day off, holiday or paid vacation.

4. No age restrictions, or only age restrictions making ineligible for coverage debtors sixty-five or over at the time the indebtedness is incurred or debtors who will have attained age sixty-six or over on the maturity date of the indebtedness.

5. A daily benefit equal in amount to one-thirtieth of the monthly benefit payable under the policy for the indebtedness.

6. A definition of "disability" which provides that during the first twelve months of disability the insured shall be unable to perform the duties of his occupation at the time the disability occurred, and thereafter the duties of any occupation for which the insured is reasonably fitted by education, training or experience.

7. A provision written in connection with an open-end credit plan which may provide for the cessation of insurance or reduction in the amount of insurance upon attainment of an age not less than sixty-five.

F. Joint coverage on any of the bases in this section shall not exceed 165 percent of the rates applicable to that type of coverage. (1992, c. 586; 1995, c. 167.)

§ **38.2-3728. Use of rates.** — A. Use of prima facie rates. An insurer that files rates or has rates on file that are not in excess of the prima facie rates set forth in § 38.2-3726 or published as set forth in § 38.2-3727, to the extent adjusted pursuant to § 38.2-3730, may use those rates without further proof of their reasonableness.

B. Use of rates higher than prima facie rates. An insurer may file for approval of and use rates that are higher than the prima facie rates set forth in § 38.2-3726 or published as set forth in § 38.2-3727, to the extent adjusted by § 38.2-3730. In order to use these higher rates, it shall be demonstrated to the satisfaction of the Commission that the use of such higher rates will result in a ratio of claims incurred to premiums earned (assuming the use of such higher rates) that is not less than the loss ratios as required by § 38.2-3725 D and E for those accounts to which such higher rates apply and that such upward deviations will not result on a statewide basis for that insurer of a ratio of claims incurred to premiums earned of less than the expected loss ratio underlying the current prima facie rate developed or adjusted pursuant to § 38.2-3730. Deviations effective for 1993 and 1994 for credit life insurance shall be derived based upon a fifty percent loss ratio.

If rates higher than the prima facie rates provided for in §§ 38.2-3726 and 38.2-3727, to the extent adjusted pursuant to § 38.2-3730, are filed for approval, the filing shall specify the account or accounts to which such rates apply. Such rates may be applied on an equitable basis approved by the Commission to only one or more accounts specified by the insurer for which the experience has been less favorable than expected.

C. Approval period of deviated rates.

1. A deviated rate will be in effect for a period of time not longer than the experience period used to establish such rate. In no event will deviated rates remain in effect after the effective date that new prima facie rates are effective as set forth in § 38.2-3730.

2. Notwithstanding subsection A of this section, the prima facie rates shall be employed in the event that the account becomes insured by another insurer.

D. As used in this section:

1. "Experience" means "earned premiums" and "incurred claims" during the experience period.

2. "Experience period" means the most recent period of time for which experience is reported, but not for a period longer than three full years.

3. "Incurred Claims" means total claims paid during the experience period, adjusted for the change in claim reserve. (1992, c. 586.)

§ **38.2-3729. Refunds.** — A. Each individual policy or group certificate shall provide that, in the event of termination of the insurance prior to the scheduled maturity date of the indebtedness, any refund of an amount paid by the debtor for insurance shall be paid or credited promptly to the person entitled thereto.

B. If a creditor requires a debtor to make any payment for credit life insurance or credit accident and sickness insurance and an individual policy or group certificate of insurance is not issued, the creditor shall immediately give written notice to such debtor and shall promptly make an appropriate credit to the account.

C. Refund formulas which any insurer desires to use for decreasing term credit life insurance and credit accident and sickness insurance with terms of more than sixty-one months must develop refunds which are at least as favorable to the debtor as refunds based on the actuarial method. Refund formulas for decreasing term credit life insurance and credit accident and sickness insurance with terms of sixty-one months or less must develop refunds which are at least as favorable to the debtor as refunds based on the Rule of 78 or the actuarial method, whichever method is consistent with the original method of premium calculation. The actuarial method will result in refunds equal to the premium cost of scheduled benefits subsequent to the date of cancellation or termination, computed at the schedule of premium rates in effect on the date of issue. The refund of premiums for level term credit life insurance shall be no less than the pro rata unearned gross premium. Refund formulas must be filed with and approved by the Commission prior to use.

D. The requirements of subsection C of this section that refund formulas be filed with the Commission shall be considered fulfilled if the refund formulas are set forth in the individual policy or group certificate filed with the Commission.

E. Refunds may be computed:

1. On a daily basis; or

2. From the end of the loan month if sixteen days or more of a loan month have been earned, provided that, if fifteen days or less of a loan month have been earned, the refund is computed from the beginning of the loan month.

F. No refund of one dollar or less need be made.

G. Refunds shall be made in accordance with this chapter without regard as to whether or not the refund has been requested by the debtor.

H. Voluntary prepayment of indebtedness. If a debtor prepays the indebtedness other than as a result of death:

1. Any credit life insurance covering such indebtedness shall be terminated and an appropriate refund of the credit life insurance premium shall be paid to the debtor in accordance with this section; and

2. Any credit accident and sickness insurance covering such indebtedness shall be terminated and an appropriate refund of the credit accident and sickness insurance premium shall be paid to the debtor in accordance with this section. If a claim under such coverage is in progress at the time of prepayment, the amount of refund may be determined as if the prepayment did not occur until the payment of benefits terminates. No refund need be paid during any period of disability for which credit accident and sickness benefits are payable. A refund shall be computed as if prepayment occurred at the end of the disability period.

I. Involuntary prepayment of indebtedness. If an indebtedness is prepaid by the proceeds of a credit life insurance policy covering the debtor, then it shall be the responsibility of the insurer to see that the following are paid to the insured debtor, if living, or the beneficiary, other than the creditor, named by the debtor or to the debtor's estate:

1. An appropriate refund of the credit accident and sickness insurance premium in accordance with this section; and

2. The amount of benefits in excess of the amount required to repay the indebtedness after crediting any unearned interest or finance charges. (1960, c. 67, § 38.1-482.8; 1982, c. 223, § 38.2-3711; 1986, c. 562; 1992, c. 586.)

§ 38.2-3730. Experience reports and adjustment of prima facie rates.

— A. Each insurer doing insurance business in this Commonwealth shall annually file with the Commission and the National Association of Insurance Commissioners a report of credit life and credit accident and sickness written on a calendar year basis. Such report shall utilize the Credit Insurance Supplement-Annual Statement Blank as then approved by the National Association of Insurance Commissioners. Such filing shall be made in accordance with and no later than the due date in the Instructions in the Annual Statement.

B. The Commission shall, on a triennial basis, publish notice and conduct a hearing to determine the actual loss ratio for each form of insurance and adjust the prima facie rates, as provided in §§ 38.2-3726 and 38.2-3727, by applying the ratio of the actual loss ratio to the loss ratio standard set forth in § 38.2-3725 to the prima facie rates. The Commission shall, after such hearing, publish the adjusted actual statewide prima facie rates to be used by insurers during the next triennium. As set forth in this section, the following formula shall be used to adjust the prima facie rates:

$$\text{PFR} \ \text{X} \ \frac{\text{Actual Loss Ratio}}{\text{Loss Ratio Standard}}$$

Where PFR is the prima facie rate as provided in §§ 38.2-3726 and 38.2-3727, the Actual Loss Ratio is the ratio of the incurred claims to the earned premiums at prima facie rates for all companies for the preceding three years as reported in the Annual Statement Supplements and the Loss Ratio Standard is the loss ratio provided in § 38.2-3725.

C. In the event that three years of experience is not available using prima facie rates published by the Commission, the Commission may adjust prima facie rates using the number of years of experience available at prima facie rates previously published by the Commission. (1992, c. 586.)

§ 38.2-3731. Claims. — A. All claims shall be promptly reported to the insurer or its designated claim representative. The insurer shall maintain adequate claim files. All claims shall be settled as soon as possible and in accordance with the terms of the insurance contract.

B. All claims shall be paid or credited by: (i) electronic means to the account of the claimant to whom payment of the claim is due pursuant to the policy provisions or to an account or person specified by such claimant; or (ii) draft drawn upon the insurer or by check of the insurer to the order of the claimant to whom payment of the claim is due pursuant to the policy provisions, or to a person specified by such claimant.

C. No plan or arrangement shall be used where any person other than the insurer or its designated claim representative shall be authorized to settle or adjust claims. The creditor shall not be designated as claim representative for the insurer in adjusting claims. A group policyholder may, by arrangement with the insurer, draw drafts or checks, or credit by electronic means in payment of claims due to the group policyholder subject to audit and review by the insurer. The insurer shall periodically review claims payments made on its behalf by claim representatives or group policyholders. (1960, c. 67, § 38.1-482.11; 1982, c. 223, § 38.2-3713; 1986, c. 562; 1992, c. 586.)

§ 38.2-3732. Insurer delegation of duties. — Any insurer that delegates to a creditor any of its duties under the laws of this Commonwealth or the regulations of this Commission shall be responsible to see that such creditor discharges such duties in accordance with said laws and regulations. A finding by the Commission that either the insurer or its delegee has failed to comply with such requirements shall subject the insurer and creditor to any and all disciplinary actions authorized under this title. Such responsibility shall include but not be limited to a determination that:

1. Proper insurance rates are being charged by the creditor;

2. Proper refunds are being made;

3. Claims are being filed and properly handled;

4. Amounts of insurance payable on death in excess of the amounts necessary to discharge indebtedness are properly distributed; and

5. The creditor is promptly and fairly processing complaints concerning its credit insurance operations and is maintaining proper procedures for and records of complaints processed. (1992, c. 586.)

§ 38.2-3733. Portion of premium may be allowed to creditor; insurance may be provided and serviced at creditor's place of business. — A. A portion of the premium for credit life insurance or credit accident and sickness insurance may be allowed by the insurer to a creditor for providing and servicing such insurance. Such portion of the premium so allowed shall not be deemed as a rebate of premium or as interest charges or consideration or an amount in excess of permitted charges in connection with the loan or other credit transaction.

B. All of the acts necessary to provide and service credit life insurance and credit accident and sickness insurance may be performed within the same place of business in which is transacted the business giving rise to the loan or other credit transaction. (1960, c. 67, § 38.1-482.9; 1982, c. 223, § 38.2-3712; 1986, c. 562; 1992, c. 586.)

Delegation of legal duties to creditor. — A section of the State Corporation Commission's "Rules Governing Credit Life Insurance" which provides that an insurer delegating legal duties to a creditor "shall be responsible to see that such creditor discharges such duties in accordance with said laws and regulations," does not prohibit an insurer's delegation of duties, contrary to subsection (B) of this section. American Bankers Life Assurance Co. v. Division of Consumer Counsel, 220 Va. 773, 263 S.E.2d 867 (1980) (decided under former § 38.2-3712).

§ 38.2-3734. License requirements. — Any person who, in this Commonwealth, on behalf of an insurer licensed in this Commonwealth, solicits, negotiates, procures or effects individual or group policies of credit life insurance or credit accident and sickness insurance, shall first apply for and obtain a license from the Commission as either a life and health insurance agent or as a credit life and health insurance agent as defined in § 38.2-1800 of this title, and shall be required to be appointed to represent such insurer in this Commonwealth as set forth in § 38.2-1833. (1992, c. 586.)

§ 38.2-3735. Disclosure and readability. — A. If a creditor makes available to the debtors more than one plan of credit life insurance or more than one plan of credit accident and sickness insurance, all debtors must be informed of all such plans for which they are eligible. In the case of credit life insurance:

1. If a creditor offers a plan of insurance that insures the actual amount of unpaid indebtedness, the creditor shall also offer to the debtor a plan of insurance that insures only the actual amount of indebtedness less any unearned interest or finance charges; and

2. In the event that a plan of insurance that insures the actual amount of unpaid indebtedness is offered, the creditor shall provide to each debtor a disclosure form which shall clearly disclose the difference in premiums charged for a contract wherein the gross indebtedness is insured versus a contract wherein only the net indebtedness is insured. This disclosure shall include the differences between the amount financed, the monthly payment and the total charge for each type of insurance. The form shall be signed and dated by the debtor and the agent, if any, soliciting the application or the creditor's representative, if any, soliciting the enrollment request. A copy of this disclosure shall be given to the debtor, and a copy shall be made a part of the creditor's loan file.

Nothing contained in this subsection shall be construed to prohibit the creditor from combining such disclosure, in order to avoid redundancy, with other forms of disclosure required under state or federal law.

B. When elective credit insurance is offered, the borrower must be given written disclosure that purchase of credit insurance is not required and is not a factor in granting credit. The disclosure shall also include notice that the borrower has the right to use alternative coverage or to buy insurance elsewhere.

C. If the debtor is given a contract which includes a single premium payment to be charged for elective credit insurance, the debtor must be given:

1. A contract which does not include the elective credit insurance premium; or

2. A disclosure form which shall clearly disclose the difference in premiums charged for a contract with credit insurance and one without credit insurance.

This disclosure shall include the difference between the amount financed, the monthly payment and the charge for each kind of insurance. The form shall be signed and dated by the debtor and the agent, if any, soliciting the application or the creditor's representative, if any, soliciting the enrollment request. A copy of this disclosure shall be given to the debtor and a copy shall be made a part of the creditor's loan file.

Nothing contained in this subsection shall be construed to prohibit the creditor from combining such disclosure, in order to avoid redundancy, with other forms of disclosure required under state or federal law.

D. If credit life insurance or credit accident and sickness insurance is required as security for any indebtedness, the debtor shall have the option of (i) furnishing the required amount of insurance through existing policies of insurance owned or controlled by him or (ii) procuring and furnishing the required coverage through any insurer authorized to transact insurance in this Commonwealth. The creditor shall inform the debtor of this option in writing and shall obtain the debtor's signature acknowledging that he understands this option. Nothing contained in this subsection shall be construed to prohibit the creditor from combining such disclosure, in order to avoid redundancy, with other forms of disclosure required under state or federal law.

E. Readability. — The Commission shall not approve any form unless the policy or certificate is written in nontechnical, readily understandable language, using words of common everyday usage

A form shall be deemed acceptable under this section if the insurer certifies that the form achieves a Flesch Readability Score of forty or more, using the Flesch Readability Formula as set forth in Rudolf Flesch, The Art of Readable Writing (1949, as revised 1974), and certifies compliance with the guidelines set forth in this section. (1992, c. 586; 1999, c. 586.)

The 1999 amendment, in subsection A, inserted "if any" in two places in the third sentence of subdivision 2, and added the concluding paragraph; in subsection C, inserted "if any" in two places in the third sentence of subdivision 2, and added the concluding paragraph; added the last sentence in subsection D; in subsection E, added the last sentence, deleted the former subdivision 1, which read: "Each insurer is required to test the readability of its policies or certificates by use of the Flesch Readability Formula, as set forth in Rudolf Flesch, The Art of Readable Writing (1949, as revised 1974)," deleted the former subdivision 2, which read: "A total readability score of forty or more on the Flesch score is required; and," deleted the former subdivision 3, which read: "All policies or certificates within the scope of this section shall be filed with the Commission, accompanied by a certificate setting forth the Flesch score and certifying compliance with the guidelines set forth in this section," and added the concluding sentence.

§ 38.2-3736. Noncontributory coverage. — If no specific charge is made to the debtor for credit life or credit accident and sickness insurance, the Commission is granted discretion in applying the provisions of this chapter. Each company must comply with § 38.2-3725 and the filing letter must specifically request an exemption from Virginia law. For purposes of this section, it will be considered that the debtor is charged a specific amount for insurance if an identifiable charge for insurance is disclosed in the credit or other instrument furnished the debtor which sets out the financial elements of the credit transactions, or if there is a differential in finance, interest, service or other similar charges made to debtors who are in like circumstances, except for their insured or noninsured status. (1992, c. 586.)

§ 38.2-3737. Application. — A. No contract of insurance upon a debtor shall be made or effectuated unless at the time of the contract, the debtor, being of lawful age and competent to contract for insurance, applies for the insurance in writing on a form approved by the Commission.

B. The application or enrollment request shall be required to:

1. Contain the name and signature of the agent or creditor's representative, if any, who solicited the application or enrollment request;

2. Contain the name and address of the insurer and creditor; the name and age of the debtor(s); the premium, rate or amount payable by the debtor separately for credit life insurance and credit accident and sickness insurance; the type of insurance coverage provided; the date of application; and separately, the amount and term, including the effective and cancellation dates, of the insurance and loan contracts; and

3. Include the disclosure requirements set forth in subsections A, B, C and D of § 38.2-3735 unless such requirements have been separately disclosed in another form or forms approved by the Commission.

C. The application or enrollment request form shall be separate and apart from the loan or credit transaction papers and will refer exclusively to insurance coverage.

D. No individual or group credit life insurance or credit accident and sickness insurance application form shall contain a question of general good health unless the application form contains appropriate specific questions concerning the applicant's health history or medical treatment history.

E. Neither this section nor subsection B of § 38.2-3735 shall apply to credit life or credit accident and sickness insurance that will insure open-end monthly outstanding balance credit transactions if the following criteria are met:

1. The credit life insurance and credit accident and sickness insurance that will insure the open-end monthly outstanding balance credit transaction are offered to the debtor after the loan or credit transaction that it will insure has been approved by the creditor and has been effective at least seven days;

2. The solicitation for the insurance is by mail or telephone. The person making the solicitation shall not condition the future use or continuation of the open-end credit upon the purchase of credit life or credit accident and sickness insurance;

3. The creditor makes available only one plan of credit life insurance and one plan of credit accident and sickness insurance to the debtor;

4. The debtor is provided written confirmation of the insurance coverage within thirty days of the effective date of such coverage. The effective date of coverage shall begin on the date the solicitation is accepted; and

5. The individual policy or certificate has printed on it a notice stating that if, during a period of at least thirty days from the date that the policy or certificate is delivered to the policyowner or certificate holder, the policy or certificate is surrendered to the insurer or its agent with a written request for cancellation, the policy or certificate shall be void from the beginning and the insurer shall refund any premium paid for the policy or certificate. This statement shall be prominently included on the face page of the policy or certificate, and shall be printed in capital letters and in bold 12-point or larger type.

F. The following shall be applicable to open-end credit transactions by mail, telephone, or brochure solicitations, that are not excluded from the requirements of this section and of subsection B of § 38.2-3735 by subsection E, where the insurer is offering only one plan of credit life insurance or one plan of credit accident and sickness insurance:

1. Section 38.2-3735 shall not apply to such transactions, provided that the following disclosures are included in such solicitations, whether as part of the application or enrollment request or separately:

a. The name and address of the insurer(s) and creditor; and

b. A description of the coverage offered, including the amount of coverage, the premium rate for the insurance coverage offered, and a description of any exceptions, limitations, or restrictions applicable to such coverage.

2. Subsections B and D of this section shall not apply to such transactions, provided that the application or enrollment request utilized as part of such transaction:

a. Is printed in a type size of not less than eight-point type, one point leaded, notwithstanding the requirements set forth in subdivision D 5 of § 38.2-3724 regarding minimum type size for policies and certificates;

b. Contains a prominent statement that the insurance offered is optional, voluntary, or not required;

c. Contains no questions relating to insurability other than the debtor's age or date of birth and, if applicable, active employment status; and

d. If the disclosures required by subdivision 1 of this subsection are not included in the application or enrollment request, makes reference to such disclosures with sufficient information so as to assist the reader in locating such disclosures within the solicitation.

3. Each insurer proposing to utilize an application or enrollment request in such transactions shall file such form for approval by the Commission. If the insurer anticipates utilizing such application or enrollment form in more than one solicitation, the insurer shall submit, as part of its filing of such form, a certification signed by an officer of the insurer, stating that any such subsequent use of the application or enrollment form will utilize the same form number and will not vary in substance from the wording and format in which the form is submitted for approval. Upon approval of such application or enrollment form by the Commission, the insurer shall be permitted to utilize such form in various solicitation materials, provided that the application or enrollment form, when incorporated into such solicitation materials, has the same form number and wording substantially identical to that contained on the approved application or enrollment form.

G. Notwithstanding the provisions of subsection A, a contract of insurance may be made or effectuated in connection with a credit transaction between a creditor regulated pursuant to Chapter 4.01 (§ 6.1-225.1 et seq.) of Title 6.1 or 12 U.S.C. § 1751 et seq. and a debtor who is of lawful age, competent to contract for the insurance and a member of the creditor if:

1. The credit transaction and the solicitation for such insurance is effected by mail, telephone or other electronic means;

2. The purchase of credit insurance is not required by the creditor and is not a factor in granting the credit;

3. The creditor or insurer, within three business days after the credit transaction is effected, transmits to the debtor, either separately or with the documents that pertain to the credit transaction, an application or enrollment request form approved by the Commission which includes or to which is attached a prominent notice that clearly advises the debtor that unless he mails the completed and signed application or enrollment request to the creditor within forty-five days following the date of the credit transaction, all such coverage requested in connection with the credit transaction will be void from the beginning; and

4. In the event the debtor does not transmit the completed and signed application or enrollment request to the creditor within the time specified in subdivision 3, the full amount of the premium charged for the insurance is returned to or credited to the account of the debtor and written notice thereof is sent to the debtor within fifteen days of the date the policy or certificate is cancelled. (1992, c. 586; 1993, c. 627; 1994, c. 202; 1995, c. 167; 1999, c. 586.)

The 1999 amendment inserted "or creditor's representative, if any" in subdivision B 1, and substituted "the insurance coverage" for "each plan of insurance" in subdivision F 1 b.

§ **38.2-3738. What laws applicable.** — In the event of conflict between the provisions of this chapter and other provisions of this title, the provisions of this chapter shall be controlling. Subdivisions 1 and 2 of § 38.2-508 shall not apply to the insurance subject to the provisions of this chapter where application of these subdivisions would conflict with the requirements of any federal agency. (1960, c. 67, § 38.1-482.1; 1972, c. 527, § 38.2-3716; 1982, c. 223; 1986, c. 562; 1992, c. 586.)

CHAPTER 38.

COOPERATIVE NONPROFIT LIFE BENEFIT COMPANIES.

ARTICLE 1.

General Provisions.

§ **38.2-3800. Scope of chapter.** — This chapter applies to cooperative nonprofit life benefit companies as defined in § 38.2-3801 and to the classes of insurance and insurance benefits those companies are authorized to provide. (1952, c. 317, § 38.1-496; 1986, c. 562.)

§ **38.2-3801. Cooperative nonprofit life benefit company defined.** — A. Any company that (i) is organized without capital stock, (ii) has a representative form of government, (iii) conducts its business under the provisions of this chapter without profit and for the sole benefit of its members and their beneficiaries, (iv) issues benefit certificates or policies of life insurance, annuities, or accident and sickness insurance, or any combination of those classes of insurance, upon its members, and (v) maintains the reserves required in this chapter on all contracts issued by it to its members, shall be a cooperative nonprofit life benefit company.

B. As used in this chapter, *"company"* means a cooperative nonprofit life benefit company as defined in subsection A of this section. (Code 1950, § 38-467; 1952, c. 317, § 38.1-497; 1986, c. 562.)

§ **38.2-3802. Continuation of existing companies.** — Any company licensed and doing business in this Commonwealth on July 1, 1952, may continue to do business in accordance with the powers contained in its certificate of incorporation, subject to the provisions of this chapter, but no such company shall be permitted to extend its powers. (1952, c. 317, § 38.1-498; 1986, c. 562.)

§ **38.2-3803. Licensing of additional companies prohibited.** — Any company that was not licensed and doing business in this Commonwealth on July 1, 1952, shall not be issued a license to do the business of insurance in this Commonwealth. On or after July 1, 1952, only a renewal of a license held by the company for the preceding year will be issued. (1952, c. 317, § 38.1-499; 1986, c. 562.)

§ **38.2-3804. What laws applicable.** — All companies shall comply with all of the provisions of this title relating to insurance companies generally. In the event of conflict between the provisions of this chapter and other provisions of this title, the provisions of this chapter shall be controlling. (1952, c. 317, § 38.1-502; 1986, c. 562.)

§ **38.2-3805. General powers of company; limitation on increase in rates.** — Each company shall make a constitution, laws or bylaws for its government, the admission of its members, the management of its affairs and the fixing and readjustment of the rates of contribution of its members. It may change, add to, or amend the constitution, laws or bylaws and shall have the other powers necessary and incidental to effect the objects and purposes of the company. It may make refunds to its members from any surplus funds of the company, but it may only increase rates or make extra assessments against members whose contracts include provisions for rate increases and extra assessments. (Code 1950, § 38-478; 1952, c. 317, § 38.1-503; 1986, c. 562.)

§ **38.2-3806. Constitution and bylaws.** — Each company shall provide in its constitution, laws or bylaws for:
1. A representative form of government for the management of the company, to be carried on either with or without a lodge, or with membership in the lodge optional;
2. A legislative or governing body composed of its officers and representatives to be elected either by the adult members or by delegates elected directly or indirectly by the adult members; and
3. The manner of selecting representatives of the members for membership in its legislative body. (Code 1950, § 38-479; 1952, c. 317, § 38.1-504; 1986, c. 562.)

§ **38.2-3807. Governing body; board of directors.** — The governing body of each company shall meet at least once every four years. Meetings of the governing body may be held in any state where the company is authorized to do business. The members of the governing body shall not vote by proxy.
A board of directors to conduct the business of the company shall be elected by the governing body for a period of not more than four years or until the next quadrennial meeting of the body. The board of directors shall elect the officers to conduct the business of the company under its direction. No officer shall be elected for a period beyond that for which the board of directors has been elected. (Code 1950, § 38-480; 1952, c. 317, § 38.1-505; 1986, c. 562.)

§ **38.2-3808. Filing copies of constitution and bylaws.** — Each company shall file with the Commission a duly certified copy of its constitution, laws or bylaws and all amendments or additions. Printed copies of the constitution, laws or bylaws, certified by the secretary or corresponding officer of the company, shall be prima facie evidence of their legal adoption and filing. (Code 1950, § 38-481; 1952, c. 317, § 38.1-506; 1986, c. 562.)

§ 38.2-3809. How a company may become legal reserve life insurer.

— Any company filing with the Commission a resolution of its board of directors or similar body, or of its legislative body, making a request to become a legal reserve life insurer, upon submitting proof satisfactory to the Commission that the request is properly authorized and that the condition of its business qualifies it under the laws of this Commonwealth to be classed as a legal reserve life insurer, shall become a legal reserve life insurer under the name and the plan provided by proper amendment of its charter or certificate of incorporation. (Code 1950, § 38-477; 1952, c. 317, § 38.1-507; 1986, c. 562.)

§ 38.2-3810. Institutions maintainable; company a charitable institution.

— Any company may maintain homes for aged members, or children's homes, hospitals or recreational centers, or any other charitable institution, and may provide for the erection of monuments or memorials to deceased members. Such a company is hereby classified as a charitable institution. (Code 1950, § 38-482; 1952, c. 317, § 38.1-508; 1986, c. 562.)

§ 38.2-3811. Benefits not subject to process.

— Any money, other benefit, charity, relief or aid to be paid, provided or rendered by any company shall not be liable to attachment, garnishment or other process, or be seized, taken, appropriated or applied by any legal or equitable process or operation of law to pay any debt or liability of a member, his beneficiary, or any other person who may have a right thereunder, either before or after payment. (Code 1950, § 38-493; 1952, c. 317, § 38.1-510; 1986, c. 562.)

§ 38.2-3812. Tax on gross premium receipts.

— The officers of each company shall, at the time of making the annual statement, file with the Commission a sworn statement of its gross premium receipts collected from members residing in this Commonwealth for the preceding year ending December 31. Each company shall pay into the state treasury by March 1 of each year, a tax of one percent on its collected gross premiums. The tax shall be in lieu of all other taxes, state, county or municipal, based on such gross premium receipts. No city, town, municipality or other subdivision of the Commonwealth shall impose any license fee on the company or any of its agents for the privilege of conducting business in any portion of this Commonwealth. In determining such gross premium receipts, the company shall not take credit for any expenditures. (Code 1950, § 38-494; 1952, c. 317, § 38.1-511; 1986, c. 562; 1987, cc. 565, 655.)

§ 38.2-3813. Suits against company.

— A suit or an action at law may be instituted against any company in any county or city in this Commonwealth. (Code 1950, § 38-495; 1950, p. 242; 1952, c. 317, § 38.1-512; 1986, c. 562.)

ARTICLE 2.

Reserves, Policies and Benefits.

§ 38.2-3814. Contracts in writing; fees.

— All contracts of any company for insurance or other benefits shall be in writing. No company or any of its officers or agents shall include in the sum charged a member, any fee, compensation, or other charge. However, a local medical examiner's fee and a policy fee on accident and sickness contracts may be charged. (Code 1950, § 38-484; 1952, c. 317, § 38.1-514; 1986, c. 562.)

§ 38.2-3815. What benefits policies may provide. — Any company may provide for (i) stipulated premiums, (ii) death, annuity, endowment and disability benefits, and (iii) cash surrender and loan values to an amount not exceeding the reserve, or its equivalent, in paid-up or extended term insurance, based upon the mortality standards set forth in this chapter. (Code 1950, § 38-483; 1952, c. 317, § 38.1-515; 1986, c. 562.)

§ 38.2-3816. Policies companies may issue; reserves required; provisions concerning increase of rates and extra assessments. — Any company may issue contracts of life, accident and sickness insurance or combinations of them. The reserves for such policies or contracts shall be based upon the American Experience Table of Mortality, with an interest assumption of no more than four percent, or some higher standard, or upon any minimum standard allowed by law in this Commonwealth for legal reserve life insurers. It may provide in its laws or bylaws and membership contracts that the rates shall not be increased or extra assessments made. (Code 1950, § 38-488; 1952, c. 317, § 38.1-516; 1986, c. 562.)

§ 38.2-3817. Paid-up insurance or extended term insurance. — Any company shall provide for automatic paid-up or extended term insurance in the event of the default in premium payments of any contract that has been in force for at least two years from the date of issue. The amount of such insurance shall not exceed the amount which the reserve that is credited to the member will purchase. The company shall carry the liability on its books. (Code 1950, § 38-486; 1952, c. 317, § 38.1-517; 1986, c. 562.)

§ 38.2-3818. Officers and members not individually liable for payment. — Officers and members of the supreme, grand or any subordinate body of any company shall not be individually liable for the payment of any disability or death or other benefits provided for in the laws, bylaws and contracts of the company. Benefits shall be payable out of the funds of the company and in the manner provided by its laws and bylaws. (Code 1950, § 38-487; 1952, c. 317, § 38.1-519; 1986, c. 562.)

CHAPTER 39.

MUTUAL ASSESSMENT LIFE, ACCIDENT AND SICKNESS INSURERS.

ARTICLE 1.

General Provisions.

§ 38.2-3900. Scope of chapter. — This chapter applies to mutual assessment life, accident and sickness insurers and to the classes of insurance written by these insurers. (1985, c. 400, § 38.1-549.1; 1986, c. 562.)

§ 38.2-3901. Definitions. — As used in this chapter:
"Mutual assessment life, accident and sickness insurance" means life, accident and sickness insurance and annuities provided by an insurer which has a right to assess its members for contributions and which is licensed under this chapter.
"Mutual assessment life, accident and sickness insurer" means a nonstock corporation that provides life, accident or sickness insurance or annuity contracts for which the following provisions are applicable:
1. All benefits payable to beneficiaries are mainly provided for by (i) assessments upon members made when needed by the insurer, or (ii) advance premiums paid at fixed dates, with the right reserved by the insurer to make additional assessments; or
2. If definite periodic premiums are used without the right to make additional assessments, premiums must be sufficient to pay average claims in accordance with standards applicable to insurers licensed pursuant to Chapter 10 (§ 38.2-1000 et seq.) of this title. (1985, c. 400, § 38.1-549.2; 1986, c. 562.)

§ 38.2-3902. Classes of insurance that may be written by mutual assessment life, accident and sickness insurers. — The following classes of insurance can be written by mutual assessment life, accident and sickness insurers:
Category A
1. Life insurance as defined in § 38.2-102;
2. Industrial life insurance as defined in § 38.2-104; and
3. Accident and sickness insurance as defined in § 38.2-109 except Medicare supplement insurance as defined in § 38.2-3600.
Category B
1. Credit life insurance as defined in § 38.2-103;
2. Variable life insurance as defined in § 38.2-105;

3. Credit accident and sickness insurance as defined in § 38.2-108; and
4. Medicare supplement insurance as defined in § 38.2-3600.
Category C
1. Annuities as defined in § 38.2-106; and
2. Variable annuities as defined in § 38.2-107. (1985, c. 400, § 38.1-549.3; 1986, c. 562.)

§ 38.2-3903. What laws applicable. — Except as provided in this section, all mutual assessment life, accident and sickness insurers shall comply with all provisions of this title relating to insurers generally. Until July 1, 1990, those classes of insurance specified in Category A of § 38.2-3902 shall be exempt from this title, except this chapter and Chapters 5 and 6 of this title. In the event of conflict between the provisions of this chapter and other provisions of this title, the provisions of this chapter shall be controlling. (1985, c. 400, § 38.1-549.4; 1986, c. 562.)

§ 38.2-3904. Conversion of mutual assessment life, accident and sickness insurers. — A. Any mutual assessment life, accident and sickness insurer which chooses to remove itself from the provisions of this chapter by becoming an insurer licensed pursuant to Chapter 10 (§ 38.2-1000 et seq.) of this title may do so by meeting the requirements of that chapter. When applying for a license pursuant to Chapter 10, an insurer shall submit an application to the Commission that shows that each requirement of Chapter 10 has been met. If the applicant does not meet these requirements, the applicant may submit for approval a plan that includes a schedule for meeting these requirements. The schedule must provide for compliance with these requirements within five years of the approval of the application. The Commission may grant an additional period in order to achieve compliance with the requirements of Chapter 10 after an informal hearing.
B. If the Commission approves the application, the insurer shall have all the rights, privileges and responsibilities of a licensed insurer not subject to the provisions of this chapter.
C. The Commission, upon failure of the applicant to comply with the terms of an approved schedule, may require the applicant to adhere to the requirements of this chapter. (1985, c. 400, § 38.1-549.5; 1986, c. 562.)

ARTICLE 2.

Organization and Licensing of Companies.

§ 38.2-3905. Incorporation of companies. — Any insurer that was licensed and transacting in this Commonwealth the business of mutual assessment life, accident and sickness insurance on July 1, 1985, may continue to transact that business in accordance with its license. (1985, c. 400, § 38.1-549.6; 1986, c. 562.)

§ 38.2-3906. Licensing of additional companies prohibited. — Any insurer that was not licensed and engaged in the business of mutual assessment life, accident and sickness insurance in this Commonwealth under the provisions of former Title 38.1 on July 1, 1952, shall not be issued a license pursuant to this chapter to transact the business of insurance in this Commonwealth. On or after that date a license shall not be issued except for renewal of a license held by the insurer for the preceding year. (1985, c. 400, § 38.1-549.7; 1986, c. 562.)

§ 38.2-3907. Directors; terms; annual meetings; voting; executive committee. — A. As provided in its certificate of incorporation and as provided in its bylaws, the management of any mutual assessment life, accident and sickness insurer shall be vested in a board of at least five directors, each of whom shall be a member of the insurer. Each director shall hold office for one year or for a longer term if specified by the bylaws, and thereafter until his successor is elected and has qualified. Vacancies on the board may be filled for the unexpired term by the remaining directors.

B. The annual meeting of the members of the insurer shall be held as provided by the certificate of incorporation or the bylaws. A quorum shall consist of the larger of ten members or the number of members specified by either the certificate of incorporation or bylaws. In all meetings of members, each member of the insurer shall be entitled to one vote, or a number of votes based upon insurance in force, the number of policies held, or the amount of premiums paid as provided in the bylaws of the insurer. Votes by proxy may be received in accordance with the certificate of incorporation or the bylaws. The date of the annual meeting shall be stated in the policy, or notice of the date and location of the annual meeting shall be provided annually.

C. Notwithstanding the provisions of the charter of any insurer to the contrary, upon a resolution adopted by the board of directors of the insurer and approved by a majority of its members present in person or by proxy, the directors of the insurer may be divided into classes, and only a portion may be elected each year. Pursuant to the provisions of § 13.1-869 the directors may appoint an executive committee to exercise the powers and perform the duties set out in that section. (1985, c. 400, § 38.1-549.8; 1986, c. 562.)

§ **38.2-3908. Officers.** — Unless the certificate of incorporation provides otherwise, the directors shall elect from their number a president and may elect a chairman, and shall also elect a secretary and a treasurer and any additional officers as they determine necessary, who may or may not be members of the insurer. The offices of secretary and treasurer may be held by one person. Unless otherwise provided in the certificate of incorporation, the term of these officers shall be not less than one year nor more than three years or until their successors are elected or qualified. (1985, c. 400, § 38.1-549.9; 1986, c. 562.)

§ **38.2-3909. Inspection of books and papers.** — The books and papers of the insurer shall be open for examination by members or their representatives at all reasonable times. (1985, c. 400, § 38.1-549.10; 1986, c. 562.)

ARTICLE 3.

Policy Provisions and Benefits.

§ **38.2-3910. Policy forms to be filed.** — Every mutual assessment life, accident and sickness insurer shall file with the Commission a copy of all policy forms and standard endorsements which the insurer intends to use. These companies shall be exempt from form approval requirements regarding those lines of insurance specified in Category A of § 38.2-3902 until July 1, 1990. (1985, c. 400, § 38.1-549.11; 1986, c. 562.)

§ **38.2-3911. Time limit on certain defenses.** — Every insurance policy or contract shall contain a provision that after two years from the effective date of the policy or contract, only fraudulent misstatements in the application may be used to void the policy or contract or deny any claim for a loss incurred or a disability that starts after the two-year period. This provision may be omitted if the incontestable clause referred to in § 38.2-3912 is included. (1985, c. 400, § 38.1-549.12; 1986, c. 562.)

§ 38.2-3912. Incontestability of policies. — Every insurance policy or contract shall contain a provision that it shall be incontestable after it has been in force during the lifetime of the insured for two years from its date of issuance, except for nonpayment of the policy's assessments or premiums. In the case of life policies and at the option of the insurer, provisions relating to benefits in the event of disability and provisions which grant additional insurance specifically against death by accident or accidental means, may be excepted in the incontestability provision. This provision may be omitted if the time limit on the certain defense clause specified in § 38.2-3911 is included. (1985, c. 400, § 38.1-549.13; 1986, c. 562; 1987, c. 520.)

§ 38.2-3913. Required grace periods. — Each insurance policy shall have a provision that the insured is entitled to a thirty-one-day period within which the payment of any premium or assessment after the first payment may be made. At the option of the insurer this may be subject to a reasonable interest charge for the number of days of grace elapsing before the payment of the premium or assessment. The provision shall also state that during the grace period the policy shall continue in full force, but if a claim arises under the policy during the grace period before the overdue premium or assessment is paid, the amount of such premium or assessment, with applicable interest, may be deducted from any amount payable under the policy in settlement. (1985, c. 400, § 38.1-549.14; 1986, c. 562.)

§ 38.2-3914. Policy to specify amount of payment and when to be paid. — Each policy shall specify the sum of money payable upon the occurrence of the insured risk. Each policy shall also state that payment shall be made within thirty days after showing proof of the occurrence of the insured risk. (1985, c. 400, § 38.1-549.15; 1986, c. 562.)

ARTICLE 4.

Insurance Transactions.

§ 38.2-3915. Assessment contract. — Contracts issued by a mutual assessment life, accident and sickness insurer shall be on forms prescribed by the insurer and shall be substantially uniform among members of the respective classes of insurance written by the insurer. Each member shall pay his pro rata share of all losses or damages sustained, expenses of operations of the insurer, and the maintenance of an adequate surplus to policyowners as determined by the board of directors. Periodic assessments may be collected as advance premiums, or by past assessments, or by both methods. The amount of assessments shall be established by the board of directors of the insurer. When a contract is subject to assessment, the contingent liability of each member of an insurer shall be clearly stated in the contract. Contracts omitting the right of contingent assessment shall be deemed to be nonassessable. (1985, c. 400, § 38.1-549.16; 1986, c. 562.)

§ 38.2-3916. Classification of risks; rates. — Any insurer writing mutual assessment life, accident and sickness insurance may classify the risks insured against, and fix the rate of assessment of premium for such insurance in accordance with the classifications. (1985, c. 400, § 38.1-549.17; 1986, c. 562.)

§ 38.2-3917. Right to limit assessment liability; when contingent assessment liability waived. — Any mutual assessment life, accident and sickness insurer having a surplus to policyowners of at least $100,000 may limit the contingent assessment liability of members, or classes of members, to an amount not more than 1 additional current annual assessment. Any insurer having surplus to policyowners of at least $300,000 may issue contracts omitting the right to make contingent assessment against members if reserves for these contracts are established and maintained in the same manner as would be required by an insurer licensed pursuant to Chapter 10 (§ 38.2-1000 et seq.) of this title. Contracts so issued shall be treated in all respects as nonassessment contracts. (1985, c. 400, § 38.1-549.18; 1986, c. 562.)

§ 38.2-3918. Notice of assessment; how given. — After an assessment is made, the insurer shall give each member subject to the assessment written notice stating the amount of the assessment and the date when payment is due. Except where the provisions of the bylaws or the policy provide otherwise, the time of payment shall not be less than thirty days nor more than sixty days from the service of the notice. This notice may be served personally or mailed with the United States Postal Service. If sent by mail, notice shall be considered given at the time of mailing and shall be sent to the member at his address shown on the insurer's records. (1985, c. 400, § 38.1-549.19; 1986, c. 562.)

§ 38.2-3919. Agents' licenses required. — A. Except as provided in subsection B, each individual who is a resident of this Commonwealth who desires to obtain a license to solicit, negotiate or effect any of the classes of insurance specified in § 38.2-3902 shall obtain that license only when that individual has passed a written examination prescribed by the Commission.

B. Any individual who is licensed prior to July 1, 1990, and whose license is restricted to the classes of insurance specified in Category A of § 38.2-3902 shall be exempted from the written examination provision noted above. (1985, c. 400, § 38.1-549.20; 1986, c. 562.)

ARTICLE 5.

Financial Provisions.

§ 38.2-3920. Surplus to policyowners. — A. A mutual assessment life, accident and sickness insurer shall have a minimum surplus to policyowners of $100,000.

B. In order to write the classes of insurance referred to in Category C of § 38.2-3902, minimum surplus to policyowners shall be $800,000. (1985, c. 400, § 38.1-549.21; 1986, c. 562.)

§ 38.2-3921. Limitation on single risk to be assumed. — No single risk shall be assumed by a mutual assessment life, accident and sickness insurer if the risk exceeds fifteen percent of the company's total surplus to policyowners. Any risk or portion of any risk that has been reinsured in accordance with § 38.2-3922 shall be deducted in determining the limitation of risk prescribed by this section. For the purposes of this section the amount of surplus to policyowners shall be determined on the basis of the last sworn statement of the insurer, or the last report of examination filed with the Commission, whichever is more recent at the time the risk is assumed. Mutual assessment life, accident and sickness insurers licensed on July 1, 1985, shall conform to this limitation by July 1, 1990. Until July 1, 1986, the single risk limit, after deducting for reinsurance, shall be twenty-five percent of surplus to policyowners. Between July 1, 1986, and July 1, 1988, single risk limits, after deducting for reinsurance, shall be twenty percent of surplus to policyowners. This section shall not apply to insurance coverages defined in §§ 38.2-108 and

38.2-109 and Medicare supplement insurance defined in § 38.2-3600. (1985, c. 400, § 38.1-549.22; 1986, c. 562.)

§ 38.2-3922. Reinsurance. — Any mutual assessment life, accident and sickness insurer may reinsure the whole or any part of its risks with any solvent insurer licensed in this Commonwealth or licensed in any other state having standards of solvency, at least equal to those required in this Commonwealth. However, the reinsurance shall be ceded without contingent liability on the part of the reinsured insurer. Any mutual assessment life, accident and sickness insurer having a surplus in excess of $800,000 may accept or assume reinsurance from any licensed insurer. (1985, c. 400, § 38.1-549.23; 1986, c. 562.)

§ 38.2-3923. Reserves required. — In addition to providing for claims incurred but not settled, mutual assessment life, accident and sickness insurers shall maintain the following reserve liabilities:
1. Life policies written with the right to make additional assessments shall have reserves established as a single group in the same manner as group annual renewable term insurance is reserved for insurers licensed pursuant to Chapter 10 (§ 38.2-1000 et seq.) of this title.
2. Life or annuity policies written without the right to make additional assessments shall have reserves established using the standard valuation provisions required of insurers licensed under Chapter 10 of this title issuing similar types of policies.
3. Accident and sickness policies shall have reserves established in accordance with regulations promulgated by the Commission for insurers licensed pursuant to Chapter 10 of this title.
4. The foregoing reserve computations for statutory accounting purposes shall be applicable to all policies hereafter in existence and shall supersede any separate reserve requirement or separate mortuary funds that have been previously used, pursuant to statute, custom or policy provision. (1985, c. 400, § 38.1-549.24; 1986, c. 562.)

CHAPTER 40.

Burial Societies.

§ 38.2-4000. Societies to which chapter applies. — The provisions of this chapter apply to every person designated as a "burial society." A *"burial society"* is any person engaged in the business of providing benefits for any payment of funeral, burial or other expenses of deceased members, by levying assessments or dues that are collected or are to be collected from the members of the society, or from the members of a class of the society. (Code 1950, § 38-143; 1952, c. 317, § 38.1-550; 1986, c. 562.)

§ 38.2-4001. Society may be incorporated. — Any existing burial society licensed and operating in this Commonwealth that is an unincorporated association may be incorporated under the provisions of Article 3 (§ 13.1-818 et seq.) of Chapter 10 of Title 13.1 and, except as otherwise provided in this title, shall be subject to all the general restrictions and shall have all the general powers imposed and conferred upon such corporations by law. All burial societies shall be under the supervision and control of the Commission. (Code 1950, §§ 38-145, 38-146; 1952, c. 317, § 38.1-551; 1956, c. 431; 1986, c. 562.)

§ 38.2-4002. Continuation of existing societies. — Any burial society that was licensed and operating as a burial society on July 1, 1952, in this Commonwealth may continue to operate as a burial society as long as it complies with the provisions of this chapter and all other applicable statutes. (1952, c. 317, § 38.1-552; 1986, c. 562.)

§ 38.2-4003. Licensing of additional societies prohibited. — Any burial society that was not licensed and operating as a burial society in this Commonwealth on July 1, 1952, shall not be issued a license as a burial society in this Commonwealth. On or after July 1, 1952, only a renewal of a license held by a society for the preceding year will be issued. (1952, c. 317, § 38.1-553; 1986, c. 562.)

§ 38.2-4004. What laws applicable. — All burial societies shall comply with all of the provisions of this title relating to insurance companies generally. In the event of conflict between the provisions of this chapter and other provisions of this title, the provisions of this chapter shall be controlling. (Code 1950, §§ 38-145, 38-146; 1952, c. 317, § 38.1-554; 1986, c. 562.)

§ 38.2-4005. License may be renewed annually. — Each license to a burial society shall expire on the June 30 next occurring after its effective date and may be renewed by the Commission annually. (Code 1950, § 38-146; 1952, c. 317, § 38.1-556; 1978, c. 4; 1986, c. 562.)

§ 38.2-4006. Annual meeting. — Each burial society shall hold, within the city or county in which the principal office is located in this Commonwealth, a stated annual meeting of its members, or representatives of local boards or subordinate bodies, subject to any regulations, restrictions and provisions the constitution or bylaws of the society may provide. (Code 1950, §§ 38-145, 38-455; 1952, c. 317, §§ 38.1-531, 38.1-555; 1986, c. 562.)

§ 38.2-4007. Adoption of bylaws. — Each burial society now authorized to do business in this Commonwealth shall, before the adoption of any bylaw or amendment, mail the proposed bylaw or amendment to the members and directors of the society, together with a notice of the time and place when the proposed bylaw or amendment will be considered. (Code 1950, §§ 38-145, 38-456; 1952, c. 317, §§ 38.1-532, 38.1-555; 1986, c. 562.)

§ 38.2-4008. Fidelity bond required. — The officers of each burial society who are charged with the duty of handling its funds shall, before receiving any funds, file with the Commission a surety bond with corporate security approved by the Commission. The bond shall be not less than $10,000 nor more than $100,000, to be fixed by the Commission. The bond shall secure to the society and its members the faithful performance of its officers' duties and a proper accounting of its funds. (Code 1950, § 38-148; 1952, c. 317, § 38.1-558; 1986, c. 562.)

§ 38.2-4009. Inspection of books and papers. — The books and papers of the burial society shall be open for examination by members or their representatives at all reasonable times. (Code 1950, §§ 38-145, 38-457; 1952, c. 317, §§ 38.1-533, 38.1-555; 1986, c. 562.)

§ 38.2-4010. Accumulation of reserve for an emergency fund. — A. In addition to provision for liability incurred on account of claims reported but not settled, claims incurred but not reported, and premiums, dues or assessments collected in advance, every company shall accumulate and maintain a reserve for an emergency fund, which in the preparation of financial statements shall be considered a liability of the corporation, of at least $10,000.

B. Each burial society shall, in each calendar year, add to that reserve for an emergency fund at least five percent of its net receipts from premiums, dues or assessments from policies of life insurance until the total accumulated reserve fund equals twenty percent of the total benefits provided in the outstanding certificates of life insurance. However, when the corporation has issued policies of life insurance on a legal reserve basis, the net receipts from those policies shall not be considered in the calculation of the reserve for an emergency fund, but the burial society shall be required to maintain only the reserve provided for in the certificates. (Code 1950, §§ 38-149, 38-461; 1952, c. 317, §§ 38.1-534, 38.1-559; 1986, c. 562.)

§ 38.2-4011. Maintenance of reserve for an emergency fund. — When the reserve for an emergency fund accumulated in accordance with the provisions of § 38.2-4010 equals the maximum amount provided in subsection B of that section, it shall be maintained at not less than that amount. However, no burial society shall be required, in any one year, to set aside more than five percent of its net receipts from premiums, dues or assessments from certificates of life insurance, other than certificates issued on a legal reserve basis. (Code 1950, § 38-462; 1952, c. 317, § 38.1-535; 1986, c. 562.)

§ 38.2-4012. Disposition of reserve for an emergency fund; discontinuance of business; receiver. — The reserve for an emergency fund required by § 38.2-4010, together with the income earned on that fund, shall be a trust fund for the payment of death claims. Whenever the reserve for an emergency fund exceeds the amount of the maximum sum provided by the certificates issued and in force by the society, the investment income generated by the reserve or an emergency fund shall be added back into that fund. It may apply that excess, or any portion of that excess, (i) in reduction of assessments upon certificate holders, or (ii) in any other equitable division or apportionment that its rules or contracts provide for the payment of claims. When any society discontinues business, delinquency proceedings against the society may be instituted and conducted as provided in Chapter 15 (§ 38.2-1500 et seq.) of this title. In the delinquency proceedings, any unexhausted portion of the reserve for an emergency fund shall be used in payment of accrued claims upon certificates. If this amount is insufficient to pay the claims in full, then the payment of the claims shall be on a pro rata basis; and if a balance remains, the payment of claims shall then be made in the order of their occurrence. Any remaining balance shall be distributed among the members in proportion to their respective premium payments during the latest full year of active business of the society. (Code 1950, § 38-464; 1952, c. 317, § 38.1-537; 1986, c. 562.)

§ **38.2-4013. Certificates of membership.** — Each burial society shall issue certificates of membership to each member of the society. Each certificate shall state the amount of the benefit payable and the name of the beneficiary. (Code 1950, § 38-150; 1952, c. 317, § 38.1-560; 1986, c. 562.)

§ **38.2-4014. Required grace period.** — Each certificate shall have a provision that the certificate holder is entitled to a grace period of thirty-one days within which the payment of any call or assessment may be paid after the first month. The provision shall also state that during the grace period the certificate shall continue in full force, but if a claim arises under the policy during the grace period but before the call or assessment is paid, the amount of the call or assessment may be deducted from the amount payable under the certificate. (Code 1950, §§ 38-145, 38-449; 1952, c. 317, §§ 38.1-543, 38.1-555; 1986, c. 562.)

§ **38.2-4015. Certificate to specify amount of payment and when to be paid.** — Each certificate issued by any burial society shall specify the sum of money payable upon the occurrence of the risk insured against. The amount payable shall not be larger than one assessment upon the entire membership. Each certificate shall also state that within thirty days after due proof of the occurrence of the insured risk, payment shall be made. (Code 1950, §§ 38-145, 38-450; 1952, c. 317, §§ 38.1-544, 38.1-555; 1986, c. 562.)

§ **38.2-4016. Payments become liens on society's property.** — Upon the occurrence of the risk insured against, the burial society shall be obligated to the beneficiary for payment of the claim unless the contract is invalid because of fraud or other reason. This indebtedness shall be a lien upon all the property, effects and bills receivable of the society. This indebtedness shall have priority over all future incurred indebtedness, except as provided in this chapter in the case of the distribution of assets of an insolvent corporation, and as to rights of third parties. (Code 1950, §§ 38-145, 38-451; 1952, c. 317, §§ 38.1-545, 38.1-555; 1986, c. 562.)

§ **38.2-4017. Notice of assessment.** — Each notice of assessment made by any burial society upon any of its members shall state the cause and purpose of the assessment. (Code 1950, §§ 38-145, 38-453; 1952, c. 317, §§ 38.1-547, 38.1-555; 1986, c. 562.)

§ **38.2-4018. Liability on officers and directors for failing to levy assessments.** — The officers or directors of any society who, after due proof of death has been filed, for sixty days refuse or neglect to levy an assessment to pay a claim not disputed by reason of fraud or validity when the death or emergency fund is insufficient to pay the claim, shall be liable to the beneficiary of the certificate. The liability of the officers or directors shall be for a sum not exceeding the face amount of the claim. (Code 1950, §§ 38-145, 38-454; 1952, c. 317, §§ 38.1-549, 38.1-555; 1986, c. 562.)

§ **38.2-4019. Beneficiaries.** — No person other than a wife, husband, relative by blood to the fourth degree, father-in-law, mother-in-law, son-in-law, daughter-in-law, stepfather, stepmother, stepchild, or child by legal adoption of the member, or one who is dependent upon the member or one who has an insurable interest in the life of the member as described in § 38.2-301, shall be named a beneficiary of the member's certificate. Within the above limitations, each member shall have the right to designate his beneficiary and to change his beneficiary, upon due notice to the society. If the beneficiary is not living or if no allowable beneficiary has been designated, any proceeds otherwise payable shall be payable to the member's estate. (Code 1950, § 38-151; 1952, c. 317, § 38.1-561; 1986, c. 562.)

§ 38.2-4020. When certificate invalid. — A certificate of membership shall be invalid if:

1. The certificate holder was ill at the time the certificate was procured;
2. Any person concerned in the procurement of the certificate had reason to believe that the illness existed at that time;
3. The illness continued to the death of the certificate holder and was a contributing cause of death;
4. Health questions were not asked on the application for coverage; and
5. The certificate holder died within sixty days from the date the certificate was issued. (Code 1950, § 38-153; 1952, c. 317, § 38.1-562; 1986, c. 562.)

§ 38.2-4021. Interest in benefits; assignability; liability to attachment, etc. — No beneficiary shall have or obtain any vested interest in a benefit until the benefit has become due and payable upon the death of the member. No certificate of membership in any burial society, nor any interest or rights in the certificate shall be assigned unless the assignment is to a person authorized by § 38.2-4019 to be named as a beneficiary except for the purpose of funding or paying for a preneed funeral contract as defined in § 54.1-2800, notwithstanding the provisions of § 38.2-4022, and so long as such assignment is revocable by the assignor. No money or other benefit provided by any burial society shall be liable to attachment, garnishment or other process, or be seized, taken, appropriated or applied by any legal or equitable process or operation of law to pay any debt or liability of a member or beneficiary, or any other person who may have a right to the benefit, either before or after payment. (Code 1950, § 38-152; 1952, c. 317, § 38.1-563; 1983, c. 94; 1986, c. 562; 1987, c. 647; 1989, c. 684.)

Law Review. — For article on the need for reform of and a proposed revision of Virginia's exemption statutes, see 37 Wash. & Lee L. Rev. 127 (1980).

§ 38.2-4022. Certain contracts with undertakers, etc., forbidden. — No burial society shall contract to pay or pay benefits provided under certificates of membership, to any official or designated undertaker or mortician or person engaged in the business of conducting and servicing funerals, so as to deprive the representatives or family of the deceased member from, or in any way control them in, obtaining funeral supplies and services in an open competitive market. (Code 1950, § 38-155; 1952, c. 317, § 38.1-565; 1986, c. 562.)

CHAPTER 41.

FRATERNAL BENEFIT SOCIETIES.

ARTICLE 1.

Structure and Purpose.

§ **38.2-4100. Fraternal benefit societies.** — Any society, order or supreme lodge without capital stock, including one exempted under the provisions of subdivision 6 of subsection A of § 38.2-4135 of this chapter, conducted solely for the benefit of its members and their beneficiaries and not for profit, operated on a lodge system with ritualistic form of work, having a representative form of government, and providing benefits in accordance with this chapter, is hereby declared to be a fraternal benefit society. (Code 1950, §§ 38-254, 38.1-569; 1952, c. 317, § 38.1-638.1; 1968, c. 654; 1986, c. 562.)

Society has only such power as is conferred by statute. — A fraternal society organized under the laws of Virginia has only such power and such authority as the statute governing its organization confers upon it. Bryant v. Tunstall, 177 Va. 1, 12 S.E.2d 784 (1941).

Beneficial and benevolent associations are not organized for the purpose of making money, but for fraternal and benevolent objects. City of Petersburg v. Petersburg Benevolent Mechanics Ass'n, 78 Va. 431 (1884); Supreme Lodge Knights of Honor v. Oeters, 95 Va. 610, 29 S.E. 322 (1898); United Moderns v. Rathbun, 104 Va. 736, 52 S.E. 552 (1906).

Chapter does not apply to Ku Klux Klan. — As the Ku Klux Klan is not a fraternal beneficiary association and does no insurance business, this chapter had no application to it. Knights of KKK v. Commonwealth ex rel. SCC, 138 Va. 500, 122 S.E. 122 (1924).

Company held not a fraternal benefit society. — See Fireman's Mut. Aid Ass'n v. Commonwealth, 166 Va. 34, 184 S.E. 189, cert. denied, 298 U.S. 677, 56 S. Ct. 941, 80 L. Ed. 1398 (1936).

§ 38.2-4101. Lodge system. — A. A society is operating on the lodge system if it has a supreme governing body and subordinate lodges into which members are elected, initiated or admitted in accordance with its laws, rules and rituals. Subordinate lodges shall be required by the laws of the society to hold regular meetings at least once each month in furtherance of the purposes of the society.

B. A society may, at its option, organize and operate lodges for children under the minimum age for adult membership. Membership and initiation in local lodges shall not be required of such children, nor shall they have a voice or vote in the management of the society. (Code 1950, §§ 38-255, 38.1-570; 1952, c. 317, § 38.1-638.2; 1968, c. 654; 1986, c. 562.)

§ 38.2-4102. Representative form of government. — A society has a representative form of government when:

1. It has a supreme governing body constituted in one of the following ways:

a. Assembly. — The supreme governing body is an assembly composed of delegates elected directly by the members or at intermediate assemblies or conventions of members or their representatives, together with other delegates as may be prescribed in the society's laws. A society may provide for election of delegates by mail. The elected delegates shall constitute a majority in number and shall not have less than two-thirds of the votes and not less than the number of votes required to amend the society's laws. The assembly shall be elected, meet at least once every four years, and elect a board of directors to conduct the business of the society between meetings of the assembly. Vacancies on the board of directors between elections may be filled in the manner prescribed by the society's laws.

b. Direct election. — The supreme governing body is a board composed of persons elected by the members, either directly or by their representatives in intermediate assemblies, and any other persons prescribed in the society's laws.

A society may provide for election of the board by mail. Each term of a board member may not exceed four years. Vacancies on the board between elections may be filled in the manner prescribed by the society's laws. Those persons elected to the board shall constitute a majority in number and not less than the number of votes required to amend the society's laws. A person filling the unexpired term of an elected board member shall be considered to be an elected member. The board shall meet at least quarterly to conduct the business of the society.

2. The officers of the society are elected either by the supreme governing body or by the board of directors.

3. Only benefit members are eligible for election to the supreme governing body, the board of directors or any intermediate assembly.

4. Each voting member shall have one vote; no vote may be cast by proxy. (Code 1950, §§ 38-256, 38.1-571; 1952, c. 317, § 38.1-638.3; 1968, c. 654; 1986, c. 562.)

§ 38.2-4103. Definitions. — As used in this chapter:

"Benefit contract" means the agreement for provision of benefits authorized by § 38.2-4116, as that agreement is described in § 38.2-4119.

"Benefit member" means an adult member who is designated by the laws or rules of the society to be a benefit member under a benefit contract.

"Certificate" means the document issued as written evidence of the benefit contract.

"Laws" means the society's articles of incorporation, constitution and bylaws, however designated.

"Lodge" means subordinate member units of the society, known as camps, courts, councils, branches or by any other designation.

"Premiums" means premiums, rates, dues or other required contributions by whatever name known, which are payable under the certificate.

"Rules" means all rules, regulations or resolutions adopted by the supreme governing body or board of directors which are intended to have general application to the members of the society.

"Society" means fraternal benefit society, unless otherwise indicated. (1986, c. 562.)

§ 38.2-4104. Purposes and powers. — A. A society shall operate for the benefit of members and their beneficiaries by:

1. Providing benefits as specified in § 38.2-4116; and

2. Operating for one or more social, intellectual, educational, charitable, benevolent, moral, fraternal, patriotic or religious purposes for the benefit of its members, which may also be extended to others. Such purposes may be carried out directly by the society, or indirectly through subsidiary corporations or affiliated organizations.

B. Every society shall have the power to adopt laws and rules for the government of the society, the admission of its members, and the management of its affairs. It shall have the power to change, alter, add to or amend such laws and rules and shall have any other powers necessary and incidental to effecting the objects and purposes of the society. (Code 1950, §§ 38-277, 38.1-593; 1952, c. 317, § 38.1-638.25; 1968, c. 654, § 38.1-638.36; 1986, c. 562.)

ARTICLE 2.

Membership.

§ 38.2-4105. Qualifications for membership. — A. A society shall specify in its laws or rules:

1. Eligibility standards for every class of membership, provided that if benefits are provided on the lives of children, the minimum age for adult membership shall be set at not less than age fifteen and not greater than age twenty-one;

2. The process for admission to membership for each membership class; and

3. The rights and privileges of each membership class, provided that only benefit members shall have the right to vote on the management of the insurance affairs of the society.

B. A society may also admit social members who shall have no voice or vote in the management of the insurance affairs of the society.

C. Membership rights in the society are personal to the member and are not assignable. (Code 1950, §§ 38-286, 38-293, 38.1-602, 38.1-609; 1952, c. 317, § 38.1-638.29; 1964, c. 355; 1968, c. 654; 1972, cc. 530, 825; 1986, c. 562.)

§ 38.2-4106. Location of office; meetings, communications to members; grievance procedures. — A. The principal office of any domestic society shall be located in this Commonwealth. The meetings of its supreme governing body may be held in any state, district, province or territory wherein such society has at least one subordinate lodge, or in any other location determined by the supreme governing body. All business transacted at such meetings shall be as valid in all respects as if such meetings were held in this Commonwealth. The minutes of the proceedings of the supreme governing body and of the board of directors shall be in the English language.

B. 1. A society may provide in its laws for an official publication in which any notice, report, or statement required by law to be given to members, including notice of election, may be published. Such required reports, notices, and statements shall be printed conspicuously in the publication. If the records of a society show that two or more members have the same mailing address, an official publication mailed to one member is deemed to be mailed to all members at the same address unless a member requests a separate copy.

2. Not later than June 1 of each year, a synopsis of the society's annual statement providing an explanation of the facts concerning the condition of the society thereby disclosed shall either (i) be printed and mailed to each benefit member of the society or (ii) published in the society's official publication.

C. A society may provide in its laws or rules for grievance or complaint procedures for members. (Code 1950, §§ 38-259, 38-318, 38.1-576, 38.1-626; 1952, c. 317, §§ 38.1-638.8, 38.1-638.47; 1968, c. 654; 1986, c. 562.)

§ **38.2-4107. No personal liability.** — A. The officers and members of the supreme governing body or any subordinate body of a society shall not be personally liable for any benefits provided by a society.

B. Any person may be indemnified and reimbursed by any society for expenses reasonably incurred by, and liabilities imposed upon, such person in connection with or arising out of any action, suit or proceeding, or threat of such, in which the person may be involved because he or she is or was a director, officer, employee or agent of the society or of any firm, corporation or organization which he or she served in any capacity at the request of the society. A person shall not be so indemnified or reimbursed in relation to any matter in (i) such action, suit or proceeding as to which he or she was finally adjudged to be or have been guilty of breach of a duty as a director, officer, employee or agent of the society or (ii) such action, suit or proceeding, or threat thereof, which has been made the subject of a compromise settlement, unless in either case the person acted in good faith for a purpose the person reasonably believed to be in or not opposed to the best interests of the society and, in a criminal action or proceeding, in addition, had no reasonable cause to believe that his or her conduct was unlawful. The determination whether the conduct of such person met the standard required in order to justify indemnification and reimbursement in relation to any matter described in (i) or (ii) of this subsection may be made only by the supreme governing body or board of directors by a majority vote of a quorum consisting of persons who were not parties to such action, suit or proceeding or by a court of competent jurisdiction. The termination of any action, suit or proceeding by judgment, order, settlement, conviction, or upon a plea of no contest, as to such person shall not in itself create a conclusive presumption that the person did not meet the standard of conduct required in order to justify indemnification and reimbursement. The foregoing right of indemnification and reimbursement shall not be exclusive of other rights to which such person may be entitled as a matter of law and shall inure to the benefit of his or her heirs, executors, and administrators.

C. A society shall have power to purchase and maintain insurance on behalf of any person who is or was a director, officer, employee or agent of the society, or who is or was serving at the request of the society as a director, officer, employee or agent of any other firm, corporation, or organization against any liability asserted against such person and incurred by him or her in any such capacity or arising out of his or her status as such, whether or not the society would have the power to indemnify the person against such liability under this section. (Code 1950, §§ 38-260, 38.1-574; 1952, c. 317, § 38.1-638.6; 1968, c. 654; 1986, c. 562.)

§ 38.2-4108. Waiver. — The laws of the society may provide that no subordinate body, nor any of its subordinate officers or members, shall have the power or authority to waive any of the provisions of the laws of the society. Such provision shall be binding on the society and every member and beneficiary of a member. (Code 1950, §§ 38-278, 38.1-594; 1952, c. 317, § 38.1-638.26; 1968, c. 654; 1986, c. 562.)

ARTICLE 3.

Governance.

§ 38.2-4109. Organization of domestic society on or after October 1, 1986. — A. On or after October 1, 1986, seven or more citizens of the United States, a majority of whom are citizens of this Commonwealth, who desire to form a fraternal benefit society, may make, sign and acknowledge before some officer competent to take acknowledgement of deeds, articles of incorporation, which shall state:

1. The proposed corporate name of the society, which shall not so closely resemble the name of any other society or insurer as to be misleading or confusing;

2. The purposes for which it is being formed and the mode in which its corporate powers are to be exercised. Such purposes shall not include more liberal powers than are granted by this chapter;

3. The names and residences of the incorporators and the names, residences and official titles of all officers, trustees, directors, or other persons who are to have and exercise the general control of the management of the affairs and funds of the society for the first year or until the ensuing election at which all such officers shall be elected by the supreme governing body, which election shall be held not later than one year from the date of issuance of the permanent certificate of authority.

B. Such articles of incorporation, duly certified copies of the society's bylaws and rules, copies of all proposed forms of certificates, applications therefor, and circulars to be issued by the society and a bond conditioned upon the return to applicants of the advanced payments if the organization is not completed within one year shall be filed with the Commission, which may require any further information it deems necessary. The bond, with sureties approved by the Commission, shall be not less than $50,000 nor more than $200,000, as required by the Commission. All documents filed are to be in the English language. If the purposes of the society conform to the requirements of this chapter and all provisions of the law have been complied with, the Commission shall so certify, retain, and file the articles of incorporation and furnish the incorporators a preliminary certificate of authority authorizing the society to solicit members as hereinafter provided.

C. No preliminary certificate of authority granted under the provisions of this section shall be valid after 1 year from its date or after such further period, not exceeding one year, as may be authorized by the Commission upon cause shown, unless the 500 required applicants have been secured and the organization has been duly completed. The articles of incorporation and all other proceedings under those articles shall become void in one year from the date of the preliminary certificate of authority, or at the expiration of the extended period, unless the society has completed its organization and received a certificate of authority to do business.

D. Upon receipt of a preliminary certificate of authority from the Commission, the society may solicit members for the purpose of completing its organization, shall collect from each applicant the amount of not less than one regular monthly premium in accordance with its table of rates, and shall issue to each such applicant a receipt for the amount collected. No society shall incur any liability other than for the return of such advance premium, nor issue any certificate, nor pay, allow, or offer or promise to pay or allow, any benefit to any person until:

1. Actual bona fide applicants for benefits have been secured on not less than 500 applicants, and any necessary evidence of insurability has been furnished to and approved by the society;

2. At least ten subordinate lodges have been established into which the 500 applicants have been admitted;

3. There has been submitted to the Commission, a list of such applicants, giving their names, addresses, date each was admitted, name and number of the subordinate lodge of which each applicant is a member, amount of benefits to be granted and their premiums; and

4. It has been shown to the Commission, by sworn statement of the treasurer, or corresponding officer of such society, that at least 500 applicants have each paid in cash at least 1 regular monthly premium, which shall total at least $150,000. Advance premiums shall be held in trust during the period of organization and, if the society has not qualified for a certificate of authority within one year, such premiums shall be returned to the applicants.

E. The Commission may examine and require any further information it deems advisable. Upon presentation of satisfactory evidence that the society has complied with all the provisions of law, the Commissioner shall issue to the society a certificate of authority to that effect and that the society is authorized to do business pursuant to the provisions of this chapter. The certificate of authority shall be prima facie evidence of the existence of the society at the date of such certificate. The Commission shall cause a record of such certificate of authority to be made. A certified copy of such record shall have the same effect as the original certificate of authority.

F. Any incorporated society authorized to do business in this Commonwealth at the time this chapter becomes effective shall not be required to reincorporate. (Code 1950, §§ 38-264 through 38-268, 38.1-582 through 38.1-587; 1952, c. 317, §§ 38.1-638.14 through 38.1-638.19; 1968, c. 654; 1975, c. 262; 1986, c. 562.)

§ 38.2-4110. Incorporation of fraternal benefit societies. — Domestic fraternal benefit societies may be incorporated under the provisions of Article 3 (§ 13.1-818 et seq.) of Chapter 10 of Title 13.1, as modified by the provisions of this title, and, except as otherwise provided in this title, shall be subject to all the general restrictions and shall have all the general powers imposed and conferred by law upon companies so incorporated. (Code 1950, §§ 38-264, 38.1-579; 1952, c. 317, § 38.1-638.11; 1956, c. 431; 1968, c. 654; 1986, c. 562.)

§ 38.2-4111. Amendments to laws. — A. A domestic society may amend its laws in accordance with the provisions of those laws by action of its supreme governing body at any regular or special meeting or, if its laws so provide, by referendum. Such referendum may be held in accordance with the provisions of its laws by the vote of the voting members of the society, by the vote of delegates or representatives of voting members, or by the vote of local lodges. A society may provide for voting by mail. No amendment submitted for adoption by referendum shall be adopted unless, within six months from the date of submission of the amendment, a majority of the members voting shall have signified their consent to such amendment by one of the methods herein specified.

B. No amendment to the laws of any domestic society shall take effect unless filed with the Commission.

C. Within ninety days from the filing specified in subsection B of this section, all such amendments, or a synopsis of the amendments, shall be furnished to all members of the society either by mail or by publication in full in the official publication of the society. The affidavit of any officer of the society or of anyone authorized by it to mail any amendments or synopsis of the amendments, stating facts which show that same have been duly addressed and mailed, shall be prima facie evidence that such amendments or their synopsis have been furnished the addressee.

D. Every foreign or alien society authorized to do business in this Commonwealth shall file with the Commission a duly certified copy of all amendments of, or additions to, its laws within ninety days after their enactment.

E. Printed copies of the laws as amended, certified by the secretary or corresponding officer of the society, shall be prima facie evidence of their legal adoption. (Code 1950, §§ 38-277, 38-279, 38.1-593, 38.1-595; 1952, c. 317, §§ 38.1-638.25, 38.1-638.27; 1968, c. 654; 1986, c. 562.)

§ **38.2-4112. Institutions.** — A society may create, maintain and operate, or may establish organizations to operate, not for profit institutions to further the purposes permitted by subdivision 2 of subsection A of § 38.2-4104. Such institutions may furnish services free or at a reasonable charge. Any real or personal property owned, held or leased by the society for this purpose shall be reported in every annual statement. No society shall own or operate funeral homes or undertaking establishments. (1968, c. 654, § 38.1-638.36; 1986, c. 562.)

§ **38.2-4113. Reinsurance.** — A. A domestic society may, by a reinsurance agreement, cede any individual risk or risks in whole or in part to an insurer, other than another fraternal benefit society, having the power to make such reinsurance and authorized to do business in this Commonwealth, or if not so authorized, one which is approved by the Commission, but no such society may reinsure substantially all of its insurance in force without the written permission of the Commission. It may take credit for the reserves on such ceded risks to the extent reinsured, but no credit shall be allowed as an admitted asset or as a deduction from liability, to a ceding society for reinsurance made, ceded, renewed, or otherwise becoming effective after the effective date of this chapter, unless the reinsurance is payable by the assuming insurer on the basis of the liability of the ceding society under the contract or contracts reinsured without diminution because of the insolvency of the ceding society.

B. Notwithstanding the limitation in subsection A, a society may reinsure the risks of another society in a consolidation or merger approved by the Commission under § 38.2-4114. (Code 1950, §§ 38-270, 38.1-575; 1952, c. 317, § 38.1-638.7; 1968, c. 654; 1986, c. 562.)

§ **38.2-4114. Consolidations and mergers.** — A. A domestic society may consolidate or merge with any other society by complying with the provisions of this section. It shall file with the Commission:

1. A certified copy of the written contract containing in full the terms and conditions of the consolidation or merger;

2. A sworn statement by the president and secretary or corresponding officers of each society showing its financial condition on a date fixed by the Commission but not earlier than December 31 next preceding the date of the contract;

3. A certificate of such officers, duly verified, that the consolidation or merger has been approved by a two-thirds vote of the supreme governing body of each society, such vote being conducted at a regular or special meeting of each such body, or, if the society's laws permit, by mail; and

4. Evidence that at least sixty days prior to the action of the supreme governing body of each society, the text of the contract has been furnished to all members of each society either by mail or by publication in full in the official publication of each society.

B. If the Commission finds that the contract conforms to the provisions of this section, that the financial statements are correct and that the consolidation or merger is just and equitable to the members of each society, the Commission shall approve the contract and issue a certificate to such effect. Upon such approval, the contract shall be effective unless any society which is a party to the contract is incorporated under the laws of any other state or territory. In such event, the consolidation or merger shall not become effective until it has been approved as provided by the laws of such state or territory and a certificate of such approval filed with the Commission. If the laws of such state or territory contain no such provision, then the consolidation or merger shall not become effective until it has been approved by the Commission of such state or territory and a certificate of such approval filed with the Commission.

C. When the consolidation or merger becomes effective, all the rights, franchises, and interests of the consolidated or merged societies in and to every species of property and things in action belonging to the societies shall be vested in the society resulting from or remaining after the consolidation or merger without any other instrument. Conveyances of real property, however, may be evidenced by proper deeds, and the title to any real estate or interest therein, vested under the laws of this Commonwealth in any of the societies consolidated or merged, shall not revert or be in anyway impaired by reason of the consolidation or merger but shall vest absolutely in the society resulting from or remaining after such consolidation or merger.

D. The affidavit of any officer of the society or of anyone authorized by it to mail any notice or document, stating that such notice or document has been duly addressed and mailed, shall be prima facie evidence that such notice or document has been furnished the addressees. (Code 1950, §§ 38-270, 38.1-575; 1952, c. 317, § 38.1-638.7; 1968, c. 654; 1986, c. 562.)

§ 38.2-4115. Conversion of fraternal benefit society into mutual life insurer. — A. Any domestic fraternal benefit society organized or operated under this chapter may, upon a two-thirds vote of its supreme governing body, amend its articles of incorporation and laws if already incorporated, or, if not incorporated, may incorporate, in a manner to transform itself into a mutual life insurer. It may use the name by which it is already known, or another name, as its supreme governing body shall determine. However, the proposed plan for reorganization or reincorporation shall be submitted to and approved by the Commission. Upon so doing, and upon procuring from the Commission a license to do the business of insurance in this Commonwealth as a mutual life insurer, it shall incur the obligations and enjoy the benefits of a mutual life insurer as if originally incorporated as a mutual life insurer. Any such corporation under its articles and bylaws as so framed or amended shall be a continuation of the original organization, and the officers of the organization shall serve through their respective terms as provided in the original articles and laws. However, their successors shall be elected and serve as the laws of this Commonwealth and the articles of incorporation or bylaws of the reorganized company provide. The incorporation, amendment or reincorporation shall not affect existing suits, rights or contracts. The organization, after reorganization, shall have the power to do business of the same nature done by it before reorganization, as well as the powers conferred in this section and contemplated by its articles of incorporation, in order to protect and perform rights and contracts existing before reorganization, but all new business written shall be as a mutual life insurer.

B. All assets, other than general or expense fund assets, belonging to any reorganized insurer, prior to reorganization or arising or accruing from benefit certificates issued prior to the reorganization, shall be used only for the benefit of the holders of the benefit certificates or their beneficiaries.

C. If at the time of reorganization, or at any time after reorganization, it appears from the last preceding annual report of any such organization, filed with the Commission, or any investigation made by the Commission, that the present value of the contributions to be received from the holders of the benefit certificates, together with all assets, other than general or expense fund assets, owned by the insurer that have been accumulated from payments made by members holding such certificates, are not equal to the present value of the benefits promised to be paid, including all matured liabilities on any benefit certificates, then the insurer so reorganized shall establish, provide for, and maintain a fund, which with the present value of contributions and assets will equal the present value of the benefits, together with all matured liabilities. The fund shall be used for the payment of matured liabilities arising on the benefit certificates when other assets applicable thereto are exhausted. The fund need not be maintained unless required by conditions expressed in this chapter.

D. Members in good standing in any society prior to reorganization shall have the right after reorganization to transfer their insurance in the society to the mutual life plan without further medical examination for the same or lesser amount, and at legal reserve or level premium rates. The interest in the assets of the society of any person so transferring, as determined by the board of directors, trustees or corresponding body, shall be transferred to, and be a part of, the assets of the insurer on the legal reserve or level premium plan.

E. The insurer so organized, and its officials, shall exercise all the rights and powers and perform all the duties conferred or imposed by law upon organizations writing the kinds of insurance written by the insurer so organized. The organization and its officials shall exercise all the rights and powers and have full authority to perform all the duties necessary to protect rights and contracts existing prior to reorganization. The Commission shall exercise the powers and discharge the duties concerning any such insurer so reorganized that are applicable to insurers writing insurance or issuing policies of the same class, organized or operating in this Commonwealth. The Commission shall issue a certificate of authority to any solvent insurer so reorganized that has fully complied with the laws of this Commonwealth to do such insurance business in this Commonwealth.

F. Any fraternal benefit society reorganized to do mutual life insurance business as provided in this chapter shall value its benefit certificates according to the standard of valuation for fraternal benefit societies used in this Commonwealth, and its legal reserve or level premium policies according to the standard of valuation for those policies in this Commonwealth. The various classes of insurance shall be governed by the law applicable to each class of insurance.

G. The expense of operation and maintenance of a reorganized insurer shall be apportioned between those holding benefit certificates issued before the reorganization and those holding policies issued after the reorganization as may be determined by the board of directors, trustees or corresponding body. (Code 1950, §§ 38-323 through 38-329, 38.1-632 through 38.1-638; 1952, c. 317, §§ 38.1-638.53 through 38.1-638.59; 1968, c. 654; 1986, c. 562.)

ARTICLE 4.

Contractual Benefits.

§ 38.2-4116. Benefits. — A. A society may apply to the Commission to provide the following contractual benefits in any form:
1. Death benefits;
2. Endowment benefits;
3. Annuity benefits;
4. Temporary or permanent disability benefits;
5. Hospital, medical or nursing benefits;
6. Monument or tombstone benefits to the memory of deceased members; and
7. Such other benefits as authorized for life insurers and which are not inconsistent with this chapter.

B. A society shall specify in its rules those persons who may be issued, or covered by, the contractual benefits in subsection A, consistent with providing benefits to members and their dependents. A society may provide benefits on the lives of children under the minimum age for adult membership upon application of an adult person. (Code 1950, §§ 38-283, 38.1-599; 1952, c. 317, § 38.1-638.31; 1968, c. 654; 1972, c. 530; 1975, c. 262; 1986, c. 562.)

§ 38.2-4117. Beneficiaries. — A. The owner of a benefit contract shall have the right at all times to change the beneficiary or beneficiaries in accordance with the laws or rules of the society unless the owner waives this right by specifically requesting in writing that the beneficiary designation be irrevocable. A society may, through its laws or rules, limit the scope of beneficiary designations and shall provide that no revocable beneficiary shall have or obtain any vested interest in the proceeds of any certificate until the certificate has become due and payable in conformity with the provisions of the benefit contract.

B. A society may provide for the payment of funeral benefits from the proceeds of a certificate of no more than $2,000 to any person equitably entitled to them because of expenses incurred by the burial of the member.

C. If, at the death of any person insured under a benefit contract, there is no lawful beneficiary to whom the proceeds are payable, the amount of such benefit, except to the extent that funeral benefits may be paid as previously provided, shall be payable to the personal representative of the deceased insured; however, if the owner of the certificate is other than the insured, the proceeds shall be payable to such owner. (Code 1950, §§ 38-284, 38.1-600; 1952, c. 317, § 38.1-638.32; 1968, c. 654; 1972, c. 530; 1986, c. 562.)

In general. — Where the charter of a benefit society designated the classes of persons who may be beneficiaries, this section was not intended to alter, modify, or repeal the charter, but merely to enumerate the objects for which a benefit association might be organized. Pettus v. Hendricks, 113 Va. 326, 74 S.E. 191 (1912).

This interpretation of the statute has met with the approval of the General Assembly. Shepherd v. Sovereign Camp of Woodmen of World, 166 Va. 488, 186 S.E. 113 (1936).

Liberal construction adopted to determine meaning of terms used to designate beneficiaries. — In determining the meaning and scope of particular terms, such as the words "children," "issue," "heirs," "devisees," "legal representatives," and "estate," as those terms are used in a member's designation of beneficiaries, or in statutes or the charter or laws of a fraternal benefit society for the purpose of designating beneficiaries, the courts adopt a liberal rule of construction, so as to effectuate the intent of the parties and the benevolent objects of the society. Shepherd v. Sovereign Camp of Woodmen of World, 166 Va. 488, 186 S.E. 113 (1936).

Beneficiary must be within class permitted by statute. — The person designated as the beneficiary under a certificate of a fraternal benefit society must be within the classes permitted by the appropriate statute and the rules and regulations of the association. Shepherd v. Sovereign Camp of Woodmen of World, 166 Va. 488, 186 S.E. 113 (1936).

A member of a fraternal benefit society has merely a power of appointment, limited to the classes of beneficiaries named in the statute, and any other designation is invalid and void. Also, the society has no authority to create a fund for other persons than those specified in this section, nor can a member direct that the fund be paid to a person outside of such classes. Bryant v. Tunstall, 177 Va. 1, 12 S.E.2d 784 (1941).

But this was not applied to foreign corporations. — Former § 38.1-600 was not intended to restrict or modify the constitution and bylaws of a Nebraska corporation which had been doing business in Virginia since 1901. Under the bylaws of the Nebraska company the right of plaintiff who was the named beneficiary, and who went to live with the assured and his wife at the age of eight, took their name, and was raised by them as their child, but no proceedings were instituted for her legal adoption, was governed by the words of the association's constitution and bylaws and not by the Virginia statute. Shepherd v. Sovereign Camp of Woodmen of World, 166 Va. 488, 186 S.E. 113 (1936).

Former § 38.1-600 did not add to the classes of beneficiaries named in the charter, constitution or bylaws of a Virginia fraternal benefit society, and conversely the charter, constitution and bylaws of a corporation, did not add to the classes enumerated in the sec-

tion. Bryant v. Tunstall, 177 Va. 1, 12 S.E.2d 784 (1941).

Charter provision for designating beneficiaries "according to its bylaws." — Where the charter of a benefit society provides that the association will "pay to the nearest relative, or such other dependent as may be designated by the member according to its bylaws, such sum of money upon the death of such member as said bylaws shall provide," the phrase "according to its bylaws" is merely intended to reserve to the association the right to prescribe a method of designation if it should see fit to do so, and the charter is, in this respect, self-executing. Pettus v. Hendricks, 113 Va. 326, 74 S.E. 191 (1912).

Right to question eligibility of beneficiary. — A person whom the assured had attempted to make the beneficiary, not being an eligible beneficiary under former § 38.1-600, had no interest in the fund and could not question the assured's wife's eligibility, and the society, having admitted its indebtedness by paying the fund into court, waived the right to question the wife's eligibility. Bryant v. Tunstall, 177 Va. 1, 12 S.E.2d 784 (1941).

The use of the restricted phrase, "children by legal adoption" is in itself a recognition of the fact that "adopted children" has a broader meaning. Shepherd v. Sovereign Camp of Woodmen of World, 166 Va. 488, 186 S.E. 113 (1936).

Example. — The holder of a certificate issued by a fraternal benefit society attempted to change the beneficiary from his wife to a person who was not dependent upon him and who was not related to him. The person whom the assured attempted to make the beneficiary was within the classes permitted by the bylaws of the society, but was not within any of the classes of beneficiaries specified in former § 38.1-600. It was held that the attempted change of beneficiary was ineffective and void, and the contract of insurance must be regarded as though the designation of the original beneficiary had never been changed. Bryant v. Tunstall, 177 Va. 1, 12 S.E.2d 784 (1941).

§ 38.2-4118. Benefits not attachable.

§ **38.2-4118. Benefits not attachable.** — No money or other benefit, charity, relief or aid to be paid, provided or rendered by any society, shall be liable to attachment, garnishment or other process, or to be seized, taken, appropriated or applied by any legal or equitable process or operation of law to pay any debt or liability of a member or beneficiary, or any other person who may have a right thereunder, either before or after payment by the society. (Code 1950, §§ 38-285, 38.1-601; 1952, c. 317, § 38.1-638.33; 1968, c. 654; 1986, c. 562.)

§ **38.2-4119. The benefit contract.** — A. Every society authorized to do business in this Commonwealth shall issue to each owner of a benefit contract a certificate specifying the amount of benefits provided thereby. The certificate, together with any attached riders or endorsements, the laws of the society, the application for membership, the application for insurance and declaration of insurability, if any, signed by the applicant, and all amendments to each, shall constitute the benefit contract, as of the date of issuance, between the society and the owner, and the certificate shall so state. A copy of the application for insurance and declaration of insurability, if any, shall be endorsed upon or attached to the certificate. All statements on the application shall be representations and not warranties. Any waiver of this provision shall be void.

B. Any changes, additions or amendments to the laws of the society duly made or enacted subsequent to the issuance of the certificate, shall bind the owner and the beneficiaries, and shall govern and control the benefit contract in all respects the same as though such changes, additions or amendments had been made prior to and were in force at the time of the application for insurance, except that no change, addition or amendment shall destroy or diminish benefits which the society contracted to give the owner as of the date of issuance.

C. Any person upon whose life a benefit contract is issued prior to attaining the age of majority shall be bound by the terms of the application and certificate and by all the laws and rules of the society to the same extent as though the age of majority had been attained at the time of application.

D. A society shall provide in its laws that if its reserves as to all or any class of certificates become impaired, its board of directors or corresponding body may require that the owner shall pay to the society his equitable proportion of such deficiency as ascertained by its board, and that if the payment is not made, either (i) it shall stand as an indebtedness against the certificate and draw interest not to exceed the rate specified for certificate loans under the certificates; or (ii) in lieu of or in combination with (i), the owner may accept a proportionate reduction in benefits under the certificate. The society may specify the manner of the election and which alternative is to be presumed if no election is made.

E. Copies of any documents mentioned in this section, certified by the secretary or corresponding officer of the society, shall be received in evidence of the terms and conditions thereof.

F. No certificate shall be delivered or issued for delivery in this Commonwealth unless a copy of the form has been filed with and approved by the Commission in the manner provided for in § 38.2-316. Every life, accident, health, or disability insurance certificate and every annuity certificate issued on or after July 1, 1986, shall meet the standard contract provision requirements not inconsistent with this chapter for like policies issued by life insurers in this Commonwealth, except that a society may provide for a grace period for payment of premiums of one full month in its certificates. The certificate shall also contain a provision stating the amount of premiums which are payable under the certificate and a provision reciting or setting forth the substance of any sections of the society's laws or rules in force at the time of issuance of the certificate which, if violated, will result in the termination or reduction of benefits payable under the certificate. If the laws of the society provide for expulsion or suspension of a member, the certificate shall also contain a provision that any member so expelled or suspended, except for nonpayment of a premium or within the contestable period for material misrepresentation in the application for membership or insurance, shall have the privilege of maintaining the certificate in force by continuing payment of the required premium.

G. Benefit contracts issued on the lives of persons below the society's minimum age for adult membership may provide for transfer of control or ownership to the insured at an age specified in the certificate. A society may require approval of an application for membership in order to effect this transfer, and may provide in all other respects for the regulation, government and control of such certificates and all rights, obligations and liabilities incident thereto. Ownership rights prior to such transfer shall be specified in the certificate.

H. A society may specify the terms and conditions on which benefit contracts may be assigned. (Code 1950, §§ 38-280, 38-282, 38-286, 38-293, 38.1-596, 38.1-598, 38.1-602, 38.1-609; 1952, c. 317, §§ 38.1-638.28 through 38.1-638.30, 38.1-638.35; 1964, c. 355; 1968, c. 654; 1972, cc. 530, 825; 1986, c. 562.)

Construction of certificates. — The beneficiary certificates of a fraternal benefit society, together with the provisions of the constitution of the society applicable thereto, in general are to be interpreted as other insurance contracts, and the rights and obligations of the parties measured accordingly. They are to be given their plain, natural, and obvious meaning and effect, when free from ambiguity. But the contract will be liberally construed to promote the benevolent objects of the society, and any doubt will be resolved in favor of the assured. Greenwood v. Royal Neighbors of Am., 118 Va. 329, 87 S.E. 581 (1916).

§ 38.2-4120. Nonforfeiture benefits, cash surrender values, certificate loans and other options.

— A. A society may grant paid-up nonforfeiture benefits, cash surrender values, certificate loans, and any other options its laws permit. Certificates issued on and after June 28, 1968, must contain at least one paid-up nonforfeiture benefit, except in the case of pure endowment, annuity or reversionary annuity contracts, reducing term insurance contracts or contracts of level term insurance for fifteen years or less expiring before age sixty-six.

B. For certificates, other than those for which reserves are computed on the Commissioners 1941 Standard Ordinary Mortality Table, the Commissioners 1941 Standard Industrial Table or the Commissioners 1958 Standard Ordinary Mortality Table, or any more recent table made applicable to life insurance companies, the value of every paid-up nonforfeiture benefit and the amount of any cash surrender value, loan or other option granted shall not be less than any excess of (1) over (2) as follows:

(1) The reserve under the certificate determined on the basis specified in the certificate; and

(2) The sum of any indebtedness to the society on the certificate, including interest due and accrued, and a surrender charge equal to $2^1/_2\%$ of the face amount of the certificate, which, in the case of insurance on the lives of persons under the minimum age for adult membership, shall be the ultimate face amount of the certificate, if death benefits provided in the certificate are graded.

C. For certificates issued on a substandard basis or for certificates with reserves computed upon the American Men Ultimate Table of Mortality, the term of any extended insurance benefit granted, including any accompanying pure endowment, may be computed upon the rates of mortality not greater than 130 percent of those shown by the mortality table specified in the certificate for the computation of the reserve.

D. For certificates with reserves computed on the Commissioners 1941 Standard Ordinary Mortality Table, the Commissioners 1941 Standard Industrial Table or the Commissioners 1958 Standard Ordinary Mortality Table, or any more recent table made applicable to life insurance companies, every paid-up nonforfeiture benefit and the amount of any cash surrender value, loan or other option granted shall not be less than the corresponding amount ascertained in accordance with the provisions of the laws of this Commonwealth applicable to life insurers issuing policies containing like insurance benefits based upon such tables. (1968, c. 654, § 38.1-638.34; 1975, c. 262; 1986, c. 562.)

ARTICLE 5.

Financial Requirements.

§ 38.2-4121. Investments. — A society shall invest its funds only in investments authorized by Chapter 14 of this title for the investment of assets of life insurers and subject to the limitations thereon. Any foreign or alien society permitted or seeking to do business in this Commonwealth which invests its funds in accordance with the laws of the state, district, territory, country or province in which it is incorporated, shall be held to meet the requirements of this section for the investment of funds. (Code 1950, §§ 38-307, 38.1-623; 1952, c. 317, § 38.1-638.43; 1968, c. 654; 1986, c. 562.)

§ 38.2-4122. Funds. — A. All assets shall be held, invested, and disbursed for the use and benefit of the society and no member or beneficiary shall have or acquire individual rights therein or become entitled to any apportionment on the surrender of any part thereof, except as provided in the benefit contract.

B. A society may create, maintain, invest, disburse, and apply any special fund or funds necessary to carry out any purpose permitted by the laws of the society.

C. A society may apply to the Commission, pursuant to resolution of its supreme governing body, to establish and operate one or more separate accounts and issue contracts on a variable basis, subject to Article 3 (§ 38.2-1443 et seq.) of Chapter 14 of this title. To the extent the society deems it necessary in order to comply with any applicable federal or state laws, or any rules issued under those laws, the society may (i) adopt special procedures for the conduct of the business and affairs of a separate account; (ii) for persons having beneficial interest therein, provide special voting and other rights, including without limitation special rights and procedures relating to investment policy, investment advisory services, selection of certified public accountants, and selection of a committee to manage the business and affairs of the account; and (iii) issue contracts on a variable basis to which subsections B and D of § 38.2-4119 of this chapter shall not apply. (Code 1950, §§ 38-301, 38.1-617; 1952, c. 317, § 38.1-638.42; 1960, c. 189; 1968, c. 654; 1986, c. 562.)

ARTICLE 6.

Regulation.

§ 38.2-4123. Exemptions. — Except as herein provided, societies shall be governed by this chapter and §§ 38.2-100 through 38.2-134, Chapters 2 through 9, §§ 38.2-1301.1, 38.2-1304, 38.2-1307 through 38.2-1315, and 38.2-1322 through 38.2-1340, Chapters 14, 15 and 18, §§ 38.2-3100 through 38.2-3125, 38.2-3127.1 and 38.2-3300 through 38.2-3317, Chapter 34, §§ 38.2-3500 through 38.2-3520, and Chapter 36 and shall be exempt from all other provisions of this title unless expressly designated therein, or unless they are specifically made applicable by this chapter. (1986, c. 562; 1987, cc. 565, 655; 1993, c. 158; 1994, c. 308.)

§ 38.2-4124. Taxation. — Every society organized or licensed under this chapter is hereby declared to be a charitable and benevolent institution, and all of its funds shall be exempt from every state, county, district, municipal and school tax other than taxes on real estate and office equipment. (Code 1950, §§ 38-262, 38.1-577; 1952, c. 317, § 38.1-638.9; 1968, c. 654; 1986, c. 562.)

Purpose of exemption. — The legislature in exempting the funds of fraternal benefit societies from taxation may have been influenced by the fact that such societies generally pay small death and burial benefits; that they serve a large class of people who, as a rule, cannot afford more expensive and adequate protection; that an important element of the body politic known as the working class is generally impelled to their membership and that such organizations need the aegis of protection that the State can properly accord to them. Fireman's Mut. Aid Ass'n v. Commonwealth, 166 Va. 34, 184 S.E. 189, cert. denied, 298 U.S. 677, 56 S. Ct. 941, 80 L. Ed. 1398 (1936).

Constitutionality. — Exemptions from taxation which are accorded some classes and withheld from other different classes do not create an inequality in a constitutional sense. Fireman's Mut. Aid Ass'n v. Commonwealth, 166 Va. 34, 184 S.E. 189, cert. denied, 298 U.S. 677, 56 S. Ct. 941, 80 L. Ed. 1398 (1936) (wherein the company was not allowed to question the constitutionality of former § 38.1-577).

§ 38.2-4125. Valuations. — A. The report of valuation shall show, as reserve liabilities, the difference between the present midyear value of the promised benefits provided in the certificates of the society in force and the present midyear value of the future net premiums as they are in practice actually collected, not including any value for the right to make extra assessments and not including any amount by which the present midyear value of future net premiums exceeds the present midyear value of promised benefits on individual certificates. At the option of any society, the valuation may show the net tabular value instead of the above value. The net tabular value as to certificates issued prior to June 28, 1969, shall be determined in accordance with the provisions of law applicable prior to June 28, 1968, and as to certificates issued on or after June 28, 1969, shall not be less than the reserves determined according to the Commissioners' reserve valuation method as defined in subsection C of this section. If the premium charged is less than the tabular net premium according to the basis of valuation used, an additional reserve equal to the present value of the deficiency in the premiums shall be set up and maintained as a liability. The reserve liabilities shall be properly adjusted in the event that the midyear or tabular values are not appropriate.

B. A society may value its certificates in accordance with valuation standards authorized by the laws of this Commonwealth for the valuation of policies issued by life insurers.

C. Reserves according to the Commissioners' reserve valuation method, for the life insurance and endowment benefits of certificates providing for a uniform amount of insurance and requiring the payment of uniform premiums shall be any excess of the present value, at the date of valuation, of the future guaranteed benefits provided for by those certificates, over the then present value of any future modified net premiums therefor. The modified net premiums for any such certificate shall be a uniform percentage of the respective contract premiums for the benefits that the present value, at the date of issue of the certificate, of all modified net premiums shall equal the sum of the then present value of the benefits provided for by the certificate and the excess of 1 over 2, as follows:

1. A net-level premium equal to the present value, at the date of issue, of the benefits provided for after the first certificate year, divided by the present value, at the date of issue, of an annual annuity of one dollar payable on each anniversary of the certificate on which a premium falls due. However, the net-level annual premium shall not exceed the net-level annual premium on the nineteen-year premium whole life plan for insurance of the same amount at any age one year higher than the age at issue of the certificate; and

2. A net one-year term premium for the benefits provided for in the first certificate year. Reserves according to the Commissioners' reserve valuation

method for (i) life insurance benefits for varying amounts of benefits or requiring the payment of varying premiums, (ii) annuity and pure endowment benefits, (iii) disability and accidental death benefits in all certificates and contracts, and (iv) all other benefits except life insurance and endowment benefits, shall be calculated by a method consistent with the principles of this subsection.

D. The present value of deferred payments due under incurred claims or matured certificates shall be deemed a liability of the society and shall be computed upon mortality and interest standards prescribed in subsections E through G of this section.

E. The valuation and underlying data shall be certified by a competent actuary or, at the expense of the society, verified by the actuary of the department of insurance of the state of domicile of the society.

F. The minimum standards of valuation for certificates issued prior to June 28, 1969, shall be those provided by the law applicable immediately prior to June 28, 1968, but not lower than the standards used in the calculating of rates for those certificates.

G. The minimum standard of valuation for certificates issued after June 28, 1969, shall be $3\frac{1}{2}$ percent interest and the following tables:

1. For certificates of life insurance, American Men Ultimate Table of Mortality, with Bowerman's or Davis' Extension thereof or with the consent of the Commission, the Commissioners 1941 Standard Ordinary Mortality Table, the Commissioners 1941 Standard Industrial Mortality Table or the Commissioners 1958 Standard Ordinary Mortality Table, using actual age of the insured for male risks and an age not more than three years younger than the actual age of the insured for female risks;

2. For annuity and pure endowment certificates, excluding any disability and accidental death benefits in the certificates, the 1937 Standard Annuity Mortality Table or the Annuity Mortality Table for 1949, Ultimate, or any modification of either of these tables approved by the Commission;

3. For total and permanent disability benefits in or supplementary to life insurance certificates, Hunter's Disability Table, or the Class III Disability Table (1926) modified to conform to the contractual waiting period, or the tables of Period 2 disablement rates and the 1930 to 1950 termination rates of the 1952 Disability Study of the Society of Actuaries with due regard to the type of benefit. Any of these tables shall, for active lives, be combined with a mortality table permitted for calculating the reserves for life insurance certificates;

4. For accidental death benefits in or supplementary to life insurance certificates, The Inter-Company Double Indemnity Mortality Table or the 1959 Accidental Death Benefits Table. Either table shall be combined with a mortality table permitted for calculating the reserves for life insurance certificates; and

5. For noncancellable accident and health benefits, the Class III Disability Table (1926) with conference modifications or, with the consent of the Commission, tables based upon the society's own experience.

H. The Commission may, in its discretion, accept other standards for valuation if it finds that the reserves produced by those standards will not be less in the aggregate than reserves computed in accordance with the minimum valuation standard prescribed in this section. The Commission may, in its discretion, vary the standards of mortality applicable to all certificates of insurance on substandard lives or other extra hazardous lives by any society licensed to do business in this Commonwealth. Whenever the mortality experience under all certificates valued on the same mortality table exceeds the expected mortality according to that table for a period of three consecutive years, the Commission may require additional reserves that it deems necessary on account of the certificates.

I. Any society, with the consent of the commissioner of insurance of the state of domicile of the society and under any conditions he may impose, may establish and maintain reserves on its certificates in excess of the reserves required by the state. However, the contractual rights of any insured member shall not be affected by the excess reserves. (Code 1950, §§ 38-316, 38.1-624; 1952, c. 317, § 38.1-638.45; 1968, c. 654; 1975, c. 262; 1986, c. 562.)

§ **38.2-4126. Reports to be filed.** — A. Every society doing business in this Commonwealth shall annually, by March 1, unless the Commission extends the time for cause shown, file with the Commission a true statement of its financial condition, transactions and affairs for the preceding calendar year. The statement shall be in general form and content as approved by the National Association of Insurance Commissioners for fraternal benefit societies or other form required by the Commission and as supplemented by additional information required by the Commission.

B. As part of the required annual statement, each society shall, by March 1, file with the Commission a valuation of its certificates in force on December 31 of the previous year, provided the Commission may, in its discretion for cause shown, extend the time of filing such valuation for not more than two calendar months. Such valuation shall be done in accordance with the standards specified in § 38.2-4125. Such valuation and underlying data shall be certified by a qualified actuary or, at the expense of the society, verified by the actuary of the department of insurance of the state of domicile of the society. (Code 1950, §§ 38-316, 38.1-624; 1952, c. 317, §§ 38.1-638.44, 38.1-638.45; 1968, c. 654; 1975, c. 262; 1986, c. 562.)

§ **38.2-4127. Annual license.** — Societies now authorized to do business in this Commonwealth may continue such business until June 30, 1987. The authority of such societies and all societies hereafter licensed may thereafter be renewed annually, but in all cases will terminate on June 30. However, a license so issued shall continue in effect until the new license is issued or specifically refused. For each such license or renewal the society shall pay the Commission twenty dollars. A duly certified copy or duplicate of such license shall be prima facie evidence that the licensee is a fraternal benefit society within the meaning of this chapter. (Code 1950, §§ 38-271, 38.1-588; 1952, c. 317, § 38.1-638.20; 1968, c. 654; 1978, c. 4; 1986, c. 562.)

§ **38.2-4128. Examination of societies; no adverse publications.** — A. The Commission, or any person the Commission may appoint, may examine any domestic, foreign or alien society doing business or applying for admission to do business in this Commonwealth in the same manner as authorized for examination of domestic, foreign or alien insurers. Requirements of notice and an opportunity to respond before findings are made public, as provided in the laws regulating insurers, shall also be applicable to the examination of societies.

B. The expense of each examination and of each valuation, including compensation and actual expense of examiners, shall be paid by the society examined or whose certificates are valued, upon statements furnished by the Commission. (Code 1950, §§ 38-319 through 38-321, 38.1-627, 38.1-629, 38.1-630; 1952, c. 317, §§ 38.1-638.48 through 38.1-638.51; 1968, c. 654; 1986, c. 562.)

§ **38.2-4129. Admission; foreign or alien society.** — No foreign or alien society shall do business in this Commonwealth without a license issued by the Commission. Any such society desiring admission to this Commonwealth shall comply substantially with the requirements and limitations of this chapter applicable to domestic societies. Any such society may be licensed to do business in this Commonwealth upon showing that its assets are invested in accordance with the provisions of this chapter and filing with the Commission:

1. A duly certified copy of its articles of incorporation;
2. A copy of its bylaws, certified by its secretary or corresponding officer;
3. A statement of its business in a form prescribed by the Commission, duly verified by an examination made by the supervising insurance official of its home state or other state, territory, province or country, satisfactory to the Commission;
4. Certification from the proper official of its home state, territory, province or country that the society is legally incorporated and licensed to do business therein;
5. Copies of its certificate forms; and
6. Such other information as the Commission may deem necessary. (Code 1950, §§ 38-272 through 38-274, 38.1-589 through 38.1-591; 1952, c. 317, §§ 38.1-638.21 through 38.1-638.23; 1956, c. 431; 1968, c. 654; 1978, c. 4; 1986, c. 562.)

§ 38.2-4130. Injunction; liquidation; receivership of domestic society. — No domestic society shall:

1. Exceed its powers;
2. Fail to comply with any provisions of this chapter;
3. Fail to fulfill its contracts in good faith;
4. Have a membership of less than 400 after an existence of 1 year or more; or
5. Conduct business fraudulently or in a manner hazardous to its members, creditors, the public or the business.

If the Commission, upon investigation, finds such deficiencies, it shall issue a written notice to the society citing the deficiencies, stating the reasons for dissatisfaction, and requiring that the deficiencies be corrected within the period it designates. The period shall be at least thirty days but not more than six months from the service of the notice. If the Commission believes the interest of the certificate holders of the society will be best served by extending the period of time beyond six months, it may do so for the period of time it considers best. If the society does not correct the deficiency to the satisfaction of the Commission, the Commission may institute delinquency proceedings against the society in the manner set out in Chapter 15 (§ 38.2-1500 et seq.) of this title. If the Commission institutes a delinquency proceeding, all the provisions of Chapter 15 of this title with respect to the rehabilitation, liquidation, conservation and reorganization of insurers generally shall be applicable to the society. (Code 1950, §§ 38-261, 38-275, 38-319, 38.1-592, 38.1-628; 1952, c. 317, §§ 38.1-638.24, 38.1-638.49; 1968, c. 654; 1986, c. 562.)

§ 38.2-4131. Suspension, revocation or refusal of license of foreign or alien society. — No foreign or alien society doing business or applying to do business in this Commonwealth shall:

1. Exceed its powers;
2. Fail to comply with any of the provisions of this chapter;
3. Fail to fulfill its contracts in good faith; or
4. Conduct its business fraudulently or in a manner hazardous to its members or creditors or the public.

If the Commission, upon investigation, finds such deficiencies, it shall notify the society in writing of its findings, and after reasonable notice require the society to show cause on a date designated in the notice why its license should not be suspended, revoked or refused. If, on the date named in the notice, the grounds for the proposed suspension, revocation or refusal of the society's license have not been removed to the satisfaction of the Commission, or the society does not present good and sufficient reasons why its authority to do business in this Commonwealth should not at that time be suspended, revoked, or refused the Commission may suspend, revoke or refuse the license of the society to do business in this Commonwealth. (Code 1950, §§ 38-322, 38.1-631; 1952, c. 317, § 38.1-638.52; 1968, c. 654; 1986, c. 562.)

§ 38.2-4132. Licensing of agents. — A. Agents of societies shall be licensed as life and health agents in accordance with Chapter 18 (§ 38.2-1800 et seq.) of this title regulating the licensing, revocation, suspension or termination of licenses of resident and nonresident agents.

B. No examination or license shall be required of any regular salaried officer, employee or member of a licensed society who devotes substantially all of his or her services to activities other than the solicitation of fraternal insurance contracts from the public, and who receives for the solicitation of such contracts no commission or other compensation directly dependent upon the amount of business obtained. (1968, c. 654, § 38.1-638.37; 1986, c. 562.)

§ 38.2-4133. Unfair methods of competition and unfair and deceptive acts and practices. — Every society authorized to do business in this Commonwealth shall be subject to the provisions of Chapter 5 (§ 38.2-500 et seq.) of this title. However, nothing in such provisions shall be construed as applying to or affecting the right of any society to determine its eligibility requirements for membership, or be construed as applying to or affecting the offering of benefits exclusively to members or persons eligible for membership in the society by a subsidiary corporation or affiliated organization of the society. (1968, c. 654, § 38.1-638.60; 1986, c. 562.)

§ 38.2-4134. Penalties. — A. Any person who willfully makes a false or fraudulent statement in or relating to an application for membership or for the purpose of obtaining money from or a benefit in any society shall upon conviction be fined not less than $100 nor more than $500 or be imprisoned not less than 30 days nor more than 1 year, or both.

B. Any person who willfully makes a false or fraudulent statement in any report or declaration required or authorized by this chapter, or of any material fact or thing contained in a statement concerning the death or disability of an insured for the purpose of procuring payment of a benefit named in the certificate, shall be guilty of perjury and shall be subject to the penalties therefor prescribed by law.

C. Any person who solicits membership for, or in any manner assists in procuring membership in, any society not licensed to do business in this Commonwealth shall upon conviction be fined not less than $50 nor more than $200.

D. Any other violation of this chapter shall be subject to § 38.2-218. (Code 1950, §§ 38-263, 38.1-578; 1952, c. 317, § 38.1-638.10; 1968, c. 654; 1986, c. 562.)

§ 38.2-4135. Exemption of certain societies. — A. Nothing contained in this chapter shall be construed to affect or apply to:

1. Grand or subordinate lodges of Masons, Odd Fellows, or Knights of Pythias, exclusive of the insurance department of the Supreme Lodge Knights of Pythias, or the Junior Order of United American Mechanics, exclusive of the beneficiary degree or insurance branch of the National Council, Junior Order of United American Mechanics;

2. Similar societies which do not issue insurance certificates;

3. An association of local lodges of a society now doing business in this Commonwealth which provides death benefits of not more than $500 to any 1 person, or disability benefits of not more than $300 in any 1 year to any 1 person, or both;

4. Contracts of reinsurance business on benefits of fraternal benefit societies in this Commonwealth;

5. Grand or subordinate lodges of societies, orders or associations now doing business in this Commonwealth which provide benefits exclusively through local or subordinate lodges;

6. Orders, societies or associations which admit to membership only persons engaged in one or more crafts or hazardous occupations, in the same or similar lines of business, insuring only their own members and their families, and the ladies' societies or ladies' auxiliaries to such orders, societies or associations;

7. Domestic societies which limit their membership to employees of a particular city or town, designated firm, business house or corporation and which provide for a death benefit of not more than $400 to any 1 person, or disability benefits of not more than $350 to any 1 person in any 1 year, or both;

8. Domestic societies or associations of a purely religious, charitable or benevolent description, which provide for a death benefit of not more than $100 or for disability benefits of not more than $150 to any 1 person in any 1 year, or both; or

9. Any association, whether a fraternal benefit society or not, which was organized before 1880 and whose members are officers or enlisted, regular or reserve, active, retired, or honorably discharged members of the Armed Forces or Sea Services of the United States, and a principal purpose of which is to provide insurance and other benefits to its members and their dependents or beneficiaries.

B. Any such society or association described in subdivisions 7 and 8 of subsection A which provides for death or disability benefits for which benefit certificates are issued, and any such society or association included in subdivision 8 of subsection A which has more than 1,000 members, shall comply with all provisions of this chapter.

C. No society which, by the provisions of this section, is exempt from the requirements of this chapter, except any society described in subdivision 6 of subsection A of this section, shall give or allow, or promise to give or allow to any person any compensation for procuring new members.

D. Every society which provides for benefits in case of death or disability resulting solely from accident, and which does not obligate itself to pay natural death or sick benefits, shall have all privileges and be subject to the applicable provisions and regulations of this chapter except that the provisions relating to medical examination, valuations of benefit certificates, and incontestability shall not apply to such society.

E. The Commission may require from any society or association, by examination or otherwise, such information as will enable the Commission to determine whether such society or association is exempt from the provisions of this chapter.

F. Societies, orders or associations exempted under the provisions of this section shall also be exempt from all other provisions of the insurance laws of this Commonwealth. (Code 1950, §§ 38-258, 38.1-573; 1952, c. 317, § 38.1-638.5; 1968, c. 654; 1986, c. 562; 1995, c. 321.)

§ 38.2-4136. Societies previously existing; reincorporation; amendments. — Any incorporated society doing business in this Commonwealth on June 19, 1914, may exercise all of the rights conferred by this chapter, and all of the rights, powers and privileges exercised or possessed by it under its charter or articles of incorporation not inconsistent with law; or, if a voluntary association, it may incorporate as provided herein. No society organized prior to June 19, 1914, shall be required to reincorporate under this section. Any society may amend its certificate of incorporation in the manner provided by law. (Code 1950, §§ 38-269, 38.1-580; 1952, c. 317, § 38.1-638.12; 1968, c. 654; 1986, c. 562.)

§ 38.2-4137. Exemption of member representatives of certain societies. — The provisions of § 38.2-4132 shall not apply to the member representatives of any society organized or licensed under this chapter which insures its members against death, dismemberment and disability resulting from accident only, and which pays no commission or other compensation for the solicitation and procurement of such contracts. (1968, c. 654, § 38.1-638.38; 1986, c. 562.)

CHAPTER 42.

HEALTH SERVICES PLANS.

ARTICLE 1.

In General.

§ 38.2-4200. Applicability of chapter. — A. Except as otherwise provided by law, no plan shall be organized, conducted or offered in this Commonwealth other than in the manner set forth in this chapter.

B. Nothing contained in this chapter shall prohibit any physician (i) as an individual, (ii) in partnership with other physicians, or (iii) as part of a professional corporation of physicians, from entering into agreements directly with his own patients, or with a parent, guardian, conservator, spouse or other family member acting in a patient's behalf, involving payment for professional services to be rendered or made available in the future. (1979, c. 721, § 38.1-813.1; 1980, c. 682; 1986, c. 562; 1997, c. 801.)

Editor's note. — Acts 1997, c. 801, cl. 2, provides: "That the provisions of this act shall become effective on January 1, 1998. The powers granted and duties imposed pursuant to this act shall apply prospectively to guardians and conservators appointed by court order entered on or after that date, or modified on or after that date if the court so directs, without regard to when the petition was filed. The procedures specified in this act governing proceedings for appointment of a guardian or conservator or termination or other modification of a guardianship shall apply on and after that date without regard to when the petition therefor was filed or the guardianship or conservatorship created."

The 1997 amendment, effective January 1, 1998, inserted "conservator" in subsection B.

§ 38.2-4201. Definitions. — As used in this chapter:

"Contract holder" means a person entering into a subscription contract with a nonstock corporation.

"Nonstock corporation" means a foreign or domestic nonstock corporation which is subject to regulation and licensing under this chapter and which offers or administers subscription contracts to contract holders as part of a plan.

"Health services plan" or *"plan"* means any arrangement for offering or administering health services or similar or related services by a nonstock corporation licensed under this chapter.

"Hospital services plan" means a health services plan for providing hospital and similar or related services.

"Medical or surgical services plan" means a health services plan for providing medical or surgical services or both, and similar or related services.

"Subscriber" means any person entitled to benefits under the terms and conditions of a subscription contract.

"Subscription contract" means a written contract which is issued to a contract holder by a nonstock corporation and which provides health services or benefits for health services on a prepaid basis. (1986, c. 562; 1988, c. 185.)

§ 38.2-4202. Hospital services plans. — A hospital or a group of hospitals may conduct through a nonstock corporation as agent for them a hospital services plan as defined in § 38.2-4201. (Code 1950, § 32-195.1; 1956, c. 268, § 38.1-810; 1960, c. 357; 1979, c. 721; 1980, c. 682; 1986, c. 562.)

Law Review. — For survey of Virginia law on insurance for the year 1969-1970, see 56 Va. L. Rev. 1356 (1970). For comment on price fixing in hospital plans and the Sherman Act, see 12 Wm. & Mary L. Rev. 676 (1971).

A Blue Cross prepaid drug plan is a similar or related service within the meaning of this section. Blue Cross v. Commonwealth, 211 Va. 180, 176 S.E.2d 439 (1970), decided under former § 32-195.1, similar to this section.

Hence, participating hospitals may conduct such a plan. Blue Cross v. Commonwealth, 211 Va. 180, 176 S.E.2d 439 (1970), decided under former § 32-195.1, similar to this section.

But not for purpose of stabilizing prices.
— Where a Blue Cross prepaid drug plan involves a combination formed for the purpose and with the effect of stabilizing the price of drugs, the plan is per se unreasonable and illegal under the Virginia Antitrust Act as well as under the Sherman Act. Blue Cross v. Commonwealth, 211 Va. 180, 176 S.E.2d 439 (1970), decided under former § 32-195.1, similar to this section.

§ 38.2-4203. Medical or surgical services plans. — A group of physicians may conduct through a nonstock corporation as agent for them a medical or surgical services plan as defined in § 38.2-4201. (Code 1950, § 32-195.2; 1956, c. 268, § 38.1-811; 1960, c. 357; 1979, c. 721; 1980, c. 682; 1986, c. 562.)

Law Review. — For note on antitrust and the Sherman Act as it applies to physicians administering Blue Shield plans, see 38 Wash. & Lee L. Rev. 460 (1981).

Antitrust law has always been sensitive to the realities of the marketplace and has been particularly watchful of organizations of the various trades or professions and Blue Shield Plans may fall within the purview of Section 1 of the Sherman Act such as where the plan attempts to eliminate competition from non-M.D. providers of psychotherapy by requiring payment for such services to be through physicians. Virginia Academy of Clinical Psychologists v. Blue Shield, 624 F.2d 476 (4th Cir. 1980), cert. denied, 450 U.S. 916, 101 S. Ct. 1360, 67 L. Ed. 2d 342 (1981).

Plans organized under this section are made up of participating physicians who as members of the plan contract to provide services to subscribers and are reimbursed by the Plan. Virginia Academy of Clinical Psychologists v. Blue Shield, 624 F.2d 476 (4th Cir. 1980), cert. denied, 450 U.S. 916, 101 S. Ct. 1360, 67 L. Ed. 2d 342 (1981).

Blue Shield Plans are not insurance companies, though they are, to a degree, insurers. Rather, they are generally characterized as prepaid health care plans, quantity purchasers of health care services. Virginia Academy of Clinical Psychologists v. Blue Shield, 624 F.2d 476 (4th Cir. 1980), cert. denied, 450 U.S. 916, 101 S. Ct. 1360, 67 L. Ed. 2d 342 (1981).

§ 38.2-4204. Merger of nonstock corporations. — A nonstock corporation operating a hospital services plan pursuant to § 38.2-4202 may be combined with a nonstock corporation operating a medical or surgical services plan pursuant to § 38.2-4203. The nonstock corporation created by such combination may be licensed to conduct a combination plan furnishing both hospital services and similar or related services and medical or surgical services, or both, and similar or related services. (1979, c. 721, § 38.1-812; 1980, c. 682; 1986, c. 562.)

§ 38.2-4204.1. Commission approval of mergers of nonstock corporations operating prepaid hospital, medical and surgical services plans. — A. Except as otherwise provided in this chapter, Article 11 (§ 13.1-894 et seq.) of Chapter 10 of Title 13.1 shall apply to mergers involving corporations licensed under this chapter.

B. Before any joint agreement for the merger of a corporation licensed under this chapter is submitted to the members, it shall first be submitted to and approved by the Commission. The Commission shall approve the agreement, unless, after giving notice and opportunity to be heard, it determines that:

1. After the merger, the new or surviving corporation would not be able to satisfy the requirements of this chapter for the issuance of a license;

2. The effect of the merger would lessen competition substantially or tend to create a monopoly in insurance, prepaid hospital, medical and surgical services plans, or health care benefit plans in this Commonwealth;

3. The financial condition of any party to the merger might jeopardize the financial stability of the new or surviving corporation, or prejudice the interest of the subscribers;

4. Any plans or proposals of the new or surviving corporation to liquidate the new or surviving corporation, sell its assets or merge it with any person, or to make any other material change in its business or corporate structure or

management, are unfair and unreasonable to the subscribers and not in the public interest;

5. The competence, experience, and integrity of those persons who would control the operation of the new or surviving corporation are such that it would not be in the interest of the subscribers and of the public to permit the merger; or

6. After the change of control, the new or surviving corporation's surplus to subscribers would not be reasonable in relation to its outstanding liabilities or adequate to its financial needs.

C. The provisions of subsection B notwithstanding, the Commission has the authority to merge two nonstock corporations licensed under this chapter where it finds that (i) one of the corporations is insolvent or is in such condition that its further transaction of business in this Commonwealth is hazardous to subscribers and the public, (ii) that the merger of such nonstock corporation into another nonstock corporation licensed under this chapter is desirable for the protection of its subscribers, and that such merger of such nonstock corporation is in the public interest, and (iii) that an emergency exists, and if the board of directors of the insolvent or financially hazardous nonstock corporation to be merged approves a plan of merger of such nonstock corporation into another nonstock corporation licensed under this chapter, compliance with the requirements of § 13.1-895 shall be dispensed with as to such nonstock corporation and the approval by the Commission of such plan of merger shall be the equivalent of approval of two-thirds of the members for all purposes of Article 11 (§ 13.1-894 et seq.) of Chapter 10 of Title 13.1. The Commission shall provide that prompt notice of its findings, and plan of merger be sent to the members of record of such corporation for the purpose of providing such members an opportunity to challenge the findings of the Commission and the plan of merger. The Commission's findings and plan of merger shall become final if a hearing before the Commission is not requested by any member in a written request delivered to the Commission within fifteen days after the notice specified herein is sent. (1986, c. 562.)

Editor's note. — This section is identical to repealed § 38.1-812.1, which was enacted by Acts 1986, c. 4, effective Feb. 19, 1986.

§ 38.2-4205. Dental and optometric services. — Dental services and optometric services may be provided by either subscription contract or endorsement in a plan. (1986, c. 562.)

§ 38.2-4206. Nonstock corporation required. — Each plan shall be conducted either by or through (i) a nonstock corporation organized pursuant to the laws of this Commonwealth or (ii) a foreign nonstock corporation that is subject to regulation and licensing under the laws of its domiciliary jurisdiction that are substantially similar to those provided by this chapter.

This section shall not apply to any foreign nonstock corporation already licensed in this Commonwealth as of July 1, 1980. (1980, c. 682, § 38.1-813.2; 1986, c. 562.)

§ 38.2-4207. Existing foreign nonstock corporation. — Any foreign nonstock corporation licensed in the Commonwealth as of July 1, 1980, may conduct a plan directly. (1980, c. 682, § 38.1-813.3; 1986, c. 562.)

§ 38.2-4208. Nonstock corporation not required to act as agent. — A. A nonstock corporation may offer or administer a plan without being required to act as an agent for providers of health care services.

B. A nonstock corporation applying for its initial license pursuant to this chapter in order to offer or administer a plan must elect in its application whether to act (i) as agent for providers of health care services, in which case §§ 38.2-4210 and 38.2-4211 shall apply, or (ii) as a nonagent, in which case the provisions of subsection D of this section shall apply.

C. A nonstock corporation operating a plan pursuant to §§ 38.2-4202, 38.2-4203, 38.2-4204 or this section prior to June 30, 1985, and any successor nonstock corporation shall continue to operate as either an agent or nonagent nonstock corporation, in accordance with the manner in which it was operating as of that date, provided that it may petition the Commission to change its status as an agent or nonagent nonstock corporation, and if it does so, it shall give notice of the petition to all interested parties. The Commission shall conduct a hearing on the petition if requested by any interested party. A nonstock corporation seeking to change its status shall make application to the Commission within ninety days following the end of any calendar year. A change in status shall only be effective as to subscriber contracts issued or renewed on and after the date of a change in status. The Commission shall enter an order in response to the nonstock corporation's petition.

D. If any nonstock corporation offers or administers a plan without acting as an agent for providers of health care services, the Commission may elect to (i) require the nonstock corporation to maintain its contingency reserves above a minimum level set by the Commission, or (ii) subject the nonstock corporation, notwithstanding the provisions of § 38.2-1700, to the requirements of Chapter 17 of this title, or (iii) both. The minimum level for contingency reserves shall not exceed forty-five days of the anticipated operating expenses and incurred claims expense generated from subscription contracts issued by the nonstock corporation, and shall be computed as the Commission requires. (Code 1950, § 32-195.5:1; 1972, c. 429, § 38.1-816; 1974, c. 54; 1979, c. 721; 1980, c. 682; 1982, c. 129; 1983, c. 464, § 38.1-813.4; 1985, c. 233; 1986, c. 562; 1988, c. 185.)

§ **38.2-4209. Preferred provider subscription contracts.** — A. As used in this section, a "preferred provider subscription contract" is a contract that specifies how services are to be covered when rendered by providers participating in a plan, by nonparticipating providers, and by preferred providers.

B. Notwithstanding the provisions of §§ 38.2-4218 and 38.2-4221, any nonstock corporation may, as a feature of its plan, offer preferred provider subscription contracts pursuant to the requirements of this section that limit the numbers and types of providers of health care services eligible for payment as preferred providers.

C. Any such nonstock corporation shall establish terms and conditions that shall be met by a hospital, physician or other type of provider listed in § 38.2-4221 in order to qualify for payment as a preferred provider under the subscription contracts. These terms and conditions shall not discriminate unreasonably against or among health care providers. No hospital, physician or type of provider listed in § 38.2-4221 willing to meet the terms and conditions offered to it or him shall be excluded. Differences in prices among hospitals or other institutional providers produced by a process of individual negotiations with the providers or based on market conditions, or price differences among providers in different geographical areas shall not be deemed unreasonable discrimination. The Commission shall have no jurisdiction to adjudicate controversies growing out of this subsection.

D. Mandated types of providers listed in § 38.2-4221 and types of providers whose services are required to be made available and which have been specifically contracted for by the holder of any subscription contract shall, to the extent required by § 38.2-4221, have the same opportunity as do doctors of medicine to qualify for payment as preferred providers.

E. Preferred provider subscription contracts shall provide for payment for services rendered by nonpreferred providers, but the payments need not be the same as for preferred providers.

F. No contract between a nonstock corporation and a provider shall include provisions which require a health care provider or health care provider group to deny covered services that such provider or group knows to be medically necessary and appropriate that are provided with respect to a specific enrollee or group of enrollees with similar medical conditions. (1983, c. 464, § 38.1-813.4; 1986, c. 562; 1999, cc. 643, 649.)

The 1999 amendments. — The 1999 amendments by cc. 643 and 649 are identical, and inserted subsection F.

This section not preempted by ERISA. — This section "regulates insurance" within the meaning of Employee Retirement Income Security Act's (ERISA) exception to its preemption clause. Therefore, this section has not been preempted by ERISA. Blue Cross & Blue Shield v. St. Mary's Hosp., 245 Va. 24, 426 S.E.2d 117 (1993).

§ 38.2-4209.1. Pharmacies; freedom of choice. — A. Notwithstanding any provision of § 38.2-4209, no corporation providing preferred provider subscription contracts shall prohibit any person receiving pharmaceutical benefits thereunder from selecting, without limitation, the pharmacy of his choice to furnish such benefits. This right of selection extends to and includes pharmacies that are nonpreferred providers and that have previously notified the corporation, by facsimile or otherwise, of their agreement to accept reimbursement for their services at rates applicable to pharmacies that are preferred providers, including any copayment consistently imposed by the corporation, as payment in full. Each corporation shall permit prompt electronic or telephonic transmittal of the reimbursement agreement by the pharmacy and ensure payment verification to the pharmacy of the terms of reimbursement. In no event shall any person receiving a covered pharmacy benefit from a nonpreferred provider which has submitted a reimbursement agreement be responsible for amounts that may be charged by the nonpreferred provider in excess of the copayment and the corporation's reimbursement applicable to all of its preferred pharmacy providers.

B. No such corporation shall impose upon any person receiving pharmaceutical benefits furnished under any such contract:

1. Any copayment, fee or condition that is not equally imposed upon all individuals in the same benefit category, class or copayment level, whether or not such benefits are furnished by pharmacists who are nonpreferred providers;

2. Any monetary penalty that would affect or influence any such person's choice of pharmacy; or

3. Any reduction in allowable reimbursement for pharmacy services related to utilization of pharmacists who are nonpreferred providers.

C. For purposes of this section, a prohibited condition or penalty shall include, without limitation: (i) denying immediate access to electronic claims filing to a pharmacy which is a nonpreferred provider and which has complied with subsection D below or (ii) requiring a person receiving pharmacy benefits to make payment at point of service, except to the extent such conditions and penalties are similarly imposed on preferred providers.

D. Any pharmacy which wishes to be covered by this section shall, if requested to do so in writing by a corporation, within thirty days of the pharmacy's receipt of the request, execute and deliver to the corporation the direct service agreement or preferred provider agreement which the corporation requires all of its preferred providers of pharmacy benefits to execute. Any pharmacy which fails to timely execute and deliver such agreement shall not be covered by this section with respect to that corporation unless and until the pharmacy executes and delivers the agreement.

E. The Commission shall have no jurisdiction to adjudicate controversies arising out of this section. (1994, c. 963; 1995, c. 467.)

Editor's note. — Acts 1995, c. 467, cl. 3, provides: "That the Joint Commission on Health Care shall conduct a three-year study of ancillary medical services insofar as the availability and quality of the same are affected by managed care, and shall include its findings thereon in its 1996, 1997 and 1998 reports to the Governor and the General Assembly."

The 1995 amendment, in subsection A, in the second sentence, substituted "and that have previously notified the corporation, by facsimile or otherwise, of their agreement" for "and that agree" and inserted "including any copayment consistently imposed by the corporation, as payment in full" and added the third and fourth sentences; added present subsections C and D; and redesignated former subsection C as present subsection E.

§ **38.2-4209.2:** Repealed by Acts 1995, c. 467.

§ **38.2-4210. Liability of participants.** — A. All hospitals, persons, nonstock corporations, and physicians participating in a plan shall be jointly and severally liable on all contracts made for the purposes of the plan by the nonstock corporation as agent for them. Each contract may be executed and signed by their agent on their behalf. A contract so signed shall be binding on the principals and not on the agent.

B. Actions for breach of these contracts may be brought against the principals by naming the agent as the sole defendant. A judgment in favor of the plaintiff may be satisfied out of the assets of the nonstock corporation or out of the assets of each of the principals.

C. Each participant shall be liable for his own torts and not for the torts of any other participant or of the agent. (Code 1950, § 32-195.4; 1956, c. 268, § 38.1-814; 1972, c. 429; 1979, c. 721; 1980, c. 682; 1986, c. 562.)

§ **38.2-4211. Change of participants.** — A. Any participating hospital, person, nonstock corporation or physician may resign from a plan at any time but will continue to be liable on each subscription contract then in effect. However, this liability shall not extend beyond the end of each such subscription contract's current contract year.

B. Hospitals, persons, nonstock corporations and physicians may be admitted to a plan at any time and will then automatically become liable on all its outstanding contracts. (Code 1950, § 32-195.5; 1956, c. 268, § 38.1-815; 1972, c. 429; 1979, c. 721; 1986, c. 562.)

§ **38.2-4212. Board of directors of nonstock corporation operating plan.** — A. Notwithstanding the provisions of §§ 13.1-853, 13.1-854 and 13.1-855, a nonstock corporation operating a plan pursuant to §§ 38.2-4202, 38.2-4203, 38.2-4204, or § 38.2-4208 shall be subject to the following:

1. The board of directors of the nonstock corporation shall consist of no more than fifteen members. However, if two or more nonstock corporations merge, the board of directors of the new or surviving nonstock corporation may consist of no more than twenty members. Further, the board of directors may be increased to a size not exceeding the aggregate number of directors on the merging nonstock corporations' boards for the balance of the year in which merger occurs and for the following five years.

2. Except as permitted by subsection B of this section, a majority of the members of the board of directors of the nonstock corporation shall be persons who are covered by subscription contracts issued by the nonstock corporation and who are not providers of health care services, or employees or salaried officers of the nonstock corporation.

B. Notwithstanding the provisions of §§ 13.1-853, 13.1-854 and 13.1-855, any nonstock corporation operating a plan pursuant to § 38.2-4203 may have a board of directors consisting of a majority of providers of health care services.

C. As used in this section, " providers of health care services" shall include, but not be limited to, physicians, pharmacists, nurses, physical therapists, hospital administrators, employees or majority or controlling stockholders of hospitals, and other persons furnishing health-related services.

D. This section shall not apply to any foreign nonstock corporation licensed in this Commonwealth on or before July 1, 1980. (Code 1950, §§ 32-195.5:1, 32-195.5:2; 1972, c. 429, §§ 38.1-816, 38.1-817; 1974, c. 54; 1979, c. 721; 1980, c. 682; 1982, c. 129; 1985, c. 233; 1986, c. 562.)

Law Review. — For note on antitrust and the Sherman Act as it applies to physicians administering Blue Shield plans, see 38 Wash. & Lee L. Rev. 460 (1981).

§ **38.2-4213. Liability of participating providers upon merger of nonstock corporation.** — If two or more nonstock corporations merge, §§ 38.2-4210 and 38.2-4211 shall not apply to the new or surviving nonstock corporation, its plans or its providers unless the nonstock corporations to be merged notify the Commission in writing at least thirty days prior to the date of the merger that the new or surviving nonstock corporation will remain subject to §§ 38.2-4210 and 38.2-4211. If notice is not given, the Commission may (i) require the new or surviving nonstock corporation to maintain its contingency reserves above minimum level, (ii) subject it, notwithstanding the provisions of § 38.2-1700, to the requirements of Chapter 17 of this title or (iii) both. The minimum level of contingency reserves shall not exceed thirty days of anticipated operating expenses and claims receipts computed as the Commission requires. If the nonstock corporation elects not to file the notice permitted by this section, the nonstock corporation and not its providers shall be liable for the obligations of the plan. (Code 1950, § 32-195.5:1; 1972, c. 429, § 38.1-816; 1974, c. 54; 1979, c. 721; 1980, c. 682; 1982, c. 129; 1985, c. 233; 1986, c. 562.)

§ **38.2-4214. Application of certain provisions of law.** — No provision of this title except this chapter and, insofar as they are not inconsistent with this chapter, §§ 38.2-200, 38.2-203, 38.2-210 through 38.2-213, 38.2-218 through 38.2-225, 38.2-230, 38.2-232, 38.2-305, 38.2-316, 38.2-322, 38.2-400, 38.2-402 through 38.2-413, 38.2-500 through 38.2-515, 38.2-600 through 38.2-620, 38.2-700 through 38.2-705, 38.2-900 through 38.2-904, 38.2-1017, 38.2-1018, 38.2-1038, 38.2-1040 through 38.2-1044, Articles 1 (§ 38.2-1300 et seq.) and 2 (§ 38.2-1306.2 et seq.) of Chapter 13, §§ 38.2-1312, 38.2-1314, 38.2-1317 through 38.2-1328, 38.2-1334, 38.2-1340, 38.2-1400 through 38.2-1444, 38.2-1800 through 38.2-1836, 38.2-3400, 38.2-3401, 38.2-3404, 38.2-3405, 38.2-3405.1, 38.2-3407.1 through 38.2-3407.6:1, 38.2-3407.9 through 38.2-3407.16, 38.2-3409, 38.2-3411 through 38.2-3419.1, 38.2-3430.1 through 38.2-3437, 38.2-3501, 38.2-3502, 38.2-3514.1, 38.2-3514.2, 38.2-3516 through 38.2-3520 as they apply to Medicare supplement policies, §§ 38.2-3522.1 through 38.2-3523.4, 38.2-3525, 38.2-3540.1, 38.2-3541, 38.2-3542, 38.2-3543.2, 38.2-3600 through 38.2-3607, Chapter 53 (§ 38.2-5300 et seq.), Chapter 58 (§ 38.2-5800 et seq.) and Chapter 59 (§ 38.2-5900 et seq.) of this title shall apply to the operation of a plan. (Code 1950, § 32-195.8; 1956, c. 268, § 38.1-818; 1960, c. 357; 1973, c. 28; 1975, c. 281; 1976, c. 355; 1977, cc. 606, 607; 1978, c. 496; 1979, cc. 47, 97, 721, 726; 1980, cc. 682, 719; 1981, c. 575; 1982, c. 577; 1983, c. 457; 1984, c. 718; 1986, cc. 550, 562; 1987, cc. 565, 655; 1989, cc. 606, 653; 1990, cc. 301, 393, 439, 531, 795, 802, 826; 1991, c. 369; 1992, c. 800; 1993, cc. 158, 306, 307; 1994, cc. 213, 320, 374, 522; 1995, cc. 420,

522; 1996, cc. 550, 776, 967; 1997, cc. 688, 807, 913; 1998, cc. 154, 891, 908; 1999, cc. 643, 649, 709, 739, 856, 857, 923.)

Editor's note. — Pursuant to § 9-77.11, effect has been given in this section, as set out above, to Acts 1986, c. 550, which amended former § 38.1-818, the comparable provision in former Title 38.1.

The 1998 amendments. — The 1998 amendment by c. 154 inserted "38.2-3522.1 through 38.2-3523.4" and inserted "38.2-3543.2."

The 1998 amendment by c. 891 deleted "and" preceding "Chapter 53" and inserted "and Chapter 58 (§ 38.2-5800 et seq.)."

The 1998 amendment by c. 908 inserted "§ 38.2-3407.12."

The 1999 amendments. — The 1999 amendment by c. 643 inserted "38.2-3407.9:01," inserted "38.2-3407.11:1," and inserted "38.2-3407.13, 38.2-3407.14, 38.2-3407.15."

The 1999 amendment by c. 649 inserted "38.2-3407.9:01," inserted "38.2-3407.11:1," inserted "38.2-3407.13, 38.2-3407.14, 38.2-3407.15," inserted "§§" preceding "38.2-3522.1," deleted "§§" preceding "38.2-3525," deleted "and" preceding "Chapter 58," and inserted "and Chapter 59 (§ 38.2-5900 et seq.)"

The 1999 amendments by cc. 709 and 739 are identical, and substituted "through 38.2-3407.13" for "38.2-3407.10, 38.2-3407.11, 38.2-3407.12."

The 1999 amendment by c. 856 inserted "38.2-3407.11:1," and substituted "38.2-3525" for "§§ 38.2-3525."

The 1999 amendment by c. 857 substituted "38.2-3407.6:1" for "38.2-3407.6," and substituted "38.2-3525" for "§§ 38.2-3525."

The 1999 amendment by c. 923, effective March 29, 1999, substituted "through 38.2-3407.13" for "38.2-3407.10, 38.2-3407.11, 38.2-3407.12," and substituted "§§ 38.2-3522.1 through 38.2-3523.4, 38.2-3525" for "38.2-3522.1 through 38.2-3523.4, §§ 38.2-3525."

§ 38.2-4214.1. Rehabilitation, liquidation, conservation. — Any rehabilitation, liquidation, or conservation of a health services plan shall be deemed to be the rehabilitation, liquidation, or conservation of an insurer and shall be subject to the provisions of Chapter 15 (§ 38.2-1500 et seq.) of Title 38.2. (1990, c. 331.)

§ 38.2-4215. Payments by nonstock corporation. — No payments shall be made by a nonstock corporation to a person included in a subscription contract unless the payment is for breach of contract or for contractually included costs incurred by that person or for services received by that person and rendered by a nonparticipating hospital or nonparticipating health care provider.

In no case shall that person be denied the right to assign his rights to benefits, except that denial may be made where the benefit is eighty percent of covered charges or greater. (Code 1950, § 32-195.8; 1956, c. 268, § 38.1-818; 1960, c. 357; 1973, c. 28; 1975, c. 281; 1976, c. 355; 1977, cc. 606, 607; 1978, c. 496; 1979, cc. 47, 97, 721, 726; 1980, cc. 682, 719; 1981, c. 575; 1982, c. 577; 1983, c. 457; 1984, c. 718; 1986, c. 562.)

Cross references. — As to denial or reduction of benefits because of existence of "other like insurance," see § 38.2-3509.

§ 38.2-4216: Repealed by Acts 1987, cc. 565, 655.

Cross references. — As to open enrollment, see now § 38.2-4216.1.

§ 38.2-4216.1. Open enrollment. — A. A nonstock corporation licensed under this chapter shall make available to citizens of the Commonwealth an open enrollment program under the terms set forth in this section.

B. As used in this section, the term:

"Comprehensive accident and sickness contracts" means contracts conforming to the requirements of subsection E which are issued to provide basic hospital and medical-surgical coverage.

"Open enrollment contracts" means comprehensive accident and sickness contracts issued pursuant to an open enrollment program by a nonstock corporation licensed pursuant to this chapter providing coverage to individuals.

C. Each nonstock corporation's open enrollment program shall provide for the issuance of open enrollment contracts without imposition by the nonstock corporation of underwriting criteria whereby coverage is denied or subject to cancellation or nonrenewal, in whole or in part because of any individual's age, health or medical history, or employment status or, if employed, industry or job classification. The open enrollment program shall make open enrollment contracts available to any individual residing in the nonstock corporation's service area within the Commonwealth; however, this subsection shall not require, and no person shall otherwise indicate, that open enrollment contracts are available to any individual who is an employee of an employer which provides, in whole or in part, hospitalization or other health coverage to its employees. Each nonstock corporation's open enrollment program shall make open enrollment contracts available on a year-round basis. The subscription charge for contracts issued pursuant to an open enrollment program shall be reasonable in relation to the benefits and deductibles provided, as determined by the Commission.

D. Each nonstock corporation must prominently advertise the availability of its open enrollment contracts at least twelve times annually in a newspaper or newspapers of general circulation throughout its service area in Virginia. The content and format of such advertising shall be generally approved by the Commission.

E. The Commission may prescribe minimum standards to govern the contents of comprehensive accident and sickness contracts issued pursuant to this section. Such minimum standards shall ensure that such contracts provide health benefit coverage for a comprehensive range of health care needs without qualifying exclusions that fail to protect the subscriber under normal circumstances. Such standards shall ensure that the option of obtaining comprehensive major medical coverage is made available to all individuals included within the definition of "open enrollment contracts" and shall allow for reasonable co-payment provisions, a range of deductibles and a range of coverages available to the consumer. Preexisting conditions may not be excluded from coverage under such contracts; however, waiting periods of up to twelve months for coverage of preexisting conditions shall be allowed. In addition, the Commission may prescribe reasonable minimum standards in order to govern the contents of policies issued to individuals who have converted from group comprehensive accident and sickness contracts to individual coverage because of termination of the individual's eligibility for group coverage.

F. If a nonstock corporation licensed under this chapter elects to discontinue its open enrollment program provided under this section, it may do so only after giving written notice to the Commission of at least twenty-four months in advance of the effective date of termination. Upon termination of the program, the nonstock corporation shall be subject to the license tax provisions of subdivision 1 of subsection A of § 58.1-2501.

G. In addition, a nonstock corporation licensed under this chapter shall provide other public services to the community including health-related educational support and training for those subscribers who, based upon such educational support and training, may experience a lesser need for health-related care and expense. (1987, cc. 565, 655; 1988, c. 185; 1997, cc. 807, 913.)

Editor's note. — Acts 1997, cc. 807 and 913, cl. 3, provide: "That the Bureau of Insurance within the State Corporation Commission, in cooperation with the Joint Commission on Health Care, monitor the impact of the provisions of this act [which, in part, amended this section] on the Commonwealth's health insurance marketplace. In monitoring the impact of this act, the State Corporation Commission shall: (i) review the federal regulations that will be promulgated to implement P.L. 104-191 (The Health Insurance Portability and Accountability Act), and determine whether any changes to this act are required by federal regulations adopted pursuant to P.L. 104-191; (ii) monitor the impact of the guaranteed issue requirements in the individual market and evaluate any specific concerns regarding such requirements identified and documented to the satisfaction of the State Corporation Commission by health insurance issuers; and (iii) recommend to the Governor and the 1998 Session of the General Assembly any revisions, corrections or improvements to the provisions of this act that would require the enactment of additional legislation."

The 1997 amendments. — The 1997 amendments by cc. 807 and 913 are identical, and in subsection B, deleted the former second sentence of the paragraph defining "Comprehensive accident and sickness contracts" which read: "Group comprehensive accident and sickness contracts must include provisions allowing individuals who leave such groups to convert to an individual policy providing an adequate level of coverage as determined by the Commission pursuant to subsection E" and deleted "and members of any group of forty-nine or fewer enrolled members, including multi-group, master-group or association-type contracts providing such coverage to individuals and members of organizations with forty-nine or fewer enrolled members" at the end of the paragraph defining "Open enrollment contracts"; in subsection C, rewrote the first sentence which formerly read: "Each nonstock corporation's open enrollment program shall provide for the issuance of open enrollment contracts without imposition by the nonstock corporation of underwriting criteria whereby coverage is denied or subject to cancellation or nonrenewal, in whole or in part because of: (i) any individual's age, health or medical history, or employment status or, if employed, industry or job classification; or (ii) in the case of any group included within the definition of 'open enrollment contracts,' because of the industry or job classification of the group, or the age, medical or health history, or insurability of any member of such group, including dependents," and in the second sentence, deleted "group included in the definition of 'open enrollment contracts' which is located in, and to any" following "available to any" and substituted "Commonwealth; however, this" for "Commonwealth; provided, however, that this"; and deleted "and groups" following "to all individuals" near the middle of the third sentence in subsection E.

§ 38.2-4217. Reports. — A. In addition to the annual statement required by § 38.2-1300, the Commission shall require each nonstock corporation to file on a quarterly basis any additional reports, exhibits or statements the Commission considers necessary to furnish full information concerning the condition, solvency, experience, transactions or affairs of the nonstock corporation. The Commission shall establish deadlines for submitting any additional reports, exhibits or statements. The Commission may require verification by any officers of the nonstock corporation the Commission designates.

B. In addition to the annual statement required by § 38.2-1300, the Commission shall require each nonstock corporation to file annually, on or before June 1, an annual statement, signed by two of its principal officers subject to § 38.2-1304, showing:

1. The number of Virginia subscribers by the following type of contract or its equivalent:

a. Individual, open enrollment;

b. Medicare, extended, under 65 disabled; and

c. Individual conversion subscribers.

2. The subscriber income and benefit payments in the aggregate for the types of contracts listed above subject to specific breakdown by type of contract as requested by the Commission; and

3. Expenditures for providing public services, in addition to open enrollment, to the community. (Code 1950, § 32-195.8:1; 1972, c. 429, § 38.1-819; 1979, c. 721; 1986, c. 562; 1987, cc. 565, 655; 1997, cc. 807, 913.)

Editor's note. — Acts 1997, cc. 807 and 913, cl. 3, provide: "That the Bureau of Insurance within the State Corporation Commission, in cooperation with the Joint Commission on Health Care, monitor the impact of the provisions of this act [which, in part, amended this section] on the Commonwealth's health insurance marketplace. In monitoring the impact of this act, the State Corporation Commission shall: (i) review the federal regulations that will be promulgated to implement P.L. 104-191 (The Health Insurance Portability and Accountability Act), and determine whether any changes to this act are required by federal regulations adopted pursuant to P.L. 104-191; (ii) monitor the impact of the guaranteed issue requirements in the individual market and evaluate any specific concerns regarding such requirements identified and documented to the satisfaction of the State Corporation Commission by health insurance issuers; and (iii) recommend to the Governor and the 1998 Session of the General Assembly any revisions, corrections or improvements to the provisions of this act that would require the enactment of additional legislation."

The 1997 amendments. — The 1997 amendments by cc. 807 and 913 are identical, and deleted former subdivision B 1 which read: "Small group, open enrollment," redesignated former subdivision B 1 c as present subdivision B 1 d and B 1 e, which read: "d. Associations;" "e. Community-rated groups of under 50 members;" and redesignated former subdivision B 1 f as present subdivision B 1 c.

§ 38.2-4218. Subscriber to have free choice of medical practitioners available. — A plan shall be organized and operated to assure that any subscriber shall have free choice of the medical practitioners available and participating in the plan. (Code 1950, § 32-195.8:2; 1972, c. 429, § 38.1-820; 1979, c. 721; 1986, c. 562.)

§ 38.2-4219. Subscriber to be advised in writing as to benefits and limitations thereon. — A nonstock corporation shall, prior to and during the term of the subscription contract, fully, fairly and currently advise the subscriber in writing of the benefits available under the contract and all limitations on the benefits available under the contract. (Code 1950, § 32-195.8:3; 1972, c. 429, § 38.1-821; 1979, c. 721; 1980, c. 682; 1986, c. 562.)

§ 38.2-4220. Interplan arrangements. — A nonstock corporation may enter into contracts with similar nonstock corporations for the interchange of services to those included in subscription contracts and may provide in subscription contracts for the substitution of services instead of those recited in its subscription contracts. However, no corporation shall enter into any contract to acquire or to attempt to acquire control, as defined in § 38.2-1322, of any person or enter into any material transaction, as defined in § 38.2-1322, if such contract or transaction would jeopardize or adversely affect the interests of the corporation's subscribers as determined by the Commission. (Code 1950, § 32-195.10; 1956, c. 268, § 38.1-823; 1979, c. 721; 1986, c. 562.)

§ 38.2-4221. Services of certain practitioners other than physicians to be covered. — A nonstock corporation shall not fail or refuse, either directly or indirectly, to allow or to pay to a subscriber for all or any part of the health services rendered by any doctor of podiatry, doctor of chiropody, optometrist, optician, chiropractor, professional counselor, psychologist, physical therapist, clinical social worker, clinical nurse specialist who renders mental health services, audiologist, speech pathologist, certified nurse midwife, or licensed acupuncturist licensed to practice in Virginia, if the services rendered (i) are services provided for by the subscription contract and (ii) are services which the doctor of podiatry, doctor of chiropody, optometrist, optician, chiropractor, professional counselor, psychologist, physical therapist, clinical social worker, clinical nurse specialist who renders mental health services, audiologist, speech pathologist, certified nurse midwife, or licensed acupuncturist is licensed to render in this Commonwealth. (Code 1950, § 32-195.10:1;

1966, c. 276, § 38.1-824; 1973, c. 428; 1979, cc. 13, 721; 1980, c. 682; 1986, c. 562; 1987, cc. 549, 551, 557; 1988, c. 522; 1989, cc. 7, 201; 1997, c. 203; 1998, c. 146.)

The 1998 amendment deleted "or" preceding "certified nurse midwife" and inserted "or licensed acupuncturist" in two places.

Law Review. — For note on antitrust and the Sherman Act as it applies to physicians administering Blue Shield plans, see 38 Wash. & Lee L. Rev. 460 (1981).

The State Corporation Commission was required to rule upon the constitutionality of this section where it sought to enforce compliance upon Blue Cross/Blue Shield by a show cause order, due process requiring that Blue Cross/Blue Shield be given a hearing and opportunity to show the invalidity of this section. Blue Cross & Blue Shield v. Commonwealth ex rel. SCC, 218 Va. 589, 239 S.E.2d 94 (1977).

Section 38.2-4228 does not deny the commission jurisdiction to pass upon the constitutionality of this section. Blue Cross & Blue Shield v. Commonwealth ex rel. SCC, 218 Va. 589, 239 S.E.2d 94 (1977).

Focus of this section is on services for medical care and the availability of such services. Virginia Academy of Clinical Psychologists v. Blue Shield, 501 F. Supp. 1232 (E.D. Va. 1980).

And this section makes more available to the public those services already determined to be advantageous to the public health and safety and represents a valid exercise of the commonwealth's police power as applied to optometrists, opticians and psychologists. Blue Cross v. Commonwealth, 221 Va. 349, 269 S.E.2d 827 (1980).

Plan may not judge necessity of service. — When psychologists perform services for which they are licensed and such services are within the terms of the contract, and prepaid medical plan may not substitute its own judgment as to the necessity of the service rendered. Virginia Academy of Clinical Psychologists v. Blue Shield, 501 F. Supp. 1232 (E.D. Va. 1980).

§ 38.2-4222. Licensing of nonstock corporations. — A. No person shall deliver or issue for delivery in this Commonwealth a subscription contract without a license issued by the Commission. Each nonstock corporation shall apply for a license and furnish any relevant information the Commission requires. Each license shall expire at midnight on the following June 30. Application for a license shall be accompanied by a nonrefundable application fee of $500.

B. The Commission may refuse to issue or renew a license to a nonstock corporation if it is not satisfied that the financial condition, the method of operation, and the manner of doing business of the nonstock corporation enable it to meet its contractual obligations to all subscribers and that the nonstock corporation has otherwise complied with all the requirements of law. (Code 1950, § 32-195.11; 1956, c. 268, § 38.1-825; 1978, c. 4; 1979, c. 721; 1980, c. 682; 1986, c. 562; 1987, cc. 565, 655; 1988, c. 185; 1994, c. 503.)

§ 38.2-4223. Renewal of license. — A. Each nonstock corporation shall renew its license with the Commission annually by July 1. The renewal license shall not be issued unless the nonstock corporation has complied with all requirements of law.

B. The Commission shall not fail or refuse to renew the license of any nonstock corporation without first giving the nonstock corporation ten days' notice of its intention not to renew the license and giving the nonstock corporation an opportunity to be heard and introduce evidence in its behalf. Any such hearing may be informal, and the required notice may be waived by the Commission and the nonstock corporation. (Code 1950, § 32-195.12; 1956, c. 268, § 38.1-826; 1978, c. 4; 1979, c. 721; 1980, c. 682; 1986, c. 562; 1987, cc. 565, 655.)

§ 38.2-4224. Licensing of agents. — Subscription contracts may be solicited only through life and health insurance agents licensed in accordance with Chapter 18 of this title. Home office salaried officers whose principal duties and responsibilities do not include the negotiation or solicitation of subscription contracts shall not be required to be licensed. (Code 1950, § 32-195.13; 1956, c. 268, § 38.1-827; 1978, c. 4; 1979, c. 721; 1980, c. 682; 1986, c. 562; 1999, c. 86.)

The 1999 amendment deleted "health agents or" following "solicited only through" in the first sentence.

§ 38.2-4225: Repealed by Acts 1987, cc. 565, 655.

§ 38.2-4226. Taxation. — Except as provided by Chapter 4 of this title, the license tax paid by a nonstock corporation under Chapter 25 of Title 58.1 shall be in lieu of all other state and local license fees or license taxes and state income taxes of the nonstock corporation. (Code 1950, § 32-195.15; 1956, c. 268, § 38.1-828; 1969, Ex. Sess., c. 26; 1979, c. 721; 1980, c. 682; 1986, c. 562; 1987, cc. 565, 655.)

§ 38.2-4227. Misleading applications or contracts. — In the operation of a plan, no person shall use any misleading subscription applications or contracts. (Code 1950, § 32-195.16; 1956, c. 268, § 38.1-829; 1960, c. 357; 1979, c. 721; 1986, c. 562.)

§ 38.2-4228. Controversies involving subscription contracts. — The Commission shall have no jurisdiction to adjudicate controversies growing out of subscription contracts. A breach of contract shall not be deemed a violation of this chapter. (Code 1950, § 32-195.20; 1956, c. 268, § 38.1-833; 1979, c. 721; 1986, c. 562.)

The sole purpose of this section is to provide that a controversy between subscribers and Blue Cross/Blue Shield, or controversies growing out of the Blue Cross/Blue Shield subscription contracts, cannot be decided by the commission but must be resolved, as are other civil controversies, in the courts throughout Virginia. Blue Cross & Blue Shield v. Commonwealth ex rel. SCC, 218 Va. 589, 239 S.E.2d 94 (1977).

The purpose of the provision reading "and a breach of contract shall not be deemed a violation of this chapter" was to assure that a mere controversy between Blue Cross/Blue Shield and a subscriber in which the subscriber alleges breach of contract, and which might be resolved adversely to Blue Cross/Blue Shield, would not result in a revocation of the license of Blue Cross/Blue Shield pursuant to former § 38.1-831. Blue Cross & Blue Shield v. Commonwealth ex rel. SCC, 218 Va. 589, 239 S.E.2d 94 (1977).

This section does not deny the commission jurisdiction to pass upon the constitutionality of § 38.2-4221. Blue Cross & Blue Shield v. Commonwealth ex rel. SCC, 218 Va. 589, 239 S.E.2d 94 (1977).

§ 38.2-4229. Reinsurance. — Any nonstock corporation licensed under this chapter may by policy, treaty or other agreement cede to any insurer reinsurance upon the whole or any part of any risk, with or without contingent liability or participation, and if a mutual insurer, with or without membership therein. (1986, c. 562.)

§ 38.2-4229.1. Conversion to domestic mutual insurer. — A. Any domestic nonstock corporation subject to the provisions of this chapter that has the surplus required by § 38.2-1030 for domestic mutual insurers issuing policies without contingent liability may, at its option and without reincorporation, convert to a domestic mutual insurer by following the procedure set forth in this section.

B. Any nonstock corporation eligible to convert to a domestic mutual insurer under subsection A of this section may effect such conversion by amending its articles of incorporation to delete any reference to this chapter and to comply with the provisions of § 38.2-1002 relating to the articles of incorporation of a domestic mutual insurer. Upon the issuance of a certificate of amendment by the Commission, the conversion shall be effective, such nonstock corporation shall become subject to all of the provisions of this title relating to domestic mutual insurers, and, except as provided in subsection D of this section, such nonstock corporation shall no longer be subject to the provisions of this chapter.

C. If any nonstock corporation converts from a health services plan organized under this chapter to a domestic mutual insurer, then at least ninety days prior to the effective date of conversion, the nonstock corporation shall comply with § 38.2-316 by filing with the Commission copies of all policies of insurance that it proposes to issue after the effective date of conversion. All subscription contracts issued and outstanding as of the effective date of conversion shall remain in force in accordance with their terms until the expiration or termination of such contracts.

D. Any nonstock corporation that offers an open enrollment program under § 38.2-4216.1 shall, directly or through a subsidiary, continue to offer such program notwithstanding its conversion to a domestic mutual insurer. If any such domestic mutual insurer converts to a stock insurer, it shall, directly or through a subsidiary, continue to offer such program notwithstanding its conversion to a stock insurer. No such insurer shall discontinue the open enrollment program required by § 38.2-4216.1 without first giving the Commission twenty-four months' prior written notice. For so long as the insurer continues to offer such open enrollment program, the license tax imposed on the direct gross premium income of the insurer and its subsidiaries from accident and sickness insurance shall be two and one-fourth percent (2.25%) on premium income from accident and sickness insurance issued to primary small employers as defined in § 38.2-3431 and three-fourths of one percent (.75%) on other premium income from accident and sickness insurance for taxable year 1997; and shall thereafter be three-fourths of one percent on premium income derived from individual accident and sickness insurance policies and from open enrollment contracts as defined in § 38.2-4216.1, and two and one-fourth percent on other premium income from accident and sickness insurance.

E. No policy of accident and sickness insurance issued by a nonstock corporation after its conversion to a domestic mutual insurer shall deny the policyholder the right to assign his benefit, except that denial may be made where the benefit is eighty percent of covered charges or greater. (1991, c. 87; 1992, c. 473; 1994, c. 294; 1997, cc. 807, 913.)

Editor's note. — Acts 1997, cc. 807 and 913, cl. 3, provide: "That the Bureau of Insurance within the State Corporation Commission, in cooperation with the Joint Commission on Health Care, monitor the impact of the provisions of this act [which, in part, amended this section] on the Commonwealth's health insurance marketplace. In monitoring the impact of this act, the State Corporation Commission shall: (i) review the federal regulations that will be promulgated to implement P.L. 104-191 (The Health Insurance Portability and Accountability Act), and determine whether any changes to this act are required by federal regulations adopted pursuant to P.L. 104-191; (ii) monitor the impact of the guaranteed issue requirements in the individual market and evaluate any specific concerns regarding such requirements identified and documented to the satisfaction of the State Corporation Commission by health insurance issuers; and (iii) recommend to the Governor and the 1998 Session of the General Assembly any revisions, corrections or improvements to the provisions of this act that would require the enactment of additional legislation."

The 1997 amendments. — The 1997 amendments by cc. 807 and 913 are identical, and in subsection D, in the third sentence, deleted "three-fourths of one percent (.75%) for taxable year 1994 and shall thereafter be" following "sickness insurance shall be" and inserted "for taxable year 1997; and shall thereafter be three-fourths of one percent on premium income derived from individual accident and sickness insurance policies and from open enrollment contracts as defined in § 38.2-4216.1, and two and one-fourth percent on other premium income from accident and sickness insurance" at the end of the sentence.

ARTICLE 2.

Holding Companies.

§ 38.2-4230. Definitions. — As used in this article:

"Affiliate" of a specific person or a person "affiliated" with a specific person means a person that directly or indirectly, through one or more intermediaries, controls, is controlled by or is under common control with the person specified.

"Control," including the terms *"controlling," "controlled by"* and *"under common control with,"* means direct or indirect possession of the power to direct or cause the direction of the management and policies of a person through (i) the ownership of voting securities, (ii) by contract other than a commercial contract for goods or nonmanagement services, or (iii) otherwise, unless the power is the result of an official position with or corporate office held by the person. Control shall be presumed to exist if any person directly or indirectly owns, controls, holds with the power to vote, or holds proxies representing collectively ten percent or more of the voting securities of any other person. This presumption may be rebutted by a showing made in the manner provided by subsection H of § 38.2-4231 that control does not exist. After giving all interested persons notice and opportunity to be heard and making specific findings to support its determination, the Commission may determine that control exists, notwithstanding the absence of a presumption to that effect.

"Holding company system" means two or more affiliated persons, one or more of which is a nonstock corporation licensed under this chapter.

"Surplus" means the excess of total admitted assets over the liabilities of a nonstock corporation licensed under this chapter, and shall include any contingency reserves maintained pursuant to § 38.2-4208 and any voluntary reserves.

"Transaction" means any (i) sale, purchase, exchange, renting or leasing arrangement, loan or extension of credit, arrangement for the assumption, extension or renewal of any obligation or liability, guaranty or surety arrangement, or investment; (ii) dividend or distribution of cash or property; (iii) reinsurance treaty or risk-sharing arrangement; (iv) management contract, service contract or cost-sharing arrangement; or (v) other arrangement, relationship or dealings that the Commission by order, rule or regulation determines to be a transaction contemplated by this article. A transaction shall not include any transaction which the Commission by rule or regulation exempts as not being material for the purpose of §§ 38.2-4231 and 38.2-4233. Any series of transactions occurring within a twelve-month period that are sufficiently similar in nature as to be reasonably construed as a single transaction and that in the aggregate exceed any minimum set forth in §§ 38.2-4231 and 38.2-4233 shall be deemed a transaction subject to the provisions of such sections.

"Voting security" means any security that enables the owner to vote for the election of directors. Voting security includes any security convertible into or evidencing a right to acquire a voting security. (1989, c. 606; 1992, c. 588.)

§ 38.2-4231. Registration of nonstock corporations that are members of holding company system. — A. Each nonstock corporation licensed under this chapter that is a member of a holding company system shall register with the Commission. Any nonstock corporation subject to registration under this section shall register within fifteen days after it becomes subject to registration, unless the Commission extends the time for registration for good cause shown.

B. 1. This section shall not apply to:

a. Any foreign nonstock corporation subject to disclosure requirements and standards adopted by statute or regulation in the jurisdiction of its domicile that are substantially similar to those contained in this section;

b. Any nonstock corporation licensed under this chapter, information, or transaction if and to the extent that the Commission exempts the same from this section; or

c. Any transaction involving less than one-sixth of one percent of admitted assets or one percent of surplus as of the immediately preceding December 31, whichever is less.

2. Any nonstock corporation licensed under this chapter that is a member of a holding company system but not subject to registration under this section may be required by the Commission to furnish a copy of the registration statement, or other information filed by the nonstock corporation, with the regulatory authority of its domiciliary jurisdiction.

C. Each nonstock corporation subject to registration under this section shall file a registration statement on a form provided by the Commission. Such statement shall contain current information on:

1. The capital structure, general financial condition, ownership, and management of the nonstock corporation and any person controlling the nonstock corporation;

2. The identity of every member of the insurance holding company system;

3. The following agreements in force, continuing relationships and transactions currently outstanding between the nonstock corporation and its affiliates:

a. Loans or extensions of credit, other investments, or purchases, sales or exchanges of securities of the affiliates by the nonstock corporation or of the nonstock corporation by its affiliates;

b. Purchases, sales, renting or leasing arrangements, or exchanges of assets;

c. Guarantees or undertakings for the benefit of an affiliate that result in an actual contingent exposure of the nonstock corporation's assets to liability;

d. All management and service contracts and all cost-sharing arrangements;

e. Reinsurance agreements or other risk-sharing arrangements;

f. Transactions not in the ordinary course of business; and

4. Other matters relating to transactions between a registered nonstock corporation and any affiliates which may be included from time to time in any registration forms adopted or approved by the Commission.

D. Each registered nonstock corporation shall report all additional transactions with affiliates and any changes in previously reported transactions with affiliates on amendment forms provided by the Commission. Each nonstock corporation shall make its report within fifteen days after the end of the month in which it learns of each additional transaction or change in a transaction. Each registered nonstock corporation shall also keep current the information required by subsection C of this section by filing an amendment to its registration statement within 120 days after the end of each fiscal year of the ultimate controlling person of the holding company system.

E. The Commission shall terminate the registration of any nonstock corporation that demonstrates it no longer is a member of a holding company system.

F. The Commission may require or allow two or more affiliated nonstock corporations subject to registration under this section to file a consolidated registration statement or consolidated reports amending their consolidated registration statement or their individual registration statements.

G. The Commission may allow a nonstock corporation which is licensed under this chapter and which is part of a holding company system, to register on behalf of any affiliated nonstock corporation required to register under subsection A of this section and to file all information and material required to be filed under this section.

H. Any person may file with the Commission a disclaimer of affiliation with any licensed nonstock corporation. The disclaimer shall fully disclose all relationships and bases for affiliation between the person and the nonstock corporation as well as the basis for disclaiming the affiliation. After a disclaimer has been filed, the nonstock corporation shall be relieved of any registration or reporting requirements under this section that may arise out of the nonstock corporation's relationship with the person unless and until the Commission disallows the disclaimer. The Commission shall disallow the disclaimer only after giving all interested parties notice and opportunity to be heard. Any disallowance shall be supported by specific findings of fact. (1989, c. 606; 1992, c. 588.)

§ 38.2-4232. Standards for transactions with affiliates; adequacy of surplus; dividends and other distributions. — A. Transactions by nonstock corporations licensed under this chapter with their affiliates shall be subject to the following standards:

1. The terms shall be fair and reasonable;

2. Charges and fees for service performed shall be reasonable;

3. Expenses incurred and payments received shall be allocated to the insurer in conformity with customary insurance accounting practices consistently applied;

4. The books, accounts, and records of each party shall disclose clearly and accurately the precise nature and details of the transactions;

5. The nonstock corporation's surplus following any transaction with affiliates involving more than one-sixth of one percent of admitted assets or one percent of surplus as of the immediately preceding December 31, whichever is less, shall be reasonable in relation to the nonstock corporation's outstanding liabilities and adequate to its financial needs; and

6. The transaction is in the best interest of the subscribers.

B. For purposes of this article, in determining whether a nonstock corporation's surplus is reasonable in relation to the nonstock corporation's outstanding liabilities and adequate to its financial needs, the following factors, among others, shall be considered:

1. The size of the nonstock corporation as measured by its assets, surplus, reserves, business in force, and other appropriate criteria;

2. The nonstock corporation's method of operation and manner of doing business;

3. The nature and extent of the nonstock corporation's risk-sharing arrangements;

4. The quality, diversification, and liquidity of the nonstock corporation's investment portfolio;

5. The recent past and projected future trend in the size of the nonstock corporation's surplus;

6. The adequacy of the nonstock corporation's reserves; and

7. The quality and liquidity of investments in subsidiaries. The Commission in its judgment may classify any investment as a nonadmitted asset for the purpose of determining the adequacy of surplus. (1989, c. 606; 1992, c. 588.)

§ 38.2-4233. Commission approval required for certain transactions. — A. Prior written approval of the Commission shall be required for any transaction between a nonstock corporation licensed under this chapter and any of its affiliates, if such transaction involves more than three-fourths of one percent of admitted assets or five percent of surplus as of the immediately preceding December 31, whichever is less. Failure of the Commission to act within sixty days after notification by the nonstock corporation shall constitute approval of the transaction.

B. Nothing contained in this section shall authorize or permit any transaction that would be otherwise contrary to law.

C. The Commission, in reviewing any transaction under this section, shall consider whether the transaction complies with the standards set forth in § 38.2-4232. The Commission shall set forth the specific reasons for the disapproval of any transaction.

D. The approval of any transaction under this section shall be deemed an amendment under subsection D of § 38.2-4231 to a nonstock corporation's registration statement without further filing.

E. The Commission shall have continuing oversight over the terms and conditions of all continuing transactions by a nonstock corporation licensed under this chapter with its affiliates. The Commission may prohibit the continuation of any continuing transaction if the Commission finds that, because of changed circumstances or material information unknown to the Commission at the time of the approval of the transaction, the transaction does not comply with the standards set forth in § 38.2-4232.

F. Existing transactions entered into between a nonstock corporation and its affiliates prior to July 1, 1989, shall be filed with the Commission for approval no later than September 1, 1989, if such transaction involves more than three-fourths of one percent of admitted assets or five percent of surplus as of the immediately preceding December 31, whichever is less. Failure of the Commission to act within 120 days after such filings shall constitute approval of such transactions. The Commission shall not disapprove any transaction entered into prior to July 1, 1989, if such transaction was lawful when entered into, but if any such transaction is found not to meet the standards of this section, such transaction shall not be renewed or extended except upon terms approved by the Commission.

G. Any nonstock corporation aggrieved by a disapproval or withdrawal of approval under this section may proceed under the provisions of § 38.2-222.

H. For the purposes of this section, a *"transaction between a nonstock corporation licensed under this chapter and any of its affiliates"* includes any transaction between a nonstock corporation licensed under this chapter and a nonaffiliate if such transaction involves (i) any loan or extension of credit where the licensee makes such loan or extension of credit with the agreement or understanding that the proceeds of such transaction, in whole or substantial part, are to be used to make any loan or extension of credit to, to purchase assets of, or to make investments in any affiliate of the licensee or (ii) any reinsurance agreement or risk-sharing arrangement, or modifications thereto, which requires as consideration the transfer of assets from a licensee to a nonaffiliate, if an agreement or understanding exists between the licensee and the nonaffiliate that any portion of such assets will be transferred to one or more affiliates of the licensee. (1989, c. 606; 1993, c. 158.)

§ 38.2-4234. Examinations. — A. In addition to the powers the Commission has under Article 4 of Chapter 13 (§ 38.2-1317 et seq.) of this title, the Commission shall also have the power to order any nonstock corporation registered under § 38.2-4231 to produce any records, books, or other information papers in the possession of the nonstock corporation or its affiliates necessary to determine the financial condition or legality of conduct of the nonstock corporation. If the nonstock corporation fails to comply with the order, the Commission shall have the power to examine its affiliates to obtain the information.

B. The Commission shall exercise its power under subsection A of this section only if the examination of the nonstock corporation under Article 4 of Chapter 13 (§ 38.2-1317 et seq.) of this title is inadequate or the interests of the subscribers of the nonstock corporation may be adversely affected.

C. The Commission may retain at the expense of the registered nonstock corporation any attorneys, actuaries, accountants and other experts reasonably necessary to assist in the conduct of the examination under subsection A of this section. Any persons so retained shall be under the direction and control of the Commission and shall act in a purely advisory capacity.

D. Each nonstock corporation producing books and papers for examination records pursuant to subsection A of this section shall be liable for and shall pay the expense of the examination in accordance with the provisions of Article 4 of Chapter 13 (§ 38.2-1317 et seq.) of this title. (1989, c. 606; 1992, c. 588.)

§ 38.2-4235. Confidential treatment of information and documents.
— All information, documents and copies obtained by or disclosed to the Commission or any other person in the course of an examination or investigation made pursuant to § 38.2-4234, and all information reported pursuant to § 38.2-4231, shall be confidential and shall not be made public by the Commission or any other person without the prior written consent of the nonstock corporation to which they pertain. However, this provision shall not apply to information given to insurance departments in other states. After the licensed nonstock corporation and its affiliates have been given notice and opportunity to be heard, the Commission may publish all or any part of the information and materials referred to in this section in any manner it considers appropriate, if it determines that the interests of subscribers or the public will be served by the publication. (1989, c. 606.)

CHAPTER 43.

HEALTH MAINTENANCE ORGANIZATIONS.

§ 38.2-4300. Definitions. — As used in this chapter:

"Basic health care services" means in and out-of-area emergency services, inpatient hospital and physician care, outpatient medical services, laboratory and radiologic services, and preventive health services. "Basic health care services" shall also mean limited treatment of mental illness and substance abuse in accordance with such minimum standards as may be prescribed by the Commission which shall not exceed the level of services mandated for insurance carriers pursuant to Chapter 34 (§ 38.2-3400 et seq.) of this title. In the case of a health maintenance organization that has contracted with this Commonwealth to furnish basic health services to recipients of medical assistance under Title XIX of the United States Social Security Act pursuant to § 38.2-4320, the basic health services to be provided by the health maintenance organization to program recipients may differ from the basic health services required by this section to the extent necessary to meet the benefit standards prescribed by the state plan for medical assistance services authorized pursuant to § 32.1-325.

"Copayment" means a payment required of enrollees as a condition of the receipt of specific health services.

"Emergency services" means those health care services that are rendered by affiliated or nonaffiliated providers after the sudden onset of a medical condition that manifests itself by symptoms of sufficient severity, including severe pain, that the absence of immediate medical attention could reasonably be expected by a prudent layperson who possesses an average knowledge of health and medicine to result in (i) serious jeopardy to the mental or physical health of the individual, (ii) danger of serious impairment of the individual's bodily functions, (iii) serious dysfunction of any of the individual's bodily organs, or (iv) in the case of a pregnant woman, serious jeopardy to the health of the fetus. Emergency services provided within the plan's service area shall include covered health care services from nonaffiliated providers only when delay in receiving care from a provider affiliated with the health maintenance organization could reasonably be expected to cause the enrollee's condition to worsen if left unattended.

"Enrollee" or *"member"* means an individual who is enrolled in a health care plan.

"Evidence of coverage" means any certificate, individual or group agreement or contract, or identification card issued in conjunction with the certificate, agreement or contract, issued to a subscriber setting out the coverage and other rights to which an enrollee is entitled.

"Health care plan" means any arrangement in which any person undertakes to provide, arrange for, pay for, or reimburse any part of the cost of any health care services. A significant part of the arrangement shall consist of arranging for or providing health care services, including emergency services and services rendered by nonparticipating referral providers, as distinguished from mere indemnification against the cost of the services, on a prepaid basis. For purposes of this section, a significant part shall mean at least ninety percent of total costs of health care services.

"Health care services" means the furnishing of services to any individual for the purpose of preventing, alleviating, curing, or healing human illness, injury or physical disability.

"Health maintenance organization" means any person who undertakes to provide or arrange for one or more health care plans.

"Limited health care services" means dental care services, vision care services, mental health services, substance abuse services, pharmaceutical

services, and such other services as may be determined by the Commission to be limited health care services. Limited health care services shall not include hospital, medical, surgical or emergency services except as such services are provided incident to the limited health care services set forth in the preceding sentence.

"Nonparticipating referral provider" means a provider who is not a participating provider but with whom a health maintenance organization has arranged, through referral by its participating providers, to provide health care services to enrollees. Payment or reimbursement by a health maintenance organization for health care services provided by nonparticipating referral providers may exceed five percent of total costs of health care services, only to the extent that any such excess payment or reimbursement over five percent shall be combined with the costs for services which represent mere indemnification, with the combined amount subject to the combination of limitations set forth in this definition and in this section's definition of health care plan.

"Participating provider" means a provider who has agreed to provide health care services to enrollees and to hold those enrollees harmless from payment with an expectation of receiving payment, other than copayments or deductibles, directly or indirectly from the health maintenance organization.

"Provider" or *"health care provider"* means any physician, hospital, or other person that is licensed or otherwise authorized in the Commonwealth to furnish health care services.

"Subscriber" means a contract holder, an individual enrollee or the enrollee in an enrolled family who is responsible for payment to the health maintenance organization or on whose behalf such payment is made. (1980, c. 720, § 38.1-863; 1986, cc. 76, 528, 562; 1990, c. 224; 1992, cc. 241, 481; 1993, c. 305; 1995, cc. 182, 345.)

Editor's note. — Pursuant to § 9-77.11, effect has been given in this section, as set out above, to Acts 1986, cc. 76 and 528, which amended former § 38.1-863, the comparable provision in former Title 38.1.

§ 38.2-4301. Establishment of health maintenance organizations. — A. No person shall establish or operate a health maintenance organization in this Commonwealth without obtaining a license from the Commission. Any person, including a foreign corporation, may apply to the Commission for a license to establish and operate a health maintenance organization in compliance with this chapter.

B. Each application for a license shall be verified by an officer or authorized representative of the applicant, shall be in a form prescribed by the Commission, and shall set forth or be accompanied by the following:

1. A copy of any basic organizational document of the applicant including, but not limited to, the articles of incorporation, articles of association, partnership agreement, trust agreement, or other applicable documents, and all amendments to those documents;

2. A copy of the bylaws, rules and regulations, or any similar document regulating the conduct of the internal affairs of the applicant;

3. A list of the names, addresses, and official positions of each member of the governing body, and a full disclosure in the application of (i) any financial interest between any officer or member of the governing body or any provider, organization or corporation owned or controlled by such person and the health maintenance organization, and (ii) the extent and nature of the financial arrangements between such persons and the health maintenance organization;

4. A copy of any contract made or to be made between any providers, sponsors or organizers of the health maintenance organization, or persons listed in subdivision 3 of this subsection and the applicant;

5. A copy of the evidence of coverage form to be issued to subscribers;

6. A copy of any group contract form that is to be issued to employers, unions, trustees, or other organizations. All group contracts shall set forth the right of subscribers to convert their coverages to an individual contract issued by the health maintenance organization;

7. Financial statements showing the applicant's assets, liabilities, and sources of financial support or, if the applicant's financial affairs are audited by independent certified public accountants, a copy of the applicant's most recent regular certified financial statement unless the Commission directs that additional or more recent financial information is required for the proper administration of this chapter;

8. A complete description of the health maintenance organization and its method of operation, including (i) the method of marketing the plan, (ii) a financial plan that includes a three-year projection of the anticipated initial operating results, (iii) a statement regarding the sources of working capital as well as any other sources of funding, and (iv) a description of any insurance, reinsurance or alternative coverage arrangements proposed;

9. A description of the mechanism by which enrollees will be given an opportunity to participate in matters of policy and operation as provided in subsection B of § 38.2-4304; and

10. Any other information the Commission may require to make the determinations required pursuant to § 38.2-4302. (1980, c. 720, § 38.1-864; 1986, c. 562; 1998, c. 891.)

The 1998 amendment, in subsection B, deleted former subdivisions 9, 10 and 11, and redesignated former subdivisions 12 and 13 as present subdivisions 9 and 10; and deleted former subsection C.

§ 38.2-4302. Issuance of license; fee; minimum net worth; impairment.

— A. The Commission shall issue a license to a health maintenance organization after the receipt of a complete application and payment of a $500 nonrefundable application fee if the Commission is satisfied that the following conditions are met:

1. The persons responsible for the conduct of the affairs of the applicant are competent, trustworthy, and reputable;

2. The health care plan constitutes an appropriate mechanism for the health maintenance organization to provide or arrange for the provision of, as a minimum, basic health care services or limited health care services on a prepaid basis, except to the extent of reasonable requirements for copayments;

3. The health maintenance organization is financially responsible and may reasonably be expected to meet its obligations to enrollees and prospective enrollees. In making this determination, the Commission may consider:

a. The financial soundness of the health care plan's arrangements for health care services and the schedule of prepaid charges used for those services;

b. The adequacy of working capital;

c. Any agreement with an insurer, a health services plan, a government, or any other organization for insuring the payment of the cost of health care services or the provision for automatic applicability of an alternative coverage if the health care plan is discontinued;

d. Any contracts with health care providers that set forth the health care services to be performed and the providers' responsibilities for fulfilling the health maintenance organization's obligations to its enrollees;

e. The deposit of a surety bond or deposit of securities in an amount satisfactory to the Commission, submitted in accordance with § 38.2-4310 as a guarantee that the obligations to the enrollees will be duly performed; and

f. The applicant's net worth which shall include minimum net worth in an amount at least equal to the sum of uncovered expenses, but not less than

$600,000, up to a maximum of $4 million; uncovered expenses shall be amounts determined for the most recently ended calendar quarter pursuant to regulations promulgated by the Commission.

4. The enrollees will be given an opportunity to participate in matters of policy and operation as required by § 38.2-4304; and

5. Nothing in the method of operation is contrary to the public interest, as shown in the information submitted pursuant to § 38.2-4301 or Chapter 58 (§ 38.2-5800 et seq.) or by independent investigation.

B. A licensed health maintenance organization shall have and maintain at all times the minimum net worth described in subdivision 3 f of subsection A of this section.

1. If the Commission finds that the minimum net worth of a domestic health maintenance organization is impaired, the Commission shall issue an order requiring the health maintenance organization to eliminate the impairment within a period not exceeding ninety days. The Commission may by order served upon the health maintenance organization prohibit the health maintenance organization from issuing any new contracts while the impairment exists. If at the expiration of the designated period the health maintenance organization has not satisfied the Commission that the impairment has been eliminated, an order for the rehabilitation or liquidation of the health maintenance organization may be entered as provided in § 38.2-4317.

2. If the Commission finds an impairment of the minimum net worth of any foreign health maintenance organization, the Commission may order the health maintenance organization to eliminate the impairment and restore the minimum net worth to the amount required by this section. The Commission may, by order served upon the health maintenance organization, prohibit the health maintenance organization from issuing any new contracts while the impairment exists. If the health maintenance organization fails to comply with the Commission's order within a period of not more than ninety days, the Commission may, in the manner set out in § 38.2-4316, suspend or revoke the license of the health maintenance organization.

3. Prior to December 31, 1999, a health maintenance organization with less than minimum net worth which is licensed on and after June 30, 1998, may continue to operate as a licensed health maintenance organization without a finding of impairment if the licensee has net worth (i) on June 30, 1998, and up to December 31, 1998, in an amount at least equal to the sum of uncovered expenses, but not less than $300,000, up to a maximum of $2 million; (ii) on December 31, 1998, and up to June 30, 1999, in an amount at least equal to the sum of uncovered expenses, but not less than $400,000, up to a maximum of $2.5 million; and (iii) on June 30, 1999, and up to December 31, 1999, in an amount at least equal to the sum of uncovered expenses, but not less than $500,000, up to a maximum of $3 million. (1980, c. 720, § 38.1-865; 1981, c. 317; 1986, c. 562; 1992, c. 481; 1998, cc. 42, 891.)

The 1998 amendments. — The 1998 amendment by c. 42, in subsection A, in subdivision 3d, deleted "and" at the end, in subdivision 3 e, added "and," and added subdivision 3 f;

and added subsection B.

The 1998 amendment by c. 891, in subsection A, in subdivision 5, inserted "or Chapter 58 (§ 38.2-5800 et seq.)."

§ 38.2-4303. Powers. — A. The powers of a health maintenance organization shall include, but shall not be limited to, the following, provided that the activities comply with all applicable state statutes and regulations:

1. The purchase, lease, construction, renovation, operation, or maintenance of hospitals, medical or other health care facilities, and their ancillary equipment and other property reasonably required for its principal office or for other purposes necessary in the transaction of the business of the organization;

2. The making of loans to (i) health care providers under contract with it in advancement of its health care plan or (ii) any corporation under its control for the purpose of acquiring or constructing medical or other health care facilities and hospitals or in advancement of its health care plan providing health care services to enrollees;

3. The furnishing of health care services through providers that are under contract with or employed by the health maintenance organization;

4. The contracting with any person for the performance on its behalf of certain functions including, but not limited to, marketing, enrollment and administration;

5. The contracting with an insurer or with a health services plan licensed in this Commonwealth, for the provision of insurance, indemnity, or reimbursement for the cost of health care services provided by the health maintenance organization;

6. The offering, in addition to basic health care services, of:

a. Additional health care services;

b. Indemnity benefits covering out-of-area services; and

c. Indemnity benefits, in addition to those relating to out-of-area services, provided through insurers or health services plans; and

7. The offering of health care plans for limited health care services.

B. 1. A health maintenance organization shall file notice with the Commission within thirty days after the exercise of any power granted in subdivision 1 or 2 of subsection A of this section that exceeds one percent of the admitted assets of the organization or five percent of net worth, whichever is less. A health maintenance organization shall file notice, with adequate supporting information, with the Commission prior to the exercise of any power granted in subdivision 1 or 2 of subsection A of this section that exceeds five percent of the admitted assets of the organization or twenty-five percent of net worth, whichever is less. Any series of transactions occurring within a twelve-month period that are sufficiently similar in nature to be reasonably construed as a single transaction shall be subject to the limitations set forth in this section. The Commission shall disapprove the exercise of power if the Commission believes such exercise of power would substantially and adversely affect the financial soundness of the health maintenance organization and endanger the health maintenance organization's ability to meet its obligations. If the Commission does not disapprove the exercise of power within thirty days of the filing, it shall be deemed approved.

2. Upon application by the health maintenance organization, the Commission may exempt from the filing requirement of subdivision 1 of subsection B of this section those activities having a minimal effect. (1980, c. 720, § 38.1-866; 1986, c. 562; 1990, c. 224; 1992, c. 481.)

§ **38.2-4304. Governing body.** — A. The governing body of any health maintenance organization may include providers of health care services, other individuals, or both, but in no event shall any class of health care provider be excluded from eligibility for membership on the governing body of any health maintenance organization.

B. The governing body shall establish a mechanism to provide the enrollees with an opportunity to participate in matters of policy and operation through (i) the establishment of advisory panels, (ii) the use of advisory referenda on major policy decisions, or (iii) the use of other mechanisms. (1980, c. 720, § 38.1-867; 1985, c. 588; 1986, c. 562.)

§ **38.2-4305. Fiduciary responsibilities.** — Any director, officer or partner of a health maintenance organization who receives, collects, disburses, or invests funds in connection with the activities of the organization shall be responsible for the funds in a fiduciary relationship with the subscribers and enrollees. (1980, c. 720, § 38.1-868; 1986, c. 562.)

§ 38.2-4306. Evidence of coverage and charges for health care services. — A. 1. Each subscriber shall be entitled to evidence of coverage under a health care plan.

2. No evidence of coverage, or amendment to it, shall be delivered or issued for delivery in this Commonwealth until a copy of the form of the evidence of coverage, or amendment to it, has been filed with and approved by the Commission, subject to the provisions of subsection C of this section.

3. No evidence of coverage shall contain provisions or statements which are unjust, unfair, untrue, inequitable, misleading, deceptive or misrepresentative.

4. An evidence of coverage shall contain a clear and complete statement if a contract, or a reasonably complete summary if a certificate, of:

a. The health care services and any insurance or other benefits to which the enrollee is entitled under the health care plan;

b. Any limitations on the services, kind of services, benefits, or kind of benefits to be provided, including any deductible or copayment feature;

c. Where and in what manner information is available as to how services may be obtained;

d. The total amount of payment for health care services and any indemnity or service benefits that the enrollee is obligated to pay with respect to individual contracts, or an indication whether the plan is contributory or noncontributory for group certificates;

e. A description of the health maintenance organization's method for resolving enrollee complaints. Any subsequent change may be evidenced in a separate document issued to the enrollee;

f. A list of providers and a description of the service area which shall be provided with the evidence of coverage, if such information is not given to the subscriber at the time of enrollment; and

g. The right of subscribers covered under a group contract to convert their coverages to an individual contract issued by the health maintenance organization.

B. 1. No schedule of charges or amendment to the schedule of charges for enrollee coverage for health care services may be used in conjunction with any health care plan until a copy of the schedule, or its amendment, has been filed with the Commission.

2. The charges may be established for various categories of enrollees based upon sound actuarial principles, provided that charges applying to an enrollee in a group health plan shall not be individually determined based on the status of his health. A certification on the appropriateness of the charges, based upon reasonable assumptions, may be required by the Commission to be filed along with adequate supporting information. This certification shall be prepared by a qualified actuary or other qualified professional approved by the Commission.

C. The Commission shall, within a reasonable period, approve any form if the requirements of subsection A of this section are met. It shall be unlawful to issue a form until approved. If the Commission disapproves a filing, it shall notify the filer. The Commission shall specify the reasons for its disapproval in the notice. A written request for a hearing on the disapproval may be made to the Commission within thirty days after notice of the disapproval. If the Commission does not disapprove any form within thirty days of the filing of such form, it shall be deemed approved unless the filer is notified in writing that the waiting period is extended by the Commission for an additional thirty days. Filing of the form means actual receipt by the Commission.

D. The Commission may require the submission of any relevant information it considers necessary in determining whether to approve or disapprove a filing made under this section. (1980, c. 720, § 38.1-869; 1986, c. 562; 1997, cc. 807, 913.)

Editor's note. — Acts 1997, cc. 807 and 913, cl. 3, provide: "That the Bureau of Insurance within the State Corporation Commission, in cooperation with the Joint Commission on Health Care, monitor the impact of the provisions of this act on the Commonwealth's health insurance marketplace. In monitoring the impact of this act, the State Corporation Commission shall: (i) review the federal regulations that will be promulgated to implement P.L. 104-191 (The Health Insurance Portability and Accountability Act), and determine whether any changes to this act are required by federal regulations adopted pursuant to P.L. 104-191; (ii) monitor the impact of the guaranteed issue requirements in the individual market and evaluate any specific concerns regarding such requirements identified and documented to the satisfaction of the State Corporation Commission by health insurance issuers; and (iii) recommend to the Governor and the 1998 Session of the General Assembly any revisions, corrections or improvements to the provisions of this act that would require the enactment of additional legislation."

§ 38.2-4306.1. Interest on claim proceeds. — A. If an action to recover the claim proceeds due under a health care plan results in a judgment against a health maintenance organization, interest on the judgment at the legal rate of interest shall be paid from the date of presentation to the health maintenance organization of proof of loss to the date judgment is entered.

B. If no action is brought, interest upon the claim proceeds paid to the subscriber, claimant, or assignee entitled thereto shall be computed daily at the legal rate of interest from the date of thirty calendar days from the health maintenance organization's receipt of proof of loss to the date of claim payment.

C. This section shall not apply to individual contracts issued prior to July 1, 1990, but shall apply to any renewals or reissues of group contracts occurring after that date.

D. This section shall not apply to claims for which payment has been or will be made directly to health care providers pursuant to a negotiated reimbursement arrangement requiring uniform or periodic interim payments to be applied against the health maintenance organization's obligation on such claims.

E. For purposes of this section, *"proof of loss"* means all necessary documentation reasonably required by the health maintenance organization to make a determination of benefit coverage. (1992, c. 23; 1996, c. 75.)

§ 38.2-4307. Annual statement. — A. Each health maintenance organization shall file a statement with the Commission annually by March 1. The statement shall be verified by at least two principal officers and shall cover the preceding calendar year. Each health maintenance organization shall also send a copy of the statement to the State Health Commissioner.

B. The statement shall be on forms prescribed by the Commission and shall include:

1. A financial statement of the organization, including its balance sheet and income statement for the preceding year;

2. Any material changes in the information submitted pursuant to subsection B of § 38.2-4301;

3. The number of persons enrolled during the year, the number of enrollees as of the end of the year and the number of enrollments terminated during the year; and

4. Any other information relating to the operations of the health maintenance organization required by the Commission pursuant to this chapter or Chapter 58 (§ 38.2-5800 et seq.) of this title.

C. If the health maintenance organization is audited annually by an independent certified public accountant, a copy of the certified audit report shall be filed annually with the Commission by June 30.

D. The Commission may extend the time prescribed for filing annual statements or other reports or exhibits of any health maintenance organization for good cause shown. However, the Commission shall not extend the time for filing annual statements beyond sixty days after the time prescribed by subsection A of this section. Any health maintenance organization which fails to file its annual statement within the time prescribed by this section shall be subject to a fine as specified in § 38.2-218.

E. The Commission may prescribe the form of the annual statement and supplemental schedules and exhibits to include additional copies in machine-readable format, and may vary the form requirements for different types of health maintenance organizations. However, as far as practicable, the form for annual statements, supplementary schedules, and exhibits shall be the same as other such forms in general use in the United States. Unless otherwise prescribed by the Commission, such annual statements shall be prepared using an annual statement convention blank developed by the National Association of Insurance Commissioners (NAIC). The annual statement, and supplementary schedules and exhibits required by this section, shall be prepared in accordance with the appropriate annual statement instructions and the accounting practices and procedures manual adopted by the NAIC, or any successor publications.

F. At the request of the Commission, a health maintenance organization that is licensed under this chapter shall annually on or before March 1 of each year, file with the NAIC a copy of its annual statement convention blank, along with such additional filings as prescribed by the Commission for the preceding year. Unless otherwise prescribed by the Commission, the information filed with the NAIC shall be in the same format and scope as that required by the Commission and shall include the signed jurat page and any actuarial certification required by the Commission. Any amendments and addenda to the annual statement filed subsequently with the Commission shall also be filed with the NAIC. (1980, c. 720, § 38.1-870; 1986, c. 562; 1987, c. 520; 1998, c. 891; 1999, c. 482.)

The **1998 amendment,** in subsection B, in subdivision 4, substituted "operations of the health maintenance organization required by the Commission pursuant to this chapter or Chapter 58 (§ 38.2-5800 et seq.)" for "the performance and utilization of the health mainte- nance organization required by the Commis- sion after consultation with the State Health Commissioner to carry out the Commission's duties under this chapter."

The **1999 amendment** added subsections E and F.

§ 38.2-4307.1. Additional reports. — A. In addition to the annual state- ment, the Commission may require a licensed health maintenance organiza- tion to file additional reports, exhibits or statements considered necessary to secure complete information concerning the condition, solvency, experience, transactions or affairs of the health maintenance organization. The Commis- sion shall establish reasonable deadlines for filing these additional reports, exhibits, or statements and may require verification by any officers of the health maintenance organization designated by the Commission.

B. The Commission may require a licensed health maintenance organiza- tion to file with the National Association of Insurance Commissioners (NAIC) a copy of its financial statement required to be filed pursuant to § 38.2-4307, on a quarterly basis. Unless otherwise prescribed by the Commission, all such financial statements, whether filed with the Commission or the NAIC, shall be prepared in accordance with applicable provisions of the annual statement instructions and the accounting practices and procedures manual adopted by the NAIC, or any successor publications. The Commission may prescribe that additional copies of financial statements and other publications be filed in machine-readable format. (1990, c. 224; 1999, c. 482.)

The 1999 amendment inserted the subsection A designator and added subsection B.

§ **38.2-4308:** Repealed by Acts 1998, c. 891.

Editor's note. — This section was also amended by Acts 1998, c. 744, at the direction of the Code Commission, the amendment was added as subsection F of § 32.1-137.6.

§ **38.2-4309. Investments.** — A health maintenance organization may invest in any Category 1 investment as defined in Chapter 14 of this title or any other investment the Commission may permit pursuant to provisions in Chapter 14 (§ 38.2-1400 et seq.) of this title. For investments made prior to July 1, 1998, by a health maintenance organization which is licensed on and after June 30, 1998, July 1, 1998 may be deemed the date of investment. (1980, c. 720, § 38.1-873; 1986, c. 562; 1998, c. 42.)

The 1998 amendment rewrote this section.

§ **38.2-4310. Protection against insolvency.** — A. Each health maintenance organization shall deposit acceptable securities with the State Treasurer in an amount satisfactory to the Commission to be held as a special fund in trust, as a guarantee that the obligations to the enrollees who are residents of this Commonwealth will be performed. The securities shall be deposited pursuant to a system of book-entry evidencing ownership interests of the securities with transfers of ownership interests effected on the records of a depository and its participants pursuant to rules and procedures established by the depository. The Commission may waive this requirement whenever the Commission is satisfied that the assets of the organization or its contract with insurers, health services plans, governments, or other organizations are reasonably sufficient to assure the performance of its obligations.

B. The Commission may require that each health maintenance organization have a plan for handling insolvency which allows for continuation of benefits for the duration of the contract period for which premiums have been paid and continuation of benefits to members who are confined on the date of insolvency in an inpatient facility until their discharge or expiration of benefits. The plan may also provide for payment of outstanding obligations to enrollees and providers. In considering such a plan, the Commission may require:

1. Insurance satisfactory in form and content to the Commission to cover the expenses to be paid for continued benefits after an insolvency;

2. Provisions in provider contracts that obligate the provider to provide services for the duration of the period after the health maintenance organization's insolvency for which premium payment has been made and until the enrollees' discharge from inpatient facilities;

3. Acceptable letters of credit;

4. A special deposit to secure providers not party to contracts under § 38.2-4311 equal to the lesser of (i) one percent of premiums determined in accordance with Chapter 4 of this title or (ii) three months' health care expenses as determined by Commission regulation attributable to providers not party to such contracts and incurred for care and treatment of enrollees who are residents of this Commonwealth; or

5. Any other arrangements to assure that benefits are continued as specified above.

C. 1. In the event of an insolvency of a health maintenance organization, all other carriers that participated in the enrollment process with the insolvent health maintenance organization at a group's last regular enrollment period shall offer such group's enrollees of the insolvent health maintenance organization a thirty-day enrollment period commencing upon a date to be prescribed by the Commission. Each carrier shall offer such enrollees of the insolvent health maintenance organization the same coverages and rates then in effect for its enrollees in such group.

2. If no other carrier had been offered to some groups enrolled in the insolvent health maintenance organization, or if the Commission determines that the other health benefit plan lacks sufficient health care delivery resources to assure that health care services shall be available and accessible to all of the group enrollees of the insolvent health maintenance organization, then the Commission may allocate equitably the insolvent health maintenance organization's group contracts for such groups among all health maintenance organizations which operate within a portion of the insolvent health maintenance organization's service area, taking into consideration the health care delivery resources of each health maintenance organization. Each health maintenance organization to which a group or groups are so allocated shall offer such group or groups the health maintenance organization's existing coverage which is most similar to each group's coverage with the insolvent health maintenance organization at rates determined in accordance with the successor health maintenance organization's existing rating methodology.

3. The Commission may also allocate equitably the insolvent health maintenance organization's nongroup enrollees which are unable to obtain other coverage among all health maintenance organizations which operate within a portion of the insolvent health maintenance organization's service area, taking into consideration the health care delivery resources of each such health maintenance organization. Each health maintenance organization to which nongroup enrollees are allocated shall offer such nongroup enrollees the health maintenance organization's existing coverage for individual or conversion coverage as determined by his type of coverage in the insolvent health maintenance organization at rates determined in accordance with the successor health maintenance organization's existing rating methodology. Successor health maintenance organizations which do not offer direct nongroup enrollment may aggregate all of the allocated nongroup enrollees into one group for rating and coverage purposes.

D. 1. Any carrier providing replacement coverage with respect to group hospital, medical or surgical expense or service benefits within a period of sixty days from the date of discontinuance of a prior health maintenance organization contract or policy providing such hospital, medical or surgical expense or service benefits shall immediately cover all employees and dependents who were validly covered under the previous health maintenance organization contract or policy at the date of discontinuance and who would otherwise be eligible for coverage under the succeeding carrier's contract, regardless of any provisions of the contract relating to active employment or hospital confinement or pregnancy.

2. Except to the extent benefits for the condition would have been reduced or excluded under the prior carrier's contract or policy, no provision in a succeeding carrier's contract of replacement coverage which would operate to reduce or exclude benefits on the basis that the condition giving rise to benefits preexisted the effective date of the succeeding carrier's contract shall be applied with respect to those employees and dependents validly covered under the prior carrier's contract or policy on the date of discontinuance.

E. Every health maintenance organization subject to the provisions of this section having physical securities deposited with the State Treasurer on or before June 30, 1992, shall deposit securities pursuant to a book-entry system as required by subsection A not later than January 1, 1993. (1980, c. 720, § 38.1-874; 1986, c. 562; 1989, c. 216; 1990, c. 224; 1992, cc. 14, 20.)

§ 38.2-4311: Repealed by Acts 1998, c. 891.

§ 38.2-4312. Prohibited practices. — A. No health maintenance organization or its representative may cause or knowingly permit the use of (i) advertising that is untrue or misleading, (ii) solicitation that is untrue or misleading, or (iii) any form of evidence of coverage that is deceptive. For the purposes of this chapter:

1. A statement or item of information shall be deemed to be untrue if it does not conform to fact in any respect that is or may be significant to an enrollee or person considering enrollment in a health care plan;

2. A statement or item of information shall be deemed to be misleading, whether or not it may be literally untrue, if the statement or item of information may be understood by a reasonable person who has no special knowledge of health care coverage as indicating (i) a benefit or advantage if that benefit or advantage does not in fact exist or (ii) the absence of any exclusion, limitation or disadvantage of possible significance to an enrollee or person considering enrollment in a health care plan if the absence of that exclusion, limitation, or disadvantage does not in fact exist; consideration shall be given to the total context in which the statement is made or the item of information is communicated; and

3. An evidence of coverage shall be deemed to be deceptive if it causes a reasonable person who has no special knowledge of health care plans to expect benefits, services, charges, or other advantages that the evidence of coverage does not provide or that the health care plan issuing the evidence of coverage does not regularly make available for enrollees covered under the evidence of coverage; consideration shall be given to the evidence of coverage taken as a whole and to the typography, format, and language.

B. The provisions of Chapter 5 (§ 38.2-500 et seq.) of this title shall apply to health maintenance organizations, health care plans, and evidences of coverage except to the extent that the Commission determines that the nature of health maintenance organizations, health care plans, and evidences of coverage render any of the provisions clearly inappropriate.

C. No health maintenance organization, unless licensed as an insurer, may use in its name, contracts, or literature (i) any of the words "insurance," "casualty," "surety," "mutual," or (ii) any other words descriptive of the insurance, casualty, or surety business or deceptively similar to the name or description of any insurance or fidelity and surety insurer doing business in this Commonwealth.

D. No health maintenance organization shall discriminate on the basis of race, creed, color, sex or religion in the selection of health care providers for participation in the organization.

E. No health maintenance organization shall unreasonably discriminate against physicians as a class or any class of providers listed in § 38.2-4221 or pharmacists when contracting for specialty or referral practitioners or providers, provided the plan covers services which the members of such classes are licensed to render. Nothing contained in this section shall prevent a health maintenance organization from selecting, in the judgment of the health maintenance organization, the numbers of providers necessary to render the services offered by the health maintenance organization.

F. No contract between a health maintenance organization and a provider shall include provisions which require a health care provider or health care provider group to deny covered services that such provider or group knows to be medically necessary and appropriate that are provided with respect to a specific enrollee or group of enrollees with similar medical conditions. (1980, c. 720, § 38.1-876; 1985, c. 588; 1986, c. 562; 1989, c. 221; 1997, c. 297; 1998, c. 891; 1999, cc. 643, 649.)

The **1998 amendment** deleted former subsection C, which read: "No health maintenance organization may cancel or refuse to renew the coverage of an enrollee on the basis of the status of the enrollee's health"; redesignated former subsections D, E and F as present subsections C, D and E; and deleted subsection G.

The **1999 amendments.** — The 1999 amendments by cc. 643 and 649 are identical, and added subsection F.

This section governs the administration of health maintenance organizations only, and not of prepaid health care plans. Keel v. Group Hospitalization Medical Servs., Inc., 695 F. Supp. 223 (E.D. Va. 1988).

§ 38.2-4312.1. Pharmacies; freedom of choice. — A. Notwithstanding any other provision in this chapter, no health maintenance organization providing health care plans shall prohibit any person receiving pharmaceutical benefits thereunder from selecting, without limitation, the pharmacy of his choice to furnish such benefits. This right of selection extends to and includes pharmacies that are not participating providers under any such health care plan and that have previously notified the health maintenance organization, by facsimile or otherwise, of their agreement to accept reimbursement for their services at rates applicable to pharmacies that are participating providers, including any copayment consistently imposed by the plan, as payment in full. Each health maintenance organization shall permit prompt electronic or telephonic transmittal of the reimbursement agreement by the pharmacy and ensure prompt verification to the pharmacy of the terms of reimbursement. In no event shall any person receiving a covered pharmacy benefit from a nonparticipating provider which has submitted a reimbursement agreement be responsible for amounts that may be charged by the nonparticipating provider in excess of the copayment and the health maintenance organization's reimbursement applicable to all of its participating pharmacy providers.

B. No such health maintenance organization shall impose upon any person receiving pharmaceutical benefits furnished under any such health care plan:

1. Any copayment, fee or condition that is not equally imposed upon all individuals in the same benefit category, class or copayment level, whether or not such benefits are furnished by pharmacists who are not participating providers;

2. Any monetary penalty that would affect or influence any such person's choice of pharmacy; or

3. Any reduction in allowable reimbursement for pharmacy services related to utilization of pharmacists who are not participating providers.

C. For purposes of this section, a prohibited condition or penalty shall include, without limitation: (i) denying immediate access to electronic claims filing to a pharmacy which is a nonparticipating provider and which has complied with subsection E below or (ii) requiring a person receiving pharmacy benefits to make payment at point of service, except to the extent such conditions and penalties are similarly imposed on participating providers.

D. The provisions of this section are not applicable to any pharmaceutical benefit covered by a health care plan when those benefits are obtained from a pharmacy wholly owned and operated by, or exclusively operated for, the health maintenance organization providing the health care plan.

E. Any pharmacy which wishes to be covered by this section shall, if requested to do so in writing by a health maintenance organization, within thirty days of the pharmacy's receipt of the request, execute and deliver to the health maintenance organization the direct service agreement or participating provider agreement which the health maintenance organization requires all of its participating providers of pharmacy benefits to execute. Any pharmacy which fails to timely execute and deliver such agreement shall not be covered by this section with respect to that health maintenance organization unless and until the pharmacy executes and delivers the agreement.

F. The Commission shall have no jurisdiction to adjudicate controversies arising out of this section. (1994, c. 963; 1995, cc. 446, 467.)

Editor's note. — Acts 1995, c. 467, cl. 3, provides: "That the Joint Commission on Health Care shall conduct a three-year study of ancillary medical services insofar as the availability and quality of the same are affected by managed care, and shall include its findings thereon in its 1996, 1997 and 1998 reports to the Governor and the General Assembly."

§ **38.2-4312.2:** Repealed by Acts 1995, c. 467.

§ **38.2-4312.3. Patient access to emergency services.** — A. A health maintenance organization shall have a system to provide to its members, on a twenty-four-hour basis: (i) access to medical care or (ii) access by telephone to a physician or licensed health care professional with appropriate medical training who can refer or direct a member for prompt medical care in cases where there is an immediate, urgent need or medical emergency. Access to a nonmedical professional who provides appropriate responses to calls from members and providers concerning after-hours care and covered benefits is not sufficient to meet the requirements of this section.

B. A health maintenance organization shall reimburse a hospital emergency facility and provider, less any applicable copayments, deductibles, or coinsurance, for medical screening and stabilization services rendered to meet the requirements of the Federal Emergency Medical Treatment and Active Labor Act (42 U.S.C. § 1395 dd) and related to the condition for which the member presented in the hospital emergency facility if (i) the health maintenance organization or its designee or the member's primary care physician or its designee authorized, directed, or referred a member to use the hospital emergency facility; or (ii) the health maintenance organization fails to have a system for provision of twenty-four-hour access in accordance with subsection A above. For purposes of (i) above, a primary care physician may include a physician with whom the primary care physician has made arrangements for on-call backup coverage.

C. Each evidence of coverage provided by a health maintenance organization shall include a description of procedures to be followed by the member for emergency services, including: (i) the appropriate use of hospital emergency facilities; (ii) the appropriate use of any urgent care facilities with which the health maintenance organization may contract; (iii) the potential responsibility of the member for payment for nonemergency services rendered in a hospital emergency facility; and (iv) the member's covered benefits for emergency services, including an explanation of the prudent layperson standard included in the definition of emergency services in § 38.2-4300. (1997, c. 139.)

§ **38.2-4313. Licensing of agents.** — Enrollee contracts may be solicited only through life and health insurance agents as provided for in Chapter 18 of this title. Home office salaried officers whose principal duties and responsibilities do not include the negotiation or solicitation of enrollee contracts shall not be required to be licensed. (1980, c. 720, § 38.1-877; 1986, c. 562; 1999, c. 86.)

The 1999 amendment deleted "licensed health agents or" following "solicited only through."

§ 38.2-4314. Powers of insurers and health services plans. — A. An insurer or a health services plan licensed in this Commonwealth may, either directly or through a subsidiary or affiliate, organize and operate a health maintenance organization under the provisions of this chapter. Notwithstanding any other law that may be inconsistent with this section, any two or more licensed insurers, health services plans, or their subsidiaries or affiliates, may jointly organize and operate a health maintenance organization.

B. An insurer or a health services plan may contract with a health maintenance organization to provide insurance or similar protection against the cost of care provided through health maintenance organizations and to provide coverage in the event of the failure of the health maintenance organization to meet its obligations. The enrollees of a health maintenance organization constitute a permissible group for purposes of laws applicable to insurers and health services plans. Under the contracts the insurer or health services plans may make benefit payments to health maintenance organizations for health care services rendered by providers under the health care plan. (1980, c. 720, § 38.1-878; 1986, c. 562.)

§ 38.2-4315. Examinations. — A. The Commission shall examine the affairs of each health maintenance organization as provided for in § 38.2-1317 at least once every five years. The Commission may examine the affairs of providers with whom any health maintenance organization has contracts, agreements, or other arrangements according to its health care plan as often as it considers necessary for the protection of the interests of the people of this Commonwealth.

B. Instead of making its own examination, the Commission may accept the report of an examination of a foreign health maintenance organization certified by the insurance supervisory official, similar regulatory agency, or the state health commissioner of another state.

C. The Commission shall coordinate such examinations with the State Health Commissioner to ensure an appropriate level of regulatory oversight and to avoid any undue duplication of effort or regulation. (1980, c. 720, § 38.1-879; 1986, c. 562; 1990, c. 224; 1997, c. 688.)

§ 38.2-4316. Suspension or revocation of license. — A. The Commission may suspend or revoke any license issued to a health maintenance organization under this chapter if it finds that any of the following conditions exist:

1. The health maintenance organization is operating significantly at variance with its basic organizational document, its health care plan, or in a manner contrary to that described in and reasonably inferred from any other information submitted under § 38.2-4301, unless amendments to those submissions have been filed with and approved by the Commission;

2. The health maintenance organization issues an evidence of coverage or uses a schedule of charges for health care services that do not comply with the requirements of § 38.2-4306;

3. The health care plan does not provide or arrange for basic health care services or limited health care services;

4. The health maintenance organization is no longer financially responsible and a reasonable expectation exists that it may be unable to meet its obligations to enrollees or prospective enrollees;

5. The health maintenance organization has failed to implement a mechanism providing the enrollees with an opportunity to participate in matters of policy and operation as provided in § 38.2-4304;

6. The health maintenance organization, or any person on its behalf, has advertised or merchandised its services in an untrue, misrepresentative, misleading, deceptive, or unfair manner;

7. The continued operation of the health maintenance organization would be hazardous to its enrollees; or

8. The health maintenance organization has otherwise failed to substantially comply with the provisions of this chapter.

B. When the license of a health maintenance organization is suspended, the health maintenance organization shall not enroll any additional enrollees during the period of the suspension except newborn children or other newly acquired dependents of existing enrollees, and shall not engage in any advertising or solicitation.

C. The Commission shall not revoke or suspend the license of a health maintenance organization upon any of the grounds set out in subsection A of this section until it has given the organization ten days' notice of the proposed revocation or suspension and the grounds for it, and has given the organization an opportunity to introduce evidence and be heard. Any hearing authorized by this section may be informal. The required notice may be waived by the Commission and the health maintenance organization.

D. When the license of a health maintenance organization is revoked, the organization shall proceed to wind up its affairs immediately following the effective date of the order of revocation. The health maintenance organization shall conduct no further business except as may be essential to the orderly conclusion of its affairs. It shall engage in no further advertising or solicitation. The Commission may, by written order, permit further operation of the organization that it finds to be in the best interests of enrollees for the purpose of giving them the greatest practical opportunity to obtain continuing health care coverage. (1980, c. 720, § 38.1-880; 1986, c. 562; 1992, c. 481; 1998, c. 891.)

The 1998 amendment, in subsection A, deleted former subdivision 4, which read: "The State Health Commissioner certifies to the Commission that the health maintenance organization is unable to fulfill its obligations to furnish quality health care services as set forth in its health care plan consistent with prevailing medical care standards and practices in the Commonwealth," redesignated former subdivisions 5 and 6 as present subdivisions 4 and 5, deleted former subdivision 7, which read: "The health maintenance organization has failed to implement the complaint system required by § 38.2-4308 to resolve valid complaints reasonably" and redesignated former subdivisions 8 through 10 as present subdivisions 6 through 8 respectively.

§ 38.2-4317. Rehabilitation, liquidation, or conservation. — A. Any rehabilitation, liquidation, or conservation of a health maintenance organization shall be deemed to be the rehabilitation, liquidation, or conservation of an insurer and shall be conducted under the supervision of the Commission. The Commission may enter an order directing the rehabilitation, liquidation, or conservation of a health maintenance organization upon any one or more grounds set out in §§ 38.2-1500 through 38.2-1521 or when, in the Commission's opinion, the continued operation of the health maintenance organization would be hazardous either to the enrollees or to the people of this Commonwealth.

B. For the purpose of determining the priority of distribution of general assets, claims of enrollees and enrollees' beneficiaries shall have the same priority as established by § 38.2-1509 for policyholders and beneficiaries of insureds of insurance companies. If an enrollee is liable to any provider for services provided pursuant to and covered by the health care plan, that liability shall have the status of an enrollee claim. Any provider who is obligated by statute or agreement to hold enrollees harmless from liability for services provided pursuant to and covered by a health care plan shall have a priority of distribution next subordinate to that of policyholders under subdivision 1 (iv) of subsection B of § 38.2-1509.

C. One or more health maintenance organizations may, subject to approval by the Commission, contract to assume all or part of the business operations, subscriber contracts and obligations of another health maintenance organization. The Commission is authorized to make known to other health maintenance organizations and other interested parties the financial condition of a health maintenance organization found by the Commission to be impaired or insolvent. (1980, c. 720, § 38.1-881; 1986, c. 562; 1989, c. 216.)

§ **38.2-4317.1. Insolvency deposit assessment.** — In the event of an insolvency of a health maintenance organization occurring after July 1, 1989, the Commission may, (i) in the absence of an assumption under subsection C of § 38.2-4317 that is satisfactory to the Commission and that occurred within sixty days after entry of an order of impairment or insolvency, and (ii) after notice and hearing, levy an assessment on premiums due by licensed health maintenance organizations on contracts issued or renewed in this Commonwealth after the date of such assessment; provided, that such assessments for all health maintenance organization insolvencies in any calendar year shall not exceed two percent of the premiums subject to such assessments. Such assessments shall be paid quarterly to the Commission, and upon receipt by the Commission shall be paid over into the deposit account of the insolvent health maintenance organization held pursuant to subsection A of § 38.2-4310 for the benefit of enrollees for use and disbursement in accordance with Commission regulations. No participating provider, as defined in § 38.2-4300, may, either directly or indirectly, receive reimbursement from any such assessments. A receiver of such an insolvent health maintenance organization appointed pursuant to § 38.2-4317 may borrow in anticipation of collection of such assessments to meet obligations under a deposit account. Any assessments levied on account of a health maintenance organization insolvency in excess of obligations to enrollees shall be ratably returned to the health maintenance organizations paying such assessments. (1989, c. 216; 1990, c. 224.)

§ **38.2-4318. License renewals.** — A. Each health maintenance organization licensed under this chapter shall renew its license with the Commission annually by July 1. The renewal license shall not be issued until the health maintenance organization has paid all fees and charges imposed on it and has complied with all other requirements of law.
B. The Commission shall not fail or refuse to renew the license of any health maintenance organization without first giving the health maintenance organization ten days' notice of its intention not to renew the license and giving it an opportunity to be heard and to introduce evidence on its behalf. Any such hearing may be informal. The required notice may be waived by the Commission and the health maintenance organization. (1980, c. 720, § 38.1-883; 1986, c. 562; 1987, c. 519.)

§ **38.2-4319. (Effective until January 1, 2000 and after July 1, 2004) Statutory construction and relationship to other laws.** — A. No provisions of this title except this chapter and, insofar as they are not inconsistent with this chapter, §§ 38.2-100, 38.2-200, 38.2-203, 38.2-210 through 38.2-213, 38.2-218 through 38.2-225, 38.2-229, 38.2-232, 38.2-305, 38.2-316, 38.2-322, 38.2-400, 38.2-402 through 38.2-413, 38.2-500 through 38.2-515, 38.2-600 through 38.2-620, Chapter 9 (§ 38.2-900 et seq.), §§ 38.2-1057, 38.2-1306.2 through 38.2-1309, Articles 4 (§ 38.2-1317 et seq.) and 5 (§ 38.2-1322 et seq.) of Chapter 13, Articles 1 (§ 38.2-1400 et seq.) and 2 (§ 38.2-1412 et seq.) of Chapter 14, §§ 38.2-1800 through 38.2-1836, 38.2-3401, 38.2-3405, 38.2-3405.1, 38.2-3407.2 through 38.2-3407.6:1, 38.2-3407.9 through 38.2-3407.16,

38.2-3411.2, 38.2-3414.1, 38.2-3418.1 through 38.2-3418.11, 38.2-3419.1, 38.2-3430.1 through 38.2-3437, 38.2-3500, 38.2-3514.1, 38.2-3514.2, §§ 38.2-3522.1 through 38.2-3523.4, 38.2-3525, 38.2-3542, 38.2-3543.2, Chapter 53 (§ 38.2-5300 et seq.), Chapter 58 (§ 38.2-5800 et seq.) and Chapter 59 (§ 38.2-5900 et seq.) of this title shall be applicable to any health maintenance organization granted a license under this chapter. This chapter shall not apply to an insurer or health services plan licensed and regulated in conformance with the insurance laws or Chapter 42 (§ 38.2-4200 et seq.) of this title except with respect to the activities of its health maintenance organization.

B. Solicitation of enrollees by a licensed health maintenance organization or by its representatives shall not be construed to violate any provisions of law relating to solicitation or advertising by health professionals.

C. A licensed health maintenance organization shall not be deemed to be engaged in the unlawful practice of medicine. All health care providers associated with a health maintenance organization shall be subject to all provisions of law.

D. Notwithstanding the definition of an eligible employee as set forth in § 38.2-3431, a health maintenance organization providing health care plans pursuant to § 38.2-3431 shall not be required to offer coverage to or accept applications from an employee who does not reside within the health maintenance organization's service area. (1980, c. 720, § 38.1-887; 1985, c. 588; 1986, c. 562; 1989, cc. 646, 653; 1990, cc. 301, 393, 439, 531, 826; 1991, cc. 103, 369; 1992, cc. 14, 23, 800; 1993, cc. 148, 158, 306, 307; 1994, cc. 213, 320, 374, 522, 699; 1995, cc. 80, 420, 522, 537; 1996, cc. 22, 155, 201, 550, 611, 776, 967; 1997, cc. 688, 807, 913; 1998, cc. 42, 43, 56, 120, 154, 625, 631, 709, 858, 891, 908; 1999, cc. 35, 643, 649, 709, 739, 856, 857, 858, 923.)

Section set out twice. — The section above is effective until January 1, 2000 and after July 1, 2004. For the version of this section effective January 1, 2000 until July 1, 2004, see the following section, also numbered 38.2-4319.

Editor's note. — Acts 1999, c. 941, cl. 4, provides: "That the Special Advisory Commission on Mandated Health Insurance Benefits, pursuant to its authority under Chapter 34 (§ 9-297 et seq.) of Title 9 of the Code of Virginia, shall collect such data, perform such studies, and convene such public hearings as are necessary to determine the effects, if any, of the coverage required under §§ 38.2-3412.1:01, 38.2-3412.1 and 38.2-4319 pursuant to this act on claims experience for and costs of policies, contracts or plans, and shall submit a written report of its findings regarding the same to the Governor and the General Assembly not later than December 1, 2001; December 1, 2002; and December 1, 2003."

The 1998 amendments. — The 1998 amendment by c. 42, in subsection A, in the first sentence, inserted "38.2-203" following "38.2-200," substituted "Articles 4 (§ 38.2-1317 et seq.) and 5 (§ 38.2-1322 et seq.) of Chapter 13, Articles 1 (§ 38.2-1400 et seq.) and 2 (38.2-1412 et seq.) of Chapter 14" for "Article 4 (§ 38.2-1317 et seq.)."

The 1998 amendment by cc. 43, 625 and 631 are identical, and in subsection A, in the first sentence, substituted "through 38.2-3418.3" for

"38.2-3418.1:1, 38.2-3418.1:2, 38.2-3418.2."

The 1998 amendment by cc. 56, 120, 709 and 858 are identical, and in the first sentence of subsection A, inserted "38.2-3418.3."

The 1998 amendment by c. 154, in the first sentence of subsection A, inserted "38.2-3522.1 through 38.2-3523.4" and inserted "38.2-3543.2."

The 1998 amendment by c. 891, in subsection A, in the first sentence, substituted "Chapter 58 (§ 38.2-5800 et seq.)" for "Chapter 54 (§ 38.2-5400 et seq.)."

The 1998 amendment by c. 908, in subsection A, in the first sentence, inserted "§ 38.2-3407.12."

The 1999 amendments. — The 1999 amendment by c. 35 substituted "38.2-3418.8" for "38.2-3418.7" in subsection A.

The 1999 amendment by c. 643, in subsection A, inserted "38.2-3407.9:01," inserted "38.2-3407.11:1," inserted "38.2-3407.14," inserted "38.2-3407.15," and substituted "38.2-3418.9" for "38.2-3418.7."

The 1999 amendment by c. 649, in subsection A, inserted "§§" preceding "38.2-1057," inserted "38.2-3407.9:01," inserted "38.2-3407.11:1, 38.2-3407.15," substituted "38.2-3418.9" for "38.2-3418.7," deleted "and" preceding "Chapter 58," and inserted "and Chapter 59 (§ 38.2-5900 et seq.)"

The 1999 amendments by cc. 709 and 739 are identical, and substituted "through 38.2-

3407.13" for "38.2-3407.10, 38.2-3407.11, 38.2-3407.12" in subsection A.

The 1999 amendment by c. 856, in subsection A, deleted "of this title" preceding "§§ 38.2-1057," and inserted "38.2-3407.11:1."

The 1999 amendment by c. 857, in subsection A, deleted "of this title" preceding "38.2-1057," and substituted "38.2-3407.6:1" for "38.2-3407.6."

The 1999 amendment by c. 858 substituted "38.2-3418.8" for "38.2-3418.7" in subsection A.

The 1999 amendment by c. 923, effective March 29, 1999, substituted "through 38.2-3407.13" for "38.2-3407.10, 38.2-3407.11, 38.2-3407.12" in subsection A.

§ **38.2-4319. (Effective January 1, 2000 until July 1, 2004) Statutory construction and relationship to other laws.** — A. No provisions of this title except this chapter and, insofar as they are not inconsistent with this chapter, §§ 38.2-100, 38.2-200, 38.2-203, 38.2-210 through 38.2-213, 38.2-218 through 38.2-225, 38.2-229, 38.2-232, 38.2-305, 38.2-316, 38.2-322, 38.2-400, 38.2-402 through 38.2-413, 38.2-500 through 38.2-515, 38.2-600 through 38.2-620, Chapter 9 (§ 38.2-900 et seq.), §§ 38.2-1057, 38.2-1306.2 through 38.2-1309, Articles 4 (§ 38.2-1317 et seq.) and 5 (§ 38.2-1322 et seq.) of Chapter 13, Articles 1 (§ 38.2-1400 et seq.) and 2 (§ 38.2-1412 et seq.) of Chapter 14, §§ 38.2-1800 through 38.2-1836, 38.2-3401, 38.2-3405, 38.2-3405.1, 38.2-3407.2 through 38.2-3407.6:1, 38.2-3407.9 through 38.2-3407.16, 38.2-3411.2, 38.2-3412.1:01, 38.2-3414.1, 38.2-3418.1 through 38.2-3418.11, 38.2-3419.1, 38.2-3430.1 through 38.2-3437, 38.2-3500, 38.2-3514.1, 38.2-3514.2, §§ 38.2-3522.1 through 38.2-3523.4, 38.2-3525, 38.2-3542, 38.2-3543.2, Chapter 53 (§ 38.2-5300 et seq.), Chapter 58 (§ 38.2-5800 et seq.) and Chapter 59 (§ 38.2-5900 et seq.) of this title shall be applicable to any health maintenance organization granted a license under this chapter. This chapter shall not apply to an insurer or health services plan licensed and regulated in conformance with the insurance laws or Chapter 42 (§ 38.2-4200 et seq.) of this title except with respect to the activities of its health maintenance organization.

B. Solicitation of enrollees by a licensed health maintenance organization or by its representatives shall not be construed to violate any provisions of law relating to solicitation or advertising by health professionals.

C. A licensed health maintenance organization shall not be deemed to be engaged in the unlawful practice of medicine. All health care providers associated with a health maintenance organization shall be subject to all provisions of law.

D. Notwithstanding the definition of an eligible employee as set forth in § 38.2-3431, a health maintenance organization providing health care plans pursuant to § 38.2-3431 shall not be required to offer coverage to or accept applications from an employee who does not reside within the health maintenance organization's service area. (1980, c. 720, § 38.1-887; 1985, c. 588; 1986, c. 562; 1989, cc. 646, 653; 1990, cc. 301, 393, 439, 531, 826; 1991, cc. 103, 369; 1992, cc. 14, 23, 800; 1993, cc. 148, 158, 306, 307; 1994, cc. 213, 320, 374, 522, 699; 1995, cc. 80, 420, 522, 537; 1996, cc. 22, 155, 201, 550, 611, 776, 967; 1997, cc. 688, 807, 913; 1998, cc. 42, 43, 56, 120, 154, 625, 631, 709, 858, 891, 908; 1999, cc. 35, 643, 649, 709, 739, 856, 857, 858, 923, 941.)

Section set out twice. — The section above is effective January 1, 2000 until July 1, 2004. For this section as in effect until January 1, 2000 and after July 1, 2004, see the preceding section, also numbered 38.2-4319.

Editor's note. — Acts 1999, cc. 35 and 858, cl. 2, provides: "That the provisions of this act shall become effective notwithstanding the provisions of § 9-299."

Acts 1999, c. 941, cl. 4, provides: "That the Special Advisory Commission on Mandated Health Insurance Benefits, pursuant to its authority under Chapter 34 (§ 9-297 et seq.) of Title 9 of the Code of Virginia, shall collect such data, perform such studies, and convene such public hearings as are necessary to determine the effects, if any, of the coverage required under §§ 38.2-3412.1:01, 38.2-3412.1 and 38.2-

4319 pursuant to this act on claims experience for and costs of policies, contracts or plans, and shall submit a written report of its findings regarding the same to the Governor and the General Assembly not later than December 1, 2001; December 1, 2002; and December 1, 2003."

Acts 1999, c. 941, cl. 5, provides that the provisions of this act shall expire on July 1, 2004.

The 1999 amendments. — The 1999 amendment by c. 35 substituted "38.2-3418.8" for "38.2-3418.7" in subsection A.

The 1999 amendment by c. 643, in subsection A, inserted "38.2-3407.9:01," inserted "38.2-3407.11:1," inserted "38.2-3407.14," inserted "38.2-3407.15," and substituted "38.2-3418.9" for "38.2-3418.7."

The 1999 amendment by c. 649, in subsection A, inserted "38.2-3407.9:01," inserted "38.2-3407.11:1, 38.2-3407.15," substituted "38.2-3418.9" for "38.2-3418.7," deleted "and" preceding "Chapter 58," and inserted "and Chapter 59 (§ 38.2-5900 et seq.)"

The 1999 amendments by cc. 709 and 739 are identical, and substituted "through 38.2-3407.13" for "38.2-3407.10, 38.2-3407.11, 38.2-3407.12" in subsection A.

The 1999 amendment by c. 856, in subsection A, deleted "of this title" preceding "§§ 38.2-1057," and inserted "38.2-3407.11:1."

The 1999 amendment by c. 857, in subsection A, deleted "of this title" preceding "38.2-1057," and substituted "38.2-3407.6:1" for "38.2-3407.6."

The 1999 amendment by c. 858 substituted "38.2-3418.8" for "38.2-3418.7" in subsection A.

The 1999 amendment by c. 923, effective March 29, 1999, substituted "through 38.2-3407.13" for "38.2-3407.10, 38.2-3407.11, 38.2-3407.12" in subsection A.

The 1999 amendment by c. 941, effective January 1, 2000, inserted "38.2-3412.1:01" near the middle of subsection A. For expiration date, see the Editor's note.

§ 38.2-4320. Authority of Commonwealth to contract with health maintenance organizations. — This Commonwealth is authorized to enter into contracts with health maintenance organizations on behalf of its employees and the citizens of the Commonwealth, including contracts to furnish health care services to recipients of medical assistance under Title XIX of the Social Security Act, 42 U.S.C. § 1396, et seq. (1980, c. 720, § 38.1-889; 1986, c. 562.)

§ 38.2-4321. Health maintenance organization affected by chapter. — Except as otherwise provided by law, no health maintenance organization shall be operated in this Commonwealth other than in the manner set forth in this chapter. (1980, c. 720, § 38.1-890; 1986, c. 562.)

§ 38.2-4322. Affiliation period. — A. A health maintenance organization which offers health insurance coverage in connection with a group health plan or group health insurance coverage and which does not impose any preexisting condition exclusion allowed under § 38.2-3432.3, with respect to any particular coverage option may impose an affiliation period for such coverage option, but only if:

1. Such period is applied uniformly without regard to any health status-related factors; and

2. Such period does not exceed two months (or three months in the case of a late enrollee).

B. An affiliation period as described in subsection A shall begin on the enrollment date.

C. An affiliation period under a plan shall run concurrently with any waiting period under the plan.

D. Defined terms as set forth in § 38.2-3431 which are used in this chapter shall have the same meaning here that they have in Chapter 34. (1997, cc. 807, 913.)

Editor's note. — Acts 1997, cc. 807 and 913, cl. 3, provide: "That the Bureau of Insurance within the State Corporation Commission, in cooperation with the Joint Commission on

Health Care, monitor the impact of the provisions of this act [which, in part, enacted this section] on the Commonwealth's health insurance marketplace. In monitoring the impact of this act, the State Corporation Commission shall: (i) review the federal regulations that will be promulgated to implement P.L. 104-191 (The Health Insurance Portability and Accountability Act), and determine whether any changes to this act are required by federal regulations adopted pursuant to P.L. 104-191;

(ii) monitor the impact of the guaranteed issue requirements in the individual market and evaluate any specific concerns regarding such requirements identified and documented to the satisfaction of the State Corporation Commission by health insurance issuers; and (iii) recommend to the Governor and the 1998 Session of the General Assembly any revisions, corrections or improvements to the provisions of this act that would require the enactment of additional legislation."

§ 38.2-4323. Alternative methods. — A health maintenance organization may use alternative methods to an affiliation period to address adverse selection provided that they are approved by the Commission prior to their use. (1997, cc. 807, 913.)

Editor's note. — Acts 1997, cc. 807 and 913, cl. 3, provide: "That the Bureau of Insurance within the State Corporation Commission, in cooperation with the Joint Commission on Health Care, monitor the impact of the provisions of this act [which, in part, enacted this section] on the Commonwealth's health insurance marketplace. In monitoring the impact of this act, the State Corporation Commission shall: (i) review the federal regulations that will be promulgated to implement P.L. 104-191 (The Health Insurance Portability and Accountability Act), and determine whether any

changes to this act are required by federal regulations adopted pursuant to P.L. 104-191; (ii) monitor the impact of the guaranteed issue requirements in the individual market and evaluate any specific concerns regarding such requirements identified and documented to the satisfaction of the State Corporation Commission by health insurance issuers; and (iii) recommend to the Governor and the 1998 Session of the General Assembly any revisions, corrections or improvements to the provisions of this act that would require the enactment of additional legislation."

CHAPTER 44.

LEGAL SERVICES PLANS.

§ 38.2-4400. Definitions. — As used in this chapter:

"Contract holder" means a person entering into a subscription contract with an organization;

"Fee discount" means predetermined amounts or reduced rates which are not substantially below the usual charge by the same attorney for those services, but not less than 70 percent of the rate usually charged non-participants for the same service, except for simple wills, simple name changes, preparation of non-complex legal documents, legal letters and calls, which may be less than 70 percent of the rate usually charged non-participants;

"Legal services organization" or *"organization"* means a person subject to regulation and licensing under this chapter who operates, conducts or administers a legal services plan;

"Legal services plan" or *"plan"* means a contractual obligation or an arrangement, whereby legal services are provided in consideration of a specified payment consisting in whole or in part of prepaid or periodic charges, regardless of whether the payment is made by the subscribers individually or by a third person for them;

"Licensed attorney" means an attorney licensed by the Virginia Board of Bar Examiners or other state licensing authority;

"Participating provider" or *"participating providers"* means a licensed attorney, group of attorneys or any other person who has agreed through an organization to provide legal services to subscribers enrolled in a legal services plan;

"Simple matters" or *"simple legal matters"* means legal matters that can be reasonably handled over the telephone, or with one or two office visits, or by a limited review of routine legal documents, and without legal representation to third parties;

"Subscriber" means any person entitled to benefits under the terms and conditions of a subscription contract;

"Subscription contract" means a written contract which is issued to a subscriber by an organization and which provides legal services or benefits for legal services. (1978, c. 658, § 38.1-791; 1986, c. 562; 1994, c. 224.)

Law Review. — For discussion of legislative developments with regard to prepaid legal services in the 1978 session of the General Assembly, see 12 U. Rich. L. Rev. 759 (1978). For survey of Virginia insurance law for the year 1977-1978, see 64 Va. L. Rev. 1477 (1978).

§ 38.2-4401. Certain contracts, etc., not deemed plans. — For the purposes of this chapter, the following are not deemed to be legal services plans:

1. Retainer contracts made by attorneys with individual clients where fees are based on estimates of the nature and amount of services that will be provided to the specific client, and similar contracts made with a group of clients involved in the same or closely related legal matters;

2. Plans providing no benefits other than a limited amount of consultation and advice on simple matters either alone or in combination with referral services or on the promise of fee discounts for other matters;

3. Plans providing limited benefits on simple legal matters on an informal basis, not involving a legally binding promise, in the context of an employment, educational or similar relationship;

4. Legal services provided by unions or employee associations to their members in matters relating to employment or occupation;

5. Legal services provided by an agency of federal or state government or a subdivision of federal or state government to its employees; or

6. Legal services insurance as provided for in §§ 38.2-127 and 38.2-300 when provided by an insurer licensed pursuant to Chapter 10 (§ 38.2-1000 et seq.) of this title. (1978, c. 658, § 38.1-802; 1986, c. 562; 1994, c. 224.)

§ 38.2-4402: Repealed by Acts 1994, c. 224.

§ 38.2-4402.1. Corporate organization required. — Each plan shall be conducted by or through (i) a nonstock or stock corporation organized pursuant to the laws of this Commonwealth or (ii) a foreign corporation that is subject to regulation and licensing under the laws of its domiciliary jurisdiction that are substantially similar to those provided by this chapter. (1994, c. 224.)

§ 38.2-4403. The Virginia State Bar may sponsor plans. — The Virginia State Bar may sponsor, and its member attorneys may, through a nonstock corporation, operate a legal services plan under the following conditions:

1. All members of the Virginia State Bar may participate in the plan.

2. No more than one-fourth of the board of directors of the nonstock corporation operating the plan may be attorneys who shall be appointed to the board by the Virginia State Bar. A majority of the members of the board shall not be providers of legal services to the plan nor employees or officers of the corporation conducting the plan. The nonprovider members of the board may not be elected or appointed by the Virginia State Bar or by attorneys participating in the plan.

3. No part of the dues paid by attorneys to the Virginia State Bar shall be used to financially support the nonstock corporation.

4. The Commission shall require quarterly compliance certification from all plans licensed pursuant to this section. (1982, c. 387, § 38.1-793.1; 1986, c. 562.)

§ 38.2-4404. Liability of participating providers. — A. Except for a plan established pursuant to § 38.2-4403, all participating providers in a plan shall be jointly and severally liable on all contracts made for the purposes of the plan by the organization as agent for them. Each contract may be executed and signed by their agent on their behalf. A contract so signed shall be binding on the participating providers and not on the agent.

B. Actions for breach of these contracts may be brought against the participating providers by naming the agent as the sole defendant. A judgment in favor of the plaintiff may be satisfied out of the assets of the legal services organization or out of the assets of each of the participating providers.

C. Each participating provider shall be liable for his own torts and not for the torts of any other participating provider or of the agent. (1978, c. 658, § 38.1-794; 1982, c. 387; 1986, c. 562; 1994, c. 224.)

§ 38.2-4405. Change of participating providers. — A. Any participating provider may resign from a plan at any time but will continue to be liable on each subscription contract while effective. However, this liability shall not extend beyond the end of each such subscription contract's current contract year.

B. Participating providers may be admitted to a plan at any time and will then automatically become liable on all its outstanding contracts. (1978, c. 658, § 38.1-795; 1986, c. 562; 1994, c. 224.)

§ 38.2-4406. Board of directors of corporation operating plan. — Notwithstanding the provisions of §§ 13.1-675 and 13.1-855, any corporation that operates any plan pursuant to the terms of this chapter shall have a board of directors consisting of no more than fifteen members of whom a majority shall be subscribers to the plan who are not providers of legal services and not employees or officers of any plan. This section does not apply to a plan operated by a group of attorneys except as provided in § 38.2-4403. (1978, c. 658, § 38.1-796; 1982, c. 387; 1986, c. 562.)

§ 38.2-4407. Board of directors of plan created by attorneys. — Notwithstanding the provisions of §§ 13.1-675, 13.1-677 and 13.1-855 to the contrary, any legal services organization operating a plan created by a group of attorneys shall have a board of directors consisting of no more than fifteen members of whom a majority may be providers of legal services. This section does not apply to a plan operated under § 38.2-4403. (1978, c. 658, § 38.1-797; 1982, c. 387; 1986, c. 562.)

§ 38.2-4408. Application of certain provisions. — No provision of this title except this chapter and insofar as they are not inconsistent with this chapter §§ 38.2-100, 38.2-200, 38.2-203, 38.2-210 through 38.2-213, 38.2-218 through 38.2-225, 38.2-229, 38.2-316, 38.2-400, 38.2-402 through 38.2-413, 38.2-500 through 38.2-515, 38.2-600 through 38.2-620, 38.2-700 through 38.2-704, 38.2-800 through 38.2-806, 38.2-1038, 38.2-1040 through 38.2-1044, Articles 1 (§ 38.2-1300 et seq.), 2 (§ 38.2-1306.2 et seq.), and 4 (§ 38.2-1317 et seq.) of Chapter 13, and 38.2-1800 through 38.2-1836, insofar as they are not inconsistent with this chapter, and § 58.1-2500 et seq. shall apply to the operation of a plan. (1978, c. 658, § 38.1-798; 1986, c. 562; 1993, c. 158; 1994, c. 224.)

§ 38.2-4408.1. Rehabilitation, liquidation, conservation. — Any rehabilitation, liquidation, or conservation of a legal services organization shall be deemed to be the rehabilitation, liquidation, or conservation of an insurer and shall be subject to the provisions of Chapter 15 (§ 38.2-1500 et seq.) of Title 38.2. (1990, c. 331; 1994, c. 224.)

§ 38.2-4409. Payments under plan. — The legal services organization shall not indemnify any subscriber for legal services rendered by any participating provider or nonparticipating attorney. (1978, c. 658, § 38.1-798; 1986, c. 562; 1994, c. 224.)

§ 38.2-4410. Quarterly reports. — In addition to the annual statement required by § 38.2-1300, the Commission shall require each organization to file on a quarterly basis any additional reports, exhibits or statements the Commission considers necessary to furnish full information concerning the condition, solvency, experience, transactions or affairs of the organization. The Commission shall establish deadlines for submitting any additional reports, exhibits or statements. The Commission may require verification by any officers of the organization the Commission designates. (1978, c. 658, § 38.1-799; 1986, c. 562.)

§ 38.2-4411. Subscriber to have free choice of participating providers available. — A legal services organization shall organize and operate a plan in a manner that assures that any subscriber to the plan shall have free choice of the participating providers available and participating in the plan. (1978, c. 658, § 38.1-800; 1986, c. 562; 1994, c. 224.)

§ 38.2-4412. Subscriber to be advised in writing as to benefits and limitations thereon. — A legal services organization shall, prior to and during the term of the subscription contract, fully, fairly, and currently advise the subscriber in writing of the benefits available under the contract and all limitations on the benefits available under the contract. (1978, c. 658, § 38.1-801; 1986, c. 562.)

§ 38.2-4413. Licensing of organization. — A. No person shall operate a legal services plan in this Commonwealth without a license issued by the

Commission. Each organization shall apply for a license and furnish any relevant information the Commission requires. Each license shall expire at midnight on the following June 30. A nonrefundable application fee of $500 shall be paid with each application for a license.

B. The Commission shall not issue to or renew a license of an organization unless it is satisfied that the financial condition, the method of operation, and the manner of doing business of the organization enable it to meet its contractual obligations to all subscribers and that the organization has otherwise complied with all the requirements of law. (1978, c. 658, § 38.1-802; 1986, c. 562.)

§ 38.2-4414. Renewal of organization license. — A. Each legal services organization shall renew its license with the Commission annually by July 1. The renewal license shall not be issued unless the organization has paid all fees and charges imposed on it, and has complied with all other requirements of law.

B. The Commission shall not fail or refuse to renew the license of any organization without first giving the organization ten days' notice of its intention not to renew the license and giving it an opportunity to be heard and to introduce evidence in its behalf. Any nonrenewal hearing may be informal. The required notice may be waived by the Commission and the organization. (1978, c. 658, § 38.1-803; 1986, c. 562.)

§ 38.2-4415. Licensing of agents. — Subscription contracts may be solicited only through licensed legal services agents as provided for in Chapter 18 of this title. Home office salaried officers whose principal duties and responsibilities do not include the negotiation or solicitation of subscription contracts shall not be required to be licensed. (1978, c. 658, § 38.1-804; 1986, c. 562.)

§ 38.2-4416. Taxation. — Except as provided by § 58.1-2501 and Chapter 4 of this title, the application fees paid by a legal services organization under this chapter shall be in lieu of all other state and local license fees or license taxes and state income taxes. (1978, c. 658, § 38.1-802; 1986, c. 562.)

§ 38.2-4417. Misleading applications or contracts. — In the operation of a plan, no person shall use any misleading subscription applications or contracts. (1978, c. 658, § 38.1-805; 1986, c. 562.)

§ 38.2-4418. Controversies involving subscription contracts. — The Commission shall have no jurisdiction to adjudicate controversies growing out of subscription contracts. A breach of contract shall not be deemed a violation of this chapter. (1978, c. 658, § 38.1-809; 1986, c. 562.)

CHAPTER 45.

DENTAL OR OPTOMETRIC SERVICES PLANS.

676

§ **38.2-4500. Applicability of chapter.** — A. Except as otherwise provided by law, no arrangement for furnishing prepaid dental services or prepaid optometric services shall be organized, conducted or offered in this Commonwealth other than in the manner set forth in this chapter.

B. Nothing contained in this chapter prohibits any dentist or optometrist individually, in partnership with other dentists or optometrists, or as part of a professional corporation of dentists or optometrists from entering into agreements directly with his own patients, or with a parent, guardian, conservator, spouse or other family member acting in a patient's behalf, involving payment for professional services to be rendered or made available in the future. (1980, c. 682, § 38.1-894; 1986, c. 562; 1997, c. 801.)

Editor's note. — Acts 1997, c. 801, cl. 2, provides: "That the provisions of this act shall become effective on January 1, 1998. The powers granted and duties imposed pursuant to this act shall apply prospectively to guardians and conservators appointed by court order entered on or after that date, or modified on or after that date if the court so directs, without regard to when the petition was filed. The procedures specified in this act governing proceedings for appointment of a guardian or conservator or termination or other modification of a guardianship shall apply on and after that date without regard to when the petition therefor was filed or the guardianship or conservatorship created."

The 1997 amendment, effective January 1, 1998, inserted "conservator" in subsection B.

§ **38.2-4501. Definitions.** — As used in this chapter:

"Contract holder" means a person entering into a subscription contract with a nonstock corporation.

"Dental services plans" means any arrangement for offering or administering prepaid dental services by a nonstock corporation licensed under this chapter.

"Nonstock corporation" means a foreign or domestic nonstock corporation which is subject to regulation and licensing under this chapter and which operates a dental services plan or an optometric services plan.

"Optometric services plan" means any arrangement for offering or administering prepaid optometric services by a nonstock corporation licensed under this chapter.

"Plan" means any dental services plan or any optometric services plan subject to regulation under this chapter.

"Subscriber" means any person entitled to benefits under the terms and conditions of a subscription contract.

"Subscription contract" means a written contract which is issued to a contract holder by a nonstock corporation and which provides dental or optometric services or benefits for dental or optometric services. (1986, c. 562.)

§ **38.2-4502. Dental services plans.** — A group of licensed dentists may conduct through a nonstock corporation as agent for them a dental services plan as defined in § 38.2-4501. (1980, c. 682, § 38.1-892; 1986, c. 562.)

§ 38.2-4503. Optometric services plans. — A group of licensed optometrists may conduct through a nonstock corporation as agent for them an optometric services plan as defined in § 38.2-4501. (1980, c. 682, § 38.1-893; 1986, c. 562.)

§ 38.2-4504. Nonstock corporation required. — Each plan shall be conducted either by or through (i) a nonstock corporation organized pursuant to the laws of this Commonwealth or (ii) a foreign nonstock corporation that is subject to regulation and licensing under the laws of its domiciliary jurisdiction that are substantially similar to those provided by this chapter. (1980, c. 682, § 38.1-895; 1986, c. 562.)

§ 38.2-4505. Liability of participants. — A. All dentists or optometrists participating in a plan shall be jointly and severally liable on all contracts made for the purpose of the plan by the nonstock corporation as agent for them. Each contract may be executed and signed by their agent on their behalf. A contract so signed shall be binding on the principals and not on the agent.

B. Actions for breach of these contracts may be brought against the principals by naming the agent as the sole defendant. A judgment in favor of the plaintiff may be satisfied out of the assets of the nonstock corporation or out of the assets of each of the principals.

C. Each participant shall be liable for his own torts and not for the torts of any other participant or of the agent. (1980, c. 682, § 38.1-896; 1986, c. 562.)

§ 38.2-4506. Terms of participation. — Each dentist or optometrist participating in any plan shall do so in accordance with the terms and conditions imposed on other participating providers under similar circumstances. Participating providers shall have the right to engage in other practice. A nonstock corporation shall not engage in the practice of dentistry or optometry. (1980, c. 682, § 38.1-897; 1986, c. 562.)

§ 38.2-4507. Change of participants. — A. Any participating dentist or optometrist may resign from a plan at any time but will continue to be liable on each subscription contract then in effect. However, this liability shall not extend beyond the end of each such subscription contract's current contract year.

B. Dentists or optometrists may be admitted to a plan at any time and will then automatically become liable on all its outstanding contracts. (1980, c. 682, § 38.1-897; 1986, c. 562.)

§ 38.2-4508. Board of directors of nonstock corporation. — Notwithstanding the provisions of § 13.1-855, a nonstock corporation shall have a board of directors consisting of at least twelve but no more than twenty members. A majority of the members of the board of directors of a nonstock corporation operating a dental services plan shall be participating dentists. A majority of the members of the board of directors of a nonstock corporation operating an optometric services plan shall be participating optometrists. (1980, c. 682, § 38.1-898; 1986, c. 562; 1987, c. 520.)

§ 38.2-4509. Application of certain laws. — A. No provision of this title except this chapter and, insofar as they are not inconsistent with this chapter, §§ 38.2-200, 38.2-203, 38.2-210 through 38.2-213, 38.2-218 through 38.2-225, 38.2-229, 38.2-316, 38.2-400, 38.2-402 through 38.2-413, 38.2-500 through 38.2-515, 38.2-600 through 38.2-620, 38.2-900 through 38.2-904, 38.2-1038, 38.2-1040 through 38.2-1044, Articles 1 (§ 38.2-1300 et seq.) and 2 (§ 38.2-

1306.2 et seq.) of Chapter 13, §§ 38.2-1312, 38.2-1314, Article 4 (§ 38.2-1317 et seq.) of Chapter 13, §§ 38.2-1400 through 38.2-1444, 38.2-1800 through 38.2-1836, 38.2-3401, 38.2-3404, 38.2-3405, 38.2-3407.10, 38.2-3407.13, 38.2-3407.14, 38.2-3407.15, 38.2-3415, 38.2-3541, 38.2-3600 through 38.2-3603, Chapter 58 (§ 38.2-5800 et seq.) and Chapter 59 (§ 38.2-5900 et seq.) of this title shall apply to the operation of a plan.

B. The provisions of subsection A of § 38.2-322 shall apply to an optometric services plan. The provisions of subsection C of § 38.2-322 shall apply to a dental services plan.

C. The provisions of Article 1.2 (§ 32.1-137.7 et seq.) of Chapter 5 of Title 32.1 shall not apply to either an optometric or dental services plan. (1980, c. 682, § 38.1-899; 1983, c. 457; 1986, c. 562; 1989, c. 653; 1993, cc. 158, 307; 1996, c. 776; 1998, cc. 42, 891; 1999, cc. 643, 649, 709, 739.)

The 1998 amendments. — The 1998 amendment by c. 42, in subsection A, inserted "38.2-203."

The 1998 amendment by c. 891, in subsection A, inserted "and Chapter 58 (§ 38.2-5800 et seq.) of this title" and added subsection C.

The 1999 amendments. — The 1999 amendment by c. 643 inserted "38.2-3407.13, 38.2-3407.15" in subsection A.

The 1999 amendment by c. 649 inserted "§§" preceding "38.2-1312," inserted "38.2-3407.13, 48.2-3407.14, 38.2-3407.15," deleted "and" preceding "Chapter 58," and inserted "and Chapter 59 (§ 38.2-5900 et seq.)".

The 1999 amendment by c. 709 in subsection A, substituted "§§" preceding "38.2-1312," inserted "§§" preceding "38.2-1400," and inserted "38.2-3407.13."

The 1999 amendment by c. 739 inserted "38.2-3407.13" in subsection A.

§ 38.2-4509.1. Rehabilitation, liquidation, conservation. — Any rehabilitation, liquidation, or conservation of a dental or optometric plan shall be deemed to be the rehabilitation, liquidation, or conservation of an insurer and shall be subject to the provisions of Chapter 15 of this title. (1990, c. 331.)

§ 38.2-4510. Quarterly reports. — In addition to the annual statement required by § 38.2-1300, the Commission shall require each nonstock corporation to file on a quarterly basis any additional reports, exhibits or statements the Commission considers necessary to furnish full information concerning the condition, solvency, experience, transactions or affairs of the nonstock corporation. The Commission shall establish deadlines for submitting additional reports, exhibits or statements. The Commission may require verification by any officers of the nonstock corporation the Commission designates. (1980, c. 682, § 38.1-900; 1986, c. 562.)

§ 38.2-4511. Corporation's contracts with participating dentists or optometrists. — Participating dentists or optometrists shall agree to (i) perform the dental services or optometric services specified by the plan at the rates of compensation determined by the nonstock corporation and filed with the Commission, and (ii) abide by the bylaws, rules and regulations of the nonstock corporation. (1980, c. 682, § 38.1-901; 1986, c. 562.)

§ 38.2-4512. Contracts between participating dentists or optometrists and subscribers. — Participating dentists or optometrists, acting through their agents, may enter into contracts with subscribers to furnish specified dental or optometric services at specified rates to a subscriber or subscriber's members, officers, or employees. Contracts may vary as to services and rates. (1980, c. 682, § 38.1-902; 1986, c. 562.)

§ 38.2-4513. Subscriber to have free choice of practitioners available. — A plan shall be organized and operated to assure that any subscriber shall have free choice of any participating dentist or optometrist who agrees to accept the subscriber as a patient for services provided by the plan. (1980, c. 682, § 38.1-903; 1986, c. 562.)

§ 38.2-4514. Subscriber to be advised in writing as to benefits and limitations thereon. — A nonstock corporation shall, prior to and during the term of the subscription contract, fully, fairly, and currently advise the subscriber in writing of the benefits available under the contract and all limitations on the benefits available under the contract. (1980, c. 682, § 38.1-903; 1986, c. 562.)

§ 38.2-4515. Geographical area. — A. Each nonstock corporation seeking to be licensed by the Commission shall specify the geographical area it desires to serve and shall satisfy the Commission that it is able to render the services of the plan.

B. The Commission may, after notice and hearing, license more than one nonstock corporation for the same geographical area unless the Commission finds that the (i) nonstock corporation's proposed method of operation or manner of doing business is not satisfactory or (ii) licensing of more than one nonstock corporation for the same geographical area will not promote the public welfare. If more than one nonstock corporation is licensed in a geographical area, the nonstock corporations in that area shall make arrangements among themselves to see that any claim filed with the wrong nonstock corporation in that area be promptly forwarded to the proper nonstock corporation, if it can be determined.

C. Subscription contracts shall not be sold to persons residing outside the area of the nonstock corporation unless they are regularly employed within the area. The subscription contract of a subscriber who neither lives nor is employed within the area shall be cancelled by notice given in accordance with the terms of the subscription contract. (1980, c. 682, § 38.1-904; 1986, c. 562.)

§ 38.2-4516. Interplan arrangements. — A nonstock corporation may enter into contracts with similar nonstock corporations or foreign companies for the interchange of services to those included in subscription contracts and may provide in subscription contracts for the substitution of the services instead of those recited in subscription contracts. (1980, c. 682, § 38.1-905; 1986, c. 562.)

§ 38.2-4517. Licensing of nonstock corporation. — A. No person shall operate a dental or optometric services plan in this Commonwealth without a license issued by the Commission. Each nonstock corporation shall apply for a license and furnish any relevant information the Commission requires. Each license shall expire at midnight on the following June 30. Application for a license shall be accompanied by a nonrefundable application fee of $500.

B. The Commission shall not issue to or renew a license of a nonstock corporation unless it is satisfied that the financial condition, the method of operation, and the manner of doing business of the nonstock corporation enable it to meet its contractual obligations to all subscribers and that the nonstock corporation has otherwise complied with all the requirements of law. (1980, c. 682, § 38.1-906; 1986, c. 562; 1987, cc. 565, 655; 1994, c. 503.)

§ 38.2-4518. Renewal of nonstock corporation license. — A. Each nonstock corporation licensed under this chapter shall renew its license annually by July 1. The renewal license shall not be issued unless the nonstock corporation has complied with all requirements of law.

B. The Commission shall not fail or refuse to renew the license of any nonstock corporation without first giving the nonstock corporation ten days' notice of its intention not to renew the license and giving it an opportunity to be heard and to introduce evidence in its behalf. Any nonrenewal hearing may be informal, and the required notice may be waived by the Commission and the nonstock corporation. (1980, c. 682, § 38.1-907; 1986, c. 562; 1987, cc. 565, 655.)

§ 38.2-4519. Licensing of agents. — Subscription contracts for dental services plans may be solicited only by licensed dental services agents as provided for in Chapter 18 of this title. Subscription contracts for optometric services plans may be solicited only by licensed optometric services agents as provided for in Chapter 18 of this title. Home office salaried officers whose principal duties and responsibilities do not include the negotiation or solicitation of subscription contracts shall not be required to be licensed. (1980, c. 682, § 38.1-908; 1986, c. 562.)

§ 38.2-4520. Corporate restrictions. — Any nonstock corporation subject to this chapter shall not engage in any other business. However, a nonstock corporation may assist in the administration of governmental health care programs in a manner provided for by contract or regulations. A nonstock corporation's charter may provide for ex officio directors and directors elected by persons or associations who are not directors or members of the nonstock corporation. (1980, c. 682, § 38.1-909; 1986, c. 562.)

§ 38.2-4521. Taxation. — Except as provided by Chapter 4 of this title, the license tax paid by a nonstock corporation under Chapter 25 of Title 58.1 shall be in lieu of all other state and local license fees or license taxes and state income taxes of the nonstock corporation. (1980, c. 682, § 38.1-909; 1986, c. 562; 1987, cc. 565, 655.)

§ 38.2-4522. Misleading applications or contracts. — In the operation of a plan, no person shall use any misleading subscription applications or contracts. (1980, c. 682, § 38.1-910; 1986, c. 562.)

§ 38.2-4523. Controversies involving subscription contracts. — The Commission shall have no jurisdiction to adjudicate controversies growing out of subscription contracts. A breach of contract shall not be deemed a violation of this chapter. (1980, c. 682, § 38.1-914; 1986, c. 562.)

CHAPTER 46.

TITLE INSURANCE.

§ 38.2-4600. Class of insurance and insurance companies to which chapter applies. — Except as otherwise provided, this chapter applies to title insurance as defined in § 38.2-123, and to title insurance companies as defined in § 38.2-4601. (1952, c. 317, § 38.1-720; 1986, c. 562.)

§ 38.2-4601. Title insurance company defined. — *"Title insurance company"* means any company licensed to transact, or transacting, title insurance. (1952, c. 317, § 38.1-721; 1986, c. 562.)

§ 38.2-4601.1. Title insurance agency or agent defined. — A "title insurance agency or agent" means any individual, corporation, partnership, or any other legal entity licensed in the Commonwealth as a title insurance agent and appointed by a title insurance company licensed in the Commonwealth, who shall perform all of the following services (for which liability arises) relevant to the issuance of title insurance policies, subject to the underwriting directives and guidelines of the agent's title insurance company. These services shall include (i) the evaluation of the title search to determine the insurability of the title; (ii) a determination of whether or not underwriting objections have been cleared; (iii) the actual issuance of a title commitment or binder and endorsements; and (iv) the actual issuance of the policy or policies and endorsements on behalf of the title insurance company. A title insurance agent holding any funds in escrow shall promptly deposit such funds in a trust account in a financial institution licensed to do business in this Commonwealth. Such trust account shall be separate from all other accounts held by the agent. (1993, c. 147; 1997, c. 426.)

§ 38.2-4602. What laws applicable. — Except as otherwise provided, and except where the context otherwise requires, all provisions of this title relating to insurance and insurers generally shall apply to title insurance and title insurance companies. (Code 1950, §§ 38-234, 38-235; 1952, c. 317, § 38.1-722; 1986, c. 562.)

§ 38.2-4603. What companies may transact title insurance. — No company other than an insurance company organized as a stock company and licensed to transact title insurance shall transact title insurance in this Commonwealth. (1952, c. 317, § 38.1-723; 1986, c. 562.)

§ 38.2-4604. Investment in plant and equipment. — Notwithstanding the provisions of Chapter 14 of this title, any domestic title insurance company may invest in title records and equipment an amount that is not in excess of fifty percent of its assets comprising its minimum capital and surplus, and any of its assets comprising its excess capital and surplus and its reserves other than unearned premium and loss reserves. (Code 1950, § 38-236; 1952, c. 317, § 38.1-724; 1983, c. 457; 1986, c. 562.)

§ 38.2-4605. Interim binders. — Binders or other temporary insurance contracts may be made and used pending the issuance of a title insurance policy. (1952, c. 317, § 38.1-725; 1986, c. 562.)

§ 38.2-4606. Forms to be filed with Commission. — All forms of title insurance policies and interim binders that are customarily used by any title insurance company in connection with the insurance of titles to property located in this Commonwealth shall be filed with the Commission. (1952, c. 317, § 38.1-726; 1986, c. 562.)

§ 38.2-4607. Maximum risk. — On and after July 1, 1952, no company transacting title insurance in this Commonwealth shall assume a single risk in an amount in excess of fifty percent of the aggregate amount of its total capital and surplus and its reserves other than its loss or claim reserves. As used in this section, *"a single risk"* means the risk or hazard attaching to or arising in connection with any one piece or parcel of property, whether or not the policy insures other property. Any risk, or portion of any risk, that has been reinsured as authorized in this title shall be deducted in determining the limitation of risk prescribed in this section. (Code 1950, § 38-167; 1952, c. 317, § 38.1-727; 1986, c. 562.)

§ 38.2-4608. Title insurance rates. — A. Title insurance risk rates shall be reasonable and adequate for the class of risks to which they apply. Risk rates shall not be unfairly discriminatory between risks involving essentially the same hazards and expense elements. The rates may be fixed in an amount sufficient to furnish a reasonable margin for profit after provision for (i) probable losses as indicated by experience within and without this Commonwealth, (ii) exposure to loss under policies, (iii) allocations to reserves, (iv) costs of participating insurance, (v) operating costs, and (vi) other items of expense fairly attributable to the operation of a title insurance business.

B. Policies may be grouped into classes for the establishment of rates. A title insurance policy that is unusually hazardous to the title insurance company because of an alleged defect or irregularity in the title insured or because of uncertainty regarding the proper interpretation or application of the law involved, may be classified separately according to the facts of each case.

C. Title insurance risk rates shall not include charges for abstracting, record searching, certificates regarding the record title, escrow services, closing services, and other related services that may be offered or furnished, or the cost and expenses of examinations of titles.

D. Any title insurance company may issue, publish and use price schedules for title insurance and for any separate or related services, or schedules setting forth one price covering the risk rate and the charges for any separate or related services. (1952, c. 317, § 38.1-728; 1986, c. 562.)

§ 38.2-4609. Loss or claim reserves. — Each title insurance company licensed in this Commonwealth shall maintain loss and loss adjustment expense reserves in an amount estimated in the aggregate as being sufficient to provide for the payment of all unpaid losses and claims under title insurance contracts of which the company has received written notice from or on behalf of the insured. (1952, c. 317, § 38.1-729; 1986, c. 562; 1990, c. 334.)

§ 38.2-4610: Repealed by Acts 1986, c. 404.

Editor's note. — Acts 1986, c. 404 repealed § 38.1-730. Pursuant to § 9-77.11, this section, which is the comparable provision in Title 38.2, is also repealed.

§ 38.2-4610.1. Unearned premium reserve. — A. A domestic title insurance company shall establish and maintain an unearned premium reserve computed in accordance with this section, and all sums attributed to such reserve shall at all times and for all purposes be considered and constitute unearned portions of the original premiums. This reserve shall be reported as a liability of the title insurance company in its financial statements.

B. The unearned premium reserve shall be maintained by the title insurance company for the protection of holders of title insurance policies. Except as provided in this section, assets equal in value to the unearned premium reserve are not subject to distribution among creditors or stockholders of the title insurance company until all claims of policyholders or claims under reinsurance contracts have been paid in full, and all liability on the policies or reinsurance contracts has been paid in full and discharged or lawfully reinsured.

C. A foreign or alien title insurance company licensed to transact title insurance business in this Commonwealth shall maintain at least the same reserves on title insurance policies issued on properties located in this Commonwealth as are required of domestic title insurance companies, unless the laws of the jurisdiction of domicile of the foreign or alien title insurance company require a higher amount.

D. The unearned premium reserve shall consist of:

1. The amount of the unearned premium reserve on June 30, 1986; and

2. A sum equal to $1.50 for each policy, contract or agreement of title insurance covering a single risk written after June 30, 1986, plus a sum equal to $12^1/_2$ cents of each $1,000 of net retained liability under each such policy, contract or agreement of title insurance on a single risk written after June 30, 1986.

E. Amounts placed in the unearned premium reserve in any year in accordance with subdivision 2 of subsection D of this section shall be deducted in determining the net profit of the title insurance company for that year.

F. A title insurance company shall release from the unearned premium reserve a sum equal to ten percent of the amount added to the reserve during a calendar year on July 1 of each of the five years following the year in which the sum was added, and shall release from the unearned premium reserve a sum equal to $3^1/_3$ percent of the amount added to the reserve during that year on each succeeding July 1 until the entire amount for that year has been released. The amount of the unearned premium reserve maintained before July 1, 1986, shall be released in accordance with the law in effect when the respective sums were reserved. (1986, c. 404, § 38.1-730.1.)

Editor's note. — This section was enacted as § 38.1-730.1 by Acts 1986, c. 404. Pursuant to § 9-77.11, this section has been incorporated into Title 38.2 as § 38.2-4610.1.

The provisions of this section are within the legislative power. Early v. Lawyers Title

Ins. Corp., 132 F.2d 42 (4th Cir. 1942).

"Unearned premiums," as used in this section, must be given its ordinary meaning. Early v. Lawyers Title Ins. Corp., 132 F.2d 42 (4th Cir. 1942).

§ 38.2-4610.2. Loss reserves. — A. Each title insurance company licensed in this Commonwealth shall annually evaluate the adequacy of its total recorded loss reserves. Total recorded loss reserves are the sum of claim reserves held under § 38.2-4609 and unearned premium reserves held under § 38.2-4610.1. The evaluation of reserve adequacy shall be prepared by a qualified actuary and shall be based on a comparison of total recorded reserves to a projection of ultimate losses not yet paid. The actuary shall certify the results of his evaluation in a report complying with such applicable title insurance annual statement instructions as may be issued by the National Association of Insurance Commissioners.

B. A domestic title insurance company shall record an additional reserve to the extent the projection of ultimate losses not yet paid set forth in the report of the qualified actuary exceeds total recorded loss reserves held by the company. For purposes of calculating any additional reserve required, a domestic title insurance company may discount the projection of ultimate losses not yet paid to reflect the time value of money. The interest rate used by the actuary to reflect the time value of money shall be based on a portfolio interest rate approach with appropriate provision for risk margins and subject to published actuarial standards for discounting reserves.

C. A foreign or alien title insurance company licensed in this Commonwealth shall record an additional reserve to the extent the projection of ultimate losses set forth in the report of the qualified actuary exceeds all recorded reserves held by the company as reported in its most recent statutory statement filed with the Commission, including reserves held under subsection C of § 38.2-4610.1 and all reserves held under the laws of the jurisdiction of the domicile of the foreign or alien title insurance company or any other jurisdiction. (1996, c. 494.)

§§ 38.2-4611, 38.2-4612: Repealed by Acts 1986, c. 404.

Editor's note. — Acts 1986, c. 404 repealed §§ 38.1-731 and 38.1-732. Pursuant to § 9-77.11, repeals were implemented in the comparable provisions in Title 38.2, §§ 38.2-4611 and 38.2-4612.

§ 38.2-4613. Unearned premium reserve to be held and administered for benefit of policyholders. — A. The reserve required under § 38.2-4610.1 shall be for the security of policyholders of the title insurance company as provided in this section.

B. If an order of rehabilitation or liquidation of any title insurance company is entered by a court of competent jurisdiction, the rehabilitator or receiver, with the approval of the court, or the Commission if it has been directed to rehabilitate or liquidate the title insurance company under the provisions of Chapter 15 of this title, may (i) use assets equal to the unearned premium reserve to pay any claims for losses sustained by policyholders prior to the time reinsurance is effected to the extent that those losses are in excess of the loss or claim reserves available for their payment, (ii) enter into contracts for the reinsurance of the obligations under the outstanding title insurance policies of the company in accordance with their terms and conditions, and (iii) use assets equal to the unearned premium reserve to pay the cost of reinsurance. After the payments authorized by this subsection have been made, assets equal to any balance in the unearned premium reserve shall become general assets of the company.

C. If no such contract of reinsurance is effected, assets equal to the unearned premium reserve may be applied by the rehabilitator or receiver with the approval of the court, or by the Commission, in the following order of preference: (i) all expenses incurred under this section in connection with the receivership or rehabilitation proceedings, (ii) all allowed and unpaid claims for losses sustained by policyholders pending at the time fixed by the court or the Commission for the filing of claims, and (iii) all allowed claims for losses asserted within twenty years from the date of the entry of the order of rehabilitation or liquidation, which claims shall be paid in the order of the date of their allowance by the court or the Commission. Assets equal to any balance in the unearned premium reserve after payment of all allowed claims shall become general assets of the company. All title records that the rehabilitator, or the receiver, or the Commission if appointed to rehabilitate or liquidate the company, deems necessary to carry out the provisions of this section shall be preserved for twenty years.

D. In proceedings for the rehabilitation or liquidation of a title insurance company that has not been declared insolvent, no assets of the company shall be distributed to its stockholders until all claims allowed in the proceedings have been paid in full. If the proposed distribution is within twenty years from the date of the entry of the order of rehabilitation or liquidation, the distribution may be made if general assets of the title insurance company sufficient to fund the unearned premium reserve to the required amount as of the date of the entry of such order are first transferred to the unearned premium reserve. Upon the expiration of twenty years from the date of the order, assets equal to any balance in the unearned premium reserve after payment of all allowed claims asserted within the twenty-year period shall become general assets of the company. (1952, c. 317, § 38.1-733; 1986, cc. 404, 562.)

Editor's note. — Pursuant to § 9-77.11, effect has been given in this section, as set out above, to Acts 1986, c. 404, which amended former § 38.1-733, the comparable provision in former Title 38.1.

§ 38.2-4614. Prohibition against payment or receipt of title insurance kickbacks, rebates, commissions and other payments; penalty. — A. 1. No person selling real property, or performing services as a real estate agent, attorney, or lender incident to any real estate settlement or sale, shall pay or receive, directly or indirectly, any kickback, rebate, commission, thing of value or other payment pursuant to any agreement or understanding, oral or otherwise, that business incident to the issuance of any title insurance be referred to any title insurance company, title insurance agency or agent. No title insurance company, title insurance agency or agent shall give any such kickback, rebate, commission, thing of value or other payment pursuant to any such agreement or understanding. For purposes of this section, *"thing of value"* means any payment, advance, funds, loan, service or other consideration. This section shall not prevent any federally insured lenders, holding companies to which they belong, or subsidiaries of such lenders or holding companies from being licensed by the Commission as title insurance agents or agencies and receiving commissions from the sale of the title insurance policies in their capacities as title insurance agents or agencies.

2. Nothing in this section shall be construed to prohibit (i) payments of sums spent for bona fide advertising and marketing promotions otherwise permissible under the provisions of the Real Estate Settlement Procedures Act, 12 U.S.C. § 2601 et seq. or (ii) providing educational materials or classes, wherein such materials or classes are provided to a group of persons or entities pursuant to a bona fide marketing or educational effort.

B. Any person who knowingly and willfully violates this section shall be guilty of a misdemeanor and subject to a fine of not more than $1,000 for each violation. Any criminal charge brought under this section shall be by indictment pursuant to Chapter 14 (§ 19.2-216 et seq.) of Title 19.2.

C. No person shall be in violation of this section solely by reason of ownership in a title insurance company, title insurance agency or agent as defined in this chapter, wherein such person receives returns on investments arising from the ownership interest. In addition, this section shall not prohibit the payment to any person of a bona fide salary or compensation or other payment for services actually performed for the business of the title insurance company, title insurance agency or agent. (1975, c. 184, § 38.1-733.1; 1986, c. 562; 1987, c. 174; 1993, c. 147; 1996, c. 883.)

§ 38.2-4615. Exchange of information. — A. In order to further more equitable adoption, use and adjustment of risk rates and premiums and forms of temporary insurance policies and contracts, the Commission and title insurance companies may (i) exchange information and experience data with each other, and with the insurance supervisory officers and insurers of other states, and with national organizations and associations, including duly licensed rating organizations, and (ii) may consult and cooperate with them with respect to risk rates, premiums, and forms of policies and contracts.

B. Any two or more licensed title insurance companies may act in concert with each other and with others with respect to any or all matters pertaining to the making of risk rates or premiums, or the preparation of forms of title insurance policies, underwriting rules and practices, surveys and investigations, or the furnishing of loss or expense statistics, or other information or data relating thereto. (1952, c. 317, § 38.1-734; 1986, c. 562.)

Law Review. — For survey of Virginia law on insurance for the year 1974-1975, see 61 Va. L. Rev. 1759 (1975). For survey of Virginia law on property for the year 1974-1975, see 61 Va. L. Rev. 1834 (1975).

§ 38.2-4616. Notification to buyers of the availability of owner's title insurance.

— In connection with any transaction involving the purchase or sale of an interest in residential real property in this Commonwealth, the settlement agent as defined in § 6.1-2.10, before the disbursement of any funds, shall obtain from the purchaser a statement in writing that he has been notified by the settlement agent that the purchaser may wish to obtain owner's title insurance coverage including affirmative mechanics' lien coverage, if available, and of the general nature of such coverage, and that the purchaser does or does not desire such coverage. The notification shall include language that the value of subsequent improvements to the property may not be covered.

The failure of a settlement agent to provide the information requested by this section shall not of itself be deemed to create a cause of action that would not otherwise exist. (1992, c. 733.)

CHAPTER 47.

INSURANCE PREMIUM FINANCE COMPANIES.

§ 38.2-4700. What persons deemed insurance premium finance companies.

— A. Any person engaged in whole or in part in financing premiums for insurance on subjects of insurance resident, located or to be performed in this Commonwealth shall be an insurance premium finance company subject to this chapter. Any person who acquires agreements for this financing from an insurance premium finance company shall be deemed an insurance premium finance company subject to this chapter.

B. No person shall be deemed an insurance premium finance company by reason of any transaction lawful under the laws of this Commonwealth without regard to the provisions of this chapter. No bank, trust company, savings institution, industrial loan association, credit union, consumer finance company licensed under Chapter 6 (§ 6.1-244 et seq.) of Title 6.1, licensed insurance agent extending credit as authorized in § 38.2-1806, or insurer shall be licensed under the provisions of this chapter, nor be subject to the restrictions and obligations imposed by this chapter. (1964, c. 147, § 38.1-735; 1986, c. 562; 1996, c. 77.)

§ 38.2-4701. License required; application; fee. — No person shall act as an insurance premium finance company in this Commonwealth until that person has obtained a license from the Commission as provided in this chapter. Application for a license shall be made in writing in the form prescribed by the Commission and shall be accompanied by a nonrefundable application fee of $500. (1964, c. 147, § 38.1-736; 1981, c. 107; 1986, c. 562.)

§ 38.2-4702. Investigation of applicant; issuance of license. — Upon the filing of an application and the payment of the application fee, the Commission shall make an investigation of the applicant. The Commission shall issue a license, expiring on June 30 immediately following the date of issuance, if it finds that (i) the application is in proper form and the required fee has been paid; (ii) the financial responsibility, experience, character, and general fitness of the applicant indicate that the business will be operated lawfully, honestly, fairly and efficiently within the purpose of this chapter, the same criteria being applicable to members of the applicant if the applicant is a partnership or association and to officers and directors of the applicant if the applicant is a corporation; (iii) if the applicant is a corporation, it is a corporation of this Commonwealth or a foreign corporation that has a certificate of authority to transact business in this Commonwealth; and (iv) the applicant has assets equal to or greater than its liabilities and has working capital sufficient for the operation of its business. (1964, c. 147, § 38.1-737; 1981, c. 107; 1986, c. 562.)

Law Review. — For article, "Uniform Consumer Credit Code—A Prospect for Consumer Credit Reform in Virginia," see 28 Wash. & Lee L. Rev. 75 (1971).

§ 38.2-4703. Renewal of license. — Subject to the provisions of § 38.2-4704, a licensed insurance premium finance company may renew its license on July 1 of each year, upon payment of a nonrefundable annual license fee of $200, unless the license has been surrendered, suspended or revoked. (1964, c. 147, § 38.1-738; 1975, c. 175; 1981, c. 107; 1986, c. 562.)

§ 38.2-4704. Suspension, revocation or failure to renew license; imposition of penalty. — The Commission may suspend, revoke or refuse to renew a license of any insurance premium finance company whenever it finds that:
1. The licensee has (i) failed to pay the annual license fee, (ii) violated or failed to comply with any of the provisions of this chapter or with any rule or regulation made by the Commission pursuant to this chapter, or (iii) violated or failed to comply with any order, demand, ruling, provision or requirement of the Commission lawfully made pursuant to or within the authority of this chapter; or
2. The licensee no longer meets the standards required for the initial issuance of a license. (1964, c. 147, § 38.1-739; 1986, c. 562.)

§ 38.2-4705. Maximum interest rate and maximum service charge on premium finance agreement. — A. The Commission shall periodically investigate the economic conditions and other factors relating to and affecting the business of insurance premium finance companies. The Commission shall ascertain all pertinent facts necessary to determine what maximum interest rate and what maximum service charge shall be permitted. Upon the basis of those facts and subject to this chapter, the Commission shall determine and fix by regulation or order the maximum interest rate and maximum service charge that may be charged in advance upon the amount financed by any insurance premium finance company.

B. The Commission shall initially fix the maximum interest rate at one percent per month charged in advance upon the entire amount financed payable in installments, and shall initially fix the maximum service charge at fifteen dollars. Thereafter, the maximum interest rate and maximum service charge shall be determined by the Commission after giving due consideration to such factors as (i) prevailing market interest rates, (ii) other relevant cost indices, and (iii) the industry-wide experience of premium finance companies operating in this Commonwealth. Before redetermining the maximum interest rate or maximum service charge, the Commission shall give all licensees notice and opportunity to be heard and to introduce evidence with respect to the maximum interest rate or service charge.

C. Interest at the authorized rate may be charged from the effective date of the premium finance agreement or the inception date of the insurance contract for which the premiums are being financed, whichever is earlier, through the date when the final installment of the premium finance agreement is payable. Interest charged under a premium finance agreement shall not be fully earned at the inception of the agreement. The insurance premium finance company may earn interest through the date the principal amount financed under a premium finance agreement has been paid in full for any reason. Upon such payment in full, a refund credit of any unearned interest shall be due the insured and shall be computed on a short rate or prorata basis as set forth in the agreement, provided that the interest charged does not exceed the maximum interest rate established by the Commission pursuant to subsection A. The service charge received by an insurance premium finance company shall be fully earned upon its receipt and no portion of the service charge need be refunded upon prepayment of the loan for any reason. Only one service charge shall be made for each premium finance agreement, and no insurance agent or insurance premium finance company shall induce any person to enter into more than one premium finance agreement for the purpose of obtaining more than one service charge. Notwithstanding the foregoing, one additional charge not to exceed ten dollars may be charged if additional premiums are added to an existing finance agreement at the insured's request. Such additional charge may be applied only once during the term of any premium finance agreement. No part of any charges shall be paid to any insurance agent by an insurance premium finance company, nor shall any insurance premium finance company pay, allow or give, or offer to pay, allow or give, directly or indirectly, to any insurance agent, any valuable consideration as an inducement to finance the premium of any insurance policy. No insurance agent shall accept any valuable consideration as an inducement to finance the premium of any insurance policy. No person shall be in violation of this section solely by reason of ownership in an insurance premium finance company.

D. Notwithstanding the foregoing, the Commission by rule or order may exempt any premium finance agreement, any class of premium finance agreements or any market segment from any of the provisions of this section, if it finds their application unnecessary to achieve the purposes of this chapter. (1981, c. 107, § 38.1-740.1; 1986, c. 562; 1994, cc. 8, 123.)

§ 38.2-4706. Default charge; bad check charge. — A. If any installment under a premium finance agreement is not paid in full within seven days after it is due, Sundays and holidays included, the insurance premium finance company may charge and collect a default charge not to exceed five percent of the installment. The default charge shall be collected only once on any installment.

B. An insurance premium finance company may charge and collect a fee, not in excess of twenty dollars, for each check returned to the insurance premium finance company because the drawer had no account or insufficient funds in the payor bank. (1981, c. 107, § 38.1-740.2; 1986, c. 562; 1994, c. 123.)

§ 38.2-4707. Forms of premium finance agreements and related forms to be approved by Commission; false or misleading statements or omissions prohibited. — No form of premium finance agreement or any related form shall be used until it is approved by the Commission. No such form shall contain any statements that are materially false or misleading or omit statements necessary to prevent the form from being in any material way false or misleading. (1964, c. 147, § 38.1-741; 1981, c. 107; 1986, c. 562.)

§ 38.2-4708. Examination of books and records of company; bond; rules and regulations; order by Commission to remedy concerns. — A. 1. The Commission is empowered to examine the books and records of an insurance premium finance company.

2. The Commission is empowered to require an insurance premium finance company to enter into bond with surety approved by the Commission, in the amount determined as reasonable by the Commission, and conditioned to protect its customers and the public in the manner required by law. The aggregate liability of the surety for all breaches of the conditions of the bond shall in no event exceed the penalty of the bond. The surety on the bond shall have the right to cancel the bond upon thirty days' notice in writing to the Commission and shall be relieved of liability for any breach of condition occurring after the effective date of the cancellation.

3. Any rules and regulations issued by the Commission with respect to the operation of insurance premium finance companies may include, without limitation, rules and regulations for the cancellation of policies by insurance premium finance companies, for the notice required to be given to the insured and the insurer, and for the mutual obligations and duties of insurers and insurance premium finance companies with regard to the cancellation of policies and the required notice.

B. If the Commission finds (i) that an insurance premium finance company's financial condition, method of operation or manner of doing business does not satisfy the Commission that the company can meet its obligations to all customers or (ii) that the company's continued operation in this Commonwealth is hazardous to customers and creditors in this Commonwealth and to the public, it may order the company to take appropriate action within a specified time to remedy the concerns of the Commission. The Commission shall give the insurance premium finance company ten days' notice of its finding and shall grant it the opportunity to be heard and to introduce evidence on its behalf. Any hearing with regard to the order may be informal, and the required notice may be waived with the mutual consent of the Commission and the company. (1964, c. 147, § 38.1-742; 1981, c. 107; 1986, c. 562.)

§ 38.2-4709. Disposition of license and other fees. — The Commission shall collect and pay directly into the state treasury licensing fees and all other fees. These fees shall be credited to the fund for the maintenance of the Bureau of Insurance. (1964, c. 147, § 38.1-743; 1981, c. 107; 1986, c. 562.)

§ 38.2-4710. Penalty for engaging in business without license. — Any person engaging in the business of financing insurance premiums in this Commonwealth without obtaining a license as required under this chapter shall be subject to a fine of not more than $100 for each day that person operates without a license. The fine shall be imposed and judgment entered by the Commission after ten days' notice has been given to the defendant by rule to show cause. (1964, c. 147, § 38.1-744; 1986, c. 562.)

§ 38.2-4711. Exemptions. — This chapter shall not apply to the inclusion of a charge for insurance in a sale of property, goods or services payable in installments, or in a loan made for purposes other than the financing of insurance premiums only. (1964, c. 147, § 38.1-745; 1981, c. 107; 1986, c. 562.)

§ 38.2-4712. Validity of secured transactions. — No filing of the premium finance agreement or recording of a premium finance transaction shall be necessary to validate the agreement as a secured transaction. (1964, c. 147, § 38.1-745; 1981, c. 107; 1986, c. 562.)

CHAPTER 48.

SURPLUS LINES INSURANCE LAW.

§ 38.2-4800. Property and casualty insurance agents may be licensed as surplus lines brokers for certain insurance from unlicensed insurers. — The Commission may issue a surplus lines broker's license to any person licensed as a property and casualty insurance agent for the procuring of insurance of the classes enumerated in §§ 38.2-109 through 38.2-122 and §§ 38.2-124 through 38.2-134 from insurers not licensed to transact insurance business in this Commonwealth. However, nothing in this chapter shall apply to the solicitation, negotiation, or effecting of the contracts of insurance cited in subsection C of § 38.2-1802. (Code 1950, § 38.1-314.1; 1960, c. 503; 1979, c. 513, § 38.1-327.46; 1982, c. 264; 1984, c. 719; 1986, c. 562; 1987, c. 519; 1988, c. 828.)

§ 38.2-4801. Applications for surplus lines brokers' licenses. — Every original applicant for a surplus lines broker's license shall apply for such license on a form prescribed by the Commission, signed by the applicant, and containing any information the Commission requires. (Code 1950, § 38.1-314.2; 1960, c. 503; 1979, c. 513, § 38.1-327.47; 1986, c. 562.)

§ 38.2-4802. Fees for surplus lines brokers' licenses. — The nonrefundable application processing fee and the annual nonrefundable renewal application processing fee for each surplus lines broker's license shall be fifty dollars. The fee shall be paid when the application for license is filed and then prior to March 15 of each subsequent year. However, the fee for any license applied for after September 15 shall be twenty-five dollars. All fees shall be collected by the Commission and paid into the state treasury to the credit of the fund for the maintenance of the Bureau of Insurance as provided in subsection B of § 38.2-400. (Code 1950, § 38.1-314.3; 1960, c. 503; 1979, c. 513, § 38.1-327.48; 1986, c. 562; 1994, c. 316; 1999, c. 44.)

The **1999 amendment,** in the first sentence, substituted "nonrefundable application processing fee and the annual nonrefundable renewal application processing fee" for "annual fee."

§ 38.2-4803. Term of licenses; renewal. — Every license issued pursuant to this chapter shall be for a term expiring on March 15 next following the date of its issuance and may be renewed for the ensuing license year, upon the filing of an application in the form prescribed by the Commission and payment of the nonrefundable renewal application processing fee prescribed in § 38.2-4802. (Code 1950, § 38.1-314.4; 1960, c. 503; 1979, c. 513, § 38.1-327.49; 1986, c. 562; 1999, c. 44.)

The **1999 amendment** inserted "nonrefundable renewal application processing."

§ 38.2-4803.1. Requirement to report to Commission. — A. Each licensed surplus lines broker shall report within thirty days to the Commission any change in his residence or name. Any licensed surplus lines broker who has moved his residence from this Commonwealth shall have all licenses immediately terminated by the Commission.

B. Each licensed surplus lines broker convicted of a felony shall report within thirty days to the Commission the facts and circumstances regarding the criminal conviction. (1999, c. 59.)

§ 38.2-4804. Applicants to file bond with Commission. — Prior to issuance of a license, the applicant shall file with the Commission, and thereafter for as long as the license remains in effect he shall keep in force, a bond in favor of this Commonwealth in the amount of $25,000 with corporate sureties licensed by the Commission. The bond shall be conditioned that the broker will conduct business under the license in accordance with the provisions of the surplus lines insurance law and that he will promptly remit the taxes provided by such law. The bond shall not be terminated unless at least thirty days' prior written notice of the termination is filed with the Commission. (Code 1950, § 38.1-314.5; 1960, c. 503; 1979, c. 513, § 38.1-327.50; 1986, c. 562.)

§ 38.2-4805. Accepting and placing surplus lines business. — No surplus lines broker shall accept surplus lines business from any person other than an applicant for insurance or a duly licensed property and casualty insurance agent nor shall such surplus lines broker compensate any person other than a duly licensed property and casualty insurance agent for such business. No person other than an applicant for insurance or a duly licensed property and casualty insurance agent shall place surplus lines business with a surplus lines broker licensed under this chapter nor shall any person other than a duly licensed property and casualty insurance agent accept compensation for such business. (Code 1950, § 38.1-314.6; 1960, c. 503; 1977, c. 318; 1979, c. 513, § 38.1-327.51; 1986, c. 562; 1987, c. 520.)

§ 38.2-4806. Affidavits that insurance is unprocurable from licensed insurers required; notice to insured. — A. For all policies of insurance procured under this chapter, the surplus lines broker procuring such policies shall execute an affidavit in form and content as prescribed by the Commission stating that the surplus lines broker was unable, after diligent effort, to procure in a form and at a premium acceptable to the insured the amount of such insurance from an insurer licensed in this Commonwealth to transact insurance business of the class within which such insurance is included. The affidavit shall also affirm that the insured was given the notice required and prescribed under subsection B of this section and shall be filed with the Commission within thirty days after the end of the calendar quarter in which any such insurance has been procured. The affidavit shall accompany the reports required by subsection D of this section and subsection A of § 38.2-4807 and shall be considered a sworn statement as to the validity and accuracy of such reports.

"Class" of insurance shall mean those classes enumerated in §§ 38.2-109 through 38.2-122 and §§ 38.2-124 through 38.2-134. For business that is referred from a licensed property and casualty insurance agent, a surplus lines broker shall be deemed to have made "diligent effort," as required in the preceding paragraph whenever the risk or portion of risk placed with a nonlicensed insurer has been rejected or declined by three insurers licensed to transact such class of insurance. For business that is originated by a surplus lines broker, *"diligent effort"* means a good faith search for insurance among admitted insurers resulting in declinations of coverage by three unaffiliated admitted insurers licensed and authorized to write in this Commonwealth the insurance coverage sought.

A company is authorized to write the insurance coverage sought when it is licensed for that class of insurance in this Commonwealth and has complied with the applicable provisions of Chapters 3, 19, 20 and 26 of this title concerning rules, rates and policy forms providing the insurance coverage sought, unless such insurance has been exempted from filing by Commission order.

B. A notice in a form prescribed by the Commission shall be given to the insured under the provisions of a policy procured pursuant to this chapter by the surplus lines broker procuring the policy or by any duly licensed property and casualty insurance agent placing surplus lines business with the surplus lines broker. The notice shall contain, but not be limited to, statements that the policy is being procured from or has been placed with an insurer approved by the Commission for issuance of surplus lines insurance in this Commonwealth, but not licensed or regulated by the Commission and that there is no protection under the Virginia Property and Casualty Insurance Guaranty Association, established under Chapter 16 of this title, against financial loss to claimants or policyholders because of the insolvency of an unlicensed insurer. The notice shall also set forth the name, license number and mailing address of the broker. The notice shall be given prior to placement of the insurance. In the event coverage must be placed and become effective within twenty-four hours after referral of the business to the surplus lines broker, the notice may be given promptly following such a placement. In addition, a copy of the notice shall be affixed to the policy.

C. The requirement of a diligent search among companies licensed and authorized to write the class of insurance sought may be waived by a commercial insured. For purposes of this section, a "commercial insured" is an insured (i) who procures the insurance of any risk or risks by use of the services of a full-time employee acting as an insurance manager or buyer, (ii) whose aggregate annual premiums for insurance on all risks total at least $75,000 or (iii) who has at least twenty-five full-time employees. Such waiver shall be in writing on a form prescribed by the Commission and shall be signed by the commercial insured. One copy of the signed waiver shall be retained by the surplus lines broker for the time period specified in § 38.2-4807 and one copy shall be attached to the affidavit forwarded to the Commission as prescribed in subsection A of this section.

D. Within thirty days after the end of each calendar quarter, each person licensed under this chapter shall file a report with the Commission summarizing the business transacted during that quarter. Such report shall be on a form prescribed by the Commission and shall include for each surplus lines policy written the direct gross premium, the policy number, the name of the insured, the policy period and the name of the insurer from which coverage has been procured and any other information required by the Commission. (Code 1950, § 38.-314.7; 1960, c. 503; 1979, c. 513, § 38.1-327.52; 1981, c. 241; 1984, c. 719; 1986, c. 562; 1987, c. 519; 1988, c. 828; 1996, c. 240.)

§ 38.2-4807. Licensees to keep records and file annual statement of policies. — A. Every person licensed pursuant to this chapter shall keep in his office a complete record of, and file on a form prescribed by the Commission in the office of the Commission annually on or before March 1, subject to § 38.2-1304 a statement setting forth (i) each policy of insurance procured by him under this chapter during the previous calendar year; (ii) the name and address of the insurer or insurers; (iii) the inception and expiration dates of each policy; (iv) the perils insured against; (v) the location of each risk so insured and the premium rate and the gross premium charged for each such policy of insurance; (vi) the amount of premium returned; and (vii) any other information the Commission requires.

B. The record of each policy of insurance shall be kept open at all reasonable times to examination by the Commission without notice for a period of not less than five years following termination of the policy. (Code 1950, § 38.1-314.8; 1960, c. 503; 1979, c. 513, § 38.1-327.53; 1986, c. 562.)

§ 38.2-4808. Effect of payment to surplus lines broker. — A. No surplus lines broker may accept a payment of premium for issuance of surplus lines insurance before placing the insurance with an eligible surplus lines insurer.

B. A payment of premium to a surplus lines broker shall be deemed to be payment to the insurer notwithstanding any policy conditions or stipulations to the contrary. (1986, c. 562.)

§ 38.2-4809. Licensees to pay assessments and license taxes on insurers. — A. 1. Every person licensed or required to be licensed under this chapter shall be subject to the annual assessment, penalties, and other provisions of §§ 38.2-400 and 38.2-403 and shall also be subject to the annual taxes, license taxes, penalties, and other provisions of Article 1 (§ 58.1-2500 et seq.) of Chapter 25 of Title 58.1 on each policy of insurance procured by him during the preceding calendar year with an insurer not licensed to transact insurance business in this Commonwealth.

2. If any person overestimates and overpays the assessment or annual taxes, the Commission shall order a refund of the amount of the overpayment to the person. The overpayment shall be refunded out of the state treasury on the order of the Commission upon the Comptroller.

B. Each person licensed or required to be licensed under this chapter whose annual premium tax liability can reasonably be expected to exceed $1,500 shall file a quarterly tax report with the Commission. Such report shall be on a form prescribed by the Commission. This report shall be filed no later than thirty days after the end of each calendar quarter. Notwithstanding any provision to the contrary, each such person shall pay the premium tax owed for the direct gross premiums adjusted for additional and returned premiums shown by each quarterly tax report when such report is filed with the Commission.

C. In addition to other penalties provided by law, any person licensed or required to be licensed under this chapter who willfully fails or refuses to pay the full amount of the tax or assessment required by this chapter, either by himself or through his agents or employees, or who makes a false or fraudulent return with intent to evade the tax or assessment hereby levied, or who makes a false or fraudulent claim for refund shall be guilty of a Class 1 misdemeanor.

D. If any person licensed or required to be licensed under this chapter charges and collects from the insured the taxes and assessments required by this section, such person shall be a fiduciary to this Commonwealth for any taxes and assessments owed to this Commonwealth under this chapter. (Code 1950, § 38.1-314.9; 1960, c. 503; 1979, c. 513, § 38.1-327.54; 1986, c. 562; 1987, c. 519; 1988, c. 153.)

Cross references. — As to punishment for Class 1 misdemeanors, see § 18.2-11.

§ 38.2-4810. Issuance and delivery of surplus lines policies; prior authority or information required. — Each policy or other written evidence of insurance procured pursuant to this chapter shall be delivered promptly to the Insured. No surplus lines broker shall issue or deliver any policy or other written evidence of insurance or represent that insurance will be or has been granted by an unlicensed insurer unless (i) he has prior written authority from such insurer for the insurance, (ii) he has received information from the insurer in the regular course of business that the insurance has been granted, or (iii) an insurance policy providing the insurance actually has been issued by the insurer and delivered to the Insured. (Code 1950, § 38.1-314.10; 1960, c. 503; 1979, c. 513, § 38.1-327.55; 1984, c. 719; 1986, c. 562.)

§ 38.2-4811. Surplus lines coverage to be placed only with unlicensed insurers approved by Commission. — A. No surplus lines broker shall procure a policy of insurance with any insurer not licensed to transact insurance business in this Commonwealth, unless such unlicensed insurer has prior approval of the Commission to issue surplus lines insurance.

B. Any unlicensed insurer wishing to be approved by the Commission to issue surplus lines coverage may receive such approval upon providing:

1. Satisfactory evidence of good repute and financial integrity; and

2. Proof that it qualifies under a, b or c of this subdivision:

a. Has capital and surplus or its equivalent under the laws of its domiciliary jurisdiction, which equal the greater of (i) the minimum capital and surplus requirements under §§ 38.2-1028, 38.2-1029, 38.2-1030 or § 38.2-1031, or (ii) $15 million except that nonadmitted insurers already qualified under this chapter shall have $5 million up to and including June 30, 1996; $10 million after June 30, 1996; $12.5 million after June 30, 1997; and $15 million after June 30, 1998.

After June 30, 1995, the requirements of subdivision 2 a of this subsection may be satisfied by an unlicensed insurer possessing less than the aforementioned capital and surplus upon an affirmative finding of acceptability by the Commission. The finding shall be based upon such factors as quality of management, capital and surplus of any parent company, company underwriting profit and investment income trends, and company record and reputation within the industry. In no event, however, shall the Commission make an affirmative finding of acceptability when the surplus lines insurer's capital and surplus is less than $4.5 million. In addition, an alien insurer may qualify under this paragraph if it maintains in the United States an irrevocable trust fund in a qualified U.S. financial institution on behalf of U.S. policyholders of not less than $2.5 million. This trust fund shall consist of cash, securities, letters of credit, or investments of substantially the same character and quality as those which are eligible investments for the capital and statutory reserves of admitted insurers authorized to write like classes of insurance in this Commonwealth. Such trust fund, which shall be included in any calculation of capital and surplus or its equivalent, shall have an expiration date which at no time shall be less than five years; and

b. In the case of any Lloyd's or other similar group, including incorporated and individual unincorporated underwriters, the incorporated members of which shall not be engaged in any business other than underwriting as a member of the group and shall be subject to the same level of solvency regulation and control by the group's domiciliary regulator as are the unincorporated members, maintains a trust fund of not less than fifty million dollars as security to the full amount thereof for all policyholders and creditors in the United States of each member of the group, and such trust shall likewise comply with the terms and conditions established in subdivision 2 a of this subsection for alien insurers; and

c. In the case of an "insurance exchange" created by the laws of individual states, maintains capital and surplus, or the substantial equivalent of capital and surplus, of not less than $50 million in the aggregate. For insurance exchanges which maintain funds for the protection of all insurance exchange policyholders, each individual syndicate shall maintain minimum capital and surplus, or the substantial equivalent of capital and surplus, of not less than $3 million. If the insurance exchange does not maintain funds for the protection of all insurance exchange policyholders, each individual syndicate shall meet the minimum capital and surplus requirements of subdivision 2 a of this subsection.

C. Any such unlicensed insurer shall cause to be provided to the Commission not later than six months after the close of the period reported upon a copy of its current annual statement certified by the insurer. The report shall be:

1. Filed with and approved by the regulatory authority in the domicile of the nonadmitted insurer; or

2. Certified by an accounting or auditing firm licensed in the jurisdiction of the insurer's domicile.

In the case of an insurance exchange, such report may be an aggregate combined statement of all underwriting syndicates operating during the period reported upon.

The Commission, at its discretion, may extend the period for filing an annual statement by a maximum of two months.

D. If at any time the Commission has reason to believe that an eligible surplus lines insurer (i) is in unsound financial condition, (ii) is no longer eligible under subdivision 2 of subsection B above, (iii) has willfully violated the laws of this Commonwealth, or (iv) does not make reasonably prompt payment of just losses and claims in this Commonwealth or elsewhere, the Commission may declare it ineligible. The Commission shall promptly mail notice of all such declarations to each surplus lines licensee. (Code 1950, § 38.1-314.11; 1960, c. 503; 1979, c. 513, § 38.1-327.56; 1984, c. 719; 1986, c. 562; 1994, c. 647; 1995, c. 60.)

§ 38.2-4812. Surplus lines insurers subject to Unlicensed Insurers Process. — Every insurer issuing surplus lines coverage under this chapter shall be subject to the provisions of §§ 38.2-801 through 38.2-807. (Code 1950, § 38.1-314.12; 1960, c. 503; 1979, c. 513, § 38.1-327.57; 1986, c. 562; 1988, c. 153.)

§ 38.2-4813. Commission to make rules and regulations. — The Commission may make, approve and adopt reasonable rules and regulations consistent with this chapter to effect the purposes of this chapter. (Code 1950, § 38.1-314.14; 1960, c. 503; 1979, c. 513, § 38.1-327.58; 1984, c. 719; 1986, c. 562.)

§ 38.2-4814. Penalties. — Any violation of this chapter shall be punished as provided for in §§ 38.2-218 and 38.2-1831. (Code 1950, § 38.1-314.15; 1960, c. 503; 1979, c. 513, § 38.1-327.59; 1986, c. 562.)

§ 38.2-4815. Effect on other provisions of Title 38.2. — Except as is otherwise provided herein, the provisions relating to the licensing and control of surplus lines brokers shall have no effect on or in any way alter any of the other provisions of this title. (Code 1950, § 38.1-314.16; 1960, c. 503; 1979, c. 513, § 38.1-327.60; 1986, c. 562.)

CHAPTER 49.

CONTINUING CARE PROVIDER REGISTRATION AND DISCLOSURE.

§ 38.2-4900. Definitions. — As used in this chapter:
"Continuing care" means providing or committing to provide board, lodging and nursing services to an individual, other than an individual related by blood or marriage, (i) pursuant to an agreement effective for the life of the individual or for a period in excess of one year, including mutually terminable contracts, and (ii) in consideration of the payment of an entrance fee. A contract shall be deemed to be one offering nursing services, irrespective of whether such services are provided under such contract, if nursing services are offered to the resident entering such contract either at the facility in question or pursuant to arrangements specifically offered to residents of the facility.

"Continuing care" also means providing or committing to provide lodging to an individual, other than an individual related by blood or marriage, (i) pursuant to an agreement effective for the life of the individual or for a period in excess of one year, including mutually terminable contracts, (ii) in consideration of the payment of an entrance fee, and (iii) where board and nursing services are made available to the resident by the provider, either directly or indirectly through affiliated persons, or through contractual arrangements, whether or not such services are specifically offered in the agreement for lodging.

"Entrance fee" means an initial or deferred transfer to a provider of a sum of money or other property made or promised to be made in advance or at some future time as full or partial consideration for acceptance of a specified individual as a resident in a facility. A fee which in the aggregate is less than the sum of the regular periodic charges for one year of residency shall not be considered to be an entrance fee except as provided in subsection A of § 38.2-4904.1.

"Facility" means the place or places in which a person undertakes to provide continuing care to an individual.

"Provider" means any person, corporation, partnership or other entity that provides or offers to provide continuing care to any individual in an existing or proposed facility in this Commonwealth. Two or more related individuals, corporations, partnerships or other entities may be treated as a single provider if they cooperate in offering services to the residents of a facility.

"Resident" means an individual entitled to receive continuing care in a facility.

"Solicit" means all actions of a provider or his agent in seeking to have individuals enter into a continuing care agreement by any means such as, but not limited to, personal, telephone or mail communication or any other communication directed to and received by any individual, and any advertisements in any media distributed or communicated by any means to individuals. (1985, c. 554, § 38.1-955; 1986, cc. 562, 598; 1993, c. 683.)

Editor's note. — Pursuant to § 9-77.11, effect has been given in this section, as set out above, to Acts 1986, c. 598, which amended former § 38.1-955, the comparable provision in former Title 38.1.

Acts 1997, c. 568, cl. 2, provides: "That the Joint Commission on Health Care, in conjunction with the Commissioner of Health or his designee and the Commissioner of Insurance or his designee, shall study the management of applications for nursing facility projects in continuing care retirement communities under the Commonwealth's Medical Facilities Certificate of Public Need law and regulations, including, but not limited to (i) whether such projects should be included or exempted from the Request for Applications (RFA) process established pursuant to § 32.1-102.3:2; (ii) the different forms of continuing care contracts being offered by continuing care providers in Virginia and the effect of such contracts on the utilization of nursing facility beds in continuing care retirement communities; (iii) the impact of increases in nursing facility beds in continuing care retirement communities, if any, on the occupancy rates and charges of existing nursing homes and certified nursing facilities in the Commonwealth; (iv) the impact, if any, of nursing facility beds in continuing care retirement communities on Virginia Medicaid expenditures; and (v) the appropriateness of the present registration law, Chapter 49 (§ 38.2-4900 et seq.) of Title 38.2, for continuing care providers and the need for any modifications to such law, particularly in view of the changing configurations in the continuing care market. The Joint Commission shall report its preliminary findings by December 1, 1997, and shall complete its work in time to submit its findings and recommendations to the Governor and the 1998 Session of the General Assembly as provided in the procedures of the Division of Legislative Automated Systems for the processing of legislative documents."

Law Review. — For comment, "Continuing Care Retirement Communities: A Promise Falling Short," see 8 Geo. Mason L. Rev. 47 (1985).

§ 38.2-4901. Registration. — A. Except as provided in § 38.2-4912, no provider shall engage in the business of providing or offering to provide continuing care at a facility in this Commonwealth unless the provider has registered with the Commission with respect to such facility.

B. A registration statement shall be filed with the Commission by the provider on forms prescribed by the Commission and shall include:

1. All information required by the Commission pursuant to its enforcement of this chapter; and

2. The initial disclosure statement required by § 38.2-4902.

C. Registration shall be approved or disapproved in writing by the Commission within ninety days of the filing. (1985, c. 554, § 38.1-956; 1986, c. 562.)

Law Review. — For comment, "Continuing Care Retirement Communities: A Promise Falling Short," see 8 Geo. Mason L. Rev. 47 (1985).

§ 38.2-4902. Disclosure statement. — A. The disclosure statement of each facility shall contain all of the following information unless such information is contained in the continuing care contract and a copy of that contract is attached to and made a part of the initial disclosure statement:

1. The name and business address of the provider and a statement of whether the provider is a partnership, foundation, association, corporation or other type of business or legal entity.

2. Full information regarding ownership of the property on which the facility is or will be operated and of the buildings in which it is or will be operated.

3. The names and business addresses of the officers, directors, trustees, managing or general partners, and any person having a ten percent or greater equity or beneficial interest in the provider, and a description of such person's interest in or occupation with the provider.

4. For (i) the provider, (ii) any person named in response to subdivision 3 of this subsection or (iii) the proposed management, if the facility will be managed on a day-to-day basis by a person other than an individual directly employed by the provider:

a. A description of any business experience in the operation or management of similar facilities.

b. The name and address of any professional service, firm, association, foundation, trust, partnership or corporation or any other business or legal entity in which such person has, or which has in such person, a 10 percent or greater interest and which it is presently intended will or may provide goods, leases or services to the provider of a value of $500 or more, within any year, including:

(1) A description of the goods, leases or services and the probable or anticipated cost thereof to the provider;

(2) The process by which the contract was awarded;

(3) Any additional offers that were received; and

(4) Any additional information requested by the Commission detailing how and why a contract was awarded.

c. A description of any matter in which such person:

(1) Has been convicted of a felony or pleaded nolo contendere to a criminal charge, or been held liable or enjoined in a civil action by final judgment, if the crime or civil action involved fraud, embezzlement, fraudulent conversion, misappropriation of property or moral turpitude; or

(2) Is subject to an injunctive or restrictive order of a court of record, or within the past five years had any state or federal license or permit suspended or revoked as a result of an action brought by a governmental agency or

department, arising out of or relating to business activity or health care, including without limitation actions affecting a license to operate a foster care facility, nursing home, retirement home, home for the aged or facility registered under this chapter or similar laws in another state; or

(3) Is currently the subject of any state or federal prosecution, or administrative investigation involving allegations of fraud, embezzlement, fraudulent conversion, or misappropriation of property.

5. A statement as to:

a. Whether the provider is or ever has been affiliated with a religious, charitable or other nonprofit organization, the nature of any such affiliation, and the extent to which the affiliate organization is or will be responsible for the financial and contractual obligations of the provider.

b. Any provision of the federal Internal Revenue Code under which the provider is exempt from the payment of income tax.

6. The location and description of the real property of the facility, existing or proposed, and to the extent proposed, the estimated completion date or dates of improvements, whether or not construction has begun and the contingencies under which construction may be deferred.

7. The services provided or proposed to be provided under continuing care contracts, including the extent to which medical care is furnished or is available pursuant to any arrangement. The disclosure statement shall clearly state which services are included in basic continuing care contracts and which services are made available by the provider at extra charge.

8. A description of all fees required of residents, including any entrance fee and periodic charges. The description shall include (i) a description of all proposed uses of any funds or property required to be transferred to the provider or any other person prior to the resident's occupancy of the facility and of any entrance fee, (ii) a description of provisions for the escrowing and return of any such funds, assets or entrance fee, the manner and any conditions of return and to whom earnings on escrowed funds are payable and (iii) a description of the manner by which the provider may adjust periodic charges or other recurring fees and any limitations on such adjustments. If the facility is already in operation, or if the provider operates one or more similar facilities within this Commonwealth, there shall be included tables showing the frequency and average dollar amount of each increase in periodic rates at each facility for the previous five years or such shorter period that the facility has been operated by the provider.

9. Any provisions that have been made or will be made to provide reserve funding or security to enable the provider to fully perform its obligations under continuing care contracts, including the establishment of escrow accounts, trusts or reserve funds, together with the manner in which such funds will be invested and the names and experience of persons who will make the investment decisions. The disclosure statement shall clearly state whether or not reserve funds are maintained.

10. Certified financial statements of the provider, including (i) a balance sheet as of the end of the two most recent fiscal years and (ii) income statements of the provider for the two most recent fiscal years or such shorter period that the provider has been in existence.

11. A pro forma income statement for the current fiscal year.

12. If operation of the facility has not yet commenced, a statement of the anticipated source and application of the funds used or to be used in the purchase or construction of the facility, including:

a. An estimate of the cost of purchasing or constructing and equipping the facility including such related costs as financing expense, legal expense, land costs, occupancy development costs and all other similar costs that the provider expects to incur or become obligated for prior to the commencement of operations.

b. A description of any mortgage loan or other long-term financing intended to be used for any purpose in the financing of the facility and of the anticipated terms and costs of such financing, including without limitation, all payments of the proceeds of such financing to the provider, management or any related person.

c. An estimate of the percentage of entrance fees that will be used or pledged for the construction or purchase of the facility, as security for long-term financing or for any other use in connection with the commencement of operation of the facility.

d. An estimate of the total entrance fees to be received from or on behalf of residents at or prior to commencement of operation of the facility.

e. An estimate of the funds, if any, which are anticipated to be necessary to fund start-up losses and provide reserve funds to assure full performance of the obligations of the provider under continuing care contracts.

f. A projection of estimated income from fees and charges other than entrance fees, showing individual rates presently anticipated to be charged and including a description of the assumptions used for calculating the estimated occupancy rate of the facility and the effect on the income of the facility of any government subsidies for health care services to be provided pursuant to the continuing care contracts.

g. A projection of estimated operating expenses of the facility, including (i) a description of the assumptions used in calculating any expenses and separate allowances for the replacement of equipment and furnishings and anticipated major structural repairs or additions and (ii) an estimate of the percentage of occupancy required for continued operation of the facility.

h. Identification of any assets pledged as collateral for any purpose.

i. An estimate of annual payments of principal and interest required by any mortgage loan or other long-term financing.

13. A description of the provider's criteria for admission of new residents.

14. A description of the provider's policies regarding access to the facility and its services for nonresidents.

15. Any other material information concerning the facility or the provider that may be required by the Commission or included by the provider.

16. The procedure by which a resident may file a complaint or disclose any concern.

B. The disclosure statement shall state on its cover that the filing of the disclosure statement with the Commission does not constitute recommendation or endorsement of the facility by the Commission.

C. A copy of the standard form or forms for continuing care contracts used by the provider shall be attached as an exhibit to each disclosure statement.

D. If the Commission determines that the disclosure statement does not comply with the provisions of this chapter, it shall have the right to take action pursuant to § 38.2-4915. (1985, c. 554, § 38.1-957; 1986, cc. 562, 598; 1992, c. 139.)

Editor's note. — Pursuant to § 9-77.11, effect has been given in this section, as set out above, to Acts 1986, c. 598, which amended former § 38.1-957, the comparable provision in former Title 38.1.

Law Review. — For comment, "Continuing Care Retirement Communities: A Promise Falling Short," see 8 Geo. Mason L. Rev. 47 (1985).

§ 38.2-4903. Availability of disclosure statement to prospective residents.

— At least three days prior to the execution of a continuing care contract or the transfer of any money or other property to a provider by or on behalf of a prospective resident, whichever first occurs, the provider shall deliver to the person with whom the contract is to be entered into a copy of a disclosure statement with respect to the facility in question meeting all requirements of this chapter as of the date of its delivery. (1985, c. 554, § 38.1-958; 1986, c. 562.)

§ **38.2-4904. Annual disclosure statements.** — A. Within four months following the end of the provider's fiscal year, each provider shall file with the Commission and make available by written notice to each resident at no cost an annual disclosure statement which shall contain the information required for the initial disclosure statement set forth in § 38.2-4902.

B. The annual disclosure statement shall also be accompanied by a narrative describing any material differences between:

1. The prior fiscal year's pro forma income statement, and
2. The actual results of operations during that fiscal year.

C. The annual disclosure statement shall describe the disposition of any real property acquired by the provider from residents of the facility.

D. In addition to filing the annual disclosure statement, the provider shall amend its currently filed disclosure statement at any other time if, in the opinion of the provider, an amendment is necessary to prevent the disclosure statement from containing any material misstatement of fact or failing to state any material fact required to be stated therein. Any such amendment or amended disclosure statement shall be filed with the Commission before it is delivered to any resident or prospective resident and is subject to all the requirements of this chapter, and the provider shall notify each resident of the existence of such amendment or amended disclosure statement.

E. If the Commission determines that the disclosure statement does not comply with the provisions of this chapter, it shall have the right to take action pursuant to § 38.2-4915. (1985, c. 554, § 38.1-959; 1986, c. 562.)

Law Review. — For comment, "Continuing Care Retirement Communities: A Promise Falling Short," see 8 Geo. Mason L. Rev. 47 (1985).

§ **38.2-4904.1. Escrow of entrance fee to continuing care providers and others.** — A. A provider shall maintain in escrow with a bank or trust company, or other escrow agent approved by the Commission, all entrance fees or portions thereof in excess of $1,000 per person received by the provider prior to the date the resident is permitted to occupy a unit in the facility. Funds or assets deposited therein shall be kept and maintained in an account separate and apart from the provider's business accounts. For the purposes of this section only, the term "entrance fee" shall include within its meaning any advanced payment or series of advanced payments totaling $5,000 or more and the term "provider" shall include any person or entity that would be included in the definition thereof in § 38.2-4900 if such fee of $5,000 or more constituted an entrance fee for the purposes of the definition of "continuing care" in § 38.2-4900.

B. All funds or assets deposited in the escrow account shall remain the property of the prospective resident until released to the provider in accordance with this section. The funds or assets shall not be subject to any liens, judgments, garnishments or creditor's claims against the provider or facility. The escrow agreement may provide that charges by the escrow agent may be deducted from the funds or assets if such provision is disclosed in the disclosure statement.

C. All funds or assets deposited in escrow pursuant to this section shall be released to the provider when the provider presents to the escrow agent evidence that a unit has been occupied by the resident or a unit of the type reserved is available for immediate occupancy by the resident or prospective resident on whose behalf the fee was received.

D. Notwithstanding any other provision of this section, all funds or assets deposited in escrow pursuant to this section shall be released according to the terms of the escrow agreement to the prospective resident from whom it was received (i) if such funds or assets have not been released within three years after placement in escrow or within three years after construction has started, whichever is later (but in any event within six years after placement in escrow unless specifically approved by the Commission), or within such longer period as determined appropriate by the Commission in writing, (ii) if the prospective resident dies before occupying a unit, (iii) if the construction of a facility, not yet operating is stopped indefinitely before the facility is completed or (iv) upon rescission of the contract pursuant to provisions in the contract or in this chapter. If construction of the unit to be reserved has not started within three years after the deposit of funds or assets into an escrow account, the prospective resident may require the return of such funds or assets unless the Commission determines that construction will begin in a reasonable period of time and the extension of such three-year period is appropriate. However, funds or assets subject to release under item (i) of this subsection or under subsection C of this section may be held in escrow for an additional period at the mutual consent of the provider and the prospective resident; however, the prospective resident may consent to such additional period only after his deposit has been held in escrow for at least two years. Item (i) above shall not apply if fees are refundable within thirty days of request for refund.

E. Unless otherwise specified in the escrow agreement, funds or assets in an escrow account pursuant to this section may be held in the form received or if invested shall be invested in instruments authorized for the investment of public funds as set forth in Chapter 18 (§ 2.1-327 et seq.) of Title 2.1 and not in default as to principal or interest.

F. This section shall not apply to entrance fees for initial occupancy of units under construction on June 30, 1986.

G. This section shall not apply to application or reservation fees whether or not such fees are considered to be a portion of the entrance fee, provided such application or reservation fees are not in excess of $1,000 per person. (1986, c. 598, § 38.1-959.1.)

Editor's note. — This section was enacted as § 38.1-959.1 by Acts 1986, c. 598. Pursuant to § 9-77.11, this section has been incorporated into Title 38.2 as § 38.2-4904.1.

§ 38.2-4905. Resident's contract. — A. In addition to other provisions considered proper to effect the purpose of any continuing care contract, each contract executed on or after the effective date of this chapter shall:

1. Provide for the continuing care of only one resident, or for two or more persons occupying space designed for multiple occupancy, under appropriate regulations established by the provider.

2. Show the value of all property transferred, including donations, subscriptions, fees and any other amounts paid or payable by, or on behalf of, the resident or residents.

3. Specify all services which are to be provided by the provider to each resident including, in detail, all items that each resident will receive and whether the items will be provided for a designated time period or for life. Such items may include, but are not limited to, food, shelter, nursing care, drugs, burial and incidentals.

4. Describe the physical and mental health and financial conditions upon which the provider may require the resident to relinquish his space in the designated facility.

5. Describe the physical and mental health and financial conditions required for a person to continue as a resident.

6. Describe the circumstances under which the resident will be permitted to remain in the facility in the event of financial difficulties of the resident.

7. State (i) the current fees that would be charged if the resident marries while at the designated facility, (ii) the terms concerning the entry of a spouse to the facility and (iii) the consequences if the spouse does not meet the requirements for entry.

8. Provide that the provider shall not cancel any continuing care contract with any resident without good cause. Good cause shall be limited to: (i) proof that the resident is a danger to himself or others; (ii) nonpayment by the resident of a monthly or periodic fee; (iii) repeated conduct by the resident that interferes with other residents' quiet enjoyment of the facility; (iv) persistent refusal to comply with reasonable written rules and regulations of the facility; (v) a material misrepresentation made intentionally or recklessly by the resident in his application for residency, or related materials, regarding information which, if accurately provided, would have resulted in either a failure of the resident to qualify for residency or a material increase in the cost of providing to the resident the care and services provided under the contract; or (vi) material breach by the resident of the terms and conditions of the continuing care contract. If a provider seeks to cancel a contract and terminate a resident's occupancy, the provider shall give the resident written notice of, and a reasonable opportunity to cure within a reasonable period, whatever conduct is alleged to warrant the cancellation of the agreement. Nothing herein shall operate to relieve the provider from duties under Chapter 13.2 (§ 55-248.2 et seq.) of Title 55 when seeking to terminate a resident's occupancy.

9. Provide in clear and understandable language, in print no smaller than the largest type used in the body of the contract, the terms governing the refund of any portion of the entrance fee and the terms under which such fee can be used by the provider.

10. State the terms under which a contract is cancelled by the death of the resident. The contract may contain a provision to the effect that, upon the death of the resident, the money paid for the continuing care of such resident shall be considered earned and become the property of the provider.

11. Provide for at least thirty days' advance notice to the resident, before any change in fees, charges or the scope of care or services may be effective, except for changes required by state or federal assistance programs.

12. Provide that charges for care paid in one lump sum shall not be increased or changed during the duration of the agreed upon care, except for changes required by state or federal assistance programs.

B. A resident shall have the right to rescind a continuing care contract, without penalty or forfeiture, within seven days after making an initial deposit or executing the contract. A resident shall not be required to move into the facility designated in the contract before the expiration of the seven-day period.

C. If a resident dies before occupying the facility, or is precluded through illness, injury or incapacity from becoming a resident under the terms of the continuing care contract, the contract is automatically rescinded and the resident or his legal representative shall receive a full refund of all money paid to the provider, except those costs specifically incurred by the provider at the request of the resident and set forth in writing in a separate addendum, signed by both parties to the contract.

D. No standard continuing care contract form shall be used in this Commonwealth until it has been submitted to the Commission. If the Commission determines that the contract does not comply with the provisions of this chapter, it shall have the right to take action pursuant to § 38.2-4915 to prevent its use. The failure of the Commission to object to or disapprove of any contract shall not be evidence that the contract does or does not comply with the provisions of this chapter. However, individualized amendments to any standard form need not be filed with the Commission. (1985, c. 554, § 38.1-960; 1986, cc. 562, 598.)

Editor's note. — Pursuant to § 9-77.11, effect has been given in this section, as set out above, to Acts 1986, c. 598, which amended former § 38.1-960, the comparable provision in former Title 38.1.

Law Review. — For comment, "Continuing Care Retirement Communities: A Promise Falling Short," see 8 Geo. Mason L. Rev. 47 (1985).

§ 38.2-4906. Sale or transfer of ownership or change in management.

— A. No provider and no person or entity owning a provider shall sell or transfer, directly or indirectly, more than fifty percent of the ownership of the provider or of a continuing care facility without giving the Commission written notice of the intended sale or transfer at least thirty days prior to the consummation of the sale or transfer. A series of sales or transfers to one person or entity, or one or more entities controlled by one person or entity, consummated within a six-month period that constitute, in the aggregate, a sale or transfer of more than fifty percent of the ownership of a provider or of a continuing care facility shall be subject to the foregoing notice provisions.

B. A provider or continuing care facility that shall change its chief executive officer, or its management firm if managed under a contract with a third party, shall promptly notify the Commission and the residents of each such change. (1985, c. 554, § 38.1-961; 1986, c. 562.)

§ 38.2-4907. Financial instability.

— The Commission may act as authorized by § 38.2-4915 to protect residents or prospective residents when the Commission determines that:

1. A provider has been or will be unable to meet the pro forma income or cash flow projections previously filed by the provider and such failure may endanger the ability of the provider to perform fully its obligation pursuant to its continuing care contracts; or

2. A provider is bankrupt, insolvent, under reorganization pursuant to federal bankruptcy laws or in imminent danger of becoming bankrupt or insolvent. (1985, c. 554, § 38.1-962; 1986, c. 562.)

§ 38.2-4908. Waivers.

— No act, agreement or statement of any resident or by an individual purchasing care for a resident under any agreement to furnish care to the resident shall constitute a valid waiver of any provision of this chapter intended for the benefit or protection of the resident or the individual purchasing care for the resident. (1985, c. 554, § 38.1-963; 1986, c. 562.)

§ 38.2-4909. Untrue, deceptive or misleading advertising.

— The provisions of § 18.2-216 shall apply to all providers. (1985, c. 554, § 38.1-964; 1986, c. 562.)

§ 38.2-4910. Right of organization.

— A. Residents shall have the right of self-organization. No retaliatory conduct shall be permitted against any resident for membership or participation in a residents' organization or for filing any complaint. The provider shall be required to provide to the organization a copy of all submissions to the Commission.

B. The board of directors, its designated representative or other such governing body of a continuing care facility shall hold meetings at least quarterly with the residents or representatives elected by the residents of the continuing care facility for the purpose of free discussion of issues relating to the facility. These issues may include income, expenditures and financial matters as they apply to the facility and proposed changes in policies, programs, facilities and services. Residents shall be entitled to seven days' notice of each meeting. (1985, c. 554, § 38.1-965; 1986, c. 562; 1992, c. 139.)

§ **38.2-4911. Civil liability.** — A. A person contracting with a provider for continuing care may terminate the continuing care contract and such provider shall be liable to the person contracting for continuing care for repayment of all fees paid to the provider, facility or person violating this chapter, together with interest thereon at the legal rate for judgments, court costs and reasonable attorney's fees, less the reasonable value of care and lodging provided to the resident prior to the termination of the contract, and for damages if after the effective date of this chapter such provider or a person acting on his behalf, with or without actual knowledge of the violation, enters into a contract with such person:

1. For continuing care at a facility which has not registered under this chapter; or

2. Without having first provided to such person a disclosure statement not (i) containing any untrue statement of a material fact or (ii) omitting a material fact required to be stated therein or necessary in order to make the statements made therein not misleading, in light of the circumstances under which they are made.

B. A person who willfully or recklessly aids or abets a provider in the commission of any act prohibited by this section shall be liable as set out in subsection A of this section.

C. The Commission shall have no jurisdiction to adjudicate controversies concerning continuing care contracts. A breach of contract shall not be deemed a violation of this chapter. Termination of a contract pursuant to subsection A of this section shall not preclude the resident's seeking any other remedies available under any law. (1985, c. 554, § 38.1-966; 1986, c. 562.)

§ **38.2-4912. Special provisions for existing providers; rights of residents with certain existing providers.** — A. Providers existing prior to July 1, 1986, shall comply with its provisions within six months of July 1, 1986. However, the Commission may extend the period within which an existing facility shall comply with this chapter for an additional six months with good cause shown.

B. Continuing care contracts entered into prior to the effective date of this chapter or prior to registration of the provider shall be valid and binding upon both parties in accordance with their terms. (1985, c. 554, § 38.1-967; 1986, c. 562.)

§ **38.2-4913. Regulations.** — A. The Commission shall have the authority to adopt, amend or repeal rules and regulations that are reasonably necessary for the enforcement of the provisions of this chapter. The Commission may issue regulations setting forth those transactions which shall require the payment of fees by a provider and the fees which shall be charged.

B. Any provider may be given a reasonable time, not to exceed 120 days from the date of publication of any applicable rules and regulations or amendments thereto adopted pursuant to this chapter, within which to comply with the rules and standards. (1985, c. 554, § 38.1-968; 1986, c. 562.)

§ **38.2-4914. Investigations and subpoenas.** — A. The Commission may make public or private investigations within or outside of this Commonwealth it deems necessary to determine whether any person has violated any provision of this chapter or any rule, regulation or order promulgated by the Commission.

B. For the purpose of any investigation or proceeding under this chapter, the Commission or any officer designated by it may administer oaths and affirmations, subpoena witnesses, compel their attendance, take evidence and require the production of any books, papers, correspondence, memoranda, agreements or other documents or records which the Commission deems relevant or material to the inquiry. (1985, c. 554, § 38.1-969; 1986, c. 562.)

§ 38.2-4915. Cease and desist orders; injunctions. — Whenever it appears to the Commission that any person has engaged in, or is about to engage in, any act or practice constituting a violation of this chapter or any rule, regulation or order issued under this chapter, the Commission may:

1. Issue an order directed at any such person requiring him to cease and desist from engaging in such act or practice.

2. Upon a proper showing, issue a permanent or temporary injunction, or a restraining order to enforce compliance with this chapter or any rule, regulation or order issued under this chapter. (1985, c. 554, § 38.1-970; 1986, c. 562.)

Law Review. — For comment, "Continuing Care Retirement Communities: A Promise Falling Short," see 8 Geo. Mason L. Rev. 47 (1985).

§ 38.2-4916. Penalties. — A. Any person who willfully and knowingly violates any provision of this chapter, or any rule, regulation or order issued under this chapter, shall be subject to payment of a fine as provided in § 38.2-218.

B. Nothing in this chapter limits the power of the Commonwealth to punish any person for any conduct which constitutes a crime under any other statute. (1985, c. 554, § 38.1-971; 1986, c. 562.)

§ 38.2-4917. Certain providers exempted. — Notwithstanding any provisions to the contrary, this chapter shall not apply to providers that do not charge an entrance fee and which only accept assignments of government transfer payments, contributions from charitable organizations and third-party health care coverages as their regular periodic charges. (1986, c. 265, § 38.1-972.)

Editor's note. — This section was enacted as § 38.1-972 by Acts 1986, c. 265. Pursuant to § 9-77.11, this section has been incorporated into Title 38.2 as § 38.2-4917.

CHAPTER 50.

VIRGINIA BIRTH-RELATED NEUROLOGICAL INJURY COMPENSATION ACT.

§ 38.2-5000. Short title. — The provisions of this chapter shall be known and may be cited as the Virginia Birth-Related Neurological Injury Compensation Act. (1987, c. 540.)

Law Review. — For comment on Virginia's Birth-Related Neurological Injury Compensation Act, see 22 U. Rich. L. Rev. 431 (1988). As to the Virginia Birth-Related Neurological Injury Compensation Act, see 22 U. Rich. L. Rev. 717 (1988). For article, "Market and Regulatory Approaches to Medical Malpractice: The Virginia Obstetrical No-Fault Statute," see 74 Va. L. Rev. 1451 (1988). For article, "Pragmatic Constraints on Market Approaches: A Response to Professor Epstein," see 74 Va. L. Rev. 1475 (1988). For note, "Will Tort Reform Combat the Medical Malpractice Insurance Availability and Affordability Problems That Virginia's Physicians Are Facing," see 44 Wash. & Lee L. Rev. 1463 (1988). For survey on medical malpractice in Virginia for 1989, see 23 U. Rich. L. Rev. 731 (1989).

Constitutionality. — This chapter does not violate the Anti-Discrimination Clause in Va. Const., Art. I, § 11. This clause is not applicable because it applies only to "governmental discrimination upon the basis of religious conviction, race, color, sex, or national origin." King v. Virginia Birth-Related Neurological Injury Comp. Program, 242 Va. 404, 410 S.E.2d 656 (1991).

This chapter does not violate Va. Const., Art. IV, §§ 14 or 15. King v. Virginia Birth-Related Neurological Injury Comp. Program, 242 Va. 404, 410 S.E.2d 656 (1991).

Purpose bears reasonable relationship to assessments provision and assessments not arbitrary. — The purpose of this chapter, which is to make medical malpractice insurance coverage available to licensed physicians, bears a reasonable relationship to the provision for assessments, and the assessments are neither arbitrary nor discriminatory in a manner prohibited by the State or federal Constitutions. King v. Virginia Birth-Related Neurological Injury Comp. Program, 242 Va. 404, 410 S.E.2d 656 (1991).

§ 38.2-5001. Definitions. — As used in this chapter:

"Birth-related neurological injury" means injury to the brain or spinal cord of an infant caused by the deprivation of oxygen or mechanical injury occurring in the course of labor, delivery or resuscitation in the immediate post-delivery period in a hospital which renders the infant permanently motorically disabled and (i) developmentally disabled or (ii) for infants sufficiently developed to be cognitively evaluated, cognitively disabled. In order to constitute a "birth-related neurological injury" within the meaning of this chapter, such disability shall cause the infant to be permanently in need of assistance in all activities of daily living. This definition shall apply to live births only and shall not include disability or death caused by genetic or congenital abnormality, degenerative neurological disease, or maternal substance abuse. The definition provided here shall apply retroactively to any child born on and after January 1, 1988, who suffers from an injury to the brain or spinal cord caused by the deprivation of oxygen or mechanical injury occurring in the course of labor, delivery or resuscitation in the immediate postdelivery period in a hospital.

"Claimant" means any person who files a claim pursuant to § 38.2-5004 for compensation for a birth-related neurological injury to an infant. Such claims may be filed by any legal representative on behalf of an injured infant; and, in the case of a deceased infant, the claim may be filed by an administrator, executor, or other legal representative.

"Commission" means the Virginia Workers' Compensation Commission.

"Participating hospital" means a hospital licensed in Virginia which at the time of the injury (i) had in force an agreement with the Commissioner of Health or his designee, in a form prescribed by the Commissioner, whereby the hospital agreed to participate in the development of a program to provide obstetrical care to patients eligible for Medical Assistance Services and to patients who are indigent, and upon approval of such program by the Commissioner of Health, to participate in its implementation, (ii) had in force an agreement with the State Department of Health whereby the hospital agreed to submit to review of its obstetrical service, as required by subsection C of § 38.2-5004, and (iii) had paid the participating hospital assessment pursuant to § 38.2-5020 for the period of time in which the birth-related neurological injury occurred. The term also includes employees of such hospitals, excluding physicians or nurse-midwives who are eligible to qualify as participating physicians, acting in the course of and in the scope of their employment.

"Participating physician" means a physician licensed in Virginia to practice medicine, who practices obstetrics or performs obstetrical services either full or part time or, as authorized in the plan of operation, a licensed nurse-midwife who performs obstetrical services, either full or part time, within the scope of such licensure and who at the time of the injury (i) had in force an agreement with the Commissioner of Health or his designee, in a form prescribed by the Commissioner, whereby the physician agreed to participate in the development of a program to provide obstetrical care to patients eligible for Medical Assistance Services and to patients who are indigent, and upon approval of such program by the Commissioner of Health, to participate in its implementation, (ii) had in force an agreement with the Board of Medicine whereby the physician agreed to submit to review by the Board of Medicine as required by subsection B of § 38.2-5004, and (iii) had paid the participating physician assessment pursuant to § 38.2-5020 for the period of time in which the birth-related neurological injury occurred.

"Program" means the Virginia Birth-Related Neurological Injury Compensation Program established by this chapter. (1987, c. 540; 1989, c. 523; 1990, cc. 234, 534; 1994, c. 872; 1995, c. 302; 1999, c. 806.)

Editor's note. — Acts 1989, c. 463, cl. 1, effective March 22, 1989, provides as follows:

"§ 1. Any physician who is otherwise eligible to become a participating physician under the Virginia Birth-Related Neurological Injury Compensation Act, but who did not meet the requirements of § 38.2-5020 on or before January 1, 1989, may become a participating physician by filing the agreements required by § 38.2-5001 and by paying an assessment to the Program on or before May 15, 1989. The amount of this assessment shall be determined by the Board of Directors of the Program on a prorated basis for the months remaining in 1989 at the time the assessment is paid. A physician who satisfies the conditions imposed by this section shall be considered a participating physician in the Program for the remainder

of 1989, beginning on the first day of the first month following the receipt by the Program of the required agreements and prorated assessment.

"§ 2. Any hospital which is otherwise eligible to become a participating hospital under the Virginia Birth-Related Neurological Injury Compensation Act, but which did not meet the requirements of § 38.2-5020 on or before January 1, 1989, may become a participating hospital by filing the agreements required by § 38.2-5001 and by paying an assessment to the Program on or before May 15, 1989. The amount of this assessment shall be determined by the Board of Directors of the Program on a prorated basis for the months remaining in 1989 at the time the assessment is paid. A hospital satisfying the conditions imposed by this section shall be considered a participating hospital in the Program for the remainder of 1989, beginning on the first day of the first month following the receipt by the Program of the required agreements and prorated assessment."

The 1999 amendment added the fourth sentence in the paragraph defining "Birth-related neurological injury."

Law Review. — For comment on Virginia's Birth-Related Neurological Injury Compensation Act, see 22 U. Rich. L. Rev. 431 (1988). For note, "Will Tort Reform Combat the Medical Malpractice Insurance Availability and Affordability Problems That Virginia's Physicians Are Facing," see 44 Wash. & Lee L. Rev. 1463 (1988).

§ 38.2-5002. Virginia Birth-Related Neurological Injury Compensation Program; exclusive remedy; exception. — A. There is hereby established the Virginia Birth-Related Neurological Injury Compensation Program.

B. Except as provided in subsection D, the rights and remedies herein granted to an infant on account of a birth-related neurological injury shall exclude all other rights and remedies of such infant, his personal representative, parents, dependents or next of kin, at common law or otherwise arising out of or related to a medical malpractice claim with respect to such injury.

C. Notwithstanding anything to the contrary in this section, a civil action shall not be foreclosed against a physician or a hospital where there is clear and convincing evidence that such physician or hospital intentionally or willfully caused or intended to cause a birth-related neurological injury, provided that such suit is filed prior to and in lieu of payment of an award under this chapter. Such suit shall be filed before the award of the Commission becomes conclusive and binding as provided for in § 38.2-5011.

D. Notwithstanding anything to the contrary in this section, a civil action arising out of or related to a birth-related neurological injury under this chapter, brought by an infant, his personal representative, parents, dependents, or next of kin, shall not be foreclosed against a nonparticipating physician or hospital, provided that (i) no participating physician or hospital shall be made a party to any such action or related action, and (ii) the commencement of any such action, regardless of its outcome, shall constitute an election of remedies, to the exclusion of any claim under this chapter; provided that if claim is made, accepted and benefits are provided by the Fund established under this Virginia Birth-Related Neurological Injury Compensation Program, the Fund shall have the right, and be subrogated, to all of the common law rights, based on negligence or malpractice, which the said infant, his personal representative, parents, dependents or next of kin may have or may have had against the non-participating physician or hospital, as the case may be. (1987, c. 540; 1990, c. 535.)

Law Review. — For comment on Virginia's Birth-Related Neurological Injury Compensation Act, see 22 U. Rich. L. Rev. 431 (1988). For note, "Will Tort Reform Combat the Medical Malpractice Insurance Availability and Affordability Problems That Virginia's Physicians Are Facing," see 44 Wash. & Lee L. Rev. 1463 (1988).

Infant who suffers injury must file claim with Workers' Compensation Commission. — An infant who suffers a neurological injury as defined by the act must file a claim with the Workers' Compensation Commission, which has exclusive jurisdiction to decide all claims made pursuant to the act. Gibson v. Riverside Hosp., 250 Va. 140, 458 S.E.2d 460 (1995).

§ 38.2-5003. Virginia Workers' Compensation Commission authorized to hear and determine claims. — The Virginia Workers' Compensation Commission is authorized to hear and pass upon all claims filed pursuant to this chapter. The Commission may exercise the power and authority granted to it in Chapter 2 of Title 65.2 as necessary to carry out the purposes of this chapter.

When a circuit court refers a civil action to the Commission pursuant to § 8.01-273.1 for the purposes of determining whether the cause of action satisfies the requirements of this chapter, the Commission shall set the matter for hearing pursuant to § 38.2-5006. The Commission shall communicate its decision to the referring circuit court in due course. (1987, c. 540; 1999, c. 822.)

The 1999 amendment added the second paragraph.

Infant who suffers injury must file claim with Workers' Compensation Commission. — An infant who suffers a neurological injury as defined by the act must file a claim with the Workers' Compensation Commission, which has exclusive jurisdiction to decide all claims made pursuant to the act. Gibson v. Riverside Hosp., 250 Va. 140, 458 S.E.2d 460 (1995).

§ 38.2-5004. Filing of claims; review by Board of Medicine; review by Department of Health; filing of responses. — A. 1. In all claims filed under this chapter, the claimant shall file with the Commission a petition, setting forth the following information:

a. The name and address of the legal representative and the basis for his representation of the injured infant;

b. The name and address of the injured infant;

c. The name and address of any physician providing obstetrical services who was present at the birth and the name and address of the hospital at which the birth occurred;

d. A description of the disability for which claim is made;

e. The time and place where the birth-related neurological injury occurred;

f. A brief statement of the facts and circumstances surrounding the birth-related neurological injury and giving rise to the claim;

g. All available relevant medical records relating to the person who allegedly suffered a birth-related neurological injury and an identification of any unavailable records known to the claimant and the reasons for their unavailability;

h. Appropriate assessments, evaluations, and prognoses and such other records and documents as are reasonably necessary for the determination of the amount of compensation to be paid to, or on behalf of, the injured infant on account of a birth-related neurological injury;

i. Documentation of expenses and services incurred to date, which indicates whether such expenses and services have been paid for, and if so, by whom; and

j. Documentation of any applicable private or governmental source of services or reimbursement relative to the alleged impairments.

2. The claimant shall furnish the Commission with as many copies of the petition as required for service upon the Program, any physician and hospital named in the petition, the Board of Medicine and the Department of Health, along with a fifteen dollar filing fee. Upon receipt of the petition the Commission shall immediately serve the Program by service upon the agent designated to accept service on behalf of the Program in the plan of operation by registered or certified mail, and shall mail copies of the petition to any physician and hospital named in the petition, the Board of Medicine and the Department of Health.

B. Upon receipt of the petition, the Board of Medicine shall evaluate the claim, and if it determines that there is reason to believe that the alleged injury resulted from, or was aggravated by, substandard care on the part of the physician, it shall take any appropriate action consistent with the authority granted to the Board in §§ 54.1-2911 through 54.1-2928.

C. Upon receipt of the petition, the Department of Health shall evaluate the claim, and if it determines that there is reason to believe that the alleged injury resulted from, or was aggravated by, substandard care on the part of the hospital at which the birth occurred, it shall take any appropriate action consistent with the authority granted to the Department of Health in Title 32.1.

D. The Program shall have thirty days from the date of service in which to file a response to the petition, and to submit relevant written information relating to the issue of whether the injury alleged is a birth-related neurological injury, within the meaning of this chapter. (1987, c. 540; 1989, c. 523.)

Law Review. — For comment on Virginia's Birth-Related Neurological Injury Compensation Act, see 22 U. Rich. L. Rev. 431 (1988). For note, "Will Tort Reform Combat the Medical Malpractice Insurance Availability and Affordability Problems That Virginia's Physicians Are Facing," see 44 Wash. & Lee L. Rev. 1463 (1988).

§ 38.2-5004.1. Notification of possible beneficiaries. — When a claim is made to an insurance company licensed to do business in the Commonwealth of Virginia or to any self-insurer, alleging that a possible birth-related neurological injury or a severe adverse outcome related to a birth has occurred, such insurance company or self-insurer shall report such claim to the Program on a form provided by the Program. Upon receipt of such report, the Program shall inform the parent or parents or guardians of the child on whose behalf such claim has been made of the Program's existence and eligibility requirements. No liability or inference of liability or eligibility shall attach to the making of such report. The making of such report shall not be admissible in any court. (1999, c. 825.)

§ 38.2-5005. Tolling of statute of limitations. — The statute of limitations with respect to any civil action that may be brought by or on behalf of an injured infant allegedly arising out of or related to a birth-related neurological injury shall be tolled by the filing of a claim in accordance with this section, and the time such claim is pending shall not be computed as part of the period within which such civil action may be brought. (1987, c. 540; 1989, c. 523.)

§ 38.2-5006. Hearing; parties. — A. Immediately after a petition has been received, the Commission shall set the date for a hearing, which shall be held no sooner than 45 days and no later than 120 days after the filing of the petition, and shall notify the parties to the hearing of the time and place of such hearing. The hearing shall be held in the city or county where the birth-related neurological injury occurred, or in a contiguous city or county, unless otherwise agreed to by the parties and authorized by the Commission.
B. The parties to the hearing required under this section shall include the claimant and the Program. (1987, c. 540; 1989, c. 523.)

§ 38.2-5007. Interrogatories and depositions. — Any party to a proceeding under this chapter may, upon application to the Commission setting forth the materiality of the information requested, serve interrogatories or cause the depositions of witnesses residing within or without the Commonwealth to be taken, the costs to be taxed as expenses incurred in connection with the filing of a claim, in accordance with subdivision 2 of § 38.2-5009. Such depositions shall be taken after notice and in the manner prescribed by law, for depositions in actions at law, except that they shall be directed to the Commission, the Commissioner or the Deputy Commissioner before whom the proceedings may be pending. (1987, c. 540; 1989, c. 523.)

§ 38.2-5008. Determination of claims; presumption; finding of Virginia Workers' Compensation Commission binding on participants; medical advisory panel. — A. The Commission shall determine, on the basis of the evidence presented to it, the following issues:
1. Whether the injury claimed is a birth-related neurological injury as defined in § 38.2-5001. A rebuttable presumption shall arise that the injury

alleged is a birth-related neurological injury where it has been demonstrated, to the satisfaction of the Virginia Workers' Compensation Commission, that the infant has sustained a brain or spinal cord injury caused by oxygen deprivation or mechanical injury, and that the infant was thereby rendered permanently motorically disabled and (i) developmentally disabled or (ii) for infants sufficiently developed to be cognitively evaluated, cognitively disabled.

If either party disagrees with such presumption, that party shall have the burden of proving that the injuries alleged are not birth-related neurological injuries within the meaning of the chapter.

2. Whether obstetrical services were delivered by a participating physician at the birth.

3. Whether the birth occurred in a participating hospital.

4. How much compensation, if any, is awardable pursuant to § 38.2-5009.

5. If the Commission determines (i) that the injury alleged is not a birth-related neurological injury as defined in § 38.2-5001, or (ii) that obstetrical services were not delivered by a participating physician at the birth and that the birth did not occur in a participating hospital, it shall dismiss the petition and cause a copy of its order of dismissal to be sent immediately to the parties by registered or certified mail.

6. All parties are bound for all purposes including any suit at law against a participating physician or participating hospital, by the finding of the Virginia Workers' Compensation Commission (or any appeal therefrom) with respect to whether such injury is a birth-related neurological injury.

B. The deans of the medical schools of the Commonwealth shall develop a plan whereby each claim filed with the Commission is reviewed by a panel of three qualified and impartial physicians. This panel shall file its report and recommendations as to whether the injury alleged is a birth-related neurological injury as defined in § 38.2-5001 with the Commission at least ten days prior to the date set for hearing pursuant to § 38.2-5006. At the request of the Commission, at least one member of the panel shall be available to testify at the hearing. The Commission must consider, but shall not be bound by, the recommendation of the panel. (1987, c. 540; 1989, c. 523; 1990, cc. 534, 535.)

Law Review. — For comment on Virginia's Birth-Related Neurological Injury Compensation Act, see 22 U. Rich. L. Rev. 431 (1988). For note, "Will Tort Reform Combat the Medical Malpractice Insurance Availability and Affordability Problems That Virginia's Physicians Are Facing," see 44 Wash. & Lee L. Rev. 1463 (1988).

§ 38.2-5009. Commission awards for birth-related neurological injuries; notice of award.

— Upon determining (i) that an infant has sustained a birth-related neurological injury and (ii) that obstetrical services were delivered by a participating physician at the birth or that the birth occurred in a participating hospital, the Commission shall make an award providing compensation for the following items relative to such injury:

1. Actual medically necessary and reasonable expenses of medical and hospital, rehabilitative, residential and custodial care and service, special equipment or facilities, and related travel, such expenses to be paid as they are incurred. However, such expenses shall not include:

a. Expenses for items or services that the infant has received, or is entitled to receive, under the laws of any state or the federal government except to the extent prohibited by federal law;

b. Expenses for items or services that the infant has received, or is contractually entitled to receive, from any prepaid health plan, health maintenance organization, or other private insuring entity;

c. Expenses for which the infant has received reimbursement, or for which the infant is entitled to receive reimbursement, under the laws of any state or federal government except to the extent prohibited by federal law; and

d. Expenses for which the infant has received reimbursement, or for which the infant is contractually entitled to receive reimbursement, pursuant to the provisions of any health or sickness insurance policy or other private insurance program.

2. Expenses of medical and hospital services under subdivision 1 of this section shall be limited to such charges as prevail in the same community for similar treatment of injured persons of a like standard of living when such treatment is paid for by the injured person.

3. Loss of earnings from the age of eighteen are to be paid in regular installments beginning on the eighteenth birthday of the infant. An infant found to have sustained a birth-related neurological injury shall be conclusively presumed to have been able to earn income from work from the age of eighteen through the age of sixty-five, if he had not been injured, in the amount of fifty percent of the average weekly wage in the Commonwealth of workers in the private, nonfarm sector. The provisions of § 65.2-531 shall apply to any benefits awarded under this subdivision.

4. Reasonable expenses incurred in connection with the filing of a claim under this chapter, including reasonable attorneys' fees, which shall be subject to the approval and award of the Commission.

5. A copy of the award shall be sent immediately by registered or certified mail to the parties. (1987, c. 540; 1989, c. 523; 1990, c. 535; 1999, c. 823.)

The **1999 amendment** added the third sentence in subdivision 3.

Law Review. — For comment on Virginia's Birth-Related Neurological Injury Compensation Act, see 22 U. Rich. L. Rev. 431 (1988).

§ 38.2-5010. Rehearing on Commission determination or award. — A. If an application for review is made to the Commission within twenty days from the date of a determination pursuant to subdivisions A 1 through A 3 of § 38.2-5008, or within twenty days from the date of an award by the Commission pursuant to § 38.2-5009, the full Commission, excluding any member of the Commission who made the determination or award, if the first hearing was not held before the full Commission, shall review the evidence. If deemed advisable and as soon as practicable, the Commission instead may hear the parties, their representatives and witnesses and shall make a determination or award, as appropriate. Such review or determination, together with a statement of the findings of fact, rulings of law and other matters pertinent to the questions at issue, shall be filed with the record of the proceedings and shall be sent immediately to the parties.

B. The legal representative of a child who was born between January 1, 1988, and July 1, 1990, may file an application for review by July 1, 2000, upon meeting the following conditions: (i) a claim was timely filed for such child and was dismissed, upon an application for review, on the basis of a determination pursuant to subdivision A 1 of § 38.2-5008 that, although the child's injuries were caused by deprivation of oxygen or mechanical injury occurring in the course of labor, delivery or resuscitation in the immediate postdelivery period in a hospital, such injuries had not rendered the child permanently nonambulatory, aphasic, incontinent, and in need of assistance in all phases of daily living as required by the definition of "birth-related neurological injury" as such definition was in effect prior to July 1, 1990, and (ii) the panel required by subsection B of § 38.2-5008 had reported to the Commission in the hearing held pursuant to the dismissed claim that such injuries did meet the definition as effective on July 1, 1990, i.e., that the injuries had rendered the child permanently motorically disabled and developmentally disabled or, if the child is sufficiently developed to be cognitively evaluated, cognitively disabled, and permanently in need of assistance in all activities of daily living. Such application for review may be filed regardless of whether or not the legal representative has filed for review of the dismissed claim by the Commission. Such review shall only be filed for live births and shall not be filed for claims dismissed as caused by genetic or congenital abnormalities, degenerative neurological diseases, or maternal substance abuse.

The full Commission shall review the evidence and make a determination on the petition as though the definition in effect on July 1, 1990, had been in effect on the date of the child's birth and no previous review or dismissal had occurred. (1987, c. 540; 1999, c. 806.)

The 1999 amendment added the subsection A designator and added subsection B.

§ 38.2-5011. Conclusiveness of determination or award; appeal. —

A. The determination of the Commission pursuant to subdivisions A 1 through A 3 of § 38.2-5008, or the award of the Commission, as provided in § 38.2-5009, if not reviewed within the time prescribed by § 38.2-5010, or a determination or award of the Commission upon such review, as provided in § 38.2-5010, shall be conclusive and binding as to all questions of fact. No appeal shall be taken from the decision of one commissioner until a review of the case has been held before the full Commission, as provided in § 38.2-5010. Appeals shall lie from the full Commission to the Court of Appeals in the manner provided in the Rules of the Supreme Court.

B. The notice of appeal shall be filed with the clerk of the Commission within thirty days from the date of such determination or award or within thirty days after receipt by registered or certified mail of such determination or award whichever occurs last. A copy of the notice of appeal shall be filed in the office of the clerk of the Court of Appeals as provided in the Rules of the Supreme Court.

C. Cases so appealed shall be placed upon the privileged docket of the Court and be heard at the next ensuing term thereof. In case of an appeal from an award of the Commission to the Court of Appeals, the appeal shall operate as a suspension of the award, and the Program shall not be required to make payment of the award involved in the appeal until the questions at issue therein shall have been fully determined in accordance with the provisions of this chapter. (1987, c. 540; 1989, c. 523.)

§ 38.2-5012. Enforcement, etc., of orders and awards. — The Commission has full authority to enforce its orders and protect itself from deception. While the language of this section is permissive and provides that a party may enforce an award in court, it must be read and considered in pari materia with the Commission's power pursuant to § 65.2-202 to punish for disobedience of its orders. (1987, c. 540.)

§ 38.2-5013. Limitation on claims. — Any claim under this chapter that is filed more than ten years after the birth of an infant alleged to have a birth-related neurological injury is barred; however an application for review filed in accordance with the provisions of § 38.2-5010 B may be filed by July 1, 2000, for a child whose birth occurred more than ten years prior to such application, if the dismissed claim upon which the application is filed was filed before the child's tenth birthday. (1987, c. 540; 1999, c. 806.)

The 1999 amendment added "however an application for review filed in accordance with the provisions of § 38.2-5010 B may be filed by July 1, 2000, for a child whose birth occurred more than ten years prior to such application, if the dismissed claim upon which the application is filed was filed before the child's tenth birthday."

Law Review. — For note, "Will Tort Reform Combat the Medical Malpractice Insurance Availability and Affordability Problems That Virginia's Physicians Are Facing," see 44 Wash. & Lee L. Rev. 1463 (1988).

§ **38.2-5014. Scope.** — This chapter applies to all claims for birth-related neurological injuries occurring in this Commonwealth on and after January 1, 1988. The chapter shall not apply to disability or death caused by genetic or congenital abnormalities. (1987, c. 540.)

Law Review. — For comment on Virginia's Birth-Related Neurological Injury Compensation Act, see 22 U. Rich. L. Rev. 431 (1988). For note, "Will Tort Reform Combat the Medical Malpractice Insurance Availability and Affordability Problems That Virginia's Physicians Are Facing," see 44 Wash. & Lee L. Rev. 1463 (1988).

§ **38.2-5015. Birth-Related Neurological Injury Compensation Fund; assets of the Fund.** — There is established the Birth-Related Neurological Injury Compensation Fund to finance the Virginia Birth-Related Neurological Injury Compensation Program created by this chapter. The assets of the Fund administered by the board of directors of the Program are trust funds and shall be used solely in the interest of the recipients of awards pursuant to § 38.2-5009 and to administer the Program. (1987, c. 540; 1999, c. 826.)

The 1999 amendment added the second sentence.
Law Review. — For comment on Virginia's Birth-Related Neurological Injury Compensation Act, see 22 U. Rich. L. Rev. 431 (1988). For note, "Will Tort Reform Combat the Medical Malpractice Insurance Availability and Affordability Problems That Virginia's Physicians Are Facing," see 44 Wash. & Lee L. Rev. 1463 (1988).

§ **38.2-5016. Board of directors; appointment; vacancies; term.** — A. The Birth-Related Neurological Injury Compensation Program shall be governed by a board of seven directors.

B. Except as provided in subsection C, directors shall be appointed for a term of three years or until their successors are appointed and have qualified.

C. 1. The directors shall be appointed by the Governor as follows:

a. Three citizen representatives. The term of the member appointed in 1999 shall commence when appointed and shall end on July 1, 2002. When the terms of the other two representatives expire, one shall be appointed for a term of two years ending July 1, 2003, and one shall be appointed for a term of three years ending July 1, 2004. In selecting citizen representatives, consideration shall be given to (i) persons who have experience in finance and investment; (ii) parents; and (iii) persons who have worked closely with persons who might qualify as claimants. Citizen representatives shall not have children or relatives who are claimants or who have been awarded benefits under the Act;

b. One representative of participating physicians. The initial term of the member appointed in 1999 shall commence when appointed and shall be for one year;

c. One representative of participating hospitals. The initial term of the member appointed in 1999 shall commence when appointed and shall be for two years;

d. One representative of liability insurers. The initial term of the member appointed in 1999 shall commence when appointed and shall be for three years; and

e. One representative of physicians other than participating physicians. The initial term of the member appointed in 1999 shall commence when appointed and shall be for three years.

2. The Governor may select the representative of the participating physicians from a list of at least three names to be recommended by the Virginia

Society of Obstetrics and Gynecology; the representative of participating hospitals from a list of at least three names to be recommended by the Virginia Hospital Association; the representative of liability insurers from a list of at least three names, one of which is recommended by the American Insurance Association, one by the Alliance of American Insurers, and one by the National Association of Independent Insurers; and the representative of physicians other than participating physicians from a list of at least three names to be recommended by the Medical Society of Virginia. In no case shall the Governor be bound to make any appointment from among the nominees of the respective associations.

D. The Governor shall promptly notify the appropriate association, which may make nominations, of any vacancy other than by expiration among the members of the board representing a particular interest and like nominations may be made for the filling of the vacancy.

E. The directors shall act by majority vote with four directors constituting a quorum for the transaction of any business or the exercise of any power of the Program. The directors shall serve without salary, but each director shall be reimbursed for actual and necessary expenses incurred in the performance of his official duties as a director of the Program. The directors shall not be subject to any personal liability with respect to the administration of the Program or the payment of any award.

F. The board shall have the power to (i) administer the Program, (ii) administer the Birth-Related Neurological Injury Compensation Fund, which shall include the authority to purchase, hold, sell or transfer real or personal property and the authority to place any such property in trust for the benefit of claimants who have received awards pursuant to § 38.2-5009, (iii) appoint a service company or companies to administer the payment of claims on behalf of the Program, (iv) direct the investment and reinvestment of any surplus in the Fund over losses and expenses, provided any investment income generated thereby remains in the Fund, and (v) reinsure the risks of the Fund in whole or in part. The board shall discharge its duties with respect to the Fund solely in the interest of the recipients of awards pursuant to § 38.2-5009 and shall invest the assets of the Fund with the care, skill, prudence, and diligence under the circumstances then prevailing that a prudent person acting in a like capacity and familiar with such matters would use in the conduct of an enterprise of a like character and with like aims. Any decisions regarding the investment of the assets of the Fund shall be based on the advice of one or more investment advisors retained by the board from a list provided by the chief investment officer of the Virginia Retirement System. The board shall report annually to the Speaker of the House of Delegates and to the Chairman of the Senate Rules Committee regarding the investment of the Fund's assets. No later than October 1, 1994, the board shall establish a procedure in the plan of operation for notice to be given to obstetrical patients concerning the no-fault alternative for birth-related neurological injuries provided in this chapter, such notice to include a clear and concise explanation of a patient's rights and limitations under the program. The board shall also have the power to reduce for a stated period of time the annual participating physician assessment described in subsection A of § 38.2-5020 and the annual participating hospital assessment described in subsection C of § 38.2-5020 after the State Corporation Commission determines the Fund is actuarially sound in conjunction with actuarial investigations conducted pursuant to § 38.2-5021. (1987, c. 540; 1989, c. 523; 1994, c. 872; 1996, c. 232; 1997, c. 399; 1999, c. 824.)

The 1999 amendment inserted "Except as provided in subsection C" at the beginning of subsection B, added the second through fifth sentences in subdivision C 1 a; added the sec- ond sentence in subdivisions C 1 b through C 1 e; and substituted "four" for "five" in the first sentence of subsection E.

§ 38.2-5017. Plan of operation. — A. On or before September 30, 1987, the directors of the Program shall submit to the State Corporation Commission for review a proposed plan of operation consistent with this chapter.

B. The plan of operation shall provide for the efficient administration of the Program and for the prompt processing of claims made against the Fund pursuant to an award under this chapter. The plan shall contain other provisions including:

1. Establishment of necessary facilities;

2. Management of the Fund;

3. Appointment of servicing carriers or other servicing arrangements to administer the processing of claims against the Fund;

4. Initial and annual assessment of the persons and entities listed in § 38.2-5020 to pay awards and expenses, which assessments shall be on an actuarially sound basis subject to the limits set forth in § 38.2-5020; and

5. Any other matters necessary for the efficient operation of the Program.

C. The plan of operation shall be subject to approval by the State Corporation Commission after consultation with representatives of interested individuals and organizations. If the State Corporation Commission disapproves all or any part of the proposed plan of operation, the directors shall within thirty days submit for review an appropriate revised plan of operation. If the directors fail to do so, the State Corporation Commission shall promulgate a plan of operation. The plan of operation approved or promulgated by the State Corporation Commission shall become effective and operational upon order of the State Corporation Commission.

D. Amendments to the plan of operation may be made by the directors of the Program, subject to the approval of the State Corporation Commission. (1987, c. 540; 1994, c. 872.)

§ 38.2-5018. Assessments to be held in restricted cash account. — All assessments paid pursuant to the plan of operation, shall be held in a separate restricted cash account under the sole control of an independent fund manager to be selected by the directors. The Fund, and any income from it, shall be disbursed for the payment of awards as provided in this chapter and for the payment of the expenses of administration of the Fund and the Program, including the reasonable expenses of the Commission. (1987, c. 540; 1989, c. 523; 1990, c. 244.)

Law Review. — For note, "Will Tort Reform Combat the Medical Malpractice Insurance Availability and Affordability Problems That Virginia's Physicians Are Facing," see 44 Wash. & Lee L. Rev. 1463 (1988).

§ 38.2-5019: Repealed by Acts 1989, c. 523.

§ 38.2-5020. Assessments. — A. A physician who otherwise qualifies as a participating physician pursuant to this chapter may become a participating physician in the Program for a particular calendar year by paying an annual participating physician assessment to the Program in the amount of $5,000 on or before December 1 of the previous year, in the manner required by the plan of operation. The board may authorize a prorated participating physician or participating hospital assessment for a particular year in its plan of operation, but such prorated assessment shall not become effective until the physician or hospital has given at least thirty days' notice to the Program of the request for a prorated assessment.

B. Notwithstanding the provisions of subsection A of this section, a participating hospital with a residency training program accredited to the American Council for Graduate Medical Education may pay an annual participating physician assessment to the Program for residency positions in the hospital's residency training program, in the manner provided by the plan of operation. However, any resident in a duly accredited family practice or obstetrics residency training program at a participating hospital shall be considered a participating physician in the Program and neither the resident nor the hospital shall be required to pay any assessment for such participation. No resident shall become a participating physician in the Program, however, until thirty days following notification by the hospital to the Program of the name of the resident or residents filling the particular position for which the annual participating physician assessment payment, if required, has been made.

C. A hospital that otherwise qualifies as a participating hospital pursuant to this chapter may become a participating hospital in the Program for a particular year by paying an annual participating hospital assessment to the Program, on or before December 1 of the previous year, amounting to fifty dollars per live birth for the prior year, as reported to the Department of Health in the Annual Survey of Hospitals. The participating hospital assessment shall not exceed $150,000 for any participating hospital in any twelve-month period.

D. All licensed physicians practicing in the Commonwealth on September 30 of a particular year, other than participating physicians, shall pay to the Program an annual assessment of $250 for the following year, in the manner required by the plan of operation.

Upon proper certification to the Program, the following physicians shall be exempt from the payment of the annual $250 assessment:

1. A physician who is employed by the Commonwealth or federal government and whose income from professional fees is less than an amount equal to ten percent of the annual salary of the physician.

2. A physician who is enrolled in a full-time graduate medical education program accredited by the American Council for Graduate Medical Education.

3. A physician who has retired from active clinical practice.

4. A physician whose active clinical practice is limited to the provision of services, voluntarily and without compensation, to any patient of any clinic which is organized in whole or in part for the delivery of health care services without charge as provided in § 54.1-106.

E. Taking into account the assessments collected pursuant to subsections A through D of this section, if required to maintain the Fund on an actuarially sound basis, all insurance carriers licensed to write and engaged in writing liability insurance in the Commonwealth of a particular year, shall pay into the Fund an assessment for the following year, in an amount determined by the State Corporation Commission pursuant to subsection A of § 38.2-5021, in the manner required by the plan of operation. Liability insurance for the purposes of this provision shall include the classes of insurance defined in §§ 38.2-117 through 38.2-119 and the liability portions of the insurance defined in §§ 38.2-124, 38.2-125 and 38.2-130 through 38.2-132.

1. All annual assessments against liability insurance carriers shall be made on the basis of net direct premiums written for the business activity which forms the basis for each such entity's inclusion as a funding source for the Program in the Commonwealth during the prior year ending December 31, as reported to the State Corporation Commission, and shall be in the proportion that the net direct premiums written by each on account of the business activity forming the basis for their inclusion in the Program bears to the aggregate net direct premiums for all such business activity written in this Commonwealth by all such entities. For purposes of this chapter *"net direct premiums written"* means gross direct premiums written in this Commonwealth on all policies of liability insurance less (i) all return premiums on the policy, (ii) dividends paid or credited to policyholders, and (iii) the unused or unabsorbed portions of premium deposits on liability insurance.

2. The entities listed in this subsection shall not be individually liable for an annual assessment in excess of one quarter of one percent of that entity's net direct premiums written.

3. Liability insurance carriers shall be entitled to recover their initial and annual assessments through (i) a surcharge on future policies, (ii) a rate increase applicable prospectively, or (iii) a combination of the two, at the discretion of the State Corporation Commission.

F. On and after January 1, 1989, a participating physician covered under the provisions of this section who has paid an annual assessment for a particular calendar year to the Program and who retires from the practice of medicine during that particular calendar year shall be entitled to a refund of one-half of his or her annual assessment for the calendar year if he or she retires on or before July 1 of that year.

G. Whenever the State Corporation Commission determines the Fund is actuarially sound in conjunction with actuarial investigations conducted pursuant to § 38.2-5021, it shall enter an order suspending the assessment required under subsection D. An annual assessment up to $250 shall be reinstated whenever the State Corporation Commission determines that such assessment is required to maintain the Fund's actuarial soundness. (1987, c. 540; 1989, cc. 361, 463, 523; 1990, c. 498; 1991, c. 486; 1992, cc. 414, 767; 1994, c. 872.)

Editor's note. — Acts 1989, c. 463, cl. 1, effective March 22, 1989, provides as follows:

"§ 1. Any physician who is otherwise eligible to become a participating physician under the Virginia Birth-Related Neurological Injury Compensation Act, but who did not meet the requirements of § 38.2-5020 on or before January 1, 1989, may become a participating physician by filing the agreements required by § 38.2-5001 and by paying an assessment to the Program on or before May 15, 1989. The amount of this assessment shall be determined by the Board of Directors of the Program on a prorated basis for the months remaining in 1989 at the time the assessment is paid. A physician who satisfies the conditions imposed by this section shall be considered a participating physician in the Program for the remainder of 1989, beginning on the first day of the first month following the receipt by the Program of the required agreements and prorated assessment.

"§ 2. Any hospital which is otherwise eligible to become a participating hospital under the Virginia Birth-Related Neurological Injury

Compensation Act, but which did not meet the requirements of § 38.2-5020 on or before January 1, 1989, may become a participating hospital by filing the agreements required by § 38.2-5001 and by paying an assessment to the Program on or before May 15, 1989. The amount of this assessment shall be determined by the Board of Directors of the Program on a prorated basis for the months remaining in 1989 at the time the assessment is paid. A hospital satisfying the conditions imposed by this section shall be considered a participating hospital in the Program for the remainder of 1989, beginning on the first day of the first month following the receipt by the Program of the required agreements and prorated assessment."

Law Review. — For comment on Virginia's Birth-Related Neurological Injury Compensation Act, see 22 U. Rich. L. Rev. 431 (1988). For note, "Will Tort Reform Combat the Medical Malpractice Insurance Availability and Affordability Problems That Virginia's Physicians Are Facing," see 44 Wash. & Lee L. Rev. 1463 (1988).

§ 38.2-5020.1. Credits against malpractice insurance premiums. — A. Each insurer issuing or issuing for delivery in the Commonwealth any personal injury liability policy which provides medical malpractice liability coverage for the obstetrical practice of any participating physician under this chapter shall provide a credit on such physician's annual medical malpractice liability insurance premium in an amount that will produce premiums that are neither inadequate, excessive nor unfairly discriminatory, as required by § 38.2-1904, and as determined by the Commission.

B. Each insurer issuing or issuing for delivery in the Commonwealth any personal injury liability policy which provides medical malpractice liability coverage for the obstetrical services of any participating hospital under this chapter shall provide a credit on such hospital's annual medical malpractice liability insurance premium in an amount that will produce premiums that are neither inadequate, excessive nor unfairly discriminatory, as required by § 38.2-1904, and as determined by the Commission. (1990, c. 498.)

§ 38.2-5021. Actuarial investigation, valuations, gain/loss analysis; notice if assessments prove insufficient. — A.

The Bureau of Insurance of the State Corporation Commission shall undertake an actuarial investigation of the requirements of the Fund based on the Fund's experience in the first year of operation, including without limitation the assets and liabilities of the Fund. Pursuant to such investigation, the State Corporation Commission shall establish the rate of contribution of the entities listed in subsection E of § 38.2-5020 for the tax year beginning January 1, 1989.

Following the initial valuation, the State Corporation Commission shall cause an actuarial valuation to be made of the assets and liabilities of the Fund no less frequently than biennially. Pursuant to the results of such valuations, the State Corporation Commission shall prepare a statement as to the contribution rate applicable to contributors listed in subsection E of § 38.2-5020. However, at no time shall the rate be greater than one quarter of one percent of net direct premiums written.

B. In the event that the State Corporation Commission finds that the Fund cannot be maintained on an actuarially sound basis subject to the maximum assessments listed in § 38.2-5020, the Commission shall promptly notify the Speaker of the House of Delegates, the President of the Senate, the board of directors of the Program, and the Virginia Workers' Compensation Commission. (1987, c. 540; 1989, c. 523.)

Law Review. — For note, "Will Tort Reform Combat the Medical Malpractice Insurance Availability and Affordability Problems That Virginia's Physicians Are Facing," see 44 Wash. & Lee L. Rev. 1463 (1988).

CHAPTER 51.

RISK RETENTION GROUPS AND PURCHASING GROUPS.

§ 38.2-5100. Purpose. — The purpose of this chapter is to regulate the formation and operation of risk retention groups and purchasing groups in this Commonwealth formed pursuant to the provisions of the federal Liability Risk

Retention Act of 1986 to the extent permitted by such law. (1987, c. 585; 1992, c. 588.)

Virginia regulates the operation of risk retention groups within the Commonwealth. National Home Ins. Co. v. SCC, 838 F. Supp. 1104 (E.D. Va. 1993).

Jurisdiction over out of state risk retention group. — Where State Corporation Commission administered all laws regulating corporations operating in the state and had specific regulatory jurisdiction over risk retention groups plainly, then, the SCC had subject matter jurisdiction over a Colorado-based risk retention group. National Home Ins. Co. v. SCC, 838 F. Supp. 1104 (E.D. Va. 1993).

§ 38.2-5101. Definitions. — As used in this chapter:

"Commissioner" means the commissioner, director, or superintendent of insurance in a state other than the Commonwealth of Virginia.

"Completed operations liability" means liability arising out of the installation, maintenance, or repair of any product at a site which is not owned or controlled by (i) any person who performs that work or (ii) any person who hires an independent contractor to perform that work; but shall include liability for activities which are completed or abandoned before the date of the occurrence giving rise to the liability.

"Domicile," for purposes of determining the state in which a purchasing group is domiciled, means (i) for a corporation, the state in which the purchasing group is incorporated; and (ii) for an unincorporated entity, the state of its principal place of business.

"Hazardous financial condition" means that, based on its present or reasonably anticipated financial condition, a risk retention group, although not yet financially impaired or insolvent, is unlikely to be able (i) to meet obligations to policyholders with respect to known claims and reasonably anticipated claims or (ii) to pay other obligations in the normal course of business.

"Insurance" means primary insurance, excess insurance, reinsurance, surplus lines insurance, and any other arrangement for shifting and distributing risk which is determined to be insurance under the laws of this Commonwealth.

"Liability" means legal liability for damages, including costs of defense, legal costs and fees, and other claims expenses, because of injuries to other persons, damage to their property, or other damage or loss to such other persons resulting from or arising out of (i) any business, whether profit or nonprofit, trade, product, services, including professional services, premises, or operations or (ii) any activity of any state or local government, or any agency or political subdivision thereof. Liability does not include personal risk liability and an employer's liability with respect to its employees other than legal liability under the federal Employers Liability Act (45 U.S.C. 51 et seq.).

"Personal risk liability" means liability for damages because of injury to any person, damage to property, or other loss or damage resulting from any personal, familial, or household responsibilities or activities.

"Plan of operation" or *"feasibility study"* means an analysis which presents the expected activities and results of a risk retention group including, at a minimum:

1. Information sufficient to verify that its members are engaged in businesses or activities similar or related with respect to the liability to which such members are exposed by virtue of any related, similar or common business, trade, product, services, premises or operations;

2. For each state in which it intends to operate, the coverages, deductibles, coverage limits, rates, and rating classification systems for each line of insurance the group intends to offer;

3. Historical and expected loss experience of the proposed members and national experience of similar exposures, to the extent this experience is reasonably available;

4. Pro forma financial statements and projections;

5. Appropriate opinions by a qualified independent casualty actuary, including a determination of minimum premium or participation levels required to commence operations and to prevent a hazardous financial condition;

6. Identification of management, underwriting and claims procedures, marketing methods, managerial oversight methods, investment policies, and reinsurance agreements;

7. Identification of each state in which the risk retention group has obtained, or sought to obtain, a charter and license, and a description of its status in each such state; and

8. Such other matters as may be prescribed by the commissioner or commission for liability insurance companies authorized by the insurance laws of the state in which the risk retention group is chartered.

"Product liability" means liability for damages because of any personal injury, death, emotional harm, consequential economic damage, or property damage, including damages resulting from the loss of use of property, arising out of the manufacture, design, importation, distribution, packaging, labeling, lease, or sale of a product, but does not include the liability of any person for those damages if the product involved was in the possession of such a person when the incident giving rise to the claim occurred.

"Purchasing group" means any group which:

1. Has as one of its purposes the purchase of liability insurance on a group basis;

2. Purchases such insurance only for its group members and only to cover their similar or related liability exposure, as described in subdivision 3;

3. Is composed of members whose businesses or activities are similar or related with respect to the liability to which members are exposed by virtue of any related, similar, or common business, trade, product, services, premises, or operations; and

4. Is domiciled in any state.

"Risk retention group" means any corporation or other limited liability association:

1. Whose primary activity consists of assuming and spreading all, or any portion, of the liability exposure of its group members;

2. Which is organized for the primary purpose of conducting the activity described under subdivision 1;

3. Which (i) is chartered and licensed as a liability insurance company and authorized to engage in the business of insurance under the laws of any state or (ii) before January 1, 1985, was chartered or licensed and authorized to engage in the business of insurance under the laws of Bermuda or the Cayman Islands and, before such date, had certified to the insurance commissioner of at least one state that it satisfied the capitalization requirements of such state, except that any such group shall be considered to be a risk retention group only if it has been engaged in business continuously since such date and only for the purpose of continuing to provide insurance to cover product liability or completed operations liability;

4. Which does not exclude any person from membership in the group solely to provide for members of such a group a competitive advantage over such a person;

5. Which (i) has as its members only persons who have an ownership interest in the group and which has as its owners only persons who are members who are provided insurance by the risk retention group or (ii) has as its sole member and sole owner an organization which is owned by persons who are provided insurance by the risk retention group;

6. Whose members are engaged in businesses or activities similar or related with respect to the liability of which such members are exposed by virtue of

any related, similar, or common business, trade, product, services, premises, or operations;

7. Whose activities do not include the provision of insurance other than (i) liability insurance for assuming and spreading all or any portion of the liability of its group members and (ii) reinsurance with respect to the liability of any other risk retention group, or any members of such other group, which is engaged in businesses or activities so that such group or member meets the requirement described in subdivision 6 from membership in the risk retention group which provides such reinsurance; and

8. The name of which includes the phrase "Risk Retention Group" and does not include deceptive or misleading words, designations or phrases.

"*State*" means any state of the United States or the District of Columbia. (1987, c. 585; 1992, c. 588.)

§ 38.2-5102. Risk retention groups chartered in this Commonwealth.

— A. A risk retention group seeking to be chartered in this Commonwealth shall be chartered and licensed as a liability insurance company authorized by the insurance laws of this Commonwealth to write only liability insurance pursuant to this chapter and, except as provided elsewhere in this chapter, shall comply with (i) all of the laws, rules, regulations and requirements applicable to such insurers chartered and licensed in this Commonwealth and with (ii) § 38.2-5103 to the extent such requirements are not a limitation on laws, rules, regulations or requirements of this Commonwealth.

B. Notwithstanding any other provision to the contrary, all risk retention groups chartered in this Commonwealth shall file with the Commission and the National Association of Insurance Commissioners (NAIC), an annual statement in a form prescribed by the NAIC and in diskette form, if required by the Commission, and completed in accordance with its instructions and the NAIC Accounting Practices and Procedures Manual.

C. Before it may offer insurance in any state, each risk retention group shall also submit for approval to the Commission a plan of operation or feasibility study. The risk retention group shall submit an appropriate revision in the event of any subsequent material change in any item of the plan of operation or feasibility study, within ten days of any such change. The group shall not offer any additional kinds of liability insurance, in this Commonwealth or any other state, until a revision of the plan or study is approved by the Commission.

D. At the time of filing its application for licensure, the risk retention group shall provide to the Commission in summary form the following information: the identity of the initial members of the group, the identity of those individuals who organized the group or who will provide administrative services or otherwise influence or control the activities of the group, the amount and nature of initial capitalization, the coverages to be afforded, and the states in which the group intends to operate. (1987, c. 585; 1992, c. 588.)

§ 38.2-5103. Risk retention groups not chartered in this Commonwealth.

— Risk retention groups chartered in states other than this Commonwealth and seeking to do business as a risk retention group in this Commonwealth shall observe and abide by the laws of this Commonwealth as follows:

1. Before offering insurance in this Commonwealth, a risk retention group shall submit to the Commission on a form prescribed by the Commission:

a. A statement identifying the state or states in which the risk retention group is chartered and licensed as a liability insurance company, date of chartering, its principal place of business, and such other information including information on its membership, as the Commission may require to verify that the risk retention group is qualified under the definition set forth in this chapter;

b. A copy of its plan of operations or a feasibility study and revisions of such plan or study submitted to its state of domicile; however, the provision relating to the submission of a plan of operation or a feasibility study shall not apply with respect to product liability or completed operations liability as defined in this chapter which was offered before October 27, 1986, by any risk retention group which had been chartered and operating for not less than three years before such date;

c. A copy of any revision to its plan of operation or feasibility study required by this chapter at the same time that the revision is submitted to the Commissioner of its chartering state; and

d. A statement of registration which designates the clerk of the Commission as its agent for the purpose of receiving service of legal documents or process.

2. Any risk retention group doing business in this Commonwealth shall submit to the Commission:

a. A copy of the group's financial statement submitted to its state of domicile, which shall be certified by an independent public accountant and contain a statement of opinion on loss and loss adjustment expense reserves made by a member of the American Academy of Actuaries or a loss reserve specialist who is qualified under criteria established by the National Association of Insurance Commissioners;

b. A copy of each examination of the risk retention group as certified by the commissioner or public official conducting the examination;

c. Upon request by the Commission, a copy of any information or document pertaining to any outside audit performed with respect to the risk retention group; and

d. Such information as may be required to verify its continuing qualification as a risk retention group under the definition set forth in this chapter.

3. All premiums paid for coverages within this Commonwealth to risk retention groups shall be subject to taxation, including the assessment set forth in § 38.2-400, at the same rate and subject to the same interest, fines and penalties for nonpayment as applicable to foreign admitted insurers. Each risk retention group shall pay the taxes for risks insured within the Commonwealth. Further, each risk retention group shall report all premiums paid to it for risks insured within this Commonwealth.

4. Any risk retention group, its agents and representatives, shall comply with § 38.2-510.

5. Any risk retention group shall comply with the provisions of §§ 38.2-500, 38.2-501, 38.2-502, 38.2-503, 38.2-504, 38.2-506, and 38.2-512 regarding deceptive, false, or fraudulent acts or practices. However, the provisions of this subdivision do not relieve a risk retention group from the requirements of any other state statutes regarding deceptive, false, or fraudulent acts or practices.

6. Any risk retention group must submit to an examination by the Commission to determine its financial condition if the commissioner of the jurisdiction in which the group is chartered has not initiated an examination or does not initiate an examination within sixty days after a request by the Commission. Any such examination shall be coordinated to avoid unjustified repetition and conducted in an expeditious manner and in accordance with the NAIC's Examiner Handbook.

7. Every application form for insurance from a risk retention group and any policy issued by a risk retention group shall contain in ten point type on the front page and the declaration page, the following notice:

NOTICE

This policy is issued by your risk retention group. Your risk retention group may not be subject to all of the insurance laws and regulations of your state.

725

State insurance insolvency guaranty funds are not available for your risk retention group.

8. The following acts by a risk retention group are hereby prohibited:

a. The solicitation or sale of insurance by a risk retention group to any person who is not eligible for membership in such group; and

b. The solicitation or sale of insurance by, or operation of, a risk retention group that is in a hazardous financial condition or is financially impaired.

9. No risk retention group shall be allowed to do business in this Commonwealth if an insurance company is directly or indirectly a member or owner of such risk retention group, other than in the case of a risk retention group all of whose members are insurance companies.

10. The terms of any insurance policy provided by a risk retention group shall not provide or be construed to provide insurance policy coverage prohibited generally by the laws of this Commonwealth or declared unlawful by the Supreme Court of Virginia. For the purpose of this subdivision, a risk retention group shall comply with §§ 38.2-227, 38.2-2200, 38.2-2204 and any other applicable laws of this Commonwealth.

11. A risk retention group not chartered in this Commonwealth and doing business in this Commonwealth shall comply with a lawful order issued in a voluntary dissolution proceeding or in a delinquency proceeding commenced by a state insurance commissioner or the Commission if there has been a finding of financial impairment after an examination under this section. (1987, c. 585; 1992, c. 588.)

§ **38.2-5104. Associations.** — A. The provisions of Chapter 16 of Title 38.2 shall not apply to a risk retention group.

B. A risk retention group shall participate in any mechanisms established pursuant to § 38.2-2015 for the equitable apportionment of liability insurance losses and expenses. (1987, c. 585.)

§ **38.2-5105. Countersignatures not required.** — A policy of insurance issued to a risk retention group, a purchasing group, or to any member of such groups shall not be required to be countersigned as otherwise provided in § 38.2-1803. (1987, c. 585.)

§ **38.2-5106. Purchasing groups; exemption from certain laws relating to the group purchase of insurance.** — Any purchasing group meeting the criteria established under the provisions of the federal Liability Risk Retention Act of 1986 shall be exempt from any law of this Commonwealth relating to the creation of groups for the purchase of insurance, prohibition of group purchasing, or any law that would discriminate against a purchasing group or its members. A purchasing group shall be subject to all other applicable laws of this Commonwealth. (1987, c. 585.)

§ **38.2-5107. Insurers; exemptions from certain laws relating to the group purchase of insurance.** — A. An insurer shall be exempt from any law of this Commonwealth which prohibits providing, or offering to provide, to a purchasing group or its members advantages based on their loss and expense experience not afforded to other persons with respect to rates, policy forms, coverages, or other matters.

B. Any insurer who transacts the business of insurance in this Commonwealth with a purchasing group or its members shall comply with the provisions of § 38.2-1024 and all other statutes in Title 38.2 which are applicable to licensed insurers, unless the insurer has received prior approval of the Commission to issue surplus lines insurance pursuant to Chapter 48 of this title. (1987, c. 585.)

§ 38.2-5108. Notice and registration requirements of purchasing groups. — A. A purchasing group which intends to do business in this Commonwealth shall furnish notice to the Commission, on forms prescribed by the Commission, which shall:

1. Identify the state in which the group is domiciled;

2. Identify all other states in which the group intends to do business;

3. Specify the lines and classifications of liability insurance which the purchasing group intends to purchase;

4. Identify the insurance company from which the group intends to purchase its insurance, the domicile of such company, and the business address of such company;

5. Specify the method by which, and the person(s), if any, through whom insurance will be offered to its purchasing groups located in this Commonwealth;

6. Identify the principal place of business of the group including the business address of the group; and

7. Provide such other information as may be required by the Commission to verify that the purchasing group is qualified under the definition set forth in this chapter.

B. A purchasing group shall, within ten days, notify the Commission of any changes in any items set forth in subsection A of this section.

C. The purchasing group shall register with and designate the clerk of the Commission as its agent solely for the purpose of receiving service of legal documents or process, except that such requirements shall not apply in the case of a purchasing group:

1. Which (i) was domiciled before April 1, 1986, and (ii) is domiciled on and after October 27, 1986, in any state of the United States;

2. Which (i) before October 27, 1986, purchased insurance from an insurance carrier licensed in any state and (ii) since October 27, 1986, purchases its insurance from an insurance carrier licensed in any state;

3. Which was a purchasing group under the requirements of the Product Liability Risk Retention Act of 1981 before October 27, 1986; and

4. Which does not purchase insurance that was not authorized for purposes of an exemption under that Act, as in effect before October 27, 1986.

D. Each purchasing group that is required to give notice pursuant to subsection A of this section shall also furnish such information as may be required by the Commission to (i) verify that the entity qualifies as a purchasing group; (ii) determine where the purchasing group is located; and (iii) determine appropriate tax treatment.

E. Any purchasing group which was doing business in Virginia prior to the enactment of this subsection shall, within thirty days after July 1, 1992, furnish notice to the Commission pursuant to the provisions of subsection A of this section and furnish such information as may be required pursuant to subsections B and C of this section. (1987, c. 585; 1992, c. 588.)

§ 38.2-5109. Restrictions on insurance purchased by purchasing groups. — A. A purchasing group may not purchase insurance from a risk retention group that is not chartered in a state or from an insurer not admitted in the state in which the purchasing group is located, unless the purchase is effected through a licensed agent or broker acting pursuant to the surplus lines laws and regulations of such state.

B. No purchasing group may purchase insurance providing for a deductible or self-insured retention applicable to the group as a whole; however, coverage may provide for a deductible or self-insured retention applicable to individual members. (1987, c. 585; 1992, c. 588.)

§ 38.2-5110. Commission's authority regarding risk retention groups and purchasing groups. — The Commission is authorized to make use of any of the powers established under Titles 12.1 and 38.2 to enforce the laws of this Commonwealth so long as those powers are not specifically preempted by the Product Liability Risk Retention Act of 1981, as amended by the Risk Retention Amendments of 1986. This includes, but is not limited to, the Commission's power to investigate, issue subpoenas, conduct depositions and hearings, issue orders, and impose penalties. The Commission shall be deemed a state court of competent jurisdiction, independent of its Bureau of Insurance, in all judicial proceedings to enforce the provisions of this chapter. (1987, c. 585; 1995, c. 843.)

§ 38.2-5111. Penalties. — A risk retention group which violates any provision of this chapter will be subject to fines and penalties applicable to licensed insurers generally, including revocation of its license or the right to do business in this Commonwealth. (1987, c. 585.)

§ 38.2-5112. Duty on agents or brokers. — Any person acting, or offering to act, as an agent or surplus lines broker for a risk retention group or purchasing group, which solicits members, sells insurance coverage, purchases coverage for its members located within this Commonwealth or otherwise does business in this Commonwealth shall, before commencing any such activity, comply with the applicable provisions of Chapters 18 and 48 of this title, relating to property and casualty insurance agents and surplus lines brokers. (1987, c. 585.)

§ 38.2-5113. Financial responsibility policy form or coverage requirements. — Any risk retention group and any insurer who transacts the business of insurance in this Commonwealth with a purchasing group or its members shall not be exempt from the policy form or coverage requirements of this Commonwealth's motor vehicle financial responsibility insurance law. For the purpose of this section, any risk retention group and any insurer who transacts the business of insurance in this Commonwealth with a purchasing group or its members shall comply with §§ 38.2-2200 through 38.2-2207, §§ 38.2-2209, 38.2-2211, 38.2-2216, and §§ 38.2-2218 through 38.2-2225 and any other applicable law of this Commonwealth. (1987, c. 585.)

§ 38.2-5114. Application of other state laws to persons or corporations. — Nothing in this chapter shall be construed to affect the applicability of state laws which are generally applicable to persons or corporations. (1987, c. 585.)

§ 38.2-5115. Binding effect of orders issued in U.S. District Court. — An order issued by any district court of the United States enjoining a risk retention group from soliciting or selling insurance, or operating, in any state, or in all states or in any territory or possession of the United States upon a finding that such a group is in a hazardous financial condition shall be enforceable in the courts of the state. (1987, c. 585.)

CHAPTER 52.

Long-Term Care Insurance.

§ **38.2-5200. Definitions.** — As used in this chapter:

"Applicant" means in the case of an individual long-term care insurance policy, the person who seeks to contract for such benefits, or in the case of a group long-term care insurance policy, the proposed certificateholder.

"Certificate" means any certificate or evidence of coverage issued under a group long-term care insurance policy, which policy has been delivered or issued for delivery in this Commonwealth.

"Group long-term care insurance" means a long-term care insurance policy delivered or issued for delivery in this Commonwealth to any group which complies with § 38.2-3521.1.

"Long-term care insurance" means any insurance policy or rider advertised, marketed, offered or designed to provide coverage for not less than twelve consecutive months for each covered person on an expense incurred, indemnity, prepaid, or other basis, for one or more necessary or medically necessary diagnostic, preventive, therapeutic, rehabilitative, maintenance, personal care, mental health or substance abuse services, provided in a setting other than an acute care unit of a hospital. Such term includes group and individual annuities and life insurance policies or riders that provide directly or that supplement long-term care insurance. Long-term care insurance may be issued by insurers, fraternal benefit societies, health services plans, health maintenance organizations, cooperative nonprofit life benefit companies or mutual assessment life, accident and sickness insurers to the extent they are otherwise authorized to issue life or accident and sickness insurance. Health maintenance organizations, cooperative nonprofit life benefit companies and mutual assessment life, accident and sickness insurers may apply to the Commission for approval to provide long-term care insurance.

"Policy" means any individual or group policy of insurance, contract, subscriber agreement, certificate, rider or endorsement delivered or issued for delivery in this Commonwealth by an insurer, fraternal benefit society, health services plan, health maintenance organization or any similar organization. (1987, c. 586; 1990, c. 285.)

§ **38.2-5201. What laws applicable.** — All policies and certificates shall comply with all of the provisions of this title relating to insurance policies and certificates generally, except Article 2 (§ 38.2-3408 et seq.) of Chapter 34 and Chapter 36 of this title. In the event of conflict between the provisions of this chapter and other provisions of this title, the provisions of this chapter shall be controlling. (1987, c. 586; 1990, c. 285.)

§ **38.2-5202. Standards for policy provisions.** — A. The Commission may adopt regulations to establish specific standards for policy provisions of long-term care insurance policies. These standards shall be in addition to and in accordance with applicable laws of this Commonwealth. The standards shall address terms of renewability, nonforfeiture provisions if applicable, initial and subsequent conditions of eligibility, continuation or conversion, nonduplication of coverage provisions, coverage of dependents, preexisting conditions, termination of insurance, probationary periods, limitations, exceptions, reductions, elimination periods, requirements for replacement, recurrent conditions, and definitions of terms and may address any other standards considered appropriate by the Commission.

B. Regulations issued by the Commission shall:

1. Recognize the unique, developing and experimental nature of long-term care insurance;

2. Recognize the appropriate distinctions necessary between group and individual long-term care insurance policies;

3. Recognize the unique needs of both those individuals who have reached retirement age and those preretirement individuals interested in purchasing long-term care insurance products; and

4. Recognize the appropriate distinctions necessary between long-term care insurance and accident and sickness insurance policies, prepaid health plans, and other health service plans. (1987, c. 586; 1990, c. 285.)

§ 38.2-5203. Prohibited provisions. — No long-term care insurance policy may:

1. Be cancelled, nonrenewed, or otherwise terminated on the grounds of the age or the deterioration of the mental or physical health of the insured individual or certificateholder;

2. Contain a provision establishing any new waiting period in the event existing coverage is converted to or replaced by a new or other form within the same company, except with respect to an increase in benefits voluntarily selected by the insured individual or group policyholder; or

3. Provide coverage for skilled nursing care only or provide significantly more coverage for skilled care in a facility than coverage for lower levels of care. (1987, c. 586; 1990, c. 285.)

§ 38.2-5204. Preexisting conditions. — A. No long-term care insurance policy or certificate shall use a definition of "preexisting condition" which is more restrictive than the following: *"preexisting condition"* means the existence of symptoms which would cause an ordinary prudent person to seek diagnosis, care or treatment, or a condition for which medical advice or treatment was recommended by, or received from a provider of health care services, within six months preceding the effective date of coverage of an insured person.

B. No long-term care insurance policy may exclude coverage for a loss or confinement which is the result of a preexisting condition for a period of confinement longer than six months following the effective date of coverage of an insured person.

C. The Commission may extend the limitation periods set forth in subsections A and B of this section as to specific age group categories or specific policy forms upon findings that the extension is in the best interest of the public.

D. The definition of "preexisting condition" does not prohibit an insurer from using an application form designed to elicit the complete health history of an applicant, and, on the basis of the answers on that application, underwriting in accordance with that insurer's established underwriting standards for long-term care insurance policies. Unless otherwise provided in the policy or certificate, a preexisting condition, regardless of whether it is disclosed on the application, need not be covered until the waiting period described in subsection A or B expires. No long-term care insurance policy or certificate may exclude or use waivers or riders of any kind to exclude, limit, or reduce coverage or benefits for specifically named or described preexisting diseases or physical conditions beyond the waiting period described in subsection A or B. (1987, c. 586; 1990, c. 285.)

§ 38.2-5205. Prior institutionalization. — A. No long-term care insurance policy may be delivered or issued for delivery in this Commonwealth if such policy conditions eligibility (i) for any benefits provided in an institutional care setting on the receipt of a higher level of institutional care or (ii) for any benefits on a prior hospitalization requirement.

B. A long-term care insurance policy containing any limitations or conditions for eligibility other than those prohibited in subsection A shall clearly label such limitations or conditions, including any required number of days of confinement, in a separate paragraph of the policy or certificate entitled "Limitations or Conditions on Eligibility for Benefits."

C. A long-term care insurance policy containing a benefit advertised, marketed or offered as a home health care or home care benefit may not condition receipt of benefits on a prior institutionalization requirement.

D. A long-term care insurance policy which conditions eligibility of noninstitutional benefits on the prior receipt of institutional care shall not require a prior institutional stay of more than thirty days for which benefits are paid. (1987, c. 586; 1990, c. 285.)

§ 38.2-5206. Rates. — A. Long-term care benefits provided either in a policy or by rider may be required to meet loss ratio standards now in effect, or as may be established in the future, contained in regulations addressing individual or group accident and sickness insurance issued by the State Corporation Commission.

B. The regulation promulgated under this section shall recognize the unique, developing and experimental nature of long-term care insurance and shall recognize the unique needs of those individuals who have reached retirement age and the needs of those preretirement individuals interested in purchasing long-term care insurance policies.

C. A certificate by a qualified actuary or other qualified professional approved by the Commission as to the adequacy of the rates and reserves shall be filed with the Commission along with adequate supporting information. (1987, c. 586; 1990, c. 286.)

§ 38.2-5207. Disclosure. — In order to provide for fair disclosure in the sale of long-term care insurance policies:

1. An outline of coverage shall be delivered to an applicant for an individual long-term care insurance policy at the time of application for an individual policy. In the case of direct response solicitation, the insurer shall deliver the outline of coverage upon the applicant's request, but regardless of request shall make such delivery no later than at the time of policy delivery. The Commission shall prescribe a standard format, including style, arrangement, and overall appearance, and the content of an outline of coverage. In the case of agent solicitations, an agent shall deliver the outline of coverage prior to the presentation of an application or enrollment form. In the case of direct response solicitations, the outline of coverage shall be presented in conjunction with any application or enrollment form.

Such outline of coverage shall include:

a. A description of the principal benefits and coverage provided in the policy;

b. A statement of the exclusions, reductions and limitations contained in the policy;

c. A statement of the renewal provisions, including any reservation in the policy of a right to change premiums. Continuation or conversion provisions of group coverage shall be specifically described;

d. A statement that the outline of coverage is a summary of the policy issued or applied for and that the policy should be consulted to determine governing contractual provisions;

e. A description of the terms under which the policy may be returned and premium refunded; and

f. A brief description of the relationship of cost of care and benefits.

2. A certificate delivered or issued for delivery in this Commonwealth shall include:

a. A description of the principal benefits and coverage provided in the policy;

b. A statement of the exclusions, reductions and limitations contained in the policy; and

c. A statement that the group master policy should be consulted to determine governing contractual provisions.

3. The Commission shall adopt and publish a Long-Term Care Insurance Consumer Guide. After adoption and publication by the Commission, a copy of the Consumer Guide shall be provided at the time of delivery of the policy or certificate. (1987, c. 586; 1990, c. 285.)

§ 38.2-5207.1. Disclosure; life insurance policies. — Whenever an individual life insurance policy which provides long-term care benefits within the policy or by rider is delivered, it shall be accompanied by a policy summary. In the case of direct response solicitations, the insurer shall deliver the policy summary upon the applicant's request, but regardless of request shall make such delivery no later than at the time of policy delivery. In addition to complying with all applicable requirements, the summary shall also include:

1. An explanation of how the long-term care benefit interacts with other components of the policy, including deductions from death benefits;

2. An illustration of the amount of benefits, the length of benefit, and the guaranteed lifetime benefits, if any, for each covered person; and

3. Any exclusions, reductions, and limitations on benefits of long-term care.

If applicable to the policy type, the summary shall also include (i) a disclosure of the effects of exercising other rights under the policy, (ii) a disclosure of guarantees related to long-term care costs of insurance charges, and (iii) current and projected maximum lifetime benefits. (1990, c. 285.)

§ 38.2-5207.2. Long-term care benefits; monthly report. — Whenever long-term care benefits being paid are funded through a life insurance policy by acceleration of the death benefit, a monthly report shall be provided to the policyholder. Such report shall include:

1. Any long-term care benefits paid out during the month;

2. An explanation of any changes in the policy, e.g., death benefits or cash values, due to long-term care benefits being paid out; and

3. The amount of long-term care benefits existing or remaining. (1990, c. 285.)

§ 38.2-5208. Right to return; free look provision. — Long-term care insurance policies and certificates shall have a notice prominently printed on the first page or attached thereto stating in substance that the policyholder or insured person has the right to return the policy or certificate within thirty days of its delivery and to have the premium refunded if, after examination of the policy or certificate, the policyholder or insured person is not satisfied for any reason. A policy or certificate returned pursuant to the notice shall be void from its inception upon the mailing or delivery of the policy or certificate to the insurer or its agent. (1987, c. 586; 1990, c. 285.)

CHAPTER 53.

PRIVATE REVIEW AGENTS.

§§ 38.2-5300 through 38.2-5309: Repealed by Acts 1998, c. 129.

Cross references. — As to private review agents, see Article 2.1 of Chapter 5, Title 32.1, § 32.1-138.6 et seq.

Editor's note. — Acts 1998, c. 129, cl. 3 provides: "That regulations promulgated by the Virginia State Corporation Commission pursuant to Chapter 53 (§§ 38.2-5300 through 38.2-5309) of Title 38.2 of the Code prior to the effective date of this act [July 1, 1998] regarding private review agents shall continue in effect and shall be deemed to be the regulations of the Department of Health until the earlier of (i) the effective date of the regulations promulgated by the Department of Health pursuant to this act or (ii) January 1, 2000."

Acts 1998, c. 129, cl. 4 provides: "That all records necessary for administration of this act shall be transferred by the Virginia State Corporation Commission to the Department of Health on or before the effective date of this act [July 1, 1998]."

CHAPTER 54.

UTILIZATION REVIEW STANDARDS AND APPEALS.

§§ 38.2-5400 through 38.2-5409: Repealed by Acts 1998, c. 891.

Editor's note. — Sections 38.2-5400 and 38.2-5401 were also amended by Acts 1998, c. 129. At the direction of the Code Commission, the amendments were implemented in §§ 32.1-137.7 and 32.1-137.8, respectively.

CHAPTER 55.

RISK-BASED CAPITAL ACT FOR INSURERS.

§ 38.2-5500. Applicability. — The provisions of this chapter shall be known as The Risk-Based Capital Act for Insurers and may be referred to herein as "the Act." The Act shall apply to all insurers licensed in this Commonwealth to transact the business of insurance pursuant to provisions in Chapter 10 (§ 38.2-1000 et seq.), 11 (§ 38.2-1100 et seq.), 12 (§ 38.2-1200 et seq.) or 25 (§ 38.2-2500 et seq.). (1995, c. 789.)

Editor's note. — The section numbers of this chapter were assigned by the Code Commission, the 1995 act having designated the provisions as §§ 38.2-5401 through 38.2-5414.

§ 38.2-5501. Definitions. — As used in this chapter, the following terms shall have the following meanings:

"Adjusted RBC Report" means an RBC report which has been adjusted by

the Commission in accordance with subsection E of § 38.2-5502.

"Corrective Order" means an order issued by the Commission specifying corrective actions which the Commission has determined are required.

"Delinquency proceeding" means any proceeding commenced against an insurer for the purpose of liquidating, rehabilitating, reorganizing or conserving an insurer pursuant to the provisions of Chapter 15 (§ 38.2-1500 et seq.).

"Domestic insurer" means any domestic company which has obtained a license to engage in insurance transactions in this Commonwealth in accordance with the applicable provisions of Chapter 10 (§ 38.2-1000 et seq.).

"Foreign insurer" means any company not domiciled in this Commonwealth which has obtained a license to engage in insurance transactions in this Commonwealth in accordance with the applicable provisions in Chapter 10 (§ 38.2-1000 et seq.).

"Life and health insurer" and *"life or health insurer"* mean any domestic insurer or foreign insurer, whether known as a life insurer or a property and casualty insurer or a reciprocal, which is authorized to write any class of life insurance, annuities, or accident and sickness insurance, and is not writing a class of insurance set forth in §§ 38.2-110 through 38.2-132.

"NAIC" means the National Association of Insurance Commissioners.

"Negative Trend," with respect to a life insurer, health insurer or life and health insurer, means a negative trend over a period of time, as determined in accordance with the "Trend Test Calculation" included in the RBC Instructions.

"Property and casualty insurer" means any domestic insurer or foreign insurer which is authorized under any chapter of this title to write any class of insurance except a class of life insurance or annuities, provided that "property and casualty insurer" shall not include monoline mortgage guaranty insurers, financial guaranty insurers and title insurers, nor shall it include any insurer which is authorized to write a class of insurance set forth in §§ 38.2-110 through 38.2-132 but is writing only accident and sickness insurance.

"RBC" means risk-based capital.

"RBC Instructions" means the RBC Report including risk-based capital instructions adopted by the NAIC, as such RBC Instructions may be amended by the NAIC from time to time in accordance with the procedures adopted by the NAIC.

"RBC Level" means an insurer's Company Action Level RBC, Regulatory Action Level RBC, Authorized Control Level RBC, or Mandatory Control Level RBC where:

1. *"Company Action Level RBC"* means, with respect to any insurer, the product of 2.0 and its Authorized Control Level RBC;

2. *"Regulatory Action Level RBC"* means the product of 1.5 and its Authorized Control Level RBC;

3. *"Authorized Control Level RBC"* means the number determined under the risk-based capital formula in accordance with the RBC Instructions;

4. *"Mandatory Control Level RBC"* means the product of 0.70 and the Authorized Control Level RBC.

"RBC Plan" means a comprehensive financial plan containing the elements specified in subsection B of § 38.2-5503. If the Commission rejects the RBC Plan, and it is revised by the insurer, with or without the Commission's recommendation, the plan shall be called the "Revised RBC Plan."

"RBC Report" means the report required in § 38.2-5502.

"Total Adjusted Capital" means the sum of:

1. An insurer's statutory capital and surplus as determined in accordance with statutory accounting applicable to the annual financial statements required to be filed under § 38.2-1300; and

2. Such other items, if any, as the RBC Instructions may provide. (1995, c. 789.)

§ 38.2-5502. RBC Reports. — A. Every domestic insurer shall, on or prior to each March 1, the "filing date," prepare and submit to the Commission a report of its RBC Levels as of the end of the calendar year just ended, in a form and containing such information as is required by the RBC Instructions. In addition, every domestic insurer shall file its RBC Report:

1. With the NAIC in accordance with the RBC Instructions; and

2. With the insurance commissioner in any state in which the insurer is authorized to do business, if the insurance commissioner has notified the insurer of its request in writing, in which case, the insurer shall file its RBC Report not later than the later of:

a. Fifteen days from the receipt of notice to file its RBC Report with that state; or

b. The filing date.

B. A life and health insurer's RBC shall be determined in accordance with the formula set forth in the RBC Instructions. The formula shall take into account, and may adjust for the covariance between, the following risks:

1. The risk with respect to the insurer's assets;

2. The risk of adverse insurance experience with respect to the insurer's liabilities and obligations;

3. The interest rate risk with respect to the insurer's business; and

4. All other business risks and such other relevant risks as are set forth in the RBC Instructions.

Each risk shall be determined in each case by applying the factors in the manner set forth in the RBC Instructions.

C. A property and casualty insurer's RBC shall be determined in accordance with the formula set forth in the RBC Instructions. The formula shall take into account, and may adjust for the covariance between, the following risks:

1. Asset risk;

2. Credit risk;

3. Underwriting risk; and

4. All other business risks and such other relevant risks as are set forth in the RBC Instructions.

Each risk shall be determined in each case by applying the factors in the manner set forth in the RBC Instructions.

D. An excess of capital over the amount produced by the risk-based capital requirements contained in this Act and the formulas, schedules and instructions referred to in this Act is desirable in the business of insurance. Accordingly, insurers should seek to maintain capital above the RBC levels required by this Act. Additional capital is used and useful in the insurance business and helps to secure an insurer against various risks inherent in, or affecting, the business of insurance and not accounted for or only partially measured by the risk-based capital requirements contained in this Act.

E. If a domestic insurer files an RBC Report which in the judgment of the Commission is inaccurate, then the Commission shall adjust the RBC Report to correct the inaccuracy and shall notify the insurer of the adjustment. The notice shall contain a statement of the reason for the adjustment. An RBC Report as so adjusted is referred to as an "Adjusted RBC Report." (1995, c. 789.)

§ 38.2-5503. Company Action Level Event. — A. *"Company Action Level Event"* means any of the following events:

1. The filing of an RBC Report by an insurer which indicates that:

a. The insurer's Total Adjusted Capital is greater than or equal to its Regulatory Action Level RBC but less than its Company Action Level RBC; or

b. If a life and health insurer, the insurer has Total Adjusted Capital which is greater than or equal to its Company Action Level RBC but less than the product of its Authorized Control Level RBC and 2.5 and has a negative trend;

2. The notification by the Commission to the insurer of an Adjusted RBC Report that indicates the event in subdivision A 1 a or A 1 b, provided the insurer does not challenge the Adjusted RBC Report under § 38.2-5507; or

3. If, pursuant to § 38.2-5507, the insurer challenges an Adjusted RBC Report that indicates the event in subdivision A 1 a or A 1 b, the notification by the Commission to the insurer that the Commission has, after a hearing, rejected the insurer's challenge.

B. In the event of a Company Action Level Event, the insurer shall prepare and submit to the Commission an RBC Plan which shall:

1. Identify the conditions in the insurer which contribute to the Company Action Level Event;

2. Contain proposals of corrective actions which the insurer intends to take and would be expected to result in the elimination of the Company Action Level Event;

3. Provide projections of the insurer's financial results in the current year and at least the four succeeding years, both in the absence of proposed corrective actions and giving effect to the proposed corrective actions, including projections of statutory operating income, net income, capital and surplus. If appropriate, the projections for both new and renewal business shall include separate projections for each major line of business and separately identify each significant income, expense and benefit component;

4. Identify the key assumptions impacting the insurer's projections and the sensitivity of the projections to the assumptions; and

5. Identify the quality of, and problems associated with, the insurer's business, including but not limited to its assets, anticipated business growth and associated surplus strain, extraordinary exposure to risk, mix of business and use of reinsurance, if any, in each case.

C. The RBC Plan shall be submitted:

1. Within forty-five days of the Company Action Level Event; or

2. If the insurer challenges an Adjusted RBC Report pursuant to § 38.2-5507, within forty-five days after notification to the insurer that the Commission has, after a hearing, rejected the insurer's challenge.

D. Within sixty days after the submission by an insurer of an RBC Plan to the Commission, the Commission shall notify the insurer whether the RBC Plan shall be implemented or is, in the judgment of the Commission, unsatisfactory. If the Commission determines the RBC Plan is unsatisfactory, the notification to the insurer shall set forth the reasons for the determination, and may set forth proposed revisions which will render the RBC Plan satisfactory, in the judgment of the Commission. Upon notification from the Commission, the insurer shall prepare a Revised RBC Plan, which may incorporate by reference any revisions proposed by the Commission, and shall submit the Revised RBC Plan to the Commission:

1. Within forty-five days after the notification from the Commission; or

2. If the insurer challenges the notification from the Commission under § 38.2-5507, within forty-five days after a notification to the insurer that the Commission has, after a hearing, rejected the insurer's challenge.

E. In the event of a notification by the Commission to an insurer that the insurer's RBC Plan or Revised RBC Plan is unsatisfactory, the Commission may at the Commission's discretion, subject to the insurer's right to a hearing under § 38.2-5507, specify in the notification that the notification constitutes a Regulatory Action Level Event.

F. Every domestic insurer that files an RBC Plan or Revised RBC Plan with the Commission shall file a copy of the RBC Plan or Revised RBC Plan with the insurance commissioner in any state in which the insurer is authorized to do business if:

1. Such state has an RBC provision substantially similar to subsection A of § 38.2-5508; and

2. The insurance commissioner of that state has notified the insurer of its request for the filing in writing, in which case the insurer shall file a copy of the RBC Plan or Revised RBC Plan in that state no later than the later of:

a. Fifteen days after the receipt of notice to file a copy of its RBC Plan or Revised RBC Plan with the state; or

b. The date on which the RBC Plan or Revised RBC Plan is filed under subsection C of § 38.2-5504. (1995, c. 789.)

§ 38.2-5504. Regulatory Action Level Event. — A. *"Regulatory Action Level Event"* means, with respect to any insurer, any of the following events:

1. The filing of an RBC Report by the insurer which indicates that the insurer's Total Adjusted Capital is greater than or equal to its Authorized Control Level RBC but less than its Regulatory Action Level RBC;

2. The notification by the Commission to an insurer of an Adjusted RBC Report that indicates the event in subdivision A 1, provided the insurer does not challenge the Adjusted RBC Report under § 38.2-5507;

3. If, pursuant to § 38.2-5507, the insurer challenges an Adjusted RBC Report that indicates the event in subdivision A 1, the notification by the Commission to the insurer that the Commission has, after a hearing, rejected the insurer's challenge;

4. The failure of the insurer to file an RBC Report by the filing date, unless the insurer has provided an explanation for such failure which is satisfactory to the Commission and has cured the failure within ten days after the filing date;

5. The failure of the insurer to submit an RBC Plan to the Commission within the time period set forth in subsection C of § 38.2-5503;

6. Notification by the Commission to the insurer that:

a. The RBC Plan or Revised RBC Plan submitted by the insurer is, in the judgment of the Commission, unsatisfactory; and

b. Such notification constitutes a Regulatory Action Level Event with respect to the insurer, provided the insurer has not challenged the determination under § 38.2-5507;

7. If, pursuant to § 38.2-5507, the insurer challenges a determination by the Commission under subdivision A 6, the notification by the Commission to the insurer that the Commission has, after a hearing, rejected such challenge;

8. Notification by the Commission to the insurer that the insurer has failed to adhere to its RBC Plan or Revised RBC Plan, but only if such failure has a substantial adverse effect on the ability of the insurer to eliminate the Company Action Level Event in accordance with its RBC Plan or Revised RBC Plan and the Commission has so stated in the notification, provided the insurer has not challenged the determination under § 38.2-5507; or

9. If, pursuant to § 38.2-5507, the insurer challenges a determination by the Commission under subdivision A 8, the notification by the Commission to the insurer that the Commission has, after a hearing, rejected the challenge.

B. In the event of a Regulatory Action Level Event, the Commission shall:

1. Require the insurer to prepare and submit an RBC Plan or, if applicable, a Revised RBC Plan;

2. Perform such examination or analysis as the Commission deems necessary of the assets, liabilities and operations of the insurer including a review of its RBC Plan or Revised RBC Plan; and

3. Subsequent to the examination or analysis, issue a corrective order specifying such corrective actions as the Commission shall determine are

required. In determining corrective actions, the Commission may take into account such factors as are deemed relevant with respect to the insurer based upon the Commission's examination or analysis of the assets, liabilities and operations of the insurer, including, but not limited to, the results of any sensitivity tests undertaken pursuant to the RBC Instructions.

C. The RBC Plan or Revised RBC Plan shall be submitted:

1. Within forty-five days after the occurrence of the Regulatory Action Level Event;

2. If the insurer challenges an Adjusted RBC Report pursuant to § 38.2-5507 and the challenge is not frivolous in the judgment of the Commission, within forty-five days after the notification to the insurer that the Commission has, after a hearing, rejected the insurer's challenge; or

3. If the insurer challenges a Revised RBC Plan under § 38.2-5507 and the challenge is not frivolous in the judgment of the Commission, within forty-five days after notification to the insurer that the Commission has, after a hearing, rejected the insurer's challenge.

D. The Commission may retain actuaries and investment experts and other consultants as may be necessary in the judgment of the Commission to review the insurer's RBC Plan or Revised RBC Plan, examine or analyze the assets, liabilities and operations of the insurer and formulate the corrective order with respect to the insurer. The fees, costs and expenses relating to consultants shall be borne by the affected insurer or such other party as directed by the Commission. (1995, c. 789.)

§ **38.2-5505. Authorized Control Level Event.** — A. *"Authorized Control Level Event"* means any of the following events:

1. The filing of an RBC Report by the insurer which indicates that the insurer's Total Adjusted Capital is greater than or equal to its Mandatory Control Level RBC but less than its Authorized Control Level RBC;

2. The notification by the Commission to the insurer of an Adjusted RBC Report that indicates the event in subdivision A 1, provided the insurer does not challenge the Adjusted RBC Report under § 38.2-5507;

3. If, pursuant to § 38.2-5507, the insurer challenges an Adjusted RBC Report that indicates the event in subdivision A 1, the notification by the Commission to the insurer that the Commission has, after a hearing, rejected the insurer's challenge;

4. The failure of the insurer to respond, in a manner satisfactory to the Commission, to a corrective order, provided the insurer has not challenged the corrective order under § 38.2-5507; or

5. If the insurer has challenged a corrective order under § 38.2-5507 and the Commission has, after a hearing, rejected the challenge or modified the corrective order, the failure of the insurer to respond, in a manner satisfactory to the Commission, to the corrective order subsequent to rejection or modification by the Commission.

B. In the event of an Authorized Control Level Event with respect to an insurer, the Commission shall:

1. Take such actions as are required under § 38.2-5504 regarding an insurer with respect to which a Regulatory Action Level Event has occurred; or

2. If the Commission deems it to be in the best interests of the policyholders and creditors of the insurer and of the public, take such actions as are necessary to cause the insurer to be placed under regulatory control under the provisions of Chapter 15 (§ 38.2-1500 et seq.). In the event the Commission takes such actions, the Authorized Control Level Event shall be deemed an indication of a hazardous financial condition which serves as sufficient grounds for the Commission to commence delinquency proceedings, and the receiver appointed in conjunction with such proceedings shall have the rights, powers

and duties with respect to the insurer as are set forth in Chapter 15 or any order of liquidation, rehabilitation or conservation entered pursuant thereto. In the event the Commission takes actions under this subdivision pursuant to an Adjusted RBC Report, the insurer shall be entitled to such protections as are afforded to insurers under the appropriate provisions of this title pertaining to summary proceedings. (1995, c. 789.)

§ **38.2-5506. Mandatory Control Level Event.** — A. *"Mandatory Control Level Event"* means any of the following events:
1. The filing of an RBC Report which indicates that the insurer's Total Adjusted Capital is less than its Mandatory Control Level RBC;
2. The notification by the Commission to the insurer of an Adjusted RBC Report that indicates the event in subdivision A 1, provided the insurer does not challenge the Adjusted RBC Report under § 38.2-5507; or
3. If, pursuant to § 38.2-5507, the insurer challenges an Adjusted RBC Report that indicates the event in subdivision A 1, notification by the Commission to the insurer that the Commission has, after a hearing, rejected the insurer's challenge.
B. In the event of a Mandatory Control Level Event:
1. With respect to a life or health insurer, the Commission shall take actions as are necessary to place the insurer under regulatory control pursuant to the provisions of Chapter 15 (§ 38.2-1500 et seq.). In that event, the Mandatory Control Level Event shall be deemed an indication of a hazardous financial condition which serves as sufficient grounds for the Commission to commence delinquency proceedings, and the receiver appointed in conjunction with such proceedings, shall have the rights, powers and duties with respect to the insurer as are set forth in Chapter 15 or any order of liquidation, rehabilitation or conservation entered thereunder. If the Commission takes actions pursuant to an Adjusted RBC Report, the insurer shall be entitled to such protections as are afforded to insurers under the appropriate provisions of this title pertaining to summary proceedings. Notwithstanding any of the foregoing, the Commission may forego action for up to ninety days after the Mandatory Control Level Event if the Commission finds there is a reasonable expectation that the Mandatory Control Level Event may be eliminated within the ninety-day period.
2. With respect to a property and casualty insurer, the Commission shall take actions as are necessary to place the insurer under regulatory control pursuant to the provisions of Chapter 15, or, in the case of an insurer which is writing no business and which is running-off its existing business, may allow the insurer to continue to run-off under the supervision of the Commission. In either event, the Mandatory Control Level Event shall be deemed an indication of a hazardous financial condition which serves as sufficient grounds for the Commission to commence delinquency proceedings, and the receiver appointed in conjunction with such a proceedings, shall have the rights, powers and duties with respect to the insurer as are set forth in Chapter 15 or any order of liquidation, rehabilitation, or conservation entered thereunder. If the Commission takes actions pursuant to an Adjusted RBC Report, the insurer shall be entitled to such protections as are afforded to insurers under the appropriate provisions of this title pertaining to summary proceedings. Notwithstanding any of the foregoing, the Commission may forego action for up to ninety days after the Mandatory Control Level Event if the Commission finds there is a reasonable expectation that the Mandatory Control Level Event may be eliminated within the ninety-day period. (1995, c. 789.)

§ **38.2-5507. Hearings.** — A. An insurer shall have the right to a confidential hearing, on a record before the Commission, at which the insurer may challenge any determination or action by the Commission, upon:

1. Notification to an insurer by the Commission of an Adjusted RBC Report;

2. Notification to an insurer by the Commission that (i) the insurer's RBC Plan or Revised RBC Plan is unsatisfactory and (ii) such notification constitutes a Regulatory Action Level Event with respect to such insurer;

3. Notification to an insurer by the Commission that the insurer has failed to adhere to its RBC Plan or Revised RBC Plan and that such failure has a substantial adverse effect on the ability of the insurer to eliminate the Company Action Level Event with respect to the insurer in accordance with its RBC Plan or Revised RBC Plan; or

4. Notification to an insurer by the Commission of a Corrective Order with respect to the insurer.

B. The insurer shall notify the Commission of its request for a hearing within five days after the notification by the Commission under subdivision 1, 2, 3 or 4 of subsection A. Upon receipt of the insurer's request for a hearing, the Commission shall set a date for the hearing, which date shall be no less than ten nor more than thirty days after the date of the insurer's request. (1995, c. 789.)

§ 38.2-5508. Confidentiality; prohibition on announcements; prohibition on use in ratemaking. — A. All RBC Plans and RBC Reports, to the extent the information therein is not required to be set forth in a publicly available annual statement schedule, which are filed with the Commission with respect to any domestic insurer or foreign insurer, constitute information that might be damaging to the insurer if made available to its competitors, and therefore shall be kept confidential by the Commission. This information shall not be made public nor shall it be subject to subpoena, other than by the Commission and then only for the purpose of enforcement actions taken by the Commission pursuant to this Act or any other provision of the insurance laws of this Commonwealth. As used in this subsection, RBC Reports and RBC Plans shall include the results or report of any examination or analysis of an insurer performed by the Commission pursuant to the provisions of this Act or by the insurance regulatory officials of another state pursuant to the provisions of a substantially similar risk-based capital statute.

B. The comparison of an insurer's Total Adjusted Capital to any of its RBC Levels is a regulatory tool which may indicate the need for possible corrective action with respect to the insurer, and is not intended as a means to rank insurers generally. Therefore, except as otherwise required under the provisions of this Act, the making, publishing, disseminating, circulating or placing before the public, or causing, directly or indirectly to be made, published, disseminated, circulated or placed before the public, in a newspaper, magazine or other publication, or in the form of a notice, circular, pamphlet, letter or poster, or over any radio or television station, or in any other way, an advertisement, announcement or statement containing an assertion, representation or statement ranking any insurer relative to other insurers solely on the basis of comparisons between Total Adjusted Capital and RBC Levels or any component derived in the calculation of RBC Levels, by any insurer agent, broker or other person engaged in any manner in the insurance business would be misleading and is therefore prohibited. If any materially false statement comparing an insurer's Total Adjusted Capital to its RBC Levels, or any of them, or a misleading comparison of any other amount to the insurer's RBC Levels is published in any written publication and the insurer is able to demonstrate to the Commission with substantial proof the falsity or misleading nature of such statement, as the case may be, then the insurer may publish an announcement in a written publication if the sole purpose of the announcement is to rebut the materially false or misleading statement.

C. RBC Instructions, RBC Reports, Adjusted RBC Reports, RBC Plans and Revised RBC Plans are intended solely for use by the Commission in monitoring the solvency of insurers and the need for possible corrective action with respect to insurers and shall not be used by the Commission for ratemaking nor considered or introduced as evidence in any rate proceeding nor used by the Commission to calculate or derive any elements of an appropriate premium level or rate of return for any line of insurance which an insurer or any affiliate is authorized to write. (1995, c. 789.)

§ **38.2-5509. Supplemental provisions; rules; exemption.** — A. The provisions of this Act are supplemental to any other provisions of the laws of this Commonwealth, and shall not preclude or limit any other powers or duties of the Commission, the Commissioner of Insurance, or any of the Commission's employees or agents under such laws, including, but not limited to, the provisions of §§ 38.2-1038 and 38.2-1040 and Chapter 15 (§ 38.2-1500 et seq.) and any regulations issued thereunder.

B. The Commission may adopt reasonable rules necessary for the implementation of this Act.

C. The Commission may exempt from the application of this Act any domestic property and casualty insurer which:

1. Writes direct business only in this Commonwealth;

2. Writes direct annual premiums of $2 million or less; and

3. Assumes no reinsurance in excess of five percent of direct premium written.

D. The Commission may exempt from the application of this Act an insurer organized and operating under the laws of this Commonwealth and licensed pursuant to the provisions of Chapter 25 (§ 38.2-2500 et seq.) of this title. (1995, c. 789.)

§ **38.2-5510. Foreign insurers.** — A. Any foreign insurer shall, upon the written request of the Commission, submit to the Commission an RBC Report as of the end of the calendar year just ended not later than the later of:

1. The date an RBC Report would be required to be filed by a domestic insurer under this Act; or

2. Fifteen days after the request is received by the foreign insurer.

Any foreign insurer shall, at the written request of the Commission, promptly submit to the Commission a copy of any RBC Plan that is filed with the insurance commissioner of any other state.

B. In the event of a Company Action Level Event, Regulatory Action Level Event or Authorized Control Level Event with respect to any foreign insurer as determined under the RBC statute applicable in the state of domicile of the insurer, or, if no RBC provision is in force in that state, under the provisions of this Act, if the insurance commissioner of the state of domicile of the foreign insurer fails to require the foreign insurer to file an RBC Plan in the manner specified under the RBC statute, or, if no RBC provision is in force in the state, under § 38.2-5503 hereof, the Commission may require the foreign insurer to file an RBC Plan with the Commission. In such event, the failure of the foreign insurer to file an RBC Plan with the Commission shall be grounds to order the insurer to cease writing new insurance business in this Commonwealth or to suspend, revoke or refuse to issue a license pursuant to § 38.2-1040.

C. In the event of a Mandatory Control Level Event with respect to any foreign insurer, if no domiciliary receiver has been appointed with respect to the foreign insurer under the rehabilitation and liquidation statute applicable in the state of domicile of the foreign insurer, the Commission may deem such insurer in a condition where any further transaction of business will be hazardous to its policyholders, creditors, members, subscribers, stockholders, or to the public, and an action may be instituted and conducted pursuant to the provisions of Chapter 15 (§ 38.2-1500 et seq.), and the occurrence of the Mandatory Control Level Event shall be considered adequate grounds for the application for such action. (1995, c. 789.)

§ **38.2-5511. Immunity.** — There shall be no liability on the part of, and no cause of action shall arise against, the Commission, the Commissioner of Insurance, or any of the Commission's employees or agents, acting in good faith, for any action taken by them in the performance of their powers and duties under this Act. (1995, c. 789.)

§ **38.2-5512. Severability clause.** — If any provision of this Act, or the application thereof to any person or circumstance, is held invalid, such determination shall not affect the provisions or applications of this Act which can be given effect without the invalid provision or application, and to that end the provisions of this Act are severable. (1995, c. 789.)

§ **38.2-5513. Notices.** — All notices by the Commission to an insurer which may result in regulatory action hereunder shall be effective upon dispatch if transmitted by registered or certified mail, or in the case of any other transmission shall be effective upon the insurer's receipt of such notice. (1995, c. 789.)

§ **38.2-5514. Phase-in provision.** — For RBC Reports required to be filed by insurers with respect to 1994, the following requirements shall apply in lieu of the provisions of §§ 38.2-5503, 38.2-5504, 38.2-5505 and 38.2-5506:

1. In the event of a Company Action Level Event with respect to a domestic insurer, the Commission shall take no regulatory action hereunder.

2. In the event of a Regulatory Action Level Event under subdivision A 1, A 2 or A 3 of § 38.2-5504, the Commission shall take the actions required under § 38.2-5503.

3. In the event of a Regulatory Action Level Event under subdivision 4, 5, 6, 7, 8 or 9 of subsection A of § 38.2-5504 or an Authorized Control Level Event, the Commission shall take the actions required under § 38.2-5504 with respect to the insurer.

4. In the event of a Mandatory Control Level Event with respect to an insurer, the Commission shall take the actions required under § 38.2-5505 with respect to the insurer. (1995, c. 789.)

CHAPTER 56.

The Virginia Medical Savings Account Act.

§ **38.2-5600. The Virginia Medical Savings Account Plan established; plan to be established upon Congressional authorization; state agency actions required.** — For the purpose of providing the Commonwealth's people with a future that includes affordable health care, there is hereby established the Virginia Medical Savings Account Plan. Upon the passage of federal legislation authorizing the components of the Plan, the state agencies named in this chapter shall take action to implement the Plan as follows:

1. The Department of Medical Assistance Services shall develop and implement a plan to utilize medical savings accounts for provision of primary and acute care to the working poor and individuals who are eligible to receive medical assistance services as defined in the federal legislation or in any regulations promulgated to implement such legislation. Further, upon the effective date of this chapter, the Department shall develop a plan and apply for a waiver from the Health Care Finance Administration to implement a medical savings account demonstration project to provide health care services to the working poor and certain individuals eligible for medical assistance services.

2. The Bureau of Insurance within the State Corporation Commission shall provide the General Assembly and the Departments of Medical Assistance Services and Workers' Compensation a report on the available plans/policies for high-deductible, indemnity health insurance policies or other comparable insurance mechanisms for providing low-cost catastrophic care. The Bureau shall also, in developing this report, advise the Departments on inclusion of the essential health services used as the basis for certain managed-care commercial health insurance coverage.

3. The Department of Workers' Compensation shall develop and implement a plan to utilize medical savings accounts for provision of acute care to the employees who are eligible to receive services through workers' compensation insurance. The Department shall concentrate its focus on containing costs for employers while ensuring adequate care for injured or sick workers. The Department shall cooperate with the Department of Taxation in developing a system for voluntary employer contributions to medical savings accounts and reasonable tax deductions for these contributions.

4. The Department of Taxation shall, consistent with federal law and regulation, develop and present to the General Assembly a system for refundable tax credits which shall include a sliding scale for the working poor as defined in federal or state law and a system of tax credits, including innovative uses of such tax credits, for employers voluntarily contributing to employee medical savings accounts and health care providers who participate in providing care to medical savings account holders at a reduced price or without compensation. (1995, c. 650.)

Editor's note. — The numbers of §§ 38.2-5600 through 38.2-5603 were assigned by the Code Commission, the 1995 act having assigned no numbers.

§ 38.2-5601. Components of the Virginia Medical Savings Account Plan.

— Upon the passage of federal legislation authorizing the components of the Plan, the Departments of Medical Assistance Services, Workers' Compensation, and Taxation and the Bureau of Insurance shall develop the Virginia Medical Savings Account Plan. The Plan shall set forth the requirements for establishing medical savings accounts, which shall include, but not be limited to:

a. Definitions of eligible participants.

b. Criteria for accounts, including such matters as trustees, maximum amounts, contracts for managing debit cards, etc.

c. Use of direct debit cards and methods for ensuring their use solely for payment for necessary health care services.

d. Programs to educate recipients in handling health care services in a cost-effective manner while ensuring that necessary care is obtained.

e. Integration of existing coverage.

f. A system of refundable tax credits, which has been coordinated with the Virginia Department of Taxation.

g. A system for withholding the amounts (refundable tax credits) to be deposited to the medical savings accounts.

h. A system for calculating individual need for health care services in order to ensure that adequate sums are calculated for the care of individuals with greater need.

i. A system for providing a viable sliding scale for refundable tax credits for the working poor.

j. A system for allowing voluntary employer contributions to the medical savings accounts and tax deductions for such contributions.

k. A system for allowing tax credits for health care practitioners providing services to holders of medical savings accounts at reduced cost or without compensation.

l. A cafeteria menu of insurance plans to provide high-deductible, indemnity health insurance policies.

m. Any other specific provisions necessary to the efficient implementation of the Virginia Medical Savings Account Plan. (1995, c. 650.)

§ **38.2-5602. Operation of medical savings accounts.** — Upon the authorization in federal law to establish medical savings accounts and upon development and enactment of the Plan described in § 38.2-5601 of this chapter, medical savings accounts may be established in the Commonwealth. (1995, c. 650.)

§ **38.2-5603. Role of the Joint Commission on Health Care.** — The Joint Commission on Health Care shall monitor the development of the Plan required in § 38.2-5601 and make recommendations to the designated agencies on modifications of the Plan. Periodic reports shall be provided to the Commission by the designated agencies as the Commission may require. (1995, c. 650.)

CHAPTER 57.

VIATICAL SETTLEMENTS ACT.

§ **38.2-5700. Definitions.** — As used in this chapter:

"Viatical settlement" means compensation or other valuable consideration paid to the viator in return for the viator's assignment, transfer, sale, devise or bequest of the death benefit or ownership of a life insurance policy or certificate to the viatical settlement provider which compensation or other valuable consideration is less than the expected death benefit of the life insurance policy or certificate.

"Viatical settlement broker" means any person who, for another and for a fee, commission or other valuable consideration, offers or advertises the availability of viatical settlements, introduces viators to viatical settlement providers, or offers or attempts to negotiate viatical settlements between a viator and one or more viatical settlement providers; however, "viatical settlement broker" does not include an attorney, accountant or financial planner who is not paid by the viatical settlement provider and who is retained to represent the viator.

"Viatical settlement contract" means a written agreement between a viatical settlement provider and a person who owns a life insurance policy or who owns or is covered under a group policy insuring the life of a person who has a catastrophic or life-threatening illness or condition; under the terms of the agreement, the viatical settlement provider will pay compensation or other valuable consideration, which is less than the expected death benefit of the insurance policy or certificate, in return for the viator's assignment, transfer, sale, devise or bequest of the death benefit or ownership of the insurance policy or certificate to the viatical settlement provider. "Viatical settlement contracts" do not include accelerated death benefit provisions contained in life insurance policies, whether issued with the original policy or as a rider, according to the regulations promulgated by the Commission.

"Viatical settlement provider" means a person that conducts the business of viatical settlements directly or indirectly as agent or attorney-in-fact for one or more persons entering into or attempting to enter into a viatical settlement contract. "Viatical settlement provider" does not include: (i) any bank, savings bank, savings institution, credit union or other licensed lending institution which takes an assignment of a life insurance policy as collateral for a loan; (ii) the issuer of a life insurance policy which makes a policy loan on a policy that it has issued, permits surrender of the policy or pays other policy benefits, including accelerated benefits according to regulations promulgated by the Commission; or (iii) any individual who enters into only one agreement in a calendar year for the transfer of the death benefit or ownership of the insurance policy or certificate for any value less than the expected death benefit.

"Viaticated policy" means a life insurance policy or a certificate of life insurance issued under a group life insurance policy that has been acquired or transferred pursuant to the terms of a viatical settlement contract.

"Viator" means the owner of a life insurance policy or the holder of a certificate issued under a group life insurance policy insuring the life of a person with a catastrophic or life threatening illness or condition who enters into an agreement under the terms of which the viatical settlement provider will pay compensation or other valuable consideration, which compensation or other valuable consideration is less than the expected death benefit of the insurance policy or certificate, in return for the assignment, transfer, sale, devise or bequest of the death benefit or ownership of the insurance policy or certificate to the viatical settlement provider. "Viator" does not include a viatical settlement provider or any subsequent owner of a viaticated policy. (1997, c. 814.)

§ 38.2-5701. License required for viatical settlement providers; Commission's authority; conditions; bonds; etc. — A. On and after January 1, 1998, no person shall act as a viatical settlement provider or enter into or solicit a viatical settlement contract while acting as a viatical settlement provider without first obtaining a license from the Commission.

1. Any person seeking to be licensed as a viatical settlement provider in this Commonwealth shall apply for such license in a form acceptable to the Commission and shall pay to the Commission a nonrefundable application fee in an amount prescribed by the Commission. Such fee shall be not less than

$500 and not more than $1,500. The application fee required by this subdivision shall be collected by the Commission, paid directly into the state treasury, and credited to the "Bureau of Insurance Special Fund — State Corporation Commission" for the maintenance of the Bureau of Insurance as provided in subsection B of § 38.2-400.

2. Every licensed viatical settlement provider shall pay to the Commission a nonrefundable biennial renewal fee in an amount prescribed by the Commission. Such fee shall be not less than $500 and not more than $1,500. Each license shall expire on June 30 of the appropriate year. Prior to April 1 of the renewal year, each licensed viatical settlement provider shall submit to the Commission a renewal application form and fee in the manner and form prescribed by the Commission. The renewal fee required by this subdivision shall be collected by the Commission and paid directly into the state treasury and credited to the "Bureau of Insurance Special Fund — State Corporation Commission" for the maintenance of the Bureau of Insurance as provided in subsection B of § 38.2-400.

B. A licensed insurer shall be prohibited from transacting the business of a viatical settlement provider.

C. The Commission may require the applicant to disclose fully the identities of all stockholders, partners, officers and employees, and may, in the exercise of its discretion, refuse to issue a license in the name of any firm, partnership, limited liability company or corporation if not satisfied that any officer, employee, stockholder or partner thereof who may materially influence the applicant's conduct meets the standards of this chapter.

D. A license issued to any partnership, limited liability company or corporation authorizes all members, officers, and designated employees to transact or conduct the business of viatical settlement provider under the license, and all such persons shall be named in the application and any application supplements.

E. Upon the filing of an application and the payment of the nonrefundable application processing fee, the Commission shall make such investigation of each applicant as the Commission may determine to be appropriate and may issue a license if it finds that the applicant: (i) has provided a detailed plan of operation; (ii) is competent and trustworthy; (iii) indicates its intention to act in good faith within the confines of the license; (iv) has a good business reputation; (v) if an individual, has had experience, training or education which qualifies him for licensure; (vi) if a resident partnership, limited liability company or corporation, has recorded the existence of the partnership, limited liability company or corporation pursuant to law; (vii) if a corporation, has specific authority to act as a viatical settlement provider in its charter; and (viii) if a nonresident partnership, limited liability company or corporation, has furnished proof of its authority to transact business in Virginia.

F. If the applicant for a viatical settlement provider license is a nonresident, such applicant, as a condition precedent to receiving or holding a license, shall designate a resident of this Commonwealth as the person upon whom any process, notices or order, required or permitted by law to be served upon such nonresident viatical settlement provider may be served; and such licensee shall promptly notify the clerk of the Commission in writing of every change in its designated agent for service of process, and such change shall not become effective until acknowledged by the Commission. Whenever a nonresident viatical settlement provider transacting business in this Commonwealth fails to appoint or maintain a registered agent in this Commonwealth, or whenever its registered agent cannot with reasonable diligence be found at the registered office, the clerk of the Commission shall be an agent of the nonresident upon whom service may be made in accordance with § 12.1-19.1.

G. The Commission may deny an application for a license or may suspend or revoke a license of or refuse to issue a new license to any viatical settlement provider if the Commission finds that the applicant or licensee has (i) made any material misrepresentation on the application; (ii) been guilty of fraudulent or dishonest practices; (iii) been subject to a final administrative action or has otherwise been shown to be untrustworthy or incompetent to act as a viatical settlement provider; (iv) demonstrated a pattern of unreasonable payments to viators; (v) been convicted of a felony or any misdemeanor involving moral turpitude; or (vi) violated any provisions of this chapter or other applicable provisions of this title.

H. If the Commission is of the opinion that any applicant for a viatical settlement provider's license is not of good character or does not have a good reputation for honesty, it may refuse to issue the license, subject to the right of the applicant to demand a hearing on the application. The Commission shall not suspend or revoke an existing license until the licensee is given an opportunity to be heard before the Commission. If the Commission refuses to issue a new license or proposes to suspend or revoke an existing license, it shall give the applicant or licensee at least ten days' notice in writing of the time and place of the hearing, if a hearing is requested. The notice shall contain a statement of the objections to the issuance of the license, or the reason for its proposed suspension or revocation as the case may be. The notice may be given to the applicant or licensee by registered or certified mail, sent to the last known address of record pursuant to § 38.2-5703, or the last known business address if the address of record is incorrect, or in any other lawful manner the Commission prescribes. The Commission may summon witnesses to testify with respect to the applicant or licensee, and the applicant or licensee may introduce evidence in his or its behalf. No applicant to whom a license is refused after a hearing, nor any licensee whose license is revoked, shall apply again for a license until after the time, not exceeding two years, the Commission prescribes in its order.

I. All viatical settlement providers shall be bonded, and the bonds shall be filed with the Commission, as may be required by the Commission pursuant to § 38.2-5706. (1997, c. 814; 1998, c. 11.)

Editor's note. — Acts 1997, c. 814, cl. 2, provides: "That the biennial licensure fees required by § 38.2-5701 for the initial licensure period ending June 30, 1999, shall not be prorated."

The 1998 amendment, in subsection A, in subdivisions 1 and 2, added the last sentence and rewrote subsection F.

§ 38.2-5702. License required for viatical settlement brokers; Commission's authority; conditions; etc. — A. No person shall act as a viatical settlement broker, or solicit a viatical settlement contract while acting as a viatical settlement broker, on or after January 1, 1998, without first obtaining a license from the Commission.

1. Application for a viatical settlement broker's license shall be made to the Commission in the manner, in the form, and accompanied by the nonrefundable license processing fee prescribed by the Commission. A license issued at any time prior to August 1, 1998, will expire on July 31, 1999, unless renewed as set forth herein. The license processing fee required by this subdivision shall be collected by the Commission, paid directly into the state treasury, and credited to the "Bureau of Insurance Special Fund — State Corporation Commission" for the maintenance of the Bureau of Insurance as provided in subsection B of § 38.2-400.

2. Before August 1 of each year commencing August 1, 1999, each viatical settlement broker shall remit the nonrefundable renewal fee and renewal form prescribed by the Commission for the renewal of the license, unless the license has been terminated, suspended or revoked on or before July 31 of such year. Viatical settlement broker's licenses may be renewed for a one-year period

ending on the following July 31 if the required renewal form and renewal fee have been received by the Commission. Unless the required renewal form and fee are received by the Commission by July 31 of such year, the viatical settlement broker's license shall expire. The renewal fee required by this subdivision shall be collected by the Commission, paid directly into the state treasury, and credited to the "Bureau of Insurance Special Fund — State Corporation Commission" for the maintenance of the Bureau of Insurance as provided in subsection B of § 38.2-400.

B. Each applicant for a viatical settlement broker's license shall provide satisfactory evidence that no disciplinary action has resulted in the suspension or revocation of any federal or state license.

C. Applicants for a nonresident viatical settlement broker's license shall designate the clerk of the Commission as agent for service of process in the manner, and with the same legal effect, provided for by this title for designation of service of process upon unauthorized insurers; and also shall furnish the clerk of the Commission with the name and address of a resident of this Commonwealth upon whom notices or orders of the Commission or process affecting such nonresident viatical settlement broker may be served. Such licensee shall promptly notify the clerk of the Commission in writing of every change in its designated agent for service of process, and such change shall not become effective until acknowledged by the Commission.

D. The Commission may deny an application for a license or may suspend or revoke a license of or refuse to issue a new license to any viatical settlement broker, if the Commission finds that the applicant or licensee has (i) made any material misrepresentation on the application; (ii) been guilty of fraudulent or dishonest practices; (iii) been subject to a final administrative action or has otherwise been shown to be untrustworthy or incompetent to act as a viatical settlement broker; (iv) placed or attempted to place a viatical settlement with a viatical settlement provider not licensed in this Commonwealth; (v) been convicted of a felony or any misdemeanor involving moral turpitude; or (vi) violated any provisions of this chapter or other applicable provisions of this title.

E. If the Commission is of the opinion that any applicant for a viatical settlement broker's license is not of good character or does not have a good reputation for honesty, it may refuse to issue the license, subject to the right of the applicant to demand a hearing on the application. The Commission shall not suspend or revoke an existing license until the licensee is given an opportunity to be heard before the Commission. If the Commission refuses to issue a new license or proposes to suspend or revoke an existing license, it shall give the applicant or licensee at least ten days' notice in writing of the time and place of the hearing, if a hearing is requested. The notice shall contain a statement of the objections to the issuance of the license, or the reason for its proposed suspension or revocation as the case may be. The notice may be given to the applicant or licensee by registered or certified mail, sent to the last known address of record pursuant to § 38.2-5703, or the last known business address if the address of record is incorrect, or in any other lawful manner the Commission prescribes. The Commission may summon witnesses to testify with respect to the applicant or licensee, and the applicant or licensee may introduce evidence in his or her behalf. No applicant to whom a license is refused after a hearing, nor any licensee whose license is revoked, shall apply again for a license until after the time, not exceeding two years, the Commission prescribes in its order.

F. In the absence of a written agreement making the broker the viator's agent, viatical settlement brokers are presumed to be agents of viatical settlement providers.

G. A viatical settlement broker shall not, without the written agreement of the viator obtained before performing any services in connection with a viatical settlement, seek or obtain any compensation from the viator. (1997, c. 814; 1998, c. 11.)

The 1998 amendment, in subsection A, in subdivisions 1 and 2, added the last sentence; and in subsection D, in clause (iii), substituted "broker" for "provider" and in clause (iv), substituted "placed or attempted to place a viatical settlement with a viatical settlement provider not licensed in this Commonwealth" for "demonstrated a pattern of unreasonable payments to viators."

§ 38.2-5703. Requirement to report to Commission. — A. Each licensed viatical settlement provider and viatical settlement broker shall report, in writing, any change in business or residence address or name within thirty days to the Commission.

B. Each licensed viatical settlement provider and viatical settlement broker convicted of a felony shall report within thirty days to the Commission the facts and circumstances regarding the criminal conviction. (1997, c. 814; 1999, c. 59.)

The 1999 amendment inserted the subsection A designation, and added subsection B.

§ 38.2-5704. Commission approval required for viatical settlement contract forms; examinations and inspections; etc. — A. No viatical settlement provider may, on or after January 1, 1998, use any viatical settlement contract in this Commonwealth unless such contract has been filed with and approved by the Commission in accordance with § 38.2-316, as well as all applicable regulations.

B. Each licensee shall file with the Commission by March 1 of each year an annual statement in the form required by the Commission. The Commission (i) may, when it deems it reasonably necessary to protect the public interest, examine and inspect the business and affairs of any licensee or applicant for a license; (ii) shall have the right to examine and investigate the business affairs of any licensee or applicant engaged or alleged to be engaged in the business of viatical settlements in this Commonwealth, including all brokers, to determine whether the person has engaged or is engaging in any violation of this title; and (iii) shall have the right to examine all records relating to the writing or alleged writing of viatical settlement contracts by any such person in this Commonwealth to determine whether the person is now or has been violating any of the provisions of this title. Any licensed viatical settlement provider or broker or any person purporting to be a licensed viatical settlement provider or broker, or any person whose actions have led any other person to believe that he is a licensed viatical settlement provider or broker, who refuses to permit the Commission or any of its employees or agents, including employees of the Bureau of Insurance, to make an examination or who fails or refuses to comply with the provisions of this section may, after notice and an opportunity to be heard, be subject to any of the penalties relating to agents or companies licensed by the Commission provided in this title, including the suspension or revocation of his or its license. The expenses incurred in the examination and inspection shall be paid by the licensee or applicant. Records of all transactions of viatical settlement contracts shall be maintained by the licensee and shall be available to the Commission for inspection during reasonable business hours. The Commission shall hold the names and individual identifiers for all viators as confidential and shall not disclose these names and individual identifiers, unless otherwise required by law. (1997, c. 814.)

§ 38.2-5705. Disclosures required of viatical settlement providers; informed consent; unconditional refund. — A. Viatical settlement providers shall advise the viator in writing, at the time of solicitation for the viatical settlement, and again at the time the viatical settlement contract is signed by all parties, of the following:

1. That there are alternatives to viatical settlement contracts for persons with catastrophic or life-threatening illnesses offered by the issuer of the life insurance policy, and that the viator should communicate with the insurance company to review all possible alternatives;

2. That some or all of the compensation of the viatical settlement may be taxable, and that assistance from a personal tax advisor should be obtained;

3. That the viatical settlement may be subject to the claims of creditors;

4. That receipt of compensation through a viatical settlement may affect the insured's eligibility for medical assistance services or other government benefits or entitlements, and that advice from the appropriate agencies should be obtained;

5. That the viator has the right to rescind a viatical settlement contract within thirty days of the date the agreement was executed by the parties or within fifteen days of the receipt of the viatical settlement proceeds by the viator, whichever occurs sooner, as provided in subsection C; and

6. The date by which the viatical settlement funds will be available to the viator and the source of the funds.

The viatical settlement provider shall retain a signed disclosure form from the viator, acknowledging the viator's understanding of the information required by this subsection.

B. Prior to entering into any viatical settlement contract with any person with a catastrophic or life-threatening illness or condition, a viatical settlement provider shall obtain (i) a written statement from a licensed physician that the person is of sound mind and under no constraint or undue influence and (ii) a witnessed document in which the viator consents to the viatical settlement contract, acknowledges the catastrophic or life-threatening illness, represents that he has a full and complete understanding of the viatical settlement contract and a full and complete understanding of the benefits of the life insurance policy, releases his medical records, and acknowledges that he has entered into the viatical settlement contract freely and voluntarily.

All medical information solicited or obtained by any licensee shall be confidential and shall only be released as provided by law.

C. All viatical settlement contracts executed in this Commonwealth shall contain an unconditional refund provision of at least thirty days from the date of the contract or fifteen days of the receipt of the viatical settlement proceeds, whichever occurs first. In the event of a refund, the amount refunded shall not be less than the value of the insurance contract as determined on the date the viatical settlement contract was signed. Immediately upon receipt from the viator of documents to effect the transfer of the death benefit or ownership of the life insurance policy or certificate, the viatical settlement provider shall pay the proceeds of the settlement to an escrow or trust account managed by a trustee or escrow agent in a qualified financial institution eligible, under the definition at § 38.2-1316.1, to act as a fiduciary of a trust, pending acknowledgment of the transfer by the issuer of the policy. The trustee or escrow agent shall be required to transfer the proceeds due to the viator immediately upon receipt of acknowledgment of the transfer from the insurer. Failure to tender the viatical settlement by the date disclosed to the viator shall render the contract null and void, unless the viator chooses to honor the contract on a later date when the viatical settlement is tendered. (1997, c. 814.)

§ 38.2-5706. Commission's authority. — Pursuant to the authority granted by § 38.2-223, the Commission may promulgate such rules and regulations as it may deem necessary to implement this chapter, including, but not limited to:

1. Establishing standards for evaluating reasonableness of payments under viatical settlement contracts. This authority includes, but is not limited to, regulation of discount rates used to determine the amount paid in exchange for assignment, transfer, sale, devise or bequest of a benefit under a life insurance policy; and

2. Setting the amount of any bond required for viatical settlement providers pursuant to § 38.2-5701. (1997, c. 814.)

§ **38.2-5707. Unfair trade practices.** — A violation of this chapter shall be considered an unfair trade practice pursuant to Chapter 5 (§ 38.2-500 et seq.) of this title and shall be subject to the penalties contained in that chapter. (1997, c. 814.)

CHAPTER 58.

MANAGED CARE HEALTH INSURANCE PLANS.

§ **38.2-5800. Definitions.** — As used in this chapter:

"Accident and sickness insurance company" means a person subject to licensing in accordance with provisions in Chapter 10 (§ 38.2-1000 et seq.) or Chapter 41 (§ 38.2-4100 et seq.) of this title seeking or having authorization (i) to issue accident and sickness insurance as defined in § 38.2-109, (ii) to issue the benefit certificates or policies of accident and sickness insurance described in § 38.2-3801, or (iii) to provide hospital, medical and nursing benefits pursuant to §§ 38.2-4116 and 38.2-4123.

"Affiliated provider" means any provider that is employed by or has entered into a contractual agreement either directly or indirectly with a health carrier to provide health care services to members of a managed care health insurance plan for which the health carrier is responsible under this chapter.

"Basic health care services" means emergency services, inpatient hospital and physician care, outpatient medical services, laboratory and radiological services, and preventive health services. *"Basic health care services"* shall also mean limited treatment of mental illness and substance abuse as set forth in § 38.2-3412.1 or in the case of a health maintenance organization shall be in accordance with such minimum standards set by the Commission which shall not exceed the level of services mandated for insurance carriers pursuant to Chapter 34 (§ 38.2-3400 et seq.) of this title.

"Copayment" means a payment required of covered persons as a condition of the receipt of specific health services.

"Covered person" means an individual, whether a policyholder, subscriber, enrollee, or member of a managed care health insurance plan (MCHIP) who is entitled to health care services or benefits provided, arranged for, paid for or reimbursed pursuant to an MCHIP.

"Evidence of coverage" includes any certificate, individual or group agreement or contract, or identification card or related documents issued in

conjunction with the certificate, agreement or contract, issued to a subscriber setting out the coverage and other rights to which a covered person is entitled.

"Health care services" means the furnishing of services to any individual for the purpose of preventing, alleviating, curing, or healing human illness, injury or physical disability.

"Health carrier" means an entity subject to Title 38.2 that contracts or offers to contract to provide, deliver, arrange for, pay for or reimburse any of the costs of health care services, including an entity providing a plan of health insurance, health benefits or health services, an accident and sickness insurance company, a health maintenance organization, or a nonstock corporation offering or administering a health services plan, a hospital services plan, or a medical or surgical services plan, or operating a plan subject to regulation under Chapter 45 (§ 38.2-4500 et seq.) of this title.

"Health maintenance organization" means a person licensed pursuant to Chapter 43 (§ 38.2-4300 et seq.) of this title.

"Limited health care services" means dental care services, vision care services, mental health services, substance abuse services, pharmaceutical services, and such other services as may be determined by the Commission to be limited health care services. Limited health care services shall not include hospital, medical, surgical or emergency services except as such services are provided incident to the limited health care services set forth in the preceding sentence.

"Managed care health insurance plan" or *"MCHIP"* means an arrangement for the delivery of health care in which a health carrier undertakes to provide, arrange for, pay for, or reimburse any of the costs of health care services for a covered person on a prepaid or insured basis which (i) contains one or more incentive arrangements, including any credentialing requirements intended to influence the cost or level of health care services between the health carrier and one or more providers with respect to the delivery of health care services and (ii) requires or creates benefit payment differential incentives for covered persons to use providers that are directly or indirectly managed, owned, under contract with or employed by the health carrier. Any health maintenance organization as defined in § 38.2-4300 or health carrier that offers preferred provider contracts or policies as defined in § 38.2-3407 or preferred provider subscription contracts as defined in § 38.2-4209 shall be deemed to be offering one or more MCHIPs. For the purposes of this definition, the prohibition of balance billing by a provider shall not be deemed a benefit payment differential incentive for covered persons to use providers who are directly or indirectly managed, owned, under contract with or employed by the health carrier. A single managed care health insurance plan may encompass multiple products and multiple types of benefit payment differentials; however, a single managed care health insurance plan shall encompass only one provider network or set of provider networks.

"Medical necessity" or *"medically necessary"* means appropriate and necessary health care services which are rendered for any condition which, according to generally accepted principles of good medical practice, requires the diagnosis or direct care and treatment of an illness, injury, or pregnancy-related condition, and are not provided only as a convenience.

"Network" means the set of providers directly or indirectly managed, owned, under contract with or employed directly or indirectly by a health carrier for the purpose of delivering health care services to the covered persons of an MCHIP.

"Provider" or *"health care provider"* means any hospital, physician, or other person authorized by statute, licensed or certified to furnish health care services.

"Service area" means a clearly defined geographic area in which a health carrier has directly or indirectly arranged for the provision of health care

services to be generally available and readily accessible to covered persons of an MCHIP. (1998, c. 891.)

Editor's note. — Acts 1998, c. 891, cl. 3 provides: "That the Commissioner of the Department of Health shall report annually to the Joint Commission on Health Care the status of this legislation, including, but not limited to (i) the criteria developed by which managed care health insurance plans are reviewed and evaluated; (ii) the number of quality assurance certificates issued by the Department; (iii) the number of quality assurance certificates denied by the Department and the reasons for the denial; (iv) the status of the periodic reviews for complaint investigations and compliance with the quality of care certificate standards established by this bill; and (v) the number and amount of civil penalties which were imposed during that year for noncompliance."

§ 38.2-5801. General provisions. — A. No person shall operate an MCHIP in this Commonwealth unless the health carrier who directly or indirectly manages, owns, contracts with, or employs the providers for the plan is licensed in accordance with provisions in this title as an insurance company, a health maintenance organization, or a nonstock corporation organized in accordance with provisions in Chapter 42 (§ 38.2-4200 et seq.) or Chapter 45 (§ 38.2-4500 et seq.) of this title. Such health carrier shall be deemed responsible for the MCHIP and its compliance with this chapter and the provisions of Title 32.1 concerning quality assurance of MCHIPs. A health carrier may be responsible for more than one MCHIP; however, no MCHIP shall have more than one responsible health carrier.

B. Except as provided in subsection C, no person shall operate an MCHIP in this Commonwealth unless the health carrier responsible for the MCHIP holds an active or temporarily suspended certificate of quality assurance issued by the Department of Health.

C. 1. A health maintenance organization applying for licensure under this title on or after July 1, 1998, or whose application for such licensure is pending before the Commission on July 1, 1998, shall request its initial certificate of quality assurance prior to licensing and a copy of its request shall be included with and made a part of the licensing application and material filed with the Commission pursuant to § 38.2-4301 and subsection B of § 38.2-5802. Until July 1, 2000, (i) issuance of a license under § 38.2-4302 shall be contingent upon receipt of notice from the State Health Commissioner that the health maintenance organization's description of its complaint system has been reviewed and approved by the State Health Commissioner and (ii) upon issuance of the license such health maintenance organization shall be deemed in compliance with subsection B provided no certificate of quality assurance has been issued to the health maintenance organization which has been revoked or not renewed by the State Health Commissioner. Effective July 1, 2000, issuance of a license under § 38.2-4302 shall be contingent upon the Department of Health's issuance of a certificate of quality assurance.

2. Until July 1, 2000, a health maintenance organization licensed under this title on and before July 1, 1998, shall be deemed in compliance with the provisions of this section if (i) a request for initial certification has been filed with the Department of Health on or before December 1, 1998, and is pending before the State Health Commissioner and (ii) no certificate has been issued to the health maintenance organization which has been revoked or not renewed by the State Health Commissioner.

3. A health carrier, other than a health maintenance organization, responsible for an MCHIP pursuant to this chapter, shall request its initial certificate of quality assurance from the Department of Health on or before December 1, 1998, or becoming responsible for a MCHIP under this title. Until July 1, 2000, such health carrier shall be deemed in compliance with the provisions of this section if (i) a request for initial certification is pending before the Department

of Health and (ii) no certificate has been issued to the health carrier which has been revoked or not renewed by the State Health Commissioner.

D. The provisions of this chapter shall apply to all health carriers and all MCHIPs operating in this Commonwealth unless an exemption is recognized in accordance with § 38.2-3420; and, except as otherwise provided in this chapter, the provisions of this chapter shall be supplemental and in addition to those otherwise applicable under this title or Title 32.1. (1998, c. 891.)

§ 38.2-5802. Establishment of an MCHIP. — A. A health carrier, when applying for initial licensing under this title and with each request for renewal that is to be effective on or after July 1, 1999, shall describe and categorize generally its transactions and operations in this Commonwealth that influence the cost or level of health care services between the health carrier and one or more providers with respect to the delivery of health care services through its MCHIPs. Descriptions and categorization shall identify generally the arrangements that the health carrier has with providers with respect to the delivery of health care services. Descriptions of incentive arrangements shall include compensation methodology and incentives. The descriptions of incentive arrangements shall not include amounts of compensation and values of incentives. Renewal filings shall clearly identify new matter and material changes of information disclosed in the preceding filing.

B. A health carrier applying to the Department of Health for initial certification of quality assurance shall simultaneously file a copy of its request for certification with the Commission and shall include the list of providers required by § 38.2-5805. Such filings shall be assessed by the Department of Health.

C. In addition to items specified in subsection B, the initial filing under this chapter by a health carrier subject to subsection B of § 38.2-5801 shall include any forms of contracts, including any amendments thereto, made with health care providers enabling the health carrier to provide health care services through its MCHIPs to covered persons. Individual provider contracts and contracts with persons outside this Commonwealth shall not be filed with the Commission unless requested by the Commission or necessary to explain or fully disclose pursuant to subsection D operational changes that are materially at variance with the information currently on file with the Commission. The health carrier shall maintain a complete file of all contracts made with health care providers which shall be subject to examination by the Commission. The contracts shall be retained in the file for a period of at least five years after their expiration. Notwithstanding the provisions of Chapter 21 (§ 2.1-340 et seq.) of Title 2.1 of the Code of Virginia, such contracts shall be confidential and shall not be subject to discovery upon subpoena.

D. No MCHIP shall be operated in a manner that is materially at variance with the information submitted pursuant to this section. Any change in such information which would result in operational changes that are materially at variance with the information currently on file with the Commission shall be subject to the Commission's prior approval. If the Commission fails to act on a notice of material change within thirty days of its filing, the proposed changes shall be deemed approved. A material change in the MCHIP's health care delivery system shall be deemed to result in operational changes that are materially at variance with the information on file with the Commission. The Commission may determine that other changes are material and may require disclosure to secure full and accurate knowledge of the affairs and condition of the health carrier.

E. A health carrier shall give notice to the State Health Commissioner of the filings it makes with the Commission pursuant to this section.

F. The provisions of this section are applicable generally for all health carriers subject to licensure under this title. The provisions of this section shall be applied specifically as follows: (i) the provisions of subsection A are applicable for each health carrier requesting renewal of a license on or after July 1, 1998, and also for each health carrier applying for initial licensing on or after July 1, 1998; (ii) the provisions of subsection B shall be applied to any health carrier that files an application with the Department of Health for initial certification of quality assurance; (iii) the provisions of subsection C become applicable as soon as a health carrier makes a filing pursuant to this section; (iv) the filing requirements described in subsection D are applicable for all material filed with the Commission pursuant to this section, and shall be applied also when a health carrier proposes material changes to information of the type described in this section which previously had been filed with the Commission pursuant to provisions of Chapter 43 (§ 38.2-4300 et seq.) of this title; and (v) the provisions of subsection E are applicable whenever a health carrier makes a filing pursuant to this section. (1998, c. 891; 1999, c. 20.)

The 1999 amendment, in subsection C, inserted "a" preceding "period of at least" in the fourth sentence, and inserted "of the Code of Virginia" in the fifth sentence; and added a new subsection F.

§ **38.2-5803. Disclosures and representations to enrollees.** — A. The following shall be provided to the MCHIP's covered persons at the time of enrollment or at the time the contract or evidence of coverage is issued and shall be made available upon request or at least annually:

1. A list of the names and locations of all affiliated providers.

2. A description of the service area or areas within which the MCHIP shall provide health care services.

3. A description of the method of resolving complaints of covered persons, including a description of any arbitration procedure if complaints may be resolved through a specified arbitration agreement.

4. Notice that the MCHIP is subject to regulation in this Commonwealth by both the State Corporation Commission Bureau of Insurance pursuant to Title 38.2 and the Virginia Department of Health pursuant to Title 32.1.

B. The following shall apply to MCHIPs that require a covered person to select a primary care physician with respect to the offer of basic health care services by the MCHIP:

1. At the time of enrollment each covered person shall have the right to select a primary care physician from among the health carrier's affiliated primary care physicians for the MCHIP, subject to availability.

2. Any covered person who is dissatisfied with his primary care physician shall have the right to select another primary care physician from among the affiliated primary care physicians, subject to availability. The health carrier may impose a reasonable waiting period for this transfer. (1998, c. 891.)

§ **38.2-5804. Complaint system.** — A. A health carrier subject to subsection B of § 38.2-5801 shall establish and maintain for each of its MCHIPs a complaint system approved by the Commission and the State Health Commissioner to provide reasonable procedures for the resolution of written complaints in accordance with requirements in or established pursuant to provisions in this title and Title 32.1 and shall include the following:

1. A record of the complaints shall be maintained for no less than five years.

2. Such health carrier shall provide complaint forms and/or written procedures to be given to covered persons who wish to register written complaints. Such forms or procedures shall include the address and telephone number of the managed care licensee to which complaints shall be directed and the mailing address, telephone number, and electronic mail address of the Managed Care Ombudsman, and shall also specify any required limits imposed by

or on behalf of the MCHIP. Such forms and written procedures shall include a clear and understandable description of the covered person's right to appeal adverse decisions pursuant to § 32.1-137.15.

B. The Commission, in cooperation with the State Health Commissioner, shall examine the complaint system. The effectiveness of the complaint system of the managed care health insurance plan licensee in allowing covered persons, or their duly authorized representatives, to have issues regarding quality of care appropriately resolved under this chapter shall be assessed by the State Health Commissioner pursuant to provisions in Title 32.1 and the regulations promulgated thereunder. Compliance by the health carrier and its managed care health insurance plans with the terms and procedures of the complaint system, as well as the provisions of this title, shall be assessed by the Commission.

C. The health carrier for each MCHIP shall submit to the Commission and the State Health Commissioner an annual complaint report in a form prescribed by the Commission and the Board of Health. The complaint report shall include (i) a description of the procedures of the complaint system, (ii) the total number of complaints handled through the grievance or complaint system, (iii) the disposition of the complaints, (iv) a compilation of the nature and causes underlying the complaints filed, (v) the time it took to process and resolve each complaint, and (vi) the number, amount, and disposition of malpractice claims adjudicated during the year with respect to any of the MCHIP's affiliated providers.

D. The provisions of Chapter 5 (§ 38.2-500 et seq.) of this title shall apply to the health carrier, its MCHIPs, and evidence of coverage and representations thereto, except to the extent that the Commission determines that the nature of the health carrier, its MCHIP, and evidences of coverage and representations thereto render any of the provisions clearly inappropriate. (1998, c. 891; 1999, cc. 643, 649.)

The 1999 amendments. — The 1999 amendments by cc. 643 and 649 are identical, and, in subdivision A 2, in the second sentence, inserted "of the managed care licensee" and inserted "and the mailing address, telephone number, and electronic mail address of the Managed Care Ombudsman," and added the last sentence.

§ **38.2-5805. Provider contracts.** — A. Each health carrier subject to subsection B of § 38.2-5801 shall file with the Commission a list of the current providers who have executed a contract directly with the health carrier or indirectly through an intermediary organization for the purpose of providing health care services pursuant to an MCHIP or for the benefit of a covered person of an MCHIP. The list shall include the names and localities of the providers. The list shall be updated by the health carrier at least annually and more frequently as required by the Commission in accordance with provisions in this title or by the State Health Commissioner in accordance with provisions in Title 32.1.

B. Every contract with a provider of health care services enabling an MCHIP to provide health care services shall be in writing.

C. When the health carrier is a health maintenance organization, the contracts with providers enabling the MCHIP to provide health care services to the covered persons shall contain a "hold harmless" clause setting forth that, in the event such health carrier fails to pay for health care services as set forth in the contract, the covered persons shall not be liable to the provider for any sums owed by the health carrier. The following requirements shall apply to such contracts:

1. Such contracts shall require that if the provider terminates the agreement, the provider shall give the health carrier at least sixty days' advance notice of termination.

2. No provider party to such a contract, or agent, trustee or assignee thereof, may maintain any action at law against a covered person to collect sums owed by the health carrier.

3. If there is an intermediary organization enabling a health carrier subject to subsection B of § 38.2-5801 to provide health care services by means of the intermediary organization's own contracts with health care providers, the contracts between the intermediary organization and its providers shall be in writing.

4. The contracts shall set forth that, in the event either the health carrier or the intermediary organization fails to pay for health care services as set forth in the contracts between the intermediary organization and its providers, or in the contract between the intermediary organization and the health carrier, the covered person shall not be liable to the provider for any sums owed by either the intermediary organization or the health carrier.

5. No provider party to such a contract, or agent, trustee or assignee thereof, may maintain any action at law against a covered person to collect sums owed by the health carrier or the intermediary organization.

6. An agreement to provide health care services between an intermediary organization and a health carrier subject to subsection B of § 38.2-5801 shall require that if the intermediary organization terminates the agreement, the intermediary organization shall give the health carrier at least sixty days' advance notice of termination.

7. An agreement to provide health care services between an intermediary organization and a provider shall require that if the provider terminates the agreement, the provider shall give the intermediary organization at least sixty days' advance notice of termination.

8. Each such health carrier and intermediary organization shall be responsible for maintaining its executed contracts enabling it to provide health care services. These contracts shall be available for the Commission's review and examination for a period of five years after the expiration of any such contract.

9. The "hold harmless" clause required by this section shall read essentially as set forth in this subdivision. The health carrier may use a corresponding provision of different wording approved by the Commission that is not less favorable in any respect to the covered persons.

Hold Harmless Clause

[Provider] hereby agrees that in no event, including, but not limited to nonpayment by the MCHIP or its health carrier, the insolvency of the [health carrier], or breach of this agreement, shall [Provider] bill, charge, collect a deposit from; seek compensation, remuneration or reimbursement from; or have any recourse against subscribers or persons other than the health carrier for services provided pursuant to this Agreement. This provision shall not prohibit collection of any applicable copayments or deductibles billed in accordance with the terms of the subscriber agreement for the MCHIP.

[Provider] further agrees that (i) this provision shall survive the termination of this Agreement regardless of the cause giving rise to such termination and shall be construed to be for the benefit of the plan's subscribers and (ii) this provision supersedes any oral or written agreement to the contrary now existing or hereafter entered into between [Provider] and the subscriber or persons acting on the subscriber's behalf.

10. If there is an intermediary organization between the health carrier and the health care providers, the hold harmless clause set forth in subdivision 5 shall be amended to include nonpayment by the plan, the health carrier, and the intermediary organization and shall be included in any contract between the intermediary organization and health care providers and in any contract

between the health carrier on behalf of the MCHIP and the intermediary organization.

D. The Commission may specify for each type of health carrier other than a health maintenance organization the circumstances, if any, under which a health carrier for an MCHIP shall contract with a provider with the "hold harmless" clause described in subsection C. The Commission may specify also the extent to which certain accounting treatment, reserves, net worth or surplus shall be required for liabilities arising from provider contracts without the "hold harmless" clause. (1998, c. 891.)

§ 38.2-5806. Prohibited practices. — A. No MCHIP licensee may cancel or refuse to renew the coverage of a covered person for basic health care services on the basis of the status of the covered person's health.

B. The following provisions shall apply whenever an MCHIP provides a covered person who is also a resident of a continuing care facility with coverage for Medicare benefits and the covered person's primary care physician determines that it is medically necessary for the covered person to be referred to a skilled nursing unit:

1. The health carrier shall not require that the covered person relocate to a skilled nursing unit outside the continuing care facility if (i) the continuing care facility's skilled nursing unit is certified as a Medicare skilled nursing facility and (ii) the continuing care facility agrees, as to such skilled nursing unit, to become a contracting provider in accordance with the health carrier's standard terms and conditions for its participating providers.

2. A continuing care facility that satisfies clauses (i) and (ii) of subdivision 1 shall not be obligated to accept as a skilled nursing unit patient any one other than a resident of the continuing care facility; and neither the health carrier nor the continuing care facility shall be allowed to include the skilled nursing unit or facilities on the list required by § 38.2-5802 or to advertise in any other way that the facility's skilled nursing unit is a participating provider with respect to coverage offered by the MCHIP for Medicare benefits or skilled nursing unit facilities for other than the continuing care facility's residents.

As used in this subsection, "Medicare benefits" means medical and health products, benefits and services offered in accordance with Title XVIII of the United States Social Security Act (42 U.S.C. § 1395 et seq.) and "continuing care facility" means a continuing care retirement community regulated pursuant to Chapter 49 (§ 38.2-4900 et seq.) of this title.

C. The following shall apply in accordance with provisions in Title 32.1 or regulations promulgated thereunder:

1. Where complaints of a covered person may be resolved through a specified arbitration agreement, the covered person shall be advised in writing of his rights and duties under the agreement at the time the complaint is registered.

2. No contract or evidence of coverage that entitles covered persons to resolve complaints through an arbitration agreement shall limit or prohibit such arbitration for any claims asserted having a monetary value of $250 or more.

3. If the covered person agrees to binding arbitration, his written acceptance of the arbitration agreement shall not be executed prior to the time the complaint is registered nor subsequent to the time an initial resolution is made, and the agreement shall be accompanied by a statement setting forth in writing the terms and conditions of binding arbitration. (1998, c. 891.)

§ 38.2-5807. Access to care. — Access to care shall be assessed by the Department of Health in accordance with provisions in Article 1.1 (§ 32.1-137.1 et seq.) of Chapter 5 of Title 32.1 concerning quality assurance. (1998, c. 891.)

§ 38.2-5808. Examinations. — A. In lieu of or in addition to making its own examination of an MCHIP and its health carrier, the Commission may accept the report of an examination of the health carrier or other person responsible for the MCHIP under the laws of another state certified by the insurance supervisory official, similar regulatory agency, or the state health commissioner of another state.

B. The Commission shall coordinate examinations of an MCHIP and its health carrier with the State Health Commissioner's examination or review of the health carrier to ensure an appropriate level of regulatory oversight and to avoid any undue duplication of effort or regulation.

C. The Commission shall accept a current certificate of quality assurance issued by the Department of Health as evidence of compliance by the certificate holder with any provision in this chapter authorizing or requiring assessment by the Department of Health, by the State Health Commissioner, or pursuant to regulations promulgated by the State Health Commissioner. (1998, c. 891.)

§ 38.2-5809. Suspension or revocation of license. — The Commission may suspend or revoke any license issued to a health carrier if it finds that any of the following conditions exist:

1. The State Health Commissioner certifies to the Commission pursuant to § 32.1-137.5 that the health carrier or its MCHIP is unable to fulfill its obligations to furnish quality health care services as set forth in Article 1.1 (§ 32.1-137.1 et seq.) of Chapter 5 of Title 32.1. The suspension of a certificate of quality assurance shall not be deemed such a certification by the State Health Commissioner.

2. The State Health Commissioner notifies the Commission that the health carrier has failed to implement the complaint system required by Title 32.1 and § 38.2-5804 to resolve valid complaints reasonably.

3. The Commission determines that a certificate of quality assurance issued to the health carrier has been revoked by the State Health Commissioner, or a request for renewal of such certificate has been denied or disapproved by the State Health Commissioner. (1998, c. 891.)

§ 38.2-5810. Statutory construction and relationship to other laws. — A. Neither the health carrier nor the MCHIP shall be deemed to be engaged in the practice of medicine solely by virtue of its compliance with this chapter. All health care providers associated with an MCHIP shall be subject to all provisions of law.

B. Notwithstanding the definition of an eligible employee as set forth in § 38.2-3431, a health carrier providing an MCHIP subject to § 38.2-3431 shall not be required to offer coverage to or accept applications from an employee who does not reside within the MCHIP's service area. (1998, c. 891.)

§ 38.2-5811. Controversies involving contracts. — The Commission shall have no jurisdiction to adjudicate controversies between an MCHIP and its covered persons, and a breach of contract shall not be deemed a violation of this chapter. (1998, c. 891.)

CHAPTER 59.

INDEPENDENT EXTERNAL REVIEW OF ADVERSE UTILIZATION REVIEW DECISIONS.

§ 38.2-5900. Application of chapter; definitions.

— This chapter shall apply to all utilization review entities established pursuant to Article 1.2 (§ 32.1-137.7 et seq.) of Chapter 5 of Title 32.1. The definitions in § 32.1-137.7 shall have the same meanings ascribed to them in § 32.1-137.7 when used in this chapter. (1999, cc. 643, 649.)

Effective date. — This section is effective July 1, 1999.

§ 38.2-5901. (Delayed effective date — See note) Review by the Bureau of Insurance.

— A. A covered person or a treating health care provider, with the consent of the covered person, may in accordance with this section appeal to the Bureau of Insurance for review of any final adverse decision concerning a health service costing more than $500, determined in accordance with regulations adopted by the Commission. The appeal shall be filed within thirty days of the final adverse decision, shall be in writing on forms prescribed by the Bureau of Insurance, shall include a general release executed by the covered person for all medical records pertinent to the appeal, and shall be accompanied by a fifty-dollar nonrefundable filing fee. The fee shall be collected by the Commission and paid directly into the state treasury and credited to the fund for the maintenance of the Bureau of Insurance as provided in subsection B of § 38.2-400. The Commission may, for good cause shown, waive the filing fee upon a finding that payment of the filing fee will cause undue financial hardship for the covered person. The Bureau of Insurance shall provide a copy of the written appeal to the utilization review entity which made the final adverse decision.

B. The Bureau of Insurance or its designee shall conduct a preliminary review of the appeal to determine (i) whether the applicant is a covered person or a treating health care provider with the consent of the covered person, (ii) whether the benefit or service that is the subject of the application reasonably appears to be a covered service costing more than $500, (iii) whether all complaint and appeal procedures available under Article 1.2 (§ 32.1-137.7 et seq.) of Chapter 5 of Title 32.1 have been exhausted, and (iv) whether the application is otherwise complete and filed in compliance with this section. Such preliminary review shall be conducted within five working days of receipt of all information and documentation necessary to conduct a preliminary review. The Bureau of Insurance shall not accept for review any application which fails to meet the criteria set forth in this subsection. Within three working days of completion of the preliminary review, the Bureau of Insurance or its designee shall notify the applicant and the utilization review entity in writing whether the appeal has been accepted for review, and if not accepted, the reasons therefor.

C. The covered person, the treating health care provider, and the utilization review entity shall provide copies of the medical records relevant to the final adverse decision to the Bureau of Insurance within ten working days after the Bureau of Insurance has mailed written notice of its acceptance of the appeal. The confidentiality of such medical records shall be maintained in accordance with the confidentiality and disclosure laws of the Commonwealth. The Bureau of Insurance or its designee may, if deemed necessary, request additional medical records from the covered person, any treating health care provider or the utilization review entity. Failure to comply with such request within ten working days from the date of such request may result in dismissal of the appeal or reversal of the final adverse decision in the discretion of the Commissioner of Insurance.

D. The Commissioner of Insurance, upon good cause shown, may provide an extension of time for the covered person, the treating health care provider, the utilization review entity and the Commission to meet the established time requirements set forth in this section. (1999, cc. 643, 649.)

Editor's note. — Acts 1999, cc. 643 and 646, cl. 3, provides: "This act shall take effect on July 1, 1999; however, the appeal processes set forth in Chapter 59 of Title 38.2 of this act shall not take effect until the earlier of (i) ninety days following the promulgation of regulations by the State Corporation Commission as set forth in § 38.2-5905 or (ii) July 1, 2000."

§ 38.2-5902. (Delayed effective date — See note) Appeals; impartial health entity. — A. The Bureau of Insurance shall contract with one or more impartial health entities for the purpose of performing the review of final adverse decisions. The Commission shall adopt regulations to assure that the impartial health entity conducting the review has adequate standards, credentials and experience for such review. The impartial health entity shall examine the final adverse decision to determine whether the decision is objective, clinically valid, compatible with established principles of health care, and appropriate under the terms of the contractual obligations to the covered person. The impartial health entity shall review the written appeal; the response of the utilization review entity; any affidavits which either the covered person, the treating health care provider, or the utilization review entity may file with the Bureau of Insurance; and such medical records as the impartial health entity shall deem appropriate. The impartial health entity shall issue its written recommendation affirming, modifying or reversing the final adverse decision within thirty working days of the acceptance of the appeal by the Bureau of Insurance. The Commissioner of Insurance, based upon such recommendation, shall issue a written ruling affirming, modifying or reversing the final adverse decision. Such written ruling shall not be construed as a final finding, order or judgment of the Commission, and shall be exempt from the application of the Administrative Process Act (§ 9-6.14:1 et seq.). The Commissioner's written ruling shall carry out the recommendations of the impartial health entity unless the impartial health entity exceeded its authority or acted arbitrarily or capriciously. The written ruling of the Commissioner shall bind the covered person and the issuer of the covered person's policy or contract for health benefits to the extent to which each would have been obligated by a judgment entered in an action at law or in equity with respect to the issues which the impartial review entity may examine when reviewing a final adverse decision under this section. The impartial health entity shall not be affiliated or a subsidiary of, nor owned or controlled by, a health plan, a trade association of health plans, or a professional association of health care providers.

B. The Bureau of Insurance shall contract with one or more impartial health entities such as medical peer review organizations and independent utilization review companies. Prior to assigning an appeal to an impartial health entity, the Bureau of Insurance shall verify that the impartial health entity conducting the review of a final adverse decision has no relationship or association with (i) the utilization review entity, or any officer, director or manager of such utilization review entity, (ii) the covered person, (iii) the treating health care provider, or any of its employees or affiliates, (iv) the medical care facility at which the covered service would be provided, or any of its employees or affiliates, or (v) the development or manufacture of the drug, device, procedure or other therapy which is the subject of the final adverse decision. The impartial health entity shall not be a subsidiary of, nor owned or controlled by, a health plan, a trade association of health plans, or a professional association of health care providers.

C. There shall be no liability on the part of and no cause of action shall arise against any officer or employee of an impartial health entity for any actions taken or not taken or statements made by such officer or employee in good faith in the performance of his powers and duties.

D. Any managed care health insurance plan licensee that is required to provide previously denied services as a result of the review by the impartial health entity shall be subject to payment of such fees as the Commission shall deem appropriate to cover the costs of the review. (1999, cc. 643, 649.)

Editor's note. — Acts 1999, cc. 643 and 646, cl. 3, provides: "This act shall take effect on July 1, 1999; however, the appeal processes set forth in Chapter 59 of Title 38.2 of this act shall not take effect until the earlier of (i) ninety days following the promulgation of regulations by the State Corporation Commission as set forth in § 38.2-5905 or (ii) July 1, 2000."

§ 38.2-5903. (Delayed effective date — See note) Assessment to fund appeals. — A. Each licensed insurer writing insurance as defined in § 38.2-109, each health maintenance organization organized in accordance with the provisions of Chapter 43 (§ 38.2-4300 et seq.), and each nonstock corporation organized in accordance with the provisions of Chapter 42 (§ 38.2-4200 et seq.) or Chapter 45 (§ 38.2-4500 et seq.) shall pay, in addition to any other assessments provided in this title, an assessment in an amount not to exceed 0.015 percent of the direct gross premium income for such insurance written during the preceding calendar year. The assessment shall be apportioned and assessed and paid as prescribed by § 38.2-403.

B. The assessments made by the Commission under subsection A and paid into the state treasury shall be deposited to a special fund designated "Bureau of Insurance Special Fund—State Corporation Commission," and out of such special fund and the unexpended balance thereof shall be appropriated the sums necessary for the regulation, supervision and examination of all entities subject to regulation under this title. (1999, cc. 643, 649.)

Editor's note. — Acts 1999, cc. 643 and 646, cl. 3, provides: "This act shall take effect on July 1, 1999; however, the appeal processes set forth in Chapter 59 of Title 38.2 of this act shall not take effect until the earlier of (i) ninety days following the promulgation of regulations by the State Corporation Commission as set forth in § 38.2-5905 or (ii) July 1, 2000."

§ 38.2-5904. Office of the Managed Care Ombudsman established; responsibilities. — A. The Office of the Managed Care Ombudsman is hereby created within the Bureau of Insurance. The Managed Care Ombudsman shall promote and protect the interests of covered persons under managed health insurance plans in the Commonwealth. All state agencies shall assist and cooperate with the Managed Care Ombudsman in the performance of his duties under this chapter. The definitions in § 32.1-137.7 shall have the same meanings ascribed to them in § 32.1-137.7 when used in this section.

B. The Managed Care Ombudsman shall:

1. Assist covered persons in understanding their rights and the processes available to them according to their managed health insurance plan.

2. Answer inquiries from covered persons and other citizens by telephone, mail, electronic mail and in person.

3. Provide to covered persons and other citizens information concerning managed care health insurance plans and other utilization review entities upon request.

4. Develop information on the types of managed health insurance plans available in the Commonwealth, including mandated benefits and utilization review procedures and appeals.

5. Make available, either separately or through an existing Internet website utilized by the Bureau of Insurance, information as set forth in subdivision 4 and such additional information as he deems appropriate.

6. In conjunction with complaint and inquiry data maintained by the Bureau of Insurance, maintain data on inquiries received, the types of assistance requested, any actions taken and the disposition of each such matter.

7. Upon request, assist covered persons in using the procedures and processes available to them from their managed health insurance plan, including all utilization review appeals. Such assistance may require the review of insurance and health care records of a covered person, which shall be done only with that person's express written consent. The confidentiality of any such medical records shall be maintained in accordance with the confidentiality and disclosure laws of the Commonwealth.

8. Ensure that covered persons have access to the services provided through the Office and that the covered persons receive timely responses from the representatives of the Office to the inquiries.

9. Provide assessments of proposed and existing managed care health insurance laws and other studies of managed care health insurance plan issues upon request by any of the standing committees of the General Assembly having jurisdiction over insurance or health or the Joint Commission on Health Care.

10. Monitor changes in federal and state laws relating to health insurance.

11. Report annually on his activities to the standing committees of the General Assembly having jurisdiction over insurance and over health and the Joint Commission on Health Care by December 1 of each year, which report shall include a summary of significant new developments in federal and state laws relating to health insurance each year.

12. Carry out activities as the Commission determines to be appropriate. (1999, cc. 643, 649.)

Effective date. — This section is effective July 1, 1999.

§ **38.2-5905. Regulations.** — The Commission shall promulgate regulations effectuating the purpose of this chapter. Such regulations shall include (i) provisions for expedited consideration of appeals in cases involving emergency health care and (ii) standards, credentials and qualifications for impartial health entities. (1999, cc. 643, 649.)

Editor's note. — Acts 1999, cc. 643 and 649, cl. 2, provides: "That the State Corporation Commission shall promulgate the first set of regulations to implement the provisions of Chapter 59 of Title 38.2 of this act to be effective within 280 days of the enactment of this provision."

Effective date. — This section is effective July 1, 1999.

Title 39.
Justices of the Peace.

[Repealed.]

§§ 39-1 through 39-13: Repealed by Acts 1968, c. 639.

Cross references. — For present provisions
as to magistrates, see §§ 19.2-26 through 19.2-
48.1.

Title 39.1.

Justices of the Peace.

[Repealed.]

§§ 39.1-1 through 39.1-25: Repealed by Acts 1973, c. 545.

Cross references. — For present provisions as to magistrates, see §§ 19.2-26 through 19.2-48.1.

Title 40.

Labor and Employment.

[Repealed.]

§§ 40-1 through 40-146: Repealed by Acts 1970, c. 321.

Cross references. — As to repeal of Title 40, enactment of Title 40.1, and transition provisions, see notes under § 40.1-1.

Title 40.1.

Labor and Employment.

Chap. 1. Department of Labor and Industry, §§ 40.1-1 through 40.1-11.1.

CHAPTER 1.

DEPARTMENT OF LABOR AND INDUSTRY.

§ 40.1-1. Department continued; powers and duties generally; delegation of authority concerning occupational health. — The Department of Labor and Industry, hereinafter referred to as the Department, is continued as a department of the state government; the Department shall be responsible for discharging the provisions of Title 40.1. All powers and duties conferred and imposed on the Bureau of Labor and Industry by any other law are hereby conferred upon and vested in the Department of Labor and Industry. The Department shall be responsible for administering and enforcing occupational safety and occupational health activities as required by the Federal Occupational Safety and Health Act of 1970 (P.L. 91-596), in accordance with the state plan for enforcement of that act; however, nothing in the occupational safety and health provisions of this title or regulations adopted hereunder shall apply to working conditions of employees or duties of employers with respect to which the Federal Occupational Safety and Health Act of 1970 does not apply by virtue of § 4 (b) (1) of the federal act. (Code 1950, § 40-1; 1962, c. 66; 1970, c. 321; 1972, c. 567; 1973, c. 425; 1979, c. 354; 1984, c. 590; 1985, c. 449; 1995, c. 373.)

Cross references. — As to the Migrant and Seasonal Farmworkers Board, see §§ 9-149 through 9-152.

Editor's note. — At its regular session of 1968 the General Assembly directed the Code Commission to revise certain titles of the Code, including Title 40, relating to labor and employment. In August of 1969 the Commission sent to the Governor and General Assembly its report containing the proposed revision of Title 40, which was published as House Document 4 of the 1970 session. This report contains revisor's notes and other explanatory matter which, while valuable, are too lengthy for inclusion here. The Commission's draft of the revision of Title 40, as amended by the General Assembly, became chapter 321 of the Acts of 1970. It repeals Title 40 of the Code and enacts in lieu thereof a new Title 40.1. As required by § 9-77.11, the Code Commission has incorporated in Title 40.1 the amendments to Title 40 enacted at the 1970 session of the General Assembly.

Some of the cases cited in the notes under the various sections of this title were decided under corresponding provisions of former law.

The term "this act of the General Assembly", as used in this section, was added by Acts 1973, c. 425.

Transition provisions. — Acts 1970, c. 321, §§ 2-5, provide as follows:

"2. All acts and parts of acts, all sections of the Code of Virginia, and all provisions of municipal charters inconsistent with the provisions of this act are, except as otherwise provided, repealed to the extent of such inconsistency.

"3. The repeal of Title 40 effective October 1, 1970, shall not affect any act or offense done or committed, or any penalty or forfeiture incurred, or any right established, accrued or accruing on or before such date, or any prosecu-

tion, suit or action pending on that date. Except as in this act otherwise provided, neither the repeal of Title 40 nor the enactment of Title 40.1 shall apply to offenses committed prior to October 1, 1970, and prosecutions for such offenses shall be governed by the prior law, which is continued in effect for that purpose. For the purposes of this act, an offense was committed prior to October 1, 1969, if any of the essential elements of the offense occurred prior thereto.

"4. Whenever in Title 40.1 any of the conditions, requirements, provisions or contents of any section, article or chapter of Title 40 as such title existed prior to October 1, 1970, are transferred in the same or in modified form to a new section, article or chapter of Title 40.1 and whenever any such former section, article or chapter of Title 40 is given a new number in Title 40.1, all references to any such former section, article or chapter of Title 40 appearing in the Code of Virginia shall be construed to apply to the new and renumbered section, article or chapter containing such conditions, requirements, provisions or contents or portions thereof.

"5. It is the intention of the General Assembly that this act shall be liberally construed to effect the purposes set out herein, and if any clause, sentence, paragraph or section of this act shall ever be declared unconstitutional, it shall be deemed severable, and the remainder of this act shall continue in full force and effect."

Law Review. — For article, "Labor Law in Virginia," see 25 Wash. & Lee L. Rev. 193 (1968). For survey of Virginia administrative law and utility regulation for the year 1978-1979, see 66 Va. L. Rev. 193 (1980). For series of articles on testing for drug abuse in the workplace, see 12 Geo. Mason L. Rev. 491 et seq. (1990).

§ 40.1-2. Definitions. — As used in this title, unless the context clearly requires otherwise, the following terms have the following meanings:

"Board" means the Safety and Health Codes Board.

"Department" means the Department of Labor and Industry.

"Commissioner" means the Commissioner of Labor and Industry.

"Commission" means the Safety and Health Codes Board.

"Employer" means an individual, partnership, association, corporation, legal representative, receiver, trustee, or trustee in bankruptcy doing business in or operating within this Commonwealth who employs another to work for wages, salaries, or on commission and shall include any similar entity acting directly or indirectly in the interest of an employer in relation to an employee.

"Employee" means any person who, in consideration of wages, salaries or commissions, may be permitted, required or directed by any employer to engage in any employment directly or indirectly.

"Business establishment" means any proprietorship, firm or corporation where people are employed, permitted or suffered to work, including agricultural employment on a farm.

"Female" or *"woman"* means a female eighteen years of age or over.

"Machinery" means machines, belts, pulleys, motors, engines, gears, vats, pits, elevators, conveyors, shafts, tunnels, including machinery being operated on farms in connection with the production or harvesting of agricultural products.

"Employ" shall include to permit or suffer to work. (Code 1950, § 40-1.1; 1962, c. 66; 1966, c. 90; 1970, c. 321; 1972, c. 567; 1973, c. 425; 1985, c. 448.)

Law Review. — For article, "The Law of Wrongful Discharge in Virginia," see 10 Geo. Mason L. Rev. 133 (1988).

Children Labor Law directed at employment for compensation. — The definitions in this section indicate strongly that the statutes included within the Child Labor Law are directed toward employment for compensation. Lovisi v. Commonwealth, 212 Va. 848, 188 S.E.2d 206, cert. denied, 407 U.S. 922, 92 S. Ct. 2469, 32 L. Ed. 2d 808 (1972).

Applied in Makarov v. Commonwealth, 217 Va. 381, 228 S.E.2d 573 (1976).

§ 40.1-2.1. Application of title to Commonwealth and its agencies, etc.; safety and health program for public employees. — The provisions of this title and any rules and regulations promulgated pursuant thereto shall not apply to the Commonwealth or any of its agencies, institutions, or political subdivisions, or any public body, unless, and to the extent that, coverage is extended by specific regulation of the Commissioner or the Safety and Health Codes Board. The Commissioner is authorized to establish and maintain an effective and comprehensive occupational safety and health program applicable to employees of the Commonwealth, its agencies, institutions, political subdivisions, or any public body. Such program shall be subject to any State plan submitted to the federal government for State enforcement of the Federal Occupational Safety and Health Act of 1970 (P.L. 91-596), or any other regulation promulgated under Title 40.1. The Commissioner shall establish procedures for enforcing the program which shall include provisions for fair hearings including judicial review and sanctions to be applied for violations. (1973, c. 425.)

§ 40.1-3. Title provides for safety, health and welfare of employees. — The provisions of this title are intended to provide solely for the safety, health and welfare of employees and the benefits thereof shall not run to any other person nor shall a third party have any right of action for breach of any provision of this title except as herein otherwise specifically provided. (Code 1950, § 40-1.2; 1962, c. 66; 1970, c. 321.)

§ 40.1-4: Repealed by Acts 1984, c. 734.

Cross references. — For section requiring the Department to submit an annual report to the Governor and the General Assembly, see now § 40.1-4.1.

§ 40.1-4.1. Annual report. — The Department shall submit an annual report to the Governor and General Assembly which contains statistical information derived from its programs and activities. The annual report shall be distributed in accordance with the provisions of § 2.1-467. (1984, c. 734.)

§ 40.1-5. Governor to appoint Commissioner of Labor and Industry. — The Governor shall appoint, by and with the consent of the General Assembly, some suitable person identified with the labor interests of the Commonwealth, who shall be designated Commissioner of Labor and Industry. The Commissioner shall, upon the request of the Governor, furnish such information as he may require. The Commissioner shall serve at the pleasure of the Governor for a term coincident with that of the Governor. (Code 1950, § 40-3; 1962, c. 66; 1970, c. 321; 1978, c. 372.)

§ 40.1-6. Powers and duties of Commissioner. — The Commissioner shall:

(1) Have general supervision and control of the Department.

(2) Enforce the provisions of this title and shall cause to be prosecuted all violations of law relating to employers or business establishments before any court of competent jurisdiction.

(3) Make such rules and regulations as may be necessary for the enforcement of this title and procedural rules as are required to comply with the Federal Occupational Safety and Health Act of 1970 (P.L. 91-596). All such rules and regulations shall be subject to Chapter 1.1:1 (§ 9-6.14:1 et seq.) of Title 9.

(4) In the discharge of his duties, have power to take and preserve testimony, examine witnesses and administer oaths and to file a written or printed list of relevant interrogatories and require full and complete answers to the same to be returned under oath within thirty days of the receipt of such list of questions.

(5) Have power to appoint such representatives as may be necessary to aid him in his work; their duties shall be prescribed by the Commissioner.

(6) [Repealed.]

(7) Have power to require that accident, injury and occupational illness records and reports be kept at any place of employment and that such records and reports be made available to the Commissioner or his duly authorized representatives upon request. Further, he may require employers to develop, maintain and make available such other records and information as are deemed necessary for the proper enforcement of this title.

(8) Have power, upon presenting appropriate credentials to the owner, operator, or agent in charge:

(a) To enter without delay and at reasonable times any business establishment, construction site, or other area, workplace or environment where work is performed by an employee of any employer in this Commonwealth; and

(b) To inspect and investigate during regular working hours and at other reasonable times, and within reasonable limits and in a reasonable manner, without prior notice, unless such notice is authorized by the Commissioner or his representative, any such business establishment or place of employment and all pertinent conditions, structures, machines, apparatus, devices, equipment, and materials therein, and to question privately any such employer, officer, owner, operator, agent, or employee. If such entry or inspection is refused, prohibited or otherwise interfered with, the Commissioner shall have power to seek from a court having equity jurisdiction an order compelling such entry or inspection.

(9) Make rules and regulations governing the granting of temporary or permanent variances from all standards promulgated by the Board under this title. Any interested or affected party may appeal to the Board, the Commissioner's determination to grant or deny such a variance. The Board may, as it sees fit, adopt, modify or reject the determination of the Commissioner.

(10) All information reported to or otherwise obtained by the Commissioner, the Board or the agents or employees of either which contains or might reveal a trade secret shall be confidential and shall be limited to those persons who need such information for purposes of enforcement of this title. The Commissioner shall have authority to issue orders to protect the confidentiality of such information. Violations of such orders shall be punishable as civil contempt upon application to the Circuit Court of the City of Richmond. It shall be the duty of each employer to notify the Commissioner, or his representatives, of the existence of trade secrets where he desires the protection provided herein.

(11) Serve as executive officer of the Virginia Safety and Health Codes Board

and of the Apprenticeship Council and see that the rules, regulations and policies that they promulgate are carried out.

(12) Establish the Interagency Migrant Worker Policy Committee, comprised of representatives from state agencies, including the Virginia Workers' Compensation Commission, whose services and jurisdictions involve migrant and seasonal farmworkers and their employees. The committee shall coordinate its activities with the Migrant and Seasonal Farmworkers Board established in § 9-149. (Code 1950, § 40-4; 1962, c. 66; 1970, c. 321; 1972, c. 567; 1973, c. 425; 1984, cc. 590, 734; 1987, c. 165; 1997, c. 919; 1998, c. 97.)

Editor's note. — Acts 1995, c. 120, cl. 1, provides: "The Commissioner of the Department of Labor and Industry shall issue certificates of completion to individuals completing apprenticeship programs within the Commonwealth that are (i) registered with the Bureau of Apprenticeship Training, United States Department of Labor, and (ii) sponsored by the United States military installations within the Commonwealth closed or scheduled for closure under the federal Defense Base Closure and Realignment Act of 1990, as amended."

Acts 1997, c. 919, cl. 2, provides: "That the membership of the Interagency Migrant Worker Policy Committee, created pursuant to executive order, as it exists on the effective date of this act [July 1, 1997], shall be transferred to the Interagency Migrant Worker Policy Committee created by this act."

The 1998 amendment, in subdivision 11, deleted "shall" preceding "see that the rules," and in subdivision 12, in the first sentence, substituted "Establish the" for "Establish an," and inserted "including the Virginia Workers' Compensation Commission."

Law Review. — For article, "Enforcement of Occupational Safety and Health Laws in Virginia: A New Beginning," see 12 U. Rich. L. Rev. 535 (1978).

§ 40.1-7. Attorney for the Commonwealth to prosecute on request of Commissioner. — The attorney for the Commonwealth of the proper county or city, upon the request of the Commissioner, or any of his authorized representatives, shall prosecute any violation of law or rule or regulation adopted thereunder which it is made the duty of the Commissioner to enforce. (Code 1950, § 40-5; 1962, c. 66; 1970, c. 321.)

§ 40.1-8. Other officers to furnish information. — All State, county, town and city officers shall furnish the Commissioner, upon his request, such statistical or other information as may be in their possession as such officers which will assist the Department in the discharge of its duties. (Code 1950, § 40-6; 1962, c. 66; 1970, c. 321.)

§ 40.1-9. How Department maintained. — The Department shall be maintained from such appropriations as the General Assembly may make for the purpose. The compensation of the Commissioner and of all other employees of the Department shall be fixed and paid in accordance with law. (Code 1950, § 40-7; 1962, c. 66; 1970, c. 321.)

§ 40.1-10. Offenses in regard to examinations, inspections, etc. — If any person who may be sworn to give testimony shall willfully fail or refuse to answer any legal and proper question propounded to him concerning the subject of such examination as indicated in § 40.1-6, or if any person to whom a written or printed list of such interrogatories has been furnished by the Commissioner shall neglect or refuse to answer fully and return the same under oath, or if any person in charge of any business establishment shall refuse admission to, or obstruct in any manner the inspection or investigation of such establishment or the proper performance of the authorized duties of the Commissioner or any of his representatives, he shall be guilty of a misdemeanor. Such person, upon conviction thereof, shall be fined not exceeding $100 nor less than $25 or imprisoned in jail not exceeding 90 days, or both. (Code 1950, § 40-8; 1962, c. 66; 1970, c. 321.)

Law Review. — For article, "Enforcement of Occupational Safety and Health Laws in Virginia: A New Beginning," see 12 U. Rich. L. Rev. 535 (1978).

§ 40.1-11. Using or revealing information gathered.

— Neither the Commissioner nor any employee of the Department shall make use of or reveal any information or statistics gathered from any person, company or corporation for any purposes other than those of this title. (Code 1950, § 40-9; 1962, c. 66; 1970, c. 321; 1984, c. 590.)

§ 40.1-11.1. Employment of illegal immigrants.

— It shall be unlawful and constitute a Class 1 misdemeanor for any employer or any person acting as an agent for an employer, or any person who, for a fee, refers an alien who cannot provide documents indicating that he or she is legally eligible for employment in the United States for employment to an employer, or an officer, agent or representative of a labor organization to knowingly employ, continue to employ, or refer for employment any alien who cannot provide documents indicating that he or she is legally eligible for employment in the United States.

Permits issued by the United States Department of Justice authorizing an alien to work in the United States shall constitute proof of eligibility for employment.

All employment application forms used by State and local governments and privately owned businesses operating in the Commonwealth on and after January 1, 1978, shall ask prospective employees if they are legally eligible for employment in the United States.

The provisions of this section shall not be deemed to require any employer to use employment application forms. (1977, c. 438; 1979, c. 472.)

Cross references. — As to punishment for Class 1 misdemeanors, see § 18.2-11.

Law Review. — For survey of Virginia commercial law for the year 1976-77, see 63 Va. L. Rev. 1377 (1977).

CHAPTER 2.

EMPLOYMENT AGENCIES.

§§ 40.1-12 through 40.1-21: Repealed by Acts 1978, c. 840.

Cross references. — For present provisions as to employment agencies, see § 54.1-1300 et seq. See also the Editor's note under § 54.1-1300.

CHAPTER 3.

PROTECTION OF EMPLOYEES.

ARTICLE 1.

General Provisions.

§ 40.1-22. Safety and Health Codes Commission continued as Safety and Health Codes Board. — (1) The Safety and Health Codes Commission is continued and shall hereafter be known as the Safety and Health Codes Board. The Board shall consist of fourteen members, twelve of whom shall be appointed by the Governor. One member shall, by reason of previous vocation, employment or affiliation, be chosen to represent labor in the manufacturing industry; one member shall, by reason of previous vocation, employment or affiliation, be chosen to represent labor in the construction industry; one member shall, by reason of previous vocation, employment or affiliation, be chosen to represent industrial employers; one member shall be chosen from and be a representative of the general public; one member shall be a representative of agricultural employers; one member shall, by reason of previous vocation, employment or affiliation, be chosen to represent agricultural employees; one member shall, by reason of previous vocation, employment or affiliation, be chosen to represent construction industry employers; one member shall be a representative of an insurance company; one member shall be a labor representative from the boiler pressure vessel industry; one member shall be a labor representative knowledgeable in chemicals and toxic substances; one member shall be an employer representative of the boiler pressure vessel industry; one member shall be an industrial representative knowledgeable in chemical and toxic substances, and the Director of the Department of Environmental Quality or his duly authorized representative shall be a member ex officio with full membership status. The Commissioner of Health or his duly authorized representative shall also be a member ex officio with full membership status.

(2) The first appointive members shall be appointed as follows: one for a term of four years, one for a term of three years, one for a term of two years, and one for a term of one year. Of the members appointed to represent the construction industry, one shall be appointed for the term of two years and one shall be appointed for the term of four years. Succeeding appointments shall be for terms of four years each but other vacancies shall be filled by appointment for the unexpired term.

(3) The Board shall annually select a chairman from its members. The Board shall meet at least once every six months; other meetings may be held upon call of the chairman or any three members of the Board. Five members of the Board shall constitute a quorum.

(4) The Board shall study and investigate all phases of safety in business establishments, the application of this title thereto, and shall serve as advisor to the Commissioner.

(5) The Board, with the advice of the Commissioner, is hereby authorized to adopt, alter, amend, or repeal rules and regulations to further, protect and promote the safety and health of employees in places of employment over which it has jurisdiction and to effect compliance with the Federal Occupational Safety and Health Act of 1970 (P.L. 91-596), and as may be necessary to carry out its functions established under this title. The Commissioner shall enforce such rules and regulations. All such rules and regulations shall be designed to protect and promote the safety and health of such employees. In making such rules and regulations to protect the occupational safety and health of employees, the Board shall adopt the standard which most adequately assures, to the extent feasible, on the basis of the best available evidence, that no employee will suffer material impairment of health or functional capacity. However, such standards shall be at least as stringent as

the standards promulgated by the Federal Occupational Safety and Health Act of 1970 (P.L. 91-596). In addition to the attainment of the highest degree of health and safety protection for the employee, other considerations shall be the latest available scientific data in the field, the feasibility of the standards, and experience gained under this and other health and safety laws. Whenever practicable, the standard promulgated shall be expressed in terms of objective criteria and of the performance desired. Such standards when applicable to products which are distributed in interstate commerce shall be the same as federal standards unless deviations are required by compelling local conditions and do not unduly burden interstate commerce.

(6) Chapter 1.1:1 (§ 9-6.14:1 et seq.) of Title 9 shall apply to the adoption of rules and regulations under this section and to proceedings before the Board.

(6a) The Board shall provide, without regard to the requirements of Chapter 1.1:1 (§ 9-6.14:1 et seq.) of Title 9, for an emergency temporary standard to take immediate effect upon publication in a newspaper of general circulation, published in the City of Richmond, Virginia, if it determines that employees are exposed to grave danger from exposure to substances or agents determined to be toxic or physically harmful or from new hazards, and that such emergency standard is necessary to protect employees from such danger. The publication mentioned herein shall constitute notice that the Board intends to adopt such standard within a period of six months. The Board by similar publication shall prior to the expiration of six months give notice of the time and date of, and conduct a hearing on, the adoption of a permanent standard. The emergency temporary standard shall expire within six months or when superseded by a permanent standard, whichever occurs first, or when repealed by the Board.

(7) Any person who may be adversely affected by a standard issued under this title may challenge the validity of such standard in the Circuit Court of the City of Richmond by declaratory judgment. The determination of the Safety and Health Codes Board shall be conclusive if supported by substantial evidence in the record considered as a whole. Adoption of a federal occupational safety and health standard shall be deemed to be sufficient evidence to support promulgation of such standard. The filing of a petition for declaratory judgment shall not operate as a stay of the standard unless the court issues a preliminary injunction. (Code 1950, § 40-20; 1962, c. 66; 1968, c. 272; 1970, cc. 321, 649; 1972, c. 567; 1973, c. 425; 1974, c. 195; 1976, c. 607; 1979, c. 656; 1980, c. 728; 1984, c. 590; 1985, c. 448; 1987, c. 165; 1988, c. 467.)

Cross references. — As to compensation and expenses of boards, commissions and similar bodies, see §§ 2.1-20.2 through 2.1-20.4.

Law Review. — For article, "Enforcement of Occupational Safety and Health Laws in Virginia: A New Beginning," see 12 U. Rich. L. Rev. 535 (1978). For note on employee drug testing, see 74 Va. L. Rev. 969 (1988). For article, "State Criminal Prosecutions: Putting Teeth in the Occupational Safety and Health Act," see 12 Geo. Mason L. Rev. 737 (1990).

Constitutionality. — Subsection (5) of this section contains sufficient legislative standards and limitations to direct the board in the exercise of the authority delegated to it by the legislature. Accordingly, the judgment of the trial court holding this subsection unconstitutional was reversed. Bell v. Dorey Elec. Co., 248

Va. 378, 448 S.E.2d 622 (1994).

Duty of employer in preventing hazards. — An employer need not take steps to prevent hazards which are not generally foreseeable, including idiosyncratic behavior of an employee, but at the same time an employer must do all it feasibly can to prevent foreseeable hazards. Floyd S. Pike Elec. Contractor v. Commissioner, Dep't of Labor & Indus., 222 Va. 317, 281 S.E.2d 804 (1981).

Safety regulations governing installation of electrical transmission lines were not designed to make the employer an insurer of an employee's safety. A safe workplace is not necessarily risk-free. Floyd S. Pike Elec. Contractor v. Commissioner, Dep't of Labor & Indus., 222 Va. 317, 281 S.E.2d 804 (1981).

§ 40.1-22.1. Governor authorized to enter certain agreements. — The Governor of Virginia is hereby authorized to enter into:

1. Such agreements with the United States Occupational Safety and Health Administration as are necessary to provide training for the employees of the Virginia Department of Labor and Industry and other appropriate agencies of the Commonwealth to assist in the enforcement of Public Law 91-596.

2. Reciprocal agreements with the appropriate authorities of any state within the United States and of the District of Columbia, with respect to the collection of claims for wages and other demands upon claims filed with the Department of Labor and Industry. (1976, c. 607; 1997, c. 282.)

Law Review. — For article, "Enforcement of Occupational Safety and Health Laws in Virginia: A New Beginning," see 12 U. Rich. L. Rev. 535 (1978).

§§ 40.1-23 through 40.1-25.1: Repealed by Acts 1988, c. 340, effective January 1, 1989.

§ 40.1-26: Repealed by Acts 1979, c. 631.

§ 40.1-27. Preventing employment by others of former employee. — No person doing business in this Commonwealth, or any agent or attorney of such person after having discharged any employee from the service of such person or after any employee shall have voluntarily left the service of such person shall willfully and maliciously prevent or attempt to prevent by word or writing, directly or indirectly, such discharged employee or such employee who has voluntarily left from obtaining employment with any other person. For violation of this section the offender shall be guilty of a misdemeanor and shall, on conviction thereof, be fined not less than $100 nor more than $500. But this section shall not be construed as prohibiting any person from giving on application for any other person a truthful statement of the reason for such discharge, or a truthful statement concerning the character, industry and ability of such person who has voluntarily left. (Code 1950, § 40-22; 1970, c. 321.)

Law Review. — For note, "Erosion of the Employment-at-Will Doctrine: Recognition of an Employee's Right to Job Security," see 43 Wash. & Lee L. Rev. 593 (1986). For comment, "Potential Employer Liability for Employee References," see 21 U. Rich. L. Rev. 427 (1987). For article, "The Law of Wrongful Discharge in Virginia," see Geo. Mason L. Rev. 133 (1988).

This section establishes criminal penalties for willful and malicious prevention of employment by others of former employee. Haigh v. Matsushita Elec. Corp. of Am., 676 F. Supp. 1332 (E.D. Va. 1987).

§ 40.1-27.1. Discharge of employee for absence due to work-related injury prohibited. — It shall be an unfair employment practice for an employer who has established an employment policy of discharging employees who are absent from work for a specified number of days to include in the computation of an employee's work absence record any day that such employee is absent from work due to a compensable absence under Title 65.2; provided, that such compensable absences can be calculated into an employee's work record for purposes of discharge after all steps of the excessive absenteeism policy have been exhausted. An employer shall not be held in violation of this section if the employee's absence exceeds six months or if the employer's circumstances have changed during such employee's absence so as to make it impossible or unreasonable not to discharge such employee. (1989, c. 572.)

Law Review. — For survey on employment law in Virginia for 1989, see 23 U. Rich. L. Rev. 607 (1989).

§ 40.1-28. Unlawful to require payment for medical examination as condition of employment.

— It shall be unlawful for any employer to require any employee or applicant for employment to pay the cost of a medical examination or the cost of furnishing any medical records required by the employer as a condition of employment.

Any employer who violates the provisions of this section shall be subject to a civil penalty not to exceed $100 for each violation. A penalty determination by the Commissioner shall be final, unless within fifteen days after receipt of such notice the person charged with the violation notifies the Commissioner by certified mail that he intends to contest the proposed penalty before the appropriate general district court.

Civil penalties owed under this section shall be paid to the Commissioner for deposit into the general fund of the Treasury of the Commonwealth. The Commissioner shall prescribe procedures for the payment of proposed penalties which are not contested by employers. (Code 1950, § 40-22.1; 1952, c. 525; 1962, c. 66; 1970, c. 321; 1973, c. 425; 1982, c. 84.)

Cross references. — For provisions as to enforcement of this title and rules and regulations adopted pursuant thereto, and penalties for violations, see § 40.1-49.4.

§ 40.1-28.1. Employers to allow employees at least one day of rest in each week.

— Except in an emergency, every employer shall allow each person employed by him in connection with any business or service at least twenty-four consecutive hours of rest in each calendar week in addition to the regular periods of rest normally allowed or legally required in each working day. (1974, c. 330.)

§ 40.1-28.2. Employees entitled to choose Sunday as day of rest.

— Every nonmanagerial person employed by any employer shall, as a matter of right, be entitled to choose Sunday as a day of rest in accordance with § 40.1-28.1 and upon the filing of written notice by the employee with the employer that such employee chooses Sunday as a day of rest, no employer shall, in any manner, discharge, discipline or penalize such employee for exercising his rights under this section and the provisions of this section may not be waived on an application for employment. (1974, c. 330.)

§ 40.1-28.3. Employees entitled to choose Saturday as day of rest.

— Any nonmanagerial employee who conscientiously believes that the seventh day of the week ought to be observed as a Sabbath, and actually refrains from all secular business and labor on that day, shall be entitled to choose the seventh day of the week as his day of rest in accordance with § 40.1-28.1 and upon the filing of written notice by the employee with the employer that such employee chooses the seventh day of the week as a day of rest, no employer shall, in any manner, discharge, discipline or penalize such employee for exercising his rights under this section. (1974, c. 330.)

§ 40.1-28.4. Penalties for violation of §§ 40.1-28.1 through 40.1-28.3; investigations.

— Any employer who violates §§ 40.1-28.1, 40.1-28.2 or § 40.1-28.3 shall be guilty of a misdemeanor and shall, upon conviction thereof, be fined not less than $250 nor more than $500 for each offense. Moreover, in the event such employer compels a nonmanagerial employee to work on his chosen day of rest in violation of the heretofore stated sections, such employer shall be liable to such employee for wages at the rate of three times the employee's regular rate of pay for all hours worked by such employee on his chosen day of rest.

Nothing contained herein shall be construed to permit any fine or penalty against any supervisory employee or agent who has been caused, directed or authorized by his employer to violate any provision of the heretofore stated sections, in which case the employer shall be subject to the sanctions prescribed by this section.

The Commissioner of Labor and Industry shall be authorized to conduct investigations of possible violations and thereafter, if compliance is not achieved, report any findings to the appropriate attorney for the Commonwealth. (1974, c. 330; 1975, c. 70.)

§ 40.1-28.5. Exceptions to application of §§ 40.1-28.1 through 40.1-28.4. — The provisions of §§ 40.1-28.1 through 40.1-28.4 shall not apply to persons engaged in any of the industries or businesses enumerated in § 18.2-341 A (1) through (19), except (15). (1974, c. 330; 1978, c. 193.)

§ 40.1-28.6. Equal pay irrespective of sex. — No employer having employees shall discriminate, within any establishment in which such employees are employed, between employees on the basis of sex by paying wages to employees in such establishment at a rate less than the rate at which he pays wages to employees of the opposite sex in such establishment for equal work on jobs the performance of which requires equal skill, effort, and responsibility, and which are performed under similar working conditions, except where such payment is made pursuant to (i) a seniority system; (ii) a merit system; (iii) a system which measures earnings by quantity or quality of production; or (iv) a differential based on any other factor other than sex.

For purposes of administration and enforcement, any amounts owing to any employee which have been withheld in violation of this section shall be deemed to be unpaid wages or unpaid overtime compensation and the employee whose wages have been wrongfully withheld in violation of this section shall have a right of action therefor to recover damages to the extent of two times the amount of wages so withheld.

This section shall not apply to employers covered by the Fair Labor Standards Act of 1938 as amended. Every action under this section shall be brought within two years next after the right to bring the same shall have accrued; provided, however, that nothing herein shall be construed to give rise to a cause of action for work performed prior to July 1, 1974. (1974, c. 405.)

The number of this section was assigned by the Virginia Code Commission, the number in the 1974 act having been 40.1-28.1.

Law Review. — For article, "The Status of the At-Will Employment Doctrine in Virginia after Bowman v. State Bank of Keysville," see 20 U. Rich. L. Rev. 267 (1986). For article, "The Law of Wrongful Discharge in Virginia," see 10 Geo. Mason L. Rev. 133 (1988).

Applicability. — This section deals only with equal pay for equal work and was not applicable to an action alleging not unequal pay but a discriminatory discharge. Barlow v. AVCO Corp., 527 F. Supp. 269 (E.D. Va. 1981).

§ 40.1-28.7: Repealed by Acts 1985, c. 421.

Cross references. — For present provisions as to remedies for the violation of rights of disabled persons, see § 51.5-46.

ARTICLE 1.1.

Virginia Minimum Wage Act.

§ 40.1-28.8. Short title. — This article shall be known as the Virginia Minimum Wage Act. (1975, c. 530.)

The numbers of §§ 40.1-28.8 through 40.1-28.12 were designated by the Virginia Code Commission, the numbers in the 1975 act having been 40.1-28.7 through 40.1-28.11.

§ 40.1-28.9. Definition of terms. — As used in this article:

A. *"Employer"* includes any individual, partnership, association, corporation, business trust, or any person or groups of persons acting directly or indirectly in the interest of an employer in relation to an employee;

B. *"Employee"* includes any individual employed by an employer, except the following:

1. Any person employed as a farm laborer or farm employee;

2. Any person employed in domestic service or in or about a private home or in an eleemosynary institution primarily supported by public funds;

3. Any person engaged in the activities of an educational, charitable, religious or nonprofit organization where the relationship of employer-employee does not, in fact, exist, or where the services rendered to such organizations are on a voluntary basis;

4. Newsboys, shoe-shine boys, caddies on golf courses, babysitters, ushers, doormen, concession attendants and cashiers in theaters;

5. Traveling salesmen or outside salesmen working on a commission basis; taxicab drivers and operators;

6. Any person under the age of eighteen in the employ of his father, mother or legal guardian;

7. Any person confined in any penal, corrective or mental institution of the State or any of its political subdivisions;

8. Any person employed by a boys' and/or girls' summer camp;

9. Any person under the age of sixteen, regardless of by whom employed;

10. Any person who normally works and is paid based on the amount of work done;

11. Any person who shall have reached his or her sixty-fifth birthday;

12. Any person whose employment is covered by the Fair Labor Standards Act of 1938 as amended;

13. Any person whose earning capacity is impaired by physical or mental deficiency;

14. Students and apprentices participating in a bona fide educational or apprenticeship program;

15. Any person employed by an employer who does not have four or more persons employed at any one time; provided that husbands, wives, sons, daughters and parents of the employer shall not be counted in determining the number of persons employed;

16. Any person who is less than eighteen years of age and who is currently enrolled on a full-time basis in any secondary school, institution of higher education or trade school, provided the person is not employed more than twenty hours per week;

16A. Any person of any age who is currently enrolled on a full-time basis in any secondary school, institution of higher education or trade school and is in a work-study program or its equivalent at the institution at which he or she is enrolled as a student;

17. Any person who is less than eighteen years of age and who is under the jurisdiction and direction of a juvenile and domestic relations district court.

C. *"Wages"* means legal tender of the United States or checks or drafts on banks negotiable into cash on demand or upon acceptance at full value; provided, wages may include the reasonable cost to the employer of furnishing meals and for lodging to an employee, if such board or lodging is customarily furnished by the employer, and used by the employee.

D. In determining the wage of a tipped employee, the amount paid such employee by his employer shall be deemed to be increased on account of tips by an amount determined by the employer, except in the case of an employee who establishes by clear and convincing evidence that the actual amount of tips received by him was less than the amount determined by the employer. In such case, the amount paid such employee by his employer shall be deemed to have been increased by such lesser amount. (1975, c. 530; 1976, c. 442; 1977, c. 432.)

Editor's note. — Acts 1993, c. 930, cl. 3, as amended by Acts 1994, c. 564, cl. 2, and Acts 1996, c. 616, c. 4, provides that the amendment to this section by Acts 1993, c. 930, cl. 1, shall become effective June 1, 1998, "if state funds are provided, including all local costs, to carry out the purposes of this bill by the General Assembly." The funding was not provided.

§ 40.1-28.10. Minimum wages. — Every employer shall pay to each of his employees wages at a rate not less than the federal minimum wage and a training wage as prescribed by the U.S. Fair Labor Standards Act (29 U.S.C. § 201 et seq.) (1975, c. 530; 1976, c. 736; 1978, c. 371; 1980, c. 532; 1991, cc. 547, 596; 1997, c. 544.)

§ 40.1-28.11. Penalties. — Whoever knowingly and intentionally violates any provisions of this article shall be punished by a fine of not less than $10 nor more than $200. (1975, c. 530.)

§ 40.1-28.12. Employee's remedies. — Any employer who violates the minimum wage requirements of this law shall be liable to the employee or employees affected in the amount of the unpaid minimum wages, plus interest at eight per centum per annum upon such unpaid wages as may be due the plaintiff, said interest to be awarded from the date or dates said wages were due the employee or employees. The court may, in addition to any judgment awarded to the employee or employees, require defendant to pay reasonable attorney's fees incurred by the employee or employees. (1975, c. 530.)

ARTICLE 2.

Pay; Assignment of Wages; Sale of Merchandise to Employees.

§ 40.1-29. Time and medium of payment; withholding wages; written statement of earnings; agreement for forfeiture of wages; penalty for violation of section; proceedings to enforce compliance. — A. 1. All employers operating a business shall establish regular pay periods and rates of pay for employees except executive personnel. All such employers shall pay salaried employees at least once each month and employees paid on an hourly rate at least once every two weeks or twice in each month, except that a student who is currently enrolled in a work-study program or its equivalent administered by any secondary school, institution of higher education or trade school may be paid once each month if the institution so chooses. Upon termination of employment an employee shall be paid all wages or salaries due him for work performed prior thereto; such payment shall be made on or before the date on which he would have been paid for such work had his employment not been terminated.

2. Any such employer who knowingly fails to make payment of wages in accordance with subsection A of this section shall be subject to a civil penalty

not to exceed $1,000 for each violation. The Commissioner shall notify any employer who he alleges has violated any provision of this section by certified mail. Such notice shall contain a description of the alleged violation. Within fifteen days of receipt of notice of the alleged violation, the employer may request an informal conference regarding such violation with the Commissioner. In determining the amount of any penalty to be imposed, the Commissioner shall consider the size of the business of the employer charged and the gravity of the violation. The decision of the Commissioner shall be final.

B. Payment of wages or salaries shall be (i) in lawful money of the United States, (ii) by check payable at face value upon demand in lawful money of the United States or (iii) by electronic automated fund transfer in lawful money of the United States into an account in the name of the employee at a financial institution designated by the employee.

Failure of the employee to designate a financial institution shall require payment of wages and salaries to be made in accordance with (i) or (ii) of this subsection.

C. No employer shall withhold any part of the wages or salaries of any employee except for payroll, wage or withholding taxes or in accordance with law, without the written and signed authorization of the employee. An employer, upon request of his employee, shall furnish the latter a written statement of the gross wages earned by the employee during any pay period and the amount and purpose of any deductions therefrom.

D. No employer shall require any employee, except executive personnel, to sign any contract or agreement which provides for the forfeiture of the employee's wages for time worked as a condition of employment or the continuance therein, except as otherwise provided by law.

E. An employer who willfully and with intent to defraud violates this section shall be guilty of a misdemeanor.

F. The Commissioner may require a written complaint of the violation of this section and, with the written and signed consent of an employee, may institute proceedings on behalf of an employee to enforce compliance with this section, and to collect any moneys unlawfully withheld from such employee which shall be paid to the employee entitled thereto. In addition, following the issuance of a final order by the Commissioner cr a court, the Commissioner may engage private counsel, approved by the Attorney General, to collect any moneys owed to the employee or the Commonwealth. Upon entry of a final order of the Commissioner, or upon entry of a judgment, against the employer, the Commissioner or the court shall assess attorney's fees of one-third of the amount set forth in the final order or judgment.

G. In addition to being subject to any other penalty provided by the provisions of this section, any employer who fails to make payment of wages in accordance with subsection A of this section shall be liable for the payment of all wages due, plus interest at an annual rate of eight percent accruing from the date the wages were due.

H. Civil penalties owed under this section shall be paid to the Commissioner for deposit into the general fund of the State Treasurer. The Commissioner shall prescribe procedures for the payment of proposed assessments of penalties which are not contested by employers. Such procedures shall include provisions for an employer to consent to abatement of the alleged violation and pay a proposed penalty or a negotiated sum in lieu of such penalty without admission of any civil liability arising from such alleged violation.

Final orders of the Commissioner, the general district courts or the circuit courts may be recorded, enforced and satisfied as orders or decrees of a circuit court upon certification of such orders by the Commissioner or the court as appropriate. (Code 1950, § 40-24; 1962, c. 66; 1966, c. 88; 1968, c. 262; 1970, c. 321; 1972, c. 848; 1977, c. 308; 1979, c. 50; 1989, c. 583; 1991, c. 499; 1993, c. 600.)

Cross references. — For statute relating to employee trusts, see § 55-13.1.

Law Review. — For survey of Virginia criminal law for the year 1976-77, see 63 Va. L. Rev. 1396 (1977). For survey on employment law in Virginia for 1989, see 23 U. Rich. L. Rev. 607 (1989).

Constitutionality. — Prior to the 1977 amendment to this section, which inserted "willfully and with intent to defraud" in former subsection (d), this section on its face dealt with a naked civil debt and there was no indication that the General Assembly implicitly meant to include proof of an intent to defraud as an essential element of the offense. For these reasons the second sentence of former subsection (a) and former subsection (d) were held unconstitutional. Makarov v. Commonwealth, 217 Va. 381, 228 S.E.2d 573 (1976).

Applied in Terry v. Gordon's Jewelry Co., 7 Bankr. 880 (Bankr. E.D. Va. 1980).

§ **40.1-30. Registration of certain nonresident employers with Department.** — (a) Any employer domiciled without this Commonwealth and performing any demolition, excavation, installation, paving, repair, maintenance, erection or construction work within this Commonwealth for a fixed price, commission, fee or percentage, when the cost of the undertaking, order, contract or subcontract is not less than $300 nor more than $60,000, shall, prior to the commencement of each such undertaking or the performance of each such order, contract or subcontract, register with the Department, at Richmond, on such form as may be prescribed by said Department, providing thereon the employer's name and address, the name and address of the employer's chief officer or owner, the name and address of the person in charge of the work being done, the type of work to be done, the date work will commence, the specific location of the work, the name of the person, firm, corporation, partnership or association for whom the work is being performed, the cost of the undertaking or the amount of the order, contract or subcontract and the approximate number of persons employed by the employer in said undertaking or performance, including the rates of pay and the number of persons employed at each rate and shall be submitted to the Department with a United States postal service money order or check drawn in favor of the State Treasurer in the amount of $100 for annual registration or $25 for registration for a specific job. Provided, however, nothing in this section shall apply to any such contractor who is registered under the provisions of Title 54.1, Chapter 11. Provided further, that any such employer may apply to the Department for annual registration which, if granted, shall relieve such employer from registration of each specific contract. Annual registration may be granted if the Department shall ascertain that such employer has a permanent and definite place of business outside this Commonwealth.

(b) Any employer failing to register with the Department as required by this section shall be guilty of a misdemeanor and upon conviction shall be fined not less than $100 nor more than $500. Each day's failure to register shall constitute a separate offense.

(c) This section shall be enforceable by the Commissioner and all officers empowered to enforce the criminal laws of this Commonwealth. (Code 1950, § 40-24.1; 1966, c. 614; 1968, c. 106; 1970, c. 321; 1972, c. 241; 1979, c. 484.)

§ **40.1-31. Assignment of wages and salaries; requirements.** — No assignment, transfer, pledge or hypothecation of wages or salary due or to become due to any person shall be valid and enforceable against any employer of the assignor, except with the express consent in writing of such employer given to the creditor or assignee, unless and until all of the following requirements have been fully met:

(1) Such assignment is printed in type not smaller than pica, is a separate instrument not incorporated in or made a part of any other contract or instrument, and is plainly designated "Wage Assignment."

(2) Such assignment is executed in triplicate and in person by the assignor, is dated on the date on which it is executed, one executed copy thereof is

delivered to the assignor, and one executed copy is mailed to the employer therein named within fifteen days after the execution thereof; provided, however, that such copy mailed to the employer shall be for his information only, and shall not be construed as giving such employer legal notice of the assignee's intention to enforce the terms thereof or as constituting the notice referred to in § 8.01-13.

(3) The name of employer of the assignor is written therein before the signing thereof and the total amount, if any, which is to be secured thereby is plainly stated therein.

(4) The assignor is, at the time of the execution of the assignment, employed by the employer therein named.

(5) Ten days before any notice of the assignee's intention to enforce the terms of the assignment is served upon the employer, the assignee gives the assignor notice in writing sent by mail to his last known address that default has been made in his obligation.

(6) Notice of the assignee's intention to enforce the terms of an assignment has been served on the employer by an officer or other person authorized to serve civil process. Such notice shall be valid to make the assignment effective only from the time it is served.

(7) Whenever the assignor changes his employment after executing an assignment contemplated by this section then any assignee who has otherwise fully complied with the provisions of this section may enforce his assignment against the new employer of the assignor provided that he mails a copy of the assignment to the new employer within fifteen days after learning of such change of employment and gives the same notice or notices to the new employer as is required to be given to the original employer and complies with the conditions of subdivision (5) hereof. (Code 1950, § 40-30; 1970, c. 321.)

Cross references. — As to validity of assignment of earnings to satisfy or retire support debt or obligation, see § 63.1-272.

Law Review. — For article, "Uniform Consumer Credit Code—A Prospect for Consumer Credit Reform in Virginia," see 28 Wash. & Lee L. Rev. 75 (1971).

This section is confined to wages or salary due or to become due by any employer. Knight v. Peoples Nat'l Bank, 182 Va. 380, 29 S.E.2d 364 (1944).

Its application is optional with the employer. — The application of this section, making unenforceable against any employer any assignment of wages or salary except with the consent of the employer, is optional with the employer. Knight v. Peoples Nat'l Bank, 182 Va. 380, 29 S.E.2d 364 (1944).

And its dominant purpose is the protection of his interest rather than the protection of the interest of the employee. Knight v. Peoples Nat'l Bank, 182 Va. 380, 29 S.E.2d 364 (1944).

It was not intended as a weapon for another creditor of the assignor to fight his way to a more favorable position in line of payment. Knight v. Peoples Nat'l Bank, 182 Va. 380, 29 S.E.2d 364 (1944).

The unearned salary or wages of municipal and state employees can be assigned if, at the time of the assignment, the assignor be employed, although it may not be necessary that his employment be for any particular time. Knight v. Peoples Nat'l Bank, 182 Va. 380, 29 S.E.2d 364 (1944).

A municipality is not an employer of a tax assessor appointed by a court, within the meaning of this section. Knight v. Peoples Nat'l Bank, 182 Va. 380, 29 S.E.2d 364 (1944).

§ 40.1-32. Partial assignments invalid. — No partial assignment of wages shall be enforceable at law or in equity; provided, however, that an assignment of all wages over and above the exemption provided in § 34-29 shall not be considered a partial assignment under the provisions of this section. (Code 1950, § 40-31; 1970, c. 321.)

Cross references. — As to validity of assignment of earnings to satisfy or retire support debt or obligation, see § 63.1-272.

§ 40.1-33. Certain assignments not affected. — The two preceding sections (§§ 40.1-31, 40.1-32) shall not be construed to apply to assignments of salaries, wages and income for the benefit of creditors as provided for in §§ 55-161 to 55-167. (Code 1950, § 40-32; 1970, c. 321.)

Cross references. — As to validity of assignment of earnings to satisfy or retire support debt or obligation, see § 63.1-272.

ARTICLE 3.

Employment of Women Generally.

§§ 40.1-34 through 40.1-38: Repealed by Acts 1974, c. 272.

ARTICLE 4.

Sanitary Provisions.

§ 40.1-39: Repealed by Acts 1979, c. 354.

§ 40.1-40: Repealed by Acts 1985, c. 449.

ARTICLE 5.

Safety Provisions.

§§ 40.1-41 through 40.1-43: Repealed by Acts 1979, c. 354.

§ 40.1-44: Repealed by Acts 1973, c. 425.

§ 40.1-44.1. Rules and regulations relating to tramways and other hauling and lifting devices. — (a) The Safety and Health Codes Board in the adoption of rules and regulations under this title shall adopt such reasonable rules and regulations as are designed to protect the safety and health of the employees engaged in the construction, maintenance, repair and operation of tramways or any other hauling or lifting device used as a public or employee conveyance, and to protect the safety and health of the public or the employees when using such conveyance in, about, or in connection with recreational areas, excluding vehicular travel covered by ICC, SCC, motor vehicle codes and §§ 40.1-128 through 40.1-134.

(b) The rules and regulations adopted by the Safety and Health Codes Board pursuant to subsection (a) of this section shall be enforced as specified in §§ 40.1-49.3 through 40.1-49.7. (1972, c. 602; 1973, c. 425; 1979, c. 406.)

Editor's note. — Sections 40.1-128 through 40.1-134, referred to in subsection (a), were repealed by Acts 1991, c. 152.

§§ 40.1-45 through 40.1-48: Repealed by Acts 1979, c. 354.

§ 40.1-49: Repealed by Acts 1973, c. 425.

Cross references. — For present provisions as to enforcement of this title and rules and regulations adopted pursuant thereto, and penalties for violations, see § 40.1-49.4.

§ 40.1-49.1: Repealed by Acts 1976, c. 607.

Cross references. — For present provisions covering the subject matter of the repealed section, see § 40.1-49.4.

§ 40.1-49.2: Repealed by Acts 1979, c. 354.

Cross references. — For present section covering the subject matter of the repealed section, see § 40.1-49.4.

§ 40.1-49.3. Definitions. — For the purposes of §§ 40.1-49.4, 40.1-49.5, 40.1-49.6, 40.1-49.7, and 40.1-51.1 through 40.1-51.3 the following terms shall have the following meanings:

"Commission" means the Virginia Workers' Compensation Commission.

"Commissioner" means the Commissioner of Labor and Industry. Except where the context clearly indicates the contrary, any reference to Commissioner shall include his authorized representatives.

"Employee" means an employee of an employer who is employed in a business of his employer.

"Employer" means any person or entity engaged in business who has employees, but does not include the United States.

"Occupational safety and health standard" means a standard which requires conditions, or the adoption or use of one or more practices, means, methods, operations, or processes, reasonably necessary or appropriate to provide safe or healthful employment and places of employment.

"Serious violation" means a violation deemed to exist in a place of employment if there is a substantial probability that death or serious physical harm could result from a condition which exists, or from one or more practices, means, methods, operations, or processes which have been adopted or are in use, in such place of employment unless the employer did not, and could not with the exercise of reasonable diligence, know of the presence of the violation.

"Person" means one or more individuals, partnerships, associations, corporations, business trusts, legal representatives, or any organized group of persons.

"Circuit court" means the circuit court of the city or county wherein the violation of this title or any standard, rule or regulation issued pursuant thereto is alleged to have occurred. Venue shall be determined in accordance with the provisions of §§ 8.01-257 through 8.01-267. (1979, c. 354; 1992, c. 777.)

Law Review. — For survey of Virginia administrative law and utility regulation for the year 1978-1979, see 66 Va. L. Rev. 193 (1980).

Applied in Floyd S. Pike Elec. Contractor v. Commissioner, Dep't of Labor & Indus., 222 Va. 317, 281 S.E.2d 804 (1981).

§ 40.1-49.4. Enforcement of this title and standards, rules or regulations for safety and health; orders of Commissioner; proceedings in circuit court; injunctions; penalties. — A. 1. If the Commissioner has reasonable cause to believe that an employer has violated any safety or health provision of Title 40.1 or any standard, rule or regulation adopted pursuant thereto, he shall with reasonable promptness issue a citation to the employer. Each citation shall be in writing and shall describe with particularity the nature of the violation or violations, including a reference to the provision of this title or the appropriate standards, rules or regulations adopted pursuant thereto, and shall include an order of abatement fixing a reasonable time for abatement of each violation.

2. The Commissioner may prescribe procedures for calling to the employer's attention de minimis violations which have no direct or immediate relationship to safety and health.

3. No citation may be issued under this section after the expiration of six months following the occurrence of any alleged violation.

4. (a) The Commissioner shall have the authority to propose civil penalties for cited violations in accordance with subsections G, H, I, and J of this section. In determining the amount of any proposed penalty he shall give due consideration to the appropriateness of the penalty with respect to the size of the business of the employer being charged, the gravity of the violation, the good faith of the employer, and the history of previous violations. In addition, the Commissioner shall have authority to assess interest on all past-due penalties and administrative costs incurred in the collection of penalties for such violations consistent with § 2.1-732.

(b) After, or concurrent with, the issuance of a citation and order of abatement, and within a reasonable time after the termination of an inspection or investigation, the Commissioner shall notify the employer by certified mail or by personal service of the proposed penalty or that no penalty is being proposed. The proposed penalty shall be deemed to be the final order of the Commissioner and not subject to review by any court or agency unless, within fifteen working days from the date of receipt of such notice, the employer notifies the Commissioner in writing that he intends to contest the citation, order of abatement or the proposed penalty or the employee or representative of employees has filed a notice in accordance with subsection B of this section and any such notice of proposed penalty, citation or order of abatement shall so state.

B. Any employee or representative of employees of an employer to whom a citation and order of abatement has been issued may, within fifteen working days from the time of the receipt of the citation and order of abatement by the employer, notify the Commissioner, in writing, that they wish to contest the abatement time before the circuit court.

C. If the Commissioner has reasonable cause to believe that an employer has failed to abate a violation for which a citation has been issued within the time period permitted for its abatement, which time shall not begin to run until the entry of a final order in the case of any contest as provided in subsection E of this section initiated by the employer in good faith and not solely for delay or avoidance of penalties, a citation for failure to abate will be issued to the employer in the same manner as prescribed by subsection A of this section. In addition, the Commissioner shall notify the employer by certified mail or by personal service of such failure and of the penalty proposed to be assessed by reason of such failure. If, within fifteen working days from the date of receipt of the notice of the proposed penalty, the employer fails to notify the Commissioner that he intends to contest the citation or proposed assessment of penalty, the citation and assessment as proposed shall be deemed a final order of the Commissioner and not subject to review by any court or agency.

D. Civil penalties owed under this section shall be paid to the Commissioner for deposit into the general fund of the Treasurer of the Commonwealth. The Commissioner shall prescribe procedures for the payment of proposed assessments of penalties which are not contested by employers. Such procedures shall include provisions for an employer to consent to abatement of the alleged violation and pay a proposed penalty or a negotiated sum in lieu of such penalty without admission of any civil liability arising from such alleged violation.

Final orders of the Commissioner or the circuit courts may be recorded, enforced and satisfied as orders or decrees of a circuit court upon certification of such orders by the Commissioner or the court as appropriate.

E. Upon receipt of a notice of contest of a citation, proposed penalty, order of abatement or abatement time pursuant to subdivision A 4 (b), subsection B or C of this section, the Commissioner shall immediately notify the attorney for the Commonwealth for the jurisdiction wherein the violation is alleged to have occurred and shall file with the circuit court a bill of complaint. Upon issuance and service of a subpoena in chancery, the circuit court shall promptly set the matter for hearing without a jury. The circuit court shall thereafter issue a written order, based on findings of fact and conclusions of law, affirming, modifying or vacating the Commissioner's citation or proposed penalty, or directing other appropriate relief, and such order shall become final twenty-one days after its issuance. The circuit court shall provide affected employees or their representatives and employers an opportunity to participate as parties to hearings under this subsection.

F. 1. In addition to the remedies set forth above, the Commissioner may file a bill of complaint with the clerk of the circuit court having equity jurisdiction over the employer or the place of employment involved asking the court to temporarily or permanently enjoin any conditions or practices in any place of employment which are such that a danger exists which could reasonably be expected to cause death or serious physical harm immediately or before the imminence of such danger can be eliminated through the enforcement procedures otherwise provided by this title. Any order issued under this section may require such steps to be taken as may be necessary to avoid, correct or remove such imminent danger and prohibit the employment or presence of any individual in locations or under conditions where such imminent danger exists, except individuals whose presence is necessary to avoid, correct or remove such imminent danger or to maintain the capacity of a continuous process operation to resume normal operations without a complete cessation of operations, or where a cessation of operations is necessary, to permit such to be accomplished in a safe and orderly manner. No order issued without prior notice to the employer shall be effective for more than five working days. Whenever and as soon as the Commissioner concludes that conditions or practices described in this subsection exist in any place of employment and that judicial relief shall be sought, he shall immediately inform the affected employer and employees of such proposed course of action.

2. Any court described in this section shall also have jurisdiction, upon petition of the Commissioner or his authorized representative, to enjoin any violations of this title or the standards, rules or regulations promulgated thereunder.

3. If the Commissioner arbitrarily or capriciously fails to seek relief under subdivision 1 of this subsection, any employee who may be injured by reason of such failure, or the representative of such employee, may bring an action against the Commissioner in a circuit court of competent jurisdiction for a writ of mandamus to compel the Commissioner to seek such an order and for such further relief as may be appropriate.

G. Any employer who has received a citation for a violation of any safety or health provision of this title or any standard, rule or regulation promulgated pursuant thereto and such violation is specifically determined not to be of a serious nature may be assessed a civil penalty of up to $7,000 for each such violation.

H. Any employer who has received a citation for a violation of any safety or health provision of this title or any standard, rule or regulation promulgated pursuant thereto and such violation is determined to be a serious violation shall be assessed a civil penalty of up to $7,000 for each such violation.

I. Any employer who fails to abate a violation for which a citation has been issued within the period permitted for its abatement (which period shall not begin to run until the entry of the final order of the circuit court) may be assessed a civil penalty of not more than $7,000 for each day during which such violation continues.

J. Any employer who willfully or repeatedly violates any safety or health provision of this title or any standard, rule or regulation promulgated pursuant thereto may be assessed a civil penalty of not more than $70,000 for each such violation.

K. Any employer who willfully violates any safety or health provisions of this title or standards, rules or regulations adopted pursuant thereto, and that violation causes death to any employee, shall, upon conviction, be punished by a fine of not more than $70,000 or by imprisonment for not more than six months, or by both such fine and imprisonment. If the conviction is for a violation committed after a first conviction of such person, punishment shall be a fine of not more than $140,000 or by imprisonment for not more than one year, or by both such fine and imprisonment.

L. In any proceeding before a judge of a circuit court parties may obtain discovery by the methods provided for in the Rules of the Supreme Court of Virginia.

M. No fees or costs shall be charged the Commonwealth by a court or any officer for or in connection with the filing of the complaint, pleadings, or other papers in any action authorized by this section or § 40.1-49.5.

N. Every official act of the circuit court shall be entered of record and all hearings and records shall be open to the public, except any information subject to protection under the provisions of § 40.1-51.4:1.

O. The provisions of Chapter 30 (§ 59.1-406 et seq.) of Title 59.1 shall be considered safety and health standards of the Commonwealth and enforced as to employers pursuant to this section by the Commissioner of Labor and Industry. (1979, c. 354; 1982, c. 412; 1989, c. 341; 1991, c. 153; 1992, c. 777.)

Law Review. — For survey of Virginia administrative law and utility regulation for the year 1978-1979, see 66 Va. L. Rev. 193 (1980).

Regulations governing installation of electrical transmission lines. — Citation and civil penalty held justified in case involving violation of regulations governing installation of electrical transmission lines. See Floyd S. Pike Elec. Contractor v. Commissioner, Dep't of Labor & Indus., 222 Va. 317, 281 S.E.2d 804 (1981).

§ 40.1-49.5. Appeals to Court of Appeals. — Appeals shall lie from the order of the circuit court to the Court of Appeals in a manner provided by § 17.1-405 and the rules of the Supreme Court. (1979, c. 354; 1992, c. 777; 1993, c. 526.)

Law Review. — For survey of Virginia administrative law and utility regulation for the year 1978-1979, see 66 Va. L. Rev. 193 (1980).

§ 40.1-49.6. Same; attorneys for Commonwealth. — A. In any proceeding pursuant to the enforcement of the safety and health provisions of Title 40.1, the attorneys for the Commonwealth are hereby directed to appear and represent the Commonwealth before the circuit court in any civil or criminal matter involving any violation of such provisions in their respective jurisdictions.

B. The Office of the Attorney General shall provide one or more assistants who will be available to consult with and assist any attorney for the Commonwealth or his assistant in the preparation of any prosecution for violations of the occupational safety and health laws, standards, rules or regulations of the

Commonwealth in order to establish uniform guidelines of prosecutorial and settlement policies and procedures in such cases. (1979, c. 354; 1992, c. 777.)

Law Review. — For survey of Virginia administrative law and utility regulation for the year 1978-1979, see 66 Va. L. Rev. 193 (1980).

§ 40.1-49.7. Same; publication of orders. — The Commissioner of Labor shall be responsible for the printing, maintenance, publication and distribution of all final orders of the circuit courts. Every attorney for the Commonwealth's office shall receive at least one copy of each such order. (1979, c. 354; 1992, c. 777.)

Law Review. — For survey of Virginia administrative law and utility regulation for the year 1978-1979, see 66 Va. L. Rev. 193 (1980).

§ 40.1-49.8. Inspections of workplace. — In order to carry out the purposes of the occupational safety and health laws of the Commonwealth and any such rules, regulations, or standards adopted in pursuance of such laws, the Commissioner, upon representing appropriate credentials to the owner, operator, or agent in charge, is authorized, with the consent of the owner, operator, or agent in charge of such workplace as described in subdivision (1) of this section, or with an appropriate order or warrant:

(1) To enter without delay and at reasonable times any factory, plant, establishment, construction site, or other area, workplace or environment where work is performed by an employee of an employer; and

(2) To inspect, investigate, and take samples during regular working hours and at other, reasonable times, and within reasonable limits and in a reasonable manner, any such place of employment and all pertinent conditions, structures, machines, apparatus, devices, equipment, and materials therein, and to question privately any such employer, owner, operator, agent or employee. (1979, c. 533; 1987, c. 643.)

Law Review. — For survey of Virginia administrative law and utility regulation for the year 1978-1979, see 66 Va. L. Rev. 193 (1980).

Warrant application must provide judicial officer with factual allegations sufficient to justify an independent determination that the inspection program is based on reasonable standards and that the standards are being applied to a particular employer in a neutral and nondiscriminatory manner. Mosher Steel-Virginia v. Teig, 229 Va. 95, 327 S.E.2d 87 (1985).

If an administrative inspection is not based on specific evidence of an existing violation, the Fourth Amendment requires a showing that reasonable legislative or administrative standards for inspection are satisfied with respect to the particular establishment to be inspected. Mosher Steel-Virginia v. Teig, 229 Va. 95, 327 S.E.2d 87 (1985).

Affidavit must describe procedure for selection for inspection. — In addition to describing the procedure by which an employer is selected for an administrative inspection, the affidavit must provide the specific facts underlying each step of the selection process. Mosher Steel-Virginia v. Teig, 229 Va. 95, 327 S.E.2d 87 (1985).

Contesting validity of warrant. — An employer need not make a showing to contest the validity of a warrant and its underlying plan for a general inspection by adducing evidence beyond the limits of the supporting affidavit. Mosher Steel-Virginia v. Teig, 229 Va. 95, 327 S.E.2d 87 (1985).

Employer may challenge, in a declaratory judgment proceeding the constitutionality of a warrant authorizing inspection of the employer's manufacturing facility to determine whether the facility is being operated in compliance with the occupational safety and health laws (§ 40.1-1, et seq.). Mosher Steel-Virginia v. Teig, 229 Va. 95, 327 S.E.2d 87 (1985).

§ 40.1-49.9. Issuance of warrant. — Administrative search warrants for inspections of workplaces, based upon a petition demonstrating probable cause and supported by an affidavit, may be issued by any judge having authority to issue criminal warrants whose territorial jurisdiction encompasses the workplace to be inspected or entered, if he is satisfied from the petition and affidavit that there is reasonable and probable cause for the issuance of an administrative search warrant. No administrative search warrant shall be issued pursuant to this chapter except upon probable cause, supported by affidavit, particularly describing the place, things or persons to be inspected or tested and the purpose for which the inspection, testing or collection of samples for testing is to be made. Probable cause shall be deemed to exist if either (i) reasonable legislative or administrative standards for conducting such inspection, testing or collection of samples for testing are satisfied with respect to the particular place, thing, or person, or (ii) there is cause to believe that there is a condition, object, activity, or circumstance which legally justifies such inspection, testing or collection of samples for testing. The supporting affidavit shall contain either a statement that consent to inspect, test or collect samples for testing has been sought and refused or facts or circumstances reasonably justifying the failure to seek such consent in order to enforce effectively the occupational safety and health laws, regulations or standards of the Commonwealth which authorize such inspection, testing or collection of samples for testing. In the case of an administrative search warrant based on legislative or administrative standards for selecting workplaces for inspection, the affidavit shall contain factual allegations sufficient to justify an independent determination by the judge that the inspection program is based on reasonable standards and that the standards are being applied to a particular workplace in a neutral and fair manner. For example, if a selection is based on a particular industry's high hazard ranking, the affidavit shall disclose the method used to establish that ranking, the numerical basis for that ranking. and the relevant inspection history of the workplace to be inspected and the status of all other workplaces within the same territorial region which are subject to inspection pursuant to the legislative or administrative standards used by the Commissioner. The affidavit shall not be required to disclose the actual schedule for inspections or the underlying data on which the statistics were based, provided that such statistics are derived from reliable, neutral third parties. The issuing judge may examine the affiant under oath or affirmation to verify the accuracy of any matter in the affidavit. (1987, c. 643.)

§ 40.1-49.10. Duration of warrant. — Any administrative search warrant issued shall be effective for the time specified therein, but not for a period of more than fifteen days, unless extended or renewed by the judicial officer who signed and issued the original warrant. The warrant shall be executed and shall be returned to the judicial officer by whom it was issued within the time specified in the warrant or within the extended or renewed time. The return shall list any records removed or samples taken pursuant to the warrant. After the expiration of such time, the warrant, unless executed, shall be void. (1987, c. 643.)

§ 40.1-49.11. Conduct of inspection, testing, or collection of samples for analysis. — No warrant shall be executed in the absence of the owner, operator or agent in charge of the particular place, things or persons unless specifically authorized by the issuing judicial officer upon showing that such authority is reasonably necessary to effect the purposes of a law or regulation being enforced. An entry pursuant to this warrant shall not be made forcibly, except that the issuing officer may expressly authorize a forcible entry (i) where facts are shown sufficient to create a reasonable suspicion of an immediate threat to an employee's health or safety, or (ii) where facts are shown establishing that reasonable attempts to serve a previous warrant have been unsuccessful. If forcible entry is authorized, the warrant shall be issued jointly to the Commissioner and to a law-enforcement officer who shall accompany the Commissioner's representative during the execution. (1987, c. 643.)

§ **40.1-49.12. Review by courts.** — A. No court of the Commonwealth shall have jurisdiction to hear a challenge to the warrant prior to its return to the issuing judge, except as a defense in a contempt proceeding, unless the owner or custodian of the place to be inspected makes by affidavit a substantial preliminary showing accompanied by an offer of proof that (i) a false statement, knowingly and intentionally, or with reckless disregard for the truth, was included by the affiant in his affidavit for the administrative search warrant and (ii) the false statement was necessary to the finding of probable cause. The court shall conduct such expeditious in camera review as the court may deem appropriate.

B. After the warrant has been executed and returned to the issuing judge, the validity of the warrant may be reviewed either as a defense to any citation issued by the Commissioner or otherwise by declaratory judgment action brought in a circuit court. In any such action, the review shall be confined to the face of the warrant and affidavits and supporting materials presented to the issuing judge unless the employer whose workplace has been inspected makes by affidavit a substantial showing accompanied by an offer of proof that (i) a false statement, knowingly and intentionally, or with reckless disregard for the truth, was made in support of the warrant and (ii) the false statement was necessary to the finding of probable cause. The reviewing court shall not conduct a de novo determination of probable cause, but only determine whether there is substantial evidence in the record supporting the decision to issue the warrant. (1987, c. 643.)

§ **40.1-50:** Repealed by Acts 1985, c. 449.

§ **40.1-51. State Health Commissioner to provide advice and aid; rules and regulations; duties of Corporation Commission not affected.** — The State Health Commissioner shall be responsible for advising and providing technical aid to the Commissioner on matters pertaining to occupational health on request. The Department of Labor and Industry shall be responsible for drafting and submitting to the Virginia Safety and Health Codes Board for adoption rules and regulations pertaining to control measures to protect the health of workers. In formulating rules and regulations pertaining to health, the Department of Labor and Industry shall request the advice and technical aid of the Department of Health.

This act shall not be interpreted to change, affect, or transfer to the Department or to the Commissioner the duties imposed upon the State Corporation Commission by §§ 27-61 through 27-90. (Code 1950, § 40-62.2; 1950, p. 636; 1970, c. 321; 1972, c. 567; 1985, c. 449.)

Editor's note. — The words "This act" in the second paragraph of this section, as amended, refer to the 1972 amendatory act, which also amended §§ 40.1-1, 40.1-2, 40.1-6, 40.1-22 and former §§ 40.1-23, 40.1-24, 40.1-40 and 40.1-49.

Law Review. — For note on employee drug testing, see 74 Va. L. Rev. 969 (1988).

§ **40.1-51.1. Duties of employers.** — A. It shall be the duty of every employer to furnish to each of his employees safe employment and a place of employment which is free from recognized hazards that are causing or are likely to cause death or serious physical harm to his employees, and to comply with all applicable occupational safety and health rules and regulations promulgated under this title.

B. Every employer shall provide to employees by such suitable means as shall be prescribed in rules and regulations of the Safety and Health Codes Board, information regarding their exposure to toxic materials or harmful physical agents and prompt information when they are exposed to concentration or levels of toxic materials or harmful physical agents in excess of those prescribed by the applicable safety and health standards and shall provide employees or their representatives with the opportunity to observe monitoring or measuring of exposures. Every employer shall also inform any employee who is being exposed of the corrective action being taken and shall provide former employees with access to information about their exposure to toxic materials or harmful physical agents.

C. Every employer cited for a violation of any safety and health provisions of this title or standards, rules and regulations promulgated thereunder shall post a copy of such citation at the site of the violations so noted as prescribed in the rules and regulations of the Safety and Health Codes Board.

D. Every employer shall report to the Virginia Department of Labor and Industry within eight hours any work-related incident resulting in a fatality or in the in-patient hospitalization of three or more persons as prescribed in the rules and regulations of the Safety and Health Codes Board.

E. Every employer, through posting of notices or other appropriate means, shall keep his employees informed of their rights and responsibilities under this title and of specific safety and health standards applicable to his business establishment.

F. An employer representative shall be given the opportunity to accompany the safety and health inspectors on safety or health inspections.

G. Nothing in this section shall be construed to limit the authority of the Commissioner pursuant to § 40.1-6 or the Board pursuant to § 40.1-22 to promulgate necessary rules and regulations to protect and promote the safety and health of employees. (1972, c. 602; 1973, c. 425; 1976, c. 607; 1979, c. 354; 1995, c. 373.)

Law Review. — For survey of Virginia administrative law and utility regulation for the year 1978-1979, see 66 Va. L. Rev. 193 (1980).

§ **40.1-51.1:1:** Repealed by Acts 1979, c. 354.

§ **40.1-51.2. Rights and duties of employees.** — (a) It shall be the duty of each employee to comply with all occupational safety and health rules and regulations issued pursuant to this chapter and any orders issued thereunder which are applicable to his own action and conduct.

(b) Employees or their representatives may bring to the attention of their employer any hazardous conditions that exist or bring the matter to the attention of the Commissioner or his authorized representative, without first bringing the matter to the attention of their employer. Upon receipt of any complaint of hazardous conditions, the Commissioner or his authorized representative shall cause an inspection to be made as soon as practicable. Within two working days after making the oral complaint the employee or the employee representative shall file a written complaint with the Commissioner on a form prescribed by the Commissioner, if at that time, the Commissioner or his authorized representative has not caused the hazardous condition to be corrected. A copy of such written complaint shall be made available to the employer by the Commissioner at the time of such inspection. The name or names of individuals bringing such matters to the attention of the Commissioner shall be held in confidence upon request of such individuals.

(c) [Repealed.]

(d) A representative of the employees selected by the employees shall be given an opportunity to accompany the Commissioner or his authorized representative during the physical inspection of the work place for the purpose of aiding such inspection. Where there is no authorized employee representative, the Commissioner or his authorized representative shall consult with a reasonable number of employees concerning matters of health and safety at the work place. No person shall discharge or in any manner discriminate against an employee representative for his participation in any safety and health inspection.

(e) The employer and the complaining employee, employees or employee representative shall be notified in writing by the Commissioner or his authorized representative of any decision concerning a complaint, of the reasons for such decision and of the rights of the parties to redress pursuant to § 40.1-49.4 of the Code. (1972, c. 602; 1973, c. 425; 1976, c. 607.)

Law Review. — For note on employee drug testing, see 74 Va. L. Rev. 969 (1988). For 1991 survey on employment law, see 25 U. Rich. L. Rev. 759 (1991).

§ 40.1-51.2:1. Discrimination against employee for exercising rights prohibited. — No person shall discharge or in any way discriminate against an employee because the employee has filed a safety or health complaint or has testified or otherwise acted to exercise rights under the safety and health provisions of this title for themselves or others. (1979, c. 354.)

Law Review. — For survey of Virginia administrative law and utility regulation for the year 1978-1979, see 66 Va. L. Rev. 193 (1980). For note, "Erosion of the Employment-at-Will Doctrine: Recognition of an Employee's Right to Job Security," see 43 Wash. & Lee L. Rev. 593 (1986). For article, "The Law of Wrongful Discharge in Virginia," see 10 Geo. Mason L. Rev. 133 (1988).

§ 40.1-51.2:2. Remedy for discrimination. — A. Any employee who believes that he or she has been discharged or otherwise discriminated against by any person in violation of § 40.1-51.2:1 may, within thirty days after such violation occurs, file a complaint with the Commissioner alleging such discharge or discrimination. Upon receipt of such complaint, the Commissioner shall cause such investigation to be made as he deems appropriate. If, upon such investigation, he determines that the provisions of § 40.1-51.2:1 have been violated, he shall attempt by conciliation to have the violation abated without economic loss to the employee. In the event a voluntary agreement cannot be obtained, the Commissioner shall bring an action in a circuit court having jurisdiction over the person charged with the violation. The court shall have jurisdiction, for cause shown, to restrain violations and order appropriate relief, including rehiring or reinstatement of the employee to his former position with back pay plus interest at a rate not to exceed eight percent per annum.

B. Should the Commissioner, based on the results of his investigation of the complaint, refuse to issue a charge against the person that allegedly discriminated against the employee, the employee may bring action in a circuit court having jurisdiction over the person allegedly discriminating against the employee, for appropriate relief. (1979, c. 354.)

Law Review. — For article, "Enforcement of Occupational Safety and Health Laws in Virginia: A New Beginning," see 12 U. Rich. L. Rev. 535 (1978).

§ 40.1-51.3. Duties of health and safety inspectors. — (a) It shall be the duty of all safety and health inspectors to inspect all places of business covered by the State Plan developed in accordance with the Federal Occupational Safety and Health Act of 1970 (P.L. 91-596) for conformity with the provisions of this title and with all safety and health standards, rules and regulations promulgated under this title.

(b) [Repealed.] (1972, c. 602; 1979, c. 354.)

Law Review. — For survey of Virginia administrative law and utility regulation for the year 1978-1979, see 66 Va. L. Rev. 193 (1980).

For note on employee drug testing, see 74 Va. L. Rev. 969 (1988).

§ 40.1-51.3:1. Penalty for giving advance notice of safety or health inspection under this title. — Any person who gives advance notice of any safety or health inspection to be conducted under the provisions of this title without authority of the Commissioner or his authorized representative shall be guilty of a misdemeanor and upon conviction shall be punished by a fine of not less than $100 nor more than $1,000, or by imprisonment for not more than six months, or by both such fine and imprisonment. (1973, c. 425; 1994, c. 28.)

Law Review. — For article, "Enforcement of Occupational Safety and Health Laws in Virginia: A New Beginning," see 12 U. Rich. L. Rev. 535 (1978).

§ 40.1-51.3:2. Evidence of civil penalty against employer under state, federal, etc., safety codes inadmissible in personal injury or property damage trial. — In the trial of any action to recover for personal injury or property damage sustained by any party, in which action it is alleged that an employer acted in violation of or failed to act in accordance with any provision of this chapter or any state or federal occupational safety, health and safety standards act, the fact of the issuance of a citation, the voluntary payment of a civil penalty by a party charged with a violation, or the judicial assessment of a civil penalty under this chapter or any such state or federal occupational safety, health and safety standards act, shall not be admissible in evidence. (1974, c. 516.)

Law Review. — For survey of Virginia law on evidence for the year 1973-1974, see 60 Va. L. Rev. 1543 (1974). For survey of Virginia law on torts for the year 1973-1974, see 60 Va. L. Rev. 1615 (1974).

§ 40.1-51.4: Repealed by Acts 1979, c. 354.

§ 40.1-51.4:1. Confidentiality of trade secrets. — All information reported to or otherwise obtained by the Commissioner or his authorized representative in connection with any inspection or proceeding under this title which contains or which might reveal a trade secret referred to in § 1905 of Title 18 of the United States Code shall be considered confidential for the purpose of that section, except that such information may be disclosed to the Commissioner or his authorized representatives concerned with carrying out any provisions of this title or any proceeding under the aforementioned title. In any such proceeding, the court, the Safety and Health Codes Board or the Commissioner shall issue such orders as may be appropriate to protect the confidentiality of trade secrets. (1976, c. 607; 1994, c. 28.)

§ 40.1-51.4:2. Penalty for making false statements, etc. — Any person who knowingly makes any false statement, representation or certification in any application, record, report, plan, or other document filed or required to be maintained under this title shall upon conviction be punished by a fine of not more than $10,000, or by imprisonment for not more than six months or by both. (1976, c. 607; 1994, c. 28.)

Law Review. — For article, "Enforcement of Occupational Safety and Health Laws in Virginia: A New Beginning," see 12 U. Rich. L. Rev. 535 (1978).

§ 40.1-51.4:3. Prohibition of use of certain questions on polygraph tests for employment.

— No employer shall, as a condition of employment, require a prospective employee to answer questions in a polygraph test concerning the prospective employee's sexual activities unless such sexual activity of the prospective employee has resulted in a conviction of a violation of the criminal laws of this Commonwealth. Any written record of the results of a polygraph examination given to a prospective employee by an employer shall be destroyed or maintained on a confidential basis by the employer giving the examination and shall be open to inspection only upon agreement of the employee tested.

Violation of this section shall constitute a Class 1 misdemeanor. (1977, c. 521; 1990, c. 368.)

Cross references. — As to punishment for Class 1 misdemeanors, see § 18.2-11.
Law Review. — For article, "The Polygraph in the Workplace," see 18 U. Rich. L. Rev. 43 (1983). For article, "Common Law Remedies of Employees Injured by Employer Use of Polygraph Testing," see 22 U. Rich. L. Rev. 51 (1987).

§ 40.1-51.4:4. Prohibition of use of polygraphs in certain employment situations.

— A. As used in this section, the term "lie detector test" means any test utilizing a polygraph or any other device, mechanism or instrument which is operated, or the results of which are used or interpreted by an examiner for the purpose of purporting to assist in or enable the detection of deception, the verification of truthfulness, or the rendering of a diagnostic opinion regarding the honesty of an individual.

B. Notwithstanding the provisions of § 40.1-2.1, it shall be unlawful for any law-enforcement agency or regional jail to require any employee to submit to a lie detector test, or to discharge, demote or otherwise discriminate against any employee for refusal or failure to take a lie detector test, except that the chief executive officer of a law-enforcement agency or the superintendent of a regional jail may, by written directive, require an employee to submit to a lie detector test related to a particular internal administrative investigation concerning allegations of misconduct or criminal activity. No employee required to submit to a lie detector test shall be discharged, demoted or otherwise discriminated against solely on the basis of the results of the lie detector test.

C. Any person who believes that he has been discharged, demoted or otherwise discriminated against by any person in violation of this section may, within ninety days after such alleged violation occurs, file a complaint with the Commissioner. Upon a finding by the Commissioner of a violation of this section, the Commissioner shall order, in the event of discharge or demotion, reinstatement of such person to his former position with back pay plus interest at a rate not to exceed eight percent per annum. Such orders of the Commissioner which have become final under the Virginia Administrative Process Act (§ 9-6.14:1 et seq.) may be recorded, enforced and satisfied as orders or decrees of a circuit court upon certification of such orders by the Commissioner. The Commissioner, or his authorized representative, shall have the right to petition circuit court for injunctive or such other relief as may be necessary for enforcement of this section. No fees or costs shall be charged the Commonwealth by a court or any officer for or in connection with the filing of the complaint, pleadings, or other papers in any action authorized by this section. (1994, c. 561; 1998, c. 140.)

The 1998 amendment, in the first sentence of subsection B, inserted "or regional jail" and inserted "or the superintendent of a regional jail."

CHAPTER 3.1.

BOILER AND PRESSURE VESSEL SAFETY ACT.

ARTICLE 1.

In General.

§ 40.1-51.5. Short title; definitions. — As used in this chapter, which may be cited as the Boiler and Pressure Vessel Safety Act, the following terms shall have the meanings set forth in this section unless the context requires a different meaning:

(a) *"Boiler"* means a closed vessel in which water is heated, steam is generated, steam is superheated, or any combination thereof, under pressure or vacuum for use externally to itself by the direct application of heat from the combustion of fuels, or from electricity or nuclear energy. The term "boiler" shall include fired units for heating or vaporizing liquids other than water where these units are separate from processing systems and are complete within themselves.

1. *"Power boiler"* means a boiler in which steam or other vapor is generated at a pressure of more than fifteen pounds per square inch gauge pressure.

2. *"High pressure, high temperature water boiler"* means a water boiler operating at pressures exceeding 160 pounds per square inch gauge pressure or temperatures exceeding 250° Fahrenheit.

3. *"Heating boiler"* means a steam or vapor boiler operating at pressures not exceeding 15 pounds per square inch gauge pressure, or a hot water boiler operating at pressures not exceeding 160 pounds per square inch gauge pressure or temperature not exceeding 250° Fahrenheit.

(b) *"Unfired pressure vessel"* means a vessel in which the pressure is obtained from an external source or by the application of heat from an indirect source or from a direct source, other than those vessels defined in subdivision (a) of this section.

(c) *"Certificate inspection"* means an inspection, the report of which is used by the Chief Inspector to decide whether or not a certificate as provided by § 40.1-51.10 may be issued. This certificate inspection shall be an internal inspection when construction permits; otherwise, it shall be as complete an inspection as possible.

(d) *"Board"* means the Safety and Health Codes Board.

(e) *"Owner-user inspection agency"* means any person, firm, partnership or corporation registered with the Chief Inspector and approved by the Board as being legally responsible for inspecting pressure vessels which they operate in Virginia.

(f) *"Examining Board"* means persons appointed by the Chief Inspector to monitor examinations of inspectors.

(g) *"Water heater"* means a vessel used to supply (i) potable hot water or (ii) both space heat and potable water in combination which is directly heated by the combustion of fuels, by electricity or any other source and withdrawn for use external to the system at pressures not to exceed 160 pounds per square inch, or temperatures of 210° Fahrenheit.

(h) *"Contract fee inspector"* means any certified boiler inspector contracted to inspect boilers or pressure vessels on an independent basis by the owner or operator of the boiler or pressure vessel. (1972, c. 237; 1974, c. 195; 1986, c. 211; 1993, c. 543; 1996, c. 294.)

The numbers of §§ 40.1-51.5 through 40.1-51.19 were assigned by the Virginia Code Commission, the numbers in the 1972 act having been 40.1-51.1 through 40.1-51.14.

§ 40.1-51.6. Safety and Health Codes Board to formulate rules, regulations, etc.; cost of administration.

— A. The Board is authorized to formulate definitions, rules, regulations and standards which shall be designed for the protection of human life and property from the unsafe or dangerous construction, installation, inspection, operation, maintenance and repair of boilers and pressure vessels in this Commonwealth.

In promulgating such rules, regulations and standards, the Board shall consider any or all of the following:

1. Standards, formulae and practices generally accepted by recognized engineering and safety authorities and bodies.

2. Previous experiences based upon inspections, performance, maintenance and operation.

3. Location of the boiler or pressure vessel relative to persons.

4. Provisions for operational controls and safety devices.

5. Interrelation between other operations outside the scope of this chapter and those covered by this chapter.

6. Level of competency required of persons installing, constructing, maintaining or operating any equipment covered under this chapter or auxiliary equipment.

7. Federal laws, rules, regulations and standards.

B. The Commissioner shall ensure that the costs of administering this chapter shall not exceed revenues generated from fees collected pursuant to the provisions of this chapter. (1972, c. 237; 1973, c. 425; 1985, c. 40.)

§ 40.1-51.7. Installations, repairs and alterations to conform to rules and regulations; existing installations. — (a) No boiler or pressure vessel which does not conform to the rules and regulations of the Board governing new construction and installation and which has been certified by the Board shall be installed or operated in this Commonwealth after twelve months from July 1, 1973. Prior to such date no boiler or pressure vessel shall be installed and operated unless it is in conformity with the rules and regulations established pursuant to this chapter which were in existence on July 1, 1972.

(b) This chapter shall not be construed as in any way preventing the use, sale or reinstallation of a boiler or pressure vessel constructed prior to July 1, 1972, provided it has been made to conform to the rules and regulations of the Board governing existing installations prior to its reinstallation or operation.

(c) Repairs and alterations shall conform to the rules and regulations set forth by the Board. (1972, c. 237; 1974, c. 195; 1986, c. 211.)

§ 40.1-51.8. (Effective until July 1, 2000) Exemptions. — The provisions of this chapter shall not apply to any of the following:

1. Boilers or unfired pressure vessels owned or operated by the federal government or any agency thereof;

2. Boilers or fired or unfired pressure vessels used in private residences or apartment houses of less than four apartments;

3. Boilers of railroad companies maintained on railborne vehicles or those used to propel waterborne vessels;

4. Hot water supply boilers, water heaters, and unfired pressure vessels used as hot water supply storage tanks heated by steam or any other indirect means when the following limitations are not exceeded:

   a. A heat input of 200,000 British thermal units per hour;

   b. A water temperature of 210° Fahrenheit;

   c. A water-containing capacity of 120 gallons.

5. Unfired pressure vessels containing air only which are located on vehicles or vessels designed and used primarily for transporting passengers or freight;

6. Unfired pressure vessels containing air only, installed on the right-of-way of railroads and used directly in the operation of trains;

7. Unfired pressure vessels used for containing water under pressure when either of the following are not exceeded:

   a. A design pressure of 300 psi; or

   b. A design temperature of 210° Fahrenheit.

8. Unfired pressure vessels containing water in combination with air pressure, the compression of which serves only as a cushion, that do not exceed:

   a. A design pressure of 300 psi;

   b. A design temperature of 210° Fahrenheit; or

   c. A water-containing capacity of 120 gallons.

9. Unfired pressure vessels containing air only, providing the volume does not exceed eight cubic feet nor the operating pressure is not greater than 175 pounds;

10. Unfired pressure vessels having an operating pressure not exceeding fifteen pounds with no limitation on size;

11. Pressure vessels that do not exceed:

    a. Five cubic feet in volume and 250 pounds per square inch gauge pressure;

    b. One and one-half cubic feet in volume and 600 pounds per square inch gauge pressure; and

c. An inside diameter of six inches with no limitations on gauge pressure.

12. Pressure vessels used for transportation or storage of compressed gases when constructed in compliance with the specifications of the United States Department of Transportation and when charged with gas marked, maintained, and periodically requalified for use, as required by appropriate regulations of the United States Department of Transportation; all others shall be used in accordance with Chapter 7 (§ 27-86 et seq.) of Title 27;

13. Unfired pressure vessels used in and as a part of electric substations owned or operated by an electric utility, provided such electric substation is enclosed, locked, and inaccessible to the public; or

14. Coil type hot water boilers without any steam space where water flashes into steam when released through a manually operated nozzle, unless steam is generated within the coil or unless one of the following limitations is exceeded:

a. Three-fourths inch diameter tubing or pipe size with no drums or headers attached;

b. Nominal water containing capacity not exceeding six gallons; and

c. Water temperature not exceeding 350° Fahrenheit. (1972, c. 237; 1977, c. 301; 1978, c. 355; 1986, c. 211; 1988, c. 289; 1990, c. 226; 1993, c. 543.)

Section set out twice. — The section above is effective until July 1, 2000. For the version of this section effective July 1, 2000, see the following section, also numbered 40.1-51.8.

§ 40.1-51.8. (Effective July 1, 2000) Exemptions. — The provisions of this article shall not apply to any of the following:

1. Boilers or unfired pressure vessels owned or operated by the federal government or any agency thereof;

2. Boilers or fired or unfired pressure vessels used in private residences or apartment houses of less than four apartments;

3. Boilers of railroad companies maintained on railborne vehicles or those used to propel waterborne vessels;

4. Antique or model boilers as defined in § 40.1-51.19:1;

5. Hot water supply boilers, water heaters, and unfired pressure vessels used as hot water supply storage tanks heated by steam or any other indirect means when the following limitations are not exceeded:

a. A heat input of 200,000 British thermal units per hour;

b. A water temperature of 210° Fahrenheit;

c. A water-containing capacity of 120 gallons;

6. Unfired pressure vessels containing air only which are located on vehicles or vessels designed and used primarily for transporting passengers or freight;

7. Unfired pressure vessels containing air only, installed on the right-of-way of railroads and used directly in the operation of trains;

8. Unfired pressure vessels used for containing water under pressure when either of the following are not exceeded:

a. A design pressure of 300 psi; or

b. A design temperature of 210° Fahrenheit;

9. Unfired pressure vessels containing water in combination with air pressure, the compression of which serves only as a cushion, that do not exceed:

a. A design pressure of 300 psi;

b. A design temperature of 210° Fahrenheit; or

c. A water-containing capacity of 120 gallons;

10. Unfired pressure vessels containing air only, providing the volume does not exceed eight cubic feet nor the operating pressure is not greater than 175 pounds;

11. Unfired pressure vessels having an operating pressure not exceeding fifteen pounds with no limitation on size;

12. Pressure vessels that do not exceed:

a. Five cubic feet in volume and 250 pounds per square inch gauge pressure;

b. One and one-half cubic feet in volume and 600 pounds per square inch gauge pressure; and

c. An inside diameter of six inches with no limitations on gauge pressure;

13. Pressure vessels used for transportation or storage of compressed gases when constructed in compliance with the specifications of the United States Department of Transportation and when charged with gas marked, maintained, and periodically requalified for use, as required by appropriate regulations of the United States Department of Transportation; all others shall be used in accordance with Chapter 7 (§ 27-86 et seq.) of Title 27;

14. Unfired pressure vessels used in and as a part of electric substations owned or operated by an electric utility, provided such electric substation is enclosed, locked, and inaccessible to the public; or

15. Coil type hot water boilers without any steam space where water flashes into steam when released through a manually operated nozzle, unless steam is generated within the coil or unless one of the following limitations is exceeded:

a. Three-fourths inch diameter tubing or pipe size with no drums or headers attached;

b. Nominal water containing capacity not exceeding six gallons; and

c. Water temperature not exceeding 350° Fahrenheit. (1972, c. 237; 1977, c. 301; 1978, c. 355; 1986, c. 211; 1988, c. 289; 1990, c. 226; 1993, c. 543; 1999, c. 335.)

Section set out twice. — The section above is effective July 1, 2000. For this section as in effect until July 1, 2000, see the preceding section, also numbered 40.1-51.8.

The 1999 amendment, effective July 1, 2000, substituted "article" for "chapter" in the introductory language, added subdivision 4, and renumbered former subdivisions 4 through 14 as 5 through 15.

§ 40.1-51.9. Employment and appointment of inspectors and other personnel; inspections; reports. — The Commissioner is authorized to employ persons to enforce the provisions of this chapter and the regulations of the Board. He shall be authorized to require examinations or other information which he deems necessary to aid him in determining the fitness, competency, and professional or technical expertise of any applicant to perform the duties and tasks to be assigned.

The Commissioner is authorized to appoint a Chief Inspector and to certify special inspectors who shall meet all qualifications set forth by the Commissioner and the Board. Special inspectors shall be authorized to inspect specified premises and without cost or expense to the Commonwealth. Reports of all violations of the regulations or of this chapter shall be immediately made to the Commissioner. Other reports shall be made as required by the Commissioner. (1972, c. 237; 1974, c. 195; 1995, c. 97.)

§ 40.1-51.9:1. Examination of inspectors; certificate of competency required. — A. All applicants for the position of inspector authorized by § 40.1-51.9 shall be required to have successfully completed an examination monitored by the Examining Board and to have received a certificate of competency from the Commissioner prior to commencing their duties. A fee as set under subsection A of § 40.1-51.15 shall be charged each applicant taking the inspector's examination.

B. Each inspector holding a valid certificate of competency and who conducts inspections, as provided by this chapter, shall be required to obtain an identification card biennially, not later than June 30 of the year in which the identification card is required. Application for the identification card shall be made on forms furnished by the Department upon request. Each application shall be submitted to the Department, accompanied by a post-office money order or check drawn to the order of the Treasurer of Virginia in the amount as set under subsection A of § 40.1-51.15. (1974, c. 195; 1986, c. 266; 1997, c. 212.)

The 1997 amendment, effective January 1, 1998, substituted "fee as set under subsection A of § 40.1-51.15" for "fee of fifty dollars" in the second sentence of subsection A and substituted "amount as set under subsection A of § 40.1-51.15" for "amount of ten dollars" at the end of subsection B.

§ 40.1-51.9:2. Financial responsibility requirements for contract fee inspectors. — A.

Contract fee inspectors inspecting or certifying regulated boilers or pressure vessels in the Commonwealth shall maintain evidence of their financial responsibility, including compensation to third parties, for bodily injury and property damage resulting from, or directly relating to, an inspector's negligent inspection or recommendation for certification of a boiler or pressure vessel.

B. Documentation of financial responsibility, including documentation of insurance or bond, shall be provided to the Chief Inspector within thirty days after certification of the inspector. The Chief Inspector may revoke an inspector's certification for failure to provide documentation of financial responsibility in a timely fashion.

C. The Safety and Health Codes Board is authorized to promulgate regulations requiring contract fee inspectors, as a condition of their doing business in the Commonwealth, to demonstrate financial responsibility sufficient to comply with the requirements of this chapter. Regulations governing the amount of any financial responsibility required by the contract fee inspector shall take into consideration the type, capacity and number of boilers or pressure vessels inspected or certified.

D. Financial responsibility may be demonstrated by self-insurance, insurance, guaranty or surety, or any other method approved by the Board, or any combination thereof, under the terms the Board may prescribe. A contract fee inspector whose financial responsibility is accepted by the Board under this subsection shall notify the Chief Inspector at least thirty days before the effective date of the change, expiration, or cancellation of any instrument of insurance, guaranty or surety.

E. Acceptance of proof of financial responsibility shall expire on the effective date of any change in the inspector's instrument of insurance, guaranty or surety, or the expiration date of the inspector's certification. Application for renewal of acceptance of proof of financial responsibility shall be filed thirty days before the date of expiration.

F. The Chief Inspector, after notice and opportunity for hearing, may revoke his acceptance of evidence of financial responsibility if he determines that acceptance has been procured by fraud or misrepresentation, or a change in circumstances has occurred that would warrant denial of acceptance of evidence of financial responsibility under this section or the requirements established by the Board pursuant to this section.

G. It is not a defense to any action brought for failure to comply with the requirement to provide acceptable evidence of financial responsibility that the person charged believed in good faith that the owner or operator of an inspected boiler or pressure vessel possessed evidence of financial responsibility accepted by the Chief Inspector or the Board. (1996, c. 294.)

§ 40.1-51.10. Right of access to premises; certification and recertification; inspection requirements. — A.

The Commissioner, his agents or special inspectors shall have free access, during reasonable hours to any premises in the Commonwealth where a boiler or pressure vessel is being constructed, operated or maintained, or is being installed to conduct a variance review, an owner-user inspection agency audit, an emergency repair review, an accident investigation, a violation follow-up, and a secondhand or used boiler review for the purpose of ascertaining whether such boiler or pressure vessel is being constructed, operated or maintained in accordance with this chapter.

B. On and after January 1, 1973, no boiler or pressure vessel used or proposed to be used within this Commonwealth, except boilers or pressure vessels exempted by this chapter, shall be installed, operated or maintained unless it has been inspected by the Commissioner, his agents or special inspectors as to construction, installation and condition and shall be certified. A fee as set under subsection A of § 40.1-51.15 shall be charged for each inspection certificate issued. In lieu of such fees both for certification and recertification, an authorized owner-user inspection agency shall be charged annual filing fees as set under subsection A of § 40.1-51.15.

C. Recertification shall be required as follows:

1. Power boilers and high pressure, high temperature water boilers shall receive a certificate inspection annually and shall also be externally inspected annually while under pressure if possible;

2. Heating boilers shall receive a certificate inspection biennially;

3. Pressure vessels subject to internal corrosion shall receive a certificate inspection biennially;

4. Pressure vessels not subject to internal corrosion shall receive a certificate inspection at intervals set by the Board, but internal inspection shall not be required of pressure vessels, the content of which are known to be noncorrosive to the material of which the shell, heads or fittings are constructed, either from the chemical composition of the contents or from evidence that the contents are adequately treated with a corrosion inhibitor, provided that such vessels are constructed in accordance with the rules and regulations of the Board;

5. Nuclear vessels within the scope of this chapter shall be inspected and reported in such form and with such appropriate information as the Board shall designate;

6. A grace period of two months beyond the periods specified in subdivisions 1, 2, 3 and 4 of this subsection may elapse between certificate inspections. The Chief Inspector may extend a certificate for up to three additional months beyond such grace period subject to a satisfactory external inspection of the object and receipt of a fee as set under subsection A of § 40.1-51.15 for each month of inspection beyond the grace period.

D. Inspection requirements for operating equipment shall be in accordance with generally accepted practice and compatible with the actual service conditions and shall include but not be limited to the following criteria:

1. Previous experience, based on records of inspection, performance and maintenance;

2. Location, with respect to personnel hazard;

3. Qualifications and competency of inspection and operating personnel;

4. Provision for related safe operation controls; and

5. Interrelation with other operations outside of the scope of this chapter.

E. Based upon documentation of such actual service conditions by the owner or user of the operating equipment, the Board may, in its discretion, permit variations in the inspection requirements as provided in this section.

F. If, at the discretion of the Commissioner, a hydrostatic test shall be deemed necessary, it shall be made by the owner or user of the boiler or pressure vessel.

G. All boilers, other than cast iron sectional boilers, and pressure vessels to be installed in this Commonwealth after the six-month period from the date upon which the rules and regulations of the Board shall become effective shall be inspected during construction as required by the applicable rules and regulations of the Board. (1972, c. 237; 1974, c. 195; 1976, c. 288; 1986, c. 266; 1988, c. 289; 1992, c. 3; 1993, c. 544; 1995, c. 97; 1997, c. 212.)

The 1997 amendment, effective January 1, 1998, in subsection B, substituted "fee as set under subsection A of § 40.1-51.15" for "twenty dollar fee" in the second sentence and substituted "set under subsection A of § 40.1-51.15" for "set forth in § 40.1-51.11:1" at the end of the third sentence, and substituted "fee as set under subsection A of § 40.1-51.15" for "fee of twenty dollars" near the end of subdivision C 6.

§ 40.1-51.10:1. Issuance of certificates; charges.

— The Commissioner may designate special inspectors and contract fee inspectors to issue inspection certificates for boilers and pressure vessels they have inspected. If no defects are found or when the boiler or pressure vessel has been corrected in accordance with regulations, the designated special inspector or contract fee inspector shall issue a certificate on forms furnished by the Department. The designated special inspector or contract fee inspector shall collect the inspection certificate fee required under § 40.1-51.10 at the time of the issuance of the certificate and forward the fee and a duplicate of the certificate to the chief inspector immediately.

Each designated special inspector or contract fee inspector may charge a fee as set under subsection A of § 40.1-51.15 for each certificate issued, but the charge shall not be mandatory. No charge shall be made unless the inspector has previously contracted therefor. (1997, c. 212.)

Editor's note. — Acts 1997, c. 212, cl. 4, provides: "That, by October 1, 1997, the Safety and Health Codes Board shall promulgate regulations governing the use of Commonwealth inspectors to inspect uninsured boilers or pressure vessels when contract fee inspectors are unavailable and to set fees for such inspections conducted by Commonwealth inspectors."

Effective date. — This section is effective January 1, 1998.

§ 40.1-51.11. Suspension of inspection certificate; emergency powers of Board.

— (a) The Commissioner or his authorized representative may at any time suspend an inspection certificate when, in his opinion, the boiler or pressure vessel for which it was issued, cannot be operated without menace to the public safety, or when the boiler or pressure vessel is found not to comply with the rules and regulations herein provided. Each suspension of an inspection certificate shall continue in effect until such boiler or pressure vessel shall have been made to conform to the rules and regulations of the Board, and until such inspection certificate shall have been reinstated. No boiler or pressure vessel shall be operated during the period of suspension.

(b) Notwithstanding any other provision of this chapter to the contrary, the Board, upon finding that the particular boiler or pressure vessel poses an immediate danger to human life because of failure to comply with provisions of law or regulation, shall have all powers provided in § 40.1-49.4 F 1. (1972, c. 237; 1981, c. 39.)

§ 40.1-51.11:1. Owner-user inspection agencies.

— Any person, firm, partnership or corporation operating pressure vessels in this Commonwealth may seek approval and registration as an owner-user inspection agency by filing an application with the chief inspector on forms prescribed and available from the Department, and request approval by the Board. Each application shall be accompanied by a fee as set under subsection A of § 40.1-51.15 and a bond in the penal sum of $5,000 which shall continue to be valid during the time the approval and registration of the company as an owner-user inspection agency is in effect. Applicants meeting the requirements of the rules and regulations for approval as owner-user inspection agencies will be approved and registered by the Board. The Board shall withdraw the approval and registration as an owner-user inspection agency of any person, firm, partnership or corporation which fails to comply with all rules and regulations applicable to owner-user inspection agencies. Each owner-user inspection agency shall file an annual statement as required by the rules and regulations, accompanied by a filing fee as set under subsection A of § 40.1-51.15. (1974, c. 195; 1986, c. 266; 1997, c. 212.)

The 1997 amendment, effective January 1, 1998, substituted "fee as set under subsection A of § 40.1-51.15" for "fee of $25" in the second sentence and rewrote the last sentence which formerly read: "Each owner-user inspection agency shall file an annual statement as required by the rules and regulations, accompanied by a filing fee in accordance with the following schedule: (a) For statements covering not more than twenty-five vessels — seven dollars per vessel. (b) For statements covering more than 25, but less than 101 vessels — $200. (c) For statements covering more than 100, but less than 501 vessels — $400. (d) For statements covering more than 500 vessels — $800."

§ 40.1-51.12. Violation for operating boiler or pressure vessel without inspection certificate; civil penalty. — A. After twelve months following July 1, 1972, it shall be unlawful for any person, firm, partnership or corporation to operate in this Commonwealth a boiler or pressure vessel without a valid inspection certificate. Any owner, user, operator or agent of any such person who actually operates or is responsible for operating such boiler or pressure vessel thereof who operates a boiler or pressure vessel without such inspection certificate, or at a pressure exceeding that specified in such inspection certificate shall be in violation of this section and subject to a civil penalty not to exceed $100. Each day of such violation shall be deemed a separate offense.

B. All procedural rights guaranteed to employers pursuant to § 40.1-49.4 shall apply to penalties under this section.

C. Investigation and enforcement for violations of this section shall be carried out by the Department of Labor and Industry. Civil penalties imposed for violations of this section shall be paid into the general fund. (1972, c. 237; 1995, c. 97.)

§ 40.1-51.13. Posting of certificate. — Certificates shall be posted in the room containing the boiler or pressure vessel inspected. If the boiler or pressure vessel is not located within the building the certificate shall be posted in a location convenient to the boiler or pressure vessel inspected, or in any place where it will be accessible to interested parties. (1972, c. 237; 1990, c. 226.)

§ 40.1-51.14. When inspection certificate for insured boiler or pressure vessel invalid. — No inspection certificate issued for an insured boiler or pressure vessel based upon a report of a special inspector shall be valid after the boiler or pressure vessel for which it was issued shall cease to be insured by a company duly authorized to issue policies of insurance in this Commonwealth. (1972, c. 237.)

§ 40.1-51.15. Fees. — A. The Safety and Health Codes Board shall establish fees required under this chapter. Following the close of any biennium, when the account for the Safety and Health Codes Board shows expenses allocated to it for the past biennium to be more than ten percent greater or less than moneys collected on behalf of the Board, it shall revise the fees levied by it for licensure and renewal thereof so that the fees are sufficient but not excessive to cover expenses. Such revisions, and the underlying rationale, shall be included in the Department's Annual Report submitted pursuant to § 40.1-4.1.

B. The owner or user of a boiler or pressure vessel required by this chapter to be reviewed shall pay directly to the Commissioner, upon completion of inspection, fees in accordance with the following schedule:

1. Conducting or participating in reviews and surveys of boiler or pressure vessel manufacturers or repair organizations for the purpose of national accreditation, shall be charged a fee as set under subsection A per review or survey.

2. a. All other inspections, including variance reviews, emergency repair reviews, and reviews of secondhand or used boilers or pressure vessels made by the Commissioner or his appointed representative shall be charged a fee as set under subsection A.

b. *"Secondhand"* shall mean an object which has changed ownership and location after primary use.

C. The Commissioner shall transfer all fees so received to the State Treasurer for deposit into the general fund of the state treasury. (1972, c. 237; 1985, c. 40; 1986, c. 266; 1988, c. 289; 1993, c. 544; 1995, c. 97; 1997, c. 212.)

Editor's note. — Acts 1997, c. 212, cl. 3, provides: "That, by October 1, 1997, the Safety and Health Codes Board shall promulgate regulations to establish the fees and charges required in this act."

Acts 1997, c. 212, cl. 4, provides: "That, by October 1, 1997, the Safety and Health Codes Board shall promulgate regulations governing the use of Commonwealth inspectors to inspect uninsured boilers or pressure vessels when contract fee inspectors are unavailable and to set fees for such inspections conducted by Commonwealth inspectors."

The 1997 amendment, effective January 1, 1998, added present subsection A; redesignated former subsection A as present subsection B; substituted "a fee as set under subsection A" for "at a rate of $600" in present subdivision B 1; substituted "a fee as set under subsection A" for "for at the rate of not less than $100 for one-half day of four hours, and $200 for one full day of eight hours, plus all expenses, including traveling and lodging" in present subdivision B 2 a; and redesignated former subsection B as present subsection C.

§ 40.1-51.15:1. Only one inspection necessary.
— Inspection under the provisions of this chapter shall constitute compliance with and shall be in lieu of any boiler or pressure vessel inspection required by Chapter 6 (§ 36-97 et seq.) of Title 36. (1980, c. 464; 1992, c. 3.)

§ 40.1-51.16. Appeals.
— Any person aggrieved by an order or an act of the Board or Commissioner under this chapter may appeal such order or act to the Board pursuant to the provisions of the Administrative Process Act (§ 9-6.14:1 et seq.). Final orders of the Board may be appealed pursuant to the Administrative Process Act. (1972, c. 237; 1986, c. 615; 1988, c. 289.)

§ 40.1-51.17. Effect of chapter on local ordinances and regulations.
— Nothing in this chapter shall be construed as repealing any valid local ordinance or regulation now in effect adopted pursuant to general law or charter provision; provided, however, that if any such ordinance or regulation is less strict than any standard rule or regulation promulgated or adopted by the Board, then such ordinance or regulation shall be superseded by the applicable standard or regulation of the Board except as provided in § 40.1-51.19. (1972, c. 237.)

§ 40.1-51.18: Not set out.

§ 40.1-51.19. Variances. — Upon application pursuant to the provisions of subdivision (9) of § 40.1-6, the Commissioner may allow variances from a specific regulation provided the applicant proves by clear and convincing evidence his boiler or pressure vessel meets substantially equivalent operating criteria and standards. (1972, c. 237; 1990, c. 226.)

ARTICLE 2.

Antique and Model Boilers.

(This article is effective July 1, 2000)

§ 40.1-51.19:1. (Effective July 1, 2000) Definitions. — As used in this article:

"Antique boiler" means any boiler used solely for demonstration, exhibition, ceremonial or educational purposes, including but not limited to, historical artifacts such as portable and stationary show boilers, farm traction engines and locomotives.

"Model boiler" means any boiler fabricated to demonstrate an original design or to reproduce or replicate a historic artifact, and used primarily for demonstration, exhibition or educational purposes. (1999, c. 335.)

Effective date. — This section is effective
July 1, 2000.

§ 40.1-51.19:2. (Effective July 1, 2000) Applicability. — Antique and model boilers may continue in operation but shall be in compliance with the provisions of this article by July 1, 2000. (1999, c. 335.)

Effective date. — This section is effective
July 1, 2000.

§ 40.1-51.19:3. (Effective July 1, 2000) Inspection and testing. — A. An antique or model boiler shall be inspected every two years. It shall be the duty of the owner of any antique or model boiler to obtain and display an inspection certificate.

B. The inspection of every antique or model boiler shall include an examination of or for the following:

1. The fusible plug.

2. The safety valve or valves. Such valve or valves shall be (i) rated by the American Society of Mechanical Engineers (ASME), (ii) set at or below the maximum allowable working pressure, and (iii) sealed in a manner that does not allow tampering with the valve without destroying the seal.

3. Internal corrosion.

4. Leakage.

5. The boiler power piping, up to and including the first valve.

C. An antique or model boiler shall be subjected to nondestructive testing, at the owner's expense, to determine the maximum allowable working pressure in accordance with Boiler and Pressure Vessel rules and regulations (16 VAC 25-50-10 et seq.).

D. All antique and model boilers shall pass a hydrostatic test at one and one-half maximum allowable working pressure, conducted in the presence of an inspector, at the time of certification and as frequently as deemed necessary based on inspections or other evidence. An antique or model boiler that does not meet the requirements of the ASME code and is not certified in the Commonwealth, shall, at the owner's expense, be tested to twice the maximum allowable working pressure and, to be operated, shall have a successful (i) complete radiographic or ultrasonic examination of the long or longitudinal seam; (ii) ultrasonic examination for metal thickness, and for the purpose of calculating the maximum allowable working pressure, the thinnest reading shall be used; and (iii) dye penetrant examination for cracks with a magnetic particle, ultrasonic, or radiographic examination of areas where dye penetrant testing shows possible cracks.

The requirements of this subsection for full radiographic or ultrasonic examination may be waived after the initial inspection if the inspector finds that the general standards of subsection B are met and the safety valve or valves are set at the maximum allowable working pressure determined by calculations from the ultrasonic results, or 100 pounds per square inch, whichever is lower. (1999, c. 335.)

Effective date. — This section is effective July 1, 2000.

§ 40.1-51.19:4. (Effective July 1, 2000) Operations and maintenance.
— A. An antique or model boiler must be attended by a person reasonably competent to operate such boiler when in operation. For the purposes of this section, an antique or model boiler may be considered as not being in operation when all of the following conditions exist:

1. The water level is at least one-third of the water gauge glass;
2. The header or dome valve is in a closed position;
3. The fire is banked and the draft doors closed or the fire is extinguished;
4. The boiler pressure is at least twenty pounds per square inch below the lowest safety valve set pressure.

B. All welding performed on antique or model boilers shall be done by an "R" stamp holder in accordance with the inspection code of the National Board of Boiler and Pressure Vessel Inspectors.

C. Repairs to longitudinal riveted joints are prohibited. (1999, c. 335.)

Effective date. — This section is effective July 1, 2000.

§ 40.1-51.19:5. (Effective July 1, 2000) Civil penalty. — A. It shall be
unlawful for any person, firm, partnership or corporation to operate in the Commonwealth an antique or model boiler without a valid certificate. Any such person shall be subject to a civil penalty as provided by § 40.1-51.12.

B. Any owner or user who leaves or causes to leave an antique or model boiler unattended while in operation shall be in violation of this article and subject to a civil penalty not to exceed $100. Any owner or user who leaves or causes to leave an antique or model boiler unattended while in operation at an event to which members of the general public are invited shall be in violation of this article and subject to a civil penalty not to exceed $5,000. Each instance of such violation shall be deemed a separate offense. (1999, c. 335.)

Effective date. — This section is effective July 1, 2000.

CHAPTER 3.2.

ASBESTOS NOTIFICATION.

Sec.
40.1-51.20.   Duties of licensed asbestos and certified lead contractors.

Sec.
40.1-51.21.   Annual inspections.
40.1-51.22.   Enforcement of chapter.

§ 40.1-51.20. Duties of licensed asbestos and certified lead contractors. — A. A licensed asbestos contractor and any certified lead contractor shall notify the Department of Labor and Industry at least twenty days prior to commencement of each asbestos or lead project. Notification shall be sent in a manner prescribed by the Department of Labor and Industry. The Department of Labor and Industry shall have the authority to waive all or any part of the twenty-day notice.

B. A licensed asbestos contractor or certified lead contractor shall obtain an asbestos or lead project permit from the Department of Labor and Industry prior to commencing each asbestos or lead project in accordance with this chapter and shall pay directly to the Commissioner a fee as established by the Safety and Health Codes Board pursuant to the Administrative Process Act (§ 9-6.14:1 et seq.). The fees shall be sufficient but not excessive to cover the cost of administering the program. All fees collected pursuant to this section shall be paid into a special fund in the state treasury to the credit of the Department of Labor and Industry and shall be used in carrying out the Department's mission under this chapter.

The provisions of this subsection shall not apply to asbestos projects in residential buildings as defined by the Board in regulations adopted pursuant to the Administrative Process Act (§ 9-6.14:1 et seq.).

C. A licensed asbestos contractor or certified lead contractor shall keep a record of each asbestos or lead project performed and shall make the record available to the Departments of Professional and Occupational Regulation and of Labor and Industry upon request. Records required by this section shall be kept for at least thirty years. The records shall include:

1. The name, address, and asbestos or lead supervisor's license or certification number of the individual who supervised the asbestos or lead project and each employee or agent who worked on the project;

2. The location and description of the project and the amount of asbestos or lead material that was removed;

3. The starting and completion dates of each project and a summary of the procedures that were used to comply with all federal and state standards; and

4. The name and address of each disposal site where waste containing asbestos or lead was deposited, the results of the lead toxicity characteristic test, and the disposal site receipts. (1992, c. 477; 1995, cc. 543, 585; 1996, cc. 180, 846.)

Editor's note. — Acts 1995, c. 585, cl. 2, provides: "That, notwithstanding the provisions of subsection B of § 54.1-503 as in effect on January 1, 1995, no person shall be required to hold a certificate as a lead contractor, professional, or worker to perform lead inspections, evaluation, or abatement activities until one hundred and twenty days after the effective date of the Virginia Board for Asbestos Licensing and Lead Certification's initial regulations."

The 1995 amendments. — The 1995 amendments by cc. 543 and 585, effective March 24, 1995, are identical, and rewrote

subsection A which formerly read: "A licensed asbestos contractor or RFS contractor shall notify the Department of Labor and Industry at least twenty days prior to commencement of each asbestos project he plans to undertake. Notification shall be sent by certified mail or hand delivered to the Department of Labor and Industry. The Department of Labor and Industry shall have the authority to waive all or any part of the twenty-day notice"; inserted "or lead" following "asbestos" throughout the section; substituted "licensed RFS contractor or certified lead contractor" for "or RFS contractor" in the first sentence of the first paragraph in subsection B; inserted "asbestos projects in" in the second paragraph of the subsection; in the first sentence of subsection C, substituted "licensed RFS contractor or certified lead contractor" for "or RFS contractor" and substituted "Departments of Professional and Occupational Regulation" for "Departments of Commerce"; substituted "or lead supervisor's license or certification number" for "worker's license number" in subdivision C 1; and, in subdivision C 4, deleted "asbestos" preceding "disposal site" and inserted "the results of the lead toxicity characteristic test."

Search warrant not required for inspection. — The defendant had no reasonable expectation of privacy in those records that it is required to maintain because it is involved in the removal and disposal of asbestos, an industry that is heavily regulated by statute and by regulation; thus defendant's claim that the citations were not valid because a search warrant was required to lawfully search these records was unsupportable. Abateco Servs., Inc. v. Bell, 23 Va. App. 504, 477 S.E.2d 795 (1996).

§ 40.1-51.21. Annual inspections. — At least once a year, during an actual project, the Department of Labor and Industry shall conduct an on-site unannounced inspection of each licensed asbestos contractor's, licensed RFS contractor's, and certified lead contractor's procedures in regard to installing, removing and encapsulating asbestos and lead. The Commissioner or an authorized representative shall have the power and authority to enter at reasonable times upon any property for this purpose. (1992, c. 477; 1995, cc. 543, 585.)

Where defendant acknowledged the contractual provision addressing a warrantless search, but failed to comply with its contractual obligation and stated that it had no intention of complying, the evidence supported a willful violation of the contract and this section. Abateco Servs., Inc. v. Bell, 23 Va. App. 504, 477 S.E.2d 795 (1996).

Inspections can be more than once per year. — The plain meaning of the statute is that the department of Labor and Industry must inspect once per year, but can inspect more than once per year, contrary to the defendant's interpretation. Abateco Servs., Inc. v. Bell, 23 Va. App. 504, 477 S.E.2d 795 (1996).

§ 40.1-51.22. Enforcement of chapter. — A. Any person who commits the following violations of this chapter shall be subject to a civil penalty of up to $1,000 for an initial violation and $5,000 for each subsequent violation:

1. Failure to provide the notification required by § 40.1-51.20;

2. Improper notification as required by § 40.1-51.20. Improper notification shall include, but not be limited to, failing to provide required fees, intentionally failing to complete all required sections of the form, failing to properly amend a notification and providing information on the form; or

3. Any violations of safety or health provisions of Title 40.1 or any standard, rule or regulation adopted pursuant thereto, discovered during an inspection conducted pursuant to § 40.1-51.21 shall be enforced separately pursuant to § 40.1-49.4.

All procedural rights guaranteed to employers pursuant to § 40.1-49.4 shall apply to the penalties set under this section.

B. Investigation and enforcement for violations of this chapter shall be carried out by the Department of Labor and Industry. Prosecutions under this chapter shall be the responsibility of the Office of the Attorney General of Virginia. Civil penalties imposed for violation of this chapter shall be paid into the general fund. (1992, c. 477.)

CHAPTER 3.3.

Virginia Asbestos NESHAP Act.

§ **40.1-51.23. Definitions.** — As used in this chapter, which may be cited as the Virginia Asbestos NESHAP Act, the following terms shall have the meanings set forth in this section unless the context requires a different meaning:

"Asbestos" means any material containing more than one percent of asbestos by weight, which is friable or which has a reasonable chance of becoming friable in the course of ordinary or anticipated building use.

"Board" means the Safety and Health Codes Board.

"Commissioner" means the Commissioner of Labor and Industry or his authorized representative.

"Department" means the Department of Labor and Industry.

"National Emissions Standards for Hazardous Air Pollutants" or *"NESHAP"* means those portions of the regulations contained in 40 CFR Part 61 under the federal Clean Air Act which deal with the demolition and renovation of asbestos facilities. The following list of sections of the CFR are included in the Board's authority but do not limit it: §§ 61.140; 61.141; 61.145; 61.146; 61.148; 61.150, except subsection (a) (4); 61.154, except subsection (d); and 61.156.

"Owner" means any person who owns, leases, operates, controls, or supervises the facility being demolished, renovated, sprayed, or insulated; any person who owns, leases, operates, controls, or supervises the demolition, renovation, spraying, or insulation operation; or both. (1992, c. 541.)

The numbers of §§ 40.1-51.23 through 40.1-51.41 were assigned by the Virginia Code Commission, the numbers in the 1992 act having been 40.1-51.20 through 40.1-51.38.

§ **40.1-51.24. Department authorized to enter certain agreements.** — The Department is hereby authorized to:

1. Make and enter into all contracts and agreements necessary or incidental to the performance of the Department's duties and the execution of its powers under this chapter including, but not limited to, contracts with the United States, other states, agencies, and governmental subdivisions of the Commonwealth.

2. Accept grants from the United States government, its agencies and instrumentalities, and any other source. To these ends, the Department shall have the power to comply with such conditions and execute such agreements as may be necessary and desirable. (1992, c. 541.)

§ 40.1-51.25. Safety and Health Codes Board to formulate rules, regulations, etc.

— A. The Board is authorized to formulate definitions, rules, regulations and standards which shall be designed to ensure the proper demolition and renovation of asbestos facilities and effect compliance with the asbestos NESHAP requirements of the federal Environmental Protection Agency. Such standards shall be at least as stringent as the asbestos regulations passed pursuant to § 112 of the Clean Air Act. The regulations shall not promote or encourage any substantial degradation of present air quality in any air basin or region which has an air quality superior to that stipulated in the regulations of the Department of Air Pollution Control. Any regulations adopted by the Board to have general effect in part or all of the Commonwealth shall be filed in accordance with the Virginia Register Act (§ 9-6.15 et seq.).

B. The Board in making regulations and in approving variances, and the courts in granting injunctive relief under the provisions of this chapter, shall consider facts and circumstances relevant to the reasonableness of the activity involved and the regulations proposed to control it, including:

1. The character and degree of injury to, or interference with, safety, health, or the reasonable use of property which is caused or threatened to be caused;

2. The social and economic value of the activity involved;

3. The suitability of the activity to the area in which it is located; and

4. The scientific and economic practicality of reducing or eliminating the discharge resulting from such activity. (1992, c. 541.)

§ 40.1-51.26. Commissioner of Labor and Industry to enforce laws.

— The Commissioner of Labor and Industry shall have the authority to:

1. Supervise, administer, and enforce the provisions of this chapter and regulations of the Board;

2. Receive complaints as to asbestos NESHAP violations;

3. Hold or cause to be held hearings and enter orders diminishing or abating the causes of air pollution and orders to enforce regulations pursuant to § 40.1-51.28;

4. Institute legal proceedings, including suits for injunctions for the enforcement of his orders, regulations of the Board, and for the enforcement of penalties;

5. Investigate any violations of this chapter and regulations;

6. Require that asbestos NESHAP records and reports be made available upon request, and require owners to develop, maintain, and make available such other records and information as are deemed necessary for the proper enforcement of this chapter and regulation; and

7. Upon presenting appropriate credentials to the owner, operator, or agent in charge:

a. Enter without delay and at reasonable times any business establishment, construction site, or other area, workplace, or environment in this Commonwealth, subject to federal security requirements; and

b. Inspect and investigate during regular working hours and at other reasonable times, and within reasonable limits and in a reasonable manner, without prior notice, unless such notice is authorized by the Commissioner or his representative, any such business establishment or place of employment and all pertinent conditions, structures, machines, apparatus, devices, equipment, and materials therein, and question privately any such employer, officer, owner, operator, agent, or employee. If such entry or inspection is refused, prohibited, or otherwise interfered with, the Commissioner shall have the power to seek an order compelling such entry or inspection, pursuant to § 40.1-49.9. (1992, c. 541.)

Editor's note. — Acts 1992, c. 541, which enacted this chapter, in cl. 2 provides that the 1992 act shall become effective on July 1, 1992, except that the Commissioner shall not be required to implement its provisions until October 1, 1992.

§ 40.1-51.27. Inspections, investigations, etc. — The Commissioner is authorized to make or cause to be made, such investigations and inspections and do such other things as are reasonably necessary to carry out the provisions of this chapter. (1992, c. 541.)

§ 40.1-51.28. Issuance of special orders. — A. The Commissioner shall have the power to issue special orders to:

1. Owners who are permitting or causing asbestos NESHAP violations, to cease and desist from such violation;

2. Owners who have violated or failed to comply with the terms and provisions of any order of the Commissioner, to comply with such terms and provisions;

3. Owners who have contravened duly adopted asbestos NESHAP standards and regulations, to cease such contravention and to comply with air quality standards and policies; and

4. Require any owner to comply with the provisions of this chapter.

B. Such special orders are to be issued only after a hearing with reasonable notice to the affected owners of the time, place and purpose thereof, and they shall become effective not less than five days after service as provided in subsection C. Should the Commissioner find that any such owner is unreasonably affecting the public health, safety or welfare, the health of animal or plant life, or property, after a reasonable attempt to give notice, he shall declare a state of emergency and may issue without a hearing an emergency special order directing the owner to cease such pollution immediately, and shall within ten days hold a hearing, after reasonable notice as to the time and place thereof to the owner to affirm, modify, amend or cancel such emergency special order. If the Commissioner finds that an owner who has been issued a special order or an emergency special order is not complying with the terms thereof, he may proceed in accordance with § 40.1-51.35 or § 40.1-51.39.

C. Any special order issued under the provisions of this section need not be filed with the Secretary of the Commonwealth, but the owner to whom such special order is directed shall be notified by certified mail, return receipt requested, sent to the last known address of such owner, or by personal delivery by an agent of the Commissioner, and the time limits specified shall be counted from the date of receipt.

D. Nothing in this section or in § 40.1-51.26 shall limit the Commissioner's authority to proceed against such owner directly under § 40.1-51.35 or § 40.1-51.39 without the prior issuance of an order, special, or otherwise. (1992, c. 541.)

§ 40.1-51.29. Decision of Commissioner pursuant to hearing. — Any decision by the Commissioner rendered pursuant to hearings under § 40.1-51.28 shall be reduced to writing and shall contain the explicit findings of fact and conclusions of law upon which the decision is based. Certified copies of the written decisions shall be delivered or mailed by certified mail to the parties affected by it. Failure to comply with this section shall render such decision invalid. (1992, c. 541.)

§ 40.1-51.30. Appeal to Board. — Any owner aggrieved by a final decision of the Commissioner under § 40.1-51.28 may file a notice of appeal to the Board within fifteen days. Such notice shall be in writing and addressed to the Commissioner. (1992, c. 541.)

§ 40.1-51.31. Penalties for noncompliance; judicial review. — A. The Board is authorized to promulgate regulations providing for the determination of a formula for the basis of the amount of any noncompliance penalty to be assessed by a court pursuant to subsection B hereof, in conformance with the requirements of § 120 of the federal Clean Air Act, as amended, and any regulations promulgated thereunder. Any regulations promulgated pursuant to this section shall be in accordance with the provisions of the Administrative Process Act (§ 9-6.14:1 et seq.).

B. Upon a determination of the amount by the Commissioner, the Commissioner shall petition the circuit court of the county or city wherein the owner subject to such noncompliance assessment resides, regularly or systematically conducts affairs or business activities, or where such owner's property affected by the administrative action is located for an order requiring payment of a noncompliance penalty in a sum the court deems appropriate.

C. Any order issued by a court pursuant to this section may be enforced as a judgment of the court. All sums collected, less the assessment and collection costs, shall be paid into the general fund of the state treasury.

D. Any penalty assessed under this section shall be in addition to permits, fees, orders, payments, sanctions, or other requirements under this chapter and shall in no way affect any civil or criminal enforcement proceedings brought under other provisions of this chapter. (1992, c. 541.)

§ 40.1-51.32. Owners to furnish plans, specifications and information. — Every owner which the Commissioner has reason to believe is causing, or may be about to cause, an asbestos NESHAP problem shall on request of the Commissioner furnish such plans, specifications and information as may be required by the Commissioner in the discharge of his duties under this chapter. Any information, except emission data, as to secret processes, formulae or methods of manufacture or production shall not be disclosed in a public hearing and shall be kept confidential. If samples are taken for analysis, a duplicate of the analytical report shall be furnished promptly to the person from whom such sample is requested. (1992, c. 541.)

§ 40.1-51.33. Protection of trade secrets. — Any information, except emissions data, reported to or otherwise obtained by the Commissioner which contains or might reveal a trade secret shall be confidential and shall be limited to those persons who need such information for purposes of enforcement of this chapter or the federal Clean Air Act or regulations and orders of the Commissioner. It shall be the duty of each owner to notify the Commissioner of the existence of trade secrets when he desires the protection provided herein. (1992, c. 541.)

§ 40.1-51.34. Right of entry. — Whenever it is necessary for the purposes of this chapter, the Commissioner may at reasonable times enter any establishment or upon any property, public or private, subject to federal security requirements, to obtain information or conduct surveys or investigations. (1992, c. 541.)

§ 40.1-51.35. Compelling compliance with regulations and orders of Board; penalty for violations. — A. Any owner violating or failing, neglecting or refusing to obey any asbestos NESHAP regulation or order of the Commissioner may be compelled to comply by injunction, mandamus or other appropriate remedy.

B. Without limiting the remedies which may be obtained under this section, any owner violating or failing, neglecting or refusing to obey any Board regulation or order or any provision of this chapter shall be subject, in the discretion of the court, to a civil penalty not to exceed $25,000 for each violation. Each day of violation shall constitute a separate offense. In determining the amount of any civil penalty to be assessed pursuant to this subsection, the court shall consider, in addition to such other factors as it may deem appropriate, the size of the owner's business, the severity of the economic impact of the penalty on the business, and the seriousness of the violation. Such civil penalties shall be paid into the state treasury.

C. With the consent of an owner who has violated or failed, neglected or refused to obey any asbestos NESHAP regulation or order or any provision of this chapter, the Commissioner may provide, in any order issued by the Commissioner against the owner, for the payment of civil charges in specific sums, not to exceed the limit of subsection B. Such civil charges shall be in lieu of any civil penalty which could be imposed under subsection B and shall be paid into the state treasury. (1992, c. 541.)

§ **40.1-51.36. Judicial review of regulations of Board.** — The validity of any regulation may be determined through judicial review in accordance with the provisions of the Administrative Process Act (§ 9-6.14:1 et seq.). (1992, c. 541.)

§ **40.1-51.37. Appeal from decision of Board.** — Any owner aggrieved by a final decision of the Board under § 40.1-51.30 or of the Commissioner under subdivision 4 of § 40.1-51.26 is entitled to judicial review thereof in accordance with the provisions of the Administrative Process Act (§ 9-6.14:1 et seq.). (1992, c. 541.)

§ **40.1-51.38. Appeal to Court of Appeals.** — The Commonwealth or any party aggrieved by any final decision of the judge shall have, regardless of the amount involved, the right to appeal to the Court of Appeals. The procedure shall be the same as that provided by law concerning appeals and supersedeas. (1992, c. 541.)

§ **40.1-51.39. Penalties; chapter not to affect right to relief or to maintain action.** — A. Any owner violating any provision of this chapter, Board regulation, or order of the Commissioner shall upon conviction be guilty of a misdemeanor and shall be subject to a fine of not more than $1,000 for each violation within the discretion of the court. Each day of continued violation after conviction shall constitute a separate offense.

B. Nothing in this chapter shall be construed to abridge, limit, impair, create, enlarge or otherwise affect substantively or procedurally the right of any person to damages or other relief on account of injury to persons or property. (1992, c. 541.)

§ **40.1-51.40. Duty of attorney for the Commonwealth.** — It shall be the duty of every attorney for the Commonwealth to whom the Commissioner has reported any violation of this chapter or any regulation or order of the Board, to cause proceedings to be prosecuted without delay for the fines and penalties in such cases. (1992, c. 541.)

§ **40.1-51.41. Local ordinances.** — A. Existing local ordinances adopted prior to July 1, 1972, shall continue in force; however, in the event of a conflict between a Board regulation, promulgated pursuant to this chapter, and a local ordinance, the Board regulation shall govern, except when the conflicting local ordinance is more stringent.

B. The governing body of any locality proposing to adopt an ordinance, or an amendment to an existing ordinance, relating to areas covered by asbestos NESHAP after June 30, 1972, shall first obtain the approval of the Board as to the provisions of the ordinance or amendment. The Board shall not approve any local ordinance less stringent than the pertinent regulations of the Board. (1992, c. 541.)

CHAPTER 4.

Labor Unions, Strikes, etc.

ARTICLE 1.

In General.

§ 40.1-52. Authority of labor unions to own, encumber and sell real estate. — The trustees of any unincorporated association organized for mutual benefit and chartered as a labor union for the purpose of collective bargaining and other lawful functions of labor unions, as defined by the laws of this Commonwealth, and having a duly authorized charter as a local labor union, from either a state or national labor organization, shall have the right to own, possess, improve, sell or mortgage real estate. Such real estate can be acquired for any lawful purpose whatsoever.

Property acquired by an unincorporated association under the provisions of this section can be sold, mortgaged or the title transferred by such trustees in the same manner and to the same extent as if such trustees were natural persons acting for themselves in their individual capacity, under the laws of this Commonwealth.

The provisions of this section shall apply to any real estate acquired prior to July 1, 1997, by any such unincorporated association, provided such real estate is real estate that could be legally acquired by such unincorporated association, if acquired after such date. (Code 1950, § 40-63; 1966, c. 382; 1970, c. 321; 1997, c. 761.)

§ 40.1-53. Preventing persons from pursuing lawful vocations, etc.; illegal picketing; injunction. — No person shall singly or in concert with others interfere or attempt to interfere with another in the exercise of his right to work or to enter upon the performance of any lawful vocation by the use of force, threats of violence or intimidation, or by the use of insulting or threatening language directed toward such person, to induce or attempt to induce him to quit his employment or refrain from seeking employment.

No person shall engage in picketing by force or violence, or picket alone or in concert with others in such manner as to obstruct or interfere with free ingress or egress to and from any premises, or obstruct or interfere with free use of public streets, sidewalks or other public ways.

Any person violating any of the provisions of this section shall be guilty of a misdemeanor, and punished accordingly.

Notwithstanding the punishments herein provided any court of general equity jurisdiction may enjoin picketing prohibited by this section, and in addition thereto, may enjoin any picketing or interference with lawful picketing when necessary to prevent disorder, restrain coercion, protect life or property, or promote the general welfare. (Code 1950, § 40-64; 1952, c. 674; 1970, c. 321; 1974, c. 254.)

Cross references. — As to picketing of dwelling places, see §§ 18.2-418 and 18.2-419.

Constitutionality. — On its face, this section infringes no right protected by U.S. Const., Amend. I. United Steelworkers v. Dalton, 544 F. Supp. 282 (E.D. Va. 1982).

Section not overbroad on its face. — Because this section prohibits only language calculated to coerce, intimidate, or lead to violence, it is not overbroad on its face. The statute does not infringe rights under U.S. Const., Amend. I. For the same reason, the statute is not preempted by § 8(a)(1) of the Labor Management Relations Act. United Steelworkers v. Dalton, 544 F. Supp. 282 (E.D. Va. 1982).

Purpose of section. — The plain purpose of this section is to protect the inherent right to work from the "clear and present danger" of destruction by those who, by the use of force, threats, violence, intimidation, or insulting words, would prevent the exercise of that right. McWhorter v. Commonwealth, 191 Va. 857, 63 S.E.2d 20 (1951); United Steelworkers v. Dalton, 544 F. Supp. 282 (E.D. Va. 1982).

Plain purpose of Virginia' picketing and right to work statute is to protect the right to work from infringement by the use of force, threats, violence, intimidation, or insulting words. Kaufhold v. Bright, 835 F. Supp. 294 (W.D. Va. 1993).

The prohibition of this section is within a narrow scope. McWhorter v. Commonwealth, 191 Va. 857, 63 S.E.2d 20 (1951); United Steelworkers v. Dalton, 544 F. Supp. 282 (E.D. Va. 1982).

Section does not provide for a civil action for damages. It is a quasi-criminal statute, the violation of which is punishable as a misdemeanor. In addition to providing for criminal penalties, it also provides for injunctive relief. Crawford v. United Steel Workers, 230 Va. 217, 335 S.E.2d 828 (1985), cert. denied, 475 U.S. 1095, 106 S. Ct. 1490, 89 L. Ed. 2d 892 (1986); Kaufhold v. Bright, 835 F. Supp. 294 (W.D. Va. 1993).

Picketing is subject to regulation by State. — The pattern which emerges to shape the boundaries of state action seems to be that picketing is subject to regulation by the State, either by legislation or by court action. But such regulation must have a reasonable basis in prevention of disorder, restraint of coercion, protection of life or property, or promotion of the general welfare. The instrument of state action, whether judicial process or legislative enactment, must be specifically directed to acts or conduct which overstep legal limits, and not include those which keep within the protected area of free speech. Edwards v. Commonwealth, 191 Va. 272, 60 S.E.2d 916 (1950); McWhorter v. Commonwealth, 191 Va. 857, 63 S.E.2d 20 (1951).

Section was not designed to end picketing. — There is nothing in this section which supports the assertion that it was designed to end the practice, common to labor disputes, known as picketing. It does not prohibit peaceful picketing or peaceful persuasion in connection with labor disputes which are protected under the constitutional guaranty of freedom of speech. McWhorter v. Commonwealth, 191 Va. 857, 63 S.E.2d 20 (1951).

It is not the public policy of this State to prohibit all picketing. Only certain types are prohibited by the picketing statute. Painters & Paperhangers Local 1018 v. Rountree Corp., 194 Va. 148, 72 S.E.2d 402 (1952).

The prohibition in this section is not directed against those in the picket line alone, but outlaws interference with the right to work by "any person singly or in concert with another." McWhorter v. Commonwealth, 191 Va. 857, 63 S.E.2d 20 (1951).

Section does not violate right of free speech. — The prohibition in this section against the interference with the right to work by the use of force, threats, violence, intimidation, or insulting words, acts which are inherently wrong and liable to bring about an immediate breach of the peace, is within the police power of the State and does not trespass upon the constitutional right of freedom of speech. McWhorter v. Commonwealth, 191 Va. 857, 63

S.E.2d 20 (1951). See Painters & Paperhangers Local 1018 v. Rountree Corp., 194 Va. 148, 72 S.E.2d 402 (1952).

The right or privilege of free speech has its limitations, and it is not violated by a state statute which makes it a crime to address any offensive, derisive, or annoying word to any person lawfully in a public place, or to call him by an offensive or derisive name, which has a direct tendency to cause acts of violence by the person to whom individually the remark is addressed. McWhorter v. Commonwealth, 191 Va. 857, 63 S.E.2d 20 (1951).

For case citing San Diego Bldg. Trades Council v. Garmon, 359 U.S. 236, 79 S. Ct. 733, 3 L. Ed. 2d 775 (1959), which held that when an activity is arguably subject to § 7 or § 8 of the National Labor Relations Act, as amended by the Taft-Hartley Act, the states as well as the federal courts must defer to the exclusive competence of the National Labor Relations Board, as authority for reversal, see Waxman v. Virginia, 371 U.S. 4, 83 S. Ct. 46, 9 L. Ed. 2d 50 (1962).

It is not aimed at the use of insulting words or language as such. It does not prohibit or punish the use of offensive words by one picket toward another picket, or toward one not connected with the particular industrial plant concerned in a labor dispute. Nor does it confine those on the picket line to language suitable only to the drawing room or the parlor car. McWhorter v. Commonwealth, 191 Va. 857, 63 S.E.2d 20 (1951); United Steelworkers v. Dalton, 544 F. Supp. 282 (E.D. Va. 1982).

Focus is on intimidating or coercive language. — This section is not aimed at merely insulting language. The statute's focus is on language which the user intends to be, or is in and of itself, intimidating or coercive. Proscribed is the use of words through which the speaker intends to convey a threat of impending harm. United Steelworkers v. Dalton, 544 F. Supp. 282 (E.D. Va. 1982).

"Insulting or threatening language" construed. — The words "insulting or threatening language" cannot be read in a vacuum. They must be read in the context of the sentence of which they are a part. These words are preceded by the words "by the use of force, threats of violence or intimidation." Such words precedent color the meaning of the words that follow. Read as a whole, the language of the statute prohibits the use of language violent in nature; language which can be construed as expressing an actual intention of inflicting injury. United Steelworkers v. Dalton, 544 F. Supp. 282 (E.D. Va. 1982).

Profane language used in labor dispute held not to support liability under § 8.01-45. Crawford v. United Steel Workers, 230 Va. 217, 335 S.E.2d 828 (1985), cert. denied, 475 U.S. 1095, 106 S. Ct. 1490, 89 L. Ed. 2d 892 (1986).

Use of police power not precluded by Labor Management Relations Act. — The hurling of insults is protected under the Labor Management Relations Act, 29 U.S.C. § 141 et seq. The existence of the LMRA, however, does not preclude the states from the exercise of their usual police power. The states remain free to act to protect the public peace and order. United Steelworkers v. Dalton, 544 F. Supp. 282 (E.D. Va. 1982).

Fighting words not protected by Labor Management Relations Act. — Violent or intimidating language — fighting words — are not protected under the Labor Management Relations Act, 29 U.S.C. § 141 et seq. As this section is addressed to unprotected conduct, it does not interfere with the federal scheme. The LMRA does not preempt Virginia's right to prohibit such conduct. United Steelworkers v. Dalton, 544 F. Supp. 282 (E.D. Va. 1982).

Conduct constituting violation of section. — The defendant, along with her companions, lay down in front of one of the main entrances to and exits from a large industrial plant in such a manner as to block completely the use of the gate by both pedestrian and vehicular traffic in the operation of the plant. Clearly such conduct on the part of the defendant was in violation of this section. Hubbard v. Commonwealth, 207 Va. 673, 152 S.E.2d 250 (1967).

Evidence sufficient to show use of insulting words. — See McWhorter v. Commonwealth, 191 Va. 857, 63 S.E.2d 20 (1951).

Violation not shown. — In Painters & Paperhangers Local 1018 v. Rountree Corp., 194 Va. 148, 72 S.E.2d 402 (1952) it was held that the record failed to disclose any violation of the picketing statute.

§ 40.1-54. Payment of certain charges by carriers or shippers to or for benefit of labor organization. — (1) As used in this section, the term *"labor organization"* means any organization of any kind, or any agency or employee representation committee or plan, in which employees participate and which exists for the purpose, in whole or in part, of dealing with employers concerning grievances, labor disputes, wages, rates of pay, hours of employment, or conditions of work.

(2) It shall be unlawful for any carrier or shipper of property, or any association of such carriers or shippers, to agree to pay, or to pay, to or for the benefit of a labor organization, directly or indirectly, any charge by reason of the placing upon, delivery to, or movement by rail, or by a railroad car, of a motor vehicle, trailer, or container which is also capable of being moved or propelled upon the highways, and any such agreement shall be void and unenforceable.

(3) It shall be unlawful for any labor organization to accept or receive from any carrier or shipper of property, or any association of such carriers or shippers, any payment described above.

(4) Any corporation, association, organization, firm or person who agrees to pay, or who does pay, or who agrees to receive, or who does receive, any payment described hereinabove shall be guilty of a misdemeanor and shall be fined not less than $100 nor more than $1,000 for each offense. Each act of violation, and each day during which such an agreement remains in effect, shall constitute a separate offense. (Code 1950, § 40-64.1; 1962, c. 376; 1970, c. 321.)

§ 40.1-54.1. Public policy as to strikes and work stoppages at hospitals. — It is hereby declared to be the public policy of the Commonwealth that hospitals shall be free from strikes, and work stoppages. (Code 1950, § 40-64.2; 1970, c. 720.)

The number of this section was assigned by the Virginia Code Commission, the number in the 1970 Act having been 40-64.2.

§ 40.1-54.2. Strikes and work stoppages at hospitals prohibited; penalty. — No employee of any hospital shall engage in any strike or work stoppage at such hospital which in any way interferes with the operation of such hospital.

Any person violating any of the provisions of this section shall be guilty of a misdemeanor and punished accordingly.

Notwithstanding the penalties herein provided, any court of general equity jurisdiction may enjoin conduct proscribed by this section. (Code 1950, § 40-64.3; 1970, c. 720.)

The number of this section was assigned by the Virginia Code Commission, the number in the 1970 Act having been 40-64.3.

ARTICLE 2.

Strikes by Government Employees.

§ 40.1-55. Employee striking terminates, and becomes temporarily ineligible for, public employment. — Any employee of the Commonwealth, or of any county, city, town or other political subdivision thereof, or of any agency of any one of them, who, in concert with two or more other such employees, for the purpose of obstructing, impeding or suspending any activity or operation of his employing agency or any other governmental agency, strikes or willfully refuses to perform the duties of his employment shall, by such action, be deemed to have terminated his employment and shall thereafter be ineligible for employment in any position or capacity during the next twelve months by the Commonwealth, or any county, city, town or other political subdivision of the Commonwealth, or by any department or agency of any of them. (Code 1950, § 40-65; 1970, c. 321.)

Law Review. — For article discussing public sector collective bargaining, see 15 Wm. & Mary L. Rev. 57 (1973). For comment, "Public Sector Collective Bargaining and Sunshine Laws — A Needless Conflict," see 18 Wm. & Mary L. Rev. 159 (1976). For comment on public employee collective bargaining in Virginia, see 11 U. Rich. L. Rev. 431 (1977). For comment, "'Working to the Contract' in Virginia: Legal Consequences of Teachers' Attempts to Limit Their Contractual Duties," see 16 U. Rich. L. Rev. 449 (1982).

§ 40.1-56. Department head, etc., to notify employee of such termination, etc. — In any such case the head of any department of the state government, or the mayor of any city or town, or the chairman of the board of supervisors or other governing body of any county, or the head of any other such employing agency, in which such employee was employed, shall forthwith notify such employee of the fact of the termination of his employment and at the same time serve upon him in person or by registered mail a declaration of his ineligibility for reemployment as before provided. Such declaration shall state the fact upon which the asserted ineligibility is based. (Code 1950, § 40-66; 1970, c. 321.)

§ 40.1-57. Appeal by employee from declaration of ineligibility. — In the event that any such employee feels aggrieved by such declaration of ineligibility he may within ninety days after the date thereof appeal to the circuit court of the county or the circuit court of the city in which he was employed by filing a petition therein for a review of the matters of law and fact involved in or pertinent to the declaration of ineligibility. A copy of the petition shall be served upon or sent by registered mail to the official signing the declaration, who may file an answer thereto within ten days after receiving the same. The court or the judge thereof in vacation shall, as promptly as practicable, hear the appeal de novo and notify the employee and the signer of the declaration of ineligibility of the time and place of hearing. The court shall hear such testimony as may be adduced by the respective parties and render judgment in accordance with the law and the evidence. Such judgment shall be final. (Code 1950, § 40-67; 1970, c. 321.)

§ 40.1-57.1. Appeal by employer for reemployment of terminated employee. — Notwithstanding any provision of law to the contrary, in the event that the employer of an individual terminated under this article deems it necessary for the protection of the public welfare that such individual be reemployed within the twelve months following his termination, the employer may, within ninety days after the date of the declaration of ineligibility, appeal to the circuit court of the county or the circuit court of the city in which the individual was employed by filing a petition therein setting forth the reasons why the public welfare requires reemployment. A copy of the petition shall be served upon or sent by registered mail to the former employee, who may file an answer therein ten days after receiving the same. The court or the judge thereof in vacation shall notify the employer and former employee of the time and place of the hearing on the appeal, such hearing to be de novo and to be held as promptly as possible. The court shall hear such testimony as may be adduced by the respective parties and render judgment in accordance with the law and the evidence. Such judgment shall be final. (1972, c. 792.)

Law Review. — For article discussing public sector collective bargaining, see 15 Wm. & Mary L. Rev. 57 (1973).

ARTICLE 2.1.

Collective Bargaining for Governmental Employees.

§ 40.1-57.2. Prohibition against collective bargaining. — No state, county, municipal, or like governmental officer, agent or governing body is vested with or possesses any authority to recognize any labor union or other employee association as a bargaining agent of any public officers or employees, or to collectively bargain or enter into any collective bargaining contract with any such union or association or its agents with respect to any matter relating to them or their employment or service. (1993, cc. 868, 879.)

§ 40.1-57.3. Certain activities permitted. — Nothing in this article shall be construed to prevent employees of the Commonwealth, its political subdivisions, or of any governmental agency of any of them from forming associations for the purpose of promoting their interests before the employing agency. (1993, cc. 868, 879.)

ARTICLE 3.

Denial or Abridgement of Right to Work.

§ 40.1-58. Policy of article. — It is hereby declared to be the public policy of Virginia that the right of persons to work shall not be denied or abridged on account of membership or nonmembership in any labor union or labor organization. (Code 1950, § 40-68; 1970, c. 321.)

Law Review. — For article, "Current Trends in Labor Law in Virginia," see 42 Va. L. Rev. 691 (1956). For article discussing public sector col-

lective bargaining, see 15 Wm. & Mary L. Rev. 57 (1973).

This article does not violate any provision of the federal or Virginia Constitutions. Finney v. Hawkins, 189 Va. 878, 54 S.E.2d 872 (1949).

The Virginia Right to Work Law is not incorporated by the federal Assimilative Crimes Act because the policy of the Virginia statute conflicts with federal law. King v. Gemini Food Servs., Inc., 438 F. Supp. 964 (E.D. Va. 1976), aff'd, 562 F.2d 297 (4th Cir. 1977).

And therefore does not apply to federal enclaves. — The Virginia Right to Work Law is not assimilated into federal law by the federal Assimilative Crimes Act and therefore does not apply to federal enclaves. King v. Gemini Food Servs., Inc., 438 F. Supp. 964 (E.D. Va. 1976), aff'd, 562 F.2d 297 (4th Cir. 1977).

Washington Metropolitan Area Transit Authority compact is federal law and thus controlling by its terms over the Virginia Right-to-Work Statute by way of the Supremacy Clause. Malone v. Washington Metro. Area Transit Auth., 622 F. Supp. 1422 (E.D. Va. 1985).

Virginia has delegated power to enforce Right-to-Work Law on WMATA employees. — Under the Washington Metropolitan Area Transit Authority compact, Virginia has delegated its power to enforce its Right-to-Work Law on WMATA employees. The WMATA compact clearly grants the Authority the power to enter into collective bargaining agreements with a union local over employees' working conditions. Implicit in its right to enter into collective bargaining agreements, WMATA has the authorization to enter into a union shop agreement. Malone v. Washington Metro. Area Transit Auth., 622 F. Supp. 1422 (E.D. Va. 1985).

Federal statutes, 10 U.S.C. §§ 974 and 3634, relating to outside employment of military personnel do not violate the Virginia right to work laws. Jenkins v. Rumsfeld, 412 F. Supp. 1177 (E.D. Va. 1976).

Picketing in violation of article. — The State, consistently with the Constitution of the United States, may enjoin peaceful picketing when it is carried on for purposes in conflict with the Virginia Right to Work Statute. Locan Union 10, United Ass'n of Journeymen Plumbers & Steamfitters v. Graham, 345 U.S. 192, 73 S. Ct. 585, 97 L. Ed. 946 (1953).

Finding that picketing was carried on for purposes in conflict with the provisions of the Right to Work Statute of the State was held to have a reasonable basis in the evidence. Local Union 10, United Ass'n of Journeymen Plumbers & Steamfitters v. Graham, 345 U.S. 192, 73 S. Ct. 585, 97 L. Ed. 946 (1953).

Violation not shown. — In Painters & Paperhangers Local 1018 v. Rountree Corp., 194 Va. 148, 72 S.E.2d 402 (1952) it was held that the record failed to disclose any violation of the Virginia Right to Work Statute.

No error in reinstatement and back pay award. — Trial court did not err in awarding airport authority employee who was fired after joining the union back pay and ordering his reinstatement; the award was equitable and consistent with the relief authorized by the right to work law. Norfolk Airport Auth. v. Nordwall, 246 Va. 391, 436 S.E.2d 436 (1993).

§ 40.1-58.1. Application of article to public employers and employees.

— As used in this article, the words, *"person," "persons," "employer," "employees," "union," "labor union," "association," "organization"* and *"corporation"* shall include but not be limited to public employers, public employees and any representative of public employees in this Commonwealth. The application of this article to public employers, public employees and their representatives shall not be construed as modifying in any way the application of § 40.1-55 to government employees. (1973, c. 79.)

Law Review. — For article discussing public sector collective bargaining, see 15 Wm. & Mary L. Rev. 57 (1973). For comment, "Public Sector Collective Bargaining and Sunshine Laws — A Needless Conflict," see 18 Wm. & Mary L. Rev. 159 (1976). For comment on public employee collective bargaining in Virginia, see 11 U. Rich. L. Rev. 431 (1977).

The legislature of Virginia has the right to and has determined not to recognize

union representation of public employees. Such determination is not in conflict with the Labor Management Relations Act, §§ 1, 7, as amended, 29 U.S.C. §§ 151, 157. In the absence of legislation a local government has no authority to recognize a labor organization as representative of city employees. It is not a matter of constitutional right, but legislative. Teamsters Local Union 822 v. City of Portsmouth, 423 F. Supp. 954 (E.D. Va. 1975), aff'd, 534 F.2d 328 (4th Cir. 1976).

§ 40.1-59. Agreements or combinations declared unlawful. — Any

agreement or combination between any employer and any labor union or labor organization whereby persons not members of such union or organization shall be denied the right to work for the employer, or whereby such membership is made a condition of employment or continuation of employment by such employer, or whereby any such union or organization acquires an employment monopoly in any enterprise, is hereby declared to be against public policy and an illegal combination or conspiracy. (Code 1950, § 40-69; 1970, c. 321.)

Law Review. — For survey of Virginia law on business associations for the year 1970-1971, see 57 Va. L. Rev. 1541 (1971).

Intent of § 14 (b) of the Taft-Hartley Act is to permit state regulation of union-security agreements which otherwise would be allowed under § (8)(a)(3) of the act. State regulation of such agreements, whether oral or written, is not only consistent with the intent of the act, but also consistent with the language of § 14 (b). Moore v. Plumbers & Steamfitters Local 10, 211 Va. 520, 179 S.E.2d 15 (1971).

State court has jurisdiction to entertain an action if it involves a consummated union-security agreement, oral or written, between the employer and the union. Moore v. Plumbers & Steamfitters Local 10, 211 Va. 520, 179 S.E.2d 15 (1971).

Allegation sufficient to withstand motion to dismiss. — A worker's allegation that the employer and the union had acted in concert to deny him employment because he was not a member of the union was a sufficient allegation of the existence of a union-security agreement between the employer and the union to withstand the assault of a demurrer or motions to dismiss on the grounds that the worker's action was based on an unfair labor practice under the National Labor Relations Act, and that the said act gave sole and exclusive jurisdiction to the National Labor Relations Board. Moore v. Plumbers & Steamfitters Local 10, 211 Va. 520, 179 S.E.2d 15 (1971).

§ 40.1-60. Employers not to require employees to become or remain members of union. — No person shall be required by an employer to become or remain a member of any labor union or labor organization as a condition of employment or continuation of employment by such employer. (Code 1950, § 40-70; 1970, c. 321.)

§ 40.1-61. Employers not to require abstention from membership in union. — No person shall be required by an employer to abstain or refrain from membership in any labor union or labor organization as a condition of employment or continuation of employment. (Code 1950, § 40-71; 1970, c. 321.)

Courts may not intervene in cases committed to jurisdiction of NLRB. — Since both this section and § 8 (a)(3) of the National Labor Relations Act of 1935 are aimed at proscribing the same practices, the danger that conflicting remedies might be brought to bear on the same activity precludes either federal or State courts from intervening in such cases, which are committed to the jurisdiction of the National Labor Relations Board. Bukovac v. Daniel Constr. Co., 469 F. Supp. 176 (W.D. Va. 1979).

This section had no bearing on a constitutional claim seeking to have declared in-valid resolutions of the York County Board of Supervisors which prohibit supervisors in the fire department from belonging to a union in which rank and file fire fighters are members. York County Fire Fighters Ass'n, Local 2498 v. County of York, 589 F.2d 775 (4th Cir. 1978).

No error in reinstatement and back pay award. — Trial court did not err in awarding airport authority employee who was fired after joining the union back pay and ordering his reinstatement; the award was equitable and consistent with the relief authorized by the right to work law. Norfolk Airport Auth. v. Nordwall, 246 Va. 391, 436 S.E.2d 436 (1993).

§ 40.1-62. Employer not to require payment of union dues, etc. — No employer shall require any person, as a condition of employment or continuation of employment, to pay any dues, fees or other charges of any kind to any labor union or labor organization. (Code 1950, § 40-72; 1970, c. 321.)

Virginia has delegated power to enforce Right-to-Work Law on WMATA employees. — Under the Washington Metropolitan Area Transit Authority compact, Virginia has delegated its power to enforce its Right-to-Work Law on WMATA employees. The WMATA compact clearly grants the Authority the power to enter into collective bargaining agreements with a union local over employees' working conditions. Implicit in its right to enter into collective bargaining agreements, WMATA has the authorization to enter into a union shop agreement. Malone v. Washington Metro. Area Transit Auth., 622 F. Supp. 1422 (E.D. Va. 1985).

§ 40.1-63. Recovery by individual unlawfully denied employment. — Any person who may be denied employment or be deprived of continuation of his employment in violation of §§ 40.1-60, 40.1-61 or § 40.1-62 or of one or more of such sections, shall be entitled to recover from such employer and from any other person, firm, corporation or association acting in concert with him by appropriate action in the courts of this Commonwealth such damages as he may have sustained by reason of such denial or deprivation of employment. (Code 1950, § 40-73; 1970, c. 321.)

§ 40.1-64. Application of article to contracts. — The provisions of this article shall not apply to any lawful contract in force on April 30, 1947, but they shall apply in all respects to contracts entered into thereafter and to any renewal or extension of an existing contract. (Code 1950, § 40-74; 1970, c. 321.)

§ 40.1-65. Agreement or practice designed to cause employer to violate article declared illegal. — Any agreement, understanding or practice which is designated to cause or require any employer, whether or not a party thereto, to violate any provision of this article is hereby declared to be an illegal agreement, understanding or practice and contrary to public policy. (Code 1950, § 40-74.1; 1954, c. 431; 1970, c. 321.)

§ 40.1-66. Conduct causing violation of article illegal; peaceful solicitation to join union. — Any person, firm, association, corporation, or labor union or organization engaged in lockouts, layoffs, boycotts, picketing, work stoppages or other conduct, a purpose of which is to cause, force, persuade or induce any other person, firm, association, corporation or labor union or organization to violate any provision of this article shall be guilty of illegal conduct contrary to public policy; provided that nothing herein contained shall be construed to prevent or make illegal the peaceful and orderly solicitation and persuasion by union members of others to join a union, unaccompanied by any intimidation, use of force, threat of use of force, reprisal or threat of reprisal, and provided that no such solicitation or persuasion shall be conducted so as to interfere with, or interrupt the work of any employee during working hours. (Code 1950, § 40-74.2; 1954, c. 431; 1970, c. 321.)

Law Review. — For article discussing public sector collective bargaining, see 15 Wm. & Mary L. Rev. 57 (1973).

Profane language used in labor dispute held not to support liability under § 8.01-45.

Crawford v. United Steel Workers, 230 Va. 217, 335 S.E.2d 828 (1985), cert. denied, 475 U.S. 1095, 106 S. Ct. 1490, 89 L. Ed. 2d 892 (1986).

§ 40.1-67. Injunctive relief against violation; recovery of damages. — Any employer, person, firm, association, corporation, labor union or organization injured as a result of any violation or threatened violation of any provision of this article or threatened with any such violation shall be entitled to injunctive relief against any and all violators or persons threatening violation, and also to recover from such violator or violators, or person or persons, any and all damages of any character cognizable at common law resulting from such violations or threatened violations. Such remedies shall be independent of and in addition to the penalties and remedies prescribed in other provisions of this article. (Code 1950, § 40-74.3; 1954, c. 431; 1970, c. 321.)

Profane language used in labor dispute held not to support liability under § 8.01-45. Crawford v. United Steel Workers, 230 Va. 217, 335 S.E.2d 828 (1985), cert. denied, 475 U.S. 1095, 106 S. Ct. 1490, 89 L. Ed. 2d 892 (1986).

§ 40.1-68. Service of process on clerk of State Corporation Commission as attorney for union. — Any labor union or labor organization doing business in this Commonwealth, all of whose officers and trustees are nonresidents of this Commonwealth, shall by written power of attorney, filed with the Department of Labor and Industry and the State Corporation Commission, appoint the clerk of the State Corporation Commission its attorney or agent upon whom all legal process against the union or organization may be served, and who shall be authorized to enter an appearance on its behalf. The manner of service of process on the clerk of the State Corporation Commission, the mailing thereof to the labor union or organization, the fees therefor, the effect of judgments, decrees and orders, and the procedure in cases where no power of attorney is filed as required, shall be the same as provided for in cases of foreign corporations. (Code 1950, § 40-74.4; 1954, c. 431; 1956, c. 430; 1970, c. 321.)

§ 40.1-69. Violation a misdemeanor. — Any violation of any of the provisions of this article by any person, firm, association, corporation, or labor union or organization shall be a misdemeanor. (Code 1950, § 40-74.5; 1954, c. 431; 1970, c. 321; 1973, c. 425.)

Cross references. — For present provisions as to enforcement of this title and rules and regulations adopted pursuant thereto, and pen- alties for violations, see § 40.1-49.4.
Applied in Old Dominion Branch 496 v. Austin, 213 Va. 377, 192 S.E.2d 737 (1972).

Article 4.

Mediation and Conciliation of Labor Disputes.

§ 40.1-70. Department designated agency to mediate disputes. — The Department is hereby designated as the state agency authorized to mediate and conciliate labor disputes. (Code 1950, § 40-95.1; 1952, c. 697; 1970, c. 321.)

§ 40.1-71. Notice of proposed termination or modification of collective bargaining contract; notice prior to work stoppage; injunctions and penalties. — Whenever there is in effect a collective bargaining contract covering employees of any utility engaged in the business of furnishing water, light, heat, gas, electric power, transportation or communication, the utility or the collective bargaining agent recognized by the utility and its employees shall not terminate or modify such contract until the party desiring such termination or modification serves written notice upon the Department of the proposed termination or modification at least thirty days prior to the expiration date thereof or, in the event such contract contains no expiration date, at least thirty days prior to the date it is proposed to make such termination or modification; provided, however, that a party having given notice of modification as provided herein shall not be required to give a notice of termination of the same contract.

Where there is no collective bargaining contract in effect, the utility or its employees shall give at least thirty days' notice to the Department prior to any work stoppage which would affect the operations of the utility engaged in the business of furnishing any of the utilities as described in this section.

If the utility or its employees, or the collective bargaining agent recognized by the utility and its employees, as the case may be, fails to give thirty days' notice as required by this section, the utility or its employees or such collective bargaining agent, as the case may be, may file a bill of complaint with the clerk of the circuit court having equity jurisdiction over the place of employment asking the court to temporarily enjoin such termination, modification or work stoppage until the proper notice has been served and the thirty-day period has been observed. The court shall have the authority to impose against any person who violates the notice provisions of this section a fine of up to $100 for each day such termination, modification or work stoppage continues until proper notice has been served and observed or against the collective bargaining agent the court shall have the authority to impose a fine of up to $1,000 for each day such termination or modification continues until proper notice has been served and observed. (Code 1950, § 40-95.2; 1952, c. 697; 1966, c. 92; 1970, c. 321; 1979, c. 515.)

§ 40.1-72. Commissioner to notify Governor of disputes; mediation and conciliation. — Upon receipt of notice of any labor dispute affecting operation of the utility, the Commissioner shall forthwith notify the Governor and inform him of the nature of the dispute. If the Governor deems it necessary the Commissioner, or his designated agent, shall offer to meet and confer with the parties in interest and undertake to mediate and conciliate their differences. If the Governor deems it advisable, it shall be the duty of the utility and its employees, or designated representatives, to meet and confer with the Commissioner or his agent, at a time and place designated by the Commissioner, for the purpose of mediating and conciliating their differences. (Code 1950, § 40-95.3; 1952, c. 697; 1966, c. 92; 1970, c. 321.)

§ 40.1-73. Commissioner to keep Governor informed of negotiations, etc. — The Commissioner shall keep the Governor fully informed as to the progress of the negotiations between the utility and its employees and shall report as soon as practical whether in his judgment a strike or lockout appears to be probable in any such dispute or, if a strike or lockout begins, whether continuation thereof is probable. (Code 1950, § 40-95.4; 1952, c. 697; 1970, c. 321.)

§ 40.1-74. Right of entry. — In order to carry out the duties imposed by this article, the Commissioner or his designated agent shall have the right to enter upon the property of the utility. (Code 1950, § 40-95.5; 1952, c. 697; 1970, c. 321.)

§ 40.1-75. Article not applicable when National Railway Labor Act applies. — Nothing in this article shall apply to any utility to which the National Railway Labor Act is applicable. (Code 1950, § 40-95.6; 1952, c. 697; 1970, c. 321.)

ARTICLE 5.

Registration of Labor Unions, Labor Associations and Labor Organizations.

§§ 40.1-76, 40.1-77: Repealed by Acts 1991, c. 443.

CHAPTER 5.

CHILD LABOR.

§ 40.1-78. Employment of children under fourteen and sixteen. —

A. No child under fourteen years of age shall be employed, permitted or suffered to work in, about or in connection with any gainful occupation except as specified in this chapter.

B. No child under sixteen years of age shall be employed, permitted or suffered to work in, about or in connection with any gainful occupation during school hours unless he has reached the age of fourteen and is enrolled in a regular school work-training program and a work-training certificate has been issued for his employment as provided in § 40.1-88.

C. Nothing in this section shall affect the provisions of §§ 40.1-100 A, 40.1-100.1, 40.1-100.2, 40.1-101 and 40.1-102. (Code 1950, § 40-96; 1956, c. 567; 1960, c. 434; 1968, c. 264; 1970, c. 321; 1991, c. 511.)

Cross references. — As to issuance by judges of juvenile and domestic relations courts of special work permits to children not qualified to obtain work permits under other provisions of law, see § 16.1-241, subdivision (H).

In general. — The Child Labor Law, as enacted in 1914 and codified in the Code of 1919 as § 1809 et seq., has been amended and other statutes for the protection of infants have been since enacted, from time to time. See Michie's Code 1942, and Michie's Suppl. 1948, §§ 1808a to 1808q, codified as this chapter. These statutes forbid the employment of infants within certain ages in gainful occupations (with some exceptions), or within designated hours, except upon terms stated in the statutes, and annex

penalties upon employers, parents, guardians, etc., for their violation (§ 40.1-113). These penalties are the means provided by law for enforcement of obedience to the statutes. Prior to the enactment in 1918 of the Workers' Compensation Act (now codified as § 65.2-100 et seq.), if these statutes were violated, there was no remedy against the wrongdoer except to enforce the penalties and a common-law action by the injured party, aided by the provisions of § 8.01-221. This common-law action was subject to all the common-law defenses. Humphrees v. Boxley Bros. Co., 146 Va. 91, 135 S.E. 890 (1926).

For other decisions relating to actions under the Child Labor Law, see Standard

Red Cedar Chest Co. v. Monroe, 125 Va. 442, 99 S.E. 589 (1919); Miller Mfg. Co. v. Loving, 125 Va. 255, 99 S.E. 591 (1919); Ocean Accident & Guarantee Corp. v. Washington Brick & Terra Cotta Co., 148 Va. 829, 139 S.E. 513 (1927); Miller Mfg. Co. v. Aetna Life Ins. Co., 150 Va. 495, 143 S.E. 747 (1928).

The principal object of the Child Labor Law is the protection of the infant. He is also entitled to the equal protection of the law with adults; and if benefits and protection are afforded to adults by the Workers' Compensation Act (now § 65.2-100 et seq.), they should be extended to infants also whenever it can be done consistently with the language and spirit of such laws. The care and welfare of the infant should be carefully borne in mind in the interpretation of these statutes. Humphrees v. Boxley Bros. Co., 146 Va. 91, 135 S.E. 890 (1926).

The object of a child labor statute is to preserve the lives and limbs of children. Standard Red Cedar Chest Co. v. Monroe, 125 Va. 442, 99 S.E. 589 (1919).

This section should be construed in harmony with the intention of the legislature as expressed in § 40.1-113. Clover Creamery Co. v. Kanode, 142 Va. 542, 129 S.E. 222 (1925).

Relative duty of proprietor and parent to prevent employment. — This section provides that no child under 14 years of age shall be employed, "permitted or suffered to work," etc. These words do not impose upon the proprietor of a business the duty to prevent, or use reasonable care to prevent, the child from engaging in the business. The section only prohibits the employment of the child and the phrase "permitted or suffered to work" was intended to make the parent or other person in control, acquiescing in the employment, equally guilty with the proprietor of the business. Clover Creamery Co. v. Kanode, 142 Va. 542, 129 S.E. 222 (1925).

Proprietor's liability as dependent upon knowledge. — Construing this section in the light of the other provisions of the Child Labor Law, it is manifest that the words "permitted or suffered to work" impose no duty or obligation upon the proprietor except where, after acquiring knowledge that a child within the prohibited age has been employed in his business, he permits or suffers him to remain in his service. Clover Creamery Co. v. Kanode, 142 Va. 542, 129 S.E. 222 (1925).

It cannot be said that the proprietor has "permitted or suffered a child to work" in his business, when he has no knowledge that the child is engaged in his service. The words "suffered" and "permitted" necessarily imply knowledge. Clover Creamery Co. v. Kanode, 142 Va. 542, 129 S.E. 222 (1925).

When employer guilty of actionable negligence under former statute. — Under § 1809 of the Code of 1919 (similar to this section) the employment of a child by a factory owner to work in his factory, with knowledge of the fact that he was within the prohibited age, was to be regarded per se as the proximate cause of an injury received by the child in the course of his employment. And where a child was knowingly employed contrary to the provisions of the statute and was injured in such employment, the employer was guilty of actionable negligence as a matter of law. The unlawful hiring constitutes the causal connection between the violation of the statute and the injury. Standard Red Cedar Chest Co. v. Monroe, 125 Va. 442, 99 S.E. 589 (1919).

Ratification of illegal employment by acquiescence. — Acquiescence by the master in the illegal employment of a child by his servant constitutes ratification and makes the employment by the servant the employment of the master. Clover Creamery Co. v. Kanode, 142 Va. 542, 129 S.E. 222 (1925).

Defendant's servant permitting child to assist in the delivery of milk. — A servant permitted a child to ride in defendant's milk wagon and assist him in the delivery of milk, and gave him presents. While thus assisting defendant's servant the child was run over and killed. Defendant had in force a rule prohibiting its drivers, who had neither authority nor necessity for employing assistants, from allowing boys to ride on its wagons or assist in the delivery of milk. This rule was enforced by defendant. Defendant had no knowledge that the driver had violated the rule by permitting the child to ride on the wagon or assist in the delivery of the milk. It was held that the act of the driver in securing the child to assist him was beyond the scope of his authority and defendant not having ratified such employment was not bound by the act of his servant, and the defendant having no knowledge of the driver's act, could not be said to have "permitted or suffered" the child to work in his service. Clover Creamery Co. v. Kanode, 142 Va. 542, 129 S.E. 222 (1925).

Liability imposed upon employers by the Workers' Compensation Act is in aid of the Child Labor Law, rather than as opposed to it. And infants, whether lawfully employed or not, are within the language and intent of the Act. Humphrees v. Boxley Bros. Co., 146 Va. 91, 135 S.E. 890 (1926); Nolde Bros. v. Chalkley, 184 Va. 553, 35 S.E.2d 827 (1945), aff'd on rehearing, 185 Va. 96, 38 S.E.2d 73 (1945).

And the remedy afforded by the Workers' Compensation Act is exclusive of all other remedies against the employer (at least where the Act applies). Hence, an infant injured while in employment covered by the Act cannot maintain a common-law action against his employer. Humphrees v. Boxley Bros. Co., 146 Va. 91, 135 S.E. 890 (1926); Nolde Bros. v.

Chalkley, 184 Va. 553, 35 S.E.2d 827 (1945), aff'd on rehearing, 185 Va. 96, 38 S.E.2d 73 (1945).

An illegal contract of employment can be pleaded in bar of an action for damages against the employer, where the remedy should be under the Workers' Compensation Act. Nolde Bros. v. Chalkley, 184 Va. 553, 35 S.E.2d 827 (1945), aff'd on rehearing, 185 Va. 96, 38 S.E.2d 73 (1945).

§ 40.1-79: Repealed by Acts 1991, c. 511.

Cross references. — For present provision relating to exemptions from chapter generally, see § 40.1-79.01.

§ 40.1-79.01. Exemptions from chapter generally. — A. Nothing in this chapter, except the provisions of §§ 40.1-100 A, 40.1-100.1, 40.1-100.2, and 40.1-103, shall apply to:

1. A child engaged in domestic work when such work is performed in connection with the child's own home and directly for his parent or a person standing in place of his parent;

2. A child employed in occasional work performed outside school hours where such work is in connection with the employer's home but not in connection with the employer's business, trade, or profession;

3. A child twelve or thirteen years of age employed outside school hours on farms, in orchards or in gardens with the consent of his parent or a person standing in place of his parent;

4. A child between the ages of twelve and eighteen employed as a page or clerk for either the House of Delegates or the Senate of Virginia;

5. A child participating in the activities of a volunteer rescue squad;

6. A child under sixteen years of age employed by his parent in an occupation other than manufacturing; or

7. A child thirteen years of age or older employed by an eleemosynary organization or unit of state or local government as a referee for sports programs sponsored by that eleemosynary, state, or local organization or by an organization of referees sponsored by an organization recognized by the United States Olympic Committee under 36 U.S.C. § 391.

B. Nothing in this chapter, except §§ 40.1-100.1, 40.1-100.2, and 40.1-103, shall be construed to apply to a child employed by his parent or a person standing in place of his parent on farms, in orchards or in gardens owned or operated by such parent or person. (1991, c. 511; 1998, c. 30.)

The 1998 amendment, in subsection A, in subdivision 5, deleted "or" at the end, in subdivision 6, added "or" and added subdivision 7.

Application of § 40.1-103. — The language of this section implies that § 40.1-103 is applicable to a person standing in loco parentis. Lovisi v. Commonwealth, 212 Va. 848, 188 S.E.2d 206, cert. denied, 407 U.S. 922, 92 S. Ct. 2469, 32 L. Ed. 2d 808 (1972). (decided under former § 40.1-79).

§ 40.1-79.1. Exemptions from chapter generally; local ordinance authorizing participation in volunteer fire company activities. — A. Any county, city or town may authorize by ordinance any person sixteen years of age or older, with parental or guardian approval, to work with or participate fully in all activities of a volunteer fire company, provided such person has attained certification under National Fire Protection Association 1001, level one, fire fighter standards, as administered by the Department of Fire Programs.

B. Any trainer or instructor of such persons mentioned in subsection A of this section and any member of a paid or volunteer fire company who supervises any such persons shall be exempt from the provisions of § 40.1-103 when engaged in activities of a volunteer fire company, provided that the volunteer fire company or the governing body of such county, city or town has purchased insurance which provides coverage for injuries to or the death of such persons in their performance of activities under this section. (1982, c. 344; 1983, c. 123; 1991, c. 511.)

§ **40.1-80:** Repealed by Acts 1991, c. 511.

Cross references. — For present provision relating to employment of children, see § 40.1-80.1.

§ **40.1-80.1. Employment of children.** — A. Except as provided in §§ 40.1-79.01, 40.1-88, 40.1-102, and 40.1-109, no child under sixteen years of age shall be employed, permitted or suffered to work in, about or in connection with any gainful occupation more than the number of hours per week or more than the number of hours per day or during the hours of the day that the Commissioner shall determine by regulations to be detrimental to the lives, health, safety or welfare of children. These regulations shall incorporate the standards contained in regulations promulgated by the United States Secretary of Labor pursuant to the Fair Labor Standards Act (29 U.S.C. § 201 et seq.) concerning the number of hours per week, hours per day, and the hours of the day that children under the age of sixteen may work in, about, or in connection with, any gainful occupation.

B. No child shall be employed or permitted to work for more than five hours continuously without an interval of at least thirty minutes for a lunch period, and no period of less than thirty minutes shall be deemed to interrupt a continuous period of work. (1991, c. 511.)

§ **40.1-81:** Repealed by Acts 1972, c. 480.

§ **40.1-81.1. Records to be kept by employers.** — Every employer employing minors under sixteen years of age shall keep a time book or time cards or other appropriate records for such minor employees which shall show the beginning and ending time of work each day together with the amount of time designated as a free-from-duty meal period, which is deductible from the schedule of hours of work. The record for the preceding twelve months for each such minor employee shall be kept on the premises for a period of thirty-six months from the date of the latest work period recorded for the minor employee involved. (1972, c. 480; 1982, c. 134; 1991, c. 511.)

§ **40.1-82:** Repealed by Acts 1979, c. 219.

§ **40.1-83:** Repealed by Acts 1991, c. 511.

§ **40.1-84. Employment certificate required.** — No child under sixteen years of age shall be employed, permitted or suffered to work, in, about or in connection with any gainful occupation with the exception of volunteer work or work on farms, orchards and in gardens and except as provided in §§ 40.1-79.01, 40.1-101, and 40.1-102 unless the person, firm or corporation employing such child, procures and keeps on file and accessible to any school attendance officer, representative of the Department or other authorized persons, charged with the enforcement of this chapter, the employment certificate as hereinafter provided, issued for such child. (Code 1950, § 40-100; 1960, c. 434; 1966, c. 603; 1970, c. 321; 1972, cc. 480, 824; 1974, cc. 283, 525; 1979, c. 219; 1991, c. 511.)

Liability of employer when certificate not obtained. — Under former wording of this section, it was held that the employment of a boy over 14 and under 16 years of age without having procured the required certificate was a tort, and an injury to the child occurring in the performance of duties under such employment was to be referred to the unlawful employment as the proximate cause of such injury. In such case it was also held that the doctrine of contributory negligence was applicable in an action for such injury. Miller Mfg. Co. v. Loving, 125 Va. 255, 99 S.E. 591 (1919); Miller Mfg. Co. v. Aetna Life Ins. Co., 150 Va. 495, 143 S.E. 747 (1928).

Where the defendant employed the plaintiff and permitted him to be put to work at a dangerous machine, with knowledge of the fact that he was between the ages of 14 and 16 years, without having obtained the required employment certificate, such hiring constituted an offense for which the defendant was liable to a fine, and, under § 8.01-221 and the decisions, to damages for any injury suffered by the plaintiff in the course of his employment, unless his right of action was barred by his own contributory negligence (or the case was covered by former Title 65.1 (now Title 65.2)). Miller Mfg. Co. v. Loving, 125 Va. 255, 99 S.E. 591 (1919).

Liability of employer's insurer. — When a statute forbids the employment of a child under 14 years of age in any event and also of one under 16 years of age, unless the employer procures and keeps on file and accessible to a factory inspector, or any other authorized officer, the required certificate, in either event the employer is debarred from making the defense that no negligence is shown, and the insurer is not liable. The employment is the act guarded against by the exception in the policy. Miller Mfg. Co. v. Aetna Life Ins. Co., 150 Va. 495, 143 S.E. 747 (1928).

§ 40.1-85. Kinds of employment certificates. — Employment certificates shall be of two kinds: work-training certificate and vacation or part-time employment certificate. (Code 1950, § 40-100.1; 1970, c. 321; 1982, c. 135; 1991, c. 511.)

§ 40.1-86: Repealed by Acts 1979, c. 219.

§ 40.1-87. Vacation or part-time employment certificate. — A vacation or part-time employment certificate shall permit the employment of a child between fourteen and sixteen years of age only during school vacation periods or on days when school is not in session, or outside school hours on school days. (Code 1950, § 40-100.3; 1958, c. 164; 1970, c. 321; 1979, c. 219; 1982, c. 136; 1991, c. 511.)

§ 40.1-88. Work-training certificate. — A work-training certificate shall permit the employment of a child between fourteen and sixteen years of age during school hours when enrolled in a regular school work-training program pursuant to a written agreement containing the same provisions as specified in § 40.1-89. (Code 1950, § 40-100.4; 1970, c. 321; 1979, c. 219; 1982, c. 670.)

§ 40.1-89. Same; employment not allowed; revocation of certificate. — No child shall be employed pursuant to a work-training certificate as provided in § 40.1-88 where such employment requires such child to work in any occupation which is deemed hazardous under § 40.1-100 A or regulations promulgated thereunder. However, a child sixteen or seventeen years of age may be employed in certain such occupations as part of a work-training program in accordance with rules and regulations promulgated by the Commissioner. No child shall work in a work-training program except pursuant to a written agreement which shall provide: (1) that the work of such child shall be incidental to his training, shall be intermittent and for short periods of time and shall be under the direct and close supervision of a competent and experienced person; (2) that safety instruction shall be given by the school and correlated with on-the-job training given by the employer; and (3) that a schedule of organized and progressive work processes to be performed shall have been prepared. Such written agreement shall set forth the name of the child so employed and shall be signed by the employer and the coordinator of schools having jurisdiction. Copies of such agreement shall be retained by the school and the employer, and a copy thereof shall be filed with the Department.

Any such work-training certificate or written agreement may be revoked at any time that it shall appear that reasonable precautions for the safety of such child have not been observed. (Code 1950, § 40-100.4:1; 1960, c. 434; 1968, c. 277; 1970, c. 321; 1982, c. 252; 1991, c. 511.)

§§ **40.1-90, 40.1-91:** Repealed by Acts 1991, c. 511.

§ **40.1-92. Issuance of certificates.** — Employment certificates shall be issued only by the division superintendent of schools, or by any person designated by him and only upon application in person of the child desiring employment, accompanied by the parent, guardian or custodian of such child. In lieu of a personal appearance, such parent, guardian, or custodian may submit a notarized statement granting permission for the employment of the child. The division superintendent of schools shall designate one person to grant such permits in every city or county. The person issuing such certificate shall have authority to administer the oath provided for therein, or to make any investigation or examination necessary for the issuance thereof. No fee shall be charged for issuing any such certificate nor for administering any oath or rendering any services in respect thereto. The officer issuing the certificate shall retain a copy of each such certificate and all documents connected therewith shall be mailed to the Commissioner by the end of the week in which the same shall have been issued for review and approval. The Commissioner shall file and preserve such certificates and documents. (Code 1950, § 40-101; 1960, c. 434; 1970, c. 321; 1979, c. 219; 1991, c. 511.)

§ **40.1-93. Proof required for employment certificate.** — The person authorized to issue an employment certificate shall not issue such certificate until he has received, examined, approved and filed the following papers:

1. Except for work coming within one of the exceptions in § 40.1-79.01, a statement signed by the prospective employer, or someone duly authorized on his behalf, stating that he expects to give such child present employment, setting forth the specific nature of the occupation in which he intends to employ such child, and the number of hours per day and of days per week which said child shall be employed and of the period for lunch.

2. Proof of age as provided in § 40.1-94. (Code 1950, § 40-102; 1960, c. 434; 1970, c. 321; 1972, c. 480; 1991, c. 511.)

§ **40.1-94. Proofs of age.** — The evidence of age required by this chapter shall consist of one of the following proofs of age, which shall be required in the order herein designated:

(1) A birth certificate or attested transcript issued by a registrar of vital statistics or other officer charged with the duty of recording births.

(2) A baptismal record or duly certified transcript thereof showing the date of birth and place of baptism of the child.

(3) Other documentary proof of age specified by the Commissioner. (Code 1950, § 40-103; 1970, c. 321.)

§ **40.1-95:** Repealed by Acts 1991, c. 511.

§ **40.1-96. Contents of employment certificates.** — The employment certificate required to be issued shall state the name, sex, date of birth and place of residence of the child. It shall certify that all the conditions and requirements for issuing an employment certificate under the provisions of this chapter have been fulfilled and shall be signed by the person issuing it. It shall state the kind of evidence of age accepted for the employment certificate. Except for work coming within one of the exceptions in § 40.1-79.01, the certificate shall show the name and address of the employer for whom and the nature of the specific occupation in which the employment certificate authorizes the child to be employed and shall be valid only for the occupation so designated. It shall bear a number, shall show the date of its issue, and shall be signed by the child for whom it is issued in the presence of the person issuing it. It shall be issued in triplicate, one copy to be mailed to the employer, one copy to be sent to the Commissioner and one copy to be retained and kept on file by the issuing officer. (Code 1950, § 40-105; 1960, c. 434; 1970, c. 321; 1978, c. 596; 1991, c. 511.)

§ **40.1-97:** Repealed by Acts 1972, c. 480.

§§ **40.1-98, 40.1-99:** Repealed by Acts 1991, c. 511.

§ **40.1-100. Certain employment prohibited or limited.** — A. No child under eighteen years of age shall be employed, permitted or suffered to work:

1. In any mine, quarry, tunnel, underground scaffolding work; in or about any plant or establishment manufacturing or storing explosives or articles containing explosive components; in any occupation involving exposure to radioactive substances or to ionizing radiations including X-ray equipment;

2. At operating or assisting to operate any grinding, abrasive, polishing or buffing machine, any power-driven metal forming, punching or shearing machine, power-driven bakery machine, power-driven paper products machine, any circular saw, band saw or guillotine shear, or any power-driven woodworking machine;

3. In oiling or assisting in oiling, wiping and cleaning any such machinery;

4. In any capacity in preparing any composition in which dangerous or poisonous chemicals are used;

5. In any capacity in the manufacturing of paints, colors, white lead, or brick tile or kindred products, or in any place where goods of alcoholic content are manufactured, bottled, or sold for consumption on the premises except in places where the sale of alcoholic beverages is merely incidental to the main business actually conducted, or to deliver alcoholic goods;

6. In any capacity in or about excavation, demolition, roofing, wrecking or shipbreaking operations;

7. As a driver or a helper on a truck or commercial vehicle of more than two axles. The provisions of this paragraph shall not apply to the drivers of school buses;

8. In logging or sawmilling, or in any lath mill, shingle mill or cooperage-stock mill, or in any occupation involving slaughtering, meatpacking, processing or rendering;

9. In any occupation determined and declared hazardous by rules and regulations promulgated by the Commissioner of Labor and Industry.

Notwithstanding the provisions of this section, children sixteen years of age or older who are serving a voluntary apprenticeship as provided in Chapter 6 (§ 40.1-117 et seq.) of this title may be employed in any occupation in accordance with rules and regulations promulgated by the Commissioner.

B. Except as part of a regular work-training program in accordance with §§ 40.1-88 and 40.1-89, no child under sixteen years of age shall be employed, permitted or suffered to work:

1. In any manufacturing or mechanical establishment, in any commercial cannery; in the operation of any automatic passenger or freight elevator; in any

dance studio; or in any hospital, nursing home, clinic, or other establishment providing care for resident patients as a laboratory helper, therapist, orderly, or nurse's aide; in the service of any veterinarian while treating farm animals or horses; in any warehouse; in processing work in any laundry or dry cleaning establishment; in any undertaking establishment or funeral home; in any curb service restaurant, in hotel and motel room service; in any brick, coal or lumber yard or ice plant or in ushering in theaters. Children fourteen years of age or more may be engaged in office work of a clerical nature in bona fide office rooms in the above types of establishments.

2. In any scaffolding work or construction trade; or in any outdoor theater, cabaret, carnival, fair, floor show, pool hall, club, or roadhouse; or as a lifeguard at a beach.

C. Children fourteen years of age or more may be employed by dry cleaning or laundry establishments in branch stores where no processing is done on the premises, and in hospitals, nursing homes, and clinics where they may be engaged in kitchen work, tray service or room and hall cleaning. Children fourteen years of age or more may be employed in bowling alleys completely equipped with automatic pin setters, but not in or about such machines, and in soda fountains, restaurants and hotel and motel food service departments. Children fourteen years of age or more may work as gatekeepers and in concessions at swimming pools and may be employed by concessionaires operating on beaches where their duties and work pertain to the handling and distribution of beach chairs, umbrellas, floats and other similar or related beach equipment.

D. Notwithstanding any other provision of this chapter:

1. Children sixteen years of age or more employed on farms, in gardens or in orchards may operate, assist in operating, or otherwise perform work involving a truck, excluding a tractor trailer, or farm vehicle as defined in § 46.2-1099, in their employment;

2. Children fourteen years of age or more employed on farms, in gardens or in orchards may perform work as a helper on a truck or commercial vehicle in their employment, while engaged in such work exclusively on a farm, in a garden or in an orchard. (Code 1950, § 40-109; 1956, cc. 443, 463; 1958, c. 321; 1960, c. 434; 1964, c. 503; 1968, c. 278; 1970, c. 321; 1972, c. 824; 1973, c. 13; 1979, cc. 219, 348; 1991, c. 511; 1994, c. 156.)

Cross references. — As to punishment for Class 6 felonies, see § 18.2-10. As to prohibition of persons under 18 from working in or around mines or quarries, see § 45.1-161.11.

Law Review. — For survey of Virginia criminal law for the year 1978-1979, see 66 Va. L. Rev. 241 (1980).

§ 40.1-100.1. Employment where hazard capable of causing serious physical harm or death.
— No person shall employ, suffer, or permit a child to work in any gainful occupation that exposes such child to a recognized hazard capable of causing serious physical harm or death to such child. Any person violating this section shall be subject to a civil monetary penalty in accordance with § 40.1-113 of this chapter. (1991, c. 511.)

§ 40.1-100.2. Employment involving sexually explicit visual material prohibited.
— A person under eighteen years of age shall not perform in or be a subject of sexually explicit visual material. As used in this section, *"sexually explicit visual material"* means a picture, photograph, drawing, sculpture, motion picture film or similar visual representation which is obscene for children, as defined in § 18.2-374.1, and which depicts nudity, sexual excitement, sexual conduct, sexual intercourse or sadomasochistic abuse, as defined in § 18.2-390, or a book, magazine or pamphlet which

contains such a visual representation. An undeveloped photograph or similar visual material may be sexually explicit material notwithstanding that processing or other action is necessary to make its sexually explicit content apparent. A person who employs, permits or suffers a person to be employed or work in violation of this section is guilty of a Class 6 felony. (1991, c. 511.)

Cross references. — As to punishment for Class 6 felonies, see § 18.2-10.

§ 40.1-101. Qualifications as to theaters. — Notwithstanding the provisions of §§ 40.1-100 and 40.1-100.1, a child under sixteen years of age, whether a resident or nonresident of the Commonwealth, may be employed, permitted or suffered to participate in the presentation of a drama, play, performance, concert or entertainment, provided the management of the theater or other public place where such performance is to be held in the Commonwealth shall secure a permit from the Commissioner; provided, that no such permit shall be required for any nonprofit dance or music recital, nor for any television or radio broadcast in which the children participating are selected by the television or radio broadcasting station for sustaining noncommercial programs. (Code 1950, § 40-110; 1960, c. 434; 1970, c. 321; 1973, c. 13; 1979, c. 348; 1991, c. 511.)

§ 40.1-102. Issuance of theatrical permit. — No permit shall be issued unless the Commissioner is satisfied that the environment in which the drama, play, performance, concert or entertainment is to be produced is a proper environment for the child and that the conditions of such employment are not detrimental to the health or morals of such child and that the child's education will not be neglected or hampered by its participation in such drama, play, performance, concert or entertainment. Applications for permits and every permit granted shall specify the name, age and sex of each child, together with such other facts as may be necessary for the proper identification of each child and the dates when, and the theaters or other places of amusement in which such drama, play, performance, concert or entertainment is to be produced and shall specify the name of the drama, play, performance, concert or entertainment in which each child is permitted to participate. Such application shall be filed with the Commissioner not less than five days before the date of such drama, play, performance, concert or entertainment. A permit shall be revocable by the Commissioner should it be found that the environment in which the drama, play, performance, concert or entertainment is being produced is not a proper environment for the child and that the conditions of such employment are detrimental to the health or morals of such child. The Commissioner shall prescribe and supply the forms required for carrying out the provisions of this section. (Code 1950, § 40-111; 1960, c. 434; 1970, c. 321.)

§ 40.1-103. Cruelty and injuries to children. — It shall be unlawful for any person employing or having the custody of any child willfully or negligently to cause or permit the life of such child to be endangered or the health of such child to be injured, or willfully or negligently to cause or permit such child to be placed in a situation that its life, health or morals may be endangered, or to cause or permit such child to be overworked, tortured, tormented, mutilated, beaten or cruelly treated. Any person violating this section shall be guilty of a Class 6 felony. (Code 1950, § 40-112; 1970, c. 321; 1991, c. 511.)

Cross references. — As to punishment for a misdemeanor, see § 18.2-11. As to exemption from this section of trainers, instructors, or supervisors of persons 16 years of age or older who are authorized by local ordinance to participate in volunteer fire company activities, see § 40.1-79.1. As to punishment for Class 6 felonies, see § 18.2-10.

Statute language unconstitutionally vague and inclusive. — Where the instant charges arose from a perception by law enforcement officials that the conduct of the defendants may have threatened the "life, health or morals" of children under the statute, use of the term "may" by the legislature criminalizes any act which presents a "possibility" of physical or moral harm to the child, thus the vague and inclusive statutory language clearly failed to adequately inform law enforcement of the precise conduct prohibited and is thus unconstitutional. Commonwealth v. Carter, 21 Va. App. 150, 462 S.E.2d 582 (1995).

Retroactive application of *Carter*. — A new rule for prosecutions under this section—the ruling in Commonwealth v. Carter, 21 Va. App. 150, 462 S.E.2d 582 (1995) declaring provisions of this section unconstitutionally void for vagueness—applied retroactively. Therefore, defendant who was indicted, his jury instructed and he ultimately convicted on precisely that unconstitutional provision had his conviction overturned. Herrera v. Commonwealth, 24 Va. App. 490, 483 S.E.2d 492 (1997).

Evidence insufficient. — Where no evidence showed that either appellant or her boyfriend ingested the drugs before or while operating the vehicle, or that the children understood their mother had just purchased illegal drugs and the moral significance associated thereto, defendant's conviction was not supported by sufficient evidence of actions that may have endangered her children. Riggs v. Commonwealth, No. 1892-95-2 (Ct. of Appeals Sept. 10, 1996).

The negligence required in a criminal proceeding must be more than the lack of ordinary care and precaution; it must be something more than mere inadvertence or misadventure; it is a recklessness or indifference incompatible with a proper regard for human life. Thus, where neither jury instruction defined criminal negligence, they invited the imposition of criminal liability upon a finding of simple negligence, which constituted reversible error. Mosby v. Commonwealth, 23 Va. App. 53, 473 S.E.2d 732 (1996).

Evidence sufficient to support conviction. — Where the child was taken out into a temperature of forty-eight degrees and the child was clothed only in a "sleeper" that was not snapped and did not cover the child's bare feet, the evidence was sufficient to support defendant's conviction for negligently causing or permitting the life of the child to be endangered or the health of the child to be injured. Morrison v. Commonwealth, No. 0035-96-1 (Ct. of Appeals Dec. 10, 1996).

Defendant is entitled to the benefit of a strict construction of this section, which is a criminal statute. Lovisi v. Commonwealth, 212 Va. 848, 188 S.E.2d 206, cert. denied, 407 U.S. 922, 92 S. Ct. 2469, 32 L. Ed. 2d 808 (1972).

But words are to be given their ordinary meaning unless it is apparent that the legislative intent is otherwise. Lovisi v. Commonwealth, 212 Va. 848, 188 S.E.2d 206, cert. denied, 407 U.S. 922, 92 S. Ct. 2469, 32 L. Ed. 2d 808 (1972).

The word "custody" has been defined generally as "the care and keeping of anything." Lovisi v. Commonwealth, 212 Va. 848, 188 S.E.2d 206, cert. denied, 407 U.S. 922, 92 S. Ct. 2469, 32 L. Ed. 2d 808 (1972).

"Custody" not limited to legal custody. — In its language this section is unambiguous, justifying no limitation of the meaning of "custody" to legal custody. To give it such a restrictive definition would eliminate, among others, teachers, athletic instructors and baby-sitters, all of whom might have temporary custody of children, from the purview of the statute. Lovisi v. Commonwealth, 212 Va. 848, 188 S.E.2d 206, cert. denied, 407 U.S. 922, 92 S. Ct. 2469, 32 L. Ed. 2d 808 (1972).

And section applies to person standing in loco parentis. — This section is applicable to a person standing in loco parentis. Lovisi v. Commonwealth, 212 Va. 848, 188 S.E.2d 206, cert. denied, 407 U.S. 922, 92 S. Ct. 2469, 32 L. Ed. 2d 808 (1972).

The terms "willfully" and "negligently" as used in this statute are concepts of longstanding recognition and legal definition; likewise criminal liability for willful and culpably negligent conduct is an established principle. These standards are solidly established and are not impermissibly vague. Mosby v. Commonwealth, 23 Va. App. 53, 473 S.E.2d 732 (1996).

Although defendant failed to raise constitutionality of provision of this section he was convicted under at trial or on appeal, court of appeals could consider issue sua sponte with regard to trial court's jurisdiction to convict defendant. Herrera v. Commonwealth, 24 Va. App. 490, 483 S.E.2d 492 (1997).

Double jeopardy. — Because the two statutes require proof of additional facts, and they therefore constitute two distinct offenses, the double jeopardy clause was not offended by defendant's convictions under § 18.2-47 and this section. Long v. Commonwealth, No. 0399-95-1 (Ct. of Appeals Dec. 5, 1995).

§ 40.1-104. Age certificates. — An age certificate shall be issued, upon request of the employer or the worker, for a person sixteen years of age or over. It shall be issued by the person authorized to issue employment certificates under the provisions of this chapter upon presentation of the same evidence of age as required for an employment certificate. The age certificate shall show the person's name and address, his date of birth and signature, the signature of the person issuing the certificate and the evidence accepted as proof of age.

An employment or age certificate duly issued shall be conclusive evidence of the age of the person for whom issued in any proceeding involving the employment of the person under any of the labor laws of this Commonwealth as to any act occurring subsequent to its issuance and prior to its revocation. (Code 1950, § 40-113; 1970, c. 321; 1972, c. 824; 1979, c. 219.)

§ 40.1-105: Repealed by Acts 1991, c. 511.

§§ 40.1-106 through 40.1-108: Repealed by Acts 1979, c. 219.

§ 40.1-109. Newspaper carriers on regular routes; hours. — Notwithstanding the other provisions of this chapter, any child between twelve and sixteen years of age may daily engage in the occupation of distributing newspapers on regularly established routes between the hours of four o'clock ante meridian and seven o'clock post meridian, excluding the time public schools are actually in session. (Code 1950, § 40-118; 1960, c. 434; 1962, c. 352; 1970, c. 321; 1972, c. 807; 1973, c. 13; 1979, c. 219; 1982, c. 83; 1991, c. 511.)

§ 40.1-110: Repealed by Acts 1979, c. 219.

§ 40.1-111: Repealed by Acts 1991, c. 511.

§ 40.1-112. Solicitation generally. — A. In order to provide for enforcement of the child labor laws and the protection of employees, it shall be unlawful for any person, firm or corporation, except a nonprofit organization as defined in § 501 (c) (3) of the United States Internal Revenue Code, to engage in or to employ any person for, or suffer or permit any person in his employment to work in, any trade in any street or public place, including but not limited to candy sales or soliciting for commercial purposes, selling, or obtaining subscription contracts or orders for books, magazines or other periodical publications other than newspapers, without obtaining from the Commissioner a permit to conduct such business. No permit shall be required for the placement of advertisements or literature on or near a business or private residence, if there is no attempt, in person, to solicit business or make a sale at the time of the placement of the material.

B. Such permits shall be valid from the date of issuance until June 30 next following the date of issuance. Applications may be made not more than thirty days prior to the requested date of issuance on forms furnished by the Commissioner, and the applicant shall supply such information as is required concerning his place or places of business, the prospective number of his employees, and the proposed hours of work and rate of compensation for such employees. A separate permit shall be required for each place of business which the applicant operates within this Commonwealth.

C. Each permittee shall maintain such records as may be prescribed by the Commissioner showing the name, residence address and age of each employee, the hours worked by each employee, the place where such work was performed, and the compensation paid and payable to such employee. Such records shall be available for inspection by the Commissioner or a representative designated by him during business hours.

D. No child shall be employed or permitted to work by or for any permittee unless all the following conditions are satisfied:

1. The child is at least sixteen years of age;

2. The permittee has a permanent business address within this Commonwealth; and

3. The child works at all times under the immediate supervision of an adult.

E. No child shall be required, permitted or directed to make any false statement representing himself, his employer or products or services in his employment.

F. Any person violating any provision or condition of this section shall be guilty of a Class 1 misdemeanor for each such violation. Any violation of this section by a permittee or with his knowledge and consent shall in addition be grounds for revocation of the permit. (Code 1950, § 40-118.3; 1964, c. 315; 1966, c. 603; 1968, c. 743; 1970, c. 321; 1973, c. 13; 1979, c. 219; 1982, c. 137; 1991, c. 511; 1998, c. 157.)

Cross references. — As to punishment for Class 2 misdemeanors, see § 18.2-11. As to punishment for Class 1 misdemeanors, see § 18.2-11.

The 1998 amendment, in subsection A, in the first sentence, substituted "or soliciting for commercial purposes, selling" for "solicitation, sale," and deleted "of" preceding "subscription," and added the second sentence; and in the last sentence of subsection B, substituted "business which the applicant" for "business or location at which applicant."

Law Review. — For survey of Virginia criminal law for the year 1978-1979, see 66 Va. L. Rev. 241 (1980).

§ 40.1-113. Child labor offenses; civil penalties. — A. Whoever employs, procures, or, having under his control, permits a child to be employed, or issues an employment certificate in violation of any of the provisions of this chapter other than §§ 40.1-100.2, 40.1-103 and 40.1-112, shall be subject to a civil penalty not to exceed $1,000 for each violation. In determining the amount of such penalty, the appropriateness of such penalty to the size of the business of the person charged and the gravity of the violation shall be considered. The determination by the Commissioner shall be final, unless within fifteen days after receipt of such notice the person charged with the violation notifies the Commissioner by certified mail that he intends to contest the proposed penalty before the appropriate general district court.

B. Civil penalties owed under this section shall be paid to the Commissioner for deposit into the general fund of the treasury of the Commonwealth. The Commissioner shall prescribe procedures for the payment of proposed penalties which are not contested by employers. (Code 1950, § 40-119; 1964, c. 504; 1970, c. 321; 1973, c. 425; 1979, c. 348; 1982, c. 416; 1991, c. 511.)

Cross references. — For provisions as to enforcement of this title and rules and regulations adopted pursuant thereto, and penalties for violations, see § 40.1-49.4.

Classes of persons liable. — This section imposes a penalty upon only four classes of persons, namely, the proprietor of the business (or his agent) who employs the child, the person who procures the employment of the child, the parent (or other person in control) who permits the child to be employed, and the official who issues the false employment certificate. Clover Creamery Co. v. Kanode, 142 Va. 542, 129 S.E. 222 (1925).

Section 40.1-78 should be construed in harmony with the legislative intent as expressed in this section. Clover Creamery Co. v. Kanode, 142 Va. 542, 129 S.E. 222 (1925).

§ 40.1-114. Enforcement of child labor law. — The Commissioner with the assistance of state and local law-enforcement officers, shall enforce the provisions of this chapter and shall have authority to appoint such represen-

tatives as may be necessary to secure the enforcement of this chapter. He shall make all necessary rules and regulations for carrying out the purposes of this chapter, and shall prescribe and supply to the proper officials blanks for employment certificates and such other forms as may be required for carrying out the provisions of this chapter. (Code 1950, § 40-120; 1970, c. 321; 1979, c. 219.)

§ **40.1-115. School attendance.** — Nothing contained in this chapter shall be construed as qualifying in any way the provisions of the compulsory education laws of this Commonwealth, nor as authorizing the employment of any child who is absent unlawfully from school. (Code 1950, § 40-121; 1970, c. 321.)

§ **40.1-116. Curfew ordinances not affected.** — Nothing in this chapter shall be construed to permit the violation of a curfew ordinance of any city. (Code 1950, § 40-122; 1970, c. 321.)

CHAPTER 6.

VOLUNTARY APPRENTICESHIP.

§ **40.1-117. Apprenticeship Council; membership and terms of office; meetings and duties.** — A. The Governor shall appoint an Apprenticeship Council, composed of four representatives each from employer and employee organizations respectively, and all of whom shall be familiar with apprenticeable occupations. The Commissioner of the Virginia Employment Commission, the Chancellor of the Virginia Community College System, or their designated representatives, and a local superintendent from a school division that provides apprenticeship-related instruction, shall be members, ex officio, of the Council. At the beginning of each year the Governor shall designate one member to serve as chairman. Each member shall be appointed for a term of three years. Any member appointed to fill a vacancy occurring prior to the expiration of the term of his predecessor shall be appointed for the remainder of such term. All members, including ex officio members, shall have voting privileges.

B. The Apprenticeship Council shall meet at the call of the chairman of the Council and shall formulate policies for the effective administration of this chapter.

C. The Apprenticeship Council shall establish standards for apprentice agreements which shall not be lower than those prescribed by this chapter and those established pursuant to Article 3 (§ 54.1-1128 et seq.) of Chapter 11 of Title 54.1, and shall perform such other functions as may be necessary to carry out the intent and purposes of this chapter. Not less than once a year the Council shall make a report of its activities and findings to the General

Assembly and to the public. (Code 1950, § 40-123; 1968, c. 273; 1970, c. 321; 1978, c. 206; 1980, c. 728; 1981, c. 331; 1987, c. 165; 1992, c. 231.)

Cross references. — As to compensation and expenses of boards, commissions and similar bodies, see §§ 2.1-20.2 through 2.1-20.4.

§ 40.1-118. Authority of Council. — The Council may:

1. Determine standards for apprentice agreements, which standards shall not be lower than those prescribed by this chapter;

2. Appoint the secretary of the Apprenticeship Council to act as secretary of each state joint apprenticeship committee;

3. Approve, if in their opinion approval is for the best interest of the apprentice, any apprentice agreement which meets the standards established under this chapter;

4. Terminate or cancel any apprentice agreement in accordance with the provisions of such agreement;

5. Keep a record of apprentice agreements and their disposition;

6. Issue certificates of journeymanship upon the completion of the apprenticeship;

7. Perform such other duties as are necessary to carry out the intent of this chapter;

8. Review decisions of local and state joint apprenticeship committees adjusting apprenticeship disputes pursuant to § 40.1-119 c 3;

9. Initiate deregistration proceedings when the apprenticeship program is not conducted, operated and administered in accordance with the registered provisions except that deregistration proceedings for violation of equal opportunity requirements shall be processed in accordance with the provisions of the Virginia State Plan for Equal Employment Opportunity in Apprenticeship; and

10. Advise the State Board for Community Colleges on policies to coordinate apprenticeship-related instruction delivered by state and local public education agencies. (Code 1950, § 40-124; 1970, c. 321; 1978, c. 206; 1990, c. 614; 1996, cc. 134, 486.)

§ 40.1-119. Local and state joint apprenticeship committees. — A. A

local joint apprenticeship committee may be appointed in any trade or group of trades in a city or trade area, by the Apprenticeship Council, whenever the apprentice training needs of such trade or group of trades justify such establishment. Sponsors not signatory to a bargaining agreement may operate an individual apprenticeship program or, at the option and under guidelines prescribed by a joint committee, participate in an apprenticeship program operated by a joint apprenticeship committee.

B. When two or more local joint apprenticeship committees have been established in the state for a trade or group of trades or at the request of any trade or group of trades, the Apprenticeship Council may appoint a state apprenticeship committee for such trade or group of trades. Such local and state joint apprenticeship committees shall be composed of an equal number of employer and employee representatives chosen from names submitted by the respective employer and employee organizations in such trade or group of trades. In a trade or group of trades in which there is no bona fide employer or employee organization, the committee shall be appointed from persons known to represent the interests of employers and of employees respectively.

C. The functions of a local joint apprenticeship committee shall be:

1. To cooperate with school authorities in regard to the education of apprentices;

2. In accordance with standards established by the Apprenticeship Council, to establish local standards of apprenticeship regarding schedule of operations,

application of wage rates, working conditions for apprentices, and the number of apprentices which shall be employed locally in the trade; and

3. To adjust apprenticeship disputes.

D. The functions of a state trade apprenticeship committee shall be to assist in an advisory capacity in the development of statewide standards of apprenticeship and in the development of local standards and local committees. (Code 1950, § 40-125; 1970, c. 321; 1990, c. 614.)

§ **40.1-120. Definitions.** — As used in this chapter, the following terms shall have the following meanings unless the context indicates otherwise:

"Apprenticeable occupation" means a skilled trade having the following characteristics:

1. It is customarily learned in a practical way through a structured systematic program of on-the-job supervised work experience;

2. It is clearly identifiable and recognized throughout an industry;

3. It involves manual, mechanical or technical skills which require a minimum of 2,000 hours of on-the-job work experience of new apprenticeable trades not otherwise established; and

4. It requires related instruction to supplement the on-the-job work experience.

"Apprentice" means a person at least sixteen years of age who is covered by a written agreement with an employer and approved by the Apprenticeship Council. The agreement shall provide for not less than 2,000 hours of reasonably continuous employment in new apprenticeable trades not otherwise established for such person, for his participation in an approved schedule of work experience through employment, and for the amount of related instruction required in the craft or trade.

"Employer" means any person or organization employing a registered apprentice who is party to an apprenticeship agreement with a sponsor.

"Joint apprenticeship committee" means a group equally representative of management and labor representatives which works under a bargaining agreement and is established to carry out the administration of an apprenticeship training program.

"Sponsor" means either an individual employer, a group of employers, or an association or organization operating an apprenticeship program, and in whose name the program is registered. (Code 1950, § 40-126; 1960, c. 336; 1970, c. 321; 1978, c. 206; 1990, c. 614.)

§ **40.1-121. Requisites of apprentice agreement.** — Every apprentice agreement entered into under this chapter shall contain:

1. The names, signatures, and addresses of the contracting parties;

2. The date of birth of the apprentice;

3. A statement of the trade, craft, or business which the apprentice is to be taught, and the time at which the apprenticeship will begin and end;

4. A statement showing the number of hours to be spent by the apprentice in work and the number of hours to be spent in related or supplemental instruction;

5. A statement setting forth a schedule of the processes in the trade or industry division in which the apprentice is to be taught and the approximate time to be spent at each process;

6. A statement of the graduated scale of wages to be paid the apprentice and whether the required schooltime shall be compensated;

7. A statement providing for a period of probation of not less than 500 hours of employment and instruction extending over not less than four months, during which time the apprentice agreement shall be terminated by the Council at the request in writing of either party, and providing that after such

probationary period the apprentice agreement may be terminated by the Council by mutual agreement of all parties thereto, or cancelled by the Council for good and sufficient reason;

8. A provision that an employer who is unable to fulfill his obligation under the apprentice agreement may with the approval of the Council transfer such contract to any other employer if (i) the apprentice consents, (ii) such other employer agrees to assume the obligations of the apprentice agreement, and (iii) the transfer is reported to the registration agency within thirty days of the transfer; and

9. Such additional terms and conditions as may be prescribed or approved by the Council not inconsistent with the provisions of this chapter. (Code 1950, § 40-127; 1960, c. 336; 1970, c. 321; 1990, c. 614.)

§ **40.1-122. Approval of agreement by Council; signing.** — No apprentice agreement under this chapter shall be effective until approved by the Council. Every apprentice agreement shall be signed by the employer, or by an association of employers or an organization of employees as provided in § 40.1-124, and by the apprentice, and, if the apprentice is a minor, by the minor's father or mother, provided, that if both father and mother be dead or legally incapable of giving consent or have abandoned their children, then by the guardian of the minor. (Code 1950, § 40-128; 1970, c. 321; 1974, c. 272.)

§ **40.1-123. Agreement binding after apprentice's majority.** — When a minor enters into an apprentice agreement under this chapter for a period of training extending into his majority, the apprentice agreement shall likewise be binding for such a period as may be covered during the apprentice's majority. (Code 1950, § 40-129; 1970, c. 321.)

§ **40.1-124. Agreement signed by organization of employers or of employees.** — For the purpose of providing greater diversity of training or continuity of employment, any apprentice agreement made under this chapter may in the discretion of the Council be signed by an association of employers or an organization of employees instead of by an individual employer. In such a case the apprentice agreement shall expressly provide that the association of employers or organization of employees does not assume the obligation of an employer but agrees to use its best endeavors to procure employment and training for such apprentice with one or more employers who will accept full responsibility, as herein provided, for all the terms and conditions of employment and training set forth in the agreement between the apprentice and employer association or employee organization during the period of each such employment. The apprentice agreement in such a case shall also expressly provide for the transfer of the apprentice, subject to the approval of the Council, to such employer or employers as shall sign a written agreement with the apprentice, and if the apprentice is a minor with his parent or guardian, as specified in § 40.1-122, contracting to employ the apprentice for the whole or a definite part of the total period of apprenticeship under the terms and conditions of employment and training set forth in the agreement entered into between the apprentice and the employer association or employee organization. (Code 1950, § 40-130; 1970, c. 321.)

§ **40.1-125. Commissioner to administer chapter.** — The Commissioner, with the advice and guidance of the Council, shall be responsible for administering the provisions of this chapter. (Code 1950, § 40-131; 1970, c. 321.)

§ **40.1-126. Operation and application of chapter.** — Nothing in this chapter or in any apprentice agreement approved under this chapter shall invalidate any apprenticeship provision in any collective agreement between employers and employees establishing higher apprenticeship standards regarding ratios of apprentices to journeymen, probationary periods, or length of the program. But none of the terms or provisions of this chapter shall apply to any person, firm, corporation, or craft unless, until and only so long as such person, firm, corporation, or craft voluntarily elects that the terms and provisions of this chapter shall apply. (Code 1950, § 40-132; 1970, c. 321; 1990, c. 614.)

§ 40.1-127: Reserved.

CHAPTER 7.

Passenger Tramway Safety.

§§ 40.1-128 through 40.1-134: Repealed by Acts 1991, c. 152.

Cross references. — As to present provision relating to amusement devices which include passenger tramways, see § 36-98.3.

CHAPTER 8.

Register of Safety and Health Law Violators.

§§ 40.1-135 through 40.1-138: Not effective.

Editor's note. — These sections were enacted by Acts 1991, c. 662, cl. 1, and Acts 1991, c. 662, cl. 2, as amended by Acts 1992, c. 798, cl. 1, provided that the provisions of the 1991 act would not become effective unless reenacted by the 1993 Session of the General Assembly. The 1991 act was not reenacted at the 1993 Session.

Title 41.
Land Office.

[Repealed.]

§§ 41-1 through 41-89: Repealed by Acts 1970, c. 291.

Cross references. — As to repeal of Title 41, enactment of Title 41.1, and transition provisions, see notes under § 41.1-1.

Title 41.1.
Land Office.

§ **41.1-1. Librarian of Virginia in charge of Land Office.** — The Librarian of Virginia shall be in charge of and keep and preserve all records of the Land Office. (Code 1950, § 41-1; 1952, c. 185; 1970, c. 291; 1998, c. 427.)

Editor's note. — At its regular session of 1968, the General Assembly directed the Code Commission to revise certain titles, including Title 41, relating to the Land Office. In October of 1969, the Commission sent to the Governor and General Assembly its report containing the proposed revision of Title 41, which was published as House Document 9 of the 1970 session. The Commission's draft of the revision of Title 41, became chapter 291 of the Acts of 1970. It repeals Title 41 and enacts in lieu thereof a new Title 41.1.

Some of the cases cited in the notes under the various sections of this title were decided under corresponding provisions of former law.

Transition provisions. — Acts 1970, c. 291, §§ 4 and 5, provide as follows:

"4. Whenever in Title 41.1 any of the conditions, requirements, provisions or contents of any section, article or chapter of Title 41, as such title existed prior to October 1, 1970, are transferred in the same or in modified form to a new section, article or chapter, and whenever any such former section, article or chapter is given a new number in Title 41.1, all references to any such former section, article or chapter of Title 41 appearing elsewhere in this Code than in this title shall be construed to apply to the new or renumbered section, article or chapter containing such conditions, requirements, provisions or contents or portions thereof.

"5. It is the intention of the General Assembly that this act shall be liberally construed to effect the purposes set out herein, and if any clause, sentence, paragraph or section of this act shall ever be declared unconstitutional, it shall be deemed severable, and the remainder of this act shall continue in full force and effect."

The 1998 amendment deleted "State" preceding "Librarian" and inserted "of Virginia."

§ **41.1-2. Act changing name of Denny Martin taken as true; records, etc., of Northern Neck and other lands.** — In all suits, either at law or in equity, in which title to any land is derived or sought to be derived from Lord Fairfax, through Denny Martin Fairfax, it shall not be necessary in order to make out a chain of title, to prove the act of Parliament authorizing Denny Martin, the devisee of Lord Fairfax, to take the name of Fairfax, but the same shall be presumed and taken to be true to the same extent as if a properly authenticated copy of such act had been adduced in evidence.

The records, documents, and entries of land granted by the former lord proprietor of the Northern Neck, and of all land granted, or to be granted, by the Commonwealth, shall be in the keeping of the Librarian of Virginia in the Land Office in the City of Richmond. (Code 1950, § 41-2; 1970, c. 291; 1998, c. 427.)

The 1998 amendment, in the second paragraph, deleted "State" preceding "Librarian" and inserted "of Virginia."

§ 41.1-3. Grants of certain lands, etc., to be void; such lands, etc., under control of Governor.

— No grant shall be valid or effectual in law to pass any estate or interest in (i) any lands unappropriated or belonging to the Commonwealth, which embrace the old magazine at Westham, or any stone quarry now worked by the Commonwealth, or any lands which are within a mile of such magazine, or any such quarry; (ii) any ungranted beds of bays, rivers, creeks and the shores of the sea under § 28.2-1200; (iii) any natural oyster bed, rock, or shoal, whether such bed, rock, or shoal shall ebb bare or not; (iv) any islands created in the navigable waters of the Commonwealth through the instrumentality of dredging or filling operations; (v) any islands which rise from any lands which are property of the Commonwealth under § 28.2-1201; or (vi) any ungranted shores of the sea, marsh or meadowlands as defined in § 28.2-1500. Every such grant for any such lands, islands, bed, rock, or shoal shall be absolutely void; however, this section shall not be construed to affect the title to grants issued prior to March 15, 1932. Such magazine and every such stone quarry and the lands of the Commonwealth adjacent to or in their neighborhood, shall be under the control of the Governor, who may make such regulations concerning the same as he may deem best for the interests of the Commonwealth. (Code 1950, § 41-8; 1970, c. 291; 1991, c. 378; 1995, c. 850.)

Law Review. — For article, "Public Access to Virginia's Tidelands: A Framework for Analysis of Implied Dedications and Public Prescriptive Rights," see 24 Wm. & Mary L. Rev. 669 (1983).

Common-law and statutory antecedents discussed. — See Bradford v. Nature Conservancy, 224 Va. 181, 294 S.E.2d 866 (1982).

Applicant must comply with all requirements before title vests in him. — It appeared that appellees' predecessor in title duly made entry on the land in 1887, pursuant to a land office treasury warrant. The county surveyor made the necessary legal survey and the affidavit required by former § 41-8. Before the applicant made the affidavit required of him by former § 41-8 and filed his proof with the application with the Register of the Land Office (now State Librarian), the General Assembly withdrew the land from patent. It was held that appellants must prevail as the patent granted to appellees' predecessor in title was void. Powell v. Field, 155 Va. 612, 155 S.E. 819

(1930), appeal dismissed, 284 U.S. 589, 52 S. Ct. 139, 76 L. Ed. 508 (1931).

But once vested, State can reclaim only by eminent domain. — Where valid grants are once made by the State the property granted can only be resumed by it when needed for the public use, under the right of eminent domain, upon making compensation. Miller v. Commonwealth, 159 Va. 924, 166 S.E. 557 (1932).

Grants prior to 1932 not ratified. — Under this statutory scheme grants issued in accordance with this section are ratified, but expressly excluded from the operation of this section are grants issued prior to 1932. The retroactivity provisions of § 41.1-6, therefore, do not apply to a grant of 1901. Nature Conservancy v. Machipongo Club, Inc., 419 F. Supp. 390 (E.D. Va. 1976), modified on other grounds, 571 F.2d 1294 (4th Cir.), 579 F.2d 873 (4th Cir.), cert. denied, 439 U.S. 1047, 99 S. Ct. 724, 58 L. Ed. 2d 706 (1978).

§ 41.1-4: Repealed by Acts 1995, c. 850.

§ **41.1-4.1:** Repealed by Acts 1992, c. 836.

§ **41.1-5. Circuit courts authorized to dispose of waste and unappropriated lands.** — The circuit courts of the counties and cities in which waste and unappropriated lands are alleged to lie are vested with authority to sell and dispose thereof in proceedings brought under §§ 41.1-16 through 41.1-20; however, no sale or disposition shall be made of lands mentioned in § 28.2-1200 or of lands as to which a grant could not have been issued by the Librarian of Virginia under § 41.1-3. (Code 1950, § 41-8.2; 1952, c. 185; 1970, c. 291; 1991, c. 378; 1995, c. 850; 1998, c. 427.)

The **1998 amendment** deleted "State" preceding "Librarian" and inserted "of Virginia."

§ **41.1-6. Ratification of grants issued pursuant to § 41.1-3.** — Any grants for land heretofore issued by the Librarian of Virginia pursuant to § 41.1-3 are hereby ratified and confirmed and title is confirmed in the grantees thereof. (Code 1950, § 41-8.3; 1966, c. 427; 1970, c. 291; 1998, c. 427.)

The **1998 amendment** deleted "State" preceding "Librarian," inserted "of Virginia" and deleted "(§ 41-8 of the Code of 1950)" following "§ 41.1-3."

Applicability to grants from 1948 to 1954. — By its terms, this section only applies to grants issued by the State Librarian, who only held the power to issue grants between 1948 and 1954. This section, enacted in 1966, applies only to grants made during that time. Bradford v. Nature Conservancy, 224 Va. 181, 294 S.E.2d 866 (1982).

§ **41.1-7. Copies of unsigned grants admissible in evidence; Commonwealth's right relinquished when certain taxes paid; correction of record.** — Where the records in the Land Office disclose the fact that the land warrants used as the foundation for a grant of any of the public lands of the Commonwealth, subject to grant, were fully paid for and that the right to such grant was finally and fully completed in the manner prescribed by law and a grant therefor made out and spread upon the record book in the Land Office, in due form of law and regular in every respect only that the name of the then Governor of Virginia was not recorded at the foot thereof on the record book, it shall be the duty of the Librarian of Virginia, upon the request of any person interested, to furnish a copy of such grant as it appears of record in the Land Office, together with a certificate to the effect that the land warrants upon which such grant was founded, were fully paid for; that the right to such grant had been finally and fully completed in the manner prescribed by law, and that the grant was regular in every respect except only that the signature of the Governor did not appear at the foot thereof on the record. Such copy and certificate shall be received in evidence in any legal proceeding in which the title to the land described in such grant, or any part thereof, is brought in controversy, and shall be prima facie evidence of title to such land; and when the land embraced in such grant, or any part thereof, shall have been regularly on the proper land books and the taxes and levies regularly assessed thereon and paid by the claimants thereof, claiming under such grant, for a continuous period of ten years, any title which may rest in the Commonwealth, to so much of the land as has been so on the land books and upon which the taxes and levies shall have been so paid, shall be relinquished to the person so claiming the same, and any such claimant of such land, on which the taxes and levies shall have been so paid, may file a petition in the circuit court of the county or city in which such land lies, after ten days' notice in writing to the attorney for the Commonwealth for such county or city who shall appear and defend the same on behalf of the Commonwealth and the county or city; and upon satisfactory proof of the fact that such land has so been on the land books of the county or city and all the taxes and levies regularly paid thereon for the period of time hereinbefore specified, and the production before the court of the copy of such grant and the certificate of the Librarian of Virginia, hereinbefore provided for, the court shall make an order which shall recite and set forth all of such facts so proved and shown, which order, when so made and entered of record on the proper order book of the court, shall operate to effectually relinquish to the person so claiming such land through and under such grant, whatever right and title may rest in the Commonwealth, thereto; and a copy of such order shall be conclusive evidence of the better right of the claimant under such grant, in any caveat proceeding, or in any other controversy between such claimant and any other person claiming under a location of such land or any part thereof, made after the date of such order.

But nothing contained in this section shall in any manner affect any right adverse to any person claiming under such grant, which vested prior to June 22, 1926, nor divest the right or title, if any, of any junior grantee of any part of the land embraced within the exterior bounds of such grant, claiming under a junior grant which was regularly issued prior to June 22, 1926, or anyone holding or claiming through or under such junior grantee, but in any controversy between such adverse claimants or junior grantees, or persons claiming or holding through or under them, and any person holding or claiming through or under such grant as is first herein mentioned, the contesting parties shall be left to the strength of their respective rights and titles according to the nature of the case, independent of this section, and just as if it had not been enacted.

If it shall appear from the original of any such grant as is first hereinbefore referred to, that such original was actually signed by the Governor, the Librarian of Virginia shall, upon the presentation to him in the Land Office, of such original grant so signed, correct the record thereof so as to conform to such original grant, and affix thereto the date of such correction and a certificate of the fact that such original, duly signed by the Governor, had been presented to him. (Code 1950, § 41-9; 1970, c. 291; 1998, c. 427.)

The 1998 amendment deleted "State" preceding "Librarian" and inserted "of Virginia" throughout this section.

§ 41.1-8. When grant invalid; when Commonwealth's right relinquished to land settled on. — No grant of any land which shall have been settled continuously for five years previously, upon which taxes shall have been paid at any time within such five years by the person having settled the same, or any person claiming under him, shall be valid; and any title which the Commonwealth may have to such land shall be relinquished to the person in possession of the land claiming the same under such settlement and payment to the extent of the boundary line enclosing the same. But such boundary line shall not include more than 1,500 acres; and any person who has made such settlement and paid such taxes, or anyone claiming under him, may have the land surveyed, and prove the settlement and payment before the circuit court of the county where the land, or a greater part thereof, lies, whereupon such court shall order the plat and certificate of survey to be recorded. Such record shall be conclusive evidence in any controversy between the claimant thereunder and any person claiming under a location of the land made after the date of such order. This section shall relate as well to land forfeited for nonpayment of taxes, or for the failure to have the same entered on the commissioner's books, or both those causes, and to land escheated or escheatable, as to waste and unappropriated lands. (Code 1950, § 41-39; 1970, c. 291.)

This statute is an exception to the doctrine that no time runs against the crown. Levasser v. Washburn, 52 Va. (11 Gratt.) 572 (1854). See to the same effect, Tichanal v. Roe, 41 Va. (2 Rob.) 288 (1843); Gore v. Lawson, 35 Va. (8 Leigh) 458 (1836); Shanks v. Lancaster, 46 Va. (5 Gratt.) 110 (1848).

Land settled continuously for more than five years. — In a suit to have set aside — so far as it had effect upon the title to the coal estate — a grant under the provisions of § 2504 of the Code of 1942 regulating the purchase of waste and unappropriated lands, the evidence showed that the land so granted was settled continuously for more than five years prior to the date of the grant. Hence, under the terms of this section, the land was not waste or unappropriated and the grant was void as to the surface estate; and this result inured to the benefit of the owner of the coal estate, for the owner of the surface is presumed to hold possession for the benefit of the owner of the minerals. Clevinger v. Bull Creek Coal Co., 199 Va. 216, 98 S.E.2d 670 (1957).

Privity of estate in computing period. — Where the tenant has entered upon and improved the land and paid the taxes thereon, it is competent for him to connect his possession with the possession of those under whom he claims, the same never having been interrupted, in computing the statutory period. Tichanal v. Roe, 41 Va. (2 Rob.) 288 (1843).

A court order in pursuance of this section is only intended to affect those who have become locators since the date of the order, and not those who have previously acquired rights. Hurley v. Charles, 110 Va. 27, 65 S.E. 468 (1909).

Evidence of court right when records burned. — In an action for cutting and removing timber, it was held that where plaintiff's predecessor in title secured a court right to the land under this section, but the evidence of the title was destroyed by burning of clerk's office, the plaintiff was not required to show upon what evidence the court right was granted, the presumption being that it was granted on proper proof. Honaker Lumber Co. v. Kiser, 134 Va. 50, 113 S.E. 718 (1922).

Plaintiff suing for trespass and relying on a court right for land, under this section, could prove what his grantor's lawyer did and the fees paid him with reference to obtaining the court right, to sustain his contention that it was granted. Honaker Lumber Co. v. Kiser, 134 Va. 50, 113 S.E. 718 (1922).

§ 41.1-9. Lost records and papers in chains of title; bill in equity to establish ownership. — If any record or paper constituting a link in the chain of title to any tract or parcel of land in this Commonwealth, has been or shall be lost or destroyed, and no authenticated copy thereof can be found, it shall be lawful for the person or persons, claiming the ownership of such tract or parcel of land, to file in the circuit court of the county, or circuit court of the city, in which such land, or the greater part thereof, is situated, a bill in equity, setting forth the circumstances of such loss or destruction, and giving a history of the title and possession of such tract or parcel of land, and a full description thereof, with the names of the persons in possession of the conterminous parcels. All persons appearing to have an interest in such lands, or to be in possession thereof, or of any adjoining parcel, shall be either plaintiffs or defendants, and the proceedings to mature the cause shall be the same as in other suits in equity, except that in every case there shall be an order of publication, setting forth briefly the purpose of the proceeding and notifying all persons interested to appear and look after their interests. (Code 1950, § 41-68; 1970, c. 291.)

Bona fide adverse settlers are necessary parties to a suit under this section. Buchanan Co. v. Heirs of Smith, 115 Va. 704, 80 S.E. 794 (1914).

Evidence. — Courts of equity, in exercising their jurisdiction to set up a lost instrument which is to constitute a muniment of title, require strong and conclusive proof of its former existence, its loss, and its contents. Barley v. Byrd, 95 Va. 316, 28 S.E. 329 (1897).

In a suit to set up a lost deed made a century ago, the court held that a memorandum in the handwriting of the grantee's attorney is not in itself evidence of the execution of the deed. Barley v. Byrd, 95 Va. 316, 28 S.E. 329 (1897).

§ 41.1-10. Same; order of court for survey. — When the suit is ready for hearing, the court may make an order of survey, to be executed by such person as the court may appoint, requiring a complete survey and plat of the land in question to be made and returned, showing its connection with conterminous tracts, and any other circumstances necessary for its thorough identification. (Code 1950, § 41-69; 1970, c. 291.)

§ **41.1-11. Same; when and how testimony taken.** — Upon the return of such survey and plat, testimony may be taken as in other suits in equity, but no notice of the taking of such testimony need be given to any defendant who has not appeared and answered the bill. (Code 1950, § 41-70; 1970, c. 291.)

§ **41.1-12. Same; ownership certified by court; order as to costs.** — If, upon such survey and plat, and upon the other facts in the cause, the court shall be clearly satisfied of the ownership of the tract or parcel of land shown by such survey and plat, and that there is no controversy about such ownership, it shall certify the same of record, and shall make such order concerning the costs as may seem proper. (Code 1950, § 41-71; 1970, c. 291.)

Applied in Barley v. Byrd, 95 Va. 316, 28 S.E. 329 (1897).

§ **41.1-13. Bill in equity for repeal of grant.** — The Commonwealth, or any other party desiring to repeal, in whole or in part, any grant of land because it was obtained by fraud, or issued contrary to law, or to the prejudice of such party's equitable right, may file a bill in equity for that purpose in the circuit court of the county, or the circuit court of the city, in which the land, or some part thereof, lies, exhibiting with the bill a certified copy of the patent, and making all proper parties. (Code 1950, § 41-75; 1970, c. 291.)

Complainant must show that he is prejudiced by grant. — This section does not confer the right upon a private citizen to maintain a suit in equity or otherwise, to set aside a grant from the State to a third person, unless he can show that he has a right therein which has been prejudiced by the grant. Meredith v. Triple Island Gunning Club, 113 Va. 80, 73 S.E. 721 (1912).

But may sue though he has only part of legal title. — A party claiming title to land, to which he has the legal title to one-third and an equitable title to the other two-thirds, may go into equity to restrain waste upon the land and to set aside a conveyance from the board of public works of Virginia to a purchaser of the land, the same having been previously legally granted by a valid grant. Garrison v. Hall, 75 Va. 150 (1881).

While public officers are presumed to act lawfully, this presumption is rebuttable. Were it not, no grant from the Commonwealth could be voided once it was made, since the fact of issuance would be proof of validity. This, however, is not the case, since this section sets forth a means for challenging the validity of grants. Bradford v. Nature Conservancy, 224 Va. 181, 294 S.E.2d 866 (1982).

§ **41.1-14. Nature of proceedings for repeal of grant.** — The proceedings thereupon shall be as in other suits in equity, and on the final hearing the court shall make such decree as law and equity may require. (Code 1950, § 41-76; 1970, c. 291.)

§ **41.1-15. Recording decree of repeal.** — Any decree for such repeal, in whole or in part, shall be certified to the Librarian of Virginia, and shall thereupon be recorded by the Librarian of Virginia in the manner prescribed in § 55-186.2. (Code 1950, § 41-77; 1970, c. 291; 1982, c. 565; 1998, c. 427.)

The 1998 amendment deleted "State" preceding "Librarian" and inserted "of Virginia" in two places.

§ 41.1-16. Sale of wastelands; proceeding by citizen resident; motion and deposit for costs; parties; copy of plat.

— Any citizen, resident of this Commonwealth, who has reason to believe that there are waste and unappropriated lands in this Commonwealth (not being excluded under § 41.1-3 from grant), shall have the right to file a proceeding in the name of the county or city seeking the sale and disposition of such land. The venue for such a proceeding shall be as specified in subdivision 3 of § 8.01-261. The proceeding shall be instituted by motion signed by the party who institutes the proceeding, or on his behalf, and shall be accompanied with a deposit to cover the costs of the proceeding but in no event to exceed $100. Each landowner adjoining the tract in question shall be made a party to the proceedings.

He shall file with the motion a copy of a plat prepared by a licensed land surveyor giving the metes and bounds of the land alleged to be waste and unappropriated. A copy of the motion and plat shall be served upon each of the landowners adjoining the tract in question. (Code 1950, § 41-84; 1952, c. 185; 1970, c. 291; 1977, c. 624; 1995, c. 850.)

Law Review. — For article discussing common-law principles underlying public interests in tidal water resources, see 23 Wm. & Mary L. Rev. 835 (1982).

Section 8.01-238 may not be used to defeat landowner's effort to show that grant under former § 41-84 (now this section) is void and to have a valid claim of equity confirm his title. Johnson v. Buzzard Island Shooting Club, Inc., 232 Va. 32, 348 S.E.2d 220 (1986).

All lands that have never been patented are to be considered waste and unappropriated, susceptible to location and to being sold under the statute. Black v. Eagle, 248 Va. 48, 445 S.E.2d 662 (1994).

The mere fact of public use and a claim of possessory rights does not provide anyone, including the Virginia Outdoors Federation (VOF), with a valid claim of ownership of land of this type in disregard of the law relating to waste and unappropriated land. Black v. Eagle, 248 Va. 48, 445 S.E.2d 662 (1994).

§ 41.1-17. Same; time and place of hearing.

— Upon the docketing of the motion, the court shall set a time and place to hear the merits of the proceeding. Such hearing shall be held not less than thirty nor more than sixty days from the date upon which the same was filed. (Code 1950, § 41-85; 1952, c. 185; 1970, c. 291.)

§ 41.1-18. Same; subsequent proceedings; disposition of proceeds of sale.

— Thereafter the proceedings shall conform, mutatis mutandis, to the provisions of Article 4 (§ 58.1-3965 et seq.) of Chapter 39 of Title 58.1 but on the motion of any party the sale of such land shall be public. From the proceeds of sale, after the expenses of suit and other costs incident to the sale, the person instituting the proceeding shall be reimbursed his deposit and costs expended up to the time the proceeding is docketed; but if such proceeds be insufficient to pay the expenses of suit and other costs incidental to the sale, the deficiency shall be paid by the person, county or city instituting the suit. The remainder left from the proceeds of sale after the payment of costs, expenses of suit and other expenses of sale shall be paid into the treasury of the county or city, as the case may be. (Code 1950, § 41-87; 1952, c. 185; 1970, c. 291.)

§ 41.1-19. Same; proceedings by governing body of county or city.

— The governing body of the county or city in which any waste or unappropriated land lies may, without deposit of costs, initiate proceedings under this chapter to have such lands sold under the provisions hereof. (Code 1950, § 41-88; 1952, c. 185; 1970, c. 291.)

§ 41.1-20. Same; sale extinguishes title and interest of Commonwealth.

— All right, title and interest of the Commonwealth, except as shown by an instrument recorded in the clerk's office of the court of the city or county in which deeds are admitted to record in which land is sold under the provisions hereof shall be extinguished by such sale. (Code 1950, § 41-89; 1952, c. 185; 1970, c. 291.)

Title 42.
Libraries.

[Repealed.]

§§ 42-1 through 42-67: Repealed by Acts 1970, c. 606.

Cross references. — As to repeal of Title 42, enactment of Title 42.1, and transition provisions, see notes under § 42.1-1.

Title 42.1.

Libraries.

CHAPTER 1.

State Library and Library Board.

ARTICLE 1.

In General.

§ **42.1-1. The Library of Virginia.** — The Library of Virginia is hereby declared an educational institution and an institution of learning. The Library of Virginia shall be the library agency of the Commonwealth, the archival agency of the Commonwealth, and the reference library at the seat of government. It shall have the following powers and duties:

(1) [Repealed.]

(2) To accept gifts, bequests and endowments for the purposes which fall within the general legal powers and duties of The Library of Virginia. Unless otherwise specified by the donor or legator, the Library may either expend both the principal and interest of any gift or bequest or may invest such sums as the Board deems advisable, with the consent of the State Treasurer, in securities in which sinking funds may be invested. The Library shall be deemed to be an institution of higher education within the meaning of § 23-9.2;

(3) To purchase and maintain a general collection of books, periodicals, newspapers, maps, films, audiovisual materials and other materials for the use of the people of the Commonwealth as a means for the promotion of knowledge within the Commonwealth. The scope of the Library's collections shall be determined by the Library Board on recommendation of the Librarian of Virginia, and, in making these decisions, the Board and Librarian of Virginia shall take into account the book collections of public libraries and college and university libraries throughout the Commonwealth and the availability of such collections to the general public. The Board shall make available for circulation to libraries or to the public such of its materials as it deems advisable;

(4) To give assistance, advice and counsel to other agencies of the Commonwealth maintaining libraries and special reference collections as to the best means of establishing and administering such libraries and collections. It may establish in The Library of Virginia a union catalogue of all books, pamphlets and other materials owned and used for reference purposes by all other agencies of the Commonwealth and of all books, pamphlets and other materials maintained by libraries in the Commonwealth which are of interest to the people of the whole Commonwealth;

(5) To fix reasonable penalties for damage to or failure to return any book, periodical or other material owned by the Library, or for violation of any rule or regulation concerning the use of books, periodicals, and other materials in custody of the Library;

(6) To give direction, assistance and counsel to all libraries in the Commonwealth, to all communities which may propose to establish libraries, and to all persons interested in public libraries, as to means of establishment and administration of such libraries, selection of books, retrieval systems, cataloguing, maintenance, and other details of library management, and to conduct such inspections as are necessary;

(7) To engage in such activities in aid of city, county, town, regional and other public libraries as will serve to develop the library system of the Commonwealth;

(8) To administer and distribute state and federal library funds in accordance with law and its own regulations to the city, county, town and regional libraries of the Commonwealth; and

(9) To enter into contracts with other states or regions or districts for the purpose of providing cooperative library services.

Wherever in this title and the Code of Virginia the terms "State Library" or "Library" appear, they shall mean The Library of Virginia. (Code 1950,

§ 42-33; 1970, c. 606; 1984, cc. 389, 734; 1986, c. 565; 1987, c. 458; 1994, c. 64; 1998, c. 427.)

Editor's note. — At its 1970 session the General Assembly, by Acts 1970, c. 606, repealed Title 42 and enacted in its place a new Title 42.1.

Transition provisions. — Acts 1970, c. 606, §§ 5-8, provide:

"5. The repeal of Title 42 shall not affect any act or offense done or committed, or any penalty or forfeiture incurred, or any right established, accrued or accruing on or before the effective date of its repeal [June 26, 1970], or any prosecution, suit or action pending on that date. Except as in this act otherwise provided, neither the repeal of Title 42 of the Code of Virginia nor the enactment of Title 42.1 shall apply to offenses committed prior to the effective date thereof, and prosecutions for such offenses shall be governed by the prior law, which is continued in effect for that purpose. For the purposes of this act, an offense was committed prior to such date if any of the essential elements of the offense occurred prior thereto.

"6. Whenever in Title 42.1 any of the conditions, requirements, provisions or contents of any section, article or chapter of Title 42, as such title existed prior to the effective date of this act, are transferred in the same or in modified form to a new section, article or chapter of Title 42.1, and whenever any such former section, article or chapter of Title 42 is given a new number in Title 42.1 or in Title 10 (now Title 10.1), all references to any such former section, article or chapter of Title 42 appearing elsewhere in the Code of Virginia than in Title 42.1 shall be construed to apply to the new or renumbered section, article or chapter containing such conditions, requirements, provisions or contents or portions thereof.

"7. It is the intention of the General Assembly that this act shall be liberally construed to effect the purposes set out herein, and if any clause, sentence, paragraph or section of this act shall ever be declared unconstitutional, it shall be deemed severable, and the remainder of this act shall continue in full force and effect.

"8. It is the intention of the General Assembly that the repeal of §§ 42-66 through 42-67 and the enactment of §§ 10-145.2 through 10-145.8 (now repealed), shall not affect the transfer of powers from the State Library Board to the Virginia Historic Landmarks Commission (now Board) accomplished by § 10-144 (now repealed), but such powers shall remain in the Virginia Historic Landmarks Commission."

The 1998 amendment, in the second sentence of subdivision (3), deleted "State" preceding "Librarian" and inserted "of Virginia" in two places.

§ 42.1-2. The Library of Virginia under direction of Library Board; membership; chairman and vice-chairman; committees and advisory bodies.

— The Library of Virginia shall be directed by a board, consisting of fifteen members, to be appointed by the Governor, which shall be and remain a corporation under the style of "The Library Board," sometimes in this chapter called the Board. Prior to such appointments the Board may submit to the Governor lists of candidates based upon interest and knowledge, geographic representation, participation in community affairs, and concern for the welfare of the Commonwealth. In no case shall the Governor be bound to make any appointment from among the nominees of the Board. The Board shall meet and organize by electing from its number a chairman and vice-chairman. It shall have the power to appoint such committees and advisory bodies as it deems advisable. (Code 1950, § 42-34; 1968, c. 122; 1970, c. 606; 1986, c. 565; 1987, c. 458; 1994, c. 64.)

§ 42.1-2.1. Executive committee.

— The Board may also provide for an executive committee, composed of not fewer than five Board members, which committee may exercise powers vested in and perform duties imposed upon the Board by this chapter to the extent designated and permitted by the Board. (1986, c. 565.)

§ 42.1-3. Terms of office of members of Board; vacancies.

— Members serving on the Board on June 30, 1986, shall continue in their respective terms, and the Governor shall appoint the following additional members: one member for a one-year term, one member for a three-year term, two members for four-year terms, and two members for five-year terms. Thereafter, all appointments shall be for five-year terms beginning on July 1 of the year of appointment, provided that appointments to fill vacancies shall be for the unexpired term.

No person shall be eligible to serve as a member of the Board for more than two successive full terms. (Code 1950, § 42-35; 1968, c. 122; 1970, c. 606; 1986, c. 565.)

§ **42.1-3.1. Authority of Board generally.** — The Board shall be vested with full authority (i) to establish policy concerning what books and other library materials are to be kept, housed, or exhibited by The Library of Virginia; (ii) to enter into agreements with institutions and organizations with purposes similar to its own; (iii) to adopt and amend bylaws; (iv) to charge for such services as deemed proper; and (v) to do such other things as it deems proper to promote education in the realm of history and library and archival science throughout the Commonwealth through The Library of Virginia.

The Board is hereby authorized to sell, grant, and convey or to change the form of investments or control of any funds, securities or other property, provided such action is not inconsistent with the terms of the instrument under which the property may have been acquired.

The Board may confer the honorary degree of patron of letters on any person who has, in its opinion, made an outstanding contribution in the realm of history, or library or archival science. (1986, c. 565; 1994, c. 64.)

§ **42.1-4:** Repealed by Acts 1986, c. 565, effective April 7, 1986.

§ **42.1-5. Expenses of members of Board.** — The members of the Board shall receive no compensation for their services as such; but reasonable expenses incurred as members of the Board in the discharge of their duties shall be paid out of the Library funds. (Code 1950, § 42-37; 1970, c. 606.)

§ **42.1-6. Minutes and records of Board.** — The Board shall keep minutes of all its proceedings, which shall be signed by the chairman and attested by the secretary, and a record of all receipts and disbursements, all of which shall be preserved as public records. (Code 1950, § 42-38; 1970, c. 606.)

§ **42.1-7:** Repealed by Acts 1985, c. 397.

§ **42.1-8. Rules and regulations.** — The Board shall make rules and regulations, not inconsistent with law, for the government and use of The Library of Virginia, and may by general or special regulation determine what books and other possessions of the Library may not be removed therefrom. (Code 1950, § 42-41; 1970, c. 606; 1994, c. 64.)

§ **42.1-9. When Library to be kept open.** — The Library of Virginia shall be kept open for such days and hours each day as may be prescribed for other state agencies at the seat of government. But the Board may, in its discretion, prescribe additional hours in which the Library shall be kept open. (Code 1950, § 42-43; 1970, c. 606; 1994, c. 64.)

§ **42.1-10. Acquisition of books and other library matter.** — The Library may from time to time acquire books and other library matter by gift, purchase, exchange or loan. And the Library shall cause to be procured, from time to time, as opportunity may offer, a copy of any book, pamphlet, manuscript, or other library material, relating to the history of Virginia, not now in The Library of Virginia, which can be obtained on reasonable terms. (Code 1950, § 42-44; 1970, c. 606; 1994, c. 64.)

§ 42.1-11. Editing and publishing state records and other special matter; list of publications. — The Board may edit, or cause to be edited, arranged and published, as the funds at its disposal permit, the state records now or hereafter deposited in The Library of Virginia and such other special matter as it deems of sufficient value.

The Board may cause to be printed any manuscript relating to the history of Virginia which has not been published, including such portions of the executive journals and letter books, and of the legislative papers, as the Board may deem proper, and shall cause the papers so to be printed to be arranged for that purpose and preserved for reference; and shall cause the records in the Library pertaining to the various wars in which the Commonwealth has been engaged to be edited, arranged, and published so as to show the service of citizens of the Commonwealth in such wars.

The Library may expend funds to list its publications in appropriate commercial listings. (Code 1950, § 42-45; 1956, c. 169; 1970, c. 606; 1994, c. 64.)

§ 42.1-12. Fees for copies made by Library staff. — The Library may, in its discretion, charge and collect such fees as it may deem reasonable for copies or extracts from any books, papers, records, documents or manuscripts in the Library, made by the Library staff, for persons applying for the same. The Librarian of Virginia shall keep an accurate account of all such fees and pay the same into the general fund of the state treasury. (Code 1950, § 42-46; 1970, c. 606; 1998, c. 427.)

The **1998 amendment,** in the second sentence, deleted "State" preceding "Librarian" and inserted "of Virginia."

ARTICLE 2.

State Librarian, Assistants and Employees.

§ 42.1-13. Appointment; terms of office; employment; duties. — The Board shall appoint a librarian, to be known as the Librarian of Virginia, who shall serve at the pleasure of the Board. The Librarian of Virginia shall appoint principal assistants and approve the appointment of other employees. The terms of office and employment of such assistants and employees shall be subject to the personnel regulations of the Commonwealth.

The Librarian of Virginia shall supervise the administration of The Library of Virginia. The Librarian of Virginia shall make requests for appropriations of necessary funds and approve all expenditures of Library funds. Such expenditures shall be made as provided by law. (Code 1950, § 42-48; 1970, c. 606; 1984, c. 444; 1985, c. 397; 1986, c. 565; 1994, c. 64; 1996, c. 812; 1998, c. 427.)

The **1998 amendment** deleted "State" preceding "Librarian" and inserted "of Virginia" throughout this section.

§ 42.1-14. Compensation. — The Librarian of Virginia, assistants and employees shall be paid such salaries from appropriations out of the public treasury as are provided by law. (Code 1950, § 42-49; 1970, c. 606; 1998, c. 427.)

The 1998 amendment deleted "State" preceding "Librarian" and inserted "of Virginia."

§ 42.1-15. Duties of Librarian of Virginia. — The Librarian of Virginia shall have charge of The Library of Virginia. He shall see that the Library is properly kept and that its contents are properly preserved and cared for.

He shall be secretary of the Board, and shall perform all duties belonging to that position. He shall keep a record of all proceedings of the Board and such financial records as are required by the Commonwealth. (Code 1950, § 42-50; 1970, c. 606; 1994, c. 64; 1998, c. 427.)

Cross references. — As to State Librarian being in charge of Land Office, see § 41.1-1.

The 1998 amendment, in the first sentence of the first paragraph, deleted "State" preceding "Librarian" and inserted "of Virginia."

§ 42.1-15.1. Qualifications required to hold professional librarian position. — Public libraries serving a political subdivision or subdivisions having over 5,000 population and libraries operated by the Commonwealth or under its authority, shall not employ, in the position of librarian or in any other full-time professional librarian position, a person who does not meet the qualifications established by the State Library Board.

A professional librarian position as used in this section is one that requires a knowledge of books and of library technique equivalent to that required for graduation from any accredited library school or one that requires graduation from a school of library science accredited by the American Library Association.

No public funds shall be paid to any person whose employment does not comply with this section.

This section shall not apply to law libraries organized pursuant to Chapter 4 (§ 42.1-60 et seq.) of this title, libraries in colleges and universities or to public school libraries. (1988, c. 716.)

§ 42.1-16. Bond of Librarian of Virginia. — The Librarian of Virginia shall give bond to the Commonwealth in the sum of $2,000, with sureties approved by the State Treasurer, subject to the approval of the Governor, for the faithful discharge of his duties and the delivery over to his successor of all the property of the Commonwealth in his possession, which bond shall be recorded by the Secretary of the Commonwealth and deposited with the Comptroller. (Code 1950, § 42-51; 1970, c. 606; 1998, c. 427.)

The 1998 amendment deleted "State" preceding "Librarian" and inserted "of Virginia."

§ 42.1-17. Cities and towns to furnish copies of official publications. — The mayor of each city and town in the Commonwealth shall send regularly at the time of publication to The Library of Virginia two copies of each of the official publications of such city or town, and also two copies of each publication of former years of which the supply has not been exhausted. Official publications for the purpose of this section shall embrace printed reports, in pamphlet or book form, of the officials of the city or town, printed volumes of ordinances and such other special publications as the city or town may authorize to be printed. (Code 1950, § 42-52; 1970, c. 606; 1994, c. 64.)

§ 42.1-18. Exchanges; donation, etc., of duplicate material. — The Library may arrange for the exchange of the Virginia publications with such states and institutions, the general government and other governments, societies and others, as it sees fit. Publications received on exchange are to become the property of The Library of Virginia, except statute and law books, which shall be placed in the Law Library. The Library may also, when deemed advantageous, donate, exchange or sell any or all duplicate material now or hereafter the property of The Library of Virginia, and other printed material not within the scope of its collections. The Librarian of Virginia shall keep an accurate account of all such sales and pay the money arising therefrom into the general fund of the state treasury. (Code 1950, § 42-56; 1970, c. 606; 1994, c. 64; 1998, c. 427.)

The 1998 amendment inserted "of Virginia" in the last sentence.

§ **42.1-19. Establishment of depository system; sending state publications to members.** — The Library of Virginia shall establish a depository system and send to the members thereof copies of state publications furnished pursuant to § 2.1-467.2. (Code 1950, § 42-57; 1970, c. 606; 1981, c. 234; 1994, c. 64.)

ARTICLE 3.

Public Records.

§§ **42.1-20 through 42.1-28:** Repealed by Acts 1976, c. 746.

Cross references. — For the Virginia Public Records Act, see § 42.1-76 et seq.

ARTICLE 3.1.

Return of Public Records.

§§ **42.1-29 through 42.1-29.2:** Repealed by Acts 1976, c. 746.

Cross references. — For the Virginia Public Records Act, see § 42.1-76 et seq.

ARTICLE 4.

Historical Material Relating to World War II.

§ **42.1-30. Virginia World War II History Commission abolished; duties transferred to Librarian of Virginia.** — The Virginia World War II History Commission, heretofore created and existing, is hereby abolished and its duty of collecting, assembling, editing and publishing such information and material with respect to the contribution to World War II made by Virginia and Virginians as is most worthy of preservation shall hereafter be performed by the Librarian of Virginia. The Virginia World War II History Commission shall deliver to the Librarian of Virginia all material, records and information collected, assembled and compiled by it in the performance of its duties. (Code 1950, § 42-64; 1970, c. 606; 1998, c. 427.)

Editor's note. — The Commission was created by Acts 1944, p. 200, codified as §§ 585(a1) through 585(a3) of Michie Suppl. 1946.

The 1998 amendment deleted "State" preceding "Librarian" and inserted "of Virginia" in two places.

§ 42.1-31. Counties and cities may submit material. — Any county or city of the Commonwealth may assemble and submit to the Librarian of Virginia information and material relating to its contribution and that of its citizens to World War II, and the governing body of any county or city may appropriate for this purpose such funds as it deems necessary. (Code 1950, § 42-65; 1970, c. 606; 1998, c. 427.)

The **1998 amendment** deleted "State" preceding "Librarian" and inserted "of Virginia."

§ 42.1-32: Reserved.

ARTICLE 5.

Networking.

§ 42.1-32.1. Declaration of intent. — It is hereby declared to be the policy of the Commonwealth, as part of its provision for public education, to promote the cooperation and networking of all public, academic, special and school libraries throughout the Commonwealth. It is the further intent of this article that none of its provisions shall be construed to interfere with the autonomy of the governing boards of institutions of higher education and the governing boards of public, special and school libraries. (1983, c. 537.)

§ 42.1-32.2. Grants for establishment of library network. — In order to assist in the development of library cooperation and a library network, the Board shall grant from such appropriations as are made to it for this purpose, funds to assist libraries in preparing for networking and in supporting a library network. The Board shall seek the advice of the State Networking Users Advisory Board, as defined in § 42.1-32.7, to guide it in its allocation of such grants and in the establishment of standards and priorities for the network. (1983, c. 537.)

§ 42.1-32.3. Standards for networking. — Libraries receiving such aid, as is provided by the Board for networking, shall be committed to the standards and priorities established by the Board for interlibrary lending policies between network members, to cooperation in establishing collection development policies and resource sharing for the greatest good of all library users, and to the provision of comprehensive and cost-effective library services to the citizens of Virginia. (1983, c. 537.)

§ 42.1-32.4. Computer programs and data bases property of the Commonwealth. — All computer programs and data bases created pursuant to programs supported by grants made for networking shall be the property of the Commonwealth and shall be made available to all libraries of the network equally. (1983, c. 537.)

§ 42.1-32.5. Board to establish standards for grants. — The Board shall establish standards under which a library shall be eligible for grants for networking. (1983, c. 537.)

§ 42.1-32.6. Establishment and operation of communication centers and other networking services. — The Board may establish and operate or may contract for the establishment and operation of one or more automated communication centers and other networking services, based on a plan approved by the Board and the Governor after consultation with the Users Board. (1983, c. 537.)

§ **42.1-32.7. State Networking Users Advisory Board.** — The State Networking Users Advisory Board shall be composed of nine members, to be appointed by the Governor as follows: one academic librarian serving in a public four-year institution of higher education; one academic librarian serving in a private four-year institution of higher education; one academic librarian serving in the Virginia Community College System; one public school librarian; one private school librarian; one librarian serving in a large public library system; one librarian serving in a small public library system; one librarian serving in a library having a specialized focus, such as, but not limited to, a corporate, legal, or medical library; and one librarian serving in an institutional library, such as, but not limited to, a state correctional institution, a mental health facility, or other agency of state government. The terms of office of the Board shall be three years. No person shall serve more than two successive full terms. Any vacancy occurring other than by expiration of term shall be filled for the unexpired term. Members shall hold office after the expiration of their terms until their successors are duly appointed and have qualified. Appointments to fill an unexpired term shall not be considered a full term. The State Networking Users Advisory Board shall advise the Librarian of Virginia and the State Library Board in the development and direction of the network and its policies, standards, funding levels and requirements for use, after receiving the input of other libraries. The State Networking Users Advisory Board shall meet no less than twice annually. (1983, c. 537; 1985, c. 448; 1986, c. 513; 1991, c. 50; 1998, c. 427.)

The 1998 amendment, in the next-to-last sentence, deleted "State" preceding "Librarian" and inserted "of Virginia."

CHAPTER 2.

LOCAL AND REGIONAL LIBRARIES.

§ **42.1-33. Power of local governments to establish and support libraries.** — The governing body of any city, county or town shall have the power to establish a free public library for the use and benefit of its residents. The governing body shall provide sufficient support for the operation of the library by levying a tax therefor, either by special levy or as a fund of the general levy of the city, county or town. The word "support" as used in this chapter shall include but is not limited to, purchase of land for library buildings, purchase or erection of buildings for library purposes, purchase of library books, materials and equipment, compensation of library personnel, and all maintenance expenses for library property and equipment. Funds appropriated or contributed for public library purposes shall constitute a separate fund and shall not be used for any but public library purposes. (1970, c. 606.)

§ 42.1-34. Power of local governments to contract for library service. — Any city, town or county shall have the power to enter into contracts with adjacent cities, counties, towns, or state-supported institutions of higher learning to receive or to provide library service on such terms and conditions as shall be mutually acceptable, or they may contract for a library service with a library not owned by a public corporation but maintained for free public use. The board of trustees of a free public library may enter into contracts with county, city or town school boards and boards of school trustees to provide library service for schools. Any city or county governing body contracting for library service shall, as a part of such contract, have the power to appoint at least one member to the board of trustees or other governing body of the library contracting to provide such service. Any city or county thus contracting for library service shall be entitled to the rights and benefits of regional free library systems established in accordance with the provisions of § 42.1-37. The board of trustees or other governing body of any library established under the provisions of § 42.1-33 may also, with the approval of and on terms satisfactory to the State Library Board, extend its services to persons in adjacent areas of other states. (1970, c. 606.)

§ 42.1-35. Library boards generally. — A. The management and control of a free public library system shall be vested in a board of not less than five members or trustees. They shall be appointed by the governing body, chosen from the citizens at large with reference to their fitness for such office. However, one board member or trustee may be a member or an employee of the local governing body. Initially members shall be appointed as follows: one member for a term of one year, one member for a term of two years, one member for a term of three years, and the remaining members for terms of four years; thereafter all members shall be appointed for terms of four years. The governing body of any county or city entitled to representation on a library board of a library system of another jurisdiction pursuant to § 42.1-34 shall appoint a member to serve for a term of four years, or until the contract is terminated, whichever is shorter. Vacancies shall be filled for unexpired terms as soon as possible in the manner in which members of the board are regularly chosen. A member shall not receive a salary or other compensation for services as a member but necessary expenses actually incurred shall be paid from the library fund. However, the governing body of Fairfax County may pay members of its library board such compensation as it may deem proper. A member of a library board may be removed for misconduct or neglect of duty by the governing body making the appointment. The members shall adopt such bylaws, rules and regulations for their own guidance and for the government of the free public library system as may be expedient. They shall have control of the expenditures of all moneys credited to the library fund. The board shall have the right to accept donations and bequests of money, personal property, or real estate for the establishment and maintenance of such free public library systems or endowments for same.

B. Notwithstanding the provisions of subsection A relating to the terms of library board members, a local governing body may alter the composition of its library board to create staggered terms of service in which approximately the same number of terms expire annually. To achieve this goal, the local governing body shall appoint in any year in which multiple terms expire members for terms of one, two, three, and four years as appropriate. Thereafter, all members shall be appointed for terms of four years. Vacancies shall be filled for unexpired terms as soon as possible in the manner in which members of the board are regularly chosen. (1970, c. 606; 1974, c. 84; 1985, c. 278; 1998, c. 212.)

Editor's note. — Acts 1998, c. 212, cl. 2 provides: "That this act shall not be construed to affect existing appointments for which the terms have not expired."

The 1998 amendment added the subsection A designation; and added subsection B.

Library board and its members were entitled to absolute immunity for their decision to adopt a policy on internet sexual harassment, as this was essentially a discretionary exercise of rulemaking authority, and as such, it is properly treated as legislative in nature. Mainstream Loudoun v. Board of Trustees, 2 F. Supp. 2d 783 (E.D. Va. 1998).

However, board and members were not entitled to legislative immunity in their enforcement role. Therefore, plaintiffs were able to properly sue Library Board and its individual members for declaratory and injunctive relief under U.S.C. § 1983 to prevent them from enforcing a policy on internet sexual harassment. Mainstream Loudoun v. Board of Trustees, 2 F. Supp. 2d 783 (E.D. Va. 1998).

§ 42.1-36. Boards not mandatory. — The formation and creation of boards shall in nowise be considered or construed in any manner as mandatory upon any city or town with a manager, or upon any county with a county manager, county executive, urban county manager or urban county executive form of government or Chesterfield County, by virtue of this chapter. (1970, c. 606; 1978, c. 6.)

§ 42.1-36.1. Power and duty of library boards and certain governing bodies regarding acceptable Internet use policies. — A. On or before December 1, 1999, and biennially thereafter, (i) every library board established pursuant to § 42.1-35 or (ii) the governing body of any county, city, or town which, pursuant to § 42.1-36, has not established a library board pursuant to § 42.1-35, shall file with the Librarian of Virginia an acceptable use policy for the international network of computer systems commonly known as the Internet. At a minimum, the policy shall contain provisions which (i) are designed to prohibit use by library employees and patrons of the library's computer equipment and communications services for sending, receiving, viewing, or downloading illegal material via the Internet, (ii) seek to prevent access by library patrons under the age of eighteen to material which is harmful to juveniles, and (iii) establish appropriate measures to be taken against persons who violate the policy. The library board or the governing body may include such other terms, conditions, and requirements in the library's policy as it deems appropriate, such as requiring written parental authorization for Internet use by juveniles or differentiating acceptable uses between elementary, middle, and high school students.

B. The library board or the governing body shall take such steps as it deems appropriate to implement and enforce the library's policy which may include, but are not limited to, (i) the use of software programs designed to block access by (a) library employees and patrons to illegal material or (b) library patrons under the age of eighteen to material which is harmful to juveniles or (c) both; (ii) charging library employees to casually monitor patrons' Internet use; or (iii) installing privacy screens on computers which access the Internet.

C. On or before December 1, 2000, and biennially thereafter, the Librarian of Virginia shall submit a report to the Chairmen of the House Committee on Education, the House Committee on Science and Technology, and the Senate

Committee on Education and Health which summarizes the acceptable use policies filed with the Librarian pursuant to this section and the status thereof. (1999, c. 64.)

§ 42.1-37. Establishment of regional library system. — Two or more political subdivisions, (counties or cities), by action of their governing bodies, may join in establishing and maintaining a regional free library system under the terms of a contract between such political subdivisions; provided, that in the case of established county or city free library systems, the library boards shall agree to such action. (1970, c. 606.)

§ 42.1-38. Agreements to create regional boards. — Two or more political subdivisions (counties or cities) which have qualified for participation in the state's regional library program, have been recognized as a region by the State Library Board, and have made the minimum local appropriation of funds as may now or hereafter be recommended by the Board, are hereby empowered and authorized to execute contracts with each other to create a regional library board to administer and control the regional library services within the region. Each jurisdiction shall, as a part of such contract, have the power to appoint at least one member to the regional library board. (1970, c. 606.)

§ 42.1-39. Regional library boards generally. — The members of the board of a regional library system shall be appointed by the respective governing bodies represented. If the board of the regional library system is composed of two or more members from each county, city and town that is a part thereof, then each governing body represented on the board may appoint a member or an employee of the governing body to the board. Such members shall in the beginning draw lots for expiration of terms, to provide for staggered terms of office, and thereafter the appointment shall be for a term of four years. Vacancies shall be filled for unexpired terms as soon as possible in the manner in which members are regularly chosen. No appointive member shall be eligible to serve more than two successive terms. A member shall not receive a salary or other compensation for services as member, but necessary expenses actually incurred shall be paid from the library fund. A regional board member may be removed for misconduct or neglect of duty by the governing body making the appointment. The board members shall elect officers and adopt such bylaws, rules and regulations for their own guidance and for the government of the regional free library system as may be expedient. They shall have control of the expenditure of all moneys credited to the regional free library fund. The regional board shall have the right to accept donations and bequests of money, personal property, or real estate for the establishment and maintenance of such regional free library system or endowments for same. (1970, c. 606; 1985, c. 278.)

§ 42.1-40. Powers of regional library board. — The regional library board shall have authority to execute contracts with the State Library Board, with the library boards of the respective jurisdictions, and any and all other agencies for the purpose of administering a public library service within the region, including contracts concerning allocation and expenditure of funds, to the same extent as the library board of any one of the jurisdictions which are parties to the agreement would be so authorized. In addition, to effectuate the purposes of this chapter, a regional library board is empowered to sell the surplus assets, including real estate, of the said regional library board if the net proceeds therefrom are used for public library services within the region. (1970, c. 606; 1986, c. 247.)

§ 42.1-41. Funds and expenses of regional library system. — The expenses of the regional library system shall be apportioned among the participating political subdivisions on such basis as shall be agreed upon in the contract. The treasurer of the regional library board shall have the custody of the funds of the regional free library system; and the treasurers or other financial officers of the participating jurisdictions shall transfer quarterly to him all moneys collected or appropriated for this purpose in their respective jurisdictions. Such funds shall be expended only for the library service for which the county or city contracted and for no other purpose. The regional library board shall furnish a detailed report of receipts and disbursements of all funds at the regular meeting of the governing body of every participating jurisdiction after the close of the state's fiscal year. It shall make a similar report to The Library of Virginia. The treasurer of the board shall be bonded for an amount to be determined by the board. The board may authorize the treasurer to pay bond premiums from state aid library funds. (1970, c. 606; 1994, c. 64.)

§ 42.1-42. Withdrawal from regional library system. — No county or city participating in a regional library system shall withdraw therefrom without two years' notice to the other participating counties and cities without the consent of such other participating political subdivisions. (1970, c. 606.)

§ 42.1-43. Appropriation for free library or library service conducted by company, society or organization. — The governing body of any county, city or town in which no free public library system as provided in this chapter shall have been established, may, in its discretion, appropriate such sums of money as to it seems proper for the support and maintenance of any free library or library service operated and conducted in such county, city or town by a company, society or association organized under the provisions of §§ 13.1-801 through 13.1-980. (1970, c. 606.)

§ 42.1-44. Cooperative library system for Henrico and Chesterfield Counties and City of Richmond. — Notwithstanding the repeal of Title 42, §§ 42-12.1 to 42-12.5 of Chapter 2.1 of former Title 42 are continued in effect and are incorporated into this title by reference. (1970, c. 606.)

Editor's note. — Sections 42-12.1 through 42-12.5, referred to above, authorize the establishment by contract of a cooperative free public library service or system for the City of Richmond and Henrico and Chesterfield Counties and were added to the Code by Acts 1964, c. 347.

§ 42.1-45. Transfer of properties, etc., of public free library to governing body of city in which it is situated. — The board of directors or trustees of any public free library established pursuant to Chapter 13, Acts of Assembly, 1924, approved February 13, 1924, may lease, convey, or transfer any interest to its properties, real or personal, to the governing body of the political subdivision in which such library be situated in order that such library may become a part of the public library system of such city, subject to such restrictions and conditions as may be agreed to by such board of directors or trustees and such governing body. (1970, c. 367.)

The number of this section was assigned by the Virginia Code Commission, the 1970 act having assigned no number.

CHAPTER 3.

STATE AND FEDERAL AID.

§ 42.1-46. Library policy of the Commonwealth. — It is hereby declared to be the policy of the Commonwealth, as a part of its provision for public education, to promote the establishment and development of public library service throughout its various political subdivisions. (Code 1950, § 42-23; 1970, c. 606.)

§ 42.1-47. Grants for development of library service. — In order to provide state aid in the development of public library service throughout the Commonwealth, the Library Board, in this chapter sometimes called the Board, shall grant from such appropriations as are made for this purpose funds to provide library service. (Code 1950, § 42-24; 1952, c. 494; 1970, c. 606.)

§ 42.1-48. Grants to improve standards. — In order to encourage the maintenance and development of proper standards, including personnel standards, and the combination of libraries or library systems into larger and more economical units of service, grants of state aid from funds available shall be made by the Board to any free public library or library system which qualifies under the standards set by the Board. The grants to each qualifying library or system in each fiscal year shall be as follows:

(a) Forty cents of state aid for every dollar expended, or to be expended, exclusive of state and federal aid, by the political subdivision or subdivisions operating or participating in the library or system. The grant to any county or city shall not exceed $250,000;

(b) A per capita grant based on the population of the area served and the number of participating counties or cities: Thirty cents per capita for the first 600,000 persons to a library or system serving one city or county, and an additional ten cents per capita for the first 600,000 persons for each additional city or county served. Libraries or systems serving a population in excess of 600,000 shall receive ten cents per capita for the excess; and

(c) A grant of ten dollars per square mile of area served to every library or library system, and an additional grant of twenty dollars per square mile of area served to every library system serving more than one city or county.

The Board may establish procedures for the review and timely adjustment of such grants when the political subdivision or subdivisions operating such library or library system are affected by annexation. (Code 1950, § 42-26; 1952, c. 494; 1958, c. 513; 1960, c. 234; 1970, c. 606; 1978, c. 565; 1989, c. 85; 1990, c. 48.)

§ 42.1-49. Grants to municipal libraries. — Every qualifying municipal library serving an area containing less than 5,000 population shall receive its proper share, but not less than $400. (1970, c. 606.)

§ 42.1-50. Limitation of grants; proration of funds. — The total amount of grants under §§ 42.1-48 and 42.1-49 shall not exceed the amount expended, exclusive of state and federal aid, by the political subdivision or subdivisions operating the library. If the state appropriations provided for grants under §§ 42.1-48 and 42.1-49 are not sufficient to meet approved applications, the Library Board shall prorate the available funds in such manner that each application shall receive its proportionate share of each type of grant. Applications must be received prior to June one of each calendar year. (Code 1950, § 42-25; 1952, c. 494; 1958, c. 426; 1970, c. 606.)

§ 42.1-51. Obligations of libraries and systems receiving aid. — The obligations of the various library systems and libraries receiving state aid, shall consist of establishing and maintaining an organization as approved by the Board, provided that personnel standards of such library systems and libraries shall conform to the provisions of § 42.1-15.1. All books and bookmobiles purchased with state aid funds shall, if the Board so determines, become the property of The Library of Virginia in the case of any library system or library which does not meet its obligations as determined by the Board. (Code 1950, § 42-27; 1952, c. 494; 1970, c. 606; 1988, c. 716; 1994, c. 64.)

§ 42.1-52. Standards of eligibility for aid; reports on operation of libraries; supervision of services. — The Board shall establish standards under which library systems and libraries shall be eligible for state aid and may require reports on the operation of all libraries receiving state aid.

As long as funds are available, grants shall be made to the various libraries, library systems or contracting libraries applying for state aid in the order in which they meet the standards established by the Board.

In the event that any library meets the standards of the State Library Board but is unable to conform to § 42.1-15.1 relating to the employment of qualified librarians, the Library Board may, under a contractual agreement with such library, provide professional supervision of its services and may grant state aid funds to it in reduced amounts under a uniform plan to be adopted by the State Library Board. (Code 1950, § 42-28; 1960, c. 235; 1970, c. 606; 1988, c. 716.)

§ 42.1-53: Repealed by Acts 1999, c. 24.

§ 42.1-54. Procedure for purchase of books, materials and equipment and payment on salaries. — All proposals for books, materials and equipment to be purchased with state aid funds and all proposals for aid in the payment of salaries of certified librarians shall be submitted for approval to The Library of Virginia by the libraries, library systems or contracting libraries applying for state aid, in form prescribed by the Board, and those approved may be ordered by the libraries, library systems or contracting libraries. Payments and disbursements from the funds appropriated for this purpose shall be made by the State Treasurer upon the approval of the duly authorized representative of the Board, to the libraries, library systems or contracting libraries within thirty days of the beginning of each quarter. (Code 1950, § 42-30; 1952, c. 494; 1956, c. 168; 1970, c. 606; 1987, c. 458; 1994, c. 64.)

§ 42.1-55. Free service available to all. — The service of books in library systems and libraries receiving state aid shall be free and shall be made available to all persons living in the county, region, or municipality. (Code 1950, § 42-31; 1970, c. 606.)

§ 42.1-56. Meaning of term "books." — The term *"books"* as used in this chapter may be interpreted in the discretion of the Board to mean books, magazines, newspapers, appropriate audiovisual materials and other printed matter. (Code 1950, § 42-32; 1952, c. 494; 1970, c. 606.)

§ 42.1-57. Authority of Library Board to accept and distribute federal funds. — The Library Board is empowered, subject to approval of the Governor, to accept grants of federal funds for libraries and to allocate such funds to libraries under any plan approved by the Board and the appropriate federal authorities. Such allocations shall not be subject to the restrictions of this chapter. (Code 1950, § 42-32.1; 1964, c. 325; 1970, c. 606; 1972, c. 167.)

§ 42.1-58. Agreements providing for expenditure of federal and matching funds. — The Library Board and the cities and counties of the Commonwealth are authorized to enter into agreements providing for the supervision of the expenditure of federal funds allocated to such cities and counties and matching funds provided by such political subdivisions. Such agreement shall set forth the standards and conditions with respect to the expenditure of such funds. (Code 1950, § 42-32.2; 1964, c. 324; 1970, c. 606.)

§ 42.1-59: Reserved.

CHAPTER 4.

LAW LIBRARIES.

§ 42.1-60. State Law Library managed by Supreme Court. — There shall be a State Law Library at Richmond, with a branch thereof at Staunton, maintained as at present, which shall be managed by the Supreme Court. The Court shall appoint the librarian and other employees to hold office during the pleasure of the Court; provided, however, that the clerk at Staunton shall act as law librarian there without additional compensation therefor. (Code 1950, § 42-13; 1970, c. 606; 1977, c. 397.)

§ 42.1-61. Books constituting Library. — The State Law Library shall consist of the books now in the law libraries at Richmond and Staunton, with such additions as may be made thereto. (Code 1950, § 42-14; 1970, c. 606.)

§ 42.1-62. Additions to Library. — The Supreme Court shall, from time to time, make additions to the State Law Library by purchases, and may lease or purchase computer terminals for the purpose of retrieving available legal reference data, with funds at its disposal for these purposes, and may cause books to be transferred from one law library to another. All law books acquired by the Commonwealth by gift, or by exchange, from the United States, or other states and countries, shall be placed in the Library. The Director of the Department of Purchases and Supply shall have placed in the State Law Library at Richmond, and in the branch thereof at Staunton, a copy of every law book required by §§ 17.1-319 and 30-34.5. (Code 1950, § 42-15; 1970, c. 606; 1977, c. 397.)

§ 42.1-63. Regulation of Library; computer expenses. — The Supreme Court shall have the power to make and enforce such rules and orders for the regulation of the State Law Library, and the use thereof, as may to it seem proper. Such rules and orders may provide for the assessment and collection of fees for the use of computer research services other than for valid state uses, which shall include official use by attorneys for the Commonwealth and public defenders, and their assistants. Such fees shall be assessed in the amount necessary to cover the expenses of such services and those collected and hereby appropriated to the Court to be paid as part of the cost of maintaining such computer research capabilities. (Code 1950, § 42-16; 1970, c. 606; 1977, c. 397; 1989, c. 704.)

§ 42.1-64. Who may use Library. — The Governor and other state officers at the seat of government, the Reporter of the Supreme Court, members of the General Assembly, judges of courts, and practicing attorneys in good standing, and such other persons as the Supreme Court shall designate, shall have the use of the State Law Library, under such rules and regulations as the Court shall make. (Code 1950, § 42-17; 1970, c. 606; 1977, c. 397.)

§ 42.1-65. Local law libraries in charge of circuit court clerks; computer research services; expenses. — A. If the members of the bar practicing in any county or city of the Commonwealth shall procure by voluntary contribution a law library of the value of $500, at the least, for the use of the courts held in such county or city, and of the bar practicing therein, it shall be the duty of the circuit court of such county or city to require its clerk to take charge of the library so contributed and to keep the same in the courthouse or clerk's office building according to the rules prescribed by the bar and approved by the court.

B. If the members of the bars practicing in two or more adjoining counties or cities of the Commonwealth shall jointly procure by voluntary contribution a law library of the value of $500, at the least, for the joint use of the courts held in such counties and cities, and of the bars practicing therein, it shall be the joint duty of the circuit courts of such counties and cities to require one of its clerks to take charge of the library so contributed and to keep the same in the most convenient courthouse or clerk's office building according to the rules jointly prescribed by the bars and jointly approved by the courts.

C. Such local and regional law libraries may purchase or lease computer terminals for the purpose of retrieving available legal reference data, and if so, the library rules shall provide for the assessment and collection of fees for the use of computer research services other than for official use of the courts, attorneys for the Commonwealth and public defenders, and their assistants, and counties and cities serviced by such libraries, which fees shall be sufficient to cover the expenses of such services. Such libraries, pursuant to rules of the Supreme Court and at costs to such libraries, may have access to computer research services of the State Law Library. (Code 1950, § 42-18; 1962, c. 515; 1970, c. 606; 1977, c. 397; 1989, c. 704.)

§ 42.1-66. Circuit courts to enforce rules for government of such libraries. — The observance of the rules so prescribed and approved may be enforced by a circuit court sitting within the area served by the particular local or regional library by such summary process and judgment as shall be provided by such rules. (Code 1950, § 42-19; 1962, c. 515; 1970, c. 606; 1977, c. 397.)

§§ 42.1-67 through 42.1-69: Repealed by Acts 1977, c. 397.

Cross references. — As to assessment for law library as part of costs in civil actions and contributions from bar associations, see § 42.1-70.

§ 42.1-70. Assessment for law library as part of costs in civil actions; contributions from bar associations. — Any county, city or town may, through its governing body, assess, as part of the costs incident to each civil action filed in the courts located within its boundaries, a sum not in excess of four dollars.

The imposition of such assessment shall be by ordinance of the governing body, which ordinance may provide for different sums in circuit courts and district courts, and the assessment shall be collected by the clerk of the court in which the action is filed, and remitted to the treasurer of such county, city or town and held by such treasurer subject to disbursements by the governing body for the acquisition of law books, law periodicals and computer legal research services and equipment for the establishment, use and maintenance of a law library which shall be open for the use of the public at hours convenient to the public. In addition to the acquisition of law books, law periodicals and computer legal research services and equipment, the disbursements may include compensation to be paid to librarians and other necessary staff for the maintenance of such library and acquisition of suitable quarters for such library. The compensation of such librarians and the necessary staff and the cost of suitable quarters for such library shall be fixed by the governing body and paid out of the fund created by the imposition of such assessment of cost. Such libraries, pursuant to rules of the Supreme Court and at costs to such libraries, may have access to computer research services of the State Law Library. Disbursements may be made to purchase or lease computer terminals for the purpose of retaining such research services. The assessment provided for herein shall be in addition to all other costs prescribed by law, but shall not apply to any action in which the Commonwealth or any political subdivision thereof or the federal government is a party and in which the costs are assessed against the Commonwealth, political subdivision thereof, or federal government. The governing body is authorized to accept contributions to the fund from any bar association.

Any such library established in the County of Wythe shall be located only in a town which is the seat of the county government. (Code 1950, § 42-19.4; 1964, c. 439; 1964, Ex. Sess., c. 26; 1966, c. 225; 1970, c. 606; 1972, c. 343; 1977, c. 397; 1981, c. 48; 1982, c. 607; 1983, cc. 309, 355; 1984, c. 16; 1985, c. 381; 1988, c. 571.)

§ 42.1-71. Establishment of regional law libraries by governing bodies. — Any two or more adjoining counties or cities assessing costs as provided in § 42.1-70 may jointly establish a regional law library, and each such regional library shall be open to the public. (1977, c. 145.)

CHAPTER 5.

OFFENSES.

§ 42.1-72. Injuring or destroying books and other property of libraries. — Any person who willfully, maliciously or wantonly writes upon, injures, defaces, tears, cuts, mutilates, or destroys any book or other library property belonging to or in the custody of any public, county or regional library, The Library of Virginia, other repository of public records, museums or any library or collection belonging to or in the custody of any educational, eleemosynary, benevolent, hereditary, historical library or patriotic institution, organization or society, shall be guilty of a Class 1 misdemeanor. (Code 1950, § 42-20; 1970, c. 606; 1975, c. 318; 1994, c. 64.)

Cross references. — As to punishment for Class 1 misdemeanors, see § 18.2-11.

§ 42.1-73. Concealment of book or other property while on premises of library; removal of book or other property from library. — Whoever, without authority, with the intention of converting to his own or another's use, willfully conceals a book or other library property, while still on the premises of such library, or willfully or without authority removes any book or other property from any of the above libraries or collections shall be deemed guilty of larceny thereof, and upon conviction thereof shall be punished as provided by law. Proof of the willful concealment of such book or other library property while still on the premises of such library shall be prima facie evidence of intent to commit larceny thereof. (Code 1950, § 42-21; 1970, c. 606; 1975, c. 318.)

§ 42.1-73.1. Exemption from liability for arrest of suspected person; electronic article surveillance devices. — A library or agent or employee of the library causing the arrest of any person pursuant to the provisions of § 42.1-73, shall not be held civilly liable for unlawful detention, slander, malicious prosecution, false imprisonment, false arrest, or assault and battery of the person so arrested, whether such arrest takes place on the premises of the library or after close pursuit from such premises by such agent or employee, if, in causing the arrest of such person, the library or agent or employee of the library had at the time of such arrest probable cause to believe that the person committed willful concealment of books or other library property.

The activation of an electronic article surveillance device as a result of a person exiting the premises or an area within the premises of a library where an electronic article surveillance device is located shall constitute probable cause for the detention of such person by such library or agent or employee of the library, provided that such person is detained only in a reasonable manner and only for such time as is necessary for an inquiry into the circumstances surrounding the activation of the device, and provided that clear and visible notice is posted at each exit and location within the premises where such device is located indicating the presence of an anti-theft device. For purposes of this section, *"electronic article surveillance device"* means an electronic device designed and operated for the purpose of detecting the removal from the premises or a protected area within such premises, of any specially marked or tagged book or other library property. (1975, c. 318; 1986, c. 33.)

§ 42.1-74. Failure to return book or other library property. — Any person having in his possession any book or other property of any of the above libraries or collections, which he shall fail to return within thirty days after receiving notice in writing from the custodian, shall be guilty of a misdemeanor and punished according to law; provided, however, that if such book should be lost or destroyed, such person may, within thirty days after being so notified, pay to the custodian the value of such book, the value to be determined by the governing board having jurisdiction. (Code 1950, § 42-22; 1970, c. 606.)

§ 42.1-74.1. "Book or other library property" defined. — The terms *"book or other library property"* as used in this chapter shall include any book, plate, picture, photograph, engraving, painting, drawing, map, newspaper, magazine, pamphlet, broadside, manuscript, document, letter, public record, microform, sound recording, audiovisual materials in any format, magnetic or other tapes, electronic data processing records, artifacts, or other documentary, written, or printed material, regardless of physical form or characteristics, belonging to, on loan to, or otherwise in the custody of any library, museum, repository of public or other records institution as specified in § 42.1-72. (1975, c. 318.)

CHAPTER 6.

INTERSTATE LIBRARY COMPACT.

Sec.
42.1-75. Compact entered into and enacted
            into law.

§ 42.1-75. Compact entered into and enacted into law. — The Interstate Library Compact is enacted into law and entered into by this State in the form substantially as follows:

The contracting states solemnly agree:

Article I

Policy and Purpose

Because the desire for the services provided by libraries transcends governmental boundaries and can most effectively be satisfied by giving such services to communities and people regardless of jurisdictional lines, it is the policy of the states party to this compact to cooperate and share their responsibilities; to authorize cooperation and sharing with respect to those types of library facilities and services which can be more economically or efficiently developed and maintained on a cooperative basis, and to authorize cooperation and sharing among localities, states and others in providing joint or cooperative library services in areas where the distribution of population or of existing and potential library resources make the provision of library service on an interstate basis the most effective way of providing adequate and efficient service.

Article II

Definitions

As used in this compact:

(a) *"Public library agency"* means any unit or agency of local or State government operating or having power to operate a library.

(b) *"Private library agency"* means any nongovernmental entity which operates or assumes a legal obligation to operate a library.

(c) *"Library agreement"* means a contract establishing an interstate library district pursuant to this compact or providing for the joint or cooperative furnishing of library services.

Article III

Interstate Library Districts

(a) Any one or more public library agencies in a party state in cooperation with any public library agency or agencies in one or more other party states may establish and maintain an interstate library district. Subject to the provisions of this compact and any other laws of the party states which pursuant hereto remain applicable, such district may establish, maintain and operate some or all of the library facilities and services for the area concerned in accordance with the terms of a library agreement therefor. Any private library agency or agencies within an interstate library district may cooperate therewith, assume duties, responsibilities and obligations thereto, and receive benefits therefrom as provided in any library agreement to which such agency or agencies become party.

(b) Within an interstate library district, and as provided by a library agreement, the performance of library functions may be undertaken on a joint or cooperative basis or may be undertaken by means of one or more arrangements between or among public or private library agencies for the extension of library privileges to the use of facilities or services operated or rendered by one or more of the individual library agencies.

(c) If a library agreement provides for joint establishment, maintenance or operation of library facilities or services by an interstate library district, such district shall have power to do any one or more of the following in accordance with such library agreement:

1. Undertake, administer and participate in programs or arrangements for securing, lending or servicing of books and other publications, any other materials suitable to be kept or made available by libraries, library equipment or for the dissemination of information about libraries, the value and significance of particular items therein, and the use thereof.

2. Accept for any of its purposes under this compact any and all donations, and grants of money, equipment, supplies, materials, and services, (conditional or otherwise), from any state or the United States or any subdivision or agency thereof, or interstate agency, or from any institution, person, firm or corporation, and receive, utilize and dispose of the same.

3. Operate mobile library units or equipment for the purpose of rendering bookmobile service within the district.

4. Employ professional, technical, clerical and other personnel and fix terms of employment, compensation and other appropriate benefits; and where desirable, provide for the in-service training of such personnel.

5. Sue and be sued in any court of competent jurisdiction.

6. Acquire, hold, and dispose of any real or personal property or any interest or interests therein as may be appropriate to the rendering of library service.

7. Construct, maintain and operate a library, including any appropriate branches thereof.

8. Do such other things as may be incidental to or appropriate for the carrying out of any of the foregoing powers.

Article IV

Interstate Library Districts, Governing Board

(a) An interstate library district which establishes, maintains or operates any facilities or services in its own right shall have a governing board which shall direct the affairs of the district and act for it in all matters relating to its business. Each participating public library agency in the district shall be represented on the governing board which shall be organized and conduct its business in accordance with provision therefor in the library agreement. But in no event shall a governing board meet less often than twice a year.

(b) Any private library agency or agencies party to a library agreement establishing an interstate library district may be represented on or advise with the governing board of the district in such manner as the library agreement may provide.

Article V

State Library Agency Cooperation

Any two or more state library agencies of two or more of the party states may undertake and conduct joint or cooperative library programs, render joint or cooperative library services, and enter into and perform arrangements for the cooperative or joint acquisition, use, housing and disposition of items or collections of materials which, by reason of expense, rarity, specialized nature, or infrequency of demand therefor would be appropriate for central collection and shared use. Any such programs, services or arrangements may include provision for the exercise on a cooperative or joint basis of any power exercisable by an interstate library district and an agreement embodying any such program, service or arrangement shall contain provisions covering the subjects detailed in Article VI of this compact for interstate library agreements.

Article VI

Library Agreements

(a) In order to provide for any joint or cooperative undertaking pursuant to this compact, public and private library agencies may enter into library agreements. Any agreement executed pursuant to the provisions of this compact shall, as among the parties to the agreement:

1. Detail the specific nature of the services, programs, facilities, arrangements or properties to which it is applicable.

2. Provide for the allocation of costs and other financial responsibilities.

3. Specify the respective rights, duties, obligations and liabilities of the parties.

4. Set forth the terms and conditions for duration, renewal, termination, abrogation, disposal of joint or common property, if any, and all other matters which may be appropriate to the proper effectuation and performance of the agreement.

(b) No public or private library agency shall undertake to exercise itself, or jointly with any other library agency, by means of a library agreement any power prohibited to such agency by the constitution or statutes of its state.

(c) No library agreement shall become effective until filed with the compact administrator of each state involved, and approved in accordance with Article VII of this compact.

Article VII

Approval of Library Agreements

(a) Every library agreement made pursuant to this compact shall, prior to and as a condition precedent to its entry into force, be submitted to the attorney general of each state in which a public library agency party thereto is situated, who shall determine whether the agreement is in proper form and compatible with the laws of his state. The attorneys general shall approve any agreement submitted to them unless they shall find that it does not meet the conditions set forth herein and shall detail in writing addressed to the governing bodies of the public library agencies concerned the specific respects in which the proposed agreement fails to meet the requirements of law. Failure to disapprove an agreement submitted hereunder within ninety days of its submission shall constitute approval thereof.

(b) In the event that a library agreement made pursuant to this compact shall deal in whole or in part with the provision of services or facilities with regard to which an officer or agency of the state government has constitutional or statutory powers of control, the agreement shall, as a condition precedent to its entry into force, be submitted to the state officer or agency having such power of control, and shall be approved or disapproved by him or it as to all matters within his or its jurisdiction in the same manner and subject to the same requirements governing the action of the attorneys general pursuant to paragraph (a) of this article. This requirement of submission and approval shall be in addition to and not in substitution for the requirement of submission to and approval by the attorneys general.

Article VIII

Other Laws Applicable

Nothing in this compact or in any library agreement shall be construed to supersede, alter or otherwise impair any obligation imposed on any library by otherwise applicable law, nor to authorize the transfer or disposition of any property held in trust by a library agency in a manner contrary to the terms of such trust.

Article IX

Appropriations and Aid

(a) Any public library agency party to a library agreement may appropriate funds to the interstate library district established thereby in the same manner and to the same extent as to a library wholly maintained by it and, subject to the laws of the state in which such public library agency is situated, may pledge its credit in support of an interstate library district established by the agreement.

(b) Subject to the provisions of the library agreement pursuant to which it functions and the laws of the states in which such district is situated, an interstate library district may claim and receive any state and federal aid which may be available to library agencies.

Article X

Compact Administrator

Each state shall designate a compact administrator with whom copies of all library agreements to which his state or any public library agency thereof is party shall be filed. The administrator shall have such other powers as may be conferred upon him by the laws of his state and may consult and cooperate with the compact administrators of other party states and take such steps as may effectuate the purposes of this compact. If the laws of a party state so provide, such state may designate one or more deputy compact administrators in addition to its compact administrator.

Article XI

Entry Into Force and Withdrawal

(a) This compact shall enter into force and effect immediately upon its enactment into law by any two states. Thereafter, it shall enter into force and effect as to any other state upon the enactment thereof by such state.

(b) This compact shall continue in force with respect to a party state and remain binding upon such state until six months after such state has given notice to each other party state of the repeal thereof. Such withdrawal shall not be construed to relieve any party to a library agreement entered into pursuant to this compact from any obligation of that agreement prior to the end of its duration as provided therein.

Article XII

Construction and Severability

This compact shall be liberally construed so as to effectuate the purposes thereof. The provisions of this compact shall be severable and if any phrase, clause, sentence or provision of this compact is declared to be contrary to the constitution of any party state or of the United States or the applicability thereof to any government, agency, person or circumstance is held invalid, the validity of the remainder of this compact and the applicability thereof to any government, agency, person or circumstance shall not be affected thereby. If this compact shall be held contrary to the constitution of any state party thereto, the compact shall remain in full force and effect as to the remaining states and in full force and effect as to the state affected as to all severable matters. (1970, c. 267.)

The number of this section was assigned by the Virginia Code Commission, the 1970 act having assigned no number.

CHAPTER 7.

VIRGINIA PUBLIC RECORDS ACT.

§ 42.1-76. Legislative intent; title of chapter. — The General Assembly intends by this chapter to establish a single body of law applicable to all public officers and employees on the subject of public records management and preservation and to ensure that the procedures used to manage and preserve public records will be uniform throughout the Commonwealth.

This chapter may be cited as the Virginia Public Records Act. (1976, c. 746.)

Law Review. — For survey of Virginia law on evidence for the year 1978-1979, see 66 Va. J. Rev. 293 (1980).

§ 42.1-77. Definitions. — As used in this chapter:

"Agency" means all boards, commissions, departments, divisions, institutions, authorities, or parts thereof, of the Commonwealth or its political subdivisions and includes the offices of constitutional officers.

"Archival quality" means a quality of reproduction consistent with established standards specified by state and national agencies and organizations responsible for establishing such standards, such as the Association for Information and Image Management, the American Standards Association, and the National Bureau of Standards.

"Board" means the State Library Board.

"Council" means the State Public Records Advisory Council.

"Custodian" means the public official in charge of an office having public records.

"Data" means symbols, or representations, of facts or ideas that can be communicated, interpreted, or processed by manual or automated means.

"Database" means a set of data, consisting of one file or a group of integrated files, maintained as an information system managed by a database management system.

"Database management system" means a set of software programs that controls the organization, storage and retrieval of data in a database. It also controls the security and integrity of the database.

"Electronic record" means any information that is recorded in machine readable form.

"Electronic records system" means any information system that produces, processes, or stores records by using a computer, and is also called an automated information system.

"Information system" means the organized collection, processing, transmission, and dissemination of information in accordance with defined procedures, whether automated or manual.

"Librarian of Virginia" means the State Librarian of Virginia or his designated representative.

"Public official" means all persons holding any office created by the Constitution of Virginia or by any act of the General Assembly, the Governor and all other officers of the executive branch of the state government, and all other officers, heads, presidents or chairmen of boards, commissions, departments, and agencies of the state government or its political subdivisions.

"Public record" means recorded information that documents a transaction or activity by or with any public officer, agency or employee of the state government or its political subdivisions. Regardless of physical form or characteristic, the recorded information is a public record if it is produced, collected, received or retained in pursuance of law or in connection with the transaction of public business.

The medium on which such information is recorded may be, but is not limited to paper, film, magnetic, optical or solid state devices which can store electronic signals, tapes, mylar, linen, silk or vellum. The general types of records may be, but are not limited to books, papers, letters, documents, printouts, photographs, films, tapes, microfiche, microfilm, photostats, sound recordings, maps, drawings, and any representations held in computer memory.

Nonrecord materials, meaning reference books and exhibit materials made or acquired and preserved solely for reference use or exhibition purposes, extra copies of documents preserved only for convenience or reference, and stocks of publications, shall not be included within the definition of public records as used in this chapter.

"Archival records" means all noncurrent records of continuing and enduring value useful to the citizens of the Commonwealth and necessary to the administrative functions of public agencies in the conduct of services and activities mandated by law. In appraisal of public records deemed archival, the terms "administrative," "legal," "fiscal," and "historical" shall be defined as:

1. *"Administrative value"*: Records shall be deemed of administrative value if they have continuing utility in the operation of an agency.

2. *"Legal value"*: Records shall be deemed of legal value when they document actions taken in the protection and proving of legal or civil rights and obligations of individuals and agencies.

3. *"Fiscal value"*: Records shall be deemed of fiscal value so long as they are needed to document and verify financial authorizations, obligations and transactions.

4. *"Historical value"*: Records shall be deemed of historical value when they contain unique information, regardless of age, which provides understanding of some aspect of the government and promotes the development of an informed and enlightened citizenry.

"Medical records" means the documentation of health care services, whether physical or mental, rendered by direct or indirect patient-provider interaction which is used as a mechanism for tracking the patient's health care status. Medical records may be technologically stored by computerized or other electronic process, or through microfilm or other similar photographic form or chemical process. Notwithstanding the authority provided by this definition to store medical records on microfilm or other similar photographic form or chemical process, prescription dispensing records maintained in or on behalf of any pharmacy registered or permitted in Virginia shall only be stored in compliance with §§ 54.1-3410, 54.1-3411 and 54.1-3412.

"Official records" means public records.

"Persons under a disability" means persons so defined under subsection A of § 8.01-229.

"Preservation" means maintaining archival records in their original physical form by stabilizing them chemically or strengthening them physically to ensure their survival as long as possible in their original form. It also means the reformatting of written, printed, electronic or visual archival information to extend the life of the information.

"Retention and disposition schedule" means an approved timetable stating the retention time period and disposition action of records series.

"Software programs" means the written specifications used to operate an electronic records system as well as the documentation describing implemen-

tation strategies. (1976, c. 746; 1977, c. 501; 1981, c. 637; 1987, c. 217; 1990, c. 778; 1994, cc. 390, 955; 1998, cc. 427, 470.)

The 1998 amendments. — The 1998 amendment by c. 427, in the paragraph defining "State Librarian," deleted "State" preceding "Librarian" and inserted "of Virginia" in two places.

The 1998 amendment by c. 470, effective April 14, 1998, in the paragraph defining "Medical records" added the last sentence.

The trial court correctly concluded that each praecipe was a forged public record, purportedly documenting the Commonwealth's motion to nolle prosequi a pending criminal prosecution, clearly the pursuit of "public business" by a "public officer;" thus defendant's actions involving the praecipes supported his convictions. Chellman v. Commonwealth, No. 1630-95-4 (Ct. of Appeals Mar. 25, 1997).

§ 42.1-78. Confidentiality safeguarded. — Any records made confidential by law shall be so treated. Records which by law are required to be closed to the public shall not be deemed to be made open to the public under the provisions of this chapter. Records in the custody of The Library of Virginia which are required to be closed to the public shall be open for public access 100 years after the date of creation of the record. No provision of this chapter shall be construed to authorize or require the opening of any records ordered to be sealed by a court. All records deposited in the archives that are not made confidential by law shall be open to public access. (1976, c. 746; 1979, c. 110; 1990, c. 778; 1994, c. 64.)

§ 42.1-79. Records management function vested in Board; State Library Board to be official custodian; State Archivist. — The archival and records management function shall be vested in the State Library Board. The State Library Board shall be the official custodian and trustee for the Commonwealth of all public records of whatever kind which are transferred to it from any public office of the Commonwealth or any political subdivision thereof. As the Commonwealth's official repository of public records, The Library of Virginia shall assume administrative control of such records on behalf of the Commonwealth.

The Librarian of Virginia shall name a State Archivist who shall perform such functions as the Librarian of Virginia assigns. (1976, c. 746; 1986, c. 565; 1990, c. 778; 1994, c. 64; 1998, c. 427.)

The 1998 amendment, in the second paragraph, deleted "State" preceding "Librarian" and inserted "of Virginia" in two places.

§ 42.1-79.1. Retention and disposition of medical records. — The medical records of all persons not under a disability shall be retained by all public agencies acting as custodians of medical records for ten years following the last date of treatment or contact. Such agencies shall retain the medical records of minors and persons under a disability for a minimum of five years following the age of majority or the removal of the disability, or ten years following the last date of treatment or contact, whichever comes later. Such agencies shall retain the medical records of deceased persons for a minimum of five years following the date of death.

Agencies of the Commonwealth which generate medical records shall notify patients at time of discharge the specific retention period that applies to their records. Such agencies shall be encouraged to destroy such medical records upon expiration of the required retention period. Such agencies may, at their discretion, retain summaries of destroyed medical records.

Medical records submitted to The Library of Virginia for retention and disposition in accordance with the terms of this section are presumed to be inactive. It shall be the duty of the originating agency to (i) designate medical records of minors, persons under a disability, or deceased persons prior to submission to The Library of Virginia for retention and disposition, and (ii) to make a verifiable attempt to notify patients that their records will be destroyed after the appropriate retention period. Unless notified otherwise by the originating agency, the Librarian of Virginia shall begin to count the required retention period from the first date of submission. Prior to destroying any medical records, the Librarian of Virginia or his designee shall notify the originating agency that the retention period has run out and that, unless the agency reclaims the medical records, the records will be destroyed.

No employee of The Library of Virginia or any agency acting in accordance with the terms of this section shall be liable, civilly or criminally, for the destruction of medical records.

The provisions of this section shall not supersede the provisions of § 16.1-306 or any other laws of this Commonwealth pertaining to the retention and disposition of records generated by agencies other than those agencies originating medical records. (1987, c. 217; 1994, cc. 64, 955; 1998, c. 427.)

The **1998 amendment,** in the third paragraph, deleted "State" preceding "Librarian" and inserted "of Virginia" in two places.

§ 42.1-80. State Public Records Advisory Council continued; members; chairman and vice-chairman; compensation. — The State Public Records Advisory Council is continued. The Council shall consist of twelve members. The Council membership shall include the Secretary of the Commonwealth, the Librarian of Virginia, the Attorney General, the State Health Commissioner, the Commonwealth Transportation Commissioner, the Director of the Department of Information Technology, the Auditor of Public Accounts, the Executive Secretary of the Supreme Court, the Director of the Department of Technology Planning, or their designated representatives and three members to be appointed by the Governor from the Commonwealth at large. The gubernatorial appointments shall include two clerks of courts of record and a member of a local governing body. Those members appointed by the Governor shall remain members of the Council for a term coincident with that of the Governor making the appointment, or until their successors are appointed and qualified. The Council shall elect annually from its membership a chairman and vice-chairman. Members of the Council shall receive no compensation for their services but shall be paid their reasonable and necessary expenses incurred in the performance of their duties. (1976, c. 746; 1977, c. 501; 1984, c. 720; 1985, c. 448; 1990, c. 778; 1994, c. 955; 1998, c. 427; 1999, cc. 412, 421, 433.)

The **1998 amendment,** in the third sentence, deleted "State" preceding "Librarian" and inserted "of Virginia."

The **1999 amendments.** — The 1999 amendments by cc. 412, 421 and 433 are iden-

tical, and substituted "Department of Technology Planning" for "Council on Information Management" preceding "or their designated" in the second sentence.

§ 42.1-81. Powers and responsibilities of Council. — The Council shall propose to the State Library Board rules, regulations, and standards, not inconsistent with law, for the purpose of establishing uniform guidelines for the management and preservation of public records throughout the Commonwealth. The Council shall have the power to appoint such subcommittees and advisory bodies as it deems advisable. The Council shall be assisted in the execution of its responsibilities by the Librarian of Virginia. (1976, c. 746; 1990, c. 778; 1998, c. 427.)

The 1998 amendment, in the last sentence, deleted "State" preceding "Librarian" and inserted "of Virginia."

§ 42.1-82. Duties and powers of Library Board. — The State Library Board shall with the advice of the Council:

1. Issue regulations to facilitate the creation, preservation, storage, filing, reformatting, management, and destruction of public records by all agencies. Such regulations shall establish procedures for records management containing recommendations for the retention, disposal or other disposition of public records; procedures for the physical destruction or other disposition of public records proposed for disposal; and standards for the reproduction of records by photocopy or microphotography processes with the view to the disposal of the original records. Such standards shall relate to the quality of film used, preparation of the records for filming, proper identification of the records so that any individual document or series of documents can be located on the film with reasonable facility, and that the copies contain all significant record detail, to the end that the photographic or microphotographic copies shall be of archival quality.

2. Issue regulations specifying permissible qualities of paper, ink, and other materials to be used by agencies for public record purposes. The Board shall determine the specifications for and shall select and make available to all agencies lists of approved papers, photographic materials, ink, or other writing materials for archival public records, and only those approved may be purchased for use in the making of such records. These regulations and specifications shall also apply to clerks of courts of record.

3. Provide assistance to agencies in determining what records no longer have administrative, legal, fiscal, or historical value and should be destroyed or disposed of in another manner. Each public official having in his custody official records shall assist the Board in the preparation of an inventory of all public records in his custody and in preparing a suggested schedule for retention and disposition of such records. No land or personal property book shall be destroyed without being first offered to The Library of Virginia for preservation.

All records created prior to the Constitution of 1902 that are declared archival may be transferred to the archives. (1976, c. 746; 1977, c. 501; 1981, c. 637; 1990, c. 778; 1994, cc. 64, 955.)

§ 42.1-83. Program for inventorying, scheduling, microfilming records; records of counties, cities and towns; storage of records. — The State Library Board shall formulate and execute a program to inventory, schedule, and microfilm official records of counties, cities and towns which it determines have permanent value and to provide safe storage for microfilm copies of such records, and to give advice and assistance to local officials in their programs for creating, preserving, filing and making available public records in their custody.

Original archival public records shall be either stored in The Library of Virginia or in the locality at the decision of the local officials responsible for maintaining public records. Original archival public records shall be returned to the locality upon the written request of the local officials responsible for maintaining local public records. Microfilm shall be stored in The Library of Virginia but the use thereof shall be subject to the control of the local officials responsible for maintaining local public records. (1972, c. 555; 1976, c. 746; 1994, cc. 64, 955.)

§ 42.1-84. Same; records of agencies and subdivisions not covered under § 42.1-83. — The State Library Board may formulate and execute a program of inventorying, repairing, and microfilming for security purposes the public records of the agencies and subdivisions not covered under the program established under § 42.1-83 which it determines have permanent value, and of providing safe storage of microfilm copies of such records. (1976, c. 746.)

§ 42.1-85. Duties of Librarian of Virginia; agencies to cooperate; agencies to designate records officer. — The Librarian of Virginia shall administer a records management program for the application of efficient and economical management methods to the creation, utilization, maintenance, retention, preservation, and disposal of public records consistent with rules, regulations, or standards promulgated by the State Library Board, including operations of a records center or centers. It shall be the duty of the Librarian of Virginia to establish procedures and techniques for the effective management of public records, to make continuing surveys of paper work operations, and to recommend improvements in current records management practices, including the use of space, equipment, and supplies employed in creating, maintaining, and servicing records.

It shall be the duty of any agency with public records to cooperate with the Librarian of Virginia in conducting surveys and to establish and maintain an active, continuing program for the economical and efficient management of the records of such agency.

Each state agency and political subdivision of this Commonwealth shall designate as many as appropriate, but at least one, records officer to serve as a liaison to The Library of Virginia for the purposes of implementing and overseeing a records management program, and coordinating legal disposition, including destruction of obsolete records. Designation of state agency records officers shall be by the respective agency head. Designation of a records officer for political subdivisions shall be by the governing body or chief administrative official of the political subdivision. (1976, c. 746; 1990, c. 778; 1994, c. 64; 1998, c. 427.)

The **1998 amendment** deleted "State" preceding "Librarian" and inserted "of Virginia" throughout this section.

§ 42.1-86. Program to select and preserve important records; availability to public; security copies. — In cooperation with the head of each agency, the Librarian of Virginia shall establish and maintain a program for the selection and preservation of public records considered essential to the operation of government and for the protection of the rights and interests of persons. He shall provide for preserving, classifying, arranging, and indexing so that such records are made available to the public and shall make security copies or designate as security copies existing copies of such essential public records. Security copies shall be of archival quality and shall be made by photographic, photostatic, microfilm, microcard, miniature photographic, or other process which accurately reproduces and forms a durable medium. Security copies shall have the same force and effect for all purposes as the original record and shall be as admissible in evidence as the original record whether the original record is in existence or not. Security copies shall be preserved in the place and manner prescribed by the State Library Board and the Governor. Public records deemed unnecessary for the transaction of the business of any agency, yet deemed to be of administrative, legal, fiscal, or historical value, may be transferred with the consent of the Librarian of

Virginia to the custody of The Library of Virginia. (1976, c. 746; 1980, c. 365; 1990, c. 778; 1994, c. 64; 1998, c. 427.)

The 1998 amendment, in the first and last sentences, deleted "State" preceding "Librarian" and inserted "of Virginia."

§ 42.1-86.1. Disposition of public records. — No agency shall destroy or discard public records without a retention and disposition schedule approved by the Librarian of Virginia as provided in § 42.1-82. No agency shall sell or give away public records. (1990, c. 778; 1998, c. 427.)

The 1998 amendment, in the first sentence, deleted "State" preceding "Librarian" and inserted "of Virginia."

§ 42.1-87. Where records kept; duties of agencies; repair, etc., of record books; agency heads not divested of certain authority. — Custodians of archival public records shall keep them in fire-resistant, environmentally controlled, physically secure rooms designed to ensure proper preservation and in such arrangement as to be easily accessible. Current public records should be kept in the buildings in which they are ordinarily used. It shall be the duty of each agency to cooperate with The Library of Virginia in complying with rules and regulations promulgated by the Board. Each agency shall establish and maintain an active and continuing program for the economic and efficient management of records.

Each agency shall develop and implement a program for the management of records created, received, maintained, used, or stored on electronic media. Each agency shall schedule the retention and disposition of all electronic records, as well as related access documentation and indexes and shall ensure the implementation of their provisions in accordance with procedures established under § 42.1-82. Procedures governing access to electronic records shall be in accordance with the Virginia Freedom of Information Act, the Virginia Privacy Protection Act, the Intellectual Property Act and any other provision of law as may be applicable and shall be enumerated in the retention and disposition schedule.

Record books should be copied or repaired, renovated or rebound if worn, mutilated, damaged or difficult to read. Whenever the public records of any public official are in need of repair, restoration or rebinding, a judge of the court of record or the head of such agency or political subdivision of the Commonwealth may authorize that the records in need of repair be removed from the building or office in which such records are ordinarily kept, for the length of time necessary to repair, restore or rebind them, provided such restoration and rebinding preserves the records without loss or damage to them. Before any restoration or repair work is initiated, a treatment proposal from the contractor shall be submitted and reviewed in consultation with The Library of Virginia. Any public official who causes a record book to be copied shall attest it and shall certify an oath that it is an accurate copy of the original book. The copy shall then have the force of the original.

Nothing in this chapter shall be construed to divest agency heads of the authority to determine the nature and form of the records required in the administration of their several departments or to compel the removal of records deemed necessary by them in the performance of their statutory duty. Whenever legislation affecting public records management and preservation is under consideration, The Library of Virginia shall review the proposal and advise the General Assembly on the effects of its proposed implementation. (1976, c. 746; 1994, cc. 64, 955.)

§ 42.1-88. Custodians to deliver all records at expiration of term; penalty for noncompliance. — Any custodian of any public records shall, at the expiration of his term of office, appointment or employment, deliver to his successor, or, if there be none, to The Library of Virginia, all books, writings, letters, documents, public records, or other information, recorded on any medium kept or received by him in the transaction of his official business; and any such person who shall refuse or neglect for a period of ten days after a request is made in writing by the successor or Librarian of Virginia to deliver the public records as herein required shall be guilty of a Class 3 misdemeanor. (1976, c. 746; 1994, c. 64; 1998, c. 427.)

Cross references. — As to punishment for Class 3 misdemeanors, see § 18.2-11.

The 1998 amendment, near the end of the paragraph, deleted "State" preceding "Librarian" and inserted "of Virginia."

§ 42.1-89. Petition and court order for return of public records not in authorized possession. — The Librarian of Virginia or his designated representative such as the State Archivist or any public official who is the custodian of public records in the possession of a person or agency not authorized by the custodian or by law to possess such public records shall petition the circuit court in the city or county in which the person holding such records resides or in which the materials in issue, or any part thereof, are located for the return of such records. The court shall order such public records be delivered to the petitioner upon finding that the materials in issue are public records and that such public records are in the possession of a person not authorized by the custodian of the public records or by law to possess such public records. If the order of delivery does not receive compliance, the plaintiff shall request that the court enforce such order through its contempt power and procedures. (1975, c. 180; 1976, c. 746; 1998, c. 427.)

The 1998 amendment, in the first sentence, deleted "State" preceding "Librarian" and inserted "of Virginia."

§ 42.1-90. Seizure of public records not in authorized possession. — A. At any time after the filing of the petition set out in § 42.1-89 or contemporaneous with such filing, the person seeking the return of the public records may by ex parte petition request the judge or the court in which the action was filed to issue an order directed at the sheriff or other proper officer, as the case may be, commanding him to seize the materials which are the subject of the action and deliver the same to the court under the circumstances hereinafter set forth.

B. The judge aforesaid shall issue an order of seizure upon receipt of an affidavit from the petitioner which alleges that the material at issue may be sold, secreted, removed out of this Commonwealth or otherwise disposed of so as not to be forthcoming to answer the final judgment of the court respecting the same; or that such property may be destroyed or materially damaged or injured if permitted to remain out of the petitioner's possession.

C. The aforementioned order of seizure shall issue without notice to the respondent and without the posting of any bond or other security by the petitioner. (1975, c. 180; 1976, c. 746.)

§ 42.1-91. Development of disaster plan. — The Library of Virginia shall develop a plan to ensure preservation of public records in the event of disaster or emergency as defined in § 44-146.16. This plan shall be coordinated with the Department of Emergency Services and copies shall be distributed to all agency heads. The personnel of the Library shall be responsible for coordinating emergency recovery operations when public records are affected. Each agency shall ensure that a plan for the protection and recovery of public records is included in its comprehensive disaster plan. (1981, c. 637; 1994, cc. 64, 955.)

Title 43.

Mechanics' and Certain Other Liens.

CHAPTER 1.

Mechanics' and Materialmen's Liens.

§ 43-1. Definitions. — As used in this chapter, the term *"general contractor"* includes contractors, laborers, mechanics, and persons furnishing materials, who contract directly with the owner, and the term *"subcontractor"* includes all such contractors, laborers, mechanics, and persons furnishing materials, who do not contract with the owner but with the general contractor. As used in this chapter, the term *"owner"* shall not be construed to mean any person holding bare legal title under an instrument to secure a debt or indemnify a surety. As used in this chapter, the term *"mechanics' lien agent"* means a person (i) designated in writing by the owner of real estate or a person authorized to act on behalf of the owner of such real estate and (ii) who consents in writing to act, as the owner's designee for purposes of receiving notice pursuant to § 43-4.01. Such person shall be an attorney at law licensed to practice in the Commonwealth, a title insurance company authorized to write title insurance in the Commonwealth or one of its subsidiaries or licensed title insurance agents, or a financial institution authorized to accept deposits and to hold itself out to the public as engaged in the banking or savings institution business in the Commonwealth or a service corporation, subsidiary or affiliate of such financial institution. Any such person may perform mechanics' lien agent services as any legal entity. Provided that nothing herein shall be construed to affect pending litigation. (Code 1919, § 6426; 1922, p. 867; 1932, p. 332; 1977, c. 294; 1992, cc. 779, 787; 1994, c. 382.)

Cross references. — As to meaning of the word "judgment" when used in this title, see § 8.01-426.

Law Review. — For survey of Virginia commercial law for the year 1970-1971, see 57 Va. L. Rev. 1527 (1971). For survey of Virginia law on business associations for the year 1970-1971, see 57 Va. L. Rev. 1541 (1971). For survey of Virginia commercial law for the year 1972-1973, see 59 Va. L. Rev. 1426 (1973). For survey of Virginia commercial law for the year 1975-1976, see 62 Va. L. Rev. 1375 (1976). For note, "Constitutionality of Mechanics' Liens Statutes," see 34 Wash. & Lee L. Rev. 1067 (1977). For survey on creditors' rights in Virginia for 1989, see 23 U. Rich. L. Rev. 561 (1989). For article, "Perfection and Enforcement of A Mechanic's Lien in Virginia: A Defense Lawyer's Perspective," see 25 U. Rich. L. Rev. 291 (1991).

"General contractor" broadly defined. — For purposes of the mechanic's lien provisions of this title, the term "general contractor" is definitionally broader than its colloquial counterpart. West Alexandria Properties, Inc. v. First Va. Mtg. & Real Estate Inv. Trust, 221 Va.

134, 267 S.E.2d 149 (1980).

There may be more than one general contractor. — Where several contractors contracted directly with the owner, under the statutory definition they were all general contractors. Northern Va. Sav. & Loan Ass'n v. J.B. Kendall Co., 205 Va. 136, 135 S.E.2d 178 (1964).

A person making improvements to land is deemed a general contractor if that person is in contractual privity with the owner. West Alexandria Properties, Inc. v. First Va. Mtg. & Real Estate Inv. Trust, 221 Va. 134, 267 S.E.2d 149 (1980).

Joint venturer could not enforce a mechanic's lien for value of work done on co-joint venturer's portion of land, which had been dedicated to the public, where the remaining land of the co-joint venturer had been transferred to a third party in fee simple and who was never in contractual privity with the joint venturer seeking to enforce the lien. West Alexandria Properties, Inc. v. First Va. Mtg. & Real Estate Inv. Trust, 221 Va. 134, 267 S.E.2d 149 (1980).

§ 43-2. Structures, materials, etc., deemed permanently annexed to freehold.

— For the purpose of this chapter, a well, excavation, sidewalk, driveway, pavement, parking lot, retaining wall, curb and/or gutter, breakwater (either salt or fresh water), underground or field-constructed above-ground storage tank and connected dispensing equipment, water system, drainage structure, filtering system (including septic or waste disposal systems) or swimming pool shall be deemed a structure permanently annexed to the freehold, and all shrubbery, earth, sod, sand, gravel, brick, stone, tile, pipe or other materials, together with the reasonable rental or use value of equipment and any surveying, grading, clearing or earth moving required for the improvement of the grounds upon which such building or structure is situated shall be deemed to be materials furnished for the improvement of such building or structure and permanently annexed to the freehold. (Code 1919,

§ 6426; 1922, p. 867; 1932, p. 332; 1962, c. 152; 1968, c. 568; 1976, c. 213; 1996, c. 513.)

Only those items specifically enumerated in this section are deemed a structure permanently annexed to the freehold and, therefore, subject to lien rights. Because subdivision streets are not enumerated in this section such streets are not permanently annexed to the freehold. Likewise, the roads upon which plaintiff performed its work in the instant case cannot be deemed permanently an- nexed to the freehold under this section because roads are not specifically enumerated in this statute. Dominion Trust Co. v. Kenbridge Constr. Co., 248 Va. 393, 448 S.E.2d 659 (1994).

No contractor's lien on land not worked. — The liberalizing provisions of this section have never extended a contractor's lien rights to land upon which he did no work. Rosser v. Cole, 237 Va. 572, 379 S.E.2d 323 (1989).

§ 43-3. Lien for work done and materials furnished; waiver of right to file or enforce lien. — A. All persons performing labor or furnishing materials of the value of fifty dollars or more, for the construction, removal, repair or improvement of any building or structure permanently annexed to the freehold, and all persons performing any labor or furnishing materials of like value for the construction of any railroad, shall have a lien, if perfected as hereinafter provided, upon such building or structure, and so much land therewith as shall be necessary for the convenient use and enjoyment thereof, and upon such railroad and franchises for the work done and materials furnished. But when the claim is for repairs or improvements to existing structures only, no lien shall attach to the property repaired or improved unless such repairs or improvements were ordered or authorized by the owner, or his agent.

If the building or structure being constructed, removed or repaired is part of a condominium as defined in § 55-79.41 or under the Horizontal Property Act (§§ 55-79.1 through 55-79.38), any person providing labor or furnishing material to one or more units or limited common elements within the condominium pursuant to a single contract may perfect a single lien encumbering the one or more units which are the subject of the contract or to which those limited common elements pertain, and for which payment has not been made. All persons providing labor or furnishing materials for the common elements pertaining to all the units may perfect a single lien encumbering all such condominium units. Whenever a lien has been or may be perfected encumbering two or more units, the proportionate amount of the indebtedness attributable to each unit shall be the ratio that the percentage liability for common expenses appertaining to that unit computed pursuant to § 55-79.83 D bears to the total percentage liabilities for all units which are encumbered by the lien. The lien claimant shall release from a perfected lien an encumbered unit upon request of the unit owner as provided in § 55-79.46 B upon receipt of payment equal to that portion of the indebtedness evidenced by the lien attributable to such unit determined as herein provided. In the event the lien is not perfected, the lien claimant shall upon request of any interested party execute lien releases for one or more units upon receipt of payment equal to that portion of the indebtedness attributable to such unit or units determined as herein provided but no such release shall preclude the lien claimant from perfecting a single lien against the unreleased unit or units for the remaining portion of the indebtedness.

B. Any person providing labor or materials for site development improvements or for streets, stormwater facilities, sanitary sewers or water lines for the purpose of providing access or service to the individual lots in a development or condominium units as defined in § 55-79.41 or under the Horizontal Property Act (§§ 55-79.1 through 55-79.38) shall have a lien on each individual lot in the development for that fractional part of the total cost of such labor or materials as is obtained by using "one" as the numerator and the number of lots as the denominator and in the case of a condominium on each individual unit in an amount computed by reference to the liability of that unit for common expenses appertaining to that condominium pursuant to § 55-79.83 D; provided, however, no such lien shall be valid as to any lot or condominium unit unless the person providing such labor or materials shall, prior to the sale of such lot or condominium unit, file with the clerk of the circuit court of the jurisdiction in which such land lies a document setting forth a full disclosure of the nature of the lien to be claimed, the amount claimed against each lot or condominium unit and a description of the development or condominium, and shall, thereafter, comply with all other applicable provisions of this chapter. *"Site development improvements"* means improvements which are provided for the development, such as project site grading, rather than for an individual lot.

Nothing contained herein shall be construed to prevent the filing of a mechanic's lien under the provisions of subsection A hereof.

C. Any right to file or enforce any mechanic's lien granted hereunder may be waived in whole or in part at any time by any person entitled to such lien. (Code 1919, § 6426; 1922, p. 867; 1932, p. 332; 1968, c. 568; 1979, cc. 360, 542; 1980, c. 449; 1992, cc. 72, 779, 787.)

Cross references. — As to priorities between mechanics' liens and liens of employees, suppliers, etc., see note to § 43-24. As to liens on franchises and property of transportation, mining and manufacturing companies, see §§ 43-24 through 43-26.

Law Review. — For comment on mechanics' liens in Virginia, see 17 Wash. & Lee L. Rev. 307 (1960). For survey of Virginia commercial law for the year 1974-1975, see 61 Va. L. Rev. 1668 (1975). For survey of Virginia commercial law for the year 1975-1976, see 62 Va. L. Rev. 1375 (1976). For comment discussing the application of the blanket lien with respect to multi-unit development in Virginia, see 13 U. Rich. L. Rev. 637 (1979). For comment, "United States v. Kimbell Foods, Inc.: A Problem or Solution in Resolving Lien Priority Disputes?," see 36 Wash. & Lee L. Rev. 1203 (1979). For survey of Virginia commercial law for the year 1978-1979, see 66 Va. L. Rev. 217 (1980). For article on title examination in Virginia, see 17 U. Rich. L. Rev. 229 (1983). As to waiver of liens, see 22 U. Rich. L. Rev. 517 (1988). For survey on construction law in Virginia for 1989, see 23 U. Rich. L. Rev. 541 (1989). For article, "Perfection and Enforcement of A Mechanic's Lien in Virginia: A Defense Lawyer's Perspective," see 25 U. Rich. L. Rev. 291 (1991).

I. GENERAL CONSIDERATION.

This chapter is not contrary to the Fourteenth Amendment to the United States Constitution. Virginia Dev. Co. v. Crozer Iron Co., 90 Va. 126, 17 S.E. 806 (1893), aff'd on rehearing, 19 S.E. 782 (1894); Millhiser Mfg. Co. v. Gallego Mills Co., 101 Va. 579, 44 S.E. 760 (1903).

This section does not violate the due process clause of the Fourteenth Amendment. In re Thomas A. Cary, Inc., 412 F. Supp. 667 (E.D. Va. 1976), aff'd sub nom. National Permanent Fed. Sav. & Loan Ass'n v. Virginia Concrete Co., 562 F.2d 47 (4th Cir.), aff'd, 562 F.2d 48 (4th Cir. 1977).

This and the sections following relate to the executorial enforcement of liens for work done and materials furnished in the construction, repair, or improvement of any building or structure permanently annexed to the freehold, whether performed by general contractors or subcontractors. Boston Blower Co. v. Carman Lumber Co., 94 Va. 94, 26 S.E. 390 (1896).

A lien created by this section is one in derogation of the common law. American Std. Homes Corp. v. Reinecke, 245 Va. 113, 425 S.E.2d 515 (1993).

The mechanics' lien is a creature of statute, with foundation in a contract, with which it must correspond. Sergeant v. Denby, 87 Va. 206, 12 S.E. 402 (1890). See N.J. Steigleder & Son v. Allen, 113 Va. 686, 75 S.E. 191 (1912); Wallace v. Brumback, 177 Va. 36, 12 S.E.2d 801 (1941).

The very existence of a mechanics' lien on land, as well as the jurisdiction of the court to enforce it, depends upon statute and not upon equitable or ethical rules, so that neither the conscience of the chancellor nor the length of his foot can supplement the statute and vest the court with any jurisdiction except that which is based upon the provisions of this chapter fairly construed. Feuchtenberger v. Williamson, Carroll & Saunders, 137 Va. 578, 120 S.E. 257 (1923). See Wallace v. Brumback, 177 Va. 36, 12 S.E.2d 801 (1941).

A mechanic's lien must be based on a contract, either oral or written, with which it must conform: although the lien is a creature of the statute, it must have its foundation in a contract. Hence it must correspond with the contract, as has been decided by other courts in analogous cases upon statutes similar to ours. United States v. 5.382 Acres, 871 F. Supp. 880 (W.D. Va. 1994), aff'd, 61 F.3d 901 (4th Cir. 1995).

Though it is analogous to common-law vendor's lien. — The lien is created by performing labor on, or furnishing materials used for the construction of, a building or structure. It is analogous to the common-law vendor's lien, binding the building and the enhanced value of the freehold created by its construction. Kinnier Co. v. Cofer, 13 Va. L. Reg. (n.s.) 238 (1927).

Policy. — In enacting the mechanics' liens statute, Virginia has enunciated its policy consideration that materialmen and suppliers should be paid or have the recourse of lodging a lien against the property. In re Thomas A. Cary, Inc., 412 F. Supp. 667 (E.D. Va. 1976), aff'd sub nom. National Permanent Fed. Sav. & Loan Ass'n v. Virginia Concrete Co., 562 F.2d 47 (4th Cir.), aff'd, 562 F.2d 48 (4th Cir. 1977).

Intent of section. — This section, authorizing a lien upon a building or structure and the land therewith necessary for use and enjoyment of the premises for labor performed and material furnished in construction, is intended to give those who have enhanced the value of a building the security of a lien on it to the extent they have added value but not to give a lien upon property not benefitted by labor or materials. This policy becomes particularly important when interests of other claimants are impinged upon by a joint lien. United Masonry, Inc. v. Jefferson Mews, Inc., 218 Va. 360, 237 S.E.2d 171 (1977).

The mechanics' lien is designed to give security to those adding value to property, by a pledge of the interest of the employer. Merchants & Mechanics Sav. Bank v. Dashiell, 66 Va. (25 Gratt.) 616 (1874); Bristol Iron & Steel Co. v. Thomas, 93 Va. 396, 25 S.E. 110 (1896).

The object of the law is to give to those who, by their labor and material, have enhanced the value of a building or structure the security of a lien thereon to the extent that they have added to its value, but not to give a lien upon property not benefitted. Gilman v. Ryan, 95 Va. 494, 28 S.E. 875 (1898).

The essence of the mechanics' lien laws is to protect materialmen when they have provided supplies and have not been compensated. In re Thomas A. Cary, Inc., 412 F. Supp. 667 (E.D. Va. 1976), aff'd sub. nom. National Permanent Fed. Sav. & Loan Ass'n v. Virginia Concrete Co., 562 F.2d 47 (4th Cir.), aff'd, 562 F.2d 48 (4th Cir. 1977).

It is not the contract for erecting a building which creates the lien under this section, but use of the materials furnished and expended by the contractor. Weaver v. Harland Corp., 176 Va. 224, 10 S.E.2d 547 (1940).

Construction of chapter. — Although there is a diversity of opinion as to whether mechanics' lien statutes should receive a strict or liberal construction, the correct rule of construction as to this chapter is that there must be a substantial compliance with the requirement of that portion of the chapter which relates to the creation of the lien, but that the provisions with respect to its enforcement should be liberally construed. H.N. Francis & Co. v. Hotel Rueger, Inc., 125 Va. 106, 99 S.E. 690 (1919). See Clement v. Adams Bros.-Paynes Co., 113 Va. 546, 75 S.E. 294 (1912).

The remedial portions of this chapter, which provide for enforcing the mechanics' lien after it is perfected, should be liberally construed, but the other portions, upon which the right to the existence of the lien depends, being in derogation of the common law, should be strictly construed. This rule of construction is not abrogated by § 43-15. Clement v. Adams Bros.-Paynes Co., 113 Va. 546, 75 S.E. 294 (1912). See also Shackleford v. Beck, 80 Va. 573 (1885); Virginia Dev. Co. v. Crozer Iron Co., 90 Va. 126, 17 S.E. 806 (1893), aff'd on rehearing, 19 S.E. 782 (1894); Bristol Iron & Steel Co. v. Thomas, 93 Va. 396, 25 S.E. 110 (1896).

Mechanics' lien and lien under § 43-24 distinguished. — The difference between a mechanics' lien and a lien under § 43-24 is that the mechanics' lien under this section is put upon the building or structure and so much of the land therewith as shall be necessary for the convenient use and enjoyment thereof, while § 43-24 puts a lien upon all the real and personal property of the company which is used in operating the same. The conflict of these liens, therefore, would only be as to such buildings or structures and lands as are used in operating the company. Building Supplies Corp. v. Willcox, 284 F. 113 (4th Cir. 1922).

Interest allowed in excess of legal rate on debts underlying liens. — Materialman's right to a mechanic's lien included interest on the unpaid cost of material furnished at a rate fixed in its contract in excess of the legal rate.

American Std. Homes Corp. v. Reinecke, 245 Va. 113, 425 S.E.2d 515 (1993).

Chancellor did not err in excluding attorney's fees as an element of the liens enforced by the final decree. The General Assembly expressly approved inclusion of interest as an element of the claim in the perfection and enforcement of a mechanic's lien. The legislature was at liberty to do, but did not do, the same for attorney's fees. American Std. Homes Corp. v. Reinecke, 245 Va. 113, 425 S.E.2d 515 (1993).

Joinder of all parties with interest in subject matter. — Where actions are filed by subcontractors against non-debtor owners and where general contractor files a bankruptcy petition, an owner might be prejudiced if the determination of the amount owing to the general contractor, that must be made in order to enforce a subcontractor's mechanic's lien, can be relitigated in a later proceeding; thus a general contractor would be a party who should be joined if feasible, and perhaps one in whose absence the case should be dismissed; although an action pursuant to this section is equitable and Rule 3:9A would not be directly applicable, it appears that the equity practice in Virginia is to require the joinder of all parties with an interest in the subject matter of the enforcement action. Middleton & Dugger Plumbing & Heating v. Richardson Bldrs., Inc., 123 Bankr. 736 (Bankr. W.D. Va. 1990).

Applied in Pioneer Nat'l Title Ins. Co. v. Cranwell, 235 Va. 597, 369 S.E.2d 678 (1988).

II. PROPERTY SUBJECT TO LIEN.

Property exempt from sale under execution. — Property which is exempt from seizure and sale under execution on grounds of public necessity must for the same reason be equally exempt from the operation of the mechanics' lien law, unless it appears by the law itself that the contrary was intended. And for this to be the case something more must appear than the ordinary provisions that the claim is to be a lien against a particular class of property enforceable as judgment rendered in other civil actions. These provisions do not apply to public buildings erected by states, cities and counties for public uses, unless the statute expressly so provides. Manly Mfg. Co. v. Broaddus, 94 Va. 547, 27 S.E. 438 (1897); Phillips v. Rector & Visitors of Univ. of Va., 97 Va. 472, 34 S.E. 66 (1899). See also Legg v. County School Bd., 157 Va. 295, 160 S.E. 60 (1931).

The mechanics' lien statutes have no application to contracts with the Commonwealth, or political subdivisions thereof, for the construction of public improvements, and do not give a subcontractor any lien on sums due by the Commonwealth or a political subdivision thereof to the contractor for the construction of public improvements. Bowers v. Town of Martinsville, 156 Va. 497, 159 S.E. 196 (1931).

A building owned by a municipal corporation is not subject to a mechanics' lien. London Bros. v. National Exch. Bank, 121 Va. 460, 93 S.E. 699 (1917).

A board of supervisors of a county cannot give a lien upon a public building. Manly Mfg. Co. v. Broaddus, 94 Va. 547, 27 S.E. 438 (1897).

Authority to issue bonds does not authorize liens. Phillips v. Rector & Visitors of Univ. of Va., 97 Va. 472, 34 S.E. 66 (1899).

Church property is included. — There is no reason arising out of the nature of church property in general for excepting it from the general terms of this section. That a church is embraced in the language "any building" is not open to doubt. Cain v. Rea, 159 Va. 446, 166 S.E. 478 (1932).

One who built roads or streets in a subdivision had no lien rights upon the subdivision lots, or the buildings thereon, until the General Assembly enacted subsection (b) and this is the first and only example in the mechanic's lien statutes of a provision for an extraterritorial lien, and it is carefully conditioned to minimize danger to purchasers without notice and other innocent third parties. Rosser v. Cole, 237 Va. 572, 379 S.E.2d 323 (1989).

By its nature, a joint lien confesses an inability to attribute the materials with particularity. In re Thomas A. Cary, Inc., 412 F. Supp. 667 (E.D. Va. 1976), aff'd sub nom. National Permanent Fed. Sav. & Loan Ass'n v. Virginia Concrete Co., 562 F.2d 47 (4th Cir.), aff'd, 562 F.2d 48 (4th Cir. 1977).

If a joint lien is filed, the premise underlying the filing is that the materials may not be segregated and allocated to a specific lot or structure. In re Thomas A. Cary, Inc., 412 F. Supp. 667 (E.D. Va. 1976), aff'd sub nom. National Permanent Fed. Sav. & Loan Ass'n v. Virginia Concrete Co., 562 F.2d 47 (4th Cir.), aff'd, 562 F.2d 48 (4th Cir. 1977).

Lien filed by construction corporation was not over-inclusive. — Where development group argued that lien was over-inclusive because its property was not a single parcel, but rather two separate non-contiguous parcels, and that construction corporation could have described the property subject to its lien, the memorandum of mechanic's lien filed by construction corporation was not over-inclusive. A lienor, such as construction corporation, was entitled to rely upon the land records. Blue Ridge Constr. Corp. v. Stafford Dev. Group, 244 Va. 361, 421 S.E.2d 199 (1992).

Contract for two houses may create joint lien. — Where the owner bargained with the general contractor to build two houses on two distinct lots, for an entire price, and the contractor bargained with the subcontractor to furnish materials for the entire work, and the work was done and the materials furnished accordingly, the lien of the general contractor and of the subcontractor was joint on both houses. Sergeant v. Denby, 87 Va. 206, 12 S.E. 402 (1890).

Except where interests of third persons are involved. — Where the interests of other lien creditors would be prejudiced thereby, a lien for the entire amount due for work done on, or materials furnished for, several buildings or lots cannot attach to, or be enforced against, part of the buildings or lots, and where it is sought to enforce the lien on less than the whole number of buildings or lots, each building is subject to the lien only to the extent of what was done or furnished therefor, and each lot only to the extent of what was done or furnished for the building or improvement thereon. The lien is properly confined to the building upon which the work was done, although the original contract embraced other buildings. Weaver v. Harland Corp., 176 Va. 224, 10 S.E.2d 547 (1940).

Joint lien cannot attach to separate buildings under separate contracts. — Where separate buildings are constructed under separate contracts no lien can attach to all the buildings. Gilman v. Ryan, 95 Va. 494, 28 S.E. 875 (1898).

Or where there is a separate estimate for each building. Gilman v. Ryan, 95 Va. 494, 28 S.E. 875 (1898).

Where several buildings are under construction, it is sufficient if lienors keep accounts from which it can be determined what labor and material is supplied to each house on which a lien is claimed. And where they receive payment without direction as to application, they are free to apply such payment as they wish, failing which the law will apply the payment to the earliest item of debt. Northern Va. Sav. & Loan Ass'n v. J.B. Kendall Co., 205 Va. 136, 135 S.E.2d 178 (1964).

The nature of the development of a subdivision provides impediments to the use of a single lien. In re Thomas A. Cary, Inc., 412 F. Supp. 667 (E.D. Va. 1976), aff'd sub nom. National Permanent Fed. Sav. & Loan Ass'n v. Virginia Concrete Co., 562 F.2d 47 (4th Cir.), aff'd, 562 F.2d 48 (4th Cir. 1977).

Joint lien for materials supplied in bulk to subdivisions. — Where subcontractors supply material in bulk to a subdivision and the nature thereof precludes allocating the material to a particular lot or building, filing of a joint lien is appropriate on the basis of policy considerations and where no subsequent release of the lien on a particular lot or building occurs. In re Thomas A. Cary, Inc., 412 F. Supp. 667 (E.D. Va. 1976), aff'd sub nom. National

Permanent Fed. Sav. & Loan Ass'n v. Virginia Concrete Co., 562 F.2d 47 (4th Cir.), aff'd, 562 F.2d 48 (4th Cir. 1977).

Memorandum of joint lien claiming unapportioned amount. — Where work was done and materials furnished for a condominium under two separate and distinct contracts which added disproportionate values to the properties liened, a memorandum which failed to apportion the amounts due between the several properties benefitted was defective and the lien void. United Masonry, Inc. v. Jefferson Mews, Inc., 218 Va. 360, 237 S.E.2d 171 (1977).

A memorandum of lien failed to comply with this section when an unapportioned amount was claimed upon all units of a condominium, whereas one contract was for work on 132 units and another was for work on common element of entire 264-unit project, and the memorandum did not seek to secure only a claim to extent plaintiff had added value but instead attempted to lien property not benefitted by work. United Masonry, Inc. v. Jefferson Mews, Inc., 218 Va. 360, 237 S.E.2d 171 (1977).

Attachment of blanket lien where condominium units unbuilt. — While a blanket mechanic's lien recorded when 132 units of a condominium were built and 132 units remained unbuilt could not be enforced against the unbuilt units, the joint lien did attach to the land on which these units would stand and directly affected the whole project. United Masonry, Inc. v. Jefferson Mews, Inc., 218 Va. 360, 237 S.E.2d 171 (1977).

Lien may attach to severable machinery and apparatus. — All machinery and apparatus of a permanent character and essential to the purposes of the building, although severable without lasting injury to it or the building, may be subjected to a valid mechanics' lien. Haskin Wood Vulcanizing Co. v. Cleveland Ship-Building Co., 94 Va. 439, 26 S.E. 878 (1897).

And machinery may be subjected without subjecting the buildings where it is located. Haskins Wood Vulcanizing Co. v. Cleveland Ship-Building Co., 94 Va. 439, 26 S.E. 878 (1897).

Structure of permanent character. — The requirements of this section had been complied with, and the structure was of a permanent character within the meaning of this section. Haskins Wood Vulcanizing Co. v. Cleveland Ship-Building Co., 94 Va. 439, 26 S.E. 878 (1897).

Entire lot in town considered necessary for convenient use and enjoyment of building. Pairo v. Bethell, 75 Va. 825 (1881).

The lien on a deed of trust recorded before land is improved is a first lien on the land and a lien on the improvements subordinate to a mechanic's lien; the mechanic's lien is a first lien on the improvements and a subordinate lien on so much of the land as is necessary for the use and enjoyment of the improvements. Walt Robbins, Inc. v. Damon Corp., 232 Va. 43, 348 S.E.2d 223 (1986).

Because the claimant did no work on any part of the lots, his lien rights would not extend to them under the provisions of subsection (a) unless his rights are extended by other provisions of law. Rosser v. Cole, 237 Va. 572, 379 S.E.2d 323 (1989).

Removal of cabinets irrelevant. — Where the seller furnished materials for building project and the cabinets were delivered, accepted, installed, and added value to the structure, the fact that the cabinets were removed before the memorandum was filed was irrelevant. The legislature could not have intended that a supplier's mechanic lien may be avoided simply by removing from the building the materials furnished and incorporated in it. Moore & Moore Gen. Contractors v. Basepoint, Inc., 253 Va. 304, 485 S.E.2d 131 (1997).

III. ESTATE OR INTEREST SUBJECT TO LIEN.

This section is to be read with § 43-21. — While this section gives to a materialman who perfects his lien within the prescribed time and in the proper manner a lien upon the building "and so much land therewith as shall be necessary for the convenient use and enjoyment thereof," it must be read in connection with § 43-21, which deals with conflicting liens on the land affected. Federal Land Bank v. Clinchfield Lumber & Supply Co., 171 Va. 118, 198 S.E. 437 (1938). See Feuchtenberger v. Williamson, Carroll & Saunders, 137 Va. 578, 120 S.E. 257 (1923).

Interest of person not ordering work is unaffected. — If this section could be construed as authorizing a lien on the interest of a person not ordering the work to be done, it would seem that the provision would be unconstitutional as taking private property without the owner's consent. Feuchtenberger v. Williamson, Carroll & Saunders, 137 Va. 578, 120 S.E. 257 (1923).

Mere knowledge of owner is insufficient to work estoppel. — While the owner of land may by conduct estop himself from denying that a building contractor who has erected a structure on the land has a lien thereon, yet the owner's mere knowledge that the contractor was building on the land by direction of the owner's vendee under a contract to convey is not alone sufficient to establish such an estoppel. Feuchtenberger v. Williamson, Carroll & Saunders, 137 Va. 578, 120 S.E. 257 (1923).

An equitable interest or estate in land is subject to a mechanics' lien, unless the statute expressly excludes such a construction.

Feuchtenberger v. Williamson, Carroll & Saunders, 137 Va. 578, 120 S.E. 257 (1923).

A mechanics' lien may be perfected on an equitable as well as on a legal estate. Wallace v. Brumback, 177 Va. 36, 12 S.E.2d 801 (1941); Blanton v. Owen, 203 Va. 73, 122 S.E.2d 650 (1961).

But lien survives or perishes with estate. — When mechanics' liens are entered against an equitable estate, their value depends upon that particular estate, and they survive or perish with it. Feuchtenberger v. Williamson, Carroll & Saunders, 137 Va. 578, 120 S.E. 257 (1923).

IV. WHO MAY SUBJECT PROPERTY TO LIEN.

Section applies to all persons performing labor. — The language of this section is general in its terms and embraces all persons who perform "any labor" in the construction of a building. Cain v. Rea, 159 Va. 446, 166 S.E. 478 (1932).

An architect is embraced in the protecting provisions of this section. Cain v. Rea, 159 Va. 446, 166 S.E. 478 (1932).

As between the owner and subcontractor it is not necessary to have the owner's consent. By the building contract the general contractor becomes, to a certain extent, the agent of the owner to procure the necessary labor and material for the construction of the building and use the same therein. Kinnier Co. v. Cofer, 13 Va. L. Reg. (n.s.) 238 (1927).

Optional remedies of subcontractor. — The subcontractor, under the provisions of § 43-18, may rely on the general contractor's lien or, under the provisions of this section and §§ 43-4 and 43-7, he may file and undertake to enforce his own independent lien. VNB Mtg. Corp. v. Lone Star Indus., Inc., 215 Va. 366, 209 S.E.2d 909 (1974).

Subcontractors and materialmen are not deprived of their independent liens unless they either expressly waived their lien rights or expressly accepted, or by clear implication, agreed to be bound by the general contractor's stipulation in the general contract against liens. VNB Mtg. Corp. v. Lone Star Indus., Inc., 215 Va. 366, 209 S.E.2d 909 (1974).

A joint venturer may be a general contractor within the compass of the mechanic's lien laws. West Alexandria Properties, Inc. v. First Va. Mtg. & Real Estate Inv. Trust, 221 Va. 134, 267 S.E.2d 149 (1980).

Joint venturer could not enforce a mechanic's lien for value of work done on co-joint venturer's portion of land, which had been dedicated to the public, where the remaining land of the co-joint venturer had been transferred to a third party in fee simple and who was never in contractual privity with the joint venturer seeking to enforce the lien. West Alexandria Properties, Inc. v. First Va. Mtg. & Real Estate Inv. Trust, 221 Va. 134, 267 S.E.2d 149 (1980).

V. REQUISITES OF LIEN.

Lien is inchoate but may be perfected. — The liens created by this section, while inchoate, are potential liens, which may be perfected within the time and in the manner provided by the succeeding sections of this chapter. DeWitt v. Coffey, 150 Va. 365, 143 S.E. 710 (1928).

All the statutory provisions for mechanics' liens are indispensable, and the omission of any one of them is fatal. Coleman v. Pearman, 159 Va. 72, 165 S.E. 371 (1932), overruled on other grounds, Mills v. Moore's Super Stores, 217 Va. 276, 227 S.E.2d 719 (1976).

The terms of the statute must be met before its benefits can be enjoyed. Coleman v. Pearman, 159 Va. 72, 165 S.E. 371 (1932), overruled on other grounds, Mills v. Moore's Super Stores, 217 Va. 276, 227 S.E.2d 719 (1976).

Knowledge of purchaser or lienor is insufficient. — Knowledge by a purchaser or lienor of the construction of the building cannot take the place of the statutory requirements. Wallace v. Brumback, 177 Va. 36, 12 S.E.2d 801 (1941).

Contract may be written or oral. — Merchants & Mechanics Sav. Bank v. Dashiell, 66 Va. (25 Gratt.) 616 (1874).

Blanket lien filed upon a building was invalid and unenforceable because the supplier failed to apportion in the lien memorandum the amount of its claim for the work and materials furnished by it on each of 10 lots described in the memorandum; where there was a series of individual but related transactions reflected in the invoices, delivery tickets, and work orders, and where there were documents which could be identified with charges for individual units, those charges should have been aggregated for the filing of memoranda of lien of specific units. Addington-Beaman Lumber Co. v. Lincoln Sav. & Loan Ass'n, 241 Va. 436, 403 S.E.2d 688 (1991).

Mechanic's lien held invalid. — Because the contractor's memorandum of mechanic's lien failed to correspond to his contract, failed to describe the land and improvements upon which his lien rights existed, and purported to cover property to which his lien rights did not extend, it was invalid. Rosser v. Cole, 237 Va. 572, 379 S.E.2d 323 (1989).

VI. RELEASE AND MERGER.

Releases are the fatal defect to a claim that the materials may not be attributed to a specific property. In re Thomas A. Cary, Inc., 412 F. Supp. 667 (E.D. Va. 1976), aff'd sub

nom., National Permanent Fed. Sav. & Loan Ass'n v. Virginia Concrete Co., 562 F.2d 47 (4th Cir.), aff'd, 562 F.2d 48 (4th Cir. 1977).

Release of part of property does not destroy lien as to remainder. — The release of a mechanics' lien as to part of the property covered thereby does not destroy the lien on the rest of the property; but where one building is released, an item for work or materials thereon cannot be included in a lien on the remaining buildings. Weaver v. Harland Corp., 176 Va. 224, 10 S.E.2d 547 (1940).

Unless interests of other lien creditors are prejudiced. — The release of a portion of the properties embraced by the lien may preclude its successful assertion against the remainder. This is only true where the interest of other lien creditors are affected; it would not be so in the case of the owner and the lienor. If it were not so the mechanics' lien lienors could so shift their liens as to burden unduly some of the lien subjects and to relieve others, to the extent of imperiling the interests of other lien creditors, which would not be consonant with the intent and spirit of this chapter and would be offensive to good conscience and equity. Weaver v. Harland Corp., 176 Va. 224, 10 S.E.2d 547 (1940).

Where lienor failed to perfect the lien upon one of the lots of a subdivision he sought to encumber, and where the chancellor released the lien as to that lot, this shifted the full burden of the lienor's claim to the remaining lots. But, when such a shift in the burden occurs, the lien is enforceable only when there were no third persons whose interests were injuriously affected by the shift, and here the secured creditor under deed of trust had a valuable interest in the lots; thus, the chancellor erred in overruling the creditor's demurrer to the lienor's bill of complaint to enforce the lien. United Va. Mtg. Corp. v. Haines Paving Co., 221 Va. 1047, 277 S.E.2d 187 (1981).

Acceptance of deed of trust may be merger. — The acceptance of a deed of trust on the property covered by a mechanics' lien, to secure the amount due, is a merger of the lien. Wroten v. Armat, 72 Va. (31 Gratt.) 228 (1879).

Agreement to waive lien must be supported by consideration. — Although a person entitled to a mechanic's lien may waive that right in whole or part, the general rule is that an agreement to waive or release a mechanic's lien must be supported by consideration to be valid and binding. United Masonry, Inc. v. Riggs Nat'l Bank, 233 Va. 476, 357 S.E.2d 509 (1987).

Sufficient consideration to waive or release a mechanic's lien exists if the promisee is induced by the waiver to do something that he is not legally bound to do or refrains from doing anything he has a legal right to do, or if the promisee acts in reliance upon the waiver to his detriment. United Masonry, Inc. v. Riggs Nat'l Bank, 233 Va. 476, 357 S.E.2d 509 (1987).

The cash payments that the contractor received, coupled with the inducement to the construction lender and title insurance company to continue construction advances, constituted sufficient consideration for the waiver of all lien rights acquired for work and materials furnished prior to a specified date. United Masonry, Inc. v. Riggs Nat'l Bank, 233 Va. 476, 357 S.E.2d 509 (1987).

§ 43-4. Perfection of lien by general contractor; recordation and notice.

— A general contractor, or any other lien claimant under §§ 43-7 and 43-9, in order to perfect the lien given by § 43-3, provided such lien has not been barred by § 43-4.01 C, shall file a memorandum of lien at any time after the work is commenced or material furnished, but not later than ninety days from the last day of the month in which he last performs labor or furnishes material, and in no event later than ninety days from the time such building, structure, or railroad is completed, or the work thereon otherwise terminated. The memorandum shall be filed in the clerk's office in the county or city in which the building, structure or railroad, or any part thereof is located. The memorandum shall show the names of the owner of the property sought to be charged, and of the claimant of the lien, the amount and consideration of his claim, and the time or times when the same is or will be due and payable, verified by the oath of the claimant, or his agent, including a statement declaring his intention to claim the benefit of the lien, and giving a brief description of the property on which he claims a lien. It shall be the duty of the clerk in whose office the memorandum is filed to record and index the same as provided in § 43-4.1, in the name of the claimant of the lien and of the owner of the property. From the time of such recording and indexing all persons shall be deemed to have notice thereof. The cost of recording the memorandum shall be taxed against the person found liable in any judgment or decree enforcing such lien. The lien claimant may file any number of memoranda but no memorandum filed pursuant to this chapter shall include sums due for labor or materials furnished more than 150 days prior to the last day on which labor was performed or material furnished to the job preceding the filing of such memorandum. However, any memorandum may include (i) sums withheld as retainages with respect to labor performed or materials furnished at any time before it is filed, but not to exceed ten percent of the total contract price and (ii) sums which are not yet due because the party with whom the lien claimant contracted has not yet received such funds from the owner or another third party. The time limitations set forth herein shall apply to all labor performed or materials furnished on construction commenced on or after July 1, 1980. (Code 1919, § 6427; 1940, p. 401; 1968, c. 568; 1976, c. 413; 1980, c. 491; 1992, cc. 779, 787; 1999, c. 533.)

Cross references. — As to curing of errors and inaccuracies in memorandum, see § 43-15. As to oaths, see §§ 49-4 through 49-10.

The 1999 amendment, in the next-to-last sentence, inserted "(i)" preceding "sums withheld" and inserted "and (ii) sums which are not yet due because the party with whom the lien claimant contracted has not yet received such funds from the owner or another third party."

Law Review. — For survey of Virginia commercial law for the year 1970-1971, see 57 Va. L. Rev. 1527 (1971); for the year 1974-1975, see 61 Va. L. Rev. 1668 (1975); for the year 1975-1976, see 62 Va. L. Rev. 1375 (1976); for the year 1976-77, see 63 Va. L. Rev. 1377 (1977). For survey of Virginia law on business associations for the year 1977-1978, see 64 Va. L. Rev. 1375 (1978). For survey of Virginia commercial law for the year 1977-1978, see 64 Va. L. Rev. 1383 (1978). For comment discussing the application of the blanket lien with respect to multiunit development in Virginia, see 13 U. Rich. L. Rev. 637 (1979). For comment,"United States v. Kimbell Foods, Inc.: A Problem or Solution in Resolving Lien Priority Disputes?," see 36 Wash. & Lee L. Rev. 1203 (1979). For article on title examination in Virginia, see 17 U. Rich. L. Rev. 229 (1983).

I. General Consideration.
II. Time of Filing.
III. The Memorandum and Affidavit; Recordation and Indexing Thereof.

I. GENERAL CONSIDERATION.

The provisions of this chapter are, each and all, indispensable to the creation of the lien; hence if any one of them is not complied with, no lien is acquired. Trustees Franklin St. Church v. Davis, 85 Va. 193, 7 S.E. 245 (1888). But see note to § 43-3, "General Consideration," I.

Perfection statute contrasted with enforcement statutes. — A lien created by § 43-3 is one in derogation of the common law. Once perfected in accordance with this section, the lien can be enforced by suit brought as provided in §§ 43-17 and 43-22. In Virginia provisions of the enforcement statutes are to be construed liberally while the requirements of the perfection statute are to be construed strictly. American Std. Homes Corp. v. Reinecke, 245 Va. 113, 425 S.E.2d 515 (1993).

Interest allowed in excess of legal rate on debts underlying liens. — Materialman's right to a mechanic's lien included interest on the unpaid cost of material furnished at a rate fixed in its contract in excess of the legal rate. American Std. Homes Corp. v. Reinecke, 245 Va. 113, 425 S.E.2d 515 (1993).

Chancellor did not err in excluding attorney's fees as an element of the liens enforced by the final decree. The General Assembly expressly approved inclusion of interest as an element of the claim in the perfection and enforcement of a mechanic's lien. The legislature was at liberty to do, but did not do, the same for attorney's fees. American Std. Homes Corp. v. Reinecke, 245 Va. 113, 425 S.E.2d 515 (1993).

A substantial compliance with this section is essential to the creation of the lien. Gilman v. Ryan, 95 Va. 494, 28 S.E. 875 (1898).

Or lien will be lost. — While one who purchases property pending the construction of a building takes it subject to the risk that a lien may thereafter be perfected thereon, unless the lien is perfected within the proper time and in the proper manner it is lost. Wallace v. Brumback, 177 Va. 36, 12 S.E.2d 801 (1941).

Actual notice to purchaser is insufficient. — Actual notice of a contractor's claim will not affect a purchaser, if this section has not been complied with. Shackleford v. Beck, 80 Va. 573 (1885).

Duty to place lien only upon property worked and no more. — Where a mechanic files a memorandum of mechanic's lien against two or more parcels but has not worked on all the parcels and where the mechanic attempts to enforce that lien against the several properties, that lien must be declared invalid in its

entirety since it is the mechanic's duty to place his lien upon the property on which he worked and no more. Woodington Elec., Inc. v. Lincoln Sav. & Loan Ass'n, 238 Va. 623, 385 S.E.2d 872 (1989).

It rests upon the claimant of the lien to show compliance with all essential requirements of this section. Shackleford v. Beck, 80 Va. 573 (1885); Trustees Franklin St. Church v. Davis, 85 Va. 193, 7 S.E. 245 (1888).

A mechanic's lien, although a statutory creation, necessarily has its foundation in a contract, and it is a contractor's performance under the contract that gives rise to the inchoate lien. United Masonry, Inc. v. Riggs Nat'l Bank, 233 Va. 476, 357 S.E.2d 509 (1987).

Debtor not divested of property by mere filing and recordation. — It does not appear that the mere filing and recordation of the lien operates to divest the debtor of his property. W.T. Jones & Co. v. Foodco Realty, Inc., 318 F.2d 881 (4th Cir. 1963).

Effect of filing and recording against claim of United States. — As against claim of United States, the interim steps of filing and recording the lien, without obtaining a final judgment enforcing the lien against the property, serve "merely as a caveat of a more perfect lien to come." W.T. Jones & Co. v. Foodco Realty, Inc., 318 F.2d 881 (4th Cir. 1963).

Effect of releasing portion of property subject to blanket lien. — The release of a portion of property subject to a blanket lien will release all of the property subject to the blanket lien if third-party interests are injuriously affected by the release. Pic Constr. Co. v. First Union Nat'l Bank, 218 Va. 915, 241 S.E.2d 804 (1978).

Optional remedies of subcontractor. — The subcontractor, under the provisions of § 43-18, may rely on the general contractor's lien or, under the provisions of this section and §§ 43-3 and 43-7, he may file and undertake to enforce his own independent lien. VNB Mtg. Corp. v. Lone Star Indus., Inc., 215 Va. 366, 209 S.E.2d 909 (1974).

Subcontractors and materialmen are not deprived of their independent liens unless they either expressly waived their lien rights or expressly accepted, or by clear implication, agreed to be bound by the general contractor's stipulation in the general contract against liens. VNB Mtg. Corp. v. Lone Star Indus., Inc., 215 Va. 366, 209 S.E.2d 909 (1974).

A person making improvements to land is deemed a general contractor if that person is in contractual privity with the owner. West Alexandria Properties, Inc. v. First Va. Mtg. & Real Estate Inv. Trust, 221 Va. 134, 267 S.E.2d 149 (1980).

Relation back of perfection may defeat rights of bankruptcy trustee. — So long as state law permits a relation-back type of perfection which would defeat an intervening lien creditor, 11 U.S.C. § 546(b) allows the creditor to perfect and allows the relation-back feature to defeat the rights of the bankruptcy trustee. The Virginia mechanic's lien statutes allow for such a relation back. H.T. Bowling, Inc. v. Bain, 52 Bankr. 58 (Bankr. W.D. Va. 1985), aff'd in part and rev'd in part, 64 Bankr. 581 (W.D. Va. 1986).

Single continuing account found. — Materials and deliveries were identifiable to specific projects under "running accounts," thus constituting a single continuing contract for each parcel. United Sav. Ass'n of Texas v. Jim Carpenter Co., 252 Va. 252, 475 S.E.2d 788 (1996).

Applied in Pulaski Nat'l Bank v. Tilghman Moyer Co., 104 F.2d 471 (4th Cir. 1939); In re Romanac, 245 F. Supp. 882 (W.D. Va. 1965); E.E. Stump Well Drilling, Inc. v. Willis, 230 Va. 445, 338 S.E.2d 841 (1986); Pioneer Nat'l Title Ins. Co. v. Cranwell, 235 Va. 597, 369 S.E.2d 678 (1988); Quantum Dev. Co. v. Luckett, 242 Va. 159, 409 S.E.2d 121 (1991); Harrison & Bates, Inc. v. Featherstone Assocs., 253 Va. 364, 484 S.E.2d 883 (1997).

II. TIME OF FILING.

Attachment of inchoate lien prior to 1980 amendment. — See Hadrup v. Sale, 201 Va. 421, 111 S.E.2d 405 (1959); W.T. Jones & Co. v. Foodco Realty, Inc., 318 F.2d 881 (4th Cir. 1963).

When time period began to run prior to 1980 amendment. — See Boston & Co. v. C & O R.R., 76 Va. 180 (1882); Osborne v. Big Stone Gap Colliery Co., 96 Va. 58, 30 S.E. 446 (1898); Northern Va. Sav. & Loan Ass'n v. J.B. Kendall Co., 205 Va. 136, 135 S.E.2d 178 (1964).

Time of "completion" may be fixed by contract. — See Trustees Franklin St. Church v. Davis, 85 Va. 193, 7 S.E. 245 (1888); Cain v. Rea, 159 Va. 446, 166 S.E. 478 (1932), decided prior to the 1980 amendment to this section.

In the absence of evidence that a contractor acted in bad faith to delay the completion of work on a project, the contractor is required to file his memorandum for mechanic's lien 90 days from the date of completion. Dominion Trust Co. v. Kenbridge Constr. Co., 248 Va. 393, 448 S.E.2d 659 (1994).

Work is not "otherwise terminated" by sale. — There is nothing in the statute to indicate that work on a building is "otherwise terminated" by a mere sale. Such a construction would impose an undue hardship upon the contractor and is not in keeping with the language or spirit of the statute. Hadrup v. Sale,

201 Va. 421, 111 S.E.2d 405 (1959).

Conveyance of a house and lot did not "otherwise terminate" the work upon a building within the meaning of this section and make it necessary for a lien to be filed. Hadrup v. Sale, 201 Va. 421, 111 S.E.2d 405 (1959).

Work "otherwise terminated." — Where the evidence showed that work under the contract ceased on Sept. 18, when the general contractor was experiencing severe financial problems and construction of the defendant's residence was approximately two-thirds completed, the work was "otherwise terminated" on that date, within the meaning of this section. Mills v. Moore's Super Stores, 217 Va. 276, 227 S.E.2d 719 (1976).

Where the owner abdicated responsibility in favor of a trusteeship composed of its principal creditors, work was "otherwise terminated" as of that date. Northern Va. Sav. & Loan Ass'n v. J.B. Kendall Co., 205 Va. 136, 135 S.E.2d 178 (1964). The time period for filing a memorandum is now 90 days. — Editor's note.

Furnishing of replacement materials did not advance date on which lien could be claimed. — Chancellor erred in confirming the commissioner's finding that "the furnishing of the replacement materials advanced the date ... on which the lien could be claimed." Because liens for the materials furnished under the material order contract were never perfected within the time prescribed by this section, they were unenforceable. American Std. Homes Corp. v. Reinecke, 245 Va. 113, 425 S.E.2d 515 (1993).

Time limit not extended where trustees completed project. — Work performed under contract with trustees committed to finish project abandoned by owner does not extend statutory time limit for filing memorandum of lien for work performed under contract with owner. American Std. Homes Corp. v. Reinecke, 245 Va. 113, 425 S.E.2d 515 (1993).

Where there were three separate construction contracts, and the contractor did not begin construction under the latter two contracts until after July 1, 1980, the filing requirements of this section applied, and the liens claimed for labor and materials furnished under those contracts were not timely filed. United Masonry, Inc. v. Riggs Nat'l Bank, 233 Va. 476, 357 S.E.2d 509 (1987).

Perfection from date of injunction. — Where federal district court effectively enjoined would-be mechanic's lienors from perfecting their liens within the period prescribed by this section, the time of perfection, for purposes of determining priority as to fund paid into court, would be the dates of the injunctive orders. Glen Constr. Co. v. Bank of Vienna, 410 F. Supp.

402 (E.D. Va. 1976), rev'd on other grounds, 557 F.2d 1050 (4th Cir. 1977).

III. THE MEMORANDUM AND AFFIDAVIT; RECORDATION AND INDEXING THEREOF.

Provision was intended for protection of purchasers. — The provision for the recordation and indexing of the memorandum was intended for the protection of a purchaser who might acquire the property after the perfection of the mechanics' lien, or a subsequent lienor who might be affected thereby. Wallace v. Brumback, 177 Va. 36, 12 S.E.2d 801 (1941). See Shackleford v. Beck, 80 Va. 573 (1885).

It must be read in connection with §§ 55-80 through 55-105. — The provision for the recordation of the memorandum and the indexing of the same must be read in connection with and as a part of the registry statutes, §§ 55-80 through 55-105, relating to the recordation of certain writings in order to give constructive notice thereof to interested parties. The provision was intended to conform the recordation or registration of mechanics' liens with the recordation or registration of deeds of trust and like liens which are required to be indexed in the same manner under the registry statutes. Wallace v. Brumback, 177 Va. 36, 12 S.E.2d 801 (1941).

Acknowledgment is not required. — Section 55-106, providing that writings shall be acknowledged before being admitted to record, does not apply to mechanics' liens filed under this section. Sprenkle v. Dillard, 10 Va. L. Reg. 431 (1904).

Perfection of a mechanics' lien is a one-step process in Virginia. Upon the filing of a memorandum in accordance with this section, the creditor's lien is perfected. Section 43-17 is merely a statute of limitations governing the period within which a lienor must file a claim to collect on his perfected lien. H.T. Bowling, Inc. v. Bain, 64 Bankr. 581 (W.D. Va. 1986).

Filing of complaint to enforce perfected lien violated automatic stay in bankruptcy. — Since the filing of a bill of complaint in the state court to enforce a mechanics' lien constitutes an attempt to enforce a perfected mechanics' lien, and not a step in the perfection process, the contractor plainly violated the automatic stay of 11 U.S.C. § 362 by filing the bill of complaint. Section 362 treats enforcement of liens much differently than their perfection. Specifically, § 362(a)(4) prohibits the filing of suit to enforce any lien against property of the debtor's estate. H.T. Bowling, Inc. v. Bain, 64 Bankr. 581 (W.D. Va. 1986).

Purpose and character of description of property. — The object of requiring a description of the property is to inform the owner upon which part of his property the lien is claimed, and to give notice thereof to purchasers and creditors, so that they may identify the property and protect themselves against the lien. If the property can be reasonably identified by the description given, it is all that the law requires. Taylor v. Netherwood, 91 Va. 88, 20 S.E. 888 (1895).

A memorandum of mechanic's lien must contain "a brief description of the property" on which the lien is claimed. The purpose of the description is to enable an owner, purchaser, or creditor to identify the property on which the lien is claimed. If the property can be "reasonably identified," the description is sufficient. Penrod & Stauffer Bldg. Sys. v. Metro Printing & Mailing Servs., Inc., 229 Va. 150, 326 S.E.2d 662 (1985).

"Owner" means owner at time of recordation of memorandum. — The owner of the property referred to in this section, providing that in order to perfect a mechanics' lien there must be filed a memorandum showing the name of the owner of the property sought to be charged, means the person who owns the property, or the interest therein to be affected, at the time of the recordation of the memorandum of the mechanics' lien. Wallace v. Brumback, 177 Va. 36, 12 S.E.2d 801 (1941).

A bill to enforce mechanics' liens was properly dismissed where the recorded memoranda of the liens had named the original owners as the owners of the properties, whereas they should have named the owners of the properties at the time the memoranda were filed. Wallace v. Brumback, 177 Va. 36, 12 S.E.2d 801 (1941).

A trustee in a deed of trust was not an "owner," within the meaning of this section, so that the failure to name such trustee, or trustees, in a memorandum for mechanics' lien did not invalidate the lien. Loyola Fed. Sav. & Loan Ass'n v. Herndon Lumber & Millwork, Inc., 218 Va. 803, 241 S.E.2d 752 (1978).

The filing of a memorandum of mechanic's lien is a judicial proceeding entitling the filer to an absolute privilege against slander. Donohoe Constr. Co. v. Mount Vernon Assocs., 235 Va. 531, 369 S.E.2d 857 (1988).

A general contractor may perfect his lien without giving notice to the owner, the filing of the required memorandum for recordation in the clerk's office being sufficient. Coleman v. Pearman, 159 Va. 72, 165 S.E. 371 (1932), overruled on other grounds, Mills v. Moore's Super Stores, 217 Va. 276, 227 S.E.2d 719 (1976).

The president of a corporation is not necessarily its agent for the purpose of making the affidavit required by this section. Clement v. Adams Bros.-Paynes Co., 113 Va. 546, 75 S.E. 294 (1912).

The holding in Clement v. Adams Bros.-

Paynes Co., 113 Va. 546, 75 S.E. 294 (1912), should be read in the light of § 49-7, subsequently enacted. — Editor's note.

But affidavit signed as "president and agent" is sufficient. — Where one signed an affidavit as "president and agent" of a corporation claiming a mechanics' lien, it sufficiently appears that the affiant was acting as the agent of the corporation, and the affidavit is sufficient to support the lien. John Diebold & Sons' Stone Co. v. Tatterson, 115 Va. 766, 80 S.E. 585 (1914).

Where the memorandum stated that the property was owned by one of two named persons or by "person unknown," this was a sufficient statement as to the ownership of the property, since one of the persons named was under contract to purchase the land and thus was equitable owner. Blanton v. Owen, 203 Va. 73, 122 S.E.2d 650 (1961).

Memorandum of joint lien claiming

unapportioned amount. — Where work was done and materials furnished for a condominium under two separate and distinct contracts which added disproportionate values to the properties liened, a memorandum which failed to apportion the amounts due between the several properties benefitted was defective and the lien void. United Masonry, Inc. v. Jefferson Mews, Inc., 218 Va. 360, 237 S.E.2d 171 (1977).

A memorandum of lien failed to comply with § 43-3 when an unapportioned amount was claimed upon all units of a condominium, whereas one contract was for work on 132 units and another was for work on common element of entire 264-unit project, and the memorandum did not seek to secure only a claim to extent plaintiff had added value but instead attempted to lien property not benefitted by work. United Masonry, Inc. v. Jefferson Mews, Inc., 218 Va. 360, 237 S.E.2d 171 (1977).

§ 43-4.01. Posting of building permit; identification of mechanics' lien agent in building permit; notice to mechanics' lien agent; effect of notice.

— A. The building permit for any one- or two-family residential dwelling unit issued pursuant to the Uniform Statewide Building Code shall be conspicuously and continuously posted on the property for which the permit is issued until all work is completed on the property. The permit shall be posted on the property before any labor is performed or any material furnished on the property for which the building permit is issued.

B. If, at the time of issuance, the building permit contains the name, mailing address, and telephone number of the mechanics' lien agent as defined in § 43-1, any person entitled to claim a lien under this title may notify the mechanics' lien agent that he seeks payment for labor performed or material furnished by registered or certified mail or by physical delivery. Such notice shall contain (i) the name, mailing address, and telephone number of the person sending such notice, (ii) the building permit number on the building permit, (iii) a description of the property as shown on the building permit, and (iv) a statement that the person filing such notice seeks payment for labor performed or material furnished. A return receipt or other receipt showing delivery of the notice to the addressee or written evidence that such notice was delivered by the postal service or other carrier to but not accepted by the addressee shall be prima facie evidence of receipt. An inaccuracy in the notice as to the description of the property shall not bar a person from claiming a lien under this title or filing a memorandum or otherwise perfecting or enforcing a lien as provided in subsection C if the property can otherwise be reasonably identified from the description.

C. Except as provided otherwise in this subsection, no person other than a person claiming a lien under subsection B of § 43-3 may claim a lien under this title or file a memorandum or otherwise perfect and enforce a lien under this title with respect to a one- or two-family residential dwelling unit if such person fails to notify any mechanics' lien agent identified on the building permit in accordance with subsection B above (i) within thirty days of the first date that he performs labor or furnishes material to or for the building or structure or (ii) within thirty days of the date such a permit is issued, if such labor or materials are first performed or furnished by such person prior to the issuance of a building permit. However, the failure to give any such notices within the appropriate thirty-day period as required by the previous sentence shall not bar a person from claiming a lien under this title or from filing a memorandum or otherwise perfecting and enforcing a lien under this title, provided that such lien is limited to labor performed or materials furnished on or after the date a notice is given by such person to the mechanics' lien agent in accordance with subsection B above. A person performing labor or furnishing materials with respect to a one- or two-family residential dwelling unit on which a building permit is not posted at the time he first performs his labor or first furnishes his material shall determine from appropriate authorities whether a permit of the type described in subsection B above has been issued and the date on which it is issued.

No person shall be required to comply with this subsection as to any memorandum of lien which is recorded prior to the issuance of a building permit nor shall any person be required to comply with this subsection when the building permit does not designate a mechanics' lien agent.

D. Unless otherwise agreed in writing, the only duties of the mechanics' lien agent shall be to receive notices delivered to him pursuant to subsection B and to provide any notice upon request to a settlement agent, as defined in § 6.1-2.10, involved in a transaction relating to the residential dwelling unit.

E. Mechanics' lien agents are authorized to enter into written agreements with third parties with regard to funds to be advanced to them for disbursement, and the transfer, disbursement, return and other handling of such funds shall be governed by the terms of such written agreements.

F. A mechanics' lien agent as defined in § 43-1 may charge a reasonable fee for services rendered in connection with administration of notice authorized herein and the disbursement of funds for payment of labor and materials for the construction or repair of improvements on real estate. (1992, cc. 779, 787.)

§ 43-4.1. Liens to be recorded in deed books and indexed in general index of deeds. — Notwithstanding the provision of any other section of this title, or any other provision of law requiring documents to be recorded in the miscellaneous lien book or the deed books in the clerk's office of any court, on and after July 1, 1964, all memoranda or notices of liens, in the discretion of the clerk, shall be recorded in the deed books in such clerk's office, and shall be indexed in the general index of deeds, and such general index shall show the type of such lien. (1960, c. 81; 1964, c. 338; 1968, c. 568; 1985, c. 392.)

Law Review. — For article on title examination in Virginia, see 17 U. Rich. L. Rev. 229 (1983).

Applied in E.E. Stump Well Drilling, Inc. v.

Willis, 230 Va. 445, 338 S.E.2d 841 (1986); Pioneer Nat'l Title Ins. Co. v. Cranwell, 235 Va. 597, 369 S.E.2d 678 (1988).

§ 43-5. Sufficiency of memorandum and affidavit required by § 43-4. — The memorandum and affidavit required by § 43-4 shall be sufficient if substantially in form and effect as follows:

Memorandum for Mechanic's Lien Claimed by General Contractor.

Name of owner: ....
Address of owner: ....
Name of claimant: ....
Address of claimant: ....
1. Type of materials or services furnished: ....
....
....
2. Amount claimed: $ ....
3. Type of structure on which work done or materials furnished: ....
....

900

4. Brief description and location of real property: ....
....
5. Date from which interest on the above amount is claimed:
Date: ....
.... (Name of claimant).

Affidavit.

State of Virginia,
County (or city) of ...., to wit:
    I, ... (notary or other officer) for the county (or city) afore-
said, do certify that .... claimant, or ...., agent for
claimant, this day made oath before me in my county (or city) aforesaid that
.... (the owner) is justly indebted to claimant in the sum of
.... dollars, for the consideration stated in the foregoing memorandum,
and that the same is payable as therein stated.
    Given under my hand this the .... day of ...., 19....
....(Notary Public or
                                                Magistrate, et cetera.)
(Code 1919, § 6427; 1940, p. 402; 1968, c. 568.)

Law Review. — For survey on creditors' rights in Virginia for 1989, see 23 U. Rich. L. Rev. 561 (1989).

Relation back of perfection may defeat rights of bankruptcy trustee. — So long as state law permits a relation-back type of perfection which would defeat an intervening lien creditor, 11 U.S.C. § 546(b) allows the creditor to perfect and allows the relation-back feature to defeat the rights of the bankruptcy trustee. The Virginia mechanics' lien statutes allow for such a relation back. H.T. Bowling, Inc. v. Bain, 52 Bankr. 58 (Bankr. W.D. Va. 1985), aff'd in part and rev'd in part, 64 Bankr. 581 (W.D. Va. 1986).

§ 43-6: Repealed by Acts 1968, c. 568.

§ 43-7. Perfection of lien by subcontractor; extent of lien; affirmative defense; provisions relating to time-share estates. — A. Any subcontractor, in order to perfect the lien given him by § 43-3 shall comply with § 43-4, and in addition give notice in writing to the owner of the property or his agent of the amount and character of his claim. But the amount for which a subcontractor may perfect a lien under this section shall not exceed the amount in which the owner is indebted to the general contractor at the time the notice is given, or shall thereafter become indebted to the general contractor upon his contract with the general contractor for such structure or building or railroad. It shall be an affirmative defense or affirmative partial defense, as the case may be, to a suit to perfect a lien of a subcontractor that the owner is not indebted to the general contractor or is indebted to the general contractor for less than the amount of the lien sought to be perfected.

B. Where the property referred to in subsection A hereof is a time-share unit, as defined by § 55-362, the word "agent," as used in subsection A, shall be deemed to include the developer, during the developer control period, or the time-share estate owners' association, after the developer control period.

Within ten days of receipt of the notice, the developer or the time-share estate owners' association shall mail by first class mail a copy of the notice to all time-share estate owners whose interests are affected by the subcontractor's lien on the time-share unit. Failure on the part of the developer or time-share estate owners' association to so notify the appropriate time-share estate owners within the time period set forth above shall result in the developer's or the association's being liable for the full amount of the subcontractor's claim, but such failure shall not affect the validity of any lien perfected under this section. Assessments levied by the estate owners' association to pay the liability hereby imposed shall be made only against the time-share estate owners of record in the time-share estate project at the time the liability was incurred.

C. Where the property referred to in subsection A hereof is a time-share unit, as defined by § 55-362, the memorandum required to be filed pursuant to § 43-4 need show only the name of the developer during the developer control period, or the time-share estate owners' association, after the developer control period. (Code 1919, § 6428; 1979, c. 412; 1984, c. 521.)

Law Review. — For survey of Virginia commercial law for the year 1970-1971, see 57 Va. L. Rev. 1527 (1971); for the year 1974-1975, see 61 Va. L. Rev. 1668 (1975); for the year 1975-1976, see 62 Va. L. Rev. 1375 (1976). For survey of Virginia practice and pleading for the year 1975-1976, see 62 Va. L. Rev. 1460 (1976). For survey of Virginia law on business associations for the year 1977-1978, see 64 Va. L. Rev. 1375 (1978). For survey of Virginia commercial law for the year 1978-1979, see 66 Va. L. Rev. 217 (1980).

I. General Consideration.
II. Notice.

I. GENERAL CONSIDERATION.

Optional remedies of subcontractor. — The subcontractor, under the provisions of § 43-18, may rely on the general contractor's lien or, under the provisions of this section and §§ 43-3 and 43-4, he may file and undertake to enforce his own independent lien. VNB Mtg. Corp. v. Lone Star Indus., Inc., 215 Va. 366, 209 S.E.2d 909 (1974).

Subcontractors and materialmen are not deprived of their independent liens unless they either expressly waived their lien rights or expressly accepted, or by clear implication, agreed to be bound by the general contractor's stipulation in the general contract against liens. VNB Mtg. Corp. v. Lone Star Indus., Inc., 215 Va. 366, 209 S.E.2d 909 (1974).

This section was designed to protect subcontractors, and create a liability which would not otherwise exist. Coleman v. Pearman, 159 Va. 72, 165 S.E. 371 (1932), overruled on other grounds, Mills v. Moore's Super Stores, 217 Va. 276, 227 S.E.2d 719 (1976).

But the terms of the section must be met before its benefits can be enjoyed. Coleman v. Pearman, 159 Va. 72, 165 S.E. 371 (1932), overruled on other grounds, Mills v. Moore's Super Stores, 217 Va. 276, 227 S.E.2d 719 (1976).

Substantial compliance is essential. — A substantial compliance with this section is essential to the creation of the lien. Gilman v. Ryan, 95 Va. 494, 28 S.E. 875 (1898).

There must be a substantial compliance with that portion of this chapter which relates to the creation of the lien, although the provisions with respect to its enforcement should be liberally construed. H.N. Francis & Co. v. Hotel Rueger, Inc., 125 Va. 106, 99 S.E. 690 (1919).

See Clement v. Adams Bros.-Paynes Co., 113 Va. 546, 75 S.E. 294 (1912); Maddux v. Buchanan, 121 Va. 102, 92 S.E. 830 (1917); Coleman v. Pearman, 159 Va. 72, 165 S.E. 371 (1932), overruled on other grounds, Mills v. Moore's Super Stores, 217 Va. 276, 227 S.E.2d 719 (1976).

The limitations of this section are for the protection of the owner from double liability. Concrete Ready-Mix of Lynchburg, Inc. v. County Green Ltd. Partnership, 438 F. Supp. 701 (W.D. Va. 1977), rev'd on other grounds, 604 F.2d 289 (4th Cir. 1979).

The statutory limitation of the owner's liability is designed to relieve the owner of the possibility of having to make double payment under the contract. Sinicrope v. Black Diamond Sav. & Loan Ass'n, 21 Bankr. 476 (Bankr. W.D. Va. 1982).

Under this section, the "owner" is the same person who is referred to in § 43-4. Wallace v. Brumback, 177 Va. 36, 12 S.E.2d 801 (1941).

Owner's liability on mechanics' liens is limited by statute to the amount of the retainage. Sinicrope v. Black Diamond Sav. & Loan Ass'n, 21 Bankr. 476 (Bankr. W.D. Va. 1982).

Surety's liability not affected. — The limitation of the owner's liability to the amount remaining unpaid under the contract in no way affects the liability of the surety. Sinicrope v. Black Diamond Sav. & Loan Ass'n, 21 Bankr. 476 (Bankr. W.D. Va. 1982).

Mechanics' liens cannot be perfected against public buildings and other public improvements. Thomas Somerville Co. v. Broyhill, 200 Va. 358, 105 S.E.2d 824 (1958).

Work must be performed or material furnished. — Before a subcontractor is entitled to claim a lien on a building he must, under his contract with the general contractor, have performed some work or furnished some material for which the general contractor is under contractual obligation to pay. John T. Wilson Co. v. McManus, 162 Va. 130, 173 S.E. 361 (1934).

It is apparent from the language of § 43-4 that no lien can be perfected under this section before the work for which the subcontractor engages is done, i.e., before his contract is completed. Moore v. Rolin, 89 Va. 107, 15 S.E. 520 (1892).

Owner must be indebted to general contractor. — Where it satisfactorily appears from the evidence that there was no time after notice to the defendant owner of the claim of the subcontractors when he was indebted in any amount to the general contractor, the owner was under no liability towards the subcontractors. Maddux v. Buchanan, 121 Va. 102, 92 S.E. 830 (1917).

The owner, at or after the time it was notified of the lienor's claim, was not indebted to the general contractor. It follows that the trial court did not err in ruling that the mechanic's lien could not be enforced against the owner's property. Henderson & Russell Assocs. v. Warwick Shopping Center, Inc., 217 Va. 486, 229 S.E.2d 878 (1976).

And general contractor must be indebted to subcontractor. — If the general contractor is not indebted to the subcontractor, the subcontractor is not entitled to a lien. John T. Wilson Co. v. McManus, 162 Va. 130, 173 S.E. 361 (1934).

Extent of lien is limited by amount of indebtedness. — A well-defined legislative policy in Virginia, as expressed in this section and §§ 43-9, 43-11 and 43-16, is that generally the extent of the liability of an owner to a subcontractor or subcontractors is limited to the amount in which the owner is indebted to the general contractor at the time notice to the owner is given by the subcontractor or subcontractors. This policy likely found its source in what is known as the "New York System," under which the lien of a subcontractor or materialman depends on, and is limited by, the amount remaining due the general contractor at or subsequent to notice by the subcontractor served on the owner. Nicholas v. Miller, 182 Va. 831, 30 S.E.2d 696 (1944). See Maddux v. Buchanan, 121 Va. 102, 92 S.E. 830 (1917).

The maximum amount for which the subcontractor is entitled to claim a lien is governed by the condition of accounts between the owner and the general contractor at the time notice is given. John T. Wilson Co. v. McManus, 162 Va. 130, 173 S.E. 361 (1934).

Under this section, a subcontractor may perfect his own lien, but the amount secured by this lien cannot exceed the amount in which the owner is indebted to the general contractor at

the time the notice is given, or shall thereafter become indebted to the general contractor upon his contract. Knight v. Ferrante, 202 Va. 243, 117 S.E.2d 283 (1960).

The lien of a subcontractor is limited to the amount in which the owner is indebted to the general contractor, at or after the time the owner is given notice of the subcontractor's claim. Henderson & Russell Assocs. v. Warwick Shopping Center, Inc., 217 Va. 486, 229 S.E.2d 878 (1976).

And subcontractor is bound by terms of general contract as to payment. — The settled general rule is that a subcontractor is charged with notice and bound by the terms of the general contract, and this rule applies especially to the mode and terms of payment agreed upon between the owner and the general contractor. Maddux v. Buchanan, 121 Va. 102, 92 S.E. 830 (1917).

But owner cannot defeat lien by giving contractor his negotiable notes. — The intent of the provision "But the amount for which a subcontractor may perfect a lien under this section shall not exceed the amount in which the owner is indebted to the general contractor at the time the notice is given," was to limit the owner's liability to the contract price of the building subject to any payments made to the general contractor for labor and materials furnished and used as its construction progressed; but the owner cannot deprive subcontractors of the lien given them by this chapter by giving to the general contractor, in payment for labor and materials, his personal obligation, evidenced by his negotiable notes. Kinnier Co. v. Cofer, 13 Va. L. Reg. (n.s.) 238 (1927).

When the owner gives the general contractor his notes for the purpose of raising money to secure labor and purchase material for the construction of a building, and the general contractor negotiates the notes to a person who knows their purpose, it seems that this section gives the holder notice of the rights of the subcontractors, and he is bound to see to the application of the proceeds of the notes. He cannot accept the notes in discharge of an antecedent debt of the general contractor. Kinnier Co. v. Cofer, 13 Va. L. Reg. (n.s.) 238 (1927).

Failure to allege indebtedness of owner to general contractor does not render the bill demurrable. Blanton v. Owen, 203 Va. 73, 122 S.E.2d 650 (1961).

Liens of subcontractors not defeated by stipulation in general contract. — The fact that the contract stipulated that the final payment to the general contractor was not to be due until he had delivered to the owner a complete release of all liens or receipts in full covering all labor and materials for which a lien could be filed, and that this had not been done, did not defeat the liens of the subcontractors.

Knight v. Ferrante, 202 Va. 243, 117 S.E.2d 283 (1960).

Price of material guaranteed by owner credited on balance due contractor. — Under this section, where the owner guarantees the amount of material used by the contractors in the construction of a house, he is entitled to credit of that amount on balance due the contractor as against a mechanics' lien filed thereafter. Thomas & Co. v. McCauley, 143 Va. 451, 130 S.E. 396 (1925). See Schrieber, Sons & Co. v. Citizens Bank, 99 Va. 257, 38 S.E. 134 (1901).

Extra work as separate transaction. — Extra work not covered or contemplated by the original contract, though performed by the same general contractor, is to be considered a separate and distinct transaction in controversy between the owner and the subcontractor. Schrieber, Sons & Co. v. Citizens Bank, 99 Va. 257, 38 S.E. 134 (1901).

Retention of percentage by owner for owner's benefit alone. — The reservation by the owner of a percentage of the cost of construction of a building until its completion, with the right to supply any deficiency and deduct the cost from any money due or to become due under the contract, is for the benefit of the owner alone, and not for subcontractors who may be thereafter employed. Thus the amount of a subcontractor's lien cannot be determined by the amount of the reserved sum, where orders drawn upon the owner by the general contractor in favor of subcontractors were paid by the owner before the lien in question was perfected, notwithstanding the fact that, under the terms of the contract, the reserved sum was not due and payable to the general contractor until after the date on which the lien was perfected. Schrieber, Sons & Co. v. Citizens Bank, 99 Va. 257, 38 S.E. 134 (1901).

Liability of owner to contractor's employee. — Where owner had paid contractor more than contract called for, owner was not liable to contractor's employee for wages or because of a mechanics' lien filed by him. Monk v. Walters, 195 Va. 246, 78 S.E.2d 202 (1953).

Action for defamation lies for premature filing of lien. — Where a subcontractor files a mechanics' lien before completion of the work, he is liable to an action for damages for injuries thereby done the contractor. In such an action, however, the declaration should charge some special damage to the plaintiff, as the language of the alleged lien does not necessarily import injurious defamation. Moore v. Rolin, 89 Va. 107, 15 S.E. 520 (1892).

And note induced by threat to file lien prematurely is without consideration. — Where subcontractors had no right, in view of this section, to file a mechanics' lien, a note given because of a threat that they would file such a lien was without consideration. Hooff v. Paine, 172 Va. 481, 2 S.E.2d 313 (1939).

Relation back of perfection may defeat rights of bankruptcy trustee. — So long as state law permits a relation-back type of perfection which would defeat an intervening lien creditor, 11 U.S.C. § 546(b) allows the creditor to perfect and allows the relation-back feature to defeat the rights of the bankruptcy trustee. The Virginia mechanics' lien statutes allow for such a relation back. H.T. Bowling, Inc. v. Bain, 52 Bankr. 58 (Bankr. W.D. Va. 1985), aff'd in part and rev'd in part, 64 Bankr. 581 (W.D. Va. 1986).

Evidence insufficient to support affirmative defense of payment. — Where owner asserted that debt arose under a separate oral contract for work which did not include work performed by subcontractors, the evidence reflected that these subcontractors provided goods both for the construction of the sewer outfall and for Section 1 work. More importantly, considering (1) the lack of differentiation between the two contracts in the record-keeping methods utilized by the owner and general contractor, (2) the subcontractors' lack of knowledge and control over the allocation of goods and services to a specific contract, and (3) the language in the release for both the sewer outfall and Section 1 payments that materials were provided for "the utilities for the entire subdivision," the trial court did not err in holding that there was only one contract as to the owner and the subcontractors and that owner failed to establish its affirmative defense of full or partial payment to the subcontractor's lien. Thompson v. Air Power, Inc., 248 Va. 364, 448 S.E.2d 598 (1994).

Applied in Southern Residence Corp. v. City Supply Co., 160 Va. 660, 169 S.E. 579 (1933); Surf Realty Corp. v. Standing, 195 Va. 431, 78 S.E.2d 901 (1953); In re Romanac, 245 F. Supp. 882 (W.D. Va. 1965); Waterval v. William Doolan Elevator Serv., Inc., 212 Va. 114, 181 S.E.2d 637 (1971); Glen Constr. Co. v. Bank of Vienna, 410 F. Supp. 402 (E.D. Va. 1976); Kayhoe Constr. Corp. v. United Va. Bank, 220 Va. 285, 257 S.E.2d 837 (1979); Penrod & Stauffer Bldg. Sys. v. Metro Printing & Mailing Servs., Inc., 229 Va. 150, 326 S.E.2d 662 (1985); E.E. Stump Well Drilling, Inc. v. Willis, 230 Va. 445, 338 S.E.2d 841 (1986).

II. NOTICE.

The notice required by this section affords protection to the owner who is not in privity of contract with the subcontractor, so that he may not be required to pay twice for the same work and materials. Concrete Ready-Mix of Lynchburg, Inc. v. County Green Ltd. Partnership, 438 F. Supp. 701 (W.D. Va. 1977), rev'd on other grounds, 604 F.2d 289 (4th Cir. 1979).

Only when the owner receives the notice to which he is entitled does he incur a

legal obligation to the subcontractor. Mills v. Moore's Super Stores, 217 Va. 276, 227 S.E.2d 719 (1976).

Actual knowledge of owner is no substitute for written notice. — If a subcontractor desires to obtain a lien, or to bind the owner personally, he is required by the express terms of this section and § 43-11 to give written notice of the amount and character of his claim. Knowledge acquired by the owner through other means than a written notice from the subcontractor, cannot be substituted for the statutory requirement, in the absence of affirmative evidence showing that the giving of written notice was waived. Failure to perform this essential requirement of this section is fatal to the establishment of the lien. Coleman v. Pearman, 159 Va. 72, 165 S.E. 371 (1932), overruled on other grounds, Mills v. Moore's Super Stores, 217 Va. 276, 227 S.E.2d 719 (1976).

There is no requirement in this section that written notice to the owner shall be given within any specified time. Mills v. Moore's Super Stores, 217 Va. 276, 227 S.E.2d 719 (1976).

Sufficient compliance with notice requirements. — Where the first notices to the owners were served by two subcontractors more than 60 days after the work was terminated, but before the chancery suit was instituted to enforce the liens and additional notices were served after the suit was commenced, but before there was any change of position by the owners, there was sufficient compliance by these subcontractors with the notice requirements of this section. Mills v. Moore's Super Stores, 217 Va. 276, 227 S.E.2d 719 (1976) (decided under former § 43-7).

§ 43-8. Sufficiency of memorandum, affidavit and notice required by § 43-7. — The memorandum, affidavit and notice required by § 43-7 shall be sufficient if substantially in form and effect as follows:

Memorandum for Mechanic's Lien Claimed by Subcontractor.

Name of owner: ....
Address of owner: ....
Name of general contractor (if any): ....
Name of claimant: ....
Address of claimant: ....
1. Type of materials or services furnished: ....
....
2. Amount claimed: $...
3. Type of structure on which work done or materials furnished: ....
4. Brief description and location of real property: ....
....
5. Date from which interest on above amount is claimed:
Date: ....
..............................(Name of claimant).

Affidavit.

State of Virginia,
County (or city) of .... to wit:
I, ... (notary or other officer) for the county (or city) aforesaid, do certify that ...., claimant, or ...., agent for claimant, this day made oath before me in my county (or city) aforesaid that .... is justly indebted to claimant in the sum of .... dollars, for the consideration stated in the foregoing memorandum, and that the same is payable as therein stated.
Given under my hand this the ...... day of ...., 19....
.... (Notary Public or
Magistrate, et cetera.)

Notice.

To .... (owner).

You are hereby notified that .... (general contractor) is indebted
to me in the sum of .... dollars ($..........) with interest thereon from
the .... day of ...., 19..., for work done (or materials furnished, as the
case may be,) in and about the construction (or removal, etc.,) of a
.... (describe structure, whether dwelling, store, or etc.,)
which he has contracted to construct (or remove, etc.,) for you or on property
owned by you in the county (or city) of ...., and that I have duly
recorded a mechanic's lien for the same.

Given under my hand this the .... day of ...., 19....

.... (Subcontractor).

(Code 1919, § 6428; 1968, c. 568.)

Law Review. — For survey of Virginia practice and pleading for the year 1975-1976, see 62 Va. L. Rev. 1460 (1976). For survey on creditors' rights in Virginia for 1989, see 23 U. Rich. L. Rev. 561 (1989).

Relation back of perfection may defeat rights of bankruptcy trustee. — So long as state law permits a relation-back type of perfection which would defeat an intervening lien creditor, 11 U.S.C. § 546(b) allows the creditor to perfect and allows the relation-back feature to defeat the rights of the bankruptcy trustee. The Virginia mechanics' lien statutes allow for such a relation back. H.T. Bowling, Inc. v. Bain, 52 Bankr. 58 (Bankr. W.D. Va. 1985), aff'd in part and rev'd in part, 64 Bankr. 581 (W.D. Va. 1986).

§ 43-9. Perfection of lien by person performing labor or furnishing materials for a subcontractor; extent of lien. — Any person performing labor or furnishing materials for a subcontractor, in order to perfect the lien given him by § 43-3, shall comply with the provisions of § 43-4, and in addition thereto give notice in writing to the owner of the property, or his agent, and to the general contractor, or his agent, of the amount and character of his claim. But the amount for which a lien may be perfected by such person shall not exceed the amount for which such subcontractor could himself claim a lien under § 43-7. (Code 1919, § 6429.)

Law Review. — For survey of Virginia commercial law for the year 1970-1971, see 57 Va. L. Rev. 1527 (1971); for the year 1975-1976, see 62 Va. L. Rev. 1375 (1976). For survey of Virginia practice and pleading for the year 1975-1976, see 62 Va. L. Rev. 1460 (1976). For survey of Virginia commercial law for the year 1977-1978, see 64 Va. L. Rev. 1383 (1978).

The language of this section is plain and unambiguous, and its meaning reasonably clear. John T. Wilson Co. v. McManus, 162 Va. 130, 173 S.E. 361 (1934).

Sub-subcontractors are placed on same basis as subcontractors. — By this section the legislature has placed those who under agreement with a subcontractor perform work or furnish material used in the building on the same basis as a subcontractor. John T. Wilson Co. v. McManus, 162 Va. 130, 173 S.E. 361 (1934).

Lien must be filed within time prescribed by § 43-4. — A claim of mechanics' lien filed by a sub-subcontractor more than 60 days after work on a building has terminated and the owner has accepted it, and settled with the general contractor, comes too late. The filing of the claim within the time prescribed by § 43-4 is one of the essential requisites in perfecting the lien. If not so filed no lien is acquired. Furst-Kerber Cut Stone Co. v. Wells, 116 Va. 95, 81 S.E. 22 (1914).

General contractor must be indebted to subcontractor. — By virtue of the last sentence of this section, one furnishing materials or performing labor for a subcontractor is not entitled to lien unless the general contractor is indebted at the time the notice is served, or thereafter becomes indebted, to the subcontractor under the contract. John T. Wilson Co. v. McManus, 162 Va. 130, 173 S.E. 361 (1934).

Under this section, the "owner" is the same person who is referred to in § 43-4. Wallace v. Brumback, 177 Va. 36, 12 S.E.2d 801 (1941).

Mechanics' liens cannot be perfected against public buildings and other public improvements. Thomas Somerville Co. v. Broyhill, 200 Va. 358, 105 S.E.2d 824 (1958).

Effect of failure to perfect lien. — If a materialman fails to perfect a mechanics' lien on the building into which his materials are placed, the amount due him therefor by a subcontractor is a general unsecured debt due to the materialman, and upon the bankruptcy of the subcontractor, the amount due him by the general contractor passes to his trustee as assets of the bankrupt. Furst-Kerber Cut Stone Co. v. Wells, 116 Va. 95, 81 S.E. 22 (1914).

Relation back of perfection may defeat rights of bankruptcy trustee. — So long as state law permits a relation-back type of perfection which would defeat an intervening lien creditor, 11 U.S.C. § 546(b) allows the creditor to perfect and allows the relation-back feature to defeat the rights of the bankruptcy trustee. The Virginia mechanics' lien statutes allow for

such a relation back. H.T. Bowling, Inc. v. Bain, 52 Bankr. 58 (Bankr. W.D. Va. 1985), aff'd in part and rev'd in part, 64 Bankr. 581 (W.D. Va. 1986).

Applied in Glen Constr. Co. v. Bank of Vienna, 410 F. Supp. 402 (E.D. Va. 1976); Kayhoe Constr. Corp. v. United Va. Bank, 220 Va. 285, 257 S.E.2d 837 (1979); E.E. Stump Well Drilling, Inc. v. Willis, 230 Va. 445, 338 S.E.2d 841 (1986).

§ 43-10. Sufficiency of memorandum, affidavit and notice required by § 43-9. — The memorandum, affidavit and notice required by § 43-9 shall be sufficient if substantially in form and effect as follows:

Memorandum for Mechanic's Lien Claimed by Sub-subcontractor.

Name of owner: ....
Address of owner: ....
Name of general contractor (if any) and subcontractor:
....
Name of claimant: ....
Address of claimant: ....
1. Type of materials or services furnished: ....
....
2. Amount claimed: $ ....
3. Type of structure on which work done or materials furnished: ....
4. Brief description and location of real property: ....
....
5. Date from which interest on above amount is claimed:
Date: ....

             .... (Name of claimant).
             .... *(Signature of claimant or agent for claimant).*

Affidavit.

State of Virginia,
County (or city) of ...., to wit:
    I, ...(notary or other officer) for the county (or city) aforesaid do certify that .... claimant, or ...., agent for claimant, this day made oath before me in my county (or city) aforesaid that ....is justly indebted to claimant in the sum of ....dollars for the consideration stated in the foregoing memorandum, and that the same is payable as therein stated.
    Given under my hand this the .... day of ...., 19....
             .... (Notary Public or
             Magistrate, et cetera.)

Notice.

To .... (owner) and ....
             (general contractor):
    You are hereby notified that ...., a subcontractor under you, said ....(general contractor) for the construction (or removal, etc.,) of a ....(describe structure) for you, or on property owned by you, said ....(owner) is indebted to me in the sum of .... dollars ($ ....) with interest thereon from the .day of ...., 19....., for work done (or materials furnished) in and about the construction (or removal, etc.,) of said ....(naming

structure), situate in the county (or city) of ....Virginia, and that I have duly recorded a mechanic's lien for the same.

Given under my hand this the .... day of ...., 19.......
.... (Sub-subcontractor).
(Code 1919, § 6429; 1968, c. 568; 1984, c. 647.)

Law Review. — For survey of Virginia practice and pleading for the year 1975-1976, see 62 Va. L. Rev. 1460 (1976). For survey on creditors' rights in Virginia for 1989, see 23 U. Rich. L. Rev. 561 (1989).

Relation back of perfection may defeat rights of bankruptcy trustee. — So long as state law permits a relation-back type of perfection which would defeat an intervening lien creditor, 11 U.S.C. § 546(b) allows the creditor to perfect and allows the relation-back feature to defeat the rights of the bankruptcy trustee. The Virginia mechanic's lien statutes allow for such a relation back. H.T. Bowling, Inc. v. Bain, 52 Bankr. 58 (Bankr. W.D. Va. 1985), aff'd in part and rev'd in part, 64 Bankr. 581 (W.D. Va. 1986).

§ 43-11. How owner or general contractor made personally liable to subcontractor, laborer or materialman.

— Any subcontractor or person furnishing labor or material to the general contractor or subcontractor, may give notice in writing to the owner or his agent or the general contractor, stating the nature and character of his contract and the probable amount of his claim, and if such subcontractor, or person furnishing labor or material shall at any time after the work is done or material furnished by him and before the expiration of thirty days from the time such building or structure is completed or the work thereon otherwise terminated furnish the owner thereof or his agent and also the general contractor, or the general contractor alone in case he is the only one notified, with a correct account, verified by affidavit, of his claim against the general contractor or subcontractor, for work done or materials furnished and of the amount due, the owner, or the general contractor, if he alone was notified, shall be personally liable to the claimant for the amount due to the subcontractor or persons furnishing labor or material by the general contractor or subcontractor, provided the same does not exceed the sum in which the owner is indebted to the general contractor at the time the notice is given or may thereafter become indebted by virtue of his contract with the general contractor, or in case the general contractor alone is notified the sum in which he is indebted to the subcontractor at the time the notice is given or may thereafter become indebted by virtue of his contract with the general contractor. But the amount which a person supplying labor or material to a subcontractor can claim shall not exceed the amount for which such subcontractor could file his claim.

Any bona fide agreement for deductions by the owner because of the failure or refusal of the general contractor to comply with his contract shall be binding upon such subcontractor, laborer or materialman.

The provisions of this section are subject to the qualification that before any such personal liability of the owner or general contractor herein provided for shall be binding the notice herein required, with such return thereon as is sufficient under § 8.01-325, shall be recorded and indexed as provided in § 43-4.1 in the appropriate clerk's office; or the notice herein required shall be mailed by registered or certified mail to and received by the owner or general contractor upon whom personal liability is sought to be imposed, and a return receipt therefor showing delivery to the addressee shall be prima facie evidence of receipt. (1924, p. 658; Michie Code 1942, § 6429a; 1968, c. 568.)

Law Review. — For survey of Virginia commercial law for the year 1975-1976, see 62 Va. L. Rev. 1375 (1976).

This section must be construed in con-nection with §§ 43-19 through 43-21. DeWitt v. Coffey, 150 Va. 365, 143 S.E. 710 (1928).

There is no conflict between this section

and §§ 43-19 through 43-21. DeWitt v. Coffey, 150 Va. 365, 143 S.E. 710 (1928).

This section is not exclusive. — The subcontractor can, by mutual agreement with the owner, still have the latter guarantee his account, and if the owner does so, he is entitled to deduct the amount so guaranteed from the contract price, both as against the general contractor and the other subcontractors. This rule applies especially when it is reasonably necessary to do so in order to complete the building, and this is true even when it would result in a preference of one subcontractor over another. Nicholas v. Miller, 182 Va. 831, 30 S.E.2d 696 (1944).

Laborers and materialmen may obtain additional security in three ways. — Laborers and materialmen unwilling to extend credit to a general contractor may obtain additional security: (1) by taking the steps prescribed by this section to fasten personal responsibility upon the owner; (2) by filing separate and independent liens under § 43-7; (3) by taking advantage of a lien perfected by the general contractor. Coleman v. Pearman, 159 Va. 72, 165 S.E. 371 (1932), overruled on other grounds, Mills v. Moore's Super Stores, 217 Va. 276, 227 S.E.2d 719 (1976).

The methods open to materialmen for obtaining additional security for their claims out of the funds due or to become due under a building contract are: (1) by taking the steps prescribed in this section to fasten personal liability upon the owner; (2) by filing separate and independent liens under § 43-9; and (3) by taking advantage of a lien perfected by the general contractor. Perrin & Martin, Inc. v. United States, 233 F. Supp. 1016 (E.D. Va. 1964).

Deduction of obligation owner required to incur to complete building. — While it is true that under this section the owner, under certain conditions, may be made personally liable to a subcontractor, yet this liability is not permitted to exceed the sum in which the owner is indebted to the general contractor at the time he receives notice of the mechanics' lien, and such indebtedness excludes the obligation the owner may have been required to incur in order to complete the building, so that what remains in the owner's hands after deducting such an obligation is applicable to the liens of the subcontractors, under this section. Nicholas v. Miller, 182 Va. 831, 30 S.E.2d 696 (1944). See § 43-16.

Applied in Spring Constr. Co. v. Harris, 614 F.2d 374 (4th Cir. 1980); Penrod & Stauffer Bldg. Sys. v. Metro Printing & Mailing Servs., Inc., 229 Va. 150, 326 S.E.2d 662 (1985).

§ 43-12: Repealed by Acts 1968, c. 568.

§ 43-13. Funds paid to general contractor or subcontractor must be used to pay persons performing labor or furnishing material. — Any contractor or subcontractor or any officer, director or employee of such contractor or subcontractor who shall, with intent to defraud, retain or use the funds, or any part thereof, paid by the owner or his agent, the contractor or lender to such contractor or by the owner or his agent, the contractor or lender to a subcontractor under any contract for the construction, removal, repair or improvement of any building or structure permanently annexed to the freehold, for any other purpose than to pay persons performing labor upon or furnishing material for such construction, repair, removal or improvement, shall be guilty of larceny in appropriating such funds for any other use while any amount for which the contractor or subcontractor may be liable or become liable under his contract for such labor or materials remains unpaid, and may be prosecuted upon complaint of any person or persons who have not been fully paid any amount due them.

The use by any such contractor or subcontractor or any officer, director or employee of such contractor or subcontractor of any moneys paid under the contract, before paying all amounts due or to become due for labor performed or material furnished for such building or structure, for any other purpose than paying such amounts, shall be prima facie evidence of intent to defraud. (1932, p. 483; Michie Code 1942, § 6429b; 1968, c. 568; 1980, c. 390; 1982, c. 391; 1992, c. 713; 1998, c. 754.)

The 1998 amendment, in the first paragraph, substituted "contractor or subcontractor" for "contractor, subcontractor" in three places, deleted "or owner-developer, as defined in § 54.1-1100" preceding "or any officer," and deleted "or owner-developer" preceding "who shall, with intent," deleted "or owner-developer" preceding "or by the owner," deleted "or owner developer" preceding "may be liable"; and in the second paragraph, substituted "contractor or subcontractor" for "contractor, subcontractor" in two places, and deleted "or owner-developer" following "contractor or subcontractor" in two places.

Law Review. — For survey of Virginia commercial law for the year 1975-1976, see 62 Va. L. Rev. 1375 (1976).

Object of section. — This section has for its object additional protection and security to subcontractors, laborers, or materialmen furnishing labor or material for work undertaken by the contractor, as well as to relieve the owner of claims, liens, and litigation. Overstreet v. Commonwealth, 193 Va. 104, 67 S.E.2d 875 (1951).

This section was enacted in the exercise of the police power, in that its object is the prevention of fraud, and it becomes a part of every contract covered by its terms. Overstreet v. Commonwealth, 193 Va. 104, 67 S.E.2d 875 (1951).

The object of this section is to prevent the misappropriation of funds, and it is not designed to imprison for debt. Overstreet v. Commonwealth, 193 Va. 104, 67 S.E.2d 875 (1951).

The purpose of this section is not for collection of the debt but punishment for the fraud. Salecki v. Virginia, 51 Bankr. 364 (Bankr. E.D. Va. 1985).

This section does not expressly provide for any private right of action imposing civil liability, and a private right of action cannot be implied by the provisions of this section. Vansant & Gusler, Inc. v. Washington, 245 Va. 356, 429 S.E.2d 31 (1993).

This section is a criminal statute. This statute extends the definition of larceny in Virginia beyond the traditional common law meaning. Specifically, this section determines that a contractor's use of funds for a purpose other than to pay the provider of materials is prima facie evidence of larceny. The purpose of the statute is to punish fraud; prosecution of a contractor for violating this code section does not affect the debt itself. Builders Supply Co. v. Lane, 115 Bankr. 81 (Bankr. E.D. Va. 1990).

This section does not interfere with the liberty to contract, since contractors enter into their engagements with the knowledge of the statute just as they enter into their engagements with the knowledge of other statutes relating to mechanics' and materialmen's liens. Overstreet v. Commonwealth, 193 Va. 104, 67 S.E.2d 875 (1951).

It is the intent to defraud and not the indebtedness which is made the determining feature in establishing guilt under this section. Overstreet v. Commonwealth, 193 Va. 104, 67 S.E.2d 875 (1951); Perrin & Martin,

Inc. v. United States, 233 F. Supp. 1016 (E.D. Va. 1964).

A prosecution under this section does not affect the debt owed by the contractor. Overstreet v. Commonwealth, 193 Va. 104, 67 S.E.2d 875 (1951).

Intent of second paragraph. — The second paragraph of this section was intended to relieve the Commonwealth from the necessity of producing further specific proof of intent to defraud, when circumstances reveal personal use of moneys paid under contract by the contractor. Overstreet v. Commonwealth, 193 Va. 104, 67 S.E.2d 875 (1951).

Former penalty provisions construed. — See Overstreet v. Commonwealth, 193 Va. 104, 67 S.E.2d 875 (1951).

Interpretation of civil statutes not changed by Overstreet v. Commonwealth. — Overstreet v. Commonwealth, 193 Va. 104, 67 S.E.2d 875 (1951), does not, by the application of a criminal statute, change the Supreme Court's interpretation of civil statutes governing the relationship of subcontractors and materialmen. Perrin & Martin, Inc. v. United States, 233 F. Supp. 1016 (E.D. Va. 1964).

Funds not held in trust. — Funds retained by a contractor from payments made by the owner and owing to the subcontractors are not held in trust for the benefit of the subcontractors. Glen Constr. Co. v. Bank of Vienna, 410 F. Supp. 402 (E.D. Va. 1976), rev'd on other grounds, 557 F.2d 1050 (4th Cir. 1977).

While this criminal statute creates a moral obligation, it contains no language creating a legal trust for the benefit of materialmen and laborers. Nor does it purport to affect or extend the rights and remedies otherwise available in a civil proceeding to materialmen and workmen under the mechanics' lien statutes. Kayhoe Constr. Corp. v. United Va. Bank, 220 Va. 285, 257 S.E.2d 837 (1979).

Therefore, a general contractor would not be entitled under a trust theory to recovery on behalf of two unpaid suppliers of a subcontractor of payments received by the subcontractor as partial payments to the suppliers but paid by the subcontractor to the bank. Kayhoe Constr. Corp. v. United Va. Bank, 220 Va. 285, 257 S.E.2d 837 (1979).

Bankruptcy court refused to enjoin a prosecution under this section against a debtor, where the court was unable to conclude that the Commonwealth was using a criminal proceeding to compel payment of a debt discharged in bankruptcy. Salecki v. Virginia, 51 Bankr. 364 (Bankr. E.D. Va. 1985).

Where criminal action under this section is instituted some time prior to filing of bankruptcy petition, a rational conclusion may be reached that its purpose was not to force collection of the debt. Where the criminal action is instituted at approximately the same time the rationalization is less clear and not as compelling. Salecki v. Virginia, 51 Bankr. 364 (Bankr. E.D. Va. 1985).

Applied in Moseley Assocs. v. Lieberman, 14

Bankr. 881 (Bankr. E.D. Va. 1981); Greenwalt v. Commonwealth, 224 Va. 498, 297 S.E.2d 709 (1982).

§ 43-13.1. Use of lien waiver form; forgery or signing without authority.

— Any person who knowingly presents a waiver of lien form to an owner, his agent, contractor, lender, or title company for the purpose of obtaining funds or title insurance and who forges or signs without authority the name of any person listed thereon shall be guilty of a felony and punished as provided in § 18.2-172. (1968, c. 568.)

§ 43-13.2. When affidavit of payment required of owner prior to sale.

— A person who is both the owner of a one- or two-family residential dwelling unit and either a developer of such property, a contractor in connection with the development or improvement of such property or a contractor or subcontractor furnishing labor or material in connection with the development or improvement of such property shall, at the time of settlement on the sale of such property, provide the purchaser with an affidavit stating either (i) that all persons performing labor or furnishing materials in connection with the improvements on such property and with whom such owner is in privity of contract have been paid in full or (ii) the name, address and amount payable or claimed to be payable to any person so performing labor or furnishing materials and with whom such owner is in privity of contract. Willful failure to provide such statement or any willful material misrepresentation with respect to such a statement which causes a monetary loss to a financial institution, title company, contractor, subcontractor, supplier, owner, mechanics' lien agent or any other person or institution shall be punishable as a Class 5 felony. (1992, cc. 779, 787.)

Cross references. — As to punishment for Class 5 felonies, see § 18.2-10.

Effective date. — This section is effective June 1, 1992.

§ 43-13.3. Affidavit of payment required of owner prior to sale or refinance; penalty.

— Any person who is the owner of a one-family or two-family residential dwelling unit not included within the scope of § 43-13.2 shall, at the time of settlement on the sale of such property, provide the purchaser, or lender in the case of a permanent loan or refinance, with an affidavit stating either (i) that all persons performing labor or furnishing materials in connection with any improvements on such property within 120 days prior to the date of settlement and with whom such owner is in privity of contract have been paid in full, or (ii) the name, address and amount payable or claimed to be payable to any person so performing labor or furnishing materials and with whom such owner is in privity of contract. Any willful material misrepresentation in the affidavit which causes a monetary loss to any financial institution, title company, or purchaser shall be punishable as a Class 3 misdemeanor. (1994, c. 388.)

Cross references. — As to punishment for Class 3 misdemeanors, see § 18.2-11.

§ 43-14: Repealed by Acts 1968, c. 568.

§ 43-14.1. Service of notices.

— Any notice authorized or required by this chapter, except the notice required by § 43-11, may be served by any sheriff or constable who shall make return of the time and manner of service; or any such notice may be served by certified or registered mail and a return receipt therefor shall be prima facie evidence of receipt. (1968, c. 568; 1971, Ex. Sess., c. 155.)

For injunction against state criminal proceedings under this section to issue, extraordinary circumstances must be present, such as where injunction is necessary in aid of a court's jurisdiction or to effect or protect judgments; situations when an individual facing prosecution in state court can prove he will suffer irreparable damages, i.e., where ". . . the danger of irreparable loss is both great and immediate . . ."; or, finally, where the threat to the plaintiff's federally protected rights cannot be eliminated by his defense against a single criminal prosecution. Bratten v. Sciortino, 55 Bankr. 577 (Bankr. E.D. Va. 1985).

§ 43-15. Inaccuracies in memorandum or description not affecting lien.

— No inaccuracy in the memorandum filed, or in the description of the property to be covered by the lien, shall invalidate the lien, if the property can be reasonably identified by the description given and the memorandum conforms substantially to the requirements of §§ 43-5, 43-8 and 43-10, respectively, and is not wilfully false. (Code 1919, § 6431.)

Law Review. — For article on title examination in Virginia, see 17 U. Rich. L. Rev. 229 (1983).

Purpose of the description is to enable an owner, purchaser, or creditor to identify the property on which the lien is claimed. Penrod & Stauffer Bldg. Sys. v. Metro Printing & Mailing Servs., Inc., 229 Va. 150, 326 S.E.2d 662 (1985).

Defects not mentioned in this section are not cured. — The legislature in this section having designated but two defects that could be disregarded, it would seem that, under the doctrine of inclusio unius, exclusio alterius, it intended that defects not mentioned were to be regarded. Clement v. Adams Bros.-Paynes Co., 113 Va. 546, 75 S.E. 294 (1912).

Duty to place lien only upon property worked and no more. — Where a mechanic files a memorandum of mechanic's lien against two or more parcels but has not worked on all the parcels and where the mechanic attempts to enforce that lien against the several properties, that lien must be declared invalid in its entirety since it is the mechanic's duty to place his lien upon the property on which he worked and no more. Woodington Elec., Inc. v. Lincoln Sav. & Loan Ass'n, 238 Va. 623, 385 S.E.2d 872 (1989).

Substantial compliance is essential. — To obtain the benefit of this section the provisions of §§ 43-5, 43-8 and 43-10 must be substantially complied with. H.N. Francis & Co. v. Hotel Rueger, Inc., 125 Va. 106, 99 S.E. 690 (1919).

By this section a substantial compliance is declared to be sufficient, but nothing less than a substantial compliance will answer. Gilman v. Ryan, 95 Va. 494, 28 S.E. 875 (1898).

§ 43-16. What owner may do when contractor fails or refuses to complete building, etc.

— If the owner is compelled to complete his building, structure, or railroad, or any part thereof undertaken by a general contractor in consequence of the failure or refusal of the general contractor to do so, the amount expended by the owner for such completion shall have priority over all mechanics' liens which have been or may be placed on such building, structure, or railroad by such general contractor, a subcontractor under him, or any person furnishing labor or materials to either of them. (Code 1919, § 6432.)

The legislative intent implicit in this section is to permit an owner who has not completed a building project that has been abandoned by a defaulting contractor to set off against withheld funds the cost of completion. Henderson & Russell Assocs. v. Warwick Shopping Center, Inc., 217 Va. 486, 229 S.E.2d 878 (1976).

Owner's right does not depend upon contract. — Independent of any contract stipulation, the owner may supply any deficiencies in the performance of agreements in a building contract and deduct the cost from any money due or to become due to the contractor, and under this section the owner has this right as against mechanics' liens. Thomas & Co. v. McCauley, 143 Va. 451, 130 S.E. 396 (1925).

Amount guaranteed by owner to subcontractor to complete building has priority. — If a subcontractor is unwilling to continue his work on the building because of the credit standing of the general contractor, under this section the owner may complete the building, and may obligate himself to the subcontractor to do so, in order that the work may go on, and the amount for which the owner is required to so obligate himself takes priority over all other mechanics' liens. Nicholas v. Miller, 182 Va. 831, 30 S.E.2d 696 (1944); Anderson v. White, 183 Va. 302, 32 S.E.2d 72 (1944).

Surety who completes contract does not take priority over lienors. — Where a surety under its contract of suretyship, upon default of its principal, a building contractor, completes the contract, the surety's relation to the owner is identical with that of the original contractor, and in such a case it is the right as well as the duty of the owner to prevent any diversion of the funds from those who had perfected statutory liens upon the structure. Their right to have their liens discharged out of the unpaid balance in the hands of the owner is as clear against the surety as it would have been against the contractor principal. Electric Transmission Co. v. Pennington Gap Bank, Inc., 137 Va. 94, 119 S.E. 99 (1923).

For he succeeds to rights of contractor, not owner. — A surety succeeds to the rights of the contractor, and it cannot consistently be held that he at the same time succeeds to the rights of the owner, to use the balance due and to become due on the contract by it for the completion of the structure according to the contract, to the exclusion of mechanics' liens, as the interest of the surety as the successor of the contractor is adverse to the interest of the owner. Electric Transmission Co. v. Pennington Gap Bank, Inc., 137 Va. 94, 119 S.E. 99 (1923).

Owner must adduce evidence as to cost of completion. — In order for an owner to take advantage of the provisions of this section, he must adduce evidence as to the cost of completion, whether or not the building has been completed. Henderson & Russell Assocs. v. Warwick Shopping Center, Inc., 217 Va. 486, 229 S.E.2d 878 (1976).

The burden is on the owner to go forward with the evidence and show what claims, if any, he has against the remaining fund. If the owner completes the building and shows that the cost of doing so has exhausted the fund, the liens of the subcontractors would be wiped out under the express terms of this section. But where the owner did not complete the building and did not offer any evidence as to the cost of completion, there was no evidence that the owner had any setoff or counterclaims against the funds which he was withholding from the general contractor. In the absence of such evidence the lower court correctly held that the owner was indebted to the general contractor in a sum exceeding the aggregate amount of the subcontractors' claims. Knight v. Ferrante, 202 Va. 243, 117 S.E.2d 283 (1960).

Equitable interest must be recorded. — The mechanics' lien statutes and the recording statutes must be read together, with the result that the owner of an equitable interest is protected by this section only if the contract or other document evidencing his interest is recorded. Where owner of equitable interest did not record her contract before mechanics' lien was filed, she was not eligible for the priority granted by this section. E.E. Stump Well Drilling, Inc. v. Willis, 230 Va. 445, 338 S.E.2d 841 (1986).

Applied in Southern Residence Corp. v. City Supply Co., 160 Va. 660, 169 S.E. 579 (1933).

§ 43-17. Limitation on suit to enforce lien. — No suit to enforce any lien perfected under §§ 43-4, 43-5 and 43-7 to 43-10 shall be brought after six months from the time when the memorandum of lien was recorded or after sixty days from the time the building, structure or railroad was completed or the work thereon otherwise terminated, whichever time shall last occur; provided, however, that the filing of a petition to enforce any such lien in any suit wherein such petition may be properly filed shall be regarded as the institution of a suit under this section; and, provided further, that nothing herein shall extend the time within which such lien may be perfected. (Code 1919, § 6433; 1926, p. 43; 1956, c. 399.)

Cross references. — As to limitation of actions generally, see §§ 8.01-228 through 8.01-256.

Perfection statute contrasted with enforcement statutes. — A lien created by § 43-3 is one in derogation of the common law. Once perfected in accordance with § 43-4, the lien can be enforced by suit brought as provided in this section and § 43-22. In Virginia provisions of the enforcement statutes are to be construed liberally while the requirements of the perfection statute are to be construed strictly. American Std. Homes Corp. v. Reinecke, 245 Va. 113, 425 S.E.2d 515 (1993).

Expiration of right. — Where a statute creates a right unknown at common law and makes a time limitation the essence of the right as well as a constriction upon the remedy, the right expires upon the expiration of the limitation; and the expiration of the right is an absolute defense which can be asserted either by demurrer or by plea of the statute of limitations. Neff v. Garrard, 216 Va. 496, 219 S.E.2d 878 (1975).

The filing of a mechanic's lien is a judicial proceeding entitling filer to an absolute privilege against slander. Donohoe Constr. Co. v. Mount Vernon Assocs., 235 Va. 531, 369 S.E.2d 857 (1988).

The mechanics' lien itself is not self-enforcing and is extinguished unless the lienholder files a bill in equity within six months and obtains a decree against the debtor's property. W.T. Jones & Co. v. Foodco Realty, Inc., 318 F.2d 881 (4th Cir. 1963).

Both perfection and enforcement must be timely. — A duly perfected mechanic's lien will be extinguished unless the suit to enforce is timely filed. Similarly, the suit to enforce will be dismissed unless there has been a timely perfection of the lien. Accordingly, both perfection and enforcement must meet the statutory requisites before a claimant can recover under the mechanic's lien statute. Donohoe Constr. Co. v. Mount Vernon Assocs., 235 Va. 531, 369 S.E.2d 857 (1988).

Section applies in suit by owner to determine validity of liens. — Where a subcontractor's lien was barred by this section his claim could not be allowed in a suit brought by the owner of the building to determine the validity of certain claims for a mechanics' lien, to which suit the subcontractor was a party, he not having been a party to earlier suits brought to establish mechanics' liens, and the account of liens ordered in these suits not having been made until after his lien was barred. H.N. Francis & Co. v. Hotel Rueger, Inc., 125 Va. 106, 99 S.E. 690 (1919).

Allegation of timely perfection of lien. — A bill to enforce a mechanics' lien contains a sufficient allegation that the lien was perfected before the expiration of 30 (now 90) days from the termination of the work, when it alleges that the lien was filed as provided for in §§ 43-3 and 43-4, and the copy of the record of the lien exhibited with the bill shows a part performance within 30 (now 90) days of the recordation of the lien. Richlands Flint Glass Co. v. Hiltebeitel, 92 Va. 91, 22 S.E. 806 (1895).

Bill to enforce lien is not part of perfection. — Filing of a bill to enforce the mechanic's lien within the time specified is not part of the perfection process. Virginia law as applied in a bankruptcy situation does not require the commencement of an action in order to perfect a mechanic's lien. Therefore, an action to enforce the lien would not be exempt from the automatic stay provisions in bankruptcy. H.T. Bowling, Inc. v. Bain, 52 Bankr. 58 (Bankr. W.D. Va. 1985), aff'd in part and rev'd in part, 64 Bankr. 581 (W.D. Va. 1986).

A creditor may plead the statute of limitations in a suit to enforce a mechanics' lien. McCartney v. Tyrer, 94 Va. 198, 26 S.E. 419 (1897); Monk v. Exposition Deepwater Pier Corp., 111 Va. 121, 68 S.E. 280 (1910).

But the right must be barred as between the lienor and the debtor. Monk v. Exposition Deepwater Pier Corp., 111 Va. 121, 68 S.E. 280 (1910).

Time of impleading subsequent lienors is immaterial. — If a suit to enforce a mechanics' lien is brought within due time against the debtor upon whose property the lien rests, the failure to implead subsequent lienors within six months does not defeat the lien so far as such encumbrances are concerned. They are proper but not necessary parties to such suits, and may be brought in at a subsequent time. Monk v. Exposition Deepwater Pier Corp., 111 Va. 121, 68 S.E. 280 (1910).

Statute is not suspended by suit to enforce another lien. — The institution of a suit in equity which was not a general creditors' suit or a general creditors' lien suit, but had for its sole object the enforcement of a mechanics' lien and other alleged rights of the plaintiff, did not suspend the running of limitations as to another mechanics' lienor who was not made a party and did not in any way become a party until it filed its petition to enforce its lien more than six months after the entire amount covered by its lien became due and payable. Richmond Eng'r & Mfg. Corp. v. Loth, 135 Va. 110, 115 S.E. 774 (1923).

Unless lienor is made a party. — A suit by a subcontractor suspends the running of limitations as to the general contractor and all claiming under him, where he is made a party and his recorded lien properly set forth in bill. Spiller v. Wells, 96 Va. 598, 32 S.E. 46 (1899).

Intervening petition in suit of another. — When read together, it is clear that this section and § 43-22 require that a lienor's intervening petition in a suit to enforce a mechanics' lien be filed within the limitation period provided in this section. Commonwealth Mechanical Contractors v. Standard Fed. Sav. & Loan, 222 Va. 330, 281 S.E.2d 811 (1981).

Where appellant mechanics' lienors sought to enforce their liens over two years after the filing of their memoranda of mechanics' liens by filing intervening petitions in a pending suit by appellee lienor which named them as defendants, the trial court properly sustained appellee lienor's demurrer to the petitions. The enforcement of appellants' liens was barred because the intervening petitions were not filed within the limitation period set out in this section. Commonwealth Mechanical Contractors v. Standard Fed. Sav. & Loan, 222 Va. 330, 281 S.E.2d 811 (1981).

Being named as a defendant. — Merely being named as a defendant in an enforcement action of another lienor is not the equivalent of either filing an independent suit or intervening in the suit of another; there is no relevant difference between being a named party defendant in a bill to enforce a mechanic's lien and being a named defendant in interpleader action; neither constitutes an affirmative act on the part of the lienor to enforce its lien, and neither complies with the statutory requirements. Isle of Wight Materials Co. v. Cowling Bros., 246 Va. 103, 431 S.E.2d 42 (1993).

Being named party defendant not suit. — Although the filing of an intervening petition in a suit filed by another lienor is the equivalent of instituting a suit under this section, being named a party defendant in a suit by a lienor is not. Commonwealth Mechanical Contractors v. Standard Fed. Sav. & Loan, 222 Va. 330, 281 S.E.2d 811 (1981).

Beneficiary of an inferior deed of trust is a necessary party in mechanic lien holder's suit to enforce its mechanic's lien and was required to be named as a defendant within the statutory time period; failure to do so defeats mechanic lien holder's suit to enforce its mechanic's lien. James T. Bush Constr. Co. v. Patel, 243 Va. 84, 412 S.E.2d 703 (1992).

Beneficiary of a superior deed of trust had substantial interest in being given opportunity to challenge lien. — Because the proceeds from a judicial sale of property may be insufficient to satisfy both a mechanic's lien and a deed of trust lien, the beneficiary of a superior deed of trust had a substantial interest in being given the opportunity to challenge the validity of the mechanic's lien, or otherwise to litigate the elements of the lien. James T. Bush Constr. Co. v. Patel, 243 Va. 84, 412 S.E.2d 703 (1992).

"Payable" as used in this section obviously refers to the time when the obligation to pay is immediate, after which the debt is past due, interest runs and action may be brought. Southern Materials Co. v. Marks, 196 Va. 295, 83 S.E.2d 353 (1954).

Rule that running account falls due on date of last item held inapplicable. — Where an account showed seven items, the last dated August 3, 1949, but complainant's vice-president testified that this last item was due on September 1, 1949, and this was corroborated by admissions in defendant's answer and by invoice rendered, which allowed discount if paid by August 25, the usual rule that a running account falls due on the date of its last item was inapplicable, and suit brought on February 21, 1950, was brought within the six-month period set by this section. Southern Materials Co. v. Marks, 196 Va. 295, 83 S.E.2d 353 (1954).

Bill not demurrable. — Where the bill alleged the date on which the memorandum of lien was filed, and suit was instituted within six months of that date, the bill was not subject to demurrer on the grounds that it failed to allege compliance with this section. Blanton v. Owen, 203 Va. 73, 122 S.E.2d 650 (1961).

Perfection of a mechanics' lien is a one-step process in Virginia. Upon the filing of a memorandum in accordance with § 43-4, the creditor's lien is perfected. This section is merely a statute of limitations governing the period within which a lienor must file a claim to collect on his perfected lien. H.T. Bowling, Inc. v. Bain, 64 Bankr. 581 (W.D. Va. 1986).

Filing of complaint to enforce perfected lien violated automatic stay in bankruptcy. — Since the filing of a bill of complaint in the state court to enforce a mechanics' lien constitutes an attempt to enforce a perfected mechanics' lien, and not a step in the perfection process, the contractor plainly violated the automatic stay of 11 U.S.C. § 362 by filing the bill of complaint. Section 362 treats enforcement of liens much differently than their perfection. Specifically, § 362(a)(4) prohibits the filing of suit to enforce any lien against property of the debtor's estate. H.T. Bowling, Inc. v. Bain, 64 Bankr. 581 (W.D. Va. 1986).

Applied in In re Romanac, 245 F. Supp. 882 (W.D. Va. 1965); Mendenhall v. Douglas L. Cooper, Inc., 239 Va. 71, 387 S.E.2d 468 (1990); McCoy v. Chrysler Condo Dev. Ltd. Partnership, 239 Va. 321, 389 S.E.2d 905 (1990); Heyward & Lee Constr. Co. v. Sands, 249 Va. 54, 453 S.E.2d 270 (1995).

§ 43-17.1. Hearing on validity of lien. — Any party, having an interest in real property against which a lien has been filed, may, upon a showing of good cause, petition the court of equity having jurisdiction wherein the building, structure, other property, or railroad is located to hold a hearing to determine the validity of any perfected lien on the property. After reasonable notice to the lien claimant and any party to whom the benefit of the lien would inure and who has given notice as provided in § 43-18 of the Code of Virginia, the court shall hold a hearing and determine the validity of the lien. If the court finds that the lien is invalid, it shall forthwith order that the memorandum or notice of lien be removed from record. (1975, c. 380.)

Where the grantor of property subject to a mechanics' lien conveyed the property with special warranty of title, the warranty had the effect under § 55-69 of a covenant to defend the grantee from those claiming through the grantor, and since the lienor was a party claiming through the grantor, the grantor had a sufficient interest within the meaning of this section to oppose the lien. Pic Constr. Co. v. First Union Nat'l Bank, 218 Va. 915, 241 S.E.2d 804 (1978).

Lien filed by construction corporation was not over-inclusive. — Where development group argued that lien was over-inclusive because its property was not a single parcel, but rather two separate noncontiguous parcels, and that construction corporation could have described the property subject to its lien, the memorandum of mechanic's lien filed by construction corporation, was not over-inclusive. A lienor, such as construction corporation, was entitled to rely upon the land records. Blue Ridge Constr. Corp. v. Stafford Dev. Group, 244 Va. 361, 421 S.E.2d 199 (1992).

Lien held invalid. — Because the contractor's memorandum of mechanics' lien failed to correspond to his contract, failed to describe the land and improvements upon which his lien rights existed, and purported to cover property to which his lien rights did not extend, it was invalid. Rosser v. Cole, 237 Va. 572, 379 S.E.2d 323 (1989).

Applied in United Va. Mtg. Corp. v. Haines Paving Co., 221 Va. 1047, 277 S.E.2d 187 (1981).

§ 43-18. Lien of general contractor to inure to benefit of subcontractor.

— The perfected lien of a general contractor on any building or structure shall inure to the benefit of any subcontractor, and of any person performing labor or furnishing materials to a subcontractor who has not perfected a lien on such building or structure, provided such subcontractor, or person performing labor or furnishing materials shall give written notice of his claim against the general contractor, or subcontractor, as the case may be, to the owner or his agent before the amount of such lien is actually paid off or discharged. (Code 1919, § 6434.)

Law Review. — For survey of Virginia commercial law for the year 1974-1975, see 61 Va. L. Rev. 1668 (1975). For survey on creditors' rights in Virginia for 1989, see 23 U. Rich. L. Rev. 561 (1989).

This section secures to the subcontractor the benefit of the lien given the general contractor, provided notice is given by former before lien is discharged. Shenandoah Valley R.R. v. Miller, 80 Va. 821 (1885).

But subcontractor is not obliged to claim through general contractor. — Under this section the subcontractor may claim through the general contractor, but he is not obliged to do so. Under § 43-7, the subcontractor may perfect his own independent lien. Knight v. Ferrante, 202 Va. 243, 117 S.E.2d 283 (1960).

The subcontractor, under the provisions of this section, may rely on the general contractor's lien or, under the provisions of §§ 43-3, 43-4 and 43-7, he may file and undertake to enforce his own independent lien. VNB Mtg. Corp. v. Lone Star Indus., Inc., 215 Va. 366, 209 S.E.2d 909 (1974).

Subcontractors and materialmen are not deprived of their independent liens unless they either expressly waived their lien rights or expressly accepted, or by clear implication, agreed to be bound by the general contractor's stipulation in the general contract against liens. VNB Mtg. Corp. v. Lone Star Indus., Inc., 215 Va. 366, 209 S.E.2d 909 (1974).

§ 43-19. Validity and priority of lien not affected by assignments.

— Every assignment or transfer by a general contractor, in whole or in part, of his contract with the owner or of any money or consideration coming to him under such contract, or by a subcontractor of his contract with the general contractor, in whole or in part, or of any money or consideration coming to him under his contract with the general contractor, and every writ of fieri facias, attachment or other process against the general contractor or subcontractor to subject or encumber his interest arising under such contract, shall be subject to the liens given by this chapter to laborers, mechanics, and materialmen. No such assignment or transfer shall in any way affect the validity or the priority of satisfaction of liens given by this chapter. (Code 1919, § 6435.)

Cross references. — As to priority of mechanics' lien generally, see §§ 43-20, 43-21, and notes. As to assignment of supply and labor liens, see also § 43-26.

Section is considered written into assignments. — The words of this section as to assignments by a contractor are written into such assignments as effectually as if the assignment in terms stated as a condition precedent that it should be void and ineffective until after the payment in full of all debts due by the assignor to subcontractors, supply men and laborers for the construction of the building, and the section in its legal effect is a direction to the owner thus to distribute the fund. DeWitt v. Coffey, 150 Va. 365, 143 S.E. 710 (1928).

It applies to contract of suretyship with option to complete. — This section, which preserves the validity and priority of the liens of laborers, mechanics and materialmen against assignments or transfers by a contractor either of any part of his contract with the owner, or of any money or consideration coming to him under such contract, applies to a contract of suretyship by which the surety is given the option of completing the contract on default of the contractor. Electric Transmission Co. v. Pennington Gap Bank, Inc., 137 Va. 94, 119 S.E. 99 (1923).

And to assignment to subcontractors. — Under this section, every assignment of every kind by a general contractor to any party of any funds due, or to become due, to the general contractor under a contract for the erection of a building is subject to the mechanics' liens given by this chapter, even though the assignees involved are subcontractors. Anderson v. White, 183 Va. 302, 32 S.E.2d 72 (1944).

Assignments given to subcontractors for work performed on the building, or supplies furnished, are not excepted. Anderson v. White, 183 Va. 302, 32 S.E.2d 72 (1944).

Priority of inchoate but potential liens is preserved. — This section is without meaning or effect unless it preserves the priority of the inchoate but potential liens created by the chapter, because liens which attached before the assignment need no such protection. DeWitt v. Coffey, 150 Va. 365, 143 S.E. 710 (1928). But see Fairbanks, Morse & Co. v. Town of Cape Charles, 144 Va. 56, 131 S.E. 437 (1926), in which it was held that this section applied only to subcontractors who had perfected their liens on the structures erected.

This section protects inchoate liens. Perrin & Martin, Inc. v. United States, 233 F. Supp. 1016 (E.D. Va. 1964).

But assignment is good against subcontractors who have no potential liens. — Assignments are not void as to subcontractors who have permitted the time given by § 43-4 to expire without taking the necessary steps to perfect their liens, and thus have no potential right to perfect liens. Coleman v. Pearman, 159 Va. 72, 165 S.E. 371 (1932), overruled on other grounds, Mills v. Moore's Super Stores, 217 Va. 276, 227 S.E.2d 719 (1976).

Disbursements before lien notice not affected. — In the absence of fraud or wrongful conversion, this section does not affect disbursements against the contract price made before lien notice is given. Kayhoe Constr. Corp. v. United Va. Bank, 220 Va. 285, 257 S.E.2d 837 (1979).

Subcontractors entitled to protection despite assignment. — Under the facts of the case, the subcontractors, who, so far as the evidence showed, contracted with the assignee in good faith, are not to be denied the protection of this chapter merely because the owners did not know of the assignment. Mills v. Moore's Super Stores, 217 Va. 276, 227 S.E.2d 719 (1976).

§ 43-20. Extent of lien where owner has less than fee in land. —

Subject to the provisions of § 43-3, if the person who shall cause a building or structure to be erected or repaired owns less than a fee simple estate in the land, then only his interest therein shall be subject to liens created under this chapter. When the vendee under a contract for the sale of real estate causes a building or structure to be erected or repaired on the land which is the subject of the contract and the owner has actual knowledge of such erection or repairs, the interest of the owner in the land shall be subject to liens created under this chapter; and for the purposes of § 43-21, the interest of such an owner in the land, to the extent of the unpaid purchase price, shall be deemed to be a recorded purchase money deed of trust lien created at the time the contract of sale was fully executed. As used in this section, "a contract for the sale of real estate" shall not include a lease of real estate containing an option to purchase the leased real estate or an option to purchase real estate unless the option is enforceable against the optionee. (Code 1919, § 6436; 1924, p. 413; 1968, c. 568; 1980, c. 574.)

§ 43-21. Priorities between mechanics' and other liens. — No lien or encumbrance upon the land created before the work was commenced or materials furnished shall operate upon the building or structure erected thereon, or materials furnished for and used in the same, until the lien in favor of the person doing the work or furnishing the materials shall have been satisfied; nor shall any lien or encumbrance upon the land created after the work was commenced or materials furnished operate on the land, or such building or structure, until the lien in favor of the person doing the work or furnishing the materials shall have been satisfied.

Unless otherwise provided in the subordination agreement, if the holder of the prior recorded lien of a purchase money deed of trust subordinates to the lien of a construction money deed of trust, such subordination shall be limited to the construction money deed of trust and said prior lien shall not be subordinate to mechanics' and materialmen's liens to the extent of the value of the land by virtue of such agreement.

In the enforcement of the liens acquired under the previous sections of this chapter, any lien or encumbrance created on the land before the work was commenced or materials furnished shall be preferred in the distribution of the proceeds of sale only to the extent of the value of the land estimated, exclusive of the buildings or structures, at the time of sale, and the residue of the proceeds of sale shall be applied to the satisfaction of the liens provided for in the previous sections of this chapter. Provided that liens filed for performing labor or furnishing materials for the repair or improvement of any building or structure shall be subject to any encumbrance against such land and building or structure of record prior to the commencement of the improvements or repairs or the furnishing of materials or supplies therefor. Nothing contained in the foregoing proviso shall apply to liens that may be filed for the construction or removal of any building or structure. (Code 1919, § 6436; 1924, p. 413; 1968, c. 568.)

Law Review. — For article, "Virginia Mechanics' Liens: A Precarious Priority," see 21 Wash. & Lee L. Rev. 235 (1964). For survey of Virginia commercial law for the year 1970-71, see 57 Va. L. Rev. 1527 (1971). For survey of Virginia law on business associations for the year 1970-1971, see 57 Va. L. Rev. 1541 (1971). For survey of Virginia commercial law for the year 1975-1976, see 62 Va. L. Rev. 1375 (1976).

Under this section, a mechanics' lien has preference over other liens. When another lien or encumbrance is created before the work is commenced or the materials furnished it does not operate on the building until the mechanics' lien is satisfied; if created after the work is commenced or the materials furnished it does not operate on the land or building until the mechanics' lien is satisfied. Kinnier Co. v. Cofer, 13 Va. L. Reg. (n.s.) 238 (1927). See also DeWitt v. Coffey, 150 Va. 365, 143 S.E. 710 (1928); Rust v. Indiana Flooring Co., 151 Va. 845, 145 S.E. 321 (1928).

This section modifies § 55-96. — The effect of this section is to modify the registry law as contained in § 55-96 so far as to give priority to a mechanics' lien on the lands of the grantee who has failed to record his deed over judgments subsequently obtained against his grantor. Pace v. Moorman, 99 Va. 246, 37 S.E. 911 (1901).

Priority of lien created on land before work was begun. — Under this section, where a lien was created on the land before the work for which the mechanics' lien is claimed was begun or the materials were furnished, the former lien is the first lien on the land and the second lien on the building or structure. Federal Land Bank v. Clinchfield Lumber & Supply Co., 171 Va. 118, 198 S.E. 437 (1938).

A deed of trust recorded before the work began is entitled to priority to the extent of the estimated value of the property without the improvements for which the lien is claimed. Fidelity Loan & Trust Co. v. Dennis, 93 Va. 504, 25 S.E. 546 (1896); Hudson v. Barham, 101 Va. 63, 43 S.E. 189 (1903).

A mechanics' lien was not entitled to priority over a claim of the United States based on an unpaid Small Business Administration loan. W.T. Jones & Co. v. Foodco Realty, Inc., 318 F.2d 881 (4th Cir. 1963).

Section ineffective against claims of United States. — However effective this section may be on its face to secure their liens against competing nonfederal claims, it is ineffective against claims of the United States. W.T. Jones & Co. v. Foodco Realty, Inc., 318 F.2d 881 (4th Cir. 1963).

Hence, when the Small Business Administration has joined a private bank in making a construction loan secured by a recorded deed of trust and the borrower becomes insolvent, the SBA's interest in the unpaid balance of the loan

is not subordinate to mechanics' liens accorded priority over deeds of trust by state law. W.T. Jones & Co. v. Foodco Realty, Inc., 318 F.2d 881 (4th Cir. 1963).

And state laws purporting to fix priorities among lienholders must yield to the federal insolvency statute (31 U.S.C. § 191) in any nonbankruptcy insolvency proceeding where it is applicable and seasonably invoked by the United States. W.T. Jones & Co. v. Foodco Realty, Inc., 318 F.2d 881 (4th Cir. 1963).

Federal common law prevails. — Federal common law, by which "the first in time is the first in right," prevails over state law in matters affecting the priority of claims of the United States. W.T. Jones & Co. v. Foodco Realty, Inc., 318 F.2d 881 (4th Cir. 1963).

Even if "federal common law" is inapplicable, a debt owing to the United States would be in any event paramount to mechanics' liens by virtue of the federal insolvency statute (31 U.S.C. § 191). W.T. Jones & Co. v. Foodco Realty, Inc., 318 F.2d 881 (4th Cir. 1963).

Effect of filing and recording against claim of United States. — As against claim of United States, the interim steps of filing and recording the lien, without obtaining a final judgment enforcing the lien against the property, serve "merely as a caveat of a more perfect lien to come." W.T. Jones & Co. v. Foodco Realty, Inc., 318 F.2d 881 (4th Cir. 1963).

Whether a vendor's or a mechanics' lien has priority is a question that may be affected by extraneous circumstances, and in such case where the master's report of the liens and their priorities is confirmed without exception thereto, the court will not give relief against alleged errors therein on a bill of review. Phipps v. Wise Hotel Co., 116 Va. 739, 82 S.E. 681 (1913).

Extinguishing priority does not extinguish claim. — The remedy of the mechanics' lien statute is to grant a priority, but the extinguishing of such priority does not in and of itself extinguish the claim. United States Elevator Corp. v. 1616 Reminc Ltd. Partnership, 9 Bankr. 679 (Bankr. E.D. Va. 1981).

Duty to place lien only upon property worked and no more. — Where a mechanic files a memorandum of mechanic's lien against two or more parcels but has not worked on all the parcels and where the mechanic attempts to enforce that lien against the several properties, that lien must be declared invalid in its entirety since it is the mechanics' duty to place his lien upon the property on which he worked and no more. Woodington Elec., Inc. v. Lincoln Sav. & Loan Ass'n, 238 Va. 623, 385 S.E.2d 872 (1989).

Mechanics' lienor cannot demand release of prior lien. — The mortgagor, as owner of the land, had no right to tender to the mortgagee the estimated value of the land necessary for the enjoyment of the building and demand a release of the mortgage thereon, nor did the holder of the mechanics' lien have any such right, either under the express language of this section or within its implied intent. Federal Land Bank v. Clinchfield Lumber & Supply Co., 171 Va. 118, 198 S.E. 437 (1938).

Liens against legal and equitable titles. — If the owner of the full equitable estate in land causes buildings to be erected thereon, for the cost of which a mechanic records a lien, such lien, by the terms of this section, takes priority, as to both land and buildings, over all liens thereafter acquired on the land, and also over all judgments thereafter recovered against the equitable owner's grantor, who holds the mere legal title to the land. If the mechanics' lien has been enforced by the sale of the property, the purchaser has the right to stand in the shoes of the mechanic before the sale. Pace v. Moorman, 99 Va. 246, 37 S.E. 911 (1901).

Lien for loan of money cannot be novated into mechanics' lien. — The theory of the mechanics' lien law is based upon an equitable vendor's lien, and, as a lien for the loan of money is solely a matter of collateral contract, it cannot be novated into a mechanics' lien by applying the money to payment for labor and material. W.T. Jones & Co. v. Foodco Realty, Inc., 206 F. Supp. 878 (W.D. Va. 1962), aff'd, 318 F.2d 881 (4th Cir. 1963).

Bulkhead as new structure. — Evidence supported the Commissioner's findings that a bulkhead constructed following severe storm damage to a motel was not for the purpose of repairing damages to the previously existing building, but was in fact a new structure erected on the premises for the express purpose of protecting the motel building against future damage arising out of an excessive high tide or a storm, and that the value of the property exclusive of the land was increased thereby by an amount in excess of the claims of the mechanics' lienors, thus entitling the mechanics' liens to the priority over existing liens and encumbrances established by this section. Strauss v. Princess Anne Marine & Bulkheading Co., 209 Va. 217, 163 S.E.2d 198 (1968).

How value of land without improvements estimated. — Where a mechanics' lien is recorded on property upon which there is a deed of trust recorded before work began on the building or structure placed thereon, the deed of trust creditor is entitled to priority of satisfaction to the extent of the estimated value of the property without the improvements for which the lien is claimed. The value is to be estimated as of the date of sale, and may be fixed directly by the court upon the testimony of witnesses, or by reference to a commissioner. Fidelity Loan & Trust Co. v. Dennis, 93 Va. 504, 25 S.E. 546 (1896). See also Hudson v. Barham, 101 Va. 63, 43 S.E. 189 (1903).

The lien on a deed of trust recorded before land is improved is a first lien on the land and a lien on the improvements subordinate to a mechanic's lien; the mechanic's lien is a first lien on the improvements and a subordinate lien on so much of the land as is necessary for the use and enjoyment of the improvements. Walt Robbins, Inc. v. Damon Corp., 232 Va. 43, 348 S.E.2d 223 (1986).

Applied in Crook, Horner & Co. v. Old Point Comfort Hotel Co., 54 F. 604 (E.D. Va. 1893); York Fed. Sav. & Loan Ass'n v. William A. Hazel, Inc., 256 Va. 599, 506 S.E.2d 315 (1998).

§ 43-22. How liens enforced. — The liens created and perfected under this chapter may be enforced in a court of equity by a bill filed in the county or city wherein the building, structure, or railroad, or some part thereof is situated, or wherein the owner, or if there be more than one, any of them, resides. The plaintiff shall file with his bill an itemized statement of his account, showing the amount and character of the work done or materials furnished, the prices charged therefor, the payments made, if any, the balance due, and the time from which interest is claimed thereon, the correctness of which account shall be verified by the affidavit of himself, or his agent. When suit is brought for the enforcement of any such lien against the property bound thereby, all parties entitled to such liens upon the property or any portion thereof may file petitions in such suit asking for the enforcement of their respective liens to have the same effect as if an independent suit were brought by each claimant. (Code 1919, § 6437; 1920, p. 485.)

Cross references. — As to limitation on suits to enforce mechanics' liens, see § 43-17. For rule of court on intervenors in equity suits generally, which excepts from its operation intervenors in mechanics' lien suits, see Rule 2:15.

Law Review. — For survey of Virginia commercial law for the year 1970-1971, see 57 Va. L. Rev. 1527 (1971); for the year 1975-1976, see 62 Va. L. Rev. 1375 (1976).

Perfection statute contrasted with enforcement statutes. — A lien created by Code

§ 43-3 is one in derogation of the common law. Once perfected in accordance with § 43-4, the lien can be enforced by suit brought as provided in § 43-17 and this section. In Virginia provisions of the enforcement statutes are to be construed liberally while the requirements of the perfection statute are to be construed strictly. American Std. Homes Corp. v. Reinecke, 245 Va. 113, 425 S.E.2d 515 (1993).

A proceeding under this section is analogous to a lien creditors' suit, and is controlled by the same consideration, and is subject to similar rules of equitable practice. Monk v. Exposition Deepwater Pier Corp., 111 Va. 121, 68 S.E. 280 (1910).

The mechanics' lien itself is not self-enforcing and is extinguished unless the lienholder files a bill in equity within six months and obtains a decree against the debtor's property. W.T. Jones & Co. v. Foodco Realty, Inc., 318 F.2d 881 (4th Cir. 1963).

A mechanic's lien is enforceable only under the conditions established by statute and, in the absence of compliance with those statutory provisions, a court has no jurisdiction to enforce the mechanic's lien. Isle of Wight Materials Co. v. Cowling Bros., 246 Va. 103, 431 S.E.2d 42 (1993).

The claim of mechanics' lien creditors is not a personal claim but is against the building and can only be enforced in a court of equity in the manner prescribed by this section. Nicholas v. Harrisonburg Bldg. & Supply Co., 181 Va. 207, 24 S.E.2d 452 (1943).

Suit is not one against other lien creditors. — A suit under this section to enforce a mechanics' lien is not a suit against other lien creditors, even when convened as parties defendant. They are impleaded as matter of convenience. The suit is analogous to a lien creditors' suit. Monk v. Exposition Deepwater Pier Corp., 111 Va. 121, 68 S.E. 280 (1910).

They are proper, but not necessary, parties. All known lien creditors, and all disclosed by the records, may be made parties, but a failure to do so is not fatal to the proceedings. Monk v. Exposition Deepwater Pier Corp., 111 Va. 121, 68 S.E. 280 (1910).

Bill must show on its face that suit was brought in time. — A bill to enforce the lien which does not show on its face that suit was brought within the time prescribed by § 43-17 is demurrable. Savings Bank v. Powhatan Clay Mfg. Co., 102 Va. 274, 46 S.E. 294 (1904).

Unless fact appears in record. — Where the record shows that a suit to enforce a mechanics' lien was brought within the time fixed by § 43-17, that fact need not be alleged in the bill, as the court will take judicial notice of the time when the suit was instituted. Sands v. Stagg, 105 Va. 444, 52 S.E. 633 (1906).

The filing of a memorandum of mechanic's lien is a judicial proceeding entitling filer to an absolute privilege against slander. Donohoe Constr. Co. v. Mount Vernon Assocs., 235 Va. 531, 369 S.E.2d 857 (1988).

Allegation of timely perfection of lien. — A bill to enforce a mechanics' lien contains a sufficient allegation that the lien was perfected before the expiration of 30 (now 60) days from the termination of the work, when it alleges that the lien was filed as provided for in §§ 43-3 and 43-4, and the copy of the record of the lien exhibited with the bill shows a part performance within 30 (now 60) days of the recordation of the lien. Richlands Flint Glass Co. v. Hiltebeitel, 92 Va. 91, 22 S.E. 806 (1895).

Limitation on lienor's intervening petition. — When read together, it is clear that § 43-17 and this section require that a lienor's intervening petition in a suit to enforce a mechanics' lien be filed within the limitation period provided in § 43-17. Commonwealth Mechanical Contractors v. Standard Fed. Sav. & Loan, 222 Va. 330, 281 S.E.2d 811 (1981).

Where appellant mechanics' lienors sought to enforce their liens over two years after the filing of their memoranda of mechanics' liens by filing intervening petitions in a pending suit by appellee lienor which named them as defendants, the trial court properly sustained appellee lienor's demurrer to the petitions. The enforcement of appellants' liens was barred because the intervening petitions were not filed within the limitation period set out in § 43-17. Commonwealth Mechanical Contractors v. Standard Fed. Sav. & Loan, 222 Va. 330, 281 S.E.2d 811 (1981).

Being named as a defendant. — Merely being named as a defendant in an enforcement action of another lienor is not the equivalent of either filing an independent suit or intervening in the suit of another; there is no relevant difference between being a named party defendant in a bill to enforce a mechanic's lien and being a named defendant in interpleader action; neither constitutes an affirmative act on the part of the lienor to enforce its lien, and neither complies with the statutory requirements. Isle of Wight Materials Co. v. Cowling Bros., 246 Va. 103, 431 S.E.2d 42 (1993).

Being named defendant not suit under § 43-17. — Although the filing of an intervening petition in a suit filed by another lienor is the equivalent of instituting a suit under § 43-17, being named a party defendant in a suit by a lienor is not. Commonwealth Mechanical Contractors v. Standard Fed. Sav. & Loan, 222 Va. 330, 281 S.E.2d 811 (1981).

Each separate house and lot is separate debtor. — Where each of several mechanics' liens is separate and distinct and asserted against separate parcels of real estate, the ultimate validity of each lien is dependent upon when the specific building upon which the work was done was completed or the work thereon otherwise terminated. Each house and lot, and none other, stands as a separate debtor — an in rem defendant — against which liability for the work done on that particular building can be enforced. Shelton v. Ogus, 201 Va. 417, 111 S.E.2d 408 (1959).

Trustee in an antecedent deed of trust recorded on unimproved land is necessary party in suit to enforce mechanic's lien on the improvements. Walt Robbins, Inc. v. Damon Corp., 232 Va. 43, 348 S.E.2d 223 (1986).

And the beneficiary of the antecedent deed of trust was a necessary party to the suits to enforce the mechanic's liens. Walt Robbins, Inc. v. Damon Corp., 232 Va. 43, 348 S.E.2d 223 (1986).

Chancellor must have jurisdiction over person of trustee before divesting him of title. — If legal title is vested in the trustee of an antecedent deed of trust, and the property is to be sold free of the trust lien, the chancellor must have jurisdiction over the person of the trustee before he can enter a decree divesting him of title. Walt Robbins, Inc. v. Damon Corp., 232 Va. 43, 348 S.E.2d 223 (1986).

The filing of the memorandum is not a proceeding at which parties with adverse interests may challenge the validity of the lien. Indeed, it is not a "proceeding" at all. A suit to enforce that lien is, however, such a proceeding. Walt Robbins, Inc. v. Damon Corp., 232 Va. 43, 348 S.E.2d 223 (1986).

The object of the memorandum is to register the claimant's lien and to put potential purchasers of the property on notice of the existence of the lien. Walt Robbins, Inc. v. Damon Corp., 232 Va. 43, 348 S.E.2d 223 (1986).

Lack of particularity in the account is not jurisdictional. It is a long-settled practice in this jurisdiction that when a defendant is not satisfied with the alleged particulars of the plaintiff's claim, he may ask for, and usually obtains, under the direction of the court further particulars of the claim. Where the owners sought no further particulars of the subcontractors' claims, but in effect moved to strike the bill on the ground of the alleged insufficiency of the accounts, the lower court properly overruled that motion. Knight v. Ferrante, 202 Va. 243, 117 S.E.2d 283 (1960).

Misdescription in account disregarded as surplusage. — Where the account inaccurately described the dwelling as "one-story" rather than "two-story," the mistake was disregarded as surplusage, since there was no doubt as to the dwelling on which the work had been done. Knight v. Ferrante, 202 Va. 243, 117 S.E.2d 283 (1960).

Filing verification after demurrer. — The complainant's filing of the verifying affidavit required by this section after defendant filed a demurrer but before the court acted upon the demurrer served to overcome the objection. Herbert Bros. v. McCarthy Co., 220 Va. 907, 265 S.E.2d 685 (1980).

Account held sufficient. — The account clearly itemized the things contracted for and supplied. The law does not require anything further. Rust v. Indiana Flooring Co., 151 Va. 845, 145 S.E. 321 (1928).

Where the account, read in connection with the further allegations in the bill, sufficiently established that the work and materials were contracted for as an entirety, it met the requirement of this section. Knight v. Ferrante, 202 Va. 243, 117 S.E.2d 283 (1960).

How land necessary for use and enjoyment described. — The quantity of land necessary to the convenient use of the building is sufficiently described by reference to an exhibit filed with the bill, giving an adequate description of it. Richlands Flint Glass Co. v. Hiltebeitel, 92 Va. 91, 22 S.E. 806 (1895).

Court of equity will give complete relief. — Where a court of equity takes cognizance of a suit to enforce a mechanics' lien, the entire case will be considered and a decree rendered according to equity and the right of the cause. Bailey Constr. Co. v. Purcell, 88 Va. 300, 13 S.E. 456 (1891).

A court of equity, in a suit to enforce a mechanics' lien, should proceed to determine all of the questions before it. Bailey Constr. Co. v. Purcell, 88 Va. 300, 13 S.E. 456 (1891); Rison v. Moon, 91 Va. 384, 22 S.E. 165 (1895); Johnston & Grommett Bros. v. Bunn, 108 Va. 490, 62 S.E. 341 (1908).

It may enter a personal decree. — In a proceeding in equity to enforce a mechanics' lien it may turn out when the evidence is taken that the complainants in the bill are not entitled to a lien upon the specific property in question; but, if it appears that the complainants are entitled to recover from the defendants, the court can proceed to enter a personal decree against the defendants for the amount due, although the complainants may have failed to establish their right to a lien. Johnston & Grommett Bros. v. Bunn, 108 Va. 490, 62 S.E. 341 (1908). See also Taylor v. Netherwood, 91 Va. 88, 20 S.E. 888 (1895).

Priority of federal law. — United States' lien, secured by its deed of trust, has priority over a mechanics' lien asserted under this section. J.S. Purcell Lumber Corp. v. Henson, 405 F. Supp. 1130 (E.D. Va. 1975).

When carpenters, plumbers and building supply houses extend credit on a construction project financed by federal money, their rights and priorities under state law are superseded by a federal law of priority. J.S. Purcell Lumber Corp. v. Henson, 405 F. Supp. 1130 (E.D. Va. 1975).

Applied in Mann v. Clowser, 190 Va. 887, 59 S.E.2d 78 (1950); Southern Materials Co. v.

Marks, 196 Va. 295, 83 S.E.2d 353 (1954); Rohanna v. Vazzana, 196 Va. 549, 84 S.E.2d 440 (1954); Globe Iron Constr. Co. v. First Nat'l Bank, 205 Va. 841, 140 S.E.2d 629 (1965).

§ 43-23. Priority among liens perfected under this chapter. — There shall be no priority among the liens created and perfected under this chapter, except that the lien of a subcontractor shall be preferred to that of his general contractor; the lien of persons performing labor or furnishing materials for a subcontractor, shall be preferred to that of such subcontractor; and liens filed by persons performing manual labor shall have priority over materialmen to the extent of the labor performed during the thirty days immediately preceding the date of the performance of the last labor. (Code 1919, § 6437; 1920, p. 485.)

Assignment to subcontractor is void as to other subcontractors. — Assignments received by subcontractors from the general contractor before he defaulted in the performance of his contract, which assignments were upon the owner for amounts due for labor and materials furnished, were clearly prohibited by this section and § 43-19 insofar as other subcontractors were concerned, and there was no priority by reason of them. Anderson v. White, 183 Va. 302, 32 S.E.2d 72 (1944).

§ 43-23.1. Forfeiture of lien. — Any person who shall, with intent to mislead, include in his memorandum of lien work not performed upon, or materials not furnished for, the property described in his memorandum shall thereby forfeit any right to a lien under this chapter. (1968, c. 568; 1976, c. 253.)

Purpose of 1976 amendment. — When the General Assembly amended this section by substituting the words "with intent to mislead" for the word "knowingly," the amendment did not constitute a substantive change in the statute. Rather, the amendment was enacted simply to reinforce the original legislative intent by clarifying an after-discovered semantical ambiguity. Prior to the amendment, "knowingly" meant more than "with knowledge." Rather, "knowingly" in this context was an antonym of "innocently" and a synonym of "designedly" and "with intent to mislead." First Nat'l Bank v. Roy N. Ford Co., 219 Va. 942, 252 S.E.2d 354 (1979).

A lienor may not enforce a lien against one project for the cost of labor or materials furnished on another. First Nat'l Bank v. Roy N. Ford Co., 219 Va. 942, 252 S.E.2d 354 (1979).

Forfeiture not warranted. — The act of a subcontractor in including in his memorandum of mechanic's lien debts due on projects other than the project in question did not constitute a forfeiture of the subcontractor's right to a mechanic's lien under this section where the statement of account filed prior to the memorandum contained data which corresponded fully with invoices and with the amount claimed in memorandum and where no evidence of an intent to mislead was produced. First Nat'l Bank v. Roy N. Ford Co., 219 Va. 942, 252 S.E.2d 354 (1979).

Beneficiary of antecedent deed of trust entitled to notice and opportunity to challenge. — Because the proceeds of a judicial sale under a decree enforcing a mechanic's lien may prove to be insufficient to pay both lien creditors in full, the beneficiary of an antecedent deed of trust has a property right which entitles him to notice and an opportunity to challenge the perfection of the mechanics' lien or to invoke the forfeiture provisions of this section. Walt Robbins, Inc. v. Damon Corp., 232 Va. 43, 348 S.E.2d 223 (1986).

§ 43-23.2. Remedies cumulative. — The remedies afforded by this chapter shall be deemed cumulative in nature and not be construed to be in lieu of any other legal or equitable remedies. (1968, c. 568.)

Chancellor did not err in excluding attorney's fees as an element of the liens enforced by the final decree. The General Assembly expressly approved inclusion of interest as an element of the claim in the perfection and enforcement of a mechanic's lien. The legislature was at liberty to do, but did not do, the same for attorney's fees. American Std. Homes Corp. v. Reinecke, 245 Va. 113, 425 S.E.2d 515 (1993).

CHAPTER 2.

LIENS ON FRANCHISES AND PROPERTY OF TRANSPORTATION, ETC., COMPANIES.

§ 43-24. Liens of employees, suppliers, etc. — All conductors, brakemen, engine drivers, firemen, captains, stewards, pilots, clerks, depot or office agents, storekeepers, mechanics, traveling representatives or laborers, and all persons furnishing railroad iron, engines, cars, fuel and all other supplies necessary to the operation of any railway, canal or other transportation company, and all clerks, mechanics, traveling representatives, foremen, and laborers, and superintendents to the extent of not more than twenty-five dollars per week, who furnish their services or labor to any one or more individuals trading under a real or fictitious name, or names, or to any partnership or other unincorporated body of persons, engaged in mining or manufacturing, or to any mining or manufacturing company, whether such railway, canal or other transportation or mining or manufacturing company be chartered under or by the laws of this Commonwealth, or be chartered elsewhere and be doing business within the limits of this Commonwealth, shall have a prior lien on the franchises, gross earnings and on all the real and personal property of such individual, partnership, unincorporated association or company which is used in operating the same, to the extent of the moneys due them by the individual, partnership, unincorporated association or company for such wages or supplies, which lien shall be superior to, and have priority over, any amount due by such individual, partnership, unincorporated association or company for rents, or royalties.

No mortgage, deed of trust, sale, hypothecation or conveyance executed since the first day of May, 1888, shall defeat or take precedence over such lien. The lien secured by this section to parties furnishing supplies, shall be subordinate to that allowed to clerks, mechanics, foremen, superintendents, and laborers for services furnished as aforesaid.

If any person entitled to a lien as well under § 43-3 as under this section, shall perfect his lien given by either section, he shall not be entitled to the benefit of the other.

No right to or remedy upon a lien which has already accrued to any person shall be extended, abridged or otherwise affected hereby. (Code 1919, § 6438; 1922, p. 13; 1932, p. 596; 1938, p. 17.)

I. General Consideration.
II. Against Whom Lien May Be Filed.
III. Who May Subject Property to Lien.
IV. Supplies and Labor for Which Lien May Exist.
V. Priorities.
VI. Effect of Bankruptcy.

I. GENERAL CONSIDERATION.

Construction of chapter. — There must be a substantial compliance with the requirement of that portion of this chapter which relates to the creation of the laborer's lien, but the provisions with respect to its enforcement should be liberally construed. Mathews v. Meyers, 151 Va. 426, 145 S.E. 352 (1928). See Wright v. Chase Nat'l Bank, 92 F.2d 271 (4th Cir. 1937).

Necessity for section. — In the nature of things, those who work for corporations seldom have possession of products of their labor, and unless the statutory lien given by this section attaches to them, the remedy designed by the legislature for their protection is in most instances but a shadow. Mathews v. Meyers, 151 Va. 426, 145 S.E. 352 (1928).

This section is not contrary to the Fourteenth Amendment to the United States

Constitution as being special and class legislation. Virginia Dev. Co. v. Crozer Iron Co., 90 Va. 126, 17 S.E. 806 (1893), aff'd on rehearing, 19 S.E. 782 (1894); First Nat'l Bank v. William R. Trigg Co., 106 Va. 327, 56 S.E. 158 (1907), appeal dismissed, 218 U.S. 693, 31 S. Ct. 218, 54 L. Ed. 1212 (1910). See also Robert Bunts Eng'g & Equip. Co. v. Palmer, 169 Va. 206, 192 S.E. 789 (1937).

But it is unconstitutional as to liens existing prior to its date, and valid as to those arising thereafter. Citizens' & Marine Bank v. Mason, 2 F.2d 352 (4th Cir. 1924); Mathews v. Meyers, 151 Va. 426, 145 S.E. 352 (1928).

It did not impair the charter right of a corporation to issue bonds and secure the same, where the corporation was organized prior to the effective date of this section, and the charter was taken subject to the general law then in effect and any changes that might be made therein; hence bondholders who took the bonds after the enactment of the section were bound by its provisions as to priority of liens. Virginia Dev. Co. v. Crozer Iron Co., 90 Va. 126, 17 S.E. 806 (1893), aff'd on rehearing, 19 S.E. 782 (1894).

For the history of this section, see Newgass v. Atlantic & D. Ry., 56 F. 676 (E.D. Va. 1893); Building Supplies Corp. v. Willcox, 284 F. 113 (4th Cir. 1922).

Supply lien not inconsistent with lien of car-trust contract. — A lien for the purchase money of rolling stock reserved under a car-trust contract, recorded pursuant to former § 55-89, was in no wise inconsistent with the existence of a supply lien under this section. Newgass v. Atlantic & D. Ry., 56 F. 676 (E.D. Va. 1893).

Applied in In re Stunzi U.S.A., Inc., 7 Bankr. 401 (Bankr. W.D. Va. 1980).

II. AGAINST WHOM LIEN MAY BE FILED.

Section applies only to companies strictly engaged in businesses named. — The legislature, in placing railroad, canal and other transportation companies and mining and manufacturing companies all in one section, plainly had in mind corporations extensive in character, and at least those actually and chiefly so engaged, and not such as might incidentally, from a technical viewpoint, be engaged partially in manufacturing something used, or capable of being used, in connection with the business in hand. "Mining or manufacturing companies" in this section manifestly was intended to apply to companies strictly engaged in the businesses named, which considered along with other portions of the section applicable to railroad, canal, and other transportation companies, clearly indicated the actual engaging in one of the five things named in

the section, to wit, operating a railroad, canal, or transportation company, or a mining or manufacturing business. Citizens' & Marine Bank v. Mason, 2 F.2d 352 (4th Cir. 1924).

But "manufacturing company" may buy and sell raw material. — A company whose general business, well recognized and understood, was that of the manufacture of rough lumber into flooring, ceiling, box shooks and other dressed material, was a manufacturing company within the meaning of this section, notwithstanding that it bought and sold rough lumber as an incident in connection with its regular business. In re W. Norfolk Lumber Co., 112 F. 759 (E.D. Va. 1902).

A boilermaker is a manufacturer. First Nat'l Bank v. William R. Trigg Co., 106 Va. 327, 56 S.E. 158 (1907), appeal dismissed, 218 U.S. 693, 31 S. Ct. 218, 54 L. Ed. 1212 (1910).

And a shipbuilding company may be a manufacturing company. — A company which manufactured ships of all sorts and sizes, and all necessary fittings and furniture therefor, and in addition did a considerable amount of original and repair work for other manufacturing concerns, was held to be a manufacturing company within the meaning of this section. First Nat'l Bank v. William R. Trigg Co., 106 Va. 327, 56 S.E. 158 (1907), appeal dismissed, 218 U.S. 693, 31 S. Ct. 218, 54 L. Ed. 1212 (1910).

A bottling company is not a manufacturing company within the meaning of this section. Citizens' & Marine Bank v. Mason, 2 F.2d 352 (4th Cir. 1924).

III. WHO MAY SUBJECT PROPERTY TO LIEN.

The principal officers of a company are not within the provisions of this section. Wilson v. Hall, 81 F.2d 918 (4th Cir. 1936).

The manager of a manufacturing company is not a "laborer" or "traveling representative" entitled to a preferred lien for salary under this section, although he spent about half his time traveling. Wright v. Chase Nat'l Bank, 92 F.2d 271 (4th Cir. 1937).

Nor is the president and general manager. — The president of a manufacturing company is not given priority of lien to secure his salary by this section. And to designate him as general manager does not change his official relation to the company, nor does it bring him within any of the classes to whom priority is given. Seventh Nat'l Bank v. Shenandoah Iron Co., 35 F. 436 (C.C.W.D. Va. 1887).

Nor the secretary and treasurer. — Claims for salaries by the manager and the secretary and treasurer of a corporation were properly disallowed as labor claims, these officers not being within the provisions of this section giving labor claims a priority. Fidelity

Ins., Trust & Safe-Deposit Co. v. Roanoke Iron Co., 81 F. 439 (W.D. Va. 1896).

A telegraph company is not a laborer. — A telegraph company rendering services to a railroad is not a laborer within the intent and reason of this section and § 43-25. Newgass v. Atlantic & D. Ry., 72 F. 712 (E.D. Va. 1894).

"Laborers" and contractors distinguished. — Where the lien claimant laid the track, constructed the overhead line and strung the necessary feeder wire for an electric railway, under an agreement with the railway whereby payment was to be made at a fixed price per foot or mile, the railway furnishing all the materials and the lien claimant furnishing all his own tools and labor, the claimant was a contractor, and not a laborer, and did not come within the purview of this section. Frick Co. v. Norfolk & O.V.R.R., 86 F. 725 (4th Cir. 1898).

Persons who contracted to move their sawmill upon the property of a lumber company, and there to log, mill out and rack certain lumber, at a stated sum per thousand feet, were contractors, and not "laborers" within the meaning of this section. Tucker v. Bryan, 217 F. 576 (4th Cir. 1913).

IV. SUPPLIES AND LABOR FOR WHICH LIEN MAY EXIST.

Medical services to employee are not supplies necessary to operation of railroad. — The claim of a hospital for medical services and board rendered to an employee of a railroad company who was injured and disabled in its service does not fall within the terms of this section. The hospital did not furnish "supplies necessary to the operation of the railroad." Newgass v. Atlantic & D. Ry., 56 F. 676 (E.D. Va. 1893).

Nor are permanent buildings forming part of railway plant. — Claims for material and labor furnished to an electric railway for the construction of a carbarn, train sheds, power and boiler houses, a workshop and a car depot, are not claims for supplies necessary to the operation of the railway. These are supplies and labor furnished for the construction of permanent buildings which are properly part of the railway plant. The buildings are not in themselves supplies necessary to the operation of the railway. They are buildings erected for the protection and preservation of the cars, engines and other machinery, just as roundhouses and car sheds are used by steam railroads for the protection and preservation of their locomotives and coaches. Their character as property is distinct from that of necessary supplies as defined by this section. Frick Co. v. Norfolk & O.V.R.R., 86 F. 725 (4th Cir. 1898).

A hotel operated by a railroad is a distinct piece of property and cannot be confounded with the railroad proper in such a way as to bring the cost of its construction, repair and furnishing under the head of labor and supplies necessary to the operation of the railroad, giving it a prior lien as such. Frick Co. v. Norfolk & O.V.R.R., 86 F. 725 (4th Cir. 1898).

Engines for the purpose of generating electricity, furnishing the propelling power for an electric railway, are "engines ... necessary to the operation" of such a railway. Frick Co. v. Norfolk & O.V.R.R., 86 F. 725 (4th Cir. 1898).

Cars supplied under "car-trust" contract are "furnished". — Cars supplied to a railroad under a "car-trust" contract, recorded pursuant to former § 55-89, were "furnished" to the railroad within the meaning of this section, notwithstanding that the contract spoke of the transaction as a lease and the vendor's name appeared as owner on plates attached to the cars. Newgass v. Atlantic & D. Ry., 56 F. 676 (E.D. Va. 1893).

V. PRIORITIES.

Preference given is unconditional. — The preference this section gives the general creditor against the corpus of a railroad's assets is unconditional. Southern Ry. v. Flournoy, 301 F.2d 847 (4th Cir. 1962).

Laborers' liens are prior lien on all employer's property. — Laborers' liens, pursuant to this section and § 43-25, are made a prior lien on all the employer's property. Textile Banking Co. v. Widener, 265 F.2d 446 (4th Cir. 1959).

Superior to factor's lien and lien of Reconstruction Finance Corporation. — A factor's lien upon a bankrupt's inventories and accounts receivable, and the lien of the Reconstruction Finance Corporation, which held a deed of trust on the bankrupt's land, plant and machinery, were subordinate to laborers' liens. In re Lincoln Indus., Inc., 166 F. Supp. 240 (W.D. Va. 1958), modified, Textile Banking Co. v. Widener, 265 F.2d 446 (4th Cir. 1959).

The lien conferred by this section has priority over a mechanics' lien under § 43-3 for furnishing materials for the original construction of the same property. Building Supplies Corp. v. Willcox, 284 F. 113 (4th Cir. 1922).

The difference between the lien under this section and the mechanics' lien is that the mechanics' lien under § 43-3 is put upon the building or structure and so much of the land therewith as shall be necessary for the convenient use and enjoyment thereof, while this section puts the lien upon all the real and personal property of the company which is used in operating the same. The conflict between these liens, therefore, would only be as to such buildings or structures and lands as are used in operating the company. Building Supplies Corp. v. Willcox, 284 F. 113 (4th Cir. 1922).

Supplier's lien prevails over earlier mortgage. — This section gives a lien on the franchises, gross earnings and on all the real and personal property of a railroad, notwithstanding any earlier mortgage, for supplies furnished on accounts becoming due and payable within 90 days before the filing of a memorandum of lien. Southern Ry. v. Flournoy, 301 F.2d 847 (4th Cir. 1962).

But lien attaches only to such interest as employer has acquired. — The prior lien given to employees under this section attaches to only such interest in the property as the employer has acquired; it is superior to only those encumbrances placed upon the property by the employer itself; if the employer has acquired property subject to encumbrances placed upon it by the former owner, or has given a purchase-money mortgage, these encumbrances are not affected by the liens conferred by this section. M.A. Furbush & Son Mach. Co. v. Liberty Woolen Mills, 81 F. 425 (W.D. Va. 1896).

When lien superior to purchase-money deed of trust. — Where a deed and a deed of trust of standing timber permitted the timber to be cut and manufactured, and provided that the vendees should pay the vendors so much per thousand feet upon the timber cut and account monthly, laborers had the right to assume that there had been no default in the payments on the purchase price since operations were carried on without protest, and the laborer's lien under this section on the sawed lumber was superior to the lien of the deed of trust for the purchase money. Mathews v. Meyers, 151 Va. 426, 145 S.E. 352 (1928).

Contract passing title to brokers. — Under the terms of a contract between an iron company and its brokers, iron produced by the company was shipped to the brokers accompanied by bills of lading in their name, and the brokers were to advance a percentage of the market price, and were to hold the iron and sell it in their discretion. The first proceeds of sale were to go to their advances, then all charges were to be deducted, and, after an account for these was made up, the iron company had a right to the net balance, if any. It was held that the title to the iron so shipped passed to the brokers and out of the iron company, and the iron did not constitute part of the personal property of the iron company so as to be subject to the lien conferred by this section. Fidelity Ins., Trust & Safe-Deposit Co. v. Roanoke Iron Co., 81 F. 439 (W.D. Va. 1896).

Prior assignment of chose in action is superior. — A valid assignment of a chose in action made by a manufacturing company is superior to liens under this section for labor furnished more than two years thereafter. S.H. Hawes & Co. v. William R. Trigg Co., 110 Va. 165, 65 S.E. 538 (1909), rev'd in part, on other

grounds, and aff'd in part, United States v. Ansonia Brass & Copper Co., 218 U.S. 452, 31 S. Ct. 49, 54 L. Ed. 1107 (1910).

The bona fide holder for value of warehouse and storage receipts has priority over a claimant asserting a lien which attached after the transfer and delivery of the receipts. Millhiser Mfg. Co. v. Gallego Mills Co., 101 Va. 579, 44 S.E. 760 (1903).

Lien does not attach to vessel becoming property of United States as fast as built. — Where, under the terms of a contract between the United States and a shipbuilding company, title to a vessel under construction passed to the United States as fast as the work progressed and payments under the contract were made, the vessel was not subject to the lien provided by this section. United States v. Ansonia Brass & Copper Co., 218 U.S. 452, 31 S. Ct. 49, 54 L. Ed. 1107 (1910), rev'g in part and aff'g in part, S.H. Hawes & Co. v. William R. Trigg Co., 110 Va. 165, 65 S.E. 538 (1909).

But it is superior to contractual lien of United States on vessel under construction. — Where the only lien which the United States could assert on a vessel in the course of construction by a manufacturing company was one reserved under the contract as collateral security for installment payments made during construction, such lien was inferior and subordinate to the lien given by this section. United States v. Ansonia Brass & Copper Co., 218 U.S. 452, 31 S. Ct. 49, 54 L. Ed. 1107 (1910), rev'g in part and aff'g in part, S.H. Hawes & Co. v. William R. Trigg Co., 110 Va. 165, 65 S.E. 538 (1909).

Receiver's certificates. — One who has perfected a lien upon the property of a corporation pursuant to this section cannot, without notice, representation and an opportunity to be heard, be deprived of his lien by the decree of a court of chancery ordering the issuance of receiver's certificates and making such certificates preferred liens upon the property. Osborne v. Big Stone Gap Colliery Co., 96 Va. 58, 30 S.E. 446 (1898).

VI. EFFECT OF BANKRUPTCY.

Lien will be recognized in court of bankruptcy. — The liens given by this section will be recognized and enforced by a court of bankruptcy, although perfected within four months prior to the adjudication. In re W. Norfolk Lumber Co., 112 F. 759 (E.D. Va. 1902).

The lien attaches at the time the supplies are furnished, and is not destroyed by the adjudication in bankruptcy of the debtor intervening between the time when the last item on the account for supplies is due and the filing and recording of the claim. Mott v. Wissler Mining Co., 135 F. 697 (4th Cir. 1905).

§ 43-25. Perfection and enforcement of lien.

§ **43-25. Perfection and enforcement of lien.** — No person shall be entitled to the lien given by § 43-24 unless he shall, within ninety days after the last item of his bill becomes due and payable for which such supplies are furnished or service rendered, file in the clerk's office of the circuit court of the county or circuit court of the city in which is located the chief office in this Commonwealth of the company against which the claim is, or in the clerk's office of the Circuit Court of the City of Richmond when such office is in the city, or within that time shall file with the receiver, trustee or assignee of such company, a memorandum of the amount and consideration of his claim, and the time or times when the same is, or will become due and payable, verified by affidavit, which memorandum, if filed with the clerk or in his office, the clerk shall forthwith record in the miscellaneous lien book and index the same in the name of the claimant and also in the name of the company against which the claim is, as required by § 43-4. Any such lien may be enforced in a court of equity. (Code 1919, § 6439; 1928, p. 760.)

Cross references. — For requirement that liens be recorded in the general deed book and indexed in the general index of deeds, see § 43-4.1.

Substantial compliance is required. — While the provisions of this chapter should be liberally construed, there must be a substantial compliance with the requirements of this section, which relates to the creation of the lien. Wilson v. Hall, 81 F.2d 918 (4th Cir. 1936).

An affidavit made before a notary public in another state and not verified as required by § 49-5 in such cases is not a nullity, and the omission to have an officer of a court of record of the state where the affidavit was made certify that the notary was authorized to administer the oath can be supplied. Fidelity Ins., Trust & Safe-Deposit Co. v. Roanoke Iron Co., 81 F. 439 (W.D. Va. 1896).

Time of filing memorandum is governed by date when claim matures. — The time within which the memorandum must be filed is governed by the date when the claim matures; the date of furnishing the supplies is immaterial. If the claim is payable in installments, this section means that the memorandum must be filed within 90 days after the last installment is due. Newgass v. Atlantic & D. Ry., 56 F. 676 (E.D. Va. 1893).

But time is not extended by acceptance of note for wages. — This section does not contemplate that a company may give its note, due 60 days or one or two years after date, for the amount due its laborer, and that then, when the note is due, 90 days shall be allowed thereafter in which to file a memorandum claiming a lien; it means that a claim for a lien shall be made within 90 days from the time the labor was performed — from the day the laborer was entitled to demand his wages. Liberty Perpetual Bldg. & Loan Co. v. M.A. Furbush & Son Mach. Co., 80 F. 631 (4th Cir. 1897).

And memorandum may be filed before claim becomes due. — The language of this section, "within ninety days after the last item of his bill becomes due and payable," is not used to designate the beginning and the end of the period in which the memorandum may be filed, but to fix a period not later than or beyond which the memorandum cannot be filed. A lien claimant who has extended credit may file his memorandum from the time the supplies are furnished, although the term of credit has not expired. In re W. Norfolk Lumber Co., 112 F. 759 (E.D. Va. 1902).

Lien relates back to date supplies were furnished. — The lien dates from the time of furnishing the supplies, and it may be claimed at any time after the supplies are furnished, whether the goods are sold for cash or on credit, provided the claim is filed not later than 90 days after the last item of the account becomes due and payable. If the claim is filed within that time, the lien secured relates back to the time the supplies were furnished. In re W. Norfolk Lumber Co., 112 F. 759 (E.D. Va. 1902).

Time runs from last item of continuous contract. — If the supplies are furnished under a single contract, and are in fulfillment thereof, the items of the account are continuous, and the lien claimant has 90 days from the due date of the last item within which to file his memorandum and perfect his lien. On the other hand, if the several items of the account, or a portion of them, are furnished under separate contracts, then the lien should be filed 90 days from the due date of the last item under each independent contract. Frick Co. v. Norfolk & O.V.R.R., 86 F. 725 (4th Cir. 1898); First Nat'l Bank v. William R. Trigg Co., 106 Va. 327, 56 S.E. 158 (1907), appeal dismissed, 218 U.S. 693, 31 S. Ct. 218, 54 L. Ed. 1212 (1910).

Limitation is suspended by order of reference to master. — An order of reference to a master suspends the running of the statutory limitation of 90 days within which the memorandum must be filed in order to secure a lien. Seventh Nat'l Bank v. Shenandoah Iron Co., 35 F. 436 (C.C.W.D. Va. 1887); Newgass v. Atlantic

& D. Ry., 56 F. 676 (E.D. Va. 1893); Fidelity Ins., Trust & Safe-Deposit Co. v. Roanoke Iron Co., 81 F. 439 (W.D. Va. 1896).

But not by pendency of suit and appointment of receivers. — The limitation in this section is not suspended by the pendency of a suit in which receivers have been appointed. Seventh Nat'l Bank v. Shenandoah Iron Co., 35 F. 436 (C.C.W.D. Va. 1887).

Claims are enforceable in bankruptcy. — When a lien for wages has been perfected in the manner prescribed by this section it is enforceable under § 67d of the Bankruptcy Act, which provides for the preservation and enforcement of liens given in good faith and not repugnant to the Bankruptcy Act. Harrington v. Sencindiver, 173 Va. 33, 3 S.E.2d 381 (1939).

And memorandum may be filed after adjudication. — The lien given by § 43-24 attaches at the time the supplies are furnished, and is not destroyed by the adjudication in

bankruptcy of the debtor intervening between the time when the last item on the account for supplies is due and the filing and recording of the claim. Mott v. Wissler Mining Co., 135 F. 697 (4th Cir. 1905).

Effect of failure to perfect lien against bankrupt. — Where wage claims are not perfected in the manner prescribed by this section, such claims are not enforceable in bankruptcy as prior liens on the property of a corporation. But failure to perfect the liens under this section does not mean that the wage claims are not entitled to priority under the Bankruptcy Act and under the provisions of the deed of assignment. Harrington v. Sencindiver, 173 Va. 33, 3 S.E.2d 381 (1939).

Applied in Textile Banking Co. v. Widener, 265 F.2d 446 (4th Cir. 1959); Southern Ry. v. Flournoy, 301 F.2d 847 (4th Cir. 1962); In re Stunzi, U.S.A., Inc., 7 Bankr. 401 (Bankr. W.D. Va. 1980).

§ 43-26. Assignee's rights. — Any assignee of such a claim as is mentioned in the preceding sections may file the memorandum and make the oath required by such sections, and shall have the same rights as his assignor. (Code 1919, § 6440.)

Cross references. — As to protection of assignee, transferee or indorsee of debt secured by mechanics' lien, see § 43-65.

CHAPTER 3.

LIENS FOR ADVANCES.

§ 43-27: Repealed by Acts 1964, c. 219.

§ 43-27.1. When clerk may destroy crop lien agreement and crop lien book. — Any agreement evidencing a lien on crops required by § 43-27 to be docketed in a clerk's office may be destroyed by such clerk after twenty-four months from the date the same is docketed in his office. Any "Crop Lien Book," together with the index thereto, required by § 43-27 to be kept in a clerk's office, may be destroyed by such clerk after twenty-four months from the date the last entry has been made therein, provided the same is replaced with a similar book and index for the recordation of current liens. (1962, c. 109.)

Editor's note. — Section 43-27, referred to in two places above, was repealed by Acts 1964, c. 219. For provisions as to future advances, see now § 8.9-204.

§ 43-28: Repealed by Acts 1964, c. 219.

§ 43-29. Liens of landlords and farmers for advances to tenants and laborers.

— (1) *Provision for lien; enforcement and priority.* — If any owner or occupier of land contract with any person to cultivate or raise livestock on such land as his tenant for rent either in money or a share of the crop or livestock; or if any person engaged in the cultivation of land contract with any laborer thereon for a share of the crop or the livestock raised thereon as his wages; and such owner or occupier of the land, or such person engaged in the cultivation of land, shall make any advances in money, supplies, or other thing to such tenant or laborer, he shall have a lien to the extent of such advances on all the crops or livestock, or the share of such laborer in the crops or livestock that are made or seeded or raised, grown or fed on the land during the year in which the advances are made, which shall be prior to all other liens on such crops or livestock or such portion thereof, or share therein. And he shall have the same remedy for the enforcement of such lien by distress when the claim is due, or by attachment when the claim is not yet payable, as is given a landlord for the recovery of rent under § 55-230; provided, that he or his agent, shall, before suing out the distress warrant, make affidavit before the justice of the peace issuing the same to the amount of his claim, that it is then due and is for advances made under contract to a tenant cultivating or raising livestock on his land, or a laborer working or raising livestock on the same; and before suing out the attachment, make the like affidavit, and also at what time the claim will become payable, and that the debtor intends to remove, or is removing from such land such crops or livestock, or his portion thereof, or share therein, so that there will not be left enough to satisfy the claim. The person, whose crops or livestock are so distrained or attached, shall have all the rights and be entitled to all the remedies allowed a tenant against a distress or attachment for rent.

(2) *When verified statement of advances required.* — However, when the crops or livestock are subject to a lien of a fieri facias or attachment, whether a levy be actually made or not, it shall be the duty of the person claiming a lien under this section, upon the request of the sheriff, or any other party in interest, to render to the sheriff of the county wherein the crops or livestock are raised or grown, a complete and itemized statement under oath of the claims for advances, showing the nature of the claims, the dates of advancement and the respective amounts. And in case the person claiming advances fails to render to the sheriff of such county the verified itemized statement above provided for within ten days after the request has been made, he shall forever lose the benefit of the lien on the crops or livestock for advances granted him under this section.

(3) *When further showing as to advances required.* — If the execution creditor or attachment creditor desires to contest the validity of the claims for advances, he may cause the clerk of the circuit court of the county in which such crops are grown or livestock raised to summon the person claiming the lien for advances to appear before such court and show to the satisfaction of the court that such money, supplies or other things of value were advanced for the purpose of, and were necessary in and about the cultivation of the crops or the raising of the livestock upon which the lien is claimed. (Code 1919, § 6454; 1930, p. 946; 1942, p. 294; 1956, c. 80.)

Cross references. — As to protection of assignee, transferee or indorsee of debt secured by crop lien, see § 43-65.

§ 43-30. Lien of landlord and other recorded liens not affected by lien given under § 43-27; nor is right to claim exemption.

— The lien provided for in § 43-27 shall not affect in any manner the rights of the landlord to his proper share of rents, or his lien for rent or advances, or his right of distress or attachment for the same, nor any lien existing at the time of making the agreement mentioned in such section, which is required by law to be recorded and shall have been admitted to record. Nor shall it affect the right of the party to whom the advances have been made, to claim such part of his crops as is exempt from levy or distress for rent. (Code 1919, § 6455.)

Editor's note. — Section 43-27, referred to above, was repealed by Acts 1964, c. 219. For provisions as to future advances, see now § 8.9-204.

CHAPTER 4.

LIENS OF INNKEEPERS, LIVERY STABLE, GARAGE AND MARINA KEEPERS, MECHANICS AND BAILEES.

§ 43-31. Lien of innkeepers, etc. — Every innkeeper and the keeper of a boardinghouse or house of private entertainment shall have a lien upon, and may retain possession of, the baggage and other property of his guest or boarder brought upon his premises, and also upon the property of the employer of such guest or boarder, controlled and brought upon the premises by such guest or boarder in the course of his employment, for the proper charges due from such guest for his board and lodging. (Code 1919, § 6444.)

Law Review. — For note, "Effect of the Uniform Commercial Code on Virginia Law," see 20 Wash. & Lee L. Rev. 267 (1963). For case comment on the innkeeper's lien and due process, see 5 U. Rich. L. Rev. 447 (1971); 28 Wash. & Lee L. Rev. 481 (1971).

For the history of this section, see Talbott v. Southern Seminary, Inc., 131 Va. 576, 109 S.E. 440 (1921).

This section gives an undisputed possessory lien to the benefitted party. Epperley v. Woodyard, 4 Bankr. 124 (Bankr. W.D. Va. 1980).

Boardinghouse defined. — A boardinghouse is not in common parlance, or any legal meaning either, a private house where one or more boarders are kept occasionally only and upon special considerations, but it is a quasi-public house where boarders are generally and habitually kept, and which is held out and known as a place of entertainment of that kind. Talbott v. Southern Seminary, Inc., 131 Va. 576, 109 S.E. 440 (1921).

"Boardinghouse" and "house of private entertainment" are the same. — As used in this section the terms "boardinghouse" and "house of private entertainment" mean the same thing. Talbott v. Southern Seminary, Inc., 131 Va. 576, 109 S.E. 440 (1921).

This section does not give a lien to a boarding school on the baggage or property of its pupils. Talbott v. Southern Seminary, Inc., 131 Va. 576, 109 S.E. 440 (1921).

§ 43-32. Lien of keeper of livery stable, garage, marina, etc. — A. Every keeper of a livery stable, hangar, tie-down, marina, or garage, and every person pasturing or keeping any horses or other animals, vehicles, boats, aircraft, or harness, shall have a lien upon such horses and other animals, vehicles, boats, aircraft, and harness, for the amount which may be due him for the keeping, supporting, and care thereof, until such amount is paid.

B. In the case of any boat, aircraft, or vehicle subject to a chattel mortgage, security agreement, deed of trust, or other instrument securing money, the keeper of the marina, hangar, tie-down, or garage shall have a lien thereon for his reasonable charges for storage under this section not to exceed $300 and for alteration and repair under § 43-33 not to exceed $ 625. However, in the case of a storage lien, to obtain the priority for an amount in excess of $150, the person asserting the lien shall give written notice by certified mail, return receipt requested, to any secured party of record at the Department of Motor Vehicles or the Department of Game and Inland Fisheries. If the secured party does not, within seven days of receipt of the notice, take or refuse redelivery to it or its designee, the lienor shall be entitled to priority for the full $300. Notwithstanding a redelivery, the vehicle or watercraft shall be subject to subsection D.

C. In addition, any person furnishing services involving the towing and recovery of a boat, aircraft or vehicle, shall have a lien for all normal costs incident thereto, if the person asserting the lien gives written notice within seven days of receipt of the boat, aircraft or vehicle by certified mail, return receipt requested, to all secured parties of record at the Department of Motor Vehicles or the Department of Game and Inland Fisheries.

D. In addition, any keeper shall be entitled to a lien against any proceeds remaining after the satisfaction of all prior security interests or liens, and may retain possession of such property until such charges are paid.

E. Any lien created under this section shall not extend to any personal property which is not attached to or considered to be necessary for the proper operation of any motor vehicle, and it shall be the duty of any keeper of such personal property to promptly return it to the owner.

F. For the purposes of this section, in the case of a truck or combination of vehicles, the owner or in the case of a rented or leased vehicle, the lessee of the truck or tractor truck shall be liable for the costs of the towing, recovery, and storage of the cargo and of any trailer or semitrailer in the combination. Nothing in this subsection, however, shall bar the owner of the truck or tractor truck from subsequently seeking to recover from the owner of any trailer, semitrailer, or cargo all or any portion of these towing, recovery, and storage costs. (Code 1919, § 6445; 1968, c. 320; 1970, c. 56; 1976, c. 77; 1977, c. 382; 1981, c. 453; 1984, c. 396; 1988, c. 120; 1990, c. 665; 1992, c. 403; 1999, c. 533.)

The 1999 amendment, in subsection B, in the first sentence, substituted "$625" for "$500," and substituted "subsection D" for "subsection C" in the last sentence; and redesignated former subsections B through E as subsections C through F.

Law Review. — For note, "Effect of the Uniform Commercial Code on Virginia Law," see 20 Wash. & Lee L. Rev. 267 (1963). For survey of recent legislation on liens, as to keepers of garages and marinas, see 5 U. Rich. L. Rev. 198 (1970). For survey of Virginia commercial law for the year 1969-1970, see 56 Va. L. Rev. 1387 (1970).

This section gives an undisputed posses-sory lien to the benefitted party limited only to the amounts set forth as to prior existing en-cumbrances. Epperley v. Woodyard, 4 Bankr.

124 (Bankr. W.D. Va. 1980).

Section 46.1-73 (now § 46.2-640) contains specific provision with respect to the pri-ority of a lien shown on the certificate of title to a motor vehicle and is controlling as to the priority of such a lien over a storage lien as well as, to a limited extent, a repair lien claimed against such vehicle. Checkered Flag Motor Car Co. v. Grulke, 209 Va. 427, 164 S.E.2d 660 (1968). See First Va. Bank v. Sutherland, 217 Va. 588, 231 S.E.2d 706 (1977).

The language "shall have priority over any other liens," in § 46.1-73 (now § 46.2-640) is obviously broad enough to include storage liens and necessarily subordinates such latter liens to a lien shown on a certificate of title. Check-ered Flag Motor Car Co. v. Grulke, 209 Va. 427, 164 S.E.2d 660 (1968). See First Va. Bank v.

Sutherland, 217 Va. 588, 231 S.E.2d 706 (1977).

Priority of lien over homestead deed. — See Epperley v. Woodyard, 4 Bankr. 124 (Bankr. W.D. Va. 1980).

Underlying interest not transformed into judicial lien. — Even where enforcement of a livery stable keeper's lien, provided for by statute, contemplates effectuation through the court system, such proceedings do not transform the underlying interest into a judicial lien. O'Malley v. Rapidan River Farm, 24 Bankr. 900 (E.D. Va. 1982).

Amount to which claimant entitled

where limit increased by amendment during proceedings. — Claimant was entitled to the $150.00 amount provided under this section for alterations and repairs when the transactions took place, rather than the $500.00 amount in effect when an adversary proceeding was filed in federal bankruptcy court, since the claims for alterations and repairs to the boat giving rise to a lien arose before the passage of the 1984 amendment. Blue Ridge Recreation, Inc. v. Dean, 55 Bankr. 332 (Bankr. W.D. Va. 1985).

§ 43-33. Lien of mechanic for repairs. — Every mechanic, who shall alter or repair any article of personal property at the request of the owner of such property, shall have a lien thereon for his just and reasonable charges therefor and may retain possession of such property until such charges are paid.

And every mechanic, who shall make necessary alterations or repairs on any article of personal property which from its character requires the making of ordinary repairs thereto as a reasonable incident to its reasonable and customary use, at the request of any person legally in possession thereof under a reservation of title contract, chattel mortgage, deed of trust, or other instrument securing money, the person so in possession having authority to use such property, shall have a lien thereon for his just and reasonable charges therefor to the extent of $ 625. In addition, such mechanic shall be entitled to a lien against the proceeds, if any, remaining after the satisfaction of all prior security interests or liens, and may retain possession of such property until such charges are paid. In any action to enforce the lien hereby given all persons having an interest in the property sought to be subjected shall be made parties defendant.

If the owner of the property held by the mechanic shall desire to obtain possession thereof, he shall make the mechanic defendant in proceeding in the county or municipal court to recover the property.

The owner may give a bond payable to the court, in a penalty of the amount equal to the lien claimed by the mechanic and court costs, with security to be approved by the clerk, and conditioned for the performance of the final judgment of the court on the trial of the proceeding, and with a further condition to the effect that, if upon the hearing, the judgment of the court be that the lien of the mechanic on such property, or any part thereof, be enforced, judgment may thereupon be entered against the obligors on such bond for the amount due the mechanic and court costs, if assessed against the owner, without further or other proceedings against them thereon. Upon giving of the bond, the property shall be delivered to the owner. (Code 1919, § 6443; 1924, p. 638; 1956, c. 558; 1966, c. 458; 1968, c. 395; 1973, c. 492; 1974, c. 166; 1980, c. 598; 1984, c. 396; 1999, c. 533.)

The 1999 amendment substituted "$625" for "$500" at the end of the first sentence of the second paragraph.

Law Review. — For note, "Effect of the Uniform Commercial Code on Virginia Law," see 20 Wash. & Lee L. Rev. 267 (1963). For survey of Virginia commercial law for the year 1969-1970, see 56 Va. L. Rev. 1387 (1970).

This section gives an undisputed possessory lien to the benefitted party limited only to the amounts set forth herein as to prior existing

encumbrances. Epperley v. Woodyard, 4 Bankr. 124 (Bankr. W.D. Va. 1980).

The limitation on amount of lien is an effective provision fixing the priority between a lien for repairs and one of the listed encumbrances otherwise than is provided by § 8.9-310. Except for the $75.00 [now $300.00] statutory amount, this section places the lien for repairs in inferior position to that occupied by the encumbrance on the property. Checkered Flag Motor Car Co. v. Grulke, 209 Va. 427, 164

S.E.2d 660 (1968). See First Va. Bank v. Sutherland, 217 Va. 588, 231 S.E.2d 706 (1977).

Section 46.1-73 (now § 46.2-640) contains specific provision with respect to the priority of a lien shown on the certificate of title to a motor vehicle and is controlling as to the priority of such a lien over a storage lien as well as, to a limited extent, a repair lien claimed against such vehicle. Checkered Flag Motor Car Co. v. Grulke, 209 Va. 427, 164 S.E.2d 660 (1968). See First Va. Bank v. Sutherland, 217 Va. 588, 231 S.E.2d 706 (1977).

Priority of lien over homestead deed. — See Epperley v. Woodyard, 4 Bankr. 124 (Bankr. W.D. Va. 1980).

§ 43-34. Enforcement of liens acquired under §§ 43-31 through 43-33 and of liens of bailees. — Any person having a lien under §§ 43-31 through 43-33 and any bailee, except where otherwise provided, having a lien as such at common law on personal property in his possession which he has no power to sell for the satisfaction of the lien, if the debt for which the lien exists is not paid within ten days after it is due and the value of the property affected by the lien does not exceed $3,000, may sell such property or so much thereof as may be necessary, by public auction, for cash. The proceeds shall be applied to the satisfaction of the debt and expenses of sale, and the surplus, if any, shall be paid within thirty days of the sale to any lienholder, and then to the owner of the property. A seller who fails to remit the surplus as provided shall be liable to the person entitled to the surplus in an amount equal to twenty-five dollars for each day beyond thirty days that the failure continues.

Before making the sale, the seller shall advertise the time, place, and terms thereof in a public place. In the case of property other than a motor vehicle required to be registered in Virginia having a value in excess of $600, ten days' prior notice shall be given to any secured party who has filed a financing statement against the property, and written notice shall be given to the owner as hereinafter provided. If the property is a motor vehicle required by the motor vehicle laws of Virginia to be registered, the person having the lien shall ascertain from the Commissioner of the Department of Motor Vehicles whether the certificate of title of the motor vehicle shows a lien thereon. If the certificate of title shows a lien, the bailee proposing the sale of the motor vehicle shall notify the lienholder of record, by certified mail, at the address on the certificate of title of the time and place of the proposed sale ten days prior thereto. If the name of the owner cannot be ascertained, the name of "John Doe" shall be substituted in any proceedings hereunder and no written notice as to him shall be required to be mailed.

If the value of the property is more than $3,000 but does not exceed $ 15,000, the party having the lien, after giving notice as herein provided, may apply by petition to any general district court of the county or city wherein the property is, or, if the value of the property exceeds $ 15,000, to the circuit court of the county or city, for the sale of the property. If, on the hearing of the case on the petition, the defense, if any made thereto, and such evidence as may be adduced by the parties respectively, the court is satisfied that the debt and lien are established and the property should be sold to pay the debt, the court shall order the sale to be made by the sheriff of the county or city. The sheriff shall make the same and apply and dispose of the proceeds in the same manner as if the sale were made under a writ of fieri facias.

If the owner of the property is a resident of this Commonwealth, any notice required by this section may be served as provided in § 8.01-296 or, if the sale is to be made without resort to the courts, by personal delivery or by certified or registered mail delivered to the present owner of the property to be sold at his last known address at least ten days prior to the date of sale. If he is a nonresident or if his address is unknown, notice may be served by posting a copy thereof in three public places in the county or city wherein the property is located. For purposes of this section, a public place means a premises owned by the Commonwealth, a political subdivision thereof or an agency of either which is open to the general public.

If the property is a motor vehicle (i) for which neither the owner nor any other lienholder or secured party can be determined by the Department of Motor Vehicles through a diligent search of its records, (ii) manufactured for a model year at least six years prior to the current model year, and (iii) having a value of no more than $1,000 as determined by the provisions of § 8.01-419.1, a person having a lien on such vehicle may, after showing proof that the vehicle has been in his continuous custody for at least thirty days, apply for and receive from the Department of Motor Vehicles title to such vehicle, free of all liens and claims of ownership of others, and proceed to sell or otherwise dispose of the vehicle.

Whenever a motor vehicle is sold hereunder, the Department of Motor Vehicles shall issue a certificate of title and registration to the purchaser thereof upon his application containing the serial or motor number of the vehicle purchased together with an affidavit of the lienholder that he has complied with the provisions hereof, or by the sheriff conducting a sale that he has complied with said order.

Any garage keeper to whom a motor vehicle has been delivered pursuant to §§ 46.2-1209, 46.2-1213 or § 46.2-1215 may after thirty days from the date of delivery proceed under this section, provided that action has not been taken pursuant to such sections for the sale of such motor vehicle. (Code 1919, § 6449; 1960, c. 571; 1968, c. 605; 1971, Ex. Sess., c. 155; 1978, c. 59; 1980, c. 598; 1987, c. 37; 1988, c. 227; 1992, c. 111; 1993, c. 759; 1998, c. 868.)

The 1998 amendment, effective July 1, 1999, in the third paragraph, substituted "$15,000" for "$10,000" in two places; added the present fifth paragraph; and in the last paragraph, substituted "thirty days" for "ninety days."

Law Review. — For case comment on the innkeeper's lien and due process, see 5 U. Rich. L. Rev. 447 (1971).

The filing of a financing statement to perfect the security interest in a motor vehicle is not required. — The $600 amount mentioned in the third sentence of this section has no application to the sale of motor vehicles; that amount relates to a requirement of notice to any secured party who has filed a financing statement against the subject property. The filing of a financing statement to perfect the security interest in a motor vehicle is not required. Instead, the sale of such motor vehicles is governed by the specific provisions of the fourth and fifth sentences of this section. Newport News Shipbuilding Employees' Credit Union, Inc. v. B & L Auto Body, Inc., 241 Va. 31, 400 S.E.2d 512 (1991).

An ad in a newspaper does not qualify as advertisement "in a public place" within the meaning of this section. Newport News Shipbuilding Employees' Credit Union, Inc. v. B & L Auto Body, Inc., 241 Va. 31, 400 S.E.2d 512 (1991).

Underlying interest not transformed into judicial lien. — Even where enforcement of a livery stable keeper's lien, provided for by statute, contemplates effectuation through the court system, such proceedings do not transform the underlying interest into a judicial lien. O'Malley v. Rapidan River Farm, 24 Bankr. 900 (E.D. Va. 1982).

§ 43-34.1. Lien of keeper of hangar or tie-down on aircraft subject to a chattel mortgage. —

In the case of any aircraft subject to a chattel mortgage, security agreement, deed of trust or other instrument securing money, the keeper of the hangar or tie-down shall have a lien thereon for his usual and reasonable charges for storage, alteration or repair from the time such lien is perfected as provided herein. Such lien is nonpossessory and shall be deemed a conveyance. To perfect such lien, the following shall be required:

1. The claim of lien shall be signed, under oath, by the claimant, his agent or attorney;

2. The claim of lien shall also be filed within 120 days after completion of alterations or repair or accrual of storage charges, as personal property security interests or liens are recorded, with the State Corporation Commission in accordance with the applicable provisions of Part 4 (§ 8.9-401 et seq.) of Title 8.9; and

3. The claim of lien shall also be filed within such 120-day period with the Aircraft Registration Branch of the Federal Aviation Administration. (1993, c. 854.)

§ 43-35. How and when validity of lien, or claim of other person to property, is tried. — Any person may file his petition, at any time before the property is sold or the proceeds of sale are paid to the plaintiff under the judgment of the trial justice or court, disputing the validity of the plaintiff's lien thereon, or stating a claim thereto, or an interest in or lien on the same, and its nature; and the trial justice or the court, as the case may be, shall inquire into such claim, and if it be found that the petitioner has title to, or a lien on, or any interest in, such property or proceeds of sale, the trial justice or court shall make such order as is necessary to protect his rights. (Code 1919, § 6450.)

§ 43-36. Appeals, how taken and tried. — Any party may appeal from the judgment of the trial justice, as in case of warrants for small claims under Chapter 6 (§ 16.1-76 et seq.) of Title 16.1, and such appeal shall be heard and determined in like manner, as appeals under such chapter. (Code 1919, § 6451.)

§ 43-37. Sale of baggage and other personal property held pursuant to § 43-31 or unclaimed. — Whenever any baggage or other personal property is being held by a hotel pursuant to the lien granted by § 43-31, or where such baggage or other personal property has been voluntarily checked with a hotel, such baggage and other personal property may be sold at public auction for cash after it has been so held or checked and has remained unclaimed for more than sixty days, provided that before such sale is held written notice of such sale stating the date and place thereof and a brief description of such baggage or other personal property and the name of the owner thereof, if known, and the amount of the charges, if any, against the same, is sent by registered mail to such owner, if known, at his last known address, if known, at least ten days prior to such sale, and provided that such notice is publicly posted in the lobby of such hotel at least ten days prior to such sale. (1940, p. 269; Michie Code 1942, § 6451b.)

§ 43-38. Withdrawal from such sale upon payment of charges, interest and expenses. — Such baggage or other personal property shall be withdrawn from sale and released to the owner thereof upon payment to such hotel, at any time prior to such sale, of the debt or charges, if any, against the same, with legal interest thereon and the expenses incurred in preparation for such sale prior to such payment. (1940, p. 270; Michie Code 1942, § 6451c.)

§ 43-39. Distribution of proceeds of sale. — The proceeds of sale shall be applied to the expenses of such sale, including the expense of notices, and to the satisfaction of the debt or charges, if any, with legal interest against such baggage or other personal property. The surplus, if any, shall be paid by the hotel to the owner of such baggage or other personal property, upon written application filed with such hotel by the owner within thirty days after such sale. If no such application is so filed, then such hotel shall pay over such surplus to the State Treasurer, who shall credit the same to the Literary Fund. Compliance by a hotel with the provisions of this and the two preceding sections (§§ 43-37, 43-38) shall be a complete bar and defense to any claim that may thereafter be made by anyone against such hotel on account of such baggage or other personal property. (1940, p. 270; Michie Code 1942, § 6451d.)

§ 43-40. Subsequent payment of surplus proceeds to persons entitled thereto. — At any time within ten years after the payment into the state treasury of the surplus proceeds of any such sale as provided in the preceding section (§ 43-39), the former owner or owners of the property so sold, upon evidence of such ownership satisfactory to the Comptroller, shall be paid the principal amount of such surplus proceeds so paid into the state treasury out of any moneys held in reserve on the books of the Department of Accounts for the benefit of the Literary Fund upon warrant of the Comptroller. If any such claim be disallowed in whole or in part by the Comptroller, it may be recovered in the manner and subject to the conditions and limitations provided in §§ 8.01-192 through 8.01-195 and 8.01-255 for recovering claims against the Commonwealth. (1940, p. 270; Michie Code 1942, § 6451e.)

CHAPTER 5.

LIENS ON OFFSPRING OF CERTAIN ANIMALS.

§ 43-41. Lien on offspring of stallion or jackass. — When the owner of a mare or jennet breeds the same to any stallion or jackass whereby such mare or jennet shall become in foal and is delivered of a live colt, the owner of any such stallion or jackass shall have a lien upon the colt for a period of twelve months, or until the price agreed upon for the season or service by the owner of the stallion or jackass and the owner of the mare or jennet be paid. Such lien shall not extend for a longer period than twelve months, and after judgment has been taken for the amount of such fee, then, unless the same is paid, the officer in whose hands the fieri facias is placed for collection may proceed to levy on and sell such colt for the aforesaid fieri facias and costs, and he shall be entitled to the same fees for his services as is provided for by the existing law. (Code 1919, § 6446; Tax Code, § 439.)

§ 43-42. Recordation of lien given by preceding section. — The lien given by the preceding section (§ 43-41), if reduced to writing, shall be recorded in the miscellaneous lien book and shall be operative from the recordation thereof and if the lien is not reduced to writing, it shall, upon application of the owner of the stallion or jackass, be recorded by the clerk of the circuit court of the county in which the foal is foaled in such book in the following form:

......................(giving the name of the owner of the stallion or jackass) versus ....(giving the name of the owner of the colt). The owner of the stallion or jackass claims a lien on a colt less than twelve months old for $..........., for the get thereof. (Code 1919, § 6446; 1994, c. 432.)

Cross references. — For requirement that liens be recorded in the general deed book and indexed in the general index of deeds, see § 43-4.1.

§ 43-43. Lien on offspring of bull. — A person owning a bull in this Commonwealth shall have a lien on the get of such bull for the period of six months from the date of the birth of such get, for the price agreed upon between him and the owner of any cow served by such bull; however, this lien shall not hold good as against an innocent purchaser for value and without notice, except when the lien has been admitted to record, which may be done in the following form:

.... (giving the name of the owner of the bull) versus .... (giving the name of the owner of the calf). The owner of the bull claims a lien on a calf less than six months old for $..............., for the get thereof.

It shall be the duty of the clerk of the county in which the calf is calved to place the same on record in the miscellaneous lien book. (Code 1919, § 6447; Tax Code, § 439; 1994, c. 432.)

Cross references. — For requirement that liens be recorded in the general deed book and indexed in the general index of deeds, see § 43-4.1.

CHAPTER 6.

LIENS OF CHATTEL DEEDS OF TRUST UPON CROPS, FARM MACHINERY, ETC.

§§ 43-44 through 43-61: Repealed by Acts 1964, c. 219.

CHAPTER 7.

MISCELLANEOUS LIENS.

Sec.
43-62. Lien for farm products consigned to commission merchant.
43-63. Lien for cleaning, laundering, dyeing, pressing or storing clothing, rugs and other fabrics.

Sec.
43-63.1. Lien for furnishing ambulance service to persons injured on highways.

§ 43-62. Lien for farm products consigned to commission merchant. — Whenever any farm products shall have been consigned to any commission merchant for sale, and he shall have made sale thereof and become insolvent or die before paying over the proceeds of the sale thereof to, or on account of, the consignor or owner of the farm products, the claim of such consignor or owner, when legally proved, shall be a lien on the estate of the commission merchant subject only to such liens as were created on the estate and recorded prior to his insolvency or death.

The benefit of this section shall not accrue to any consignor or owner who, without requesting payment, shall allow such proceeds to remain with such commission merchant at interest, nor to any consignor or owner who, without requesting payment, shall allow such proceeds to remain in the hands of such commission merchant more than thirty days after becoming informed of such sale.

Jurisdiction is hereby given to courts exercising circuit court powers in chancery to enforce the provisions of this section. (Code 1919, § 6448.)

§ 43-63. Lien for cleaning, laundering, dyeing, pressing or storing clothing, rugs and other fabrics. — Every person, firm, association and corporation engaged in the business of cleaning, laundering, dyeing and pressing or storing clothing, carpets, rugs and other fabrics shall have a lien upon such clothing, carpets, rugs or other fabrics for the amount which may be due for the cleaning, dyeing, pressing or storage thereof, and may retain such clothing, carpets, rugs or other fabrics until such amount is paid.

If the debt for which a lien is given under this section be not paid within ninety days after it is due, the property subject to such lien, or so much thereof as may be necessary to satisfy such lien, may be sold by the person, firm, association or corporation holding such lien at public auction for cash, and the proceeds of such sale applied to the expenses thereof, and to pay the debt, and the surplus, if any, shall be paid to the owner of such property. Before making such sale the person, firm or corporation holding such lien shall give ten days' written notice thereof by registered mail sent to the last known post-office address of such owner, and, in addition thereto, shall advertise the time and place thereof in such manner as to give it reasonable publicity; provided that if the owner at the time of leaving such property to be cleaned, laundered, dyed, pressed or stored is given a ticket or other receipt therefor which bears on its face in type not smaller than eight point the words, "The property evidenced hereby may be sold if unclaimed after one hundred and eighty days except in the case of stored property which shall not be subject to sale until such property is unclaimed for two hundred forty days," then notice of sale by mail and other advertisement shall not be required. A copy of this section shall be prominently displayed in the place of business in which any such property is left by the owner. (1938, p. 613; Michie Code 1942, § 6451a; 1964, c. 272; 1973, c. 317.)

§ 43-63.1. Lien for furnishing ambulance service to persons injured on highways. — Whenever a person is injured on any highway in this Commonwealth and is given ambulance service as a result of such injury, the person furnishing such ambulance service shall have a lien for the amount of a just and reasonable charge for the service rendered but not to exceed fifty dollars on the claim of such injured person or of his personal representative, against the person, firm or corporation whose negligence is alleged to have caused such injuries.

No such lien shall be created or become effective unless and until a written notice setting forth the name of the person furnishing the ambulance service, the name of the injured person, and the date and place such person is alleged to have sustained injuries, shall have been served upon or given to the person, firm or corporation whose negligence is alleged to have caused such injuries or to the attorney for the injured party.

Such notice when served upon or given to either shall have the effect of making such party liable for the reasonable charges for the service rendered to the injured person to the extent of the amount paid to or received by such injured party or his personal representative exclusive of attorney's fees but not in excess of the maximum amounts prescribed herein. Provided that nothing contained herein shall be construed as imposing liability on any person, firm or corporation whose negligence is alleged to have caused injuries to the person so receiving such ambulance service or on the attorney for the injured party where no settlement is made, or in the case of an attorney, where no funds come into his hands, or where no judgment is obtained in favor of such injured party or his personal representative.

Should the person who received ambulance service question the reasonableness of the charges made therefor, he may file, in the court that would have jurisdiction of such claim if such claim were asserted against him by such person rendering the service, a petition setting forth the facts and the court shall hear and dispose of the same in a summary way after five days' notice to such claimant; and also in such case the claimant may file such petition in the court having jurisdiction if such claim were asserted against the injured party or his personal representative, and after five days' notice the court shall hear and dispose of same in a summary way.

If suit is instituted by such injured person or his personal representative, the person rendering ambulance service may, in lieu of proceeding according to the provisions of this section, file in the court wherein such suit is pending a petition to enforce the lien given hereunder, which petition shall be heard and disposed of in a summary way. (1956, c. 511.)

CHAPTER 8.

MISCELLANEOUS PROVISIONS.

§ 43-64. How notices served, acts done, etc., in case of bankruptcy, death or absconding. — Whenever any act is required to be done by, or notice is to be given to, a person mentioned in any section of this title, or of Chapter 17 (§ 8.01-426 et seq.) of Title 8.01, if such person become bankrupt, the act may be done by, or the notice given to, either the bankrupt or his trustee; or if such person die, the act may be done by, or the notice given to, his personal representative; or if he abscond, the notice may be given to any person over the age of sixteen years found at his last known place of business or residence, or if no such person be found there, by posting the same at the front door of such place of business or residence, or at some other conspicuous part of the building, or he may be proceeded against by order of publication as a nonresident of the Commonwealth. (Code 1919, § 6442; 1944, p. 338.)

§ 43-65. Protection of assignees, transferees or indorsees of debts secured by mechanics' or crop liens. — Whenever any debt secured on real estate or personal property by a mechanics' or crop lien has been assigned, transferred or indorsed to another, in whole or in part by the original payee thereof, such payee, assignee, transferee or indorsee, may cause a memorandum or statement of the assignment to such assignee, transferee, or indorsee to be entered on the margin of the page in the book where such encumbrance securing the same is recorded, which memorandum or statement shall be signed by the assignor, transferrer, or indorser, his duly authorized agent or attorney, and when so signed and the signature thereto attested by the clerk in whose office such encumbrance is recorded the same shall operate as a notice of such assignment and transfer. And where such transfer by the payee is so entered on the margin of the proper book subsequent transfers may likewise be entered in the same manner and with like effect. Provided, however, this section shall not apply to conditional sales contracts of personal property. (Code 1919, § 6457; 1932, p. 548; 1934, p. 249.)

§ 43-66. Purchaser not affected by liens of Mutual Assurance Society against Fire. — The lien of the Mutual Assurance Society against Fire on buildings in the Commonwealth of Virginia upon property insured therein for quotas assessed against the policies of such property owners shall not be valid against purchasers of such property for valuable consideration without notice of the existence of such insurance, except from the time the Society shall have complied with the provisions of this section. The Society shall have prepared and kept in the clerk's office of the Circuit Court of the City of Richmond, and of the circuit court of each county and the circuit court of each city in which the

Society insures property, a book to be called the "Mutual Assurance Society's Lien Book." Such book when left with the clerk shall become a public record and shall be kept open to the inspection of the public. The Society shall have entered in such book a brief description of the property insured by it upon which it claims a lien, the date and amount of the policy and the name of the parties to whom the policy was issued, and the date of the entry shall be made in such book. (Code 1919, § 6458.)

CHAPTER 9.

RELEASE OF LIENS.

§ 43-67. Release of mechanic's lien upon payment or satisfaction. — When payment or satisfaction has been made of a debt secured by a mechanic's lien it shall be released in the manner provided in §§ 55-66.3 and 55-66.4, insofar as appropriate. (Code 1919, § 6456; 1926, p. 80; 1930, p. 69; 1932, p. 120; 1944, p. 198.)

§ 43-68. Releases made by court. — Any person who owns or has any interest in real estate or personal property on which such lien exists may, after twenty days' notice thereof to the person entitled to such lien, apply to the circuit or corporation court of the county or corporation in whose clerk's office such encumbrance is recorded, or to the Circuit Court of the City of Richmond, if it be in the clerk's office of such court, to have the same released or discharged; and upon proof that it has been paid or discharged, or upon its appearing to the court that more than twenty years have elapsed since the maturity of the lien, raising a presumption of payment, and which is not rebutted at the hearing, or upon proof that no suit, as defined by § 43-17, has been brought to enforce the same within the time prescribed by such section; such court shall order the same to be entered by the clerk on the margin of the page in the book wherein the lien is recorded, which entry, when so made, shall operate as a release of such lien.

All releases made prior to June 24, 1944, by any court under this section upon such presumption of payment so arising and not rebutted, shall be validated. (Code 1919, § 6456; 1926, p. 81; 1930, p. 70; 1932, p. 121; 1944, p. 199.)

§ 43-69: Repealed by Acts 1994, c. 432.

§ 43-70. Release of mechanic's lien upon payment into court or filing of bond after suit brought. — In any suit brought under the provisions of § 43-22, the owner of the building and premises to which the lien, or liens, sought to be enforced shall have attached, the general contractor for such building or other parties in interest may, after five days' notice to the lienor, or lienors, apply to the court in which such suit shall be pending, or to the judge thereof in vacation, for permission to pay into court an amount of money sufficient to discharge such lien, or liens, and the costs of the suit or for permission to file a bond in the penalty of double the amount of such lien, or liens, and costs, with surety to be approved by the court, or judge, conditioned for the payment of such judgment adjudicating the lien or liens to be valid and determining the amount for which the same would have been enforceable against the real estate as may be rendered by the court upon the hearing of the case on its merits, which permission shall be granted by the court, or judge, in either such case, unless good cause be shown against the same by some party in interest.

Upon the payment of such money into court, or upon the filing of such bond, as the case may be, after the court has granted permission for the same to be done, the property affected thereby shall stand released from such lien, or liens, and the money so paid in, or the bond so filed, as the case may be, shall be subject to the final judgment of the court upon the hearing of the case on its merits. (1936, p. 492; Michie Code 1942, § 6437a; 1962, c. 166; 1976, c. 388; 1992, c. 532.)

The holder of a mechanic's lien that is "bonded off," pursuant to this section, must still establish the priority of the lien. York Fed. Sav. & Loan Ass'n v. William A. Hazel, Inc., 256 Va. 599, 506 S.E.2d 315 (1998).

Applied in VNB Mtg. Corp. v. Lone Star Indus., Inc., 215 Va. 366, 209 S.E.2d 909 (1974).

§ 43-71. Release of mechanic's lien upon payment into court or filing bond before suit. — At any time after the perfecting of any such lien and before a suit be brought for the enforcement thereof, the owner of the property affected thereby, the general contractor or other parties in interest may, after five days' notice to the lienor, apply to the court having jurisdiction of a suit for the enforcement of such lien, or to the judge thereof in vacation, for permission to make such payment into court, or to file such bond, as prescribed in § 43-70, which permission, in either such event, shall be granted by such court, or judge, unless good cause be shown against the same by some party in interest. Upon the granting of such permission, and the payment of such money into court, or the filing of such bond, as the case may be, the property affected thereby shall stand released from such lien.

Such money, or bond, as the case may be, shall be held under the control of the court and shall be subject to the final judgment of the court adjudicating the lien or liens to be valid and determining the amount for which the same would have been enforceable against the real estate in any suit or action thereafter brought for the ascertainment of the rights of the parties in interest, with respect hereto, or, shall be paid out and disposed of as the parties in interest may direct, in the event the matters in controversy with respect thereto be settled and adjusted between the parties without suit or action.

The sureties on any such bond, which may be involved in any suit or action brought under the provisions of this section, shall be made parties to such suit or action. (1936, p. 493; Michie Code 1942, § 6437b; 1962, c. 166; 1976, c. 390; 1992, c. 532.)

The legislative purpose of this section was to facilitate the financing and expedite the completion of construction and repair projects by creating an alternative security device which provides those who supply the labor and materials to those projects protection equivalent to the protection afforded by mechanic's liens. George W. Kane, Inc. v. Nuscope, Inc., 243 Va. 503, 416 S.E.2d 701 (1992).

Necessary parties. — The owner of property encumbered by a subcontractor's mechanic's lien and the trustees and the beneficiary of a deed of trust recorded prior to commencement of the improvements are not necessary parties to the subcontractor's suit to enforce its lien when that lien has been "bonded off" and released pursuant to this section. George W. Kane, Inc. v. Nuscope, Inc., 243 Va. 503, 416 S.E.2d 701 (1992).

Applied in VNB Mtg. Corp. v. Lone Star Indus., Inc., 215 Va. 366, 209 S.E.2d 909 (1974).

Title 44.

Military and Emergency Laws.

CHAPTER 1.

MILITARY LAWS OF VIRGINIA.

Article 1.

Classification of Militia.

Article 2.

General Administrative Officers.

Article 3.

National Guard in General.

ARTICLE 1.

Classification of Militia.

§ 44-1. Composition of militia. — The militia of the Commonwealth of Virginia shall consist of all able-bodied citizens of this Commonwealth and all other able-bodied persons resident in this Commonwealth who have declared their intention to become citizens of the United States, who are at least sixteen years of age and, except as hereinafter provided, not more than fifty-five years of age. The militia shall be divided into four classes, the National Guard, which includes the Army National Guard and the Air National Guard, the Virginia State Defense Force, the naval militia, and the unorganized militia. (1930, p. 948; 1942, p. 642; Michie Code 1942, § 2673(1); 1944, p. 24; 1958, c. 393; 1970, c. 662; 1973, c. 401; 1976, c. 399; 1979, c. 647; 1984, c. 765; 1989, c. 414.)

§ 44-2. Composition of National Guard. — A. The National Guard shall consist of the regularly enlisted militia and of commissioned and warrant officers, who shall be residents of the Commonwealth of Virginia and shall fall within the age limits and qualifications as prescribed in existing or subsequently amended National Guard regulations (army and air), organized, armed and equipped as hereinafter provided. Upon original enlistment members of the National Guard shall not be less than seventeen nor more than fifty-five years of age, or, in subsequent enlistments not more than sixty-four years of age. All enlistments in the National Guard of persons under the age of eighteen years made prior to June 27, 1958, shall be held, and the same are hereby declared valid and effective in all respects, if otherwise valid and effective according to the law then in force.

B. Notwithstanding the above, persons otherwise qualified but residing outside the Commonwealth of Virginia, may enlist or serve as commissioned or warrant officers in the National Guard. (1930, p. 948; Michie Code 1942, § 2673(2); 1958, c. 393; 1976, c. 399; 1979, c. 647.)

§ 44-2.1: Repealed by Acts 1989, c. 414.

Cross references. — For the Virginia State Defense Force, see now § 44-54.4 et seq.

§ 44-3. Composition of naval militia. — The naval militia shall consist of the regularly enlisted militia between the ages of eighteen and forty-five years, organized, armed, and equipped as hereinafter provided, and commissioned officers between the ages of eighteen and sixty-four years; but enlisted personnel may continue in the service after the age of forty-five years and until the age of sixty-four years, provided the service is continuous. (1930, p. 949; Michie Code 1942, § 2673(3); 1972, c. 823; 1973, c. 401.)

§ 44-4. Composition of unorganized militia. — The unorganized militia shall consist of all able-bodied persons as set out in § 44-1, except such as may be included in §§ 44-2, 44-2.1, and 44-3, and except such as may be exempted as hereinafter provided. (1930, p. 949; Michie Code 1942, § 2673(4); 1970, c. 662; 1973, c. 401; 1984, c. 765.)

Editor's note. — Section 44-2.1, which is referred to above, was repealed by Acts 1989, c. 414. For present provisions, see § 44-54.4 et seq.

§ 44-5. Exemptions from militia duty. — In addition to those exempted by the laws of the United States, the following persons shall be exempt from military duty under a state call:

(1) The officers, judicial and executive, of the governments of the United States and the Commonwealth of Virginia.

(2) The members of the General Assembly of the Commonwealth of Virginia and of the Congress of the United States.

(3) Persons in the active military or naval services of the United States.

(4) Customhouse clerks.
(5) Persons employed by the United States in the transmission of the mail.
(6) The judges and clerks of courts of record.
(7) The mayor and councilmen of incorporated cities and towns.
(8) Members of the governing bodies of counties.
(9) Sheriffs, United States district attorneys, attorneys for the Commonwealth and city attorneys.
(10) [Repealed.]
(11) Lighthouse keepers.
(12) Marine pilots.
(13) [Repealed.]
(14) All persons who because of religious belief shall claim exemption from military service, if the conscientious holding of such belief by such person shall be established under such regulations as the President of the United States shall prescribe, shall be exempted from militia service in any capacity that the President shall declare to be combatant.
(15) Such other persons as may be designated by the Governor in the best interests of the public and of the Commonwealth. (1930, p. 949; Michie Code 1942, § 2673(5); 1958, c. 393; 1976, c. 399.)

§ 44-6. Maintenance of other troops. — In time of peace the Commonwealth shall maintain only such troops as may be authorized by the President of the United States; but nothing in this chapter shall be construed as limiting the rights of the Commonwealth in the use of the Virginia National Guard or Virginia State Defense Force within or without its borders in time of peace and nothing contained in this chapter shall prevent the organization and maintenance of State Police or constabulary. (1930, p. 949; Michie Code 1942, § 2673(6); 1958, c. 393; 1984, c. 765.)

§ 44-7. Corps entitled to retain privileges. — Any corps of artillery, cavalry, or infantry existing in this Commonwealth on the passage of the act of Congress of May 8, 1972, which by the laws, customs or usages of the Commonwealth has been in continuous existence since the passage of such act, under its provisions and under the provisions of § 232 and § 1660, both inclusive, of Title 16 of the Revised Statutes of 1873: and the act of Congress of January 21, 1903, relating to the militia, shall be allowed to retain its ancient privileges, subject, nevertheless, to all duties required by law of militia; provided, that such organizations may be a part of the National Guard and entitled to all the privileges of this chapter, and shall conform in all respects to the organization, discipline and training of the National Guard in time of war; provided, further, that for the purposes of training and when on active duty in the service of the United States they may be assigned to higher units, as the President may direct, and shall be subject to the orders of officers under whom they shall be serving. (1930, p. 949; Michie Code 1942, § 2673(7).)

ARTICLE 2.

General Administrative Officers.

§ 44-8. Governor as Commander in Chief. — The Governor shall be Commander in Chief of the armed forces of the Commonwealth, and shall have power to employ such forces to repel invasion, suppress insurrection, and enforce the execution of the laws. (1930, p. 950; Michie Code 1942, § 2673(8); R. P. 1948, § 44-8; 1958, c. 393; 1964, c. 227.)

Cross references. — For constitutional authority, see Va. Const., Art. V, § 7.

§ 44-9. Commander in Chief to prescribe regulations.

— The Commander in Chief shall have the power, and it shall be his duty, from time to time, to issue such orders and to prescribe such regulations relating to the organization of the armed forces of the Commonwealth as will cause the same at all times to conform to the federal requirements of the United States government relating thereto. (1930, p. 950; Michie Code 1942, § 2673(9); R. P. 1948, § 44-9; 1958, c. 393.)

§ 44-10. Divisions of military staff.

— The military staff shall be divided into (a) the personal staff of the Governor and (b) the administrative staff.

The personal staff of the Governor shall be constituted as now prescribed by law.

The administrative staff shall be as is authorized by the Secretary of Defense of the United States and shall perform such duties as the commander in chief may direct. (1930, p. 950; Michie Code 1942, § 2673(10); R. P. 1948, § 44-10; 1958, c. 393.)

§ 44-11. Department of Military Affairs; Adjutant General.

— There is hereby created the Department of Military Affairs to which is transferred all of the functions, powers and duties of the former Division of Military Affairs.

The Governor shall appoint an Adjutant General with the rank of brigadier general, major general or lieutenant general as the Governor may prescribe, subject to confirmation by the General Assembly if in session, and if not in session, then at its next succeeding session. The Adjutant General shall not hold the rank of lieutenant general unless such rank is federally recognized. The Adjutant General shall be in direct charge of the Department of Military Affairs and shall be responsible to the Governor and commander in chief for the proper performance of his duties. All the powers conferred and the duties imposed by law upon the Adjutant General shall be exercised or performed by him under the direction and control of the Governor. The Adjutant General shall serve at the pleasure of the Governor for a term coincident with that of the Governor. No person shall be appointed Adjutant General who shall not have had at least ten years' commissioned service in the Virginia National Guard in at least field grade. The Adjutant General, while serving as such, may be a member of the Virginia National Guard.

The Adjutant General shall receive a salary prescribed by law. (1927, p. 106; 1930, p. 951; Michie Code 1942, §§ 585(62), 2673(12); 1948, p. 48; R. P. 1948, § 44-11; 1964, c. 227.)

§ 44-12. Board of Military Affairs.

— In the Department of Military Affairs there shall be a Board of Military Affairs, composed of the senior officer of the Virginia National Guard, or, whenever the Virginia National Guard is mustered into the service of the United States and until it is returned to state service, the senior officer of the Virginia State Defense Force, one military officer and one enlisted person appointed by the Adjutant General, and one military officer and one enlisted person appointed by the Governor, all of whom shall be active or retired members of the United States Armed Forces, the Reserves of the United States Armed Forces, or the National Guard. The Board of Military Affairs shall meet upon call of the Governor or the Adjutant General to advise them on military affairs. The members of the Board shall receive no compensation for their services except that, to cover attendance at meetings of the Board, the military members shall receive the pay and allowances of their rank and other members their reasonable expenses incurred. The former

Military Board is hereby abolished. (1930, p. 950; Michie Code 1942, § 2673(11); 1944, p. 24; R.P. 1948, § 44-12; 1972, c. 496; 1973, c. 401; 1984, c. 605; 1989, c. 414.)

§ 44-13. Powers of Adjutant General. — As head of the Department of Military Affairs, the Adjutant General shall have command of all of the militia of the Commonwealth, subject to the orders of the Governor as Commander in Chief, and shall distribute all orders from the Governor pertaining to the military service and shall perform all duties imposed upon him or that Department by this title in the manner prescribed by law. (1927, p. 106; 1930, p. 951; Michie Code 1942, §§ 585(62), 2673(13); R. P. 1948, § 44-13; 1958, c. 393; 1989, c. 414.)

§ 44-14. Expenditures for Department. — All payments and disbursements payable out of the appropriation to the Department of Military Affairs shall be made by the State Treasurer upon warrants of the Comptroller issued upon vouchers signed by the Adjutant General or such person as the Adjutant General may designate for such purpose. Expenditures not specifically provided for but manifestly for the benefit of the military service may be made by the Adjutant General with the concurrence of the Board of Military Affairs and the written approval of the Governor. (1930, p. 950; Michie Code 1942, § 2673(11); 1944, p. 24; R. P. 1948, § 44-13.)

§ 44-15. Reports to Secretary of Defense. — The Adjutant General shall make such returns and reports to the Secretary of Defense, or to such officers as he may designate, at such times and in such form as may from time to time be prescribed. (1930, p. 951; Michie Code 1942, § 2673(13); R. P. 1948, § 44-14; 1958, c. 393.)

§ 44-16. Records of Adjutant General. — The Adjutant General shall keep a record of all officers and enlisted personnel, and shall also keep in his office all records and papers required by law or regulations to be filed therein. (1930, p. 951; Michie Code 1942, § 2673(13); R. P. 1948, § 44-15; 1970, c. 662.)

§ 44-17. Regulations as to reports and care of property. — The Adjutant General is empowered to make such regulations pertaining to the preparation and rendering of reports and returns and to the care and preservation of public property as in his opinion the conditions demand, such regulations to be operative and in force when promulgated in the form of general orders, circulars, circular letters, or other regulations and documents. (1930, p. 951; Michie Code 1942, § 2673(13); R. P. 1948, § 44-17; 1964, c. 227.)

§ 44-18. Seal of Adjutant General. — The Adjutant General is authorized to adopt an appropriate seal for use in his office. (1930, p. 951; Michie Code 1942, § 2673(13); R. P. 1948, § 44-18.)

§ 44-19. Adjutant General to have charge of military property. — The Adjutant General shall have charge and care of all state military property and all United States military property issued to the Commonwealth of Virginia, and shall cause to be kept an accurate and careful account of all receipts and issues of the same. He shall require to be kept careful memoranda of all public military property on hand in the state arsenal or storehouses, and in the possession of the several organizations of the Virginia National Guard or issued to the Virginia State Defense Force, and shall guard such property against injury and loss to the extent of his ability. He shall require every accountable and responsible officer of the National Guard to account for every deficiency in public military property in his possession immediately after such deficiency is discovered. The Adjutant General shall have the care and control of the state military reservation near Virginia Beach, and of such other real estate as the Commonwealth may acquire for military purposes, and it shall be the duty of the Adjutant General to provide for the proper care of such property and buildings thereon. For the maintenance, upkeep and improvement of the military reservation or reservations, the Adjutant General may expend from the appropriation to the Department of Military Affairs such amounts as may be necessary. (1930, pp. 950, 952; Michie Code 1942, §§ 2673(11), 2673(13); 1944, p. 24; R. P. 1948, § 44-19; 1958, c. 393; 1989, c. 414.)

§ 44-20. Deputy Adjutant General (Army and Air) and Assistant Adjutant General (Army); assistants and clerical forces of Adjutant General. — The Adjutant General shall have a Deputy Adjutant General (Air), a Deputy Adjutant General (Army) and an Assistant Adjutant General (Army) whose grades shall not exceed that of brigadier general and he shall have other assistants and such clerical forces as may be necessary who shall serve at the pleasure of the Adjutant General, subject to the provisions of general law, and shall perform such duties as he may assign them. The Adjutant General shall have such other clerks and employees as may be necessary for the administration of his office. (1930, p. 952; Michie Code 1942, § 2673(13); R.P. 1948, § 44-20; 1964, c. 227; 1979, c. 504; 1983, c. 74.)

§ 44-21. Bonds of Adjutant General and fiscal clerks. — The Adjutant General and his fiscal clerks shall each give bond, with sufficient sureties, to be approved by the Governor, as provided by law for other state officers. The penalties of the bond shall be as follows: of the Adjutant General, $10,000, of each of his fiscal clerks, $3,000. (1930, p. 952; Michie Code 1942, § 2673(13); R. P. 1948, § 44-21; 1964, c. 227.)

§ 44-22. Auditing accounts of Adjutant General. — The office and accounts of the Adjutant General pertaining to the Commonwealth of Virginia shall be audited by the direction of the Governor in the same manner as the office and accounts of other state officers are audited, as provided by law. (1930, p. 952; Michie Code 1942, § 2673(13); R. P. 1948, § 44-22.)

§ 44-23: Repealed by Acts 1984, c. 734.

§ 44-24. United States Property and Fiscal Officer. — The Governor shall appoint, designate or detail, subject to the approval of the Secretary of Defense, an officer of the National Guard of the Commonwealth to serve as a United States Property and Fiscal Officer. Any officer of the National Guard who has been so appointed and is serving as United States Property and Fiscal Officer, may be removed for just cause by the Governor with the approval of the Secretary of Defense. The Adjutant General is hereby declared ineligible to serve as United States Property and Fiscal Officer. The duties and remuneration of said United States Property and Fiscal Officer shall be such as are prescribed by existing or subsequently amended regulations of the armed forces of the United States. (1930, p. 952; Michie Code 1942, § 2673(14); R. P. 1948, § 44-24; 1958, c. 393.)

§ 44-24.1. Adjutant General may provide group health and hospitalization insurance for employees of Department. — The Adjutant General of the Commonwealth of Virginia is hereby authorized and empowered to provide group health insurance and hospitalization benefits for the employees of the Department of Military Affairs including civilian employees of the state National Guard compensated under the provisions of 32 U.S.C. § 709, as amended, and whose compensation is solely payable from federal funds, and to enter into agreements with insurance companies and prepaid hospital and medical care plan companies to that end provided all premiums and costs of participation are contributed solely by such employees.

The Adjutant General is further authorized and empowered to deduct, or authorize the deduction by the Comptroller of, the amount of the premium and costs of participation which the employee has agreed to pay for such insurance benefits from the wages of such employee and the State Treasurer shall remit the same directly to the insurance company or prepaid hospital and medical care plan companies issuing the group insurance or plan on the receipt of the written request of such employee.

Nothing in this section shall affect any provision of §§ 38.2-3318.1 through 38.2-3339 or of Title 51. (1966, c. 402.)

The number of this section was assigned by the Virginia Code Commission, the 1966 act having assigned no number.

ARTICLE 3.

National Guard in General.

§ 44-25. Organization; composition of units. — Except as otherwise specifically provided by the laws of the United States, the organization of the National Guard, including the composition of all units thereof, shall be the same as that prescribed for the active army, air force and navy, subject in time of peace to such general exceptions as may be authorized by the Secretary of Defense. (1930, p. 952; Michie Code 1942, § 2673(15); 1958, c. 393; 1964, c. 227.)

Cross references. — As to conversion of military property by persons discharged from the National Guard, see § 18.2-111.1.

§ 44-26. Location of units and headquarters. — The Governor shall determine and fix the location of the units and headquarters of the National Guard within the Commonwealth. (1930, p. 953; Michie Code 1942, § 2673(16); 1958, c. 393.)

§ 44-27. Appointment and promotion of officers. — All officers of the National Guard shall be appointed and commissioned by the Governor as follows:

(1) Appointments of second lieutenants shall, when practicable, be made from the enlisted personnel within the organization.

(2) Commanding officers shall forward through channels the name of the best qualified enlisted person in their organization, accompanied by the necessary documents and his military records, with the commander's endorsement thereon, to the Adjutant General's office for consideration by the Governor.

(3) Original appointments in new organizations, all appointments in the headquarters and headquarters detachment, and to all staffs higher than brigade, and the appointment of brigade and higher commanders shall be made upon the recommendation of the Adjutant General.

(4) Within the organization, insofar as practicable, all appointments and promotions shall be based on professional qualifications, efficiency, length of service in grade, length of commissioned service, and demonstrated command and staff ability at the appropriate level, and will be effected only when an appropriate vacancy exists in the applicable table of organization and equipment or table of organization or distribution. (1930, p. 953; Michie Code 1942, § 2673(17); 1958, c. 393; 1964, c. 227; 1970, c. 662.)

§ 44-28. Qualifications of commanding or staff officers. — No person shall be appointed a commanding or staff officer unless such person shall have had federally recognized commissioned military service, nor shall any officer be appointed who fails to qualify as to fitness for military service under such regulations as the Secretary of Defense shall prescribe. Such officers may hold their positions until they have reached the age or length of service as prescribed in existing or subsequently amended National Guard regulations, unless separated from the service prior to that time by reason of resignation, disability, withdrawal or termination of federal recognition or commission, or upon finding of a legally convened court-martial. (1930, p. 953; Michie Code 1942, § 2673(18); 1958, c. 393; 1970, c. 662.)

§ 44-29. Qualifications of National Guard officers. — The qualifications of National Guard officers shall be as prescribed in current and subsequently amended National Guard regulations. (1930, p. 953; Michie Code 1942, § 2673(19); 1958, c. 393.)

§ 44-30. Tests as to fitness for officers; examining board. — No person shall hereafter be appointed an officer of the National Guard unless such person first shall have successfully passed such tests as to physical, moral, and professional fitness as the President shall prescribe. The examination to determine such qualifications for commission shall be conducted by a board of three commissioned officers appointed by the Secretary of Defense from the active army or the National Guard, or both. (1930, p. 954; Michie Code 1942, § 2673(20); 1958, c. 393; 1964, c. 227; 1970, c. 662.)

§ 44-31. Relative rank of officers. — Relative rank among officers of the same grade shall be determined according to current and subsequently amended Department of Defense and National Guard regulations. (1930, p. 954; Michie Code 1942, § 2673(21); 1964, c. 227.)

§ 44-32. Oath of National Guard officers. — Commissioned officers of the National Guard shall take and subscribe to the following oath of office: "I .... do solemnly swear that I will support and defend the Constitution of the United States and the Constitution of the Commonwealth of Virginia, against all enemies, foreign and domestic; that I will bear true faith and allegiance to the same; that I will obey the orders of the President of the United States and of the Governor of the Commonwealth of Virginia; that I make this obligation freely, without mental reservation or purpose of evasion, and that I will well and faithfully discharge the duties of the office of .... in the National Guard of the United States and of the Commonwealth of Virginia, upon which I am about to enter; so help me God." (1930, p. 954; Michie Code 1942, § 2673(22); 1958, c. 393.)

§ 44-32.1. Administration of oaths of office and enlistment. — Any duly commissioned officer or warrant officer of the Virginia National Guard or any commissioned officer of any of the armed services of the United States may administer the oaths of office and enlistment to prospective officers and enlisted personnel desirous of becoming members of the Virginia National Guard and the National Guard of the United States. Any duly commissioned officer of the Virginia State Guard, when called into service by the Governor, may administer oaths to prospective officers and enlisted personnel desirous of becoming members of the state guard of Virginia. (1947, p. 143; Michie Suppl. 1948, § 2673(22a); 1958, c. 393; 1979, c. 647.)

§ 44-33. Elimination and disposition of officers. — At any time the moral character, capacity, and general fitness for the service of any National Guard officer may be determined by an efficiency board of three commissioned officers senior in rank to the officer whose fitness for service shall be under investigation, said board to be appointed by the Adjutant General and convened on his order. If the findings of such board be unfavorable to such officer and be approved by the Adjutant General, such officer shall be discharged. Commissions of officers of the National Guard may be vacated upon resignation, if approved by the Adjutant General, absence without leave for three months, upon the recommendation of an efficiency board, pursuant to sentence of a court-martial, upon physical disqualification, when convicted of a felony in a civil court, when appointed or inducted into the armed forces of the United States, when federal recognition is withdrawn from such officer or from the unit to which assigned, upon reaching maximum age limitation, and when it has been determined that an officer is subversive or disloyal. Officers of the Virginia National Guard rendered surplus by the disbandment of their organization shall be placed in another unit, providing an appropriate vacancy exists, otherwise such officers shall be separated from the Virginia National Guard and automatically revert to the reserve. (1930, p. 954; Michie Code 1942, § 2673(23); 1958, c. 393; 1964, c. 227; 1970, c. 662.)

§ 44-34: Repealed by Acts 1958, c. 393.

§ 44-35. Enlistments in National Guard. — Enlistments in the National Guard shall be as prescribed in existing or subsequently amended National Guard regulations. (1930, p. 954; Michie Code 1942, § 2673(25); 1958, c. 393.)

§ 44-36. Enlistment contract and oath. — Enlisted persons shall not be recognized as members of the National Guard until they shall have signed an enlistment contract and taken and subscribed to the oath of enlistment prescribed by present or subsequently amended National Guard regulations; or such oath of enlistment as shall be prescribed by the Governor of Virginia for members of the Virginia State Defense Force. (1930, p. 955; Michie Code 1942, § 2673(26); 1958, c. 393.)

§ 44-37. Discharge of enlisted persons. — An enlisted person discharged from service in the Virginia National Guard shall receive a discharge in writing. The form and classification of such discharge shall be as prescribed by existing or subsequently amended National Guard regulations. (1930, p. 955; Michie Code 1942, § 2673(27); 1958, c. 393.)

§ 44-38. Membership continued in National Guard after termination of federal service. — When inducted into the active military service of the United States and thereafter discharged or separated from the armed forces, all persons so inducted and thereafter discharged or separated shall resume their membership in the Virginia National Guard and shall continue to serve therein as though their service had not been so interrupted. (1930, p. 955; Michie Code 1942, § 2673(28); 1958, c. 393.)

Federal service regarded as temporary. United States is regarded as temporary. City of — This section shows that the service of mem- Lynchburg v. Suttenfield, 177 Va. 212, 13 bers of the National Guard in the army of the S.E.2d 323 (1941).

§ **44-39. Uniforms, arms and equipment.** — The National Guard shall, as far as practicable, be uniformed, armed, and equipped with the same type of uniform, arms, and equipment as are or shall be provided for the armed forces of the United States. (1930, p. 955; Michie Code 1942, § 2673(29); 1958, c. 393.)

§ **44-40. Discipline and training.** — The discipline and training of the Virginia National Guard shall conform to that of the Armed Forces of the United States, and to that end, the Manual for Courts-Martial, United States, including but not limited to the Uniform Code of Military Justice as now existing or subsequently amended, is hereby incorporated as a part of the military laws of Virginia except where in conflict with other provisions of this chapter. Officers and soldiers of the National Guard shall have such powers in the performance of their duty under this title as officers and soldiers of the active armed services have in the performance of like duty under the Uniform Code of Military Justice and Manual for Courts-Martial, United States. However, should a person commit an offense punishable under the criminal laws of Virginia, then prosecution under the criminal laws shall bar prosecution under this chapter. The Adjutant General shall by regulation adapt to state usage the provisions and terminology of the Manual for Courts-Martial, United States, including but not limited to the Uniform Code of Military Justice. (1930, p. 955; Michie Code 1942, § 2673(30); 1958, c. 393; 1976, c. 399; 1984, c. 7; 1987, c. 32.)

§ **44-40.1. Persons subject to the Virginia military laws.** — All members of the Virginia National Guard are subject to the military laws of Virginia when under orders to be present for duty, not in federal service. (1976, c. 399.)

§ **44-40.2. Administration of oaths and taking of sworn statements by commissioned officers.** — In addition to those powers set forth in § 44-40, commissioned officers in the Virginia National Guard may administer oaths and take sworn statements in connection with any investigation required by law or regulation pertaining to the Virginia National Guard in the performance of their duties. (1987, c. 32.)

§ **44-41. Armory drills, inactive training, annual active duty training, etc.** — Training, including inactive training, armory drills, annual active duty for training, active duty training and other exercises, shall be conducted in accordance with existing or subsequently amended National Guard regulations. (1930, p. 955; Michie Code 1942, § 2673(31); 1958, c. 393; 1964, c. 227.)

§ **44-41.1. Failure to attend annual active duty training; etc.** — If any person, being an active member of the Virginia National Guard, in violation of valid orders, fails to initially report for annual active duty training or having initially reported absents himself from his unit without leave, upon warrant issued, after hearing, by a summary court-martial, such person shall be taken into custody by military personnel of the Virginia National Guard, or by any State Police Officer or local law-enforcement officer listed in § 44-50, and be forthwith returned to his assigned unit by such military personnel, or held by the State Police or by such local law-enforcement officers until such time as he is taken into custody by military personnel. If taken into custody by the State Police or by local law-enforcement officers, he shall be afforded reasonable opportunity to make bail or recognizance as provided in Chapter 9 (§ 19.2-119 et seq.) of Title 19.2. In no case shall he be held in custody by the State Police or by such local law-enforcement officers in excess of twenty-four hours. Upon return to his assigned unit, such person shall be subject to disciplinary proceedings.

If any active member of the Virginia National Guard fails to report for scheduled inactive duty training, he may, in the same manner, be taken into custody and returned to his unit where he shall be subject to disciplinary proceedings. (1977, c. 315; 1978, c. 342; 1983, c. 65; 1984, c. 206.)

ARTICLE 4.

National Guard Courts-Martial.

§ 44-42. Kinds of courts-martial; how constituted and powers. — In the National Guard not in federal service, there shall be general, special, and summary courts-martial, constituted like similar courts of the army and the air force. They shall have the jurisdiction and powers, except as to punishments, and shall follow the forms and procedures provided for such courts as are enumerated in the Manual for Courts-Martial United States. (1930, p. 956; Michie Code 1942, § 2673(32); 1976, c. 399.)

§ 44-43. General courts-martial; sentencing. — A. General courts-martial of the National Guard, not in federal service, may be convened by orders of the Governor or the Adjutant General of Virginia.

B. A general court-martial shall have the authority to impose any of the following fines and penalties:

1. A fine of not more than $200;
2. Forfeiture of pay and allowances;
3. A reprimand;
4. Dismissal or dishonorable discharge;
4a. Restriction to limits;
4b. Imposition of extra duty;
4c. Confinement for not more than twenty days;
5. Reduction of enlisted persons one or more pay grades; or
6. Any combination of these punishments. (1930, p. 956; Michie Code 1942, § 2673(33); 1958, c. 393; 1964, c. 227; 1976, c. 399; 1977, c. 74.)

§ 44-44. Special courts-martial. — A. In the National Guard, not in federal service, the commanding officer of each garrison, fort, post, camp, air base, auxiliary air base, or other place, where troops are on duty, or brigade, regiment, wing, group, detached battalion, separate squadron, or other detached command, may convene special courts-martial. Special courts-martial may also be convened by superior authority.

B. A special court-martial may not try a commissioned officer.

C. A special court-martial shall have the same powers of punishment as a general court-martial, except that of dismissal or dishonorable discharge. Any fine imposed by a special court-martial shall not exceed $100 nor shall any period of confinement exceed 10 days. A special court-martial may award a bad conduct discharge. (1930, p. 956; Michie Code 1942, § 2673(34); 1958, c. 393; 1964, c. 227; 1976, c. 399; 1977, c. 74.)

§ 44-45. Summary courts-martial. — A. In the National Guard, not in federal service, the commanding officer of each garrison, fort, post, camp, air base, auxiliary air base, or other place where troops are on duty, or division, brigade, regiment, wing, group, squadron, battalion or detached company, or other detachment, may convene a summary court-martial, consisting of one commissioned officer. Proceedings conducted under the provisions of this section shall be informal.

B. A summary court-martial shall have the authority to impose fines of not more than twenty-five dollars, to impose forfeitures of pay and allowances, to restrict to limits, to impose extra duty, to require confinement for not more than $2^1/_2$ days and to reduce enlisted persons one or more pay grades. (1930, p. 956; Michie Code 1942, § 2673(35); 1958, c. 393; 1964, c. 227; 1976, c. 399; 1977, c. 74.)

§ 44-46: Repealed by Acts 1977, c. 74.

Cross references. — For present provisions as to confinement by courts-martial, see §§ 44-43, 44-44, 44-45 and 44-53.

§ 44-46.1. Military judges. — A military judge shall be a commissioned officer of the National Guard, shall be so assigned as a legal officer, shall be admitted to the practice of law, and shall be certified for such duty by the Adjutant General.

The Adjutant General shall designate a military judge on a case-by-case basis to preside over courts-martial of the National Guard not in federal service. (1976, c. 399.)

§ 44-47. Process and procedure. — In the National Guard, not in federal service, military judges whenever they sit on a military court, and otherwise presidents of courts-martial and summary court officers, shall have power to issue warrants to arrest accused persons and to bring them before the court for trial whenever such persons shall have disobeyed an order in writing from the convening authority to appear before such court, a copy of the charge or charges having been delivered to the accused with such order, and to issue commitments in carrying out sentences of confinement, and to issue subpoenas and subpoenas duces tecum, and to enforce by attachment attendance of witnesses and the production of books and papers, and to sentence for a refusal to be sworn or to answer as provided in actions before civil courts. They shall also have power to punish for contempt occurring in the presence of the court. (1930, p. 957; Michie Code 1942, § 2673(37); 1976, c. 399.)

§ 44-48. Review of judgments of courts-martial; procedure. — Judgments of general, special and summary courts-martial shall be subject to review by the Adjutant General only, except that sentences of dismissal from the service or dishonorable discharge shall also be subject to review by the Governor; and such judgments may be affirmed, set aside or modified; provided, however, no higher or greater sentence, punishment, penalty, fine or forfeiture than that imposed by the court-martial shall be approved; otherwise trials and proceedings, including nonjudicial punishment, pretrial proceedings, post-trial proceedings, search and seizure proceedings and proceedings by all courts and boards, including review proceedings, shall be in accordance with the Manual for Courts-Martial United States, as now existing or subsequently amended, procedure for courts of inquiry, and retiring boards, and other procedures under military law, as may from time to time be prescribed by the appropriate secretary of the respective services. (1930, p. 957; Michie Code 1942, § 2673(38); 1964, c. 227; 1976, c. 399.)

§ 44-49. Where sentences executed. — All sentences to confinement imposed by any military court of this Commonwealth shall be executed in such penal institutions of the Commonwealth as may be appropriate for similar terms of confinement sentenced for violations of criminal laws of the Commonwealth. (1930, p. 957; Michie Code 1942, § 2673(39); 1958, c. 393; 1964, c. 227; 1976, c. 399.)

§ 44-50. How process and sentence executed. — All processes and sentences of any of the military courts of this Commonwealth shall be executed by any sheriff, deputy sheriff, sergeant, or police officer into whose hands the same may be placed for service or execution, and such officer shall make return thereof to the officer issuing or imposing the same. Such service or execution of process or sentence shall be made by such officer without tender or advancement of fee therefor, but all costs in such cases shall be paid from funds appropriated for military purposes. The actual necessary expenses of conveying a prisoner from one county or city in the Commonwealth to another, when the same is authorized and directed by the Adjutant General of the Commonwealth, shall be paid from the military fund of the Commonwealth upon a warrant approved by the Adjutant General. (1930, p. 957; Michie Code 1942, § 2673(40); 1958, c. 393; 1976, c. 399.)

§ 44-51. Certificates. — Where any sentence to fine or imprisonment shall be imposed by any military court of this Commonwealth, it shall be the duty of the military judge whenever one sits on such court, and otherwise the president of the court or summary court officer, upon the approval of the findings and sentence of such court, to make out and sign a certificate entitling the case, giving the name of the accused, the date and place of trial, the date of approval of sentence, the amount of fine, or manner, place, and duration of confinement, and deliver such certificate to the sheriff, or deputy sheriff, sergeant or police officer of the county, city or town wherein the sentence is to be executed; and it shall thereupon be the duty of such officer to carry such sentence into execution in the manner prescribed by law for the collection of fines or commitments to service of terms of imprisonment in criminal cases determined in the courts of this Commonwealth. (1930, p. 957; Michie Code 1942, § 2673(41); 1958, c. 393; 1976, c. 399.)

§ 44-52. Dismissal or dishonorable discharge. — No sentence of dismissal from the service or dishonorable discharge, imposed by a National Guard courts-martial not in federal service, shall be executed until approved by the Governor. Any officer convicted by a general courts-martial and dismissed from the service shall be forever disqualified from holding a commission in the militia. (1930, p. 958; Michie Code 1942, § 2673(42); 1976, c. 399.)

§ 44-53. Collection of fines. — For the purpose of collecting any fines or penalties imposed by a court-martial, the military judge whenever one sits on such court, and otherwise the president of the court, or the summary court officer, shall, within fifteen days after the fines or penalties have been imposed and approved, make a list of all the persons fined, describing them distinctly, and showing the sums imposed as fines or penalties on each person, and shall draw his warrant, under his official signature, directed to any marshal of the court, or to the sheriff, sergeant, or any policeman of any city or county, as the case may be, thereby commanding him to levy such fines or penalties, together with the costs, on the goods and chattels of such delinquent, and the warrant shall thereupon have the force and effect of fieri facias, but such delinquent shall not be entitled to the benefit of any exemption law of this Commonwealth, as against such warrant and the lien thereof. In default of sufficient personal property to satisfy the same, the officer executing the same shall make report accordingly to the drawing authority of the warrant which may then require the fined person to show whether or not he possesses sufficient property to satisfy the fine and if such property is found to exist and the fined person fails to deliver it over the executing officer shall be ordered to take the body of the delinquent and convey him to the jail of the city or county in which he may be found, whose jailer shall closely confine him without bail until the fine or penalty and jailer's fees be paid. No such imprisonment shall extend beyond the period of ten days. (1930, p. 958; Michie Code 1942, § 2673(44); 1976, c. 399; 1977, c. 74.)

§ 44-54. Disposition of fines. — All fines imposed by courts-martial or other military courts, whether collected by such courts or by the civil authorities, shall be turned over by the courts or by the civil officer collecting the same to the Adjutant General, who shall keep an accurate account of the same. The Adjutant General, after deducting the costs of holding the courts and the collection of the fines, shall annually turn the balance in to the treasury of the Commonwealth, to be placed to the credit of the Literary Fund. (1930, p. 958; Michie Code 1942, § 2673(43); 1958, c. 393.)

ARTICLE 4.1.

National Guard Mutual Assistance Compact.

§ 44-54.1. Compact enacted into law; terms. — The National Guard Mutual Assistance Compact is hereby enacted into law and entered into by the Commonwealth of Virginia with all other states legally joining therein, in the form substantially as follows:

NATIONAL GUARD MUTUAL ASSISTANCE COMPACT

Article I. Purposes.

The purposes of this compact are to:
1. Provide for mutual aid among the party states in the utilization of the national guard to cope with emergencies.
2. Permit and encourage a high degree of flexibility in the deployment of national guard forces in the interest of efficiency.
3. Maximize the effectiveness of the national guard in those situations which call for its utilization under this compact.
4. Provide protection for the rights of national guard personnel when serving in other states on emergency duty.

Article II. Entry into Force and Withdrawal.

(a) This compact shall enter into force when enacted into law by any two states. Thereafter, this compact shall become effective as to any other state upon its enactment thereof.
(b) Any party state may withdraw from this compact by enacting a statute repealing the same, but no such withdrawal shall take effect until one year after the governor of the withdrawing state has given notice in writing of such withdrawal to the governors of all other party states.

Article III. Mutual Aid.

(a) As used in this article:

1. *"Emergency"* means an occurrence or condition, temporary in nature, in which police and other public safety officials and locally available national guard forces are, or may reasonably be expected to be, unable to cope with substantial and imminent danger to the public safety.

2. *"Requesting state"* means the state whose governor requests assistance in coping with an emergency.

3. *"Responding state"* means the state furnishing aid, or requested to furnish aid.

(b) Upon request of the governor of a party state for assistance in an emergency, the governor of a responding state shall have authority under this compact to send without the borders of his state and place under the temporary command of the appropriate national guard or other military authorities of the requesting state all or any part of the national guard forces of his state as he may deem necessary, and the exercise of his discretion in this regard shall be conclusive.

(c) The governor of a party state may withhold the national guard forces of his state from such use and recall any forces or part or member thereof previously deployed in a requesting state.

(d) Whenever national guard forces of any party state are engaged in another state in carrying out the purposes of this compact, the members thereof so engaged shall have the same powers, duties, rights, privileges and immunities as members of national guard forces in such other state. The requesting state shall save members of the national guard forces of responding states harmless from civil liability for acts or omissions in good faith which occur in the performance of their duty while engaged in carrying out the purposes of this compact, whether the responding forces are serving the requesting state within its borders or are in transit to or from such service.

(e) Subject to the provisions of paragraphs (f), (g) and (h) of this article, all liability that may arise under the laws of the requesting state, the responding state, or a third state on account of or in connection with a request for aid, shall be assumed and borne by the requesting state.

(f) Any responding state rendering aid pursuant to this compact shall be reimbursed by the requesting state for any loss or damage to, or expense incurred in the operation of any equipment answering a request for aid, and for the cost of the materials, transportation and maintenance of national guard personnel and equipment incurred in connection with such request: Provided, that nothing herein contained shall prevent any responding state from assuming such loss, damage, expense or other cost.

(g) Each party state shall provide, in the same amounts and manner as if they were on duty within their state, for the pay and allowances of the personnel of its national guard units while engaged without the state pursuant to this compact and while going to and returning from such duty pursuant to this compact. Such pay and allowances shall be deemed items of expense reimbursable under paragraph (f) by the requesting state.

(h) Each party state providing for the payment of compensation and death benefits to injured members and the representatives of deceased members of its national guard forces in case such members sustain injuries or are killed within their own state, shall provide for the payment of compensation and death benefits in the same manner and on the same terms in case such members sustain injury or are killed while rendering aid pursuant to this compact. Such compensation and death benefits shall be deemed items of expense reimbursable pursuant to paragraph (f) of this article.

Article IV. Delegation.

Nothing in this compact shall be construed to prevent the governor of a party state from delegating any of his responsibilities or authority respecting the national guard, provided that such delegation is otherwise in accordance with law. For purposes of this compact, however, the governor shall not delegate the power to request assistance from another state.

Article V. Limitations.

Nothing in this compact shall:
1. Expand or add to the functions of the national guard, except with respect to the jurisdictions within which such functions may be performed.
2. Authorize or permit national guard units to be placed under the field command of any person not having the military or national guard rank or status required by law for the field command position in question.

Article VI. Construction and Severability.

This compact shall be liberally construed so as to effectuate the purposes thereof. The provisions of this compact shall be severable and if any phrase, clause, sentence or provision of this compact is declared to be contrary to the constitution of any state or of the United States or the applicability thereof to any government, agency, person or circumstance is held invalid, the validity of the remainder of this compact and the applicability thereof to any government, agency, person or circumstance shall not be affected thereby. If this compact shall be held contrary to the constitution of any state participating herein, the compact shall remain in full force and effect as to the remaining party states and in full force and effect as to the state affected as to all severable matters. (1968, c. 36.)

The numbers of §§ 44-54.1 through 44-54.3 were assigned by the Virginia Code Commission, the 1968 act having assigned no numbers.

§ 44-54.2. Payment of liability of State pursuant to Article III (f) of compact. — Upon presentation of a claim therefor by an appropriate authority of a state whose national guard forces have aided this State pursuant to the compact, any liability of this State pursuant to Article III (f) of the compact shall be paid out of funds appropriated to the Department of Military Affairs. (1968, c. 36; 1980, c. 221.)

§ 44-54.3. Members of National Guard deemed to be in state service when engaged pursuant to compact. — In accordance with Article III (h) of the compact, members of the National Guard forces of this Commonwealth shall be deemed to be in state service at all times when engaged pursuant to this compact, and shall be entitled to all rights and benefits provided pursuant to this title as amended. (1968, c. 36.)

ARTICLE 4.2.

Virginia State Defense Force.

§ 44-54.4. Organization; definitions. — The Virginia State Defense Force with a targeted membership of at least 1,200 shall be organized within and subject to the control of the Department of Military Affairs.

When called to state active duty, the mission of the Virginia State Defense Force shall be to (i) provide for an adequately trained organized reserve militia to assume control of Virginia National Guard facilities and to secure any federal and state property left in place in the event of the mobilization of the Virginia National Guard, (ii) assist in the mobilization of the Virginia National Guard, (iii) support the Virginia National Guard in providing family assistance to military dependents within the Commonwealth in the event of the mobilization of the Virginia National Guard, (iv) provide a military force to respond to the call of the Governor in those circumstances described in § 44-75.1.

Nothing in this article shall be construed as authorizing the Virginia State Defense Force or any part thereof to be called, ordered or in any manner drafted by federal authorities into the military service of the United States. However, no person by reason of his enlistment or appointment in the Virginia State Defense Force shall be exempted from military service under any law of the United States.

Members of the Virginia State Defense Force may serve in either of the following duty statuses:

1. *"Training duty,"* which is the normal service and training performed by the Virginia State Defense Force in order to be prepared for state active duty, and which includes but is not limited to organization, administration, recruiting, maintenance of equipment and training.

2. *"State active duty,"* which is the performance of actual military service for the Commonwealth when called by the Governor or his designee to active duty in service of the Commonwealth in accordance with Article 7 (§ 44-75.1 et seq.) of this chapter. (1989, c. 414.)

§ 44-54.5. Composition of units. — The organization and composition of units and force structure shall be as prescribed by the Adjutant General. (1989, c. 414.)

§ 44-54.6. Members, appointment and enlistment. — The age limitations of § 44-1 to the contrary notwithstanding, the Virginia State Defense Force shall consist of:

1. Such volunteers who of their own volition agree to service in conformity with regulations prescribed by the Adjutant General who are (i) citizens of the Commonwealth, (ii) at least sixteen, provided that any volunteer under the age of eighteen shall have the written consent of at least one parent or guardian, and (iii) less than sixty-five years of age may join the Virginia State Defense Force.

2. Such persons of the unorganized militia who may be drafted to fill the force structure of the Virginia State Defense Force or who may be ordered out for active duty until released from such service.

The Adjutant General may, on a case-by-case basis, authorize volunteer members of the Virginia State Defense Force to be retained beyond age sixty-five to age seventy-five.

The officers of the Virginia State Defense Force shall be appointed by the Governor in conformity with regulations prescribed by the Adjutant General.

Enlisted members shall be enlisted and retained in conformity with regulations prescribed by the Adjutant General. (1989, c. 414; 1996, c. 70.)

§ 44-54.7. Regulations. — Recruiting, enlistment, retention, organization, administration, equipment, facilities, training, discipline, discharge, dismissal, wearing of the uniform, appearance and standards of conduct shall be governed by regulations prescribed by the Adjutant General in conformity with this chapter and federal law and regulations pertaining to state defense forces. Such regulations shall, to the extent practicable, be consistent with regulations governing the Army National Guard. (1989, c. 414.)

§ 44-54.8. Administration of oaths. — All commissioned officers of the Virginia State Defense Force and such other persons or officials as the Adjutant General prescribes are hereby authorized and empowered to administer oaths and affirmations in all matters pertaining to and concerning the Virginia State Defense Force, including but not limited to the enlistment of soldiers and the appointment of officers therein. (1989, c. 414.)

§ 44-54.9. Uniform; rank in precedence; command. — The Virginia State Defense Force shall be uniformed and shall conform to standards of dress and appearance in accordance with regulations prescribed by the Adjutant General. The uniform and insignia of the State Defense Force shall include distinctive devices identifying it as a state defense force and distinguishing it from the National Guard or the armed forces of the United States. The wearing of permanent military decorations awarded in the service of the armed forces of the United States or in the national guards of the several states is authorized.

The grade structure of the Virginia State Defense Force, to the extent practicable, shall be the same as that prescribed for the Army National Guard. (1989, c. 414.)

§ 44-54.10. Discipline. — All members of the Virginia State Defense Force on training duty or state active duty shall be subject to military discipline. Infractions of military discipline by members of the Virginia State Defense Force on state active duty shall be punishable under the provisions of § 44-40 and Article 4 (§ 44-42 et seq.) of this chapter. (1989, c. 414.)

§ 44-54.11. Discharge; dismissal. — Upon expiration of the term of service for which appointed or enlisted, a member of the Virginia State Defense Force shall be entitled to a discharge. However, no member shall be discharged by reason of expiration of his term of service while on state active duty.

A member of the Virginia State Defense Force may be dismissed or discharged prior to the expiration of his term of service by sentence of a court-martial or for misconduct, inefficiency, unsatisfactory participation, personal hardship or for the convenience of the Commonwealth. Discharge proceedings shall be prescribed by the Adjutant General.

The Adjutant General may prescribe appropriate discharge certificates reflecting the character of the member's service. (1989, c. 414.)

§ 44-54.12. Arms, equipment and facilities. — The Virginia State Defense Force, to the extent authorized by the Governor and funded by the General Assembly, shall be equipped as needed for training and for state active duty. The Adjutant General, by regulation or otherwise, may authorize the use of privately owned real and personal property if deemed in the best interest of the Commonwealth.

To the extent permitted by federal law and contracts with the federal government or localities and to the extent that space is available, the Adjutant General in his discretion may authorize the use of armories and other facilities of the National Guard, other state facilities under his control, and all or portions of privately owned facilities under contract for the storage and maintenance of arms, equipment and supplies of the Virginia State Defense Force and for the assembly, drill, training and instruction of its members.

Members of the Virginia State Defense Force shall not be armed with firearms during the performance of training duty or state active duty, except under circumstances and in instances authorized by the Governor. (1989, c. 414.)

ARTICLE 5.

Naval Militia in General.

§ 44-55. Composition. — The naval militia of the Commonwealth shall be composed of able-bodied persons as set out in § 44-1, of such age as may be lawful for enrollment or appointment in the naval reserve of the United States. (1930, p. 958; Michie Code 1942, § 2673(45); 1973, c. 401.)

Cross references. — As to conversion of military property by persons discharged from the naval militia, see § 18.2-111.1.

§ 44-56. Organization. — The organization of the naval militia shall be such as is prescribed for the naval reserve, and the regulations of the United States naval reserve shall govern like matters in the naval militia, except (1) when a member of the naval reserve applies for enlistment, enrollment or appointment in the naval militia, he may be enrolled in, but not above, the rank or rating held in the naval reserve, and the age limit shall be waived, and except (2) where specifically stated otherwise in this chapter. (1930, p. 958; Michie Code 1942, § 2673(45).)

§ 44-57. Arms and equipment. — The arms and equipment of the naval militia shall be those prescribed for the naval reserve. (1930, p. 959; Michie Code 1942, § 2673(45).)

§ 44-58. Precedence of officers. — Officers of the naval militia, who are members of the naval reserve, shall take precedence among themselves in accordance with their seniority in the naval reserve. In the question of precedence with officers of other branches of the armed service of the State and of the United States, the regulations governing precedence in the armed forces of the United States will govern. (1930, p. 959; Michie Code 1942, § 2673(45).)

§ 44-59. Membership in other naval or military organizations. — No officer or enlisted person of the naval militia shall be a member of any other naval or military organization except the naval reserve of the United States. (1930, p. 959; Michie Code 1942, § 2673(46); 1973, c. 401.)

§ 44-60. Who to command. — The naval forces shall not be considered as attached to any division or brigade of the land forces of the Commonwealth, but shall be under the direct command of the Adjutant General and ultimately the Governor as commander in chief. When, however, the naval militia, or any part thereof, shall be in the field or afloat upon actual service, the senior officer present shall be in command, and whenever operating or acting in conjunction with the land forces of the militia of the Commonwealth, the senior officer present, according to relative rank of either force, shall command the whole, unless otherwise specially ordered or directed by the Governor as commander in chief or other competent military or naval authority. (1930, p. 959; Michie Code 1942, § 2673(47); 1998, c. 52.)

The 1998 amendment, in the first sentence, inserted "the Adjutant General and ultimately"; and in the second sentence, inserted "be in" and deleted "same" following "command."

§ 44-61. Discipline. — The naval militia shall be subject to the system of discipline prescribed for the United States navy and marine corps, and the naval militia officer in command of naval militia forces on shore or on any vessel of the United States navy loaned to the Commonwealth, or any vessel on which such forces are training, whether within or without the Commonwealth, or wherever, either within or without the Commonwealth, naval militia forces of the Commonwealth shall be assembled pursuant to orders, shall have power, without trial by courts-martial, to impose upon members of the naval militia the punishments which the commanding officer of the vessel of the navy is authorized by law to impose. (1930, p. 959; Michie Code 1942, § 2673(48).)

§ 44-62. Members of naval reserve. — Officers and enlisted personnel of the naval militia shall be required, in the discretion of the Secretary of the Navy, to be appointed or enlisted in the naval reserve in the grade, rank, or rating for which they may be found qualified in accordance with such special regulations as may be prescribed by the Secretary of the Navy. Unless within one year after the organization of any unit of the naval militia at least ninety-five per centum of its personnel has been appointed or enlisted in the naval reserve, it shall be disbanded, and thereafter, unless its organization, administration, and training conform to the standard prescribed by the Secretary of the Navy for such units, it shall be disbanded. (1930, p. 959; Michie Code 1942, § 2673(49); 1973, c. 401.)

§ 44-63. When relieved from service or duty. — Officers and enlisted personnel of the naval militia who are members of the naval reserve shall stand relieved from all service or duty in the naval militia when on active duty in time of war or national emergency.

A member of the naval militia who is also a member of the naval reserve and who has conformed to all the requirements of the naval reserve for maintaining efficiency in rank or rating shall be deemed thereby to have maintained his efficiency in the naval militia, and no other drills, training duty or other instruction shall be required of him. (1930, pp. 959, 960; Michie Code 1942, §§ 2673(45), 2673(50); 1973, c. 401.)

§ 44-64. Oath of officers and enlisted persons. — Every officer and enlisted person, before he enters upon his duties, shall take and subscribe before any officer authorized to administer oaths or before any duly commissioned officer in the naval militia, such oath of enlistment as may be prescribed by the Governor. Enlistments or enrollments shall be made concurrent with enlistments or enrollments in the naval reserve for a term of four years, or for a less period for persons already members of the naval reserve. (1930, p. 961; Michie Code 1942, § 2673(59); 1973, c. 401.)

§ 44-65. United States naval laws, customs and regulations. — In the interpretation of state laws governing the naval militia, the United States laws concerning the United States navy shall be followed as far as applicable, and the customs and naval reserve regulations of the United States navy shall govern in all cases not otherwise specifically provided for. (1930, p. 961; Michie Code 1942, § 2673(60).)

§ 44-66. Courts of inquiry. — Courts of inquiry in the naval militia shall be instituted, constituted, and conducted in the same manner, and shall have like powers and duties, as similar courts in the navy of the United States, except that they shall be ordered by the Governor. (1930, p. 961; Michie Code 1942, § 2673(58).)

ARTICLE 6.

Naval Militia Courts-Martial.

§ 44-67. Kinds of courts-martial. — Courts-martial in the naval militia shall consist of general courts-martial, summary courts-martial and deck courts. General courts-martial shall consist of not less than three nor more than thirteen officers, and may be convened by order of the Governor. Summary courts-martial may be ordered by the Governor or by the commanding officer of a naval militia unit. Deck courts may be ordered by a naval militia officer in command of a naval militia force on shore or on any vessel loaned to the Commonwealth or on any vessel on which such forces may be serving. (1930, p. 960; Michie Code 1942, § 2673(51).)

§ 44-68. Jurisdiction and procedure. — The courts-martial and deck courts herein provided for shall be constituted and have cognizance of the same subjects and possess like powers, except as to punishments, as similar courts-martial provided for in the navy of the United States; and the proceedings of courts-martial of the naval militia shall follow the forms and modes of procedure prescribed for such courts in the navy of the United States. (1930, p. 960; Michie Code 1942, § 2673(52).)

§ 44-69. Powers of punishment. — General courts-martial shall have power to impose fines not exceeding $200, to sentence to forfeiture of pay and allowances, to a reprimand, to dismissal or dishonorable discharge from the service, to reduction in rank or rating; or any 2 or more of such punishments may be combined in the sentences imposed by such courts.

Summary courts-martial shall have the same powers of punishment as general courts-martial, except that fines imposed by summary courts-martial shall not exceed $100.

Deck courts may impose fines not exceeding fifty dollars for any single offense; may sentence enlisted personnel to reduction in rank or rating, to forfeiture of pay and allowances, to a reprimand, to discharge with other than dishonorable discharge, or a fine in addition to any one of the other sentences specified. (1930, p. 960; Michie Code 1942, § 2673(53); 1973, c. 401.)

§ 44-70. Warrants, process and commitments; contempt. — Presidents of general courts-martial, senior members of summary courts-martial, and deck court officers of the naval militia shall have the power to issue warrants to arrest accused persons, and to bring them before the court for trial whenever such persons have disobeyed an order in writing from the convening authority to appear before such court, a copy of the charge or charges having been delivered to the accused with such order, and to issue commitments in carrying out sentences of confinement, and to issue subpoenas and subpoenas duces tecum, and to enforce by attachment attendance of witnesses and the production of books and papers, and to sentence for a refusal to be sworn or to answer, all as authorized for similar proceedings for courts-martial in the navy of the United States. They shall also have the power to punish for contempt occurring in the presence of the court. (1930, p. 960; Michie Code 1942, § 2673(54).)

§ 44-71. How processes and sentences executed. — All processes, warrants and sentences of the courts named in the preceding section (§ 44-70) shall be executed by any sheriff or deputy sheriff, or any sergeant, of any county, city or town, who shall be authorized by law to execute or serve any civil or criminal process. (1930, p. 961; Michie Code 1942, § 2673(54).)

§ 44-72. Confinement in lieu of fines. — All courts-martial of the naval militia, including deck courts, shall have the power to sentence to confinement in lieu of fines authorized to be imposed, and shall have the power to direct that upon nonpayment of a fine the person convicted shall be confined in any county or city jail; provided, that such sentences to confinement shall not exceed one day for each dollar of fine authorized; provided, further, that when naval militia forces are embarked on any vessel, the confinement in whole or in part may be had in prisons provided thereon. (1930, p. 961; Michie Code 1942, § 2673(55).)

§ 44-73. Dismissal or dishonorable discharge. — No sentence of dismissal or dishonorable discharge from the naval militia shall, except when the naval militia shall have been called into the service of the United States, be executed without the approval of the Governor. (1930, p. 961; Michie Code 1942, § 2673(56).)

§ 44-74. Disposition of fines. — All fines imposed by courts-martial shall be disposed of by the Adjutant General in accordance with the provisions of law governing the collection of fines imposed by courts-martial in the National Guard. (1930, p. 961; Michie Code 1942, § 2673(57).)

ARTICLE 7.

Regulations as to Active Service.

§ 44-75: Repealed by Acts 1988, c. 352.

§ 44-75.1. Militia state active duty. — A. The Governor or his designee may call forth the militia or any part thereof to state active duty for service in any of the following circumstances:

1. In the event of invasion or insurrection or imminent threat of either;
2. When any combination of persons becomes so powerful as to obstruct the execution of laws in any part of this Commonwealth;
3. When the Governor determines that a state agency or agencies having law-enforcement responsibilities are in need of assistance to perform particular law-enforcement functions, which functions he shall specify in his call to the militia;
4. In the event of flood, hurricane, fire or other forms of natural or manmade disaster wherein human life, public or private property, or the environment is imperiled;
5. In emergencies of lesser magnitude than those described in subdivision 4, including but not limited to the disruption of vital public services, wherein the use of militia personnel or equipment would be of assistance to one or more departments, agencies, institutions, or political subdivisions of the Commonwealth;
6. When the Governor determines that the National Guard and its assets would be of valuable assistance to state, local or federal agencies having a drug law-enforcement function to combat the flow of or use of illegal drugs in the Commonwealth, he may provide for the National Guard or any part thereof to support drug interdiction, counterdrug and demand reduction activities within the Commonwealth, or outside the Commonwealth under the National Guard Mutual Assistance Counterdrug Activities Compact. In calling forth the National Guard under this section, the Governor shall specify the type of support that the National Guard shall undertake with state, local or federal law-enforcement agencies. Once called forth by the Governor, the National Guard is also specifically authorized to enter into mutual assistance and

support agreements with any law-enforcement agencies, state or federal, operating within or outside this Commonwealth so long as those activities are consistent with the Governor's call. All activities undertaken by the National Guard in the areas of drug interdiction, counterdrug and drug demand reduction shall be reported by the Adjutant General's office to the Governor and reviewed by the Governor no less frequently than every three months; and

7. When the Governor or his designee, in consultation with the Adjutant General, determines that the militia or any part thereof is in need of specific training to be prepared for being called forth for any of the circumstances expressed in subdivisions 1 through 6 above. Such training may be conducted with a state or federal agency or agencies having the capability or responsibility to coordinate or assist with any of the circumstances set forth in subdivisions 1 through 6 above.

B. The Virginia National Guard shall be designated as a state law-enforcement agency for the sole purpose of receiving property and revenues pursuant to 18 U.S.C § 981(e) (2), 19 U.S.C. § 1616a, and 21 U.S.C. § 881(e) (1) (A). (1988, c. 352; 1993, c. 932; 1995, c. 49; 1996, cc. 71, 805.)

§ 44-75.1:1. Compact enacted into law; terms. — The National Guard Mutual Assistance Counterdrug Activities Compact is hereby enacted into law and entered into by the Commonwealth of Virginia with all other states legally joining therein, in the form substantially as follows:

INTERSTATE COMPACT ON NATIONAL GUARD COUNTERDRUG
OPERATIONS

ARTICLE I.

PURPOSE.

The purposes of this compact are to:

1. Provide for mutual assistance and support among the party states in the utilization of the National Guard in drug interdiction, counterdrug and demand reduction activities.

2. Permit the National Guard of this Commonwealth to enter into mutual assistance and support agreements, on the basis of need, with one or more law-enforcement agencies operating within this Commonwealth, for activities within this Commonwealth, or with a National Guard of one or more other states, whether said activities are within or without this Commonwealth in order to facilitate and coordinate efficient, cooperative enforcement efforts directed toward drug interdiction, counterdrug activities, and demand reduction.

3. Permit the National Guard of this Commonwealth to act as a requesting or a responding state as defined within this compact and to ensure the prompt and effective delivery of National Guard personnel, assets, and services to agencies or areas that are in need of increased support and presence.

4. Permit and encourage a high degree of flexibility in the deployment of National Guard forces in the interest of efficiency.

5. Maximize the effectiveness of the National Guard in those situations which call for its utilization under this compact.

6. Provide protection for the rights of National Guard personnel when performing duty in other states in counterdrug activities.

7. Ensure uniformity of state laws in the area of National Guard involvement in interstate counterdrug activities by incorporating said uniform laws within the compact.

ARTICLE II.

ENTRY INTO FORCE AND WITHDRAWAL.

A. This compact shall enter into force when enacted by any two states. Thereafter, this compact shall become effective as to any other state upon its enactment thereof.

B. Any party state may withdraw from this compact by enacting a statute repealing the same, but no such withdrawal shall take effect until one year after the governor of the withdrawing state has given notice in writing of such withdrawal to the governors of all other party states.

ARTICLE III.

MUTUAL ASSISTANCE AND SUPPORT.

A. As used in this article:

"*Demand reduction*" means providing available National Guard personnel, equipment, support and coordination to federal, state, local and civic organizations, institutions, and agencies for the purposes of the prevention of drug abuse and the reduction in the demand for illegal drugs.

"*Drug interdiction and counterdrug activities*" means the use of National Guard personnel, while not in federal service, in any law-enforcement support activities that are intended to reduce the supply or use of illegal drugs in the United States. These activities include, but are not limited to:

1. Providing information obtained, during either the normal course of military training or operations or during counterdrug activities, to federal, state or local law-enforcement officials that may be relevant to a violation of any federal or state law within the jurisdiction of such officials;

2. Making available any equipment, including associated supplies or spare parts, base facilities, or research facilities of the National Guard to any federal, state or local civilian law-enforcement official for law-enforcement purposes, in accordance with other applicable laws or regulations;

3. Providing available National Guard personnel to train federal, state or local civilian law-enforcement personnel in the operation and maintenance of equipment, including equipment made available above, in accordance with other applicable laws;

4. Providing available National Guard personnel to operate and maintain equipment provided to federal, state or local law-enforcement officials pursuant to activities defined and referred to in this compact;

5. Operating and maintaining equipment and facilities of the National Guard or other law-enforcement agencies used for the purposes of drug interdiction and counterdrug activities;

6. Providing available National Guard personnel to operate equipment for the detection, monitoring and communication of the movement of air, land and sea traffic; to facilitate communications in connection with law-enforcement programs; to provide transportation for civilian law-enforcement personnel; and to operate bases of operations for civilian law-enforcement personnel;

7. Providing available National Guard personnel, equipment and support for administrative, interpretive, analytic or other purposes; and

8. Providing available National Guard personnel and equipment to aid federal, state and local officials and agencies otherwise involved in the prosecution or incarceration of individuals processed within the criminal justice system who have been arrested for criminal acts involving the use, distribution or transportation of controlled substances as defined in 21 U.S.C. § 801 et seq. or otherwise by law, in accordance with other applicable law.

"*Law-enforcement agency*" means a lawfully established federal, state, or local public agency that is responsible for the prevention and detection of crime and the enforcement of penal, traffic, regulatory, game, immigration, postal, customs or controlled substances laws.

"Mutual assistance and support agreement" or *"agreement"* means an agreement between the National Guard of this Commonwealth and one or more law-enforcement agencies or between the National Guard of this Commonwealth and the National Guard of one or more other states, consistent with the purposes of this compact.

"Official" means the appointed, elected, designated or otherwise duly selected representative of an agency, institution or organization authorized to conduct those activities for which support is requested.

"Party state" refers to a state that has lawfully enacted this compact.

"Requesting state" means the party state whose governor requested assistance in the area of counterdrug activities.

"Responding state" means the party state furnishing assistance, or requested to furnish assistance, in the area of counterdrug activities.

"State" means each of the several states of the United States, the District of Columbia, the Commonwealth of Puerto Rico or a territory or possession of the United States.

B. Upon the request of a governor of a party state for assistance in the area of drug interdiction, counterdrug and demand reduction activities, the governor of a responding state shall have authority under this compact to send without the borders of his state and place under the temporary operational control of the appropriate National Guard or other military authority of the requesting state, for the purposes of providing such requested assistance, all or any part of the National Guard forces of his state as he may deem necessary, and the exercise of his discretion in this regard shall be conclusive.

C. The governor of a party state may, within his discretion, withhold the National Guard forces of his state from such use and recall any forces or part or member thereof previously deployed in a requesting state.

D. The National Guard of this Commonwealth is hereby authorized to engage in counterdrug activities and demand reduction.

E. The Adjutant General of this Commonwealth, in order to further the purposes of this compact, may enter into a mutual assistance and support agreement with one or more law-enforcement agencies of this Commonwealth, including federal law-enforcement agencies operating within this Commonwealth, or with the National Guard of one or more other party states to provide personnel, assets, and services in the area of counterdrug activities and demand reduction, provided that all parties to the agreement are not specifically prohibited by law to perform said activities.

The agreement shall set forth the powers, rights, and obligations of the parties to the agreement, where applicable, as follows:

1. Its duration;

2. The organization, composition, and nature of any separate legal entity created thereby;

3. The purpose of the agreement;

4. The manner of financing the agreement and establishing and maintaining its budget;

5. The method to be employed in accomplishing the partial or complete termination of the agreement and for disposing of property upon such partial or complete termination;

6. A provision for administering the agreement, which may include creation of a joint board responsible for such administration;

7. The manner of acquiring, holding, and disposing of real and personal property used in this agreement, if necessary;

8. The minimum standards for National Guard personnel implementing the provisions of this agreement;

9. The minimum insurance required of each party to the agreement, as necessary;

10. The chain of command or delegation of authority to be followed by National Guard personnel acting under the provisions of the agreement;

11. The duties and authority that the National Guard personnel of each party state may exercise; and

12. Any other necessary and proper matters.

Agreements prepared under the provisions of this compact are exempt from any general law pertaining to intergovernmental agreements.

F. As a condition precedent to an agreement becoming effective under this article, the agreement must be submitted to and receive the approval of the Office of the Attorney General of Virginia. The Attorney General of Virginia may delegate his approval authority to the appropriate attorney for the Virginia National Guard subject to those conditions which he decides are appropriate. Such delegation must be in writing.

1. The Attorney General, or his agent for the Virginia National Guard as stated above, shall approve an agreement submitted to him under this article unless he finds that it is not in proper form, does not meet the requirements set forth in this article, or otherwise does not conform to the laws of Virginia. If the Attorney General disapproves an agreement, he shall provide a written explanation to the Adjutant General of the National Guard.

2. If the Attorney General, or his authorized agent, does not disapprove an agreement within thirty days after its submission to him, it shall be considered approved by him.

G. Whenever National Guard forces of any party state are engaged in the performance of their duties, in the area of drug interdiction, counterdrug and demand reduction activities, pursuant to orders, they shall not be held personally liable for any acts or omissions which occur during the performance of their duty.

ARTICLE IV.

RESPONSIBILITIES.

A. Nothing in this compact shall be construed as a waiver of any benefits, privileges, immunities, or rights otherwise provided for National Guard personnel performing duty pursuant to Title 32 of the United States Code nor shall anything in this compact be construed as a waiver of coverage provided for under the Federal Tort Claims Act. In the event that National Guard personnel performing counterdrug activities do not receive rights, benefits, privileges and immunities otherwise provided for National Guard personnel as stated above, the following provisions shall apply:

1. Whenever National Guard forces of any responding state are engaged in another state in carrying out the purposes of this compact, the members thereof so engaged shall have the same powers, duties, rights, privileges and immunities as members of National Guard forces of the requesting state. The requesting state shall save and hold members of the National Guard forces of responding states harmless from civil liability, except as otherwise provided herein, for acts or omissions which occur in the performance of their duties while engaged in carrying out the purposes of this compact, whether the responding forces are serving the requesting state within the borders of the responding state or are attached to the requesting state for purposes of operational control.

2. Subject to the provisions of subdivisions 3, 4, and 5 of this section, all liability that may arise under the laws of the requesting state or the responding state, in connection with a request for assistance or support, shall be assumed and borne by the requesting state.

3. Any responding state rendering aid or assistance pursuant to this compact shall be reimbursed by the requesting state for any loss or damage to, or expense incurred in the operation of, any equipment answering a request for aid and for the cost of the materials, transportation and maintenance of National Guard personnel and equipment incurred in connection with such request; however, nothing herein contained shall prevent any responding state from assuming such loss, damage, expense, or other cost.

4. Unless there is a written agreement to the contrary, each party state shall provide, in the same amounts and manner as if its National Guard units were on duty within their own state, for pay and allowances of personnel of its National Guard units while engaged without the state pursuant to this compact and while going to and returning from such duty pursuant to this compact.

5. Each party state providing for the payment of compensation and death benefits to injured members and the representatives of deceased members of its National Guard forces, in case such members sustain injuries or are killed within their own state, shall provide for the payment of compensation and death benefits in the same manner and on the same terms in the event such members sustain injury or are killed while rendering assistance or support pursuant to this compact. Such benefits and compensation shall be deemed items of expense reimbursable pursuant to subdivision 3 of this section.

B. Officers and enlisted personnel of the National Guard performing duties subject to proper orders pursuant to this compact shall be subject to and governed by the provisions of their home state code of military justice whether they are performing duties within or without their home state. In the event that any National Guard member commits, or is suspected of committing, a criminal offense while performing duties pursuant to this compact without his home state, he may be returned immediately to his home state and the home state shall be responsible for any disciplinary action to be taken. However, nothing in this section shall abrogate the general criminal jurisdiction of the state in which the offense occurred.

ARTICLE V.

DELEGATION.

Nothing in this compact shall be construed to prevent the governor of a party state from delegating any of his responsibilities or authority respecting the National Guard, provided that such delegation is otherwise in accordance with law. For purposes of this compact, however, the governor shall not delegate the power to request assistance from another state.

ARTICLE VI.

LIMITATIONS.

Nothing in this compact shall:

1. Authorize or permit National Guard units or personnel to be placed under the operational control of any person not having the National Guard rank or status required by law for the command in question.

2. Deprive a properly convened court of jurisdiction over an offense or a defendant merely because of the fact that the National Guard, while performing duties pursuant to this compact, was utilized in achieving an arrest or indictment.

3. Authorize the National Guard to directly engage in the personal apprehension, arrest and incarceration of any individual or the physical search and seizure of any person. The National Guard may indirectly support any such

law-enforcement activities by an otherwise appropriate law-enforcement agency. The National Guard may engage in direct or indirect legal searches and seizures of any property through the use of aerial surveillance, provided that appropriate law-enforcement agents are present to provide supervision of such activity.

ARTICLE VII.
CONSTRUCTION AND SEVERABILITY.

This compact shall be liberally construed so as to effectuate the purposes thereof. The provisions of this compact shall be severable, and, if any phrase, clause, sentence or provision of this compact is declared to be contrary to the Constitution of the United States or of any state or the applicability thereof to any government, agency, person or circumstance is held invalid, the validity of the remainder of this compact and the applicability thereof to any government, agency, person or the circumstance shall not be affected thereby. If this compact shall be held contrary to the constitution of any state participating herein, the compact shall remain in full force and effect as to the remaining party states and in full force and effect as to the state affected as to all severable matters. (1993, c. 932; 1996, cc. 153, 566.)

§ **44-75.2. Militia training duty.** — Subject to the direction and orders of the Governor, the Adjutant General shall provide for the training and administration of the National Guard and the State Defense Force and shall require the members of the National Guard and the State Defense Force to attend such training when scheduled. Members of the National Guard may assist on an unpaid, volunteer basis in the training and administration of the State Defense Force. Whether training in a paid or unpaid status, members of the National Guard and State Defense Force shall at all times be subject to the orders of their respective commanders. (1988, c. 352.)

§ **44-76. Transportation, equipment and support of militia.** — Whenever the Governor shall call forth the militia, whether by virtue of the Constitution or of § 44-75.1, he shall issue such orders and take such measures for procuring and transporting the elements thereof as to him shall seem best; and for their accommodation, equipment and support, he shall appoint such a staff as to him shall seem proper. (1930, p. 962; Michie Code 1942, § 2673(62); 1958, c. 393.)

§ **44-77. Orders to officers and appointment of rendezvous.** — Such orders shall be sent to such officers and in such manner as the Governor may deem expedient, with a notification of the place of rendezvous; and the officers to whom the orders are sent shall proceed immediately to execute the same. (1930, p. 962; Michie Code 1942, § 2673(63).)

§ **44-78:** Repealed by Acts 1988, c. 352.

§ **44-78.1. Request for assistance by localities.** — In the event of the circumstances described in subdivision A 2, 4 or 5 of § 44-75.1 arise within a county, city or town of the Commonwealth, either the governing body or the chief law-enforcement officer of the county, city or town may call upon the Governor for assistance from the militia. The Governor may call forth the militia or any part thereof to provide such assistance as he may deem proper in responding to such circumstances, but in all instances the militia shall remain subject to military command and not to civilian authorities of the county, city or town receiving assistance. (1988, c. 352.)

§ 44-79: Repealed by Acts 1988, c. 352.

§ 44-80. Order in which classes of militia called into service. — The National Guard, the Virginia State Defense Force, the naval militia and the unorganized militia or any part thereof may be ordered into service by the Governor in such order as he determines. (1930, p. 963; Michie Code 1942, § 2673(66); 1964, c. 227; 1989, c. 414.)

§ 44-81. Length of service when called out. — The National Guard, the Virginia State Defense Force, the naval militia or the unorganized militia, when called into service by the Governor, shall serve for sixty days after their arrival at the place of rendezvous, unless sooner discharged. But the Governor shall, at all times, have power to retain them in service for such time as, in his judgment, may be necessary; however, except when the whole National Guard or the whole Virginia State Defense Force is not required, no individual shall be retained for a longer period than sixty days except in instances where an individual soldier or airman of the National Guard voluntarily consents to service beyond sixty days. (1930, p. 963; Michie Code 1942, § 2673(67); 1958, c. 393; 1989, c. 414; 1993, c. 112.)

§ 44-82. How troops paid while in service; transportation to be furnished; movement of troops and supplies not to be delayed. — All officers and enlisted personnel of the National Guard or naval militia, whenever called out in aid of the civil authorities, shall receive the compensation herein provided, and such compensation, and the necessary expenses incurred in furnishing supplies, subsistence, quartering, and transporting troops, shall be paid monthly by the State Treasurer out of the military contingent fund, and out of any moneys not otherwise appropriated. Such payments shall be made on warrants to be drawn by the Comptroller, on the State Treasurer, upon certificates of the officer in actual command of the troops, and upon payrolls prepared according to such forms as the state regulations shall prescribe. Such payrolls and certificates are to be transmitted to the Adjutant General through the regular military channels, and he shall approve them before such warrants shall be drawn. The Comptroller and the State Treasurer are hereby authorized and directed to draw the warrants and make the payments herein provided for in accordance with current or subsequently amended pay and allowances of United States armed forces.

The several transportation companies in this Commonwealth shall furnish transportation for troops so called out, stores, munitions and equipments, upon application of the officer in actual command, accompanied by a certificate from him of the number of personnel to be carried and their destination, and a copy of the order calling them out. For such transportation the transportation company shall be entitled to receive compensation from the Commonwealth. And it shall be the duty of the Adjutant General to contract annually with the various transportation companies of the Commonwealth, for rates of transportation, should there be occasion for it, provided, that such rates shall not exceed any maximum fixed by law.

Transportation of troops and military supplies shall be as speedy as possible and have the right-of-way over all passenger and freight traffic on transportation lines within the Commonwealth, and failure to furnish transportation when called upon, or unnecessary delay in transporting such troops and supplies, shall be punishable by a fine of not less than $1,000 or more than

$10,000. (1930, p. 963; Michie Code 1942, § 2673(68); 1958, c. 393; 1973, c. 401.)

Cross references. — As to transportation in times of peril, see §§ 44-121, 56-385.

§ 44-83. Pay and allowance of officers and enlisted persons. — When called into active state duty, not in the service of the United States, officers of the National Guard shall receive the same pay and allowances as prescribed for officers of like rank in the United States armed forces. For each day of such service, enlisted persons of the National Guard shall receive the same pay, rations and allowances as enlisted persons of like grade of the United States armed forces. When rations are not issued, the value of the same shall be commuted and paid by the Adjutant General. (1930, p. 964; Michie Code 1942, § 2673(69); 1958, c. 393; 1988, c. 352.)

§ 44-84. Regulations enforced on actual service. — Whenever any portion of the militia shall be called into service to execute the law, suppress riot or insurrection, or to repel invasion, the military justice opinions as set forth in Article 4 (§ 44-42 et seq.) of this chapter, and the regulations prescribed for the National Guard of the United States, and the regulations issued thereunder, shall be enforced and regarded as a part of this chapter until such forces shall be duly relieved from such duty. (1930, p. 964; Michie Code 1942, § 2673(70); 1958, c. 393.)

ARTICLE 8.

Unorganized Militia.

§ 44-85. Regulations and penalties. — Whenever any part of the unorganized militia is ordered out, it shall be governed by the same rules and regulations and be subject to the same penalties as the National Guard or naval militia. (1930, p. 965; Michie Code 1942, § 2673(71).)

§ 44-86. When ordered out for service. — The commander in chief may at any time, in order to execute the law, suppress riots or insurrections, or repel invasion, or aid in any form of disaster wherein the lives or property of citizens are imperiled or may be imperiled, order out the National Guard and the inactive National Guard or any parts thereof, or the whole or any part of the unorganized militia. When the militia of this Commonwealth, or a part thereof, is called forth under the Constitution and laws of the United States, the Governor shall order out for service the National Guard, or such part thereof as may be necessary; and he may likewise order out such a part of the unorganized militia as he may deem necessary. During the absence of organizations of the National Guard in the service of the United States, their state designations shall not be given to new organizations. (1930, p. 965; Michie Code 1942, § 2673(72); 1958, c. 393.)

§ 44-87. Manner of ordering out for service. — The Governor shall, when ordering out the unorganized militia, designate the number to be so called. He may order them out either by calling for volunteers or by draft. (1930, p. 965; Michie Code 1942, § 2673(73); 1944, p. 25; 1958, c. 393; 1984, c. 765.)

§ 44-88. Incorporation into the Virginia State Defense Force. — Whenever the Governor orders out the unorganized militia or any part thereof, it shall be incorporated into the Virginia State Defense Force until relieved from service. (1944, p. 25; Michie Suppl. 1946, § 2673(73); 1984, c. 765.)

§ 44-89. Draft of unorganized militia. — If the unorganized militia is ordered out by draft, the Governor shall designate the persons in each county and city to make the draft, and prescribe rules and regulations for conducting the same. (1930, p. 965; Michie Code 1942, § 2673(74).)

§ 44-90. Punishment for failure to appear. — Every member of the militia ordered out for duty, or who shall volunteer or be drafted, who does not appear at the time and place ordered, shall be liable to such punishment as a court-martial may direct. (1930, p. 965; Michie Code 1942, § 2673(75); 1958, c. 393.)

ARTICLE 9.

Pay of Militia.

§§ 44-91, 44-92: Repealed by Acts 1958, c. 393.

ARTICLE 10.

Privileges of United States Reserve, National Guard, and Naval Militia.

§ 44-93. Leaves of absence for employees of Commonwealth or political subdivisions. — All officers and employees of the Commonwealth or of any political subdivision of the Commonwealth who are former members of the armed services or members of the organized reserve forces of any of the armed services of the United States, National Guard, or naval militia shall be entitled to leaves of absence from their respective duties, without loss of seniority, accrued leave, or efficiency rating, on all days during which they are engaged in federally funded military duty, to include training duty, or when called forth by the Governor pursuant to the provisions of § 44-75.1 or § 44-78.1. There shall be no loss of pay during such leaves of absence, except that paid leaves of absence for federally funded military duty, to include training duty, shall not exceed fifteen workdays per federal fiscal year, and except that no officers or employees shall receive paid leave for more than fifteen workdays per federally funded tour of active military duty. When relieved from such duty, they shall be restored to positions held by them when ordered to duty. For the purposes of this section, with respect to employees of the Commonwealth or its political subdivisions who do not normally work approximately equal workdays on five or more days of each calendar week, the term *"workday"* shall mean $1/_{260}$ of the total working hours such employee would be scheduled to work during an entire federal fiscal year, not taking into account any state holidays, annual leave, military leave, or other absences. (1930, p. 966; Michie Code 1942, § 2673(78); 1958, c. 393; 1964, c. 227; 1966, c. 295; 1968, c. 503; 1983, c. 590; 1984, c. 540; 1985, c. 103; 1986, c. 611; 1989, cc. 414, 474; 1991, c. 653.)

Editor's note. — Acts 1991, c. 653, cl. 2 provides: "That it is the intent of the General Assembly that the act apply retroactively to any officer or employee of the Commonwealth or of any political subdivision of the Commonwealth who is at the time of enactment or was previously engaged in federally funded active military duty on or after August 1, 1990."

§ 44-94. Exemption from jury duty. — The active officers and members of the National Guard and naval militia shall be exempt from serving on juries in civil and criminal cases upon presentation to the clerk of the court of a certificate of such membership signed by the commanding officer of the unit of which the person summoned for jury service is a member. (1930, p. 966; Michie Code 1942, § 2673(79).)

§ 44-95: Repealed by Acts 1958, c. 393.

§ 44-96. Military property exempt from levy and sale. — The uniforms, arms and equipment required by law or regulations, of every commissioned and warrant officer and every enlisted person of the Virginia National Guard, Virginia State Defense Force and naval militia shall be exempt from sale under any execution, distress or other process for debt and taxes. (1930, p. 966; Michie Code 1942, § 2673(81); 1958, c. 393; 1984, c. 765.)

§ 44-97. Exemption from arrest. — No person belonging to the Virginia National Guard, Virginia State Defense Force or the naval militia shall be arrested on any process issued by or from any civil officer or court, except in cases of felony or breach of the peace, while going to, remaining at or returning from any place at which he may be required to attend for military duty; nor in any case whatsoever while actually engaged in the performance of his military duties, except with the consent of his commanding officer. (1930, p. 966; Michie Code 1942, § 2673(82); 1984, c. 765.)

§ 44-97.1. Continuance or time for filing pleading, etc., where party or attorney is on active duty in United States reserves, National Guard, or naval militia. — Any party to or attorney in an action or proceeding in any court, including the Supreme Court of Virginia, commission, or other tribunal having judicial or quasi-judicial powers or jurisdiction who has been ordered to participate in annual active duty for training or temporary active duty in the reserve forces of any of the armed services of the United States, National Guard, or naval militia shall be entitled to a continuance, not to exceed three weeks, as a matter of right during the period of such duty, provided the continuance is requested at least four days prior to the first day for which the continuance is sought. The period required by any statute or rule for the filing of any pleading or the performance of any act relating thereto shall be extended for seven days after such active duty, provided a request is made four days prior to the date the pleading or act is due. The failure of any court, commission, or other tribunal to allow such continuance when requested to do so or the returning of such filing or act during the period hereinabove specified shall constitute reversible error. This section shall not prevent the granting of temporary injunctive relief or the dissolution or extension of a temporary injunction, but the right to such relief shall remain in the sound discretion of the court or other such tribunal. (1981, c. 288; 1990, c. 790.)

§ 44-98. Interference with employment of members of Virginia National Guard, Virginia State Defense Force or naval militia. — A person, who either by himself, or with another, deprives a member of the Virginia National Guard, Virginia State Defense Force or naval militia of his employment, or prevents by himself or another, such member being employed, or obstructs or annoys such member or his employer at his trade, business or employment, because such member of such organization is such member, dissuades any person from enlistment in the Virginia National Guard, Virginia State Defense Force or naval militia by threat or injury to him in his employment, trade or business, in case he shall so enlist, shall be guilty of a misdemeanor and on conviction thereof shall be fined in a sum not exceeding

$500, or imprisonment in jail not more than 30 days, or shall suffer both fine and imprisonment. (1930, p. 967; Michie Code 1942, § 2673(83); 1958, c. 393; 1984, c. 765.)

§ 44-99. Organizations may own property; suits. — Companies or other organizations of the Virginia National Guard, Virginia State Defense Force and naval militia shall have the right to own and keep real and personal property necessary for their use, which shall belong to and be under control of the active members of the unit; and the commanding officer of any unit shall have the right and power to maintain any suit, in his own name, to recover for the use of the unit any debts or effects belonging to the unit, or damages for the injury thereof; and no suit pending in his name shall be abated by his ceasing to be the commanding officer of the unit; but upon motion of the commander succeeding him, such commander shall be admitted to prosecute the suit in like manner and with like effect as if it had been originally instituted by him. Armories owned by such units shall be exempt from all state, county and municipal taxation. (1930, p. 967; Michie Code 1942, § 2673(84); 1958, c. 393; 1984, c. 765.)

§ 44-100. No action allowed on account of military duties; counsel for members sued or prosecuted. — No action or proceeding shall be prosecuted or maintained against a member of a military court, or officer or person acting under its authority or reviewing its proceedings, on account of the approval or imposition or execution of any sentence, or the imposition or collection of fine or penalty, or the execution of any warrant, writ, execution, process, or mandate of a military court, nor shall any member of the Virginia National Guard, Virginia State Defense Force or naval militia be liable to civil action or suit or criminal prosecution for any act done while in the discharge of his military duty.

If any member of the Virginia National Guard, Virginia State Defense Force or naval militia is sued civilly or arrested, indicted or otherwise prosecuted for any act committed in the discharge of his official duty while on state duty the Adjutant General may employ special counsel approved by the Attorney General to defend such member. The compensation for special counsel employed pursuant to this section shall, subject to the approval by the Attorney General, be paid out of the funds appropriated for the administration of the Department of Military Affairs. (1930, p. 967; Michie Code 1942, § 2673(85); 1972, c. 416; 1973, c. 401; 1984, c. 765.)

§ 44-101: Repealed by Acts 1958, c. 544.

§ 44-102. Commission not to vacate civil office. — Any citizen of this Commonwealth may accept and hold a commission in the Virginia National Guard and receive pay therefrom or a commission in the Virginia State Defense Force or armed forces reserve of the United States, without thereby vacating any civil office or position or commission held by him; and the acceptance or holding of any such commission, and receiving pay therefrom shall not constitute such holding of an office of trust and profit under the government of this Commonwealth and of the United States as shall be incompatible with the holding of any civil office, legislative or judicial, or position or commission under the government of this Commonwealth. (1930, p. 968; Michie Code 1942, § 2673(87); 1958, c. 393; 1984, c. 765.)

ARTICLE 11.

Care of Military Property.

§ 44-103. Deposit in armories or headquarters for safekeeping. — All arms, equipment and ordnance stores, which shall be furnished to the several commands under the provisions of this chapter, shall be deposited in the armories or headquarters of such commands for safekeeping. (1930, p. 968; Michie Code 1942, § 2673(88).)

§ 44-104. Care required and liability of officers. — All commissioned officers of the Virginia National Guard, Virginia State Defense Force and naval militia shall exercise the strictest care and vigilance for the preservation of the uniforms, arms, supplies, equipment and military property furnished to their several commands under the provisions of this chapter. Any officer receiving public property for military use shall be responsible for the articles so received by him; and he shall not transfer such property, or any portion thereof, to another, either as a loan or permanently, without the authority of the Adjutant General, or his duly authorized representative. (1930, p. 968; Michie Code 1942, § 2673(89); 1958, c. 393; 1984, c. 765.)

§ 44-105: Repealed by Acts 1958, c. 393.

§ 44-106. Upon disbandment of organization, or call into active federal service, commanding officer to return certain property to Adjutant General. — Upon the disbandment of any organization, or call into active federal service of such organization, which has received arms, supplies or equipment from the Adjutant General, in accordance with the provisions of this chapter, the commanding officer of such organization shall be responsible for the safe return to the custody of the Adjutant General of all such public property in possession of the organization, except for such federally owned property that may be required by federal law to be retained by such organization in the federal service. (1930, p. 968; Michie Code 1942, § 2673(91); 1958, c. 393.)

§ 44-107. Use for private purposes forbidden. — No officer or enlisted person shall use, except upon military duty any article of military property belonging to the United States or to the Commonwealth. (1930, p. 969; Michie Code 1942, § 2673(92); 1958, c. 393.)

§ 44-108. Officers and enlisted persons personally liable for military property. — Every officer and enlisted person to whom any article of military property is delivered in pursuance of the provisions of this chapter shall be held personally responsible for its care, safekeeping, and return. He shall use the same for military purposes only, and upon receiving a discharge, or otherwise leaving the military service, or upon demand of his commanding officer or the Adjutant General, shall forthwith surrender and deliver such property in as good order and condition as the same was at the time he received it, reasonable fair wear and tear excepted. As insurance for compliance with the provisions of this chapter, the Adjutant General may require the bonding of any or all such officers or enlisted persons in an amount that he may deem appropriate, commensurate with the responsibilities of such officers or enlisted persons. The cost of such bonds shall be borne from funds appropriated for the operation of the Department of Military Affairs, and shall be without cost to the individual officer and/or enlisted person bonded. (1930, p. 969; Michie Code 1942, § 2673(93); 1958, c. 393.)

§ 44-109. Punishment for injuries to military property. — Whoever shall willfully or maliciously destroy, injure, or deface any arms or articles of military property belonging to the United States or to the Commonwealth, or receive any property in violation of the preceding sections of this chapter, shall be deemed guilty of a misdemeanor and be fined not exceeding double the amount of the value of the property so injured or defaced, or, in the discretion of the jury, be imprisoned in jail not less than two weeks nor more than two months. (1930, p. 969; Michie Code 1942, § 2673(94).)

§ 44-110. Punishment for sale, etc., of military property. — Whoever shall secrete, sell, dispose of, offer for sale, or in any manner pawn or pledge, or receive in pawn or pledge, or buy any of the arms, uniforms, or equipments, being the property of the United States or of the Commonwealth, knowing or having reason to believe the same to be the property of the United States or the Commonwealth, shall be deemed guilty of a misdemeanor, and shall, on conviction thereof, be imprisoned in jail for not less than 6 months nor more than 1 year, or in the discretion of the jury, be fined not less than $50 nor more than $100. (1930, p. 969; Michie Code 1942, § 2673(95).)

§ 44-111. Replacement of lost or damaged property. — Whenever any military property issued to the militia of the Commonwealth shall have been lost, damaged, or destroyed, and upon report of a disinterested survey officer of the armed forces or militia it shall appear that the loss, damage or destruction of property was due to carelessness or neglect, or that its loss, damage or destruction could have been avoided by the exercise of reasonable care, the money value of such property shall be charged against the bond of the officer or enlisted person, if bonded. If such officer or enlisted person is not bonded, the value of such property shall be charged to such officer or enlisted person, and the pay of such officer or enlisted person from both federal and state funds at any time accruing may be stopped and applied to the payment of any such indebtedness until the same is discharged. In addition thereto, any officer accountable or responsible for military property shall be liable on his bond to the Commonwealth and the United States Property and Fiscal Officer as accounting, accountable and responsible officer for any lost, damaged, or destroyed property for which he is accountable or responsible. (1930, p. 969; Michie Code 1942, § 2673(96); 1958, c. 393.)

ARTICLE 12.

Support of Militia.

§ 44-112. Requisition for federal funds. — The Governor or such other state officer as may be authorized by law, shall make requisition upon the Secretary of Defense, through the National Guard Bureau, for such state allotment from federal funds as may be necessary for the support of the militia and as may be authorized by the laws and regulations of the United States. (1930, p. 970; Michie Code 1942, § 2673(97); R. P. 1948, § 44-112; 1958, c. 393.)

§ 44-113. County, city and town appropriations. — Counties, cities and towns may appropriate such sums of money and real and personal property as they may deem proper to the various organizations of the National Guard or naval militia, when such organizations are maintained within the limits of the counties, cities and towns respectively; and counties may appropriate such sums of money and real and personal property as they may deem proper to the various organizations of the National Guard if such organizations are maintained in any incorporated town or city of the second class located within the geographical limits of such counties respectively. (1930, p. 970; 1940, p. 54; Michie Code 1942, § 2673(98); R. P. 1948, § 44-113; 1958, c. 393.)

§ 44-114. Allowances made to organizations from state appropriations. — For the necessary expenses of the maintenance of the National Guard and the naval militia, to include the providing of one flag of the Commonwealth of Virginia to the next of kin of any individual, upon his death, who was serving in or honorably served for a period of twenty years in and retired from the Virginia National Guard, the Adjutant General with the advice and approval of the Board of Military Affairs, shall annually allot to each organization or unit such amounts as may in his judgment be advisable, and as may be available from the appropriation to the Department of Military Affairs, such allotment to be based upon such scheme of distribution as may appear equitable to the Adjutant General and the Board of Military Affairs and best suited to the needs of the military forces of the Commonwealth. (1930, p. 970; Michie Code 1942, § 2673(99); R. P. 1948, § 44-114; 1999, c. 667.)

The 1999 amendment inserted "to include the providing of one flag of the Commonwealth of Virginia to the next of kin of any individual, upon his death, who was serving in or honor- ably served for a period of twenty years in and retired from the Virginia National Guard" near the beginning of the section.

ARTICLE 12.1.

Orders Inducting State Militia Into Federal Service.

§ 44-114.1. Orders transmitted to and through the Governor. — All orders from the federal government or any of its officers, agencies or departments to the state militia of Virginia, including the National Guard, the naval militia, and the unorganized militia which relate to the call, induction, drafting of Virginia state troops of any type or description, into the federal service for active duty or otherwise and withdrawing them from the control of the Governor of Virginia shall be first transmitted to and through the Governor of Virginia. The Governor, as commander in chief of the state militia, shall not approve, consent to, or concur in any such order which has not been transmitted as herein required. (1958, c. 540, § 1.)

The numbers of §§ 44-114.1 through 44-114.4 were assigned by the Virginia Code Com- mission, the 1958 act having assigned no num- bers.

§ 44-114.2. Governor to be notified of receipt of order; no action taken until his instructions complied with. — If the Adjutant General of Virginia, or during his absence, any of his assistants, or anyone else in the Department of Military Affairs of the Commonwealth of Virginia, either in a civilian or military status, shall receive an order of the nature required in § 44-114.1 to be transmitted to the Governor, he shall immediately notify the Governor of Virginia of such receipt and the contents of this order by the most expeditious means, and no action shall be taken by anyone towards notifying the individuals of organizations of the Virginia militia of the contents of such orders or directions received from the federal government on this subject by any of its agencies or representatives until the Governor has been first advised and instructions from him have been complied with fully. (1958, c. 540, § 2.)

§ 44-114.3. Orders void if transmitted to militia before Governor notified. — If the Adjutant General or anyone else in the Department of Military Affairs should receive such a message of the kind referred to in

§ 44-114.1 and fail to notify the Governor immediately, and subsequently transmits such orders, for the purpose of having such orders executed, to any personnel of the state militia, or to any person other than the Governor, then such order or orders shall be illegal, null and void. (1958, c. 540, § 3.)

§ 44-114.4. Governor not prevented from drafting into state military service. — Nothing in this article shall prevent the Governor from drafting all citizens into the state military service if he may so desire in accordance with the military laws of Virginia. (1958, c. 540, § 4; 1973, c. 401.)

ARTICLE 13.

General Provisions.

§ 44-115. Custom and usage of United States army, air force and navy; applicability of § 44-40 and Article 4 of this chapter. — All matters relating to the organization, discipline and government of the Virginia National Guard, not otherwise provided for by law or by regulations, shall be decided by the custom and usage of the United States army, air force or navy, as appropriate. In addition, all members of the Virginia State Defense Force, the naval militia, and the unorganized militia on state active duty shall be subject to military discipline. Infractions of military discipline shall be punishable under the provisions of § 44-40 and Article 4 (§ 44-42 et seq.) of this chapter. (1930, p. 970; Michie Code 1942, § 2673(100); 1964, c. 227; 1984, c. 765; 1989, c. 414.)

§ 44-116. Printing or purchase and distribution of military laws and Uniform Code of Military Justice. — The Governor shall cause to be printed or purchased and distributed, whenever he may think it necessary, so many copies of the military laws of Virginia and of the Uniform Code of Military Justice of the United States as may be determined to be sufficient. (1930, p. 970; Michie Code 1942, § 2673(101); 1958, c. 393.)

§ 44-117. Officers of Virginia Military Institute and Virginia Polytechnic Institute and State University to be officers of militia. — The officers of the Virginia Military Institute and the Commandant of Cadets and Assistant Commandants of Cadets of the Virginia Polytechnic Institute and State University shall be commissioned officers of the Virginia militia, unorganized, and subject to the orders of the Governor and the same rules and regulations as to discipline provided for other commissioned officers of the military organizations of the Commonwealth. The Governor is authorized and directed to issue commissions to the professors, assistant professors and other officers of the Virginia Military Institute, according to the rank prescribed by it; and to the Commandant of Cadets and Assistant Commandants of Cadets of the Virginia Polytechnic Institute and State University. Such persons shall be eligible to receive and to continue to hold such commissions, regardless of age, for so long as they continue to be officers, professors or assistant professors of the Virginia Military Institute or the Commandant of Cadets or Assistant Commandants of Cadets of Virginia Polytechnic Institute and State University. The governing boards of each institution shall recommend to the Governor the rank to which such eligible persons shall be commissioned, but the following determination of such rank shall be made by the Governor. Commissions in such militia issued such persons by the Governor shall not entitle any person holding the same to any pay or emolument by reason thereof unless he be assigned to duty by order of the Governor with the Virginia National Guard; and in such event, the rank of such officer shall be relatively inferior to that of all other officers of the same grade in the Virginia National Guard. (1930, p. 970; Michie Code 1942, § 2673(102); 1958, c. 393; 1978, c. 384.)

§§ 44-117.1, 44-118: Repealed by Acts 1958, c. 393.

§ 44-119. Retired list of officers, warrant officers and enlisted persons. — There shall be a retired list of officers, warrant officers and enlisted persons of the Virginia National Guard.

The following persons, upon their written applications through regular military channels to the Adjutant General, may be placed on the retired list of the Virginia National Guard:

1. Former Adjutant Generals who have resigned or been relieved;

2. Officers or enlisted persons in the guard who have been honorably discharged and have served for at least ten years in active service of the guard, or ten years computing the period served in the Virginia National Guard and the period of active service in the United States armed forces.

Officers who have served honorably and efficiently in the Virginia National Guard or the Virginia militia shall be commissioned on the retired list of the Virginia militia, unorganized, in their respective grade, or the highest grade held by them in the military service of the Commonwealth, except that officers who have to their credit fifteen years or more of exemplary service may, at the discretion of the Adjutant General, be retired with commission of the next higher grade to the highest grade held by them in the military service of the Commonwealth of Virginia.

Warrant officers and noncommissioned officers shall be placed on the retired list with the highest rank held by them in the Virginia National Guard.

Reentry into the active military service of the Commonwealth or of the United States shall discharge officers, warrant officers and enlisted persons from the retired list, and for any future retirement new application shall be made.

All officers, warrant officers and enlisted personnel heretofore placed on the retired list by virtue of the provisions of an act approved March 3, 1892, as amended, shall be transferred to and borne upon the retired list of the Virginia militia, unorganized. (1930, p. 971; Michie Code 1942, § 2673(104); 1958, c. 393; 1983, c. 157.)

§ 44-120. Protection of the uniform. — It shall be unlawful for any person, not an officer, warrant officer or enlisted person in the armed forces of the United States, to wear the duly prescribed uniform thereof, or any distinctive part of such uniform, or a uniform any part of which is similar to a distinctive part of the duly prescribed uniform of the armed forces of the United States.

The foregoing provision shall not be construed so as to prevent officers, warrant officers or enlisted persons of the National Guard, nor to prevent members of the organization known as the Boy Scouts of America, or such other organizations as the Secretary of Defense may designate, from wearing their prescribed uniforms; nor to prevent persons who in time of war have served honorably as officers of the armed forces of the United States and whose most recent service was terminated by an honorable discharge, muster out, or resignation, from wearing, upon occasions of ceremony, the uniform of the highest grade they have held in such service; nor to prevent any person who has been honorably discharged from the armed forces of the United States from wearing his uniform from the place of his discharge to his home, within three months after his discharge; nor to prevent the members of military societies composed entirely of honorably discharged officers and enlisted persons, or both, of the armed forces of the United States from wearing, upon occasions of ceremony, the uniform duly prescribed by such societies to be worn by members thereof; nor to prevent the instructors and members of the duly organized cadet corps of any educational institution offering a regular course in military instruction from wearing the uniform duly prescribed by appropriate respective authority to be worn by instructors and members of such cadet corps; nor to prevent the instructors and members of such duly organized cadet corps of such institution of learning offering a regular course in military instruction and at which an officer, warrant officer or enlisted person of the armed forces of the United States is lawfully detailed for duty as instructor in military science and tactics, from wearing the uniform duly prescribed by appropriate authority to be worn by instructors and members of such cadet corps; nor to prevent civilians attending a course of military instruction authorized and conducted by the military authorities of the United States from wearing while attending such a course the uniform authorized and prescribed by such military authorities to be worn during such course of instruction; nor to prevent any person from wearing the uniform of the armed forces of the United States, in any playhouse or theater or in motion picture films or television while actually engaged in representing therein a military character not tending to bring discredit or reproach upon the armed forces of the United States.

The uniform worn by officers, warrant officers or enlisted persons of the National Guard, or by members of military societies, or the instructors and members of the cadet corps referred to in preceding paragraph, shall include some distinctive mark or insignia approved by the Secretary of Defense, to distinguish such uniforms from the uniform of the armed forces of the United States. The members of the military societies and the instructors and members of the cadet corps hereinbefore mentioned shall not wear the insignia of rank prescribed to be worn by the officers of the armed forces of the United States, or any insignia of rank similar thereto, unless otherwise authorized.

Any person who offends against the provisions of this section shall, on conviction, be punished by a fine not exceeding $100, or by imprisonment not exceeding 30 days, or by both such fine and imprisonment. (1930, p. 971; Michie Code 1942, § 2673(105); 1958, c. 393.)

§ 44-120.1. Manufacture of Virginia military medals and decorations in United States. — Virginia military medals and decorations shall be made in the United States. Existing stocks of Virginia military medals and decorations which are of foreign origin may be consumed without violating the provisions of this act. All Virginia military medals and decorations shall have the words "Made in the USA" stamped on the reverse side. This act shall not limit the country of origin of United States military medals and decorations that are presented to members of the Virginia National Guard. (1999, c. 22.)

The number of this section was assigned by the Virginia Code Commission, the 1999 act having assigned no section number.

§ 44-121. Statute relating to transportation of troops not repealed. — Nothing contained in this chapter shall be construed as intended to repeal § 56-385, relating to transportation of troops in times of peril. (1930, p. 974; Michie Code 1942, § 2673(108).)

§ 44-122. Citation of chapter. — This chapter may be cited as the "Military Laws of Virginia." (1930, p. 973; Michie Code 1942, § 2673(107).)

CHAPTER 2.

ARMORIES, BUILDINGS AND GROUNDS.

§ 44-123. Armory Commission abolished; duties, powers and properties transferred. — The Armory Commission of Virginia heretofore created and existing is hereby abolished. All the duties and powers heretofore imposed upon and exercised by the Armory Commission are hereby transferred to and imposed upon the Department of Military Affairs as hereinafter provided. Any property, real or personal held by the Armory Commission of Virginia in its corporate name is hereby transferred to the Department of Military Affairs to be held, managed, and maintained by that Department in the name of the Commonwealth of Virginia as provided by law. (1932, p. 758; Michie Code 1942, § 2673(109); R. P. 1948, § 44-123.)

§ 44-123.1. Armory defined. — As used in this chapter, unless otherwise provided, the meaning of *"armory"* shall include training or logistical support facilities, such as, but not limited to, maintenance facilities, training areas, and facilities at the State Military Reservation, Virginia Beach, Virginia. (1976, c. 266.)

§ 44-124: Repealed by Acts 1976, c. 266.

Cross references. — As to the power of the Adjutant General to acquire and maintain property, see § 44-124.1.

§ 44-124.1. Power of Adjutant General to acquire and maintain property. — The Adjutant General may acquire for and in the name of the Commonwealth, by gift, grant, appropriation, purchase such real or personal property as is necessary for the maintenance of, the training and administration of, the logistical support of, and the safeguarding of property in the care, custody or control of the Department of Military Affairs when such real or personal property is reasonably necessary to carry out and perform the duties required by this chapter and the duties of the office of the Adjutant General. The Adjutant General may make such acquisitions in cooperation with counties, cities, or incorporated towns, private corporations, voluntary incorporated or unincorporated associations or individuals, the United States or other states or commonwealths of the United States. The Adjutant General may provide for the day-to-day operation and maintenance of said facilities to include but not limited to heat, water, light, telephone service, sewer and other costs of operation, including insurance, and may in a like manner make additions, alterations and improvements to said facilities. (1976, c. 266.)

§§ 44-125 through 44-128: Repealed by Acts 1976, c. 266.

Cross references. — As to the power of the Adjutant General to acquire and maintain property, see § 44-124.1.

§ 44-129. Joint use of public buildings for armories. — The governing body of any county, city or incorporated town, wherein a unit or units of the National Guard and naval militia of Virginia have been, or may hereafter be established, may either severally, or acting jointly with each other, or with the Adjutant General, construct or acquire by purchase, contract, lease, gift, donation or condemnation, grounds and/or buildings which shall be suitable for public assemblages, conventions, exhibitions and entertainments; provided, that such buildings, or the plans and specifications therefor, are first approved by the Adjutant General as suitable for use as armories by such National Guard units; provided further, that such governing bodies or either of them, shall have contracted with the Adjutant General for the use of such buildings as an armory by such National Guard unit or units upon terms not inconsistent with this chapter. (1932, p. 759; Michie Code 1942, § 2673(112); R. P. 1948, § 44-129.)

§ 44-130. Public grounds for armory building purposes. — Any municipality or county owning lands on which no permanent building has been actually constructed whether such lands constitute part of a park or site for some public structure, is authorized to convey the same to the Commonwealth for use as a site for an armory for the Virginia National Guard; provided, that such conveyance will not prevent the reasonable use of any such structure for the purpose for which it was constructed. (1932, p. 760; Michie Code 1942, § 2673(113); R. P. 1948, § 44-130.)

§ 44-131. Military property exempt from taxation. — All property actually used for armory and military training purposes, as hereinabove defined, shall be exempt from all taxation, impost or assessment. (1932, p. 760; Michie Code 1942, § 2673(114); R. P. 1948, § 44-131.)

§ 44-132. Power of condemnation. — The power of condemnation herein granted to the Adjutant General and to counties, cities and incorporated towns, shall be exercised in the manner prescribed in the Code of Virginia. (1932, p. 760; Michie Code 1942, § 2673(115); R. P. 1948, § 44-132.)

§ 44-133. Use of armories for meetings of veterans' associations and other organizations. — Whenever in the opinion of the Adjutant General it is practicable to do so, each armory of the National Guard shall contain a room suitable for meetings of the associations composed of veterans of the War between the States, the Spanish-American War, and the World Wars, and shall be available for such meetings under such rules and regulations as may be prescribed by the commanding officer of the National Guard unit or units using such armory. The Adjutant General may permit the use of any armory for assembly and other purposes of various patriotic and civic organizations such as Confederate Veterans, Sons of Confederate and Federal Veterans, American Legion, Veterans of Foreign Wars, Daughters of the Confederacy, Chamber of Commerce, etc., as may be deemed advisable, where the use does not interfere with the use of the armory by the National Guard unit or units occupying same. (1932, p. 760; Michie Code 1942, § 2673(116); R. P. 1948, § 44-133.)

§ **44-134. Management and care of armories and training areas.** — The Adjutant General shall be responsible for the general management and care of armories and drill and training areas, and shall have the power to adopt and prescribe such rules and regulations for the management and government and for the guidance of the organizations occupying them as may be necessary and desirable; but such rules are not to conflict with the provisions of this chapter. (1932, p. 760; Michie Code 1942, § 2673(117); R. P. 1948, § 44-134.)

§ **44-134.1:** Repealed by Acts 1981, c. 219.

Cross references. — For provisions concerning the management, harvesting, and sale of timber on state-owned land, see § 10.1-1122.

§ **44-135:** Repealed by Acts 1976, c. 266.

Cross references. — For present provisions covering the subject matter of the repealed section, see § 44-135.1.

§ **44-135.1. Armory control board for each armory; temporary renting.** — Each armory erected or provided by the Commonwealth under the provisions of this chapter, excepting those armories or logistical support facilities provided for by license agreement with the United States, shall have an armory control board appointed by the Adjutant General to consist of one or more officers of the organization or organizations quartered therein, and any other persons deemed necessary by the Adjutant General. Such board of control may rent the armory and any temporary quarters or billeting facilities thereon for temporary purposes, subject to any regulations or conditions that may be prescribed by the Adjutant General or such board of control. The money derived from the rental shall be placed in a special revenue interest-earning fund, and properly accounted for. Any nonappropriated funds and interest earned from such funds shall be used to defray the cost of operating, improving, and maintaining such armory and its facilities. Any money remaining in the fund at the end of the fiscal year shall not revert to the general fund but shall remain in the fund. (1976, c. 266; 1996, cc. 137, 802.)

§ **44-136. Sale or lease of armories.** — When the Adjutant General shall receive information from the Governor of the disbandment of an organization of the National Guard or naval militia occupying or using an armory provided by the Commonwealth under the direction of the Adjutant General, he shall determine whether such armory shall be sold or not, and if it is determined that such armory be sold after due publication as prescribed by the laws of the Commonwealth for the sale of real estate under a deed of trust, it shall be sold at public auction for the highest price to be paid for same, and upon such terms and conditions as may seem best to the Adjutant General. The proceeds of such sale shall be divided between the Commonwealth, county, city or individual, as their interest may appear.

In case an armory becomes vacant by any reason mentioned in this section, the Adjutant General may lease such armory for a period not to exceed one year, or, when duly authorized by the Governor, may lease the same for a period of years, the proceeds due the Commonwealth therefrom in either case to be turned into the state treasury to be credited to the Armory Fund. Should there be other owner or owners than the Commonwealth then the balance of the proceeds shall be equitably turned over to them as their interest may appear. During the time that the troops quartered in an armory are absent from their home station, in federal service, the armory may be leased as above provided, but not sold. (1932, p. 761; Michie Code 1942, § 2673(118); R. P. 1948, § 44-136.)

§ **44-137. City and county aid.** — Every city and county in the Commonwealth having an active National Guard or naval militia organization or organizations is authorized to render such financial assistance as it may deem wise and patriotic to such organization or organizations, either by donating land or buildings, or donating the use of land or buildings, or by contributing to their equipment and maintenance. (1932, p. 761; Michie Code 1942, § 2673(119); R. P. 1948, § 44-137; 1976, c. 266.)

§ **44-138. Maintenance funds.** — In order that there shall be provided maintenance funds for armories and other buildings erected, and areas provided for drill and training and other military purposes under the provisions of this chapter, the Adjutant General is authorized to draw a voucher for such funds, to be paid from any appropriation provided. (1932, p. 761; Michie Code 1942, § 2673(120); R. P. 1948, § 44-138.)

§ **44-139. Reversions of donations.** — In the event that any real property is donated to a National Guard or naval militia organization under the provisions of this chapter, and the organization shall fail to accept such property, or shall, after accepting it, be disbanded, the title to the property thus donated shall revert to the person, county or municipality donating the same as their interest may appear. (1932, p. 761; Michie Code 1942, § 2673(121); R. P. 1948, § 44-139.)

§ **44-140. Liberal construction.** — This chapter shall be liberally construed in favor of its purposes. (1932, p. 762; Michie Code 1942, § 2673(123); R. P. 1948, § 44-140.)

CHAPTER 3.

Civil Defense.

§§ **44-141 through 44-146.1:** Repealed by Acts 1973, c. 260.

CHAPTER 3.1.

Post-Attack Resource Management Act.

§§ **44-146.2 through 44-146.12:** Repealed by Acts 1975, c. 11.

CHAPTER 3.2.

EMERGENCY SERVICES AND DISASTER LAW.

§ **44-146.13. Short title.** — This chapter may be cited as the "Commonwealth of Virginia Emergency Services and Disaster Law of 1973." (1973, c. 260.)

Law Review. — For survey of Virginia administrative law for the year 1974-1975, see 61 Va. L. Rev. 1632 (1975).

Effect of amendments to chapter. — The amendments to this chapter were changes of form, which merely interpreted the 1973 act and made it more detailed and specific. They were not changes of substance, which add rights to, or withdraw existing rights from, an original act. Boyd v. Commonwealth, 216 Va. 16, 215 S.E.2d 915 (1975).

Acute motor vehicle fuel shortage of 1973 was a "disaster" within the meaning of this chapter. Boyd v. Commonwealth, 216 Va. 16, 215 S.E.2d 915 (1975).

§ **44-146.14. Findings of General Assembly.** — (a) Because of the ever present possibility of the occurrence of disasters of unprecedented size and destructiveness resulting from enemy attack, sabotage or other hostile action, resource shortage, or from fire, flood, earthquake, or other natural causes, and in order to insure that preparations of the Commonwealth and its political subdivisions will be adequate to deal with such emergencies, and generally to provide for the common defense and to protect the public peace, health, and safety, and to preserve the lives and property and economic well-being of the people of the Commonwealth, it is hereby found and declared to be necessary and to be the purpose of this chapter:

(1) To create a State Department of Emergency Services, and to authorize the creation of local organizations for emergency services in the political subdivisions of the Commonwealth;

(2) To confer upon the Governor and upon the executive heads or governing bodies of the political subdivisions of the Commonwealth emergency powers provided herein;

(3) To provide for rendering of mutual aid among the political subdivisions of the Commonwealth and with other states and to cooperate with the federal government with respect to the carrying out of emergency service functions.

(b) It is further declared to be the purpose of this chapter and the policy of the Commonwealth that all emergency service functions of the Commonwealth be coordinated to the maximum extent possible with the comparable functions of the federal government, other states, and private agencies of every type, and that the Governor shall be empowered to provide for enforcement by the Commonwealth of national emergency services programs, to the end that the most effective preparation and use may be made of the nation's resources and facilities for dealing with any disaster that may occur. (1973, c. 260; 1974, c. 4; 1975, c. 11.)

Importance of adequate supply of motor vehicle fuel. — The health, safety and welfare of the people of Virginia depend upon an adequate supply of motor vehicle fuel. Boyd v. Commonwealth, 216 Va. 16, 215 S.E.2d 915 (1975).

§ 44-146.15. Construction of chapter. — Nothing in this chapter is to be construed to:

(1) Limit, modify, or abridge the authority of the Governor to exercise any powers vested in him under other laws of this Commonwealth independent of, or in conjunction with, any provisions of this chapter;

(2) Interfere with dissemination of news or comment on public affairs; but any communications facility or organization, including, but not limited to, radio and television stations, wire services, and newspapers, may be required to transmit or print public service messages furnishing information or instructions in connection with actual or pending disaster;

(3) Affect the jurisdiction or responsibilities of police forces, fire-fighting forces, units of the armed forces of the United States or any personnel thereof, when on active duty; but state, local and interjurisdictional agencies for emergency services shall place reliance upon such forces in the event of declared disasters;

(4) Interfere with the course of conduct of a labor dispute except that actions otherwise authorized by this chapter or other laws may be taken when necessary to forestall or mitigate imminent or existing danger to public health or safety. (1973, c. 260.)

§ 44-146.16. Definitions. — As used in this chapter unless the context requires a different meaning:

(1) *"Natural disaster"* means any hurricane, tornado, storm, flood, high water, wind-driven water, tidal wave, earthquake, drought, fire or other natural catastrophe resulting in damage, hardship, suffering or possible loss of life;

(2) *"Man-made disaster"* means any condition following an attack by any enemy or foreign nation upon the United States resulting in substantial damage of property or injury to persons in the United States and may be by use of bombs, missiles, shell fire, nuclear, radiological, chemical or biological means or other weapons or by overt paramilitary actions; also any industrial, nuclear or transportation accident, explosion, conflagration, power failure, resources shortage or other condition such as sabotage, oil spills and other injurious environmental contaminations, which threaten or cause damage to property, human suffering, hardship or loss of life;

(2a) *"Emergency"* means a sudden and unforeseeable occurrence or condition, either as to its onset or as to its extent, of such disastrous severity or magnitude that governmental action beyond that authorized or contemplated by existing law is required because governmental inaction for the period required to amend the law to meet the exigency would work immediate and irrevocable harm upon the citizens of the Commonwealth or some clearly defined portion or portions thereof;

(3) *"Emergency services"* means the preparation for and the carrying out of functions, other than functions for which military forces are primarily responsible, to prevent, minimize and repair injury and damage resulting from natural or man-made disasters, together with all other activities necessary or incidental to the preparation for and carrying out of the foregoing functions. These functions include, without limitation, fire-fighting services, police services, medical and health services, rescue, engineering, warning services, communications, radiological, chemical and other special weapons defense, evacuation of persons from stricken areas, emergency welfare services, emergency transportation, emergency resource management, existing or properly assigned functions of plant protection, temporary restoration of public utility services, and other functions related to civilian protection. These functions also include the administration of approved state and federal disaster recovery and assistance programs;

(4) *"Major disaster"* means any natural or man-made disaster in any part of the United States, which, in the determination of the President of the United States is, or thereafter determined to be, of sufficient severity and magnitude to warrant disaster assistance above and beyond emergency services by the federal government to supplement the efforts and available resources of the several states, local governments, and relief organizations in alleviating the damage, loss, hardship, or suffering caused thereby and is so declared by him;

(5) *"State of emergency"* means the condition declared by the Governor when in his judgment, the threat or actual occurrence of a disaster in any part of the Commonwealth is of sufficient severity and magnitude to warrant disaster assistance by the Commonwealth to supplement the efforts and available resources of the several localities, and relief organizations in preventing or alleviating the damage, loss, hardship, or suffering threatened or caused thereby and is so declared by him when it is evident that the resources of the Commonwealth are adequate to cope with such disasters;

(6) *"Local emergency"* means the condition declared by the local governing body when in its judgment the threat or actual occurrence of a disaster is or threatens to be of sufficient severity and magnitude to warrant coordinated local government action to prevent or alleviate the damage, loss, hardship or suffering threatened or caused thereby; provided, however, that a local emergency arising wholly or substantially out of a resource shortage may be declared only by the Governor, upon petition of the local governing body, when he deems the threat or actual occurrence of a disaster to be of sufficient severity and magnitude to warrant coordinated local government action to prevent or alleviate the damage, loss, hardship or suffering threatened or caused thereby; provided, however, nothing in this chapter shall be construed as prohibiting a local governing body from the prudent management of its water supply, in the absence of a declared state of emergency, to prevent a water shortage;

(7) *"Local emergency organization"* means an organization created in accordance with the provisions of this chapter by local authority to perform local emergency service functions;

(8) *"Political subdivision"* means any city or county in the Commonwealth and for the purposes of this chapter, the Town of Chincoteague and any town of more than 5,000 population which chooses to have an emergency services program separate from that of the county in which such town is located;

(9) *"Interjurisdictional agency for emergency services"* is any organization established between contiguous political subdivisions to facilitate the cooperation and protection of the subdivisions in the work of disaster prevention, preparedness, response, and recovery;

(10) *"Resource shortage"*means the absence, unavailability or reduced supply of any raw or processed natural resource, or any commodities, goods or services of any kind which bear a substantial relationship to the health, safety, welfare and economic well-being of the citizens of the Commonwealth;

(11) *"Discharge"* means spillage, leakage, pumping, pouring, seepage, emitting, dumping, emptying, injecting, escaping, leaching, fire, explosion, or other releases;

(12) *"Hazardous substances"* means all materials or substances which now or hereafter are designated, defined, or characterized as hazardous by law or regulation of the Commonwealth or regulation of the United States government. (1973, c. 260; 1974, c. 4; 1975, c. 11; 1978, c. 60; 1979, c. 193; 1981, c. 116; 1984, c. 743; 1993, c. 671.)

Law Review. — For note, "Federal and State Remedies to Clean Up Hazardous Waste Sites," see 20 U. Rich. L. Rev. 379 (1986).

Acute motor vehicle fuel shortage of 1973 was a "disaster" within the meaning of this chapter. Boyd v. Commonwealth, 216 Va. 16, 215 S.E.2d 915 (1975).

§ 44-146.17. Powers and duties of Governor. — The Governor shall be Director of Emergency Services. He shall take such action from time to time as is necessary for the adequate promotion and coordination of state and local civilian activities relating to the safety and welfare of the Commonwealth in time of natural or man-made disasters.

The Governor shall have, in addition to his powers hereinafter or elsewhere prescribed by law, the following powers and duties:

(1) To proclaim and publish such rules and regulations and to issue such orders as may, in his judgment, be necessary to accomplish the purposes of this chapter including, but not limited to such measures as are in his judgment required to control, restrict, allocate or regulate the use, sale, production and distribution of food, fuel, clothing and other commodities, materials, goods, services and resources under any state or federal emergency services programs. He may direct and compel evacuation of all or part of the populace from any stricken or threatened area if this action is deemed necessary for the preservation of life or other emergency mitigation, response or recovery; prescribe routes, modes of transportation and destination in connection with evacuation; and control ingress and egress at an emergency area, the movement of persons within the area and the occupancy of premises therein. Executive orders shall have the force and effect of law and the violation thereof shall be punishable as a Class 1 misdemeanor in every case where the executive order declares that its violation shall have such force and effect. Except as to emergency plans issued to prescribe actions to be taken in the event of disasters and emergencies, no rule, regulation, or order issued under this section shall have any effect beyond June 30 next following the next adjournment of the regular session of the General Assembly but the same or a similar rule, regulation, or order may thereafter be issued again if not contrary to law;

(2) To appoint a State Coordinator of Emergency Services and authorize the appointment or employment of other personnel as is necessary to carry out the provisions of this chapter, and to remove, in his discretion, any and all persons serving hereunder;

(3) To procure supplies and equipment, to institute training programs and public information programs, and to take all other preparatory steps including the partial or full mobilization of emergency service organizations in advance of actual disaster, to insure the furnishing of adequately trained and equipped forces in time of need;

(4) To make such studies and surveys of industries, resources, and facilities in the Commonwealth as may be necessary to ascertain the capabilities of the Commonwealth and to plan for the most efficient emergency use thereof;

(5) On behalf of the Commonwealth enter into mutual aid arrangements with other states and to coordinate mutual aid plans between political subdivisions of the Commonwealth;

(6) To delegate any administrative authority vested in him under this chapter, and to provide for the further delegation of any such authority;

(7) Whenever, in the opinion of the Governor, the safety and welfare of the people of the Commonwealth require the exercise of emergency measures due to a threatened or actual disaster, he may declare a state of emergency to exist; and

(8) When necessary, to request predisaster federal assistance or the declaration of a major disaster and certify the need for federal disaster assistance and to give assurance of the expenditure of a reasonable amount of funds of the Commonwealth, its local governments, or other agencies for alleviating the damage, loss, hardship, or suffering resulting from the disaster. (1973, c. 260; 1974, c. 4; 1975, c. 11; 1981, c. 116; 1990, c. 95; 1997, c. 893.)

Cross references. — As to punishment for Class 1 misdemeanors, see § 18.2-11.

§ 44-146.17:1. Transmittal to General Assembly of rules, regulations, and orders.

— The Governor shall cause copies of any order, rule, or regulation proclaimed and published by him pursuant to § 44-146.17 to be transmitted forthwith to each member of the General Assembly. (1981, c. 160.)

§ 44-146.18. Office of Emergency Services continued as Department of Emergency Services; administration and operational control; coordinator and other personnel; powers and duties.

— (a) The State Office of Emergency Services is continued and shall hereafter be known as the Department of Emergency Services. Wherever the words "State Office of Emergency Services" are used in any law of this Commonwealth, they shall mean the Department of Emergency Services. During a declared emergency this Department shall revert to the operational control of the Governor. The Department shall have a coordinator who shall be appointed by and serve at the pleasure of the Governor and also serve as State Emergency Planning Director. The Department shall employ the professional, technical, secretarial, and clerical employees necessary for the performance of its functions.

(b) The State Department of Emergency Services shall in the administration of disaster preparedness programs:

(1) Promulgate plans and programs which are conducive to adequate disaster preparedness programs;

(2) Prepare and maintain a State Emergency Operations Plan relating to man-made and natural disaster concerns;

(3) Coordinate and administer preparedness plans and programs with the proponent federal, state and local government agencies and related groups;

(4) Provide guidance and assistance to state agencies and units of local government in designing emergency programs and plans;

(5) Make necessary recommendations to agencies of the federal, state, or local governments on preventive and preparedness measures designed to eliminate or reduce disasters and their impact;

(6) Determine requirements of the Commonwealth and its political subdivisions for those necessities needed in the event of a declared emergency which are not otherwise readily available;

(7) Assist state agencies and political subdivisions in establishing and operating training programs and programs of public information;

(8) Promulgate, prepare, maintain or coordinate emergency resource management plans and programs with federal, state and local government agencies and related groups, and make such surveys of industries, resources, and facilities within the Commonwealth, both public and private, as are necessary to carry out the purposes of this chapter;

(9) Coordinate with the federal government and any public or private agency or entity in achieving any purpose of this chapter and in implementing programs for disaster prevention, mitigation, preparation, response, and recovery; and

(10) Establish guidelines pursuant to § 44-146.28, and administer payments to eligible applicants as authorized by the Governor.

(c) The State Department of Emergency Services shall during a period of declared emergency be responsible for:

(1) The receipt, evaluation, and dissemination of intelligence pertaining to an impending or actual disaster;

(2) Providing adequate facilities for state agencies for conduct of disaster operations;

(3) Providing an adequate communications and warning system capable of notifying all political subdivisions in the Commonwealth of an impending disaster within a reasonable time;

(4) Establishing and maintaining liaison with affected political subdivisions;

(5) Determining requirements for disaster relief and recovery assistance;

(6) Coordinating disaster response actions of federal and state agencies;

(7) Providing guidance and assistance to affected political subdivisions to ensure orderly and timely recovery from disaster effects.

(d) The State Department of Emergency Services shall be provided the necessary facilities and equipment needed to perform its normal day-to-day activities and coordinate disaster-related activities of the various federal, state, and other agencies during periods of declared emergency.

(e) The State Department of Emergency Services is authorized to enter into all contracts and agreements necessary or incidental to performance of any of its duties stated in this section or otherwise assigned to it by law. (1973, c. 260; 1974, c. 4; 1975, c. 11; 1979, c. 193; 1984, c. 720; 1985, cc. 443, 447; 1997, c. 893.)

§ 44-146.18:1. Virginia Disaster Response Funds disbursements; reimbursements. — There is hereby created a nonlapsing revolving fund which shall be maintained as a separate special fund account within the state treasury, and administered by the Coordinator of Emergency Services, consistent with the purposes of this chapter. All expenses, costs, and judgments recovered pursuant to this section, and all moneys received as reimbursement in accordance with applicable provisions of federal law, shall be paid into the fund. Additionally, an annual appropriation to the fund from the general fund or other unrestricted nongeneral fund, in an amount determined by the Governor, may be authorized to carry out the purposes of this chapter. All recoveries from occurrences prior to March 10, 1983, and otherwise qualifying under this section, received subsequent to March 10, 1983, shall be paid into the fund. No moneys shall be credited to the balance in the fund until they have been received by the fund. An accounting of moneys received and disbursed shall be kept and furnished to the Governor or the General Assembly upon request.

Disbursements from the fund may be made for the following purposes and no others:

1. For costs and expenses, including, but not limited to personnel, administrative, and equipment costs and expenses directly incurred by the Department of Emergency Services or by any other state agency or political subdivi-

sion, acting at the direction of the Coordinator of Emergency Services, in and for preventing or alleviating damage, loss, hardship, or suffering caused by emergencies, resource shortages, or natural or man-made disasters; and

2. For procurement, maintenance, and replenishment of materials, equipment, and supplies, in such quantities and at such location as the Coordinator of Emergency Services may deem necessary to protect the public peace, health, and safety and to preserve the lives and property and economic well-being of the people of the Commonwealth; and

3. For costs and expenses incurred by the Department of Emergency Services or by any other state agency or political subdivision, acting at the direction of the Coordinator of Emergency Services, in the recovery from the effects of a disaster or in the restoration of public property or facilities.

The Coordinator of Emergency Services shall promptly seek reimbursement from any person causing or contributing to an emergency or disaster for all sums disbursed from the fund for the protection, relief and recovery from loss or damage caused by such person. In the event a request for reimbursement is not paid within sixty days of receipt of a written demand, the claim shall be referred to the Attorney General for collection. The Coordinator of Emergency Services shall be allowed to recover all legal and court costs and other expenses incident to such actions for collection. The Coordinator is authorized to recover any sums incurred by any other state agency or political subdivision acting at the direction of the Coordinator as provided in this paragraph. (1983, c. 48.)

Law Review. — For article, "Environmental Liens and Title Insurance," see 23 U. Rich. L. Rev. 305 (1989).

§ 44-146.18:2. Authority of Coordinator of Emergency Services in undeclared emergency. — In an emergency which does not warrant a gubernatorial declaration of a state of emergency, the Coordinator of Emergency Services, after consultation with and approval of the Secretary of Public Safety, may enter into contracts and incur obligations necessary to prevent or alleviate damage, loss, hardship, or suffering caused by such emergency and to protect the health and safety of persons and property. In exercising the powers vested by this section, the Coordinator may proceed without regard to normal procedures pertaining to entering into contracts, incurring of obligations, rental of equipment, purchase of supplies and materials, and expenditure of public funds; however, mandatory constitutional requirements shall not be disregarded. (1985, c. 443; 1990, cc. 1, 317.)

§ 44-146.19. Powers and duties of political subdivisions. — A. Each political subdivision within the Commonwealth shall be within the jurisdiction of and served by the Department of Emergency Services and be responsible for local disaster preparedness and coordination of response. Each political subdivision may maintain in accordance with state emergency preparedness plans and programs an agency of emergency services which, except as otherwise provided under this chapter, has jurisdiction over and services the entire political subdivision.

B. Each political subdivision shall have a director of emergency services who, after the term of the person presently serving in this capacity has expired and in the absence of an executive order by the Governor, shall be the following:

1. In the case of a city, the mayor or city manager, who shall have the authority to appoint a coordinator of emergency services activities with consent of council;

2. In the case of a county, a member of the board of supervisors selected by the board or the chief administrative officer for the county, who shall have the

authority to appoint a coordinator of emergency services activities with the consent of the governing body;

3. A coordinator of emergency services may be appointed by the council of any town to ensure integration of its organization into the county emergency services organization;

4. In the case of the Town of Chincoteague and of towns with a population in excess of 5,000 having an emergency services organization separate from that of the county, the mayor or town manager shall have the authority to appoint a coordinator of emergency services with consent of council;

5. In Smyth County and in York County, the chief administrative officer for the county may appoint a director of emergency services, with the consent of the governing body, who shall have the authority to appoint a coordinator of emergency services with the consent of the governing body.

C. Whenever the Governor has declared a state of emergency, each political subdivision within the disaster area may, under the supervision and control of the Governor or his designated representative, control, restrict, allocate or regulate the use, sale, production and distribution of food, fuel, clothing and other commodities, materials, goods, services and resource systems which fall only within the boundaries of that jurisdiction and which do not impact systems affecting adjoining or other political subdivisions, enter into contracts and incur obligations necessary to combat such threatened or actual disaster, protect the health and safety of persons and property and provide emergency assistance to the victims of such disaster. In exercising the powers vested under this section, under the supervision and control of the Governor, the political subdivision may proceed without regard to time-consuming procedures and formalities prescribed by law (except mandatory constitutional requirements) pertaining to the performance of public work, entering into contracts, incurring of obligations, employment of temporary workers, rental of equipment, purchase of supplies and materials, levying of taxes, and appropriation and expenditure of public funds.

D. The director of each local organization for emergency services may, in collaboration with other public and private agencies within this Commonwealth or within an adjacent state, develop or cause to be developed mutual aid arrangements for reciprocal assistance in case of a disaster too great to be dealt with unassisted. Such arrangements shall be consistent with state plans and programs and it shall be the duty of each local organization for emergency services to render assistance in accordance with the provisions of such mutual aid arrangements.

E. Each local and interjurisdictional agency shall prepare and keep current a local or interjurisdictional emergency operations plan for its area. The plan shall include, but not be limited to, responsibilities of all local agencies and shall establish a chain of command. Each political subdivision having a nuclear power station or other nuclear facility within ten miles of its boundaries shall, if so directed by the Department of Emergency Services, prepare and keep current an appropriate emergency plan for its area for response to nuclear accidents at such station or facility. (1973, c. 260; 1974, c. 4; 1975, c. 11; 1978, c. 495; 1982, c. 5; 1990, cc. 404, 945; 1993, cc. 621, 671, 781.)

§ 44-146.20. Joint action by political subdivisions. — If two or more adjoining political subdivisions find that disaster operation plans and programs would be better served by interjurisdictional arrangements in planning for, preventing, or responding to disaster in that area, then direct steps may be taken as necessary, including creation of an interjurisdictional relationship, a joint emergency services operations plan, mutual aid, or such other activities as necessary for planning and services. A determination of such findings shall be based on the factors related to the difficulty of providing emergency services on an interjurisdictional basis. (1973, c. 260.)

§ 44-146.21. Declaration of local emergency. — (a) A local emergency may be declared by the local director of emergency services with the consent of the governing body of the political subdivision. In the event the governing body cannot convene due to the disaster or other exigent circumstances, the director or any member of the governing body in the absence of the director may declare the existence of a local emergency, subject to confirmation by the governing body at its next regularly scheduled meeting or at a special meeting within fourteen days of the declaration, whichever occurs first. The governing body, when in its judgment all emergency actions have been taken, shall take appropriate action to end the declared emergency.

(b) A declaration of a local emergency as defined in § 44-146.16 (6) shall activate the response and recovery programs of all applicable local and interjurisdictional emergency operations plans and authorize the furnishing of aid and assistance thereunder.

(c) [Repealed.]

(c1) Whenever a local emergency has been declared, the director of emergency services of each political subdivision or any member of the governing body in the absence of the director, if so authorized by the governing body, may control, restrict, allocate or regulate the use, sale, production and distribution of food, fuel, clothing and other commodities, materials, goods, services and resource systems which fall only within the boundaries of that jurisdiction and which do not impact systems affecting adjoining or other political subdivisions, enter into contracts and incur obligations necessary to combat such threatened or actual disaster, protect the health and safety of persons and property and provide emergency assistance to the victims of such disaster. In exercising the powers vested under this section, under the supervision and control of the governing body, such director may proceed without regard to time-consuming procedures and formalities prescribed by law (except mandatory constitutional requirements) pertaining to the performance of public work, entering into contracts, incurring of obligations, employment of temporary workers, rental of equipment, purchase of supplies and materials, and other expenditures of public funds, provided such funds in excess of appropriations in the current approved budget, unobligated, are available. Whenever the Governor has declared a state of emergency, each political subdivision within the disaster area may, under the supervision and control of the Governor or his designated representative, enter into contracts and incur obligations necessary to combat such threatened or actual disaster beyond the capabilities of local government, protect the health and safety of persons and property and provide emergency assistance to the victims of such disaster. In exercising the powers vested under this section, under the supervision and control of the Governor, the political subdivision may proceed without regard to time-consuming procedures and formalities prescribed by law pertaining to public work, entering into contracts, incurring of obligations, employment of temporary workers, rental of equipment, purchase of supplies and materials, levying of taxes, and appropriation and expenditure of public funds.

(d) No interjurisdictional agency or official thereof may declare a local emergency. However, an interjurisdictional agency of emergency services shall provide aid and services to the affected political subdivision authorizing such assistance in accordance with the agreement as a result of a local or state declaration.

(e) None of the provisions of this chapter shall apply to the Emergency Disaster Relief provided by the American Red Cross or other relief agency solely concerned with the provision of service at no cost to the citizens of the Commonwealth. (1973, c. 260; 1974, c. 4; 1975, c. 11; 1976, c. 594; 1986, c. 24; 1990, c. 945; 1994, c. 75.)

§ 44-146.22. Development of measures to prevent or reduce harmful consequences of disasters. — In addition to disaster prevention measures included in state, local and interjurisdictional emergency operations plans, the Governor shall consider, on a continuing basis, steps that could be taken to prevent or reduce the harmful consequences of disasters. At his direction, and pursuant to any other authority, state agencies, including, but not limited to, those charged with responsibilities in connection with floodplain management, stream encroachment and flow regulation, weather modification, fire prevention and control, air quality, public works, land use and land-use planning, and construction standards, shall make studies of disaster prevention. The Governor, from time to time, shall make recommendations to the General Assembly, local governments, and other appropriate public and private entities as may facilitate measures for prevention or reduction of the harmful consequences of disasters. (1973, c. 260; 1974, c. 4; 1975, c. 11.)

§ 44-146.23. Immunity from liability. — (a) Neither the Commonwealth, nor any political subdivision thereof, nor federal agencies, nor other public or private agencies, nor, except in cases of willful misconduct, public or private employees, nor representatives of any of them, engaged in any emergency services activities, while complying with or attempting to comply with this chapter or any rule, regulation, or executive order promulgated pursuant to the provisions of this chapter, shall be liable for the death of, or any injury to, persons or damage to property as a result of such activities. The provisions of this section shall not affect the right of any person to receive benefits to which he would otherwise be entitled under this chapter, or under the Workers' Compensation Act (§ 65.2-100 et seq.), or under any pension law, nor the right of any such person to receive any benefits or compensation under any act of Congress.

(b) Any person owning or controlling real estate or other premises who voluntarily and without compensation grants a license or privilege, or otherwise permits the designation or use of the whole or any part or parts of such real estate or premises for the purpose of sheltering persons, of emergency access or of other uses relating to emergency services shall, together with his successors in interest, if any, not be liable for negligently causing the death of, or injury to any person on or about such real estate or premises or for loss of or damage to the property of any person on or about such real estate or premises during such actual or impending disaster.

(c) If any person holds a license, certificate, or other permit issued by any state, or political subdivision thereof, evidencing the meeting of qualifications for professional, mechanical, or other skills, the person may gratuitously render aid involving that skill in this Commonwealth during a disaster, and such person shall not be liable for negligently causing the death of, or injury to, any person or for the loss of, or damage to, the property of any person resulting from such gratuitous service.

(d) No person, firm or corporation which gratuitously services or repairs any electronic devices or equipment under the provisions of this section after having been approved for the purposes by the State Coordinator shall be liable for negligently causing the death of, or injury to, any person or for the loss of, or damage to, the property of any person resulting from any defect or imperfection in any such device or equipment so gratuitously serviced or repaired.

(e) Notwithstanding any law to the contrary, no individual, partnership, corporation, association, or other legal entity shall be liable in civil damages as a result of acts taken voluntarily and without compensation in the course of rendering care, assistance, or advice with respect to an incident creating a danger to person, property, or the environment as a result of an actual or threatened discharge of a hazardous substance, or in preventing, cleaning up, treating, or disposing of or attempting to prevent, clean up, treat, or dispose of any such discharge, provided that such acts are taken under the direction of state or local authorities responding to the incident. This section shall not preclude liability for civil damages as a result of gross negligence, recklessness or willful misconduct. The provisions of this section shall not affect the right of any person to receive benefits to which he would otherwise be entitled under this chapter, or under the Workers' Compensation Act (§ 65.2-100 et seq.), or under any pension law, nor the right of any such person to receive any benefits or compensation under any act of Congress. The immunity provided by the provisions of this paragraph shall be in addition to, not in lieu of, any immunities provided by § 8.01-225. (1973, c. 260; 1979, c. 193; 1984, c. 743.)

Law Review. — For comment, "'911' Emergency Assistance Call Systems: Should Local Governments Be Liable for Negligent Failure to Respond?," see 8 Geo. Mason L. Rev. 103 (1985).

§ 44-146.24. Cooperation of public agencies. — In carrying out the provisions of the chapter, the Governor, the heads of state agencies, the local directors and governing bodies of the political subdivisions of the Commonwealth are directed to utilize the services, equipment, supplies and facilities of existing departments, offices, and agencies of the Commonwealth and the political subdivisions thereof to the maximum extent practicable. The officers and personnel of all such departments, offices, and agencies are directed to cooperate with and extend such services and facilities to the Governor and to the State Department of Emergency Services upon request. (1973, c. 260; 1974, c. 4; 1975, c. 11.)

§ 44-146.25. Certain persons not to be employed or associated in emergency services organizations; loyalty oath required. — No person shall be employed or associated in any emergency services organization established under this chapter who advocates or has advocated a change by force or violence in the constitutional form of government of the United States or in this Commonwealth or the overthrow of any government in the United States by force, or violence, or who has been convicted of, or is under indictment or information charging any subversive act against the United States. Each person who is appointed to serve in an organization for emergency services shall, before entering upon his duties, take an oath, in writing, before a person authorized to administer oaths in this Commonwealth, which shall be substantially as follows:

"I .... do solemnly swear (or affirm) that I will support and defend the Constitution of the United States and the Constitution of the Commonwealth of Virginia, against all enemies foreign and domestic; that I will bear true faith and allegiance to the same; that I take this obligation freely, without any mental reservation or purpose of evasion; and that I will well and faithfully discharge the duties upon which I am about to enter.

"And I do further swear (or affirm) that I do not advocate, nor am I a member of any political party or organization that advocates the overthrow of the Government of the United States or of this State by force or violence and that during such time as I am a member of the (name of emergency services organization), I will not advocate, nor become a member of any political party or organization that advocates the overthrow of the Government of the United States or of this State by force or violence." (1973, c. 260.)

§ 44-146.26. Duties of emergency services organizations. — It shall be the duty of every organization for emergency services established pursuant to this chapter and of the officers thereof to execute and enforce such orders, rules and regulations as may be made by the Governor under authority of this chapter. Each organization shall have available for inspection at its office all such orders, rules and regulations. (1973, c. 260.)

§ 44-146.27. Supplementing federal funds; assistance of federal agencies; acceptance of gifts and services; appropriations by local governing bodies.

— A. If the federal government allots funds for the payment of a portion of any disaster programs, projects, equipment, supplies or materials or other related costs, the remaining portion may be paid with a combination of state and local funds available for this purpose and consistent with state emergency service plans and program priorities.

B. Whenever the federal government or any agency or officer thereof offers to the Commonwealth, or through the Commonwealth to any political subdivision thereof, services, equipment, supplies, materials, or funds by way of gift, grant or loan for purposes of emergency services, the Commonwealth, acting through the Governor, or such political subdivision, acting with the consent of the Governor and through its local director or governing body, may accept such offer and agree to the terms of the offer and the rules and regulations, if any, of the agency making the offer, including, but not limited to, requirements to hold and save the United States free from damages and to indemnify the federal government against any claims arising from the services, equipment, supplies, materials, or funds provided. Upon such acceptance, the Governor or local director or governing body of such political subdivision may authorize any officer of the Commonwealth or of the political subdivision, as the case may be, to receive such services, equipment, supplies, materials, or funds on behalf of the Commonwealth or such political subdivision, in accordance with the terms of the agreement, and subject to the rules and regulations, if any, of the agency making the offer.

C. Whenever any person, firm or corporation offers to the Commonwealth or to any political subdivision thereof services, equipment, supplies, materials, or funds by way of gift, grant or loan, for purposes of emergency services, the Commonwealth, acting through the Governor, or such political subdivision, acting through its local director or governing body, may accept such offer and upon such acceptance the Governor or local director or governing body of such political subdivision may authorize any officer of the Commonwealth or of the political subdivision, as the case may be, to receive such services, equipment, supplies, materials, or funds on behalf of the Commonwealth or such political subdivision, and subject to the terms of the offer.

D. The governing bodies of the counties, cities and towns are hereby authorized to appropriate funds for expenditure by any local or regional organization for emergency service established pursuant to this chapter and for local or regional disaster service activities. (1973, c. 260; 1999, cc. 6, 7.)

The 1999 amendments. — The 1999 amendments by cc. 119 and 124, effective February 12, 1999, are identical, and redesignated subsections (a) through (d) as subsections A through D; substituted "allots" for "shall allot" in subsection A; in subsection B, substituted "offers" for "shall offer," inserted the language beginning "agree to the terms" at the end of the first sentence, and substituted "in accordance with the terms of the agreement, and subject to" for "and subject to the terms of the offer and"; and substituted "offers" for "shall offer" in subsection C.

§ 44-146.28. Authority of Governor and agencies under his control in declared state of emergency.

— (a) In the case of a declaration of a state of emergency as defined in § 44-146.16, the Governor is authorized to expend from all funds of the state treasury not constitutionally restricted, a sum sufficient. Allotments from such sum sufficient may be made by the Governor to any state agency or political subdivision of the Commonwealth to carry out disaster service missions and responsibilities. Allotments may also be made by the Governor from the sum sufficient to provide financial assistance to eligible applicants located in an area declared to be in a state of emergency, but not declared to be a major disaster area for which federal assistance might be forthcoming. This shall be considered as a program of last resort for those local jurisdictions that cannot meet the full cost.

The Virginia Department of Emergency Services shall establish guidelines and procedures for determining whether and to what extent financial assistance to local governments may be provided.

The guidelines and procedures shall include, but not be limited to, the following:

(1) Participants may be eligible to receive financial assistance to cover a percentage of eligible costs if they demonstrate that they are incapable of covering the full cost. The percentage may vary, based on the Commission on Local Government's fiscal stress index. The cumulative effect of recent disasters during the preceding twelve months may also be considered for eligibility purposes.

(2) Only eligible participants that have sustained an emergency or disaster as defined in § 44-146.16 with total eligible costs of four dollars or more per capita may receive assistance. No site or facility may be included with less than $1,000 in eligible costs. However, the total cost of debris clearance may be considered as costs associated with a single site.

(3) Eligible participants shall be fully covered by all-risk property and flood insurance policies, including provisions for insuring the contents of the property and business interruptions, or shall be self-insured, in order to be eligible for this assistance. Insurance deductibles shall not be covered by this program.

(4) Eligible costs incurred by towns, public service authorities, volunteer fire departments and volunteer rescue squads may be included in a county's or city's total costs.

(5) Unless otherwise stated in guidelines and procedures, eligible costs are defined as those listed in the Public Assistance component of Public Law 93-288, as amended, excluding beach replenishment and snow removal.

(6) State agencies, as directed by the Virginia Department of Emergency Services, shall conduct an on-site survey to validate damages and to document restoration costs.

(7) Eligible participants shall maintain complete documentation of all costs in a manner approved by the Auditor of Public Accounts and shall provide copies of the documentation to the Virginia Department of Emergency Services upon request.

If a jurisdiction meets the criteria set forth in the guidelines and procedures, but is in an area that has neither been declared to be in a state of emergency nor been declared to be a major disaster area for which federal assistance might be forthcoming, the Governor is authorized, in his discretion, to make an allotment from the sum sufficient to that jurisdiction without a declaration of a state of emergency, in the same manner as if a state of emergency declaration had been made.

The Governor shall report to the Chairmen of the Senate Finance Committee, the House Appropriations Committee, and the House Finance Committee within thirty days of authorizing the sum sufficient pursuant to this section. The Virginia Department of Emergency Services shall report annually to the General Assembly on the local jurisdictions that received financial assistance and the amount each jurisdiction received.

(b) Public agencies under the supervision and control of the Governor may implement their emergency assignments without regard to normal procedures (except mandatory constitutional requirements) pertaining to the performance of public work, entering into contracts, incurring of obligations, employment of temporary workers, rental of equipment, purchase of supplies and materials and expenditures of public funds. (1973, c. 260; 1974, c. 4; 1975, c. 11; 1997, c. 893.)

§ **44-146.28:1. Compact enacted into law; terms.** — The Emergency Management Assistance Compact is hereby enacted into law and entered into by the Commonwealth of Virginia with all other states legally joining therein, in the form substantially as follows:

EMERGENCY MANAGEMENT ASSISTANCE COMPACT

ARTICLE I.

PURPOSE AND AUTHORITIES.

This compact is made and entered into by and between the participating member states which enact this compact, hereinafter called party states. For the purposes of this compact, the term "states" is taken to mean the several states, the Commonwealth of Puerto Rico, the District of Columbia, and all U.S. territorial possessions.

The purpose of this compact is to provide for mutual assistance between the states entering into this compact in managing any emergency or disaster that is duly declared by the Governor of the affected state, whether arising from natural disaster, technological hazard, man-made disaster, civil emergency aspects of resources shortages, community disorders, insurgency, or enemy attack.

This compact shall also provide for mutual cooperation in emergency-related exercises, testing, or other training activities using equipment and personnel simulating performance of any aspect of the giving and receiving of aid by party states or subdivisions of party states during emergencies, such actions occurring outside actual declared emergency periods. Mutual assistance in this compact may include the use of the states' National Guard forces, either in accordance with the National Guard Mutual Assistance Compact or by mutual agreement between states.

ARTICLE II.

GENERAL IMPLEMENTATION.

Each party state entering into this compact recognizes that many emergencies transcend political jurisdictional boundaries and that intergovernmental coordination is essential in managing these and other emergencies under this compact. Each state further recognizes that there will be emergencies which require immediate access and present procedures to apply outside resources to make a prompt and effective response to such an emergency. This is because few, if any, individual states have all the resources they may need in all types of emergencies or the capability of delivering resources to areas where emergencies exist.

The prompt, full, and effective utilization of resources of the participating states, including any resources on hand or available from the federal government or any other source, that are essential to the safety, care, and welfare of the people in the event of any emergency or disaster declared by a party state, shall be the underlying principle on which all articles of this compact shall be understood.

On behalf of the Governor of each state participating in the compact, the legally designated state official who is assigned responsibility for emergency management will be responsible for formulation of the appropriate interstate mutual aid plans and procedures necessary to implement this compact.

ARTICLE III.

PARTY STATE RESPONSIBILITIES.

A. It shall be the responsibility of each party state to formulate procedural plans and programs for interstate cooperation in the performance of the responsibilities listed in this article. In formulating such plans, and in carrying them out, the party states, insofar as practical, shall:

1. Review individual state hazards analyses and, to the extent reasonably possible, determine all those potential emergencies the party states might jointly suffer, whether due to natural disaster, technological hazard, man-made disaster, emergency aspects of resources shortages, civil disorders, insurgency, or enemy attack;

2. Review party states' individual emergency plans and develop a plan which will determine the mechanism for the interstate management and provision of assistance concerning any potential emergency;

3. Develop interstate procedures to fill any identified gaps and to resolve any identified inconsistencies or overlaps in existing or developed plans;

4. Assist in warning communities adjacent to or crossing the state boundaries;

5. Protect and assure uninterrupted delivery of services, medicines, water, food, energy and fuel, search and rescue, and critical lifeline equipment, services, and resources, both human and material;

6. Inventory and set procedures for the interstate loan and delivery of human and material resources, together with procedures for reimbursement or forgiveness; and

7. Provide, to the extent authorized by law, for temporary suspension of any statutes or ordinances that restrict the implementation of the above responsibilities.

B. The authorized representative of a party state may request assistance of another party state by contacting the authorized representative of that state. The provisions of this compact shall only apply to requests for assistance made by and to authorized representatives. Requests may be verbal or in writing. If verbal, the request shall be confirmed in writing within thirty days of the verbal request. Requests shall provide the following information:

1. A description of the emergency service function for which assistance is needed, including, but not limited to, fire services, law enforcement, emergency medical, transportation, communications, public works and engineering, building inspection, planning and information assistance, mass care, resource support, health and medical services, and search and rescue;

2. The amount and type of personnel, equipment, materials and supplies needed, and a reasonable estimate of the length of time they will be needed; and

3. The specific place and time for staging of the assisting party's response and a point of contact at that location.

C. There shall be frequent consultation between state officials who have assigned emergency management responsibilities and other appropriate representatives of the party states with affected jurisdictions and the United States Government, with free exchange of information, plans, and resource records relating to emergency capabilities.

ARTICLE IV.

LIMITATIONS.

Any party state requested to render mutual aid or conduct exercises and training for mutual aid shall take such action as is necessary to provide and make available the resources covered by this compact in accordance with the terms hereof; provided that it is understood that the state rendering aid may withhold resources to the extent necessary to provide reasonable protection for such state.

Each party state shall afford to the emergency forces of any party state, while operating within its state limits under the terms and conditions of this compact, the same powers, except that of arrest unless specifically authorized by the receiving state, duties, rights, and privileges as are afforded forces of the state in which they are performing emergency services. Emergency forces will continue under the command and control of their regular leaders, but the organizational units will come under the operational control of the emergency services authorities of the state receiving assistance. These conditions may be activated, as needed, only subsequent to a declaration of a state emergency or disaster by the governor of the party state that is to receive assistance or upon commencement of exercises or training for mutual aid and shall continue so long as the exercises or training for mutual aid are in progress, the state of emergency or disaster remains in effect, or loaned resources remain in the receiving state, whichever is longer.

ARTICLE V.

LICENSES AND PERMITS.

Whenever any person holds a license, certificate, or other permit issued by any state party to the compact evidencing the meeting of qualifications for professional, mechanical, or other skills, and when such assistance is requested by the receiving party state, such person shall be deemed licensed, certified, or permitted by the state requesting assistance to render aid involving such skill to meet a declared emergency or disaster, subject to such limitations and conditions as the Governor of the requesting state may prescribe by executive order or otherwise.

ARTICLE VI.

LIABILITY.

Officers or employees of a party state rendering aid in another state pursuant to this compact shall be considered agents of the requesting state for tort liability and immunity purposes. No party state or its officers or employees rendering aid in another state pursuant to this compact shall be liable on account of any act or omission in good faith on the part of such forces while so engaged or on account of the maintenance or use of any equipment or supplies in connection therewith. Good faith in this article shall not include willful misconduct, gross negligence, or recklessness.

ARTICLE VII.

SUPPLEMENTARY AGREEMENTS.

Inasmuch as it is probable that the pattern and detail of the machinery for mutual aid among two or more states may differ from that among the states that are party hereto, this compact contains elements of a broad base common to all states, and nothing herein shall preclude any state entering into supplementary agreements with another state or affect any other agreements already in force between states. Supplementary agreements may comprehend, but shall not be limited to, provisions for evacuation and reception of injured and other persons and the exchange of medical, fire, police, public utility, reconnaissance, welfare, transportation and communications personnel, and equipment and supplies.

ARTICLE VIII.
COMPENSATION.

Each party state shall provide for the payment of compensation and death benefits to injured members of the emergency forces of that state and representatives of deceased members of such forces in case such members sustain injuries or are killed while rendering aid pursuant to this compact, in the same manner and on the same terms as if the injury or death were sustained within their own state.

ARTICLE IX.
REIMBURSEMENT.

Any party state rendering aid in another state pursuant to this compact shall be reimbursed by the party state receiving such aid for any loss or damage to or expense incurred in the operation of any equipment and the provision of any service in answering a request for aid and for the costs incurred in connection with such requests; provided, that any aiding party state may assume in whole or in part such loss, damage, expense, or other cost, or may loan such equipment or donate such services to the receiving party state without charge or cost; and provided further, that any two or more party states may enter into supplementary agreements establishing a different allocation of costs among those states. Article VIII expenses shall not be reimbursable under this article.

ARTICLE X.
EVACUATION.

Plans for the orderly evacuation and interstate reception of portions of the civilian population as the result of any emergency or disaster of sufficient proportions to so warrant, shall be worked out and maintained between the party states and the emergency management/services directors of the various jurisdictions where any type of incident requiring evacuations might occur. Such plans shall be put into effect by request of the state from which evacuees come and shall include the manner of transporting such evacuees, the number of evacuees to be received in different areas, the manner in which food, clothing, housing, and medical care will be provided, the registration of the evacuees, the providing of facilities for the notification of relatives or friends, and the forwarding of such evacuees to other areas or the bringing in of additional materials, supplies, and all other relevant factors. Such plans shall provide that the party state receiving evacuees and the party state from which the evacuees come shall mutually agree as to reimbursement of out-of-pocket expenses incurred in receiving and caring for such evacuees, for expenditures for transportation, food, clothing, medicines and medical care, and like items. Such expenditures shall be reimbursed as agreed by the party state from which the evacuees come. After the termination of the emergency or disaster, the party state from which the evacuees come shall assume the responsibility for the ultimate support of repatriation of such evacuees.

ARTICLE XI.
IMPLEMENTATION.

A. This compact shall become effective immediately upon its enactment into law by any two states. Thereafter, this compact shall become effective as to any other state upon enactment by such state.

B. Any party state may withdraw from this compact by enacting a statute repealing the same, but no such withdrawal shall take effect until thirty days after the Governor of the withdrawing state has given notice in writing of such withdrawal to the Governors of all other party states. Such action shall not relieve the withdrawing state from obligations assumed hereunder prior to the effective date of withdrawal.

C. Duly authenticated copies of this compact and of such supplementary agreements as may be entered into shall, at the time of their approval, be deposited with each of the party states and with the Federal Emergency Management Agency and other appropriate agencies of the United States Government.

ARTICLE XII.

VALIDITY.

This compact shall be construed to effectuate the purposes stated in Article I. If any provision of this compact is declared unconstitutional, or the applicability thereof to any person or circumstances is held invalid, the constitutionality of the remainder of this compact and the applicability thereof to other persons and circumstances shall not be affected.

ARTICLE XIII.

ADDITIONAL PROVISIONS.

Nothing in this compact shall authorize or permit the use of military force by the National Guard of a state at any place outside that state in any emergency for which the President is authorized by law to call into federal service the militia, or for any purpose for which the use of the Army or the Air Force would in the absence of express statutory authorization be prohibited under § 1385 of Title 18 of the United States Code. (1995, c. 280.)

§ **44-146.29:** Expired.

Editor's note. — This section expired by its own terms 30 days after the commencement of the 1975 Session of the General Assembly. See Acts 1974, c. 4.

§§ **44-146.29:1, 44-146.29:2:** Expired.

Editor's note. — Acts 1984, c. 332, which enacted §§ 44-146.29:1 and 44-146.29:2, provided in cl. 3 that its provisions would expire upon the effective date of any act of the 1984 General Assembly creating a Department of Mines, Minerals and Energy. Acts 1984, c. 590, created such a department, effective January 1, 1985. See now § 45.1-161.1 et seq.

CHAPTER 3.3.

Transportation of Hazardous Radioactive Materials.

Sec.
44-146.30. Department of Emergency Services to monitor transportation of hazardous radioactive materials.

§ **44-146.30. Department of Emergency Services to monitor transportation of hazardous radioactive materials.** — The Coordinator of the

Department of Emergency Services, pursuant to regulations promulgated by the Virginia Waste Management Board, will maintain a register of shippers of hazardous radioactive materials and monitor the transportation within the Commonwealth of those hazardous radioactive materials, as defined by the Virginia Waste Management Board, which may constitute a significant potential danger to the citizens of the Commonwealth in the event of accidental spillage or release. The regulations promulgated by the Board shall not be in conflict with federal statutes, rules, or regulations. Other agencies and commissions of the Commonwealth shall cooperate with the Virginia Waste Management Board in the formulation of regulations as herein provided. (1979, c. 434; 1984, c. 745; 1988, c. 30.)

Editor's note. — Acts 1988, c. 30, cl. 2 provides: "That regulations promulgated by the Board of Health governing transportation of hazardous radioactive materials shall remain in force as regulations of the Virginia Waste Management Board until any such regulation is amended, modified, or repealed by the Vir-

ginia Waste Management Board."

Law Review. — For article discussing issues relating to toxic substances litigation, focusing on the Fourth Circuit, see 16 U. Rich. L. Rev. 247 (1982). For note, "The Role of Localities in the Transportation and Disposal of Nuclear Wastes," see 18 U. Rich. L. Rev. 655 (1984).

CHAPTER 3.4.

FUNDING FOR STATE AND LOCAL GOVERNMENT RADIOLOGICAL EMERGENCY
PREPAREDNESS.

§ 44-146.31. Definitions. — As used in this chapter, unless the context requires a different meaning:

"Nuclear power station" means a facility producing electricity through the utilization of nuclear energy for sale to the public which is required to be licensed by the Nuclear Regulatory Commission and includes all units of the facility at a single site.

"Person" means any individual, corporation, partnership, firm, association, trust, estate, public or private institution, group, agency, political subdivision or agency thereof, and any legal successor, representative, agent or agency of the foregoing.

"Department" means the Department of Emergency Services. (1982, c. 222.)

§ 44-146.32. One-time and annual fees. — A. For each nuclear power station in commercial operation on July 1, 1982, the person owning the station shall pay to the Department, within ninety days of such date, a one-time fee of $55,000.

B. For each nuclear power station commencing commercial operation after July 1, 1982, the person owning the station shall pay to the Department a one-time fee of $55,000 not less than one year prior to the scheduled commencement of operation.

C. For each nuclear power station that on July 1 of each year is validly licensed to operate by the Nuclear Regulatory Commission, the person owning the station shall pay to the Department not later than August 1 of that year an annual fee in an amount based upon the projected annual cost of administering the state and local governments' radiological emergency preparedness programs for the station.

D. The Department shall send timely invoices for such fees to the persons responsible for their payment. However, failure of the Department to send the invoices in a timely manner shall not relieve the responsible persons of their obligation to pay such fees. (1982, c. 222; 1984, c. 322; 1988, c. 56.)

§ **44-146.33. Radiological Emergency Preparedness Fund.** — All moneys received by the Department under this chapter shall be deposited in the state treasury and set apart in a special fund to be known as the "Radiological Emergency Preparedness Fund." Moneys deposited in this fund shall be expended by the Department to the extent appropriated only to support the activities of state agencies and the local governments in establishing, maintaining and operating such emergency plans, programs and capabilities to deal with nuclear accidents as are required by the Nuclear Regulatory Commission and the Federal Emergency Management Agency with respect to nuclear power stations. (1982, c. 222.)

CHAPTER 3.5.

VIRGINIA HAZARDOUS MATERIALS EMERGENCY RESPONSE PROGRAM.

§ **44-146.34. Purpose; definitions.** — A. The purpose of this chapter is to provide for the development and implementation of a program to protect the environment and the health, safety, and welfare of the people of the Commonwealth from the threats and potential threats of accidents or incidents involving hazardous materials. This program shall be known as the Virginia Hazardous Materials Emergency Response Program.

B. As used in this chapter, unless the context requires otherwise:

"Coordinator" means the Coordinator of the Department of Emergency Services.

"Department" means the Department of Emergency Services.

"Hazardous materials" means substances or materials which may pose unreasonable risks to health, safety, property, or the environment when used, transported, stored or disposed of, which may include materials which are solid, liquid or gas. Hazardous materials may include toxic substances, flammable and ignitable materials, explosives, corrosive materials, and radioactive materials and include (i) those substances or materials in a form or quantity which may pose an unreasonable risk to health, safety, or property when transported, and which the Secretary of Transportation of the United States has so designated by regulation or order; (ii) hazardous substances as defined or designated by law or regulation of the Commonwealth or law or regulation of the United States government; and (iii) hazardous waste as defined or designated by law or regulation of the Commonwealth.

"Political subdivision" means any city or county in the Commonwealth, and for the purposes of this chapter, any town with a population of more than 5,000

which chooses to have an emergency services program separate from that of the county in which the town is located.

"Transport" or *"transportation"* means any movement of property by any mode and any packing, loading, unloading, or storage incidental thereto. (1987, c. 492.)

§ 44-146.35. Powers and duties of the Department of Emergency Services. — In carrying out the purposes set forth in this chapter the Department shall have the authority to:

1. Coordinate the development of hazardous materials training programs and hazardous materials emergency response programs and plans with state and local government agencies and related groups. Those state agencies and local government agencies shall retain the statutory responsibilities assigned elsewhere in this Code.

2. Administer the implementation of the Virginia Hazardous Materials Emergency Response Program. The Department shall consider the recommendations of the Hazardous Materials Emergency Response Advisory Council in implementing the Program. (1987, c. 492.)

§ 44-146.36. Coordinator to enter into agreements with political subdivisions; immunity from liability. — A. The Coordinator may enter into agreements with political subdivisions to provide hazardous materials emergency response within a specific geographical area of the Commonwealth on a state and political subdivision cost-sharing basis. The cost-sharing agreements shall be negotiated with political subdivisions by the Coordinator.

B. Neither the Commonwealth, nor any political subdivision thereof, nor federal agencies, nor other public or private agencies, nor public or private employees, nor representatives of any of them, engaged in any emergency services activities while complying with or attempting to comply with this chapter or any regulation or executive order promulgated pursuant to the provisions of this chapter, shall be liable for the death of or injury to any person or damage to property as a result of such activities, except where such death, injury or damage results from gross negligence, recklessness or willful misconduct. The provisions of this section shall not affect the right of any person to receive benefits to which he would otherwise be entitled under this chapter, or under the Workers' Compensation Act (§ 65.2-100 et seq.), or under any pension law, nor the right of any such person to receive any benefits or compensation under any act of Congress. (1987, c. 492; 1989, c. 378.)

§ 44-146.37. Disbursements made from Virginia Disaster Response Fund. — A. Disbursements for costs and expenses, including, but not limited to equipment, material, hazardous materials emergency response operations and immediate accident or incident site cleanup costs and expenses in preventing or alleviating damage, loss, hardship, or suffering caused by accidents or incident, involving hazardous materials, shall be made from the Virginia Disaster Response Fund in accordance with the provisions of § 44-146.18:1.

B. The Coordinator shall promptly seek reimbursement from any party causing or contributing to an accident or incident involving hazardous materials for all sums disbursed from the Virginia Disaster Response Fund for the protection, relief, and recovery from loss or damage caused by such party.

C. The Coordinator is also authorized to recover any sums expended by any other state agency or political subdivision for preventing or alleviating damage, loss, hardship, or suffering caused by accidents or incidents involving hazardous materials. To recover such sums the Coordinator shall provide documentation that the costs were incurred whether or not they were actually disbursed from the Virginia Disaster Response Fund. (1987, c. 492.)

Law Review. — For article, "Environmental Liens and Title Insurance," see 23 U. Rich. L. Rev. 305 (1989).

§ 44-146.38. Political subdivisions to appoint hazardous materials coordinator.

— Each political subdivision shall appoint a hazardous materials coordinator. In appointing the hazardous materials coordinator, political subdivisions shall consider the requisite qualifications for hazardous materials coordinators as established by the Coordinator upon recommendation of the State Hazardous Materials Emergency Response Advisory Council. The hazardous materials coordinator shall coordinate the hazardous materials emergency response program within the political subdivision. (1987, c. 492.)

§ 44-146.39. State Hazardous Materials Emergency Response Advisory Council created; membership; responsibilities.

— A. There is hereby created the State Hazardous Materials Emergency Response Advisory Council, hereinafter referred to in this chapter as the "Council." The Council shall consist of such state agency heads or their designated representatives as the Governor shall appoint and nine other members appointed by the Governor. Those nine members shall be representative of local government, industry, the general public, and environmental and emergency response interests. The Governor shall designate a chairman from among the Council members and the Council shall meet at the call of the chairman. Upon initial appointment three of the nine nonstate agency representatives shall be appointed for three-year terms, three for two-year terms, and three for one-year terms. Thereafter, each shall be appointed for a term of three years.

B. The Department of Emergency Services shall provide staff support for the Council. State agencies shall cooperate in providing assistance and advice upon request of the Council to the Coordinator. Expenses incurred as a result of Council functions shall be paid by the Department of Emergency Services from an appropriation for that purpose.

C. The Council shall provide programmatic advice to the Coordinator in the development and implementation of the Virginia Hazardous Materials Emergency Response Program. The Council shall study and make recommendations on all aspects of the Virginia Hazardous Materials Emergency Response Program including, but not limited to, planning, organization, equipment, training, funding, accident prevention and enforcement of regulations.

D. The Council shall provide advice to the Virginia Emergency Response Council. (1987, c. 492.)

§ 44-146.40. Virginia Emergency Response Council created; membership; responsibilities; immunity for local councils.

— A. There is hereby created the Virginia Emergency Response Council to carry out the provisions of Title 3, Public Law 99-499.

B. The Virginia Emergency Response Council shall consist of such state agency heads or designated representatives with technical expertise in the emergency response field as the Governor shall appoint. The Governor shall designate a chairman from among its members.

C. The Virginia Emergency Response Council, known as the "Virginia Council," shall designate an appropriate state agency to receive funds provided under Title 3, Public Law 99-499.

D. The Virginia Emergency Response Council shall seek advice on policy and programmatic matters from the Hazardous Materials Emergency Response Advisory Council.

E. The Virginia Council shall adopt rules and procedures in accordance with the provisions of the Administrative Process Act, Chapter 1.1:1 (§ 9-6.14:1 et seq.) of Title 9 for the conduct of its business.

F. Any person appointed by the Virginia Emergency Response Council as a member of a local emergency planning committee shall be immune from civil liability for any official act, decision or omission done or made in performance of his duties as a member of such local council, provided that the act, decision or omission was not done or made in bad faith or with malicious intent or does not constitute gross negligence. No member of any emergency planning committee nor any state agency on behalf of such member need make a payment into the state insurance fund under § 2.1-526.8 for this purpose.

G. Any joint emergency planning committee serving any county operating under the urban county executive form of government and serving a city with a population between 19,500 and 20,000 shall have the authority to require any facility within its emergency planning district to submit the information required and participate in the emergency planning provided for in Subtitle A of Title 3 of Public Law 99-499. For the purposes of this subsection, *"facility"* shall include any development or installation having an aggregate storage capacity of at least one million gallons of oil as defined in § 62.1-44.34:10, or the potential for a sudden release of 10,000 pounds or more of any other flammable liquid or gas not exempt from the provisions of § 327 of Title 3 of Public Law 99-499. This requirement shall not occur until after public notice and the opportunity to comment. The committee shall notify the facility owner or operator of any requirement to comply with this subsection. (1987, c. 492; 1992, cc. 633, 656; 1994, c. 691.)

CHAPTER 4.

Air Raid Precautions.

§ **44-147. Authorization of precautions.** — (a) Whenever a state of war exists between the United States and any foreign country, and whenever, in the opinion of the Governor, the Commonwealth is in grave peril, the Governor is authorized to establish air raid precautions; and pursuant thereto to order blackouts in such areas, under such conditions, at such times and for such periods as he deems advisable or upon the request of any federal military or naval authority, and also to regulate and prohibit during such blackouts the movement of vehicular traffic on public highways and streets and to make such regulations as he deems necessary to insure the success of such blackouts and the protection of life and property during the same.

(b) All political subdivisions of this Commonwealth are authorized and directed to enforce the orders and regulations of the Governor issued or made pursuant to this chapter; and they are further authorized to order blackouts in their own jurisdictions whenever they are requested by proper federal military or naval authority and to make reasonable regulations to insure the success of the same and the protection of life and property, provided that such regulations do not conflict with any regulations of the Governor. (1942, p. 368; Michie Code 1942, § 2673(132); 1952, c. 359.)

§ 44-148. Nonliability for damages. — Neither the Commonwealth nor any political subdivision thereof shall be liable for any damage to persons or property caused directly or indirectly by an authorized blackout, or any other air raid precaution or anything incidental thereto. (1942, p. 368; Michie Code 1942, § 2673(133).)

§ 44-149. Appointment of special officers. — The Governor may authorize appropriate local authorities to appoint citizens of the United States as air raid wardens, fire watchers, auxiliary fire fighters, and policemen, and he shall prescribe the powers, duties, rights, privileges and immunities of persons so appointed. In the absence of an agreement therefor, such appointee shall serve without compensation. (1942, p. 368; Michie Code 1942, § 2673(134); 1977, c. 326.)

§ 44-150. Violations of regulations. — Any person violating any regulation made pursuant to this chapter shall upon conviction thereof be punishable by a fine not exceeding $1,000 or imprisonment for not exceeding 30 days, or both. (1942, p. 369; Michie Code 1942, § 2673(135).)

§ 44-151. When chapter in effect. — This chapter shall be in effect only during such time as a state of war exists between the United States and a foreign country, and whenever, in the opinion of the Governor, the Commonwealth is in grave peril. (1942, p. 369; Michie Code 1942, § 2673(136); 1952, c. 359.)

CHAPTER 5.

MOBILIZATION OF FIRE FIGHTERS.

§ 44-152. Outside service by fire departments. — Whenever a state of war exists between the United States and any foreign country and at the request of the chief executive of any county, city or town in this Commonwealth the head of any other fire department may, or if so ordered by the Governor shall, detail, assign and make available for duty and use in such county, town or city any part of the officers, fire fighters, forces, fire-fighting apparatus or other equipment under his command or control. (1942, p. 369; Michie Code 1942, § 2673(137); 1977, c. 326.)

§ 44-153. Powers, duties, rights, privileges and immunities. — Whenever all or any part of the regular fire-fighting forces of any county, town or city in this Commonwealth are engaged in rendering services pursuant to this chapter, the officers and members of such fire-fighting forces shall have the same powers, duties, rights, privileges and immunities as if they were performing their duties in the political subdivision in which they are normally employed. (1942, p. 369; Michie Code 1942, § 2673(138).)

§ 44-154. Loss, damages, expense or cost. — The county, town or city in which any equipment is used pursuant to this chapter shall be liable for any loss or damage thereto and to the supplies therefor and shall pay any expenses incurred in the operation and maintenance thereof, including the cost of all materials and supplies therefor. No claim for any such loss, damage, expense or cost shall be allowed unless, within sixty days after the same has been sustained or incurred, a written notice of such claim, under oath and itemizing the same, is served by mail or otherwise upon the treasurer of such county, town or city where such equipment was so used. (1942, p. 369; Michie Code 1942, § 2673(139).)

§ 44-155. Liability for acts or omissions. — Neither the Commonwealth nor the political subdivision of the Commonwealth whose fire-fighting forces are engaged pursuant to this chapter shall be liable or accountable in any way for or on account of any act or omission on the part of an officer or member of such forces while engaged pursuant to this chapter or for or on account of the operation, maintenance or use of any apparatus, equipment or supplies in connection therewith, nor shall any fire commissioner, fire chief or other superior officer or head of a fire department, fire company or other fire-fighting forces, acting pursuant to this chapter, be held liable or accountable in any way for or on account of any act or omission on the part of any of his subordinates without the political subdivision of their appointment while such subordinates are under the command of an officer other than himself. (1942, p. 369; Michie Code 1942, § 2673(140).)

§ 44-156. Reimbursement for salaries and expenses. — The political subdivision in which aid or assistance is given pursuant to this chapter shall reimburse the political subdivision furnishing such aid and assistance for any moneys paid for the salaries or other compensation of employees furnished under this chapter during the time they shall not be performing their duties in the political subdivision by which they are employed or act and shall defray the actual traveling and maintenance expenses of such employees while they are rendering such aid and assistance. The provisions of this section and the term "employee" as used herein shall mean and apply with equal effect to paid and volunteer fire fighters. (1942, p. 370; Michie Code 1942, § 2673(141); 1977, c. 326.)

§ 44-157. Temporary substitute fire-fighting forces. — Whenever all or any part of the regular fire-fighting forces of any county, city or town in the Commonwealth are engaged in rendering aid and assistance, pursuant to this chapter, substitute fire fighters, not exceeding the number of regular fire fighters engaged in rendering such aid and assistance, may be appointed in the same manner as provided by law for the appointment of such regular fire fighters. Except in the case of a volunteer fire company, the compensation of such substitute fire fighters shall be fixed at a sum not greater than the lowest rate of pay for a regular fire fighter in such fire department, company or fire-fighting force. Each person appointed under this section shall be vested with the same powers and charged with the same duties as if he were a regular member of such fire department, company or fire-fighting force. No appointment under this section shall continue for more than two days after the regular fire fighters for whom they are substituting have returned to duty. The compensation of any substitute fire fighter appointed pursuant to this section and any allowable expense actually and necessarily incurred by him in the performance of his duties shall be charged against the county, city or town in and for which he was appointed and shall be audited and allowed in the same manner as other charges against the county, city or town are audited and allowed. (1942, p. 370; Michie Code 1942, § 2673(142); 1977, c. 326.)

§ 44-158. Rules and regulations. — The Governor is hereby authorized and empowered to prescribe all necessary and reasonable rules and regulations in order to carry out the provisions of this chapter. (1942, p. 370; Michie Code 1942, § 2673(143).)

§ 44-159. When chapter in effect. — This chapter shall be in effect only during the time a state of war exists between the United States and any foreign country. (1942, p. 370; Michie Code 1942, § 2673(144).)

CHAPTER 6.

EMERGENCY FAIR RENT ACT.

§§ 44-160 through 44-203: Repealed by Acts 1950, p. 188.

CHAPTER 7.

MISCELLANEOUS LAWS.

§ 44-204. Leaves of absence for employees of Commonwealth or political subdivisions. — All officers and employees of the Commonwealth, or of any political subdivision of the Commonwealth who are members of the Virginia State Defense Force or National Defense Executive Reserve shall be entitled to leaves of absence from their respective duties without loss of pay, seniority, accrued leave or efficiency rating on all days during which they shall be engaged in training approved by the Governor or his designee, not to exceed fifteen workdays per federal fiscal year. When relieved from such duty, they shall be restored to positions held by them when ordered to duty. (1938, p. 573; Michie Code 1942, § 2673(124); 1964, c. 227; 1986, c. 611.)

§ 44-205. Traffic regulations. — (1) *Powers of Governor.* — Whenever a state of war exists between the United States and any foreign country, the Governor alone, or through such state departments and agencies as he shall designate, is hereby authorized to:
(a) Cooperate with the agencies of other states and of the federal government in the furtherance of national defense by the formulation and execution of plans for the rapid and safe movement over public highways and streets of troops, vehicles of a military nature, materials for national defense, and all other traffic;
(b) Coordinate the activities of the departments or agencies of this Commonwealth and its political subdivisions concerned directly or indirectly with public highways and streets in a manner which will best effectuate any plan

for the rapid and safe movement over the same of troops, vehicles of a military nature, and materials for national defense;

(c) Promulgate rules and regulations and do any and all other things by him deemed necessary and desirable for the control of traffic over public highways and streets to accomplish the purposes of this section.

(2) *Powers of political subdivisions.* — The chief executive of the governing body of each political subdivision of this Commonwealth is hereby authorized and directed upon request of the Governor to cooperate with him and any state department or agency designated by him in carrying out the purposes of this section.

(3) *When section in effect.* — This section shall be in effect only during the time a state of war exists between the United States and any foreign country. (1942, p. 367; Michie Code 1942, § 2673(180).)

§ 44-206. Issuing agents for sale of obligations of United States. — Notwithstanding the provisions of any other laws, all individuals, partnerships, associations or corporations organized, operating or doing business under the laws of this Commonwealth are hereby authorized, during the continuance of any emergency proclaimed by the President of the United States or of a state of war between the United States and a foreign nation or nations, and for such time thereafter as may be expedient or necessary, and upon designation by and qualification with the Secretary of the Treasury of the United States or under his authority, to act as issuing agents for the sale and issue of obligations of the United States. (1942, p. 394; Michie Code 1942, § 2673(181).)

§ 44-207. Laws continued in effect. — The following laws are continued in effect subject to such limitations as to duration as are contained therein:

(1) *Health and sanitation areas.* — Chapter 216 of the Acts of 1942, approved March 13, 1942, codified as §§ 2673(145)-2673(151) of Michie Code 1942, relating to special emergency health and sanitation areas.

(2) *Motor vehicle tires.* — Chapter 319 of the Acts of 1942, approved March 30, 1942, codified as § 2673(182) of Michie Code 1942, relating to acquisition of motor vehicle tires.

(3) *Powers of attorney and agency agreements.* — Chapter 111 of the Acts of 1944, approved March 2, 1944, codified as § 2673(184) of Michie Suppl. 1946, relating to powers of attorney or agency agreements executed by persons in military service or absent from United States in connection with war work.

§ 44-208. Securing site of structural failure, fire, explosion, or industrial or transportation accident. — The official in charge of the investigation of any structural failure, fire, explosion, or industrial or transportation accident which results in the loss of human life, except when caused by a natural disaster or war, may secure for no more than twelve hours so much of the site where it occurred as, in his opinion, may be necessary to gather evidence regarding the cause of the occurrence. No owner or lessee of the site may be denied entrance except to prevent the destruction of evidence.

In cases of fire from any cause, the chief or other authorized officer of any fire department or fire company in command at the fire shall have the rights and authority granted to him and his subordinates upon his order or direction by § 27-17.1. Nothing in this section shall limit or otherwise affect the authority of, or be construed to deny access to such site by, any person charged by law with the responsibility of investigating any such accident. (1982, c. 213.)